Twentieth-Century American Poetry

Edited by

Dana Gioia

David Mason
Colorado College

Meg Schoerke
San Francisco State University

with D.C. Stone

Boston   Burr Ridge, IL   Dubuque, IA   Madison, WI   New York
San Francisco   St. Louis   Bangkok   Bogotá   Caracas   Kuala Lumpur
Lisbon   London   Madrid   Mexico City   Milan   Montreal   New Delhi
Santiago   Seoul   Singapore   Sydney   Taipei   Toronto

McGraw-Hill Higher Education

A Division of The **McGraw-Hill** Companies

TWENTIETH-CENTURY AMERICAN POETRY
Published by McGraw-Hill, a business unit of The McGraw-Hill Companies, Inc., 1221 Avenue of the Americas, New York, NY, 10020. Copyright © 2004, by Dana Gioia, David Mason, and Meg Schoerke. All rights reserved. No part of this publication may be reproduced or distributed in any form or by any means, or stored in a database or retrieval system, without the prior written consent of The McGraw-Hill Companies, Inc., including, but not limited to, in any network or other electronic storage or transmission, or broadcast for distance learning.

Some ancillaries, including electronic and print components, may not be available to customers outside the United States.

This book is printed on acid-free paper.

1 2 3 4 5 6 7 8 9 0 FGR/FGR 0 9 8 7 6 5 4 3

ISBN 0-07-240019-6

President of McGraw-Hill Humanities/Social Sciences: *Steve Debow*
Executive editor: *Lisa Moore*
Senior developmental editor: *Jane Carter*
Executive marketing manager: *David S. Patterson*
Senior media producer: *Todd Vaccaro*
Senior project manager: *Jean Hamilton*
Production supervisor: *Janean A. Utley*
Senior designer: *Gino Cieslik*
Lead supplement producer: *Marc Mattson*
Associate photo research coordinator: *Natalia C. Peschiera*
Associate art editor: *Cristin C. Yancey*
Permissions: *Marty Granahan*
Cover design: *Gino Cieslik*
Cover photo: *Charles Sheeler.* Canyons, 1951. © *Museo Thyssen-Bornemisza. Madrid.*
Typeface: *9.5/11.5 Sabon*
Compositor: *Thompson Type*
Printer: *Quebecor World Fairfield Inc.*

Library of Congress Cataloging-in-Publication Data
   Twentieth-century American poetry / edited by Dana Gioia, David Mason, Meg Schoerke.
        p. cm.
     Includes index.
     ISBN 0-07-240019-6 (alk. paper)
1. American poetry—20th century. I. Gioia, Dana. II. Mason, David, 1954- III.
   Schoerke, Meg.
   PS323.5.T88 2004
   811.5'08—dc22

                                                                     2003061449
www.mhhe.com

To our teachers,
living and dead,
including a few immortals

About the Editors

Born in Los Angeles in 1950, **Dana Gioia** attended Stanford University and Harvard University, where he studied with Elizabeth Bishop and Robert Fitzgerald, earning a master's degree in comparative literature. Returning to Stanford for his master's in business administration, he then worked in New York for fifteen years, writing on nights and weekends, before giving up business to write full time. Gioia has published three books of poems—*Daily Horoscope* (1986), *The Gods of Winter* (1991), and *Interrogations at Noon* (2001), which won the American Book Award—and has edited a dozen anthologies of poetry and fiction, including two anthologies of Italian poetry and a translation of *Mottetti* (1990) by the Italian Nobel laureate Eugenio Montale. He is also the author of "Can Poetry Matter?" (originally published in *Atlantic* in 1991 and collected in *Can Poetry Matter?: Essays on Poetry and American Culture*, 1992). Reissued in honor of its tenth anniversary, this essay continues to stimulate debate over the role poetry plays in the United States today. A prolific critic and reviewer, Gioia is a frequent commentator on American culture for BBC Radio, and he recently completed *Nosferatu* (2001), an opera libretto, for composer Alva Henderson. He was selected in 2003 to direct the National Endowment for the Arts. He now lives in Washington, D.C., and northern California.

David Mason grew up in Washington State and has lived in many other places, including Greece, New York, Minnesota, and Colorado. He received his bachelor's degree at the Colorado College and his Ph.D. from the University of Rochester. Among his collections of poems are two award-winning books—*The Buried Houses* and *The Country I Remember*—and two chapbooks—*Small Elegies* and *Land without Grief*. With Mark Jarman he co-edited *Rebel Angels: Twenty-five Poets of the New Formalism*, and with the late John Frederick Nims, *Western Wind: An Introduction to Poetry*. He is also author of a collection of essays entitled *The Poetry of Life and the Life of Poetry*. His poems, stories, translations, essays, and memoirs have appeared in a variety of periodicals, including the *New York Times, Hudson Review, Sewanee Review, Poetry, Irish Times, American Scholar, Grand Street,* and *Shenandoah.* Mason has been a Fulbright Fellow to Greece and currently teaches at the Colorado College. He lives in the mountains outside Colorado Springs.

Raised in the Philadelphia and Chicago areas, **Meg Schoerke** did undergraduate work at Northwestern University and earned M.A., M.F.A., and Ph.D degrees from Washington University in St. Louis. Her poems and reviews have appeared in journals such as the *American Scholar, TriQuarterly,* and *Hudson Review,* and she has contributed essays to a variety of books on twentieth-century American poetry. Her collections of poems include *Anatomical Venus* (2004) and a chapbook, *Beyond Mourning.* She is Associate Professor of English at San Francisco State University and lives in San Francisco.

Contents

Early Modernism:
From Imagism to High Modernism
Historical and Critical Overview   82

EZRA POUND (1885–1972)   **168**

H. D. [HILDA DOOLITTLE] (1886–1961)   **203**

The Harlem Renaissance
Historical and Critical Overview   304

Modern Alternatives: Romantics and Neoclassicists
Historical and Critical Overview   350

Mid-Century Poets
Historical and Critical Overview   440

Open Form:
Objectivists, Black Mountain Poets, San Francisco Renaissance, and Beats
Historical and Critical Overview   572

Postwar Formalism and Its Discontents: From Formalism to Feminism and the Confessional Mode

Historical and Critical Overview 664

ANTHONY HECHT (b. 1923)   **696**

RICHARD HUGO (1923–1982)   **705**

LOUIS SIMPSON (b. 1923)   **708**

DONALD JUSTICE (b. 1925)   **715**

CAROLYN KIZER (b. 1925)   **721**

MAXINE KUMIN (b. 1925)   **727**

American Internationalism:
Surrealism, Deep Image Poetry, and the
New York School
Historical and Critical Overview   776

Return to Realism:
Regionalism and Cultural Identity
Historical and Critical Overview   842

Contemporary Voices
Historical and Critical Overview   896

Chronological List of Poets

Preface

HISTORICAL VIEWS

Make it new.
—*Ezra Pound*

The root meaning of *anthology* is "word-bloom" or "a garland of words," implying a harvest of the most beautiful verbal flowers one has been able to gather. In reality anthologies are rougher bouquets with weeds and thorns mixed in. Any anthology that tries to represent the diverse achievements of American poetry in the twentieth century will necessarily be full of various and surprising plants—from spikey wildflowers to hothouse blossoms generously intermixed with familiar garden varieties. At least such fragrant profusion has been our aim. As we looked at other anthologies covering this period in American poetry, we found ourselves, both as poets and readers, dissatisfied with much of what we saw. Frequently the books take too narrow a view—often dropping remarkable individual poets or even poetic schools that do not fit into conventional accounts of literary history. If modern American poetry is anything, it is not uniform, monochromatic, or predictable. There seems a genuine need for a book inclusive enough to represent the many different, even irreconcilable impulses that enliven modern American poetry. Together with its companion volume, *Twentieth-Century American Poetics*, we hope our anthology will provide the best general survey available for students, professors, and anyone else who would like to read and understand modern poetry with its massive engagement of traditions and innovations.

Anthologists must choose not only what to include, but how to arrange their fistfuls of stems and leaves. The organization of this book is historical but not strictly chronological. We have arranged the volume to help the reader understand the complex and shifting shape of the art in a period of unprecedentedly rapid change and experimentation. The result is a book organized partly by chronology, and partly by poetic schools or movements. We have divided the anthology into ten sections using broad critical or historical categories like Early Modernism or Harlem Renaissance as headings. We consider this arrangement both practical and illuminating.

Each of the anthology's ten sections is prefaced by an Historical and Critical Overview intended to place poets in the context of their times, as well as in the light of debates about the nature and purposes of the art. Within these sections, poets are presented in chronological order, and each poet's work is again prefaced by a critical biography. We are aware of the limitations of such arrangements, and our headnotes often make connections across these categories, bridging perceptual gaps that remain in any purely chronological survey.

The opening section, for example, begins with Stephen Crane, the only poet in the book whose short life was over just before the twentieth century officially began. Although slightly outside the stated period of the anthology, his work presents certain tendencies that appear truer to the twentieth century than to the nineteenth—not only his use of free verse, but also his dark, surreal imagery. We recognize that poets like Edwin Arlington Robinson and Robert Frost overlapped with the Modernists of the following sections—Frost was a friend of Ezra Pound, in fact—but we have placed them in a distinct section of their own because of their formal difference, as well as their commonality with popular regionalists of the time. Other critics have responded similarly to this problem. *The Princeton Encyclopedia of Poetry and Poetics* (1993) calls such poets as Robinson, Frost, and even Ransom "premoderns": "Like their modernist contemporaries, they felt the increasing gravity and precariousness of the human predicament. . . . But the strongly regional conservatism of these three made them resist breaking the old forms and reject the formal experimentation that impelled modernism internationally."

We agree with many critics that Modernism (which we capitalize because it now seems a definable, historically bound literary movement) was the crucible in which much great twentieth-century poetry was formed, and we explore the range and complexity of this poetry in two of the next sections, Early Modernism and Modernist Alternatives. As the latter chapter demonstrates, Modernism was by no means a unified or monopolistic enterprise. Competing aesthetics thrived in the period. Poets as dissimilar as Hart Crane, Edna St. Vincent Millay, Dorothy Parker, and Melvin Tolson were all contemporaries. Sandwiched between these two sections is The Harlem Renaissance, which was perhaps the most significant alternative realization of American Modernism. This movement combined both traditional and experimental methods with the hugely important component of racial identity.

By this point in the book, discerning readers will have discovered a great many of the personalities and forces that would contribute to American poetry after World War II as well. Notice how Frost and Ransom influence Richard Wilbur, Anthony Hecht, and some of the New Formalists; how Gertrude Stein and Laura Riding influence the Language poets; how William Carlos Williams and Robinson Jeffers gave new energy to American regionalism; how the Harlem Renaissance made a diverse array of identity poetries possible. Whatever the weaknesses of a historical approach to poetry, these connections and others like them are often helpful as we try to understand the new. In "Speaking of Poetry," John Peale Bishop wrote:

The ceremony must be found

Traditional, with all its symbols
ancient as the metaphors in dreams;
strange, with never before heard music; continuous
until the torches darken at the bedroom doors.

American poetry in the twentieth century has been all of these—traditional, ancient, strange, with never before heard music—and our anthology recognizes that the torches are still lit.

CRITICAL VIEWS

. . . the rest is criticism.

—*Randall Jarrell*

Bringing our historical survey closer to the present day was one of our hardest tasks. In many cases, critical consensus about recent poetry was unavailable or too tentative to be useful. Chronology alone made strange bedfellows of some poets, and no doubt we did not completely escape such arrangements in our critical criteria as well. We use the term *Mid-Century Poets* to describe the large and influential group of poets including Robert Lowell, Randall Jarrell, Elizabeth Bishop, Gwendolyn Brooks, and Weldon Kees, who combined certain Modernist procedures with generally traditional notions of form. We employ this conventional term from a number of critical studies and anthologies, but we note, too, that it represents a sort of literary historical fiction since it ignores other Mid-Century poets like Robert Duncan and Lorine Niedecker, who were also writing at the same time. We group many of these writers in the section Open Form, realizing that here, too, is a risk of giving the message that other Mid-Century poets were not also experimenting with free verse. Yet placing poets together in groups that share some affinities allows the reader or student to see key resemblances and common concerns. Again, in our Historical and Critical Overviews we have striven to place these issues in context. While the grouping of poets in categories may be problematic, it helps teachers and readers clarify the arguments and issues that made the century so exciting.

When we rehearsed these arguments ourselves, we raised the very issues still vociferously debated among American poets and readers. What, for example, makes American poetry *American?* In a recent interview, the poet Judith Ortiz Cofer observed, "The Library of Congress defines as an American writer a person writing in English within the boundaries of the United States who's an American citizen." Sensible enough, but sometimes Americans choose not to write in English, as readers will see in a few pages of the present volume. And quite often they choose to live outside the country, sometimes for most of their adults lives, as in the case of Pound, Eliot, Stein, H. D., Plath, and Stevenson. There is also the question of what is poetry. What is the "poetic"? What forms might poetry take? What diction? Are any of these questions answerable beyond the subjective response of an individual's taste?

Such questions involve American poets in the most fundamental issues of the art. What gets said *about* poetry is often intriguing, angering, hilarious, exalted, or trivial, just like poetry itself. Our critical overviews attempt to clarify the *isms*, the revolutions and reactions of twentieth-century American poetry: Realism, Naturalism, Feminism, Imagism, Vorticism, Modernism, Regionalism, Internationalism, Objectivism, Multiculturalism, Formalism, and so on. We should be clear that poems do not exist merely to illustrate such critical categories. Rather, poems *exist.* The critical categories are tentative ways of understanding the existence.

When we arrived at the task of grouping the most recent poets, we struggled to find a title that would represent all the visible trends and tendencies, and finally resorted to a simple inclusive description, Contemporary Voices. Of course, many of the poets in sections preceding the final one are contemporary as well, and our critical headnote for Contemporary Voices endeavors to clarify several major trends of our time, all of which have their roots in the work of earlier generations.

ADDING AND SUBTRACTING

> Only a certain
> claque of beasts
> is part of the
> crèche racket. . . .
>
> — *Kay Ryan*

Anthologists begin with the hope of making a clear, cogent, and inclusive canon of poetry, but end in despair at all the excellent work they must exclude. This is a very large book, but is too small to include everything the editors wanted. The first version of the anthology was, in fact, nearly twice its current size. The most difficult part of our job over the last three years has been choosing what to use, only to find ourselves later cutting much of it out.

We began with a few simple rules. We would only select poems to which the editors had a strong and genuine response. No poem would be included if it was not approved by at least two of the three editors. We also wanted to represent the true variety of American poetry, which meant including many types of poems—epigrams, narratives, and satires—often left out of academic textbooks. We would also include only poets who had published at least one full-length book of poems. Whenever possible we met in person for the work, usually at Dana Gioia's house in northern California, where we read, wrote, debated, revised, researched, argued, stormed, slammed doors, wept (or nearly wept), laughed, feasted, starved, riffled the medicine chest, consoled each other, consumed a vineyard and coffee plantation or two, and generally badgered each other until the work was done.

There were moments of discovery and joy in nearly every part of the process. We are especially proud to be the first anthology ever to include poems by John Allen Wyeth, an utterly forgotten writer who is arguably the best American poet of World War I. We are also proud to include Yone Noguchi, the first significant Asian American poet, who brought the influence of Japanese poetry to many American writers (including Ezra Pound) and himself wrote lovely poems in English. And we delight, too, in the perversity of the Spectra poets, the national literary hoax perpetrated by Witter Bynner and Arthur Davison Ficke. We are pleased to restore neglected figures like Melvin Tolson, Laura Riding, John Peale Bishop, Weldon Kees, Thomas McGrath, Jack Spicer, Samuel Menashe, and Josephine Miles to their rightful places among their contemporaries.

That each of us was forced to exclude poets we love has been undeniably painful. In some cases, the pain will no doubt be increased by encounters and arguments with our friends and fellow poets. Anthologists cannot afford to be cowards. Such agony goes with the job and is only made more inevitable by the attempt to make a book of reasonable size that represents so vital and diverse a period in American poetry. Virtually every reader of this book will regret some of our omissions, to put it politely, and we can console our readers and ourselves only with the promise that those excluded poems are still out there to be sought in bookstores, libraries, and, we hope, other anthologies. This book is less unwieldy than some, less driven by a single ideological or aesthetic agenda. It attempts to be thorough, broad-minded, and fair, which is all any anthologist can hope to do.

Finally, two of the editors who have published full-length books of poems debated whether or not to include themselves. It was decided finally that each would choose poems by and write the headnote for the other.

Dana Gioia
David Mason
Meg Schoerke

Acknowledgments

Oh, it's the shared comedy of the worst
blessed; the sound leading the hand;
a wordlife running from mind to mind. . . .

— *Anne Stevenson*

This book would never have been finished at all without the superhuman labor of Mary Gioia, who typed and collated huge portions of text, checked and rechecked facts, remained friends with two of the editors, and stayed married to the third. No expression of gratitude we offer will be commensurate with her spirit and her work.

Dan Stone wrote a number of author headnotes, checked texts, proofread drafts, helped Mary Gioia with fact-checking, taped and numbered pages, and generally proved himself a professional writer and editor every step of the way. Ultimately, his contribution was so significant that we decided to add his name to the title page.

David Mason also wishes to thank his wife, Anne Lennox, and several colleagues who helped: Jane Hilberry, Claire Garcia, Ruth Barton, Daniel Tynan, John Simons, and Barry Sarchett. Colby Cedar Smith helped with research in the early stages. The Colorado College provided a two-year MacArthur Professorship which made much of this work possible.

Meg Schoerke acknowledges the support of San Francisco State University, whose grant of a semester's sabbatical enabled her to complete this anthology. She is grateful for the computer expertise and critical eye of Mark Seiden and the aid of Purdue University reference librarian Robert Freeman. She also thanks her mother, Donna S. White, for keeping the faith, and Anne-Marie Cusac, Susan Koppelman, Brighde Mullins, Catherine Rankovic, and Loretta Stec, for their sustaining support and friendship. Finally, she was helped at crucial junctures by Stephen Arkin, Rosemary Catacalos, Lois Lyles, and Christine Ruotolo.

We would like to thank our editors: Sarah Touborg, who gently prodded us for more than two years; Lisa Moore, who continued the prodding and encouragement after Sarah moved on; and Jane Carter, who plunged into the details of the book. We would also like to thank our patient project manager, Jean Hamilton; the production supervisor, Janean Utley; the permissions editor, Marty Granahan; the copy editor, Michelle (Lulos) Livingston; the proofreader, Lauren Milantoni; and the designer, Gino Cieslik.

Finally, at each of this book's evolutionary stages portions of it were sent out for review by teachers of poetry, and we would like to thank the following for their helpful reactions:

Jonathan N. Barron, University of Southern Mississippi
James Bobrick, University of Massachusetts—Dartmouth
Kenneth Chamlee, Brevard College
Joanne Craig, Bishop's University

Martha B. Crowe, East Tennessee State University
Peter Van Egmond, University of Maryland
Norman Finkelstein, Xavier University
Jeffrey Gray, Seton Hall
Charles O. Hartman, Connecticut College
Henry D. Herring, College of Wooster
George B. Hutchinson, Indiana University
Linda A. Kinnahan, Duquesne University
Thomas Wayne Koontz, Ball State
Philip Kuberski, Wake Forest University
Linda Leavell, Oklahoma State
Jeredith Merrin, Ohio State
Charles T. Molesworth, Queens College, City University of New York
Kay Murphy, University of New Orleans
John T. Newcomb, West Chester University
Suzanne Paola, Western Washington University
Barbara Perkins, formerly of University of Michigan
George Perkins, formerly of University of Michigan
Stephen Ratcliffe, Mills College
John Ridland, UC Santa Barbara
Camille Roman, Washington State University
Reginald Shepherd, Cornell University
Ernest Smith, University of Central Florida
Thomas R. Smith, Penn State
Alan Soldofsky, San Jose State University
Philip Tabakow, Bridgewater State College
Jon Thompson, North Carolina State University
Michael Thurston, Smith College
Mark Vinz, Minnesota State University

Realism and Naturalism

Unknown girl, photographed in Colorado in the 1890s.

HISTORICAL AND CRITICAL OVERVIEW

> It takes a great deal of history to produce a little literature.
> —*Henry James*

Consider the nation in which twentieth-century American poetry developed. The United States in 1900 may have been a smaller country than the one we inhabit now, but to its citizens it was a vast, complex, and rapidly changing nation. Its population was 76 million—less than one-quarter of our present number. It was already predominantly urban; the flight to the cities had begun and only one-third of its people still lived on farms. If by 1890 more people lived in the United States than in France and England combined, there was also a great deal more land to make room for them in the forty-five contiguous states. 1890 was the year in which the first posthumous collection of Emily Dickinson's poems was published (in highly edited form) by Thomas Wentworth Higginson and Mabel Loomis Todd. It was also the year in which the United States Seventh Cavalry took its revenge for the Battle of the Little Big Horn by slaughtering three hundred men, women, and children at Wounded Knee in South Dakota. Custer's Last Stand had taken place in 1876, the same year in which Alexander Graham Bell called to his assistant, Watson, via a crude prototype of the telephone.

In other words, we cannot talk about the twentieth century without talking about the century that preceded it, a time of immense progress and often violent national struggle for self-definition. The Civil War of 1861–1865 cost over 600,000 lives—greater than the American casualties in World War I, World War II, and the Korean War combined. This terrible national catastrophe left cultural, social, and economic scars that in some ways last to this day, particularly in issues of racial equality, states' rights, and federal authority. As the French aristocrat Alexis de Tocqueville had earlier predicted, race relations would remain a major American problem. In 1865 the Thirteenth Amendment to the constitution outlawed slavery, but in the same year the Ku Klux Klan was formed, and a year earlier the Sand Creek Massacre, in which hundreds of Cheyenne Indians were killed, took place in what would become the state of Colorado. The Fourteenth Amendment of 1868 extended voting rights to any male citizen twenty-one years of age or older, including former slaves, but in many states such citizens were prevented from voting by the poll tax (an obstacle removed by the Twenty-fourth Amendment almost a century later).

In 1870 the population of the United States had only been 39 million; by 1900 it had nearly doubled. Immigration had been encouraged by the Homestead Act of 1862, and the railroads and mines sought new labor. Most early immigrants were northern European. They were followed by southern and eastern Europeans, usually Catholics and Jews who also faced discrimination based upon religion and ethnicity. With astonishing rapidity the European poor sought new lives in America. By 1900, for instance, the five boroughs of New York City contained more Italians than Rome. But not all foreigners were welcomed. In 1882, Chinese immigrants (many of whom had originally come to work in mining or railroading) were formally barred from entering the United States; Japanese immigration was also limited in the early twentieth century. Yet many who came here found great opportunity and a government that was often reluctant to meddle with commerce.

No survey of modern American poetry can be entirely divorced from these developments and others. In the following sections of this review we will notice the contexts—social, economic, and literary—in which poetry was being written.

Of course the art itself cannot be entirely understood in these contexts, but the emergence of modern American poetry in all its range and complexity is partly a function of the personalities and the times that produced it.

The Gilded Age

God gave me my money.
—*John D. Rockefeller, Sr.*

Named after the 1873 novel Mark Twain wrote with Charles Dudley Warner, the late nineteenth century was "The Gilded Age" of the Robber Barons, successful businessmen with controlling interests in the new industrial economy—railroads, shipping, banking, mining, and steel. These powerful magnates included Jay Gould, Leland Stanford, Henry Clay Frick, Andrew Carnegie, J. P. Morgan, and John D. Rockefeller. The sometimes brutal manipulations of these competitive industrialists no doubt contributed to the rise of labor politics, the formation of unions like the United Mine Workers, and the efforts of labor activists like Mother Jones and anarchists like Emma Goldman. But the Robber Barons also became the country's first great philanthropists, endowing libraries, museums, and universities in many parts of the nation. The paradoxical phenomenon of a vast fortune ruthlessly assembled then voluntarily given away became a distinctively American tradition.

It was an era of conspicuous prosperity, hard poverty, economic and geographical expansion, class warfare and ethnic confrontation—in short, America was a young nation enduring growing pains on a very large scale. The first transcontinental railroad was completed in 1869, and by 1885 there were four separate lines running from coast to coast. Peoples' lives were steadily improved by new technologies. The 1870s saw Edison's phonograph and electric light bulb (moving pictures came two decades later), though a generation would pass before these inventions were commonly used. In 1917, for example, only one quarter of American households had electricity; within three years that number had doubled. Again and again we see inventions of the nineteenth century that transformed the twentieth—from radio telegraphy to the automobile. When cars were driven onstage in Irish playwright George Bernard Shaw's *Man and Superman* (1905), they would have seemed almost as rare as space shuttles, but by 1909 Henry Ford was mass-producing the Model T and inventing the paternal corporation. The Wright brothers made their motorized flight at Kitty Hawk in 1903, and within six years Louis Blériot had flown across the English Channel.

This time of expansiveness and hope was also an era of pessimism in some quarters. In 1893, the Chicago World's Fair represented high hopes for the Western Hemisphere; that same year, the Gold Panic shook the markets and brought on recession. The young Californian Jack London found himself among the unemployed, was jailed for vagrancy and thereafter became a committed socialist. In 1898 the United States won a rapid war with Spain, and soon found itself a colonial power in the Philippines, Guam, and Puerto Rico. A hero of the Spanish-American War, Theodore Roosevelt became vice president under William McKinley in 1900. But early in his administration McKinley was assassinated by an anarchist in Buffalo, New York. Roosevelt served out the term, winning a second term for himself. Among his many accomplishments, Teddy Roosevelt helped found the National Park System, enforced the Sherman Antitrust Act (alienating powerful business interests in the process), and defended coal miners striking against mine owners for better working conditions. There were also natural disasters like the San Francisco earthquake and fire in 1906; but in the same year, following the publication of Upton Sinclair's novel, *The Jungle,* new laws concerning the inspection of food processing plants were passed. Still, nearly two million children were at work, often in appalling conditions, unprotected by child labor laws.

Cultural Change

Unreal city . . .
—*T. S. Eliot*

In 1910 the nation's population had expanded to 92 million. New York City had nearly four million inhabitants, Chicago about half that number, although in many parts of America you could still walk for days without meeting a soul. Roads were narrow and often rough. Journeys by wagon or early automobile were not easy. American literature reflected a smaller, more parochial society in many ways. Regionalism—always a force in American writing—was particularly strong as the twentieth century began. We had the San Francisco of Frank Norris, Ambrose Bierce and Jack London, the Chicago of Upton Sinclair and Theodore Dreiser, the New England of Edwin Arlington Robinson and Sarah Orne Jewett. Chicago also boasted one of America's great architects, Louis Sullivan, whose functional buildings contained elaborate Art Nouveau ornamentation. (Sullivan's student, Frank Lloyd Wright, would develop a Modernist style, as different from Sullivan's as Picasso from John Singer Sargent.) It was a time of Sousa marches, Puccini operas, Joplin rags, and early jazz. The ideas of Darwin and Marx were widely influential, and Freudian psychology was on its way. *The Interpretation of Dreams* appeared in 1900; that same year the American historian Henry Adams saw the hall of dynamos at the World's Fair in Paris and was convinced of a major cultural seachange, as he later reported in *The Education of Henry Adams* (1907):

> To Adams, the dynamo became a symbol of infinity. As he grew accustomed to the great gallery of machines, he began to feel the forty-foot dynamos as a moral force, much as the early Christians felt the Cross. The planet itself seemed less impressive, in its oldfashioned, deliberate, annual or daily revolution, than this huge wheel, revolving within arm's-length at some vertiginous speed, and barely murmuring—scarcely humming an audible warning to stand a hair's-breadth further for respect of power—while it would not wake the baby lying close against its frame. Before the end, he began to pray to it; inherited instinct taught the natural expression of man before silent and infinite force.

Within a few years, Modernist movements like the Futurists would express similar devotion to and fascination with the machine.

Growth of Communication

All I know is what I see in the papers.
—*Will Rogers*

Education was available to many Americans, and newspapers proliferated. Many of the best-known writers of the time were found in newspaper pages, but also in magazines like *Century, Harper's, Scribner's, Atlantic, Bedford's Monthly, Collier's* and the *Saturday Evening Post.* This "print culture" transmitted information and ideas rapidly across the English-speaking world. If it moved more slowly than television or the Internet, it reached as large an audience with a speed never before seen in human society. News could now not only be telegraphed from coast to coast, but numerous cables had been laid across the Atlantic Ocean's floor to connect Europe and North America. A new class of professional writers called *reporters* now worked by the thousands across North America and Europe to provide the steady stream of news required by the journalistic media. Newspapers published several editions each day to keep up with the constant flow of information.

Print culture had the power of bestowing immediate fame on the objects of its attention. Editors read other newspapers and reprinted items that interested them, including poems and short stories. When the California poet Edwin Markham, for example, published "The Man with the Hoe" in a newspaper in 1899, it was soon reprinted in thousands of other newspapers, frequently translated. By the time "The Man with the Hoe" became the title poem of a book published that same year, Markham was an international celebrity. Eventually that one poem earned its author a very real fortune, roughly $250,000. A new literature of social protest and unflinching realism was in its ascendancy—fueled by a popular press of unprecedented reach and power.

American Writers at the Turn of the Century

> . . . I ran against a Prejudice
> That quite cut off the view.
> —*Charlotte Perkins Gilman*

In 1900, Doubleday published Theodore Dreiser's first novel, *Sister Carrie*, often called the first major work of American Naturalism. It tells the story of a woman's rise as an actress, her affair with a married man, and his ultimate dissolution. The novel also contains passages of gritty urban life. However, the publishers withdrew the book almost immediately because Mrs. Doubleday considered it scandalous. Stephen Crane also wrote about low life in *Maggie: A Girl of the Streets* (1893), as did Jack London in *The People of the Abyss* (1903). Realistic voices came from other quarters as well: Booker T. Washington's autobiography, *Up from Slavery* appeared in 1901, followed by W. E. B. DuBois's groundbreaking book *The Souls of Black Folk* (1903). Feminist works like Charlotte Perkins Gilman's "The Yellow Wallpaper" (1892) and Kate Chopin's *The Awakening* (1899) gained influence with later generations. Edith Wharton's novels sold very well in her own lifetime, though she was not taken as seriously as she deserved to be by literary critics until feminism made new readings of her work available.

Not all writings of the period, however, were realistic. For example, in 1902, Owen Wister, a Harvard classmate of Teddy Roosevelt, published *The Virginian,* an adventure story set in Wyoming cattle country, which sold so well that it was reprinted fourteen times in eight months and helped establish some of the mythology of the Western genre, including the melodramatic conflict between good and evil. There were other kinds of fantasy as well, like the regional caricatures in the stories of Bret Harte and the poems of James Whitcomb Riley, Eugene Field, and Paul Laurence Dunbar.

American poetry at the turn of the century still enjoyed a lively popularity with a mass audience, who read it eagerly in newspapers, magazines, anthologies, and books. But poetry's cultural position as either a type of entertainment or inspirational literature limited its artistic vitality. This was a period mostly of charming small talents, and it conspicuously lacked major vision and innovation. In retrospect it seems, despite its regional variety, like an interim period between the great nineteenth century poets and the Modernist explosion that followed World War I. Consider the six most significant American poets of the mid-nineteenth century: William Cullen Bryant, Ralph Waldo Emerson, Henry Wadsworth Longfellow, Walt Whitman, John Greenleaf Whittier, and Emily Dickinson. By 1893, all of them were dead, and Dickinson's work would not even be known in a reliable edition until 1955. These important writers of the nineteenth century were followed by regional Populists of the 1890s (including Riley, Field, and Dunbar) and also by the rather more effete Harvard poets: George Santayana, Trumbull Stickney, and William Vaughan Moody. Ella Wheeler Wilcox provided spiritual uplift and consolation to a huge readership. Even rebellion was genial. The popular "Vagabond" poets, Richard Hovey and Bliss Carman, celebrated youthful freedom like polite college boys on a vacation spree.

There were other poets at work: we could list the vitriolic verses of Ambrose Bierce, the surreal free verse of Stephen Crane, the realistic vignettes of Hamlin Garland, the social satire of Charlotte Perkins Gilman, the novelistic lyrics of Edwin Arlington Robinson. But Robinson, the one inarguably major poet in this group, worked in almost complete obscurity for the first half of his life, and Crane died young, while more fanciful "newspaper poets" published widely. The popular editorial taste was not ready for their brooding vision and dark humor. What made Robinson unique in some ways was that he took the approach of the best fiction writers and distilled it in poetry. Robinson brought a new kind of Realism to American poetry, modernizing its diction and approach to character, and became the first great American poet of the new century.

Naturalism and Realism

> Words, as is well known, are the great foes of reality.
> —*Joseph Conrad*

When we speak of Realism in literature, we must distinguish it from Naturalism. These theories were initially understood in relation to fiction, but would also become important determinants of poetic practice. Naturalism and Realism eschew idealized subjects for stories about realistic characters in representative situations. Both styles pay close attention to details of individual psychology, economic identity, and social milieu. Both models avoid impossibly noble heroes and heroines. Realism refers mostly to an *attitude* toward reality—a determination to reflect the actual shape and texture of life—and this attitude is present in many kinds of writing. The central impulse of Realism—from Jane Austen to Henry James—was to contrast and compare the inner psychological situation of its characters with their external social and economic realities. Realism recognized the complexity of the human condition, influenced by both internal and external forces. Many Realist works contain fantastic elements—as in Charles Dickens, Honoré de Balzac, or Henry James—but such work remains realistic in the way human psychology or social situations are viewed or in the plausibility of certain story elements.

Naturalism, by contrast, is a particular variety of Realist literature which emphasizes how human beings are often passive victims of social forces, economic conditions, and natural impasses. Naturalism is specifically rooted in the late nineteenth century's claims of scientific objectivity and social activism. French novelist Émile Zola (1840–1902) urged writers to imitate scientists by observing reality without requiring explanations. Implicit in Zola's philosophy (and in the work of most later

Naturalists) was the conviction that the novelist must show many unpleasant truths, including the gritty particulars of poverty, labor, crime, politics, and sexuality. Yet Zola's purported objectivity displayed his own leftist political convictions and passionate desire to effect social change. William Dean Howells, one of the period's most substantial American Realist writers, who greatly admired Zola, wrote that novels were "the sincere and conscientious endeavor to picture life just as it is, to deal with character as we witness it in living people, and to record the incidents that grow out of character." Naturalistic elements can be found in the fiction of Howells, London, Crane, Sarah Orne Jewett, Frank Norris, and Dreiser, but critics also point out that the best of these fictions are richly imagined works, slanted by the personalities of their authors. Naturalistic fictions could not be called objective in the same way we call science objective (if in fact we still do). Rather, they created a stylized illusion of objectivity. Naturalistic writers tended to be Darwinian and deterministic in worldview, a stance that was well suited to the materialism of American society. They also tended to be rather bleak, which often resulted in their neglect by more conventional readers.

Realism and Naturalism in Poetry

> Poetry is a way of taking life by the throat.
> —*Robert Frost*

Although *Realism* and *Naturalism* are conventionally applied only to American fiction, the terms can be meaningfully used to analyze the poetry of the early twentieth century. The work of Edwin Arlington Robinson seems motivated by the same realistic impulse that animated the novels of Henry James and Willa Cather. While never as detailed or complex as such extended works of prose fiction, Robinson's poems carefully explore human action and motivation with similar care and exactitude. Though his style was relatively austere, he was unwilling to abandon the traditional rhyme and meter that defined poetry for so many. Asked if he ever wrote free verse, which seemed more natural than metered verse to some readers, Robinson pointedly replied, "No, I write badly enough as it is." His approach was clearly artful, self-consciously poetic, though his view of the world was never idealized. In fact, Robinson frequently made fun of idealists like his own Miniver Cheevy. Robinson's work shares the Naturalist obsession with determinism. Many of his characters are trapped in unhappy lives by circumstances beyond their control or events that happened long ago.

That consummate artist Henry James was not a popular writer at the turn of the century. It would take Modernists like Pound and Eliot and various scholars to resurrect his reputation. Yet James the critic fully understood the styles of the times, referring to Zola's "triumphant vulgarity of practice." Perhaps what James wrote of Zola's contemporary, Guy de Maupassant, resembles more the Realism we find in a poet like Robinson:

> His eye *selects* unerringly, unscrupulously, almost impudently—catches the particular thing in which the character of the object or the scene resides, and, by expressing it with the artful brevity of a master, leaves a convincing, original picture.

James refers to Maupassant's clarity of impression, and novelists Joseph Conrad and Ford Madox Ford would soon develop a theory of literary Impressionism. But Robinson's terms were more likely to be reserved and abstract than those of such writers. It is primarily his stance toward life that we would call realistic.

A more narrowly Naturalistic approach in poetry was that of Edgar Lee Masters, whose *Spoon River Anthology* appeared in 1915. Like Robinson he was interested in character, and both poets followed the example of Thomas Hardy in creating their own fictional communities, which fed their writing. But Masters populated his book with people whose lives were already over, and as a result his authorial determinism trapped them in a realm beyond choice. The destinies of his characters were shaped not by themselves but by their narrow social environment. Masters also stepped further away from obvious artifice by writing in plain free verse. He was removing signs of artifice in order to appear more the recorder or naturalist of reality.

Naturalist fiction almost inevitably explored political issues, especially the harsh social conditions that fostered individual crime and brutality. Although Markham's "The Man with the Hoe" presented a universalized worker in a seemingly timeless landscape, the poem implicitly addressed contemporary labor issues. Many of the leading women poets of the era were also overtly concerned with political and social reform. Charlotte Perkins Gilman and Sara Cleghorn both brilliantly satirized political corruption, social hypocrisy, and class prejudice. Meanwhile James Weldon Johnson and Paul Laurence Dunbar not only celebrated African American folkloric traditions but also wrote powerful indictments of fascism.

In prose, Stephen Crane was one of the major American Naturalists. His strange and idiosyncratic poems reflect that same philosophic stance, though in different ways. His imagery is often surreal or overtly symbolic, but his vision of life seems Naturalistic in its fatalism and violence. Edwin Markham might be said to idealize the man with the hoe, making him a symbol of social change, but he also recognizes how this crude and brutal peasant had been shaped by political and economic forces beyond his control. Charlotte Perkins Gilman, especially in her fiction, displayed an interest in psychological allegory. James Weldon Johnson and Paul Laurence Dunbar were concerned with conveying African American experience to an audience both white and black, while Trumbull Stickney was a Harvard classicist, perhaps just discovering a fine lyrical sensibility and psychological realism when he died suddenly at the age of thirty.

Robert Frost, on the other hand, took on some of the folksy subject matter that James Whitcomb Riley had popularized for an earlier generation, but squeezed the sentimentality out of it. Frost deepened Robinson's realistic technique and perfected the Americanization of diction, meter, and rhyme. Like Robinson's, his dark vision was leavened with mordant humor. Like Robinson, he was a regional writer—known as a New Englander, though he spent his first eleven years in California. Steeped in the pastoral tradition of Latin poetry, Frost made it conform to a toughness in his own spirit that was suited to the modern age. Together, Robinson and Frost were the giants of Realism in American poetry.

There are two deliberate eccentricities in the selection of poets that follows. First, we begin with Stephen Crane even though other poets are represented in chronological order. This is because Crane's poetry is so suggestive of major trends in twentieth-century American literature. In its violence, its lack of sentimentality in scene and diction, and its pioneering use of free verse, Crane's poetry prefigures much that would follow it. Second, we include in this section only two poets who were involved as combatants in World War I—Alan Seeger and John Allan Wyeth, Jr. This does not mean that no other American poets served in some capacity during that war. On the contrary, E. E. Cummings, John Crowe Ransom, John Peale

Bishop, and Archibald MacLeish were all involved, not to mention novelists like Hemingway and Dos Passos. In British poetry there was a vast literature arising out of World War I, which includes major figures like Wilfred Owen, Robert Graves, and Edward Thomas. German, French, and Canadian poetry have similar traditions, but there is nothing comparable in American literature.

The literary effects of World War I are visible mostly in poets associated with Modernism, and they generally approach it in broader cultural terms. Seeger's poetic stance, as well as his death in 1916, however, connects him to the earlier period. He was a combatant, indeed a casualty. His poem, "I Have a Rendezvous with Death," like Markham's "The Man with the Hoe," is very much a realistic public poem of a sort that became rarer after the war. Wyeth is a new discovery, an outstanding war poet who had been entirely overlooked by posterity. Although his work has a Modernist aspect, his Naturalist sensibility and formal metrics also link him to Robinson and Frost. His innovative work makes an illuminating contrast to Seeger's traditional stance and style.

These poets of Realism and Naturalism overlapped with the Imagists and High Modernists, of course, and figures like Frost lived to see several more generations of American poets come along. He would publish in magazines like *Poetry* (established in 1912), where his early work was reviewed by Ezra Pound. But the Modernists were altogether different in their approaches to versification, style, and subject matter. They also professed a different idea of the audience for poetry. While it may have taken Frost and Robinson many years to find a large audience for their work, they had always written for the intelligent general reader rather than a literary elite. What we cannot forget when we look at American poetry in the twentieth century is the richness of these conflicting designs, as well as others we have yet to mention.

◄ STEPHEN CRANE ►
(1871–1900)

Although Stephen Crane published all of his poetry by the final year of the nine-teenth century, his innovative and idiosyncratic verse marks an obvious beginning for twentieth-century American poetry. Its bitter irony, violent imagery, and philo-sophical pessimism stand in sharp contrast to the easy musicality, public tone, and religious optimism of the popular poetry of his era. Crane's influences are often evident. He emulates Ambrose Bierce's savage satire, Emily Dickinson's suggestive concision, and Walt Whitman's prophetic tone. But what strikes one most force-fully about Crane's verse is its precocious originality. His compressed and fantas-tic free-verse poems seem virtually unprecedented in American literature. Some of his poems read like brief existential parables, others like nightmarish visions. He was a new and revolutionary voice in American poetry.

Born in Newark, New Jersey, Stephen Crane was the fourteenth and final child of a Methodist minister who died when the author was still a boy. As a teenager Crane worked for an older brother's news agency and later left college to become a reporter in New York City. His first novel, *Maggie: A Girl of the Streets,* pri-vately published under a pseudonym in 1893, drew on his impoverished years in Manhattan's seedy Bowery district. While the novel did not sell well, it was no-ticed by some influential critics like William Dean Howells and Hamlin Garland who later welcomed Crane's classic novel of the Civil War, *The Red Badge of Courage,* when it appeared in 1895.

In 1895 Crane also published *The Black Riders,* the first of his two books of poems. The poems were printed in an unorthodox manner for the time—entirely in capital letters without individual titles or punctuation. This singular design height-ened the unusual style of Crane's unrhymed and unmetered verse. *The Black Riders* proved a controversial volume. Many reviewers heaped abuse on Crane's bleak or-phic poems, calling them "absurd" and "lunatic," "garbage" and "rot." Their odd visual appearance on the page also left them open to imitation and parody. Nearly one hundred parodies—not all unfriendly—appeared in the months after publica-tion. Meanwhile other critics ardently defended Crane's force and originality. The public debate over *The Black Riders,* combined with the phenomenal sales of *The Red Badge of Courage,* made the young Crane internationally famous.

Flushed with his new success, Crane continued his journalistic career, gaining ever greater notoriety while also discovering material he would use in his short stories. In January 1897, while aboard a ship running contraband arms to Cuban revolutionaries, Crane was shipwrecked off the coast of Florida. His newspaper account of his survival, published on the front page of the *New York Press,* was followed by his fictional version of the same event, entitled "The Open Boat." In the story, the correspondent's realization that "nature does not regard him as im-portant, and that she feels she would not maim the universe by disposing of him," both captures the antiromantic stance of Naturalism and looks ahead to the exis-tential despair and cosmic irony more commonly associated with writers of the next century. This Naturalist fatalism is also reflected almost everywhere in his poetry. Crane took his poetry seriously. In 1896 he claimed that "Personally, I like my little book of poems, *The Black Riders,* better than I do *The Red Badge of Courage.*" In the poems, Crane added, "I aim to give my ideas of life as a whole."

Crane's health, seriously weakened by his strenuous work as a reporter during the Greco-Turkish War of 1897 and the Spanish-American War of 1898, began to fail. Diagnosed as tubercular, he moved to England in 1899 with his common-law wife, Cora Taylor. (He had met Taylor in Jacksonville, Florida, where she was the madam of Hotel de Dream, a brothel.) In England the nearly penniless couple settled in Brede Place, a centuries-old unheated manor house outside Rye in rural Sussex. Henry James lived nearby, and he frequently visited the younger writer. Crane also enjoyed brief but intense literary friendships with Joseph Conrad, H. G. Wells, and Ford Madox Ford. Despite his poor health, Crane wrote furiously to meet expenses. In England he also published his second and last volume of verse, *War Is Kind* (1899). Ravaged by tuberculosis and malaria, he died in a German sanitarium at the age of twenty-eight.

With the possible exceptions of John Keats and Arthur Rimbaud, no literary career has been so brief and yet so influential as that of Stephen Crane. His novels and short stories rank as classics of American Naturalism. As an experimental poet, he pioneered free verse and plainspoken idiom. If Crane's influence on subsequent American poetry was limited, that was largely a matter of timing. His poems were initially published too early to be part of the Modernist movement, and they were republished too late (in 1930) for their novelty to be appreciated. Techniques that were radically innovative at the end of the nineteenth century had become common practice in the twentieth. Consequently, Crane's poetry has occupied an uncertain place in the American canon. Since his poems do not fit easily into the established major trends of modern American poetry, many anthologists omit them entirely or reprint minimal selections.

Perhaps Crane's sheer originality has made his poetic oeuvre problematic. His work displays exceptional strength, but in some ways remains the poetry of a young man who did not realize the full possibilities of his idiom. "His inventions, though tersely and concretely phrased," remarked literary historian David Perkins, "are without density or manifold interaction in the phrasing; they arrest attention but do not hold it."

Others disagree with critics who denigrate Crane's poetry. John Berryman, who wrote a critical biography of Crane, called him "the important American poet between Walt Whitman and Emily Dickinson on one side and his tardy developing contemporaries Edwin Arlington Robinson and Robert Frost with Ezra Pound on the other." Berryman saw Crane not as an experimentalist but as a primitive visionary whose poetry "has the inimitable sincerity of a frightened savage anxious to learn what his dream means."

These two views of Crane's poetry will never be reconciled. Critics who prize dense verbal texture will always be troubled by Crane's simplicity and directness, but these same attributes will appeal to those who respond to his imagistic and mythic power. More than a century after its publication, Crane's poetry continues to impress readers with its imaginative force and epigrammatic concision. His two books may only suggest his ultimate potential as a poet, but they remain vivid and incisive.

◄━━━►

Black riders came from the sea

Black riders came from the sea.
There was clang and clang of spear and shield,
And clash and clash of hoof and heel,
Wild shouts and the wave of hair
In the rush upon the wind: 5
Thus the ride of sin.

1895

In the desert

In the desert
I saw a creature, naked, bestial,
Who, squatting upon the ground,
Held his heart in his hands,
And ate of it.   5
I said, "Is it good, friend?"
"It is bitter—bitter," he answered;
"But I like it
"Because it is bitter,
"And because it is my heart."   10

1895

I stood upon a high place

I stood upon a high place,
And saw, below, many devils
Running, leaping,
And carousing in sin.
One looked up, grinning,   5
And said, "Comrade! Brother!"

1895

I saw a man pursuing the horizon

I saw a man pursuing the horizon;
Round and round they sped.
I was disturbed at this;
I accosted the man.
"It is futile," I said,   5
"You can never ———"
"You lie," he cried,
And ran on.

1895

I met a seer

I met a seer.
He held in his hands
The book of wisdom.
"Sir," I addressed him,
"Let me read." 5
"Child———" he began.
"Sir," I said,
"Think not that I am a child,
"For already I know much
"Of that which you hold. 10
"Aye, much."

He smiled.
Then he opened the book
And held it before me.—
Strange that I should have grown so suddenly blind. 15

1895

On the horizon the peaks assembled

On the horizon the peaks assembled;
And as I looked,
The march of the mountains began.
As they marched, they sang,
"Aye! We come! We come!" 5

1895

I walked in a desert

I walked in a desert.
And I cried,
"Ah, God, take me from this place!"
A voice said, "It is no desert."
I cried, "Well, but——— 5
"The sand, the heat, the vacant horizon."
A voice said, "It is no desert."

1895

A man feared that he might find an assassin

A man feared that he might find an assassin;
Another that he might find a victim.
One was more wise than the other.

1895

Do not weep, maiden, for war is kind

Do not weep, maiden, for war is kind.
Because your lover threw wild hands toward the sky
And the affrighted steed ran on alone,
Do not weep.
War is kind.   5

    Hoarse, booming drums of the regiment
    Little souls who thirst for fight,
    These men were born to drill and die
    The unexplained glory flies above them
    Great is the battle-god, great, and his kingdom———   10
    A field where a thousand corpses lie.

Do not weep, babe, for war is kind.
Because your father tumbled in the yellow trenches,
Raged at his breast, gulped and died,
Do not weep.   15
War is kind.

    Swift, blazing flag of the regiment
    Eagle with crest of red and gold,
    These men were born to drill and die
    Point for them the virtue of slaughter   20
    Make plain to them the excellence of killing
    And a field where a thousand corpses lie.

Mother whose heart hung humble as a button
On the bright splendid shroud of your son,
Do not weep.   25
War is kind.

1899

The wayfarer

    The wayfarer
    Perceiving the pathway to truth
    Was struck with astonishment.
    It was thickly grown with weeds.
    "Ha," he said,   5
    "I see that none has passed here
    "In a long time."
    Later he saw that each weed
    Was a singular knife.
    "Well," he mumbled at last,   10
    "Doubtless there are other roads."

1899

A man said to the universe

A man said to the universe:
"Sir, I exist!"
"However," replied the universe,
"The fact has not created in me
"A sense of obligation."   5

1899

My Cross!¹

Your cross?
The real cross
Is made of pounds,
Dollars or francs.
Here I bear my palms for the silly nails   5
To teach the lack
—The great pain of lack—
Of coin.

[1899] 1957

A man adrift on a slim spar

A man adrift on a slim spar
A horizon smaller than the rim of a bottle
Tented waves rearing lashy dark points
The near whine of froth in circles.
                                        God is cold.   5

The incessant raise and swing of the sea
And growl after growl of crest
The sinkings, green, seething, endless
The upheaval half-completed.
                                        God is cold.   10

The seas are in the hollow of The Hand;
Oceans may be turned to a spray
Raining down through the stars
Because of a gesture of pity toward a babe.
Oceans may become grey ashes,   15
Die with a long moan and a roar
Amid the tumult of the fishes
And the cries of the ships,
Because The Hand beckons the mice.

A horizon smaller than a doomed assassin's cap,   20
Inky, surging tumults

1. The cross in Crane's poem is both the Christian symbol and a reference to William Jennings Bryan's celebrated speech at the 1896 Democratic convention denouncing the U.S. Treasury's gold standard. "You shall not crucify mankind," he said, "upon a cross of gold."

A reeling, drunken sky and no sky
A pale hand sliding from a polished spar.
                              God is cold.

The puff of a coat imprisoning air.   25
A face kissing the water-death
A weary slow sway of a lost hand
And the sea, the moving sea, the sea.

                              God is cold.

                                        [1899] 1929

❖◄ EDWIN MARKHAM ►◦
(1852–1940)

Edwin Markham was born in Oregon City in the Oregon Territory. His pioneer parents had already separated by the time of his birth, and his mother soon took the three youngest of her six children to an isolated California ranch near Sacramento. Markham was raised in the strict Disciples of Christ sect, which took a dim view of literature and the other arts. His domineering and miserly mother demanded that he quit school to work at fifteen, which prompted the young poet to run away from home for two months until she relented. He earned a teacher's certificate at California College in Vacaville and California State Normal School (now California State University) in San Jose—always moving with his mother who lived with him until her death in 1891. He married for the first of three times in 1875 and taught at various northern California high schools while drifting in and out of several spiritualist sects and numerous love affairs. In 1878 he became a disciple of Thomas Lake Harris, who headed a religious cult in Santa Rosa called the Brotherhood of the New Life. Harris's credo of Christian socialism and mystical sexuality became Markham's lifelong philosophy. While supporting himself as a teacher, Markham gradually discovered himself as a writer and developed influential friendships with the Naturalist fiction writers then working in San Francisco, including Jack London, Frank Norris, and Ambrose Bierce. (Norris used Markham as the model for Presley, the protagonist of his classic 1901 novel *The Octopus*.)

The central moment in Markham's life came unexpectedly at a 1898 New Year's Eve party. The forty-six-year-old author read his new poem inspired by the French artist Jean-François Millet's painting *The Man with the Hoe*, which depicts a bent and brutish peasant in a field. Half naturalistic and half visionary, Markham's poem dramatized the oppression of labor and predicted the violent consequences of its liberation. The editor of the *San Francisco Examiner* heard Markham's recitation, and on January 18, 1899, he published the poem on the front page of William Randolph Hearst's influential newspaper. "The Man with the Hoe" created an immediate public sensation. It was eventually reprinted in over ten thousand journals. Its reception made Markham world-famous as "the bard of labor." It also reportedly made him rich. (He eventually made a quarter million dollars from the poem—an enormous sum by the standards of the time.) The poem, he later remarked, was "a chance stroke: I caught the eye and ear of the world."

Moving to New York, Markham became a noted literary figure. In 1910 he helped found the Poetry Society of America. Hailed as America's "greatest living poet," he traveled the country in a four-month celebrity speaking tour. In 1922 at the invitation of former President William Howard Taft, the tall bearded Markham read his poem, "Lincoln, the Man of the People" at the dedication of the Lincoln Memorial in Washington. In 1930 Staten Island declared his birthday a public holiday; schools were closed annually so that children could parade through the streets in Markham's honor. His eightieth birthday was celebrated at Carnegie Hall, and thirty-five nations sent representatives to salute the poetic patriarch of the international labor movement. Crippled by a stroke in 1938, he died two years later in Staten Island.

Markham's work reflects the end of the nineteenth century tradition of the poet as a public figure. His work also shows the close connection that once existed in America between poetry and journalism. Newspapers were the primary publishers of poetry, which still commanded a large readership eager to discover new talent. Markham directly addressed the political issues of his time—from the Russian Revolution to drug addiction—and mastered an elevated but accessible style. He also wrote important articles and books on political issues, most notably *Children in Bondage* (1914), which helped foster child-labor reform legislation.

Markham represented the new democratic spirit of the American West. At the height of Markham's fame, his friend Bierce, San Francisco's most mordant literary critic, speculated that "The Man with the Hoe" would eventually kill him as a poet. Bierce's warning proved sadly true. Markham never developed into a major poet, but his signature poem still ranks as the high point of American Naturalism in verse.

The Man with the Hoe

Written after seeing Millet's World-Famous Painting[1]

> God made man in His own image,
> in the image of God made He him.
> —*Genesis*

Bowed by the weight of centuries he leans
Upon his hoe and gazes on the ground,
The emptiness of ages in his face,
And on his back the burden of the world.
Who made him dead to rapture and despair,   5
A thing that grieves not and that never hopes,
Stolid and stunned, a brother to the ox?
Who loosened and let down this brutal jaw?
Whose was the hand that slanted back this brow?
Whose breath blew out the light within this brain?   10

---

1. *The Man with the Hoe* (1800), a painting by Jean François Millet (1814–1875), a French painter known for peasant subjects.

Is this the Thing the Lord God made and gave
To have dominion over sea and land;
To trace the stars and search the heavens for power;
To feel the passion of Eternity?
Is this the Dream He dreamed who shaped the suns   15
And pillared the blue firmament with light?
Down all the stretch of Hell to its last gulf
There is no shape more terrible than this—
More tongued with censure of the world's blind greed—
More filled with signs and portents for the soul—   20
More fraught with menace to the universe.

What gulfs between him and the seraphim!
Slave of the wheel of labor, what to him
Are Plato and the swing of Pleiades?
What the long reaches of the peaks of song,   25
The rift of dawn, the reddening of the rose?
Through this dread shape the suffering ages look;
Time's tragedy is in that aching stoop;
Through this dread shape humanity betrayed,
Plundered, profaned and disinherited,   30
Cries protest to the Judges of the World,
A protest that is also prophecy.

O masters, lords and rulers in all lands,
Is this the handiwork you give to God,
This monstrous thing distorted and soul-quenched?   35
How will you ever straighten up this shape;
Touch it again with immortality;
Give back the upward looking and the light;
Rebuild in it the music and the dream;
Make right the immemorial infamies,   40
Perfidious wrongs, immedicable woes?

O masters, lords and rulers in all lands,
How will the Future reckon with this Man?
How answer his brute question in that hour
When whirlwinds of rebellion shake the world?   45
How will it be with kingdoms and with kings—
With those who shaped him to the thing he is—
When this dumb Terror shall reply to God,
After the silence of the centuries?

                                                            1899

Outwitted

He drew a circle that shut me out—
Heretic, rebel, a thing to flout.
But Love and I had the wit to win:
We drew a circle that took him in!

                                                            1914

CHARLOTTE PERKINS GILMAN
(1860–1935)

Charlotte Perkins Gilman was born in Hartford, Connecticut. Her father was the writer Frederick Beecher Perkins (a nephew of reformer-novelist Harriet Beecher Stowe, the author of *Uncle Tom's Cabin,* and abolitionist minister Henry Ward Beecher), but he abandoned his family shortly after his daughter's birth. Raised in meager surroundings, the young Gilman adopted her intellectual Beecher aunts as role models.

As her mother moved from one relation to another, Gilman's early education was neglected, and at fifteen she had had only four years of formal schooling. Nevertheless, in 1878 she entered the Rhode Island School of Design to study commercial art. In 1884 she married Charles Walter Stetson, an artist. After the birth of their daughter Katherine in 1885, she experienced severe depression. The rest cure her doctor prescribed became the basis of her famous story, "The Yellow Wallpaper," which powerfully combined elements of Gothic fiction with a subversive feminist perspective.

In 1888 she left Stetson and moved with her daughter to Pasadena, California; her first marriage eventually ended in an amicable divorce.

Gilman now began a literary career in earnest. A celebrated essayist and public speaker, Gilman became an important early figure in American feminism. In 1891 she moved to Oakland, California, to become more closely involved with the reform movements emerging in the Bay Area, especially the Nationalist Party, a xenophobic socialist group. She helped organize the California Women's Congress in 1894 and 1895. Her constant travel, however, made it difficult to care for her daughter, and in 1894 she reluctantly relinquished custody of Katherine to Stetson. Her study *Women and Economics* (1898) stressed the importance of both sexes having a place in the working world. Her feminist-utopian novel, *Herland* (1915), described a thriving nation of women without men. In 1900 Gilman was married a second time—more happily—to her cousin George Houghton Gilman. After his sudden death in 1934, Gilman discovered she had inoperable breast cancer. After finishing her autobiography, she killed herself with chloroform in Pasadena.

Although Gilman's work had been praised by influential critics like William Dean Howells, her writing had already fallen into obscurity by the time of her death. By mid-century, her critical reputation was so marginal that her name did not even appear in most literary reference works. In 1973, however, a new edition of "The Yellow Wallpaper" appeared with an afterword by Elaine Hedges that proclaimed Gilman's tale a feminist masterpiece—an assertion subsequent critics have endorsed.

Gilman is now remembered for her short stories, but in her own lifetime she was better known for poetry than fiction. Her first book, *In This Our World* (1893), was a collection of verse; she eventually published over five hundred poems. Her verse usually had a strong didactic tone, and she frequently wrote on political subjects like women's suffrage, world peace, labor reform, and even meat-packing safety. Gilman's best poetry, however, was satiric. Her keen eye for social hypocrisy and sharp sense of humor enlivened her often didactic subjects. Like Edwin Markham, Gilman represents an older tradition of public and political poetry that would slowly disappear as the twentieth century progressed.

An Obstacle

I was climbing up a mountain path
  With many things to do,
Important business of my own,
  And other people's too,
When I ran against a Prejudice   5
  That quite cut off the view.

My work was such as could not wait,
  My path quite clearly showed,
My strength and time were limited,
  I carried quite a load;   10
And there that hulking Prejudice
  Sat all across the road.

I spoke to him politely,
  For he was huge and high,
And begged that he would move a bit   15
  And let me travel by.
He smiled, but as for moving!—
  He didn't even try.

And when I reasoned quietly
  With that colossal mule: 20
My time was short—no other path—
  The mountain winds were cool.
I argued like a Solomon;
  He sat there like a fool.

Then I flew into a passion,   25
  I danced and howled and swore.
I pelted and belabored him
  Till I was stiff and sore;
He got as mad as I did—
  But he sat there as before.   30

And then I begged him on my knees;
  I might be kneeling still
If so I hoped to move that man
  Of obdurate ill-will—
As well invite the monument   35
  To vacate Bunker Hill.

So I sat before him helpless,
  In an ecstasy of woe—
The mountain mists were rising fast,
  The Sun was sinking slow—   40
When a sudden inspiration came,
  As sudden winds do blow.

I took my hat, I took my stick,
  My load I settled fair,

I approached that awful incubus 45
    With an absent-minded air—
And I walked directly through him,
    As if he wasn't there.

1893

Whatever Is

Whatever is we only know
As in our minds we find it so;
    No staring fact is half so clear
    As one dim, preconceived idea—
No matter how the fact may glow. 5

Vainly may Truth her trumpet blow
To stir our minds; like heavy dough
    They stick to what they think—won't hear
    Whatever is.

Our ancient myths in solid row 10
Stand up—we simply have to go
    And choke each fiction old and dear
    Before the modest facts appear;
Then we may grasp, reluctant, slow,
    Whatever is. 15

1903

◆►◄ EDGAR LEE MASTERS ►◄◆
(1868–1950)

Masters's vision of small-town America, often compared to those of Sherwood Anderson, Sinclair Lewis, and Thornton Wilder, had its roots in his own childhood. Born in Garnett, Kansas, he grew up in two Illinois towns, Petersburg and Lewistown, spending much of his time on his grandparents' farm—his "nurturing spot of earth." Though he would publish two dozen volumes of poetry, biographies of Mark Twain, Walt Whitman, Vachel Lindsay, and Abraham Lincoln, in addition to novels, plays, and other works, Masters's reputation rests solely on one book, *Spoon River Anthology* (1915), which is very much founded upon his childhood. "Like a hawk that circles around the old tree," he once wrote, "I have circled over the old haunts. . . ."

    Masters had a patchwork education, with only one year of college, but was fortunate in that certain teachers and acquaintances made their libraries available to him. He had the autodidact's fascination with learning, and after a few years of working as a printer he succumbed to family pressure and went to work in his father's law firm. In 1891 he was admitted to the bar in Illinois, and by 1898 he was a successful Chicago attorney. That year he published his first collection of poems and married Helen Jenkins, with whom he would have three children. Two more collections followed that continued to show the influence of such figures as Whitman and Swinburne.

By 1912, when Theodore Dreiser published *The Financier,* Masters had absorbed the influence of naturalistic fiction and had begun to read the contemporary free verse of Carl Sandburg and others in *Poetry* magazine. He had also, a few years earlier, been introduced to J. W. Mackail's *Select Epigrams from the Greek Anthology,* a book that profoundly influenced many modern poets. It was given to Masters by William Morris Reedy, whose magazine *Reedy's Mirror,* published the Spoon River poems in serialization.

In these poems, Masters thought back on the lives of people he had known or had heard about in childhood and used them to populate his fictional cemetery. The poems are free-verse epitaphs, but they are also small bits of dramatic or narrative speech. Masters once wrote that the Spoon River poems attempt to convey "something in the human heart which gnaws without ceasing, and affects all the acts of the person. . . ." In a sense, this vision is the product of his materialism and homegrown Hellenism, his sense of life as endurance and of the individual as part of a larger and unknowable essence. He also later acknowledged the influence of Spinoza's philosophy, where metaphysics is offered in an imaginative and unconventional manner, and asserted that he was not quite the atheist he appeared to be: "I see just one force in the world, in the universe, and everything from chemical activity to spiritual aspiration is a manifestation of it."

Spoon River Anthology was a bestseller and firmly established Masters's reputation as both a serious and a popular poet. In the early 1920s he abandoned his law practice and moved to New York, hoping to live by his pen. By divorcing his wife in 1923, however, he put himself in financial straits, and when he married the independent-minded, twenty-six-year-old Ellen Coyne in 1926, his life soon sank into constant domestic turmoil. His last twenty-five years were productive, but Masters could never match the critical and financial success of his one great book and in his disappointment he often turned to other women to buoy his spirits. These years of struggle are recalled in a brilliant book, *Last Stands,* by Hilary Masters, the son born to Ellen Coyne when the poet was sixty years old.

Nevertheless, *Spoon River Anthology,* a wholly American book published at a time when the European formalism of Eliot and Pound was in its ascendancy, is much more than a period piece. Its characters remain vital and distinctive, and its vision of loss and endurance, conveyed by the ghostly voices of the dead, continues to move readers.

FROM Spoon River Anthology

The Hill

Where are Elmer, Herman, Bert, Tom and Charley,
The weak of will, the strong of arm, the clown, the
*   boozer, the fighter?*
All, all, are sleeping on the hill.

One passed in a fever,
One was burned in a mine,
One was killed in a brawl,
One died in a jail,

5

One fell from a bridge toiling for children and wife—
All, all are sleeping, sleeping, sleeping on the hill.

Where are Ella, Kate, Mag, Lizzie and Edith,   10
The tender heart, the simple soul, the loud, the proud,
   the happy one?—
All, all, are sleeping on the hill.

One died in a shameful child-birth,
One of a thwarted love,
One at the hands of a brute in a brothel,   15
One of a broken pride, in the search for heart's desire,
One after life in far-away London and Paris
Was brought to her little space by Ella and Kate and
   Mag—
All, all are sleeping, sleeping, sleeping on the hill.

Where are Uncle Isaac and Aunt Emily,   20
And old Towny Kincaid and Sevigne Houghton,
And Major Walker who had talked
With venerable men of the revolution?—
All, all, are sleeping on the hill.

They brought them dead sons from the war,   25
And daughters whom life had crushed,
And their children fatherless, crying—
All, all are sleeping, sleeping, sleeping on the hill.

Where is Old Fiddler Jones
Who played with life all his ninety years,   30
Braving the sleet with bared breast,
Drinking, rioting, thinking neither of wife nor kin,
Nor gold, nor love, nor heaven?
Lo! He babbles of the fish-frys of long ago,
Of the horse-races of long ago at Clary's Grove,   35
Of what Abe Lincoln said
One time at Springfield.

                                            1915

Anne Rutledge[1]

Out of me unworthy and unknown
The vibrations of deathless music;
"With malice toward none, with charity for all."[2]
Out of me the forgiveness of millions toward millions,

1. The real Anne Rutledge was said to be beloved of the young Abraham Lincoln. Dead at nineteen, she was buried in the Oakland Cemetery in Petersburg, Illinois.
2. Quoted from Lincoln's second Inaugural Address, March 4, 1865, promising liberal terms to the defeated South; Lincoln was assassinated one month later.

And the beneficent face of a nation   5
Shining with justice and truth.
I am Anne Rutledge who sleep beneath these weeds,
Beloved in life of Abraham Lincoln,
Wedded to him, not through union,
But through separation.   10
Bloom forever, O Republic,
From the dust of my bosom!

                                                                1915

Editor Whedon

To be able to see every side of every question;
To be on every side, to be everything, to be nothing long;
To pervert truth, to ride it for a purpose,
To use great feelings and passions of the human family
For base designs, for cunning ends,   5
To wear a mask like the Greek actors—
Your eight-page paper—behind which you huddle,
Bawling through the megaphone of a big type:
"This is I, the giant."
Thereby also living the life of a sneak-thief,   10
Poisoned with the anonymous words
Of your clandestine soul.
To scratch dirt over scandal for money,
And exhume it to the winds for revenge,
Or to sell papers,   15
Crushing reputations, or bodies, if need be,
To win at any cost, save your own life.
To glory in demoniac power, ditching civilization,
As a paranoiac boy puts a log on the track
And derails the express train.   20

                                                                1915

Knowlt Hoheimer[3]

I was the first fruits of the battle of Missionary Ridge.
When I felt the bullet enter my heart
I wished I had staid at home and gone to jail
For stealing the hogs of Curl Trenary,
Instead of running away and joining the army.   5
Rather a thousand times the county jail
Than to lie under this marble figure with wings,
And this granite pedestal
Bearing the words, *"Pro Patria."*[4]
What do they mean, anyway?   10

                                                                1915

3. In November 1863, the Union Army attacked the Confederates on Missionary Ridge, near Chattanooga, Tennessee; it was a costly but decisive victory for the North.
4. Latin, "For Country" (compare Horace, *Odes,* 3.2).

Lucinda Matlock[5]

I went to the dances at Chandlerville,
And played snap-out at Winchester.
One time we changed partners,
Driving home in the moonlight of middle June,
And then I found Davis.   5
We were married and lived together for seventy years,
Enjoying, working, raising the twelve children,
Eight of whom we lost
Ere I had reached the age of sixty.
I spun, I wove, I kept the house, I nursed the sick,   10
I made the garden, and for holiday
Rambled over the fields where sang the larks,
And by Spoon River gathering many a shell,
And many a flower and medicinal weed—
Shouting to the wooded hills, singing to the green valleys. 15
At ninety-six I had lived enough, that is all,
And passed to a sweet repose.
What is this I hear of sorrow and weariness,
Anger, discontent and drooping hopes?
Degenerate sons and daughters,   20
Life is too strong for you—
It takes life to love Life.

1915

Petit, the Poet

Seeds in a dry pod, tick, tick, tick,
Tick, tick, tick, like mites in a quarrel—
Faint iambics that the full breeze wakens—
But the pine tree makes a symphony thereof.
Triolets, villanelles, rondels, rondeaus,   5
Ballades by the score with the same old thought:
The snows and the roses of yesterday are vanished;
And what is love but a rose that fades?
Life all around me here in the village:
Tragedy, comedy, valor and truth,   10
Courage, constancy, heroism, failure—
All in the loom, and oh what patterns!
Woodlands, meadows, streams and rivers—
Blind to all of it all my life long.
Triolets, villanelles, rondels, rondeaus,   15
Seeds in a dry pod, tick, tick, tick,
Tick, tick, tick, what little iambics,
While Homer and Whitman roared in the pines?

1915

---

5. This poem was based on the life of Masters's paternal grandmother.

━━━━●━◄ EDWIN ARLINGTON ROBINSON ►━●━━━━
(1869–1935)

When Edwin Arlington Robinson was born in the small village of Head Tide, Maine, his father had only recently prospered through investments in timber. Before their third son was a year old, his parents moved the family to a larger community, Gardiner—the "Tilbury Town" of Robinson's poems. Edwin, nicknamed "Win" by family, disliked his name and perceived that his older brothers, Dean and Herman, were nearer to his parents' affections. He always felt like an outsider, remarking years later that "I could never have done *anything* but write poetry." Dean was the only son to finish college, but afterwards, while practicing as a doctor, he became hopelessly addicted to morphine and moved back home, where he remained dependent on the family for the rest of his life. Herman was for a time a successful banker. He married Emma Shepherd, with whom Win had also been in love. This romantic disappointment proved one of the central events in the poet's life. Robinson would never marry.

From an early age Robinson knew he wanted to be a poet. Though his family did not particularly encourage this ambition, he was never forced by them to find a career. His strongest early support in these endeavors came when, at fifteen, he met Dr. Alanson Tucker Schumann, who had set aside his medical practice to follow poetry and who quickly recognized Win's great talent. Dean's addiction and Herman's marriage to Emma were only two of the traumatic events in Robinson's youth. An ear injury, sustained at the age of twelve when a teacher struck him (apparently for daydreaming), flared up, forcing Robinson to see a specialist's care in Boston. The visit turned out to be fortunate; with family help, he used this opportunity to study for two years at Harvard. But his father's sudden death and the resulting financial difficulties, worsened by Herman's own heavy drinking, ended that idyllic period in Robinson's life.

Robinson lived mostly at home until he was nearly thirty, working about the house and reading deeply both fiction and poetry. He also cared for members of his family. His mother died in 1896, shortly before he received copies of *The Torrent and the Night Before,* his first, privately printed collection of poems. The following year, Robinson published a revised version under the title *The Children of the Night.* These early, self-published volumes contained some of the best poems ever written by an American, including "Luke Havergal," "Richard Cory," and "Reuben Bright." That year, after quarreling with Herman, Robinson left Gardiner, eventually settling in New York City. These were difficult times. Perhaps alluding to another early poem, "George Crabbe," Robinson would later say, "Nobody devoted as much as an inch to me. I did not exist." Dean died of a morphine overdose, Herman ruined his marriage and career through his alcoholism, and Edwin often lived hand-to-mouth, working odd jobs and drinking heavily himself.

Captain Craig (1902) was Robinson's first book with a commercial publisher (though it was partially financed by friends). Despite good reviews, the volume did little to further Robinson's reputation or relieve his financial distress. The following year he took a job in the bowels of the New York subway, then being built, working long days as a time checker for twenty cents an hour. Though he bore his deprivations with surprisingly good humor, it must have looked as though he was headed for disaster until he was rescued from poverty in a remarkable and unprecedented way. President Theodore Roosevelt, who had been given *The Children of the Night* by one of his sons, invited Robinson to the White House for a lengthy conversation. Shocked by the poet's poverty and obscurity, Roosevelt made a point of helping him. The President not only published a famous review of Robinson's long out-of-print book, but also secured him a job at the New York Custom House—a sinecure that allowed the poet time to write. His only job responsibility was to come to the Custom House each morning and leave a newspaper on his chair to prove he had been there. No other American President has ever been so directly responsible for the well-being of American poetry.

When Taft was elected in 1908, Robinson was informed that he would have to do real work at the Custom House, and he resigned in frustration. That same year, Herman died. Again Robinson tried to make a living by his pen, and again he fell into financial difficulty. He was forty-one when he published *The Town Down the River* (1910), still surviving partly on loans from loyal friends. In 1911 he began spending his summers at the MacDowell Colony in New Hampshire; this would become an annual ritual until the year before his death. When his friend Hays Gardiner died in 1913, leaving him $4,000, Robinson resolved to change his life. He stopped drinking and took up alcohol again only in protest when Prohibition became law. He was also writing regularly, buoyed by the MacDowell visits and an ever wider circle of literary friends. In 1921 his *Collected Poems* received the first of the three Pulitzer Prizes he would win. Though much of his best work was now behind him, Robinson continued to publish long poems, including a bestselling trilogy based on Arthurian legend—*Merlin* (1917), *Lancelot* (1920), and *Tristram* (1923). In January 1935 he was diagnosed with inoperable cancer. That April in his hospital bed Robinson completed the corrections to his last book, *King Jasper* (1935), a few hours before he sank into a final coma.

A yearning for the legendary past does occur in some of Robinson's poems, though this longing is treated tragicomically in lyrics like "Miniver Cheevy" and briefer narratives like "Isaac and Archibald." Robinson's poetry is often pessimistic, concerned as it is with death, suicide, prostitution, addiction, and assorted other problems, yet one can also find in it surprising comedy. In "Mr. Flood's Party" one finds a drunken sentimentalist who, like Cheevy, ebbs and floods quite a bit in his thinking, but here Robinson exactly captures the sad hilarity of a drunk's conversation with himself.

Although he failed as a fiction writer, Robinson was a great creator of characters in verse, often catching them at a climactic moment of their lives. In "Reuben Bright," for example, he presents the definitive gesture of a man who has no language sufficient for his grief. Robert Frost understood this aspect of Robinson's poetry, noting in his great introduction to Robinson's *King Jasper* a distinction "between griefs and grievances" and arguing that Robinson was profound because he understood this distinction. "His theme was unhappiness itself," Frost wrote, "but his still was as happy as it was playful."

The skill Frost refers to is not only the formal mastery we see in a villanelle like "The House on the Hill" or in Robinson's many sonnets. It also has to do with the modernization of diction. In his best poems, Robinson steers clear of the flowery artificiality of much poetry written in his lifetime and finds a plain American style capable of exploring a range of characters and ideas, both literary and extraliterary. Robinson and Frost were modern in their point of view without being merely despairing: "But for me," Frost wrote, "I don't like grievances. I find

I gently let them alone whenever published. What I like is griefs and I like them Robinsonianly profound."

Along with Thomas Hardy, Frost is perhaps the poet closest to Robinson in sensibility. They share a novelistic interest in the dark and often contradictory motivations of the human heart and a penetrating gift of psychological analysis that also links them to other writers of the era such as Theodore Dreiser, Jack London, and Stephen Crane. The vision in Robinson's poems is more tragic than pathetic, more resilient than carping. His influence upon later poets—not only Frost, but also Yvor Winters, James Wright, and many others—has been deep and continuous. Robinson is the first great modern American poet.

⊷◈⊶

The Clerks

I did not think that I should find them there
When I came back again; but there they stood,
As in the days they dreamed of when young blood
Was in their cheeks and women called them fair.
Be sure, they met me with an ancient air,—   5
And yes, there was a shop-worn brotherhood
About them; but the men were just as good,
And just as human as they ever were.

And you that ache so much to be sublime,
And you that feed yourselves with your descent,   10
What comes of all your visions and your fears?
Poets and kings are but the clerks of Time,
Tiering the same dull webs of discontent,
Clipping the same sad alnage[1] of the years.

1897

George Crabbe[2]

Give him the darkest inch your shelf allows,
Hide him in lonely garrets, if you will,—
But his hard, human pulse is throbbing still
With the sure strength that fearless truth endows.
In spite of all fine science disavows,   5
Of his plain excellence and stubborn skill
There yet remains what fashion cannot kill,
Though years have thinned the laurel from his brows.

---

1. An old word for a measure of cloth.
2. A British poet (1754–1832) best known for *The Village* (1783) and *The Borough* (1810), which portray small-town English life of his era in starkly realistic terms. Crabbe, who rejected both the neoclassical pastoralism and Romantic idealism of country life in favor of "fearless truth" (to use Robinson's phrase), became a standard of artistic integrity for the American poet.

Whether or not we read him, we can feel
From time to time the vigor of his name 10
Against us like a finger for the shame
And emptiness of what our souls reveal
In books that are as altars where we kneel
To consecrate the flicker, not the flame.

1897

Reuben Bright

Because he was a butcher and thereby
Did earn an honest living (and did right),
I would not have you think that Reuben Bright
Was any more a brute than you or I;
For when they told him that his wife must die, 5
He stared at them, and shook with grief and fright,
And cried like a great baby half that night,
And made the women cry to see him cry.

And after she was dead, and he had paid
The singers and the sexton and the rest, 10
He packed a lot of things that she had made
Most mournfully away in an old chest
Of hers, and put some chopped-up cedar boughs
In with them, and tore down the slaughter-house.

1897

How Annandale Went Out[3]

"They called it Annandale—and I was there
To flourish, to find words, and to attend:
Liar, physician, hypocrite, and friend,
I watched him; and the sight was not so fair
As one or two that I have seen elsewhere: 5
An apparatus not for me to mend—
A wreck, with hell between him and the end,
Remained of Annandale; and I was there.

"I knew the ruin as I knew the man;
So put the two together, if you can, 10
Remembering the worst you know of me.
Now view yourself as I was, on the spot—
With a slight kind of engine. Do you see?
Like this . . . You wouldn't hang me? I thought not."

1910

3. This poem, which seems deliberately obscure at first, describes the death of an inexplicably ruined man named Annandale. Robinson wrote two other poems. The first, "The Book of Annandale" (1902), shows a young man about to begin what seems like a happy marriage. The second, "Annandale Again" (1932) describes his devastating injury in an automobile crash—the incident that stands behind this poem from 1910.

Miniver Cheevy

Miniver Cheevy, child of scorn,
    Grew lean while he assailed the seasons;
He wept that he was ever born,
    And he had reasons.

Miniver loved the days of old   5
    When swords were bright and steeds were prancing;
The vision of a warrior bold
    Would set him dancing.

Miniver sighed for what was not,
    And dreamed, and rested from his labors;   10
He dreamed of Thebes and Camelot,
    And Priam's neighbors.[4]

Miniver mourned the ripe renown
    That made so many a name so fragrant;
He mourned Romance, now on the town,   15
    And Art, a vagrant.

Miniver loved the Medici,[5]
    Albeit he had never seen one;
He would have sinned incessantly
    Could he have been one.   20

Miniver cursed the commonplace
    And eyed a khaki suit with loathing;
He missed the medieval grace
    Of iron clothing.

Miniver scorned the gold he sought,   25
    But sore annoyed was he without it;
Miniver thought, and thought, and thought,
    And thought about it.

Miniver Cheevy, born too late,
    Scratched his head and kept on thinking;   30
Miniver coughed, and called it fate,
    And kept on drinking.

                                                           1910

The House on the Hill

They are all gone away,
    The House is shut and still,
There is nothing more to say.

---

4. Thebes: A city in ancient Greece and the setting of many famous Greek myths; Camelot: Legendary site of King Arthur's court; Priam: The last king of Troy, his "neighbors" would have included Helen of Troy, Aeneas, and other famous figures.
5. The Medici: The ruling family of Florence during the High Renaissance and renowned patrons of the arts.

Through broken walls and gray
   The winds blow bleak and shrill: 5
They are all gone away.

Nor is there one to-day
   To speak them good or ill:
There is nothing more to say.

Why is it then we stray   10
   Around the sunken sill?
They are all gone away,

And our poor fancy-play
   For them is wasted skill:
There is nothing more to say.   15

There is ruin and decay
   In the House on the Hill:
They are all gone away,
There is nothing more to say.

                            1897

Luke Havergal

Go to the western gate, Luke Havergal,
There where the vines cling crimson on the wall,
And in the twilight wait for what will come.
The leaves will whisper there of her, and some,
Like flying words, will strike you as they fall;   5
But go, and if you listen she will call.
Go to the western gate, Luke Havergal—
Luke Havergal.

No, there is not a dawn in eastern skies
To rift the fiery night that's in your eyes;   10
But there, where western glooms are gathering,
The dark will end the dark, if anything:
God slays Himself with every leaf that flies,
And hell is more than half of paradise.
No, there is not a dawn in eastern skies—   15
In eastern skies.

Out of a grave I come to tell you this,
Out of a grave I come to quench the kiss
That flames upon your forehead with a glow
That blinds you to the way that you must go.   20
Yes, there is yet one way to where she is,
Bitter, but one that faith may never miss.
Out of a grave I come to tell you this—
To tell you this.

There is the western gate, Luke Havergal,   25
There are the crimson leaves upon the wall.
Go, for the winds are tearing them away,—
Nor think to riddle the dead words they say,
Nor any more to feel them as they fall;
But go, and if you trust her she will call.   30
There is the western gate, Luke Havergal—
Luke Havergal.

                                                                    1897

Richard Cory

Whenever Richard Cory went down town,
We people on the pavement looked at him:
He was a gentleman from sole to crown,
Clean favored, and imperially slim.

And he was always quietly arrayed,   5
And he was always human when he talked;
But still he fluttered pulses when he said,
"Good-morning," and he glittered when he walked.

And he was rich—yes, richer than a king—
And admirably schooled in every grace: 10
In fine, we thought that he was everything
To make us wish that we were in his place.

So on we worked, and waited for the light,
And went without the meat, and cursed the bread;
And Richard Cory, one calm summer night,   15
Went home and put a bullet through his head.

                                                                    1897

Another Dark Lady[6]

Think not, because I wonder where you fled,
That I would lift a pin to see you there;
You may, for me, be prowling anywhere,
So long as you show not your little head:
No dark and evil story of the dead   5
Would leave you less pernicious or less fair—
Not even Lilith,[7] with her famous hair;
And Lilith was the devil, I have read.

I cannot hate you, for I loved you then.
The woods were golden then. There was a road   10

---

6. The first "dark lady" was the beloved but unfaithful woman in Shakespeare's sonnets.
7. The female demon who, according to Rabbinical lore, was supposed to have been Adam's first wife in Eden. In another story, King Solomon had Lilith's hair bound to diminish her sexual power.

Through beeches; and I said their smooth feet showed
Like yours. Truth must have heard me from afar,
For I shall never have to learn again
That yours are cloven as no beech's are.

1916

Bewick Finzer

Time was when his half million drew
    The breath of six per cent;
But soon the worm of what-was-not
    Fed hard on his content;
And something crumbled in his brain   5
    When his half million went.

Time passed, and filled along with his
    The place of many more;
Time came, and hardly one of us
    Had credence to restore,   10
From what appeared one day, the man
    Whom we had known before.

The broken voice, the withered neck,
    The coat worn out with care,
The cleanliness of indigence,   15
    The brilliance of despair,
The fond imponderable dreams
    Of affluence,—all were there.

Poor Finzer, with his dreams and schemes,
    Fares hard now in the race,   20
With heart and eye that have a task
    When he looks in the face
Of one who might so easily
    Have been in Finzer's place.

He comes unfailing for the loan   25
    We give and then forget;
He comes, and probably for years
    Will he be coming yet,—
Familiar as an old mistake,
    And futile as regret.   30

1916

Eros Turannos[8]

She fears him, and will always ask
    What fated her to choose him;

8. The title is Greek for "love the tyrant."

She meets in his engaging mask
   All reasons to refuse him;
But what she meets and what she fears
Are less than are the downward years,
Drawn slowly to the foamless weirs
   Of age, were she to lose him.

Between a blurred sagacity
   That once had power to sound him,
And Love, that will not let him be
   The Judas that she found him,
Her pride assuages her almost,
As if it were alone the cost.—
He sees that he will not be lost,
   And waits and looks around him.

A sense of ocean and old trees
   Envelops and allures him;
Tradition, touching all he sees,
   Beguiles and reassures him;
And all her doubts of what he says
Are dimmed with what she knows of days—
Till even prejudice delays
   And fades, and she secures him.

The falling leaf inaugurates
   The reign of her confusion;
The pounding wave reverberates
   The dirge of her illusion;
And home, where passion lived and died,
Becomes a place where she can hide,
While all the town and harbor side
   Vibrate with her seclusion.

We tell you, tapping on our brows,
   The story as it should be,—
As if the story of a house
   Were told, or ever could be;
We'll have no kindly veil between
Her visions and those we have seen,—
As if we guessed what hers have been,
   Or what they are or would be.

Meanwhile we do no harm; for they
   That with a god have striven,
Not hearing much of what we say,
   Take what the god has given;
Though like waves breaking it may be,
Or like a changed familiar tree,
Or like a stairway to the sea
   Where down the blind are driven.

1916

The Mill

The miller's wife had waited long,
   The tea was cold, the fire was dead;
And there might yet be nothing wrong
   In how he went and what he said:
"There are no millers any more,"   5
   Was all that she had heard him say;
And he had lingered at the door
   So long that it seemed yesterday.

Sick with fear that had no form
   She knew that she was there at last;   10
And in the mill there was a warm
   And mealy fragrance of the past.
What else there was would only seem
   To say again what he had meant;
And what was hanging from a beam   15
   Would not have heeded where she went.

And if she thought it followed her,
   She may have reasoned in the dark
That one way of the few there were
   Would hide her and would leave no mark: 20
Black water, smooth above the weir
   Like starry velvet in the night,
Though ruffled once, would soon appear
   The same as ever to the sight.

                                   1920

Mr. Flood's Party

Old Eben Flood, climbing alone one night
Over the hill between the town below
And the forsaken upland hermitage
That held as much as he should ever know
On earth again of home, paused warily.   5
The road was his with not a native near;
And Eben, having leisure, said aloud,
For no man else in Tilbury Town to hear:

"Well, Mr. Flood, we have the harvest moon
Again, and we may not have many more;   10
The bird is on the wing, the poet says,
And you and I have said it here before.
Drink to the bird." He raised up to the light
The jug that he had gone so far to fill,
And answered huskily: "Well, Mr. Flood,   15
Since you propose it, I believe I will."

Alone, as if enduring to the end
A valiant armor of scarred hopes outworn,

He stood there in the middle of the road
Like Roland's ghost[9] winding a silent horn.   20
Below him, in the town among the trees,
Where friends of other days had honored him,
A phantom salutation of the dead
Rang thinly till old Eben's eyes were dim.

Then, as a mother lays her sleeping child   25
Down tenderly, fearing it may awake,
He set the jug down slowly at his feet
With trembling care, knowing that most things break;
And only when assured that on firm earth
It stood, as the uncertain lives of men   30
Assuredly did not, he paced away,
And with his hand extended paused again:

"Well, Mr. Flood, we have not met like this
In a long time; and many a change has come
To both of us, I fear, since last it was   35
We had a drop together. Welcome home!"
Convivially returning with himself,
Again he raised the jug up to the light;
And with an acquiescent quaver said:
"Well, Mr. Flood, if you insist, I might.   40

"Only a very little, Mr. Flood—
For auld lang syne. No more, sir; that will do."
So, for the time, apparently it did,
And Eben evidently thought so too;
For soon amid the silver loneliness   45
Of night he lifted up his voice and sang,
Secure, with only two moons listening,
Until the whole harmonious landscape rang—

"For auld lang syne." The weary throat gave out,
The last word wavered, and the song was done.   50
He raised again the jug regretfully
And shook his head, and was again alone.
There was not much that was ahead of him,
And there was nothing in the town below—
Where strangers would have shut the many doors   55
That many friends had opened long ago.

                                                    1921

---

9. In the medieval French romance, *The Song of Roland,* the title character was one of Charlemagne's paladins or knights errant. Roland possessed an enchanted ivory horn that could be heard for hundreds of miles. In his last battle Roland refuses to blow the horn for help until the moment before his own death.

New England

Here where the wind is always north-north-east
And children learn to walk on frozen toes,
Wonder begets an envy of all those
Who boil elsewhere with such a lyric yeast
Of love that you will hear them at a feast   5
Where demons would appeal for some repose,
Still clamoring where the chalice overflows
And crying wildest who have drunk the least.

Passion is here a soilure of the wits,
We're told, and Love a cross for them to bear;   10
Joy shivers in the corner where she knits
And Conscience always has the rocking-chair,
Cheerful as when she tortured into fits
The first cat that was ever killed by Care.

1925

The Sheaves

Where long the shadows of the wind had rolled,
Green wheat was yielding to the change assigned;
And as by some vast magic undivined
The world was turning slowly into gold.
Like nothing that was ever bought or sold   5
It waited there, the body and the mind;
And with a mighty meaning of a kind
That tells the more the more it is not told.

So in a land where all days are not fair,
Fair days went on till on another day   10
A thousand golden sheaves were lying there,
Shining and still, but not for long to stay—
As if a thousand girls with golden hair
Might rise from where they slept and go away.

1925

◄ JAMES WELDON JOHNSON ►
(1871–1938)

In his introduction to *The Book of American Negro Poetry* (1922), James Weldon Johnson celebrates "this power of the Negro to suck up the national spirit from the soil and create something artistic and original, which, at the same time, possesses the note of universal appeal," and he credits the achievement to "a remarkable racial gift of adaptability; it is a transfusive quality." In his life and work, Johnson himself was remarkably adaptable, skilled in fusing a variety of styles in his poetry and successful in pursuing careers as a poet, novelist, autobiographer, journalist, songwriter, teacher, lawyer, diplomat, and leader of the National Association for the Advancement of Colored People (NAACP).

Born in Jacksonville, Florida, in 1871, Johnson grew up in a middle-class African American family and attended the Stanton school, one of the largest public schools in the state. At the age of sixteen, he matriculated at Atlanta University and, after graduating in 1894, returned to Stanton to serve as principal. While directing the school, he studied law and became the first African American to pass the Florida bar examination. He also started a newspaper, the *Daily American,* which served the Jacksonville African American community from 1895 to 1896. In 1897 Johnson began collaborating with his brother Rosamond, a graduate of the New England Conservatory of Music, and wrote a number of popular songs, including "Lift Ev'ry Voice and Sing," which became known as "the Negro National Anthem." After moving to New York in 1901, Johnson continued to write songs, many of which became hits popularized by touring Broadway musicals. Diplomatic appointments to serve as the U.S. consul to Venezuela (1906–1909) and to Nicaragua (1909–1912) gave him time to pursue literary endeavors. While in Central America he completed a novel, *Autobiography of an Ex-Colored Man,* which was published anonymously in 1912. Returning to the United States in 1913, Johnson again turned to journalism as a writer of editorials for *New York Age.* He also wrote poetry, which appeared in *Fifty Years and Other Poems* (1917). Beginning in 1916, as field secretary for the NAACP, Johnson became adept at political organizing: from 1920 to 1930, as general secretary, he refined the NAACP into a catalyst for legal action and public protest against racism.

Johnson's political commitments, however, did not diminish his literary energy. By the end of the 1920s he had become a leading figure of the Harlem Renaissance through his poetry, anthologies, and reviews, as well as his mentorship of younger writers. In a series of anthologies, *The Book of American Negro Poetry* (1922), *The Book of American Negro Spirituals* (1925), and *The Second Book of American Negro Spirituals* (1926), Johnson showcased the vitality of African American poetry, particularly its roots in music. His own poetry of this period, *God's Trombones: Seven Negro Sermons in Verse* (1927), pays homage to spirituals and adopts the colloquial language and rolling rhythms of African American preaching. These poems, which achieved great popularity at the time, also participate in the Modernist trend toward loosened form, for Johnson turns from the rhyme and meter and dialect poetry of his first collection to a supple vernacular speech that builds momentum through incremental repetitions and varied line lengths. *God's Trombones* fulfills the challenge Johnson proposes in his introduction to *The Book of American Negro Poetry:*

> What the colored poet in the United States needs to do is something like what Synge did for the Irish; he needs to find a form that will express the racial spirit by symbols from within rather than by symbols from without. . . . He needs a form that is freer and larger than dialect, but which will still hold the racial flavor; a form expressing the imagery, the idioms, the peculiar turns of thought, and the distinctive humor and pathos, too, of the Negro, but which will also be capable of voicing the deepest and highest human emotions and aspirations, and allow of the widest range of subjects and the widest scope of treatment.

In 1930 Johnson accepted a professorship at Fisk University, where he completed his autobiography, *Along This Way* (1933); a call for integration, *Negro Ameri-*

cans, What Now? (1934); and *Saint Peter Relates an Incident: Selected Poems*
(1935). He died in an automobile accident in June 1938.

O Black and Unknown Bards

O Black and unknown bards of long ago,
How came your lips to touch the sacred fire?
How, in your darkness, did you come to know
The power and beauty of the minstrel's lyre?
Who first from midst his bonds lifted his eyes?   5
Who first from out the still watch, lone and long,
Feeling the ancient faith of prophets rise
Within his dark-kept soul, burst into song?

Heart of what slave poured out such melody
As "Steal away to Jesus"? On its strains   10
His spirit must have nightly floated free,
Though still about his hands he felt his chains.
Who heard great "Jordan roll"? Whose starward eye
Saw chariot "swing low"? And who was he
That breathed that comforting, melodic sigh,   15
"Nobody knows de trouble I see"?[1]

What merely living clod, what captive thing,
Could up toward God through all its darkness grope,
And find within its deadened heart to sing
These songs of sorrow, love, and faith, and hope?   20
How did it catch that subtle undertone,
That note in music heard not with the ears?
How sound the elusive reed, so seldom blown,
Which stirs the soul or melts the heart to tears?

Not that great German master[2] in his dream   25
Of harmonies that thundered 'mongst the stars
At the creation, ever heard a theme
Nobler than "Go down, Moses." Mark its bars,
How like a mighty trumpet-call they stir
The blood. Such are the notes that men have sung,   30
Going to valorous deeds; such tones there were
That helped make history when Time was young.

There is a wide, wide wonder in it all,
That from degraded rest and service toil
The fiery spirit of the seer should call   35

1. "Steal Away to Jesus," "Roll, Jordan, Roll," "Swing Low, Sweet Chariot," and "Go Down, Moses"
(l. 28) are all Negro spirituals.
2. Gottfried Wilhelm Leibnitz (1646–1716), philosopher and mathematician.

These simple children of the sun and soil.
O black slave singers, gone, forgot, unfamed,
You—you alone, of all the long, long line
Of those who've sung untaught, unknown, unnamed,
Have stretched out upward, seeking the divine.   40

You sang not deeds of heroes or of kings;
No chant of bloody war, no exulting pæan
Of arms-won triumphs; but your humble strings
You touched in chord with music empyrean.
You sang far better than you knew; the songs   45
That for your listeners' hungry hearts sufficed
Still live,—but more than this to you belongs:
You sang a race from wood and stone to Christ.

1908

The Creation

And God stepped out on space,
And he looked around and said:
I'm lonely—
I'll make me a world.

And far as the eye of God could see   5
Darkness covered everything,
Blacker than a hundred midnights
Down in a cypress swamp.

Then God smiled,
And the light broke,   10
And the darkness rolled up on one side,
And the light stood shining on the other,
And God said: That's good!

Then God reached out and took the light in his hands,
And God rolled the light around in his hands   15
Until he made the sun;
And he set that sun a-blazing in the heavens.
And the light that was left from making the sun
Got gathered it up in a shining ball
And flung it against the darkness,   20
Spangling the night with the moon and stars.
Then down between
The darkness and the light
He hurled the world;
And God said: That's good!   25

Then God himself stepped down—
And the sun was on his right hand,
And the moon was on his left;
The stars were clustered about his head,

And the earth was under his feet.   30
And God walked, and where he trod
His footsteps hollowed the valleys out
And bulged the mountains up.

Then he stopped and looked and saw
That the earth was hot and barren.   35
So God stepped over to the edge of the world
And he spat out the seven seas—
He batted his eyes, and the lightnings flashed—
He clapped his hands, and the thunders rolled—
And the waters above the earth came down,   40
The cooling waters came down.

Then the green grass sprouted,
And the little red flowers blossomed,
The pine tree pointed his finger to the sky,
And the oak spread out his arms,   45
The lakes cuddled down in the hollows of the ground,
And the rivers ran down to the sea;
And God smiled again,
And the rainbow appeared,
And curled itself around his shoulder.   50

Then God raised his arm and he waved his hand
Over the sea and over the land,
And he said: Bring forth! Bring forth!
And quicker than God could drop his hand,
Fishes and fowls   55
And beasts and birds
Swam the rivers and the seas,
Roamed the forests and the woods,
And split the air with their wings.
And God said: That's good!   60

Then God walked around,
And God looked around
On all that he had made.
He looked at his sun,
And he looked at his moon,   65
And he looked at his little stars;
He looked on his world
With all its living things,
And God said: I'm lonely still.

Then God sat down—   70
On the side of a hill where he could think;
By a deep, wide river he sat down;
With his head in his hands,
God thought and thought,
Till he thought: I'll make me a man!   75

Up from the bed of the river
God scooped the clay;
And by the bank of the river
He kneeled him down;
And there the great God Almighty   80
Who lit the sun and fixed it in the sky,
Who flung the stars to the most far corner of the night,
Who rounded the earth in the middle of his hand;
This Great God,
Like a mammy bending over her baby,   85
Kneeled down in the dust
Toiling over a lump of clay
Till he shaped it in his own image;

Then into it he blew the breath of life,
And man became a living soul.   90
Amen. Amen.

                                                                 1920

⚬◄ PAUL LAURENCE DUNBAR ►⚬
(1872–1906)

The first African American poet to achieve widespread fame, Paul Laurence Dunbar was born in Dayton, Ohio—the only child of Matilda Murphy and Joshua Dunbar, both of whom had been slaves. His father escaped to Canada before the Civil War and later served in the Massachusetts 55th Regiment. While Dunbar was still an infant, his parents separated; they divorced in 1876. A remarkable and supportive woman, Dunbar's mother, who worked in a laundry, taught her son to read before he entered Dayton public schools. When he began to write at an early age, she encouraged his efforts. At age sixteen, Dunbar published poems in the *Dayton Herald,* and while still in high school he collaborated with his classmate Orville Wright on a short-lived newspaper, the *Tattler.* By the time he graduated from high school with the class of 1891 (in which he was the only black student), Dunbar had edited the school paper and been elected both class president and class poet.

Fulfilling employment, however, was not readily available for a young African American. For a while he worked as an elevator operator in Dayton, but he continued to write and publish his work in newspapers. In 1892 he was invited by a former teacher to address the Western Association of Writers, and soon after he received an encouraging letter about his poems from James Whitcomb Riley, who, along with Robert Burns, was one of Dunbar's early models. Encouraged by this recognition, Dunbar borrowed money to publish his first book of poems, *Oak and Ivy* (1893). His early poems were often written in African American dialect. Though such dialect had previously appeared in the work of white writers like Stephen Foster, Joel Chandler Harris, and Mark Twain, Dunbar fast became known as the most significant African American writer to take part in the late nineteenth-century vogue for regionalism and dialect, as he did in "Song of Summer":

Dreamin' by de rivah side
  Wif de watahs glist'nin',
Feelin' good an' satisfied
  Ez you lay a-list'nin'
To the little naked boys
  Splashin' in de watah,
Hollerin' fo' to spress deir joys
  Jes' lak youngsters ought to.

The Dixie depicted in such poems is obviously a fiction and owed as much to the minstrel show as it did to observed life.

After a brief time of employment as a page at the Dayton courthouse, Dunbar was hired by the famous abolitionist Frederick Douglass in 1893 for the World's Columbia Exposition in Chicago; he was a clerk in the Haiti Building. While there he became acquainted with more black writers, including Ida B. Wells and Angelina Grimke. As his circle of friends and patrons widened, his work appeared in more prominent periodicals like the *Century* and the *New York Times*. Dunbar's first full-length collection of poems, *Majors and Minors,* appeared in 1895 and was praised at length in *Harper's* by one of America's most prominent men of letters, William Dean Howells, who considered Dunbar "the only man of pure African blood and of American civilization to feel the negro [*sic*] life aesthetically and express it lyrically." While inaccurate in many ways, Howells's assessment propelled Dunbar to greater fame, earning him a contract with a commercial publisher for his next book of poems, *Lyrics of Lowly Life* (1896), for which Howells provided an introduction. Dunbar was also in demand as a performer of his poetry. After a successful tour of England he moved to Washington, D.C., where he clerked in the reading room at the Library of Congress, still continuing to pursue his own writing. In 1898 he married the poet and teacher Alice Ruth Moore and published a novel, *The Uncalled,* as well as a collection of stories, *Folks from Dixie.* Revenue from these books and his public appearances allowed Dunbar to quit his job and write full time.

Despite these public successes, Dunbar's personal life was increasingly troubled. His heavy drinking contributed to a bout of pneumonia, and in 1899 he was diagnosed with tuberculosis, then often a death sentence. In order to recuperate, he moved to Colorado, where he wrote three more novels, in addition to collections of stories and poems. After separating from his wife in 1902, Dunbar spent his last years living with his mother in a Dayton house that he had built for her. His final collection of poems, *Lyrics of Sunshine and Shadow,* appeared in 1905.

In many ways, Dunbar's poetry was close to the work of those whites who had fantasized about African American culture. He, too, created a fictionalized Dixie, though he had heard stories of the South from his mother. But Dunbar's facility with traditional verse forms (as in his rondeau "We Wear the Mask") and his ability to write either in dialect or in standard English helped clear the way for writers like Claude McKay and Langston Hughes. Although he was not usually as frank as later writers about racial issues in America, he certainly did not avoid them. Long after Dunbar's death, Maya Angelou found the title for her autobiography, *I Know Why the Caged Bird Sings,* in Dunbar's poem "Sympathy." Dunbar's work was in its way an important addition to African American literature, just as it was a significant example of American regional populism.

We Wear the Mask

We wear the mask that grins and lies,
It hides our cheeks and shades our eyes,—
This debt we pay to human guile;
With torn and bleeding hearts we smile,
And mouth with myriad subtleties.   5

Why should the world be otherwise,
In counting all our tears and sighs?
Nay, let them only see us, while
   We wear the mask.

We smile, but, O great Christ, our cries   10
To thee from tortured souls arise.
We sing, but oh the clay is vile
Beneath our feet, and long the mile;
But let the world dream otherwise,
   We wear the mask!   15

1895

Sympathy

I know what the caged bird feels, alas!
   When the sun is bright on the upland slopes;
When the wind stirs soft through the springing grass,
And the river flows like a stream of glass;
   When the first bird sings and the first bud opes,   5
And the faint perfume from its chalice[1] steals—
   I know what the caged bird feels!

I know why the caged bird beats his wing
   Till its blood is red on the cruel bars;
For he must fly back to his perch and cling   10
When he fain would be on the bough a-swing;
   And a pain still throbs in the old, old scars
And they pulse again with a keener sting—
   I know why he beats his wing!

I know why the caged bird sings, ah me,   15
   When his wing is bruised and his bosom sore,—
When he beats his bars and he would be free;
It is not a carol of joy or glee,
   But a prayer that he sends from his heart's deep core,
But a plea, that upward to Heaven he flings—   20
   I know why the caged bird sings!

1899

---

1. Suggests that the flower is like a cup.

The Debt

This is the debt I pay
Just for one riotous day,
Years of regret and grief,
Sorrow without relief.

Pay it I will to the end—   5
Until the grave, my friend,
Gives me a true release—
Gives me the clasp of peace.

Slight was the thing I bought,
Small was the debt I thought,   10
Poor was the loan at best—
God! but the interest!

1903

The Poet

He sang of life, serenely sweet,
    With, now and then, a deeper note.
    From some high peak, nigh yet remote,
He voiced the world's absorbing beat.

He sang of love when earth was young,   5
    And Love, itself, was in his lays,[2]
    But ah, the world, it turned to praise
A jingle in a broken tongue.

1903

To a Captious Critic

Dear critic, who my lightness so deplores,
Would I might study to be prince of bores,
Right wisely would I rule that dull estate—
But, sir, I may not; till you abdicate.

1903

◦━◀ TRUMBULL STICKNEY ▶━◦
(1874–1904)

Brilliant, cosmopolitan, and tragically short-lived, Joseph Trumbull Stickney was born of American parents in Geneva, Switzerland. Raised almost entirely in Europe, he was educated until age twelve by his father, a professor of classics. In 1891 Stickney entered Harvard where he became part of an influential circle of young poets that included William Vaughn Moody, George Cabot Lodge, and George

2. Songs.

Santayana. After graduating, he studied at the Sorbonne in Paris where he became the first Anglo-Saxon to earn a doctorate in literature. In 1902 his *Dramatic Verses* appeared in a limited edition. It would be the only collection of his poems issued in his lifetime, though he also published a study in French of the ancient Greek dramatist Euripides. Stickney returned to Harvard in 1903 to teach Greek, but the next year he was diagnosed with a brain tumor. He went blind but continued to write until his death on October 11, 1904. "He was thirty years old," wrote his friend Lodge, "by far the most promising man I have ever known." Stickney had virtually no literary reputation at the time of his death beyond the esteem of his friends. Despite a memorial volume published by his Harvard colleagues, *The Poems of Trumbull Stickney* (1905), his poetry remained uncelebrated for decades. By mid-century, however, his work was reassessed by influential arbiters of taste like Van Wyck Brooks, Conrad Aiken, and Edmund Wilson. Slowly Stickney emerged as one of the few distinctive and memorable American poets of his generation.

Stickney's style and forms were traditional, but his voice—lucid, lyric, and elegiac—still seems markedly personal. His sensibility was deeply romantic, full of unrealized and unrealizable longing, but his language stayed simple, direct, and understated. His best work was written late in his brief life, and it suggests how much unfulfilled promise remained at his death. The other "Harvard Poets" of his generation now survive only as literary footnotes; but Stickney's finest poems, especially "Mnemosyne" remain hauntingly fresh and expressive.

Mnemosyne[1]

It's autumn in the country I remember.

How warm a wind blew here about the ways
And shadows on the hillside lay to slumber
During the long sun-sweetened summer-days.

It's cold abroad the country I remember.   5

The swallows veering skimmed the golden grain
At midday with a wing aslant and limber;
And yellow cattle browsed upon the plain.

It's empty down the country I remember.

I had a sister lovely in my sight: 10
Her hair was dark, her eyes were very sombre;
We sang together in the woods at night.

It's lonely in the country I remember.

The babble of our children fills my ears,
And on our hearth I stare the perished ember   15
To flames that show all starry thro' my tears.

---

1. The name of a Greek goddess who represents memory; she gave birth to the Muses.

It's dark about the country I remember.

There are the mountains where I lived. The path
Is slushed with cattle-tracks and fallen timber,
The stumps are twisted by the tempests' wrath.   20

But that I knew these places are my own,
I'd ask how came such wretchedness to cumber
The earth, and I to people it alone.

It rains across the country I remember.

1902

Near Helikon[2]

By such an all-embalming summer day
As sweetens now among the mountain pines
Down to the cornland yonder and the vines,
To where the sky and sea are mixed in gray,
How do all things together take their way   5
Harmonious to the harvest, bringing wines
And bread and light and whatsoe'er combines
In the large wreath to make it round and gay.
To me my troubled life doth now appear
Like scarce distinguishable summits hung   10
Around the blue horizon: places where
Not even a traveller purposeth to steer,—
Whereof a migrant bird in passing sung,
And the girl closed her window not to hear.

1903

Sir, say no more

Sir, say no more.
Within me 't is as if
The green and climbing eyesight of a cat
Crawled near my mind's poor birds.

1904

◄ ROBERT FROST ►
(1874–1963)

Robert Frost stands as the preeminent contrarian of twentieth-century American
poetry. His achievement contradicts most easy definitions of modern poetry, and
yet no satisfactory explanation of American Modernism can afford to ignore his
work. Aside from a few parodies of his friend Ezra Pound, Frost wrote exclusively

---

2. The mountain in Greece beloved of the Muses.

Robert Frost, Franconia, New Hampshire (1915).

in meter and mastered traditional forms like the sonnet, ballad, couplet, and blank verse. "I'd as soon write free verse," he famously quipped, "as play tennis with the net down." His use of poetic language was spare and understated but like his masters—Henry Wadsworth Longfellow, Thomas Hardy, and E. A. Robinson—Frost wrote for the ear. His poems were meant to be spoken and heard—even memorized—unlike the visual prosody that emerged among his younger contemporaries like William Carlos Williams and Ezra Pound. Yet Frost's worldview is indisputably modern. An agnostic, he saw humanity as alone in a universe seemingly devoid of meaning yet fraught with the terror of pain or extinction.

Frost was the most famous and popular American poet of the twentieth century. Alone among his poetic contemporaries, he achieved the difficult feat of combining immense popularity with nearly universal critical esteem. No modern American poet was so abundantly honored in his own lifetime. Frost won every prize the nation had to offer, including four Pulitzer Prizes—a record no other poet or novelist has ever matched and an achievement all the more remarkable when one observes that he did not win his first Pulitzer until he was forty-nine. By the end of his long lifetime, Frost had become a national icon: His later books became best-sellers. Universities competed for his presence. Buildings were named in his honor. His poems entered the curriculum at every level of education from grammar school to graduate school. His later birthdays became public events accompanied by press conferences, formal banquets, and government proclamations. A frequent guest on television and radio, Frost was the only living poet most Americans knew by name. The height of his celebrity came when the eighty-six-year-old poet read at John F. Kennedy's 1961 presidential inauguration. Televised live into homes and classrooms, it became the most famous public appearance by any American writer.

Robert Lee Frost, the great poet of rural New England, was born in San Francisco in 1874. His childhood was not only West Coast but urban. The future farmer grew up in the apartments and hotels of California's biggest city, within sight of the Pacific Ocean. He spent his first eleven years in San Francisco's extraordinarily constant climate where he never saw snow or dramatic seasonal change. The first woodlands he visited were not the birch forests he would eventually immortalize in verse but the Pacific live oaks, madrones, and redwoods of the Napa Valley. Frost's mother, Isabelle Moodie, was a Scottish immigrant. Born near Edinburgh, she had been raised with relations in Ohio, but she never lost her Scottish accent. The future poet laureate of Vermont, his only connection to New England came from his father, William Prescott Frost, who had been born in New Hampshire, but had fled the state at an early age. William Frost was no ordinary Yankee. During the Civil War he had traveled south to fight under Robert E. Lee for the Confederacy, but had been arrested in Philadelphia and sent home. He remained a Copperhead Rebel sympathizer till the end and christened his only son Robert Lee Frost, an ironic name for the great bard of Yankee New England. In California the hard-drinking temperamental William Frost worked in journalism and politics but achieved little success in either field.

Frost's California childhood came abruptly to an end in 1885 when his father died at thirty-four from tuberculosis. The elder Frost left no insurance. The poet's mother had nowhere to turn except her husband's family. Taking William Frost's body with them, she and her children traveled by train to Lawrence, Massachusetts, where the young poet spent the next decade in poverty, moving between a series of dreary mill towns in pursuit of financial security.

When the eleven-year-old Frost followed his father's body to Massachusetts, he saw the region with fresh and foreign eyes. Unlike a native, he took nothing in this new landscape for granted. The flora, fauna, weather, and folkways of the Northeast were new to him. And yet their connection to his dead father gave them a deep resonance. Frost's position was, therefore, half-in and half-outside the region. As a newcomer, he had to make conscious sense of a place in ways that a native never bothers. Frost was an elective New Englander, and a convert is always more passionate about a new faith than someone born to the religion.

The young Frost was a brilliant student—a relentless competitor both in the classroom and on the playing field. He graduated from high school at the top of his class and was covaledictorian with Elinor White, the young woman he would eventually marry. Frost even won a scholarship to nearby Dartmouth College. But at this point something happened to Frost that no biographer has ever adequately explained. His ferociously competitive instincts suddenly turned inward. He no longer cared much for external measures of success; he had set his eyes on literary greatness, which he instinctively knew would take decades of dedication to achieve. Except for marriage and providing his growing family with the bare necessities, Frost stayed remarkably aloof from the worldly preoccupations of most ambitious young men.

Within a few weeks of starting, Frost had dropped out of Dartmouth (He would leave Harvard the same way five years later.) He found the academic work easy but uncongenial. Instead, he devoted himself to courting the wary and often reluctant Elinor. It took three years to convince her to marry him. Whatever his faults as a husband, Frost never wavered in his love for his wife. They were married forty-three years and had six children together.

For the next sixteen years, he eked out a living mostly as a chicken farmer with a few short stints as a schoolteacher. (His grandfather gave him a small farm under the condition that he work it for ten years.) Frost wrote constantly but published almost nothing. He liked farming, but he wasn't very good at it, especially since he often slept till noon. He was an excellent—if also unorthodox—teacher, but he refused to stay in the profession for very long, since it made writing difficult.

The turning point in Frost's public life occurred in 1912 when he sold his farm and took his family to England. He was thirty-eight years old with no poetic reputation whatsoever. He had never held a steady job for any length of time and had never published a book. But after twenty years of writing in isolation, Frost felt the time had finally come to make his mark on the literary world. But Frost had long wagered his life for just this moment. Almost immediately the wager paid off. Frost had his first book of poems, *A Boy's Will* (1913), accepted by a small but established London firm. (It was reprinted two years later in the United States.) He also met many writers at the newly opened Poetry Bookshop in London. Among these new acquaintances was the American Modernist, Ezra Pound, who championed his fellow expatriate and helped make Frost's debut volume a critical success. He also met W. B. Yeats, Ford Madox Ford, and Robert Bridges, but most importantly, he met Edward Thomas, with whom he would have the closest literary friendship of his life. Frost inspired Thomas to shift from nature writing to poetry, and Thomas's friendship helped Frost mature and deepen as a poet.

During his two years in England, Frost not only wrote some of the best poems of his life but paradoxically some of the most American—like "Birches," "Home Burial," "Mending Wall," "After Apple Picking," and "The Road Not Taken." Living in England somehow gave him the clarity to understand his homeland. In 1914 his second book, *North of Boston,* appeared, and the forty-year-old poet was now established. When a New York publisher offered to print a U.S. edition, Frost told his wife, "Now we can go home." He returned to America a celebrated poet. As a writer, all of his sacrifices had now paid off. His public reputation would never stop growing, but his private sorrow had only just begun.

If Frost was by nature a family man, his domestic life was marked by enormous suffering and loss. The couple's first son died of typhoid fever in childhood. Another daughter died at birth. Frost's only sister went insane, a fate later shared by one of his daughters. His youngest daughter died agonizingly in childbirth. His second son committed suicide. Only one of his six children—his daughter Lesley—lived out a natural and healthy life. Under the burden of such private sorrow, it hardly seems surprising that Frost would carefully create a happier public image. Literary fame gradually became his one refuge from personal agony.

Frost never allowed the public to view these private sorrows. His poetry seems so compellingly personal that one forgets how seldom it is overtly autobiographical. His most painful poems, like "Home Burial" or " 'Out, Out—,' " are mostly narratives, which distance their tragedies by placing them in fictive lives. Fear, guilt, and suffering cast their shadows everywhere across his poetry, but in art, as in life, Frost kept those dark themes in such careful balance that they did not overwhelm him.

Frost's relations with his wife were loving but difficult. He was a steadfast and faithful husband, but his own melancholy and self-absorption strained the marriage. She also came to blame his slowness in summoning a doctor for the death of their first son. When she was on her deathbed in 1938, Frost waited outside the bedroom wanting her to call him in as a sign that she forgave all the suffering he had caused throughout their forty-three-year marriage. For two days he intermittently paced the hallway, but Elinor never requested to see him. By the time the doctor asked him to enter, his wife was unconscious. Her final rejection weighed on Frost the rest of his life. His sense of personal failure deepened two years later when Carol killed himself. "I took the wrong way with him," wrote Frost to a friend. "I tried many ways and every single one was wrong." The poet's later years were marked by public fame and increasing emotional isolation. He died at eighty-eight in 1963.

Frost's greatness as a lyric poet has never seriously been questioned. He perfected a compressed but accessible style that combined evocative musicality with spiritual profundity. His best work has an extraordinarily meaningful complexity in which he often explores two opposing ideas with balanced intelligence, intensity, and invention. Frost's great preeminence, however, rests on the breadth of his accomplishment. He did distinguished work in lyric, narrative, and didactic poetry, and he mastered the tragic, comic, pastoral, and satiric modes with equal genius. No other major modern American poet matched his versatility. Only in dramatic verse did his genius falter the level of mere talent as in his verse plays, *A Masque of Reason* (1945) and *A Masque of Mercy* (1947).

Frost's narrative poetry was especially distinguished and innovative. He took the stark, naturalist style of E. A. Robinson and developed it into a more suggestive and elliptical mode. His best narrative poems, like "Home Burial" and "The Death of the Hired Man," present compelling stories in which far more is suggested than is ever overtly revealed. Frost had a genius for creating powerful and individual characters. He once claimed that he never took sides in his poems, and his narratives—as well as his many lyrics—often take the form of passionate but unresolved (indeed often unresolvable) arguments. Deeply read in Greek and Latin poetry, Frost cast many poems as eclogues, a classical form that was originally a rustic dialogue between two shepherds. Even a meditative lyric like "Mending Wall" employs dialogue and dialectic as its main devices in depicting opposing views of the wall held by two neighbors. The poem provokes and prolongs a deep but amicable dispute that the narrator cannot resolve but only explicate. This avoidance of easy resolution is, like the unsentimental diction of his poems, a mark of the modern in Frost. From Emerson and Dante he borrowed the metaphysical image of a man lost in the woods, often in Frost a cold and unknowable place. Despite this apparent perdition, Frost's worldview and technique can be absolutely playful, and his resolute spirit is part of what makes Frost a perennially attractive poet.

-◦-◀─▶-◦-

Mowing

There was never a sound beside the wood but one,
And that was my long scythe whispering to the ground.
What was it it whispered? I knew not well myself;

Perhaps it was something about the heat of the sun,
Something, perhaps, about the lack of sound—   5
And that was why it whispered and did not speak.
It was no dream of the gift of idle hours,
Or easy gold at the hand of fay or elf:
Anything more than the truth would have seemed too weak
To the earnest love that laid the swale in rows,   10
Not without feeble-pointed spikes of flowers
(Pale orchises), and scared a bright green snake.
The fact is the sweetest dream that labor knows.
My long scythe whispered and left the hay to make.

                                                       1913

My November Guest

My Sorrow, when she's here with me,
    Thinks these dark days of autumn rain
Are beautiful as days can be;
She loves the bare, the withered tree;
    She walks the sodden pasture lane.   5

Her pleasure will not let me stay.
    She talks and I am fain to list:
She's glad the birds are gone away,
She's glad her simple worsted grey
    Is silver now with clinging mist.   10

The desolate, deserted trees,
    The faded earth, the heavy sky,
The beauties she so truly sees,
She thinks I have no eye for these,
    And vexes me for reason why.   15

Not yesterday I learned to know
    The love of bare November days
Before the coming of the snow,
But it were vain to tell her so,
    And they are better for her praise.   20

                                                       1913

Storm Fear

When the wind works against us in the dark,
And pelts with snow
The lower chamber window on the east,
And whispers with a sort of stifled bark,
The beast,   5
"Come out! Come out!"—
It costs no inward struggle not to go,
Ah, no!

I count our strength,
Two and a child,   10
Those of us not asleep subdued to mark
How the cold creeps as the fire dies at length,—
How drifts are piled,
Dooryard and road ungraded,
Till even the comforting barn grows far away,   15
And my heart owns a doubt
Whether 'tis in us to arise with day
And save ourselves unaided.

                                                            1913

The Tuft of Flowers

I went to turn the grass once after one
Who mowed it in the dew before the sun.

The dew was gone that made his blade so keen
Before I came to view the levelled scene.

I looked for him behind an isle of trees;   5
I listened for his whetstone on the breeze.

But he had gone his way, the grass all mown,
And I must be, as he had been,—alone,

"As all must be," I said within my heart,
"Whether they work together or apart."   10

But as I said it, swift there passed me by
On noiseless wing a bewildered butterfly,

Seeking with memories grown dim o'er night
Some resting flower of yesterday's delight.

And once I marked his flight go round and round,   15
As where some flower lay withering on the ground.

And then he flew as far as eye could see,
And then on tremulous wing came back to me.

I thought of questions that have no reply,
And would have turned to toss the grass to dry;   20

But he turned first, and led my eye to look
At a tall tuft of flowers beside a brook,

A leaping tongue of bloom the scythe had spared
Beside a reedy brook the scythe had bared.

I left my place to know them by their name,   25
Finding them butterfly weed when I came.

The mower in the dew had loved them thus,
By leaving them to flourish, not for us,

Nor yet to draw one thought of ours to him,
But from sheer morning gladness at the brim.   30

The butterfly and I had lit upon,
Nevertheless, a message from the dawn,

That made me hear the wakening birds around,
And hear his long scythe whispering to the ground,

And feel a spirit kindred to my own;   35
So that henceforth I worked no more alone;

But glad with him, I worked as with his aid,
And weary, sought at noon with him the shade;

And dreaming, as it were, held brotherly speech
With one whose thought I had not hoped to reach.   40

"Men work together," I told him from the heart,
"Whether they work together or apart."

                                                    1913

After Apple-Picking

My long two-pointed ladder's sticking through a tree
Toward heaven still,
And there's a barrel that I didn't fill
Beside it, and there may be two or three
Apples I didn't pick upon some bough.   5
But I am done with apple-picking now.
Essence of winter sleep is on the night,
The scent of apples: I am drowsing off.
I cannot rub the strangeness from my sight
I got from looking through a pane of glass   10
I skimmed this morning from the drinking trough
And held against the world of hoary grass.
It melted, and I let it fall and break.
But I was well
Upon my way to sleep before it fell,   15
And I could tell
What form my dreaming was about to take.
Magnified apples appear and disappear,
Stem end and blossom end,
And every fleck of russet showing clear.   20
My instep arch not only keeps the ache,
It keeps the pressure of a ladder-round.
I feel the ladder sway as the boughs bend.
And I keep hearing from the cellar bin
The rumbling sound   25
Of load on load of apples coming in.
For I have had too much

Of apple-picking: I am overtired
Of the great harvest I myself desired.
There were ten thousand thousand fruit to touch,   30
Cherish in hand, lift down, and not let fall.
For all
That struck the earth,
No matter if not bruised or spiked with stubble,
Went surely to the cider-apple heap   35
As of no worth.
One can see what will trouble
This sleep of mine, whatever sleep it is.
Were he not gone,
The woodchuck could say whether it's like his   40
Long sleep, as I describe its coming on,
Or just some human sleep.

1914

The Death of the Hired Man

Mary sat musing on the lamp-flame at the table
Waiting for Warren. When she heard his step,
She ran on tip-toe down the darkened passage
To meet him in the doorway with the news
And put him on his guard. "Silas is back."   5
She pushed him outward with her through the door
And shut it after her. "Be kind," she said.
She took the market things from Warren's arms
And set them on the porch, then drew him down
To sit beside her on the wooden steps.   10

"When was I ever anything but kind to him?
But I'll not have the fellow back," he said.
"I told him so last haying, didn't I?
'If he left then,' I said, 'that ended it.'
What good is he? Who else will harbour him   15
At his age for the little he can do?
What help he is there's no depending on.
Off he goes always when I need him most.
'He thinks he ought to earn a little pay,
Enough at least to buy tobacco with,   20
So he won't have to beg and be beholden.'
'All right,' I say, 'I can't afford to pay
Any fixed wages, though I wish I could.'
'Someone else can.' 'Then someone else will have to.'
I shouldn't mind his bettering himself   25
If that was what it was. You can be certain,
When he begins like that, there's someone at him
Trying to coax him off with pocket-money,—
In haying time, when any help is scarce.
In winter he comes back to us. I'm done."   30

"Sh! Not so loud: he'll hear you," Mary said.

"I want him to: he'll have to soon or late."

"He's worn out. He's asleep beside the stove.
When I came up from Rowe's I found him here,
Huddled against the barn-door fast asleep,   35
A miserable sight, and frightening, too—
You needn't smile—I didn't recognise him—
I wasn't looking for him—and he's changed.
Wait till you see."

                    "Where did you say he'd been?"

"He didn't say. I dragged him to the house,   40
And gave him tea and tried to make him smoke.
I tried to make him talk about his travels.
Nothing would do: he just kept nodding off."

"What did he say? Did he say anything?"

"But little."

                    "Anything? Mary, confess   45
He said he'd come to ditch the meadow for me."

"Warren!"

                    "But did he? I just want to know."

"Of course he did. What would you have him say?
Surely you wouldn't grudge the poor old man
Some humble way to save his self-respect.   50
He added, if you really care to know,
He meant to clear the upper pasture, too.
That sounds like something you have heard before?
Warren, I wish you could have heard the way
He jumbled everything. I stopped to look   55
Two or three times—he made me feel so queer—
To see if he was talking in his sleep.
He ran on Harold Wilson—you remember—
The boy you had in haying four years since.
He's finished school, and teaching in his college.   60
Silas declares you'll have to get him back.
He says they two will make a team for work:
Between them they will lay this farm as smooth!
The way he mixed that in with other things.
He thinks young Wilson a likely lad, though daft   65
On education—you know how they fought
All through July under the blazing sun,
Silas up on the cart to build the load,
Harold along beside to pitch it on."

"Yes, I took care to keep well out of earshot."   70

"Well, those days trouble Silas like a dream.
You wouldn't think they would. How some things linger!
Harold's young college boy's assurance piqued him.
After so many years he still keeps finding
Good arguments he sees he might have used.   75
I sympathise. I know just how it feels
To think of the right thing to say too late.
Harold's associated in his mind with Latin.
He asked me what I thought of Harold's saying
He studied Latin like the violin   80
Because he liked it—that an argument!
He said he couldn't make the boy believe
He could find water with a hazel prong—
Which showed how much good school had ever done him.
He wanted to go over that. But most of all   85
He thinks if he could have another chance
To teach him how to build a load of hay—"

"I know, that's Silas' one accomplishment.
He bundles every forkful in its place,
And tags and numbers it for future reference,   90
So he can find and easily dislodge it
In the unloading. Silas does that well.
He takes it out in bunches like big birds' nests.
You never see him standing on the hay
He's trying to lift, straining to lift himself."   95

"He thinks if he could teach him that, he'd be
Some good perhaps to someone in the world.
He hates to see a boy the fool of books.
Poor Silas, so concerned for other folk,
And nothing to look backward to with pride,   100
And nothing to look forward to with hope,
So now and never any different."

Part of a moon was falling down the west,
Dragging the whole sky with it to the hills.
Its light poured softly in her lap. She saw it   105
And spread her apron to it. She put out her hand
Among the harp-like morning-glory strings,
Taut with the dew from garden bed to eaves,
As if she played unheard some tenderness
That wrought on him beside her in the night.   110
"Warren," she said, "he has come home to die:
You needn't be afraid he'll leave you this time."

"Home," he mocked gently.

                              "Yes, what else but home?

It all depends on what you mean by home.
Of course he's nothing to us, any more   115

Than was the hound that came a stranger to us
Out of the woods, worn out upon the trail."

"Home is the place where, when you have to go there,
They have to take you in."

                              "I should have called it
Something you somehow haven't to deserve."   120

Warren leaned out and took a step or two,
Picked up a little stick, and brought it back
And broke it in his hand and tossed it by.
"Silas has better claim on us you think
Than on his brother? Thirteen little miles   125
As the road winds would bring him to his door.
Silas has walked that far no doubt to-day.
Why didn't he go there? His brother's rich,
A somebody—director in the bank."

"He never told us that."

                        "We know it though."   130

"I think his brother ought to help, of course.
I'll see to that if there is need. He ought of right
To take him in, and might be willing to—
He may be better than appearances.
But have some pity on Silas. Do you think   135
If he had any pride in claiming kin
Or anything he looked for from his brother,
He'd keep so still about him all this time?"

"I wonder what's between them."

                         "I can tell you.
Silas is what he is—we wouldn't mind him—   140
But just the kind that kinsfolk can't abide.
He never did a thing so very bad.
He don't know why he isn't quite as good
As anybody. Worthless though he is,
He won't be made ashamed to please his brother."   145

"*I* can't think Si ever hurt anyone."

"No, but he hurt my heart the way he lay
And rolled his old head on that sharp-edged chair-back.
He wouldn't let me put him on the lounge.
You must go in and see what you can do.   150
I made the bed up for him there to-night.
You'll be surprised at him—how much he's broken.
His working days are done; I'm sure of it."

"I'd not be in a hurry to say that."

"I haven't been. Go, look, see for yourself.   155
But, Warren, please remember how it is:
He's come to help you ditch the meadow.
He has a plan. You mustn't laugh at him.
He may not speak of it, and then he may.
I'll sit and see if that small sailing cloud   160
Will hit or miss the moon."

            It hit the moon.
Then there were three there, making a dim row,
The moon, the little silver cloud, and she.

Warren returned—too soon, it seemed to her,
Slipped to her side, caught up her hand and waited.   165

"Warren?" she questioned.

             "Dead," was all he answered.

                    1914

Home Burial

He saw her from the bottom of the stairs
Before she saw him. She was starting down,
Looking back over her shoulder at some fear.
She took a doubtful step and then undid it
To raise herself and look again. He spoke   5
Advancing toward her: "What is it you see
From up there always—for I want to know."
She turned and sank upon her skirts at that,
And her face changed from terrified to dull.
He said to gain time: "What is it you see,"   10
Mounting until she cowered under him.
"I will find out now—you must tell me, dear."
She, in her place, refused him any help
With the least stiffening of her neck and silence.
She let him look, sure that he wouldn't see,   15
Blind creature; and a while he didn't see.
But at last he murmured, "Oh," and again, "Oh."

"What is it—what?" she said.

                 "Just that I see."

"You don't," she challenged. "Tell me what it is."

"The wonder is I didn't see at once.   20
I never noticed it from here before.
I must be wonted[1] to it—that's the reason.
The little graveyard where my people are!

---

1. Accustomed.

So small the window frames the whole of it.
Not so much larger than a bedroom, is it?   25
There are three stones of slate and one of marble,
Broad-shouldered little slabs there in the sunlight
On the sidehill. We haven't to mind *those*.
But I understand: it is not the stones,
But the child's mound—"

                  "Don't, don't, don't, don't," she cried.   30

She withdrew shrinking from beneath his arm
That rested on the banister, and slid downstairs;
And turned on him with such a daunting look,
He said twice over before he knew himself:
"Can't a man speak of his own child he's lost?"   35

"Not you! Oh, where's my hat? Oh, I don't need it!
I must get out of here. I must get air.
I don't know rightly whether any man can."

"Amy! Don't go to someone else this time.
Listen to me. I won't come down the stairs."   40
He sat and fixed his chin between his fists.
"There's something I should like to ask you, dear."

"You don't know how to ask it."

                    "Help me, then."

Her fingers moved the latch for all reply.

"My words are nearly always an offence.   45
I don't know how to speak of anything
So as to please you. But I might be taught
I should suppose. I can't say I see how.
A man must partly give up being a man
With women-folk. We could have some arrangement   50
By which I'd bind myself to keep hands off
Anything special you're a-mind to name.
Though I don't like such things 'twixt those that love.
Two that don't love can't live together without them.
But two that do can't live together with them."   55
She moved the latch a little. "Don't—don't go.
Don't carry it to someone else this time.
Tell me about it if it's something human.
Let me into your grief. I'm not so much
Unlike other folks as your standing there   60
Apart would make me out. Give me my chance.
I do think, though, you overdo it a little.
What was it brought you up to think it the thing
To take your mother-loss of a first child
So inconsolably—in the face of love.   65
You'd think his memory might be satisfied—"

"There you go sneering now!"

            "I'm not, I'm not!
You make me angry. I'll come down to you.
God, what a woman! And it's come to this,
A man can't speak of his own child that's dead."   70

"You can't because you don't know how to speak.
If you had any feelings, you that dug
With your own hand—how could you?—his little grave;
I saw you from that very window there,
Making the gravel leap and leap in air,   75
Leap up, like that, like that, and land so lightly
And roll back down the mound beside the hole.
I thought, Who is that man? I didn't know you.
And I crept down the stairs and up the stairs
To look again, and still your spade kept lifting.   80
Then you came in. I heard your rumbling voice
Out in the kitchen, and I don't know why,
But I went near to see with my own eyes.
You could sit there with the stains on your shoes
Of the fresh earth from your own baby's grave   85
And talk about your everyday concerns.
You had stood the spade up against the wall
Outside there in the entry, for I saw it."

"I shall laugh the worst laugh I ever laughed.
I'm cursed. God, if I don't believe I'm cursed."   90

"I can repeat the very words you were saying.
'Three foggy mornings and one rainy day
Will rot the best birch fence a man can build.'
Think of it, talk like that at such a time!
What had how long it takes a birch to rot   95
To do with what was in the darkened parlour.
You *couldn't* care! The nearest friends can go
With anyone to death, comes so far short
They might as well not try to go at all.
No, from the time when one is sick to death,   100
One is alone, and he dies more alone.
Friends make pretence of following to the grave,
But before one is in it, their minds are turned
And making the best of their way back to life
And living people, and things they understand.   105
But the world's evil. I won't have grief so
If I can change it. Oh, I won't, I won't!"

"There, you have said it all and you feel better.
You won't go now. You're crying. Close the door.
The heart's gone out of it: why keep it up.   110
Amy! There's someone coming down the road!"

"*You*—oh, you think the talk is all. I must go—
Somewhere out of this house. How can I make you—"

"If—you—do!" She was opening the door wider.
"Where do you mean to go? First tell me that.   115
I'll follow and bring you back by force. I *will!*—"

                                                                                1914

Mending Wall

Something there is that doesn't love a wall,
That sends the frozen-ground-swell under it,
And spills the upper boulders in the sun;
And makes gaps even two can pass abreast.
The work of hunters is another thing: 5
I have come after them and made repair
Where they have left not one stone on a stone,
But they would have the rabbit out of hiding,
To please the yelping dogs. The gaps I mean,
No one has seen them made or heard them made,   10
But at spring mending-time we find them there.
I let my neighbour know beyond the hill;
And on a day we meet to walk the line
And set the wall between us once again.
We keep the wall between us as we go.   15
To each the boulders that have fallen to each.
And some are loaves and some so nearly balls
We have to use a spell to make them balance:
"Stay where you are until our backs are turned!"
We wear our fingers rough with handling them.   20
Oh, just another kind of out-door game,
One on a side. It comes to little more:
There where it is we do not need the wall:
He is all pine and I am apple orchard.
My apple trees will never get across   25
And eat the cones under his pines, I tell him.
He only says, "Good fences make good neighbours."
Spring is the mischief in me, and I wonder
If I could put a notion in his head:
"*Why* do they make good neighbours? Isn't it   30
Where there are cows? But here there are no cows.
Before I built a wall I'd ask to know
What I was walling in or walling out,
And to whom I was like to give offence.
Something there is that doesn't love a wall,   35
That wants it down." I could say "Elves" to him,
But it's not elves exactly, and I'd rather
He said it for himself. I see him there

Bringing a stone grasped firmly by the top
In each hand, like an old-stone savage armed.   40
He moves in darkness as it seems to me,
Not of woods only and the shade of trees.
He will not go behind his father's saying,
And he likes having thought of it so well
He says again, "Good fences make good neighbours."   45

1914

The Wood-Pile

Out walking in the frozen swamp one grey day,
I paused and said, "I will turn back from here.
No, I will go on farther—and we shall see."
The hard snow held me, save where now and then
One foot went through. The view was all in lines   5
Straight up and down of tall slim trees
Too much alike to mark or name a place by
So as to say for certain I was here
Or somewhere else: I was just far from home.
A small bird flew before me. He was careful   10
To put a tree between us when he lighted,
And say no word to tell me who he was
Who was so foolish as to think what *he* thought.
He thought that I was after him for a feather—
The white one in his tail; like one who takes   15
Everything said as personal to himself.
One flight out sideways would have undeceived him.
And then there was a pile of wood for which
I forgot him and let his little fear
Carry him off the way I might have gone,   20
Without so much as wishing him good-night.
He went behind it to make his last stand.
It was a cord of maple, cut and split
And piled—and measured, four by four by eight.
And not another like it could I see.   25
No runner tracks in this year's snow looped near it.
And it was older sure than this year's cutting,
Or even lasts year's or the year's before.
The wood was grey and the bark warping off it
And the pile somewhat sunken. Clematis²   30
Had wound strings round and round it like a bundle.
What held it though on one side was a tree
Still growing, and on one a stake and prop,
These latter about to fall. I thought that only
Someone who lived in turning to fresh tasks   35

2. A flowering vine.

Could so forget his handiwork on which
He spent himself, the labour of his axe,
And leave it there far from a useful fireplace
To warm the frozen swamp as best it could
With the slow smokeless burning of decay.   40

1914

Birches

When I see birches bend to left and right
Across the lines of straighter darker trees,
I like to think some boy's been swinging them.
But swinging doesn't bend them down to stay.
Ice-storms do that. Often you must have seen them   5
Loaded with ice a sunny winter morning
After a rain. They click upon themselves
As the breeze rises, and turn many-colored
As the stir cracks and crazes their enamel.
Soon the sun's warmth makes them shed crystal shells   10
Shattering and avalanching on the snow-crust—
Such heaps of broken glass to sweep away
You'd think the inner dome of heaven had fallen.
They are dragged to the withered bracken by the load,
And they seem not to break; though once they are bowed 15
So low for long, they never right themselves:
You may see their trunks arching in the woods
Years afterwards, trailing their leaves on the ground
Like girls on hands and knees that throw their hair
Before them over their heads to dry in the sun.   20
But I was going to say when Truth broke in
With all her matter-of-fact about the ice-storm
I should prefer to have some boy bend them
As he went out and in to fetch the cows—
Some boy too far from town to learn baseball,   25
Whose only play was what he found himself,
Summer or winter, and could play alone.
One by one he subdued his father's trees
By riding them down over and over again
Until he took the stiffness out of them,   30
And not one but hung limp, not one was left
For him to conquer. He learned all there was
To learn about not launching out too soon
And so not carrying the tree away
Clear to the ground. He always kept his poise   35
To the top branches, climbing carefully
With the same pains you use to fill a cup
Up to the brim, and even above the brim.
Then he flung outward, feet first, with a swish,
Kicking his way down through the air to the ground.   40

So was I once myself a swinger of birches.
And so I dream of going back to be.
It's when I'm weary of considerations,
And life is too much like a pathless wood
Where your face burns and tickles with the cobwebs   45
Broken across it, and one eye is weeping
From a twig's having lashed across it open.
I'd like to get away from earth awhile
And then come back to it and begin over.
May no fate willfully misunderstand me   50
And half grant what I wish and snatch me away
Not to return. Earth's the right place for love:
I don't know where it's likely to go better.
I'd like to go by climbing a birch tree,
And climb black branches up a snow-white trunk   55
Toward heaven, till the tree could bear no more,
But dipped its top and set me down again.
That would be good both going and coming back.
One could do worse than be a swinger of birches.

1916

"Out, Out—"[3]

The buzz-saw snarled and rattled in the yard
And made dust and dropped stove-length sticks of wood,
Sweet-scented stuff when the breeze drew across it.
And from there those that lifted eyes could count
Five mountain ranges one behind the other   5
Under the sunset far into Vermont.
And the saw snarled and rattled, snarled and rattled,
As it ran light, or had to bear a load.
And nothing happened: day was all but done.
Call it a day, I wish they might have said   10
To please the boy by giving him the half hour
That a boy counts so much when saved from work.
His sister stood beside them in her apron
To tell them "Supper." At the word, the saw,
As if to prove saws knew what supper meant,   15
Leaped out at the boy's hand, or seemed to leap—
He must have given the hand. However it was,
Neither refused the meeting. But the hand!
The boy's first outcry was a rueful laugh,
As he swung toward them holding up the hand   20
Half in appeal, but half as if to keep

3. The title of this poem echoes the words of Shakespeare's Macbeth on receiving news that his queen is dead: "Out, out, brief candle! / Life's but a walking shadow, a poor player / That struts and frets his hour upon the stage / And then is heard no more. It is a tale / Told by an idiot, full of sound and fury, / Signifying nothing" (*Macbeth* V, v. 23–28).

The life from spilling. Then the boy saw all—
Since he was old enough to know, big boy
Doing a man's work, though a child at heart—
He saw all spoiled. "Don't let him cut my hand off—   25
The doctor, when he comes. Don't let him, sister!"
So. But the hand was gone already.
The doctor put him in the dark of ether.
He lay and puffed his lips out with his breath.
And then—the watcher at his pulse took fright.   30
No one believed. They listened at his heart.
Little—less—nothing!—and that ended it.
No more to build on there. And they, since they
Were not the one dead, turned to their affairs.

                                                    1916

The Oven Bird[4]

There is a singer everyone has heard,
Loud, a mid-summer and a mid-wood bird,
Who makes the solid tree trunks sound again.
He says that leaves are old and that for flowers
Mid-summer is to spring as one to ten.   5
He says the early petal-fall is past
When pear and cherry bloom went down in showers
On sunny days a moment overcast;
And comes that other fall we name the fall.
He says the highway dust is over all.   10
The bird would cease and be as other birds
But that he knows in singing not to sing.
The question that he frames in all but words
Is what to make of a diminished thing.

                                                    1916

The Road Not Taken[5]

Two roads diverged in a yellow wood,
And sorry I could not travel both
And be one traveler, long I stood
And looked down one as far as I could
To where it bent in the undergrowth;   5

Then took the other, as just as fair,
And having perhaps the better claim,
Because it was grassy and wanted wear;

---

4. The title refers to a wood warbler that builds its domed nest on the ground.
5. According to Frost biographer Lawrance Thompson, this poem was inspired by walks Frost took with his friend, the English poet Edward Thomas: "After one of their best flower-gathering walks, he had said to Thomas, 'No matter which road you take, you'll always sigh and wish you'd taken another.' "

Though as for that the passing there
Had worn them really about the same,   10

And both that morning equally lay
In leaves no step had trodden black.
Oh, I kept the first for another day!
Yet knowing how way leads on to way,
I doubted if I should ever come back.   15

I shall be telling this with a sigh
Somewhere ages and ages hence:
Two roads diverged in a wood, and I—
I took the one less traveled by,
And that has made all the difference.   20

                                        1916

Fire and Ice

Some say the world will end in fire,
Some say in ice.
From what I've tasted of desire
I hold with those who favor fire.
But if it had to perish twice,   5
I think I know enough of hate
To say that for destruction ice
Is also great
And would suffice.

                                        1923

The Need of Being Versed in Country Things

The house had gone to bring again
To the midnight sky a sunset glow.
Now the chimney was all of the house that stood,
Like a pistil after the petals go.

The barn opposed across the way,   5
That would have joined the house in flame
Had it been the will of the wind, was left
To bear forsaken the place's name.

No more it opened with all one end
For teams that came by the stony road   10
To drum on the floor with scurrying hoofs
And brush the mow with the summer load.

The birds that came to it through the air
At broken windows flew out and in,
Their murmur more like the sigh we sigh   15
From too much dwelling on what has been.

Yet for them the lilac renewed its leaf,
And the aged elm, though touched with fire;
And the dry pump flung up an awkward arm;
And the fence post carried a strand of wire.   20

For them there was really nothing sad.
But though they rejoiced in the nest they kept,
One had to be versed in country things
Not to believe the phoebes wept.

                                                              1923

Nothing Gold Can Stay

Nature's first green is gold,
Her hardest hue to hold.
Her early leaf's a flower;
But only so an hour.
Then leaf subsides to leaf.   5
So Eden sank to grief,
So dawn goes down to day.
Nothing gold can stay.

                                                              1923

Stopping by Woods on a Snowy Evening

Whose woods these are I think I know.
His house is in the village though;
He will not see me stopping here
To watch his woods fill up with snow.

My little horse must think it queer   5
To stop without a farmhouse near
Between the woods and frozen lake
The darkest evening of the year.

He gives his harness bells a shake
To ask if there is some mistake.   10
The only other sound's the sweep
Of easy wind and downy flake.

The woods are lovely, dark and deep.
But I have promises to keep,
And miles to go before I sleep,   15
And miles to go before I sleep.

                                                              1923

To Earthward

Love at the lips was touch
As sweet as I could bear;
And once that seemed too much;
I lived on air

That crossed me from sweet things,   5
The flow of—was it musk
From hidden grapevine springs
Down hill at dusk?

I had the swirl and ache
From sprays of honeysuckle   10
That when they're gathered shake
Dew on the knuckle.

I craved strong sweets, but those
Seemed strong when I was young;
The petal of the rose   15
It was that stung.

Now no joy but lacks salt
That is not dashed with pain
And weariness and fault;
I crave the stain   20

Of tears, the aftermark
Of almost too much love,
The sweet of bitter bark
And burning clove.

When stiff and sore and scarred   25
I take away my hand
From leaning on it hard
In grass and sand,

The hurt is not enough:
I long for weight and strength   30
To feel the earth as rough
To all my length.

                        1923

Acquainted with the Night

I have been one acquainted with the night.
I have walked out in rain—and back in rain.
I have outwalked the furthest city light.

I have looked down the saddest city lane.
I have passed by the watchman on his beat   5
And dropped my eyes, unwilling to explain.

I have stood still and stopped the sound of feet
When far away an interrupted cry
Came over houses from another street,

But not to call me back or say good-bye;   10
And further still at an unearthly height,
One luminary clock against the sky

Proclaimed the time was neither wrong nor right
I have been one acquainted with the night.

1928

Once by the Pacific

The shattered water made a misty din.
Great waves looked over others coming in,
And thought of doing something to the shore
That water never did to land before.
The clouds were low and hairy in the skies,   5
Like locks blown forward in the gleam of eyes.
You could not tell, and yet it looked as if
The shore was lucky in being backed by cliff,
The cliff in being backed by continent;
It looked as if a night of dark intent   10
Was coming, and not only a night, an age.
Someone had better be prepared for rage.
There would be more than ocean-water broken
Before God's last *Put out the Light*[6] was spoken.

1928

Desert Places

Snow falling and night falling fast oh fast
In a field I looked into going past,
And the ground almost covered smooth in snow,
But a few weeds and stubble showing last.

The woods around it have it—it is theirs.   5
All animals are smothered in their lairs.
I am too absent-spirited to count;
The loneliness includes me unawares.

And lonely as it is that loneliness
Will be more lonely ere it will be less—   10
A blanker whiteness of benighted snow
With no expression, nothing to express.

They cannot scare me with their empty spaces
Between stars—on stars where no human race is.
I have it in me so much nearer home   15
To scare myself with my own desert places.

1936

---

6. Before killing Desdemona, Shakespeare's Othello says, "Yet she must die, else she'll betray more men. /
Put out the light, and then put out the light" (*Othello* V, ii, 6–7). Frost also echoes the Book of Genesis 1:1–5.

Design

I found a dimpled spider, fat and white,
On a white heal-all,[7] holding up a moth
Like a white piece of rigid satin cloth—
Assorted characters of death and blight
Mixed ready to begin the morning right,   5
Like the ingredients of a witches' broth—
A snow-drop spider, a flower like froth,
And dead wings carried like a paper kite.

What had that flower to do with being white,
The wayside blue and innocent heal-all?   10
What brought the kindred spider to that height,
Then steered the white moth thither in the night?
What but design of darkness to appall?[8]—
If design govern in a thing so small.

1936

Neither Out Far Nor in Deep

The people along the sand
All turn and look one way.
They turn their back on the land.
They look at the sea all day.

As long as it takes to pass   5
A ship keeps raising its hull;
The wetter ground like glass
Reflects a standing gull.

The land may vary more;
But wherever the truth may be—   10
The water comes ashore,
And the people look at the sea.

They cannot look out far.
They cannot look in deep.
But when was that ever a bar   15
To any watch they keep?

1936

Provide Provide

The witch that came (the withered hag)
To wash the steps with pail and rag,
Was once the beauty Abishag,[9]

7. A plant in the mint family said to have healing powers.
8. To make white.
9. The beautiful young woman who nursed King David in his old age.

The picture pride of Hollywood.
Too many fall from great and good   5
For you to doubt the likelihood.

Die early and avoid the fate.
Or if predestined to die late,
Make up your mind to die in state.

Make the whole stock exchange your own!   10
If need be occupy a throne,
Where nobody can call *you* crone.

Some have relied on what they knew;
Others on being simply true.
What worked for them might work for you.   15

No memory of having starred
Atones for later disregard,
Or keeps the end from being hard.

Better to go down dignified
With boughten friendship at your side   20
Than none at all. Provide, provide!

1936

Come In

As I came to the edge of the woods,
Thrush music—hark!
Now if it was dusk outside,
Inside it was dark.

Too dark in the woods for a bird   5
By sleight of wing
To better its perch for the night,
Though it still could sing.

The last of the light of the sun
That had died in the west   10
Still lived for one song more
In a thrush's breast.

Far in the pillared dark
Thrush music went—
Almost like a call to come in   15
To the dark and lament.

But no, I was out for stars:
I would not come in.
I meant not even if asked,
And I hadn't been.   20

1942

The Gift Outright

The land was ours before we were the land's.
She was our land more than a hundred years
Before we were her people. She was ours
In Massachusetts, in Virginia,
But we were England's, still colonials,   5
Possessing what we still were unpossessed by,
Possessed by what we now no more possessed.
Something we were withholding made us weak
Until we found it was ourselves
We were withholding from our land of living,   10
And forthwith found salvation in surrender.
Such as we were we gave ourselves outright
(The deed of gift was many deeds of war)
To the land vaguely realizing westward,
But still unstoried, artless, unenhanced,   15
Such as she was, such as she would become.

1942

The Silken Tent

She is as in a field a silken tent
At midday when a sunny summer breeze
Has dried the dew and all its ropes relent,
So that in guys it gently sways at ease,
And its supporting central cedar pole,   5
That is its pinnacle to heavenward
And signifies the sureness of the soul,
Seems to owe naught to any single cord,
But strictly held by none, is loosely bound
By countless silken ties of love and thought   10
To everything on earth the compass round,
And only by one's going slightly taut
In the capriciousness of summer air
Is of the slightest bondage made aware.

1942

Directive

Back out of all this now too much for us,
Back in a time made simple by the loss
Of detail, burned, dissolved, and broken off
Like graveyard marble sculpture in the weather,
There is a house that is no more a house   5
Upon a farm that is no more a farm
And in a town that is no more a town.
The road there, if you'll let a guide direct you
Who only has at heart your getting lost,

May seem as if it should have been a quarry—   10
Great monolithic knees the former town
Long since gave up pretense of keeping covered.
And there's a story in a book about it:
Besides the wear of iron wagon wheels
The ledges show lines ruled southeast northwest,   15
The chisel work of an enormous Glacier
That braced his feet against the Arctic Pole.
You must not mind a certain coolness from him
Still said to haunt this side of Panther Mountain.
Nor need you mind the serial ordeal[1]   20
Of being watched from forty cellar holes
As if by eye pairs out of forty firkins.[2]
As for the woods' excitement over you
That sends light rustle rushes to their leaves,
Charge that to upstart inexperience.   25
Where were they all not twenty years ago?
They think too much of having shaded out
A few old pecker-fretted apple trees.
Make yourself up a cheering song of how
Someone's road home from work this once was,   30
Who may be just ahead of you on foot
Or creaking with a buggy load of grain.
The height of the adventure is the height
Of country where two village cultures faded
Into each other. Both of them are lost.   35
And if you're lost enough to find yourself
By now, pull in your ladder road behind you
And put a sign up CLOSED to all but me.
Then make yourself at home. The only field
Now left's no bigger than a harness gall.[3]   40
First there's the children's house of make believe,
Some shattered dishes underneath a pine,
The playthings in the playhouse of the children.
Weep for what little things could make them glad.
Then for the house that is no more a house,   45
But only a belilaced cellar hole,
Now slowly closing like a dent in dough.
This was no playhouse but a house in earnest.
Your destination and your destiny's
A brook that was the water of the house,   50
Cold as a spring as yet so near its source,
Too lofty and original to rage.
(We know the valley streams that when aroused
Will leave their tatters hung on barb and thorn.)

1. Refers to the trials a knight might undergo on a quest.
2. Small wooden casks.
3. A sore from wearing a harness.

I have kept hidden in the instep arch   55
Of an old cedar at the waterside
A broken drinking goblet like the Grail[4]
Under a spell so the wrong ones can't find it,
So can't get saved, as Saint Mark says they mustn't.[5]
(I stole the goblet from the children's playhouse.)   60
Here are your waters and your watering place.
Drink and be whole again beyond confusion.

1947

 SARAH N. CLEGHORN
(1876–1959)

Sarah Norcliffe Cleghorn was born in Norfolk, Virginia, but she spent her early years in Wisconsin and Minnesota. When she was nine, her mother died, and the young Sarah moved to Manchester, Vermont, to live with two aunts who raised her as a Quaker. Except for one year at Radcliffe, she spent most of her life in Manchester. Like Edwin Markham, Cleghorn was a Christian socialist who became active in progressive causes, including child-labor regulation, prison reform, and pacifism. But Cleghorn most often used satire to achieve her didactic ends. Her widely reprinted short poem, "The Golf Links," delivers a powerful critique of child-labor conditions and upper-class hypocrisy through a quietly savage humor. Cleghorn so consistently universalized her radical political messages, which in her hands seem based on common sense and common decency rather than partisan politics, that she won the admiration of writers like Robert Frost, whose conservative temperament was antithetical to her reformist idealism. (Frost even wrote the preface to her 1936 autobiography, *Threescore*.) Cleghorn's poetry was collected in *Portraits and Protests* (1917), and *Poems of Peace and Freedom* (1945). She died in Philadelphia. Cleghorn is admittedly a minor poet and critics and anthologists have ignored her work, but she remains a brilliant miniaturist whose concise and pointed satires still have the power to sting.

The Golf Links

The golf links lie so near the mill
    That almost every day
The laboring children can look out
    And see the men at play.

1917

---

4. The cup from which Jesus drank at the Last Supper. In Arthurian romance, knights went in quest of the Grail, believing it could heal the kingdom.
5. Mark 16:16; "He that believeth and is baptized shall be saved, but he that believeth not shall be damned."

The Survival of the Fittest[1]

"The unfit die: the fit both live and thrive."
Alas, who say so?—They who do survive.

So when her bonfires lighted hill and plain,
Did Bloody Mary think on Lady Jane.[2]

So Russia thought of Finland, while her heel   5
Fell heavier on the prostrate commonweal.[3]

So Booth of Lincoln thought; and so the High
Priests let Barabbas live, and Jesus die.[4]

1917

ALAN SEEGER
(1888–1916)

The son of wealthy parents from old New England families, Alan Seeger was born in New York City and raised mostly on Staten Island (although his family spent two years in Mexico). He attended the Hackley School, an elite private academy, and Harvard, where he became editor of the *Harvard Monthly*. He moved to Paris in 1912 and soon adopted France as his second home. When World War I broke out in 1914, the young poet decided to enlist in the French Foreign Legion. (America did not enter the war until 1917.) "It was unthinkable," Seeger wrote about being an American in wartime Paris, "to leave the danger to them and accept only the pleasures oneself." Stationed on the front line of battle, he understood that he would probably be killed, but he insisted that "Had I had the choice I would be nowhere else in the world than where I am." He was killed with most of his battalion a few months later in an attack on a German position in Belloy-en-Santerre. Ironically, he died on July 4. Three days earlier he had written, "I Have a Rendezvous with Death," which would quickly become the most famous American poem of World War I. (It was also the favorite poem of President John F. Kennedy.) Seeger was awarded a posthumous *Croix de Guerre*. His work was collected a few months after his death in *Poems* (1916), but his reputation rested almost entirely on a single poem whose romantic idealism offered traditional consolation to a public appalled by the horrors of modern warfare.

---

1. The title is a phrase coined by Herbert Spencer (1820–1903) and echoed by Charles Darwin (1809–1882) in his book *On the Origin of Species* (1859).
2. Queen Mary Tudor (1516–1558) was known for her persecution of Protestants; Lady Jane Grey, titular queen of England for nine days after the death of Edward VI, was beheaded in 1554.
3. Finland was dominated by Russia for most of the nineteenth century, achieving autonomy only after the Russian Revolution in March 1917.
4. So Booth of Lincoln thought: John Wilkes Booth (1838–1865) assassinated Abraham Lincoln (1809–1865); Barabbas: Pilate offered to free one of his prisoners, Jesus or Barabbas, and the assembled crowd chose Barabbas (see Matthew 27:15–21, John 18:39–40).

I Have a Rendezvous with Death

I have a rendezvous with Death
At some disputed barricade,
When Spring comes back with rustling shade
And apple-blossoms fill the air—
I have a rendezvous with Death   5
When Spring brings back blue days and fair.

It may be he shall take my hand
And lead me into his dark land
And close my eyes and quench my breath—
It may be I shall pass him still.   10
I have a rendezvous with Death
On some scarred slope of battered hill,
When Spring comes round again this year
And the first meadow-flowers appear.

God knows 'twere better to be deep   15
Pillowed in silk and scented down,
Where love throbs out in blissful sleep,
Pulse nigh to pulse, and breath to breath,
Where hushed awakenings are dear . . .
But I've a rendezvous with Death   20
At midnight in some flaming town,
When Spring trips north again this year,
And I to my pledged word am true,
I shall not fail that rendezvous.

1916

◄ JOHN ALLAN WYETH, JR. ►
(1894–1981)

John Allan Wyeth, perhaps the finest American soldier poet of World War I, was born in New York City, the third child of a noted surgeon. His father John Allan Wyeth, Sr., a former Confederate soldier and published poet, was a founder of New York Polyclinic Hospital and Medical School. Wyeth attended the Lawrenceville School, a private preparatory school in New Jersey, where he was president of the drama club and class poet. In 1911 he entered Princeton where his literary acquaintances included fellow undergraduate Edmund Wilson, who said that Wyeth was the "only aesthete" in the class of 1915. After graduating Wyeth went on to earn a master's degree from Princeton in 1917. Wyeth enlisted in the army later that year to fight in World War I. His fluent knowledge of French led him to an assignment in the Corps of Interpreters with the 33rd Division. By May 1918 he was in France and soon involved in the late battles on the Somme and Verdun. Eventually the 33rd division became part of the Army of Occupation in Germany. Discharged in 1919, Wyeth taught French at St. Paul's school before quitting to become a painter. He spent the next two decades mostly in Europe. He returned to the United States in later life and converted to Catholicism. He died at eighty-six in Princeton.

Wyeth's literary importance rests solely on one remarkable and neglected book of poems, *This Man's Army: A War in Fifty-Odd Sonnets* (1928). This striking, naturalistic sonnet sequence chronicles the movements of an American troop division from receiving sailing orders and embarkation in France through the battles across the western front. With slangy dialogue and vivid description, the poems present the war in brief, memorable scenes. Each sonnet begins by creating a narrative scene but ultimately rises to a lyrical conclusion. Wyeth's poems are also technically innovative. For the book-length sequence, he created a new rhyme scheme based on the Petrarchan sonnet but better adapted to the paucity of English-language rhymes. While formal, Wyeth's language is as fresh, varied, and contemporary as that of most free-verse poets of the period. There are no inversions, no forced rhymes or stale language. (Most of the poetry by our soldiers was written in a more traditional romantic style, as in the work of Alan Seeger.) Wyeth's sonnets have the narrative vitality and stark realism of prose but with the concision and lyricality of poetry. There is nothing quite like *This Man's Army* elsewhere in modern American poetry. It is comparable in scope and quality to the best British poetry from the Great War. Long neglected, it deserves careful reassessment. Wyeth never wrote another volume of poetry. *This Man's Army* is out of print.

◦—◀▶—◦

The Train from Brest[1]

A haze of dusk behind low roofs of thatch
and sloping moors and barren gouty trees—
dim roads and earth-walled fields—the steady flight
of blinking poles and the rhythmic sweep of wires.
Darkness outside—   5
     "Hey Tommy, gimme a match—
now gimme a Lucky."[2]
     "You're sorta hard to please—
you don't want much."
      —"Somebody turn off the light
I want to sleep."
      "Hell—with these frog flat tires?"[3]
A stifling blackness—sweat, and the jiggling scratch
of cloth on your neck and tickling under the knees,   10
and the clank of iron beating a rackety tune—
and like a secret calling in the night
waking to see the black cathedral spires
of Chartres[4] against a low-hung lazy moon.

               1928

1. This port city on the west coast of France was the disembarkation point for U.S. troops during World War I.
2. Lucky Strike, a brand of cigarettes.
3. Frog: Slang for Frenchman; flat tires: Suggests that it is a bumpy train ride.
4. Notre Dame de Chartres, a thirteenth-century Gothic cathedral.

Corbie to Sailly-le-Sec[5]

High staggering walls, and plank-spiked piles of brick
and plaster—jagged gables wrenched apart,
and tall dolls' houses cleanly split in two—
Rooms gaping wide on every cloven floor,
pictures askew that made your throat go thick,   5
and humble furniture that tore your heart.
"By God let's get out of here!"
                              We motored through
to the poplar marsh along the river's shore.
Sailly-le-Sec—her church one candlestick
on a broken altar, and beyond it, part   10
of a rounded apse—a dusty village husk
of rubble and tile. Low hills ahead, all blue,
and twinkling with the phosphorescent soar
of rockets leaping in the fringe of dusk.

                                              1928

War in Heaven

A reek of steam—the bath-house rang with cries.
"Come across with the soap."
                              "Like hell, what makes you think
it's yours?"
              "Don't turn *off the water,* that ain't fair
I'm all *covered* with soap."
                              "Hurry up, get out of the way."
"Thank God you're takin' a bath."
                              "He wants to surprise   5
us."
       "Oh is that so, well anyway I don't stink
like you."
          "Air raid!"
                         We ran into the square,
naked and cold like souls on Judgment Day.
Over us, white clouds blazoned on blue skies,
and a green balloon[6] on fire—we watched it shrink   10
into flame and a fall of smoke. Around us, brute
guns belching puffs of shrapnel in the air,
where one plane swooping like a bird of prey
spat fire into a dangling parachute.

                                              1928

5. Two towns near Amiens in France, site of one of the last major battles in World War I.
6. A barrage balloon used for observation.

Early Modernism: From Imagism to High Modernism

BLAST

EDITED BY
WYNDHAM LEWIS.

To be published Quarterly.　　　First Number will contain

MANIFESTO.

Story by Wyndham Lewis.

Poems by Ezra Pound.

Reproductions of Drawings, Paintings, and Sculpture
by
Etchells, Nevinson, Lewis, Hamilton, Brzeska, Wadsworth, Epstein, Roberts, etc., etc.

Twenty Illustrations.

Price 2s. 6d.　Annual Subscription 10s. 6d.
America 65 cents.　　　,,　　　$2.50.

Discussion of Cubism, Futurism, Imagisme and all Vital Forms of Modern Art.

THE CUBE.　　THE PYRAMID.

Putrifaction of Guffaws Slain by Appearance of BLAST.

Advertisement for BLAST (1914).

HISTORICAL AND CRITICAL OVERVIEW

> Progress is a comfortable disease.
> —*E. E. Cummings*

America in the period surrounding World War I remained a vibrant and conflicted nation. Largely convinced in its isolationism, it could not ultimately deny its increasing power on the world scene, which had for centuries been dominated by Europe. The Chinese Revolution of 1911, the rise of Russian communism, nationalist movements in the Balkans and other eastern European countries as well as in Ireland, would all have an impact on American life and politics. Global events in the world of ideas were likewise unavoidable. The influence of nineteenth-century thinkers like Darwin and Marx grew in literary and intellectual circles. Conflict over Darwin's ideas would eventually lead to the Scopes Trial (1925), pitting the theory of evolution against religious fundamentalism. Marxist ideology drove American labor politics as new unions were formed and strikes and demonstrations staged. By 1920 the Socialists polled nearly a million votes in a national election, and that same year the arrest of two immigrant anarchists, Nicola Sacco and Bartolomeo Vanzetti, for robbery and murder, became a cause célèbre. While Marx's ideas had stressed economic conditions as determinants of human life, the increasingly popular theories of Sigmund Freud provided a new vocabulary for discussing human psychology. Published at the end of the nineteenth century, *The Interpretation of Dreams* developed a theory of the unconscious, a hidden realm of reality inaccessible to conventional thought. Freud's basic notion that human sexuality was a dominant impulse and that its suppression through learned social norms contributed to neuroses was taken up by many artists and thinkers in a broad critique of civilization itself. Sexuality and the unconscious were increasingly perceived as better guides to the truth than social custom and traditional morality. Darwinism, Marxism, and Freudianism provided categories of thought that, for many, would only be confirmed by the wholesale disaster of world war, as if civilization were nothing more than the "restraint" of our savage impulses, or a chosen lie, as Joseph Conrad had suggested in his influential novella, *Heart of Darkness* (1899).

Of course, Americans also had cause for optimism. The technology of flight improved and the Panama Canal opened. The State of Massachusetts introduced a minimum wage law for working women and children. In 1913 the Armory Show brought exciting new art from Europe to a few American cities, and by 1915 Ford had produced its millionth automobile. However, 1915 was also the year of the sinking of a British passenger ship, the *Lusitania,* in which 128 Americans lost their lives, and that same year the revival of the Ku Klux Klan reaffirmed racist elements and religious intolerance in the country. South of the border, Mexico was engulfed in a decade-long revolution. Writers like John Reed reported on the war, and Ambrose Bierce disappeared into Mexico early in 1914. When Pancho Villa raided American soil, the United States responded in 1916 with an expeditionary force under the command of General John "Blackjack" Pershing, who would eventually command U.S. troops abroad.

World War I

A war to end all wars.
—*H. G. Wells*

The war in Europe had begun in August 1914, but the initial U.S. response was to maintain its traditional neutrality concerning foreign conflicts. By 1917, however, when the Germans instigated a strategy of unrestricted submarine warfare, President Woodrow Wilson was forced to act. It was "a war against all nations," he declared in a speech to Congress. "Armed neutrality" would no longer suffice, and "civilization itself" was "in the balance." America entered the war. Eventually the nation sent more than two million troops overseas, almost three-quarters of whom saw combat. More than one hundred thousand American lives were lost. But for Europe, of course, the impact of World War I was far more devastating. By some estimates there were as many as thirteen million military deaths. Just after the war, Winston Churchill described its horrors in almost surreal terms:

> No truce or parley mitigated the strife of the armies. The wounded died between the lines: the dead mouldered into the soil. Merchant ships and neutral ships and hospital ships were sunk on the seas and all on board left to their fate, or killed as they swam. Every effort was made to starve whole nations into submission without regard to age or sex. Cities and monuments were smashed by artillery. Bombs from the air were cast down indiscriminately. Poison gas in many forms stifled or seared the soldiers. Liquid fire was projected upon their bodies. Men fell from the air in flames, or were smothered often slowly in the dark recesses of the sea. . . . When all was over, Torture and Cannibalism were the only two expedients that the civilized, scientific, Christian States had been able to deny themselves: and they were of doubtful utility.

Whatever natural savagery had been let loose by human kind, the technological advances of the modern age had only made a more efficient nightmare. In England a whole generation of young men had been decimated. Among the British poets who died in the war were Rupert Brooke, Wilfred Owen, Edward Thomas, T. E. Hulme, and Isaac Rosenberg. Siegfried Sassoon, Robert Graves, and Ivor Gurney were either wounded or shell-shocked. "There died a myriad," wrote Ezra Pound, who lost several friends in the conflict, including the young sculptor Henri Gaudier-Brzeska.

Although America's involvement in the war lasted less than two years, its effect on our literature was enormous. The war not only helped shape the fiction of Dos Passos and Hemingway, but also the poetry of T. S. Eliot, especially *The Waste Land*. The vast and barbaric destruction filled some poets like Robinson Jeffers with skepticism about human progress and others like Archibald MacLeish with a passion for progressive political reform. Woodrow Wilson had entered the war with honorable ideals, and at its close gave another speech outlining the Fourteen Points of his vision for peace. But the deep-rooted cynicism and hatred exacerbated by the war among the European powers would prove too much for American idealism. In 1919 the Treaty of Versailles produced a crippled Germany and guaranteed that war would come again. Throughout the 1920s and '30s there were poems and novels expressing dread of impending conflict, a sense that society was morally bankrupt or spiritually ill, doomed to erupt again in senseless conflict. Even more devastating than the war was the influenza outbreak of 1918 and 1919. This pandemic killed twenty million people worldwide, including six hundred thousand in the United States alone.

By 1920 the population of the United States had topped 100 million. The Eighteenth Amendment of 1919 created Prohibition, making it illegal to manufacture or sell alcohol. One result of this was the rise of organized crime, which made enormous sums of money selling and distributing bootleg liquor. The gangster became a frequent figure in American literature and movies. In 1920 the first commercial radio broadcasts were made, and American women were finally given the right to vote by the Nineteenth Amendment. More women entered colleges and universities as well as the work force. The 1920s are often characterized as a period of greater sexual liberation—what F. Scott Fitzgerald would eventually dub the Jazz Age. American cities were also being transformed by the migration of African Americans from the rural south to the industrial north and midwest, a subject we will discuss further when we come to the Harlem Renaissance.

Modernism

> The French fathered the Modern Movement, which slowly moved beyond the channel and then across the Irish Sea until the Americans finally took it over, bringing to it their own demonic energy, extremism and taste for the colossal.
>
> —*Cyril Connolly*

In the arts, the period we are describing usually comes under the rubric of Modernism, a term as difficult to define as it is to date. What we can say is that Modernism was an international phenomenon, in some ways an extension of Romanticism and in some ways a reaction against it. It transformed all the arts, but poetry stood with painting very much at the center of the movement. Looking back on the period in "A Note on Poetry" (1946), the critic Randall Jarrell would describe Modernist poetry in the following terms:

> Very interesting language, a great emphasis on connotation, "texture"; extreme intensity, forced emotion—violence; a good deal of obscurity; emphasis on sensation, perceptual nuances; emphasis on details, on the part rather than on the whole; experimental or novel qualities of some sort; a tendency toward external formlessness . . . : an extremely personal style—*refine your singularities;* lack of restraint—all tendencies are forced to their limits; there is a good deal of emphasis on the unconscious, dream structure, the thoroughly subjective; the poet's attitudes are usually anti-scientific, anti-common-sense, anti-public—he is, essentially, removed; poetry is primarily lyric, intensive—the few long poems are aggregations of lyric details; poems usually have, not a logical, but the more or less associational structure of dramatic monologue.

Of all the artistic revolutions in history, Modernism was the first that involved—for many, but not all artists—a breakdown in the reliance upon traditional forms. Many composers abandoned traditional notions of melody, rhythm, and harmony; some even rejected tonality itself. Novelists sought new narrative structures that did not rely on chronology and plot. Painters and sculptors abandoned verisimilitude and played with multiple perspectives. Poets more often wrote what came to be called free verse. While Modernist artists were often well schooled in history and tradition, their art bore less physical resemblance to the art of previous generations. In nineteenth-century France such tendencies were seen in the prose poems of Baudelaire and Rimbaud, in Verlaine's *Les poètes maudits* with their cultivated decadence, and in "Art for art's sake"—attitudes that would influence figures like Oscar Wilde and the early Yeats. As an extension of Romanticism, Modernism was often antibourgeois and alienated from society at large.

No single definition adequately describes the complex and often contradictory Modernist phenomenon. The remainder of this historical note will examine several of the major strains that characterized the movement. But first an exemplary anecdote. One event that signaled a cultural change was the 1896 Paris premiere of Alfred Jarry's play, *Ubu Roi*. The first word of the play, *"Merde!"* ("Shit!"), proclaimed the author's intent to shock and confront the audience. The avant-garde artist and the middle-class public were now at war over the control of art. Though he alluded to Shakespeare's *Macbeth* and other canonical works, Jarry turned the theater into a space of such grotesque absurdity that the art was permanently transformed. At least it seemed so to William Butler Yeats, who attended the opening with his friend Arthur Symons. "After Stéphane Mallarmé," he wrote, listing French writers and artists of the time, "after Paul Verlaine, after Gustave Moreau, after Puvis de Chavannes, after our own verse, after all the subtle colours and nervous rhythm, after the faint mixed tints of Conder, what more is possible? After us the Savage God." Art, it seemed, had become a barbaric response to an empty civilization.

Futurism and the Avant-Garde

> The essential elements of our poetry
> will be courage, daring, and revolt.
> —F. T. Marinetti

The early twentieth century witnessed the rise of a series of new movements in the arts, such as Fauvism, Futurism, Cubism, and Expressionism, each focused on some particular innovation or aesthetic. Each new movement was Modernist, but no single trend fully characterized or exhausted the possibilities of Modernism itself. Although some of these movements centered on the visual arts, poets took a keen interest in each development. After settling in Paris in 1903, Gertrude Stein met Picasso, Braque, and Matisse, visual artists who worked at the forefront of some of these movements. Stein not only collected their work, she also began writing drama, poetry, and prose that reflected the influence of these experiments in the visual arts. In general, artists were more concerned than ever before with formal experimentation. Bohemia—unlike the modern university—did not require specialization, and different kinds of artists mixed freely. Some poets even worked in different media: E. E. Cummings and Wyndham Lewis painted; Pound composed music.

In 1909, the Italian painter and poet F. T. Marinetti published his "Manifesto of Futurism," declaring, "We stand on the last promontory of the centuries! . . . Why should we look back, when what we want is to break down the mysterious doors of the Impossible? Time and Space died yesterday. We already live in the absolute, because we have created eternal, omnipresent speed." Marinetti's brand of Modernism was destructive of the past. "We want to demolish the museums, libraries. . . ."

This radical and apocalyptic proclamation of newness as an absolute virtue had extraordinary international impact on modern aesthetics. While Futurism itself was short-lived as a separate movement, its manifesto remained the ideological matrix of subsequent avant-garde and experimental movements. Marinetti's later career also reveals the fallacy of those who associate radical aesthetic positions with revolutionary politics. He became an enthusiastic fascist and supporter of the Italian dictator Benito Mussolini. "We want to glorify war," he had announced in 1909, "the only hygiene of the world." His later career sadly confirmed the truth of that youthful boast.

Other Modernist artists were more playful in their subversion of the old order. The term *collage,* coined by poet Guillaume Apollinaire to describe certain works of Picasso, became a common label for the fragmentary assemblages of modern art. The principles of collage, especially in juxtaposing fragments or borrowed materials, expanded the technique of modern poetry, especially in the work of Eliot, Pound, Williams, and Moore. (In cinema, the word *montage* was later applied by Sergei Eisenstein to describe a linear assembly and juxtaposition of disparate images that intensified narrative experience.) Music by Debussy and Scriabin pushed tonality to the point where traditional harmony broke down. Their work suggested the atonality that would be extended by the Viennese composers, Arnold Schoenberg, Anton Webern, and Alban Berg into Serialism, a new method of organizing musical sounds. This radical and highly intellectual style, which was announced as the "music of the future," used *tone-rows,* or twelve-note themes to organize sound rather than conventional tonality.

Impersonality and objectivity became key goals among artists. In a statement written from the trenches and then published by Ezra Pound as a memorial, Gaudier-Brzeska described his artistic intentions: "I shall derive my emotions solely from the arrangement of surfaces, I shall present my emotions by the arrangement of my surfaces, the planes and lines by which they are defined." This manipulation and reconception of forms became the defining characteristic of Modernist arts. Time, space, and point-of-view were all now understood to be relative to the experience of the individual, and belief in universal, communicable properties for the arts was increasingly questioned. Modernism brought a new intensity—often a new difficulty—to the experience of the audience. Just as surely, it both expressed and contributed to a broad sense of alienation in the twentieth century.

Imagism

> It is better to present one Image in a lifetime than to produce voluminous works.
>
> —*Ezra Pound*

London before the Great War was a place where American and British poets met and influenced each other. (Ezra Pound, Robert Frost, T. S. Eliot, Yone Noguchi, H. D., and Conrad Aiken all took up residence in or near London during these years.) In 1908, T. E. Hulme joined the Poets' Club and began postulating a poetry of "visual, concrete language" and free verse. Translations of Japanese tanka and haiku had recently come into vogue. Noguchi had first visited in England in 1902 and published a well-received pamphlet, *From the Eastern Sea,* which was admired by Thomas Hardy and George Meredith. By 1911 he had begun corresponding with Pound about Japanese poetry, who until then knew little about haiku. In 1913 Noguchi returned to lecture at Oxford's Magdalen College.

Japanese poetry proved highly influential on Hulme's thinking. Within a year, Hulme had met F. S. Flint, another British poet who advocated "unrimed cadence," and the two became part of yet another poetry group meeting at London's

Café Tour d'Eiffel, where they began to formulate the ideas that would become the core of a still nameless movement. On April 22, 1909, Pound joined the group, reciting his "Sestina: Altaforte" to them. Flint would later recall that Pound seemed not to have read any French poetry written after the sixteenth century, but Pound's passion and charisma soon made him one of the ringleaders of the group, which advocated a new minimalist aesthetic that stressed, in Hulme's words, "absolutely accurate presentation and no verbiage." Demonstrating the new creed of compression, the January 1912 issue of *New Age* contained five short poems entitled "The Complete Poetical works of T. E. Hulme." The longest of them was only nine lines; Pound reprinted them as an appendix in *Ripostes,* a volume of essays.

Not only did Pound take up the new method, but he gave it a strikingly apt name—Imagism—and enunciated its principles. Meeting in a Kensington restaurant with the American poet Hilda Doolittle (to whom he had once been engaged) and her new British fiancé, Richard Aldington, he declared that they were *Imagistes.* Later, in the British Museum tea shop, Pound decisively renamed one of the new movement's central poets. Reading a manuscript of Doolittle's poems, he made a few quick revisions and then wrote at the bottom of the page, "H. D. *Imagiste."* That master stroke of literary publicity permanently changed both Doolittle's life and the course of modern poetry.

The most famous statement of Imagist principles, and one of the most influential passages in all of modern poetry criticism, appeared in Pound's column in *Poetry* (March 1913). Entitled "A Few Don'ts," it called for a poetry of objects written in a direct style, pared down to its most essential words and presented in "the sequence of the musical phrase" rather than "the sequence of the metronome." Pound erroneously suggested that meter was mechanistically regular, like the ticking of a clock, but his formulation was hugely important in the conceptualization of free verse in English.

The Imagist poem tended to be short, spare, and concrete, with no overt statement of emotions—almost an arrangement of surfaces, like the sculpture of Gaudier-Brzeska. By far the most famous Imagist poem was Pound's "In a Station of the Metro," its two lines juxtaposing distinct images in a manner like that of a Japanese haiku:

> The apparition of these faces in the crowd:
> Petals on a wet, black bough.

Though Pound had given modern poetry one of its most famous mottoes, "Make it new," he was also an idiosyncratic scholar of the past. Unlike the Futurist Marinetti, he never advocated the eradication of traditional monuments; instead his slogan expressed his disillusionment with lackluster poems of the late nineteenth century. "As to Twentieth century poetry," he wrote, "it will, I think, move against poppy-cock, it will be harder and saner. . . . It will be as much like granite as it can be. . . ."

In 1914 Pound compiled the first anthology of the movement: *Des Imagistes,* which contained work by Pound, H. D., Flint, Aldington, William Carlos Williams, James Joyce, and Amy Lowell. When Lowell took over the editorship of the anthologies, Pound moved on, deriding her efforts as "Amygism." With Pound no longer at the helm, the movement gradually lost momentum, and the individual poets gradually went their different ways. Although it lasted less than a decade,

Imagism had a profound effect on twentieth-century poetry. To this day, among many poets, "direct treatment of the thing" is favored over most symbolism, concrete diction over abstract, free verse over metered. Though H. D., William Carlos Williams, and Pound himself would extend their range as poets, the Imagist aesthetic stood at the core of nearly everything they wrote.

Other poets not formally involved in the Imagist movement shared many of its principles. Noguchi must be seen as a seminal influence on the group, though he had gone back to Japan by the time the first anthology was published. Adelaide Crapsey, who died without taking part in the movement, wrote short poems that were essentially Imagistic. Janet Lewis and Yvor Winters's early work was also a product of Imagist principles. The principles Pound outlined in his columns for *Poetry* magazine expressed a modern desire to avoid embroidered abstractions, poetic diction, and didacticism. They epitomized modern poetry's antipoetic stance. Where English-language poetry is concerned, Imagism was the most influential single movement of the Modernist era.

Vorticism and After

> WE ONLY WANT THE WORLD TO LIVE,
> and feel its crude energy flowing through us.
> —*Wyndham Lewis*

What Pound moved on to was a short-lived movement he called Vorticism in collaboration with British writer and artist Wyndham Lewis, who edited the visually stunning magazine *Blast*—festooned with revolutionary claims about new art. *Blast* lasted for only two issues, but its striking design, distinguished contributors, and aggressive editorials made it one of the most memorable little magazines of the century. The contributors included Pound, Eliot, Ford Madox Ford, and Rebecca West, but it was mostly a showpiece for Lewis's powerful art and dense writing. Reviewing the first of these in *Poetry,* Harriet Monroe observed that its intention was "to blow away, in thick black capitals half an inch high, the Victorian Vampire." But revolutionary rhetoric was not enough to hold the loose-knit Vorticists together as a movement. Lewis considered Pound "a charitable egoist," and Pound was too restless to submit to another artist's will. Vorticism was never so clearly defined or so influential as Imagism had been. The movement never articulated a clear set of ideas except for a general commitment to artistic innovation, an idealization of creative energy, an impatience with realism, and a sense of unity among the various arts.

By 1914 Pound had met T. S. Eliot, who was writing his own poetry partly influenced by French Symbolism. Pound was aware that *vers libre* had swept through the literary world so rapidly and completely that it was practiced nearly everywhere. In his Imagist manifesto he had already declared, "Indeed *vers libre* has become as prolix and as verbose as any of the flaccid varieties that preceded it." Pound with his proselytizing energy, and Eliot with his fastidious mind, became the two most important critics of their generation. They were also two of the writers who have been commonly referred to as High Modernists, meaning that their desire to make art new was accompanied by serious erudition and the most ambitious artistic standards. Their poetry exhibited this erudition through its complex patterns of literary references, suggesting to many a contempt for the nonscholarly reader. Some of the best critical essays Eliot wrote were partly in explanation or defense of such difficulty in art, not only his own poetry, but in great poets of the English Renaissance and great modern novels like James Joyce's *Ulysses*. "I know," he wrote, "that some of the poetry to which I am most devoted is poetry which I did not understand at first reading; some is poetry which I am not sure I understand yet. . . ."

The careers of Pound and Eliot—like their counterparts in other arts such as Igor Stravinsky or Pablo Picasso—demonstrate an impatience with stylistic stability. No sooner did they master and popularize one style than they moved on to another. Pound and Eliot, for example, tired of free verse once it caught on, and during the Great War both composed poems in rhymed quatrains. Eliot's included "Sweeney Among the Nightingales," while Pound's would eventually result in "Hugh Selwyn Mauberley." Despite their use of traditional forms, these poems remained densely allusive and difficult. A few years later both poets were again composing mostly in free verse. In Modernist aesthetics, which prized experimentation, innovation, and originality, constant innovation became the sign for artistic greatness and integrity.

Symbolism

> All art constantly aspires towards the condition of music.
> —*Walter Pater*

As we have said, Modernism was a complex movement that evades any single simple definition. It had the capacity to contain and utilize seemingly opposed ideas. While Imagism emerged as a dominant aesthetic among many in Pound's London circle, an almost contradictory impulse—Symbolism—took hold among other poets in the same milieu. Symbolism originated in nineteenth-century France and was led by the poets Charles Baudelaire, Arthur Rimbaud, Stéphane Mallarmé, Paul Verlaine, and Paul Valéry. Influenced by Edgar Allan Poe's theory of poetry as necessarily concise, intense, and lyrical, these writers developed a new style of verse that was subtle, indirect, and sensuously beautiful. Symbolist poetry tried to emulate music—both in its careful craftsmanship and evocative power. Verlaine began his *Art Poetique* (1874) with the statement "De la musique avant toute chose" ("Music above all things").

Symbolist poetry developed the lyric mode to its extreme possibilities. It avoided direct statement, narrative exposition, basic description, and didacticism. Instead Symbolist poetry cultivated complex and subtle effects. It spoke to the reader's intuition, imagination, and emotions rather than his or her rational mind. Symbolism, Mallarmé asserted, was the aesthetic of "evoking an object little by little so as to reveal a mood." It sought to arouse a response below the ordinary level of consciousness. The Symbolist poem was deeply musical and verbally complex—communicating its aims indirectly through suggestion and association rather than direct exposition. The poet operated as a sort of secular priest who had both the ability to perceive reality deeply and to express it by creating symbols that evoke it in readers.

Symbolism first entered English-language literature through the so-called "Decadent" poets of the 1890s. This loosely connected group, which included Ernest Dowson, Aubrey Beardsley, Oscar Wilde, T. Sturge Moore, and Arthur Symons, held an aesthetic creed that rejected overt moralism in poetry (though it often nonetheless creeped into their work). They read and translated the French

Symbolists, and their work influenced younger writers including W. B. Yeats. Symons wrote a pioneering study, *The Symbolist Movement in Literature* (1899), which among its many enduring effects decisively renamed the tendency from "decadent" to "symbolist." The book was enlarged in two later editions (1908 and 1919) and exercised huge influence on subsequent writers.

The young Eliot read Symons's book in 1908 and became deeply immersed in the authors and ideas it presented. He especially admired Baudelaire, Valéry, and Jules Laforgue, a charming minor poet whose urbane and sardonic voice Eliot emulated in early poems like "The Love Song of J. Alfred Prufrock." What Eliot took most importantly from Symbolism was the idea that a poem did not overtly state its aims and ideas; rather the poem used words, images, verbal pattern, and musical effect to evoke the desired response in the reader. Eliot's mastery of the Symbolist mode can perhaps be seen in its purest form in his "Preludes."

Other American Modernists deeply influenced by the Symbolist aesthetic include Wallace Stevens, Conrad Aiken, John Peale Bishop, Allen Tate, Yvor Winters, and Hart Crane. Stevens's statement that "French and English constitute a single language," is an extreme but suggestive statement of the debt these poets felt to the Symbolist movement, but Crane's poetic practice is probably most revealing. Crane adopted a Symbolist aesthetic for his poetry by studying both Eliot and Eliot's sources: Baudelaire, Rimbaud, and Valéry. His work vividly illustrates one of the chief aspects of Modernist poetry—the dominance of the lyric mode. Crane pushed the possibilities of suggestion to the furthest limits in his densely textured poems that radiate so many associations to defy any single interpretation.

Visual vs. Auditory Prosody

> I do not believe that writing is music. I do not believe writing would gain in quality or force by seeking to attain the conditions of music.
> —*William Carlos Williams*

Prosody is a literary term for the rules and theory of versification—the principles by which poets arrange language into lines of verse and then build those lines into complete poems. Although prosody is in some sense theoretical, it is also quite practical since it deals with the concrete matters of poetic composition like lineation, rhythm, rhyme, and stanza. The Modernist revolution in prosody is often described as a shift from traditional rhyme and meter to unrhymed free verse—an evolution from an old system to a new one. That conventional explanation, however, is too reductive and inaccurate to bear serious examination. The real practice of Modernist American poets was more complex, varied, and interesting.

There had been free verse before Modernism. Walt Whitman and Stephen Crane wrote almost exclusively in free verse, and even Henry Wadsworth Longfellow and Emily Dickinson occasionally worked in unmetered lines. Meanwhile High Modernists like Stevens, Pound, Eliot, Crane, and Cummings continued to use rhyme and meter along with free verse. Much early free verse like H. D.'s "Helen" employs rhyme without the support of meter. While free verse gained prominence in the Modernist era, it never replaced traditional meters. Traditional meter and free verse coexisted—although not always easily—throughout the period. American Modernism both radically changed and expanded notions of prosody in unprecedented ways.

Until Modernism, traditional English-language versification had been based on sound. Poetry was understood as a heightened sort of speech that arranged sound for special expressive effect and memorability. There were several systems of arranging language for auditory effect that went from the highly patterned and regular (like accentual syllabic verse in which both syllable count and stress pattern were controlled as in Shakespeare's sonnets) to the less regularly patterned (like the stress verse of nursery rhymes). Even free verse like the Psalms in the King James Bible or Walt Whitman's *Leaves of Grass* arranged auditory elements to announce the composition's identity as poetry. A native speaker of English could intuitively recognize the formal conventions and hear the language as poetry.

Modernism did not reject auditory prosody, but it developed a rival system based on the visual appearance of the poem on the printed page. If auditory poetry was originally the product of preliterate, oral cultures, the new verse was the result of the typographic print culture of books, newspapers, and journals. Modernist poets like Williams, Cummings, Moore, H. D., and Pound consciously shaped their poems to be seen on printed pages. The visual arrangement of type on the white space of the page became the canvas on which they worked. The development of visual prosody was not surprising since the Modernists were the first generation of poets in history who had grown up with typewriters. (The shift-key typewriter was invented in 1878 and made it possible for a poet to predict more or less what a new poem would look like on a printed page.)

Poets like Williams began to arrange their lines on the page in ways that created visual rhythms unlike anything in traditional auditory verse. Cummings and Pound experimented with expressive visual arrangements that were sometimes impossible to read aloud. Cummings's witty poem "r-p-o-p-h-e-s-s-a-g-r," for example, has no real existence off the page. It is an entirely visual poem. (The letters of the poem jump around the page until they eventually spell "grasshopper"—a purely typographic trick.) Eventually this visual prosody was taken to its logical extreme in "concrete" poetry, which used typographic arrangement to make designs out of letters and words.

Although the split between auditory and visual prosody may seem abstract, it rests on a simple and practical distinction. When the author arranges language for expressive effect in the poem, is the primary focus on sight or sound? The techniques can easily be—and commonly are—mixed. The visual arrangement of typographic words on a page affects how we read them aloud, and traditional metrical poets often design their auditory lines in special ways for the page. But among the Modernists one can often discern the main organizing principle of each poem.

Another effect of defining the printed page as a visual field on which to organize the poem was the development of the prose poem. This form was first popularized by the French Symbolists, especially Baudelaire and Rimbaud, and it represents the logical extension of free verse. If metrical language is no longer the necessary building block of the poem, and the raw material of the art is heightened figurative language, why should prose not be a suitable medium for poetry? Eliot published a prose poem, "Hysteria," in his first book, but he rarely used the form thereafter. Williams and Stein were the most assiduous experimenters of the new form, which also had a profound effect on Modernist fiction, especially in the work of James Joyce, John Dos Passos, Djuna Barnes, and Jean Toomer, often blurring traditional distinctions between prose and poetry.

Not all innovation concerned free verse. Another meter that began to be used by the Modernists was syllabic verse. This system, which was the standard measure in

Romance-language literature such as French, Italian, and Spanish, determines line length by counting a regular pattern of syllables. Syllabic verse had been used in English during the Renaissance but never fully established itself because native speakers of English cannot—unlike Romance language speakers—easily hear syllable count. By the late sixteenth century, purely syllabic verse was replaced in English by accentual-syllabic verse, which marks the syllable count by strong accentual stresses. Until its revival by poets like Marianne Moore and Robert Bridges in the early twentieth century, syllabic verse had remained quite rare. Modernist poets reintroduced syllabic verse as a variety of visual meter—a formal alternative to free verse. The form of syllabic verse could not be easily heard when the poem was read aloud, but it was unmistakable on the printed page, especially when written in complicated stanza patterns like Moore's "The Fish" or "Those Various Scalpels." Moore's syllabic poems, which seem consciously designed to exhibit their extravagant patterns, provided a formal but still Modernist alternative to free verse.

The Modernist Long Poem

> . . . Ecstasy affords
> the occasion and expediency determines the form.
> —*Marianne Moore*

Although early Modernism celebrated compression and intensity, the more ambitious poets could not put aside the traditional desire to write long poems. Since classical times the supreme test for the poet had been to write an epic. This ancient ambition, however, posed particular problems to Modernists that had not faced earlier poets. "A long poem does not exist," Poe had written in 1848, stating that the lyrical intensity necessary to make a poem successful "cannot be sustained throughout a composition of any great length." Poe's dictum had become a cornerstone of Symbolist aesthetics, and it was reflected in even more radical form in Imagism's insistence on evocative brevity. The High Modernist style tended to be dense, allusive, and self-reflective—hardly the most accessible approach for long works. Meanwhile Modernism's dedication to the lyrical mode had relegated narrative poetry to a secondary position. The narrative mode, which had been the most common structure for earlier long poems, seemed old-fashioned and insufficiently intense for the new avant garde. Besides, popular prose fiction appeared to have supplanted the poet's traditional role as storyteller. Yet literary ambition craved a larger scope. How did the Modernist poets negotiate this difficult feat?

Pound's restless search for a suitable long form typified the Modernist response. His solution was to combine the lyric intensity of the Imagist tradition with some non-narrative means of unifying the work, usually by grouping individual poems around a single character or historical milieu to create a cumulative effect. In *Cathay* (1915), a book of free verse translations from Chinese, Pound arranged the individual poems in a way that evoked British wartime experience as well as the literal meaning of the ancient Chinese sources. *Homage to Sextus Propertius* (1917) took the Latin elegies of the Roman poet, Sextus Propertius, and rearranged them into an extended dramatic monologue divided into lyric sections. Propertius became a persona for Pound, and decadent Imperial Rome merged into contemporary London, capital of the decaying British Empire. In his two Mauberly sequences Pound created another alter ego, a talented but passive modern poet who was destroyed by the age. Although in retrospect these powerful and original poems seem at the center of Pound's achievement, he considered them stepping stones to his major life work, *The Cantos,* his long and ultimately unfinished Modernist epic. In mid-career Pound gradually abandoned all other poetry to focus solely on *The Cantos* for the rest of his life.

Still unfinished at Pound's death in 1971, *The Cantos* would literally have no ending. Steeped in the narrative tradition of Homer, Ovid, Dante, and Browning, Pound would also squeeze in *The Confucian Odes,* Hesiod, Anglo-Saxon poetry, Li Po, Cavalcanti, Villon, Shakespeare, and his own contemporary politics and economic theories. As early as 1917 he was writing to James Joyce, "I have begun an endless poem, of no known category." Even he cannot have known how true that would prove. Twenty years later he wrote, hopefully, "when I get to [the] end, pattern *ought* to be discoverable. Stage set à la Dante is *not* modern truth. It may be O.K. but *not* as modern man's. . . ." Ultimately, even Pound's genius could not find closure, and the poem became victim to his growing obsessions and eccentricities. Despite their brilliant passages and patterns of thought, *The Cantos* transgressed most previous notions of comprehensibility. Pound wanted to create an epic, "a poem containing history," which resembled the epics of Homer, Virgil, and Dante as a major work that encompasses and exemplifies the issues and achievements of a cultural era. If *The Cantos* is ultimately a magnificent and mesmerizing failure, it nonetheless demonstrated, as Margaret Dickie observed, "the possibilities of the Modernist long poem." Its influence upon subsequent American poets—Charles Olson, Robert Duncan, and others—was profound, and the poem's fascination for scholars and other serious readers continues to this day.

The challenge for Modernists was in how to sustain a long poem without relying on conventional narrative, which was associated with the popular poetry of the late nineteenth century. The Modernist long poem tended to be a sequence of more or less lyrical or Imagistic sections, often layered with mythological, historical, and literary allusions. Building on the Imagist experience, Modernist poets made a religion of compression and placed high value on the most distilled writing. This was the principle behind Pound's editing of Eliot's *The Waste Land,* as he wrote in a famous letter: "The thing now runs from April . . . to shantih without [a] break. That is 19 pages, and let us say the longest poem in the English langwidge. Don't try to bust all records by prolonging it three pages further."

Published in 1922, the same year as James Joyce's novel *Ulysses,* Eliot's *The Waste Land* achieved an immediate international celebrity, and it became the quintessential long poem of the Modernist movement. (Its influence was not confined to the English-speaking world, but galvanized poets from Greece and Italy to India and Sri Lanka.) Although only of medium length by traditional standards, *The Waste Land* defined the stylistic possibilities of the extended Modernist poem and vividly embodied the density, compression, allusion, and discontinuity of the new movement. Eliot's poem also reflects the impact of new technology, specifically cinema and recorded music. The poem moves forward in quick cinematic cuts from one scene (and set of characters) to another; it also interrupts the action with snatches of borrowed songs—from opera to jazz. Its heterogeneous mix of characters, styles, and sources astonished and baffled its first readers just as its classical allusions to Greek, Latin, and Sanskrit exasperated American poets like Williams, who railed against its example for decades. While *The Waste Land* did not exhaust the possibilities of the Modernist narrative, it became the landmark by which other poems—rightly or wrongly—were evaluated.

Wallace Stevens shared the Modernist fascination with the long poem, but unlike Pound he did not focus on the all-encompassing epic enterprise. Instead he concentrated on works of medium length. Stevens alternated long and short poems across his long career. No major Modernist except Jeffers worked so consistently in extended forms. Stevens had no imaginative interest in Jeffers' narrative mode or Pound's historical subjects. He was fundamentally a philosophical poet interested in exploring certain obsessive themes in his work, primarily the search for meaning in a world without gods and the role of the imagination in creating new values. These themes link Stevens to the Romantic tradition of S. T. Coleridge and William Wordsworth as well as the revolutionary skepticism of Friedrich Nietzsche. If Stevens brought philosophical seriousness to the long poem, he also brought wit and wild imagination. One sees Stevens's lively engagement in the form even from his letters. "I find that prolonged attention to a single subject," he wrote editor Harriet Monroe, "has the same results that prolonged attention to a señora has, according to the authorities. All manner of favors drop from it. Only it requires a skill in the varying of the serenade." Stevens's first book, *Harmonium* (1923), contained two extended poems, "The Comedian as the Letter C" and "Le Monocle de Mon Oncle," but his major efforts came in mid-career—*Owl's Clover* (1936), "The Man with the Blue Guitar" (1937), and *Notes Toward a Supreme Fiction* (1942). These profoundly original works combine the intellectual depth of great didactic poetry with the imaginative force and evocative power of the lyric mode. There are no long poems of equal philosophical distinction to be found elsewhere in Modernist American poetry.

Robinson Jeffers was the only major Modernist who characteristically wrote long narrative poems. In the thirty years from *Tamar* (1924) to *Hungerfield* (1954), he created over a dozen major verse narratives. His exploration of narrative verse, however, had little effect on his contemporaries. Frost and Robinson, members of an older generation, continued to publish narrative poems well into the High Modernist era. *Tristam* (1927), the final volume of Robinson's Arthurian trilogy not only won the 1928 Pulitzer Prize but also became a best-seller. The next year Stephen Vincent Benét won the Pulitzer for his best-selling historical poem, *John Brown's Body* (1929), and Archibald MacLeish captured the Pulitzer for his epic poem, *Conquistador* (1932).

Although the long narrative poem never entirely disappeared—and its public appeal continued to be strong—most Modernists did not use narrative organization in their longer poems. Instead they most preferred to build a poem as a sequence of compressed lyrical moments and scenes. *The Waste Land* explored themes of miscommunication, sterility, fragmentation, and loss. *The Cantos* were a new attempt to create "the tale of the tribe" without merely telling it, by reflecting the multiple codes of more than one civilization. William Carlos Williams's long poem, *Paterson*, was also a collage, this time united mostly by American mythologies, texts, images, and personalities. Like *The Cantos*, *Paterson* remained unfinished at its author's death.

Other long poems did reach completed form. Pound's fellow Imagist, H. D., made her own response to the challenge of writing the long poem. She began by writing prose fiction and verse drama, even participating in cinema. These experiences, plus her psychoanalysis with Freud, led her to experiment with a new sort of epic symbolism in pursuit of psychological wholeness. In the forties, she wrote not one but three long poems: *The Walls Do Not Fall* (1944), *Tribute to the Angels* (1945), and *The Flowering of the Rod* (1946). (In almost the same time period, Eliot composed his religious meditations, *Four Quartets*). H. D.'s final epic work, *Helen in Egypt,* was published in 1961. All of these poems comprised sequences of lyrical passages; unifying narratives were implied rather than overt.

There were still more Modernist experiments with the long poem. In addition to poetic sequences, there were Marianne Moore's mid-length meditation, *Marriage* (1923), William Carlos Williams's mixture of didactic prose and Imagistic lyrics in *Spring and All* (1923), and his later poems in the "variable foot," like "Asphodel: That Greeny Flower." Hart Crane's *The Bridge* (1930), which will be discussed in the critical note on Modernist Alternatives, explored lyric organization for the extended poem. Modernist long poems usually required new ways of reading, more intense forms of exegesis. But at the same time they offered levels of complexity and interest that were unavailable by other means. They were alternative reflections of the new difficulties presented both by Modernism and by modern life.

The Literary Magazines

> Of all the literary scenes.
> Saddest this sight to me:
> The graves of little magazines
> Who died to make verse free.
> —*Keith Preston*

Unlike the Realists and Naturalists, Modernist poets rarely published in the popular newspapers and magazines of their time. Indeed, Modernism was largely responsible for the growth of a new kind of periodical, the small literary magazine. Published on a monthly, quarterly, or even annual basis, literary magazines made no attempt to reach a mass audience, but instead fostered the most rigorous, occasionally experimental ideals. Sometimes, like *Blast* (with only two issues, June 1914 and July 1915), they lived just long enough to garner notice and publish a few important works. Wallace Thurman's *Fire!!,* a defining small magazine of the Harlem Renaissance, for instance, published only one issue in 1927 before vanishing. Some magazines, like Eliot's the *Criterion* (1922–1939), exercised immense influence for a decade or two. By contrast, the *Dial* had great longevity. First published in 1880, it was taken over by two adherents of Modernism, Scofield Thayer and James Sibley Watson, in 1919, and went on to publish Thomas Mann, W. B. Yeats, William Carlos Williams, Marianne Moore, E. E. Cummings, D. H. Lawrence, H. D., and many other important writers of the time. For the four years from 1925 to its demise in 1929, it was edited by Moore, who also contributed some of her best criticism to the magazine, including important reviews of Stein, Stevens, and Williams.

Founded in 1912 by poet Harriet Monroe, *Poetry: A Magazine of Verse* is the one major periodical of the Modernist era that is still publishing today. Although the concept of an all-poetry journal is common today, *Poetry* was the first journal in the English-speaking world devoted solely to verse. That specialization was in itself an important sign of the times—of both the journal's dedication to poetry and its lack of interest in the general reader. Among *Poetry*'s early contributors were Pound, Frost, H. D., Lindsay, Sandburg, Eliot, and Williams. With Pound as its European correspondent, *Poetry* helped keep the transatlantic energies of Modernism alive.

Pound was also very influential at *The Little Review*, edited by Margaret Anderson until the late twenties. Without such magazines and such courageous editors, sometimes risking legal difficulties to publish Modernist literature (*The Little Review* was fined for obscenity after publishing excerpts from James Joyce's *Ulysses*), the movement could not have had so great and enduring an impact. These so-called little magazines were the places in which Modernist poets found their first readers and established some critical consensus about how the new literature might be read. If Modernism was in part the moment at which poetry began to be separated from a large popular audience, it also represented a high water mark in American literature, often sustained by small magazines and publishers.

Modernists in America

> America, my country, is almost a
> continent and hardly yet a nation.
> —*Ezra Pound*

From February 17 to March 15, 1913, the International Exhibition of Modern Art was held at the Sixty-ninth Street Armory in New York City. Eventually, the Armory Show, as it came to be called, was seen by some three hundred thousand Americans in New York, Chicago, and Boston. Roughly one-third of the paintings and sculptures exhibited were by Europeans like Marcel Duchamp, Henri Matisse, and Constantin Brancusi. For many Americans, the exhibition was their first taste of European Modernism, and its effect was profound—not only on painters like Georgia O'Keefe and Arthur Dove, but also on poets. Remembering the show years later, William Carlos Williams wrote, "There was at that time a great surge of interest in the arts generally before the First World War. New York was seething with it. Painting took the lead. It came to a head for us in the famous Armory Show of 1913. I went to it and gaped along with the rest at a 'picture' in which an electric bulb kept going on and off. . . ." Williams befriended several American artists who used Modernist techniques, and his knowledge of painting helped define his poetic technique.

While Stein, Pound, Eliot, and H. D. looked to Europe (and sometimes Asia) for cultural models, there were more Modernists who, like Williams, drew their inspiration from America. The meditative free and blank verse poems of Wallace Stevens and the intricate syllabics of Marianne Moore provided transformations of ordinary life, a project not unrelated to the often antipoetic free verse of Williams. Though Williams's father was English, his mother Puerto Rican, and though he had lived in Europe several times, he consciously based his approach on American speech and opposed the Eurocentrism of some of his friends. If Pound was the single greatest influence upon modern free verse in English, Williams's influence was nearly as strong; he experimented with new ideas about the measure and the line, and was militantly American in his choice of subject matter and diction.

Successful, self-contained, and introspective, Stevens was personally indifferent to appeals of literary nationalism. He alone among all the major Modernist poets never went to Europe, although he was a lifelong Francophile who bought books and paintings from Paris by mail. Stevens added a philosophical depth and playful elegance to American poetry. In some ways more rarified and intense than other poets, he was a high priest of the imagination. "I have no life except in poetry," Stevens wrote, and much of his work negotiates the terrain between reality and imagination. E. E. Cummings often traveled to Europe, but he centered his life in New York and New England as part of an American avant garde. Moore, too, lived a somewhat circumscribed life, yet she wrote as wittily about America's pastime, baseball, as she did about animals. To the figures of Williams, Stevens, Cummings, and Moore we can add Frost and Jeffers, who in different ways contributed to a vital Modernism at home in America. Though Frost was not overtly a Modernist in his formal techniques, a poem like "Home Burial" showed a despair at human miscommunication that is surprisingly close to what we find in Eliot. Out in California, Jeffers pioneered his own brand of narrative verse, full of tragic grandeur and psychological insight.

While Modernism often made extreme demands on its audience, and some Modernist poets wrote for an increasingly specialized audience, the populist Modernism of Vachel Lindsay and Carl Sandburg was broadly accessible. Both poets were formally experimental, both rooted in the American Midwest, with its regionalist and populist traditions. The desire to make art new was not always accompanied by an elitist program. If you open the early volumes of *Poetry*—or other magazines like the *Little Review,* the *Criterion,* or the *Dial*—you can see how varied and complex a time this was, how broad an umbrella the term *Modernism* implies. It actually refers to many movements, each with its manifesto, its adherents and critics. Pessimism and disillusionment were commonly found in Modernist poetry, but not always. The breakdown of traditional forms was commonly found, but not always. Immersion in ancient or primitive cultures was common, but not universal. Still, despite its contradictory nature, Modernism was a profoundly serious attempt to revitalize the arts, and it left American poets with a problem: where could they go next?

◄ AMY LOWELL ►
(1874–1925)

The youngest of five children, Amy Lowell was born into an elite Boston family whose ancestors included nineteenth-century textile magnates and the poet James Russell Lowell. She grew up on her family's Brookline estate, Sevenels, which she inherited after her father's death in 1900. She was educated, first, at home by governesses and, later, at private schools, but disdaining rote curriculum, she mostly pursued her own course of reading in her family's extensive private library. At age seventeen she entered Boston's social life as a debutante, attending sixty dinners given in her honor. Entranced by the theater, she considered becoming an actress in her early twenties, but a severe weight problem, glandular in origin, made a stage career impossible.

Until 1910, Lowell engaged in activities typical of an upper-class woman—travel to Europe, projects for civic improvement, and parties at Sevenels. But she also devoted an increasing number of hours to writing poetry. In 1910 the *Atlantic Monthly* accepted four sonnets, and in 1912 she published her first collection, *A Dome of Many-Coloured Glass,* whose poems reflect her immersion in the work of Keats and Shelley. The year 1912 marked a watershed for Lowell not only because of the publication of her first book, but also because she met Ada Dwyer Russell, a professional actress who soon gave up her career to live with Lowell at Sevenels. Lowell's prolific production over the next decade, in which she averaged a book per year, is due in part to her sustaining relationship with Russell, who helped manage Sevenels and offered supportive criticism.

The year 1912 was also a landmark year for American letters, for the journal *Poetry* was founded in Chicago. Inspired by the magazine's advocacy of "the New Poetry," especially the poems of H. D. (Hilda Doolittle) and the expositions of the new movement, Imagism, contributed by F. S. Flint and Ezra Pound, Lowell experienced a shift of sensibility as powerful as a religious conversion. In the summer of 1913, she set off for London to introduce herself to Pound, H. D., Flint, and their Imagist cohorts. By the time she returned to the United States in midsummer, the conversion was complete: her new poems were spare and direct, written in end-stopped free verse with lines carefully aligned to match the clauses of her sentences. The next year, Lowell's new poems appeared in *Poetry,* the *Egoist,* and Pound's anthology, *Des Imagistes,* as well as in her second book, *Sword Blades and Poppy Seed.* But when she took a second trip to London in July 1914, Pound had christened a new movement, "Vorticism." Lowell felt that in calling for a poetry of explosive energy Pound had abandoned the smooth perfection of Imagism. Concerned that the cause would lapse, Lowell decided to edit further Imagist anthologies herself, and by the time she left England in September 1914, she had secured the support of the other Imagist poets—with the exception of Pound, who scoffed at Lowell's determination to promote a movement he considered moribund. Lowell went on to edit three more Imagist anthologies.

Through her poetry collections, anthologies, extensive public appearances, and two books of criticism, Lowell helped popularize the Modernist movement in the United States—so much so that by the late teens *vers libre,* or free verse, had become so commonplace that it could be found not just in bohemian literary journals but also in mainstream magazines. Although Pound disparaged Lowell's version of the movement as "Amygism," her advocacy made modern poetry palatable to large numbers of readers.

Despite her championship of Imagism, her nine books of poetry contain a wide spectrum of styles: narrative poems, experiments in the rhythmical prose that she called "polyphonic," haiku, long-lined descriptive poems in the mode of Whitman and Sandburg, and lyric monologues such as the immensely popular "Patterns," whose astute combination of antiwar sentiments with a criticism of Victorian moral strictures articulated feelings experienced by many American women during World War I. Lowell's many evocations of female beauty also place her in a tradition of lesbian love poets.

Despite the coded eroticism of some of her love poetry, her books were accessible to a wide audience, which set her work apart from the dense and allusive poetry that Pound, Marianne Moore, and other Modernists went on to write. In the early twenties, she and Pound had become such implacable foes that she automatically dismissed writers he supported, such as T. S. Eliot and James Joyce. By then she had turned her critical energy back to her first inspiration, John Keats, and wrote a two-volume biography of the poet based in part on an extensive selection of his manuscripts that she had purchased over the years.

At the time of her death in 1925 from a cerebral hemorrhage, she was recognized as an important woman of letters, a status she had achieved through a brief thirteen years of hard work and energetic self-promotion. In 1926, she was awarded the Pulitzer Prize posthumously, for *What's O'Clock*. After her death, Lowell was remembered more for biographical details, such as her obesity and fondness for cigars, than for her poetry, although "Patterns" remained a consistently popular anthology piece. By the close of the century, however, feminist scholars had drawn attention to her role in the development of modern American poetry, and more of Lowell's work was restored to the canon.

◄◦───◄ ▶───◦►

Patterns

I walk down the garden paths,
And all the daffodils
Are blowing, and the bright blue squills.[1]
I walk down the patterned garden-paths
In my stiff, brocaded gown.   5
With my powdered hair and jeweled fan,
I too am a rare
Pattern. As I wander down
The garden paths.

My dress is richly figured,   10
And the train
Makes a pink and silver stain
On the gravel, and the thrift

---

1. Bulbous plants of the lily family.

Of the borders.
Just a plate of current fashion,   15
Tripping by in high-heeled, ribboned shoes.
Not a softness anywhere about me,
Only whalebone and brocade.
And I sink on a seat in the shade
Of a lime tree. For my passion   20
Wars against the stiff brocade.
The daffodils and squills
Flutter in the breeze
As they please.
And I weep;   25
For the lime-tree is in blossom
And one small flower has dropped upon my bosom.

And the plashing of waterdrops
In the marble fountain
Comes down the garden-paths.   30
The dripping never stops.
Underneath my stiffened gown
Is the softness of a woman bathing in a marble basin,
A basin in the midst of hedges grown
So thick, she cannot see her lover hiding,   35
But she guesses he is near,
And the sliding of the water
Seems the stroking of a dear
Hand upon her.
What is Summer in a fine brocaded gown!   40
I should like to see it lying in a heap upon the ground.
All the pink and silver crumpled up on the ground.

I would be the pink and silver as I ran along the paths,
And he would stumble after,
Bewildered by my laughter.   45
I should see the sun flashing from his sword-hilt and the buckles on his shoes.
I would choose
To lead him in a maze along the patterned paths,
A bright and laughing maze for my heavy-booted lover.
Till he caught me in the shade,   50
And the buttons of his waistcoat bruised my body as he clasped me,
Aching, melting, unafraid.
With the shadows of the leaves and the sundrops,
And the plopping of the waterdrops,
All about us in the open afternoon—   55
I am very like to swoon
With the weight of this brocade,
For the sun sifts through the shade.

Underneath the fallen blossom
In my bosom,   60

Is a letter I have hid.
It was brought to me this morning by a rider from the Duke.
"Madam, we regret to inform you that Lord Hartwell
Died in action Thursday se'nnight."[2]
As I read it in the white, morning sunlight,   65
The letters squirmed like snakes.
"Any answer, Madam," said my footman.
"No," I told him.
"See that the messenger takes some refreshment.
No, no answer."   70
And I walked into the garden,
Up and down the patterned paths,
In my stiff, correct brocade.
The blue and yellow flowers stood up proudly in the sun,
Each one.   75
I stood upright too,
Held rigid to the pattern
By the stiffness of my gown.
Up and down I walked,
Up and down.   80

In a month he would have been my husband.
In a month, here, underneath this lime,
We would have broke the pattern;
He for me, and I for him,
He as Colonel, I as Lady,   85
On this shady seat.
He had a whim
That sunlight carried blessing
And I answered, "It shall be as you have said."
Now he is dead.   90

In Summer and in Winter I shall walk
Up and down
The patterned garden-paths
In my stiff, brocaded gown.
The squills and daffodils   95
Will give place to pillared roses, and to asters, and to snow.
I shall go
Up and down,
In my gown.
Gorgeously arrayed,   100
Boned and stayed.
And the softness of my body will be guarded from embrace
By each button, hook, and lace.
For the man who should loose me is dead,

---

2. An archaic form of "seven and a night," or one week ago.

Fighting with the Duke in Flanders,[3]   105
In a pattern called a war.
Christ! What are patterns for?

1916

A Decade

When you came, you were like red wine and honey,
And the taste of you burnt my mouth with its sweetness.
Now you are like morning bread,
Smooth and pleasant.
I hardly taste you at all, for I know your savor;   5
But I am completely nourished.

1919

A Lover

If I could catch the green lantern of the firefly
I could see to write you a letter.

1919

The Pond

Cold, wet leaves
Floating on moss-colored water,
And the croaking of frogs—
Cracked bell-notes in the twilight.

1919

Opal

You are ice and fire,
The touch of you burns my hands like snow.
You are cold and flame.
You are the crimson of amaryllis,
The silver of moon-touched magnolias.   5
When I am with you,
My heart is a frozen pond
Gleaming with agitated torches.

1919

3. A medieval European country; in modern times the word refers to an area comprising parts of France, Belgium, and the Netherlands—the site of many bloody battles during World War I when this poem was written.

GERTRUDE STEIN
(1874–1946)

Born in Allegheny, Pennsylvania, Gertrude Stein was the youngest of the five children of Daniel Stein, a prosperous Jewish businessman, and his wife Amelia Keyser Stein. The family moved to Europe in 1875, and Stein was raised first in Vienna and then in Passy, France; consequently, she first spoke German and French, rather than English, which she did not learn until the family returned to the United States in 1879. After a year in Baltimore, the family relocated to Oakland, California, where Daniel Stein became vice president of the Omnibus Cable Company, which operated San Francisco's streetcars. His profits allowed him to rent a ten-acre farm just outside Oakland and to pamper his children. Before her college years, Stein's formal education was uneven, divided between studying with governesses and sporadic attendance at various schools; she never officially graduated from high school.

In 1888 her mother died of cancer, and when Daniel Stein died three years later, Gertrude's oldest brother, Michael, took over the care of his four siblings. After discovering that his father had left the family in debt, Michael took a job as a branch manager of the Central Pacific Railway, eventually earning enough money to ensure that his brothers and sisters would never have to work for a living.

In 1892 Stein moved to Baltimore to live with an aunt, and a year later entered Radcliffe College, choosing to be near her brother Leo, who was studying at Harvard with the psychologist William James. Gertrude found James's ideas cogent and attractive. His calls for detailed empirical observation and for open-minded attitudes would serve as core principles that enabled her to question poetic conventions. In 1898 she began studies in medicine at Johns Hopkins University, a prerequisite for advanced work in psychology. She left Hopkins in 1901, having failed four courses, and began to travel with Leo, visiting Morocco, Spain, France, Italy, and England. In 1903 Stein decided to make France her permanent home and settled in Paris with Leo, who had become a patron of the arts. In 1907 Stein met and fell in love with Alice B. Toklas, an American visitor, who, recognizing genius, decided to dedicate her life to Stein. In 1910 Toklas moved into Gertrude and Leo's Paris apartment and, three years later, Leo moved out, taking his half of the art collection. For the next thirty-six years, the two women were inseparable. Alice served as Gertrude's secretary, housekeeper, loyal reader, and best critic.

The 1903 move to France coincided with Stein's choice to dedicate herself to writing. For the next fifty years, until her death in 1946, she wrote nearly every day. Her writing challenged not only traditional assumptions about poetry, but about the nature of language itself, yet the strangeness of her experiments was often buffered by sly humor. Stein's exposure to modern art and friendships with painters fueled her writing. She remarked in 1946 that "Cezanne conceived the idea that in composition one thing was as important as another thing. Each part is as important as the whole, and that impressed me enormously." This revolutionary principle of composition governs her early prose works, Q.E.D. (1903–4; published 1950), which traces a lesbian love triangle; Three Lives (1909), which looks at three working-class women; and The Making of Americans (1903–11; published 1925), the history of an American family. In word-portraits of friends and in the "still lifes" of Tender Buttons: Objects, Food, Rooms (1914), Stein concentrated on capturing the essence of a person or thing, as a means of detaching the

Pablo Picasso, *Portrait of Gertrude Stein* (1906).

thing from the language ordinarily used to represent it. In a lecture that she delivered during the mid-1930s, she emphasized that "in *Tender Buttons* I was making poetry . . . but in prose I no longer needed the help of nouns and in poetry I did need the help of nouns. Was there not a way of naming things that would not invent names, but mean names without naming them."

Much of Stein's poetry, including parts of *Tender Buttons,* explores the possibilities of lesbian eroticism through intricately coded appraisals of publicly unnamable feelings and experiences. In "Patriarchal Poetry," a long piece that blurs the boundaries between poetry and essay (1923; published 1953), Stein mocks linguistic hierarchies that she attributes to a male-centered poetic tradition, and a great deal of her experimentation was motivated by feminist skepticism.

During the 1920s, Stein gradually began to receive recognition for her work, due in part to the agency of other writers. Hemingway provided the impetus for the publication of *The Making of Americans.* The British poet Edith Sitwell arranged for Stein to lecture in 1926 at Oxford and Cambridge, and the Hogarth Press published the lectures, along with several portraits and a landscape play, under the title, *Composition as Explanation* (1926). Stein also regularly published work in avant-garde magazines and also in more widely circulated magazines such as *Vanity Fair* and the *Little Review.* In 1927 she collaborated with the composer Virgil Thomson on an opera, *Four Saints in Three Acts.*

In 1933 Stein finally achieved the popular success she had sought. In *What Are Masterpieces,* she wryly observed that: "For a very long time everybody refuses and then almost without a pause everybody accepts. In the history of the refused in the arts and literature the rapidity of the change is always startling." In a short six weeks, she wrote *The Autobiography of Alice B. Toklas* (1933), a memoir of the couple's years together seen from Alice's perspective. The book was serialized in the *Atlantic Monthly,* became a Literary Guild selection, and was the first publication to generate income for Stein. She followed the success of the *Autobiography* with a lecture tour through the United States in 1934–35—the first time she had returned in over thirty years. The *Autobiography*'s popularity also led to a book contract with Random House, that Stein amply fulfilled by publishing one new book each year until the end of the decade.

During World War II, Stein continued to write, even though she and Alice had to give up their Paris apartment and retreat to the south of France, where villagers sheltered them from the Nazis. After the war, Stein became a popular figure among American GIs in France, whose voices she sought to render in one of her last books, *Brewsie and Willie* (1946). That same year, shortly after finishing *The Mother of Us All,* an opera libretto for Thomson based on the life of Susan B. Anthony, Stein died of intestinal cancer.

In the 1950s Yale University Press published many of the works that she had left in manuscript form at the time of her death, adding eight more volumes to the already formidable accumulation of poetry, essays, prose fiction, portraits, memoirs, plays, and opera libretti that she had published during her life.

◄●──◄▶──●►

FROM Tender Buttons

Objects Food Rooms

A BLUE COAT

A blue coat is guided guided away, guided and guided away, that is the particular color that is used for that length and not any width not even more than a shadow.

A PIANO

If the speed is open, if the color is careless, if the selection of a strong scent is not awkward, if the button holder is held by all the waving color and there is no color, not any color. If there is no dirt in a pin and there can be none scarcely, if there is not then the place is the same as up standing.

5

This is no dark custom and it even is not acted in any such a way that a restraint is not spread. That is spread, it shuts and it lifts and awkwardly not awkwardly the centre is in standing.

A PURSE

A purse was not green, it was not straw color, it was hardly seen and it had a use a long use and the chain, the chain was never missing, it was not misplaced, it showed that it was open, that is all that it showed.

A MOUNTED UMBRELLA

What was the use of not leaving it there where it would hang what was the use if there was no chance of ever seeing it come there and show that it was handsome and right in the way it showed it. The lesson is to learn that it does show it, that it shows it and that nothing, that there is nothing, that there is no more to do about it and just so much more is   5 there plenty of reason for making an exchange.

A TIME TO EAT

A pleasant simple habitual and tyrannical and authorised and educated and resumed and articulate separation. This is not tardy.

A FIRE

What was the use of a whole time to send and not send if there was to be the kind of thing that made that come in. A letter was nicely sent.

A HANDKERCHIEF

A winning of all the blessings, a sample not a sample because there is no worry.

RED ROSES

A cool red rose and a pink cut pink, a collapse and a sold hole, a little less hot.

                                                                    1914

➤ YONE NOGUCHI ➤
(1875–1947)

Yone Nogushi, the first Asian American poet of significant influence, was born in Tsushima, a small town near Nagaya, Japan. He became interested in English language and literature in public school. He later studied English at Keio University in Tokyo, but after two years he decided to immigrate to America. He arrived in San Francisco in December 1893, where he worked for a Japanese-language paper while studying American poetry. In 1896 he met the popular Western poet Joaquin Miller who encouraged his literary ambitions. For three years Noguchi lived in a hut on Miller's hillside property above Oakland, and he associated with Les Jeunes, a group of young San Francisco writers including Gelitt Burgess. Noguchi soon published two books, *Seen & Unseen* (1897) and *The Voice of the Valley* (1897), which showed the influence of Miller and Walt Whitman. Although written in slightly odd English, these early books were praised for their freshness. His next two collections of poetry, *From the Eastern Sea* (1903) and *The Summer Cloud* (1906) not only display more confidence and originality, they also incorporate more traditional Japanese elements of style and structure. *The Summer Cloud,* which presented sixty-two prose poems, also demonstrated Noguchi's early interest in literary Modernism. In 1904 Noguchi returned to Japan—leaving behind his American lover, Leonie Gilmour, and their newborn son Isamu Noguchi, who would become an internationally celebrated sculptor. Gilmour followed the poet to Tokyo where she remained with Noguchi although he soon married a Japanese woman.

Back in Japan, however, Noguchi's role in English-language poetry was not yet finished. While teaching at Keio University, he published over ninety books, which included four substantial volumes of English poetry. (He revisited the United States in 1919.) Noguchi corresponded with Ezra Pound and William Butler Yeats about Japanese literary aesthetics. Noguchi, therefore, played an important but little-known role in influencing the development of Imagism. He also helped popularize haiku as an English-language form. His volume *Japanese Hokkus* (1920), which was dedicated to Yeats, still stands as a major early milestone in the American haiku tradition. Noguchi understood his unique role as a conduit between the Japanese and English-language literary traditions. "We must lose our insularity," he wrote of Japanese literature, but he could certainly have claimed to have helped broaden the perspective of American letters.

⋯⊷━◖━⊶⋯

I Hear You Call, Pine Tree

I hear you call, pine tree, I hear you upon the hill, by the silent pond where the lotus flowers bloom, I hear you call, pine tree.

What is it you call, pine tree, when the rains fall, when the winds blow, and when the stars appear, what is it you call, pine tree?

I hear you call, pine tree, but I am blind, and do not know how to reach you, pine tree. Who will take me to you, pine tree?

5

1906

FROM Japanese Hokkus

1

Suppose the stars
Fall and break?—Do they ever sound
Like my own love song?

12

Leaves blown,
Birds flown away.

I wander in and out the Hall of Autumn.

16

Are the fallen stars
Returning up the sky?—
The dews on the grass.

48

It is too late to hear a nightingale?
Tut, tut, tut, . . . some bird sings,—
That's quite enough, my friend.

61

Like a cobweb hung upon the tree,
A prey to wind and sunlight!
Who will say that we are safe and strong?

68

Oh, How cool—
The sound of the bell
That leaves the bell itself.

1920

◦—◀ ADELAIDE CRAPSEY ▶—◦
(1878–1914)

Born in Brooklyn Heights, New York, Adelaide Crapsey was the third child of
an Episcopalian minister whose freethinking ways eventually caused him to break
from the church. The poet grew up (mostly in Rochester, New York) in a household
that honored learning. She graduated from Vassar College in 1901 and taught for
two years before traveling to study archaeology in Rome. Returning to the United
States in 1905, she gave support to her father during his ecclesiastical trial for
heresy, then traveled with him to the 1907 Hague Peace Conference. From 1909 to
1911 she was abroad again, partly in Rome, partly in England, where she began
her intensive study of prosody. Although this was the same period in which the
Imagists were beginning to formulate their ideas, Crapsey seems not to have been
aware of their work. Like them, however, she was influenced by new translations of
Japanese poetry. On her return to the United States, she taught briefly at Smith College, but she was forced to abandon teaching when it was discovered that she had
an advanced case of tuberculosis. She died of this disease at thirty-six.

    A minor but talented poet, Crapsey will always be associated with the poetic
form she invented while at Smith, the cinquain. A five-line poem with some of the
qualities of a Japanese *tanka,* the cinquain uses an ascending number of accents
per line: 1, 2, 3, 4, 1. The final line, by pulling back to only one firm stress, allows
for a kind of "turn" or a moment of surprise. Although she also wrote more traditional verse, often marred by old-fashioned diction, as well as free verse and some
prose poetry, it is a handful of her cinquains that will endure. Shortly before her
death, she noticed an advertisement for the Modernist journal *Blast* and wrote to

a friend, "Rather delightful, don't you think so—We must have it!" She did not live to see the arrival of this new movement in the arts.

❖—◆—❖

November Night

Listen . . .
With faint dry sound,
Like steps of passing ghosts,
The leaves, frost-crisp'd, break from the trees
And fall.   5

1915

Triad

These be
Three silent things:
The falling snow . . . the hour
Before the dawn . . . the mouth of one
Just dead.   5

1915

The Warning

Just now,
Out of the strange
Still dusk . . . as strange, as still . . .
A white moth flew. Why am I grown
So cold?   5

1915

❖◄ CARL SANDBURG ►❖
(1878–1967)

Carl Sandburg, the poet who would epitomize the democratic side if Modernism, was born in Galesburg, Illinois. The oldest brother in a family of seven children, Carl was the son of two poor Swedish immigrants. He was, as Daniel Hoffman has noted, the first important American poet to be raised in a household where English was a second language. Leaving school after eighth grade to help support his family, he drove a milk wagon, laid bricks, and worked on farms. At eighteen he became a hobo and wandered the United States on freight trains. When the Spanish-American War broke out in 1898, Sandburg enlisted. He served as a private in Puerto Rico but saw no combat. He did, however, write about his army experiences in long letters published by the Galesburg newspaper. After his military discharge, Sandburg enrolled in Lombard College, paying his tuition by working as a fireman in Galesburg. Philip Green Wright, a Lombard professor, became the young poet's mentor and later published Sandburg's first three volumes of verse—*In Reckless Ecstasy* (1904), *Incidentals* (1907), and *The Plaint of a Rose* (1908)—as well as *Joseffy* (1910), a promotional biography commissioned by a traveling magician. Sandburg left Lombard in 1902 and worked successively as an advertising copywriter, journalist, and political organizer for socialist and progressive parties. He also met Lillian Steichen (the sister of the celebrated photographer, Edward Steichen) whom he married in 1908.

Sandburg was slow in making a reputation as a poet, but in 1914 Chicago's *Poetry* magazine printed six poems that built his reputation as a Modernist with popular appeal. The most famous of these poems was "Chicago," an address to the "City of Big Shoulders," which would become his signature piece. "Chicago" also signaled a change in American poetry. Written in muscular free verse, it celebrated modern industrial and urban America. Few earlier poets would have exalted the beauty of slaughterhouses, railroad yards, or tool factories, but although Sandburg admitted the squalor and brutality of Chicago, he also saw it as the joyful embodiment of twentieth-century America's vibrant energy and creativity. The publication of Sandburg's *Chicago Poems* (1916) established him as a central figure in the populist side of American modern poetry. Along with Vachel Lindsay and Edgar Lee Masters, both fellow midwesterners, Sandburg created an accessible but overtly contemporary style that employed an oratorical kind of free verse. All three poets also had a novelistic or journalistic sense of generally public subject matter, and the literal content of their poems can be paraphrased in ways not always possible with, for example, the poems of Wallace Stevens or Hart Crane.

Sandburg's later books continued in the mode of *Chicago,* although the political outrage of the early book softened. *Cornhuskers* (1918), which celebrated rural life, won an unofficial Pulitzer Prize (awarded in 1919 by the Poetry Society of America to protest the Pulitzer committee's initial decision to offer no prize for verse). *Smoke and Steel* (1920), which some critics consider his finest volume, secured Sandburg's position as the bard of the Midwest and poet of the Common Man who had humanized Imagism and re-created the Whitmanian tradition.

Sandburg became one of the first poets to earn a substantial part of his living on the lecture circuit. The handsome gray-haired poet toured the country reciting poems and singing folk songs while accompanying himself on the guitar. He also compiled *The American Songbag* (1927), a popular musical compilation of ballads and folk songs. Sandburg was fascinated with Abraham Lincoln, and he eventually published a monumental six-volume biography of the fallen president. (He won the 1939 Pulitzer Prize in history for the final four volumes, *Abraham Lincoln: The War Years.*) During the Great Depression Sandburg also published *The People, Yes* (1936), a book-length free-verse poem which examined and celebrated the lives of everyday Americans.

In old age Sandburg was a beloved public figure. His *Complete Poems* (1950) won another Pulitzer. He often appeared on television and radio, where he convincingly played the role of the philosophical Common Man. On his seventy-fifth birthday, Illinois proclaimed a statewide "Carl Sandburg Day," and the king of Sweden awarded him a medal. But his greatest public honor came in 1959 on Lincoln's birthday when he addressed a joint session of the U.S. Congress. He died at eighty-nine at his home in Flat Rock, North Carolina.

Sandburg occupies a complicated position in Modernist American poetry. He was indisputably an innovator who helped shape the public's perception of twentieth-century poetry, and his poems still figure in anthologies. From *Chicago Poems* on, however, most critics have complained that his work lacked depth and complexity. While there is truth in that critique, such a view misses the great energy and immediacy of his best work. Sandburg's most persuasive defender, Mark Van Doren, suggested that "the art for him was an art of improvisation: the quick view, quickly taken." Sandburg had a genius for presenting the evocative detail and the unforgettable phrase, but he had no interest in the careful development of form or structure. As Van Doren maintains, "his best-known poems—and they are his best—tend to be short ones." Despite the Whitmanian sprawl of his longer poems, Sandburg's strength remains rooted in the Imagistic aesthetic of his early work. He was also innovative in his subject matter. As Louis D. Rubin has noted, "Sandburg's particular talent is that he opens up areas of our experience which are not ordinarily considered objects of aesthetic contemplation." Although his reputation has declined substantially since his death, Sandburg's influence remains undeniable on poets as diverse as Langston Hughes, Lawrence Ferlinghetti, Muriel Rukeyser, and Philip Levine.

✦—◆—✦

Chicago

Hog Butcher for the World,
Tool Maker, Stacker of Wheat,
Player with Railroads and the Nation's Freight Handler;
Stormy, husky, brawling,
City of the Big Shoulders: 5

They tell me you are wicked and I believe them, for I have seen your painted
    women under the gas lamps luring the farm boys.
And they tell me you are crooked and I answer: Yes, it is true I have seen the
    gunman kill and go free to kill again.
And they tell me you are brutal and my reply is: On the faces of women and
    children I have seen the marks of wanton hunger.
And having answered so I turn once more to those who sneer at this my city, and I
    give them back the sneer and say to them:
Come and show me another city with lifted head singing so proud to be alive and
    coarse and strong and cunning.   10
Flinging magnetic curses amid the toil of piling job on job, here is a tall bold
    slugger set vivid against the little soft cities;
Fierce as a dog with tongue lapping for action, cunning as a savage pitted against
    the wilderness,
    Bareheaded,
    Shoveling,
    Wrecking,   15
    Planning,
    Building, breaking, rebuilding,
Under the smoke, dust all over his mouth, laughing with white teeth,
Under the terrible burden of destiny laughing as a young man laughs,
Laughing even as an ignorant fighter laughs who has never lost a battle,   20

Bragging and laughing that under his wrist is the pulse, and under his ribs the
   heart of the people,
      Laughing!
Laughing the stormy, husky, brawling laughter of Youth, half-naked, sweating,
   proud to be Hog Butcher, Tool Maker, Stacker of Wheat, Player with
   Railroads and Freight Handler to the Nation.

1916

Fog

The fog comes
on little cat feet.
It sits looking
over harbor and city
on silent haunches   5
and then moves on.

1916

Limited

I am riding on a limited express, one of the crack trains of the nation.
Hurtling across the prairie into blue haze and dark air go fifteen all-steel coaches
   holding a thousand people.
(All the coaches shall be scrap and rust and all the men and women laughing in
   the diners and sleepers shall pass to ashes.)
I ask a man in the smoker where he is going and he answers: "Omaha."

1916

Window

Night from a railroad car window
Is a great, dark, soft thing
Broken across with slashes of light.

1916

Cool Tombs

When Abraham Lincoln was shoveled into the tombs, he forgot the copperheads[1]
   and he assassin . . . in the dust, in the cool tombs.

And Ulysses Grant[2] lost all thought of con men and Wall Street, cash and collateral
   turned ashes . . . in the dust, in the cool tombs.

Pocahontas' body, lovely as a poplar, sweet as a red haw in November or a
   pawpaw[3] in May, did she wonder? does she remember? . . . in the dust, in the
   cool tombs?

1. During the Civil War, slang for Northerners who sympathized with the South.
2. Grant's presidency was marred by scandal; he went bankrupt after leaving office.
3. Pocahontas: Daughter of Indian chief Powhatan in seventeenth-century Virginia who saved John
Smith from execution by her father; red haw: A type of hawthorn tree; pawpaw: Fruit of the papaya.

Take any streetful of people buying clothes and groceries, cheering a hero or
  throwing confetti and blowing tin horns . . . tell me if the lovers are losers . . .
  tell me if any get more than the lovers . . . in the dust . . . in the cool tombs.

                                                                    1918

Grass

Pile the bodies high at Asterlitz and Waterloo.[4]
Shovel them under and let me work—
            I am the grass; I cover all.

And pile them high at Gettysburg[5]
And pile them high at Ypres and Verdun.[6]   5
Shovel them under and let me work.
Two years, ten years, and passengers ask the conductor:
            What place is this?
            Where are we now?

            I am the grass.   10
            Let me work.

                                                                    1918

Cahoots[7]

Play it across the table.
What if we steal this city blind?
If they want any thing let 'em nail it down.

Harness bulls, dicks, front office men,[8]
And the high goats[9] up on the bench,   5
Ain't they all in cahoots?
Ain't it fifty-fifty all down the line,
Petemen, dips, boosters,[1] stick-ups and guns—
            what's to hinder?

            Go fifty-fifty.   10
If they nail you call in a mouthpiece.[2]
Fix it, you gazump, you slant-head,[3] fix it.
            Feed 'em. . . .

Nothin' ever sticks to my fingers, nah, nah,
            nothin' like that,   15

4. Two battles fought by Napoleon—the first a victory (1805), the second a defeat (1815).
5. A major battle (1863) in the American Civil War.
6. Major World War I battles.
7. This poem is in the slang-filled voice of a big city politico.
8. Thugs, detectives, and those who put on a show of legitimacy.
9. Judges; in cahoots: in league with each other.
1. Safe-crackers.
2. Lawyer.
3. Idiot.

But there ain't no law we got to wear mittens[4]—
  huh—is there?
Mittens, that's a good one—mittens!
There oughta be a law everybody wear mittens.

1920

➤◄ VACHEL LINDSAY ►◄
(1879–1931)

Nicholas Vachel Lindsay was born in Springfield, Illinois (the hometown of Abraham Lincoln). The future poet's father, a Scottish doctor, assisted at his son's birth. Lindsay grew up in a comfortable and prosperous home, located across the street from the governor's mansion. His early life was dominated by his eccentric and idealistic mother, a fundamentalist Christian, who experienced mystical visions. His parents wanted him to become a doctor, and Lindsay studied medicine at Hiram College for three years but eventually quit in 1900 to study drawing at the Art Institute of Chicago. In New York he studied with painter Robert Henri who encouraged him to pursue poetry.

Lindsay lived in such poverty in Manhattan that one night he decided to sell his poems door-to-door. The experiment was not a success. His poetic peddling earned him only thirteen cents. A little later he embarked on his first "tramp" across the United States. Starting in Jacksonville, Florida, the penniless poet walked from town to town, farm to farm, performing his poems and selling broadsides and pamphlets of his work in exchange for food and lodging. (In 1912 he entitled one book *Rhymes to be Traded for Bread.*) The first "tramp" already suggests how much Lindsay modeled his literary career after the itinerant revivalists and evangelists he saw as a youth with his mother. Returning to Springfield in 1908, he developed the theory of "New Localism," a democratic vision of regional art where every town and village would develop and support its local talent.

Lindsay's public breakthrough came in 1912 when Harriet Monroe, the editor of *Poetry,* a new journal dedicated entirely to verse, solicited some work from the Springfield author. He sent her "General William Booth Enters into Heaven," an exuberantly original and visionary celebration of the recently deceased founder of the Salvation Army. Published in the January 1913 issue of *Poetry,* the popular poem soon became the title piece of his first full-length collection, *General William Booth Enters into Heaven and Other Poems* (1913), which also included some earlier work from Lindsay's privately printed pamphlets, flyers, and broadsides. Lindsay's success was both real and immediate. "A fine brave poem . . . that makes the heart leap," said novelist William Dean Howells. *The Congo and Other Poems* (1914) further built his reputation. Lindsay started giving public recitations of his work, and he soon developed the confidence and the oratorical power of a fine actor. His fame proved both a blessing and a curse. He briefly became the most famous American Modernist—a colorful and charming eccentric in the eyes of middle-class Americans—and his "higher vaudeville" concept of performing poetry earned him a living, but his touring sapped his energy and turned his attention away from writing.

---

4. To keep from taking bribes.

(In his emphasis on oral recitation Lindsay both anticipated and influenced later trends like the Beats, Cowboy Poets, slam poets, and performance artists.) Lindsay was also greatly interested in the new arts of his time. His book, *The Art of the Moving Picture* (1915), was one of the first serious studies of cinema.

Despite his growing fame, Lindsay still lived in Springfield with his mother. He fell in love with the poet Sara Teasdale. She liked her improvident suitor but would not marry him. After the death of his mother in 1922, Lindsay collapsed. Eventually in 1925 the poet married Elizabeth Connor with whom he had two children. But by then the peak of his popularity had passed, and Lindsay could not support his family. His mental condition suffered, aggravated by epilepsy, a disorder he had kept secret for years. His reading tours declined in popularity, but the remaining few left him ever more exhausted. His despondency grew until he killed himself on December 5, 1931, by drinking a bottle of Lysol.

With Carl Sandburg and Edgar Lee Masters, Lindsay formed the so-called "Middle Western School" of Modernism, which was actively promoted by Chicago's *Poetry* magazine. Populist and oral, this accessible branch of Modernist poetry reached its peak in the decade from 1915 to 1925. Of the Chicago trio, Lindsay seems the most conspicuously gifted and original, although he lacked the ability to develop his talents—a situation not helped by his constant touring and the audience's pressure to hear his most famous early poems. "I was born a creator," he complained, "not a parrot."

There had never been anything like Lindsay's poetry before in American literature. It mostly used traditional meters as its rhythmic base, but it played with them with astonishing freedom. Lindsay's poetry especially delighted in syncopating traditional meters by adding extra stressed syllables that give the language a special intensity (as in the line "Booth died blind and still by faith he trod.") The total effect is much like the early jazz of Lindsay's era in which European meters are overlaid with African polyrhythmic syncopation. Lindsay has had few direct successors, but his work unforgettably embodies the broad and democratic possibilities of early Modernism.

◄◦━━◖━━◦►

General William Booth[1] Enters into Heaven

(To be sung to the tune of "The Blood of the Lamb"
with indicated instrument)

I

(Bass drum beaten loudly.)
Booth led boldly with his big bass drum—
(Are you washed in the blood of the Lamb?)[2]
The Saints smiled gravely and they said: "He's come."

---

1. William Booth (1829–1912) was an English revivalist preacher, founder and general of the Salvation Army. An indefatigable traveler and speaker for his cause, he was an honored public figure by the time of his death.
2. A hymn written by Elisa A. Hoffman.

(Are you washed in the blood of the Lamb?)
Walking lepers followed, rank on rank,   5
Lurching bravos from the ditches dank,
Drabs from the alleyways and drug fiends pale—
Minds still passion-ridden, soul-powers frail:—
Vermin-eaten saints with moldy breath,
Unwashed legions with the ways of Death—   10
(Are you washed in the blood of the Lamb?)

   (Banjos.)
Every slum had sent its half-a-score
The round world over. (Booth had groaned for more.)
Every banner that the wide world flies
Bloomed with glory and transcendent dyes.   15
Big-voiced lasses made their banjos bang,
Tranced, fanatical they shrieked and sang:—
"Are you washed in the blood of the Lamb?"
Hallelujah! It was queer to see
Bull-necked convicts with that land make free.   20
Loons with trumpets blowed a blare, blare, blare
On, on upward thro' the golden air!
(Are you washed in the blood of the Lamb?)

II

   (Bass drum slower and softer.)
Booth died blind and still by faith he trod,
Eyes still dazzled by the ways of God.   25
Booth led boldly, and he looked the chief
Eagle countenance in sharp relief,
Beard a-flying, air of high command
Unabated in that holy land.

   (Sweet flute music.)
Jesus came from out the court-house door,   30
Stretched his hands above the passing poor.
Booth saw not, but led his queer ones there
Round and round the mighty court-house square.
Then, in an instant all that blear review
Marched on spotless, clad in raiment new.   35
The lame were straightened, withered limbs uncurled
And blind eyes opened on a new, sweet world.

   (Bass drum louder.)
Drabs and vixens in a flash made whole!
Gone was the weasel-head, the snout, the jowl!
Sages and sibyls now, and athletes clean,   40
Rulers of empires, and of forests green!

   Grand chorus of all instruments. Tambourines to the foreground.)
The hosts were sandalled, and their wings were fire!
(Are you washed in the blood of the Lamb?)
But their noise played havoc with the angel-choir.

(Are you washed in the blood of the Lamb?)   45
Oh, shout Salvation! It was good to see
Kings and Princes by the Lamb set free.
The banjos rattled and the tambourines
Jing-jing-jingled in the hands of Queens.

   (Reverently sung, no instruments.)
And when Booth halted by the curb for prayer   50
He saw his Master thro' the flag-filled air.
Christ came gently with a robe and crown
For Booth the soldier, while the throng knelt down
He saw King Jesus. They were face to face,
And he knelt a-weeping in that holy place.   55
Are you washed in the blood of the Lamb?

                                    1913

Factory Windows Are Always Broken

    Factory windows are always broken.
    Somebody's always throwing bricks,
    Somebody's always heaving cinders,
    Playing ugly Yahoo[1] tricks.

    Factory windows are always broken.   5
    Other windows are let alone.
    No one throws through the chapel-window
    The bitter, snarling derisive stone.

    Factory windows are always broken.
    Something or other is going wrong,   10
    Something is rotten—I think, in Denmark.[2]
    End of the factory-window song.

                                      1914

The Voyage

    What is my mast? A pen.
    What are my sails? Ten crescent moons.
    What is my sea? A bottle of ink.
    Where do I go? To heaven again.
    What do I eat? The amaranth flower,   5
    While the winds through the jungles think old tunes.
    I eat that flower with ivory spoons
    While the winds through the jungles play old tunes;
    The songs the angels used to sing
    When heaven was not old autumn, but spring—   10
    The bold, old songs of heaven and spring.

                                      1929

---

1. A brutish person, slang adopted from Swift's *Gulliver's Travels.*
2. Allusion to Shakespeare's *Hamlet* (I, iv, 90), when the ghost has been seen but the royal crime not yet discovered.

◦─◄ WALLACE STEVENS ►─◦
(1879–1955)

Wallace Stevens was born in Reading, Pennsylvania, the second of five children in a family of Dutch-German ancestry. His father was a prosperous and practical lawyer, his mother a former schoolteacher who loved poetry and read the Bible to her children each night. Although in later life Stevens became passionately interested in genealogy, he rarely mentioned his own childhood, which seems to have been conventional middle-class, Presbyterian, and provincial. In high school he played football, took the classical curriculum, which included Greek and Latin, and failed to pass one year. Finally graduating in 1897 (in the same class as his younger brother), Stevens entered Harvard University as a special student, which allowed him to attend classes at a reduced tuition but not qualify for a degree. At Harvard he studied French, German, and English literature while also publishing stories and poems in campus magazines. ("Some of one's early things give one the creeps," he later commented on his undergraduate writing.) In his third and last year Stevens was elected president of the *Harvard Advocate,* the college literary magazine.

A formative experience in his Cambridge years was meeting the Spanish-born and Harvard-educated philosopher and poet, George Santayana (1863–1952). Stevens never took a course from Santayana, but he visited the brilliant man of letters numerous times and even read early poems to him. Santayana's ideas on aesthetics, philosophy, and religion influenced Stevens throughout his life, and his late poem, "To an Old Philosopher in Rome," sympathetically portrays Santayana's final years.

Stevens was an intensely private man who avoided publicity and preferred to speak in abstract universal terms. (His published poetry and prose never indulges in direct autobiography.) In later life he seemed a remote and Olympian figure in American poetry—working in a corporate office in commercial Hartford, Connecticut, avoiding literary circles, and hardly socializing even with business associates. Not surprisingly, a mythology arose about Stevens as the businessman-poet, a unique and solitary figure, half-playful aesthete and half-stolid burgher. While there is some truth to this image of the mysteriously divided man, it describes the staid and narrow life of the older Stevens, not the unsettled and urban existence of the aspiring poet.

When Stevens left Harvard in 1900, he intended to be a writer. Moving to New York, he started first as a reporter for the *New York Tribune* and then as an editor for *World's Work.* He fell in love with the cosmopolitan life of New York, which always remained his favorite city. His father strongly disapproved of Stevens's artistic aspirations. When the young poet wrote home suggesting he should quit journalism and dedicate himself solely to literature, his father returned the letter torn in half. Family pressure continued until 1901 when the young poet reluctantly agreed to enter New York Law School from which he graduated two years later. Now began a crucial period of Stevens's life that was not well understood by early critics who viewed the poet only in his reclusive later years. Between 1903 and 1916 Stevens lived mostly in Manhattan, worked at various legal jobs, and actively mixed in bohemian cultural life. In the salons of Manhattan, Stevens met many major modernists, including fellow poet William Carlos Williams, the artist Marcel Duchamp, and the composer Edgard Varèse. During this period Stevens's business career was not successful; he drifted through five law firms and four insurance companies in fourteen years. He did, however, begin writing the brilliantly original poems that would eventually fill his book, *Harmonium* (1923).

The other major event of the New York years was Stevens's long courtship, troubled engagement, and difficult marriage to Elsie Viola Kachel Moll. He met the eighteen-year-old salesclerk on a visit home in 1904, and quickly fell in love with "the prettiest girl in Reading." Over the next four years he courted her through letters and occasional visits. When they became formally engaged on Christmas 1908, his father objected to Elsie's social background. (She had only a grammar school education, and the elder Stevens suspected that she had been born illegitimate.) The young poet stood loyally by his fiancée and cut off relations with his family. He never spoke to his father again. The couple was married in 1909, but differences in their temperaments and tastes soon caused difficulties. They never enjoyed a happy relationship, although the exact nature of their problems remains obscure, since both husband and wife displayed a discretion that bordered on secrecy. In later years they lived in separate sections of their large Hartford house. They also delayed their first and only child for fifteen years—until Stevens had published his first book.

Stevens tasted failure often in these early years, and in 1916 the thirty-six-year-old found himself once again without a job when his employer went bankrupt. Reluctantly leaving New York, he accepted a position in Connecticut at Hartford Accident and Indemnity to head their surety claims department. He now settled into the second and final phase of his professional and artistic life. He would never leave the city or the company. Hartford would nourish the reclusive and meditative side of his personality, and his new career was so secure and remunerative that it sheltered him from economic worry, even during the harsh Depression years. Stevens now focused more seriously on his writing, and at the age of forty-three, he published his first book, *Harmonium*.

Harmonium is not merely the most astonishing and ample first book by any American modernist poet; it ranks with Walt Whitman's *Leaves of Grass* as one of the greatest poetic debuts in American literature—with both eccentricities and originality equal to Whitman's. Simply to list some of the poems from *Harmonium* gives an idea of the book's extraordinary level of achievement: "The Snow Man," "The Emperor of Ice-Cream," "Disillusionment at Ten O'Clock," "Sunday Morning," "Anecdote of the Jar," "Peter Quince at the Clavier," and "Thirteen Ways of Looking at a Blackbird." These canonic works in modern poetry all first appeared in this debut volume whose contents ranged from the ornate and intricate texture of "Sunday Morning," a triumph of both philosophical inquiry and lyricality, to the Imagist lucidity of "Thirteen Ways of Looking at a Blackbird," which transcends the usual slightness of Imagist poetry by creating a sequence of interrelated short poems exploring the same ideas.

Harmonium was a commercial failure, earning Stevens only $6.70 in his first royalty check, but it announced him as a major poet. The poet was not immune to the disappointment of *Harmonium*'s modest impact, but he was supremely confident of his own artistic development. Always cautious, he waited until he was fifty-five to publish a second volume, *Ideas of Order* (1935), which appeared first in a small limited edition that he expanded into a full-length trade book the next year.

His business career and family life now firmly settled, Stevens finally began publishing regularly. Over the remaining twenty years of his life he issued a series of

books of notable artistic ambition, intellectual seriousness, and poetic distinction—
Owl's Clover (1936), *The Man with the Blue Guitar* (1937), *Parts of a World*
(1942), *Notes Toward a Supreme Fiction* (1942), *Esthétique du Mal* (1945), *Transport to Summer* (1947), *Auroras of Autumn* (1950), and *The Collected Poems*
(1954), as well as *The Necessary Angel* (1951), a volume of "Essays on Reality and
the Imagination." There was no falling off in his later years—a common fault among
poets—and his last poems rank among his finest work. Some of these volumes appeared only in limited editions, but having already waited so long to pursue a public
literary career, Stevens was indifferent to fame and expected no financial reward
from poetry. Until his final years, he declined most invitations for readings, lectures,
recordings, and interviews. Literary honors came too late to matter greatly—a
Bollingen Prize (1950), two National Book Awards (1951 and 1955), and a Pulitzer
Prize (1955) that was announced a few weeks after he was diagnosed with incurable
stomach cancer.

Stevens's later years reveal a well-ordered life of artistic dedication, personal
prosperity, and self-imposed emotional deprivation. Inured to his joyless marriage,
Stevens led a reclusive life outside the office. He and his wife were never seen together in public, and he drank mostly at his club to avoid her censure. He had no
intimate friends, and almost none of his acquaintances were allowed in his house.
His copious correspondence shows how few people, including old friends, he addressed on a first-name basis. The office provided him with his social existence,
and he did not retire until his final illness. On his deathbed he had several conversations with the hospital's Catholic chaplain and reportedly requested and received baptism—an incident which his daughter disputed, but which, if true, can
be interpreted (depending on the critic) as either a denial or vindication of his lifelong obsession with the idea of God in an apparently godless universe.

The quality and originality of Stevens's poetry has been appreciated from the
beginning. Even before the publication of *Harmonium,* Yvor Winters presciently
declared "Sunday Morning" one of the great poems of the century. But most early
critics tended to see Stevens as an aesthete, or "poet's poet"—elegant, sophisticated, ingenious, and slightly precious. In a review of *Harmonium,* for example,
Edmund Wilson declared him "impervious to life," and as late as 1946 Horace
Gregory and Marya Zaturenska declared in their *A History of American Poetry:
1900–1940,* that Stevens did not write intellectual or philosophical poetry, but "a
kind of poetry that employs to the utmost the resources of poetic intelligence and
wit." Although this opinion seems superficial in retrospect, Gregory and Zaturenska's judgment does suggest something essential about Stevens's art. He brought a
playful extravagance usually associated with nonsense verse into meditative lyric
poetry. Who but Stevens would write a startling poem about poverty and death in
the high burlesque manner of "The Emperor of Ice-Cream" or lodge the hymn to
beauty that concludes "Peter Quince at the Clavier" with the boisterous clowning
of Hebrew Susanna's inexplicable Byzantine attendants? Even the titles of Stevens's
poems announce a rude comic vigor seemingly at cross-purposes with his earnestness—"No Possum, No Sop, No Taters," "So-and-So Reclining on Her Couch,"
"Le Monocle de Mon Oncle," "Invective against Swans." Yet it is precisely this irreverent exuberance that enlivens and personalizes Stevens's otherwise intellectual
and often seraphic imagination. The comic mode is not a secondary element in
Stevens's work; it is the integrating and humanizing vision that informs his work,
the underlying worldview that nourished the generosity of his imagination.

Stevens's unique contribution to Modernism can be seen more easily if his work is compared to the poetry of Pound, Moore, or Eliot, which during his lifetime generally defined the High Modernist style. Pound, Moore, and Eliot pioneered the use of collage, quotation, and cinematic montage in verse. Their work customarily incorporates dramatically different material (often in foreign languages or contrasting diction) into a heterogeneous and purposely discontinuous whole. Pound's polyglot *Cantos* are an extreme example of this Modernist reaction against the smooth stylistic homogeneity of Victorian poets like Tennyson and Swinburne. Stevens, however, created an astonishingly cohesive yet inclusive style that could take the most disparate material and refine it through a powerfully unifying sensibility. His sadly beautiful meditative lyric "Autumn Refrain," for example, begins with the unlikely line, "The skreek and skritter of the evening gone." Yet those grating neologisms almost immediately become an indispensable part of the dark and noble poem. In Stevens the poetic imagination subsumes and transforms all material.

Abstract, austere, impersonal, and analytical, Stevens is nonetheless the most Romantic of the High Modernists. His sensibility was fixated on the central themes of Wordsworth and Coleridge—the relation between intellect and reality, the growth of poetic imagination as an instrument of perception and creativity, and the correspondence between the mind and the natural world. Although some early poems like "Thirteen Ways of Looking at a Blackbird" reflect the methods of Imagism, Stevens was never a true member of that school. His imagination was too expansive and abundant, his need to pursue intellectual development too strong. Stevens also maintained a career-long fascination with longer forms. *Harmonium* contains three extended poems—the briefest, "Sunday Morning," resembles one of Keats's or Wordsworth's great romantic odes, and the others, "Le Monocle de Mon Oncle" and "The Comedian as the Letter C," presage the long poems he would regularly publish across his career culminating in *Notes Toward a Supreme Fiction*, perhaps the greatest ars poetica of American Modernism.

Stevens's poetic career began late, and during his lifetime he was overshadowed by Pound, Frost, Jeffers, and especially Eliot. Since his death, however, no American poet—not even Williams—has proved so influential on younger writers. His expansive style and inclusive imagination appealed to writers as diverse as Elizabeth Bishop, Weldon Kees, Donald Justice, John Ashbery, May Swenson, James Merrill, W. S. Merwin, and Charles Wright. In contemporary poetry he has influenced both Language Poets and New Formalists. Among critics no Modernist is more highly regarded or widely discussed, and there exists a veritable industry of Stevens scholarship. But amidst the myriad of influences and commentary, the magisterial, mysterious, and ironic author abides "beyond the last thought," untouched and independent, the pure poet of the Modernist imagination.

◄◦─◄▌►─◦►

The Snow Man[1]

One must have a mind of winter
To regard the frost and the boughs
Of the pine-trees crusted with snow;

1. In a letter dated April 18, 1944, Stevens wrote, "I shall explain The Snow Man as an example of the necessity of identifying oneself with reality in order to understand and enjoy it."

And have been cold a long time
To behold the junipers shagged with ice,   5
The spruces rough in the distant glitter

Of the January sun; and not to think
Of any misery in the sound of the wind,
In the sound of a few leaves,

Which is the sound of the land   10
Full of the same wind
That is blowing in the same bare place

For the listener, who listens in the snow,
And, nothing himself, beholds
Nothing that is not there and the nothing that is.   15

1923

Nuances of a Theme by Williams

It's a strange courage
you give me, ancient star:

Shine alone in the sunrise
toward which you lend no part![2]

I

Shine alone, shine nakedly, shine like bronze,   5
that reflects neither my face nor any inner part
of my being, shine like fire, that mirrors nothing.

II

Lend no part to any humanity that suffuses
you in its own light.
Be not chimera[3] of morning,   10
Half-man, half-star.
Be not an intelligence,
Like a widow's bird
Or an old horse.

1923

A High-Toned Old Christian Woman

Poetry is the supreme fiction, madame.
Take the moral law and make a nave[4] of it
And from the nave build haunted heaven. Thus,
The conscience is converted into palms,

2. The four lines of "El Hombre" (1917) by William Carlos Williams.
3. Fire-breathing monster of Greek mythology or phantasm.
4. The long, central hall of a church where the congregation sits.

Like windy citherns[5] hankering for hymns.   5
We agree in principle. That's clear. But take
The opposing law and make a peristyle,
And from the peristyle project a masque[6]
Beyond the planets. Thus, our bawdiness,
Unpurged by epitaph, indulged at last,   10
Is equally converted into palms,
Squiggling like saxophones. And palm for palm,
Madame, we are where we began. Allow,
Therefore, that in the planetary scene
Your disaffected flagellants, well-stuffed,   15
Smacking their muzzy[7] bellies in parade,
Proud of such novelties of the sublime,
Such tink and tank and tunk-a-tunk-tunk,
May, merely may, madame, whip from themselves
A jovial hullabaloo among the spheres.   20
This will make widows wince. But fictive things
Wink as they will. Wink most when widows wince.

                                                                          1923

The Emperor of Ice-Cream

Call the roller of big cigars,
The muscular one, and bid him whip
In kitchen cups concupiscent curds.
Let the wenches dawdle in such dress
As they are used to wear, and let the boys   5
Bring flowers in last month's newspapers.
Let be be finale of seem.
The only emperor is the emperor of ice-cream.

Take from the dresser of deal,
Lacking the three glass knobs, that sheet   10
On which she embroidered fantails[8] once
And spread it so as to cover her face.
If her horny feet protrude, they come
To show how cold she is, and dumb.
Let the lamp affix its beam.   15
The only emperor is the emperor of ice-cream.

                                                                          1923

5. Stringed, pear-shaped instruments.
6. Peristyle: A colonnade surrounding a courtyard; masque: An elaborate poetic drama to be performed at court, usually to musical accompaniment.
7. Flagellants: People who whip themselves in religious penance; muzzy: Dull, spiritless, stupid.
8. Deal: cheap wood; fantails: Fantailed pigeons.

Tea at the Palaz of Hoon

Not less because in purple I descended
The western day through what you called
The loneliest air, not less was I myself.

What was the ointment sprinkled on my beard?
What were the hymns that buzzed beside my ears?   5
What was the sea whose tide swept through me there?

Out of my mind the golden ointment rained,
And my ears made the blowing hymns they heard.
I was myself the compass of that sea:

I was the world in which I walked, and what I saw   10
Or heard or felt came not but from myself;
And there I found myself more truly and more strange.

1923

Disillusionment of Ten O'Clock

The houses are haunted
By white night-gowns.
None are green,
Or purple with green rings,
Or green with yellow rings,   5
Or yellow with blue rings.
None of them are strange,
With socks of lace
And beaded ceintures.[9]
People are not going   10
To dream of baboons and periwinkles.
Only, here and there, an old sailor,
Drunk and asleep in his boots,
Catches tigers
In red weather.   15

1923

Sunday Morning[1]

I

Complacencies of the peignoir,[2] and late
Coffee and oranges in a sunny chair,
And the green freedom of a cockatoo
Upon a rug mingle to dissipate

9. Belts.
1. In a letter dated March 31, 1928, Stevens wrote, "The poem is simply an explanation of paganism, although, of course, I did not think that I was expressing paganism when I wrote it."
2. Negligée.

The holy hush of ancient sacrifice. 5
She dreams a little, and she feels the dark
Encroachment of that old catastrophe,
As a calm darkens among water-lights.
The pungent oranges and bright, green wings
Seem things in some procession of the dead, 10
Winding across wide water, without sound.
The day is like wide water, without sound,
Stilled for the passing of her dreaming feet
Over the seas, to silent Palestine,
Dominion of the blood and sepulchre.[3] 15

II

Why should she give her bounty to the dead?
What is divinity if it can come
Only in silent shadows and in dreams?
Shall she not find in comforts of the sun,
In pungent fruit and bright, green wings, or else 20
In any balm or beauty of the earth,
Things to be cherished like the thought of heaven?
Divinity must live within herself:
Passions of rain, or moods in falling snow;
Grievings in loneliness, or unsubdued 25
Elations when the forest blooms; gusty
Emotions on wet roads on autumn nights;
All pleasures and all pains, remembering
The bough of summer and the winter branch.
These are the measures destined for her soul. 30

III

Jove[4] in the clouds had his inhuman birth.
No mother suckled him, no sweet land gave
Large-mannered motions to his mythy mind.
He moved among us, as a muttering king,
Magnificent, would move among his hinds,[5] 35
Until our blood, commingling, virginal,
With heaven, brought such requital to desire
The very hinds discerned it, in a star.
Shall our blood fail? Or shall it come to be
The blood of paradise? And shall the earth 40
Seem all of paradise that we shall know?
The sky will be much friendlier then than now,
A part of labor and a part of pain,
And next in glory to enduring love,
Not this dividing and indifferent blue. 45

3. Christ's tomb was in Palestine; the blood may refer both to his crucifixion and to the wine of the Last Supper.
4. Jove, or Zeus, was the son of a Titan and was suckled by a goat.
5. Servants or rustics.

IV

She says, "I am content when wakened birds,
Before they fly, test the reality
Of misty fields, by their sweet questionings;
But when the birds are gone, and their warm fields
Return no more, where, then, is paradise?"   50
There is not any haunt of prophesy,
Nor any old chimera[6] of the grave,
Neither the golden underground, nor isle
Melodious, where spirits gat them home,
Nor visionary south, nor cloudy palm   55
Remote on heaven's hill, that has endured
As April's green endures; or will endure
Like her remembrance of awakened birds,
Or her desire for June and evening, tipped
By the consummation of the swallow's wings.   60

V

She says, "But in contentment I still feel
The need of some imperishable bliss."
Death is the mother of beauty; hence from her,
Alone, shall come fulfillment to our dreams
And our desires. Although she strews the leaves   65
Of sure obliteration on our paths,
The path sick sorrow took, the many paths
Where triumph rang its brassy phrase, or love
Whispered a little out of tenderness,
She makes the willow shiver in the sun   70
For maidens who were wont to sit and gaze
Upon the grass, relinquished to their feet.
She causes boys to pile new plums and pears
On disregarded plate.[7] The maidens taste
And stray impassioned in the littering leaves.   75

VI

Is there no change of death in paradise?
Does ripe fruit never fall? Or do the boughs
Hang always heavy in that perfect sky,
Unchanging, yet so like our perishing earth,
With rivers like our own that seek for seas   80
They never find, the same receding shores
That never touch with inarticulate pang?
Why set the pear upon those river-banks

6. Fire-breathing monster of Greek mythology or phantasm.
7. The common, household silver.

Or spice the shores with odors of the plum?
Alas, that they should wear our colors there,   85
The silken weavings of our afternoons,
And pick the strings of our insipid lutes![8]
Death is the mother of beauty, mystical,
Within whose burning bosom we devise
Our earthly mothers waiting, sleeplessly.   90

VII

Supple and turbulent, a ring of men
Shall chant in orgy on a summer morn
Their boisterous devotion to the sun,
Not as a god, but as a god might be,
Naked among them, like a savage source.   95
Their chant shall be a chant of paradise,
Out of their blood, returning to the sky;
And in their chant shall enter, voice by voice,
The windy lake wherein their lord delights,
The trees, like serafin,[9] and echoing hills,   100
That choir among themselves long afterward.
They shall know well the heavenly fellowship
Of men that perish and of summer morn.
And whence they came and whither they shall go
The dew upon their feet shall manifest.   105

VIII

She hears, upon that water without sound,
A voice that cries, "The tomb in Palestine
Is not the porch of spirits lingering.
It is the grave of Jesus, where he lay."
We live in an old chaos of the sun,   110
Or old dependency of day and night,
Or island solitude, unsponsored, free,
Of that wide water, inescapable.
Deer walk upon our mountains, and the quail
Whistle about us their spontaneous cries;   115
Sweet berries ripen in the wilderness;
And, in the isolation of the sky,
At evening, casual flocks of pigeons make
Ambiguous undulations as they sink,
Downward to darkness, on extended wings.   120

1923

8. Stringed instruments commonly used in the Renaissance.
9. Seraphim, angels of the Lord.

Bantams in Pine-Woods

Chieftain Iffucan of Azcan[1] in caftan
Of tan with henna hackles, halt!

Damned universal cock, as if the sun
Was blackamoor to bear your blazing tail.

Fat! Fat! Fat! Fat! I am the personal.   5
Your world is you. I am my world.

You ten-foot poet among inchlings. Fat!
Begone! An inchling bristles in these pines,

Bristles, and points their Appalachian tangs,
And fears not portly Azcan nor his hoos.   10

1923

Anecdote of the Jar

I placed a jar in Tennessee,
And round it was, upon a hill.
It made the slovenly wilderness
Surround that hill.

The wilderness rose up to it,   5
And sprawled around, no longer wild.
The jar was round upon the ground
And tall and of a port in air.

It took dominion everywhere.
The jar was gray and bare.   10
It did not give of bird or bush,
Like nothing else in Tennessee.

1923

To the One of Fictive Music[2]

Sister and mother and diviner love,
And of the sisterhood of the living dead
Most near, most clear, and of the clearest bloom,
And of the fragrant mothers the most dear
And queen, and of diviner love the day   5
And flame and summer and sweet fire, no thread
Of cloudy silver sprinkles in your gown
Its venom of renown, and on your head
No crown is simpler than the simple hair.

1. Stevens's invention.
2. Although wary of explanations, Stevens wrote of this poem, "It is not only children who live in a world of the imagination. But after living there to the degree that a poet does, the desire to get back to the everyday world becomes so keen that one turns away from the imaginative world in a most definite and determined way. Another way of putting it is that, after writing a poem, it is a good thing to walk round the block. . . ."

Now, of the music summoned by the birth   10
That separates us from the wind and sea,
Yet leaves us in them, until earth becomes,
By being so much of the things we are,
Gross effigy and simulacrum, none
Gives motion to perfection more serene   15
Than yours, out of our imperfections wrought,
Most rare, or ever of more kindred air
In the laborious weaving that you wear.

For so retentive of themselves are men
That music is intensest which proclaims   20
The near, the clear, and vaunts the clearest bloom,
And of all vigils musing the obscure,
That apprehends the most which sees and names,
As in your name, an image that is sure,
Among the arrant spices of the sun,   25
O bough and bush and scented vine, in whom
We give ourselves our likest issuance.

Yet not too like, yet not so like to be
Too near, too clear, saving a little to endow
Our feigning with the strange unlike, whence springs   30
The difference that heavenly pity brings.
For this, musician, in your girdle fixed
Bear other perfumes. On your pale head wear
A band entwining, set with fatal stones.
Unreal, give back to us what once you gave: 35
The imagination that we spurned and crave.

                                        1923

Peter Quince at the Clavier[3]

I

Just as my fingers on these keys
Make music, so the self-same sounds
On my spirit make a music, too.

Music is feeling, then, not sound;
And thus it is that what I feel,   5
Here in this room, desiring you,

Thinking of your blue-shadowed silk,
Is music. It is like the strain
Waked in the elders by Susanna;[4]

3. The title pairs one of Shakespeare's comic rustics in *A Midsummer Night's Dream* with a delicate-sounding early version of the piano—an absurd combination.
4. The story of Susanna and the elders appears in the Apocrypha, in Daniel, 13; she is falsely accused of lying naked with a young man by two old men whose advances she rejected, and the young Daniel proves her innocence.

Of a green evening, clear and warm,   10
She bathed in her still garden, while
The red-eyed elders, watching, felt

The basses of their beings throb
In witching chords, and their thin blood
Pulse pizzicati[5] of Hosanna.   15

II

In the green water, clear and warm,
Susanna lay.
She searched
The touch of springs,
And found   20
Concealed imaginings.
She sighed,
For so much melody.

Upon the bank, she stood
In the cool   25
Of spent emotions.
She felt, among the leaves,
The dew
Of old devotions.

She walked upon the grass,   30
Still quavering.
The winds were like her maids,
On timid feet,
Fetching her woven scarves,
Yet wavering.   35

A breath upon her hand
Muted the night.
She turned—
A cymbal crashed,
And roaring horns.   40

III

Soon with a noise like tambourines,
Came her attendant Byzantines.[6]

They wondered why Susanna cried
Against the elders by her side;

And as they whispered, the refrain   45
Was like a willow swept by rain.

---

5. Music played by plucking strings.
6. The phrase is nonsense if we note that people of Byzantium would not have lived in Susanna's time.

Anon, their lamps' uplifted flame
Revealed Susanna and her shame.

And then, the simpering Byzantines
Fled, with a noise like tambourines.   50

IV

Beauty is momentary in the mind—
The fitful tracing of a portal;
But in the flesh it is immortal.

The body dies; the body's beauty lives.
So evenings die, in their green going,   55
A wave, interminably flowing.
So gardens die, their meek breath scenting
The cowl of winter, done repenting.
So maidens die, to the auroral
Celebration of a maiden's choral.   60

Susanna's music touched the bawdy strings
Of those white elders; but, escaping,
Left only Death's ironic scraping.
Now, in its immortality, it plays
On the clear viol of her memory,   65
And makes a constant sacrament of praise.

1923

Thirteen Ways of Looking at a Blackbird

I

Among twenty snowy mountains,
The only moving thing
Was the eye of the blackbird.

II

I was of three minds,
Like a tree   5
In which there are three blackbirds.

III

The blackbird whirled in the autumn winds.
It was a small part of the pantomime.

IV

A man and a woman
Are one.   10
A man and a woman and a blackbird
Are one.

V

I do not know which to prefer,
The beauty of inflections
Or the beauty of innuendos,   15
The blackbird whistling
Or just after.

VI

Icicles filled the long window
With barbaric glass.
The shadow of the blackbird   20
Crossed it, to and fro.
The mood
Traced in the shadow
An indecipherable cause.

VII

O thin men of Haddam,[7]   25
Why do you imagine golden birds?
Do you not see how the blackbird
Walks around the feet
Of the women about you?

VIII

I know noble accents
And lucid, inescapable rhythms;   30
But I know, too,
That the blackbird is involved
In what I know.

IX

When the blackbird flew out of sight,   35
It marked the edge
Of one of many circles.

X

At the sight of blackbirds
Flying in a green light,
Even the bawds of euphony   40
Would cry out sharply.

XI

He rode over Connecticut
In a glass coach.

---

7. In a letter of July 1, 1953, Stevens explained, "The thin men of Haddam are entirely fictitious although some years ago one of the citizens of that place wrote to me to ask what I had in mind. I just liked the name."

Once, a fear pierced him,
In that he mistook   45
The shadow of his equipage
For blackbirds.

XII

The river is moving.
The blackbird must be flying.

XIII

It was evening all afternoon.   50
It was snowing
And it was going to snow.
The blackbird sat
In the cedar-limbs.

1923

To the Roaring Wind

What syllable are you seeking,
Vocalissimus,
In the distances of sleep?
Speak it.

1923

The Man Whose Pharynx Was Bad[8]

The time of year has grown indifferent.
Mildew of summer and the deepening snow
Are both alike in the routine I know.
I am too dumbly in my being pent.

The wind attendant on the solstices   5
Blows on the shutters of the metropoles,
Stirring no poet in his sleep, and tolls
The grand ideas of the villages.

The malady of the quotidian . . .
Perhaps, if summer ever came to rest   10
And lengthened, deepened, comforted, caressed
Through days like oceans in obsidian

Horizons full of night's midsummer blaze;
Perhaps, if winter once could penetrate
Through all its purples to the final slate,   15
Persisting bleakly in an icy haze;

8. The title of this poem could suggest that the man has a sore throat, but compare the poem's opening lines with those of Shakespeare's Sonnet 73: "That time of year thou mayst in me behold / When yellow leaves, or none, or few, do hang / Upon those boughs which shake against the cold, / Bare ruined choirs, where late the sweet birds sang."

One might in turn become less diffident—
Out of such mildew plucking neater mould
And spouting new orations of the cold.
One might. One might. But time will not relent.   20

[1921] 1931, 1957

Evening without Angels

> *the great interests of man: air and
> light, the joy of having a body, the
> voluptuousness of looking.*
> —*Mario Rossi*[9]

Why seraphim like lutanists arranged
Above the trees? And why the poet as
Eternal *chef d'orchestre?*[1]

        Air is air.
Its vacancy glitters round us everywhere.
Its sounds are not angelic syllables   5
But our unfashioned spirits realized
More sharply in more furious selves.

        And light
That fosters seraphim and is to them
Coiffeur of haloes, fecund jeweller—
Was the sun concoct for angels or for men?   10
Sad men made angels of the sun, and of
The moon they made their own attendant ghosts,
Which led them back to angels, after death.

Let this be clear that we are men of sun
And men of day and never of pointed night,   15
Men that repeat antiquest sounds of air
In an accord of repetitions. Yet,
If we repeat, it is because the wind
Encircling us, speaks always with our speech.

Light, too, encrusts us making visible   20
The motions of the mind and giving form
To moodiest nothings, as, desire for day
Accomplished in the immensely flashing East,
Desire for rest, in that descending sea
Of dark, which in its very darkening   25
Is rest and silence spreading into sleep.

. . . Evening, when the measure skips a beat
And then another, one by one, and all

9. From Mario Rossi's *Pilgrimage in the West* (1933).
1. Conductor.

To a seething minor swiftly modulate.
Bare night is best. Bare earth is best. Bare, bare,   30
Except for our own houses, huddled low
Beneath the arches and their spangled air,
Beneath the rhapsodies of fire and fire,
Where the voice that is in us makes a true response,
Where the voice that is great within us rises up,   35
As we stand gazing at the rounded moon.

                                                        1936

The Idea of Order at Key West

She sang beyond the genius[2] of the sea.
The water never formed to mind or voice,
Like a body wholly body, fluttering
Its empty sleeves; and yet its mimic motion
Made constant cry, caused constantly a cry,   5
That was not ours although we understood,
Inhuman, of the veritable ocean.

The sea was not a mask. No more was she.
The song and water were not medleyed sound
Even if what she sang was what she heard,   10
Since what she sang was uttered word by word.
It may be that in all her phrases stirred
The grinding water and the gasping wind;
But it was she and not the sea we heard.

For she was the maker of the song she sang.   15
The ever-hooded, tragic-gestured sea
Was merely a place by which she walked to sing.
Whose spirit is this? we said, because we knew
It was the spirit that we sought and knew
That we should ask this often as she sang.   20

If it was only the dark voice of the sea
That rose, or even colored by many waves;
If it was only the outer voice of sky
And cloud, of the sunken coral water-walled,
However clear, it would have been deep air,   25
The heaving speech of air, a summer sound
Repeated in a summer without end
And sound alone. But it was more than that,
More even than her voice, and ours, among
The meaningless plungings of water and the wind,   30
Theatrical distances, bronze shadows heaped
On high horizons, mountainous atmospheres
Of sky and sea.

2. Local spirit or deity.

It was her voice that made
The sky acutest at its vanishing.
She measured to the hour its solitude.   35
She was the single artificer of the world
In which she sang. And when she sang, the sea,
Whatever self it had, became the self
That was her song, for she was the maker. Then we,
As we beheld her striding there alone,   40
Knew that there never was a world for her
Except the one she sang and, singing, made.

Ramon Fernandez,[3] tell me, if you know,
Why, when the singing ended and we turned
Toward the town, tell why the glassy lights,   45
The lights in the fishing boats at anchor there,
As the night descended, tilting in the air,
Mastered the night and portioned out the sea,
Fixing emblazoned zones and fiery poles,
Arranging, deepening, enchanting night.   50

Oh! Blessed rage for order, pale Ramon,
The maker's rage to order words of the sea,
Words of the fragrant portals, dimly-starred,
And of ourselves and of our origins,
In ghostlier demarcations, keener sounds.   55

                                                      1936

A Postcard from the Volcano

Children picking up our bones
Will never know that these were once
As quick as foxes on the hill;

And that in autumn, when the grapes
Made sharp air sharper by their smell   5
These had a being, breathing frost;

And least will guess that with our bones
We left much more, left what still is
The look of things, left what we felt

At what we saw. The spring clouds blow   10
Above the shuttered mansion-house,
Beyond our gate and the windy sky

---

3. Stevens insisted in a letter that this name did not refer to any actual person.

Cries out a literate despair.
We knew for long the mansion's look
And what we said of it became   15

A part of what it is . . . Children,
Still weaving budded aureoles,[4]
Will speak our speech and never know,

Will say of the mansion that it seems
As if he that lived there left behind   20
A spirit storming in blank walls,

A dirty house in a gutted world,
A tatter of shadows peaked to white,
Smeared with the gold of the opulent sun.

                                          1936

FROM Notes toward a Supreme Fiction[5]

To Henry Church

And for what, except for you, do I feel love?
Do I press the extremest book of the wisest man
Close to me, hidden in me day and night?
In the uncertain light of single, certain truth,
Equal in living changingness to the light   5
In which I meet you, in which we sit at rest,
For a moment in the central of our being,
The vivid transparence that you bring is peace.

It Must Be Abstract

I

Begin, ephebe,[6] by perceiving the idea
Of this invention, this invented world,   10
The inconceivable idea of the sun.

You must become an ignorant man again
And see the sun again with an ignorant eye
And see it clearly in the idea of it.

Never suppose an inventing mind as source   15
Of this idea nor for that mind compose
A voluminous master folded in his fire.

4. Haloes.
5. Compare this poem with "A High-Toned Old Christian Woman," p. 122.
6. In ancient Greece, a young male citizen.

How clean the sun when seen in its idea,
Washed in the remotest cleanliness of a heaven
That has expelled us and our images . . .   20

The death of one god is the death of all.
Let purple Phoebus[7] lie in umber harvest,
Let Phoebus slumber and die in autumn umber,

Phoebus is dead, ephebe. But Phoebus was
A name for something that never could be named.   25
There was a project for the sun and is.

There is a project for the sun. The sun
Must bear no name, gold flourisher, but be
In the difficulty of what it is to be.

II

It is the celestial ennui of apartments   30
That sends us back to the first idea, the quick
Of this invention; and yet so poisonous

Are the ravishments of truth, so fatal to
The truth itself, the first idea becomes
The hermit in a poet's metaphors,   35

Who comes and goes and comes and goes all day.
May there be an ennui of the first idea?
What else, prodigious scholar, should there be?

The monastic man is an artist. The philosopher
Appoints man's place in music, say, today.   40
But the priest desires. The philosopher desires.

And not to have is the beginning of desire.
To have what is not is its ancient cycle.
It is desire at the end of winter, when

It observes the effortless weather turning blue   45
And sees the myosotis[8] on its bush.
Being virile, it hears the calendar hymn.

It knows that what it has is what is not
And throws it away like a thing of another time,
As morning throws off stale moonlight and shabby sleep.   50

III

The poem refreshes life so that we share,
For a moment, the first idea . . . It satisfies
Belief in an immaculate beginning.

---

7. Apollo, god of poetry and the sun.
8. Plants, like the forget-me-not, of the *Myosotis* family.

And sends us, winged by an unconscious will,
To an immaculate end. We move between these points: 55
From that ever-early candor to its late plural

And the candor of them is the strong exhilaration
Of what we feel from what we think, of thought
Beating in the heart, as if blood newly came,

An elixir, an excitation, a pure power.   60
The poem, through candor, brings back a power again
That gives a candid kind to everything.

We say: At night an Arabian in my room,
With his damned hoobla-hoobla-hoobla-how,
Inscribes a primitive astronomy   65

Across the unscrawled fores the future casts
And throws his stars around the floor. By day
The wood-dove used to chant his hoobla-hoo

And still the grossest iridescence of ocean
Howls hoo and rises and howls hoo and falls.   70
Life's nonsense pierces us with strange relation.

*   *   *

[CODA]

Soldier, there is a war between the mind
And sky, between thought and day and night. It is
For that the poet is always in the sun,

Patches the moon together in his room
To his Virgilian[9] cadences, up down,   5
Up down. It is a war that never ends.

Yet it depends on yours. The two are one.
They are a plural, a right and left, a pair,
Two parallels that meet if only in

The meeting of their shadows or that meet   10
In a book in a barrack, a letter from Malay.[1]
But your war ends. And after it you return

With six meats and twelve wines or else without
To walk another room . . . Monsieur and comrade,
The soldier is poor without the poet's lines,   15

His petty syllabi, the sounds that stick,
Inevitably modulating, in the blood.
And war for war, each has its gallant kind.

9. Rhythms like those of the Roman poet Virgil (70–19 B.C.E.), who wrote of rural life, but also of war
and the founding of Rome in *The Aeneid.*
1. Malay Peninsula in Southeast Asia.

How simply the fictive hero becomes the real;
How gladly with proper words the soldier dies,   20
If he must, or lives on the bread of faithful speech.

                                                        1942

The Course of a Particular

Today the leaves cry, hanging on branches swept by wind,
Yet the nothingness of winter becomes a little less.
It is still full of icy shades and shapen snow.

The leaves cry . . . One holds off and merely hears the cry.
It is a busy cry, concerning someone else.   5
And though one says that one is part of everything,

There is a conflict, there is a resistance involved;
And being part is an exertion that declines:
One feels the life of that which gives life as it is.

The leaves cry. It is not a cry of divine attention,   10
Nor the smoke-drift of puffed-out heroes, nor human cry.
It is the cry of leaves that do not transcend themselves,

In the absence of fantasia, without meaning more
Than they are in the final finding of the ear, in the thing
Itself, until, at last, the cry concerns no one at all.   15

                                                        1951 [1957]

Final Soliloquy of the Interior Paramour[2]

Light the first light of evening, as in a room
In which we rest and, for small reason, think
The world imagined is the ultimate good.

This is, therefore, the intensest rendezvous.
It is in that thought that we collect ourselves,   5
Out of all the indifferences, into one thing:

Within a single thing, a single shawl
Wrapped tightly round us, since we are poor, a warmth,
A light, a power, the miraculous influence.

Here, now, we forget each other and ourselves.   10
We feel the obscurity of an order, a whole,
A knowledge, that which arranged the rendezvous.

Within its vital boundary, in the mind.
We say God and the imagination are one . . .
How high that highest candle lights the dark.   15

_____
2. A lover.

Out of this same light, out of the central mind,
We make a dwelling in the evening air,
In which being there together is enough.

1954

Of Modern Poetry

The poem of the mind in the act of finding
What will suffice. It has not always had
To find: the scene was set; it repeated what
Was in the script.
                    Then the theatre was changed
To something else. Its past was a souvenir.   5

It has to be living, to learn the speech of the place.
It has to face the men of the time and to meet
The women of the time. It has to think about war
And it has to find what will suffice. It has
To construct a new stage. It has to be on that stage   10
And, like an insatiable actor, slowly and
With meditation, speak words that in the ear,
In the delicatest ear of the mind, repeat,
Exactly, that which it wants to hear, at the sound
Of which, an invisible audience listens,   15
Not to the play, but to itself, expressed
In an emotion as of two people, as of two
Emotions becoming one. The actor is
A metaphysician in the dark, twanging
An instrument, twanging a wiry string that gives   20
Sounds passing through sudden rightnesses, wholly
Containing the mind, below which it cannot descend,
Beyond which it has no will to rise.
                              It must
Be the finding of a satisfaction, and may
Be of a man skating, a woman dancing, a woman   25
Combing. The poem of the act of the mind.

1954

The Plain Sense of Things

After the leaves have fallen, we return
To a plain sense of things. It is as if
We had come to an end of the imagination,
Inanimate in an inert savoir.

It is difficult even to choose the adjective   5
For this blank cold, this sadness without cause.
The great structure has become a minor house.
No turban walks across the lessened floors.

The greenhouse never so badly needed paint.
The chimney is fifty years old and slants to one side.   10
A fantastic effort has failed, a repetition
In a repetitiousness of men and flies.

Yet the absence of the imagination had
Itself to be imagined. The great pond,
The plain sense of it, without reflections, leaves,   15
Mud, water like dirty glass, expressing silence

Of a sort, silence of a rat come out to see,
The great pond and its waste of the lilies, all this
Had to be imagined as an inevitable knowledge,
Required, as a necessity requires.   20

1954

Of Mere Being

The palm at the end of the mind,
Beyond the last thought, rises
In the bronze decor,

A gold-feathered bird
Sings in the palm, without human meaning,   5
Without human feeling, a foreign song.

You know then that it is not the reason
That makes us happy or unhappy.
The bird sings. Its feathers shine.

The palm stands on the edge of space.   10
The wind moves slowly in the branches.
The bird's fire-fangled feathers dangle down.

[1955] 1957

◄ WILLIAM CARLOS WILLIAMS ►
(1883–1963)

With the exception of a few sojourns in Europe and an education pursued in New York City and Philadelphia, William Carlos Williams spent his life in the town of his birth—Rutherford, New Jersey. Yet his background was quite cosmopolitan. He was the son of William George Williams, a cultured businessman who was born in England and came to the United States with his mother at the age of five, but chose never to abandon his British citizenship. Because his father's work as an advertising manager for a perfume manufacturer required long stretches of travel abroad, the poet was raised in Rutherford by his British grandmother, Emily Dickinson Wellcome, and his mother, Raquel Hélène Rose Hoheb Williams, a woman of Basque, Spanish, Dutch, and Jewish ancestry whom his father had met in Puerto Rico. Although she acquired some English, she preferred to speak Spanish, especially at home, and to practice the French she had learned while studying art in

Paris. Williams's interest in celebrating an American language whose vigor derives from actual speech was perhaps initiated in his childhood home, where he listened intently to the blend of languages around him. Despite his later emphasis on his American identity, he imbibed significant doses of European culture during his childhood. In 1897, when Williams was fourteen, his mother took him and his younger brother to Europe for a year-long stay and sent them to private schools, first in Geneva and then in Paris.

After their return to the United States in 1899, Williams attended Horace Mann, a prestigious private school in New York City. Williams's parents enrolled him in a course of study that emphasized science, but he excelled in his English courses, for which he read poetry from Chaucer to Tennyson and discovered the Romantics, especially John Keats, whose work he began to imitate. Along with Keatsian imitations, he filled notebooks with long-lined, cadenced effusions in the style of Whitman: "I wrote my immortal thoughts in those books, whatever they were. If I had an opinion about things about me, I'd jot it down, and occasionally it would take the loose form of verse." The pleasure he found in writing determined the course he would take for the rest of his life. In addition to a career in medicine, he would become a poet. In 1902 he enrolled in the school of dentistry at the University of Pennsylvania but soon switched to the medical school. Even in the midst of his demanding studies, he continued to write.

Williams's commitment to poetry was encouraged by his new friend Ezra Pound, whom he met in 1902 during his first semester of medical school at the University of Pennsylvania. Pound introduced Williams to other poets, such as Hilda Doolittle (H. D.), and, above all, offered astringent criticism that helped Williams drop the nineteenth-century affectations clogging his early poetry. After Williams sent him a copy of his first book, a privately published collection written in blank verse and rhymed stanzas, Pound wrote back, declaring "Individual, original it is not. Great art it is not. . . . There are fine lines in it, but nowhere I think do you add anything to the poets you have used as models. . . . You are out of touch." In subsequent letters Pound alerted Williams to the incipient Imagist movement. Williams soon changed his style so radically—going on to champion what Pound advocated in a 1913 letter as "the simple order of natural speech"—that he dumped the remaining copies of the book and never republished any of the poems. In old age he remarked that there was nothing "of the slightest value in the whole thin booklet—except the intent."

Williams's intent held firm through studies in pediatrics undertaken during the winter of 1909–10 in Germany and through the work of establishing a private practice in Rutherford after his return. Even marriage in 1912 to Florence ("Flossie") Herman, and the birth of his two sons soon after, did not diminish his efforts. His poems appeared in several of the Imagist anthologies and in little magazines such as *Poetry, Others,* and the *Egoist.* His second book, *The Tempers* (1913), was transitional, but his third book, *Al Que Quiere!* (1917), established the parameters he would explore for the rest of his career: a style grounded not on traditional metrics but on the vigor of American speech and a celebration of the particular, of quotidian details that his critics would call antipoetic, but that Williams saw as the essence of poetry, and on an emphasis on the mind and the imagination.

Williams's lifelong fascination with painting, prompted by his mother's background in the arts and his own amateur forays into painting, carried over into his poetry. He later remarked that "because of my interest in painting, the Imagists appealed to me. It was an image that I was seeking, and when Pound came along with his drive for the image it appealed to me very strongly." His friendship with the artist Charles Demuth, whom he had met in Philadelphia, helped attune him to the Modernist revolution in painting, as did his visits to the 1913 Armory Show and New York galleries. His engagement with the work of painters such as Cézanne, Matisse, Duchamp, and the Cubists taught him to think of poetry not as representational, but as a form of design that forces readers to look at both the world and their own habits of perception differently. Thus, Williams's focus on "things" in his poetry (and his well-known aphorism "no ideas but in things") involves not static depiction, but active processes of observation: the mind in motion.

Williams's work in medicine also nourished his poetry. In interviews and essays, he sometimes made analogies between the habits of observation he developed as a doctor and his aims as a poet, claiming that the poet's business is "not to talk in vague categories, but to write particularly, as a physician works, upon a patient, upon the thing before him, in the particular to discover the universal." In the midst of a thriving medical practice—between house calls, hospital visits, seeing patients in his office, and delivering babies—he claimed time to write not only poetry, but also novels, short stories, essays, plays, experimental prose, and autobiography, publishing almost fifty books during his lifetime. In the introduction to his *The Autobiography* (1951) he described his method:

> Five minutes, ten minutes, can always be found. I had my typewriter in my office desk. All I needed to do was pull up the leaf to which it was fastened and I was ready to go. I worked at top speed. If a patient came in at the door while I was in the middle of a sentence, bang would go the machine—I was a physician. When the patient left, up would come the machine. . . . Finally, after eleven at night, when the last patient had been put to bed, I could always find the time to bang out ten or twelve pages. In fact, I couldn't rest until I had freed my mind from the obsessions that had been tormenting me all day.

As Williams neared forty, he published two books of improvisatory, experimental prose, *Kora in Hell* (1920) and *The Great American Novel* (1923), a book of new poetry, *Sour Grapes* (1921), and *Spring and All* (1923), a remarkable series of poems interspersed with brusque, annunciatory, and sometimes contradictory prose meditations on his goals as an artist. Seeking "to refine, to clarify, to intensify that eternal moment in which we alone live," he concluded that "there is but a single force—the imagination."

Yet Williams also celebrated poetry's potential to "affirm reality," for he argued that the imagination's "unique power is to give created forms reality, actual existence." At the same time he stressed that the imagination does not "avoid reality, nor is it a description nor an evocation of objects or situations[;] . . . poetry does not tamper with the world but moves it—it affirms reality most powerfully." The *Spring and All* poems test these ideas. The urgency of Williams's voice, moreover, moves the poems forward through feeling, a passion for discovery similar to the enthusiasm he attributed in the essays of his next book, *In the American Grain* (1925), to the men who explored the New World.

Williams thought of himself as akin to those explorers, for he aimed to chart a "New World" in his poetry: American subjects and American speech. For him, dedication to American themes was a moral choice, and he set himself against the expatriate Modernism of T. S. Eliot, whom he thought had turned poetry in the wrong direction:

I had a violent feeling that Eliot had betrayed what I believed in. He was looking back-ward; I was looking forward. He was a conformist, with wit, learning I did not possess. He knew French, Latin, Arabic, God knows what. I was interested in that. But I felt he had rejected America and I refused to be rejected. . . . I realized the responsibility that I must accept. . . . I had envisaged a new form of poetic composition, a form for the future.

Although Williams's opposition to Eliot sprung from profound philosophical and temperamental differences—from his opposition to what he saw as Eliot's pessimism, dependence on European traditions, and adherence (even in his free verse) to an iambic norm—it also arose, as Williams freely acknowledged, from professional jealousy. After *The Waste Land* (1922), critics had canonized Eliot as the premier Modernist poet, and Williams felt overlooked.

During the Great Depression conditions worsened for Williams, as they did for most Americans. In the 1920s he had invested in the stock market, hoping that his profits would enable him to retire early. The crash of 1929 ended those hopes. As the Depression deepened, his medical practice grew even more burdensome. He often waived his fees for patients who were unable to pay, and he had to put in additional hours to make ends meet. Like many writers of the era, he grew interested in the possibilities of political poetry, and he wrote a number of poems, such as "The Yachts," that implicitly attack class injustices in America. Yet he also drew fire in leftist journals for his refusal to commit himself unreservedly to radical causes, and he remained skeptical of poetry about public events.

By the middle of the 1930s, just after he had turned fifty, he found new opportunities for publication. In 1934, the poet Louis Zukofsky arranged for the Objectivist Press to publish Williams's *Collected Poems 1921–1931*. Although the book appeared under the imprint of yet another small press, it gave Williams the chance both to consolidate his mature work and to receive homage from the Objectivists, a group of young writers led by Zukofsky, who considered Williams a crucial Modernist poet and credited him with inspiring their own poetry of concrete particulars. Only in 1938, however, when James Laughlin's New Directions press published *The Complete Collected Poems,* did Williams's work become widely available. "All my life I've been hoping to get a regular publisher to put my stuff out in a more or less uniform style," Williams wrote at the time. He found that publisher in Laughlin, who considered him the cornerstone of New Directions.

Among the many volumes that Williams published with New Directions was his long poem *Paterson,* which was released in five books, the first appearing in 1946, the last in 1958. Setting himself against *The Waste Land* and Pound's *Cantos,* yet also borrowing collage techniques from these two poems, Williams looked back to Whitman in hopes of writing an American epic both local and inclusive. His solution was to focus on a particular place, the city of Paterson, New Jersey, and to fuse that place with an Everyman figure, Dr. Paterson. Williams explained: "*Paterson* is a long poem in four parts—that a man in himself is a city, beginning, seeking, achieving and concluding his life in ways which the various aspects of a city may embody—any city, all the details of which may be made to voice his most intimate convictions." Those details include not only the characteristically rapid movements of Williams's own verse and prose, but extracts from newspapers, historical documents, and private letters from friends.

Williams not only struggled to create the right form for a long poem but also for a prosody (or "measure," as he preferred to call it) responsive to American language, for he associated traditional accentual syllabic prosody with British English. Throughout his career Williams argued that no verse is free and strove to articulate a prosodic system that matched the rhythms of American speech. Yet his impulse for invention and novelty chafed against his wish to develop a quantifiable system. As he aged and attracted followers, he increased his efforts to discover a specifically American prosody, and in his lecture "The Poem as a Field of Action" (1948) and in similar essays he envisioned an elastic system that allowed room for change. While writing *Paterson,* he hit on a concept that he would call "the variable foot," a triadic, step-down line that first emerged in "The Descent," a poem that was originally part of Book 2, and that he fully developed in late poems such as "Asphodel, That Greeny Flower." Although the step-down line seems more a style of free verse than a new system of prosody, Williams's emphasis on process and motion, on capturing the subtleties of American speech, and on using the whole page as an active field of composition influenced a wide range of poets, including Zukofsky, George Oppen, Lorine Niedecker, Charles Olson, Robert Duncan, Robert Creeley, Allen Ginsberg, Denise Levertov, and Robert Lowell.

Due in part to the advocacy of this new generation of poets, toward the end of his life Williams began to gain institutional recognition: honorary degrees, invitations to lecture, a contract with Random House, the 1953 Bollingen Prize (shared with Archibald MacLeish), and the 1963 Pulitzer Prize, awarded posthumously for *Pictures from Brueghel* (1962). Yet his late years involved hardship. Forced to give up his medical practice after a series of debilitating strokes, Williams fought to continue writing, teaching himself to type with his left hand because his right hand was incapacitated. He was offered the post of Poetry Consultant to the Library of Congress in 1952, but the appointment was revoked after the Librarian of Congress received protests from literary editors complaining about both Williams's purported communist sympathies and his public defense of Ezra Pound. His wife's devoted care during these difficult years also prompted the poet to feel intense remorse over extramarital affairs he had had during the course of their marriage. His late poems, published in *The Desert Music* (1954) and *Pictures from Brueghel* often contemplate renewal, both of love and of the power to write. These poems, the publication of a single volume edition of *Paterson* (1963), and increased attention to his early lyrics contributed to the marked rise in Williams's literary fortunes after his death.

◄○──◄▶──○►

Aux Imagistes[1]

> I think I have never been so exalted
> As I am now by you,
> O frost bitten blossoms,
> That are unfolding your wings
> From out the envious black branches.   5
>
> Bloom quickly and make much of the sunshine.
> The twigs conspire against you!

---

1. The title means "To the Imagists"; this poem was first published in the *Egoist,* December 1914, following the appearance of the first Imagist anthology earlier that year.

Hear them!
They hold you from behind!

You shall not take wing   10
Except wing by wing, brokenly,
And yet—
Even they
Shall not endure for ever.

                                                                      1914

Danse Russe[2]

If when my wife is sleeping
and the baby and Kathleen[3]
are sleeping
and the sun is a flame-white disc
in silken mists   5
above shining trees,—
if I in my north room
dance naked, grotesquely
before my mirror
waving my shirt round my head   10
and singing softly to myself:
"I am lonely, lonely.
I was born to be lonely,
I am best so!"
If I admire my arms, my face,   15
my shoulders, flanks, buttocks
against the yellow drawn shades,—

Who shall say I am not
the happy genius[4] of my household?

                                                                      1917

Dedication for a Plot of Ground

This plot of ground
facing the waters of this inlet
is dedicated to the living presence of
Emily Dickinson Wellcome[5]
who was born in England, married,   5
lost her husband and with
her five year old son
sailed for New York in a two-master,
was driven to the Azores;

2. The title means "Russian Dance"; the Ballets Russes had been in New York in 1916.
3. Kathleen was a nursemaid to the Williams children.
4. By "genius" Williams means both a highly intelligent person and, in the archaic sense, a spirit of place.
5. Williams's paternal grandmother; compare this poem with "The Last Words of My English Grandmother," p. 157.

ran adrift on Fire Island shoal,   10
met her second husband
in a Brooklyn boarding house,
went with him to Puerto Rico
bore three more children, lost
her second husband, lived hard   15
for eight years in St. Thomas,
Puerto Rico, San Domingo, followed
the oldest son to New York,
lost her daughter, lost her "baby,"
seized the two boys of   20
the oldest son by the second marriage
mothered them—they being
motherless—fought for them
against the other grandmother
and the aunts, brought them here   25
summer after summer, defended
herself here against thieves,
storms, sun, fire,
against flies, against girls
that came smelling about, against   30
drought, against weeds, storm-tides,
neighbors, weasels that stole her chickens,
against the weakness of her own hands,
against the growing strength of
the boys, against wind, against   35
the stones, against trespassers,
against rents, against her own mind.

She grubbed this earth with her own hands,
domineered over this grass plot,
blackguarded[6] her oldest son   40
into buying it, lived here fifteen years,
attained a final loneliness and—

If you can bring nothing to this place
but your carcass, keep out.

                                                        1917

El Hombre[7]

It's a strange courage
you give me ancient star:

Shine alone in the sunrise
toward which you lend no part!

                                                        1917

6. Tricked.
7. The title means "The Man" in Spanish; compare this poem with "Nuances of a Theme by Williams" by Wallace Stevens, p. 122.

Tract

I will teach you my townspeople
how to perform a funeral—
for you have it over a troop
of artists—
unless one should scour the world—   5
you have the ground sense necessary.

See! the hearse leads.
I begin with a design for a hearse.
For Christ's sake not black—
nor white either—and not polished!   10
Let it be weathered—like a farm wagon—
with gilt wheels (this could be
applied fresh at small expense)
or no wheels at all:
a rough dray to drag over the ground.   15

Knock the glass out!
My God—glass, my townspeople!
For what purpose? Is it for the dead
to look out or for us to see
how well he is housed or to see   20
the flowers or the lack of them—
or what?
To keep the rain and snow from him?
He will have a heavier rain soon:
pebbles and dirt and what not.   25
Let there be no glass—
and no upholstery, phew!
and no little brass rollers
and small easy wheels on the bottom—
my townspeople what are you thinking of?   30

A rough plain hearse then
with gilt wheels and no top at all.
On this coffin lies
by its own weight.

                    No wreaths please—   35
especially no hot house flowers.
Some common memento is better,
something he prized and is known by:
his old clothes—a few books perhaps—
God knows what! You realize   40
how we are about these things
my townspeople—
something will be found—anything
even flowers if he had come to that.
So much for the hearse.   45

For heaven's sake though see to the driver!
Take off the silk hat! In fact
that's no place at all for him—
up there unceremoniously
dragging our friend out to his own dignity!   50
Bring him down—bring him down!
Low and inconspicuous! I'd not have him ride
on the wagon at all—damn him—
the undertaker's understrapper!
Let him hold the reins   55
and walk at the side
and inconspicuously too!

Then briefly as to yourselves:
Walk behind—as they do in France,
seventh class, or if you ride   60
Hell take curtains! Go with some show
of inconvenience; sit openly—
to the weather as to grief.
Or do you think you can shut grief in?
What—from us? We who have perhaps   65
nothing to lose? Share with us
share with us—it will be money
in your pockets.

                    Go now
I think you are ready.
                                                               70

                                              1917

Portrait of a Lady

Your thighs are appletrees
whose blossoms touch the sky.
Which sky? The sky
where Watteau[8] hung a lady's
slipper. Your knees   5
are a southern breeze—or
a gust of snow. Agh! What
sort of man was Fragonard?[9]
—as if that answered
anything. Ah, yes—below   10
the knees, since the tune
drops that way, it is
one of those white summer days,
the tall grass of your ankles

---

8. Jean-Antoine Watteau (1684–1721), French painter.
9. Williams probably had mind "The Swing," a painting by Jean-Honoré Fragonard (1732–1806).

flickers upon the shore—   15
Which shore?—
the sand clings to my lips—
Which shore?
Agh, petals maybe. How
should I know?   20
Which shore? Which shore?
I said petals from an appletree.

                                                          1920

The Great Figure[1]

Among the rain
and lights
I saw the figure 5
in gold
on a red   5
firetruck
moving
tense
unheeded
to gong clangs   10
siren howls
and wheels rumbling
through the dark city.

                                                          1921

Queen-Anne's-Lace[2]

Her body is not so white as
anemone petals nor so smooth—nor
so remote a thing. It is a field
of the wild carrot taking
the field by force; the grass   5
does not raise above it.
Here is no question of whiteness,
white as can be, with a purple mole
at the center of each flower.
Each flower is a hand's span   10
of her whiteness. Wherever
his hand has lain there is

---

1. In his *Autobiography* (1948), Williams reports that he once dropped in on the studio of painter Marsden Hartley: "As I approached his number I heard a great clatter of bells and the roar of a fire engine passing the end of the street down Ninth Avenue. I turned just in time to see a golden 5 on red background flash by. The impression was so sudden and forceful that I took a piece of paper out of my pocket and wrote a short poem about it" (172). Another painter, Charles Demuth, reinterpreted Williams's poem in his painting *I Saw the Figure 5 in Gold*.
2. Refers to a common white flower. Williams once said that the woman in the poem was his wife, Flossie.

a tiny purple blemish. Each part
is a blossom under his touch
to which the fibres of her being   15
stem one by one, each to its end,
until the whole field is a
white desire, empty, a single stem,
a cluster, flower by flower,
a pious wish to whiteness gone over—   20
or nothing.

                                        1921

To Waken an Old Lady

Old age is
a flight of small
cheeping birds
skimming
bare trees   5
above a snow glaze.
Gaining and failing
they are buffeted
by a dark wind—
But what?   10
On harsh weedstalks
the flock has rested,
the snow
is covered with broken
seedhusks   15
and the wind tempered
by a shrill
piping of plenty.

                                        1921

The Widow's Lament in Springtime

Sorrow is my own yard
where the new grass
flames as it has flamed
often before but not
with the cold fire   5
that closes round me this year.
Thirtyfive years
I lived with my husband.
The plumtree is white today
with masses of flowers.   10
Masses of flowers

load the cherry branches
and color some bushes
yellow and some red
but the grief in my heart   15
is stronger than they
for though they were my joy
formerly, today I notice them
and turn away forgetting.
Today my son told me   20
that in the meadows,
at the edge of the heavy woods
in the distance, he saw
trees of white flowers.
I feel that I would like   25
to go there
and fall into those flowers
and sink into the marsh near them.

                                         1921

Spring and All

By the road to the contagious hospital[3]
under the surge of the blue
mottled clouds driven from the
northeast—a cold wind. Beyond, the
waste of broad, muddy fields   5
brown with dried weeds, standing and fallen

patches of standing water
the scattering of tall trees

All along the road the reddish
purplish, forked, upstanding, twiggy   10
stuff of bushes and small trees
with dead, brown leaves under them
leafless vines—

Lifeless in appearance, sluggish
dazed spring approaches—   15

They enter the new world naked,
cold, uncertain of all
save that they enter. All about them
the cold, familiar wind—

Now the grass, tomorrow   20
the stiff curl of wildcarrot leaf

---

3. A hospital for patients with infectious diseases.

One by one objects are defined—
It quickens: clarity, outline of leaf

But now the stark dignity of
entrance—Still, the profound change   25
has come upon them: rooted, they
grip down and begin to awaken

                                                      1923

The Right of Way

In passing with my mind
on nothing on the world

but the right of way
I enjoy on the road by

virtue of the law—   5
I saw

an elderly man who
smiled and looked away

to the north past a house—
a woman in blue   10

who was laughing and
leaning forward to look up

into the man's half
averted face

and a boy of eight who was   15
looking at the middle of

the man's belly
at a watchchain—

The supreme importance
of this nameless spectacle   20

sped me by them
without a word—

Why bother where I went?
for I went spinning on the

four wheels of my car   25
along the wet road until

I saw a girl with one leg
over the rail of a balcony

                                                      1923

To Elsie[4]

The pure products of America
go crazy—
mountain folk from Kentucky

or the ribbed north end of
Jersey   5
with its isolate lakes and

valleys, its deaf-mutes, thieves
old names
and promiscuity between

devil-may-care men who have taken   10
to railroading
out of sheer lust of adventure—

and young slatterns, bathed
in filth
from Monday to Saturday   15

to be tricked out that night
with gauds
from imaginations which have no

peasant traditions to give them
character   20
but flutter and flaunt

sheer rags—succumbing without
emotion
save numbed terror

under some hedge of choke-cherry   25
or viburnum—
which they cannot express—

Unless it be that marriage
perhaps
with a dash of Indian blood   30

will throw up a girl so desolate
so hemmed round
with disease or murder

that she'll be rescued by an
agent—   35
reared by the state and

4. A retarded woman from the State Orphanage who worked as a nursemaid for the Williams family
after Kathleen (see "Danse Russe," p. 147).

sent out at fifteen to work in
some hard-pressed
house in the suburbs—

some doctor's family, some Elsie—   40
voluptuous water
expressing with broken

brain the truth about us—
her great
ungainly hips and flopping breasts   45

addressed to cheap
jewelry
and rich young men with fine eyes

as if the earth under our feet
were   50
an excrement of some sky

and we degraded prisoners
destined
to hunger until we eat filth

while the imagination strains   55
after deer
going by fields of goldenrod in

the stifling heat of September
Somehow
it seems to destroy us   60

It is only in isolate flecks that
something
is given off

No one
to witness   65
and adjust, no one to drive the car

                                                1923

The Red Wheelbarrow

so much depends
upon

a red wheel
barrow

glazed with rain   5
water

beside the white
chickens

                                                1923

The Last Words of My English Grandmother[5]

There were some dirty plates
and a glass of milk
beside her on a small table
near the rank, disheveled bed—

Wrinkled and nearly blind   5
she lay and snored
rousing with anger in her tones
to cry for food,

Gimme something to eat—
They're starving me—   10
I'm all right I won't go
To the hospital. No, no, no

Give me something to eat
Let me take you
to the hospital, I said   15
and after you are well

you can do as you please.
She smiled, Yes
you do what you please first
then I can do what I please—   20

Oh, oh, oh! she cried
as the ambulance men lifted
her to the stretcher—
Is this what you call

making me comfortable?   25
By now her mind was clear—
Oh you think you're smart
you young people,

she said, but I'll tell you
you don't know anything.   30
Then we started.
On the way

we passed a long row
of elms. She looked at them
awhile out of   35
the ambulance window and said,

What are all those
fuzzy-looking things out there?
Trees? Well, I'm tired
of them and rolled her head away.   40

                                                         1924

5. Compare this poem with "Dedication for a Plot of Ground, p. 147.

This is Just to Say

I have eaten
the plums
that were in
the icebox

and which   5
you were probably
saving
for breakfast

Forgive me
they were delicious   10
so sweet
and so cold

1934

Flowers by the Sea

When over the flowery, sharp pasture's
edge, unseen, the salt ocean

lifts its form—chicory and daisies
tied, released, seem hardly flowers alone

but color and the movement—or the shape   5
perhaps—of restlessness, whereas

the sea is circled and sways
peacefully upon its plantlike stem

1935

The Yachts

contend in a sea which the land partly encloses
shielding them from the too-heavy blows
of an ungoverned ocean which when it chooses

tortures the biggest hulls, the best man knows
to pit against its beatings, and sinks them pitilessly.   5
Mothlike in mists, scintillant in the minute

brilliance of cloudless days, with broad bellying sails
they glide to the wind tossing green water
from their sharp prows while over them the crew crawls

ant-like, solicitously grooming them, releasing,   10
making fast as they turn, lean far over and having
caught the wind again, side by side, head for the mark.

In a well guarded arena of open water surrounded by
lesser and greater craft which, sycophant, lumbering
and flittering follow them, they appear youthful, rare   15

as the light of a happy eye, live with the grace
of all that in the mind is fleckless, free and
naturally to be desired. Now the sea which holds them

is moody, lapping their glossy sides, as if feeling
for some slightest flaw but fails completely.   20
Today no race. Then the wind comes again. The yachts

move, jockeying for a start, the signal is set and they
are off. Now the waves strike at them but they are too
well made, they slip through, though they take in canvas.

Arms with hands grasping seek to clutch at the prows.   25
Bodies thrown recklessly in the way are cut aside.
It is a sea of faces about them in agony, in despair

until the horror of the race dawns staggering the mind,
the whole sea become an entanglement of watery bodies
lost to the world bearing what they cannot hold. Broken,   30

beaten, desolate, reaching from the dead to be taken up
they cry out, failing, failing! their cries rising
in waves still as the skillful yachts pass over.

                                                    1935

The Dance

In Breughel's great picture, The Kermess,[6]
the dancers go round, they go round and
around, the squeal and the blare and the
tweedle of bagpipes, a bugle and fiddles
tipping their bellies (round as the thick-   5
sided glasses whose wash they impound)
their hips and their bellies off balance
to turn them. Kicking and rolling about
the Fair Grounds, swinging their butts, those
shanks must be sound to bear up under such   10
rollicking measures, prance as they dance
in Breughel's great picture, The Kermess.

                                                    1944

The Descent

The descent beckons
          as the ascent beckoned.
                    Memory is a kind
of accomplishment,

---

6. Pieter Breughel (more generally spelled Bruegel or Brueghel) the Elder (1525?–1569), a Flemish painter noted for scenes of peasant life; his painting *The Kermess* (1567–1568) depicts a village celebration on the feast day of a local saint.

                    a sort of renewal   5
                              even
an initiation, since the spaces it opens are new places
                    inhabited by hordes
                              heretofore unrealized,
of new kinds—   10
          since their movements
                              are toward new objectives
(even though formerly they were abandoned).

No defeat is made up entirely of defeat—since
the world it opens is always a place   15
                    formerly
                              unsuspected. A
world lost,
          a world unsuspected,
                              beckons to new places   20
and no whiteness (lost) is so white as the memory
of whiteness.

With evening, love wakens
          though its shadows
                              which are alive by reason   25
of the sun shining—
                    grow sleepy now and drop away
                              from desire.

Love without shadows stirs now
          beginning to awaken   30
                              as night
advances.

The descent
          made up of despairs
                              and without accomplishment   35
realizes a new awakening:
                    which is a reversal
of despair.
                    For what we cannot accomplish, what
is denied to love,   40
                    what we have lost in the anticipation—
                              a descent follows,
endless and indestructible

                                             1954

From Asphodel, That Greeny Flower

BOOK I

Of asphodel,[7] that greeny flower,
    like a buttercup
        upon its branching stem—
save that it's green and wooden—
    I come, my sweet,   5
        to sing to you.
We lived long together
    a life filled,
        if you will,
with flowers. So that   10
    I was cheered
        when I came first to know
that there were flowers also
    in hell.
        Today   15
I'm filled with the fading memory of those flowers
    that we both loved,
        even to this poor
colorless thing—
    I saw it   20
        when I was a child—
little prized among the living
    but the dead see,
        asking among themselves:
What do I remember   25
    that was shaped
        as this thing is shaped?
while our eyes fill
    with tears.
        Of love, abiding love   30
it will be telling
    though too weak a wash of crimson
        colors it
to make it wholly credible.
    There is something   35
        something urgent
I have to say to you
    and you alone
        but it must wait
while I drink in   40
    the joy of your approach,
        perhaps for the last time.
And so

---

7. A hardy plant of the lily family.

with fear in my heart
        I drag it out   45
and keep on talking
      for I dare not stop.
         Listen while I talk on
against time.
      It will not be   50
        for long.
I have forgot
      and yet I see clearly enough
        something
central to the sky   55
      which ranges round it.
        An odor
springs from it!
      A sweetest odor!
        Honeysuckle! And now   60
there comes the buzzing of a bee!
      and a whole flood
        of sister memories!
Only give me time,
      time to recall them   65
        before I shall speak out.
Give me time,
      time.
When I was a boy
      I kept a book   70
        to which, from time
to time,
      I added pressed flowers
        until, after a time,
I had a good collection.   75
      The asphodel,
        forebodingly,
among them.
      I bring you,
        reawakened,   80
a memory of those flowers.
      They were sweet
        when I pressed them
and retained
      something of their sweetness   85
        a long time.
It is a curious odor,
      a moral odor,
        that brings me
near to you.   90
      The color
        was the first to go.

There had come to me
    a challenge,
        your dear self,   95
mortal as I was,
    the lily's throat
        to the hummingbird!
Endless wealth,
    I thought,   100
        held out its arms to me.
A thousand topics,
    in an apple blossom.
        The generous earth itself
gave us lief.   105
    The whole world
        became my garden!
But the sea
    which no one tends
        is also a garden   110
when the sun strikes it
    and the waves
        are wakened.
I have seen it
    and so have you   115
        when it puts all flowers
to shame.
    Too, there are the starfish
        stiffened by the sun
and other sea wrack   120
    and weeds. We knew that
        along with the rest of it
for we were born by the sea,
    knew its rose hedges
        to the very water's brink.   125
There the pink mallow[8] grows
    and in their season
        strawberries
and there, later,
    we went to gather   130
        the wild plum.
I cannot say
    that I have gone to hell
        for your love
but often   135
    found myself there
        in your pursuit.
I do not like it

---

8. A plant known for its extravagant blossoms.

and wanted to be
         in heaven. Hear me out.   140
Do not turn away.

I have learned much in my life
      from books
         and out of them
about love.   145
       Death
         is not the end of it.
There is a hierarchy
     which can be attained,
        I think,   150
in its service.
       Its guerdon
         is a fairy flower;
a cat of twenty lives.
       If no one came to try it   155
         the world
would be the loser.
       It has been
         for you and me
as one who watches a storm   160
       come in over the water.
         We have stood
from year to year
       before the spectacle of our lives
         with joined hands.   165
The storm unfolds.
       Lightning
         plays about the edges of the clouds.
The sky to the north
       is placid,   170
         blue in the afterglow
as the storm piles up.
       It is a flower
         that will soon reach
the apex of its bloom.   175
       We danced,
         in our minds,
and read a book together.
       You remember?
         It was a serious book.   180
And so books
       entered our lives.
The sea! The sea!
       Always
         when I think of the sea   185
there comes to mind

                    the *Iliad*
                          and Helen's public fault
that bred it.
                    Were it not for that   190
                          there would have been
no poem but the world
          if we had remembered,
                    those crimson petals
spilled among the stones,   195
                    would have called it simply
                          murder.
The sexual orchid that bloomed then
          sending so many
                    disinterested   200
men to their graves
          has left its memory
                    to a race of fools
or heroes
          if silence is a virtue.   205
                    The sea alone
with is multiplicity
          holds any hope.
                    The storm
has proven abortive   210
          but we remain
                    after the thoughts it roused
to
          re-cement our lives.
                    It is the mind   215
the mind
          that must be cured
                    short of death's
intervention,
          and the will becomes again   220
                    a garden. The poem
is complex and the place made
          in our lives
                    for the poem.
Silence can be complex too,   225
          but you do not get far
                    with silence.
Begin again.
          It is like Homer's
                    catalogue of ships:[9]   230
it fills up the time.
          I speak in figures,

9. See *The Iliad*, Book II.

well enough, the dresses
you wear are figures also,
　　　　we could not meet   235
　　　　　　otherwise. When I speak
of flowers
　　　it is to recall
　　　　　that at one time
we were young.   240
　　　　　All women are not Helen,
　　　　　　I know that,
but have Helen in their hearts.
　　　　My sweet,
　　　　　　you have it also, therefore   245
I love you
　　　and could not love you otherwise.
　　　　　Imagine you saw
a field made up of women
　　　all silver-white.   250
　　　　　　What should you do
but love them?
　　　　The storm bursts
　　　　　or fades! it is not
the end of the world.   255
　　　　Love is something else,
　　　　　or so I thought it,
a garden which expands,
　　　though I knew you as a woman
　　　　　and never thought otherwise,   260
until the whole sea
　　　has been taken up
　　　　　and all its gardens.
It was the love of love,
　　　the love that swallows up all else,   265
　　　　　a grateful love,
a love of nature, of people,
　　　animals,
　　　　　a love engendering
gentleness and goodness   270
　　　that moved me
　　　　　and *that* I saw in you.
I should have known
　　　though I did not,
　　　　　that the lily-of-the-valley   275
is a flower makes many ill
　　　who whiff it.
　　　　　We had our children,
rivals in the general onslaught.
　　　I put them aside   280
　　　　　though I cared for them

as well as any man
        could care for his children
                according to my lights.
You understand   285
        I had to meet you
                after the event
and have still to meet you.
        Love
                to which you too shall bow   290
along with me—
        a flower
                a weakest flower
shall be our trust
        and not because   295
                we are too feeble
to do otherwise
        but because
                at the height of my power
I risked what I had to do,   300
        therefore to prove
                that we love each other
while my very bones sweated
        that I could not cry to you
                in the act.   305
Of asphodel, that greeny flower,
        I come, my sweet,
                to sing to you!
My heart rouses
        thinking to bring you news   310
                of something
that concerns you
        and concerns many men. Look at
                what passes for the new.
You will not find it there but in   315
        despised poems.
                It is difficult
to get the news from poems
        yet men die miserably every day
                for lack   320
of what is found there.
        Hear me out
                for I too am concerned
and every man
        who wants to die at peace in his bed   325
                besides.

                                            1955

EZRA POUND
(1885–1972)

Ezra Loomis Pound, the central genius and tragic figure of Modernist poetry, was born in the remote mining town of Hailey, Idaho, five years before the territory was admitted to the Union. The poet's father, Homer Pound, had obtained a political appointment from his own father, a congressman from Wisconsin, as local assayer of gold and silver and register of mining claims. The poet's mother, Isabel Weston Pound, a relative of Henry Wadsworth Longfellow, disliked Hailey, and by late 1887 the family moved back east, eventually settling in Philadelphia where Homer worked for the U.S. Mint. In 1901 the sixteen-year-old Pound enrolled at the University of Pennsylvania where the next year he met William Carlos Williams in his first year of medical school. In 1903 Pound transferred to Hamilton College, a smaller school with a superior language program, so that he could study Italian and Spanish in addition to Greek, Latin, French, German, Portuguese, and Anglo-Saxon. (He later studied Provençal and Chinese as well.) Linguistics was an exciting field at that time, as European philologists documented and analyzed the Continent's complex language families. Pound became fascinated with the Romance languages and in 1906 returned to Penn to take a master's degree in the field.

Pound's academic studies proved crucial to his artistic development. His immersion in linguistics gave his own work an international orientation, and it led him to become the most influential translator of poetry in American literature. Later specialists have sometimes criticized Pound's command of foreign languages. While it is true that he did not know all the languages he studied equally well, his range was impressive. Pound not only translated widely from eight languages, he also published in Italian and French and even composed two Cantos in Italian.

Equally important were the human relationships Pound cultivated. He had an indisputable genius not only for identifying artistic talent but also for encouraging, shaping, and promoting it. He was the great literary mentor of Modernism, often serving in important advisory roles even to his elders, like William Butler Yeats. While still a teenager he had already formed lifelong friendships with William Carlos Williams and Hilda Doolittle (later H.D.). (Pound had even hoped to marry Doolittle but was prevented by her father, who was suspicious of the brash, young bohemian.) Pound was not satisfied merely with articulating a new aesthetic in his own poetry and criticism. He wanted to create a new literary culture that embodied these values. He understood that meant convincing the most talented writers of his time to pursue Modernism and then shaping and supporting their efforts.

No writer of his time proved more influential. Pound was a decisive figure in the literary careers of T. S. Eliot, James Joyce, William Carlos Williams, H. D., the later W. B. Yeats, and the younger poets who gathered under the "Objectivist" banner (most notably Basil Bunting, George Oppen, and Louis Zukofsky). His role in Eliot's career was crucial. He took the draft of Eliot's poem "He Do the Police in Different Voices," drastically cut and reshaped it, and retitled it "The Waste Land." Pound's compressed and elliptical version of Eliot's poem became the poetic touchstone of the Modernist movement. He also influenced and championed visual artists like Jacob Epstein, Henri Gaudier-Brzeska, and Constantine Brancusi as well as the avant-garde composer George Antheil, the so-called "Bad Boy of Music." Few major writers have ever been so generous, not only with attention and energy but also with money. Although Pound lived a bohemian life of voluntary poverty, he was always ready to pass on whatever funds he had to needy friends. As Pound's lifelong mistress Olga Rudge commented, "He didn't talk about things—He wanted something *done*."

Pound first traveled to Europe on a tiny fellowship in 1906. After touring Spain and France, he returned to Penn to work on his doctorate and study Provençal and Sicilian. In the autumn of 1907, the twenty-one-year-old poet began teaching at Wabash College in Crawfordsville, Indiana. The flamboyant young bohemian was not destined to stay long in such a conservative milieu. (Tobacco and alcohol were forbidden by local law.) In February he was dismissed by the college authorities for allowing a stranded actress to spend the night in his room (while he slept on the floor). The trustees could not prove immorality, but they wanted the cigarette-smoking, free-speaking "Latin Quarter type" off campus. They offered to pay his full year's salary if he left. Pound took the money and sailed to Europe. He would spend the next thirty-seven years as an émigré in England, France, and Italy. Indiana lost a fine professor of comparative literature, and America gained a great Modernist poet.

After privately publishing his first book of poems, *A Lume Spento* ("With Candles Quenched") (1908) in Venice, Pound settled in London where he soon became the central figure in the new experimental movement. At that time Pound believed that English-language poetry was moribund, stuck in stale Romantic clichés and unable to reflect the complex reality of the modern world. Only Yeats, he felt, was a great living poet, although even he needed to develop a more contemporary idiom. In both poetry and criticism the young Pound proclaimed a program of artistic modernization. *Make It new,* the title of his 1934 critical collection, aptly summarizes the artistic battle cry of Pound's London years.

In 1912 Pound created his first and most influential literary movement, Imagism, or to use the French term initially employed, *Imagisme.* Joining Richard Aldington, T. E. Hulme, F. S. Flint, and Hilda Doolittle (whom he renamed "H. D., Imagiste"), Pound announced a new poetic credo of intensity, concision, and directness. In *Poetry* (March 1913) Pound published a manifesto, "A Few Don'ts by an Imagist," which remains one of the generative Modernist texts. Pound characterized the "new fashion in poetry" as having three principles:

1. Direct treatment of the "thing" whether subjective or objective.
2. To use absolutely no word that does not contribute to the presentation.
3. As regarding rhythm: to compose in the sequence of the musical phrase, not in sequence of a metronome.

Pound soon published an anthology, *Des Imagistes* (1914), containing work by eleven poets, including H.D., Amy Lowell, William Carlos Williams, and James Joyce. In his introduction he elaborated on the principles of the new experimental poetry to include "to use the language of common speech, but always the exact word—not the almost exact one" and "to create new rhythms." As a distinct and unified movement, Imagism lasted only two years. By 1914 Pound was plotting his next movement, Vorticism, with writer-artist Wyndham Lewis. Amy Lowell soon issued rival Imagist anthologies, which led Pound to dismiss her efforts as "Amygisme." Vorticism, however, never clearly articulated a distinct aesthetic and soon faltered, leaving behind two issues of *BLAST* (1914 and 1915), a rudely exuberant, oversized arts journal, as its chief memorial.

Pound's attention now turned to Chinese and Japanese verse—an artistic enterprise that would have profound influence on modern poetry. Significantly, Pound had rejected the Romantic assertion—found in Coleridge, Shelley, and others—that poetry is essentially untranslatable. Instead, Pound reasserted the Renaissance notion of poetic translation as a creative art that expands a national literature by introducing foreign works. Translation is not a doomed enterprise but a necessary part of literary culture. "A great age of literature," he asserted, "is perhaps always a great age of translation, or follows it." Translation became central both to Pound's own poetic development and his cultural program to modernize and reform English-language verse.

In 1913 the widow of Ernest Fenollosa, an American scholar who had worked in Tokyo to preserve Japanese culture, sent Pound her husband's extensive notes on Chinese and Japanese poetry. Fenellosa's notebooks excited Pound, who saw similarities between the East Asian conception of poetry and Imagism. He worked on the notebooks that winter while living in Stone Cottage with Yeats for whom he served as secretary. He translated several Japanese *Noh* dramas (which led Yeats to write his own *Noh*-influenced "Plays for Dancers"). He also published *Cathay* (1915), a sequence of free translations from the Chinese, which included "The River-Merchant's Wife: A Letter," which Pound biographer Humphrey Carpenter has called "the most appealing poem of Ezra's whole career." *Cathay* has exercised an enormous influence. Eliot called Pound "the inventor of Chinese poetry for our time," but its importance extends beyond translation. Pound's sharply sensory, concise, and emotionally understated free verse in *Cathay* became a model modern style for many later American poets.

In London Pound also pioneered what would become perhaps the major Modernist long poetic form, the sequence (a group of interconnected short poems arranged in sections). Pound, like most American Modernists, rejected the narrative mode as the organizing structure for longer poems. He became fascinated with the concept of creating an extended poem composed of carefully arranged and thematically unified short lyric sections. The sequence soon became the dominant structure for longer Modernist poems, and it proved indispensable to writers as different as Pound, Williams, Eliot, H.D., Wallace Stevens, Gertrude Stein, and Hart Crane. (Only Robinson Jeffers among the major Modernists worked consistently in the narrative mode.)

Pound's *Cathay* can be read as a sequence, although it is composed of discrete translations from Chinese; his two Mauberley sequences, however, demonstrate the full possibilities of this new form. "Hugh Selwyn Mauberley" (1920) describes an alter ego for Pound. Mauberley is a thirty-one-year-old American author trying to write great poetry in literary London in the era around World War I. In this poem and many others Pound adopted a persona (literally "a mask"), an invented character whose voice he *impersonates* in a way that allows him to speak indirectly about his own life and time. The most ambitious example of Pound's persona poems is "Homage to Sextus Propertius," a brilliant sequence of lyric and dramatic monologues supposedly spoken by the title character, a Roman poet living under the Caesars, re-created in a way that reflected the American writer's own life in London during the twilight years of the British Empire.

In London Pound also began what would become the central creative undertaking of his life, the *Cantos*. Begun in 1917, this Modernist epic occupied him for the remainder of his life (by 1926 he had more or less stopped writing all other poetry), but it was never finished to the author's satisfaction. *The Cantos of Ezra Pound*

(1970) contained final versions, drafts, or fragments of 115 cantos, some of which existed only as short passages. (The book omitted two overtly profascist cantos written in Italian, so the total number of sections in Pound's final version was 117.)

The *Cantos* have been controversial since their inception. Many critics offer them as conclusive evidence of the poet's genius—a modern epic, which Pound defined as "a poem including history," that addresses world culture, politics, economics, and mythology. Other critics see its nonlinear organization and densely allusive language (which contains numerous Latin, Greek, Italian, Chinese, Provençal, and French quotations in the original) as signs of Pound's decline into obscurantism and megalomania. The most reasonable reaction is probably in between. The entire poem surely fails to deliver the author's grand intention of a powerfully poetic Modernist epic that summarizes and critiques the best of world culture. In his old age Pound himself declared the work a "botch." Yet few readers who study the richly textured and carefully sculpted poem can fail to recognize the lyric power of its best sections or the intellectual energy of certain themes, especially the figure and ideas of Confucius, whose philosophy and poetry exercised a decisive influence on Pound's views. Ultimately, the *Cantos* represent a test case for the Modernist method: how effectively can a literary work communicate when it abandons the traditional techniques like narrative or linear argumentation for lyric methods of indirection, allusion, and symbolism? Successful or failed, the *Cantos* stand at the center of Modernist literature, and their considerable influence has not been limited to English-language poets.

Had Pound died at forty in 1925, he would probably be universally venerated as the central genius of American Modernism whose innovative brilliance, critical acumen, and personal generosity had refashioned poetry. But he lived for another forty-seven years. After leaving London in 1921, he lived in Paris for four years, where he moved among the American émigrés now known as "The Lost Generation," who include Ernest Hemingway, Gertrude Stein, Archibald MacLeish, and E. E. Cummings. But finding it too expensive, he and his British wife, Dorothy Shakespear, moved to Rapallo, Italy, in 1924. By now Pound had become increasingly involved in politics and economics, and the intellectual isolation of the Italian seaside town aggravated his already idiosyncratic views of modern society. He became a devoted admirer of the fascist dictator, Benito Mussolini, and he used his unreliable economic theories to vent his growing anti-Semitism. When Britain declared war on Germany and Italy in 1939, Pound's book royalties stopped and his wife's English investments were frozen.

Pound contemplated returning to the United States but instead he took a job broadcasting for the Italian government's *American Hour* radio show. Hired to talk about literary matters, Pound could not resist the opportunity to promulgate his political views. His broadcasts were self-indulgent and digressive to the point of incoherence, but there was no mistaking his devotion to fascism, his hatred of President Franklin Roosevelt, and his virulent anti-Semitism. (Pound's talks were so chaotic and bizarre that some Italian officials suspected that he was an American spy broadcasting in a secret code.) When America declared war on Italy in 1941, Pound did not cease broadcasting, nor change his citizenship, but continued praising Mussolini and eventually Hitler, while criticizing America in crude, racist terms. That same year Pound was indicted *in absentia* for treason, a capital offense. The fifty-nine-year-old poet was arrested by the U.S. Army in 1945.

After several months in a military prison near Pisa (partly confined in an open outdoor cage) during which time he wrote the "Pisan Cantos" (Nos. 74–84), Pound was flown to Washington, D.C., for trial. Through the efforts of his literary friends, he was declared unfit for trial by reason of insanity and confined to Washington's St. Elizabeths Hospital for the Criminally Insane, where he remained for the next thirteen years. During his confinement Pound received a steady stream of visitors, including Charles Olson, Elizabeth Bishop, and Marshall McLuhan. Due to the efforts of Frost, MacLeish, and Hemingway, Pound was finally discharged as "unimproved" in 1958. As soon as he was issued a passport, the seventy-two-year-old poet returned to Italy. His final years were marked by mental deterioration. He sat silently for days but occasionally broke out with normal conversation as when he reportedly told Allen Ginsberg who visited him in 1967, "The worst mistake I made was the stupid, suburban prejudice of anti-Semitism." Pound died in Venice in 1972. His body was taken by gondola to the tiny island cemetery of San Michele in the Venetian lagoon where he was buried.

Pound was, with T. S. Eliot, the generative critical intelligence of Modernism. He has been condemned—often with some justice—as an elitist, aesthete, obscurantist, fraud, egotist, racist, and totalitarian, but his central position in the renewal of English-language poetry in the early twentieth century remains indisputable. Pound's insistence on the importance of certain principles—verse technique, poetic compression, creative translation, expansion of the literary canon, and the interdependence of national literatures—has helped shape contemporary attitudes about poetry and poetics.

◄•◦•►◄▶►◄•◦•►

Sestina: Altaforte[1]

LOQUITUR: *En* Bertrans de Born.
    Dante Alighieri put this man in hell for that he was a stirrer
    up of strife.
    Eccovi!
    Judge ye!
    Have I dug him up again?
The scene is at his castle, Altaforte. "Papiols" is his jongleur.
"The Leopard," the *device* of Richard Coeur de Lion.[2]

I

Damn it all! all this our South stinks peace.
You whoreson dog, Papiols, come! Let's to music!
I have no life save when the swords clash.
But ah! when I see the standards gold, vair,[3] purple, opposing

---

1. In *The Spirit of Romance* (1910) Pound writes of "the sestina form invented by Arnout Daniel, later introduced into Italy by Dante, and into Spain, I believe, by Fernando de Herrera, 'El Divino,' a form like a thin sheet of flame folding and infolding upon itself."
2. *Loquitur:* He speaks; *En:* Sir; Bertrans de Born: A medieval knight and troubadour, best known for poems about war (see Dante, *Inferno,* Canto XXVIII); *Eccovi:* "Here you are!" (Italian); jongleur: minstrel; *device:* Heraldic emblem; Richard Coeur de Lion: Richard the Lion Hearted (1157–1199), King of England (1189–99).
3. vair: gray and white fur used for trimming garments in medieval Europe.

And the broad fields beneath them turn crimson,
Then howl I my heart nigh mad with rejoicing.   5

II

In hot summer have I great rejoicing
When the tempests kill the earth's foul peace,
And the lightnings from black heav'n flash crimson,
And the fierce thunders roar me their music   10
And the winds shriek through the clouds mad, opposing,
And through all the riven skies God's swords clash.

III

Hell grant soon we hear again the swords clash!
And the shrill neighs of destriers in battle rejoicing,
Spiked breast to spiked breast opposing!   15
Better one hour's stour[4] than a year's peace
With fat boards, bawds, wine and frail music!
Bah! there's no wine like the blood's crimson!

IV

And I love to see the sun rise blood-crimson.
And I watch his spears through the dark clash   20
And it fills all my heart with rejoicing
And pries wide my mouth with fast music
When I see him so scorn and defy peace,
His lone might 'gainst all darkness opposing.

V

The man who fears war and squats opposing   25
My words for stour, hath no blood of crimson
But is fit only to rot in womanish peace
Far from where worth's won and the swords clash
For the death of such sluts I go rejoicing;
Yea, I fill all the air with my music.   30

VI

Papiols, Papiols, to the music!
There's no sound like to swords swords opposing,
No cry like the battle's rejoicing
When our elbows and swords drip the crimson
And our charges 'gainst "The Leopard's" rush clash.   35
May God damn for ever all who cry "Peace!"

4. stour: tumult. *destriers:* war horses.

VII

And let the music of the swords make them crimson!
Hell grant soon we hear again the swords clash!
Hell blot black for alway the thought "Peace"!

1909

Portrait D'une Femme[5]

Your mind and you are our Sargasso Sea,[6]
London has swept about you this score years
And bright ships left you this or that in fee:
Ideas, old gossip, oddments of all things,
Strange spars of knowledge and dimmed wares of price.   5
Great minds have sought you—lacking someone else.
You have been second always. Tragical?
No. You preferred it to the usual thing:
One dull man, dulling and uxorious,
One average mind—with one thought less, each year.   10
Oh, you are patient, I have seen you sit
Hours, where something might have floated up.
And now you pay one. Yes, you richly pay.
You are a person of some interest, one comes to you
And takes strange gain away: 15
Trophies fished up; some curious suggestion;
Fact that leads nowhere; and a tale or two,
Pregnant with mandrakes,[7] or with something else
That might prove useful and yet never proves,
That never fits a corner or shows use,   20
Or finds its hour upon the loom of days:
The tarnished, gaudy, wonderful old work;
Idols and ambergris and rare inlays,
These are your riches, your great store; and yet
For all this sea-hoard of deciduous things,   25
Strange woods half sodden, and new brighter stuff:
In the slow float of differing light and deep,
No! there is nothing! In the whole and all,
Nothing that's quite your own.
                    Yet this is you.   30

1912

---

5. "Portrait of a Lady" (French).
6. Part of the North Atlantic so choked with seaweed that it was said to have trapped ships.
7. Narcotic plants of the nightshade family.

The Return

See, they[8] return; ah, see the tentative
Movements, and the slow feet,
The trouble in the pace and the uncertain
Wavering!
See, they return, one, and by one,   5
With fear, as half-awakened;
As if the snow should hesitate
And murmur in the wind,
               and half-turn back;
These were the 'Wing'd-with-Awe',   10
         Inviolable.

Gods of the wingèd shoe![9]
With them the silver hounds,
            sniffing the trace of air!

Haie! Haie!   15
        These were the swift to harry;
These the keen-scented;
These were the souls of blood.

Slow on the leash,
           pallid the leash-men!   20

                             1912

Alba[1]

As cool as the pale wet leaves
          of lily-of-the-valley
She lay beside me in the dawn.

                             1915

Coda

O my songs,
Why do you look so eagerly and so curiously into people's faces,
Will you find your lost dead among them?

                             1915

The Coming of War: Actæon[2]

An image of Lethe,[3]
     and the fields

---

8. The pagan gods.
9. A Homeric epithet indicating Hermes, messenger of the gods.
1. The title refers to the Provençal tradition of the "dawn poem," a time when lovers part.
2. In Ovid's *Metamorphoses,* Actæon sees the goddess Diana naked and as punishment is transformed into a stag and torn apart by hounds. Pound may have intended this as an ironic reference to young men going to fight in World War I.
3. River in ancient Greek mythology that caused all who drank from it to forget the past.

Full of faint light
    but golden,
Gray cliffs,   5
    and beneath them
A sea
Harsher than granite,
    unstill, never ceasing;
High forms   10
    with the movement of gods,
Perilous aspect;
    And one said:
"This is Actæon."
    Actæon of golden greaves![4]   15
Over fair meadows,
Over the cool face of that field,
Unstill, ever moving
Hosts of an ancient people,
The silent cortège.[5]   20

                             1915

The Garden

En robe de parade.
      —Samain[6]

Like a skein of loose silk blown against a wall
She walks by the railing of a path in Kensington Gardens,
And she is dying piece-meal
    of a sort of emotional anæmia.

And round about there is a rabble   5
Of the filthy, sturdy, unkillable infants of the very poor.
They shall inherit the earth.[7]

In her is the end of breeding.
Her boredom is exquisite and excessive.
She would like some one to speak to her,   10
And is almost afraid that I
    will commit that indiscretion.

                             1915

The Garret

Come, let us pity those who are better off than we are.
Come, my friend, and remember
    that the rich have butlers and no friends,

4. Greaves: armor worn on the shins
5. A procession, usually used in funerals.
6. From Albert Samain's *Au Jardin de l'Infante* (1893). The words mean "dressed for show."
7. See Matthew 5:5—"Blessed are the meek: for they shall inherit the earth."

And we have friends and no butlers.
Come, let us pity the married and the unmarried.   5

Dawn enters with little feet
    like a gilded Pavlova,[8]
And I am near my desire.
Nor has life in it aught better
Than this hour of clear coolness,   10
    the hour of waking together.

                            1915

Papyrus[9]

    Spring . . . .
    Too long . . . . . .
    Gongula[1] . . . . . .

                            1915

In a Station of the Metro

The apparition of these faces in the crowd;
Petals on a wet, black bough.

                            1915

The Jewel Stairs' Grievance[2]

The jewelled steps are already quite white with dew,
It is so late that the dew soaks my gauze stockings,
And I let down the crystal curtain
And watch the moon through the clear autumn.

    By Rihaku[3]

                            1915

Lament of the Frontier Guard[4]

By the North Gate, the wind blows full of sand,
Lonely from the beginning of time until now!
Trees fall, the grass goes yellow with autumn.
I climb the towers and towers
    to watch out the barbarous land: 5

---

8. Anna Pavlova, famed Russian ballerina (1885–1931).
9. The texts of some poems by Sappho (c. 620–c. 565 B.C.E., renowned poet of Lesbos in ancient Greece and one of the few female poets of the classical world) survived only in fragments on papyrus; some critics regard this as a satire of Sappho scholarship.
1. Said to be one of Sappho's followers.
2. In 1912 Pound was introduced to the widow of Ernest Fenollosa, who had been translating Chinese poetry shortly before his death; using Fenollosa's manuscripts, Pound produced the poems of *Cathay* (1915). Pound's note: "Jewel stairs, therefore a palace. Grievance, therefore there is something to complain of. Gauze stockings, therefore a court lady, not a servant who complains. Clear autumn, therefore he has no excuse on account of weather. Also she has come early, for the dew has not merely whitened the stairs, but has soaked her stockings. The poem is especially prized because she utters no direct reproach."
3. The Japanese name for the Chinese poet Li Po (701–762).
4. From *Cathay*; see note 2.

Desolate castle, the sky, the wide desert.
There is no wall left to this village.
Bones white with a thousand frosts,
High heaps, covered with trees and grass;
Who brought this to pass?   10
Who has brought the flaming imperial anger?
Who has brought the army with drums and with kettle-drums?
Barbarous kings.
A gracious spring, turned to blood-ravenous autumn,
A turmoil of wars-men, spread over the middle kingdom,   15
Three hundred and sixty thousand,
And sorrow, sorrow like rain.
Sorrow to go, and sorrow, sorrow returning.
Desolate, desolate fields,
And no children of warfare upon them,   20
          No longer the men for offence and defence.
Ah, how shall you know the dreary sorrow at the North Gate,
With Riboku's name forgotten,
And we guardsmen fed to the tigers.

     By Rihaku[5]

                                                              1915

The Rest

O helpless few in my country,
O remnant enslaved!

Artists broken against her,
A-stray, lost in the villages,
Mistrusted, spoken-against,   5

Lovers of beauty, starved,
Thwarted with systems,
Helpless against the control;

You who can not wear yourselves out
By persisting to successes,   10
You who can only speak,
Who can not steel yourselves into reiteration;

You of the finer sense,
Broken against false knowledge,
You who can know at first hand,   15
Hated, shut in, mistrusted:

Take thought:
I have weathered the storm,
I have beaten out my exile.

                                                              1915

5. See note 3, p. 177.

The River-Merchant's Wife: A Letter[6]

While my hair was still cut straight across my forehead
I played about the front gate, pulling flowers.
You came by on bamboo stilts, playing horse,
You walked about my seat, playing with blue plums.
And we went on living in the village of Chokan:[7]   5
Two small people, without dislike or suspicion.

At fourteen I married My Lord you.
I never laughed, being bashful.
Lowering my head, I looked at the wall.
Called to, a thousand times, I never looked back.   10

At fifteen I stopped scowling,
I desired my dust to be mingled with yours
Forever and forever and forever.
Why should I climb the lookout?

At sixteen you departed,   15
You went into far Ku-to-yen,[8] by the river of swirling eddies,
And you have been gone five months.
The monkeys make sorrowful noise overhead.

You dragged your feet when you went out.
By the gate now, the moss is grown, the different mosses,   20
Too deep to clear them away!
The leaves fall early this autumn, in wind.
The paired butterflies are already yellow with August
Over the grass in the West garden;
They hurt me. I grow older.   25
If you are coming down through the narrows of the river Kiang,[9]
Please let me know before hand,
And I will come out to meet you
          As far as Cho-fu-sa.[1]

          1915

Salutation

O generation of the thoroughly smug
          and thoroughly uncomfortable,
I have seen fishermen picnicking in the sun,
I have seen them with untidy families,
I have seen their smiles full of teeth   5

---

6. A free translation from the Chinese poet Li Po. Pound was fascinated by the dramatic monologues of Browning and thought this poem might have fit among them "without causing any surprise save by its simplicity and its naïve beauty."
7. A suburb of Nanking.
8. An island in the river.
9. This river is now known as Ch'u-t'ang.
1. Literally, the "long Wind Beach," hundreds of miles up river from Nanking.

                    and heard ungainly laughter.
            And I am happier than you are,
            And they were happier than I am;
            And the fish swim in the lake
                    and do not even own clothing.   10

                                                                    1915

A Pact

            I make a pact with you, Walt Whitman—
            I have detested you long enough.
            I come to you as a grown child
            Who has had a pig-headed father;
            I am old enough now to make friends.   5
            It was you that broke the new wood,
            Now is a time for carving.
            We have one sap and one root—
            Let there be commerce between us.

                                                                    1916

FROM Homage to Sextus Propertius[2]

I

Shades of Callimachus, Coan ghosts of Philetas[3]
It is in your grove I would walk,
I who come first from the clear font
Bringing the Grecian orgies[4] into Italy,
                    and the dance into Italy.   5
Who hath taught you so subtle a measure,
            in what hall have you heard it;
What foot beat out your time-bar,
            what water has mellowed your whistles?

Out-weariers of Apollo will, as we know, continue their Martian
            generalities,[5]   10
        We have kept our erasers in order.
A new-fangled chariot follows the flower-hung horses;
A young Muse with young loves clustered about her
            ascends with me into the æther, . . .
And there is no high-road to the Muses.   15

---

2. This work is based on the *Elegies* of Propertius (born between 54 and 47 B.C.E.) K. K. Ruthven writes in *A Guide to Ezra Pound's Personae* (1969), "Propertius' struggle to maintain what would now be called his artistic integrity in conditions that constantly demanded a compromise of his talents was something that appealed to Pound for obvious reasons" (84).
3. Callimachus: Cyrenaic poet (born 310 B.C.E.); Philetas: Greek poet from Cos, an island in the Aegean, who lived at roughly the same time as Callimachus.
4. In Greek *orgia* means "mysteries," but Pound may have intended the English meaning as well.
5. War propaganda.

Annalists will continue to record Roman reputations,
Celebrities from the Trans-Caucasus will belaud Roman celebrities
And expound the distentions of Empire,
But for something to read in normal circumstances?
For a few pages brought down from the forked hill unsullied?   20
I ask a wreath which will not crush my head.[6]
             And there is no hurry about it;
I shall have, doubtless, a boom after my funeral,
Seeing that long standing increases all things
                regardless of quality.   25
And who would have known the towers
           pulled down by a deal-wood horse;
Or of Achilles withstaying waters by Simois
Or of Hector spattering wheel-rims,
Or of Polydmantus, by Scamander, or Helenus and Deiphoibos?   30
Their door-yards would scarcely know them, or Paris.[7]
Small talk O Ilion, and O Troad
               twice taken by Oetian gods,[8]
If Homer had not stated your case!

And I also among the later nephews of this city   35
              shall have my dog's day,
With no stone upon my contemptible sepulchre;
My vote coming from the temple of Phoebus in Lycia, at Patara,[9]
And in the meantime my songs will travel,
And the devirginated young ladies will enjoy them   40
          when they have got over the strangeness,
For Orpheus tamed the wild beasts—
          and held up the Threician river;
And Cithaeron shook up the rocks by Thebes
        and danced them into a bulwark at his pleasure,   45
And you, O Polyphemus? Did harsh Galatea almost
Turn to your dripping horses, because of a tune, under Aetna?[1]
We must look into the matter.
Bacchus and Apollo in favour of it,

---

6. After reading a "dull" review of his work by Eliot, Pound complained of such "granite wreaths, leaden laurels. . . ."
7. towers . . . deal-wood horse: According to Homer's *Iliad* Troy was destroyed by the Greeks; the Trojan horse does not figure in Homer's epic (*deal* is cheap wood). Paris: In the *Iliad*, Book XXI, Achilles battles the rivers near Troy, the Simois and the Scamander; Hector was dragged behind Achilles' chariot (*Iliad*, Book XXII). Polydmantus, Helenus, and Deiphoibos were Trojan leaders; Helenus, Deiphoibos, and Paris were sons of Priam, King of Troy; it was Paris's seduction/abduction of Helen, wife of Menelaus, King of Sparta, that was the cause of the Trojan war, according to Homer.
8. Ilion . . . Troad: Ilion was the citadel, Troad (Troy) the city; Oetian gods: Mt. Oeta was sacred to Hecules, who died there.
9. Phoebus in Lycia, at Patara: Phoebus Apollo—god of light, music, poetry; Patara—a town in the province of Lycia, southwest of Troy.
1. Orpheus: Son of Apollo and a Muse, he was famed in Greek and Roman legend as a singer and lyrist whose music "allured the trees, the savage animals, and even the insensate rocks to follow him. . . ." (Ovid, *Metamorphoses*, Book XI); Threician: Thracian—Orpheus was from Thrace; Cithaeron: A mountain near Thebes, famous for its Dionysian rites; Polyphemus . . . Galatea: Polyphemus was the Cyclops, Galatea a sea nymph he loved; Aetna: Mt Etna, volcano in Sicily.

There will be a crowd of young women doing homage to my palaver,   50
Though my house is not propped up by Taenarian columns from
    Laconia (associated with Neptune and Cerberus),[2]
Though it is not stretched upon gilded beams:
My orchards do not lie level and wide
                    as the forests of Phaeacia,   55
                    the luxurious and Ionian,
Nor are my caverns stuffed stiff with a Marcian vintage,
My cellar does not date from Numa Pompilius,[3]
Nor bristle with wine jars,
Nor is it equipped with a frigidaire patent;   60
Yet the companions of the Muses
        will keep their collective nose in my books,
And weary with historical data, they will turn to my dance tune.

Happy who are mentioned in my pamphlets,
      the songs shall be a fine tomb-stone over their beauty.   65
          But against this?
Neither expensive pyramids scraping the stars in their route,
Nor houses modelled upon that of Jove in East Elis,
Nor the monumental effigies of Mausolus,
                are a complete elucidation of death.[4]   70

Flame burns, rain sinks into the cracks
And they all go to rack ruin beneath the thud of the years.
Stands genius a deathless adornment,
        a name not to be worn out with the years.

IX[5]

1

The twisted rhombs[6] ceased their clamour of accompaniment;
The scorched laurel lay in the fire-dust;
The moon still declined to descend out of heaven,

But the black ominous owl hoot was audible.

And one raft bears our fates   5
           on the veiled lake towards Avernus
Sails spread on cerulean waters, I would shed tears
      for two;[7]

---

2. Taenarian columns: Columns made from the dark marble quarried near Sparta, in that part of Greece called Laconia; Neptune: Poseidon, god of the sea; Cerberus: A monstrous dog who guards the entrance to Hades, which one legend placed in Laconia.
3. Numa Pompilius: A legendary king of Rome.
4. Jove in East Elis: Roman name for Zeus, King of the Gods; Elis, a state in the northwestern Peloponnesos, known for its temple to Zeus at Olympia; Mausolus: A Greek king whose grand tomb gives us our word "mausoleum."
5. This section is more concerned with Cynthia, the beloved of Propertius.
6. Rhombs: In this case, odd-shaped wheels; spinning them was said to make one lucky in love.
7. Avernus: A lake near Naples also regarded as an entrance to the Underworld; cerulean: A shade of blue.

I shall live, if she continue in life,
     If she dies, I shall go with her.
Great Zeus, save the woman,
     or she will sit before your feet in a veil,   10
     and tell out the long list of her troubles.

2

Persephone and Dis, Dis, have mercy upon her,
There are enough women in hell,
     quite enough beautiful women,
Iope, and Tyro, and Pasiphae, and the formal girls of Achaia,   15
And out of Troad, and from the Campania,[8]
Death has his tooth in the lot,
     Avernus lusts for the lot of them,
Beauty is not eternal, no man has perennial fortune,
Slow foot, or swift foot, death delays but for a season.   20

3

My light, light of my eyes,
     you are escaped from great peril,
Go back to Great Dian's dances bearing suitable gifts,
Pay up your vow of night watches
     to Dian goddess of virgins,   25
And unto me also pay debt:
The ten nights of your company you have
     promised me.

                            1917

Hugh Selwyn Mauberley[9]

Life and Contacts

"Vocat æstus in umbram"
Nemesianus Ec. IV.[1]

E. P. Ode pour L'Election de Son Sepulchre[2]

I

For three years, out of key with his time,
He strove to resuscitate the dead art

---

8. Persephone and Dis: Persephone, a young girl, was carried off into the Underworld by Pluto, or Dis, to be his wife; Iope: Daughter of Aeolus, the wind; Tyro: Young woman who loved the river Enipeus but slept with Poseidon when he adopted the river's form; Pasiphae: Wife of King Minos, mother of the minotaur; Achaia: Northeastern part of the Peloponnesos; Campania: the countryside around Naples.
9. The critic K. K. Ruthven writes that "the prototype of Mauberley was Walter Villerant, a persona Pound used when contributing 'Imaginary Letters' to the *Little Review* in 1918." This sequence Pound called "a farewell to London."
1. "Summer calls us to the shade" (Latin). From the *Eclogues* of Nemesianus, a Latin poet from Carthage who lived in the third century.
2. Ezra Pound, "Ode for the Choice of His Tomb," adapted from the title of a poem by the French poet Pierre de Ronsard (1524–1585).

Of poetry; to maintain "the sublime"
In the old sense. Wrong from the start—

No, hardly, but seeing he had been born   5
In a half savage country,[3] out of date;
Bent resolutely on wringing lilies from the acorn;
Capaneus;[4] trout for factitious bait;

Ἴδμεν γάρ τοι πάνθ', ὅσ' ἐνὶ Τ ροίη[5]
Caught in the unstopped ear;   10
Giving the rocks small lee-way
The chopped seas held him, therefore, that year.

His true Penelope was Flaubert,[6]
He fished by obstinate isles;
Observed the elegance of Circe's[7] hair   15
Rather than the mottoes on sun-dials.

Unaffected by "The march of events,"
He passed from men's memory in *l'an trentuniesme*
De son eage;[8] the case presents
No adjunct to the Muses' diadem.   20

II

The age demanded an image
Of its accelerated grimace,
Something for the modern stage,
Not, at any rate, an Attic grace;

Not, not certainly, the obscure reveries   25
Of the inward gaze;
Better mendacities
Than the classics in paraphrase!

The "age demanded" chiefly a mould in plaster,
Made with no loss of time,   30
A prose kinema,[9] not, not assuredly, alabaster
Or the "sculpture" of rhyme.

3. The United States.
4. One of the Seven Against Thebes; having defied Zeus, he was struck down.
5. "For we know everything that in Troy, . . ." from Homer's *Odyssey*, Book XII, the song of the Sirens. Odysseus had himself bound to the mast so he could hear the song that lured men to their deaths; his men stopped their ears with wax.
6. Pound suggests that *this* antihero would journey home not to his wife, as Odysseus did to Penelope, but to the aesthetic perfection of the work of French novelist Gustave Flaubert (1821–1880).
7. Circe was a sorceress who turned men into pigs; she kept Odysseus under her spell for a year.
8. In "the thirty-first year of his life" (French); this line adapted from the first line of *The Testament*, by François Villon (1431–c. 1485).
9. "Movement" (Greek); the root of our word "cinema."

III

The tea-rose tea-gown, etc.
Supplants the mousseline of Cos,[1]
The pianola "replaces"   35
Sappho's barbitos.[2]

Christ follows Dionysus,
Phallic and ambrosial
Made way for macerations;
Caliban casts out Ariel.[3]   40

All things are a flowing,
Sage Heracleitus[4] says;
But a tawdry cheapness
Shall outlast our days.

Even the Christian beauty   45
Defects—after Samothrace;[5]
We see τὸ καλόν[6]
Decreed in the market place.

Faun's flesh is not to us,
Nor the saint's vision.   50
We have the press for wafer;
Franchise for circumcision.

All men, in law, are equals.
Free of Pisistratus,[7]
We choose a knave or an eunuch   55
To rule over us.

O bright Apollo,
τίν᾽ ἄνδρα, τίν᾽ ἥρωα, τίνα θεόν,
What god, man, or hero[8]
Shall I place a tin wreath upon!   60

1. A sheer, stiff fabric for which the Greek island Cos was famed.
2. Lyre.
3. Christ follows Dionysus: Christian asceticism follows the fertility cult of ancient Greece (the word "follows" has a double meaning here); macerations: Softenings, dissolutions; Caliban casts out Ariel: The bestial figure supplants the ethereal one from Shakespeare's *The Tempest*.
4. Heracleitus: Greek pre-Socratic philosopher (535–475 B.C.E.), who said that everything is in eternal flux.
5. Samothrace: A Greek island visited by St. Paul on his way to convert the Jews of Macedonia.
6. "The Beautiful" (Greek).
7. Athenian tyrant.
8. Pound translates the Greek in the next line, a variation on a line by Pindar, the Greek lyric poet (c. 522–402 B.C.E.), who wrote "What god, what hero, what man."

IV

These fought in any case,
and some believing,
            pro domo,[9] in any case . . .

Some quick to arm,
some for adventure,   65
some from fear of weakness,
some from fear of censure,
some for love of slaughter, in imagination,
learning later . . .
some in fear, learning love of slaughter;   70

Died some, pro patria,
            non "dulce" non "et decor" . . .
walked eye-deep in hell
believing in old men's lies, then unbelieving
came home, home to a lie,   75
home to many deceits,
home to old lies and new infamy;
usury age-old and age-thick
and liars in public places.

Daring as never before, wastage as never before.   80
Young blood and high blood,
fair cheeks, and fine bodies;

fortitude as never before

frankness as never before,
disillusions as never told in the old days,   85
hysterias, trench confessions,
laughter out of dead bellies.

V

There died a myriad,
And of the best, among them,
For an old bitch gone in the teeth,   90
For a botched civilization,

Charm, smiling at the good mouth,
Quick eyes gone under earth's lid,

For two gross of broken statues,
For a few thousand battered books.   95

---

9. Roman poet Horace (65–8 B.C.E.), in his *Odes* 3.2.13, said that it is sweet and fitting to die for one's country ("Dulce et decorum est pro patria mori"); Pound says for home, *pro domo*. The passage from Horace is alluded to again in lines 71–72.

Yeux Glauques[1]

Gladstone[2] was still respected,
When John Ruskin produced
"Kings' Treasuries";[3] Swinburne
And Rossetti still abused.[4]

Fœtid Buchanan lifted up his voice　　　　　　　　　　100
When that faun's head of hers
Became a pastime for
Painters and adulterers.

The Burne-Jones cartons
Have preserved her eyes;　　　　　　　　　　　　　105
Still, at the Tate, they teach
Cophetua to rhapsodize;[5]

Thin like brook-water,
With a vacant gaze.
The English Rubaiyat was still-born[6]　　　　　　　110
In those days.

The thin, clear gaze, the same
Still darts out faun-like from the half-ruin'd face,
Questing and passive. . . .
"Ah, poor Jenny's case' . . .[7]　　　　　　　　　　115

Bewildered that a world
Shows no surprise
At her last maquero's[8]
Adulteries.

1. Reference to the "sea-green eyes" (French) of Elizabeth Siddal, the model in paintings by Dante Gabriel Rossetti, who married her two years before her death from an overdose of laudanum in 1862; this section evokes the lost London of the mid–nineteenth-century Pre-Raphaelite Brotherhood, which was formed in protest against the conventional, formulaic art produced by members of London's Royal Academy.
2. William Ewart Gladstone (1809–1898), British prime minister who epitomized Victorian propriety.
3. John Ruskin (1819–1900), great English art historian, who was contemptuous of English materialism and provincialism; "Kings' Treasuries" is a reference to the first lecture in Ruskin's book *Sesame and Lilies* (1865).
4. Algernon Charles Swinburne (1837–1909), an English poet whose early poems such as "Laus Veneris," with its suggestions of sexual passion, were considered daring, if not shocking, but whose later books became much more sedate. Dante Gabriel Rossetti (1828–1882), a poet as well as a painter, was known for the rejection of convention that inspired the formation of the Pre-Raphaelite Brotherhood. Both Swinborne and Rossetti were attacked by Robert Buchanan (1841–1901) in his book "The Fleshly School of Poetry" (1871).
5. French for *cartoons*, or preparatory drawings for paintings, by Sir Edward Burne-Jones (1833–1898), another Pre-Raphaelite painter; Elizabeth Siddal posed for his painting *King Cophetua and the Beggar Maid* (1884), which is owned by the Tate Gallery in London.
6. The Edward FitzGerald translation of *The Rubáiyát of Omar Khayyám* (1858) received little notice until Rossetti promoted it among the Pre-Raphaelites.
7. Allusion to Rossetti's poem, "Jenny," about a prostitute. Pimp, or sexual predator (French).
8. Pimp, or sexual predator (French).

"Siena Mi Fe'; Disfecemi Maremma"[9]

Among the pickled fœtuses and bottled bones,   120
Engaged in perfecting the catalogue,
I found the last scion of the
Senatorial families of Strasbourg, Monsieur Verog.

For two hours he talked of Galliffet;
Of Dowson; of the Rhymers' Club,   125
Told me how Johnson (Lionel) died
By falling from a high stool in a pub . . .[1]

But showed no trace of alcohol
At the autopsy, privately performed—
Tissue preserved—the pure mind   130
Arose toward Newman[2] as the whiskey warmed.

Dowson found harlots cheaper than hotels;
Headlam for uplift; Image impartially imbued
With raptures for Bacchus, Terpsichore and the Church.
So spoke the author of "The Dorian Mood,"[3]   135

M. Verog, out of step with the decade,
Detached from his contemporaries,
Neglected by the young,
Because of these reveries.

Brennbaum[4]

The sky-like limpid eyes,   140
The circular infant's face,
The stiffness from spats to collar
Never relaxing into grace;

The heavy memories of Horeb, Sinai and the forty years,
Showed only when the daylight fell   145

9. "Siena made me; Maremma unmade me" (from Dante's *Purgatorio*, Book V, line 133); borne in Sienna, Pia dé Tolomei is murdered by her husband in Maremma.
1. A fictional character modeled on Victor Plarr (1863–1929), a poet better known as a cataloguer of medical manuscripts and librarian of the Royal College of Surgeons. Galliffet: Gaston Alexandre de Gallifet (1830–1909), a French general in the Franco-Prussian war; Pound also refers to Gallifet in *Canto* XV. Of Dowson; of the Rhymers' Club: Ernest Dowson (1867–1900), a poet and subject of a biography by Plarr; the Rhymers' Club began in 1891 to meet at the Cheshire Cheese, a restaurant in London. William Butler Yeats was a dominant member. Johnson: Lionel Johnson (1867–1902), another poet and Rhymers' Club member; also a convert to Catholicism. Pound got the facts about his death wrong.
2. John Henry Newman (1801–1890), like Johnson, a convert to Catholicism, was made cardinal in 1879.
3. Headlam: The Reverend Steward D. Headlam (1847–1924), friend to several writers in this group; Image: Selwyn Image (1849–1930), editor of the *Hobby Horse*, a literary magazine; Terpsichore: The Muse of Dancing; "The Dorian Mood": Plarr's only collection of poems was entitled *In the Dorian Mood* (1896).
4. Usually thought to be a portrait of the critic and caricaturist Max Beerbohm (1872–1956); Pound was wrong in his assumption that Beerbohm was Jewish.

Level across the face
Of Brennbaum "The Impeccable."[5]

MR. NIXON[6]

In the cream gilded cabin of his steam yacht
Mr. Nixon advised me kindly, to advance with fewer
Dangers of delay. "Consider   150
    "Carefully the reviewer.

"I was as poor as you are;
"When I began I got, of course,
"Advance on royalties, fifty at first," said Mr. Nixon,
"Follow me, and take a column,   155
"Even if you have to work free.

"Butter reviewers. From fifty to three hundred
"I rose in eighteen months;
"The hardest nut I had to crack
"Was Dr. Dundas.   160

"I never mentioned a man but with the view
"Of selling my own works.
"The tip's a good one, as for literature
"It gives no man a sinecure.

"And no one knows, at sight, a masterpiece.   165
"And give up verse, my boy,
"There's nothing in it."

   .   .   .   .   .

Likewise a friend of Blougram's once advised me:
Don't kick against the pricks,[7]
Accept opinion. The "Nineties" tried your game   170
And died, there's nothing in it.

X

Beneath the sagging roof
The stylist[8] has taken shelter,
Unpaid, uncelebrated,
At last from the world's welter   175

Nature receives him;
With a placid and uneducated mistress
He exercises his talents
And the soil meets his distress.

---

5. Beerbohm's nickname was "The Incomparable Max."
6. Possibly Arnold Bennett (1867–1931), a commercially successful writer.
7. "It is hard for thee to kick against the pricks," says Christ to Saul (Acts 9:5).
8. Here, the example of Ford Madox Ford (1873–1939), a poet and novelist greatly admired by Pound, provides a contrast to the opportunistic Mr. Nixon.

The haven from sophistications and contentions   180
Leaks through its thatch;
He offers succulent cooking;
The door has a creaking latch.

XI

"Conservatrix of Milesien"[9]
Habits of mind and feeling,   185
Possibly. But in Ealing[1]
With the most bank-clerkly of Englishmen?

No, "Milésian" is an exaggeration.
No instinct has survived in her
Older than those her grandmother   190
Told her would fit her station.

XII

"Daphne with her thighs in bark
Stretches toward me her leafy hands,"—
Subjectively. In the stuffed-satin drawing-room
I await The Lady Valentine's commands,[2]   195

Knowing my coat has never been
Of precisely the fashion
To stimulate, in her,
A durable passion;

Doubtful, somewhat, of the value   200
Of well-gowned approbation
Of literary effort,
But never of The Lady Valentine's vocation:[3]

Poetry, her border of ideas,
The edge, uncertain but a means of blending   205
With other strata
Where the lower and higher have ending;

A hook to catch the Lady Jane's attention,
A modulation toward the theatre,
Also, in the case of revolution,   210
A possible friend and comforter.

    ·   ·   ·   ·   ·

9. Paraphrased from *Magic Stories, Strategems* (1894), a book by Rémy de Gourmount (1858–1915); *The Milesien Tales of Aristides* (c. 100 B.C.E.) were known for their lewdness.
1. A suburb of London.
2. Lines translated from "Le Château du Souvenir" ("The Castle of Memory") by Théophile Gautier; the allusion is to Daphne, who was transformed into a laurel tree to escape Apollo's embrace.
3. Lady Valentine is said to be modeled on Lady Ottoline Morrell, who hosted a salon for literary and political figures of the day.

Conduct, on the other hand, the soul
"Which the highest cultures have nourished"
To Fleet St. where
Dr. Johnson flourished;[4]   215

Beside this thoroughfare
The sale of half-hose has
Long since superseded the cultivation
Of Pierian roses.[5]

ENVOI (1919)[6]

Go, dumb-born book,   220
Tell her that sang me once that song of Lawes:
Hadst thou but song
As thou hast subjects known,
Then were there cause in thee that should condone
Even my faults that heavy upon me lie,   225
And build her glories their longevity.

Tell her that sheds
Such treasure in the air,
Recking naught else but that her graces give
Life to the moment,   230
I would bid them live
As roses might, in magic amber laid,
Red overwrought with orange and all made
One substance and one colour
Braving time.   235

Tell her that goes
With song upon her lips
But sings not out the song, nor knows
The maker of it, some other mouth,
May be as fair as hers,   240
Might, in new ages, gain her worshippers,
When our two dusts with Waller's shall be laid,
Siftings on siftings in oblivion,
Till change hath broken down
All things save Beauty alone.   245

1920

4. Samuel Johnson (1709–1784)—lexicographer, poet, essayist, and editor—had more success in the
journalistic world of Fleet Street than Lionel Johnson would later have.
5. An allusion to Sappho LXXI; at Pieria, near Mt. Olympus, the muses were worshiped.
6. A pastiche of the song, "Go, Lovely Rose," by Edmund Waller (1606–1687), which was set to music
by the composer Henry Lawes (1596–1662).

Mauberley[7]

"Vacuos exercet in aera morsus."[8]

I

Turned from the "eau-forte
Par Jacquemart"
To the strait head
Of Messalina:[9]

"His true Penelope   250
Was Flaubert,"
And his tool
The engraver's.

Firmness,
Not the full smile,   255
His art, but an art
In profile;

Colourless
Pier Francesca,
Pisanello lacking the skill   260
To forge Achaia.[1]

II

"Qu'est ce qu'ils savent de l'amour, et qu'est ce qu'ils peuvent en comprendre? S'ils ne comprennent pas la poésie, si'ils ne sentent pas la musique, qu'est ce qu'ils peuvent comprendre de cette passion en comparaison avec laquelle la rose est grossière et le parfum des violettes un tonnerre?"

—Caid Ali[2]

For three year, diabolus in the scale,
He drank ambrosia,
All passes, ANANGKE prevails,
Came end, at last, to that Arcadia.   265

---

7. A continuation of the earlier sequence.
8. "He hits the empty air" (Latin), misquoted from Ovid's *Metamorphoses*, 7.786; the allusion returns in lines 295–98.
9. Eau-forte: A process used in etching, here indicating the etching itself; Jacquemart: Jules Jaquemart (1837–1880), whose etching of Théophile Gautier appeared in *Émaux et Camées* (1881), Gautier's most influential book of poems; Messalina: Wife of Roman emperor Claudius, evidently depicted in a portrait.
1. Pier Francesca: Piero della Francesca (c. 1416–1492), Umbrian painter; Pisanello lacking the skill: Vittore Pisano (1397–1455), Veronese painter; Achaia: A region in ancient Greece, but often used (as here) to denote the country as a whole.
2. "What do they know about love, and what could they understand about it? If they don't understand poetry, if they have no feeling for music, what can they understand in comparison to which the rose is gross and the perfume of the violets thunderous?" (French); although Pound credited this to Caid Ali, he was himself the author.

He had moved amid her phantasmagoria,
Amid her galaxies,
NUKTOS' AGALMA[3]

.   .   .   .   .

Drifted . . . drifted precipitate,
Asking time to be rid of . . .   270
Of his bewilderment; to designate
His new found orchid. . . .

To be certain . . . certain . . .
(Amid ærial flowers) . . . time for arrangements—
Drifted on   275
To the final estrangement;

Unable in the supervening blankness
To sift TO AGATHON[4] from the chaff
Until he found his sieve . . .
Ultimately, his seismograph: 280

—Given that is his "fundamental passion,"
This urge to convey the relation
Of eye-lid and cheek-bone
By verbal manifestation;

To present the series   285
Of curious heads in medallion—

He had passed, inconscient, full gaze,
The wide-banded irides
And botticellian sprays implied
In their diastasis;[5]   290

Which anæsthesis, noted a year late,
Ad weighed, revealed his great affect,
(Orchid), mandate
Of Eros,[6] a retrospect.

.   .   .

Mouths biting empty air,   295
The still stone dogs,

3. diabolus in the scale: Reference to the discordant tritone, which was banned from medieval Church music; ANANGKE: "Necessity" (Greek); Arcadia: A region of the Peloponnesos associated with Pan; more generally, an idyllic pastoral landscape. Phantasmagoria: Ruthven quotes Pound from the *Little Review* (March 1918): ". . . certain men move in phantasmagoria; the images of their gods, whole countrysides, stretches of hill land and forest, travel with them; NUKTOS' AGALMA: "Night's jewel (Greek).
4. "The Good" (Greek).
5. Irides: Irises; botticellian sprays: May be an allusion to the painting *The Birth of Venus*, by Sandro Botticelli (1447–1510); diastasis: separation.
6. anaesthesis: A state of insensibility or numbness; Eros: God of Love in Greek mythology, Cupid to the Romans.

Caught in metamorphosis, were
Left him as epilogues.

"THE AGE DEMANDED"

Vide Poem II. page 184

For this agility chance found
Him of all men, unfit   300
As the red-beaked steeds[7] of
The Cytheræan for a chain bit.

The glow of porcelain
Brought no reforming sense
To his perception   305
Of the social inconsequence.

Thus, if her colour
Came against his gaze,
Tempered as if
It were through a perfect glaze   310

He made no immediate application
Of this to relation of the state
To the individual, the month was more temperate
Because this beauty had been.

    The coral isle, the lion-coloured sand   315
    Burst in upon the porcelain revery:
    Impetuous troubling
    Of his imagery.

Mildness, amid the neo-Nietzschean[8] clatter,
His sense of graduations,   320
Quite out of place amid
Resistance to current exacerbations,

Invitation, mere invitation to perceptivity
Gradually led him to the isolation
Which these presents place   325
Under a more tolerant, perhaps, examination.

By constant elimination
The manifest universe
Yielded an armour
Against utter consternation,   330

---

7. The doves that pull the chariot of Aphrodite (Venus to the Romans); Cythera is the island near which Aphrodite is said to have emerged from the sea's foam.
8. Friedrich Nietzsche (1844–1900), German philosopher.

A Minoan[9] undulation,
Seen, we admit, amid ambrosial circumstances
Strengthened him against
The discouraging doctrine of chances,

And his desire for survival,   335
Faint in the most strenuous moods,
Became an Olympian *apathein*[1]
In the presence of selected perceptions.

A pale gold, in the aforesaid pattern,
The unexpected palms   340
Destroying, certainly, the artist's urge,
Left him delighted with the imaginary
Audition of the phantasmal sea-surge,

Incapable of the least utterance or composition,
Emendation, conservation of the "better tradition,"   345
Refinement of medium, elimination of superfluities,
August attraction or concentration.

Nothing, in brief, but maudlin confession,
Irresponse to human aggression,
Amid the precipitation, down-float   350
Of insubstantial manna,
Lifting the faint susurrus[2]
Of his subjective hosannah.

Ultimate affronts to
Human redundancies;   355
Non-esteem of self-styled "his betters"
Leading, as he well knew,
To his final
Exclusion from the world of letters.

IV

    Scattered Moluccas   360
    Not knowing, day to day,
    The first day's end, in the next noon;
    The placid water
    Unbroken by the Simoon;[3]

    Thick foliage   365
    Placid beneath warm suns,
    Tawn fore-shores
    Washed in the cobalt of oblivions:

9. Of Cretan civilization.
1. "Without passion" (Greek).
2. Soft murmurs.
3. Moluccas: Islands in the South Pacific; Simoon: A hot wind.

Or through dawn-mist
The grey and rose   370
Of the juridical
Flamingoes;

A consciousness disjunct,
Being but this overblotted
Series   375
Of intermittences;

Coracle[4] of Pacific voyages,
The unforecasted beach;
Then on an oar
Read this: 380

"I was
And I no more exist;
Here drifted
An hedonist."

MEDALLION[5]

Luini[6] in porcelain!   385
The grand piano
Utters a profane
Protest with her clear soprano.

The sleek head emerges
From the gold-yellow frock   390
As Anadyomene in the opening
Pages of Reinach.[7]

Honey-red, closing the face-oval,
A basket-work of braid which seem as if they were
Spun in King Minos' hall   395
From metal, or intractable amber;

The face-oval beneath the glaze,
Bright in its suave bounding-line, as,
Beneath half-watt rays,
The eyes turn topaz.   400

1920

---

4. Small boat.
5. Implies that this poem is a pendant, or *envoi*, that is, a short stanza of conclusion.
6. Bernardino Luini (c. 1480–1532), a painter of the Italian Renaissance; Pound may have used him as an example of the lack of originality.
7. Anadyomene: Reference to Aphrodite, meaning "born of the foam" (Greek); Reinach: Salomon Reinach (1858–1932), a French scholar of archaeology, philology, and religion.

FROM The Cantos[8]

I[9]

And then went down to the ship,
Set keel to breakers, forth on the godly sea, and
We set up mast and sail on that swart ship,
Bore sheep aboard her, and our bodies also
Heavy with weeping,[1] and winds from sternward   5
Bore us out onward with bellying canvas,
Circe's this craft, the trim-coifed goddess.[2]
Then sat we amidships, wind jamming the tiller,
Thus with stretched sail, we went over sea till day's end.
Sun to his slumber, shadows o'er all the ocean,   10
Came we then to the bounds of deepest water,
To the Kimmerian lands,[3] and peopled cities
Covered with close-webbed mist, unpierced ever
With glitter of sun-rays
Nor with stars stretched, nor looking back from heaven   15
Swartest night stretched over wretched men there.
The ocean flowing backward, came we then to the place
Aforesaid by Circe.
Here did they rites, Perimedes and Eurylochus,[4]
And drawing sword from my hip[5]   20
I dug the ell-square pitkin;
Poured we libations unto each the dead,
First mead and then sweet wine, water mixed with white flour.
Then prayed I many a prayer to the sickly death's-heads;
As set in Ithaca, sterile bulls of the best   25

8. Begun in 1917 (although he would claim to have begun more than a decade earlier), Pound's long "poem including history," was left unfinished at the time of his death, despite his having worked on it and published from it for more than fifty years. Pound borrowed the term *Canto*, Italian for "song," from Dante, who divided each of the three parts of his *Divine Comedy* into thirty-four (or thirty-three) cantos, rather like chapters. Pound completed 109 of his own cantos, leaving fragments of several more. "When I get to the end," he wrote in 1937, "pattern *ought* to be discoverable." One of the most helpful books for students interested in looking for a pattern is *A Guide to the Cantos of Ezra Pound* by William Cookson (New York: Persea, 1985). It might also help to know that in a 1939 letter Pound wrote, "All typographic disposition, placings of words *on* the page, is intended to facilitate reader's intonation, whether he be reading silently to self or aloud to friends."
9. Until line 67 Pound was freely translating from the *Odyssey*, Book XI. This is the *Nekuia*, The Book of the Dead, in which Odysseus descends to Hades, and the source for such events in the epic tradition of Virgil and Dante. However, he was working not from Homer's Greek, but from a Renaissance Latin version he credits to one Andreas Divus Justinopolitanus (see Pound's "Translators of Greek: Early Translators of Homer" in *The Literary Essays of Ezra Pound* [1935]). In much of this Canto Pound uses Anglo-Saxon alliterative verse (see also his version of "The Seafarer"), thus recalling the ancient sources of poetry in English.
1. Odysseus's men are grieving not only for the loss of friends like Elpenor, who, in a drunken state, fell from Circe's roof and broke his neck (see line 42; Odyssey, Book X), but also because the journey to Hades stands between them and home.
2. The sorceress who has kept Odysseus and his men under a spell and who has now directed them to seek Tiresias, the seer, in the land of the dead for guidance on their return to Ithaka.
3. Region near the entrance to Hades; Homer spoke of the Cimmerian people as living in perpetual darkness (Book XI, lines 12–19).
4. Shipmates of Odysseus.
5. Lines 20–28 describe the rites performed to summon the dead.

For sacrifice, heaping the pyre with goods,
A sheep to Tiresias only, black and a bell-sheep.
Dark blood flowed in the fosse,
Souls out of Erebus,[6] cadaverous dead, of brides
Of youths and of the old who had borne much;   30
Souls stained with recent tears, girls tender,
Men many, mauled with bronze lance heads,
Battle spoil, bearing yet dreory[7] arms,
These many crowded about me; with shouting,
Pallor upon me, cried to my men for more beasts;   35
Slaughtered the herds, sheep slain of bronze;
Poured ointment, cried to the gods,
To Pluto the strong, and praised Proserpine;[8]
Unsheathed the narrow sword,
I sat to keep off the impetuous impotent dead,   40
Till I should hear Tiresias.
But first Elpenor came, our friend Elpenor,
Unburied,[9] cast on the wide earth,
Limbs that we left in the house of Circe,
Unwept, unwrapped in sepulchre, since toils urged other.   45
Pitiful spirit. And I cried in hurried speech:
"Elpenor, how art thou come to this dark coast?
"Cam'st thou afoot, outstripping seamen?"
          And he in heavy speech:
"Ill fate and abundant wine. I slept in Circe's ingle.[1]   50
"Going down the long ladder unguarded,
"I fell against the buttress,
"Shattered the nape-nerve, the soul sought Avernus.[2]
"But thou, O King, I bid remember me, unwept, unburied,
"Heap up mine arms, be tomb by sea-bord, and inscribed: 55
"*A man of no fortune, and with a name to come.*
"And set my oar up, that I swung mid fellows."

And Anticlea[3] came, whom I beat off, and then Tiresias Theban,
Holding his golden wand, knew me, and spoke first:
"A second time? why? man of ill star,   60
"Facing the sunless dead and this joyless region?
"Stand from the fosse, leave me my bloody bever
"For soothsay."
          And I stepped back,
And he strong with the blood, said then: "Odysseus   65

6. Pitkin appears to be Pound's word for a small pit; Tiresias is the Theban seer (see Eliot's *The Waste Land*); fosse: "ditch" (Latin). Erebus: The darkness of the Underworld.
7. Bloody.
8. Pluto: The Roman name for Hades, lord of the Underworld; Proserpine: also called Persephone, Hades' wife.
9. Because Odysseus learned of Elpenor's death too late, proper burial rites were not performed.
1. Hearth.
2. A lake near Naples, said to be an entrance to the Underworld.
3. Mother of Odysseus; Pound omits the detail in Homer of Odysseus weeping at the sight of her shade.

"Shalt return through spiteful Neptune,[4] over dark seas,
"Lose all companions." And then Anticlea came.
Lie quiet Divus.[5] I mean, that is Andreas Divus,
In officina Wecheli,[6] 1538, out of Homer.
And he sailed, by Sirens and thence outward and away   70
And unto Circe.
                Venerandam,[7]
In the Cretan's phrase, with the golden crown, Aphrodite,
Cypri munimenta sortita est, mirthful, orichalchi,[8] with golden
Girdles and breast bands, thou with dark eyelids   75
Bearing the golden bough of Argicida.[9] So that:

                                                       1917

XLV[1]

With *Usura*[2]

With usura hath no man a house of good stone
each block cut smooth and well fitting
that design might cover their face,
with usura
hath no man a painted paradise on his church wall   5
harpes et luz[3]
or where virgin receiveth message
and halo projects from incision,
with usura
seeth no man Gonzaga his heirs and his concubines[4]   10
no picture is made to endure nor to live with
but it is made to sell and sell quickly
with usura, sin against nature,
is thy bread ever more of stale rags
is thy bread dry as paper,   15
with no mountain wheat, no strong flour

---

4. Poseidon, god of the sea, who opposes Odysseus, especially since the blinding of the Cyclops; in this passage shipwreck is foretold.
5. Here, Pound addresses Andreas Divus, whose Latin translation formed the basis of this Canto.
6. At the print-shop of Wechtel, where the Divus translation was published.
7. "Worthy of reverence" (Latin).
8. Cypri . . . est: "The castles of Cyprus are her home" (Latin); orichalchi: "Made of copper" (Latin).
9. "The killer of Argus" (Latin); one of the names given to Hermes, guide to the Underworld.
1. *The Fifth Decade of Cantos* (1937) begins with Cantos 42–44, a miniature history of the founding of Pound's ideal bank, the Monte dei Paschi in Sienna in the seventeenth century. This was a bank "built for beneficence, for reconstruction," he wrote, rather than "to prey on people." In Canto 45 Pound makes his most passionate denunciation of usury, the practice of lending money at interest, which he saw as a destructive force in western civilization.
2. *With Usura* can be understood as the "title" of this Canto if we take into account Pound's stated intention that "with" in English derives from Anglo-Saxon and has an "oppositive aroma, as in 'withstand' meaning 'stand against'" (quoted in Cookson, *A Guide to the Cantos of Ezra Pound* [1985], 49).
3. "Harps and lutes" (French) from François Villon's *Le Testament*.
4. Luigi Gonzaga (1267–1360); reference to the painting *Gonzaga, His Heirs and His Concubines*, by Andrea Mantegna (1431–1506), Italian painter and engraver.

with usura the line grows thick[5]
with usura is no clear demarcation
and no man can find site for his dwelling.
Stonecutter is kept from his stone   20
weaver is kept from his loom
WITH USURA
wool comes not to market
sheep bringeth no gain with usura
Usura is a murrain,[6] usura   25
blunteth the needle in the maid's hand
and stoppeth the spinner's cunning. Pietro Lombardo[7]
came not by usura
Duccio came not by usura
nor Pier della Francesca; Zuan Bellin' not by usura   30
nor was 'La Calunnia' painted.
Came not by usura Angelico; came not Ambrogio Praedis,
Came no church of cut stone signed: *Adamo me fecit.*
Not by usura St Trophime
Not by usura Saint Hilaire,   35
Usura rusteth the chisel
It rusteth the craft and the craftsman
It gnaweth the thread in the loom
None learneth to weave gold in her pattern;
Azure hath a canker by usura; cramoisi[8] is unbroidered   40
Emerald findeth no Memling[9]
Usura slayeth the child in the womb
It stayeth the young man's courting
It hath brought palsey to bed, lyeth
between the young bride and her bridegroom   45
                CONTRA NATURAM[1]
They have brought whores for Eleusis[2]
Corpses are set to banquet
at behest of usura.

                                                                    1937

N.B. Usury: A charge for the use of purchasing power, levied without regard to production; often without regard to the possibilities of production. (Hence the failure of the Medici bank.) [*Pound's note.*]

5. Pound believed that the decline in painting corresponded to the rise in the practice of usury.
6. Plague or pestilence.
7. A list of Renaissance artists and works, including several medieval churches, follows Pietro Lombardo: Italian architect and sculptor (1435–1515).
8. Duccio: Agnostino di Duccio, Italian sculptor (1418–1481); Pier della Francesca: Piero della Francesca (1420–1492), Florentine painter; Zuan Bellin': Giovanni Bellini (1430–1516), Venetian painter; La Calunnia: "Calumny," a painting by the Florentine artist Sandro Botticelli (1444–1510); Angelico: Fra Angelico (1387–1455), Florentine painter; Ambrogio Praedis: Milanese painter (1455?–1560); *Adamo me fecit*: (Latin) A version of this phrase, "Adam made me" was carved on a pillar of the church of San Zeno, Verona; St. Trophime: Church in Arles, France; Saint Hilaire: Church in Poitiers, France; cramoisi: "Crimson fabric" (French).
9. Hans Memling (c. 1430–1494), Flemish painter.
1. "Against nature" (Latin), quoted from Aristotle's Politics, where usury is also criticized.
2. Town near Athens noted for its fertility rites.

FROM LXXXI[3]

libretto[4]

Yet
Ere the season died a-cold
Borne upon a zephyr's[5] shoulder
I rose through the aureaete sky
    Lawes and Jenkyns guard thy rest   5
    Dolmetsch ever be thy guest,
Has he tempered the viol's wood
To enforce both the grave and the acute?
Has he curved us the bowl of the lute?
    Lawes and Jenkyns guard thy rest   10
    Dolmetsch ever be thy guest[6]
Hast 'ou fashioned so airy a mood
  To draw up leaf from the root?
Has 'ou found a cloud so light
  As seemed neither mist nor shade?   15

    Then resolve me, tell me aright
    If Waller sang or Dowland played.[7]

   Your eyen two wol sleye me sodenly
   I may the beauté of hem nat susteyne[8]

And for 180 years almost nothing.   20

Ed ascoltando al leggier mormorio[9]
  there came new subtlety of eyes into my tent,
whether of spirit or hypostasis,[1]
  but what the blindfold hides
or at carneval   25
      nor any pair showed anger
  Saw but the eyes and stance between the eyes,
colour, diastasis,[2]
   careless or unaware it had not the
   whole tent's room   30
nor was place for the full Εἰδὼς[3]
interpass, penetrate
   casting but shade beyond the other lights
    sky's clear
    night's sea   35
    green of the mountain pool

---

3. *The Pisan Cantos* (LXXIV–LXXXIV) derive from Pound's incarceration in a U.S. Army internment camp at Pisa; he was held on charges of treason.
4. The text of an opera.
5. A zephyr is a westerly wind.
6. Henry Lawes (1596–1662) and John Jenkins (1592–1678), English composers who wrote for aristocratic or royal patrons; Arnold Dolmetsch (1858–1940), French musician and maker of musical instruments.
7. Edmund Waller (1606–1687), English poet; John Dowland (1563–1626), English composer.
8. Lines from "Merciless Beauty," a poem attributed to Geoffrey Chaucer (c. 1340–1400).
9. "And listening to the light murmur' (Italian).
1. Substance, in this case of the divine.
2. Separation.
3. "Knowing" (Greek).

shone from the unmasked eyes in half-mask's space.
What thou lovest well remains,

the rest is dross
What thou lov'st well shall not be reft from thee   40
What thou lov'st well is thy true heritage
Whose world, or mine or theirs

or is it of none?
First came the seen, then thus the palpable
Elysium,[4] though it were in the halls of hell,   45
What thou lovest well is thy true heritage
What thou lov'st well shall not be reft from thee

The ant's a centaur in his dragon world.
Pull down thy vanity, it is not man
Made courage, or made order, or made grace,   50
     Pull down thy vanity, I say pull down.
Learn of the green world what can be thy place
In scaled invention or true artistry,
Pull down thy vanity,

Paquin pull down!   55
The green casque has outdone your elegance.[5]

"Master thyself, then others shall thee beare"
     Pull down thy vanity
Thou are a beaten dog beneath the hail,
A swollen magpie in a fitful sun,   60
Half black half white
Nor knowst'ou wing from tail
Pull down thy vanity

How mean thy hates
Fostered in falsity,   65
          Pull down thy vanity,
Rathe[6] to destroy, niggard in charity,
Pull down thy vanity,
          I say pull down.

But to have done instead of not doing   70
          this is not vanity
To have, with decency, knocked
That a Blunt[7] should open
          To have gathered from the air a live tradition
or from a fine old eye the unconquered flame   75
This is not vanity.
     Here error is all in the not done,
all in the diffidence that faltered . . .

1948

---

4. The Greek version of Paradise, where the virtuous go when they die.
5. Paquin: a Parisian dress designer; green casque: Green helmet, perhaps a reference to forms of Nature.
6. "Quick" (Middle English).
7. Wilfred Scawen Blunt (1840–1922), an anti-Imperialist English poet; Pound, who thought him "the grandest of old men," organized a feast in his honor in 1914.

◆ H. D. [HILDA DOOLITTLE] ►
(1886–1961)

The sixth child of an artist mother and astronomer father, Hilda Doolittle, who would come to literary fame as H. D., was born in Bethlehem, Pennsylvania. Raised in the strict Moravian tradition of her mother's family, the young Hilda encountered the hymns, rituals, and beliefs, especially the direct apprehension of God's love through revelation, that would help shape the mystical concerns of her later poetry.

The Doolittle family moved to Upper Darby, Pennsylvania, in 1892 after her father was named director of the Flower Observatory at the University of Pennsylvania. Hilda attended private schools and then in 1905 enrolled as a commuter student at Bryn Mawr College, where one of her classmates was Marianne Moore, who became a lifelong friend. The young poet's studies at Bryn Mawr lasted only a year and a half, for she failed several courses due to illness and her preference for the readings recommended to her by Ezra Pound, whom she had met a few years earlier at a Halloween party. In 1908 she and Pound became engaged, but her family opposed the match. When the flamboyant young Pound asked her father for his permission, the very proper professor reportedly replied, "Why, you're nothing but a nomad!" Pound then left for Europe—effectively ending their marriage plans.

Doolittle found inspiration not only in the relationship with Pound, but in a romance she began in 1910 with a woman, Frances Gregg. After a brief time in bohemian Greenwich Village, Doolittle traveled to Europe with Gregg in 1911. She soon settled in London among writers and artists she met through Pound, who, as a self-styled impresario of Modernism, vigorously promoted poets whose work exemplified his innovative literary ideals.

Hilda Doolittle was one of the poets Pound most effectively championed. Three poems that she showed him in September, 1912, struck him as the perfect expression of the spare and direct "presentation" of intense perceptions that he saw as an antidote to Victorian poetry's excesses. Striking out her name on the manuscript, he rechristened her "H. D., *Imagiste*," thereby creating the non de plume she would use for all her mature work. Pound quickly sent the poems to Harriet Monroe, editor of *Poetry* magazine, calling them "*modern* stuff by an American, I say modern, for it is in the laconic speech of the Imagistes. . . . Objective—no slither; direct—no excessive use of adjectives, no metaphors that won't permit examination. It's straight talk, straight as the Greek!" It is hardly an exaggeration to say that both H. D. and Imagism were born at the same moment. Her early work vividly embodied all the objectives of the movement. By the time she published her first collection, *Sea Garden*, in 1916, H. D. was already celebrated—and widely imitated—as the best of the Imagists, a group of poets that included Pound, F. S. Flint, William Carlos Williams, Amy Lowell, and Richard Aldington (whom H. D. married in 1913). Although the movement was short-lived, its stress on concision and concreteness, preference for free verse over rhyme and meter, and its aim "to present an intellectual and emotional 'complex' in an instant of time" became guiding principles of Modernist poetry.

The rich compression of H. D.'s Imagist poems arises in part from her skill in fusing different, even opposing elements, such as the seascape and landscape of "Oread" or the strength and vulnerability of the "Sea Rose" and "Sea Violet." Equally, her terse descriptions invest with feeling the objects she describes yet keep the feeling taut and distanced from the self—an approach that anticipated T. S.

Eliot's concepts of "impersonality" and the "the objective correlative." In her next books, *Hymen* (1921) and *Heliodora* (1924), she honed these techniques in poems that reconsider classical women such as Euridice and Helen of Troy from a female perspective, often in monologues that both give the heroines power to speak for themselves and serve as a mask for the poet.

While embodying Imagist principles, the poems in H. D.'s first three books also announce themes she would explore in her later long poems: the complexity of female experience, the synthesis of oppositions, the reinvigoration of myth, the adoption of personae for the self, and the search for consolidating love in a fragmented world. Having perfected a powerfully lyric Imagist style, H. D.'s artistic interests gradually shifted toward epic themes—a development similar to that of her Modernist contemporaries like Pound, Eliot, and Williams. As Susan Stanford Friedman notes, however, H. D. did not "find the direction that led to her mature art with the immediacy of compatriots like Pound and Williams. While *The Cantos* and *Paterson* began to take shape in the twenties, H. D.'s route . . . was more indirect and included considerable experiments with a variety of genres and art forms as she attempted to find her 'true direction.'"

World War I precipitated personal trauma for the poet, including the stillbirth of a child in 1915 and estrangement from Aldington, the result of his bitter experiences as a soldier and his extramarital affairs. Early in 1919, pregnant again, she learned in quick succession of the deaths of her brother in France and her father from shock. Physically and emotionally exhausted, H. D. succumbed to influenza (the 1918–1919 influenza epidemic took 20 million lives). She and her daughter Perdita survived due to the care of a new love, Winnifred Ellerman, a writer who used the pseudonym Bryher, which eventually became her legal name. The daughter of a shipping magnate, Bryher was wealthy, independent, and deeply committed to the arts. The two women became lifelong companions, traveling together in Greece, Italy, Egypt, and the United States, and living in London, Berlin, Paris, and Switzerland.

In 1926, she began an affair with a filmmaker, Kenneth MacPherson, that evolved into an unorthodox living arrangement that lasted until 1933: Bryher married MacPherson, and the couple adopted H. D.'s daughter. Under MacPherson's direction, H. D. appeared in three films, which she also helped edit: *Wingbeat* (1927), *Foothills* (1928), and a full-length feature, *Borderlands* (1930), which also starred Paul Robeson. H. D.'s fascination with cinema found additional expression in *Close-Up* (1927–1933), a film journal she edited with MacPherson.

During the twenties and thirties, H. D.'s prose experiments included fictionalized autobiography, historical fiction, short stories, and a children's novel. She also wrote a verse drama, *Hippolytus Temporizes* (1927) and additional poetry that appeared in *Collected Poems* (1925) and *Red Roses for Bronze* (1931), and she translated Euripides' *Ion* (1936). In the thirties, her growing interest in psychoanalysis and the occult culminated in sessions with Sigmund Freud, an experience she detailed in *Tribute to Freud* (1956). At Freud's urging, she began to write autobiography, documenting the break-up of her marriage to Aldington in *Bid Me to Live* (published 1960), and her Moravian childhood in *The Gift* (published 1981). Freud helped her break a writing block, understand her bisexuality, and recognize that her psychic visions registered not personal, but universal human symbols.

Armed with new insight, H. D. returned to London in 1938, and her experience of the Blitz prompted *Trilogy: The Walls Do Not Fall* (1944), *Tribute to the Angels* (1945), and *The Flowering of the Rod* (1946). Her epic trilogy aims for regeneration through merging symbols from Greek, Egyptian, Christian, and occult sources. Speaking as a poet-prophet, H. D. maintains the concreteness and rhythmic intensity that she perfected in her Imagist poems, but broadens her scope in her search for a haven of spiritual integration. The quest leads to visions of "a hieratic figure, the veiled Goddess," who appears in various guises as the Virgin, St. Sophia, Psyche, Isis, Astarte, and Mary Magdalene—all symbols for the unifying love that transcends destruction.

In the aftermath of the war, however, the poem's optimism was not borne out in H. D.'s life. Afflicted with anemia and meningitis, she suffered a nervous breakdown in 1946. After recovering in a Swiss sanitarium, she spent the rest of her life in Switzerland and Italy, living alone in hotels but remaining close to Bryher, who accompanied her on several trips to the United States. Just before her death in Zurich in 1961 she published a second epic, *Helen in Egypt*. Following the legend that the Greeks and Trojans fought over a phantom Helen, H. D. describes the real Helen in Egypt during the Trojan War. Conjoining Helen's fragmented memories and dreams with elements of Greek and Egyptian mythology, H. D. dramatizes the classical heroine's quest for wholeness.

In a 1919 essay, "Notes on Thought and Vision," H. D. tells the reader, "My sign-posts are not yours, but if I blaze my own trail, it may help to give you confidence and urge you to get out of the murky, dead, old, thousand-times explored old world, the dead world of overworked emotions and thoughts." Throughout her career, H. D. was a trailblazer, striving to shake herself free of conventions that she believed were outmoded and to reinvigorate lost traditions such as classical mythology. Whether in her early Imagist work—which became a signpost for Modernists who sought to escape from Victorian poetry's "dead world of overworked thoughts and emotions"—or in her later epics—*Trilogy* and *Helen in Egypt,* which reconfigured myths from a female perspective—H. D. helped to define the course of Modernist poetry and demonstrated how women's experience could serve as an archetype of universal, human experience.

Oread[1]

Whirl up, sea—
whirl your pointed pines,
splash your great pines
on our rocks,
hurl your green over us,   5
cover us with your pools of fir.

1915

---

1. A nymph of the mountains.

Garden

I

You are clear
O rose, cut in rock,
hard as the descent of hail.

I could scrape the colour
from the petals   5
like spilt dye from a rock.

If I could break you
I could break a tree.

If I could stir
I could break a tree—   10
I could break you.

II

O wind, rend open the heat,
cut apart the heat,
rend it to tatters.

Fruit cannot drop   15
through this thick air—
fruit cannot fall into heat
that presses up and blunts
the points of pears
and rounds the grapes.   20

Cut the heat—
plough through it,
turning it on either side
of your path.

1916

Pear Tree

Silver dust
lifted from the earth,
higher than my arms reach,
you have mounted,
O silver,   5
higher than my arms reach
you front us with great mass;

no flower ever opened
so staunch a white leaf,
no flower ever parted silver   10
from such rare silver;

O white pear,
your flower-tufts
thick on the branch
bring summer and ripe fruits   15
in their purple hearts.

1916

The Pool

Are you alive?
I touch you.
You quiver like a sea-fish.
I cover you with my net.
What are you—banded one?   5

1916

Sea Rose

Rose, harsh rose,
marred and with stint of petals,
meagre flower, thin,
sparse of leaf,

more precious   5
than a wet rose
single on a stem—
you are caught in the drift.

Stunted, with small leaf,
you are flung on the sand,   10
you are lifted
in the crisp sand
that drives in the wind.

Can the spice-rose
drip such acrid fragrance   15
hardened in a leaf?

1916

Sea Violet

The white violet
is scented on its stalk,
the sea-violet
fragile as agate,
lies fronting all the wind   5
among the torn shells
on the sand-bank.

The greater blue violets
flutter on the hill,

but who would change for these   10
who would change for these
one root of the white sort?

Violet
your grasp is frail
on the edge of the sand-hill,   15
but you catch the light—
frost, a star edges with its fire.

                                                        1916

Storm

You crash over the trees,
you crack the live branch—
the branch is white,
the green crushed,
each leaf is rent like split wood.   5

You burden the trees
with black drops,
you swirl and crash—
you have broken off a weighted leaf
in the wind,   10
it is hurled out,
whirls up and sinks,
a green stone.

                                                        1916

Eurydice[2]

I

So you have swept me back,
I who could have walked with the live souls
above the earth,
I who could have slept among the live flowers
at last;   5

so for your arrogance
and your ruthlessness
I am swept back
where dead lichens drip
dead cinders upon moss of ash;   10

so for your arrogance
I am broken at last,

---

2. Beloved wife of Orpheus, Eurydice was bitten by a serpent and died. Orpheus descended into the Underworld to rescue her by charming King Hades with his music. He was allowed to lead her back to the world of the living under the condition that he not look back until he reached the upper world. Near the end of his return journey he turned around once to see if she was following, and she was lost.

I who had lived unconscious,
who was almost forgot;

if you had let me wait   15
I had grown from listlessness
into peace,
if you had let me rest with the dead,
I had forgot you
and the past.   20

II

Here only flame upon flame
and black among the red sparks,
streaks of black and light
grown colourless;

why did you turn back,   25
that hell should be reinhabited
of myself thus
swept into nothingness?

why did you turn?
why did you glance back?   30
why did you hesitate for that moment?
why did you bend your face
caught with the flame of the upper earth,
above my face?

what was it that crossed my face   35
with the light from yours
and your glance?
what was it you saw in my face?
the light of your own face,
the fire of your own presence?   40

What had my face to offer
but reflex of the earth,
hyacinth colour
caught from the raw fissure in the rock
where the light struck,   45
and the colour of azure crocuses[3]
and the bright surface of gold crocuses
and of the wind-flower,
swift in its veins as lightning
and as white.   50

---

3. In Greek myth, the flower was associated with unrequited sexual love and was used as an ingredient in love potions; azure and purple crocuses were also associated with the Underworld.

III

Saffron[4] from the fringe of the earth,
wild saffron that has bent
over the sharp edge of earth,
all the flowers that cut through the earth,
all, all the flowers are lost;   55

everything is lost,
everything is crossed with black,
black upon black
and worse than black,
this colourless light.   60

IV

Fringe upon fringe
of blue crocuses,
crocuses, walled against blue of themselves,
blue of that upper earth,
blue of the depth upon depth of flowers,   65
lost;

flowers,
if I could have taken once my breath of them,
enough of them,
more than earth,   70
even than of the upper earth,
had passed with me
beneath the earth;

if I could have caught up from the earth,
the whole of the flowers of the earth,   75
if once I could have breathed into myself
the very golden crocuses
and the red,
and the very golden hearts of the first saffron,
the whole of the golden mass,   80
the whole of the great fragrance,
I could have dared the loss.

V

So for your arrogance
and your ruthlessness
I have lost the earth   85
and the flowers of the earth,
and the live souls above the earth,
and you have passed across the light

4. The beautiful youth Crocus, in love with the perpetually coy nymph Smilax, asked the gods to save him from his agony and was turned into a saffron plant; in Ovid's version of the story, he was changed into the crocus flower (see *Metamorphosis*, Book 4).

and reached
ruthless;   90
you who have your own light,
who are to yourself a presence,
who need no presence;

yet for all your arrogance
and your glance,   95
I tell you this:

such loss is no loss,
such terror, such coils and strands and pitfalls
of blackness,
such terror   100
is no loss;

hell is no worse than your earth
above the earth,
hell is no worse,
no, nor your flowers   105
nor your veins of light
nor your presence,
a loss;

my hell is no worse than yours
though you pass among the flowers and speak   110
with the spirits above earth.

                    VI

Against the black
I have more fervour
than you in all the splendour of that place,
against the blackness   115
and the stark grey
I have more light;

and the flowers,
if I should tell you,
you would turn from your own fit paths   120
toward hell,
turn again and glance back

and I would sink into a place
even more terrible than this.

                    VII

At least I have the flowers of myself,   125
and my thoughts, no god
can take that;
I have the fervour of myself for a presence
and my own spirit for light;

and my spirit with its loss   130
knows this;
though small against the black,
small against the formless rocks,
hell must break before I am lost;

before I am lost,   135
hell must open like a red rose
for the dead to pass.

                                                                        1917

At Baia[5]

I should have thought
in a dream you would have brought
some lovely, perilous thing,
orchids piled in a great sheath,
as who would say (in a dream)   5
I send you this,
who left the blue veins
of your throat unkissed.

Why was it that your hands
(that never took mine)   10
your hands that I could see
drift over the orchid heads
so carefully,
your hands, so fragile, sure to lift
so gently, the fragile flower stuff—   15
ah, ah, how was it

You never sent (in a dream)
the very form, the very scent,
not heavy, not sensuous,
but perilous—perilous—   20
of orchids, piled in a great sheath,
and folded underneath on a bright scroll
some word:

Flower sent to flower;
for white hands, the lesser white,   25
less lovely of flower leaf,

or

Lover to lover, no kiss,
no touch, but forever and ever this.

                                                                        1921

5. A place near Cumae on the Bay of Naples famous since classical times for its warm mineral springs.

Helen[6]

All Greece hates
the still eyes in the white face,
the lustre as of olives
where she stands,
and the white hands.   5

All Greece reviles
the wan face when she smiles,
hating it deeper still
when it grows wan and white,
remembering past enchantments   10
and past ills.

Greece sees unmoved,
God's daughter, born of love,
the beauty of cool feet
and slenderest knees,   15
could love indeed the maid,
only if she were laid,
white ash amid funeral cypresses.

                                                          1924

FROM The Walls Do Not Fall

To Bryher[7]

for Karnak 1923[8]
from London 1942[9]

[1]

An incident here and there,
and rails gone (for guns)
from your (and my) old town square:

mist and mist-grey, no colour,
still the Luxor bee, chick and hare[1]   5
pursue unalterable purpose

---

6. In Greek mythology, Helen, most beautiful of all women, was the daughter of a mortal, Leda, by the god Zeus. Wife of Menelaus, king of the Greek city-state of Sparta, Helen was carried off by Paris, prince of Troy. Her kidnapping set off the long and devastating Trojan War: Menelaus and his brother Agamemnon raised an army, besieged Troy for ten years, and eventually recaptured her.
7. Bryher was the lifelong friend and sometime lover of H. D.; born Winnifred Ellerman, daugher of a British shipping magnate, she later adopted "Bryher," her pen name, as her legal surname. See pages 204–205
8. Karnak is a temple complex in Egypt, visited by H. D. and Bryher in February 1923.
9. The poem begins in bombed-out London, which H. D. fuses with the ruined Karnak temple.
1. The bee, chick, and hare are images on the Karnak temple.

in green, rose-red, lapis;
they continue to prophesy
from the stone papyrus:[2]

there, as here, ruin opens   10
the tomb, the temple; enter,
there as here, there are no doors:

the shrine lies open to the sky,
the rain falls, here, there
sand drifts; eternity endures: 15

ruin everywhere, yet as the fallen roof
leaves the sealed room
open to the air,

so, through our desolation,
thoughts stir, inspiration stalks us   20
through gloom:

unaware, Spirit announces the Presence;
shivering overtakes us,
as of old, Samuel:[3]

trembling at a known street-corner,   25
we know not nor are known;
the Pythian[4] pronounces—we pass on

to another cellar, to another sliced wall
where poor utensils show
like rare objects in a museum;   30

Pompeii has nothing to teach us,
we know crack of volcanic fissure,
slow flow of terrible lava,

pressure on heart, lungs, the brain
about to burst its brittle case   35
(what the skull can endure!):

over us, Apocryphal fire,
under us, the earth sway, dip of a floor,
slope of a pavement

where men roll, drunk   40
with a new bewilderment,
sorcery, bedevilment:

the bone-frame was made for
no such shock knit within terror,
yet the skeleton stood up to it: 45

2. A reference to the sandstone columns shaped like a papyrus scroll.
3. Old Testament prophet.
4. "Pythian" refers to the Oracle at Delphi in Greece.

the flesh? it was melted away,
the heart burnt out, dead ember,
tendons, muscles shattered, outer husk dismembered,

yet the frame held:
we passed the flame: we wonder   50
what saved us? what for?

[2]

Evil was active in the land,
Good was impoverished and sad;

Ill promised adventure,
Good was smug and fat;   55

Dev-ill was after us,
tricked up like Jehovah;

Good was the tasteless pod,
stripped from the manna-beans, pulse, lentils:

they were angry when we were so hungry   60
for the nourishment, God;

they snatched off our amulets,
charms are not, they said, grace;

but gods always face two-ways,
so let us search the old highways   65

for the true-rune, the right-spell,
recover old values;

nor listen if they shout out,
your beauty, Isis, Aset or Astarte,[5]

is a harlot; you are retrogressive,   70
zealot, hankering after old flesh-pots;

your heart, moreover,
is a dead canker,

they continue, and
your rhythm is the devil's hymn,   75

your stylus is dipped in corrosive sublimate,[6]
how can you scratch out

indelible ink of the palimpsest
of past misadventure?

1944

---

5. Isis: principle fertility goddess of ancient Egypt. Asest: another name for Isis. Astarte: Greek name for Ashtaroth, the supreme goddess of the Phoenicians.
6. Mercuric chloride.

FROM The Flowering of the Rod[7]

[6]

So I would rather drown, remembering—
than bask on tropic atolls

in the coral-seas; I would rather drown,
remembering—than rest on pine or fir-branch

where great stars pour down   5
their generating strength, Arcturus[8]

or the sapphires of the Northern Crown;[9]
I would rather beat in the wind, crying to these others:

yours is the more foolish circling,
yours is the senseless wheeling   10

round and round—yours has no reason—
I am seeking heaven;

yours has no vision,
I see what is beneath me, what is above me,

what men say is-not—I remember,   15
I remember, I remember—you have forgot:

you think, even before it is half-over,
that your cycle is at an end,

but you repeat your foolish circling—again, again, again;
again, the steel sharpened on the stone;   20

again, the pyramid of skulls;
I gave pity to the dead,

O blasphemy, pity is a stone for bread,
only love is holy and love's ecstasy

that turns and turns and turns about one centre,   25
reckless, regardless, blind to reality,

that knows the Islands of the Blest[1] are there,
for *many waters can not quench love's fire*.

1946

---

7. In Numbers 17, God causes the rod of Aaron to blossom and bear fruit. A sign of election and fertility.
8. Arcturus, "the archer," is the brightest star in the northern constellation of Boötes.
9. The constellation "Corona Borealis," in Greek mythology a crown given to Ariadne by the gods after her lover, Thesius, deserted her.
1. The greatest of paradises in ancient Greek mythology.

ROBINSON JEFFERS
(1887–1962)

John Robinson Jeffers, the great poet of the American West Coast, was born in the suburbs of Pittsburgh, Pennsylvania. His father, William Hamilton Jeffers, was a professor of Old Testament biblical theology and a Presbyterian minister. A strict disciplinarian and serious intellectual, the elder Jeffers was a middle-aged widower when he met and courted Annie Tuttle, twenty-two years his junior. Robinson was the first of their two sons. His father determined that his older son should be properly educated and gave him rigorous private lessons in Greek, Latin, and religion. In 1898 the family journeyed overseas where the young Jeffers was enrolled first in a German school in Leipzig, then the following year in a French school in Switzerland. By the time he was twelve, Jeffers was fluent in French, German, Greek, Latin, and English, but awkward among other children. Not surprisingly, the boy developed complex feelings toward his deeply loving but authoritarian father, whose image haunts the many tragic patriarchs who figure in Jeffers's later narrative poems.

Jeffers entered the University of Pittsburgh at fifteen and was awarded sophomore standing. When his father retired the next year and the family moved to Los Angeles, Jeffers transferred to Occidental College, from which he graduated in 1905 at seventeen. Entering graduate school at the University of Southern California, the precocious teenager eventually did graduate work at several universities in literature, medicine, and forestry, but gradually realized that poetry was his calling. At USC, Jeffers met Una Call Kuster, a beautiful woman who was not only three years older than he, but married to a wealthy local attorney. Robinson and Una fell irrevocably in love. After seven years of guilt-ridden romance with many renunciations, separations, reconciliations, and eventually a public scandal (reported in the *Los Angeles Times*), Una obtained a divorce on August 1, 1913. The next day she and Jeffers married.

By now Jeffers had dedicated himself fully to poetry. His first collection, *Flagons and Apples,* had appeared in 1912, but the restless young writer had already improved beyond this early volume of rhymed love lyrics. He and Una traveled north on a horse-drawn mail coach to the wild Big Sur region of coastal California where the road ended. They rented a small cabin in the village of Carmel, which they recognized as their "inevitable place." Jeffers later remembered, "For the first time in my life I could see people living—amid magnificent unspoiled scenery—as they did in the Idyls or the Sagas or in Homer's Ithaca. . . . Here was a contemporary life that was also permanent life."

The twenty-seven-year-old poet knew that he had not yet written anything of enduring value. The death of both his father and his own newborn daughter in 1914 heightened his sense of mortality. After issuing a second collection, *Californians* (1916), Jeffers published nothing for eight years. He divided his time between writing and building a stone house for his family, which now included twin sons, on a promontory overlooking the Pacific. He carefully reconsidered his aims as a poet and underwent a slow but radical transformation. He rejected rhyme and traditional meter, which inhibited him from telling a story flexibly in verse. He also rejected the obscurity of Modernist poetry. "It became clear to me," he wrote, "that poetry—if it were to survive at all—must reclaim some of the power and reality that it has so hastily surrendered to prose." He determined to write a timeless and truthful poetry purged of ephemeral things.

In 1924 Jeffers published *Tamar and Other Poems* with a small vanity press in New York. This volume pronounced Jeffers mature in style, form, subject, and theme. The book even took the characteristic shape of most of his subsequent volumes—a long narrative poem followed by a group of shorter lyric and meditative poems. *Tamar* attracted no initial notice, but a year later it was suddenly taken up by several influential critics. Jeffers produced an expanded trade edition containing what would be his most famous narrative poem, "Roan Stallion." Both public and critical opinions were extraordinary. *Roan Stallion, Tamar and Other Poems* (1925) went into multiple reprintings. Praising his narrative energy, stylistic originality, and thematic profundity, critics compared him to Sophocles and Shakespeare.

Jeffers ignored his sudden celebrity and focused on his work. Over the next ten years he wrote the most remarkable, ambitious, and odd series of narrative poems in American literature. Published in eight major collections—*The Women at Point Sur* (1927), *Cawdor* (1928), *Dear Judas* (1929), *Descent to the Dead* (1931), *Thurso's Landing* (1932), *Give Your Hearts to the Hawks* (1933), *Solstice* (1935), and *Such Counsels You Gave to Me* (1937)—these books appeared at the rate of almost one per year and add up to almost one thousand pages of verse in all. Nearly every volume centers on a long narrative, usually set in or around Big Sur. Violent, sexual, philosophical, and subversive, these verse novels are difficult to describe. Their tragic stories of family rivalry and primal emotion usually move with determined pace to a bloody finale. In sheer narrative energy and visual scope they resemble movies—not real ones but imaginary cinema where high and low art collide. The poems reveal Jeffers's obsessions, as the suffocating burden of the past (often in the form of religious dogmatism, patriotic hypocrisy, or social convention) bears down to destroy human freedom. Alternately magnificent and hyperbolic, powerful and excessive, dramatic and overblown, they are unlike anything else in Modernist American poetry.

Almost immediately Jeffers's long narrative poems divided audiences. His explicit sexuality, violent plots, and overt anti-Christianity alienated conservative readers. Leftists were dismayed by his distrust of all political programs for human improvement. Meanwhile, the New Critics perceived Jeffers's commitment to poetry of direct statement, expansive treatment, and linear narrative as a rejection of the compressed, indirect, and lyric High Modernist mode they had all championed. He rarely found a place in academic anthologies, and his critical reception increasingly tended to be hostile.

The controversy over Jeffers's narratives unfortunately overshadowed his shorter works tucked in the back pages of each new book. These lyric meditations generally written in long rhythmic free verse lines marked a new kind of nature poem that tried to describe the physical world not from a human perspective but on its own terms. Humanity existed, he insisted, as an integral part of nature, not as its master. "Not man apart," was his phrase, which became a famous rallying cry among environmentalists and conservationists, who consider him a seminal figure in the movement to protect natural habitat, wilderness, and coastal land. Jeffers's nature poetry is emotionally direct, magnificently musical, and philosophically profound. His language is strong, concise, and timeless. His ideas are boldly expressed in memorable images. The poems unfold as clearly as prose without the indirection common in the work of overtly Modernist poets like Pound, Eliot, and Moore, who were his contemporaries.

By World War II Jeffers's critical reputation had collapsed and would not rise again until after his death. The Depression and the war had made his cosmic fatalism and distrust of all political systems less palatable to intellectuals caught up in international events. To the disgust of many Americans, he opposed America's entry into World War II, warning that the conflict would turn the United States into an imperial power. Jeffers still commanded a large group of serious readers, and his books sold very well, but the literary establishment dominated by New Critics on the right and Marxists on the left had rejected him.

The poet's complete isolation from public literary life aggravated the situation. Hating big cities, Jeffers hardly stirred from Carmel. He would not teach or lecture. He scarcely answered his mail. Remote from the centers of literary power in London and New York, he seemed indifferent to his slowly declining reputation. In 1945, however, the noted actress, Judith Anderson, asked the poet to translate and adapt Euripides' classical tragedy for the modern stage. When Jeffers's *Medea* opened on Broadway in 1947, it stunned audiences and critics with its power and intensity. *New York Times* critic Brook Atkinson called it "a landmark in the theater." *Medea* played to sold-out houses, a national touring company was soon formed, and productions were staged across Europe. As its frequent revivals have demonstrated, it is one of the finest adaptations of classical drama in English.

Medea's success relieved Jeffers's financial worries, but the happiest days of his life were now behind him. After Una's slow death from cancer in 1950, Jeffers sank into a prolonged depression aggravated by heavy drinking. His eyesight failed. He continued writing but with less energy and little savor. Jeffers published only one book during the last fourteen years of his life, *Hungerfield and Other Poems* (1954). The title poem is a violent and nightmarish narrative that ends unexpectedly with an authorial interruption—Jeffers's heartbreaking invocation to his dead wife. A few days after his seventy-fifth birthday he died in his sleep at Tor House, the stone house, complete with a tower, that he had built for himself and Una and in which he had written all of his major poems.

As Scottish poet George MacBeth observed, Jeffers "is one of the few American poets of the twentieth century who can be approached in terms of his ideas rather than technique." His poetic technique was both strong and original, but once he had developed his style in the mid-1920s, he never significantly altered it. Unlike his Modernist contemporaries Wallace Stevens, Marianne Moore, and T. S. Eliot, Jeffers was not interested in poetry as an exploration of language's ability to describe its own processes. "Language itself," as Robert Hass commented, "is simply not one of Jeffers's subjects."

Jeffers's philosophy has frequently been called pessimistic, but that term seems vague and misleading, since the poet shares almost nothing in common with major philosophical pessimists like Arthur Schopenhauer, who believed the sensory world was illusory and human existence in bondage to the evils of irrational desire. Jeffers, by contrast, asserts the supreme—and joyfully beautiful—reality of the physical world. Trained in the sciences, Jeffers took a coldly rational view of humanity's small place in the cosmos. He called his new philosophical stance "Inhumanism," a term that has been much misunderstood. It does not endorse cruelty or inhumanity in the common sense of the word. Jeffers's "Inhumanism" is a simple but radical realignment of moral values, which he described as "a shifting of emphasis and significance from man to not-man." Humanity was not, he felt, the measure of all things. It was merely one species—albeit the triumphantly dominant one—but it neither understood its place nor its responsibility to the world. Overpopulation, urbanization, pollution, and industrialization would have dire consequences on the planet, Jeffers warned in his prophetic poems.

What saves Jeffers's poetry from unrelieved bitterness and nihilism is its joyful awe and, indeed, religious devotion to the natural world. Living on the edge of the Pacific, he drew wisdom, strength, and perspective from observing the forces of nature around him. In "Rock and Hawk" he offers the image of a falcon perched on a tall coastal rock as a symbol of the proper human values: "bright power, dark peace; / Fierce consciousness joined with final / Disinterestedness, / Life with calm death." That unusual combination of sensual delight and stoical resolve underlies much of Jeffers's best work. Magnificent, troubling, idiosyncratic, and uneven, Jeffers remains the great prophetic voice of American Modernism.

To the Stone-Cutters

Stone-cutters fighting time with marble, you foredefeated
Challengers of oblivion
Eat cynical earnings, knowing rock splits, records fall down,
The square-limbed Roman letters
Scale in the thaws, wear in the rain. The poet as well   5
Builds his monument mockingly;
For man will be blotted out, the blithe earth die, the brave sun
Die blind and blacken to the heart:
Yet stones have stood for a thousand years, and pained thoughts found
The honey of peace in old poems.   10

                                                                      1924

Boats in a Fog

Sports and gallantries, the stage, the arts, the antics of dancers,
The exuberant voices of music,
Have charm for children but lack nobility; it is bitter earnestness
That makes beauty; the mind
Knows, grown adult.

                    A sudden fog-drift muffled the ocean,   5
A throbbing of engines moved in it,
At length, a stone's throw out, between the rocks and the vapor,
One by one moved shadows
Out of the mystery, shadows, fishing-boats, trailing each other
Following the cliff for guidance,   10
Holding a difficult path between the peril of the sea-fog
And the foam on the shore granite.
One by one, trailing their leader, six crept by me,
Out of the vapor and into it,
The throb of their engines subdued by the fog, patient and cautious,   15
Coasting all round the peninsula
Back to the buoys in Monterey harbor. A flight of pelicans

Is nothing lovelier to look at;
The flight of the planets is nothing nobler; all the arts lose virtue
Against the essential reality   20
Of creatures going about their business among the equally
Earnest elements of nature.

                                                        1925

Shine, Perishing Republic

While this America settles in the mould of its vulgarity, heavily thickening to
    empire, And protest, only a bubble in the molten mass, pops and sighs out,
    and the mass hardens,

I sadly smiling remember that the flower fades to make fruit, the fruit rots to
    make earth.   5
Out of the mother; and through the spring exultances, ripeness and decadence;
    and home to the mother.

You making haste haste on decay: not blameworthy; life is good, be it stubbornly
    long or suddenly
A mortal splendor: meteors are not needed less than mountains: shine,   10
    perishing republic.

But for my children, I would have them keep their distance from the thickening
    center; corruption
Never has been compulsory, when the cities lie at the monster's feet there are left
    the mountains.

And boys, be in nothing so moderate as in love of man, a clever servant,
    insufferable master.
There is the trap that catches noblest spirits, that caught—they say—God, when
    he walked on earth.

                                                        1925

Fawn's Foster-Mother[1]

The old woman sits on a bench before the door and quarrels
With her meagre pale demoralized daughter.
Once when I passed I found her alone, laughing in the sun
And saying that when she was first married
She lived in the old farmhouse up Garapatas Canyon.[2]   5
(It is empty now, the roof has fallen
But the log walls hang on the stone foundation; the redwoods
Have all been cut down, the oaks are standing;
The place is now more solitary than ever before.)
"When I was nursing my second baby   10
My husband found a day-old fawn hid in a fern-brake
And brought it; I put its mouth to the breast

1. This poem is based upon a true story.
2. Located near Carmel, California.

Rather than let it starve, I had milk enough for three babies.
Hey how it sucked, the little nuzzler,
Digging its little hoofs like quills into my stomach.   15
I had more joy from that than from the others."
Her face is deformed with age, furrowed like a bad road
With market-wagons, mean cares and decay.
She is thrown up to the surface of things, a cell of dry skin
Soon to be shed from the earth's old eye-brows,   20
I see that once in her spring she lived in the streaming arteries,
The stir of the world, the music of the mountain.

                                                            1928

Hurt Hawks

I

The broken pillar of the wing jags from the clotted shoulder,
The wing trails like a banner in defeat,
No more to use the sky forever but live with famine
And pain a few days: cat nor coyote
Will shorten the week of waiting for death, there is game without talons.   5
He stands under the oak-bush and waits
The lame feet of salvation; at night he remembers freedom
And flies in a dream, the dawns ruin it.
He is strong and pain is worse to the strong, incapacity is worse.
The curs of the day come and torment him   10
At distance, no one but death the redeemer will humble that head,
The intrepid readiness, the terrible eyes.
The wild God of the world is sometimes merciful to those
That ask mercy, not often to the arrogant.
You do not know him, you communal people, or you have forgotten him;   15
Intemperate and savage, the hawk remembers him;
Beautiful and wild, the hawks, and men that are dying, remember him.

II

I'd sooner, except the penalties, kill a man than a hawk; but the great redtail
Had nothing left but unable misery
From the bones too shattered for mending, the wing that trailed under his talons
        when he moved.   20
We had fed him six weeks, I gave him freedom,
He wandered over the foreland hill and returned in the evening, asking for death,
Not like a beggar, still eyed with the old
Implacable arrogance. I gave him the lead gift in the twilight. What fell was
        relaxed.
Owl-downy, soft feminine feathers; but what   25
Soared: the fierce rush: the night-herons by the flooded river cried fear at its rising
Before it was quite unsheathed from reality.

                                                            1928

Hands

Inside a cave in a narrow canyon near Tassajara[3]
The vault of rock is painted with hands,
A multitude of hands in the twilight, a cloud of men's palms, no more,
No other picture. There's no one to say
Whether the brown shy quiet people who are dead intended   5
Religion or magic, or made their tracings
In the idleness of art; but over the division of years these careful
Signs-manual are now like a sealed message
Saying: "Look: we also were human; we had hands, not paws. All hail
You people with the cleverer hands, our supplanters   10
In the beautiful country; enjoy her a season, her beauty, and come down
And be supplanted; for you also are human."

                                                                        1929

Shane O'Neill's Cairn[4]

to U. J.

When you and I on the Palos Verdes[5] cliff
Found life more desperate than dear,
And when we hawked at it on the lake by Seattle,
In the west of the world, where hardly
Anything has died yet: we'd not have been sorry, Una,   5
But surprised, to foresee this gray
Coast in our days, the gray waters of the Moyle[6]
Below us, and under our feet
The heavy black stones of the cairn of the lord of Ulster.
A man of blood who died bloodily   10
Four centuries ago: but death's nothing, and life,
From a high death-mark on a headland
Of this dim island of burials, is nothing either.
How beautiful are both these nothings.

                                                                        1931

3. Site of hot springs in the Santa Lucia Mountains of Big Sur (in central California south of Carmel, Jeffers's home). The cave Jeffers refers to is several miles from the springs.
4. In the summer of 1929, Jeffers and his wife, Una (to whom this poem is dedicated), stayed at Dromere Cottage, Knocknacarry, County Antrim, in Northern Ireland. To one friend he wrote, "Antrim is the only county in Ulster that wasn't planted with Scotch and English Protestants, therefore it is as wild and almost as shiftless as the [American] west." He was particularly interested in Shane O'Neill, the Irish chieftain of Tyrone, who was murdered in 1567 by his rivals, the MacDonnells.
5. Peninsula south of Los Angeles.
6. River in Northern Ireland.

New Mexican Mountain

I watch the Indians dancing to help the young corn at Taos pueblo.[7] The old men squat in a ring
And make the song, the young women with fat bare arms, and a few shame-faced young men, shuffle the dance.

The lean-muscled young men are naked to the narrow loins, their breasts and backs daubed with white clay,
Two eagle-feathers plume the black heads. They dance with reluctance, they are growing civilized; the old men persuade them.

Only the drum is confident, it thinks the world has not changed; the beating heart, the simplest of rhythms,   5
It thinks the world has not changed at all; it is only a dreamer, a brainless heart, the drum has no eyes.

These tourists have eyes, the hundred watching the dance, white Americans, hungrily too, with reverence, not laughter;
Pilgrims from civilization, anxiously seeking beauty, religion, poetry; pilgrims from the vacuum.

People from cities, anxious to be human again. Poor show how they suck you empty! The Indians are emptied,
And certainly there was never religion enough, nor beauty nor poetry here . . . to fill Americans.   10

Only the drum is confident, it thinks the world has not changed. Apparently only myself and the strong
Tribal drum, and the rock-head of Taos mountain, remember that civilization is a transient sickness.

1932

November Surf

Some lucky day each November great waves awake and are drawn
Like smoking mountains bright from the west
And come and cover the cliff with white violent cleanness: then suddenly
The old granite forgets half a year's filth:
The orange-peel, egg-shells, papers, pieces of clothing, the clots   5
Of dung in corners of the rock, and used
Sheaths that make light love safe in the evenings: all the droppings of the summer
Idlers washed off in a winter ecstasy:
I think this cumbered continent envies its cliff then. . . . But all seasons
The earth, in her childlike prophetic sleep,   10
Keeps dreaming of the bath of a storm that prepares up the long coast
Of the future to scour more than her sea-lines:

---

7. The Pueblo Indians of Taos, New Mexico, built their remarkable adobe dwellings—flat-roofed, multistoried, apartmentlike homes—centuries ago; Taos pueblo is the oldest continuously inhabited pueblo in the United States. When Jeffers visited the site it was possible to walk through it.

The cities gone down, the people fewer and the hawks more numerous,
The rivers mouth to source pure; when the two-footed
Mammal, being someways one of the nobler animals, regains   15
The dignity of room, the value of rareness.

1932

Ave Caesar[8]

No bitterness: our ancestors did it.
They were only ignorant and hopeful, they wanted freedom but wealth too.
Their children will learn to hope for a Caesar.
Or rather—for we are not aquiline Romans but soft mixed colonists—
Some kindly Sicilian tyrant who'll keep   5
Poverty and Carthage off until the Romans arrive.[9]
We are easy to manage, a gregarious people,
Full of sentiment, clever at mechanics, and we love our luxuries.

1935

Love the Wild Swan

"I hate my verses, every line, every word.
Oh pale and brittle pencils ever to try
One grass-blade's curve, or the throat of one bird
That clings to twig, ruffled against white sky,
Oh cracked and twilight mirrors ever to catch   5
One color, one glinting flash, of the splendor of things.
Unlucky hunter, Oh bullets of wax,
The lion beauty, the wild-swan wings, the storm of the wings."
—This wild swan of a world is no hunter's game.
Better bullets than yours would miss the white breast,   10
Better mirrors than yours would crack in the flame.
Does it matter whether you hate your . . . self? At least
Love your eyes that can see, you mind that can
Hear the music, the thunder of the wings. Love the wild swan.

1935

Rock and Hawk

Here is a symbol in which
Many high tragic thoughts
Watch their own eyes.

This gray rock, standing tall
On the headland, where the sea-wind   5
Lets no tree grow,

---

8. "Hail, Caesar!"
9. After the first Punic War (264–241 B.C.E.) Rome annexed Sicily and quelled its local tyrants.

Earthquake-proved, and signatured
By ages of storms: on its peak
A falcon has perched.

I think, here is your emblem   10
To hang in the future sky;
Not the cross, not the hive,

But this; bright power, dark peace;
Fierce consciousness joined with final
Disinterestedness;   15

Life with calm death; the falcon's
Realist eyes and act
Married to the massive

Mysticism of stone,
Which failure cannot cast down   20
Nor success make proud.

                                                    1935

Carmel Point

The extraordinary patience of things!
This beautiful place defaced with a crop of suburban houses—
How beautiful when we first beheld it,
Unbroken field of poppy and lupin walled with clean cliffs;
No intrusion but two or three horses pasturing,   5
Or a few milch[1] cows rubbing their flanks on the outcrop rock-heads—
Now the spoiler has come: does it care?
Not faintly. It has all time. It knows the people are a tide
That swells and in time will ebb, and all
Their works dissolve. Meanwhile the image of the pristine beauty   10
Lives in the very grain of the granite,
Safe as the endless ocean that climbs our cliff.—As for us:
We must uncenter our minds from ourselves;
We must unhumanize our views a little, and become confident
As the rock and ocean that we were made from.

                                                                15
                                                    1954

◦►◄ MARIANNE MOORE ►◄◦
(1887–1972)

Marianne Craig Moore was born in the Kirkwood, Missouri, home of her grandfather, John Riddle Warner, a Presbyterian minister, where her mother, Mary Warner
Moore, had retreated after her husband was institutionalized for a nervous break-

---

1. Milkable.

down. Marianne Moore and her older brother, Warner, never knew their father. After Moore's father was released from the sanitarium, her mother never returned to him, preferring to raise the children on her own, despite the economic and social trials of such a choice. When Moore was seven, her grandfather died, and the family moved to a Pittsburgh suburb to reside with an uncle. Two years later they resettled in Carlisle, Pennsylvania, where Mrs. Moore taught English at the Metzger Institute, a preparatory school for girls that her daughter attended. These early hardships created a tight bond between the Moores that they solidified through their Presbyterian faith, an ethos of strict privacy, and a determination to bear difficulty with fortitude and equanimity. The family's fierce insularity and religious devotion provided Moore with the emotional and philosophical support that buttressed her career and motivated her ideas about art. Moore is a consummate Modernist, although her moral bent—such as her attacks on pretentious behavior and egotism, her advocacy of precision, endurance, and humility, and her insistence on hope in the face of despair—chafes against definitions of Modernism that consider experimental work incompatible with Christianity.

In 1905, Moore matriculated at Bryn Mawr College, where, denied admission to the English major, she majored in Law, History, and Politics and minored in Biology. But Moore was undissuaded from pursuing her writing. She contributed poems to the college literary magazine, *Tipyn O'Bob*, and served on its editorial board. She also took a class in "Imitative Prose," in which students were required to model their own essays on the work of seventeenth-century prose stylists such as Thomas Browne and Francis Bacon. "I was really fond of all those sermons and the antique sentence structure," she later said. Her minor in Biology also influenced her poetry. She later remarked that the habits of careful observation she had cultivated in her science courses helped foster the attentiveness to detail that characterizes her writing: "Precision, economy of statement, logic employed to ends that are disinterested, drawing and identifying, liberate—at least have some bearing on—the imagination."

After graduation in 1909 she returned to Carlisle, where she completed the business course at Carlisle Commercial College in 1910, taught stenography and typewriting at the Carlisle Indian School, and worked for women's suffrage. Meanwhile, she began to place poems in magazines such as the *Egoist, Poetry,* and *Others.* In 1916 she and her mother moved to Chatham, New Jersey. Moore made frequent trips into New York, solidifying her connections to avant-garde writers and artists. She also established friendships through correspondence, exchanging letters with H. D., whom she had known briefly at Bryn Mawr, and William Carlos Williams. In 1918 mother and daughter moved to New York, where Marianne worked half days at the Hudson Park Branch of the New York Public Library. Mrs. Moore staunchly supported her daughter's literary career, and in drafting her poems Moore found her mother's incisive criticism indispensable.

Moore's composition process was eclectic, for she often drew from the notebooks in which she meticulously recorded quotations from her diverse readings, letters she had received, lectures and sermons she had heard, and even conversations. In the poetry, Moore integrates her own words with material from the notebooks. From a paragraph-long quotation, she would lift a sentence or a phrase to splice into a poem, sometimes acknowledging her borrowings through quotation marks and citations, sometimes not. Moore stands, along with T. S. Eliot, Ezra Pound, and William Carlos Williams, as one of the poets who first developed the Modernist method of juxtaposing fragments from other sources against her own words to create a collage effect. As early as 1907—well before Eliot's quotation-laden poem, *The Waste Land,* appeared—Moore was weaving quotations into her poems. She also became notorious for her revisions, changing poems after she had published them, usually through cuts rather than additions.

In 1919 Moore began corresponding with Pound, and in 1921 with Eliot, both of whom contacted her about publishing her poems. Their initial inquiries led to supportive friendships that were sustained primarily through letters. But her first book was made possible by H. D. and her companion Bryher, who gathered many of the poems that Moore had contributed to journals in *Poems* (1921). The book's appearance came as a surprise to Moore, who felt that she was not yet ready for a collection.

In 1924, she released a longer book, *Observations,* whose chronological arrangement included fifty-two of the sixty-five poems she had published since 1915, some of them in revised versions. The book was distinctive not only because of the poetry—particularly the remarkable long poems, "Marriage" and "An Octopus"—but also because of its extensive notes and index. Her choice to write about uncommon subjects, such as a steam roller or an elephant, and her eschewal of traditional forms in favor of free verse or the intricate patterns of syllabic verse, underscored her call, in "Poetry," for poets to be " 'literalists of the imagination.' " Her work paid precise attention to literal details, but framed them in unexpected, highly subjective ways. The book won the prestigious Dial Award in 1924 and solidified Moore's reputation as a key Modernist poet.

The award also led to Moore's appointment as editor of the *Dial,* a leading arts and letters magazine. During her tenure, from 1925 to 1929, she became a powerful literary arbiter. In addition to editing, Moore dedicated herself to writing prose for the magazine: book reviews and a total of forty-two editorial columns in which she reflected not only on art and literature, but on an idiosyncratic array of subjects. Moore developed a prose style that shares many attributes with her poetry: complex syntax, frequent quotations, and electric shifts of thought that seem to launch the argument in unrelated directions but whose relevance Moore establishes as the essay develops. She continued to write prose after the *Dial* folded in 1929, publishing her essays and reviews in both mainstream and literary journals.

Although her work for the *Dial* gave her considerable power in the literary world and a venue for her essays, it left her little energy to draft poems. From 1925 until 1932 she did not publish any poetry. In 1930 Moore and her mother moved from Manhattan to Brooklyn, where distance from the literary scene enabled her to write new poems, including such important works as "The Steeple-Jack," "The Jerboa," and "The Plumet Basilisk," many of which intensified her focus on animals as analogues for virtues, such as perseverance and discipline. She positioned the group of new poems at the end of *Selected Poems* (1935). More new work appeared in *The Pangolin and Other Verse* (1936) and *What Are Years* (1941). Despite her self-imposed distance from literary life, Moore visited Manhattan often and kept up her relationships with other writers through extensive correspondence. She served as a mentor to younger women writers, particularly Elizabeth Bishop, whom she met in 1934.

The vast devastation of World War II challenged Moore to change some of her ideas about poetry, and her poems became less dense and more direct than they had been. (After the death of her mother in 1947, Moore's shift in style became even more pronounced.) Nevertheless, her *Collected Poems* (1951) won the Pulitzer Prize, the National Book Award, and the Bollingen Prize—the three most significant awards in American poetry—and Moore followed the book with four new volumes of poetry before she published *Complete Poems* (1967) on her eightieth birthday.

Moore's later poetry often featured accessible subjects such as baseball, and she became a minor celebrity, the subject of articles in popular magazines as diverse as *Life, Vogue,* and *Sports Illustrated.* She appeared as a guest on *The Tonight Show* and became friends with athletes such as Cassius Clay (Muhammad Ali). But the media tended to feature Moore as a grandmotherly eccentric rather than as a major poet, and her achievements as a Modernist innovator were ignored in favor of her interests in baseball, fashion, and zoos. Nevertheless, at the time of her death from a stroke, in 1972, readers of poetry and especially other poets considered her work indispensable and counted her among the most important American poets of the twentieth century.

◄○►━◄►━○►►

The Fish

wade
through black jade.
   Of the crow-blue mussel shells, one
     keeps
     adjusting the ash heaps;   5
   opening and shutting itself like

an
injured fan.
   The barnacles which encrust the
     side   10
     of the wave, cannot hide
   there for the submerged shafts of the

sun,
split like spun
   glass, move themselves with spotlike swift-   15
     ness
     into the crevices—
   in and out, illuminating

the
turquoise sea   20
   of bodies. The water drives a
     wedge
     of iron through the iron edge
   of the cliff, whereupon the stars,[1]

1. Starfish.

pink   25
rice grains, ink
      bespattered jelly-fish, crabs like
          green
          lilies and submarine
      toadstools, slide each on the other.   30

   All
   external
      marks of abuse are present on
          this
          defiant edifice—   35
      all the physical features of

ac-
cident—lack
      of cornice, dynamite grooves, burns
          and   40
      hatchet strokes, these things stand
      out on it; the chasm side is

dead.
Repeated
      evidence has proved that it can   45
          live
          on what cannot revive
      its youth. The sea grows old in it.

                                                    1921

Poetry

I too, dislike it: there are things that are important beyond all this fiddle.
   Reading it, however, with a perfect contempt for it, one discovers that there is in
   it after all, a place for the genuine.
      Hands that can grasp, eyes
      that can dilate, hair that can rise   5
          if it must, these things are important not because a

high sounding interpretation can be put upon them but because they are
   useful; when they become so derivative as to become unintelligible, the
   same thing may be said for all of us—that we
      do not admire what   10
      we cannot understand. The bat,
          holding on upside down or in quest of something to

eat, elephants pushing, a wild horse taking a roll, a tireless wolf under
   a tree, the immovable critic twinkling his skin like a horse that feels a flea,
          the base-
   ball fan, the statistician—case after case   15
      could be cited did
      one wish it; nor is it valid
          to discriminate against "business documents and

school-books";[2] all these phenomena are important. One must make a distinction
  however: when dragged into prominence by half poets, the result is not poetry, 20
  nor till the autocrats among us can be
    "literalists of
    the imagination"[3]—above
      insolence and triviality and can present

for inspection, imaginary gardens with real toads in them, shall we have   25
  it. In the meantime, if you demand on one hand, in defiance of their opinion—
  the raw material of poetry in
    all its rawness and
    that which is, on the other hand,
      genuine then you are interested in poetry.   30

                                      1921

Poetry[4]

I, too, dislike it.
  Reading it, however, with a perfect contempt for it, one discovers in
  it, after all, a place for the genuine.

                                      1967

Those Various Scalpels

Those
various sounds consistently indistinct, like intermingled echoes
  struck from thin glass successively at random—the
  inflection disguised: your hair, the tails of two fighting-cocks head to head in
    stone—like sculptured scimitars re-
      peating the curve of your ears in reverse order: your eyes,   5
      flowers of ice

and
snow sown by tearing winds on the cordage of disabled ships: your raised hand
  an ambiguous signature: your cheeks, those rosettes
  of blood on the stone floors of French châteaux, with regard to which guides

2. When she published this poem in *Observations* (1924), Moore added the full quotation from the *Diary of Tolstoy* in a note: "Where the boundary between prose and poetry lies, I shall never be able to understand. The question is raised in manuals of style, yet the answer to it lies beyond me. Poetry is verse: prose is not verse. Or else poetry is everything with the exception of business documents and school books."
3. In another note, Moore gives the full quotation, from W. B. Yeats's "William Blake and His Illustrations" in *Ideas of Good and Evil* (1903): "The limitation of [Blake's] view was from the very intensity of his vision; he was a too literal realist of imagination, as others are of nature; and because he believed that the figures seen by the mind's eye, when exalted by inspiration were 'external existences,' symbols of divine essences, he hated every grace of style that might obscure their lineaments."
4. Moore constantly revised her best-known poem, "Poetry"; throughout her career the poem appeared in many different versions. For its final publication in *Complete Poems* (1967), she reduced the poem to its first three lines, while including a longer version for reference in the endnotes and adding a curt explanatory note at the beginning of the book: "Omissions are not accidents."

are so affirmative: 10
   your other hand

a
bundle of lances all alike, partly hid by emeralds from Persia
   and the fractional magnificence of Florentine
   goldwork—a collection of half a dozen little objects made fine   15
     with enamel in gray, yellow, and dragonfly blue: a lemon, a

pear
and three bunches of grapes, tied with silver: your dress, a magnificent square
   cathedral of uniform
   and at the same time, diverse appearance—a species of vertical vineyard
      rustling in the storm   20
    of conventional opinion. Are they weapons or scalpels?
    Whetted

to
brilliance by the hard majesty of that sophistication which is superior to opportunity, these things are rich   25
   instruments with which to experiment but surgery is not tentative: why dissect
      destiny with instruments which
    are more highly specialized than the tissues of destiny
     itself?

                                              1921

To a Steam Roller

The illustration
is nothing to you without the application.
   You lack half wit. You crush all the particles down
     into close conformity, and then walk back and forth on them.

Sparkling chips of rock   5
are crushed down to the level of the parent block.
   Were not "impersonal judgment in æsthetic
     matters, a metaphysical impossibility," you

might fairly achieve
it. As for butterflies, I can hardly conceive   10
   of one's attending upon you, but to question
     the congruence of the complement is vain, if it exists.

                                            1921

Marriage[5]

This institution,
perhaps one should say enterprise

---

5. In her 1967 footnotes, Moore describes "Marriage" as "statements that took my fancy which I tried
to arrange plausibly."

out of respect for which
one says one need not change one's mind
about a thing one has believed in,   5
requiring public promises
of one's intention
to fulfil a private obligation:
I wonder what Adam and Eve
think of it by this time,   10
this fire-gilt steel
alive with goldenness;
how bright it shows—
"of circular traditions and impostures,
committing many spoils,"6   15
requiring all one's criminal ingenuity
to avoid!
Psychology which explains everything
explains nothing,
and we are still in doubt.   20
Eve: beautiful woman—
I have seen her
when she was so handsome
she gave me a start,
able to write simultaneously   25
in three languages—
English, German, and French—7
and talk in the meantime;
equally positive in demanding a commotion
and in stipulating quiet: 30
"I should like to be alone";
to which the visitor replies,
"I should like to be alone;
why not be alone together?"
Below the incandescent stars   35
below the incandescent fruit,
the strange experience of beauty;
its existence is too much;
it tears one to pieces
and each fresh wave of consciousness   40
is poison.
"See her, see her in this common world,"8
the central flaw
in that first crystal-fine experiment,

6. Moore's note: "Francis Bacon." Bacon (1561–1625) was an English philosopher and statesman.
7. Moore's note: "'Miss A—— will write simultaneously in three languages: English, German, and French, talking in the meantime. [She] takes advantages of her abilities in everyday life, writing her letters simultaneously with both hands; namely, the first, third, and fifth words with her left and the second, fourth, and sixth with her right hand. While generally writing outward, she is able as well to write inward with both hands.' 'Multiple Consciousness or Reflex Action of Unaccustomed Range,' *Scientific American*, January 1922.'"
8. Moore's note: "George Shock."

this amalgamation which can never be more   45
than an interesting impossibility,
describing it
as "that strange paradise
unlike flesh, stones,
gold or stately buildings,   50
the choicest piece of my life:
the heart rising
in its estate of peace
as a boat rises
with the rising of the water";[9]   55
constrained in speaking of the serpent—
shed snakeskin in the history of politeness
not to be returned to again—
that invaluable accident
exonerating Adam.   60
And he has beauty also;
it's distressing—the O thou
to whom from whom,
without whom nothing—Adam;
"something feline,   65
something colubrine"[1]—how true!
a crouching mythological monster
in that Persian miniature of emerald mines,
raw silk—ivory white, snow white,
oyster white and six others—   70
that paddock full of leopards and giraffes—
long lemon-yellow bodies
sown with trapezoids of blue.
Alive with words,
vibrating like a cymbal   75
touched before it has been struck,
he has prophesied correctly—
the industrious waterfall,
"the speedy stream
which violently bears all before it,   80
at one time silent as the air
and now as powerful as the wind."
"Treading chasms
on the uncertain footing of a spear,"[2]

9. Moore's note: "Richard Baxter, *The Saints' Everlasting Rest.* Baxter (1691–1651) was an English Puritan devotional writer.
1. Moore's note: "'We were puzzled and we were fascinated, as if by something feline, by something-colubrine. Philip Littell, reviewing Santayana's *Poems* in *The New Republic*, March 21, 1923." "Colubrine" means "snakelike." George Santayana (1963–1952) was a Spanish-American born philosopher and poet.
2. Moore's note: "'*Treading chasms* . . .' Hazlitt: 'Essay on Burke's Style.'" William Hazlitt (1778–1830) was an English essayist and literary critic. Moore does not identify the source of the quotation in lines 79–82.

forgetting that there is in woman   85
a quality of mind
which as an instinctive manifestation
is unsafe,
he goes on speaking
in a formal customary strain,   90
of "past states, the present state,
seals, promises,
the evil one suffered,
the good one enjoys,
hell, heaven,   95
everything convenient
to promote one's joy."[3]
In him a state of mind
perceives what it was not
intended that he should;   100
"he experiences a solemn joy
in seeing that he has become an idol."[4]
Plagued by the nightingale
in the new leaves,
with its silence—   105
not its silence but its silences,
he says of it:
"It clothes me with a shirt of fire."[5]
"He dares not clap his hands
to make it go on   110
lest it should fly off;
if he does nothing, it will sleep;
if he cries out, it will not understand."[6]
Unnerved by the nightingale
and dazzled by the apple,   115
impelled by "the illusion of a fire
effectual to extinguish fire,"[7]
compared with which
the shining of the earth
is but deformity—a fire   120
"as high as deep
as bright as broad
as long as life itself,"

---

3. Moore's note: "Richard Baxter."
4. Moore' note: *"A Travers Champs,"* by Anatole France in Filles et Garçons (Hachette)" *"Le petit Jean comprend qu'el est beau et cette idéé le pénéte d'un respect profound de lui-même. . . . Il goûte une joie pieuse à se sentir devenu une idole."* (French) By Anatole France (1844–1924), in "Across the Fields" in *Girls and Boys:* "Young Jean understands that he is handsome, and this idea creates in him a profound self-respect. . . . He experiences a solemn joy in seeing that he has become an idol."
5. Moore's note: "Hagop Boghossian in a poem, 'The Nightingale.'" Moore revealed in her 1924 note that the poem was written in Armenian and that Boghossian taught at Worcester College in Massachusetts.
6. Moore's note: "Edward Thomas, *Feminine Influence on the Poets* (Martin Secker, 1910)." Thomas (1878–1917) was an English poet who died in World War I.
7. Moore's note: " '*Illusion of a fire* . . .,' '*as high as deep* . . .' Richard Baxter."

he stumbles over marriage,
"a very trivial object indeed"[8]   125
to have destroyed the attitude
in which he stood—
the ease of the philosopher
unfathered by a woman.
Unhelpful Hymen![9]   130
a kind of overgrown cupid
reduced to insignificance
by the mechanical advertising
parading as involuntary comment,
by that experiment of Adam's   135
with ways out but no way in—
the ritual of marriage,
augmenting all its lavishness;
its fiddle-head ferns,
lotus flowers,[1] opuntias,[2] white dromedaries,   140
its hippopotamus—
nose and mouth combined
in one magnificent hopper—
its snake and the potent apple.
He tells us   145
that "for love that will
gaze an eagle blind,
that is with Hercules
climbing the trees
in the garden of the Hesperides,   150
from forty-five to seventy
is the best age,"[3]
commending it
as a fine art, as an experiment,
a duty or as merely recreation.   155
One must not call him ruffian
nor friction a calamity—
the fight to be affectionate:
"no truth can be fully known
until it has been tried   160

8. Moore's note: "Godwin." William Godwin (1736–1856) was an English social philosopher and the husband of Mary Wollstonecraft (1759–1797), author of *A Vindication of the Rights of Woman* (1792).
9. Greek god of marriage.
1. In Homer's *Odyssey* XI, those who ate lotus fruit forgot their homes, families, and friends, and lost all desire to return to their native countries, preferring instead to live a life of ease and idleness.
2. Prickly pear cactus.
3. Moore note: "Anthony Trollope, *Barchester Towers*." Trollope was an important Victorian novelist. Hercules was a Greek hero whose remarkable strength enabled him to complete nine labors, dangerous tasks imposed as penance after he slew his wife and children in a fit of madness. One of those labors was to steal golden apples, given to Zeus's wife Hera as a marriage gift, from the garden of the Hesperides, where they were guarded by a dragon.

by the tooth of disputation."[4]
The blue panther with black eyes,
the basalt panther with blue eyes,
entirely graceful—
one must give them the path—   165
the black obsidian Diana[5]
who "darkeneth her countenance
as a bear doth,"[6]
the spiked hand
that has an affection for one   170
and proves it to the bone,
impatient to assure you
that impatience is the mark of independence,
not of bondage.
"Married people often look that way"—[7]   175
"seldom and cold, up and down,
mixed and malarial
with a good day and a bad."[8]
We Occidentals are so unemotional,
self lost, the irony preserved   180
in "the Ahasuerus[9] tête-à-tête banquet"
with its small orchids like snakes' tongues,
with its "good monster, lead the way,"[1]
with little laughter
and munificence of humor   185
in that quixotic atmosphere of frankness
in which "four o'clock does not exist,
but at five o'clock
the ladies in their imperious humility
are ready to receive you";[2]   190
in which experience attests
that men have power
and sometimes one is made to feel it.
He says, "What monarch would not blush
to have a wife   195

4. Moore's note: "Robert of Sorbonne." Robert of Sorbonne (1201–1274) founded the famous Paris University that bears his name.
5. Roman name for Artemis, Greek virgin goddess who presided over chastity, marriage, and hunting.
6. Moore's note: "Ecclesiasticus." Moore quotes 25:24, "The wickedness of a woman changeth her face: and she darkeneth her countenance as a bear: and sheweth it like sackcloth."
7. Moore's note: "C. Bertram Hartmann." Hartmann (1892–1960) was an American painter.
8. Moore's note: " 'Seldom and cold . . .' Richard Baxter.
9. Moore's note: "George Adam Smith, Expositor's Bible." Ahasuerus is a Persian king featured in the Old Testament book of Esther. After banishing his first wife Vashti for disobeying him, he chose Esther as his next wife. At a banquet she had prepared, Esther asked him to spare the lives of her people, the Jews, whom the king's advisor Haman had planned to slaughter.
1. Moore's note: *The Tempest.*" Moore changes Stephano's charge to Caliban in II. ii. 187: "O brave monster! lead the way."
2. Moore's note: "Comtesse de Noailles, 'Le Thé,' *Feminia*, December 1921. *"Dans leur impérieuse humilité elles jouent instinctivement leurs roles sur le globe.'* " (French) "In their imperious humility, they [women] instinctively play their roles on the planet."

with hair like a shaving-brush?"[3]
The fact of woman
is "not the sound of the flute
but very poison."[4]
She says, "Men are monopolists   200
of 'stars, garters, buttons
and other shining baubles'—
unfit to be the guardians
of another person's happiness."[5]
He says, "These mummies   205
must be handled carefully—
'the crumbs from a lion's meal,
a couple of shins and the bit of an ear';[6]
turn to the letter M
and you will find   210
that 'a wife is a coffin,'[7]
that severe object
with the pleasing geometry
stipulating space not people,
refusing to be buried   215
and uniquely disappointing,
revengefully wrought in the attitude
of an adoring child
to a distinguished parent."
She says, "This butterfly,   220
this waterfly, this nomad
that has 'proposed
to settle on my hand for life'—[8]
What can one do with it?
There must have been more time   225
in Shakespeare's day
to sit and watch a play.
You know so many artists who are fools."
He says, "You know so many fools
who are not artists."   230
The fact forgot
that "some have merely rights

3. Moore's note: "What monarch . . ." From 'The Rape of the Lock,' a parody by Mary Frances Near-ing, with suggestions by M. Moore."
4. Moore's Note: "A. Mitram Rihbany, The Syrian Christ (Houghton Mifflin, 1916). Silence of women—'to an Oriental, this is as poetry set to music.'"
5. Moore's note: "Miss M. Carey Thomas, Founder's Address, Mount Holyoke, 1921: 'Men practically reserve for themselves stately funerals, splendid monuments, memorial statues, membership in acade-mies, medals, titles, honorary degrees, starts, garters, ribbons, buttons and other shining baubles, so val-ueless in themselves and yet so infinitely desirable because they are symbols of recognition by their fellow-craftsmen of difficult work well done.'" M. (Martha) Carey Thomas (1857–1935), a feminist and distinguished educator, was president of Bryn Mawr College from 1894–1922.
6. Moore's note: "Amos iii.12. Translation by George Adam Smith, Expositor's Bible."
7. Moore's note: "Ezra Pound."
8. Moore's note: "Charles Read, Christie Johnston." British novelist Charles Reade (1814–1884) pub-lished his novel Christie Johnstone in 1853.

while some has obligations,"[9]
he loves himself so much,
he can permit himself   235
no rival in that love.
She loves herself so much,
she cannot see herself enough—
a statuette of ivory on ivory,
the logical last touch   240
to an expansive splendor
earned as wages for work done:
one is not rich but poor
when one can always seem so right.
What can one do for them—   245
these savages
condemned to disaffect
all those who are not visionaries
alert to undertake the silly task
of making people noble?   250
This model of petrine[1] fidelity
who "leaves her peaceful husband
only because she has seen enough of him"—[2]
that orator reminding you,
"I am yours to command."   255
"Everything to do with love is mystery;
it is more than a day's work
to investigate this science."[3]
One sees that it is rare—
that striking grasp of opposites   260
opposed each to the other, not to unity,
which in cycloid[4] inclusiveness
has dwarfed the demonstration
of Columbus with the egg—[5]
a triumph of simplicity—   265
that charitive Euroclydon[6]
of frightening disinterestedness
which the world hates,
admitting:

9. Moore's note: " 'Asiatics have rights; Europeans have obligations.' Edmund Burke." Burke (1729–1797) was an Irish political philosopher.
1. Like St. Peter, whose name means "rock" and whose faith was rocklike. When choosing his disciples, Jesus said, "Thou art Peter, and upon this rock I will build my church" (Matt. 18). Yet on the night Jesus was condemned to death, Peter denied knowing him.
2. Moore's note: "Simone Puget, advertisement entitled 'Change of Fashion,' *English Review,* June 1914: 'Thus proceed pretty dolls when they leave their old home to renovate their frame, and dear others who may abandon their peaceful husband only because they have seen enough of him.' "
3. Moore's note: "F. C. Tilney, *Fables of La Fontaine,* 'Love and Folly,' Book XII, No. 14."
4. Circular.
5. When asked at a banquet if others would have discovered the New World had he not done so, Columbus challenged the guests to stand an egg on end. After everyone failed, he broke one end of the egg, flattening its bottom and making it stand.
6. A tempestuous Mediterranean wind referred to in Acts 27:13–14.

"I am such a cow,   270
if I had a sorrow
I should feel it a long time;
I am not one of those
who have a great sorrow
in the morning   275
and a great joy at noon";

which says: "I have encountered it
among those unpretentious
protégés of wisdom,
where seeming to parade   280
as the debater and the Roman,
the statesmanship
of an archaic Daniel Webster[7]
persists to their simplicity of temper
as the essence of the matter: 285

  'Liberty and union
  now and forever';

the Book on the writing-table;
the hand in the breast-pocket."[8]

                                     1923

An Egyptian Pulled Glass Bottle in the Shape of a Fish

Here we have thirst
and patience, from the first,
   and art, as in a wave held up for us to see
   in its essential perpendicularity;

not brittle but   5
intense—the spectrum, that
   spectacular and nimble animal the fish,
   whose scales turn aside the sun's sword by their polish.

                                 [1924] 1967

A Graveyard[9]

Man, looking into the sea—
taking the view from those who have as much right to it as you have to it
   yourself—
it is human nature to stand in the middle of a thing
but you cannot stand in the middle of this:

---

7. Daniel Webster (1782–1852) was an American politician and orator.
8. Moore's note: "Daniel Webster (statue with inscription, Central Park, New York City)." The "liberty and union" lines are from a famous 1830 Senate debate in which Webster defended Federalism against Southern proponents of states's rights.
9. When Moore published this poem in *Observations*, she change to title to "A Grave."

the sea has nothing to give but a well excavated grave.   5
The firs stand in a procession—each with an emerald turkey-foot at the top—
reserved as their contours, saying nothing;
repression, however, is not the most obvious characteristic of the sea;
the sea is a collector, quick to return a rapacious look.
There are others besides you who have worn that look—   10
whose expression is no longer a protest; the fish no longer investigate them
for their bones have not lasted;
men lower nets, unconscious of the fact that they are desecrating a grave,
and row quickly away—the blades of the oars
moving together like the feet of water-spiders as if there were no such thing as
   death.   15
The wrinkles progress upon themselves in a phalanx—beautiful under networks
   of foam,
and fade breathlessly while the sea rustles in and out of the seaweed;
the birds swim through the air at top speed, emitting cat-calls as heretofore—
the tortoise-shell scourges about the feet of the cliffs, in motion beneath them
and the ocean, under the pulsation of light-houses and noise of bell-buoys,   20
advances as usual, looking as if it were not that ocean in which dropped things
   are bound to sink—
in which if they turn and twist, it is neither with volition nor consciousness.

                                                                              1924

New York

   the savage's romance,
   accreted where we need the space for commerce—
   the center of the wholesale fur trade,
   starred with tepees of ermine and peopled with foxes,
   the long guard-hairs waving two inches beyond the body of the pelt;   5
   the ground dotted with deer-skins—white with white spots
   "as satin needle-work in a single colour may carry a varied pattern,"[1]
   and blankets of eagles' down—
   submarine forest upon submarine forest of tropical seaweed.
   It is a far cry from the "queen full of jewels"   10
   and the beau with the muff,
   from the gilt coach shaped like a perfume bottle,
   to the conjunction of the Monongahela and the Allegheny
   and the scholastic philosophy of the wilderness,
   to combat which one must stand outside and laugh   15
   since to go in is to be lost.
   It is not the dime-novel exterior,

1. In *Observations,* Moore quotes as her source for this line five paragraphs of an article from *Field and Stream* that was reprinted in the March 1918 issue of *The Literary Digest.* In *The Complete Poems,* she reduced the quotation to a single paragraph: "About the middle of June, 1916, a white fawn only a few days old was discovered in a thicket and brought to the hotel. Here, in the company of another fawn, it grew rapidly. During the earlier months this fawn had the usual row of white spots on the back and sides, and although there was no difference between these and the body color, they were conspicuous in the same way that satin needle work in a single color may carry a varied pattern. . . ."

Niagara Falls, the calico horses, and the war canoe;
it is not that "if the fur is not finer than such as one sees others wear,
one would rather be without it—"[2]   20
that estimated in raw meat and berries, we could feed the universe:
it is not the atmosphere of ingenuity,
the otter, the beaver, the puma skins
without shooting-irons or dogs;
it is not the plunder,   25
it is the "accessibility to experience."[3]

                                                            1924

Silence

My father used to say,[4]
"Superior people never make long visits,
have to be shown Longfellow's[5] grave
or the glass flowers at Harvard.
Self-reliant like the cat—   5
that takes its prey to privacy,
the mouse's limp tail hanging like a shoelace from its mouth—
they sometimes enjoy solitude,
and can be robbed of speech
by speech which has delighted them.   10
The deepest feeling always shows itself in silence;
not in silence, but restraint."
Nor was he insincere in saying, "Make my house your inn."[6]
Inns are not residences.

                                                            [1924] 1967

The Steeple-Jack[7]

Dürer[8] would have seen a reason for living
    in a town like this, with eight stranded whales
to look at; with the sweet sea air coming into your house
on a fine day, from water etched

---

2. In a note, Moore gives as her source *The Psychology of Dress* (1920) by Frank Alvah Parsons, who quotes Isabella, Duchess of Gonzala: "I wish black cloth even if it cost ten ducats a yard. If it is only as good as that which I see other people wear, I had rather be without it."
3. In a note, Moore cites Henry James as the source of this phrase, but she did not give any indication of which of James's writings she draws upon here.
4. In a note to the poem, Moore informs readers that she draws some of the phrases in this long quotation, as well as the poem's first line, from "Miss A. M. Homans," who was Professor Emeritus of Hygiene at Wellesley College.
5. Henry Wadsworth Longfellow (1807–1882), popular American poet and translator.
6. Moore reveals in a note that she quotes from the eighteenth-century Irish political philosopher Edmund Burke, as quoted in Sir James Prior's *Life of Burke* (1872); Burke remarked to a stranger whom he had just met in a bookstore, " 'Throw yourself into a coach,' said he. 'Come down and make my house your inn.' "
7. A steeple-jack builds and repairs church steeples.
8. German painter and printmaker Albrecht Dürer (1471–1558).

with waves as formal as the scales
on a fish.

One by one in two's and three's, the seagulls keep
    flying back and forth over the town clock,
or sailing around the lighthouse without moving their wings—
rising steadily with a slight
    quiver of the body—or flock
mewing where

a sea the purple of the peacock's neck is
    paled to greenish azure as Dürer changed
the pine green of the Tyrol to peacock blue and guinea
gray. You can see a twenty-five-
    pound lobster; and fish nets arranged
to dry. The

whirlwind fife-and-drum of the storm bends the salt
    marsh grass, disturbs stars in the sky and the
star on the steeple; it is a privilege to see so
much confusion. Disguised by what
    might seem the opposite, the sea-
side flowers and

trees are favored by the fog so that you have
    the tropics at first hand: the trumpet-vine,
fox-glove, giant snap-dragon, a salpiglossis that has
spots and stripes; morning-glories, gourds,
    or moon-vines trained on fishing-twine
at the back door;

cat-tails, flags, blueberries and spiderwort,
    striped grass, lichens, sunflowers, asters, daisies—
yellow and crab-claw ragged sailors with green bracts—toad-plant,
petunias, ferns; pink lilies, blue
    ones, tigers; poppies; black sweet-peas.
The climate

is not right for the banyan, frangipani, or
    jack-fruit trees; or for exotic serpent
life. Ring lizard and snake-skin for the foot, if you see fit;
but here they've cats, not cobras, to
    keep down the rats. The diffident
little newt

with white pin-dots on black horizontal spaced-
    out bands lives here; yet there is nothing that
ambition can buy or take away. The college student
named Ambrose sits on the hillside
    with his not-native books and hat
and sees boats

at sea progress white and rigid as if in
    a groove. Liking an elegance of which   50
the source is not bravado, he knows by heart the antique
sugar-bowl shaped summer-house of
    interlacing slats, and the pitch
of the church

spire, not true, from which a man in scarlet lets   55
    down a rope as a spider spins a thread;
he might be part of a novel, but on the sidewalk a
sign says C. J. Poole, Steeple-Jack,
    in black and white; and one in red
and white says   60

Danger. The church portico has four fluted
    columns, each a single piece of stone, made
modester by white-wash. This would be a fit haven for
waifs, children, animals, prisoners,
    and presidents who have repaid   65
sin-driven

senators by not thinking about them. The
    place has a school-house, a post-office in a
store, fish-houses, hen-houses, a three-masted
    schooner on   70
the stocks. The hero, the student,
    the steeple-jack, each in his way,
is at home.

It could not be dangerous to be living
    in a town like this, of simple people,   75
who have a steeple-jack placing danger-signs by the church
while he is gilding the solid-
    pointed star, which on a steeple
stands for hope.

                                         [1935] 1967

What Are Years?

        What is our innocence,
    what is our guilt? All are
        naked, none is safe. And whence
    is courage: the unanswered question,
        the resolute doubt,—   5
        dumbly calling, deafly listening—that
    in misfortune, even death,
            encourages others
            and in its defeat, stirs

        the soul to be strong? He   10
    sees deep and is glad, who

accedes to mortality
and in his imprisonment rises
upon himself as
the sea in a chasm, struggling to be   15
free and unable to be,
    in its surrendering
    finds its continuing.

    So he who strongly feels,
behaves. The very bird,   20
    grown taller as he sings, steels
his form straight up. Though he is captive,
his mighty singing
says, satisfaction is a lowly
thing, how pure a thing is joy.   25
    This is mortality,
    this is eternity.

1941

In Distrust of Merits

Strengthened to live, strengthened to die for
  medals and positioned victories?
They're fighting, fighting, fighting the blind
  man who thinks he sees,—
who cannot see that the enslaver is   5
enslaved; the hater, harmed. O shining O
    firm star, O tumultuous
    ocean lashed till small things go
  as they will, the mountainous
    wave makes us who look, know   10

depth. Lost at sea before they fought! O
  star of David, star of Bethlehem,[9]
O black imperial lion
  of the Lord—emblem
of a risen world—be joined at last, be   15
joined. There is hate's crown beneath which all is
    death; there's love's without which none
    is king; the blessed deeds bless
  the halo. As contagion
    of sickness makes sickness,   20

contagion of trust can make trust. They're
  fighting in deserts and caves, one by
one, in battalions and squadrons;
  they're fighting that I

9. Moore refers to both the Jewish and the Christian symbols, for Bethlehem is the "city of David."

may yet recover from the disease, My   25
Self; some have it lightly; some will die. "Man's
    wolf to man"[1] and we devour
      ourselves. The enemy could not
    have made a greater breach in our
      defenses. One pilot-   30

ing a blind man can escape him, but
    Job[2] disheartened by false comfort knew
that nothing can be defeating
    as a blind man who
can see. O alive who are dead, who are   35
proud not to see, O small dust of the earth
    that walks arrogantly,
      trust begets power and faith is
    an affectionate thing. We
      vow, we make this promise   40

to the fighting—it's a promise—"We'll
    never hate black, white, red, yellow, Jew,
Gentile, Untouchable."[3] We are
    not competent to
make our vows. With set jaw they are fighting,   45
fighting, fighting,—some we love whom we know,
    some we love but know not—that
      hearts may feel and not be numb.
    It cures me; or am I what
      I can't believe in? Some   50

in snow, some on crags, some in quicksands,
    little by little, much by much, they
are fighting fighting fighting that where
    there was death there may
be life. "When a man is prey to anger,   55
he is moved by outside things; when he holds
    his ground in patience patience
      patience, that is action or
    beauty," the soldier's defense
      and hardest armor for   60

the fight. The world's an orphans' home. Shall
    we never have peace without sorrow?
without pleas of the dying for
    help that won't come? O
quiet form upon the dust, I cannot   65
look and yet I must. If these great patient

---

1. From *Asinaria* by the Roman playwright Plautus (250–184 B.C.E.).
2. In the Old Testament book of Job, God tested Job's faith through a series of trials, each more severe than the one before it. When friends tried to comfort him, Job cursed their inability to see his plight.
3. Lowest caste in India.

dyings—all these agonies
   and wound bearings and bloodshed—
can teach us how to live, these
   dyings were not wasted.   70

Hate-hardened heart, O heart of iron,
   iron is iron till it is rust.
There never was a war that was
   not inward; I must
fight till I have conquered in myself what   75
causes war, but I would not believe it.
   I inwardly did nothing.
     O Iscariot-like[4] crime!
   Beauty is everlasting
     and dust is for time.   80

[1944] 1967

The Mind Is an Enchanting Thing

is an enchanted thing
   like the glaze on a
katydid-wing
     subdivided by sun
     till the nettings are legion.   5
Like Gieseking playing Scarlatti;[5]

like the apteryx-awl[6]
   as a beak, or the
kiwi's rain-shawl
     of haired feathers, the mind   10
     feeling its way as though blind,
walks along with its eyes on the ground.

It has memory's ear
   that can hear without
having to hear.   15
     Like the gyroscope's fall,
     truly unequivocal
because trued by regnant certainty,

it is a power of
   strong enchantment. It   20
is like the dove-
     neck animated by
     sun; it is memory's eye;
it's conscientious inconsistency.

4. Judas Iscariot betrayed Christ, and therefore failed to follow Christ's teachings.
5. Walter Wilhelm Gieseking (1895–1956), German pianist renowned for his interpretations of works by the Italian composer Domenico Scarlatti (1685–1757).
6. The apteryx is a flightless bird from New Zealand, with a beak shaped like an awl.

It tears off the veil; tears   25
  the temptation, the
mist the heart wears,
      from its eyes—if the heart
      has a face; it takes apart
dejection. It's fire in the dove-neck's   30

iridescence; in the
  inconsistencies
of Scarlatti.
      Unconfusion submits
      its confusion to proof; it's   35
not a Herod's oath[7] that cannot change.

                                                                    1944

◂ T. S. ELIOT ▸
(1888–1965)

Thomas Stearns Eliot was born the seventh child of Henry Ware Eliot and Charlotte Champe Stearns Eliot in St. Louis, Missouri, where his father was a prominent executive in the Hydraulic Press Brick Company. His grandfather, the Reverend William Greenleaf Eliot, had settled in St. Louis in 1834, eventually founding Washington University. The family maintained its distinguished New England connections, however: a distant cousin, Charles William Eliot, was president of Harvard University from 1869 to 1909. Eliot's mother was born in Baltimore and attended schools in Massachusetts. She taught in West Chester, Pennsylvania, and in Wisconsin, as well as at Antioch in Ohio and St. Louis Normal School, where she met her future husband. A poet and biographer, she was highly influential in the development of her son's literary sensibilities. The family summered in Maine and Massachusetts, and at seventeen Eliot went east to Milton Academy. He entered Harvard in 1906, where his classmates included the future communist John Reed, the journalist Walter Lippmann, and the poet Conrad Aiken. After taking his degree in 1909, Eliot began graduate studies in philosophy at Harvard. By then he had encouraged his teacher Irving Babbitt's dislike of Romanticism, and also, in 1908, he read Arthur Symons's highly influential study of late nineteenth-century French poetry, *The Symbolist Movement in Literature*—a book that profoundly affected his notion of poetry. He had written poetry since childhood with his mother's approval, but now the work took new directions. He wrote his first masterpiece, "The Love Song of J. Alfred Prufrock," while still at Harvard in 1910.

That same year, having earned his Master's Degree, he went to the Sorbonne in Paris. There he befriended Jean Verdenal, a brilliant young medical student, and heard the lectures of Henri Bergson on personality. Upon returning to Harvard, Eliot began his dissertation on the philosopher F. H. Bradley, author of *Appearance and Reality*. He was also studying modern poetry and learning Sanskrit.

---

7. Herod, who ruled Judea under the Romans, swore to grant Salome any request after her dancing pleased him; she asked for the head of John the Baptist.

Although Eliot's attitude toward religion was skeptical at this point, he objected to the way the Harvard Philosophy Department distanced itself from religious studies since he was already a serious student of comparative religions. He was also taking dancing lessons to compensate for his intense shyness with women. After a year's assistantship at Harvard, Eliot obtained a fellowship to travel and study in Europe. He intended to go to Germany, but the outbreak of World War I forced him instead to take up studies at Oxford.

At the time, the London literary scene was full of vitality and ferment. Ford Madox Ford was editing and writing; Yeats held forth in his *salon,* where he was visited by young poets like Ezra Pound and Robert Frost. In September 1914 Eliot met Pound in London. Pound, who had already been at the forefront of the London poetry scene for several years, quickly saw that Eliot had "modernized himself *on his own.*" By early 1915, Eliot doubted that he wanted an academic career in philosophy, writing to his friend Norbert Wiener that "all philosophy is a perversion of reality. . . ." Work on his dissertation, *Knowledge and Experience in the Philosophy of F. H. Bradley,* had been completed, but increasingly Eliot thought of himself as a poet and man of letters. The dissertation concerns knowledge as a "relational" phenomenon and the difficulty of communication between people—a major theme in Eliot's poetry. It also concerns the human desire to comprehend an absolute and the problem of doing so in a context of skepticism.

Everything in Eliot's life came to a climax in the spring of 1915: the war, which kept him in England, and eventually killed his friend Jean Verdenal, his parents' desire that he pursue an academic career, the cauldron of literary London, and even his relations with women. Although he had been in love with a young American, Emily Hale, he suddenly married an Englishwoman, Vivien Haigh-Wood, whom he hardly knew. Eliot had decided against America and his parents' wishes, and his precipitous marriage seemed partly an effort to affirm his choice.

That same month, "The Love Song of J. Alfred Prufrock" appeared in *Poetry* in Chicago; it was easily the strongest and most indelible poem in the issue, but also the strangest. A kind of interior monologue, suggestive of dream journeys and multiple anxieties, its allusiveness, apparent disconnection, and defiance of easy interpretation were utterly new. The first issue of the journal *BLAST* contained Eliot's "Preludes" and "Rhapsody on a Windy Night." His poetic career was launched.

Vivien was a vivacious, talented woman, but already so beset with nervous disorders that friends would soon refer to her as an "invalid." To support her, Eliot tried teaching at various schools and then in 1917 took a job as a clerk in the Colonial and Foreign Department of Lloyd's Bank. At the same time, he was working several hours a night on book reviews, essays, and poems. *Prufrock and Other Observations* appeared in 1917, *Poems* two years later. Both Eliot and Pound had begun to feel that contemporary vers libre was enervated and experimented with writing sharply ironic poems in rhymed quatrains. Again the work was densely allusive and violently disjunctive, requiring erudition and careful attention on the part of readers. In 1919, Eliot's father died without having seen his son since before the war, and Eliot now had to bear some responsibility for his mother as well, even while he kept up his productive literary life. He published his first book of criticism, *The Sacred Wood,* in 1920. Three essays stand out in that collection. In one of these, "The Perfect Critic," he concludes that "the critic and the creative artist should frequently be the same person." In another, "Hamlet and

His Problems," Eliot coined the term "objective correlative." Finally, in "Tradition and the Individual Talent," he developed a theory of impersonal poetry not unlike Keats's image of the poet as chameleon. Eliot would later refine or disavow this doctrine of impersonality, but its influence on the next two generations of poets cannot be overstated, and to some degree it lies at the heart of what would come to be known as the New Criticism.

For Eliot, however, this literary self-denial arose from his increasingly traumatic personal life. His marriage to Vivien was troubled by her poor health and his uncompromising fastidiousness. To meet expenses, he was working himself into a state of exhaustion. He worked six days a week at Lloyd's while also reviewing books and composing in fragments his disturbing poem *The Waste Land*—a poem that expresses his vision of a complete breakdown in human communications and sexuality. Eliot suffered his own breakdown in 1921 and was advised to take a holiday, which he began at Margate and continued in Lausanne, Switzerland, with a course of psychiatric treatment. There he quickly wrote the final section of his poem and sought the opinion of Pound, who had moved to Paris after the war. Pound's editing of *The Waste Land* is legendary. As he wrote to Eliot in December, "The thing now runs from April . . . to shantih without break. That is 19 pages, and let us say the longest poem in the English langwidge. Don't try to bust all records by prolonging it three pages further." With typical humor Pound concluded, "Complimenti, you bitch. I am wracked by the seven jealousies. . . ."

The Waste Land was published in 1922, the same years as James Joyce's *Ulysses*. Eliot's poem was notable not only for its difficulty and allusiveness (or "mythic method")—two qualities he had identified in Joyce—but also for its extraordinary compression. Critics differed on whether it was a collage of distinct voices or a kind of disturbed dramatic monologue. In either case, the poem eventually engendered as much critical commentary as any modern work of art. In 1922 Eliot had also begun to edit the *Criterion,* an important journal, and in 1925 he left banking to join the publishing firm of Faber and Faber, where he worked for the rest of his life. From his poetry, criticism, and editing he had become one of the most significant and powerful literary figures in the world. The influence of Eliot's ideas and verse was soon global, and he was able to foster the careers of other writers, such as W. H. Auden.

During the 1920s Eliot experienced a growing religious faith, and he was baptized into the Anglican Church. In 1927 he became a British subject. One can trace these developments in poems such as "The Hollow Men" (1925), "Journey of the Magi" (1928), and "Ash-Wednesday" (1930), and also in his essays collected in *For Lancelot Andrewes* (1928), where he openly proclaimed himself a royalist.

In 1932 Eliot separated from his wife, who had been hospitalized for mental illness. (She died in a sanatorium in 1947.) The following year he published more essays in *The Use of Poetry and the Use of Criticism.* Eliot was a pioneer of modern poetic drama, and in 1935 he published his first major play, *Murder in the Cathedral.* Four other plays would follow, including *The Family Reunion* (1939) and *The Cocktail Party* (1950). The 1940s saw the publication of his last major poetic work, the religious cycle entitled *Four Quartets.* There would be other books, but Eliot's major work was finished by the end of World War II. In 1948 he won the Nobel Prize, and thereafter he became more and more the literary eminence. In 1957 he married his secretary, Valerie Fletcher, who would later publish

The Waste Land: A Facsimile and Transcript of the Original Drafts Including the Annotations of Ezra Pound (1971), and Eliot's letters. She would also see the popular success that had eluded him when his light verse was set in what became the longest running musical in history, *Cats*.

As a poet Eliot was known not only for his fragmented vision, which seemed so real and accurate to readers in many parts of the world, but also for his uncanny and memorable phrasing. He was famous for the difficulty of his poetry, a position that made him uneasy as time wore on. He was also controversial for his politics—like many intellectuals of his generation he made anti-Semitic statements he later regretted. But Eliot had equal impact as a literary critic. He left behind certain phrases and formulations—about the impersonality of art, the nature of verse form, the uses of allusion, and dramatic structure—that have proved extremely helpful in critical discussion. He helped formulate a canon of literature that would reign for two or more generations, including the Metaphysical Poets like Donne, but also Dante, Milton, Dryden, Yeats, Tennyson, and Kipling. Perhaps most importantly, his criticism was written in lucid prose that could be understood by anyone with an interest in literature.

◄●━━◄●━━●►

The Love Song of J. Alfred Prufrock

S'io credessi che mia risposta fosse
A persona che mai tornasse al mondo,
Questa fiamma staria senza più scosse.
Ma per ciò che giammai di questo fondo
Non tornò vivo alcun, s'i' odo il vero,
Senza tema d'infamia ti rispondo.[1]

Let us go then, you and I,
When the evening is spread out against the sky
Like a patient etherized upon a table;
Let us go, through certain half-deserted streets,
The muttering retreats   5
Of restless nights in one-night cheap hotels
And sawdust restaurants with oyster-shells:
Streets that follow like a tedious argument
Of insidious intent
To lead you to an overwhelming question . . .   10
Oh, do not ask, "What is it?"
Let us go and make our visit.

In the room the women come and go
Talking of Michelangelo.

1. The epigraph to the poem is from Dante's *Inferno* (XXVII, 61–66): "If I thought my response would be to one who would ever return to earth, this fire would remain unmoving. But no one has ever returned from this gulf alive. If what I hear is true, I can answer you without fear of infamy."

The yellow fog that rubs its back upon the window-panes,   15
The yellow smoke that rubs its muzzle on the window-panes,
Licked its tongue into the corners of the evening,
Lingered upon the pools that stand in drains,
Let fall upon its back the soot that falls from chimneys,
Slipped by the terrace, made a sudden leap,   20
And seeing that it was a soft October night,
Curled once about the house, and fell asleep.

And indeed there will be time[2]
For the yellow smoke that slides along the street
Rubbing its back upon the window-panes;   25
There will be time, there will be time
To prepare a face to meet the faces that you meet;
There will be time to murder and create,
And time for all the works and days[3] of hands
That lift and drop a question on your plate;   30
Time for you and time for me,
And time yet for a hundred indecisions,
And for a hundred visions and revisions,
Before the taking of a toast and tea.

In the room the women come and go   35
Talking of Michelangelo.

And indeed there will be time
To wonder, "Do I dare?" and, "Do I dare?"
Time to turn back and descend the stair,
With a bald spot in the middle of my hair—   40
(They will say: "How his hair is growing thin!")
My morning coat, my collar mounting firmly to the chin,
My necktie rich and modest, but asserted by a simple pin—
(They will say: "But how his arms and legs are thin!")
Do I dare   45
Disturb the universe?
In a minute there is time
For decisions and revisions which a minute will reverse.

For I have known them all already, known them all—
Have known the evenings, mornings, afternoons,   50
I have measured out my life with coffee spoons;
I know the voices dying with a dying fall
Beneath the music from a farther room.
    So how should I presume?

And I have known the eyes already, known them all—   55
The eyes that fix you in a formulated phrase,
And when I am formulated, sprawling on a pin,

2. From Ecclesiastes 3. See also Andrew Marvell (1621–1678), "To His Coy Mistress": "Had we but
world enough and time, / This coyness, lady, were no crime."
3. "Works and Days" is the title of a poem by Hesiod (eighth century B.C.E.).

When I am pinned and wriggling on the wall,
Then how should I begin
To spit out all the butt-ends of my days and ways?   60
  And how should I presume?

And I have known the arms already, known them all—
Arms that are braceleted and white and bare
(But in the lamplight, downed with light brown hair!)
Is it perfume from a dress   65
That makes me so digress?
Arms that lie along a table, or wrap about a shawl.
  And should I then presume?
  And how should I begin?

            . . . . .

Shall I say, I have gone at dusk through narrow streets   70
And watched the smoke that rises from the pipes
Of lonely men in shirt-sleeves, leaning out of windows? . . .

I should have been a pair of ragged claws
Scuttling across the floors of silent seas.

            . . . . .

And the afternoon, the evening, sleeps so peacefully!   75
Smoothed by long fingers,
Asleep . . . tired . . . or it malingers,
Stretched on the floor, here beside you and me.
Should I, after tea and cakes and ices,
Have the strength to force the moment to its crisis?   80
But though I have wept and fasted, wept and prayed,
Though I have seen my head (grown slightly bald) brought in upon a platter,[4]
I am no prophet—and here's no great matter;
I have seen the moment of my greatness flicker,
And I have seen the eternal Footman hold my coat, and snicker,   85
And in short, I was afraid.

And would it have been worth it, after all,
After the cups, the marmalade, the tea,
Among the porcelain, among some talk of you and me,
Would it have been worth while,   90
To have bitten off the matter with a smile,
To have squeezed the universe into a ball[5]
To roll it towards some overwhelming question,
To say: "I am Lazarus,[6] come from the dead,
Come back to tell you all, I shall tell you all"—   95

---

4. At the request of Queen Herodias, King Herod ordered the beheading of the prophet John the Baptist. His head was brought to the queen upon a silver dish (Matthew 14:3–11).
5. Marvell, "To His Coy Mistress": "Let us roll all our strength and all / Our sweetness up into one ball, / And tear our pleasures with rough strife / Through the iron gates of life." Another ironic echo of the *carpe diem* (seize the day) theme.
6. In the Bible (John 11:1–44), Christ raises Lazarus from the dead. Yet another Lazarus comments on the experience of death in Luke 16:19–31.

If one, settling a pillow by her head,
    Should say: "That is not what I meant at all.
    That is not it, at all."

And would it have been worth it, after all,
Would it have been worth while,   100
After the sunsets and the dooryards and the sprinkled streets,
After the novels, after the teacups, after the skirts that trail along the floor—
And this, and so much more?—
It is impossible to say just what I mean!
But as if a magic lantern threw the nerves in patterns on a screen: 105
Would it have been worth while
If one, settling a pillow or throwing off a shawl,
And turning toward the window, should say:
    "That is not it at all,
    That is not what I meant, at all."   110
    . . . . .

No! I am not Prince Hamlet, nor was meant to be;
Am an attendant lord, one that will do
To swell a progress, start a scene or two,
Advise the prince; no doubt, an easy tool,
Deferential, glad to be of use,   115
Politic, cautious, and meticulous;
Full of high sentence, but a bit obtuse;
At times, indeed, almost ridiculous—
Almost, at times, the Fool.[7]

I grow old . . . I grow old . . .   120
I shall wear the bottoms of my trousers rolled.

Shall I part my hair behind?[8] Do I dare to eat a peach?
I shall wear white flannel trousers, and walk upon the beach.
I have heard the mermaids singing,[9] each to each.

I do not think that they will sing to me.   125

I have seen them riding seaward on the waves
Combing the white hair of the waves blown back
When the wind blows the water white and black.

We have lingered in the chambers of the sea
By sea-girls wreathed with seaweed red and brown   130
Till human voices wake us, and we drown.

                                                 1917

7. Prufrock may be referring here to Polonius, adviser to the king in *Hamlet*. The fool was a stock figure in Shakespeare's plays. In *Hamlet* the fool, Yorick, is dead, and Hamlet remembers him in a famous soliloquy.
8. Eliot's Harvard roommate, Conrad Aiken, wrote in his 1952 memoir, *Ushant*, that it was considered daring in their college days to part one's hair behind. Others have speculated that this refers to the effort to cover a bald spot.
9. One of Donne's impossible challenges in the song beginning "Go and catch a falling star" is "Teach me to hear mermaids singing."

Preludes[1]

I

The winter evening settles down
With smell of steaks in passageways.
Six o'clock.
The burnt-out ends of smoky days.
And now a gusty shower wraps   5
The grimy scraps
Of withered leaves about your feet
And newspapers from vacant lots;
The showers beat
On broken blinds and chimney-pots,   10
And at the corner of the street
A lonely cab-horse steams and stamps.

And then the lighting of the lamps.

II

The morning comes to consciousness
Of faint stale smells of beer   15
From the sawdust-trampled street
With all its muddy feet that press
To early coffee-stands.

With the other masquerades
That time resumes,   20
One thinks of all the hands
That are raising dingy shades
In a thousand furnished rooms.

III

You tossed a blanket from the bed,
You lay upon your back, and waited;   25
You dozed, and watched the night revealing
The thousand sordid images
Of which your soul was constituted;
The flickered against the ceiling.
And when all the world came back   30
And the light crept up between the shutters
And you heard the sparrows in the gutters,
You had such a vision of the street
As the street hardly understands;
Sitting along the bed's edge, where   35
You curled the papers from your hair,
Or clasped the yellow soles of feet
In the palms of both soiled hands.

1. The title suggests brief musical variations, as in Chopin.

IV

His soul stretched tight across the skies
That fade behind a city block,   40
Or trampled by insistent feet
At four and five and six o'clock;
And short square fingers stuffing pipes,
And evening newspapers, and eyes
Assured of certain certainties,   45
The conscience of a blackened street
Impatient to assume the world.

I am moved by fancies that are curled
Around these images, and cling:
The notion of some infinitely gentle   50
Infinitely suffering thing.

Wipe your hand across your mouth, and laugh;
The worlds revolve like ancient women
Gathering fuel in vacant lots.

                                                        1917

THE Boston Evening Transcript

The readers of the *Boston Evening Transcript*
Sway in the wind like a field of ripe corn.

When evening quickens faintly in the street,
Wakening the appetites of life in some
And to others bringing the *Boston Evening Transcript,*   5
I mount the steps and ring the bell, turning
Wearily, as one would turn to nod good-bye to La Rochefoucauld,[2]
If the street were time and he at the end of the street,
And I say, "Cousin Harriet, here is the *Boston Evening Transcript.*"

                                                        1917

Hysteria

As she laughed I was aware of becoming involved in her laughter and
being part of it, until her teeth were only accidental stars with a talent for
squad-drill. I was drawn in by short gasps, inhaled at each momentary recovery, lost finally in the dark caverns of her throat, bruised by the ripple
of unseen muscles. An elderly waiter with trembling hands was hurriedly   5
spreading a pink and white checked cloth over the rusty green iron table,
saying: "If the lady and the gentleman wish to take their tea in the garden,
if the lady and gentleman wish to take their tea in the garden . . ." I decided that if the shaking of her breasts could be stopped, some of the fragments of the afternoon might be collected, and I concentrated my attention   10
with careful subtlety to this end.

                                                        1917

---

2. François de La Rochefoucauld (1613–1680), French writer known for his remorseless analysis of the
human character in his *Maxims*.

La Figlia che Piange³
*O quam te memorem virgo . . .*⁴

Stand on the highest pavement of the stair—
Lean on a garden urn—
Weave, weave the sunlight in your hair—
Clasp your flowers to you with a pained surprise—
Fling them to the ground and turn   5
With a fugitive resentment in your eyes:
But weave, weave the sunlight in your hair.

So I would have had him leave,
So I would have had her stand and grieve,
So he would have left   10
As the soul leaves the body torn and bruised,
As the mind deserts the body it has used.
I should find
Some way incomparably light and deft,
Some way we both should understand,   15
Simple and faithless as a smile and shake of the hand.

She turned away, but with the autumn weather
Compelled my imagination many days,
Many days and many hours:
Her hair over her arms and her arms full of flowers.   20
And I wonder how they should have been together!
I should have lost a gesture and a pose.
Sometimes these cogitations still amaze
The troubled midnight and the noon's repose.

1917

Sweeney Among the Nightingales⁵

ὤμοι, πέπληγμαι καιρίαν πληγὴν ἔσω.⁶

Apeneck Sweeney spreads his knees
Letting his arms hang down to laugh,
The zebra stripes along his jaw
Swelling to maculate⁷ giraffe.

---

3. (Italian) "The Weeping Girl."
4. (Italian) "How may I name thee, maiden . . ." (Virgil, *Aeneid*).
5. Sweeney is an archetypal character in several Eliot poems and an unfinished play. Eliot once joked that he might have been a pugilist when younger "who then grew older and retired to keep a pub." The word "nightingales" is English slang for prostitutes. The poem also refers to a Greek myth in which King Tereus raped Philomela, the sister of his wife Procne. Tereus cut out Philomela's tongue to ensure her silence. In revenge, Procne killed her son Itys and fed his flesh to Tereus. Before Tereus could get his revenge, the gods took pity on the sisters, changing Philomela to a nightingale, Procne to a swallow.
6. (Greek) From Aeschylus's *Agàmemnon*. When he was murdered by Clytemnestra, Agamemnon cried, "Alas, I am struck a mortal blow within."
7. Spotted, not immaculate.

The circles of the stormy moon   5
Slide westward toward the River Plate,[8]
Death and the Raven[9] drift above
And Sweeney guards the hornèd gate.[1]

Gloomy Orion and the Dog[2]
Are veiled; and hushed the shrunken seas;   10
The person in the Spanish cape
Tries to sit on Sweeney's knees

Slips and pulls the table cloth
Overturns a coffee-cup,
Reorganised upon the floor   15
She yawns and draws a stocking up;

The silent man in mocha brown
Sprawls at the window-sill and gapes;
The waiter brings in oranges
Bananas figs and hothouse grapes;   20

The silent vertebrate in brown
Contracts and concentrates, withdraws;
Rachel *née* Rabinovitch
Tears at the grapes with murderous paws;

She and the lady in the cape   25
Are suspect, thought to be in league;
Therefore the man with heavy eyes
Declines the gambit, shows fatigue,

Leaves the room and reappears
Outside the window, leaning in,   30
Branches of wistaria
Circumscribe a golden grin;

The host with someone indistinct
Converses at the door apart,
The nightingales are singing near   35
The Convent of the Sacred Heart,[3]

And sang within the bloody wood[4]
When Agamemnon cried aloud

8. Rio de la Plata in South America.
9. Refers to the constellation Corvus.
1. In Book VI of Virgil's *Aeneid*, dreams pass from Hades through either the Gates of Ivory or the Gates of Horn; the true pass through the latter, the false through the former.
2. Orion the Hunter is a constellation close to Canis Major, the Dog.
3. The Sacred Heart has both pagan and Christian implications pertaining to beauty that arises from sacrifice.
4. In Sophocles's *Oedipus at Colonus,* the Grove of the Furies is said to be full of nightingales. In addition, Eliot refers to the Sacred Wood of ancient rites, where the priest-king was slain by his successor. Also referenced here are Agamemnon's murder in the bath and Orpheus's death at the hands of the women he had rejected.

And let their liquid siftings fall
To stain the stiff dishonoured shroud.   40

1919

The Waste Land[5]

"Nam Sibyllam quidem Cumis ego ipse oculis meis vidi in ampulla pendere,
et cum illi pueri dicerent: Σίβυλλα τί θέλεις; respondebat illa: ἀποθανεῖν θέλω."[6]

For Ezra Pound
il miglior fabbro.[7]

I. THE BURIAL OF THE DEAD[8]

April is the cruellest month,[9] breeding
Lilacs out of the dead land, mixing
Memory and desire, stirring
Dull roots with spring rain.
Winter kept us warm, covering   5
Earth in forgetful snow, feeding
A little life with dried tubers.
Summer surprised us, coming over the Starnbergersee[1]
With a shower of rain; we stopped in the colonnade,

---

5. Eliot's note: "Not only the title, but the plan and a good deal of the incidental symbolism of the poem were suggested by Miss Jessie L. Weston's book on the Grail legend: *From Ritual to Romance* (Macmillan). Indeed so deeply am I indebted, Miss Weston's book will elucidate the difficulties of the poem much better than my notes can do; and I recommend it (apart from the great interest of the book itself) to any who think such elucidation of the poem worth the trouble. To another work of anthropology I am indebted in general, one which has influenced our generation profoundly; I mean *The Golden Bough;* I have used especially the two volumes *Adonis, Attis, Osiris.* Anyone who is acquainted with these works will immediately recognize in the poem certain references to vegetation ceremonies." Eliot's poem depends on motifs of death and resurrection, which he draws not only from Christian sources but from a variety of world religions and mythologies, including Greece (the Adonis myth), Phrygia, an ancient region of Asia Minor (the Attis myth), and Egypt (the Osiris myth). For information about these ancient fertility cycles, in which a god must die and be reborn in order to return life to the land and the people, Eliot was indebted to Sir James Frazer's twelve volume study, *The Golden Bough* (1912). As his note attests, he also used as a source Jessie L. Weston's *From Ritual to Romance* (1920), which focuses on the Grail legends. The Holy Grail, the cup used by Christ at the Last Supper, was said to have been brought to England by Joseph of Arimathea and subsequently lost. In medieval legends, the quest for the Grail symbolizes a search for spiritual truth and wholeness. After enduring many ordeals, the knight who seeks the Grail must reach the Chapel Perilous and then ask ritual questions in order to gain his prize. Weston links the Grail story with the ancient fertility myths that Frazer discusses in his book. Thus, the Grail legends are also often intertwined with the tale of the Fisher King, whose land has been laid waste through a curse. The King, like his land and his people, is impotent; all can be restored to fertility only by a stranger who asks the right questions. In Wolfram von Eschenbach's *Parzival,* the right question is one that shows the asker's sympathy and compassion; thus Parzifal only gains the Grail and restores the King (and kingdom) by asking him not "how can I earn the Grail" but "what ails you"? At the conclusion of *The Waste Land,* Eliot merges this aspect of the Grail legends with the commands of the Thunder in Hindu legend: "give, sympathize, control." But Eliot also leaves open whether the spiritual emptiness of the modern waste land can be healed.
6. (Latin and Greek) In his *Satyricon,* chapter 48, Petronius tells that Apollo had granted eternal life to the Sibyl but not eternal youth: "For once I saw with my own eyes the Sibyl at Cumae hanging in a cage, and when the young men asked, 'Sibyl, what do you want?' she replied, 'I want to die.'"
7. (Italian) The dedication to Ezra Pound quotes from Dante's tribute to Arnaut Daniel, "the better maker."
8. The title of the burial service in the Anglican *Book of Common Prayer.*
9. Eliot's opening is a deliberate contrast to the Prologue of Chaucer's *The Canterbury Tales.*
1. Lake near Munich.

And went on in sunlight, into the Hofgarten,[2]   10
And drank coffee, and talked for an hour.
Bin gar keine Russin, stamm' aus Litauen, echt deutsch.[3]
And when we were children, staying at the arch-duke's,
My cousin's, he took me out on a sled,
And I was frightened. He said, Marie,   15
Marie, hold on tight. And down we went.
In the mountains, there you feel free.
I read, much of the night, and go south in the winter.[4]

What are the roots that clutch, what branches grow
Out of this stony rubbish? Son of man,   20
You cannot say, or guess, for you know only
A heap of broken images, where the sun beats,
And the dead tree gives no shelter, the cricket no relief,[5]
And the dry stone no sound of water. Only
There is shadow under this red rock,   25
(Come in under the shadow of this red rock),
And I will show you something different from either
Your shadow at morning striding behind you
Or your shadow at evening rising to meet you;
I will show you fear in a handful of dust.   30
        Frisch weht der Wind
        Der Heimat zu
        Mein Irisch Kind,
        Wo weilest du?[6]
"You gave me hyacinths first a year ago;   35
"They called me the hyacinth girl."[7]
—Yet when we came back, late, from the hyacinth garden,
Your arms full, and your hair wet, I could not
Speak, and my eyes failed, I was neither
Living nor dead, and I knew nothing,   40
Looking into the heart of light, the silence.
Oed' und leer das Meer.[8]

Madame Sosostris,[9] famous clairvoyante,
Had a bad cold, nevertheless

---

2. Park in Munich.
3. (German) "I'm no Russian, I'm from Lithuania, true German." Some critics note that the German spoken here is not entirely correct.
4. Lines 8–18 are said to be based on a conversation Eliot had with Countess Marie Larisch of Austria.
5. Eliot's note: "Cf Ezekiel 2:7"
6. (German) Eliot's note: "V. *Tristan und Isolde,* I, verses 5–8." In Wagner's *Tristan and Isolde,* a sailor sings these lines on the ship bearing Isolde to Cornwall and her soon-to-be husband, King Mark, whom she does not love: "The wind blows fresh / To the homeland; / My Irish lass, / Where are you lingering."
7. Hyacinths were associated with ancient fertility rites. In Greek mythology, Hyacinthus was a prince beloved of Apollo. After accidentally killing the youth in a game, Apollo caused flowers to spring up from his blood. Hyacinths came to symbolize death and resurrection.
8. (German) From *Tristan and Isolde.* Tristan has been wounded after being caught in adultery with Isolde. He hopes she will come to heal him, but the shepherd who keeps watch for her boat sings, "Desolate and empty the sea."
9. A name Eliot borrowed, in slightly altered form, from Aldous Huxley's comic novel *Crome Yellow.*

Is known to be the wisest woman in Europe,   45
With a wicked pack of cards.[1] Here, said she,
Is your card, the drowned Phoenician Sailor,[2]
(Those are pearls that were his eyes. Look!)[3]
Here is Belladonna,[4] the Lady of the Rocks,
The lady of situations.   50
Here is the man with three staves, and here the Wheel,[5]
And here is the one-eyed merchant,[6] and this card,
Which is blank, is something he carries on his back,
Which I am forbidden to see. I do not find
The Hanged Man. Fear death by water.   55
I see crowds of people, walking round in a ring.
Thank you. If you see dear Mrs. Equitone,[7]
Tell her I bring the horoscope myself:
One must be so careful these days.

Unreal City,[8]   60
Under the brown fog of a winter dawn,
A crowd flowed over London Bridge, so many,
I had not thought death had undone so many.[9]
Sighs, short and infrequent, were exhaled,[1]
And each man fixed his eyes before his feet.   65
Flowed up the hill and down King William Street,
To where Saint Mary Woolnoth kept the hours

---

1. Eliot's note: "I am not familiar with the exact constitution of the Tarot pack of cards, from which I have obviously departed to suit my own convenience. The Hanged Man, a member of the traditional pack, fits my purpose in two ways: because he is associated in my mind with the Hanged God of Frazer, and because I associate him with the hooded figure in the passage of the disciples to Emmaus in Part V. The Phoenician Sailor and the Merchant appear later; also the 'crowds of people,' and Death by Water is executed in Part IV. The Man with Three Staves (an authentic member of the Tarot pack) I associate, quite arbitrarily, with the Fisher King himself."
2. The Phoenician Sailor returns as Phlebas in Part IV. This card does not exist in the Tarot deck.
3. In Act I of Shakespeare's *The Tempest*, Ariel convinces Prince Ferdinand that his father has drowned by singing him a deceiving song: "Full fathom five thy father lies, / Of his bones are coral made, / Those are pearls that were his eyes. / Nothing of him that doth fade, / But doth suffer a sea-change, / Into something rich and strange." Thus Eliot echoes his themes of death and resurrection. See also lines 125, 191, and 257.
4. (Italian) "Beautiful Lady," an appellation given by Dante to Beatrice. It is also the name of a poisonous plant. "Lady of the Rocks" may refer either to Leonardo da Vinci's painting of the Virgin Mary, "Madonna of the Rocks, " or to da Vinci's *La Gioconda* (*Mona Lisa*), whom Walter Pater described in *The Renaissance* (1893) as "older than the rocks among which she sits."
5. The Wheel of Fortune; perhaps also a reference to the Buddhist Wheel of Karma.
6. The merchant may return as Mr. Eugenides in Part III. This card does not exist in the Tarot deck.
7. The name "Mrs. Equitone" echoes that of Eleanor of Aquitaine, who was famous for her romances. The name recurs at the conclusion of Eliot's poem.
8. Eliot's note: "Cf. Baudelaire: '*Fourmillante cité, cité pleine de rêves, / Où le spectre en plein jour raccroche le passant.*'" (French) From Charles Baudelaire's poem "*Les Sept Vieillards*" (The Seven Old Men): "Swarming city, city full of dreams, / Where the spectre in broad daylight accosts the passer-by."
9. Eliot's note: "Cf. *Inferno*, iii, 55–57: '*si lunga tratta / di gente, ch'io non avrei mai creduto / che morte tanta n'avesse disfatta.*'" (Italian) In this passage from the *Inferno*, Dante describes the souls in Limbo: "So long a train / of people, I should never have believed / that death had undone so many."
1. Eliot's note: "Cf. *Inferno*, iv, 25–27: '*Quivi, secondo che per ascoltare, / non avea pianto, ma che di sospiri, / che l'aura eterna facevan tremare.*'" Here, Dante describes the sighs of virtuous pagans who lived before Christ, and therefore exist after death in Limbo, unable to reach heaven: "Here, as much as one could tell / there was no cry louder than the sighs / that caused the everlasting air to tremble."

With a dead sound on the final stroke of nine.[2]
There I saw one I knew, and stopped him, crying: "Stetson!
"You who were with me in the ships at Mylae![3]   70
"That corpse you planted last year in your garden,
"Has it begun to sprout? Will it bloom this year?
"Or has the sudden frost disturbed its bed?
"O keep the Dog far hence, that's friend to men,
"Or with his nails he'll dig it up again![4]   75
"You! hypocrite lecteur!—mon semblable,—mon frère!"[5]

II. A GAME OF CHESS[6]

The Chair she sat in, like a burnished throne,
Glowed on the marble,[7] where the glass
Held up by standards wrought with fruited vines
From which a golden Cupidon peeped out   80
(Another hid his eyes behind his wing)
Doubled the flames of sevenbranched candelabra
Reflecting light upon the table as
The glitter of her jewels rose to meet it,
From satin cases poured in rich profusion.   85
In vials of ivory and coloured glass
Unstoppered, lurked her strange synthetic perfumes,
Unguent, powdered, or liquid—troubled, confused
And drowned the sense in odours; stirred by the air
That freshened from the window, these ascended   90
In fattening the prolonged candle-flames,[8]
Flung their smoke into the laquearia,
Stirring the pattern on the coffered ceiling.
Huge sea-wood fed with copper
Burned green and orange, framed by the coloured stone,   95
In which sad light a carvèd dolphin swam.
Above the antique mantel was displayed
As though a window gave upon the sylvan scene[9]

2. Eliot's note: "A phenomenon which I have often noticed."
3. The battle of Mylae took place during the first Punic War between Rome and Carthage. The poem also alludes here to World War I.
4. Eliot's note: "Cf. the Dirge in Webster's *White Devil*." In Act V of John Webster's 1612 play, a mother sings a dirge for her dead son and mourns "the friendless bodies of unburied men / . . . But keep the wolf far thence, that's foe to men, / For with his nails he'll dig them up again."
5. (French) Baudelaire's line from the Preface to *Les Fleurs du Mal* translates, "Hypocrite reader!—my double—my brother!"
6. In an earlier draft this section was entitled "In the Cage." The new title was borrowed from Thomas Middleton's play *A Game of Chess* (1624), while the chess game Eliot describes evokes Middleton's *Women Beware Women* (1657), in which a girl is seduced while her unwary mother-in-law plays chess in the next room. The chess moves parallel the progress of the seduction.
7. Eliot's note: "Cf. *Antony and Cleopatra*, II, ii, 190." Eliot's opening lines here echo Enobarbus's description of Cleopatra which begins: "The barge she sat in, like a burnish'd throne / Burned on the water." Eliot's lines may also be another example of the "Belladonna" theme in the poem.
8. Eliot's note: "Laqueraria. V. *Aeneid*, I, 726: "*dependent lychni laquearibus aureis incensi, et noctem flammis funalia vincunt.*" (Latin) "lamps hang from the gold paneled ceiling, and the torches conquer night with their flames." "Laqueraria" means "paneled ceiling." Eliot alludes here to the banquet given for Aeneas by Dido in Book I of Virgil's epic.
9. Eliot's note: "Sylvan scene. V. Milton, *Paradise Lost*, iv, 140." In Milton's epic, when Satan arrives in Eden he sees "A Sylvan Scene" and is overcome by the beauty of the paradise he aims to despoil.

The change of Philomel,[1] by the barbarous king
So rudely forced; yet there the nightingale[2]   100
Filled all the desert with inviolable voice
And still she cried, and still the world pursues,
"Jug Jug" to dirty ears.[3]
And other withered stumps of time
Were told upon the walls; staring forms   105
Leaned out, leaning, hushing the room enclosed.
Footsteps shuffled on the stair.
Under the firelight, under the brush, her hair
Spread out in fiery points
Glowed into words, then would be savagely still.   110

"My nerves are bad to-night. Yes, bad. Stay with me.
"Speak to me. Why do you never speak. Speak.
 "What are you thinking of? What thinking? What?
"I never know what you are thinking. Think."[4]

I think we are in rats' alley[5]   115
Where the dead men lost their bones.

"What is that noise?"
                    The wind under the door.[6]
"What is that noise now? What is the wind doing?"
                    Nothing again nothing.   120
                                        "Do
"You know nothing? Do you see nothing? Do you remember
"Nothing?"

        I remember
Those are pearls that were his eyes.[7]   125
"Are you alive, or not? Is there nothing in your head?"[8]
                                        But

O O O O that Shakespeherian Rag—[9]
It's so elegant
So intelligent   130

---

1. Eliot's note: "V. Ovid, *Metamorphoses*, vi, Philomela." Compare "Sweeney Among Nightingales" (page 258). In these lines of *The Waste Land*, Eliot also refers to Greek mythology as narrated by Ovid, in which King Tereus raped Philomela, sister of his wife, Procne. Tereus cut out Philomela's tongue to ensure her silence. In revenge, Procne killed her son, Itys, and fed his flesh to Tereus. Before Tereus could get his revenge, the gods took pity on the sisters, changing Philomela to the nightingale, Procne to the swallow.
2. Eliot's note: "Cf. Part III, l. 204" of *The Waste Land.*
3. A degraded representation, from Elizabethan times, of the nightingale's song.
4. Some readers suggest that these lines directly evoke Eliot's troubled marriage to Vivien Haigh-Wood. In *The Waste Land: A Facsimile and Transcript of the Original Drafts including the Annotations of Ezra Pound* (1971), we can see that Vivien wrote "WONDERFUL" in the margin next to this passage.
5. Eliot's note: "Cf . Part III, l. 195" of *The Waste Land.* "Rats' alley" may refer to the rat-infested trenches of World War I.
6. Eliot's note: "Cf. Webster: "Is the wind in that door still?" Eliot quotes Act 3 of Webster's *The Devil's Law Case* (1619), in which a doctor makes this comment to a fellow physician after they hear a groan from a man they had thought was dead.
7. A line from Ariel's song in *The Tempest;* see footnote to line 48.
8. Eliot's note: "Cf. Part I, l. 37, 48" of *The Waste Land.*
9. Refers to an actual song performed in Ziegfeld's Follies of 1912.

"What shall I do now? What shall I do?"
"I shall rush out as I am, and walk the street
"With my hair down, so. What shall we do tomorrow?
"What shall we ever do?"
                        The hot water at ten.   135
And if it rains, a closed car at four.
And we shall play a game of chess,[1]
Pressing lidless eyes and waiting for a knock upon the door.

When Lil's husband got demobbed,[2] I said—
I didn't mince my words, I said to her myself,   140
HURRY UP PLEASE ITS TIME[3]
Now Albert's coming back, make yourself a bit smart.
He'll want to know what you done with that money he gave you
To get yourself some teeth. He did, I was there.
You have them all out, Lil, and get a nice set,   145
He said, I swear, I can't bear to look at you.
And no more can't I, I said, and think of poor Albert,
He's been in the army four years, he wants a good time,
And if you don't give it him, there's others will, I said.
Oh is there, she said. Something o' that, I said.   150
Then I'll know who to thank, she said, and give me a straight look.
HURRY UP PLEASE ITS TIME
If you don't like it you can get on with it, I said.
Others can pick and choose if you can't.
But if Albert makes off, it won't be for lack of telling.   155
You ought to be ashamed, I said, to look so antique.
(And her only thirty-one.)
I can't help it, she said, pulling a long face,
It's them pills I took, to bring it off, she said.
(She's had five already, and nearly died of young George.)   160
The chemist[4] said it would be all right, but I've never been the same.
You *are* a proper fool, I said.
Well, if Albert won't leave you alone, there it is, I said,
What you get married for if you don't want children?
HURRY UP PLEASE ITS TIME   165
Well, that Sunday Albert was home, they had a hot gammon,[5]
And they asked me in to dinner, to get the beauty of it hot—
HURRY UP PLEASE ITS TIME
HURRY UP PLEASE ITS TIME
Goonight Bill. Goonight Lou. Goonight May. Goonight.   170

---

1. Eliot's note: "Cf. the game of chess in Middleton's *Women Beware Women*."
2. Demobilized. This is one of Pound's stringent bits of editing. Eliot had written, "When Lil's husband was coming back out of the Transport Corps."
3. This is what a barkeeper in an English pub would call out at closing time.
4. A pharmacist.
5. Ham.
6. From Ophelia's farewell speech (*Hamlet*, IV, v) before she drowns herself.

Ta ta. Goonight. Goonight.
Good night, ladies, good night, sweet ladies, good night, good night.[6]

III. THE FIRE SERMON[7]

The river's tent is broken; the last fingers of leaf
Clutch and sink into the wet bank. The wind
Crosses the brown land, unheard. The nymphs are departed.   175
Sweet Thames, run softly, till I end my song.[8]
The river bears no empty bottles, sandwich papers,
Silk handkerchiefs, cardboard boxes, cigarette ends
Or other testimony of summer nights. The nymphs are departed.
And their friends, the loitering heirs of City directors;   180
Departed, have left no addresses.
By the waters of Leman I sat down and wept . . .[9]
Sweet Thames, run softly till I end my song,
Sweet Thames, run softly, for I speak not loud or long.
But at my back in a cold blast I hear[1]   185
The rattle of the bones, and chuckle spread from ear to ear.

A rat crept softly through the vegetation
Dragging its slimy belly on the bank
While I was fishing in the dull canal
On a winter evening round behind the gashouse   190
Musing upon the king my brother's wreck[2]
And on the king my father's death before him.
White bodies naked on the low damp ground
And bones cast in a little low dry garret,
Rattled by the rat's foot only, year to year.   195
But at my back from time to time I hear[3]
The sound of horns and motors, which shall bring[4]
Sweeney to Mrs. Porter in the spring.
O the moon shone bright on Mrs. Porter
And on her daughter   200

---

7.   See Eliot's note to line 308. He had studied Buddhism at Harvard. In this sermon, Buddha advised his followers to transcend the fires of passion and become detached from earthly sensations.
8.   Eliot's note: "V. Spenser, *Prothalamion*." In l. 176, he quotes the refrain of Spenser's wedding-song in which nymphs figure as "lovely Daughters of the Flood." Eliot's poem incorporates both Thames-maidens and Wagner's Rhine-maidens from *Die Götterdämmerung*. See lines 292–306.
9.   Echoes Psalm 137, "By the waters of Babylon, there we sat down, yea, we wept, when we remembered Zion." The Swiss city of Geneva sits on Lake Leman. Eliot was recovering near there when he finished *The Waste Land*. "Leman" is also a renaissance term (now obsolete) meaning "mistress" or "lover."
1.   Echoes Andrew Marvell's "To His Coy Mistress": "But at my back I always hear / Time's wingéd chariot hurrying near . . ."
2.   Eliot's note: "Cf. *The Tempest*, I, ii." See footnote to line 48.
3.   Eliot's note: "Cf. Marvell's *To His Coy Mistress*."
4.   Eliot's note: "Cf. Day, *Parliament of Bees*: 'When of the sudden, listening you shall hear, / A noise of horns and hunting, which shall bring / Actaeon to Diana in the spring, / Where all shall see her naked skin . . .'" These lines are from a satirical masque by English poet John Day (1574?–1640). When the hunter Actaeon glimpsed the virgin goddess Diana bathing in the woods, she changed him into a stag; he was then chased down and killed by his own dogs.

They wash their feet in soda water[5]
Et O ces voix d'enfants, chantant dans la coupole![6]

Twit twit twit
Jug jug jug jug jug jug
So rudely forc'd.   205
Tereu[7]

Unreal City
Under the brown fog of a winter noon
Mr. Eugenides, the Smyrna merchant
Unshaven, with a pocket full of currants   210
C.i.f. London: documents at sight,[8]
Asked me in demotic French
To luncheon at the Cannon Street Hotel[9]
Followed by a weekend at the Metropole.[1]

At the violet hour, when the eyes and back   215
Turn upward from the desk, when the human engine waits
Like a taxi throbbing waiting,
I Tiresias, though blind, throbbing between two lives,[2]
Old man with wrinkled female breasts, can see
At the violet hour, the evening hour that strives   220
Homeward, and brings the sailor home from sea,[3]
The typist home at teatime, clears her breakfast, lights
Her stove, and lays out food in tins.
Out of the window perilously spread

5. Eliot's note: "I do not know the origin of the ballad from which these lines are taken: it was reported to me from Sydney, Australia." The song was sung by Australian troops during World War I; Mrs. Porter and her daughter were Cairo prostitutes reputed to have infected soldiers with venereal disease.
6. Eliot's note: "V. Verlaine, *Parsifal*." (French) "And O those voices of children, singing in the dome!" Verlaine's poem is about a quest for the Holy Grail, and the allusion echoes the quest motifs of *The Waste Land*. In Wagner's opera based on the same story, an enchantress washes the knight's feet so he may enter the Grail Castle. There he heals the ailing Fisher King. The opera concludes with a chorus of children praising Christ's power.
7. Another allusion to Philomela and Tereus.
8. Eliot's note: "the currants were quoted at a price 'carriage and insurance free to London'; and the Bill of Lading, etc., were to be handed to the buyer upon payment of the sight draft."
9. A London hotel used by businessmen traveling to and from the Continent. Also a clandestine meeting place for homosexuals.
1. Seaside resort hotel in Brighton.
2. Eliot's note: "Tiresias, although a mere spectator and not indeed a 'character,' is yet the most important personage in the poem, uniting all the rest. Just as the one-eyed merchant, seller of currants, melts into the Phoenician Sailor, and the latter is not wholly distinct from Ferdinand Prince of Naples, so all the women are one woman, and the two sexes meet in Tiresias. What Tiresias sees, in fact, is the substance of the poem. The whole passage from Ovid is of great anthropological interest . . . " The Latin passage he then quotes (*Metamorphoses* III, 320–338) tells the story in which Tiresias separated two copulating snakes and was transformed into a woman. Years later he repeated the gesture and was changed back into a man. Since he had been both man and woman, Jupiter and Juno asked him to settle a dispute: do men or women enjoy sex more? Tiresias answered that women do, which made Juno furious. She blinded him, but Jupiter took pity on him and gave him the gift of prophecy.
3. Eliot's note: "This may not appear as exact as Sappho's lines, but I had in mind the 'longshore' or 'dory' fisherman, who returns at nightfall." Eliot refers here to Fragment 149 by the Greek lyric poet (7th century, BC): "Evening Star, that returns home all that the shining Dawn has sent far and wide, you bring back the sheep, the goat, and the child back to the mother." Line 221 also echoes Robert Louis Stevenson's "Requiem," "Home is the sailor home from the sea."

Her drying combinations touched by the sun's last rays,   225
On the divan are piled (at night her bed)
Stockings, slippers, camisoles, and stays.
I Tiresias, old man with wrinkled dugs
Perceived the scene, and foretold the rest—
I too awaited the expected guest.   230
He, the young man carbuncular,[4] arrives,
A small house agent's clerk, with one bold stare,
One of the low on whom assurance sits
As a silk hat on a Bradford millionaire.[5]
The time is now propitious, as he guesses,   235
The meal is ended, she is bored and tired,
Endeavours to engage her in caresses
Which still are unreproved, if undesired.
Flushed and decided, he assaults at once;
Exploring hands encounter no defence;   240
His vanity requires no response,
And makes a welcome of indifference.
(And I Tiresias have foresuffered all
Enacted on this same divan or bed;
I who have sat by Thebes below the wall[6]   245
And walked among the lowest of the dead.)
Bestows one final patronising kiss,
And gropes his way, finding the stairs unlit . . .

She turns and looks a moment in the glass,
Hardly aware of her departed lover;   250
Her brain allows one half-formed thought to pass:
"Well now that's done: and I'm glad it's over."
When lovely woman stoops to folly and
Paces about her room again, alone,
She smoothes her hair with automatic hand,   255
And puts a record on the gramophone.[7]

"This music crept by me upon the waters"[8]
And along the Strand, up Queen Victoria Street.
O City city, I can sometimes hear
Beside a public bar in Lower Thames Street,   260
The pleasant whining of a mandoline
And a clatter and a chatter from within
Where fishmen lounge at noon: where the walls

4. May refer to acne, rather than to infected boils.
5. Refers to a war profiteer, thus *nouveau riche* and by implication low class.
6. Alludes to the Oedipus cycle of Sophocles; Tiresias had foretold the fall of Oedipus and Creon, two Theban kings.
7. Eliot's note: "V. Goldsmith, the song in *The Vicar of Wakefield*." In Oliver Goldsmith's novel (1766), Olivia, victim of seduction, sings "When lovely woman stoops to folly / And finds too late that men betray, / What charm can soothe her melancholy, / What art can wash her guilt away?"
8. Eliot's note: "V. *The Tempest* as above." See footnote to line 48.

Of Magnus Martyr[9] hold
Inexplicable splendour of Ionian white and gold.   265

    The river sweats[1]
    Oil and tar
    The barges drift
    With the turning tide
    Red sails   270
    Wide
    To leeward, swing on the heavy spar.
    The barges wash
    Drifting logs
    Down Greenwich reach   275
    Past the Isle of Dogs.[2]
          Weialala leia
          Wallala leialala

    Elizabeth and Leicester[3]
    Beating oars   280
    The stern was formed
    A gilded shell
    Red and gold
    The brisk swell
    Rippled both shores   285
    Southwest wind
    Carried down stream
    The peal of bells
    White towers
          Weialala leia   290
          Wallala leialala

    "Trams and dusty trees.
    Highbury bore me. Richmond and Kew
    Undid me.[4] By Richmond I raised my knees
    Supine on the floor of a narrow canoe."   295

    "My feet are at Moorgate, and my heart
    Under my feet. After the event

9.   Eliot's note: "The interior of St. Magnus Martyr is to my mind one of the finest among Wren's interiors. See *The Proposed Demolition of Nineteen City Churches:* (P. S. King & Son, Ltd.). The London church, constructed in 1676, was designed by Sir Christopher Wren.
1.   Eliot's note: "The song of the (three) Thames-daughters begins here. From line 292 to 306 inclusive they speak in turn. V. *Götterdämmerung*, III, i: the Rhine-daughters." In Wagner's 1874 opera, the Rhine daughters mourn the despoiling of their river. Eliot also includes in these lines details taken from the opening description of the Congo river in Joseph Conrad's *Heart of Darkness* (1899).
2.   A peninsula on the left bank of the Thames, opposite Greenwich.
3.   Eliot's note: "V. Froude, *Elizabeth*, Vol. I, ch. iv., letter of De Quadra to Philip of Spain: 'In the afternoon we were in a barge, watching the games on the river. (The queen) was alone with Lord Robert [Earl of Leicester] and myself on the poop, when they began to talk nonsense, and went so far that Lord Robert at last said, as I was on the spot there was no reason why they should not be married if the queen pleased."
4.   Eliot's note: "Cf. *Purgatorio*, V. 133: *Ricorditi di me, che son la Pia; / Siena mi fe', disfecemi Maremma.*" In Purgatorio V, 133 the ghost of Lady Pia de Tolomei tells Dante, Remember me, who am La Pia; Siena made me, Maremma undid me," because her husband murdered her in Maremma. Highbury is a suburb in Northeast London; Richmond and Kew are two riverside districts on the Thames.

He wept. He promised 'a new start.'
I made no comment. What should I resent?"

"On Margate Sands.[5]   300
I can connect
Nothing with nothing.
The broken fingernails of dirty hands.
My people humble people who expect
Nothing."   305
        la la

To Carthage then I came[6]

Burning burning burning burning[7]
O Lord Thou pluckest me out[8]
O Lord Thou pluckest
                                                        310

burning

IV. DEATH BY WATER[9]

Phlebas the Phoenician, a fortnight dead,
Forgot the cry of gulls, and the deep sea swell
And the profit and loss.
        A current under sea   315
Picked his bones in whispers. As he rose and fell
He passed the stages of his age and youth
Entering the whirlpool.
        Gentile or Jew
O you who turn the wheel and look to windward,   320
Consider Phlebas, who was once handsome and tall as you.

V. WHAT THE THUNDER SAID[1]

After the torchlight red on sweaty faces
After the frosty silence in the gardens
After the agony in stony places

---

5. In 1921 Eliot convalesced in Margate, a beach resort, before undergoing therapy in Switzerland.
6. Eliot's note: "V. St. Augustine's *Confessions:* "to Carthage then I came, where a cauldron of unholy loves sang all about mine ears."
7. Eliot's note: "The complete text of the Buddha's Fire Sermon (which corresponds in importance to the Sermon on the Mount) from which these words are taken, will be found translated in the late Henry Clarke Warren's *Buddhism in Translation* (Harvard Oriental Series). Mr. Warren was one of the great pioneers of Buddhist studies in the Occident."
8. Eliot's note: "From St. Augustine's *Confessions* again. The collocation of these two representatives of eastern and western asceticism, as the culmination of this part of the poem, is not an accident."
9. This section parallels the last stanza of Eliot's poem in French, "Dans le Restaurant." See Milton's "Lycidas" for an example in the pastoral tradition of death by drowning, and death that leads to resurrection. This theme is also echoed in the novels of Charles Dickens, particularly *Our Mutual Friend.*
1. Eliot's note: "In the first part of Part V three themes are employed: the journey to Emmaus, the approach to the Chapel Perilous (See Miss Weston's book) and the present decay of eastern Europe." See Luke 24:13-34 for the story of the journey to Emmaus, in which the risen Christ joins two of his disciples as they walk down a road, but they don't recognize him. Lines 322–330 allude to the events culminating in the crucifixion. With regard to the Chapel Perilous, the final stage of the Grail quest, readers might also refer to *Sir Gawain and the Green Knight.* Thunder is the voice of God, as evoked in the Hindu Upanishads.

The shouting and the crying   325
Prison and palace and reverberation
Of thunder of spring over distant mountains
He who is living is now dead
We who were living are now dying
With a little patience   330

Here is no water but only rock
Rock and no water and the sandy road
The road winding above among the mountains
Which are mountains of rock without water
If there were water we should stop and drink   335
Amongst the rock one cannot stop or think
Sweat is dry and feet are in the sand
If there were only water amongst the rock
Dead mountain mouth of carious teeth that cannot spit
Here one can neither stand nor lie nor sit   340
There is not even silence in the mountains
But dry sterile thunder without rain
There is not even solitude in the mountains
But red sullen faces sneer and snarl
From doors of mudcracked houses   345
                                    If there were water
        And no rock
        If there were rock
        And also water
        And water   350
        A spring
        A pool among the rock
        If there were the sound of water only
        Not the cicada
        And dry grass singing   355
        But sound of water over a rock
        Where the hermit-thrush sings in the pine trees[2]
        Drip drop drip drop drop drop drop
        But there is no water

Who is the third who walks always beside you?[3]   360
When I count, there are only you and I together
But when I look ahead up the white road

---

2. Eliot's note: "This is *Turdus aonalaschkae pallasii*, the hermit-thrush which I have heard in Quebec County. Chapman says (*Handbook of Birds of Eastern North America*) 'it is most at home in secluded woodland and thickety retreats. . . . Its notes are not remarkable for variety or volume, but in purity and sweetness of tone and exquisite modulation they are unequalled.' Its 'water-dripping song' is justly celebrated." Eliot also alludes to the hermit-thrush of Walt Whitman's elegy for President Lincoln, "When Lilacs Last in the Door-Yard Bloom'd."
3. Eliot's note: "The following lines were stimulated by the account of one of the Antarctic expeditions (I forget which, but I think one of Shackleton's): it was related that the party of explorers, at the extremity of their strength, had the constant delusion that there was *one more member* than could actually be counted." These lines evoke not only a passage from Ernest Shackleton's *South* (1919), but also the journey to Emmaus.

There is always another one walking beside you
Gliding wrapt in a brown mantle, hooded
I do not know whether a man or a woman   365
—But who is that on the other side of you?

What is that sound high in the air[4]
Murmur of maternal lamentation
Who are those hooded hordes swarming
Over endless plains, stumbling in cracked earth   370
Ringed by the flat horizon only
What is the city over the mountains
Cracks and reforms and bursts in the violet air
Falling towers
Jerusalem Athens Alexandria   375
Vienna London
Unreal

A woman drew her long black hair out tight
And fiddled whisper music on those strings
And bats with baby faces in the violet light   380
Whistled, and beat their wings
And crawled head downward down a blackened wall
And upside down in air were towers
Tolling reminiscent bells, that kept the hours
And voices singing out of empty cisterns and exhausted wells   385

In this decayed hole among the mountains
In the faint moonlight, the grass is singing
Over the tumbled graves, about the chapel[5]
There is the empty chapel, only the wind's home.
It has no windows, and the door swings,   390
Dry bones can harm no one.
Only a cock stood on the rooftree
Co co rico co co rico
In a flash of lightning. Then a damp gust
Bringing rain   395

Ganga[6] was sunken, and the limp leaves
Waited for rain, while the black clouds
Gathered far distant, over Himavant.[7]
The jungle crouched, humped in silence.

---

4. In his note to lines 367–377, Eliot quotes a long passage in German from Herman Hesse's *Blick ins Chaos* (1920) (*A Glimpse into Chaos*): "Already half of Europe, or at least half of Eastern Europe, is on the road toward chaos, driving drunkenly in holy madness along the edge of the abyss, and singing drunken hymns like Dmitri Karamazov sang. The citizen, offended, laughs at these songs, the saint and the prophet listen to them with tears." The quotation refers to the 1917 Russian Revolution; Dmitri Karamazov features prominently in Fyodor Dostoevski's *The Brothers Karamazov* (1880). The "maternal lamentation" in these lines may also refer to the women weeping at the crucifixion.
5. Suggests the Perilous Chapel, a fearful place that the knight must enter on his quest for the Grail. Gawain must enter such a place before he battles the Green Knight.
6. One of the sacred rivers of India, the Ganges.
7. The Himalayan mountain range.

Then spoke the thunder   400
DA[8]
Datta: what have we given?
My friend, blood shaking my heart
The awful daring of a moment's surrender
Which an age of prudence can never retract   405
By this, and this only, we have existed
Which is not to be found in our obituaries
Or in memories draped by the beneficent spider[9]
Or under seals broken by the lean solicitor
In our empty rooms   410
DA
Dayadhvam: I have heard the key[1]
Turn in the door once and turn once only
We think of the key, each in his prison
Thinking of the key, each confirms a prison   415
Only at nightfall, aethereal rumours
Revive for a moment a broken Coriolanus[2]
DA
Damyata: the boat responded
Gaily, to the hand expert with sail and oar   420
The sea was calm, your heart would have responded
Gaily, when invited, beating obedient
To controlling hands

                          I sat upon the shore
Fishing,[3] with the arid plain behind me   425
Shall I at least set my lands in order?[4]
London Bridge is falling down falling down falling down

8. Eliot's note: "'Datta, dayadhvam, damyata' (Give, sympathise, control). The fable of the meaning of the Thunder is found in the *Brihadaranyaka—Upanishad, 5,* I. A translation is found in Deussen's *Sechzig Upanishads des Veda,* p. 489." In the fable, the creator Prajapti's thunderous command "DA" is interpreted differently by gods (who hear it as "Damyatta," "control yourselves"); men (who hear it as "Datta," "give alms"); and demons (who hear it as "dayadhvam," "have compassion"). In the poem, the Russian word for "yes" is also echoed.
9. Eliot's note: "Cf. Webster, *The White Devil,* V, vi: '. . . they'll remarry / Ere the worm pierce your winding-sheet, ere the spider / Make a thin curtain for your epitaphs.' These lines condemn the inconstancy of women.
1. Eliot's note: "Cf. *Inferno,* xxxiii. 46: *'ed io sentii chiavar l'uscio di sotto / all'orrible torre.'* Also F. H. Bradley, *Appearance and Reality,* p. 346. 'My external sensations are no less private to myself than are my thoughts or my feelings. In either case my experience falls within my own circle, a circle closed on the outside; and, with all its elements alike, every sphere is opaque to the others which surround it. . . . In brief, regarded as an existence which appears in a soul, the whole world for each is peculiar and private to that soul.'" The lines from the *Inferno* are spoken by the traitor, Count Ugolino, who was imprisoned with his sons and grandsons in a tower, where they all starved to death: "And below I heard them nailing up / the door of the horrible tower."
2. Proud Roman general in the play of the same name by Shakespeare; after being exiled from Rome, Coriolanus leads the enemy in an attack on the city and is then killed by conspirators, his death cheered on by a mob.
3. Eliot's note: "V. Weston: *From Ritual to Romance;* chapter on the Fisher King."
4. In Isaiah 38:1 the Lord says, "Set thine house in order: for thou shalt die, and not live."

Poi s'ascose nel foco che gli affina[5]
Quando fiam uti chelidon[6]—O swallow swallow[7]
Le Prince d'Aquitaine à la tour abolie[8]   430
These fragments I have shored against my ruins
Why then Ile fit you. Hieronymo's mad againe.[9]
Datta. Dayadhvam. Damyata.
          Shantih shantih shantih[1]

                                 1922

The Hollow Men[2]

Mistah Kurtz—he dead.[3]

A penny for the Old Guy[4]

I

We are the hollow men
We are the stuffed men
Leaning together
Headpiece filled with straw. Alas!
Our dried voices, when   5
We whisper together
Are quiet and meaningless
As wind in dry grass
Or rats' feet over broken glass
In our dry cellar   10

Shape without form, shade without colour,
Paralysed force, gesture without motion;[5]

---

5. Eliot's note: "V. *Purgatorio*, xxvi, 148." He then quotes the Italian, "'*Ara vos prec per aquella valor / que vos guida al som de l'escalina, / sovegna vos a temps de ma dolor.' / Poi s'ascose nel foco che gli affina.*" Here, the Provencal poet Arnaut Daniel, punished in Purgatory for the sin of Lust, tells Dante, "'Now, by the power that guides you / to the summit of the stair, I pray you; / remember in due time my pain," and Dante adds "Then, in the fire that purifies them, he hid."
6. Eliot's note: "V. *Pervigilium Veneris*. Cf. Philomela in Parts II and III." (Latin) "When shall I be like the swallow?" Philomela asks in "The Vigil of Venus," the anonymous poem cited here by Eliot.
7. The phrase appears as a refrain in "The Princess," a poem by Alfred Lord Tennyson. Philomela's sister, Procne, was turned into a swallow (see footnote to line 99).
8. Eliot's note: "V. Gerard de Nerval, Sonnet *El Desdichado*." (French) In Nerval's sonnet, the poet compares himself to the disinherited "Prince of Aquitaine in the ruined tower."
9. Eliot's note: "V. Kyd's *Spanish Tragedy*." The subtitle of Thomas Kyd's 1592 play, *The Spanish Tragedy*, is *Hieronymo Is Mad Againe*. Feigning madness over murder of his son, when asked to write a play for the court Hieronymo answers "Why then Ile fit [serve] you!" He stages a work composed of fragments of poetry in different languages, and, acting one of the parts, kills his son's murderers and then himself.
1. Eliot's note: "Shantih. Repeated as here, a formal ending to an Upanishad. 'The Peace which passeth all understanding' is a feeble translation of the content of this word."
2. Derives from Shakespeare's *Julius Caesar* (IV, ii), in which Brutus meditates upon the hollow men who murdered Caesar.
3. Spoken in Joseph Conrad's *Heart of Darkness*. Kurtz's last words were "The horror—the horror!"
4. "A penny for the Old Guy" is a children's saying on Guy Fawkes Day, when stuffed effigies of Guy Fawkes, a leader in the Gunpowder Plot of 1605, are set on fire.
5. These lines recall the shades in Dante's *Inferno*. One may read the sections of this poem as fragmented reflections on the journey of Dante in the *Divine Comedy*.

Those who have crossed
With direct eyes, to death's other Kingdom
Remember us—if at all—not as lost   15
Violent souls, but only
As the hollow men
The stuffed men.

II

Eyes I dare not meet in dreams
In death's dream kingdom   20
These do not appear:
There, the eyes are
Sunlight on a broken column
There, is a tree swinging
And voices are   25
In the wind's singing
More distant and more solemn
Than a fading star.

Let me be no nearer
In death's dream kingdom   30
Let me also wear
Such deliberate disguises
Rat's coat, crowskin, crossed staves
In a field
Behaving as the wind behaves   35
No nearer—

Not that final meeting
In the twilight kingdom

III

This is the dead land
This is the cactus land   40
Here the stone images
Are raised, here they receive
The supplication of a dead man's hand
Under the twinkle of a fading star.

Is it like this   45
In death's other kingdom
Waking alone
At the hour when we are
Trembling with tenderness
Lips that would kiss   50
Form prayers to broken stone.

IV

The eyes are not here
There are no eyes here

In this valley of dying stars
In this hollow valley   55
This broken jaw of our lost kingdoms

In this last of meeting places
We grope together
And avoid speech
Gathered on this beach of the tumid river[6]   60

Sightless, unless
The eyes reappear
As the perpetual star
Multifoliate rose[7]
Of death's twilight kingdom   65
The hope only
Of empty men.

V

Here we go round the prickly pear[8]
Prickly pear prickly pear
Here we go round the prickly pear   70
At five o'clock in the morning.

Between the idea[9]
And the reality
Between the motion
And the act   75
Falls the Shadow
                    For Thine is the Kingdom[1]

Between the conception
And the creation
Between the emotion   80
And the response
Falls the Shadow
                    Life is very long[2]

Between the desire
And the spasm   85
Between the potency
And the existence
Between the essence

6. Suggests both the River Acheron in Hades and Conrad's Congo.
7. From Dante's *Paradiso*, Canto XXX, in which the Empyrean, or divine city, is depicted as a rose, its many petals containing all the blessed.
8. These lines parody the children's song, "Here we go round the mulberry bush / On a cold and frosty morning."
9. Lines 72 through 90 parallel a passage in *Julius Caesar* (II, i) when Brutus and the conspirators are plotting to assassinate Caesar.
1. From the Lord's Prayer (see I Chronicles 29:11, 15).
2. Quotes Conrad's *An Outcast of the Islands* (1896).

And the descent
Falls the Shadow   90

For Thine is the Kingdom

For Thine is
Life is
For Thine is the

This the way the world ends   95
This is the way the world ends
This is the way the world ends
Not with a bang but a whimper.[3]

1925

Journey of the Magi[4]

"A cold coming we had of it,
Just the worst time of the year
For a journey, and such a long journey:
The ways deep and the weather sharp,
The very dead of winter."[5]   5
And the camels galled, sore-footed, refractory,
Lying down in the melting snow.
There were times we regretted
The summer palaces on slopes, the terraces,
And the silken girls bringing sherbet.   10
Then the camel men cursing and grumbling
And running away, and wanting their liquor and women,
And the night-fires going out, and the lack of shelters,
And the cities hostile and the towns unfriendly
And the villages dirty and charging high prices: 15
A hard time we had of it.
At the end we preferred to travel all night,
Sleeping in snatches,
With the voices singing in our ears, saying
That this was all folly.   20

Then at dawn we came down to a temperate valley,
Wet, below the snow line, smelling of vegetation;
With a running stream and a water-mill beating the darkness,
And three trees on the low sky.[6]
And an old white horse[7] galloped away in the meadow.   25

---

3. Alludes to Kipling's poem "Danny Deever," in which the soul of Danny whimpers overhead following his execution for the murder of a fellow soldier. See Eliot's introduction to *A Choice of Kipling's Verse* (1941).
4. The story of the three wise men (Magi) is told in Matthew 2:1–12.
5. These lines are adapted from a sermon preached by Lancelot Andrewes for King James I on Christmas in 1622.
6. The three crosses on Calvary. See Luke 23:32–33.
7. In Revelation 6:2 and 19:11–14, Christ rides a white horse.

Then we came to a tavern with vine-leaves over the lintel,
Six hands at an open door dicing for pieces of silver,[8]
And feet kicking the empty wine-skins.
But there was no information, and so we continued
And arrived at evening, not a moment too soon   30
Finding the place; it was (you may say) satisfactory.

All this was a long time ago, I remember,
And I would do it again, but set down
This set down
This: were we led all that way for   35
Birth or Death? There was a Birth, certainly,
We had evidence and no doubt. I had seen birth and death,
But had thought they were different; this Birth was
Hard and bitter agony for us, like Death, our death.
We returned to our places, these Kingdoms,   40
But no longer at ease here, in the old dispensation,[9]
With an alien people clutching their gods.
I should be glad of another death.

1927

Ash-Wednesday[1]

I[2]

Because I do not hope to turn again
Because I do not hope
Because I do not hope to turn
Desiring this man's gift and that man's scope[3]
I no longer strive to strive towards such things   5
(Why should the aged eagle[4] stretch its wings?)
Why should I mourn
The vanished power of the usual reign?

Because I do not hope to know again
The infirm glory of the positive hour   10
Because I do not think
Because I know I shall not know
The one veritable transitory power
Because I cannot drink
There, where trees flower, and springs flow, for there is nothing again   15

8. There are distorted allusions here to Matthew 26:14–15 and 27:35.
9. Older, pagan religions about to be displaced by Christianity. See Ephesians 3:2–4, in which Paul refers to "the dispensation of the Grace of God."
1. Refers to the first day of Lent. On this day the priest marks the foreheads of worshippers with ashes in the form of a cross, saying, "Remember, O man, that thou are dust, and unto dust thou shalt return."
2. Originally published under the title "Perch'io non spero," quoted from Italian poet Guido Cavalcanti's poem in which an exiled lover cannot hope to see the beloved again.
3. Quotes Shakespeare's Sonnet 29.
4. The aged eagle suggests a Christian allegory of renewal through baptism.

Because I know that time is always time
And place is always and only place
And what is actual is actual only for one time
And only for one place
I rejoice that things are as they are and   20
I renounce the blessèd face
And renounce the voice
Because I cannot hope to turn again
Consequently I rejoice, having to construct something
Upon which to rejoice   25

And pray to God to have mercy upon us
And I pray that I may forget
These matters that with myself I too much discuss
Too much explain
Because I do not hope to turn again   30
Let these words answer
For what is done, not to be done again
May the judgement not be too heavy upon us

Because these wings are no longer wings to fly
But merely vans to beat the air   35
The air which is now thoroughly small and dry
Smaller and dryer than the will
Teach us to care and not to care
Teach us to sit still.

Pray for us sinners now and at the hour of our death   40
Pray for us now and at the hour of our death.[5]

II[6]

Lady, three white leopards sat under a juniper-tree[7]
In the cool of the day, having fed to satiety
On my legs my heart my liver and that which had been contained
In the hollow round of my skull. And God said   45
Shall these bones live?[8] shall these
Bones live? And that which had been contained
In the bones (which were already dry) said chirping:
Because of the goodness of this Lady
And because of her loveliness, and because   50
She honours the Virgin in meditation,
We shine with brightness. And I who am here dissembled
Proffer my deeds to oblivion, and my love
To the posterity of the desert and the fruit of the gourd.
It is this which recovers   55
My guts the strings of my eyes and the indigestible portions

5. The closing of the "Hail Mary," asking for her intercession on behalf of all sinners.
6. Originally entitled "Salutation."
7. Eliot refused to comment on the meaning of this line, though critics have noted that leopards were God's agents of destruction in Jeremiah and Hosea.
8. See Ezekiel 37:3.

Which the leopards reject. The Lady is withdrawn
In a white gown, to contemplation, in a white gown.
Let the whiteness of bones atone to forgetfulness.
There is no life in them. As I am forgotten   60
And would be forgotten, so I would forget
Thus devoted, concentrated in purpose. And God said
Prophesy to the wind, to the wind only for only
The wind will listen. And the bones sang chirping
With the burden of the grasshopper, saying   65

Lady of silences[9]
Calm and distressed
Torn and most whole
Rose of memory
Rose of forgetfulness   70
Exhausted and life-giving
Worried reposeful
The single Rose
Is now the Garden
Where all loves end   75
Terminate torment
Of love satisfied
The greater torment
Of love satisfied
End of the endless   80
Journey to no end
Conclusion of all that
Is inconclusible
Speech without word and
Word of no speech   85
Grace to the Mother
For the Garden
Where all love ends.

Under a juniper-tree the bones sang, scattered and shining
We are glad to be scattered, we did little good to each other,   90
Under a tree in the cool of the day, with the blessing of sand,
Forgetting themselves and each other, united
In the quiet of the desert. This is the land which ye
Shall divide by lot. And neither division nor unity
Matters. This is the land. We have our inheritance.   95

III[1]

At the first turning of the second stair[2]
I turned and saw below

9. Lines 66–88 echo the Catholic Litany to the Blessed Virgin Mary, which refers to her as a rose.
1. Originally entitled "Som de l'escalina," Italian for the "Summit of the Stairway," from a speech of Arnaut Daniel to Dante in Canto XXVI of *Purgatorio*. Daniel was consigned to Purgatory for lustfulness.
2. The slow ascent in lines 96–106 parallels Dante's climb up Mount Purgatory. Critics have also observed that the opening stanza in this section borrows from Henry James's ghost story, *The Turn of the Screw*.

The same shape twisted on the banister
Under the vapour in the fetid air
Struggling with the devil of the stairs who wears   100
The deceitful face of hope and of despair.

At the second turning of the second stair
I left them twisting, turning below;
There were no more faces and the stair was dark,
Damp, jaggèd, like an old man's mouth drivelling, beyond repair,   105
Or the toothed gullet of an agèd shark.

At the first turning of the third stair
Was a slotted window bellied like the fig's fruit
And beyond the hawthorn blossom and a pasture scene
The broadbacked figure drest in blue and green   110
Enchanted the maytime with an antique flute.
Blown hair is sweet, brown hair over the mouth blown,
Lilac and brown hair;
Distraction, music of the flute, stops and steps of the mind over the third stair,
Fading, fading; strength beyond hope and despair   115
Climbing the third stair.

Lord, I am not worthy
Lord, I am not worthy

      but speak the word only.

IV[3]

Who walked between the violet and the violet[4]   120
Who walked between
The various ranks of varied green
Going in white and blue, in Mary's colour,
Talking of trivial things
In ignorance and in knowledge of eternal dolour   125
Who moved among the others as they walked,
Who then made strong the fountains and made fresh the springs

Made cool the dry rock and made firm the sand
In blue of larkspur, blue of Mary's colour,
Sovegna vos[5]   130

Here are the years that walk between, bearing
Away the fiddles and the flutes, restoring
One who moves in the time between sleep and waking, wearing

White light folded, sheathed about her, folded.
The new years walk, restoring   135
Through a bright cloud of tears, the years, restoring

---

3. Originally entitled "Vestita di Color di Fiamma," Italian for "Clad in Color of Flame," like the image of Beatrice I *Purgatorio*, Canto XXX.
4. Violet is the liturgical color of penitence and intercession.
5. (Italian) "Be mindful." In Canto XXVI of *Purgatorio*, Arnaut Daniel asks Dante to remember him in his pain.

With a new verse the ancient rhyme. Redeem
The time.[6] Redeem
The unread vision in the higher dream
While jewelled unicorns draw by the gilded hearse.   140

The silent sister veiled in white and blue[7]
Between the yews, behind the garden god,
Whose flute is breathless,[8] bent her head and signed but spoke no word

But the fountain sprang up and the bird sang down
Redeem the time, redeem the dream   145
The token of the word unheard, unspoken

Till the wind shake a thousand whispers from the yew

After this our exile[9]

V[1]

If the lost word is lost, if the spent word is spent
If the unheard, unspoken   150
Word is unspoken, unheard;
Still is the unspoken word, the Word unheard,
The Word without a word, the Word within
The world and for the world;
And the light shone in darkness and   155
Against the Word the unstilled world still whirled
About the centre of the silent Word.

O my people, what have I done unto thee.[2]

Where shall the word be found, where will the word
Resound? Not here, there is not enough silence   160
Not on the sea or on the islands, not
On the mainland, in the desert or the rain land,
For those who walk in darkness
Both in the day time and in the night time
The right time and the right place are not here   165
No place of grace for those who avoid the face[3]
No time to rejoice for those who walk among noise and deny the voice

6. In his essay, "Thoughts after Lambeth," Eliot wrote, "Redeeming the time: so that the Faith may be preserved alive through the dark ages before us; to renew and rebuild civilization and save the world from suicide." He was echoing Paul in Colossians 4:5.
7. Lines 140–41 allude to the vision of Beatrice in *Purgatorio,* Canto XXX.
8. The garden god with the flute suggests both Priapus, son of Dionysus and Aphrodite and a god of fertility, and Pan, the god of shepherds and hunters. There may be a pun on "flute" here, as the attribute of Priapus was the phallus.
9. From a Roman Catholic prayer: ". . . and after this our exile show us unto the blessed fruit of the womb, Jesus."
1. Originally entitled "La Sua Volontade," Italian for "His Will," from a speech of Piccarda Donati to Dante in *Paradiso,* Canto III. The whole line in Dante translates, "And in His will is our peace."
2. A Good Friday saying of repentance.
3. In Canto IV of *Paradiso,* Dante lowers his eyes from the radiance of Beatrice.

Will the veiled sister pray for
Those who walk in darkness, who chose thee and oppose thee,
Those who are torn on the horn between season and season, time and time,
      between   170
Hour and hour, word and word, power and power, those who wait
In darkness? Will the veiled sister pray
For children at the gate
Who will not go away and cannot pray:
Pray for those who chose and oppose   175

      O my people, what have I done unto thee.

Will the veiled sister between the slender
Yew trees pray for those who offend her
And are terrified and cannot surrender
And affirm before the world and deny between the rocks   180
In the last desert between the last blue rocks
The desert in the garden the garden in the desert
Of drouth, spitting from the mouth the withered apple-seed.

      O my people.

VI

Although I do not hope to turn again   185
Although I do not hope
Although I do not hope to turn

Wavering between the profit and the loss
In this brief transit where the dreams cross
The dreamcrossed twilight between birth and dying   190
(Bless me father)[4] though I do not wish to wish these things
From the wide window towards the granite shore
The white sails still fly seaward, seaward flying
Unbroken wings

And the lost heart stiffens and rejoices   195
In the lost lilac and the lost sea voices
And the weak spirit quickens to rebel
For the bent golden-rod and the lost sea smell
Quickens to recover
The cry of quail and the whirling plover   200
And the blind eye creates
The empty forms between the ivory gates[5]
And smell renews the salt savour of the sandy earth

This is the time of tension between dying and birth
The place of solitude where three dreams cross   205
Between blue rocks

4. "Bless me, father, for I have sinned" are the opening words of confession in the Roman Catholic Church.
5. Dreams that are delusory pass through the ivory gates from the underworld (*Aeneid*, Book VI).

But when the voices shaken from the yew-tree drift away
Let the other yew be shaken and reply.

Blessèd sister, holy mother, spirit of the fountain, spirit of the garden,
Suffer us not to mock ourselves with falsehood   210
Teach us to care and not to care
Teach us to sit still
Even among these rocks,
Our peace in His will[6]
And even among these rocks   215
Sister, mother
And spirit of the river, spirit of the sea,
Suffer me not to be separated

And let my cry come unto Thee.[7]

                                                                                  1930

FROM Four Quartets

Burnt Norton[8]

τοῦ λό γον δ'ἐόντος ξυνοῦ ζώουσιν οἱ πολλοί
ὡς ἰδίαν ἔχοντες φρόνησιν.

I. p. 77. Fr. 2.

ὁδὸς ἄνω κάτω μία καὶ ὠυτή.

I. p. 89. Fr. 60.

Diels: *Die Fragmente der Vorsokratiker* (Herakleitos).[9]

I

Time present and time past
Are both perhaps present in time future,
And time future contained in time past.
If all time is eternally present
All time is unredeemable.[1]   5
What might have been is an abstraction[2]
Remaining a perpetual possibility
Only in a world of speculation.
What might have been and what has been
Point to one end, which is always present.   10

---

6. See footnote 19 about the title of Part V.
7. Psalm 102.
8. The title refers to a Gloucestershire manor where Eliot and is old flame, Emily Hale, walked in the rose garden in September 1935. Biographies of Eliot make it clear that Hale wanted him to resume their courtship, but that Eliot resisted.
9. (Greek) "Although the Law of Reason [Logos] is common, the majority of people live as though they had their own intelligence"; "The road up and the road down are one and the same." Both epigraphs are from the Greek philosopher Herakleitos, known for his paradoxical aphorisms.
1. See footnote 6 on page 281.
2. May refer to Eliot's relationship with Emily Hale.

Footfalls echo in the memory
Down the passage which we did not take
Towards the door we never opened
Into the rose-garden. My words echo
Thus, in your mind.

      But to what purpose   15
Disturbing the dust on a bowl of rose-leaves
I do not know.
    Other echoes
Inhabit the garden. Shall we follow?
Quick, said the bird, find them, find them,
Round the corner. Through the first gate,   20
Into our first world, shall we follow
The deception of the thrush? Into our first world.
There they were, dignified, invisible,
Moving without pressure, over the dead leaves,
In the autumn heat, through the vibrant air,[3]   25
And the bird called, in response to
The unheard music hidden in the shrubbery,
And the unseen eyebeam crossed, for the roses
Had the look of flowers that are looked at.
There they were as our guests, accepted and accepting. 30
So we moved, and they, in a formal pattern,
Along the empty alley, into the box circle,
To look down into the drained pool.
Dry the pool, dry concrete, brown edged,
And the pool was filled with water out of sunlight, 35
And the lotos rose, quietly, quietly,
The surface glittered out of heart of light,
And they were behind us, reflected in the pool.
Then a cloud passed, and the pool was empty.
Go, said the bird, for the leaves were full of children, 40
Hidden excitedly, containing laughter.
Go, go, go, said the bird: human kind
Cannot bear very much reality.
Time past and time future
What might have been and what has been   45
Point to one end, which is always present.

II

Garlic and sapphires in the mud
Clot the bedded axle-tree.[4]
The trilling wire in the blood
Sings below inveterate scars   50

---

3. Alludes to the ghosts in Kipling's short story "They."
4. A term deriving from the axle of a cart, but also referring to the axle of nature or Heaven, the shaft upon which the universe turns.

Appeasing long forgotten wars.
The dance along the artery
The circulation of the lymph
Are figured in the drift of stars
Ascend to summer in the tree   55
We move above the moving tree
In light upon the figured leaf
And hear upon the sodden floor
Below, the boarhound and the boar
Pursue their pattern as before   60
But reconciled among the stars.

At the still point of the turning world. Neither flesh nor fleshless;
Neither from nor towards; at the still point, there the dance is,
But neither arrest nor movement. And do not call it fixity,
Where past and future are gathered. Neither movement from nor towards, 65
Neither ascent nor decline. Except for the point, the still point,
There would be no dance, and there is only the dance.[5]
I can only say, *there* we have been: but I cannot say where.
And I cannot say, how long, for that is to place it in time.

The inner freedom from the practical desire,   70
The release from action and suffering, release from the inner
And the outer compulsion, yet surrounded
By a grace of sense, a white light still and moving,
Erhebung[6] without motion, concentration
Without elimination, both a new world   75
And the old made explicit, understood
In the completion of its partial ecstasy,
The resolution of its partial horror.
Yet the enchainment of past and future
Woven in the weakness of the changing body,   80
Protects mankind from heaven and damnation
Which flesh cannot endure.
                              Time past and time future
Allow but a little consciousness.
To be conscious is not to be in time
But only in time can the moment in the rose-garden,   85
The moment in the arbour where the rain beat,
The moment in the draughty church at smokefall
Be remembered; involved with past and future.
Only through time time is conquered.

III[7]

Here is a place of disaffection   90
Time before and time after

5. Eliot borrows the image of the dance from the poems of W. B. Yeats.
6. (German) "Exaltation."
7. Set in the London tube or subway.

In a dim light: neither daylight
Investing form with lucid stillness
Turning shadow into transient beauty
With slow rotation suggesting permanence   95
Nor darkness to purify the soul
Emptying the sensual with deprivation
Cleansing affection from the temporal.
Neither plenitude nor vacancy. Only a flicker
Over the strained time-ridden faces   100
Distracted from distraction by distraction
Filled with fancies and empty of meaning
Tumid apathy with no concentration
Men and bits of paper, whirled by the cold wind
That blows before and after time,   105
Wind in and out of unwholesome lungs
Time before and time after.
Eructation of unhealthy souls
Into the faded air, the torpid
Driven on the wind that sweeps the gloomy hills of London,   110
Hampstead and Clerkenwell, Campden and Putney,
Highgate, Primrose and Ludgate. Not here
Not here the darkness, in this twittering world.

Descend lower, descend only[8]
Into the world of perpetual solitude,   115
World not world, but that which is not world,
Internal darkness, deprivation
And destitution of all property,
Desiccation of the world of sense,
Evacuation of the world of fancy,   120
Inoperancy of the world of spirit;
This is the one way, and the other
Is the same, not in movement
But abstention from movement; while the world moves
In appetency, on its metalled ways   125
Of time past and time future.

IV

Time and the bell have buried the day,
The black cloud carries the sun away.
Will the sunflower turn to us, will the clematis
Stray down, bend to us; tendril and spray   130
Clutch and cling?
Chill
Fingers of yew[9] be curled

8. Refers to the descent into the Underworld, but may also refer to the Christian image of the Descent of the Dove, or Paraclete.
9. Yew trees are associated with graveyards, as in Tennyson's *In Memoriam.*

Down on us? After the kingfisher's wing
Has answered light to light, and is silent, the light is still   135
At the still point of the turning world.

V

Words move, music moves
Only in time; but that which is only living
Can only die. Words, after speech, reach
Into the silence. Only by the form, the pattern,   140
Can words or music reach
The stillness, as a Chinese jar still
Moves perpetually in its stillness.
Not the stillness of the violin, while the note lasts,
Not that only, but the co-existence,   145
Or say that the end precedes the beginning,
And the end and the beginning were always there
Before the beginning and after the end.
And all is always now. Words strain,
Crack and sometimes break, under the burden,   150
Under the tension, slip, slide, perish,
Decay with imprecision, will not stay in place,
Will not stay still. Shrieking voices
Scolding, mocking, or merely chattering,
Always assail them. The Word in the desert   155
Is most attacked by voices of temptation,
The crying shadow in the funeral dance,
The loud lament of the disconsolate chimera.

The detail of the pattern is movement,
As in the figure of the ten stairs.   160
Desire itself is movement
Not in itself desirable;
Love is itself unmoving,
Only the cause and end of movement,
Timeless, and undesiring   165
Except in the aspect of time
Caught in the form of limitation
Between un-being and being.
Sudden in a shaft of sunlight
Even while the dust moves   170
There rises the hidden laughter
Of children in the foliage
Quick now, here, now, always—
Ridiculous the waste sad time
Stretching before and after.   175

1942

---------------◦►◄ **E. E. CUMMINGS** ►◄◦---------------

(1894–1962)

Edward Estlin Cummings was born in Cambridge, Massachusetts, the son of a Harvard professor who became a Unitarian minister. He grew up surrounded by family members who encouraged creativity. He later observed, "Ever since I can remember I've written; & painted or made drawings." Having decided at age eight to be a poet, Cummings produced a poem a day for fourteen years, training himself in traditional forms and slowly becoming acquainted with the work of his Modernist contemporaries. When not attending Cambridge public schools, he vacationed with his family in Maine and at Joy Farm, the family summer home in New Hampshire. In 1911 he entered Harvard, where he studied Greek and other languages, discovered the poetry of Ezra Pound, and befriended writers like John Dos Passos, as well as friends of the arts like Scofield Thayer and James Sibley Watson. At his graduation in 1915, Cummings delivered a commencement address entitled "The New Art," extolling Modernist values. Although a champion of innovation, Cummings also (like Pound and Eliot) possessed a thorough grounding in traditional literature. He took his master's degree from Harvard in 1916, then worked briefly in New York City before joining the Norton Harjes Ambulance Corps and sailing for wartime France in 1917.

On board the ship he befriended another young American, William Slater Brown. It was Brown's letters home from France, criticizing the conduct of the war, that aroused the suspicions of the French censors, resulting in his arrest. Out of loyalty, Cummings refused to denounce his friend; both were sent in October 1917 to the detention center at la Ferté-Macé in Normandy, France. Although conditions in the camp were terrible, Cummings's letters home to his family were full of high spirits. His imprisonment, however, gave him a permanent distaste for authority and a sympathy for political dissent. Due to his father's strenuous efforts, Cummings was released after only three months and returned home. But with the United States now in the war, he was immediately drafted into the army—luckily, he was not sent back overseas. After the Armistice, he went back to New York City, determined to live by his art. With the exception of one year as a professor at Harvard (1952–53), Cummings pursued no other career for the rest of his life but writing and painting. It was not always an easy life in financial terms, but several times he benefited from grants and fellowships, as well as small inheritances from his family.

In 1920 he began to contribute to *The Dial,* an influential arts magazine owned by Thayer and Watson. Through this association, he met more writers, such as Marianne Moore, Kenneth Burke, and Edmund Wilson. He also conducted an affair with Thayer's wife, Elaine Orr, and in 1919 the lovers had a daughter. In 1922, Cummings published *The Enormous Room,* his jaunty, fictionalized account of his wartime imprisonment in France. The following year his first full-length collection of poems, *Tulips and Chimneys,* appeared. In the 1920s he published five more books of poems, a play entitled *Him,* and numerous articles for *Vanity Fair,* where he served as a roving correspondent. Throughout his productive life, Cummings traveled widely, maintaining for a base his apartment in New York and the family residence, Joy Farm, in New Hampshire. He married Elaine Orr in 1924, but they divorced the following year. His marriage to Anne Barton lasted from 1929 to 1932. His common law marriage to photographer Marion Morehouse lasted from 1934 until his death. Nancy Thayer did not learn that she was actually Cummings's natural daughter until 1948. It says a great deal about the poet's personal charm and good character that he remained on cordial terms with all of his wives.

Cummings's many collections of poems included *XLI Poems* (1925), *&* (1925), *is 5* (1926), *W(ViVa)* (1931), *50 Poems* (1940), *XAIPE* (1950), and *95 Poems* (1958). Some critics have noted that his approach did not change or develop significantly from book to book. Instead, what one notices about Cummings from the start is a freshness, a contagious delight, and an almost childlike playfulness. (His avoidance of capital letters contributes to this effect.) Cummings came early to a simple but radical decision about his poetics: he would work in traditional aural forms while simultaneously exploring new types of visual poetic syntax. He considered the two styles complementary, not contradictory. No other Modernist poet was consistently so stylistically inclusive. Many of his poems combine the traditional underpinnings of meter and rhyme, with fragmented typography and complex visual word play. He once wrote in a letter—in his characteristic punning manner—that "not all of my poems are to be read aloud—some . . . are to be seen and not heard." Such poems refresh language by breaking its conventional order. His poems were also full of puns and sexual jokes. Whatever forms they took, they were attempts to capture "the vivisection of the Now."

In a letter to his friend Hildegarde Watson, Cummings called himself an animist, suggesting an almost primitive desire to find the sacred vitality in things. He wrote a great many sonnets, usually with unconventional punctuation. Although his poems often expressed outrage at American politics and commercial culture, his greatest subject was love. Indeed, Cummings is one of the best-loved poets in the English language, not only for his frankness about and delight in sex, but also for his ability to express small, ordinary moments of awe between men and women. One of the least jaded of modern poets, Cummings gives credence to the powerful aspirations love creates. He also comprehends and illuminates the deadening effects of social conventions where love and sex are concerned. If there is a discernible development in his poetry from early to late, it is perhaps in his progress through the theme of love to an almost religious conception of being. In this he resembles the Metaphysical poets of seventeenth-century England.

Cummings wanted to capture the feeling of being intensely alive. He was less concerned with ideas than most other Modernists were, and he offered no formal intellectual or artistic agenda in his work. In a program note for the opening of his play, *Him* (1928), at the Provincetown Playhouse, he wrote "Relax and give the play a chance to strut its stuff—relax, stop wondering what it's all 'about'—like many strange and familiar things, Life included, this Play isn't 'about,' it simply is." When his friend Ezra Pound was accused of treason after World War II, Cummings remained loyal, and explained his loyalty in apolitical terms: "I consider that any human being alive today owes him an immeasurable debt. Why? Not because, as a reformer, he has tried to pry an unworld out of its nonexistence; but because, as a poet, he has created particular beauty in an epoch of universal ugliness." This emphasis on beauty links Cummings to the Romantics and is another way in which his overtly modern poems are profoundly traditional in their concerns. Though he received numerous honors for his work, including two Guggenheim Fellowships and the Bollingen Prize, he has always had detractors. Cummings asks us to let down our guard, to take our critical preconceptions with a grain of salt. We cannot read him in quite the same way we might read Frost or Eliot. But the vitality of his poetry pays enormous dividends to anyone who is open to it.

in Just-

in Just-
spring   when the world is mud-
luscious the little
lame balloonman

whistles   far   and wee   5

and eddieandbill come
running from marbles and
piracies and it's
spring

when the world is puddle-wonderful   10

the queer
old balloonman whistles
far   and   wee
and bettyandisbel come dancing

from hop-scotch and jump-rope and   15

it's
spring
and
     the

          goat-footed   20

balloonMan   whistles
far
and
wee

                                                        1923

Buffalo Bill 's[1]

Buffalo Bill 's
defunct
          who used to
          ride a watersmooth-silver
                              stallion   5
and break onetwothreefourfive pigeonsjustlikethat
                                        Jesus

he was a handsome man
                    and what i want to know is
how do you like your blueeyed boy   10
Mister Death

                                                        1923

1. William Cody (1846–1917) became known as "Buffalo Bill" after slaughtering thousands of buffalo for the Kansas Pacific Railroad. Later in life he enacted fictionalized versions of his exploits all over the world in his famous Wild West Show.

the Cambridge ladies who live in furnished souls

the Cambridge ladies who live in furnished souls
are unbeautiful and have comfortable minds
(also, with the church's protestant blessings
daughters, unscented shapeless spirited)
they believe in Christ and Longfellow, both dead,   5
are invariably interested in so many things—
at the present writing one still finds
delighted fingers knitting for the is it Poles?
perhaps.   While permanent faces coyly bandy
scandal of Mrs. N and Professor D   10
....the Cambridge ladies do not care,above
Cambridge if sometimes in its box of
sky lavender and cornerless,the
moon rattles like a fragment of angry candy

1923

next to of course god america i

"next to of course god america i
love you land of the pilgrims' and so forth oh
say can you see by the dawn's early my
country 'tis of centuries come and go
and are no more what of it we should worry   5
in every language even deafanddumb
thy sons acclaim your glorious name by gorry
by jingo by gee by gosh by gum
why talk of beauty what cold be more beautiful than these heroic happy dead   10
who rushed like lions to the roaring slaughter
they did not stop to think they died instead
then shall the voice of liberty be mute?"

He spoke.   And drank rapidly a glass of water.

1926

i sing of Olaf glad and big

i sing of Olaf glad and big
whose warmest heart recoiled at war:
a conscientious object-or

his wellbelovéd colonel(trig[2]
westpointer most succinctly bred)   5
took erring Olaf soon in hand;

2. Neat.

but—though an host of overjoyed
noncoms(first knocking on the head
him)do through icy waters roll
that helplessness which others stroke   10
with brushes recently employed
anent this muddy toiletbowl,
while kindred intellects evoke
allegiance per blunt instruments—
Olaf(being to all intents   15
a corpse and wanting any rag
upon what God unto him gave)
responds,without getting annoyed
"I will not kiss your fucking flag"

straightway the silver bird[3] looked grave   20
(departing hurriedly to shave)

but—though all kinds of officers
(a yearning nation's blueeyed pride)
their passive prey did kick and curse
until for wear their clarion   25
voices and boots were much the worse,
and egged the firstclassprivates on
his rectum wickedly to tease
by means of skilfully applied
bayonets roasted hot with heat—   30
Olaf(upon what were once knees)
does almost ceaselessly repeat
"there is some shit I will not eat"

our president,being of which
assertions duly notified   35
threw the yellowsonofabitch
into a dungeon,where he died

Christ(of His mercy infinite)
i pray to see;and Olaf,too

preponderatingly because   40
unless statistics lie he was
more brave than me:more blond than you.

                                          1931

somewhere i have never travelled,gladly beyond

somewhere i have never travelled,gladly beyond
any experience,your eyes have their silence:
in your most frail gesture are things which enclose me,
or which i cannot touch because they are too near

3. A colonel's insignia.

your slightest look easily will unclose me   5
though i have closed myself as fingers,
you open always petal by petal myself as Spring opens
(touching skilfully,mysteriously)her first rose

or if your wish be to close me,i and
my life will shut very beautifully,suddenly,   10
as when the heart of this flower imagines
the snow carefully everywhere descending;

nothing which we are to perceive in this world equals
the power of your intense fragility:whose texture
compels me with the colour of its countries,   15
rendering death and forever with each breathing

(i do not know what it is about you that closes
and opens;only something in me understands
the voice of your eyes is deeper than all roses)
nobody,not even the rain,has such small hands   20

                                                    1931

may i feel said he

may i feel said he
(i'll squeal said she
just oncc said he)
it's fun said she

(may i touch said he   5
how much said she
a lot said he)
why not said she

(let's go said he
not too far said she   10
what's too far said he
where you are said she)

may i stay said he
(which way said she
like this said he   15
if you kiss said she

may i move said he
is it love said she)
if you're willing said he
(but you're killing said she   20

but it's life said he
but your wife said she
now said he)
ow said she

(tiptop said he   25
don't stop said she
oh no said he)
go slow said she

(cccome?said he
ummm said she)   30
you're divine!said he
(you are Mine said she)

                                                         1935

r-p-o-p-h-e-s-s-a-g-r

                         r-p-o-p-h-e-s-s-a-g-r
              who
a)s w(e loo)k
upnowgath
              PPEGORHRASS   5
                              eringint(o-
aThe):l
       eA
          !p:
S   a   10
              (r
rIvInG   .gRrEaPsPhOs)
                              to
rea(be)rran(com)gi(e)ngly
,grasshopper;   15

                                                         1935

you shall above all things be glad and young

you shall above all things be glad and young.
For if you're young,whatever life you wear

it will become you;and if you are glad
whatever's living will yourself become.
Girlboys may nothing more than boygirls need: 5
i can entirely her only love

whose any mystery makes every man's
flesh put space on;and his mind take off time

that you should ever think,may god forbid
and(in his mercy)your true lover spare: 10
for that way knowledge lies,the foetal grave
called progress,and negation's dead undoom.

I'd rather learn from one bird how to sing
than teach ten thousand stars how not to dance

                                                         1938

anyone lived in a pretty how town

anyone lived in a pretty how town
(with up so floating many bells down)
spring summer autumn winter
he sang his didn't he danced his did.

Women and men(both little and small)   5
cared for anyone not at all
they sowed their isn't they reaped their same
sun moon stars rain

children guessed(but only a few
and down they forgot as up they grew   10
autumn winter spring summer)
that noone loved him more by more

when by now and tree by leaf
she laughed his joy she cried his grief
bird by snow and stir by still   15
anyone's any was all to her

someones married their everyones
laughed their cryings and did their dance
(sleep wake hope and then)they
said their nevers they slept their dream   20

stars rain sun moon
(and only the snow can begin to explain
how children are apt to forget to remember
with up so floating many bells down)

one day anyone died i guess   25
(and noone stooped to kiss his face)
busy folk buried them side by side
little by little and was by was

all by all and deep by deep
and more by more they dream their sleep   30
noone and anyone earth by april
wish by spirit and if by yes.

Women and men(both dong and ding)
summer autumn winter spring
reaped their sowing and went their came   35
sun moon stars rain

1940

my father moved through dooms of love

my father moved through dooms of love
through sames of am through haves of give,
singing each morning out of each night
my father moved through depths of height

this motionless forgetful where   5
turned at his glance to shining here;
that if(so timid air is firm)
under his eyes would stir and squirm

newly as from unburied which
floats the first who,his april touch   10
drove sleeping selves to swarm their fates
woke dreamers to their ghostly roots

and should some why completely weep
my father's fingers brought her sleep:
vainly no smallest voice might cry   15
for he could feel the mountains grow.

Lifting the valleys of the sea
my father moved through griefs of joy;
praising a forehead called the moon
singing desire into begin   20

joy was his song and joy so pure
a heart of star by him could steer
and pure so now and now so yes
the wrists of twilight would rejoice

keen as midsummer's keen beyond   25
conceiving mind of sun will stand,
so strictly(over utmost him
so hugely)stood my father's dream

his flesh was flesh his blood was blood:
no hungry man but wished him food;   30
no cripple wouldn't creep one mile
uphill to only see him smile.

Scorning the pomp of must and shall
my father moved through dooms of feel;
his anger was as right as rain   35
his pity was as green as grain

septembering arms of year extend
less humbly wealth to foe and friend
than he to foolish and to wise
offered immeasurable is   40

proudly and(by octobering flame
beckoned)as earth will downward climb,
so naked for immortal work
his shoulders marched against the dark

his sorrow was as true as bread: 45
no liar looked him in the head;
if every friend became his foe
he'd laugh and build a world with snow.

My father moved through theys of we,
singing each new leaf out of each tree 50
(and every child was sure that spring
danced when she heard my father sing)

then let men kill which cannot share,
let blood and flesh be mud and mire,
scheming imagine,passion willed, 55
freedom a drug that's bought and sold

giving to steal and cruel kind,
a heart to fear,to doubt a mind,
to differ a disease of same,
conform the pinnacle of am 60

though dull were all we taste as bright,
bitter all utterly things sweet,
maggoty minus and dumb death
all we inherit,all bequeath

and nothing quite so least as truth 65
—i say though hate were why mean breathe—
because my father lived his soul
love is the whole and more than all

1940

pity this busy monster,manunkind

pity this busy monster,manunkind,

not. Progress is a comfortable disease:
your victim(death and life safely beyond)

plays with the bigness of his littleness
—electrons deify one razorblade 5
into a mountainrange;lenses extend

unwish through curving wherewhen till unwish
returns on its unself.
                    A world of made
Is not a world of born—pity poor flesh

and trees,poor stars and stones,but never this 10
fine specimen of hypermagical

ultraomnipotence. We doctors know

a hopeless case if—listen:there's a hell
of a good universe next door;let's go

1944

o purple finch

"o purple finch
　　　　　　please tell me why
this summer world(and you and i
who love so much to live)
　　　　　　　　　　　　must die"

"if i
　　　should tell you anything"
(that eagerly sweet carolling   5
self answers me)
　　　　　　"i could not sing."

1963

WITTER BYNNER and ARTHUR DAVISON FICKE
(1881–1968)　　　　　　　　　(1883–1945)

Fun
Is the mastodon
Vanished complete . . .
　—*Emanuel Morgan*

In 1916, two American poets pulled off one of the century's great literary hoaxes. Witter Bynner had published two collections of his own poems after attending Harvard and working for women's suffrage. He had also translated Euripides's *Iphigenia in Taurus* for the dancer Isadora Duncan. He was a sophisticated literary man but was disillusioned with Modernist movements such as Imagism and Vorticism. Arthur Davison Ficke had known Bynner at Harvard, but he had moved back to Iowa to study law and had married Evelyn Blunt in 1907. He too had published several books in the following decade and was disgruntled at how captivated many artists were by the Modernist avant-garde.

　　Early in 1916, on his way to visit Ficke in Iowa, Bynner stopped in Chicago, where he saw a production of a one-act ballet, *Le Spectre de La Rose*. In the intermission before the next dance, he was discussing the fashion for literary movements with his companions when he spontaneously invented yet another movement, the Spectrists. He had recently been in Pittsburgh, so he told his friends that these remarkable Spectrists were Pittsburgh poets. Later in Iowa, Bynner and Ficke invented two personalities, Emanuel Morgan, a middle-aged, bearded painter-turned-poet, and Anne Knish, a beautiful and temperamental Hungarian émigré. As William Jay Smith wrote in his fascinating study, *The Spectra Hoax* (1961, 2000), the two men immediately began composing "Spectrist" poems:

> The personalities of the mythical writers became more clearly outlined in proportion to
> the "spectra" or "spectrics" produced; and these were written at a fast clip. In fact, so
> absorbed did the poets become in their productions that the constant composition and
> recitations of spectric verse became too much for Mrs. Ficke. She ordered the pair out of
> the house until they had finished their manuscript. They retired to a hotel across the river

in Moline, Illinois, where as Arthur Davison Ficke put it, from ten quarts of excellent Scotch in ten days they extracted the whole of the Spectric philosophy.

Remarkably, the two conspirators convinced their own publisher to bring out a collection, *Spectra: A Book of Poetic Experiments* (1916), with a preface by Anne Knish comparing this new poetry to "the methods of Futurist Painting." Using elaborate metaphors, Knish explained the aesthetics of the new movement in which "the theme of the poem is to be regarded as a prism, upon which the colorless white light of infinite existence falls and is broken up into glowing, beautiful, and intelligible hues." The Spectrists generally declined to give their poems titles, preferring to treat their works as musical compositions using opus numbers.

Even more remarkably, the movement was taken seriously. Bynner himself was invited to review the book by unsuspecting editors of the *New Republic,* and he obligingly heaped praise upon it. Newspapers around the country carried articles discussing the new Modernist school, and poems by Morgan and Knish appeared in leading journals such as *Others* and *Poetry.* The two authors had a hard time keeping up with demands for new Spectrist work and invited their friend Marjorie Allen Seiffert to join them under the name Elijah Hay. It was Hay who kept up a long correspondence about Spectrism with William Carlos Williams. Other poets to praise the movement included Edgar Lee Masters.

The hoax was finally exposed in 1918 with a great deal of amused coverage in the popular press. Bynner and Ficke moved on to other things, but they never quite rid themselves of Morgan and Knish. At one point they had Anne Knish die in Budapest "by an obscure disease," after which Emanuel Morgan committed suicide in Pittsburgh. Ironically, the two men each suspected that they had done some of their best work in these fictional guises. Without really undermining the legitimacy of Modernism, the Spectra hoax exposed its obsession with novelty and group psychology. By using chance and discontinuity in their compositions, the Spectrists inadvertently created some charming as well as hilarious poems, a few of which prefigure movements in postwar American poetry.

◄●━━◀▶━━●►

Anne Knish

Opus 181

Skeptical cat,
Calm your eyes, and come to me.
For long ago, in some palmèd forest,
I too felt claws curling
Within my fingers . . .   5
Moons wax and wane;
My eyes, too, once narrowed and widened . . .
Why do you shrink back?
Come to me: let me pat you—
Come, vast-eyed one . . .   10
Or I will spring upon you
And with steel-hook fingers

Tear you limb from limb. . . .

There were twins in my cradle. . . .

[Arthur Davison Ficke]
1916

Emanuel Morgan

Opus 104

How terrible to entertain a lunatic!
To keep his earnestness from coming close!

A Madagascar land-crab once
Lifted blue claws at me
And rattled long black eyes   5
That would have got me
Had I not been gay.

[Witter Bynner]
1916

Emanuel Morgan

Opus 40

Two cocktails round a smile,
    A grapefruit after grace,
Flowers in an aisle
    . . . Were your face.

A strap in a street-car   5
    A sea-fan on the sand,
A beer on a bar
    . . . Were your hand.

The pillar of a porch,
    The tapering of an egg,   10
The pine of a torch
    . . . Were your leg.—

Sun on the Hellespont,
    White swimmers in the bowl
Of the baptismal font   15
    Are your soul.

[Witter Bynner]
1916

Emanuel Morgan

Opus 15

Despair comes when all comedy
   Is tame
And there is left no tragedy
   In any name,
When the round and wounded breathing   5
   Of love upon the breast
Is not so glad a sheathing
   As an old brown vest.

Asparagus is feathery and tall,
And the hose lies rotting by the garden-wall.   10

[Witter Bynner]
1916

The Harlem Renaissance

Harlem's famous Cotton Club.

HISTORICAL AND CRITICAL OVERVIEW

The New Negro

> Harlem, I grant you, isn't typical—but it is significant, it is prophetic.
>
> —*Alain Locke*

What we now call "The Harlem Renaissance," one of the century's peaks of African American accomplishments in the arts, was known during the 1920s as "The New Negro" Movement. The term, popularized by Howard University Professor Alain Locke in his 1925 anthology of the same name, connotes the possibilities for black achievements nationwide, not simply in New York City's Harlem district. Yet Harlem was seen at the time as "the Negro Capitol," and, although its cultural flourishing mirrored the growing sense of purpose felt among African American communities throughout the United States, the district remained the center of political and artistic activity that set the foundation for African American advancements not only in the 1920s but throughout the century. "Renaissance," therefore, is an appropriate metaphor for the remarkable quantity of work produced by black artists during the 1920s; during this "rebirth" they built upon an already established heritage—in the case of poetry, not only the literary verse of writers such as Phillis Wheatley, Francis Harper, and Paul Laurence Dunbar, but the vital folk traditions of spirituals and the blues.

Certainly, writers did not have to live in Harlem to contribute to the Renaissance. Langston Hughes grew up in the Midwest and came to Harlem in 1921 at the age of 19. On the other hand, Claude McKay was born in Jamaica, moved to Harlem in 1914, at age 24, but left for Europe in 1922; he admitted in his autobiography, *A Long Way from Home* (1937): "I had done my best Harlem stuff when I was abroad, seeing it from a long perspective." Angelina Weld Grimké spent the 1920s teaching high school in Washington, D.C., though she made trips to New York. And Sterling Brown, who published his first book in 1932, taught at black colleges in the South and the Midwest until 1929, when he was hired by Howard University in Washington, D.C. Despite their varied whereabouts, these writers maintained ties to the Harlem literary scene, and their work appeared in the journals and anthologies that helped define the era. But they all belonged to what W. E. B. DuBois defined as "the Talented Tenth," the small percentage of African Americans who were the beneficiaries of a college education and "must be made leaders of thought and missionaries of culture among their people." With the exception of a few older writers, such as James Weldon Johnson, who had secured his reputation in the teens, and Angelina Weld Grimké, much of whose poetry belongs in the genteel school of "raceless" literature, the poets of the Harlem Renaissance were young. It was no accident that Locke dedicated *The New Negro* "to the younger generation," quoting a line from a spiritual: "O, rise, shine for Thy Light is a' coming." Although he was looking forward to the productivity of future generations of African Americans, he was also acknowledging the youth-driven energy of the New Negro movement in the arts.

Some historians trace the beginning of the movement to 1919, when the "Red Summer" riots resulted in the killings of hundreds of blacks across the country by white mobs. In his sonnet about the riots, "If We Must Die," Claude McKay evoked the rising mood of rebellion among the victims of white rage: "Like men we'll face the murderous, cowardly pack, / Pressed to the wall, dying, but fighting back!" During the coming decade, African American art was deeply linked to calls for an end to racist violence and the increasing political organization mobilized by groups such as the National Association for the Advancement of Colored People (in which writers as diverse as W. E. B. DuBois, James Weldon Johnson, and Walter White played major roles). Most historians agree that the Harlem Renaissance lost its momentum after the stock market crash of 1929; the Great Depression limited opportunities for all Americans, but for African Americans in particular, and there was little incentive among publishing houses to feature the work of black authors during the 1930s. Langston Hughes, in his autobiography *The Big Sea*, describes "the end of the gay times of the New Negro era in Harlem, the period that had begun to reach its end when the crash came in 1929 and the white people had much less money to spend on themselves, and practically none to spend on Negroes, for the depression brought everybody down a peg or two. And the Negroes had but few pegs to fall."

The Great Migration

> The problem of the twentieth century is the problem of the color line.
> —W. E. B. DuBois

Although the end of the Civil War promised equality to newly emancipated slaves, during the Reconstruction era white Southerners established segregation, the practice of racial separation between blacks and whites. Segregation was confirmed as legal by the U.S. Supreme Court in *Plessy v. Ferguson*, the 1896 case that upheld "separate but equal" accommodations in railroad transportation (and, by extension, in schools, restaurants, parks, and neighborhoods). The majority of southern blacks not only lived in rural poverty, but they were often prevented from voting through literacy laws, poll taxes, and other strategies devised by white politicians. Lynchings and other acts of racist violence by the Ku Klux Klan occurred with increasing frequency, threatening even the small numbers of African Americans who had achieved some degree of prosperity. During the first decade of the twentieth century, race riots in which white mobs attacked and sometimes killed blacks and destroyed black property inflamed southern and northern cities: Wilmington, North Carolina (1898), New York (1900), Atlanta (1906), and Springfield, Illinois (1908).

At the turn of the century northern cities were also segregated. Although unions denied membership to blacks, which made finding work other than domestic service or unskilled labor difficult, African Americans nonetheless began migrating away from the rural south in search of better lives. Impelled by an economic depression in the South during 1914–1915 and boll weevil infestations and flooding during the same years, and drawn by industrial opportunities made possible by the American entry into World War I in 1917, African Americans began moving in record numbers to northern cities such as New York, Chicago, Detroit, and Cleveland. In 1918 alone, almost 250,000 fled north. The exodus continued through the 1920s. Census figures show that the number of African Americans in New York City alone nearly tripled, from 91,709 in 1910 to 327,706 in 1930. In Chicago the African American population grew sixfold from 40,000 in 1910 to 240,000 in 1930. By 1920 between half a million and a million blacks had left the rural South for the urban North. Despite continuing political and economic barriers to equality, many African Americans in the 1920s felt a collective sense of self and an urge to assert their independence, feelings summed up by W. E. B. DuBois in his celebration of black soldiers returning from the Great War: "now that that war is over, we [must] marshal every ounce of our brain and brawn to fight a sterner, longer, more unbending battle against the forces of hell in our own land."

Harlem: Epicenter of the Renaissance

> I was in love with Harlem long before I got there.
> —*Langston Hughes*

Within New York City, the district of Harlem became, as the *Saturday Evening Post* noted in 1925, "the Mecca for all those who seek Opportunity with a capital O." Not only American blacks, but immigrants from the West Indies and Africa enriched the cultural climate. An area of less than 2 square miles in northern Manhattan, Harlem contained wide streets flanked by fine houses and apartment buildings, some of which were quickly sold off by their white owners once blacks gained a foothold in the area. In *Black Manhattan* (1930), James Weldon Johnson linked the security gained by ownership of property with Harlem's cultural ascendancy:

> Twenty years ago barely a half-dozen coloured individuals owned land on Manhattan. Down to fifteen years ago the amount that Negroes had acquired in Harlem was by comparison negligible. Today a very large part of the property in Harlem occupied by Negroes is owned by Negroes. . . . The Negro's situation in Harlem is without precedent in all his history in New York; never before has he been so securely anchored, never before has he had so well established a community life.

Although Johnson's optimistic vision glosses over some of the district's problems, such as overcrowding, exorbitant rents, and the limited number of black-owned retail businesses, it amply reflects the pride and sense of possibility that African Americans felt for Harlem in the 1920s. All classes were drawn there, from workers to artists and intellectuals. A common Harlem saying of the 1920s, "I'd rather be a lamppost in Harlem than the Governor of Georgia," attests to the vitality of the streets, especially Seventh Avenue, known as the "Black Broadway," home to a multitude of shops, theaters, restaurants, churches, and cabarets. In a 1927 essay, "Why I Like Harlem," the sociologist Ira De Augustine Reid praised Harlem's diversity:

> Harlem—one has to like it. And not because it is the "Mecca of the New Negro," rather because it is the "Maker of a New Negro." It is a part of all it has met—Grand Boulevard, Beale Street, St. Antoine Street, Birmingham, Atlanta, Little Rock, London, Paris, and The Islands; social leaders, bums, erudite students, fanatics, rich-man, poor-man, beggar-man, thief. An immense picture in all colors.

Harlem was both an African American community, complete with black policemen, and a cosmopolitan center whose cultural power equaled that of European cities. When Langston Hughes' father gave him the chance to attend college in Europe, Hughes turned him down, choosing Columbia University "mainly because I wanted to see Harlem. . . . More than Paris, or the Shakespeare country, or Berlin, or the Alps, I wanted to see Harlem, the greatest Negro city in the world." Harlem became the base of operations for African American political and cultural groups such as the National Urban League, the National Association for the Advancement of Colored People (NAACP), and the United Negro Improvement Association. These organizations worked for political and social change and published newspapers that denounced racial injustice and championed African American achievements, especially in the arts.

And it was for the arts—especially its music—that Harlem gained world renown. Initially, the cabarets and tearooms, like the churches, served as hubs of the community, especially for the returning soldiers: ragtime piano, blues singers, crowded dance floors, and jazz, the fast evolving hybrid of ragtime and blues, sustained Harlemites night after night. After Prohibition went into effect at midnight on January 15, 1920, speakeasies selling bootleg liquor flourished, and "rent parties," apartment parties whose admission fees helped people pay the rent, also served liquor, sometimes turning whole apartment blocks into impromptu music and dance venues. When *Shuffle Along,* the first show of the decade to be written and performed by blacks, opened in Manhattan in 1921, it created a vogue for black music and dance among whites, who began venturing up to Harlem to explore the nightlife there. Black musicals and nightclubs were the sources of all the popular dances of the 1920s, including the Charleston, the Black Bottom, and the Lindy Hop. After the white writer Carl Van Vechten published *Nigger Heaven* (1926), a controversial novel featuring Harlem cabarets, whites overran many of the Harlem clubs in such numbers that Harlem writers such as Rudolph Fisher complained that "time was when white people went to Negro cabarets to see how Negroes acted; now Negroes go to these same cabarets to see how white people act."

Some clubs adopted a "whites only policy" and catered to white expectations to see "primitivism" on display in Harlem. Others were known as "Black and Tans"—clubs that served a racially mixed clientele. The Cotton Club, for example, which was run by white mobsters, featured jungle decor and a chorus line of tall, light-skinned African American women in exotic costumes. The Cotton Club featured bands led by Duke Ellington and Cab Calloway, and singers such as Ethel Waters. Connie's Inn, another club, headlined Louis Armstrong. These performers and other important musicians such as the bands of Fletcher Henderson, King Oliver, and Chick Webb dominated other mixed race dance halls like the Roseland Ballroom and the Savoy Ballroom. Such clubs helped bring jazz into the national imagination, especially through the Columbia Broadcasting System's live radio broadcasts of Ellington's shows from the Cotton Club.

Politics, Poets, and Publications

> Black is beautiful.
> —*Marcus Garvey*

Some African Americans during the 1920s saw white praise and attention as necessary to gain ground in the struggle for equality, while others criticized artists who "sold out" to the whites and argued that the New Negro Renaissance was developed by Negroes for Negroes. These points of view reflected the different ideas voiced by African American leaders of the era. W. E. B. DuBois, through his NAACP-sponsored journal, the *Crisis,* granted the importance of attention from whites, noting that "until the art of the black folk compels recognition they will not be rated as human." Yet he emphasized that African American artists must work from their own experience and traditions as the best way of creating compelling art: "we who are dark can see America in a way that white Americans can not." Likewise, in the foreword to his landmark 1925 anthology, *The New Negro,* Alain Locke celebrated race consciousness and proclaimed: "[We] discover in the artistic self-expression of the Negro to-day a new figure on the national canvas and a new force in the foreground of affairs. Whoever wishes to see the Negro in his essential traits, in the full perspective of his achievement and possibilities, must seek the enlightenment of the self-portraiture which the present developments of Negro culture are offering." And Marcus Garvey, who advocated African nationalism through stirring speeches and publication of the international weekly, *Negro World,* turned black artists toward their African heritage. Although Garvey's separatist message was far more radical than Locke's and DuBois's efforts to strike a balance between black pride and the struggle for equality with whites, the arts were just as important to him as a means of fostering his ideals. The *Crisis, Negro World,* and *Opportunity,* the journal of the National Urban League, all published poetry. In addition, they sponsored literary contests that helped both to recognize and promote the achievements of New Negro writers.

The poets not only answered the call of leaders such as DuBois, Locke, and Garvey, but offered their own perspectives on the movement's goals. Like DuBois, James Weldon Johnson contended that young African American writers "must not be mere dilettantes; they have serious work to do. They can bring to bear a tremendous force for breaking down and wearing away the stereotyped ideas about the Negro, and for creating a higher and more enlightened opinion about the race." A staunch advocate of the new poetry, in 1922 Johnson published one of the first anthologies of the period, *The Book of American Negro Poetry,* whose importance lies not only in Johnson's collection of poets, beginning with Paul Laurence Dunbar and ending with Claude McKay and Anne Spencer, but in his definition of an African American tradition of poetry rooted in musical forms such as spirituals, ragtime, blues, and jazz. In his introduction to the book, Johnson condemned dialect poetry and called for a poetry of heightened speech. Other anthologies soon followed, including Robert T. Kerlin's *Negro Poets and Their Poems* (1923) and Countee Cullen's *Caroling Dusk* (1927). Cullen's preface stressed the diversity of styles among black poets, noting that "the poet writes out of his experience, whether it be personal or vicarious, and as these experiences differ among other poets, so do they differ among Negro poets; for the double obligation of being both Negro and American is not so unified as we are often led to believe." The New Negro movement made possible not only a poetry of protest, but a poetry of self-revelation.

By the middle of the decade, in fact, younger poets such as Cullen and Langston Hughes began to rebel against the older generation's insistence that Negro art be political in prescriptive ways. In his long poem "Heritage," Cullen questioned the mystique of Africa, and Hughes's second book, *Fine Clothes to the Jew* (1927), depicted scenes from lower class black life that angered members of the Talented Tenth who felt that New Negro writers should offer only exemplary, morally uplifting portrayals of African Americans. But Hughes was adamant about the importance of examining all aspects of black experience, and of doing so without aiming to impress a white audience. In his landmark 1926 essay, "The Negro Artist and the Racial Mountain," he argued:

> The Negro artist works against an undertow of sharp criticism and misunderstanding from his own group and unintentional bribes from the whites. "Oh, be respectable, write about nice people, show how good we are," say the Negroes. "Be stereotyped, don't go too far, don't shatter our illusions about you, don't amuse us too seriously. We will pay you," say the whites.

He concluded by allying creative freedom with racial pride and chiding black poets who turned from the richness of African American culture. In the spirit of rebellion, Hughes banded together with other young Harlem writers in 1926—including

Cullen, Gwendolyn Bennett, and fiction writers Zora Neale Hurston and Wallace Thurman—to publish an avant-garde little magazine, *Fire!!* In *The Big Sea*, Hughes explains that they hoped the magazine "would burn up a lot of the old, dead, conventional Negro-white ideas of the past" and shock the black middle class "into a realization of the existence of the younger Negro writers and artists." The magazine's stories about prostitutes and homosexuals, its stylized artwork depicting jungle scenes and nude Africans, and its celebration of jazz and paganism had the desired effect. Although it folded after the first issue due to lack of funds (and the remaining copies were, ironically, destroyed in a fire), *Fire!!* gave the young writers of the Harlem Renaissance a platform for self-declaration and a means of both aligning themselves with and differentiating themselves from the Modernist avant garde.

Styles of Poetry: Cultural and Formal Diversity

> You have definitely linked me to the purpose and vision of what is best in creative America.
>
> —*Jean Toomer*

During the years of the Harlem Renaissance, critics were divided about its relationship to Modernism. On the one hand, as Ann Douglas points out in *Terrible Honesty: Mongrel Manhattan in the 1920s* (1995), the alienation felt by many white writers of the period contrasted with the sense of purpose and self-discovery experienced by New Negro artists. In light of their own experience of racism, many African American writers found suspect the disaffection voiced in a Modernist centerpiece such as T. S. Eliot's *The Waste Land*. Moreover, the fragmentation and allusiveness of Eliot's form of Modernism, along with his insistence in "Tradition and the Individual Talent" that poetry "is an escape from emotion," conflicted with African American writers' aims of communicating with their audience. Some writers also recognized that the white fascination with black culture arose in part from longings to escape alienation. In his autobiography, *A Long Way from Home*, Claude McKay criticized "the modernistic white groups that took a significant interest in Negro art and literature," suggesting that they "were searching for a social and artistic significance in Negro art which they could not find in their own society." Yet some proponents of the New Negro Renaissance were eager to ally the movement with the spirit of the era, especially the sense of creating a new national literature in the wake of the Great War's devastation. Thus Alain Locke, in *The New Negro*, announced that "America seeking a new spiritual expansion and artistic maturity, trying to found an American literature, a national art, and national music implies a Negro-American culture seeking the same satisfactions and objectives. Separate as it may be in color and substance, the culture of the Negro is of a pattern integral with the times and with its cultural setting."

All of the poets of the Harlem Renaissance claimed the right to delineate African American experience on their own terms—so much so that one of the signal characteristics of the period is the poetry's diversity of form. Ranging from the experimental genre blending of Jean Toomer's *Cane* to the sonnets of Claude McKay and Countee Cullen, Harlem Renaissance poetry exemplifies the stylistic range that gives early twentieth-century poetry its extraordinary vitality. In fact, many Renaissance writers, including Toomer, Gwendolyn Bennett, and Angelina Weld Grimké were equally adept at writing Imagistic free verse and European forms such as the sonnet. Yet these writers, like Cullen and McKay, turned inherited forms to their own ends, using them to protest racism and develop unstereotyped, psychologically complex representations of African American life. But diversity of form is also the element that sets the New Negro poetry apart from all other poetry of the period. For the formal flexibility of Harlem Renaissance poetry is most apparent in the work of writers such as Langston Hughes and Sterling Brown, who used the vernacular traditions of spirituals, blues, jazz, and black preaching as a means of both affirming and extending a uniquely African American tradition. Through their path-breaking adaptations of folk forms and the rhythms of black music, Hughes and Brown answered James Weldon Johnson's calls for "a form expressing the imagery, the idioms, the peculiar turns of thought, and the distinctive humor and pathos" of African American culture, along with "the deepest and highest emotions and aspirations" and the "widest range of subjects and the widest scope of treatment." By linking "literary" poetry with folk traditions purged of the dialect associated with minstrelsy, Hughes and Brown renewed the language of African American poetry and widened its range of subjects in ways that black poets still draw upon today.

ANGELINA WELD GRIMKÉ
(1880–1958)

Angelina Weld Grimké had already written a great deal of well-crafted poetry in traditional forms before she began experimenting with free verse in the teens and early 1920s. Although she never published a collection, her work appeared in several defining anthologies of the Harlem Renaissance, as well as in important African American journals such as *Opportunity* and the *Crisis*. Her best lyrics conjoin Imagist techniques either with race consciousness or expressions of her love for women and create resonant, often disquieting analogies for these two poles of her experience.

Born in Boston, Grimké came from a distinguished interracial family and received a privileged education available to few African Americans of her time. Her father, Archibald Henry Grimké, was helped by his aunts, Sarah and Angelina Grimké, wealthy and influential Quaker abolitionists who not only acknowledged but also provided financial assistance for the illegitimate sons whom their brother had with his mistress, a household slave. A graduate of Lincoln University and Harvard Law School, Archibald Grimké developed a flourishing law practice and also became known as a writer, diplomat, and leader of the National Association for the Advancement of Colored People (NAACP). In 1879 he married a white woman, Sarah Stanley, over the severe objections of her father. Perhaps because she was unable to bear the social stigma of an interracial marriage, Sarah abandoned her husband in 1883, returning to her parents with her three-year-old daughter in tow. But four years later, she gave Angelina back to Archibald. Sarah died in 1898, and the child never saw her mother again. Angelina became devoted to her father, who sent her to a series of academically distinguished schools: Fairmont School in Hyde Park, Massachusetts; Carleton Academy in Northfield, Minnesota; Cushing Academy in Ashburnham, Massachusetts; and the Boston Normal School of Gymnastics, from which she graduated in 1902. She then moved to Washington, D.C., where she earned her living as a teacher, working first as a physical education teacher at the Armstrong Manual Training School and then, from 1907 until her retirement in 1926, as an English teacher at the elite Dunbar High School. In Washington she became part of a distinguished circle of African American artists and intellectuals, and during her twenties she also thrived in the intellectual milieu of Boston, where she took English classes each summer at Harvard from 1904 to 1910.

Grimké wrote plays, short stories, and essays, but her reputation rests on her evocative lyrics. She began writing early in her life, publishing he first poem in 1893 at age thirteen. In 1916, her play *Rachel* was produced in Washington by the NAACP. Exposing the evils of racism through melodramatic turns of plot and sentimental dialogue (devices common to late nineteenth- and early twentieth-century theater), the play received mixed reviews. But its historical importance was acknowledged ten years later by Alain Locke and Montgomery Gregory, who noted in *Plays of Negro Life* (1927) that it was "apparently the first successful drama written by a Negro and interpreted by Negro actors." She also published several short stories, all of which attack racism. But in her poetry, racial concerns are often understated, for Grimké aimed to evoke moods through lyrical descriptions of nature. In 1925, she wrote:

I think most [poems] that I do are the reflections of moods. These appear to me in clearly defined forms and colors—remembered from what I have seen, felt. The mood is the spiritual atmosphere. Symbolic also. I love colors and contrasts. Suggestion.

In the race poems, Grimké characteristically established a tranquil, atmospheric scene, and then breaks the mood with foreboding, even violent imagery. The love poems develop through a similar tension, for Grimké depicts lesbian love as both compelling and dangerous. During the 1920s, a small group of her poems was anthologized repeatedly, but despite the reputation she established as a well-respected "New Negro" writer, she never published a book. After her father's death in 1930, she moved to New York and virtually ceased writing, living alone in a West Side apartment for the next twenty-eight years. Oxford University Press published her *Selected Works* in 1991, thirty-three years after her death, but many of her poems and stories still remain in manuscript form among her papers at Howard University.

⊷⊷◆⊷⊷

The Black Finger

I have just seen, a beautiful thing
    Slim and still,
Against a gold, gold sky,
    A straight cypress,
    Sensitive   5
    Exquisite,
A black finger
Pointing upwards.
Why, beautiful, still finger are you black?
And why are you pointing upwards?   10

1925

Tenebris[1]

There is a tree, by day,
That, at night,
Has a shadow,
A hand huge and black,
With fingers long and black,   5
    All through the dark,
Against the white man's house
    In the little wind,
The black hand plucks and plucks
    At the bricks.   10
The bricks are the color of blood and very small.
    Is it a black hand,
    Or is it a shadow?

1927

1. (Latin) "In Darkness."

A Mona Lisa

1.

I should like to creep
Through the long brown grasses
   That are your lashes;
I should like to poise
   On the very brink   5
Of the leaf-brown pools
   That are your shadowed eyes;
I should like to cleave
   Without sound,
Their glimmering waters,   10
   Their unrippled waters,
I should like to sink down
   And down
      And down. . . .
         And deeply drown.   15

2.

Would I be more than a bubble breaking?
   Or an ever-widening circle
   Ceasing at the marge?
Would my white bones
   Be the only white bones   20
Wavering back and forth, back and forth
   In their depths?

                  1927

Fragment

I am the woman with the black black skin
I am the laughing woman with the black black face
I am living in the cellars and in every crowded place
   I am toiling just to eat
   In the cold and in the heat   5
    And I laugh
I am the laughing woman who's forgotten how to weep
I am the laughing woman who's afraid to go to sleep

              c. 1930

CLAUDE McKAY
(1889–1948)

At the age of twenty-eight, Claude McKay wrote an account of his origins:

> I was born in the heart of the little island of Jamaica on the 15th of September 1889. My grandparents were slaves, my parents free-born. My mother was very sweet-natured, fond of books; my father, honest, stern even to harshness, hard working, beginning empty-handed he coaxed a good living from the soil, bought land, and grew to be a comparatively prosperous small settler. A firm believer in education, he tried to give all his eight children the best he could afford.
>
> I was the last child and when I was nine years old my mother sent me to my eldest brother who was a schoolmaster in the northwestern part of the island.
>
> From that time on I became interested in books. . . . That was a great formative period in my life—a time of perfect freedom to play, read and think as I liked.

After an apprenticeship to a cabinetmaker, McKay joined the Jamaican Constabulary in 1909. With the encouragement of English linguist Walter Jekyll, he wrote poems in Jamaican dialect. In 1912, two collections of these were published, *Songs of Jamaica* and *Constab Ballads*. McKay soon became the Caribbean Robert Burns for his use of dialect and his populist stance. Publication of these early poems enabled him to move to America, where he studied briefly at the Tuskegee Institute in Alabama, followed by two years at Kansas State College.

In 1914 McKay moved to Harlem, working as a bartender, longshoreman, porter, and waiter. He was married briefly to Eulalie Imelda Edwards. He continued to write, publishing poems in the prominent magazine *Seven Arts* in 1917 under the pseudonym Eli Edwards. He also gravitated toward leftist literary circles, publishing in 1919 his most famous poem, "If We Must Die," in Max Eastman's Marxist newspaper, the *Liberator*. McKay's poetry appeared often in England, and in 1920 he moved there, worked on the radical *Worker's Dreadnought* and brought out a collection of poems, *Spring in New Hampshire*. But in many ways McKay was still a Jamaican poet, concerned with Pan-Africanist politics and sometimes with his own private nostalgia. In a 1922 poem entitled "The Tropics in New York" he wrote about his childhood home:

> . . . memories
> Of fruit-trees laden by low-singing rills,
> And deep dawns, and mystical blue skies
> In benediction over nun-like hills.
>
> My eyes grew dim, and I could no more gaze;
> A wave of longing through my body swept,
> And, hungry for the old, familiar ways,
> I turned aside and bowed my head and wept.

It was also in 1922—the year of T. S. Eliot's *The Waste Land* and James Joyce's *Ulysses*—that McKay published his American collection, *Harlem Shadows,* and traveled to Moscow, meeting Leon Trotsky, the Communist politician he most admired. He stayed on in Europe until 1934, mostly in Marseilles, publishing three novels: *Home to Harlem* (1928), *Banjo* (1929), and *Banana Bottom*

(1933). After his return to the United States, he married Ellen Tarry in 1938 and settled in Chicago. In his final years he renounced Communism and became a Roman Catholic. He taught in a Chicago Catholic school.

Like the younger Countee Cullen, McKay was traditional in his versification, heavily influenced by English and Scottish Romanticism. Some of his best-known poems were sonnets. Though he spent most of the Harlem Renaissance away from Harlem, he sometimes depicted urban American scenes from memory. Deracination and racism were two of his primary subjects. His descriptions in "The Lynching" can be verified by the horrifying photographs of such events in America, and in "Africa" he expressed disillusionment with Pan-African hopes: "Thou art the harlot, now thy time is done, / Of all the mighty nations of the sun." McKay hoped his poetry would have universal appeal, and it did. Although "If We Must Die" was inspired by race riots in Harlem, Winston Churchill read it to his countrymen on the radio during World War II, and the poem became a rallying cry for the English war effort.

◄•───◄▶───•►

If We Must Die[1]

If we must die, let it not be like hogs
Hunted and penned in an inglorious spot,
While round us bark the mad and hungry dogs,
Making their mock at our accursed lot.
If we must die, O let us nobly die,   5
So that our precious blood may not be shed
In vain; then even the monsters we defy
Shall be constrained to honor us though dead!
O kinsmen! we must meet the common foe!
Though far outnumbered let us show us brave,   10
And for their thousand blows deal one deathblow!
What though before us lies the open grave?
Like men we'll face the murderous, cowardly pack,
Pressed to the wall, dying, but fighting back!

1919

The Lynching[2]

His Spirit in smoke ascended to high heaven.
His father, by the cruelest way of pain,
Had bidden him to his bosom once again;
The awful sin remained still unforgiven.

---

1. Written after the riots of the "Red Summer" of 1919. As African Americans became more prosperous following World War I, they encountered the jealousy of whites in a number of American cities, including New York, Baltimore, Washington, D.C., and Chicago. Riots began with whites attacking blacks, and then escalated, sometimes including lynchings. Due to the bloodiness of these attacks, James Weldon Johnson called this the "Red Summer."
2. By some estimates there were more than two thousand lynchings of African Americans in the South during the last two decades of the nineteenth century. The resurgence of the Ku Klux Klan in 1915 brought new acts of violence.

All night a bright and solitary star   5
(Perchance the one that ever guided him,
Yet gave him up at last to Fate's wild whim)
Hung pitifully o'er the swinging char.
Day dawned, and soon the mixed crowds came to view
The ghastly body swaying in the sun.   10
The women thronged to look, but never a one
Showed sorrow in her eyes of steely blue.

And little lads, lynchers that were to be,
Danced round the dreadful thing in fiendish glee.

                                                        1920

America

Although she feeds me bread of bitterness,
And sinks into my throat her tiger's tooth,
Stealing my breath of life, I will confess
I love this cultured hell that tests my youth.
Her vigor flows like tides into my blood,   5
Giving me strength erect against her hate,
Her bigness sweeps my being like a flood.
Yet, as a rebel fronts a king in state,
I stand within her walls with not a shred
Of terror, malice, not a word of jeer.   10
Darkly I gaze into the days ahead,
And see her might and granite wonders there,
Beneath the touch of Time's unerring hand,
Like priceless treasures sinking in the sand.

                                                        1921

My Mother

The dawn departs, the morning is begun,
The Trades[3] come whispering from off the seas,
The fields of corn are golden in the sun,
The dark-brown tassels fluttering in the breeze;
The bell is sounding and children pass,   5
Frog-leaping, skipping, shouting, laughing shrill,
Down the red road, over the pasture-grass,
Up to the schoolhouse crumbling on the hill.
The older folk are at their peaceful toil,
Some pulling up the weeds, some plucking corn,   10

---

3. Trade Winds, strong subtropical winds.

And others breaking up the sun-baked soil.
Float, faintly scented breeze, at early morn
Over the earth where mortals sow and reap—
Beneath its breast my mother lies asleep.

1921

The White City

I will not toy with it nor bend an inch.
Deep in the secret chambers of my heart
I muse my life-long hate, and without flinch
I bear it nobly as I live my part.
My being would be a skeleton, a shell,   5
If this dark Passion that fills my every mood,
And makes my heaven in the white world's hell,
Did not forever feed me vital blood.
I see the mighty city through a mist—
The strident trains that speed the goaded mass,   10
The poles and spires and towers vapor-kissed,
The fortressed port through which the great ships pass,
The tides, the wharves, the dens I contemplate,
Are sweet like wanton loves because I hate.

1921

Outcast

For the dim regions whence my fathers came
My spirit, bondaged by the body, longs.
Words felt, but never heard, my lips would frame;
My soul would sing forgotten jungle songs.
I would go back to darkness and to peace,   5
But the great western world holds me in fee,[4]
And I may never hope for full release
While to its alien gods I bend my knee.
Something in me is lost, forever lost,
Some vital thing has gone out of my heart,   10
And I must walk the way of life a ghost
Among the sons of earth, a thing apart;
For I was born, far from my native clime,
Under the white man's menace, out of time.

1922

4. In a condition of servitude.

JEAN TOOMER
(1894–1967)

Born in 1894, in Washington, D.C., Nathan Eugene Toomer (who took the name "Jean" when he decided to become a writer) spent his childhood and adolescent years seeing the world from both sides of the color line. The experience eventually led him to define himself as neither black nor white but, he insisted, as "an American . . . striv[ing] for a spiritual fusion analogous to the fact of racial intermingling." Although Toomer's maternal grandfather, P. B. S. Pinchback, grounded his career as a Reconstruction-era, Louisiana politician on claims of being black, the family was racially mixed and fair enough to pass for white. Toomer grew up in white neighborhoods: first in an affluent suburb of Washington, D.C., in the Pinchback home, where his mother retreated after Toomer's father left her in 1895; then, after 1905, in New Rochelle and Brooklyn, New York, where his mother settled with her white second husband. When she died in 1909, Toomer returned to his maternal grandparents, who, because of financial setbacks, had relocated to a black neighborhood in Washington. Toomer attended a black high school and then, in 1914, matriculated at the University of Wisconsin, Madison, hoping to major in agriculture. Impelled by chronic restlessness and a yearning for perfection—forces that troubled him throughout his life—he left after one year. He subsequently enrolled in four other colleges but never took a degree. In 1919, while at the City College of New York, he settled on becoming a writer, a course that was influenced by his introduction to the Greenwich Village literary scene and his friendship with the novelist and social critic Waldo Frank, who became his mentor.

For the next two years, living with his grandparents in Washington but making occasional sojourns to New York, Toomer immersed himself in literature, reading widely and drafting a flurry of short stories, poems, essays, and reviews, but submitted few of his efforts for publication. In August 1921, he accepted an offer to serve for two months as the principal of a black school in rural Sparta, Georgia, where he suddenly understood his goals as a writer. After his return, he emphasized that "a visit to Georgia last fall was the starting point of everything of worth that I have done. I heard folk-songs come from the lips of Negro peasants. I saw the rich dusk beauty that I had heard many false accents about, and of which til then, I was somewhat skeptical. And a deep part of my nature, a part that I had repressed, sprang suddenly to life and responded to them." Some of his subsequent prose sketches, short stories, and poems set in the South found publication in literary journals, but, lacking enough material for a book, Toomer created a section of poetry and prose based on his experiences in northern cities. The resulting work, *Cane* (1923), was one of the most influential contributions to the budding Harlem Renaissance movement, for Toomer not only charted tensions between the African American experience of North and South, the urban and the rural, alienation and spiritual yearning, but he also opened new possibilities for African American literature through his intense lyricism and Modernist experimentation with form. By including in *Cane* poems of traditional form, Imagist free verse, prose poetry, narrative sketches that include poetic devices such as refrain lines, and poetry grounded on African American forms such as spirituals and work songs, Toomer inspired other black writers of the era to take risks with form and in their portrayals of African American life. Moreover, his blurring of the lines between poetry and prose reflected his opposition to inflexible categories such as "Negro" and "White." Thus, after *Cane* appeared, Toomer objected to being called a "Negro Writer," and, emphasizing that he was simply an American writer, he turned away from African American themes.

Instead, searching for spiritual balance, he became a follower of Georgei Gurdjieff, a Russian guru who promised achievement of higher consciousness through "Unitism," a system that melded elements from philosophy, psychology, dance, and eastern religions. Beginning in 1924, Toomer taught Gurdjieff's method in New York and Chicago. His writing quickly became saturated with the guru's ideology and was still immersed in "Unitism" even after he broke with Gurdjieff in 1934. In 1931, Toomer married the novelist Margery Latimer, but she died giving birth to their daughter a year later. He remarried in 1934 and settled on a farm in Doylestown, Pennsylvania, but both his domestic and intellectual life were compromised by failing health that began to overtake him in the 1940s. Despite enervation, kidney problems, and eye trouble, Toomer continued to write until his death in 1967. He had difficulty finding publication, for his work after *Cane* was often didactic. But since the rediscovery of *Cane* during the Black Arts movement of the 1960s, his reputation as an innovative Modernist and as one of the most important writers of the Harlem Renaissance has never faltered.

◄●───◄▶───●►

Seventh Street

> Money burns the pocket, pocket hurts,
> Bootleggers in silken shirts,
> Ballooned, zooming Cadillacs,
> Whizzing, whizzing down the street-car tracks.

Seventh Street is a bastard of Prohibition and the War. A crude-boned, soft-skinned wedge of nigger life breathing its loafer air, jazz songs and love, thrusting unconscious rhythms, black reddish blood into the white and whitewashed wood of Washington. Stale soggy wood of Washington. Wedges rust in soggy wood . . . Split it! In two! Again! Shred it! . . . the sun. Wedges are brilliant in the sun; ribbons of wet wood dry and blow away. Black reddish blood. Pouring for crude-boned soft-skinned life, who set you flowing? Blood suckers of the War would spin in a frenzy of dizziness if they drank your blood. Prohibition would put a stop to it. Who set you flowing? White and whitewash disappear in blood. Who set you flowing? Flowing down the smooth asphalt of Seventh Street, in shanties, brick office buildings, theaters, drug stores, restaurants, and cabarets? Eddying on the corners? Swirling like a blood-red smoke up where the buzzards fly in heaven? God would not dare to suck black red blood. A Nigger God! He would duck his head in shame and call for the Judgment Day. Who set you flowing?

> Money burns the pocket, pocket hurts,
> Bootleggers in silken shirts,
> Ballooned, zooming Cadillacs,
> Whizzing, whizzing down the street-car tracks.

1923

November Cotton Flower

Boll-weevil's[1] coming, and the winter's cold,
Made cotton-stalks look rusty, season's old,
And cotton, scarce as any southern snow,
Was vanishing; the branch, so pinched and slow,
Failed in its function as the autumn rake;   5
Drouth fighting soil had caused the soil to take
All water from the streams; dead birds were found
In wells a hundred feet below the ground—
Such was the season when the flower bloomed.
Old folks were startled, and it soon assumed   10
Significance. Superstition saw
Something it had never seen before:
Brown eyes that loved without a trace of fear,
Beauty so sudden for that time of year.

                                                    1923

Georgia Dusk

The sky, lazily disdaining to pursue
    The setting sun, too indolent to hold
    A lengthened tournament for flashing gold,
Passively darkens for night's barbecue,

A feast of moon and men and barking hounds,   5
    An orgy for some genius of the South
    With blood-hot eyes and cane-lipped scented mouth,
Surprised in making folk-song from soul sounds.

The sawmill blows its whistle, buzz-saws stop,
    And silence breaks the bud of knoll and hill,   10
    Soft settling pollen where plowed lands fulfill
Their early promise of a bumper crop.

Smoke from the pyramidal sawdust pile
    Curls up, blue ghosts of trees, tarrying low
    Where only chips and stumps are left to show   15
The solid proof of former domicile.

Meanwhile, the men, with vestiges of pomp,
    Race memories of king and caravan,
    High-priests, an ostrich, and a juju-man,[2]
Go singing through the footpaths of the swamp.   20

Their voices rise . . . the pine trees are guitars,
    Strumming, pine-needles fall like sheets of rain . . .

1. A beetle, the most notorious pest to cotton growers.
2. A conjurer.

Their voices rise . . . the chorus of the cane
Is caroling a vesper to the stars . . .

O singers, resinous and soft your songs   25
  Above the sacred whisper of the pines,
  Give virgin lips to cornfield concubines,
Bring dreams of Christ to dusky cane-lipped throngs.

1923

Reapers

Black reapers with the sound of steel on stones
Are sharpening scythes. I see them place the hones[3]
In their hip-pockets as a thing that's done,
And start their silent swinging, one by one.
Black horses drive a mower through the weeds.   5
And there, a field rat, startled, squealing bleeds.
His belly close to ground. I see the blade,
Blood-stained, continue cutting weeds and shade.

1923

◄ STERLING A. BROWN ►
(1901–1989)

Born in Washington, D.C., Sterling Allen Brown grew up in the vigorous intellectual milieu of Howard University, where his father was a professor of religion.
Brown attended the prestigious Dunbar High School and then studied at Williams
College on a scholarship for minorities, graduating Phi Beta Kappa in 1922. He
continued his academic training at Harvard, where in 1923 he received his master's degree in English. At Harvard, Brown discovered Louis Untermeyer's *Modern American Poetry* (1921), which introduced him not only to Imagist poetry but
also to the work of Edwin Arlington Robinson, Robert Frost, and Edgar Lee Masters. Their supple vernacular language, character studies, and narrative techniques
demonstrated to Brown the viability of a realist, audience-oriented poetry, and he
began to aim for similar effects in his own poetry.

   After graduating from Harvard, he taught English at Virginia Seminary and
College, Lincoln University, and Fisk University. While in the South, Brown immersed himself in the life of rural African American communities, gaining an education that he deemed far superior to the studies he pursued in college. In the midst of
people for whom spirituals, folktales, and verbal wit were a means of survival, he
encountered living traditions that he used in his poetry and would later document in
his scholarship. In a 1942 speech he explains, "I was first attracted by certain qualities that I thought the speech of the people had, and I wanted to get for my own
writing a flavor, a color, a pungency of speech. Then later, I came to something more
important—I wanted to get an understanding of people, to acquire an accuracy in

---

3. Sharpening stones.

the portrayal of their lives." In poems that were sometimes based on people he met, such as the waiter in Jefferson City, Missouri, who became the model for "Slim Greer," he not only created distinctive portraits and protested against racism, but deployed folk forms such as the blues, spirituals, ballads, and work songs, often in dialect notable for its blend of realism and musicality. As Brown notes in *Negro Poetry and Drama*, he "sought to convey the tragedy of the southern Negro [and] the dogged stoicism he has found in Negro experience." Yet that tragedy and stoicism are sharpened by humor, a laughter empowered by irony.

When the poems were collected in Brown's first book, *Southern Road* (1932), James Weldon Johnson argued that the poet's new realism in dialect left the simpering minstrel tradition far behind. He also noted that Brown "has made more than mere transcriptions of folk poetry, and he has done more than bring it to mere artistry; he has deepened its meanings and multiplied its implications. He has actually absorbed the spirit of his material, made it his own; and without diluting its primitive frankness and raciness, truly re-expressed it with artistry and magnified power." Reviewers were also moved by the book's stark power, and they recognized *Southern Road* not as the probings of a beginner, but as the work of an accomplished artist.

Brown's passion for African American literature and folklore also found expression in his distinguished academic career. As an English professor at Howard University from 1929 until his retirement in 1969, he inspired generations of students. His work as a scholar and anthologist helped to establish the field of African American literature through books such as *The Negro in American Fiction* (1937) and *Negro Poetry and Drama* (1937), which survey literature from the 1700s through the 1930s, and his landmark anthology, *The Negro Caravan: Writings by American Negroes* (1941), co-edited with Ulysses Lee and Arthur P. Davis, which collects poetry, fiction, drama, essays, speeches, and folklore and sets them in the context of American literary movements. In all three books, Brown denounces racial stereotypes and emphasizes that African American folklore is a significant *literary* achievement, and, conversely, that African American literature gains vigor from its roots in folklore.

During the Depression, Brown's literary expertise led to public service. From 1936 to 1939, he served as editor of Negro Affairs for the Works Progress Administration's Federal Writers' Project, where he oversaw the collection of ex-slave narratives, edited a guidebook on Washington, D.C., and reviewed copy for sections on African Americans to be included in the WPA's state guides. He also held a Guggenheim Fellowship (1937–1938), was appointed to the committee on Negro studies of the American Council of Learned Societies, and worked as an editor for the *Encyclopaedia Britannica*. In the following decades, he poured most of his energy into teaching at Howard University. His retirement from teaching in 1969 coincided with the Black Arts Movement's rediscovery and celebration of important African American authors, and his work claimed renewed interest. His second book of poetry, *The Last Ride of Wild Bill, and Eleven Narrative Poems*, appeared in 1975, followed by *The Collected Poems of Sterling A. Brown*, edited by the poet Michael Harper, in 1980. Since Brown's death in 1989, his reputation as a master of vernacular narrative poetry and his influence on African American poetry have continued to grow.

Memphis Blues[1]

I

Nineveh, Tyre,
Babylon,[2]
Not much lef'
Of either one.
All dese cities   5
Ashes and rust,
De win' sing sperrichals
Through deir dus' . . .
Was another Memphis
Mongst de olden days,   10
Done been destroyed
In many ways. . . .
Dis here Memphis
It may go;
Floods may drown it;   15
Tornado blow;
Mississippi wash it
Down to sea—
Like de other Memphis in
History.   20

II

Watcha gonna do when Memphis on fire,
   Memphis on fire, Mistah Preachin' Man?
Gonna pray to Jesus and nebber tire,
   Gonna pray to Jesus, loud as I can,
     Gonna pray to my Jesus, oh, my Lawd!   25

Watcha gonna do when de tall flames roar,
   Tall flames roar, Mistah Lovin' Man?
Gonna love my brownskin better'n before—
   Gonna love my baby lak a do right man,
     Gonna love my brown baby, oh, my Lawd!   30

Watcha gonna do when Memphis falls down,
   Memphis falls down, Mistah Music Man?
Gonna plunk on dat box as long as it soun',
   Gonna plunk dat box fo' to beat de ban',
     Gonna tickle dem ivories, oh, my Lawd!   35

Watcha gonna do in de hurricane,
   In de hurricane, Mistah Workin' Man?
Gonna put dem buildings up again

---

1. The ancient city of Memphis in Egypt was associated with the slavery of the Israelites. Memphis, Tennessee, was a center of the blues. Both cities are located on rivers, the former on the Nile, the latter on the Mississippi.
2. All cities associated with corruption in the Old Testament.

Gonna put em up dis time to stan',
   Gonna push a wicked wheelbarrow, oh, my Lawd!   40

Watcha gonna do when Memphis near gone,
   Memphis near gone, Mistah Drinkin' Man?
Gonna grab a pint bottle of Mountain Corn,
   Gonna keep de stopper in my han',
      Gonna get a mean jag[3] on, oh, my Lawd!   45

Watcha gonna do when de flood roll fas',
   Flood roll fas', Mistah Gamblin' Man?
Gonna pick up my dice fo' one las' pass—
   Gonna fade my way to de lucky lan',
      Gonna throw my las' seven—oh, my Lawd!   50

III

Memphis go
By Flood or Flame;
Nigger won't worry
All de same—
Memphis go   55
Memphis come back,
Ain' no skin
Off de nigger's back.
All dese cities
Ashes, rust. . . .   60
De win' sing sperrichals
Through deir dus'.

1932

Mose

Mose is black and evil
And damns his luck
Driving Mister Schwartz's[4]
Big coal truck.

He's got no gal,   5
He's got no jack,
No fancy silk shirts
For his back.

But summer evenings,
Hard luck Mose   10
Goes in for all
The fun he knows.

3. Drinking bout.
4. (German) Black.

On the corner kerb
With a sad quartette
His tenor peals   15
Like a clarinet.

O hit it Moses
Sing att thing
But Mose's mind
Goes wandering;—   20

And to the stars
over the town
Floats, from a good man
Way, way down—

A soft song, filled   25
With a misery
Older than Mose
Will ever be

                                1932

Slim Greer

Listen to the tale
Of Ole slim Greer,
Waitines' devil
Waitin' here;

    Talkinges' guy   5
    An' biggest liar,
    With always a new lie
    On the fire.

Tells a tale
Of Arkansaw   10
That keeps the kitchen
In a roar;

    Tells in a long-drawled
    Careless tone,
    As solemn as a Baptist   15
    Parson's moan.

How he in Arkansaw
Passed for white,
An' he no lighter
Than a dark midnight.   20

    Found a nice white woman
    At a dance,
    Thought he was from Spain
    Or else from France;

Nobody suspicioned   25
Ole Slim Greer's race
But a Hill Billy, always
Roun' the place,

    Who called one day
    On the trustful dame   30
    An' found Slim comfy
    When he came.

The whites lef' the parlor
All to Slim
Which didn't cut   35
No ice with him,

    An' he started a-tinklin'
    Some mo'nful blues,
    An' a-pattin' the time
    With No. Fourteen shoes.   40

The cracker listened
An' then he spat
An' said, "No white man
Could play like that. . . ."

    The white jane[5] ordered   45
    The tattler out;
    Then, female-like,
    Began to doubt,

Crept into the parlor
Soft as you please,   50
Where Slim was agitatin'
The ivories.

    Heard Slim's music—
    An' then, hot damn!
    Shouted sharp—"Nigger!"   55
    An' Slim said, "Ma'am?"

She screamed and the crackers
Swarmed up soon,
But found only echoes
Of his tune;   60

    'Cause Slim had sold out
    With lightnin' speed;
    "Hope I may die, sir—
    Yes, indeed. . . ."

                        1932

5. Woman.

Slim in Atlanta

Down in Atlanta,
  De whitefolks got laws
For to keep all de niggers
  From laughin' outdoors.

      Hope to Gawd I may die   5
        If I ain't speakin' truth
      Make de niggers do deir laughin'
        In a telefoam booth.

Slim Greer hit de town
  An' de rebs got him told,—   10
"Dontcha laugh on de street,
  If you want to die old."

      Den dey showed him de booth,
        An' a hundred shines
      In front of it, waitin'   15
        In double lines.

Slim thought his sides
  Would bust in two,
Yelled, "Lookout, everybody,
  I'm coming through!"   20

      Pulled de other man out,
        An' bust in de box,
      An' laughed four hours
        By de Georgia clocks.

Den he peeked through de door,   25
  An' what did he see?
Three hundred niggers there
  In misery.—

      Some holdin' deir sides
        Some holdin' deir jaws,   30
      To keep from breakin'
        De Georgia laws.

An' Slim gave a holler,
  An' started again;
An' from three hundred throats   35
  Come a moan of pain.

      An' everytime Slim
        Saw what was outside,
      Got to whoopin' again
        Till he nearly died.   40

An' while de poor critters
  Was waitin' deir chance,

        Slim laughed till dey sent
        Fo' de ambulance.

            De state paid de railroad   45
            To take him away;
            Den, things was as usural
            In Atlanta, Gee A.[6]

                                                                    1932

◦━◄ GWENDOLYN BENNETT ►━◦

(1902–1981)

As a poet, graphic artist, and arts columnist, Gwendolyn Bennett was an influential contributor to the Harlem Renaissance, even though she never gathered her work into a collection. Born in Giddings, Texas, Bennett moved with her parents first to Nevada, where they taught at an Indian reservation, and then to Washington, D.C., where they soon divorced. Although Mrs. Bennett gained custody of Gwendolyn, Mr. Bennett kidnapped the seven-year-old girl; moving from town to town to escape detection, father and daughter did not settle until she reached high-school age, when he married again and relocated to Brooklyn, New York. Gwendolyn flourished at Brooklyn Girls' High School, and after graduation in 1921 she studied art at Columbia University and the Pratt Institute, where she received her bachelor's degree in 1924. After a brief teaching stint at Howard University in Washington, D.C., Bennett received a scholarship to work in Paris for a year. When she returned to New York in 1926, she was poised to become a full-fledged member of the "New Negro" cultural flowering.

    The 1920s were Bennett's most productive years, for she began participating in the Harlem Renaissance arts scene even when she was a student: in 1923, she published a poem in *Opportunity* and illustrated the cover of the *Crisis*. Between 1921 and 1931, twenty-two of her poems appeared in African American journals, her designs graced the covers of *Opportunity* and *Crisis* on five occasions, and she contributed to several landmark anthologies: James Weldon Johnson's *The Book of American Negro Poetry* (1922), Alain Locke's *The New Negro* (1925), Countee Cullen's *Caroling Dusk: An Anthology of Verse by Negro Poets* (1927), and William Stanley Braithwaite's *Anthology of Magazine Verse for 1927* and *Yearbook of American Poetry* (1927). Her poetry was admired for its lyricism and its articulation of the mixed emotions experienced by urban African Americans—the newfound pride in their heritage and the bitterness at the limitations still constricting them. Bennett also became an important cultural arbiter; beginning in 1926, she worked as an assistant to the editor of *Opportunity* and began an arts column, "Ebony Flute," in which she offered monthly reports on literary and arts events and personalities in Harlem. She gave up the column in 1928, when she moved with her new husband, Alfred Jackson, to Florida.

    Feeling isolated in the South, the Jacksons returned to New York in 1930, when the vibrancy of the Harlem Renaissance had faded because of the Depres-

---

6. That is, GA, or Georgia.

sion, and Bennett never again regained the momentum she had sustained during the 1920s. Instead, she was active in arts administration and education, working for the WPA's Federal Writers' Project and Arts Project in the 1930s and guiding the Jefferson School for Democracy and the George Washington Carver School in the early 1940s. But after the House Committee on Un-American Activities unfairly accused the schools of being communist and subjected them to a strenuous investigation, Bennett fled public life and moved to Kutztown, Pennsylvania, where she and her second husband became antique dealers. Today, she is remembered not only for what James Weldon Johnson called "her delicate, poignant lyrics" but also for her versatility in combining her vocations in the visual and literary arts, and for her *Opportunity* column, which has become an important source of Harlem Renaissance cultural history.

Hatred

I shall hate you
Like a dart of singing steel
Shot through still air
At even-tide.
Or solemnly   5
As pines are sober
When they stand etched
Against the sky.
Hating you shall be a game
Played with cool hands   5
And slim fingers.
Your heart will yearn
For the lonely splendor
Of the pine tree;
While rekindled fires   5
In my eyes
Shall wound you like swift arrows.
Memory will lay its hands
Upon your breast
And you will understand   5
My hatred.

1927

To a Dark Girl

I love you for your brownness
And the rounded darkness of your breast.
I love you for the breaking sadness in your voice
And shadows where your wayward eye-lids rest.

Something of old forgotten queens   5
Lurks in the lithe abandon of your walk,
And something of the shackled slave
Sobs in the rhythm of your talk.

Oh, little brown girl, born for sorrow's mate,
Keep all you have of queenliness,   5
Forgetting that you once were slave,
And let your full lips laugh at Fate!

1927

⬥◄ LANGSTON HUGHES ►⬥
(1902–1967)

The man who would become one of the leading figures in the Harlem Renaissance and later a major American poet of civil rights protest was born James Langston Hughes in Joplin, Missouri. His father, James Hughes, was a mining company stenographer, his mother, Carrie Mercer Langston Hughes, an amateur poet and actress. His parents' marriage was troubled, and soon after the poet's birth his father left, first for Cuba and then Mexico. His mother took her son back to her hometown of Lawrence, Kansas. Langston Hughes's grandmother, with whom he lived for most of a dozen years, had once been married to a member of John Brown's abolitionist band who was killed during the raid on Harper's Ferry in 1859. Her second husband, Charles Langston, had also been an abolitionist, and after the Civil War a Republican businessman. The poet, conscious of his mixed blood and heritage, grew up with his grandmother's stories, which gave him a sense of American history. "Nobody ever cried in my grandmother's stories," he once wrote. "They worked, schemed, or fought. But no crying."

After his grandmother's death, Langston moved with his mother to Lincoln, Illinois, where she remarried. The poet now had a stepfather and stepbrother, but still felt drawn to his own father's powerful presence in Mexico. His new family moved to Cleveland, Ohio, where his stepfather worked in a steel mill. The summer before his senior year at Cleveland's Central High School, Langston went to stay with his father. He was already writing poems that displayed the influence of Walt Whitman and Carl Sandburg, and when he finished high school he was named "class poet." But after graduation, a year spent back in Mexico with his father was often disrupted by their arguments. The elder Hughes was not only disappointed by his son's desire to be a writer, but also by the subjects he chose to write about.

In *The Big Sea* (1940), the first volume of his autobiography, Hughes remembered the composition of his first literary success, a poem written while riding a train across the Mississippi in 1921:

> I looked out the window of the Pullman at the great muddy river flowing down toward
> the heart of the South, and I began to think what that river, the old Mississippi, had
> meant to Negroes in the past—how to be sold down the river was the worst fate that
> could overtake a slave in times of bondage. . . . Then I began to think about other rivers
> in our past—the Congo, and the Niger, and the Nile in Africa—and the thought came
> to me: "I've known rivers," and I put it down on the back of an envelope I had in my

Langston Hughes in the 1920s.

pocket, and within the space of ten or fifteen minutes, as the train gathered speed in the dusk, I had written this poem, which I called "The Negro Speaks of Rivers."

Published that year in the *Crisis*, the official organ of the NAACP, "The Negro Speaks of Rivers" introduced the young Hughes to a larger community of writers. He enrolled at Columbia University for a year at his father's expense, where he met W. E. B. DuBois, the founder and editor of *Crisis*, as well as the young Harlem poet Countee Cullen. Refusing his father's invitation to return to Mexico, he stayed on in New York to be a writer, continuing to absorb the cultural influences of the time, including jazz and the blues.

The 1920s were for Hughes a time of travel and frenetic literary activity. After a period doing odd jobs, he began working on merchant ships, sailing once to Africa and twice to Europe. He lived in France and Italy, then returned to live with his mother in Washington, D.C., where he held down various menial jobs. Another of his poems, "The Weary Blues," made him new literary friends, one of whom—Carl Van Vechten—arranged to have Knopf publish a book of his poetry. One day the poet Vachel Lindsay, who was on a public reading tour, happened to dine at a hotel where Hughes was a busboy. Hughes shyly left some of his poems at Lindsay's table, and the older poet, attracted by their deliberate informality, performed some of them that night, earning Hughes minor celebrity. Hughes soon had a patroness as well, a wealthy widow named Charlotte Mason, who also supported the work of Zora Neale Hurston and others. In 1929 he took a degree from Lincoln University in Pennsylvania. After a successful reading tour of Cuba, he worked on a play, *Mule Bone,* with Hurston, but a powerful disagreement caused them to break with each other and also lost Hughes the support of their patroness. Nevertheless, he continued to travel—to Haiti, Russia, California—and write at a prolific rate.

Increasingly, Hughes involved himself in leftist causes. In 1937, as a reporter covering the Spanish Civil War, he spent three months in Madrid under siege. He met Pablo Neruda and W. H. Auden in Paris and Ernest Hemingway in Spain, where he also began to translate poems by Federico García Lorca, who had been murdered by Franco's Nationalists in 1936. (He later translated Lorca's verse drama, *Blood Wedding.*) Several of his plays having been performed in New York, Hughes soon found himself writing a screenplay for a motion picture, *Way Down South* (1939).

During World War II Hughes lived in New York, publishing a weekly column in the newspaper the *Chicago Defender.* There he introduced his Harlem character, Jesse B. Semple (or "Simple"), perhaps his most popular creation. Over the years he published several collections of Semple sketches. When his musical, *Street Scene,* on which he collaborated with the German composer Kurt Weill, opened on Broadway in 1947, it was greeted with rave reviews and became a hit.

In the next decade, however, his past friendships with figures like former Communist agent Whittaker Chambers resulted in his being called before Senator Joseph McCarthy's subcommittee on un-American Activities. Hughes survived the ordeal in part by admitting that his past radicalism had been a mistake, but his leftist connections and social activism caused him problems for the rest of his life.

Hughes's populist aesthetic caused him a different sort of problem with the next generation of African American writers. In 1959 his *Selected Poems* was dismissed in the *New York Times* by novelist James Baldwin for its apparent lack of literary sophistication. In fact, Hughes's work often met with disdain, particularly by academic critics who considered it simple-minded. Nevertheless, he was clearly the most famous and popular African American poet of his generation—and in works like his long poem, *Ask Your Mama: 12 Moods for Jazz* (1961), also one of the most ambitious. Hughes created an original blend of folk tradition, jazz, and midwestern modernism in plain language that appealed to a broad readership and profoundly influenced later black writers. Hughes objected to the more militant black poets of the 1960s, such as LeRoi Jones (Imamu Amiri Baraka), and defended the nonviolent strategies of Martin Luther King, Jr.

Hughes was also one of the most innovative poets of his time, but the speed and facility with which he wrote resulted in uneven output. While his literary productions (novels, plays, poems, nonfiction, and musical collaborations), read together, can become repetitive and formulaic, Hughes was at his best a genuine populist poet in the tradition of Whitman and Sandburg, but with particular lyric gifts and subject matter rooted in black experience. Many of his poems have the lightness and transparency of song lyrics; indeed, he often wrote poetry with the intention of having it set to music.

Hughes died in 1967 of complications following prostate surgery. Thirty-two of his books were still in print. It was typical of his productive life that two more volumes appeared posthumously that same year.

The Negro Speaks of Rivers

I've known rivers:
I've known rivers ancient as the world and older than the flow of human blood in
    human veins.

My soul has grown deep like the rivers.

I bathed in the Euphrates when dawns were young.   5
I built my hut near the Congo and it lulled me to sleep.
I looked upon the Nile and raised the pyramids above it.
I heard the singing of the Mississippi when Abe Lincoln went down to New
    Orleans, and I've seen its muddy bosom turn all golden in the sunset.   10

I've known rivers:
Ancient, dusky rivers.

My soul has grown deep like the rivers.

1926

I, Too

I, too, sing America.
I am the darker brother.
They send me to eat in the kitchen
When company comes,
But I laugh,   5
And eat well,
And grow strong.

Tomorrow,
I'll be at the table
When company comes.   10
Nobody'll dare
Say to me,
"Eat in the kitchen,"
Then.

Besides,   15
They'll see how beautiful I am
And be ashamed—

I, too, am America.

1926

Negro

I am a Negro:
   Black as the night is black,
   Black like the depths of my Africa.

I've been a slave:
   Caesar told me to keep his door-steps clean.   5
   I brushed the boots of Washington.

I've been a worker:
   Under my hand the pyramids arose.
   I made mortar for the Woolworth Building.

I've been a singer: 10
   All the way from Africa to Georgia
   I carried my sorrow songs.
   I made ragtime.

I've been a victim:
   The Belgians cut off my hands in the Congo.[1]   15
   They lynch me still in Mississippi.

I am a Negro:
   Black as the night is black,
   Black like the depths of my Africa.

1926

Cross

My old man's a white old man
And my old mother's black.
If ever I cursed my white old man
I take my curses back.

If ever I cursed my black old mother   5
And wished she were in hell,
I'm sorry for that evil wish
And now I wish her well.

My old man died in a fine big house.
My ma died in a shack.   10
I wonder where I'm gonna die,
Being neither white nor black?

1926

---

1. During King Leopold of Belgium's colonial rule over the Congo, failure to pay a labor tax often resulted in having a hand cut off, or even in the offender's execution.

The Weary Blues

Droning a drowsy syncopated tune,
Rocking back and forth to a mellow croon,
   I heard a Negro play.
Down on the Lenox Avenue[2] the other night
By the pale dull pallor of an old gas light   5
   He did a lazy sway. . . .
   He did a lazy sway. . . .
To the tune o' those Weary Blues.
With his ebony hands on each ivory key
He made that poor piano moan with melody.   10
   O Blues!
Swaying to and fro on his rickety stool
He played that sad raggy tune like a musical fool.
   Sweet Blues!
Coming from a black man's soul.   15
   O Blues!
In a deep song voice with a melancholy tone
I heard that Negro sing, that old piano moan—
   "Ain't got nobody in all this world,
     Ain't got nobody but ma self.   20
     I's gwine to quit ma frownin'
     And put ma troubles on the shelf."

Thump, thump, thump, went his foot on the floor.
He played a few chords then he sang some more—
   "I got the Weary Blues   25
     And I can't be satisfied.
     Got the Weary Blues
     And can't be satisfied—
     I ain't happy no mo'
     And I wish that I had died."   30
And far into the night he crooned that tune.
The stars went out and so did the moon.
The singer stopped playing and went to bed
While the Weary Blues echoed through his head.
He slept like a rock or a man that's dead.   35

                1926

Dream Variations

   To fling my arms wide
   In some place of the sun,
   To whirl and to dance
   Till the white day is done.
   Then rest at cool evening   5

2. Avenue in New York City, now called Malcolm X Boulevard.

Beneath a tall tree
While night comes on gently,
   Dark like me—
That is my dream!

To fling my arms wide   10
In the face of the sun,
Dance! Whirl! Whirl!
Till the quick day is done.
Rest at pale evening . . .
A tall, slim tree . . .   15
Night coming tenderly
   Black like me.

                         1926

Song for a Dark Girl

Way Down South in Dixie
   (Break the heart of me)
They hung my black young lover
   To a cross roads tree.

Way Down South in Dixie   5
   (Bruised body high in air)
I asked the white Lord Jesus
   What was the use of prayer.

Way Down South in Dixie
   (Break the heart of me)   10
Love is a naked shadow
   On a gnarled and naked tree.

                         1927

Mother to Son

Well, son, I'll tell you:
Life for me ain't been no crystal stair.
It's had tacks in it,
And splinters,
And boards torn up,   5
And places with no carpet on the floor—
Bare.
But all the time
I'se been a-climbin' on,
And reachin' landin's,   10
And turnin' corners,
And sometimes goin' in the dark
Where there ain't been no light.
So boy, don't you turn back.

Don't you set down on the steps   15
'Cause you finds it's kinder hard.
Don't you fall now—
For I'se still goin', honey,
I'se still climbin',
And life for me ain't been no crystal stair.   20

1932

Park Bench

I live on a park bench.
You, Park Avenue.
Hell of a distance
Between us two.

I beg a dime for dinner—   5
You got a butler and maid.
But I'm wakin' up!
Say, ain't you afraid

That I might, just maybe,
In a year or two,   10
Move on over
To Park Avenue?

1934

50–50

I'm all alone in this world, she said,
Ain't got nobody to share my bed,
Ain't got nobody to hold my hand—
The truth of the matter's
I ain't got no man.   5

Big Boy opened his mouth and said,
Trouble with you is
You ain't got no head!
If you had a head and used your mind
You could have *me* with you   10
All the time.

She answered, Babe, what must I do?

He said, Share your bed—
And your money, too.

1942

Ku Klux

They took me out
To some lonesome place.
They said, "Do you believe
In the great white race?"

I said, "Mister,   5
To tell you the truth,
I'd believe in anything
If you'd just turn me loose."

The white man said, "Boy,
Can it be   10
You're a-standin' there
A-sassin' me?"

They hit me in the head
And knocked me down.
And then they kicked me   15
On the ground.

A klansman said, "Nigger,
Look me in the face—
And tell me you believe in
The great white race."   20

                                                    1942

Madam's Past History

My name is Johnson—
Madam Alberta K.
The Madam stands for business.
I'm smart that way.

I had a   5
HAIR-DRESSING PARLOR
Before
The depression put
The prices lower.

Then I had a   10
BARBECUE STAND
Till I got mixed up
With a no-good man.

Cause I had a insurance
The WPA[3]   15
Said, We can't use you
Wealthy that way.

---

3. Works Progress Administration, a Depression-era agency that created jobs for the unemployed.

I said,
DON'T WORRY 'BOUT ME!
Just like the song,   20
You WPA folks take care of yourself—
And I'll get along.

I do cooking,
Day's work, too!
Alberta K. Johnson—   25
Madam to you.

                                                            1949

Island

Wave of sorrow,
Do not drown me now;

I see the island
Still ahead somehow.

I see the island   5
And its sands are fair:

Wave of sorrow,
Take me there.

                                                            1950

Harlem

What happens to a dream deferred?

Does it dry up
like a raisin in the sun?
Or fester like a sore—
And then run?   5
Does it stink like rotten meat?
Or crust and sugar over—
like a syrupy sweet?

Maybe it just sags
like a heavy load.   10

Or does it explode?

                                                            1951

Theme for English B

The instructor said,

   Go home and write
   a page tonight.
   And let that page come out of you—
   Then, it will be true.   5

I wonder if it's that simple?
I am twenty-two, colored, born in Winston-Salem.
I went to school there, then Durham, then here
to this college on the hill above Harlem.[4]
I am the only colored student in my class.   10
The steps from the hill lead down into Harlem,
through a park, then I cross St. Nicholas,
Eighth Avenue, Seventh, and I come to the Y,
the Harlem Branch Y, where I take the elevator
up to my room, sit down, and write this page: 15

It's not easy to know what is true for you and me
at twenty-two, my age. But I guess I'm what
I feel and see and hear, Harlem, I hear you:
hear you, hear me—we too—you, me, talk on this page.
(I hear New York, too.) Me—who?   20
Well, I like to eat, sleep, drink, and be in love.
I like to work, read, learn, and understand life.
I like a pipe for a Christmas present,
or records—Bessie,[5] bop, or Bach.
I guess being colored doesn't make me not like   25
the same things other folks like who are other races.
So will my page be colored that I write?
Being me, it will not be white.

But it will be
a part of you, instructor.   30
You are white—
yet a part of me, as I am a part of you.
That's American.
Sometimes perhaps you don't want to be a part of me.
Nor do I often want to be a part of you.   35
But we are, that's true!
As I learn from you,
I guess you learn from me—
although you're older—and white—
and somewhat more free.   40

This is my page for English B.

1951

Homecoming

I went back in the alley
And I opened up my door.
All her clothes was gone:
She wasn't home no more.

---

4. Usually thought to refer to Columbia University, where Hughes studied for a year. However, this poem is not autobiographical. The young speaker is a character invented by the middle-aged author.
5. Bessie Smith (1898?–1937) was a popular blues singer often called the "Empress of the Blues."

I pulled back the covers,   5
I made down the bed.
A *whole* lot of room
Was the only thing I had.

1959

Dinner Guest: Me

I know I am
The Negro Problem
Being wined and dined,
Answering the usual questions
That come to white mind   5
Which seeks demurely
To probe in polite way
The why and wherewithal
Of darkness U.S.A.—
Wondering how things got this way   10
In current democratic night,
Murmuring gently
Over *fraises due bois*,[6]
"I'm so ashamed of being white."

The lobster is delicious,   15
The wine divine,
And center of attention
At the damask table, mine.
To be a Problem on
Park Avenue at eight   20
Is not so bad.
Solutions to the Problem,
Of course, wait.

1967

◄ COUNTEE CULLEN ►
(1903–1946)

Disagreements about Countee (pronounced Coun-tay) Cullen begin with his birth. So little is known about his beginnings that scholars have not even been able to decide where he was born—both New York City and Louisville, Kentucky, are often named. As James Weldon Johnson wrote, "There is not much to say about these earlier years of Cullen—unless he himself should say it." We do know that he was raised by his paternal grandmother, and that when she died in 1918, the fifteen-year-old poet (who signed his early poems Countee L. Porter) was adopted by the Reverend Frederick A. Cullen, a dynamic intellectual who had built a storefront congregation

6. (French) strawberries.

into Harlem's Salem Methodist Episcopal Church with more than 2,500 members. Dr. Cullen was a leader in the NAACP and a friend of W. E. B. DuBois. The young poet had moved into the center of black cultural life in America and would soon become one of the leading figures in the Harlem Renaissance of the 1920s.

Cullen attended DeWitt Clinton High School and, from 1922 to 1925, New York University, where he wrote many of his best-known poems. These works often display Cullen's Romanticism, particularly his fascination with Keats—in their poetic diction, their obsessions with fragile beauty, and their intimations of early death. Edna St. Vincent Millay, subject of Cullen's senior thesis, was also a strong influence on his work. Cullen was a prodigy. During his last year at New York University he published his first book, *Color* (1925), which included such poems as "Yet Do I Marvel," "Incident," "Saturday's Child," "Heritage," and "For a Lady I Know." That same year Alain Locke published his groundbreaking anthology, *The New Negro*, which prominently included Cullen's work. These volumes quickly established the young poet as an important literary figure. Cullen went to Harvard, where he took a master's degree in 1926. He also began writing a highly visible column, "The Dark Tower," for *Opportunity*, the magazine of the National Urban League. Here he gave voice to his ideas about art and race, going so far as to criticize Langston Hughes for his Modernism and incorporation of jazz rhythms in poetry.

Cullen's universalist views on art and race differed from those of most other members of the Harlem Renaissance. Already in 1924 the *Brooklyn Daily Eagle* quoted him as saying, "If I am going to be a poet at all, I am going to be a POET and not a NEGRO POET." That is, he had early on developed theories of art that transcended race. Though race consciousness is everywhere in his work, and though many of his best poems deal with racism and white smugness, Cullen wanted to be a bridge between the white and black worlds. Indeed, it has often been said that the Harlem Renaissance required the patronage of a white audience to survive, and that its financial energies were dissipated when the Great Depression of the 1930s arrived. In 1927 Cullen published his own influential anthology, *Caroling Dusk*, which he called "an anthology of verse by Negro poets rather than an anthology of Negro verse. . . ." If there was a divide in black intellectual life at the time between those who emphasized Negritude and those who emphasized unity with white America, Cullen was on the latter side. Nevertheless his work often deals frankly with racial issues and clearly articulates the author's outrage at racial and social injustice. Still, the traditional measures of his poems, coupled with his critique of important figures like Hughes, would eventually lead to the neglect of Cullen's work, largely on political grounds.

Cullen's fall from grace, however, was yet to come. In the 1920s the young poet was a major literary figure. He published his second major collection of poems, *Copper Sun*, in 1927, and won a Guggenheim Fellowship to live in France from 1928 to 1930. At this point in his life, however, there was a sharp falling off in Cullen's poetic production. His brief marriage to the daughter of W. E. B. DuBois ended in 1930 (a second marriage in 1940 proved more successful), and the poems stopped coming, as if he had outgrown the early impulses that had produced them. Though he was offered professorships at several universities, Cullen taught English, French, and creative writing at Frederick Douglass High School in New York City from 1934 to his death. He turned to translating Greek drama, and in 1935 published *The Medea and Some Poems*. The play itself he rendered as prose, but with a commission from actor John Houseman he wrote the choruses as lyrics to be set to music by Virgil Thomson. Cullen's adoptive mother had been a singer; the poet was fascinated by music all his life, and several of his poems were set to music.

Cullen was at work on a musical, *St. Louis Woman,* when he died suddenly of high blood pressure and uremic poisoning in January 1946. Two months later, the musical—which had inspired controversy for its portrayal of crime in the black community—had its Broadway premiere. It contained songs by Johnny Mercer and Harold Arlen, and made Pearl Bailey a star. But Countee Cullen died without seeing this success and would be thought of mostly as a poet of the 1920s. When the American Civil Rights movement rose to new heights in the 1950s and 1960s, Cullen's poems seemed too old-fashioned to some, and he was accused of having too easily accepted white values.

Gradually Cullen's poetic reputation has been rehabilitated. In 1971 Ishmael Reed published *Mumbo Jumbo,* an experimental novel in which Cullen figures as Nathan Brown. Reed's novel suggests that black culture needn't be seen as a unitary phenomenon, but as something diverse and multifarious enough to include Cullen and his views. Scholars and critics began to reevaluate Cullen's reputation, and he now ranks as one of the strongest voices of the Harlem Renaissance whose contributions are particularly interesting for sounding a note of dissent. Cullen's return to critical favor has also been helped by the revival of traditional poetic form at the end of the twentieth century, so that his characteristic uses of rhyme and meter no longer seem as old-fashioned as they might have appeared in 1960. Cullen was an artist of uneven output, to be sure, but in his verse, prose, and translation he holds an indelible place in the arguments of modern poetry.

━◦━━◀▶━━◦━

For a Lady I Know

She even thinks that up in heaven
    Her class lies late and snores,
While poor black cherubs rise at seven
    To do celestial chores.

1925

For Paul Laurence Dunbar[1]

Born of the sorrowful of heart,
    Mirth was a crown upon his head;
Pride kept his twisted lips apart
    In jest, to hide a heart that bled.

1925

1. Dunbar was an African American poet (1872–1906). See Dunbar headnote and introductory note on Realism and Naturalism in this book, page 6.

Heritage

(For Harold Jackman)[2]

What is Africa to me:
Copper sun or scarlet sea,
Jungle star or jungle track,
Strong bronzed men, or regal black
Women from whose loins I sprang   5
When the birds of Eden sang?
One three centuries removed
From the scenes his fathers loved,
Spicy grove, cinnamon tree,
What is Africa to me?   10

So I lie, who all day long
Want no sound except the song
Sung by wild barbaric birds
Goading massive jungle herds,
Juggernauts of flesh that pass   15
Trampling tall defiant grass
Where young forest lovers lie,
Plighting troth beneath the sky.
So I lie, who always hear,
Though I cram against my ear   20
Both my thumbs, and keep them there,
Great drums throbbing through the air.
So I lie, whose fount of pride,
Dear distress, and joy allied,
Is my somber flesh and skin,   25
With the dark blood dammed within
Like great pulsing tides of wine
That, I fear, must burst the fine
Channels of the chafing net
Where they surge and foam and fret.   30

Africa? A book one thumbs
Listlessly, till slumber comes.
Unremembered are her bats
Circling through the night, her cats
Crouching in the river reeds,   35
Stalking gentle flesh that feeds
By the river brink; no more
Does the bugle-throated roar
Cry that monarch claws[3] have leapt
From the scabbards where they slept.   40
Silver snakes that once a year

2. Harold Jackman (1900–1960), a Harlem schoolteacher and friend of Cullen.
3. Of the lion.

Doff the lovely coats you wear,
Seek no covert in your fear
Lest a mortal eye should see;
What's your nakedness to me?   45
Here no leprous flowers rear
Fierce corollas in the air;
Here no bodies sleek and wet,
Dripping mingled rain and sweat,
Tread the savage measures of   50
Jungle boys and girls in love.
What is last year's snow to me,
Last year's anything? The tree
Budding yearly must forget
How its past arose or set—   55
Bough and blossom, flower, fruit,
Even what shy bird with mute
Wonder at her travail there,
Meekly labored in its hair.
One three centuries removed   60
From the scenes his fathers loved,
Spicy grove, cinnamon tree,
What is Africa to me?

So I lie, who find no peace
Night or day, no slight release   65
From the unremittant beat
Made by cruel padded feet
Walking through my body's street.
Up and down they go, and back,
Treading out a jungle track.   70
So I lie, who never quite
Safely sleep from rain at night—
I can never rest at all
When the rain begins to fall;
Like a soul gone mad with pain   75
I must match its weird refrain;
Ever must I twist and squirm,
Writhing like a baited worm,
While its primal measures drip
Through my body, crying, "Strip!   80
Doff this new exuberance.
Come and dance the Lover's Dance!"
In an old remembered way
Rain works on me night and day.

Quaint, outlandish heathen gods   85
Black men fashion out of rods,[4]

4. Sticks.

Clay, and brittle bits of stone,
In a likeness like their own,
My conversion came high-priced;
I belong to Jesus Christ,   90
Preacher of humility;
Heathen gods are naught to me,

Father, Son, and Holy Ghost,
So I make an idle boast;
Jesus of the twice-turned cheek,   95
Lamb of God, although I speak
With my mouth thus, in my heart
Do I play a double part.
Ever at Thy glowing altar
Must my heart grow sick and falter,   100
Wishing He I served were black,
Thinking then it would not lack
Precedent of pain to guide it,
Let who would or might deride it;
Surely then this flesh would know   105
Yours had borne a kindred woe.
Lord, I fashion dark gods, too,
Daring even to give You
Dark despairing features where,
Crowned with dark rebellious hair,   110
Patience wavers just so much as
Mortal grief compels, while touches
Quick and hot, of anger, rise
To smitten cheek and weary eyes.
Lord, forgive me if my need   115
Sometimes shapes a human creed.
All day long and all night through,
One thing only must I do:
Quench my pride and cool my blood,
Lest I perish in the flood.   120
Lest a hidden ember set
Timber that I thought was wet
Burning like the dryest flax,
Melting like the merest wax,
Lest the grave restore its dead.   125
Not yet has my heart or head
In the least way realized
They and I are civilized.

1925

Incident

(For Eric Walrond)[5]

Once riding in old Baltimore,
   Heart-filled, head-filled with glee,
I saw a Baltimorean
   Keep looking straight at me.

Now I was eight and very small,   5
   And he was no whit bigger,
And so I smiled, but he poked out
   His tongue, and called me, "Nigger."

I saw the whole of Baltimore
   From May until December;   10
Of all the things that happened there
   That's all that I remember.

                         1925

Yet Do I Marvel

I doubt not God is good, well-meaning, kind,
And did He stoop to quibble could tell why
The little buried mole continues blind,
Why flesh that mirrors Him must some day die,
Make plain the reason tortured Tantalus[6]   5
Is baited by the fickle fruit, declare
If merely brute caprice dooms Sisyphus[7]
To struggle up a never-ending stair.
Inscrutable His ways are, and immune
To catechism[8] by a mind too strewn   10
With petty cares to slightly understand
What awful brain compels His awful hand.
Yet do I marvel at this curious thing:
To make a poet black, and bid him sing!

                         1925

To Certain Critics

Then call me traitor if you must,
Shout treason and default!
Say I betray a sacred trust

5. Eric Walrond (1898–1966), a writer.
6. In Greek mythology, a king and father of Pelops; as such a founding figure in the House of Atreus and in Greek tragedy.
7. Figure in mythology whose punishment after death was to roll a boulder eternally up a hillside, only to watch it tumble down again.
8. Understanding, particularly of religious scripture.

Aching beyond this vault.
I'll bear your censure as your praise,   5
For never shall the clan
Confine my singing to its ways
Beyond the ways of man.

No racial option narrows grief,
Pain is no patriot,   10
And sorrow plaits her dismal leaf
For all as lief as not.
With blind sheep groping every hill,
Searching an oriflamme,[9]
How shall the shepherd heart then thrill   15
To only the darker lamb?

                                              1929

9. A banner or ensign.

Modern Alternatives:
Romantics and Neoclassicists

A W.P.A. poster from the 1930s.

The Jazz Age

> The dinner party downstairs began with the
> popping of corks and the braying of a phonograph.
> —*Edmund Wilson,* The Twenties

When Edmund Wilson was discharged from the army on Long Island in 1919, he asked his parents to bring him works by three recent authors. Wilson was destined to become one of the strongest literary critics of the century, but at this time he still thought of himself primarily as a poet and novelist. The books he requested were the poems of Witter Bynner, Ezra Pound's *Lustra* (1916), and H. L. Mencken's *The American Language* (1919). The first two of these tell us about the growing importance of Modernism for Wilson's generation. Pound, of course, was one of the instigators of Imagism, and Bynner had already, in collusion with Arthur Davison Ficke, pulled off a great literary hoax intended to make fun of those who flocked to the avant-garde. Bynner and Ficke invented two poets—Emanuel Morgan and Anne Knish—and in 1916 published a volume under the fictitious names entitled *Spectra: A Book of Poetic Experiments.*[1] Since every new Modernist movement had to have a name, Morgan and Knish announced themselves as the "Spectrists," and their poems were widely reviewed and taken seriously by readers as sophisticated as Edgar Lee Masters, Alfred Kreymborg, and William Carlos Williams. Modernism was, in other words, a phenomenon strong and pervasive enough to be parodied.

The third book Wilson requested is also telling. H. L. Mencken's project had been to describe "certain salient differences between the English of England and the English of America as practically spoken and written—differences in vocabulary, in syntax, in the shade and habits of idiom, and even, coming to common speech, in grammar." Having arrived on the international scene through its belated participation in World War I, America was furthering its own cultural self-consciousness. It had absorbed the Modernist revolution enough to make additional native versions of it, especially in the poetic nationalism of William Carlos Williams, who argued passionately for the poetic viability of the American idiom. Modernism, in short, continued to be many different things, and it coexisted with kinds of poetry that may seem less avant-garde in formal terms.

Wilson settled in New York City and almost immediately went to work at *Vanity Fair* with his friend John Peale Bishop. Vacancies at the magazine had been created by the sudden resignations of Dorothy Parker and Robert Benchley, who within a few years would join the staff of a new journal called the *New Yorker*. It was a heady time for the popular press. While more venerable periodicals continued to publish, new magazines from *Reader's Digest* and *Time* to the *American Mercury* and the *New Yorker* were founded in the twenties, a decade that also saw the formation of the Book-of-the-Month Club as a way of marketing new fiction and nonfiction to a mass audience.

The decade also marked a period of increasing prosperity for most of the nation, despite great disparities in income and continued labor unrest. In 1920 there were over 105 million Americans, and for the first time more of them lived in towns and cities than in rural areas. The Great War had dealt a death blow to Victorian

---

1. Compare our discussion of the "Spectra hoax" on pp. 298–299.

prudery, women got the vote, and a new sexual revolution was underway. In 1921 a New York nurse, Margaret Sanger, helped found the American Birth Control League, a forerunner of Planned Parenthood. More women than ever before entered colleges and universities as well as the workplace. Though telephones were still available mostly to the affluent, new appliances like vacuum cleaners and clothes washing machines made housework easier, and a man named Clarence Birdseye perfected the technology of frozen foods. (However, 75 percent of African American women still worked in domestic service or in agricultural jobs.) By 1923 a Ford Model T cost less than three hundred dollars, making it affordable to many middle class families. New roads and industries were built around the automobile—an aspect of twentieth-century American culture that would be both liberating and alienating. The first coast-to-coast highway, Route 66, was soon completed. American cities were altered by an increasing number of skyscrapers, and the elevator became a common feature. The technology of flight also improved. In 1927 Charles Lindbergh made his famous flight from New York to Paris. In the same year, underwater telephone cables connected Europe and the United States.

New Technology: Radio, Recording, and Cinema

> The movie is not only a supreme expression of mechanism,
> but paradoxically it offers as product the most magic of
> consumer commodities, namely dreams.
> —*Marshall McLuhan*

By 1920 three new technologies had emerged that would utterly transform America's culture—radio, phonographic recording, and cinema. These new electronic media radically changed the flow of information in society not only in terms of speed and accessibility but—more significantly—in terms of basic sensory perception. For the first time since the development of mechanical printing, the printed word faced serious competition from the mass distribution of information and ideas by sound or moving image. Quickly commercialized, radio, phonographic recording, and cinema soon created mass audiences for new forms of art and entertainment designed to fit the new media.

The first radio program in the United States was an experimental broadcast on Christmas Eve, 1906, from Brant Rock, Massachusetts—using the wireless transmission system developed by the Italian physicist Guglielmo Marconi. The broadcast, which was heard mainly by ship wireless operators in the North Atlantic, featured two musical selections and a poem. The first commercial radio broadcast, however, did not occur until November 2, 1920, when KDKA in Pittsburgh announced the result of the Harding-Cox presidential election. Within two years there were 564 licensed broadcasting stations, and the audience had grown into millions of homes. Major companies like General Electric's Radio Corporation of America (RCA) and Westinghouse soon created coast-to-coast national networks broadcasting live news, music, variety shows, and drama. The ability of the national network to reach the largest audience ever assembled instantaneously with both cultural and commercial messages gave electronic media enormous influence.

By 1920 another auditory technology had already become internationally commercialized—phonographic recording. When the phonograph was originally invented in 1877 by Thomas Alva Edison, it was conceived mostly as a means of recording the spoken word. Edison even envisioned phonographic records as a medium for poetry and sent a representative to record British Poet Laureate Alfred Lord Tennyson reading his work. Largely deaf, Edison underestimated what would be the major use of his new technology, recorded music, and he never fully exploited this market. By 1905, however, the phonograph had become an international success, making distinguished performances of music readily available in the remotest places.

If the phonograph made European opera available to new mass audiences (which purchased the tenor Enrico Caruso's recordings by the millions), it had a more profound and transforming impact on popular music. The new electronic media could deliver rapid fame through new means of mechanical reproduction. Individual performers might reach larger audiences through a single successful "platter" than they might see in a whole career of live performances. Meanwhile local or regional styles of music like blues, jazz, or bluegrass could quickly become international phenomena—as well as moving across domestic barriers of race, class, and gender.

Records played a crucial role in fostering jazz. Originating in New Orleans around the turn of the twentieth century, jazz slowly made its way up the Mississippi toward Chicago, where King Oliver's Creole Jazz Band held sway in the early 1920s. The new music, however, achieved its most rapid dissemination on recordings, which not only made early masters like Louis Armstrong, Jelly Roll Morton, Sidney Bechet, and King Oliver popular artists, but also preserved their performance for posterity. They also immersed aspiring artists in the new tradition. Bix Beiderbecke, a white middle-class teenager from Iowa, could hear records of African American jazz greats from New Orleans and teach himself the essentials of jazz style without leaving home. Recordings were the ideal medium for the new art form; being a quasi-improvised and performative form, jazz is not preserved in written scores but unfolds in live performance. Without recording technology the jazz heritage would have been unavailable in permanent form and would not have achieved the huge international audience that it had by the 1920s.

F. Scott Fitzgerald called the twenties "The Jazz Age" because of its fast, freewheeling cultural changes and the ascendancy of jazz music. Early forms of jazz, such as the blues and ragtime, had been more marginal culturally, but now that jazz had more polish and cachet, it moved into the white middle class. Popular songs by Irving Berlin, the Gershwin brothers, Hoagy Carmichael and others filled the airwaves. The first great jazz composer, Duke Ellington, established his orchestra at the Cotton Club in the twenties, and soon premiered new work in Carnegie Hall, demonstrating African American music's equality with the European classical tradition.

In movies the twenties were still the era of the silent film, but the range of productions was immense—from German expressionists like F. W. Murnau and Spanish surrealists like Luis Buñuel to more mainstream filmmakers in Hollywood. This was an era of great freedom and experimentation in cinema. Longer films were made using multiple reels of film, so narrative structures grew more ambitious. Even the silent film comedians like Buster Keaton and Charlie Chaplin went well beyond the comic short subjects that defined their early careers. In 1927 the MPPDA, or Motion Picture Producers and Distributors of America (called "the Hays Office" because it was directed by the conservative Will Hays) attempted to impose censorship of sexual content on filmmakers. These rules were largely ignored until the enactment of a stringent code in 1934. Before that time, American cinema was surprisingly liberated. Theda Bara, known as "the Vamp," had been a sex symbol in early silent films, while in the twenties such figures as Clara Bow and Louise Brooks emerged—and Joan Crawford, who would also have a long career after the introduction of "talking pictures" with Al Jolson's *The Jazz Singer* in 1928. Greta Garbo began to make films in America in the twenties, while Marlene Dietrich arrived in *The Blue Angel* (1930). Early "talkies" made stars of Mae West, Jean Harlow, and such male actors as Cary Grant. Books tend to be read privately by individuals or aloud by a small family group, but cinema became a modern tribal experience, a new sort of storytelling in the dark cave of the theater, making cultural gods and goddesses of film stars.

Before feature films were run, theaters often showed newsreels depicting far-flung events. All the major governments of the thirties learned that cinema had enormous propaganda potential. The power of this new medium cannot be exaggerated. The medium of the newsreel appeared in the novels of John Dos Passos and J. T. Farrell, and images from the movies often appeared in contemporary fiction. Literature was still considered a higher calling than film, but during the lean years of the thirties and forties noted novelists William Faulkner and F. Scott Fitzgerald made their living in Hollywood. Even some poets found work in Hollywood. Stephen Vincent Benét wrote the script for D. W. Griffith's first talkie, *Abraham Lincoln* (1930), and Langston Hughes worked on the screenplay for *Way Down South* (1939).

America in the twenties was also a country under Prohibition. The Eighteenth Amendment to the Constitution had made the sale of alcohol illegal, and as a result some aspects of American culture went underground. There were illegal drinking clubs all over the country, some offering the entertainment of dancing girls called "flappers" after a recent dance craze. In the popular image, the flapper had usually bobbed her hair, adopting the latest liberated fashion. The sale and consumption of alcohol was not by any means stopped just because it was illegal. In fact, New York politician Fiorello H. LaGuardia testified before the U.S. Senate in 1926 that Prohibition had only increased whiskey consumption and the business interests of organized crime. Fitzgerald, too, noted something hollow in the romanticism of the twenties. As his character Nick Carraway said in *The Great Gatsby* (1925), "Again at eight o'clock, when the dark lanes of the Forties were five deep with throbbing taxicabs bound for the theater district, I felt a sinking in my heart."

The "Dirty Thirties": Poetry and Politics in the Great Depression

> The crisis of our time as we are beginning slowly and
> painfully to perceive is a crisis not of the hands but of the heart.
> —*Archibald MacLeish, "In Challenge, Not Defense"*

Early in 1929 the New York Stock Exchange was trading a record volume of shares. For the latter half of Calvin Coolidge's presidency (1923–1929), it seemed America's economic expansion would never end. Less than two weeks before Black Tuesday, October 26th, a *New York Times* headline blared, "STOCK PRICES WILL STAY AT HIGH LEVEL FOR YEARS TO COME." The newly elected Herbert Hoover focused his attention less on the economy than on the rise in gang-related murders (this was the year of Al Capone's St. Valentine's Day Massacre). Despite some predictions that banks had loaned more money than they could possibly cover and that too many individuals and companies had overinvested in the stock market, few were adequately prepared for the crash when it came. In the months of October and November roughly $30 billion in stock values were wiped out. The stock market continued to fall, and by 1932 stocks retained only twenty percent of their value before the drop. By 1933, nearly half of America's banks had failed. Roughly 30 percent of American workers were unemployed, and many farms went under. "During a lot of the thirties," the poet Thomas McGrath later recalled, "you'd put the seed in and be lucky to get the seed back—because it was also the drought times, Dust Bowl times." The worst drought years were 1934 to 1936, when some communities recorded dust storms lasting for weeks or months as farms in the Midwest breadbasket lost too much of their topsoil. Thus, to many people the decade came to be known as the "Dirty Thirties."

The Great Depression lasted for most of the decade until 1939. It spread from America to the entire industrialized world, and in Germany, already crippled by the Treaty of Versailles following World War I, it made Adolf Hitler seem an attractive alternative to the status quo. In the United States, a swing to the political left led to the election of Franklin Delano Roosevelt, whose New Deal transformed American politics. Inaugurated in 1933, Roosevelt would defy American tradition by serving four terms and remaining in office until his death in 1945. Facing the national crisis, he initiated a series of federal programs designed to improve conditions for American citizens; Roosevelt changed the U.S. banking system, provided new support for farms, and created Social Security. To combat unemployment, he instituted the CCC (Civilian Conservation Corps), where men and women were put to work, usually constructing buildings, roads, and trails on federal land, and the WPA (Works Progress Administration), which would employ thousands of skilled laborers.

One division of the WPA was the Federal Writers' Project, which hired out-of-work authors, including Saul Bellow, Richard Wright, Conrad Aiken, Weldon Kees, Kenneth Fearing, Ralph Ellison, Kenneth Rexroth, Lorine Niedecker, and Margaret Walker, to compile and publish guide books to the forty-eight states and other major regional attractions. A poet even played an important role in the administration; one of Roosevelt's chief public spokesmen was Archibald MacLeish, whom he helped appoint Librarian of Congress (1939–1944). In 1944, Roosevelt named MacLeish as Assistant Secretary of State for Cultural Affairs and the chairman of the Committee on War Information. After World War II he became a significant cultural ambassador through the United Nations. In his new public role, MacLeish used his poetry, drama, and criticism to further a humanitarian and progressive agenda.

American politics in the thirties emphasized lines of disagreement between the Left and the Right, lines that were clearly related to sympathies for political causes in Europe and Russia. While novelists like John Steinbeck wrote about labor unrest in America, the Spanish Civil War provided in Europe a battleground between the forces of fascism and various revolutionary parties of the Left, some of which were tied to the power struggle between Stalin and Trotsky in Russia. Hitler and Mussolini actually tested their military forces in Spain, and because a divided Left was unable to stand up to the fascist military might—while most western nations remained officially neutral—the fascist powers gained confidence. International political events were notable in the careers and works of many American poets. Although most of the older American Modernists remained on the Right (Eliot, Pound, Stevens, Moore) or professed disdain for politics (Jeffers, Cummings), many younger poets felt a passionate commitment to progressive causes, and the thirties became a period of strong political activism. Feminist politics, as well as the international struggle between fascism and the Left, also became increasingly important. As feminism was a growing political and cultural phenomenon of the Left, it was reflected in the fact that American literary life made room for increasing numbers of women writers.

The Female Lyric Tradition

> Women have no wilderness in them. . . .
> —*Louise Bogan*

While free verse in its various forms had become a dominant trend in Modernist American poetry, such age-old techniques as rhyme and meter did not disappear. Not only did Eliot, Pound, Stevens, Cummings, and Moore never entirely abandon them, but Frost famously refused to write free verse. As we continue to define Modernism by its multiplicity of forms, it is useful to observe that some of the forerunners of literary feminism in the twenties were traditionalists in terms of poetic technique. Sara Teasdale's early models were Christina Rossetti and A. E. Housman. Though Amy Lowell made fun of Teasdale's refinement in "A Critical Fable," she recognized something "bolder" in Teasdale's love poetry than in the work of earlier women poets. Regardless of Lowell's low opinion, Teasdale was a hugely popular poet—so much so that during World War II the navy christened a ship in her name.

Delicate as they sometimes were, Teasdale's lyrics were important for introducing a modern women's voice. But no poet of the time came to represent the liberated modern woman more than Edna St. Vincent Millay. Famous before she was twenty, Millay electrified readers with her bold sexuality and held the respect of critics because of her strong technique. Her apparent candor came with a toughness that few women poets of the previous generation possessed. Millay's poems mocked the sentimentality of men. In both her life and her work she was a modern lover, who continued to have affairs—with men and women—even after her marriage. Once at a cocktail party, she asked a psychologist for advice about recurring headaches, and the psychologist queried her about her love for women. Millay replied: "Oh, you mean I'm homosexual! Of course I am, and heterosexual too, but what's that got to do with my headache?" The fact that her boldness in poetry was matched by that of her life contributed to the legend of Millay as a modern romantic figure, dangerous and somehow doomed.

Yet her notoriety was both a blessing and a curse, and it exemplifies the dilemma faced by other female lyric poets who came into prominence during the 1920s. Millay was so widely celebrated as a liberated, ingenue poet that she could not escape the shackles of the stereotype as she aged and tried to broaden the scope of her work. And her popularity ultimately led critics to question the seriousness of her poetry—a fate not shared by many American male poets whose work achieved popular success. As critic Cheryl Walker argues, "the most popular among [women poets] have rarely been respectable at the highest levels of culture, unlike Henry Wadsworth Longfellow, William Cullen Bryant, Walt Whitman, Robert Frost, and T. S. Eliot, who have had both popularity and prestige." Because of Millay's popularity, along with her focus on love and her preference for traditional forms such as the sonnet, male critics in the 1930s attacked her poetry as sentimental and insufficiently modern. Although her books remained in print, her poetry was often left out of anthologies. In the last two decades of the century, however, feminist critics such as Walker set out to reclaim the work of Millay and her peers by emphasizing not only its modern cultural contexts, but also the ways in which it challenges the stereotypes by developing a double perspective. Louise Bogan deploys such a perspective in "Women," with implications that radically shift depending on whether we imagine the speaker as male or female. The poem's capacity for being viewed through multiple points of view, its irony, and its skepticism of the value of love are eminently modern.

Yet the very modern skepticism voiced by Bogan and Millay was part of their appeal for readers. Teasdale emphasized it in her introduction to the 1928 edition of her anthology, *The Answering Voice: Love Lyrics by Women*:

> Though the passion called love has not changed appreciably during recorded time, our ideas about it have changed constantly, and sometimes with great rapidity. The immediate cause of the new attitude may be traced to the growing economic independence of women consequent on education, and to the universal tendency to rationalize all emotion. . . . There is a wider range of feeling as well as a less conventional treatment in contemporary poetry. One finds little now of that ingratiating dependence on the beloved, those vows of eternal and unwavering adoration, which filled the poems of even the sincerest women of the times before our own. One finds little, too, of the pathetic despair so often present in the earlier work. Today, there is stated over and over, perhaps at times overstated, the women's fearlessness, her love of change, her almost cruelly analytical attitude.

Among the most fearless was Elinor Wylie, who adopted the persona of a woman warrior and voiced anger and scorn, as well as a desire for solitude. Dorothy Parker, on the other hand, inflected her skepticism with humor. As Edmund Wilson wrote in a review for the *New Republic* (January 19, 1927), "Dorothy Parker's unprecedented feat has been to raise to the dignity of poetry the 'wise-cracking' humor of New York." A more complex woman's voice was that of Bogan, who felt a particular need to distance herself from the romanticism of Teasdale, Millay, and Wylie. Where Millay mythologized herself, Bogan looked coolly on such revelations. She developed a harder, plainer style of formal verse, yet was capable of memorable lyricism. She was also, from the thirties until her death, the primary poetry critic for the *New Yorker*, and became one of the prominent poet-critics of her generation. By contrast, Millay left virtually no memorable criticism behind, and her letters were mostly consumed with personal matters. Although very different in taste and temperament, all of these poets were in some manner feminists, though they never associated their political ideas with such formal practices as free verse.

Symbolists, Fugitives, and New Critics

> New thresholds, new anatomies!
> —*Hart Crane*

As we noted in our section on Early Modernism, the profound lyrical gifts of Hart Crane aspired to music, and Crane frequently played the phonograph while writing—driving his neighbors to distraction. Basing his work on the Symbolist rather than the Imagist tradition, Crane created a complex and associative poetic style that operated through suggestion and allusion rather than direct statement or precise visual imagery. He was a late Romantic in his effusions and impatience with bourgeois life, a Modernist in his difficulty and broad ambitions. Like Whitman and Williams, he wanted to embrace America, and when he wrote his long poem, *The Bridge* (1933), Crane chose an American symbol, the Brooklyn Bridge, as his organizing image—and the poem employs a largely New World range of historical and mythological allusions. Unlike Whitman and Williams, however, he never abandoned traditional meter. Indeed, he was one of the most innovative metrists of his generation; his lines often seem less comprehensible to the intellect than to the ear. Like Eliot, whose poem *The Waste Land* had seemed to Williams a Eurocentric disaster, Crane reveled in densely allusive and intricately layered language. *The Bridge* is as prone to editorial footnoting as the works of Eliot and Pound.

While the second generation of Modernists emerged in the twenties, the elder High Modernists were still very much at work, some of them engaged in writing their most important poems. Conrad Aiken, who had known Eliot at Harvard, mythologized himself in the figure of Senlin, his protagonist in yet another example of the long poem. But younger American poets like Crane and John Peale Bishop were making their own variations on Modernist style. Where Crane brought a Keatsian lushness and fevered sensitivity to many of his poems, Bishop absorbed the verbal playfulness of the Modernists, and wrote poems that changed styles restlessly, sometimes resembling Pound, sometimes Frost.

A decisive figure of the time was poet-critic Allen Tate, deeply influenced by Eliot, whom he saw as the key Modernist thinker. Like many Southern intellectuals of his generation, Kentucky-born Tate was obsessed with an idealized aristocratic past. He blamed the Civil War and Reconstruction for destroying the cultivated Southern society to which he aspired. Although he spent much of his later life in the Northeast, he often privately expressed deep mistrust of "Yankees" and displayed the typical white Southern racism of the segregationist era. With his Vanderbilt professors, John Crowe Ransom and Donald Davidson, and his friend Robert Penn Warren, among others, Tate helped to form a group of Southern poets and intellectuals called the Fugitives, their name suggesting alienation from the dominant cultural forces of the United States. Backward looking, frequently reactionary, the Fugitives idealized their shared Southern agrarian heritage, which they contrasted to the dehumanizing industrialism of the North. Initially the group aired their verse and opinions in a small influential magazine, the *Fugitive,* which they published from 1922 to 1925. Not surprisingly, although Tate was able to convince his friends of Eliot's importance, it was not the revolutionary Modernist in Eliot who attracted them so much as the cultural conservative and the disaffected, erudite man of letters.

As they began to publish their own cultural manifesti in the thirties, the Fugitives seemed less and less relevant to the national, political, and literary scene, which was dominated by the Great Depression. America in the thirties leaned to the political left, while the Fugitives leaned right in their resistance to social change. The rise of Fascism in Europe, as well as the difficult economic conditions at home, caused many American intellectuals to sympathize with the Communist Party, or at least with the socialist ideals reflected in Roosevelt's New Deal policies. The Fugitives gradually abandoned their movement as their literary careers progressed. Warren moved to Baton Rouge, founding the *Southern Review* with Cleanth Brooks. (Both men would eventually teach at Yale.) Ransom took a position at Kenyon College, editing the *Kenyon Review* and becoming one of the most influential poetry teachers in the country. Tate traveled and taught at Princeton and other colleges.

Half innovative, half reactionary, the Fugitive group, which became the most influential literary coterie of its generation, is another reminder of the complex and contradictory diversity of the Modernist Movement. These feisty, brilliant, and opinionated Southerners also demonstrate how regional identity plays a recurring role in American literature. The first generation of Modernists had been noteworthy for its rootlessness. St. Louis–born Eliot lived in London and died a British subject, and Pittsburgh-born and European-educated Jeffers settled in Carmel, California. Idaho-born and Philadelphia-educated Pound moved from London to Paris to Rapallo, Italy, while his fellow Pennsylvanian H. D. also lived in England, Austria, and Switzerland. Meanwhile from Hartford, Connecticut, Stevens cultivated "an Italy of the mind," a placeless poetry rooted in the universal symbols and intellectual concepts of the imagination. Ransom, Tate, Warren, and the other Fugitives reasserted the importance of regional identity in American literary culture. Learned, innovative, and intellectually aggressive, they demonstrated that writers could be regional without being provincial, and they led the way—both creatively and critically—for the Southern literary renaissance of the next few decades which brought writers like William Faulkner, Katherine Anne Porter, Flannery O'Connor, Zora Neale Hurston, and Eudora Welty into the American canon.

Under the influence of Eliot, the Fugitives also played a major role in developing a remarkably innovative period in American literary theory and scholarship. In 1941 Ransom published *The New Criticism,* borrowing a term that may have been coined much earlier. What the term "New Criticism" came to represent was, in classrooms and in print, an elevation of poetry as the supreme verbal art and close attention to the poem as its own mode of discourse. Poets like Eliot and Pound demanded erudition of their readers. New Critics, who often employed examples from English poetry of the seventeenth and eighteenth centuries, responded with their own careful models of criticism. More recently the New Criticism has fallen out of favor in American universities, accused of isolating literary study as an abstract science, separating poems from social and political contexts. The New Critics, however, did not really make such exclusive demands; rather they sought a disciplined way of writing and talking about poetry by focusing on the text itself and emphasizing semantic and rhetorical analysis. Their methods are strikingly similar to Deconstructionists who borrowed New Critical techniques. The chief characteristic that separates New Criticism from Deconstruction is that the New Critics actually believed in the coherence, importance, and permanence of great poetry. They were for the most part practicing poets and had no motive to lower the status of their art.

With Cleanth Brooks, Warren composed the most influential poetry textbook of the mid-twentieth century, *Understanding Poetry.* Tate wrote many essays and reviews, at times imitating Eliot's cultural criticism. Ransom continued to write criticism and turned to the radical revision of his own poetry while fostering the careers of a younger generation of American poets, including Randall Jarrell and Robert Lowell. There were, of course, other important poet-critics of the time, some of them influenced by New Critical trends. While Louise Bogan wielded influence in New York, Yvor Winters became a powerful but isolated literary figure on the West Coast. Having begun as an Imagist poet, Winters transformed himself into a formalist of a very particular sort, combining classical austerity with Symbolist density. In his academic position at Stanford, Winters influenced several generations of American poets, and through his prolific criticism he debunked some of the Romantic excesses of the modern era. "Write little; do it well," he advised.

Though not as famous or influential, the poems and novels of his wife Janet Lewis made their own important contribution to literature from the American West.

Poetry and the Coming War

> There was no
> Disturbance. Even the Communists didn't protest
> And say they were Morgan hirelings. It was too hot,
> Too hot to protest, too hot to get excited. . . .
> —*Stephen Vincent Benét*

After writing his best-selling book-length poem, *John Brown's Body* (1928), Stephen Vincent Benét followed the path of many other American writers and went to Hollywood. Throughout the Depression, however, he continued to be involved in liberal causes, both as a radio commentator and as an editor. It was Benét who accepted the first books of James Agee, Muriel Ruykeyser, and Margaret Walker for the Yale Series of Younger Poets. The poetry of Edna St. Vincent Millay and Dorothy Parker also expanded to include social activism in the thirties. Some Modernist poets like Ezra Pound and Wyndham Lewis moved further to the right, even embracing fascism. Others like Wallace Stevens and Marianne Moore developed a more reserved conservatism, while the Fugitives were, in most cases, decidedly reactionary. But the thirties were a decade in which new political poets of the Left found their voices. Some of these, such as Ruykeyser, Kenneth Fearing, Kenneth Rexroth, and Thomas McGrath, we will survey in later sections of this anthology. Among the second generation of Modernists, writers like MacLeish and Millay would sacrifice some of their literary standing to their political beliefs. During World War II, MacLeish directed Roosevelt's propaganda machine, ironically called the Office of Facts and Figures. Having begun as a High Modernist capable of writing "A poem should not mean / But be," MacLeish became a public poet of liberal democracy. His book, *America Was Promises* (1939), urged readers to adhere to the New Deal. Actively seeking a popular audience, MacLeish, like Benét and others, turned to writing verse drama for radio.

Though World War II would have enormous impact on the lives and works of the Modernists, they were not the generation who fought. It was the younger generation of writers, many of whom came of age during the Depression and many of whom actually saw combat overseas, who would most come to grips with the political and social complexities of the mid-century. Still, for subsequent generations, Modernism would remain a rich and exhilarating period, offering examples and challenges they would have to face. Formal definitions of poetry would change, social definitions would change, even to the point of asking whether poetry still had an audience or purpose anymore. American poetry would become increasingly influential outside America, but would lose some of its audience at home. And American poets would continue to question their designs, both as writers and as citizens.

◄ SARA TEASDALE ►
(1884–1933)

The daughter of a successful merchant and a religious mother, Sara Teasdale grew up in St. Louis, where she was educated at home until the age of nine because her overprotective parents insisted that she was fragile and in constant danger of illness. She developed literary interests in high school and sustained them after graduation by joining a group of amateur women artists, the Potters, who published a monthly magazine, *The Potter's Wheel*. Her contributions were noticed by the editor of a weekly St. Louis newspaper, who began publishing her work. After her dramatic monologue "Guenevere" received national attention, Teasdale put together her first poetry collection, entitled *Sonnets to Duse and Other Poems* (1907), and, with the financial support of her parents, hired a small press in Boston to publish it. Encouraged by critics to whom she had sent the book, Teasdale worked hard on her writing over the next several years, despite ill health. Putnam's, a major New York publishing firm, released her second book, *Helen of Troy and Other Poems* (1911), which contains a series of monologues on love spoken by well-known women from literature, a section entitled "Love Songs," a group of sonnets and lyrics, and a verse play. The book gained notoriety for one poem, "Union Square," in which the female speaker, unable to tell a man that she loves him, envies the freedom of prostitutes unconstrained by genteel conventions in their attitudes toward love. Teasdale soon gained a reputation as a love poet who balanced nineteenth-century lyric conventions against a modern woman's yearnings for sexual freedom. In depicting female speakers torn between dreams of romance and stirrings of independence, she reflected the experience of many young women of her generation, and her books were not only commended by the critics, but were widely popular, especially during World War I and the 1920s, times when American women's roles were undergoing change.

In 1911, Teasdale decided to move to New York both to be part of the literary scene and to loosen her ties to her parents. Her career was fostered by influential new friends such as Louis Untermeyer, a noted anthologist, Harriet Monroe, editor of *Poetry* magazine, and Jessie Rittenhouse, founder of the Poetry Society of America, with whom Teasdale traveled to Europe in 1912. Teasdale continued to devote her energy to poetry, but now also wanted the emotional and financial security of marriage. Although she had strong feelings for two poets, John Hall Wheelock and Vachel Lindsay, she married a St. Louis businessman, Ernst Filsinger, in 1914. She remained close friends with Wheelock and Lindsay, however, with whom she exchanged poems and shared commentary. In her third book, *Rivers to the Sea* (1915), Teasdale abandoned the monologue in favor of love lyrics voiced with clarity, directness, and musicality. For Teasdale, poetry was a response to her experiences, yet she acknowledged that those experiences were more often internal than external, and, like many of her contemporaries, she suggested that poems arise from psychological conflict: "My theory is that poems are written because of a state of emotional irritation. . . . The emotional irritation springs, probably, from subconscious combinations of partly forgotten thoughts and feelings." Yet Teasdale also believed that the "irritation" should result in an utterance whose beauty and simplicity attest to its sincerity:

> Poetry is a concise and beautiful way of telling the truth. . . . If a writer asks himself frankly and exactly what he feels about a certain object, provided he has felt real emo-

tion in regard to it, and provided that the subject is worth the emotion, his answer to
the question, if it is simple, direct, and musical, will be a poem.

Rivers to the Sea achieved these aims so well that the first edition sold out within
three months. Teasdale followed *Love Songs* (1917), which included both new
poems and work from her previous collections; the book won the Columbia Poetry
Prize, the antecedent of the Pulitzer. She also edited *The Answering Voice* (1917),
an anthology of love poems by nineteenth- and twentieth-century women writers.

Despite her acclaim, Teasdale became depressed, for she was troubled by the
nation's war fever and disappointed by her marriage. Feeling compelled to choose
between motherhood and career, she had an abortion in 1917, and her poetry became increasingly introspective: less concerned with love than with the conflict
she experienced between freedom and limitation. *Flame and Shadow* (1920) charts
a starkly modern search for meaning in an often bleak world, and the last section,
"Songs for Myself," depicts a female speaker coming to terms with the loneliness
that often accompanies independence. Despite the sober cast to *Flame and Shadow*
and her next book, *Dark of the Moon* (1926), the press continued to characterize
Teasdale as a love poet. She withdrew into chronic illness and melancholy, retreating to New England inns for rejuvenation while her husband pursued lengthy business trips. A close friendship with a young woman, Margaret Conklin, who
eventually became her literary executor, lifted her spirits in the mid-1920s, but divorce from Filsinger in 1929 and the deaths of friends, including the gruesome
suicide of Vachel Lindsay, weighed her down and slowed her writing considerably.
In January 1933, she took an overdose of sleeping pills, and her death was
mourned nationally, for she was considered an important modern poet and her
work was immensely popular. Although her poetry subsequently fell out of favor
with academics, it never fell out of print, and recent scholarship has made a strong
case for Teasdale's enduring achievement as a lyric poet. In addition, she has begun
to be recognized for her substantial influence not only on her contemporaries—
Edna St. Vincent Millay, Elinor Wylie, and Louise Bogan—but on poets such as
John Berryman and Sylvia Plath who explored the dark reaches of the psyche.

Over the Roofs

I

Oh chimes set high on the sunny tower
　Ring on, ring on unendingly,
Make all the hours a single hour,
For when the dusk begins to flower,
　The man I love will come to me! . . .   5

But no, go slowly as you will,
　I should not bid you hasten so,
For while I wait for love to come,
Some other girl is standing dumb,
　Fearing her love will go.   10

II

Oh white steam over the roofs, blow high!
   Oh chimes in the tower ring clear and free!
Oh sun awake in the covered sky,
   For the man I love, loves me! . . .

Oh drifting steam disperse and die,   15
   Oh tower stand shrouded toward the south,—
Fate heard afar my happy cry,
   And laid her finger on my mouth.

III

The dusk was blue with blowing mist,
   The lights were spangles in a veil,   20
And from the clamor far below
   Floated faint music like a wail.

It voiced what I shall never speak,
   My heart was breaking all night long,
But when the dawn was hard and gray,   25
   My tears distilled into a song.

IV

I said, "I have shut my heart
   As one shuts an open door,
That Love may starve therein
   And trouble me no more."   30

But over the roofs there came
   The wet new wind of May,
And a tune blew up from the curb
   Where the street-pianos play.

My room was white with the sun   35
  And Love cried out to me,
"I am strong, I will break your heart
   Unless you set me free."

1915

There Will Come Soft Rains

(War Time)

There will come soft rains and the smell of the ground,
And swallows circling with their shimmering sound;

And frogs in the pools singing at night,
And wild plum-trees in tremulous white;

Robins will wear their feathery fire   5
Whistling their whims on a low fence-wire;

And not one will know of the war, not one
Will care at last when it is done.

Not one would mind, neither bird nor tree
If mankind perished utterly;   10

And Spring herself, when she woke at dawn,
Would scarcely know that we were gone.

1920

Since There Is No Escape

Since there is no escape, since at the end
    My body will be utterly destroyed,
This hand I love as I have loved a friend,
    This body I tended, wept with and enjoyed;
Since there is no escape even for me   5
    Who love life with a love too sharp to bear:
The scent of orchards in the rain, the sea
    And hours alone too still and sure for prayer—
Since darkness waits for me, then all the more
Let me go down as waves sweep to the shore   10
    In pride, and let me sing with my last breath;
In these few hours of light I lift my head;
Life is my lover—I shall leave the dead
    If there is any way to baffle death.

1920

Water Lilies

If you have forgotten water lilies floating
    On a dark lake among mountains in the afternoon shade,
If you have forgotten their wet, sleepy fragrance,
    Then you can return and not be afraid.

But if you remember, then turn away forever   5
    To the plains and the prairies where pools are far apart,
There you will not come at dusk on closing water lilies,
    And the shadow of mountains will not fall on your heart.

1920

In a Darkening Garden

Gather together, against the coming of night,
    All that we played with here,
Toys and fruits, the quill from the sea-bird's flight,
    The small flute, hollow and clear;
The apple that was not eaten, the grapes untasted—   5
    Let them be put away.
They served for us, I would not have them wasted,
    They lasted out our day.

1933

❧ ELINOR WYLIE ❧
(1885–1928)

Elinor Wylie's persistent themes—endurance, the declaration of power despite vulnerability, and the need to arm the self against an indifferent or hostile world—arise directly from her bold and contentious life, which often resembled fiction in its sensational twists and turns. Born into a prosperous family, Elinor Morton Hoyt grew up in Philadelphia, where she attended private school, and Washington, D.C., where her father served as an Assistant Attorney General under Theodore Roosevelt and then as a counselor for the State Department. Despite Elinor's intellectual precocity, her parents denied her the chance to pursue her education beyond high school, and instead groomed her to be a socialite. In 1905 she married a lawyer, Philip Hichborn, and gave birth to a son in 1907. But she soon discovered that her husband was mentally unstable, and as his illness worsened she developed the high blood pressure and severe migraines that she would experience for the rest of her life. Unwilling to keep up the social pretense of an idyllic marriage, in 1910 she fled to England with Horace Wylie, an older married man. The scandal drew front-page notice in the East Coast newspapers, and both the press and high society demonized Elinor for her actions but offered little criticism of Horace. The couple lived in England as Mr. and Mrs. Horace Waring but was forced to return to the United States in 1914, at the start of World War I. They married in 1916, after Hichborn committed suicide and Wylie's wife granted him a divorce—events that reignited the scandalmongers in the press, whose attacks on Elinor guaranteed that despite their marriage the couple would remain social pariahs.

Unlike her parents, Horace supported Elinor's literary gifts. He helped subsidize the publication of her first book, *Incidental Numbers* (1912), from a vanity press in England. But the years of social isolation, financial strain, and failed efforts to have children eroded their relationship, and Elinor put more and more energy into her writing. In 1921, she left her husband and moved to New York, where her poetry was valued and her social notoriety was an asset in bohemian circles. During the 1920s, she became one of the country's most celebrated writers—so much so that the publication of her first novel, *Jennifer Lorn* (1923), occasioned a torchlight parade through Greenwich Village. She wrote four novels and three collections of poetry: *Nets to Catch the Wind* (1921), *Black Armour* (1923), and *Trivial Breath* (1928). She also became the literary editor of *Vanity Fair* and published essays and reviews. In 1923, she divorced Horace and married the poet William Rose Benét, who had helped launch her career; but by 1927 their relationship cooled. Unwilling to risk a third divorce, she separated from Benét and returned to England, where she pursued research on her favorite poet, Percy Bysshe Shelley, whom she saw as a kindred spirit. There she fell in love with another married man, Henry de Clifford Woodhouse, but was resigned to limit their exchanges to friendship. Despite her literary success, Wylie began to feel beaten down by the strains of her life, including not only her romantic reversals but the suicide of her brother Henry in 1920 and her sister Constance in 1923. As she entered her forties she was hit by depression, debilitating migraines, and two strokes. On a Christmas visit to the United States in 1928, she died suddenly of a third stroke, at the age of forty-three. After her death, Benét released additional books of poetry, *Angels and*

Earthly Creatures (1929), *Collected Poems of Elinor Wylie* (1932), and *Last Poems of Elinor Wylie* (1943), along with the *Collected Prose of Elinor Wylie* (1933).

Wylie's achievement as a poet is succinctly described by Louise Bogan, who notes that she "brought to the feminine lyric a mature emotional richness, as well as an added brilliance of craftsmanship." That "emotional richness" is often gained when Wylie strikes a note of defiance, which she juxtaposes against an intense pleasure in perception—whether the world's bounty or an interior landscape of shifting moods. Wylie's tight lyrics, characterized by explorations of the endurance of solitary, embattled speakers, appealed to the post–World War I generation as much as the more experimental work of T. S. Eliot, for both poets balance sensuous perception against the demands of an alienated consciousness.

The Eagle and the Mole

Avoid the reeking herd,
Shun the polluted flock,
Live like that stoic bird,
The eagle of the rock.

The huddled warmth of crowds   5
Begets and fosters hate;
He keeps, above the clouds,
His cliff inviolate.

When flocks are folded warm,
And herds to shelter run,   10
He sails above the storm,
He stares into the sun.

If in the eagle's track
Your sinews cannot leap,
Avoid the lathered pack,   15
Turn from the steaming sheep.

If you would keep your soul
From spotted sight or sound,
Live like the velvet mole;
Go burrow underground.   20

And there hold intercourse
With roots of trees and stones,
With rivers at their source,
And disembodied bones.

1921

Wild Peaches

1

When the world turns completely upside down
You say we'll emigrate to the Eastern Shore
Aboard a river-boat from Baltimore;
We'll live among wild peach trees, miles from town,
You'll wear a coonskin cap, and I a gown   5
Homespun, dyed butternut's dark gold colour.
Lost, like your lotus-eating ancestor,[1]
We'll swim in milk and honey till we drown.

The winter will be short, the summer long,
The autumn amber-hued, sunny and hot,   10
Tasting of cider and of scuppernong;[2]
All seasons sweet, but autumn best of all.
The squirrels in their silver fur will fall
Like falling leaves, like fruit, before your shot.

2

The autumn frosts will lie upon the grass   15
Like the bloom on grapes of purple-brown and gold.
The misted early mornings will be cold;
The little puddles will be roofed with glass.
The sun, which burns from copper into brass,
Melts these at noon, and makes the boys unfold   20
Their knitted mufflers,[3] full as they can hold,
Fat pockets dribble chestnuts as they pass.

Peaches grow wild, and pigs can live in clover;
A barrel of salted herrings lasts a year;
The spring begins before the winter's over.   25
By February you may find the skins
Of garter snakes and water moccasins[4]
Dwindled and harsh, dead-white and cloudy-clear.

3

When April pours the colours of a shell
Upon the hills, when every little creek   30
Is shot with silver from the Chesapeake
In shoals new-minted by the ocean swell,
When strawberries go begging, and the sleek
Blue plums lie open to the blackbird's beak,
We shall live well—we shall live very well.   35

---

1. In Book XI of Homer's *Odyssey,* eaters of the lotus became forgetful, desiring only to live in idleness.
2. Sweet wine common in the American South.
3. Scarves.
4. A kind of snake.

The months between the cherries and the peaches
Are brimming cornucopias which spill
Fruits red and purple, sombre-bloomed and black;
Then, down rich fields and frosty river beaches
We'll trample bright persimmons, while you kill   40
Bronze partridge, speckled quail, and canvasback.[5]

4

Down to the Puritan marrow of my bones
There's something in this richness that I hate.
I love the look, austere, immaculate,
Of landscapes drawn in pearly monotones.   45
There's something in my very blood that owns
Bare hills, cold silver on a sky of slate,
A thread of water, churned to milky spate
Streaming through slanted pastures fenced with stones.

I love those skies, thin blue or snowy gray,   50
Those fields sparse-planted, rendering meagre sheaves;
That spring, briefer than apple-blossom's breath,
Summer, so much too beautiful to stay,
Swift autumn, like a bonfire of leaves,
And sleepy winter, like the sleep of death.   55

1921

From the Wall

Woman, be steel against loving, enfold and defend you,
Turn from the innocent look and the arrogant tongue;
You shall be coppery dross to the purses that spend you;
Lock up your years like a necklace of emeralds strung.

Lock up your heart like a jewel; be cruel and clever;   5
Woman, be strong against loving, be iron, be stone;
Never and never and never and never and never
Give for the tears of a lover a tear of your own.

Cover the clutch of your greed with a velvety gloving;
Take from the good if you can, from the vile if you must;   10
Take from the proud and alone, from the cowardly loving;
Hold out your hands for the pity; accept of the lust.

1922

---

5. A kind of duck.

Let No Charitable Hope

Now let no charitable hope
Confuse my mind with images
Of eagle and of antelope:
I am in nature none of these.

I was, being human, born alone;   5
I am, being woman, hard beset;
I live by squeezing from a stone
The little nourishment I get.

In masks outrageous and austere
The years go by in single file;   10
But none has merited my fear,
And none has quite escaped my smile.

1923

Prophecy

I shall lie hidden in a hut
    In the middle of an alder wood,
With the back door blind and bolted shut,
    And the front door locked for good.

I shall lie folded like a saint,   5
    Lapped in a scented linen sheet,
On a bedspread striped with bright-blue paint,
    Narrow and cold and neat.

The midnight will be glassy black
    Behind the panes, with wind about   10
To set his mouth against a crack
    And blow the candle out.

1923

◄ JOHN CROWE RANSOM ►
(1888–1974)

Although John Crowe Ransom was an important and pivotal figure in both modern American poetry and poetics, critics have differed over his legacy. As a literary critic, editor, and teacher, he was best known under the rubric he coined in a 1941 book, *The New Criticism*. As a poet, however, he holds an additional place as a Southern writer and an ironist of great subtlety and skill.

Born in Pulaski, Tennessee, Ransom was the son of a Methodist minister who changed congregations several times. As a result, Ransom grew up in various parts of his native state, and this made him a sharp observer of people even as he studied the Bible and other texts. He was also intensely aware of Southern history—a great-uncle had helped found the Ku Klux Klan.

At the age of fifteen, Ransom entered Vanderbilt University, where he studied classics and philosophy, two subjects that confirmed his religious skepticism. After his graduation in 1909, he taught for a year in a prep school, then a Rhodes Scholarship took him to Christ Church, Oxford. His three-year sojourn in England turned Ransom from philosophy to poetry, which he saw as a form of discourse that escaped the confining logic of prose. At age twenty-six, and without the formal credentials that an academic career would later require, Ransom joined the faculty of his alma mater. He was writing poems, most of which he would later reject for their technical clumsiness, and beginning to formulate his own aesthetic stance. A 1914 letter to his father finds him struggling to determine aspects of poetry that were fundamentally different from prose.

Ransom's reflections on poetry were interrupted by America's entrance into World War I. By 1917 he was a lieutenant in a Field Artillery Training Base in Saumur, France. He saw combat early in 1918, then was transferred back to the safety of Saumur as an instructor for the remainder of the war. While Ransom was in the service, his friend Christopher Morley helped him prepare a manuscript for publication, which, after an encouraging word from Robert Frost, was published in 1919 as *Poems about God*. Soon afterward Ransom returned to the United States and his teaching post at Vanderbilt. In 1920 he married Robb Reavill, with whom he would have three children.

The 1920s proved an important decade for Ransom. He was increasingly identified as a Southern writer, indeed a central figure of the "Southern Renaissance" that included William Faulkner, Katherine Anne Porter, Allen Tate, Thomas Wolfe, Robert Penn Warren, and Caroline Gordon. Steeped in Modernist literary ferment, these writers were also aware that they had been formed by the code of the old South with its agrarian chivalry and what Ransom called its "dynastic wound." At Vanderbilt he befriended poets Donald Davidson and Allen Tate; with these and other friends, Ransom founded a magazine called the *Fugitive* in 1922. At first the poets it included signed their poems with pen names—Ransom's was the self-mocking "Roger Prim"—but before long they identified themselves openly as an acknowledged movement. The poems the *Fugitive* published were highly literary and allusive, brainy more than emotional, pessimistic in outlook. In addition to Southern poets, the *Fugitive* published such figures as Hart Crane, Robert Graves, and Laura Riding. By 1925, when the *Fugitive* ended, Ransom had written some of his best-known poems, including "Bells for John Whiteside's Daughter," "Philomela," and "Captain Carpenter."

In a 1924 letter about poetry to Allen Tate, Ransom wrote, "The form is organic with the matter." That was the year in which he published his collections *Chills and Fever* and *Grace after Meat*. His reading in philosophy and the poetics of Coleridge led him to compose his own treatise on aesthetic theory. When that attempt proved disappointing to him, he returned to poetry, composing the poems that would be collected in *Two Gentlemen in Bonds* (1927), a book that garnered rave reviews. These poems, like those of the two earlier collections, were often erudite, though the best of them often avoided allusion and focussed on closely observed scenes. The manner was genteel, even archaic, but firmly ironic and disillusioned. Nevertheless, it was two books of social criticism that gained him broader notoriety and inaugurated another movement. In the summer of 1929 he dashed off a book entitled *God without Thunder: An Unorthodox Defense of Orthodoxy* defending Southern agrarian values, and soon after he contributed to *I'll Take My Stand*, a book in which "Twelve Southerners"—including Davidson,

Tate, and Warren—raised up an image of agrarian gentility against the industrialized and estranging North.

In 1937 Ransom left Vanderbilt for a chair at Kenyon College in Ohio, where he founded the *Kenyon Review,* which published its first issue in January 1939 and fostered the careers of such younger writers as Randall Jarrell, Robert Lowell, James Wright, and Anthony Hecht. In 1945 he published his *Selected Poems,* a book he would later revise but that already established the small canon of Ransom's poetry.

The last four decades of Ransom's life were more concerned with criticism, editing, and teaching than with the composition of new poems. *The World's Body,* a collection of essays on poetry, appeared in 1938, and three years later he published *The New Criticism.* Ransom's New Criticism, as practiced by two generations of poets and critics, was highly congenial to many poets because it valued the poem itself over most ways of contextualizing it. The New Criticism elevated poetry to a position of special status in the academy from which it has since fallen. There were other books from John Crowe Ransom, but none so influential as those he had published by the end of World War II. He became a courtly presence at Kenyon College, and after his death his ashes were interred behind its library.

Bells for John Whiteside's Daughter

There was such speed in her little body,
And such lightness in her footfall,
It is no wonder her brown study[1]
Astonishes us all.

Her wars were bruited[2] in our high window.   5
We looked among orchard trees and beyond
Where she took arms against her shadow,
Or harried unto the pond

The lazy geese, like a snow cloud
Dripping their snow on the green grass,   10
Tricking and stopping, sleepy and proud,
Who cried in goose, Alas,

For the tireless heart within the little
Lady with rod that made them rise
From their noon apple-dreams and scuttle   15
Goose-fashion under the skies!

But now go the bells, and we are ready,
In one house we are sternly stopped
To say we are vexed at her brown study,
Lying so primly propped.   20

1924

---

1. Moodiness, daydreaming.
2. Sounded.

Winter Remembered

Two evils, monstrous either one apart,
Possessed me, and were long and loath at going:
A cry of Absence, Absence, in the heart,
And in the wood the furious winter blowing.

Think not, when fire was bright upon my bricks,   5
And past the tight boards hardly a wind could enter,
I glowed like them, the simple burning sticks,
Far from my cause, my proper heat and center.

Better to walk forth in the frozen air
And wash my wound in the snows; that would be healing;   10
Because my heart would throb less painful there,
Being caked with cold, and past the smart of feeling.

And where I walked, the murderous winter blast
Would have this body bowed, these eyeballs streaming,
And though I think this heart's blood froze not fast   15
It ran too small to spare one drop for dreaming.

Dear love, these fingers that had known your touch,
And tied our separate forces first together,
Were ten poor idiot fingers not worth much,
Ten frozen parsnips hanging in the weather.   20

                                                          1924

Blue Girls

Twirling your blue skirts, travelling the sward
Under the towers of your seminary,
Go listen to your teachers old and contrary
Without believing a word.

Tie the white fillets[3] then about your hair   5
And think no more of what will come to pass
Than bluebirds that go walking on the grass
And chattering on the air.

Practise your beauty, blue girls, before it fail;
And I will cry with my loud lips and publish   10
Beauty which all our power shall never establish,
It is so frail.

For I could tell you a story which is true;
I know a woman with a terrible tongue,
Blear eyes fallen from blue,   15
All her perfections tarnished—yet it is not long
Since she was lovelier than any of you.

                                                          1927

3. Ribbons

Dead Boy

The little cousin is dead, by foul subtraction,
A green bough from Virginia's aged tree,
And none of the county kin like the transaction,
Nor some of the world of outer dark, like me.

A boy not beautiful, nor good, nor clever,   5
A black cloud full of storms too hot for keeping,
A sword beneath his mother's heart—yet never
Woman bewept her babe as this is weeping.

A pig with a pasty face, so I had said,
Squealing for cookies, kinned by poor pretense   10
With a noble house. But the little man quite dead,
I see the forebears' antique lineaments.

The elder men have strode by the box of death
To the wide flag porch, and muttering low send round
The bruit of the day. O friendly waste of breath!   15
Their hearts are hurt with a deep dynastic wound.

He was pale and little, the foolish neighbors say;
The first-fruits, saith the Preacher, the Lord hath taken;
But this was the old tree's late branch wrenched away,
Grieving the sapless limbs, the shorn and shaken.   20

                                                                     1927

Piazza Piece

—I am a gentleman in a dustcoat[4] trying
To make you hear. Your ears are soft and small
And listen to an old man not at all,
They want the young men's whispering and sighing.
But see the roses on your trellis dying   5
And hear the spectral singing of the moon;
For I must have my lovely lady soon,
I am a gentleman in a dustcoat trying.

—I am a lady young in beauty waiting
Until my truelove comes, and then we kiss.   10
But what grey man among the vines is this
Whose words are dry and faint as in a dream?
Back from my trellis, Sir, before I scream!
I am a lady young in beauty waiting.

                                                                     1927

4. Often worn in early automobiles to keep the road dust off one's clothing.

CONRAD AIKEN
(1889–1973)

Conrad Potter Aiken, a formidably talented poet, novelist, short story writer, and critic, was born in Savannah, Georgia, the eldest of four children born to a prosperous doctor and his wife, both transplanted New Englanders. The pivotal and tragic event of his youth came in 1901 when the eleven-year-old boy heard shots from the next room and discovered that his father had murdered his mother and then killed himself. Aiken's subsequent life would be scarred by this horrifying event. He was separated from his siblings and raised by relations in Massachusetts. Aiken entered Harvard in 1907 where he became a close friend of his classmate T. S. Eliot. At Harvard he studied with George Santayana, the Spanish-American philosopher, whose ideas on poetry influenced Aiken (as well as Eliot and Wallace Stevens). Aiken graduated in 1911 and soon moved to England. He returned to the United States and subsequently lived in Boston, New York, and Cape Cod. He was married three times. In old age he returned to Savannah where he died of a heart attack at eighty-four.

Aiken was an impressively prolific writer. He was only twenty-four when his first volume of poems, *Earth Triumphant* (1914), was issued. ("It was horribly bad," he later confessed.) Thereafter he published roughly one book a year until just before his death—eventually writing over fifty volumes, including five novels, five collections of short stories, and thirty-five volumes of verse. His *Selected Poems* (1929) won the Pulitzer Prize, and his *Collected Poems* (1953) received the National Book Award. He also published an unusual but compelling autobiography written in the third person, *Ushant* (1952), which in its original edition employs code names for the real people he described. (T. S. Eliot became "Tsetse," for example, and Ezra Pound was ironically named "Rabbi Ben Ezra," a sly comment on Pound's anti-Semitism.) His short stories were highly regarded and widely anthologized for many years, though they have gradually dropped from critical favor. Aiken was also a prodigious reviewer and critic.

Aiken's early poetry was undistinguished, soft Romantic musing, but he gradually developed a sinuously musical Modernist idiom. Between 1916 and 1925 he published six "symphonies," long poetic sequences that employed lyrical elements for linear narrative. The best of these early "symphonies" is probably "Senlin: A Biography" (1918), a psychological character study of a self-obsessed creative personality, which bears a strong stylistic and thematic relation to Eliot's "The Love Song of J. Alfred Prufrock." The reasons behind the resemblance between the two poems are not difficult to discover. Aiken and Eliot developed as young poets together, and they both looked to the French Symbolists as models for what modern American poetry might be. Aiken's "symphonies" are informed and skillful attempts to embody the Symbolist notion of poetry emulating the abstract beauties of music. Aiken used these complex and alluring musical structures, however, to develop philosophical themes, especially psychoanalytical ideas on love, identity, and consciousness.

Aiken's poetic reputation has always been precarious. "There is something about him that keeps him from rising, both personally and as a poet," Wallace Stevens once confided in a letter. Aiken himself joked that he had acquired a reputation as a poet without any critic ever considering what he wrote to be poetry. Aiken's poetry tended to lack the imaginative concision that creates intensity. It reaches for large philosophical themes at the expense of the small literary virtues that keep verse moving. Yet Aiken's ear was superb, and his poetry usually affords verbal music of a high order. English novelist Julian Symons aptly summarized Aiken's accomplishment, claiming that "his finest work . . . achieves in places the grandeur he was always looking for, and in others gets beyond the fluent expression of nostalgia to what comes through as genuine anguish."

Morning Song of Senlin[1]

It is morning, Senlin says, and in the morning
When the light drips through the shutters like the dew,
I arise, I face the sunrise,
And do the things my fathers learned to do.
Stars in the purple dusk above the rooftops   5
Pale in a saffron mist and seem to die,
And I myself on a swiftly tilting planet
Stand before a glass and tie my tie.

Vine leaves tap my window,
Dew-drops sing to the garden stones,   10
The robin chirps in the chinaberry tree
Repeating three clear tones.

It is morning. I stand by the mirror
And tie my tie once more.
While waves far off in a pale rose twilight   15
Crash on a white sand shore.
I stand by a mirror and comb my hair:
How small and white my face!—
The green earth tilts through a sphere of air
And bathes in a flame of space.   20

There are houses hanging above the stars
And stars hung under a sea . . .
And a sun far off in a shell of silence
Dapples my walls for me . . .

It is morning, Senlin says, and in the morning   25
Should I not pause in the light to remember god?
Upright and firm I stand on a star unstable,
He is immense and lonely as a cloud.
I will dedicate this moment before my mirror
To him alone, for him I will comb my hair.   30

---

1. Part of a long poem, Senlin was the poet's fictional alter ego.

Accept these humble offerings, cloud of silence!
I will think of you as I descend the stair.

Vine leaves tap my window,
The snail-track shines on the stones,
Dew-drops flash from the chinaberry tree   35
Repeating two clear tones.

It is morning, I awake from a bed of silence,
Shining I rise from the starless waters of sleep.
The walls are about me still as in the evening,
I am the same, and the same name still I keep.   40

The earth revolves with me, yet makes no motion,
The stars pale silently in a coral sky.
In a whistling void I stand before my mirror,
Unconcerned, and tie my tie.

There are horses neighing on far-off hills   45
Tossing their long white manes,
And mountains flash in the rose-white dusk,
Their shoulders black with rains . . .
It is morning. I stand by the mirror
And surprise my soul once more;   50
The blue air rushes above my ceiling,
There are suns beneath my floor . . .

. . . It is morning, Senlin says, I ascend from darkness
And depart on the winds of space for I know not where,
My watch is wound, a key is in my pocket,   55
And the sky is darkened as I descend the stair.
There are shadows across the windows, clouds in heaven,
And a god among the stars; and I will go
Thinking of him as I might think of daybreak
And humming a tune I know . . .   60

Vine-leaves tap at the window,
Dew-drops sing to the garden stones,
The robin chirps in the chinaberry tree
Repeating three clear tones.

                                                     1918

FROM Priapus[2] and the Pool

III

When trout swim down Great Ormond Street,[3]
And sea-gulls cry above them lightly,

---

2. Priapus was the Greek and Roman god of procreation.
3. A street in central London.

And hawthorns heave cold flagstones up
To blossom whitely,

Against old walls of houses there,   5
Gustily shaking out in moonlight
Their country sweetness on sweet air;
And in the sunlight,

By the green margin of that water,
Children dip white feet and shout,   10
Casting nets in the braided water
To catch the trout:

Then I shall hold my breath and die,
Swearing I never loved you; no,
'You were not lovely!' I shall cry,   15
'I never loved you so.'

                                                        1922

⊶ JOHN PEALE BISHOP ⊷
(1892–1944)

The poetic talents of John Peale Bishop, though highly regarded by friends like Edmund Wilson, F. Scott Fitzgerald, and Allen Tate, were overshadowed by the more productive and famous writers of his generation. Greatly influenced by other poets of his era like T. S. Eliot, Ezra Pound, and Robert Frost, Bishop only rarely found his own distinctive voice. He did, however, leave behind a few superb poems, and his influence as an editor and critic was considerable. In addition, he was one of the first significant Modernist poets to emerge from the American South.

Bishop was born a doctor's son in Charles Town (now Charleston), West Virginia, and was brought up in a prosperous, cultivated home. His mother came from an old Virginia family that had played an important role for two centuries in the colony's settlement, development, and eventual division into two states. A childhood illness set Bishop back in school; he did not enter Princeton University until he was twenty-one years old. By then he seemed to friends like Wilson already a distinguished poet. Bishop published his first collection of verse, *Green Fruit*, in 1917, the year of his graduation as well as his enlistment in the U.S. Army's expeditionary force to France.

One of his most grisly wartime duties was to serve with a reinterment camp unit stationed in Paris. By the time of his discharge in 1920, Bishop had seen much to disillusion him, but he had also fallen deeply in love with the art and culture of Europe. His 1922 marriage to heiress Margaret Grosvenor Hutchins made it possible for Bishop to live in Europe for nearly a decade. There he came to know many fellow "Lost Generation" writers, especially Hemingway, Pound, and Fitzgerald. He had already served as the model for poet Tom D'Invilliers in Fitzgerald's 1920 novel *This Side of Paradise*.

For the two years prior to his marriage, Bishop worked as managing editor of *Vanity Fair*, one of the most influential magazines of the period. He had also published stories and poems in *The Undertaker's Garland* (1922) with his friend Wilson. Bishop's next book was the collection of stories *Many Thousands Gone* (1931), followed by the poems of *Now with His Love* (1933), in which the influence of European painting was very strong. He published his highly regarded Southern novel, *Act of Darkness,* in 1935, and in the same year another collection of poems, *Minute Particulars.* In 1940 Bishop became the chief poetry reviewer for the *Nation.* His *Selected Poems* appeared the following year. Before his premature death of heart disease, he lived with his family on Cape Cod.

◄►━━◄I►━━►►

Perspectives Are Precipices

Sister Anne, Sister Anne,
Do you see anybody coming?

> I see a distance of black yews
> Long as the history of the Jews.

> I see a road sunned with white sand,   5
> Wide plains surrounding silence. And

> Far-off, a broken colonnade
> That overthrows the sun with shade.

Sister Anne, Sister Anne,
Do you see nobody coming?   10

A man

Upon that road a man who goes
Dragging a shadow by its toes.

Diminishing he goes, head bare
Of any covering even hair.   15

A pitcher depending from one hand
Goes mouth down. And dry is sand

Sister Anne, Sister Anne,
What do you see?

> His dwindling stride. And he seems blind   20
> Or worse to the prone man behind.

Sister Anne! Sister Anne!

> I see a road. Beyond nowhere
> Defined by cirrus and blue air.

> I saw a man but he is gone   25
> His shadow gone into the sun.

1933

My Grandfather Kept Peacocks

When other reasons for pride were gone
Winters he sat by the green-primed woodbox
And pine-knots flared upon a meditation
Of wild blue eyes and a grey beard stalked
On the thin despair of a dwindling hand.   5
Frost had been kind: windows gave back
A glazed white stare of crazy eyes but blind.
Carpets were windy stripes upon the floor.
The kitchen planks were wide and scoured with sand.
He could not see unless he undertook the door   10
Those arrogant birds, whom the wind balked
In their poor progress through the snow.
He could not touch the door; he did not dare
Because of a looking glass beside the door.
He would not risk the smallest crack   15
Of snow, lest death should see him there
Looking from out the glass beside the door.

1933

◦—◄ ARCHIBALD MacLEISH ►—◦
(1892–1982)

Poet, statesman, playwright, editor, and librarian, Archibald MacLeish was born in Glencoe, Illinois, the son of twice-widowed Andrew MacLeish and his third wife, Martha Hillard. His stern Glasgow-born father was an early settler of Chicago and had become a prosperous partner in a leading department store. His Vassar-educated mother, who traced her lineage to the *Mayflower,* had been a college instructor. MacLeish grew up in a large, affluent family that prized education. Initially a difficult child and mediocre student, MacLeish was sent at fifteen to start over at Hotchkiss, a preparatory school in Lakeville, Connecticut, where he soon excelled. In 1911, he entered Yale, where his achievements displayed the extraordinary diversity that distinguished his later career. Captain of the water polo team, center of the football team, chairman of the *Yale Literary Magazine,* and class poet, he also was chosen for Skull and Bones, the university's elite secret society. At graduation in 1915, fellow classmates overwhelmingly voted him "most brilliant" and "most versatile." By then MacLeish had already chosen his future wife, Ada Taylor Hitchcock, recognized his poetic vocation, and reluctantly planned a career in law.

By the time MacLeish graduated first in his class from Harvard Law School in 1919, he had become a husband, father, war veteran, and published poet. After successfully completing his first year, he had gained his father's permission to marry Ada. Their first son was born the next year. When America entered the Great War a few months later, the new father enlisted as a private in Yale's hospital unit "so as to do the right thing but not get hurt," but soon shifted to a combat unit to pursue a commission. In the meantime Yale University Press published his first collection of poems, *Tower of Ivory* (1917). He returned from the war a captain, but his beloved younger brother Kenneth had been killed in air combat. After law school, MacLeish briefly taught government at Harvard before joining the Boston law firm of Choate, Hall, and Stewart. In 1923, however, the thirty-year-old poet resigned just as the firm offered him a partnership.

With his father's promise of support, MacLeish took his family to Paris where the favorable exchange rate allowed Americans to live cheaply. Planning to stay one year to write poetry seriously, he remained for five years in "the last of the great holy cities of the arts." He befriended his fellow American émigré writers of the Lost Generation—Ernest Hemingway, John Dos Passos, F. Scott Fitzgerald, and E. E. Cummings. MacLeish followed a strict and compulsive schedule to transform himself into a modern poet. He learned Italian to read Dante and systematically studied the entire history of English-language poetry. Determined and self-critical, MacLeish developed a lucid, compressed, and sensuously evocative poetic style unlike the limp Romanticism of his early work. Producing five books in five years, he began to write the poems that would earn him a permanent place in American literature. The best poems of his Parisian period—"Memorial Rain," "The End of the World," You, Andrew Marvell," and "*Ars Poetica*"—were immediately recognized as modern classics and have never left the anthologies. Indeed, the last two lines of "*Ars Poetica*" ("A poem should not mean / But be.") might well rank as the most frequently quoted couplet in twentieth-century American poetry. The force, beauty, and originality of these poems, however, eventually worked against MacLeish; later critics carped that he never wrote this well again.

When MacLeish returned from Paris in 1928, he was widely recognized as one of America's leading poets. His fifth book of poems, *Streets in the Moon* (1926), had appeared to triumphant reviews. MacLeish and his wife bought (with the help of Ada's father) a house and farm in Conway, Massachusetts, where they would live for more than fifty years. MacLeish's critical reputation was ruffled by the publication of his book-length poem, *The Hamlet of A. MacLeish* (1928), which not only occasioned bad reviews but eventually inspired Edmund Wilson's savage 1939 parody "The Omelet of A. MacLeish." He quickly regained favor, however, with *New Found Land* (1930) and *Conquistador* (1932), a book-length narrative of Cortés's plunder of Mexico, which won the first of the poet's three Pulitzer Prizes.

The market crash of 1929 decimated MacLeish's small private income. Not wanting to return to practicing law, he accepted Henry Luce's offer to join the staff of *Fortune*, which had not yet published its first issue. *Fortune's* original staff, which included James Agee and Dwight Macdonald, remains legendary, but MacLeish, who usually worked only part-time, soon emerged as the acknowledged star. Publishing nearly one hundred major articles, he became the most influential writer at the nation's premier business magazine. His liberal perspective helped make *Fortune* sympathetic to many New Deal reforms, and the poet became increasingly drawn into public affairs, especially the fight against fascism.

In 1939 President Franklin Roosevelt asked MacLeish to become the Librarian of Congress. The poet initially refused, but Roosevelt was not to be gainsaid, for he believed MacLeish would prove valuable in Washington as an articulate and well-connected spokesman for the administration's policies. Idealistic and ambitious, the poet fell under the President's sway. For the next six years he became Roosevelt's loyal public apologist. Not without reason did one of MacLeish's key library associates refer to him as "Roosevelt's Minister of Culture." MacLeish quickly defined goals for the library, reorganized the staff, updated services, and secured significantly greater funding. He also reconceived the newly endowed position of Poetry Consultant, by creating a rotating appointment that soon became the most prestigious public position in American poetry. (Congress recognized its preeminence in 1986 by changing the consultantship's title to "Poet Laureate of the United States.")

MacLeish's new determination "to integrate the role of the poet and the public man" proved disastrous to his poetry but beneficial to his political career. The poetry he published over the next decade addressed timely public issues, but it became overly rhetorical and verbally thin. He also returned to verse drama. His 1935 play *Panic* (directed by John Houseman and starring Orson Welles) ran for only three nights but occasioned huge controversy when communist organizations packed the final performance for a special critical symposium. In collaboration with Dos Passos and Lillian Hellman, he wrote the screenplay for *The Spanish Earth* (1937), an antifascist documentary. That same year, *The Fall of the City*, the first verse play ever written for American radio, was broadcast nationally on CBS. Starring Welles and Burgess Meredith, the half-hour-long play scored a huge success and was rebroadcast a few months later from the Hollywood Bowl.

Roosevelt soon expanded the poet's role in Washington. MacLeish joined Harry Hopkins, Sam Rosenman, and Robert Sherwood to write presidential speeches. (Most of the 1941 inaugural address, for instance, was by MacLeish.) When America entered World War II, MacLeish was put in charge of the Office of Facts and Figures, a newly created bureau to disseminate accurate defense information (as well as to provide positive wartime propaganda). MacLeish was also appointed chairman of the Committee on War Information and made an overseer for the Office of Censorship. Roosevelt also asked him to supervise preparations for the nation's official history of the war. While fulfilling these important public duties, he continued as Librarian of Congress. In 1943 MacLeish joined a secret government committee to plan the postwar peace. They envisioned a central role for the still nascent United Nations, which would be officially chartered in 1945. Leaving his library post in late 1944, MacLeish became (despite opposition from conservatives in both parties) Assistant Secretary of State for Cultural and Public Affairs. A fervent "One World" internationalist, he welcomed his official task of selling the American people on the United Nations. Among his many duties, MacLeish helped write the UN charter. (The preamble is almost entirely his work.) He also headed the U.S. delegation at the founding of UNESCO and became the first American member of UNESCO's Executive Council.

A year after Roosevelt's death in 1945, MacLeish returned to private life nervously hoping he could resume writing poetry. Harvard offered him the Boylston Chair of Rhetoric and Oratory. His thirteen years at Harvard proved the happiest period of his life. He taught poetry and writing on a comfortable part-time basis. His students included Donald Hall, Robert Bly, John Simon and Edward Hoagland. In 1952 he published his *Collected Poems, 1917–1952* to exultant reviews. The book won every major prize, including the National Book Award, the Bollingen, and a second Pulitzer. A year later he was elected president of the American Academy of Arts and Letters. MacLeish also returned to the theater. In 1958 his modern version of the Job story, *J. B.*, was first staged in New Haven, Connecticut. Much revised, the verse play opened on Broadway, where it became a huge hit and ran for a year before going on a national tour. Hailed as a modern classic, *J. B.* won both a Tony Award and a Pulitzer. The play also earned the poet more money than all of his other books combined. Additional public acclaim came when his screenplay for the documentary *The Eleanor Roosevelt Story* (1965) won him an Academy Award for best feature documentary, a unique honor for an American poet. Although MacLeish's critical reputation began to decline in his later years, he remained America's most visible public poet. He died of pneumonia on April 20, 1982, a few weeks short of his ninetieth birthday.

MacLeish's enduring reputation rests mainly on his short personal lyrics rather than the long public poems of his middle years. His best work remains so strong and original that he ranks as a major figure in the second generation of American Modernist poets. With the exception of *J. B.*, his verse plays are now seldom performed, but his ambitious experiments in that genre nonetheless make him the most influential figure in modern American poetic drama. His voluminous critical prose has aged badly, but it reflects the broad and progressive concerns of his political career. No American writer of similar distinction has ever played such an important role in public life.

Ars Poetica[1]

A poem should be palpable and mute
As a globed fruit,

Dumb
As old medallions to the thumb,

Silent as the sleeve-worn stone   5
Of casement ledges where the moss has grown—

A poem should be wordless
As the flight of birds.

*

A poem should be motionless in time
As the moon climbs,   10

Leaving, as the moon releases
Twig by twig the night-entangled trees,

Leaving, as the moon behind the winter leaves,
Memory by memory the mind—

A poem should be motionless in time   15
As the moon climbs.

*

A poem should be equal to:
Not true.

1. (Latin) The "poetic art" or "art of poetry." The Latin term originated with Horace and has come to be the traditional title for discussions of the aesthetics of poetry. Here MacLeish articulates a specifically Modernist perspective.

For all the history of grief
An empty doorway and a maple leaf.   20

For love
The leaning grasses and two lights above the sea—

A poem should not mean
But be.

1926

The End of the World[2]

Quite unexpectedly as Vasserot
The armless ambidextrian was lighting
A match between his great and second toe
And Ralph the lion was engaged in biting
The neck of Madame Sossman while the drum   5
Pointed, and Teeny was about to cough
In waltz-time swinging Jocko by the thumb—
Quite unexpectedly the top blew off:

And there, there overhead, there, there, hung over
Those thousands of white faces, those dazed eyes,   10
There in the starless dark the poise, the hover,
There with vast wings across the canceled skies,
There in the sudden blackness the black pall
Of nothing, nothing, nothing—nothing at all.

1926

The Silent Slain

For Kenneth MacLeish, 1894–1918[3]

We too, we too, descending once again
The hills of our own land, we too have heard
Far off—Ah, que ce cor a longue haleine[4]—
The horn of Roland in the passages of Spain,
The first, the second blast, the failing third,   5
And with the third turned back and climbed once more
The steep road southward, and heard faint the sound
Of swords, of horses, the disastrous war,
And crossed the dark defile at last, and found
At Roncevaux upon the darkening plain   10

---

2. The proper names in this poem are fictional.
3. The poet's brother, Kenneth, was killed in World War I.
4. (Old French) "Ah, that this horn of the mighty breath." A quotation from the epic poem *The Song of Roland* (c. 1100), which describes the death of the warrior Roland at the battle of Roncevaux.

The dead against the dead and on the silent ground
The silent slain—

1926

You, Andrew Marvell[5]

And here face down beneath the sun
And here upon earth's noonward height
To feel the always coming on
The always rising of the night:

To feel creep up the curving east   5
The earthy chill of dusk and slow
Upon those under lands the vast
And ever climbing shadow grow

And strange at Ecbatan[6] the trees
Take leaf by leaf the evening strange   10
The flooding dark about their knees
The mountains over Persia change

And now at Kermanshah[7] the gate
Dark empty and the withered grass
And through the twilight now the late   15
Few travelers in the westward pass

And Baghdad[8] darken and the bridge
Across the silent river gone
And through Arabia the edge
Of evening widen and steal on   20

And deepen on Palmyra's[9] street
The wheel rut in the ruined stone
And Lebanon fade out and Crete
High through the clouds and overblown

And over Sicily the air   25
Still flashing with the landward gulls
And loom and slowly disappear
The sails above the shadowy hulls

And Spain go under and the shore
Of Africa the gilded sand   30
And evening vanish and no more
The low pale light across that land

5. English poet (1621–1676) who wrote in "To His Coy Mistress," "But at my back I always hear /
Time's wingèd chariot hurrying near."
6. Capital of ancient Media (present-day Iran).
7. A city in Iran.
8. Capital of Iraq, on the Tigris River.
9. Once a great city, now a small town near some ancient ruins in Syria.

Nor now the long light on the sea:

And here face downward in the sun
To feel how swift how secretly   35
The shadow of the night comes on . . .

1930

EDNA ST. VINCENT MILLAY
(1892–1950)

Edna St. Vincent Millay, the lyric poet whose passionate celebration of bohemian hedonism and defiant assertion of female independence made her the embodiment of the Jazz Age, was born in Rockland, Maine. The eldest of three daughters, Millay, who began writing poetry in childhood, was raised by her mother, a musician who had to abandon her art for the financial security of nursing. (Millay's parents had separated when she was seven.) After graduating from high school, Millay had no money for college; instead, with her mother's blessing, she stayed at home and wrote poetry. In 1912 her poem "Renascence" was a finalist in the national *Lyric Year* competition. When it was published as the fourth-place poem in the contest's anthology, prominent critics complained that it deserved first prize. The resulting controversy made the young poet famous. Meanwhile her recitation of the poem at a party at a local resort hotel led to a wealthy guest sponsoring Millay's admission into Barnard College in New York City. When Millay arrived in Manhattan, she was already a literary celebrity. The next year she entered Vassar, graduating in 1917.

Millay settled in Greenwich Village, moving in artistic circles that included many of the period's most influential writers and radicals—the critic Edmund Wilson, poets Witter Bynner and John Peale Bishop, and dramatists Eugene O'Neill and Floyd Dell. She wrote verse plays such as *Aria Da Capa* (1919) for the newly established Provincetown Players, the small but influential theatrical company that also produced new works by O'Neill, Susan Glaspell, E. E. Cummings, and Sherwood Anderson. Millay wrote satiric articles for popular magazines—often under a pseudonym—and her numerous love affairs with both men and women would soon become part of her public legend.

Millay's first book, *Renascence and Other Poems* (1917), appeared a few months after her college graduation. It was soon followed by *A Few Figs from Thistles* (1920) and *Second April* (1921). These early volumes gained Millay a huge readership, drawn in both by her unprecedented sexual and emotional candor and the sensuous music of her poems, which were written mostly in traditional meter and rhyme. These early poems also reveal, as critic Margaret Carter has noted, "the sadness underlying her bravado, a sadness arising from her powerlessness to resolve the conflicting demands of love and poetry." In the first few years after World War I, the concept of modern poetry had not yet became narrowly identified with the "High Modernist" mode of Eliot, Pound, Moore, and Stevens. Noting how progressive Millay's subject matter and attitudes were, critics viewed her as an important poet of the new vanguard. With her fourth volume, *The Harp Weaver* (1923), she became the first woman to win the Pulitzer Prize in poetry.

Millay was now the most famous woman poet in the United States, but her notoriety went beyond the sales and reputation of her books. As a public personality, she had come to symbolize the free-spirited and free-thinking new woman—sexually liberated, politically radical, and effortlessly urbane. The poet did little to discourage this public image, though her unconventional life often took a heavy toll in its emotional stress and economic difficulty. After many love affairs, Millay met Eugene Jan Boissevain, an Older Dutch-Irish businessman who dedicated himself to caring for her. They married in 1923, and he remained devoted to her despite her overt infidelities. Boissevain managed all the practical details of Millay's daily life, which freed her up to write without distraction or worry. The early years with Boissevain coincided with the prime of Millay's career. She also became a political activist, joining the national committee to save the anarchists Sacco and Vanzetti from the electric chair.

The height of Millay's career came with the publication of *Fatal Interview* (1931). This sequence of fifty-two Shakespearean sonnets celebrated, chronicled, and commemorated her love affair with the young poet George Dillon. Full of passionately lyrical poems such as "Love Is Not All," *Fatal Interview* became an immense popular and critical success. Edmund Wilson declared it one of the century's great volumes of poetry. Her later career, however, followed a slowly downward trajectory. Her health declined, and she began writing increasing amounts of highly uneven political poetry—"acres of bad poetry," she once called it—earnestly dedicated to fighting fascism. She spent much of her time in isolation at Steepletop, a seven-hundred-acre farm in upstate New York. In 1949 Boissevain died, and Millay never recovered emotionally from his loss. A year later the fifty-eight-year-old poet died of a heart attack at Steepletop.

By the time of her death, critical opinion had turned decisively against Millay's work, which was dismissed as sentimental in tone and old-fashioned in form. Her political verse was condemned as verbally thin and melodramatic. Her direct emotion and formal lyrics had little appeal for New Critics intent on examining and explicating complexities of language. As poet-critic John Ciardi stated condescendingly in a memorial article, "It was not as a craftsman nor an influence, but as the creator of her own legend that she was most alive for us." Her poetry, as poet Colin Falck observed, was "no longer a part of any trend or tendency." It had no apparent place in the Modernist tradition and could only be understood as artistically reactionary. More recently feminist critics have reexamined her poems and placed them in a formalist tradition of lyric women poets such as Elinor Wylie, Sara Teasdale, and Louise Bogan, which constituted an alternative to high Modernism. Feminists have also emphasized that, in breaking through barriers of subject matter for women poets, Millay opened new possibilities for later writers. The recent revival of form in American poetry has also reinforced Millay's importance as a master of formal music and one of the great sonneteers in American literature. Although still underrated and poorly understood, Millay is generally acknowledged as an important and unorthodox figure in modern American poetry.

Time Does Not Bring Relief: You All Have Lied

Time does not bring relief; you all have lied
Who told me time would ease me of my pain!
I miss him in the weeping of the rain;
I want him at the shrinking of the tide;
The old snows melt from every mountain-side,   5
And last year's leaves are smoke in every lane;
But last year's bitter loving must remain
Heaped on my heart, and my old thoughts abide.
There are a hundred places where I fear
To go,—so with his memory they brim.   10
And entering with relief some quiet place
Where never fell his foot or shone his face
I say, "There is no memory of him here!"
And so stand stricken, so remembering him.

                                                     1917

First Fig

My candle burns at both ends;
    It will not last the night;
But ah, my foes, and oh, my friends—
    It gives a lovely light!

                                                     1920

Second Fig

Safe upon the solid rock the ugly houses stand:
Come and see my shining palace built upon the sand!

                                                     1920

I Shall Forget You Presently, My Dear

I shall forget you presently, my dear,
So make the most of this, your little day,
Your little month, your little half a year,
Ere I forget, or die, or move away,
And we are done forever; by and by   5
I shall forget you, as I said, but now,
If you entreat me with your loveliest lie
I will protest you with my favourite vow.
I would indeed that love were longer-lived,
And oaths were not so brittle as they are,   10
But so it is, and nature has contrived

To struggle on without a break thus far,—
Whether or not we find what we are seeking
Is idle, biologically speaking.

1920

Recuerdo[1]

We were very tired, we were very merry—
We had gone back and forth all night on the ferry.
It was bare and bright, and smelled like a stable—
But we looked into a fire, we leaned across a table,
We lay on a hill-top underneath the moon;   5
And the whistles kept blowing, and the dawn came soon.

We were very tried, we were very merry—
We had gone back and forth all night on the ferry;
And you ate an apple, and I ate a pear,
From a dozen of each we had bought somewhere;   10
And the sky went wan, and the wind came cold,
And the sun rose dripping, a bucketful of gold.

We were very tired, we were very merry,
We had gone back and forth all night on the ferry.
We hailed, "Good morrow, mother!" to a shawl-covered head,   15
And bought a morning paper, which neither of us read;
And she wept, "God bless you!" for the apples and pears,
And we gave her all our money but our subway fares.

1920

Passer Mortuus Est[2]

Death devours all lovely things:
    Lesbia with her sparrow
Shares the darkness,—presently
    Every bed is narrow.

Unremembered as old rain   5
    Dries the sheer libation;
And the little petulant hand
    Is an annotation.

After all, my erstwhile dear,
    My no longer cherished,   10
Need we say it was not love,
    Just because it perished?

1921

1. (Spanish) "I remember."
2. (Latin) "The sparrow is dead." The Roman poet Catullus (84?–54 B.C.E.,) wrote that his beloved Lesbia's pet sparrow had died.

What Lips My Lips Have Kissed

What lips my lips have kissed, and where, and why,
I have forgotten, and what arms have lain
Under my head till morning; but the rain
Is full of ghosts tonight, that tap and sigh
Upon the glass and listen for reply,   5
And in my heart there sits a quiet pain
For unremembered lads that not again
Will turn to me at midnight with a cry.
Thus in the winter stands the lonely tree,
Nor knows what birds have vanished one by one,   10
Yet knows its boughs more silent than before:
I cannot say what loves have come and gone,
I only know that summer sang in me
A little while, that in me sings no more.

1923

Love Is Not All

Love is not all: it is not meat nor drink
Nor slumber nor a roof against the rain;
Nor yet a floating spar to men that sink
And rise and sink and rise and sink again;
Love can not fill the thickened lung with breath,   5
Nor clean the blood, nor set the fractured bone;
Yet many a man is making friends with death
Even as I speak, for lack of love alone.
It well may be that in a difficult hour,
Pinned down by pain and moaning for release,   10
Or nagged by want past resolution's power,
I might be driven to sell your love for peace,
Or trade the memory of this night for food.
It well may be. I do not think I would.

1931

Hearing Your Words, and Not a Word among Them

Hearing your words, and not a word among them
Tuned to my liking, on a salty day
When inland woods were pushed by winds that flung them
Hissing to leeward like a ton of spray,
I thought how off Matinicus[3] the tide   5
Came pounding in, came running through the Gut,
While from the Rock the warning whistle cried,

---

3. An island off the coast of Maine.

And children whimpered, and the doors blew shut;
There in the autumn when the men go forth,
With slapping skirts the island women stand   10
In gardens stripped and scattered, peering north,
With dahlia tubers dripping from the hand:
The wind of their endurance, driving south,
Flattened your words against your speaking mouth

1931

◦►◄ DOROTHY PARKER ►◄◦
(1893–1967)

The daughter of a wealthy Jewish garment manufacturer and a Scottish Protestant
mother, Dorothy Rothschild was born two months prematurely, during a hurricane, in West End, New Jersey where her family was vacationing. She was raised
in a tony neighborhood on the Upper West Side of Manhattan. When she was
quite young, her mother died, and her father soon remarried. Insisting that
Dorothy needed to be cured of her Jewishness, her stepmother sent her to a
Catholic school; as an adult, Parker claimed that the nuns asked her to leave when
she insisted that the Immaculate Conception arose from "Spontaneous Combus-
tion." Her stepmother died in 1903, but Dorothy did not escape the convent
school until 1907, when her father enrolled her in an exclusive private boarding
school, which she attended for only a year. Although she never graduated, she received a solid classical education, and by the time she left school at the age of fourteen, she had learned Latin and French, studied literature, and begun to write
poetry. After her father died in 1913, she was forced to work, and she lived quite
literally by her wits, for she soon found an entry-level writing job at *Vogue*. In
1917 she transferred to *Vanity Fair*, another magazine owned by the same company, since her acerbic contributions—such as the photo caption "Brevity is the
Soul of Lingerie"—were deemed unsuitable for a fashion venue.

In 1917, she became Mrs. Edwin Pond Parker II, wife of a hard-drinking Wall
Street broker. She later quipped that they had been married "for about five minutes" when he joined the war effort as an ambulance driver and was sent to Europe, where he was wounded. He returned in 1919, addicted to morphine, and
the marriage ultimately failed although the couple did not divorce until 1928. By
that time, Parker had established herself as a celebrated wit and best-selling poet.
Until 1920, she contributed poems and reviewed plays for *Vanity Fair*, gaining notoriety for her withering one-liners. But that notoriety cost her her job, for she
was fired in 1920 after panning plays produced by three financial backers of the
magazine. She had no trouble supporting herself for the rest of her life as a free-
lance writer, penning short stories such as "Big Blonde," which won the O. Henry
Award in 1929; book reviews, such as the acid "Constant Reader" column for the
New Yorker; plays and screenplays; and three books of verse: *Enough Rope*
(1926), *Sunset Gun* (1928), and *Death and Taxes* (1931), all of which were collected in *Not So Deep as a Well* (1936). During the 1920s, she also found ample
opportunities to display her virtuosity at coining puns, double entendres, and
sometimes defensive put-downs at frequent lunches held at the Algonquin Hotel

with a group known as the Round Table, whose core members included journalist George S. Kaufman, the satirist Robert Benchley, and Harold Ross, founding editor of the *New Yorker*. Members of the group would challenge each other to develop punning sentences from polysyllabic words, and Parker often bested her competition with responses such as "You can lead a horticulture, but you can't make her think." Her verve endeared her to high society, and she became a sought-after luminary at theatre openings, cocktail parties, and speakeasies.

But her accelerated social life in the 1920s was shadowed by personal trauma: numerous affairs which ended badly, alcoholism, several abortions, and four suicide attempts. Her life stabilized somewhat after she married Alan Campbell in 1933; after 1934, the couple split their time between New York and Hollywood, where Parker's gift for snappy repartee served her well as a writer of screenplays, most notably *A Star Is Born* (1937). Yet she was dissatisfied with her Hollywood writing, and towards the end of her life she felt prouder of the political activism she engaged in during the 1930s than of her screenplays, which she found glib. Long attracted to leftist causes, in 1936 Parker became active in the Screen Writers Guild and also helped found the Hollywood Anti-Nazi League, which lobbied against fascism. Before the decade closed, she had joined over thirty leftist organizations, donating money and allowing them to list her as a sponsor. Her pro-union views, belief in the Communist Party, and continuing support for radical causes caused her to be blacklisted by the Hollywood studios in 1950 after her name appeared in *Red Channels,* a list of "Communist Sympathizers." Although she was never openly investigated by the House Committee on Un-American Activities, her screenwriting career was over. In the last two decades of her life, writing grew increasingly difficult for her as her eyesight failed and her alcoholism worsened. She died of a heart attack in a New York hotel, leaving her estate to the National Association for the Advancement of Colored People (NAACP).

Too often dismissed as light verse, Parker's poetry reflects the temper of her times—particularly the costs and gains of the new social freedoms available to women. Although her speakers are often jaded, their sexual experience gives them the wisdom and power to attack romantic hypocrisy, whether it is committed by men or by women. Moreover, Parker achieves her epigrammatic parodies of love poetry through her skill in conforming to literary conventions—only to explode them at a poem's conclusion. Her poetry's blend of irony, baleful skepticism, and clear-sighted pessimism, along with its theme of resigned continuance in the midst of desperate conditions, could only have arisen in the twentieth century.

Comment

Oh, life is a glorious cycle of song,
A medley of extemporanea;
And love is a thing that can never go wrong;
And I am Marie of Roumania.

1926

One Perfect Rose

A single flow'r he sent me, since we met.
  All tenderly his messenger he chose;
Deep-hearted, pure, with scented dew still wet—
  One perfect rose.

I knew the language of the floweret;   5
  "My fragile leaves," it said, "his heart enclose."
Love long has taken for his amulet
  One perfect rose.

Why is it no one ever sent me yet
  One perfect limousine, do you suppose?   10
Ah no, it's always just my luck to get
  One perfect rose.

                    1926

Résumé

Razors pain you;
Rivers are damp;
Acids stain you;
And drugs cause cramp.
Guns aren't lawful;   5
Nooses give;
Gas smells awful;
You might as well live.

                    1926

Unfortunate Coincidence

By the time you swear you're his,
  Shivering and sighing,
And he vows his passion is
  Infinite, undying—
Lady, make a note of this: 5
  One of you is lying.

                    1926

Sanctuary

My land is bare of chattering folk;
  The clouds are low along the ridges,
And sweet's the air with curly smoke
  From all my burning bridges.

                    1931

◦—◄ LOUISE BOGAN ►—◦
(1897–1970)

Born in Livermore Falls, Maine, Louise Bogan (pronounced Bogán) grew up buffeted by the storms of her parents' troubled marriage. Her father, Daniel Bogan, served as a foreman of various New England mills, and the family moved frequently, living in hotels and boarding houses in New Hampshire and Massachusetts. Her mother, May Shields Bogan, engaged in extramarital affairs, which led to several prolonged disappearances from the family. Considering the effects of these disruptions in the autobiographical writings collected in *Journey Around My Room* (1980), Bogan admitted that in childhood she became "the semblance of a girl, in which some desires and illusions had been early assassinated: shot dead." The skepticism about love and the preoccupation with romantic betrayal that characterize Bogan's poetry, as well as the severe depressions that afflicted her during adulthood, were likely engendered during these difficult years.

In her education, however, Bogan found a haven against disorder. She attended a convent school from 1906 to 1908 and then studied at the prestigious Girl's Latin School in Boston, where she received a superb classical education and began to write poetry. By the time of her graduation in 1915, she had become fluent enough in traditional forms that, as she notes in *Journey Around My Room*, "I had a thick pile of manuscript, in the drawer in the dining room—and had learned every essential of my trade." After a year at Boston University, she was offered a scholarship to Radcliffe, but chose instead to marry Curt Alexander, a German native who was a corporal in the U.S. Army. When the United States declared war, Alexander was shipped to Panama in April 1917. Bogan, who was four months pregnant, joined him there and gave birth to a daughter. Miserable in Panama and disillusioned with her marriage, she returned to Massachusetts with the baby in May 1918. After a brief rapprochement with her husband, she left him in 1919 and moved to Manhattan, entrusting her daughter to her parents. Her husband's death in 1920 from pneumonia made her eligible for widow's benefits, which, along with work at Brentano's Bookstore and the New York Public Library, gave her the financial security to concentrate on poetry.

In New York, Bogan soon forged friendships with writers who helped her embark on a literary career. Her poems appeared in journals such as *Poetry, Others,* and the *Measure,* and in 1923 she published her first book, *Body of This Death,* a remarkable collection of lyrics. The following year, at the urging of Edmund Wilson, she published her first book review. By the early 1930s, she had established herself as a formidable poet and critic, but reached a crisis in her personal life. In 1925 she married the poet Raymond Holden; with her daughter in tow they later moved to a home in Hillsdale, New York. But on December 26, 1929, three months after the publication of her second book, *Dark Summer,* the house was destroyed by fire. The couple returned to New York City, but the marriage deteriorated, and Bogan was hit with depression severe enough that she required a three-month hospitalization.

After her release from the sanitarium, Bogan began to write poetry reviews for the *New Yorker,* and until 1969 she contributed biannual, omnibus reviews of new poetry, as well as incisive essays on a variety of authors, to the magazine. Along with the criticism that she published in the *New Republic* and the *Nation,* Bogan's *New Yorker* reviews earned her a reputation as one of the most powerful literary arbiters in the country, for her judgments were concise, high-minded, and never tainted by influence peddling. Bogan also opposed the ideological poetry popular during the 1930s and stood by her belief that "poetry has something to do with the imagination: I still think it ought to be well-written. I still think it is private feeling, not public speech." For Bogan "private feeling" was compromised by public enumeration, and her aversion to the self-pity that she heard in much of the Confessional poetry of the 1960s reflected her disinclination toward overt autobiography in her own verse.

That autobiographical landscape grew increasingly bleak for Bogan during the early 1930s. In the summer of 1933, returning early from a solo trip to Europe that she had funded through a Guggenheim Fellowship, she discovered that her husband had committed adultery, and the marriage blew apart. In November, suffering again from severe depression, she checked herself into New York Hospital's Westchester Division. After her release seven months later, she found the strength to pursue her work again. Although she experienced financial difficulties, including eviction from her apartment in September 1935, by the decade's close she had rebounded. In 1935 she was energized by a brief affair with the young Theodore Roethke, and in 1937, the year of her divorce, she published her third book, *The Sleeping Fury,* whose lyrics celebrated her new found equilibrium yet did not flinch from contemplating the darkness she had weathered. But *The Sleeping Fury* was to be her last book made up entirely of new poems, for the three additional poetry books that she published before her death were compilations that included only slim selections of new work. Over the next three decades Bogan poured most of her literary energy into prose, publishing essays, reviews, translations, and a book-length study of modern American poetry. She also received national recognition for her verse, serving as Consultant in Poetry to the Library of Congress in 1945–46 and sharing the 1955 Bollingen Prize with Léonie Adams. She was elected to the American Academy of Arts and Letters in 1968.

At the time of her death in 1970 from a coronary occlusion, she was best known as a critic. Yet many poets prized her lyrics, as W. H. Auden noted at her funeral, both for their technical excellence and for "her determination never to surrender to self-pity, but to wrest beauty and joy out of dark places." Bogan, who called the lyric "the most intense, the most compressed, the most purified form of language," developed a severe attitude toward her writing, for she not only pursued formal perfection, but favored subjects so psychically charged that she eschewed ordinary occasions—so much so that her collected poems, *The Blue Estuaries* (1968), contains only 107 poems. As Malcolm Cowley argued, Bogan "has done something that has been achieved by very few of her contemporaries: she has added a dozen or more to our small stock of memorable lyrics." Like many poets of her generation, Bogan works both with and against nineteenth-century conventions, fusing the emotional depth common to much Romantic poetry with Modernist irony, skepticism, and openness to the power of the unconscious. In writing of women's experience, she also set herself in the line of American female poets that begins with Anne Bradstreet and includes Bogan's contemporaries, Sara Teasdale, Elinor Wylie, and Edna St. Vincent Millay.

Never denying the primacy of personal experience to poetry, Bogan aimed to distill internal experience, rather than chronicle external events. As she wrote in 1961, "The poet represses the outright narrative of his life. He absorbs it, along with life itself. The repressed becomes the poem. Actually, I have written down my experiences in the closest detail. But the rough and vulgar facts are not there."

The Alchemist

I burned my life, that I might find
A passion wholly of the mind,
Thought divorced from eye and bone,
Ecstasy come to breath alone.
I broke my life, to seek relief   5
From the flawed light of love and grief.

With mounting beat the utter fire
Charred existence and desire.
It died low, ceased its sudden thresh.
I had found unmysterious flesh—   10
Not the mind's avid substance—still
Passionate beyond the will.

                                                                1923

The Crows

The woman who has grown old
And knows desire must die,
Yet turns to love again,
Hears the crows' cry.

She is a stem long hardened,   5
A weed that no scythe mows.
The heart's laughter will be to her
The crying of the crows,

Who slide in the air with the same voice
Over what yields not, and what yields,   10
Alike in spring, and when there is only bitter
Winter-burning in the fields.

                                                                1923

Medusa[1]

I had come to the house, in a cave of trees,
Facing a sheer sky.
Everything moved,—a bell hung ready to strike,
Sun and reflection wheeled by.

When the bare eyes were before me   5
And the hissing hair,
Held up at a window, seen through a door.
The stiff bald eyes, the serpents on the forehead
Formed in the air.

This is a dead scene forever now.   10

---

1. A female monster in Greek mythology whose horrific appearance could turn men into stone.

Nothing will ever stir.
The end will never brighten it more than this,
Nor the rain blur.

The water will always fall, and will not fall,
And the tipped bell make no sound.   15
The grass will always be growing for hay
Deep on the ground.

And I shall stand here like a shadow
Under the great balanced day,
My eyes on the yellow dust, that was lifting in the wind,   20
And does not drift away.

                                                 1923

Memory

Do not guard this as rich stuff without mark
Closed in a cedarn dark,
Nor lay it down with tragic masks and greaves,
Licked by the tongues of leaves.

Nor let it be as eggs under the wings   5
Of helpless, startled things,
Nor encompassed by song, nor any glory
Perverse and transitory.

Rather, like shards and straw upon coarse ground,
Of little worth when found,—   10
Rubble in gardens, it and stones alike,
That any spade may strike.

                                                 1923

Women

Women have no wilderness in them,
They are provident instead,
Content in the tight hot cell of their hearts
To eat dusty bread.

They do not see cattle cropping red winter grass,   5
They do not hear
Snow water going down under culverts
Shallow and clear.

They wait, when they should turn to journeys,
They stiffen, when they should bend.   10
They use against themselves that benevolence
To which no man is friend.

They cannot think of so many crops to a field
Or of clean wood cleft by an axe.
Their love is an eager meaninglessness   15
Too tense, or too lax.

They hear in every whisper that speaks to them
A shout and a cry.
As like as not, when they take life over their door-sills
They should let it go by.   20

1923

Knowledge

Now that I know
How passion warms little
Of flesh in the mould,
And treasure is brittle,—

I'll lie here and learn   5
How, over their ground,
Trees make a long shadow
And a light sound.

1923

Cassandra[2]

To me, one silly task is like another.
I bare the shambling tricks of lust and pride.
This flesh will never give a child its mother,—
Song, like a wing, tears through my breast, my side,
And madness chooses out my voice again,   5
Again. I am the chosen no hand saves:
The shrieking heaven lifted over men,
Not the dumb earth, wherein they set their graves.

1929

Henceforth, from the Mind

Henceforth, from the mind,
For your whole joy, must spring
Such joy as you may find
In any earthly thing,
And every time and place   5
Will take your thought for grace.

---

2. Trojan daughter of Priam and Hecuba, Cassandra was a prophetess cursed to have no one believe her predictions.

Henceforth, from the tongue,
From shallow speech alone,
Comes joy you thought, when young,
Would wring you to the bone,   10
Would pierce you to the heart
And spoil its stop and start.

Henceforward, from the shell,
Wherein you heard, and wondered
At oceans like a bell   15
So far from ocean sundered—
A smothered sound that sleeps
Long lost within lost deeps,

Will chime you change and hours,
The shadow of increase,   20
Will sound you flowers
Born under troubled peace—
Henceforth, henceforth
Will echo sea and earth.

1937

The Sleeping Fury[3]

You are here now,
Who were so loud and feared, in a symbol before me,
Alone and asleep, and I at last look long upon you.

Your hair fallen on your cheek, no longer the semblance of serpents,
Lifted in the gale; your mouth, that shrieked so, silent.   5
You, my scourge, my sister, lie asleep, like a child,
Who, after rage, for an hour quiet, sleeps out its tears.

The days close to winter
Rough with strong sound. We hear the sea and the forest,
And the flames of your torches fly, lit by others,   10
Ripped by the wind, in the night. The black sheep for sacrifice
Huddle together. The milk is cold in the jars.

All to no purpose, as before, the knife whetted and plunged,
The shout raised, to match the clamor you have given them.
You alone turn away, not appeased; unaltered, avenger.   15

Hands full of scourges, wreathed with your flames and adders,
You alone turned away, but did not move from my side,
Under the broken light, when the soft nights took the torches.

At thin morning you showed, thick and wrong in that calm,
The ignoble dream and the mask, sly, with slits at the eyes,   20
Pretence and half-sorrow, beneath which a coward's hope trembled.

---

3. In Greek mythology, the three Furies were merciless goddesses of vengeance and retribution.

You uncovered at night, in the locked stillness of houses,
False love due the child's heart, the kissed-out lie, the embraces,
Made by the two who for peace tenderly turned to each other.

You who know what we love, but drive us to know it;   25
You with your whips and shrieks, bearer of truth and of solitude;
You who give, unlike men, to expiation your mercy.

Dropping the scourge when at last the scourged advances to meet it,
You, when the hunted turns, no longer remain the hunter
But stand silent and wait, at last returning his gaze.   30

Beautiful now as a child whose hair, wet with rage and tears
Clings to its face. And now I may look upon you,
Having once met your eyes. You lie in sleep and forget me.
Alone and strong in my peace, I look upon you in yours.

                                                         1937

Song for the Last Act

Now that I have your face by heart, I look
Less at its features than its darkening frame
Where quince and melon, yellow as young flame,
Lie with quilled dahlias and the shepherd's crook.
Beyond, a garden. There, in insolent ease   5
The lead and marble figures watch the show
Of yet another summer loath to go
Although the scythes hang in the apple trees.

Now that I have your face by heart, I look.

Now that I have your voice by heart, I read   10
In the black chords upon a dulling page
Music that is not meant for music's cage,
Whose emblems mix with words that shake and bleed.
The staves are shuttled over with a stark
Unprinted silence. In a double dream   15
I must spell out the storm, the running stream.
The beat's too swift. The notes shift in the dark.

Now that I have your voice by heart, I read.

Now that I have your heart by heart, I see
The wharves with their great ships and architraves;   20
The rigging and the cargo and the slaves
On a strange beach under a broken sky.
O not departure, but a voyage done!
The bales stand on the stone; the anchor weeps
Its red rust downward, and the long vine creeps   25
Beside the salt herb, in the lengthening sun.

Now that I have your heart by heart, I see.

                                                         1953

Night

The cold remote islands
And the blue estuaries
Where what breathes, breathes
The restless wind of the inlets,
And what drinks, drinks   5
The incoming tide;

Where shell and weed
Wait upon the salt wash of the sea,
And the clear nights of stars
Swing their lights westward   10
To set behind the land;

Where the pulse clinging to the rocks
Renews itself forever;
Where, again on cloudless nights,
The water reflects   15
The firmament's partial setting;

—O remember
In your narrowing dark hours
That more things move
Than blood in the heart.   20

                                                        1968

◄ STEPHEN VINCENT BENÉT ►
(1898–1943)

The son of a career army officer, Stephen Vincent Benét was born in Bethlehem, Pennsylvania, and raised at army postings in New York, California, and Georgia. His older brother, William Rose Benét, was a poet and critic who would help found the *Saturday Review of Literature*. Stephen began to publish poetry while a student at Yale. He graduated in 1919 and spent much of his adult life writing and publishing at a feverish pace—more than forty books in all, including several novels and short stories like the celebrated one entitled "The Devil and Daniel Webster." Always a student of history, Benét received a Guggenheim fellowship in 1925 to write a long poem about the Civil War. The result was *John Brown's Body* (1928), which became a perennial best-seller and won the Pulitzer Prize. For the rest of his short life, Benét was one of the best-known and most highly regarded American poets.

In addition to writing books, Benét lectured, made radio broadcasts for leftist causes, and wrote for the movies in Hollywood. With his wife, Rosemary Carr (they married in 1921 and had three children) he published *A Book of Americans* (1933), a series of poems for children, including wonderfully ironic verses on figures like Cotton Mather and Daniel Boone. Much of Benét's verse came to seem dated. Its narrative clarity, somewhat innocent sense of American history, and occasionally mawkish diction did not age well. Yet in his best lyrics, as well as the high points of *John Brown's Body* and the unfinished *Western Star* (for which he

received a second, posthumous Pulitzer Prize), Benét produced popular poetry of
a very high order. In the 1970s, Dee Brown's best-selling revisionist history of the
American West took its title from the last line of Benét's "American Names."

American Names

I have fallen in love with American names,
The sharp names that never get fat,
The snakeskin-titles of mining-claims,
The plumed war-bonnet of Medicine Hat,[1]
Tucson and Deadwood and Lost Mule Flat.[2]   5

Seine and Piave[3] are silver spoons,
But the spoonbowl-metal is thin and worn,
There are English counties like hunting-tunes
Played on the keys of a postboy's horn,
But I will remember where I was born.   10

I will remember Carquinez Straits,
Little French Lick and Lundy's Lane,
The Yankee ships and the Yankee dates
And the bullet-towns of Calamity Jane.
I will remember Skunktown Plain.   15

I will fall in love with a Salem tree
And a rawhide quirt from Santa Cruz,
I will get me a bottle of Boston sea
And a blue-gum nigger to sing me blues.
I am tired of loving a foreign muse.   20

Rue des Martyrs and Bleeding-Heart-Yard,
Senlis, Pisa, and Blindman's Oast,
It is a magic ghost you guard
But I am sick for a newer ghost,
Harrisburg, Spartanburg, Painted Post.   25

Henry and John were never so
And Henry and John were always right?
Granted, but when it was time to go
And the tea and the laurels had stood all night,
Did they never watch for Nantucket Light?   30

I shall not rest quiet in Montparnasse.
I shall not lie easy at Winchelsea.
You may bury my body in Sussex grass,

1. Town in Monument Valley, Arizona.
2. Towns of the American West.
3. Rivers, one in France, the other in Italy.

You may bury my tongue at Champmédy.[4]
I shall not be there. I shall rise and pass.   35
Bury my heart at Wounded Knee.[5]

                                                                                1927

1936

All night they marched, the infantrymen under pack,
But the hands gripping the rifles were naked bone
And the hollow pits of the eyes stared, vacant and black,
When the moonlight shone.

The gas mask lay like a blot on the empty chest,   5
The slanting helmets were spattered with rust and mold,
But they burrowed the hill for the machine-gun nest
As they had of old.

And the guns rolled, and the tanks, but there was no sound,
Never the gasp or rustle of living men   10
Where the skeletons strung their wire on disputed ground. . . .
I knew them, then.

"It is seventeen years," I cried. "You must come no more.
We know your names. We know that you are the dead.
Must you march forever from France and the last, blind war?"   15
"*Fool! From the next!*" they said.

                                                                                1936

◦—◄ MELVIN B. TOLSON ►—◦
(1898–1966)

Melvin Beaunorus Tolson was born in Moberly, Missouri, to Lera Hurt Tolson
and Alonzo Tolson, a Methodist minister whose seriousness, self-motivation, and
intellectual curiosity, which included teaching himself Latin and Greek, helped
forge the mind and character of his son. Tolson's poetic abilities surfaced early. At
fourteen he published his first poem (about the sinking of the *Titanic*) in a small-
town Iowa newspaper, and he was elected senior-class poet at his Kansas City,
Missouri, high school in 1918. After a year at Fisk University, Tolson transferred
to Lincoln University in Pennsylvania, graduating with a bachelor's degree in
1923. Even before he left Lincoln, however, Tolson had to balance his literary ambitions against family responsibilities, for he had married in his junior year, and
the first of his four children was born the month he graduated. Rather than make

---

4. The last stanza uses place names from England and France until the final line.
5. The site in South Dakota of a massacre in December 1890. The Seventh Cavalry killed roughly three
hundred Sioux men, women, and children.

the pilgrimage to Harlem along with other African American writers of his generation, he secured a job teaching English at Wiley College in Marshall, Texas. At Wiley, Tolson wrote a novel (the manuscript of which is lost) and, in addition to his classroom duties, coached the school debate team, achieving unprecedented national success by besting white teams throughout the midwest, south, and west, and even defeating debaters from England's Oxford University.

In 1931 Tolson finally had the chance both to visit Harlem and to concentrate on his writing. Leaving his family with his parents in Kansas City, he accepted a fellowship to pursue a master's degree in comparative literature at Columbia University, a degree he completed only in 1940 long after his return to Wiley. Looking back on his New York year, he later admitted: "In 1932 I was a Negro poet writing Anglo-Saxon sonnets as a graduate student in an eastern university. I moved in a world of twilight haunted by the ghosts of a dead classicism." But his thesis topic, the literature of the Harlem Renaissance, and his contacts with other African American writers in Harlem soon inspired him to shift direction. In 1932 he began writing the character study poems that comprise *A Gallery of Harlem Portraits*. Tolson's range of models for the book epitomizes his eclectic blend of influences. Borrowing his overall structure from Edgar Lee Masters's *Spoon River Anthology*, Tolson also incorporated elements from Robert Browning's dramatic monologues, Walt Whitman's zesty populism, and Langston Hughes's blues variations, in drafting the 152 portraits, each probing the experiences and attitudes of a different character. Altogether, the portraits celebrate the cultural richness and racial diversity of Harlem, and the work represents one of the major expressions of the populist Modernism of the period. Written in the depth of the Great Depression when publishing opportunities were scarce, especially for African American writers, *A Gallery of Harlem Portraits* did not appear in book form until 1979. Tolson, however, did place many of the poems in journals, and the work's vitality gained him the support of fellow writers such as Hughes and critics such as V. F. Calverton, who heralded Tolson as "a bright and vivid writer who attains his best effects by understatement rather than overstatement, and who catches in a line or a stanza what most of his contemporaries have failed to capture in pages or volumes."

Returning to family life and to Wiley, Tolson, like may writers as the Depression deepened, grew increasingly radical in his politics. He was active in organizing sharecroppers for the Southern Tenant Farmers Union, and he stirred debate with his spirited defense of Hughes's controversial poem, "Good-Bye, Christ." In the *Pittsburgh Courier*, Tolson argued that Jesus Christ was a radical who "heralded the dawn of a new economic, social, and political order," and he stressed that "[Hughes] has always stood for the man lowest down and has sought to show his essential fineness of soul to those who were too high up—by the accident of fortune—to understand." The defense, along with Tolson's reputation as a formidable debater, prompted an invitation from the *Washington Tribune*, a black newspaper in Washington, D.C., to write a weekly column. In "Caviar and Cabbages," which ran from 1937 to 1944, Tolson commented on politics and culture, and he championed an apocalyptic vision in which black and white workers would join together to overcome big business and create a new world grounded on economic and social equality. Tolson also began to stress this philosophy in his poetry. His poem "Dark Symphony" imitates a symphony's shifts in mood and tempo, praises African Americans' role in American history, and sharply differentiates the moral courage of blacks from the greed of industrialists. In 1939, the poem won a national contest run by Chicago's American Negro Exposition and appeared in the *Atlantic Monthly* in 1941. The magazine's editor was so impressed by "Dark Symphony" that she arranged for Tolson to publish his first book, *Rendezvous with America* (1944), which quickly went through three editions. The book was praised by reviewers for its broad historical scope, humane vision, and mastery of technique. The acclaim brought about two important changes in Tolson's life. In 1947, he accepted a job at Langston University, in Langston, Oklahoma, where he taught until his retirement in 1965. That same year, he was also appointed poet laureate of the West African nation of Liberia by its president, William V. S. Tubman, who commissioned Tolson to write a poem for the 1956 centennial celebration.

In *Libretto for the Republic of Liberia,* completed in 1953, Tolson's style took a dramatic turn from the Populist Modernism of Masters, Hughes, and Sandburg to the High Modernist mode of Eliot, Pound, and Crane. Having steeped himself in Modernist poetry, Tolson developed a dense and highly allusive new style that expressed an African American perspective through the complex refractions of the High Modernist sensibility. The poem also gave Tolson the occasion to demonstrate how the history and egalitarian principles of Liberia exemplified his political ideals, especially his utopian hopes for universal racial and economic equality. Although the poem was praised by white critics, that praise was often laced with condescension. Allen Tate, however, in the book's introduction, remarks: "In the end I found that I was reading *Libretto for the New Republic of Liberia* not because Mr. Tolson is a Negro, but because he is a poet, not because the poem has a 'Negro subject,' but because it is about the world of all men." Tate's support certainly helped solidify Tolson's high reputation in the literary world, but his disregard of the poem's racial contexts diminishes Tolson's achievement. On the other hand, some African American critics attacked the poem as too esoteric and suggested that Tolson had abandoned himself to a white tradition. But Tolson insisted that his influences encompassed not only elements of the white canon but also African American vernacular speech. Late in his life, speaking about his influences in an interview, he noted: "I would add another group to the Metaphysical Poets and the French Symbolists: the Negro people. . . . I, as a black poet, have absorbed the Great Ideas of the Great White World, and interpreted them in the melting-pot idiom of my people. My roots are in Africa, Europe, and America." Intending to explore the history of African Americans, Tolson planned a five-book epic poem, but only completed the first part, *Harlem Gallery: Book I, The Curator* (1965), before his death. Returning to the portrait mode of his first book, Tolson presents a tour of a Harlem art gallery, whose curator is a man of "Afroirishjewish" ancestry, "an octoroon, who is a Negro in New York and a white man in Mississippi." The curator, aided by an art critic and three artists, tells the stories behind the gallery's portraits. The poem incorporates not only narratives but also debates between the curator and his peers about art and race. Like Tolson's first book, it pulses with the vitality of Harlem life and culture.

During the 1950s and 1960s, Tolson continued to receive a great deal of public recognition for his accomplishments. In 1951 he garnered *Poetry* magazine's Bess Hokin Prize, and in 1954 he became a permanent poetry fellow of Bread Loaf writers' colony in Vermont. Long interested in politics, he also began a career in public service, when in 1952 he was elected mayor of Langston, a job he performed so well that he was elected for another three terms. In 1954 Liberian president Tubman inducted him into the Liberian Knighthood of the Order of the Star of Africa. He also received academic honors, including an honorary doctorate from Lincoln University and Tuskegee Institute's Avalon Chair in Humanities. After his death in 1966 from abdominal cancer, his work fell into relative neglect because of its unusual position on the borderlines between Modernist elitism and African American populism, two traditions that some critics declared irreconcilable. By the end of the century, however, Tolson's work was rediscovered and celebrated both for its innovative merging of Modernist techniques with African American themes and traditions and for its evocations of Harlem life.

Sootie Joe

From A Gallery of Harlem Portraits

The years had rubbed out his youth,
But his fellows ranked him still
As a chimney sweep without a peer . . .
Whether he raced a weighted corset
Up and down the throat of a freakish flue,　　　　5
Or, from a chair of rope,
His eyes goggled and his mouth veiled,
He wielded his scraping knife
Through the walled-in darkness.

The soot from ancient chimneys　　　　10
Had wormed itself into his face and hands.
The four winds had belabored the grime on him.
The sun had trifled with his ebony skin
And left ashen spots.

Sometimes Sootie Joe's wealthy customers　　　　15
Heard him singing a song that gave them pause:

I's a chimney sweeper, a chimney sweeper,
I's black as the blackest night.
I's a chimney sweeper, a chimney sweeper,
And the world don't treat me right.　　　　20
But somebody hasta black hisself
For somebody else to stay white.

[1932] 1979

An Ex-Judge at the Bar

Bartender, make it straight and make it two—
One for the you in me and the me in you.
Not let us put our heads together: one
Is half enough for malice, sense, or fun.

I know, Bartender, yes, I know when the Law　　　　5
Should wag its tail or rip with fang and claw.

When Pilate[1] washed his hands, that neat event
Set for us judges a Caesarean precedent.

What I shall tell you now, as man is man,
You'll find in neither Bible nor Koran.   10
It happened after my return from France
At the bar in Tony's Lady of Romance.

We boys drank pros and cons, sang *Dixie;* and then,
The bar a Sahara, we pledged to meet again.
But lo, on the bar there stood in naked scorn   15
The Goddess Justice, like September Morn.

Who blindfolds Justice on the courthouse roof
While the lawyers weave the sleight-of-hand of proof?
I listened, Bartender, with my heart and head,
As the Goddess Justice unbandaged her eyes and said: 20

"To make the world safe for Democracy,
You lost a leg in Flanders fields—*oui, oui?*[2]
To gain the judge's seat, you twined the noose
That swung the Negro higher than a goose."

Bartender, who has dotted every *i?*   25
Crossed every *t?* Put legs on every *y?*
Therefore, I challenged her: "Lay on, Macduff,[3]
And damned be him who first cries, 'Hold, enough!' "

The boys guffawed, and Justice began to laugh
Like a maniac on a broken phonograph.   30
Bartender, make it straight and make it three—
One for the Negro . . . one for you and me.

1944

Dark Symphony[4]

I. ALLEGRO MODERATO[5]

Black Crispus Attucks[6] taught
                    Us how to die
Before white Patrick Henry's[7] bugle breath

---

1. Judge at trial and execution of Jesus (Matthew 27).
2. (French) "Yes."
3. The last words of Shakespeare's *Macbeth.*
4. Tolson's models for the symphonic structure of this poem probably included not only European classical symphonies but also Duke Ellington's *Symphony in Black* (1935), a jazz suite that served as the
basis of an Academy Award–winning film in which each musical episode was matched with images of
African American life. Ellington's composition asserted the aesthetic equality of African American jazz
with the masterpieces of European musical culture.
5. (Italian) Musical term meaning "moderately lively."
6. An escaped slave who died in the Boston Massacre of 1770.
7. Patriot whose last words are quoted in line 6.

Uttered the vertical
                    Transmitting cry: 5
"Yea, give me liberty, or give me death."

Waifs of the auction block,
                    Men black and strong
The juggernauts of despotism withstood,
Loin-girt with faith that worms   10
                    Equate the wrong
And dust is purged to create brotherhood.

No Banquo's[8] ghost can rise
                    Against us now,
Aver we hobnailed Man beneath the brute,   15
Squeezed down the thorns of greed
                    On Labor's brow,
Garroted lands and carted off the loot.

II. LENTO GRAVE[9]

The centuries-old pathos in our voices
Saddens the great white world,   20
And the wizardry of our dusky rhythms
Conjures up shadow-shapes of ante-bellum years:

Black slaves singing *One More River to Cross*
In the torture tombs of slave-ships,
Black slaves singing *Steal Away to Jesus*   25
In jungle swamps,
Black slaves singing *The Crucifixion*
In slave-pens at midnight,
Black slaves singing *Swing Low, Sweet Chariot*
In cabins of death,   30
Black slaves singing *Go Down, Moses*
In the canebrakes of the Southern Pharaohs.

III. ANDANTE SOSTENUTO[1]

They tell us to forget
The Golgotha[2] we tread . . .

We who are scourged with hate,   35
A price upon our head.
They who have shackled us
Require of us a song,
They who have wasted us
Bid us condone the wrong.   40

---

8. Character in Shakespeare's *Macbeth* who was murdered by Macbeth and later comes back as a ghost
to haunt his killer.
9. (Italian) "Slowly, solemnly."
1. (Italian) "Moderately slow and sustained."
2. The hill where Jesus was crucified.

They tell us to forget
Democracy is spurned.
They tell us to forget
The Bill of Rights is burned.
Three hundred years we slaved,   45
We slave and suffer yet:
Though flesh and bone rebel,
They tell us to forget!

Oh, how can we forget
Our human rights denied?   50
Oh, how can we forget
Our manhood crucified?
When Justice is profaned
And plea with curse is met,
When Freedom's gates are barred,   55
Oh, how can we forget?

IV. TEMPO PRIMO[3]

The New Negro[4] strides upon the continent
In seven-league boots . . .
The New Negro
Who sprang from the vigor-stout loins   60
Of Nat Turner,[5] gallows-martyr for Freedom,
Of Joseph Cinquez,[6] Black Moses of the Amistad Mutiny,
Of Frederick Douglass,[7] oracle of the Catholic Man,
Of Sojourner Truth,[8], eye and ear of Lincoln's legions,
Of Harriet Tubman,[9] Saint Bernard of the Underground Railroad.   65

The New Negro
Breaks the icons of his detractors,
Wipes out the conspiracy of silence,
Speaks to *his* America:

"My history-moulding ancestors   70
Planted the first crops of wheat on these shores,
Built ships to conquer the seven seas,
Erected the Cotton Empire,
Flung railroads across a hemisphere,
Disemboweled the earth's iron and coal,   75

Tunneled the mountains and bridged rivers,
Harvested the grain and hewed forests,

---

3. (Italian) Musical term used to indicate the same speed as the opening movement, that is, Allegro Moderato.
4. Alain Locke's 1925 anthology of poetry was called *The New Negro*.
5. Leader of a famous slave revolt.
6. Leader of the mutiny on the slave ship *Amistad* in 1839.
7. Abolitionist and orator.
8. Abolitionist and orator.
9. Escaped slave who became an abolitionist and leader in the Underground Railroad.

Sentineled the Thirteen Colonies,
Unfurled Old Glory at the North Pole,[1]
Fought a hundred battles for the Republic."   80

The New Negro:
His giant hands fling murals upon high chambers,
His drama teaches a world to laugh and weep,
His music leads continents captive,
His voice thunders the Brotherhood of Labor,   85
His science creates seven wonders,
His Republic of Letters challenges the Negro-baiters.

The New Negro,
Hard-muscled, Fascist-hating, Democracy-ensouled,
Strides in seven-league boots   90
Along the Highway of Today
Toward the Promised Land of Tomorrow!

V. LARGHETTO[2]

None in the Land can say
To us black men Today:
You send the tractors on their bloody path,   95
And create Okies for *The Grapes of Wrath*.[3]
You breed the slum that breeds a *Native Son*[4]
To damn the good earth[5] Pilgrim Fathers won.

None in the Land can say
To us black men Today: 100
You dupe the poor with rags-to-riches tales,
And leave the workers empty dinner pails.
You stuff the ballot box, and honest men
Are muzzled by your demagogic din.

None in the Land can say   105
To us black men Today:
You smash stock markets with your coined blitzkriegs,[6]
And make a hundred million guinea pigs.
You counterfeit our Christianity,
And bring contempt upon Democracy.   110

None in the land can say
To us black men Today:

---

1. Matthew Henson (1866–1955), an African American, was the first man to reach the North Pole in Robert Peary's historic 1909 expedition.
2. (Italian) "Somewhat slowly."
3. Title of John Steinbeck's 1939 novel.
4. Novel by Richard Wright, also published in 1939.
5. Refers obliquely to the best-known novel of Pearl S. Buck, *The Good Earth*.
6. (German) "Lightning wars," refers to sudden attacks at the start of World War II.

You prowl when citizens are fast asleep,
And hatch Fifth Column[7] plots to blast the deep

Foundations of the State and leave the Land   115
A vast Sahara with a Fascist brand.

VI. TEMPO DI MARCIA[8]

Out of abysses of Illiteracy,
Through labyrinths of Lies,
Across waste lands of Disease . . .
We advance!   120

Out of dead-ends of Poverty,
Through wildernesses of Superstition,
Across barricades of Jim Crowism[9] . . .
We advance!   125

With the Peoples of the World . . .
We advance!

1944

HART CRANE
(1899–1932)

Immensely gifted, Hart Crane pursued poetry with uncompromising dedication, yet his life was marred by the emotional imbalances that ultimately led to debilitating alcoholism and suicide. Born in Garrettsville, Ohio, Harold Hart Crane grew up as a pawn in marital battles waged between his mother, Grace Hart Crane, an intelligent, high-strung woman, and his father, Clarence ("C. A.") Crane, an ambitious and successful businessman. The family lived in Warren, Ohio, from 1903 until 1908, when domestic conflicts drove Grace into a sanitarium and C. A. to Chicago. Harold was sent to live with his mother's parents in Cleveland, where Grace returned in 1909 and C. A. later rejoined her. The Cranes remained there until 1916, when Grace and C. A. arranged to divorce, and their son, determined to become a poet, set off for New York City without graduating from high school. But he was never able to free himself from the family miasma; throughout his life he felt obliged to ally himself either with one parent or the other. In 1917, he sided with his mother so strongly that he chose to call himself "Hart," her maiden name, because Grace encouraged his vocation as a poet while C. A. expected him to learn the family business.

Between 1917 and 1919 Crane shuttled between Ohio and New York, where he established connections with two literary magazines, *The Little Review* and *Seven*

---

7. Refers to pro-Franco guerrillas in Madrid during the Spanish Civil War (1936–39); more generally, any group working in secret to aid an enemy of their country.
8. (Italian) "March time."
9. Refers to laws that separated whites and blacks in public places in the United States.

Arts. He remained in Cleveland from 1920 to 1923, working first for his father and then in advertising. Whenever possible, he continued the precocious pattern of reading that he had begun in his high school years; he also wrote many of the lyrics that appeared in his first book, *White Buildings* (1926). By the time he returned to New York in 1923, he had established a reputation as an important young poet, which enabled him to forge friendships with artists and writers such as Alfred Stieglitz, Jean Toomer, and Allen Tate. He soon left his job with the advertising firm of J. Walter Thompson to devote himself entirely to writing. For the rest of his life, Crane supported himself through short-term jobs, small stipends from his parents, money borrowed from friends, and occasional grants from benefactors.

Crane saw poetry in extreme terms, as an all-consuming vocation that demanded sacrifice and the utmost intensity. Consequently, his poetry places extreme demands on the reader. Crane sought to push language to its limits in an effort to voice ideas and feelings that are inexpressible—an aim that was Romantic in its ends but Modernist in its means. In a 1926 letter to Harriet Monroe, he explained that "the nuances of feeling and observation in a poem may well call for certain liberties" that go beyond the strictures of rational logic. Metaphor allows for unexpected parallels between different realms of experience, and serving as "something like short-hand as compared to usual description and dialectics," it leads both poet and reader "toward fresh concepts, more inclusive evaluations." Crane emphasized seeking (though not necessarily finding) spiritual transcendence amidst the desperate conditions of modern life. Thus, he opposed the pessimism he saw in T. S. Eliot's work and countered with a poetry of visionary possibility.

For Crane, those moments were often inspired by homoerotic relationships, and "the new *word*" that he strove to enunciate through metaphor encompassed experiences that could not be proclaimed in public. But among his literary friends he made no secret of his homosexuality, nor of the sharp emotional swings that his affairs brought on. His most important relationship, although it lasted only a year, was intense enough that Crane described it in religious terms. Emil Opffer, who worked as a ship's writer, invited Crane to share his rooms near the Brooklyn Bridge shortly after they met in 1924, and in April Crane confessed to his friend and mentor, Waldo Frank: "I have seen the Word made flesh." For Crane, the relationship veered between agonized separations when Opffer was at sea, to joyous reunions in which even a simple walk across the bridge became charged with illumination. Meditating on the view from the harbor, Crane told Frank that: "I think the sea has thrown itself upon me and been answered, at least in part, and I believe I am a little changed—not essentially, but changed and transubstantiated as anyone is who has asked a question and been answered." The relationship with Opffer culminated in the poem "Voyages," in which Crane developed complex analogies between love and the sea's overwhelming fluctuations, psychological dissolution and sensual ecstasy. Crane pursued both of these poles in his life as well as in his art. His high spirits brought him numerous friends, yet too many of his friendships soured due to the excesses of his drinking.

Although the alcoholism eventually compromised his writing, in 1926 he was at the height of his powers. Otto Kahn, a banker and patron of the arts, granted him funds to work on *The Bridge,* a sequence of poems that Crane hoped would "enunciate a new cultural synthesis" of America. In a burst of energy, he wrote the last poem, "Atlantis," first, and then worked on the beginning poems until quarrels with Allen Tate and his wife Caroline Gordon, with whom he was staying in upstate New York, forced him to relocate. From May to October, he lived on his grandparents' defunct Caribbean plantation on the Isle of Pines, off the coast of Cuba, where he completed half of the poem and a number of fine lyrics. After his return to New York, his mother's financial and emotional troubles drew his attention away from *The Bridge;* her letters often spurred his self-destructive drinking sprees. In late 1927 he lived in Pasadena as a paid companion to a wealthy invalid, but moved in the spring to Hollywood to help Grace, who was nursing her mother through a terminal illness. Eventually, the nervous collapses that afflicted his mother whenever he tried to go out at night drove him to leave for New York. After his grandmother died Grace tried to block his inheritance, and he feared that she would tell his father about his homosexuality.

When he obtained the money in December 1928, he set off for Europe, where in Paris he met Harry Crosby, owner of the Black Sun Press, whose enthusiastic agreement to publish *The Bridge* inspired Crane to finish the poem after he returned to New York. The Black Sun edition, including photographs by Walker Evans of the Brooklyn Bridge, appeared in January 1930, and an American edition followed in April. Crane binds the various poems together with recurring patterns of figurative language, and the Brooklyn Bridge becomes a symbol with which he tries to span oppositions such as space and time, faith and doubt, the Old World and the New, primitive naturalism and modern industrialism, cultural and personal memory, high rhetoric and American demotic speech, possibility and limitation. Although the book received favorable reviews in several publications, it was attacked by Yvor Winters and Allen Tate, friends to whom Crane had written often during the years he had worked on the poem, offering his thoughts on the work in progress. Both critics accused Crane of sentimentality and argued that the poem failed to cohere into a unified whole.

Crane's last years were overshadowed by alcoholism and diminished poetic production. The Depression made finding employment a hopeless task, and by the end of 1930 Crane returned to Cleveland, having reconciled with his father. For three months he helped out at the restaurant his father owned, until a Guggenheim fellowship enabled him to make more ambitious plans. In April he left for Mexico, where he intended to draft a verse drama about Cortés and Moctezuma, but instead resumed his heavy drinking. The novelist Katherine Anne Porter, a fellow Guggenheim recipient with whom he first stayed in Mexico City, recalled his nightly returns from the bars, when he stood outside of her house and raged: "with words so foul there is no question of repeating them, he cursed separately and by name the moon, and its light: the heliotrope, the heaven-tree, the sweet-by-night, the star jessamine, and their perfumes. He cursed the air we breathed together, the pool of water with its two small ducks huddled at the edge, and the vines on the wall and the house." The emotional crisis that precipitated such incidents was exacerbated in July, when he learned of his father's death from a stroke. After a trip to Cleveland for the funeral, he returned to Mexico in September and was soon caught up in his first heterosexual love affair, with Peggy Baird Cowley, who was in Mexico seeking a divorce from her husband, the writer Malcolm Cowley. Although the energy of the relationship enabled Crane to finish one important poem, "The Broken Tower," it could not stanch his feelings of financial desperation—his father's estate had been claimed by creditors. Moreover, the affair with Peggy, which he had promised her would end in marriage, conflicted with his continuing attraction to men. Deciding to return to New York City, he and Peggy set sail from Veracruz in April 1932. During the early morning of

April 27, Crane was badly beaten, perhaps by sailors whom he had solicited for sex. At noon, he returned to the stateroom that he shared with his lover, bade her good-bye, went up to the deck, and leapt into the sea.

When news of Crane's suicide reached New York, many writers felt that it symbolized the end of the previous decade's remarkable surge of literary energy. Other writers, particularly Winters, used it to cast moral aspersions on Crane's poetry. More recently, critics such as Thomas Yingling have faulted society's lack of tolerance for homosexuality. Regardless of Crane's troubled life, readers have continued to be drawn in by the intensity of his poetry, even as they acknowledge its difficulty. The poetry's complexity, and the indelible power of Crane's voice, confirm the early assessment of Allen Tate, in his review of *White Buildings,* who lauded Crane's work as "one of the finest achievements of this age."

Praise for an Urn

In Memoriam: Ernest Nelson[1]

It was a kind and northern face
That mingled in such exile guise
The everlasting eyes of Pierrot[2]
And, of Gargantua,[3] the laughter.

His thoughts, delivered to me   5
From the white coverlet and pillow,
I see now, were inheritances—
Delicate riders of the storm.

The slant moon on the slanting hill
Once moved us toward presentiments   10
Of what the dead keep, living still,
And such assessments of the soul

As, perched in the crematory lobby,
The insistent clock commented on,
Touching as well upon our praise   15
Of glories proper to the time.

Still, having in mind gold hair,
I cannot see that broken brow
And miss the dry sound of bees
Stretching across a lucid space.   20

Scatter these well-meant idioms
Into the smoky spring that fills
The suburbs, where they will be lost.
They are no trophies of the sun.

1926

Garden Abstract

The apple on its bough is her desire,—
Shining suspension, mimic of the sun.
The bough has caught her breath up, and her voice,
Dumbly articulate in the slant and rise

---

1. A friend of Crane, Nelson, who immigrated to the United States from Norway, was a painter and poet who worked as a commercial lithographer. Crane believed that Nelson, forced to give up his ideals as an artist in order to earn a living, "was one of many broken against the stupidity of American life" (*Oh My Land, My Friends: The Selected Letters of Hart Crane*, pp. 94–95. Subsequent citations from this book will appear as *Selected Letters*). In 1921, Nelson was killed by a car as he stepped off a curb, and Crane served as one of the pallbearers at his funeral.
2. (French) "Little Pierre." A mournful French clown, common in pantomime.
3. (Spanish) From *garganta*, "gullet." A giant with a voracious appetite, Gargantua was the title character of François Rabelais's satire, *Gargantua and Pantagruel* (1535).

Of branch on branch above her, blurs her eyes.   5
She is prisoner of the tree and its green fingers.

And so she comes to dream herself the tree,
The wind possessing her, weaving her young veins,
Holding her to the sky and its quick blue,
Drowning the fever of her hands in sunlight.   10
She has no memory, nor fear, nor hope
Beyond the grass and shadows at her feet.

                                                                              1926

At Melville's Tomb[4]

Often beneath the wave, wide from this ledge
The dice of drowned men's bones he saw bequeath
An embassy.[5] Their numbers as he watched,
Beat on the dusty shore and were obscured.

And wrecks passed without sound of bells,   5
The calyx[6] of death's bounty giving back
A scattered chapter, livid hieroglyph,
The portent wound in corridors of shells.

Then in the circuit calm of one vast coil,
Its lashings charmed and malice reconciled,   10
Frosted eyes there were that lifted altars;[7]
And silent answers crept across the stars.

4. Herman Melville (1819–1891), author of seafaring novels such as *Moby-Dick* and *Billy Budd*. When Crane submitted "At Melville's Tomb" in 1926 to *Poetry* magazine, the editor, Harriet Monroe, wrote back asking for clarification of the poem's metaphors, which she found confusing. In a now-famous justification of his approach to poetry, Crane wrote back, arguing that what he called "the logic of metaphor" "demands completely other faculties of recognition than the pure rationalistic associations permit" (*Selected Letters*, 279). Monroe subsequently published the poem, accompanied by her query and Crane's long letter, in the October 1926 issue of *Poetry*.

5. Crane explained to Monroe: "Dice bequeath an embassy, in the first place, by being ground (in this connection only, of course) in little cubes from the bones of drowned men by the action of the sea, and are finally thrown up on the sand, having 'numbers' but no identification. These being the bones of dead men who never completed their voyage, it seems legitimate to refer to them as the only surviving evidence of certain messages undelivered, mute evidence of certain things, experiences that the dead mariners might have had to deliver. Dice as a symbol of chance and circumstance is also implied" (*Selected Letters*, 281).

6. The sepals of a flower, which open to reveal the interior. In the letter to Monroe, Crane expanded upon this idea: "This calyx refers in a double ironic sense both to a cornucopia and the vortex made by a sinking vessel. As soon as the water has closed over a ship this whirlpool sends up broken spars, wreckage, etc., which can be alluded to as *livid hieroglyphs*, making *a scattered chapter* so far as any complete record of the recent ship and her crew is concerned. In fact, about as much definite knowledge might come from all this as anyone might gain from the roar of his own veins, which is easily heard (haven't you ever done it?) by holding a shell to one's ear" (*Selected Letters*, 281).

7. Crane wrote that this line "refers simply to a conviction that a man, not knowing perhaps a definite god yet being endowed with a reverence for deity—such a man naturally postulates a deity somehow, and the altar of that deity by the very *action* of the eyes *lifted* in searching" (*Selected Letters*, 281).

Compass, quadrant and sextant[8] contrive
No farther tides . . . High in the azure steeps
Monody shall not wake the mariner.   15
This fabulous shadow only the sea keeps.

1926

Black Tambourine[9]

The interests of a black man in a cellar
Mark tardy judgment on the world's closed door.
Gnats toss in the shadow of a bottle,
And a roach spans a crevice in the floor.

Aesop,[1] driven to pondering, found   5
Heaven with the tortoise and the hare;
Fox brush and sow ear top his grave
And mingling incantations on the air.

The black man, forlorn in the cellar,
Wanders in some mid-kingdom, dark, that lies,   10
Between his tambourine, stuck on the wall,
And, in Africa, a carcass quick with flies.

1926

Chaplinesque[2]

We make our meek adjustments,
Contented with such random consolations

---

8. A mariner's navigational tools. Crane noted "Hasn't it often occurred that instruments originally invented for record and computation have inadvertently so extended the concepts of mind and imagination that employed them, that they may metaphorically be said to have extended the original boundaries of the entity measured? This little bit of 'relativity' ought not to be discredited in poetry now that scientists are proceeding to measure the universe on principles of pure *ratio,* quite as metaphorical, so far as previous standards of scientific methods extended, as some of the axioms of Job" (*Selected Letters,* 282).

9. In a 1921 letter to his friend Gorham Munson, Crane suggested that "the word 'mid-kingdom' is perhaps the key word to what ideas there are in ['Black Tambourine']. The poem is a description and bundle of insinuations, suggestions bearing on the negro's place somewhere between man and beast. That is why Aesop is brought in, etc.—the popular conception of negro romance, the tambourine on the wall. The value of the poem is only, to me, in what a painter would call its 'tactile' quality,—an entirely aesthetic feature. A propagandist for either side of the negro question could find anything he wanted to in it. My only declaration in it is that I find the negro (in the popular mind) sentimentally or brutally 'placed' in this midkingdom [*sic*]" (*Selected Letters,* 64).

1. (620–560 B.C.E.) Greek author of animal fables such as "The Tortoise and the Hare." Historians disagree about Aesop's origins, but some claim that he was born in Africa, brought forcibly to Greece as a slave, and later freed.

2. Crane considered the silent film star Charlie Chaplin "a dramatic genius" (*Selected Letters,* 65). After seeing Chaplin's film *The Kid* in 1921, Crane wrote this poem in homage to the actor whom he saw as a symbol of the American poet. To his friend Gorham Munson, Crane admitted: "[T]he pantomime of Charlie represents fairly well the futile gesture of the poet in U.S.A. today [*sic*], perhaps elsewhere too. And yet, the heart lives on. . . ." (*Selected Letters,* 67). He further clarified his ideas in a letter to another friend, William Wright: "I am moved to put Chaplin with the poets (of today); hence the 'we.' In other words, he, especially in *The Kid* made me feel myself, as a poet, as being 'in the same boat' with him. Poetry, the human feelings, 'the kitten' is so crowded out of the humdrum, rushing, mechanical scramble of today that the man who would preserve them must duck and camouflage for dear life to keep them or keep himself from annihilation. I have since learned that I am by no means alone in seeing these things in the buffooneries of the tragedian, Chaplin . . . and in the poem I have tried to express these 'social sympathies' in words corresponding somewhat to the antics of the actor" (*Selected Letters,* 70).

As the wind deposits
In slithered and too ample pockets.

For we can still love the world, who find   5
A famished kitten on the step, and know
Recesses for it from the fury of the street,
Or warm torn elbow coverts.

We will sidestep, and to the final smirk
Dally the doom of that inevitable thumb   10
That slowly chafes its puckered index toward us,
Facing the dull squint with what innocence
And what surprise!

And yet these fine collapses are not lies
More than the pirouettes of any pliant cane;   15
Our obsequies[3] are, in a way, no enterprise.
We can evade you, and all else but the heart:
What blame to us if the heart live on.

The game enforces smirks; but we have seen
The moon in lonely alleys make   20
A grail of laughter of an empty ash can,
And through all sound of gaiety and quest
Have heard a kitten in the wilderness.

                                        1926

My Grandmother's Love Letters

There are no stars tonight
But those of memory.
Yet how much room for memory there is
In the loose girdle of soft rain.

There is even room enough   5
For the letters of my mother's mother,
Elizabeth,
That have been pressed so long
Into a corner of the roof
That they are brown and soft,   10
And liable to melt as snow.

Over the greatness of such space
Steps must be gentle.
It is all hung by an invisible white hair.
It trembles as birch limbs webbing the air.   15

And I ask myself:

---

3. Crane plays off of two meanings of this word, "excessive compliance" (as in "obsequious") and "funeral ceremonies."

"Are your fingers long enough to play
Old keys that are but echoes:
Is the silence strong enough
To carry back the music to its source   20
And back to you again
As though to her?"

Yet I would lead my grandmother by the hand
Through much of what she would not understand;
And so I stumble. And the rain continues on the roof   25
With such a sound of gently pitying laughter.

1926

Voyages[4]

I

Above the fresh ruffles of the surf
Bright striped urchins flay each other with sand.
They have contrived a conquest for shell shucks,
And their fingers crumble fragments of baked weed
Gaily digging and scattering.   5

And in answer to their treble interjections
The sun beats lightning on the waves,
The waves fold thunder on the sand;
And could they hear me I would tell them:

O brilliant kids, frisk with your dog,   10
Fondle your shells and sticks, bleached
By time and the elements; but there is a line
You must not cross nor ever trust beyond it
Spry cordage of your bodies to caresses
Too lichen-faithful from too wide a breast.   15
The bottom of the sea is cruel.

II

—And yet this great wink of eternity,
Of rimless floods, unfettered leewardings,[5]
Samite[6] sheeted and processioned where
Her undinal[7] vast belly moonward bends,   20
Laughing the wrapt inflections of our love;

---

4. Crane was inspired to write "Voyages" by a brief but intense love affair, in the spring of 1924, with the sailor Emil Opffer.
5. Movements in the direction of the "lee," an area toward which the wind blows.
6. Silk fabric interwoven with gold and silver.
7. Like an undine, a spirit of the waters. According to the medieval alchemist Paracelsus, Undine was created without a soul, but gained one after she fell in love with a mortal, married him, and bore him a child, thereby experiencing the pain and suffering of the human condition.

Take this Sea, whose diapason[8] knells
On scrolls of silver snowy sentences,
The sceptred terror of whose sessions rends
As her demeanors motion well or ill,   25
All but the pieties of lovers' hands.

And onward, as bells off San Salvador
Salute the crocus lustres of the stars,
In these poinsettia meadows of her tides,—
Adagios of islands,[9] O my Prodigal,   30
Complete the dark confessions her veins spell.

Mark how her turning shoulders wind the hours,
And hasten while her penniless rich palms
Pass superscription of bent foam and wave,—
Hasten, while they are true,—sleep, death, desire,   35
Close round one instant in one floating flower.

Bind us in time, O Seasons clear, and awe.
O minstrel galleons of Carib fire,
Bequeath us to no earthly shore until
Is answered in the vortex of our grave   40
The seal's wide spindrift gaze toward paradise.

III

Infinite consanguinity it bears—
This tendered theme of you that light
Retrieves from sea plains where the sky
Resigns a breast that every wave enthrones;   45
While ribboned water lanes I wind
Are laved and scattered with no stroke
Wide from your side, whereto this hour
The sea lifts, also, reliquary hands.

And so, admitted through black swollen gates   50
That must arrest all distance otherwise,—
Past whirling pillars and lithe pediments,
Light wrestling there incessantly with light,
Star kissing star through wave on wave unto
Your body rocking!   55

                    and where death, if shed,
Presumes no carnage, but this single change,—
Upon the steep floor flung from dawn to dawn
The silken skilled transmemberment of song;

Permit me voyage, love, into your hands . . .   60

---

8. A harmonious melody; also, the entire range of musical tones.
9. In his essay "General Aims and Theories," Crane explained this phrase: "[T]he reference is to the motion of a boat through islands clustered thickly, the rhythm of the motion, etc. And it seems a much more direct and creative statement than any more logical employment of words such as 'coasting slowly through the islands,' besides ushering in a whole world of music."

IV

Whose counted smile of hours and days, suppose
I know as spectrum of the sea and pledge
Vastly now parting gulf on gulf of wings
Whose circles bridge, I know, (from palms to the severe
Chilled albatross's white immutability)   65
No stream of greater love advancing now
Than, singing, this mortality alone
Through clay aflow immortally to you.

All fragrance irrefragably, and claim
Madly meeting logically in this hour   70
And region that is ours to wreathe again,
Portending eyes and lips and making told
The chancel port and portion of our June—

Shall they not stem and close in our own steps
Bright staves of flowers and quills today as I   75
Must first be lost in fatal tides to tell?

In signature of the incarnate word
The harbor shoulders to resign in mingling
Mutual blood, transpiring as foreknown
And widening noon within your breast for gathering   80
All bright insinuations that my years have caught
For islands where must lead inviolably
Blue latitudes and levels of your eyes,—

In this expectant, still exclaim receive
The secret oar and petals of all love.   85

V

Meticulous, past midnight in clear rime,
Infrangible and lonely, smooth as though cast
Together in one merciless white blade—
The bay estuaries fleck the hard sky limits.

—As if too brittle or too clear to touch!   90
The cables of our sleep so swiftly filed,
Already hang, shred ends from remembered stars.
One frozen trackless smile . . . What words
Can strangle this deaf moonlight? For we

Are overtaken. Now no cry, no sword   95
Can fasten or deflect this tidal wedge,
Slow tyranny of moonlight, moonlight loved
And changed . . . "There's

Nothing like this in the world," you say,
Knowing I cannot touch your hand and look   100
Too, into that godless cleft of sky
Where nothing turns but dead sands flashing.

"—And never to quite understand!" No,
In all the argosy[1] of your bright hair I dreamed
Nothing so flagless as this piracy.   105

                    But now
Draw in your head, alone and too tall here.
Your eyes already in the slant of drifting foam;
Your breath sealed by the ghosts I do not know:
Drawn in your head and sleep the long way home.   110

                    VI

Where icy and bright dungeons lift
Of swimmers their lost morning eyes,
And ocean rivers, churning, shift
Green borders under stranger skies,

Steadily as a shell secretes   115
Its beating leagues of monotone,
Or as many waters trough the sun's
Red kelson[2] past the cape's wet stone;

O rivers mingling toward the sky
And harbor of the phoenix' breast—   120
My eyes pressed black against the prow,
—Thy derelict and blinded guest

Waiting, afire, what name, unspoke,
I cannot claim: let thy waves rear
More savage than the death of kings,   125
Some splintered garland for the seer.

Beyond siroccos harvesting
The solstice thunders, crept away,
Like a cliff swinging or a sail
Flung into April's inmost day—   130

Creation's blithe and petalled word
To the lounged goddess when she rose
Conceding dialogue with eyes
That smile unsearchable repose—

Still fervid covenant, Belle Isle,[3]   135
—Unfolded floating dais before
Which rainbows twine continual hair—
Belle Isle, white echo of the oar!

1. A large ship; a fleet of ships.
2. In ship construction, a longitudinal structure attached to the keel and designed to give the ship stiffness and support.
3. Beautiful island.

The imaged Word,[4] it is, that holds
Hushed willows anchored in its glow.   140
It is the unbetrayable reply
Whose accent no farewell can know.

1926

The Wine Menagerie

Invariably when wine redeems the sight,
Narrowing the mustard scansions of the eyes,
A leopard ranging always in the brow
Asserts a vision in the slumbering gaze.

Then glozening[5] decanters that reflect the street   5
Wear me in crescents on their bellies. Slow
Applause flows into liquid cynosures:[6]
—I am conscripted to their shadows' glow.

Against the imitation onyx wainscoting
(Painted emulsion of snow, eggs, yarn, coal, manure)   10
Regard the forceps of the smile that takes her.
Percussive sweat is spreading to his hair. Mallets,
Her eyes, unmake an instant of the world . . .

What is it in this heap the serpent pries—
Whose skin, facsimile of time, unskeins   15
Octagon, sapphire transepts round the eyes;
—From whom some whispered carillon assures
Speed to the arrow into feathered skies?

Sharp to the windowpane guile drags a face,
And as the alcove of her jealousy recedes   20
An urchin who has left the snow
Nudges a cannister across the bar
While August meadows somewhere clasp his brow.

Each chamber, transept, coins some squint,
Remorseless line, minting their separate wills—   25
Poor streaked bodies wreathing up and out,
Unwitting the stigma that each turn repeals:
Between black tusks the roses shine!

New thresholds, new anatomies! Wine talons
Build freedom up about me and distill   30

4. Alluding to John 1:14 ("And the Word was made flesh, and dwelt among us"), in an ecstatic letter to Waldo Frank, written in April 1924, Crane extols his relationship with Opffer: "I have seen the Word made Flesh. I mean nothing less, and I know now that there is such a thing as indestructibility. In the deepest sense, where flesh became transformed through intensity of response to counter-response, where sex was beaten out, where a purity of joy was reached that included tears."
5. Literally, "glossy." But Crane also plays off of two other meanings of "gloze," "to flatter" and "to interpret."
6. Cynosure is the constellation Ursa Minor, which contains the North Star; a center of attraction.

This competence—to travel in a tear
Sparkling alone, within another's will.

Until my blood dreams a receptive smile
Wherein new purities are snared; where chimes
Before some flame of gaunt repose a shell   35
Tolled once, perhaps, by every tongue in hell.
—Anguished, the wit that cries out of me:

"Alas,—these frozen billows of your skill!
Invent new dominoes of love and bile . . .
Ruddy, the tooth implicit of the world   40
Has followed you. Though in the end you know
And count some dim inheritance of sand,
How much yet meets the treason of the snow.

"Rise from the dates and crumbs. And walk away,
Stepping over Holofernes'[7] shins—   45
Beyond the wall, whose severed head floats by
With Baptist John's.[8] Their whispering begins.

"—And fold your exile on your back again;
Petrushka's valentine[9] pivots on its pin."

                                                         1926

FROM The Bridge

> From going to and fro in the earth,
>   and from walking up and down in it.
>   *The Book of Job*

To Brooklyn Bridge

How many dawns, chill from his rippling rest
The seagull's wings shall dip and pivot him,
Shedding white rings of tumult, building high
Over the chained bay waters Liberty—

Then, with inviolate curve, forsake our eyes   5
As apparitional as sails that cross
Some page of figures to be filed away;
—Till elevators drop us from our day . . .

---

7. In the apocryphal Old Testament book of Judith, the heroine beguiles and then beheads the Assyrian general Holofernes.
8. Refers to the New Testament prophet John the Baptist, who was beheaded by King Herod at the request of the dancer Salome.
9. Alludes to *Petrouchka* (1911), a ballet composed by Igor Stravinsky and choreographed by Michel Fokine, which Crane saw in 1925. The lead character, Petrouchka, is a carnival puppet hopelessly in love with another puppet, the Dancer, whom Crane calls his "valentine." The Dancer, however, loves another puppet, who eventually kills Petrouchka. Crane's line not only describes the jerky movements of the ballerina who plays the Dancer, but also evokes the pain of love rejected.

I think of cinemas, panoramic sleights
With multitudes bent toward some flashing scene   10
Never disclosed, but hastened to again,
Foretold to other eyes on the same screen;

And Thee, across the harbor, silver-paced
As though the sun took step of thee, yet left
Some motion ever unspent in thy stride,—   15
Implicitly thy freedom staying thee!

Out of some subway scuttle, cell or loft
A bedlamite[1] speeds to thy parapets,
Tilting there momently, shrill shirt ballooning,
A jest falls from the speechless caravan.   20

Down Wall,[2] from girder into street noon leaks,
A rip-tooth of the sky's acetylene;
All afternoon the cloud-flown derricks turn . . .
Thy cables breathe the North Atlantic still.

And obscure as that heaven of the Jews,   25
Thy guerdon[3] . . . Accolade thou dost bestow
Of anonymity time cannot raise:
Vibrant reprieve and pardon thou dost show.

O harp and altar, of the fury fused,
(How could mere toil align thy choiring strings!)   30
Terrific threshold of the prophet's pledge,
Prayer of pariah, and the lover's cry,—

Again the traffic lights that skim thy swift
Unfractioned idiom, immaculate sigh of stars,
Beading thy path—condense eternity: 35
And we have seen night lifted in thine arms.

Under thy shadow by the piers I waited;
Only in darkness is thy shadow clear.
The City's fiery parcels all undone,
Already snow submerges an iron year . . .   40

O Sleepless as the river under thee,
Vaulting the sea, the prairies' dreaming sod,
Unto us lowliest sometime sweep, descend
And of the curveship lend a myth to God.

1930

---

1. A madman.
2. Wall Street.
3. Reward.

Royal Palm

For Grace Hart Crane[4]

Green rustlings, more-than-regal charities
Drift coolly from that tower of whispered light.
Amid the noontide's blazed asperities
I watched the sun's most gracious anchorite

Climb up as by communings, year on year   5
Uneaten of the earth or aught earth holds,
And the grey trunk, that's elephantine, rear
Its frondings sighing in aetherial folds.

Forever fruitless, and beyond that yield
Of sweat the jungle presses with hot love   10
And tendril till our deathward breath is sealed—
It grazes the horizons, launched above

Mortality—ascending emerald-bright,
A fountain at salute, a crown in view—
Unshackled, casual of its azured height   15
As though it soared suchwise through heaven too.

1933

The Broken Tower

The bell-rope that gathers God at dawn
Dispatches me as though I dropped down the knell
Of a spent day—to wander the cathedral lawn
From pit to crucifix, feet chill on steps from hell.

Have you not heard, have you not seen that corps   5
Of shadows in the tower, whose shoulders sway
Antiphonal carillons launched before
The stars are caught and hived in the sun's ray?

The bells, I say, the bells break down their tower;
And swing I know not where. Their tongues engrave   10
Membrane through marrow, my long-scattered score
Of broken intervals . . . And I, their sexton slave!

Oval encyclicals[5] in canyons heaping
The impasse high with choir. Banked voices slain!
Pagodas, campaniles[6] with reveilles outleaping—   15
O terraced echoes prostrate on the plain! . . .

And so it was I entered the broken world
To trace the visionary company of love, its voice

4. Crane's mother. He adopted her maiden name, "Hart," as his first name.
5. Letters sent to a wide circle of recipients.
6. Bell towers.

An instant in the wind (I know not whither hurled)
But not for long to hold each desperate choice.   20

My word I poured. But was it cognate, scored
Of that tribunal monarch of the air
Whose thigh embronzes earth, strikes crystal Word
In wounds pledged once to hope,—cleft to despair?

The steep encroachments of my blood left me   25
No answer (could blood hold such a lofty tower
As flings the question true?)—or is it she
Whose sweet mortality stirs latent power?—

And through whose pulse I hear, counting the strokes
My veins recall and add, revived and sure   30
The angelus[7] of wars my chest evokes:
What I hold healed, original now, and pure . . .

And builds, within, a tower that is not stone
(Not stone can jacket heaven)—but slip
Of pebbles,—visible wings of silence sown   35
In azure circles, widening as they dip

The matrix of the heart, lift down the eye
That shrines the quiet lake and swells a tower . . .
The commodious, tall decorum of that sky
Unseals her earth, and lifts love in its shower.   40

1933

◆◄ ALLEN TATE ►◆
(1899–1979)

John Orley Allen Tate was born the youngest of three sons to John Orley Tate and Eleanor Varnell Tate in Winchester, Kentucky, "the heart of bluegrass country." His mother's family hailed from Fairfax County, Virginia, however, and when his parents became estranged due to his father's business failures and erratic behavior, Tate was led to believe that he had been born in her native state. His recollections of a largely Presbyterian childhood in the South were infused with Southern aristocratic mythology, but also with shame at the interracial violence he occasionally witnessed and at his own family's declining fortunes. Although his formal schooling was sporadic, he impressed his teachers early on with his facility for memorizing poems. By the time Tate entered Vanderbilt University in 1918, both the institution and the South were changing, but he resisted those new social and cultural forces that, he believed, would rob the South of its old agrarian identity and code of honor.

At Vanderbilt he and his roommate Robert Penn Warren, joined forces with the Fugitives, a group of poets including two young professors, John Crowe Ransom and Donald Davidson. Deeply aware of their Southern heritage, these poet-critics,

---

7. A devotion of the Catholic Church, to be recited at morning, noon, and evening, that commemorates Christ's Incarnation.

who would soon become immensely influential, fell under the spell of Modernism. Tate was introduced to T. S. Eliot's work by Hart Crane, who initiated a correspondence after reading some of his poems in a New Orleans journal, the *Double-Dealer.* Tate conveyed his new enthusiasm for Eliot to the other Fugitives. At one point Warren even decorated the walls of their room with painted images from *The Waste Land.* The literary sophistication of Eliot's poetry appealed to these future priests of the New Criticism.

Poor health, including an interlude in a tuberculosis sanatorium, and a brief stint as a public school teacher, interrupted Tate's college education. In 1923, however, he finally took his degree. Soon he went to work for his brother, Ben, a successful businessman. Ill-suited to such a career, Tate later confessed, "In one day I lost the company $700 by shipping some coal to Duluth that should have gone to Cleveland. . . ." Leaving business in 1924, he married the future novelist, Caroline Gordon, and the couple moved to New York, where Tate worked as a magazine editor and book reviewer. There he befriended writers like E. E. Cummings, Kenneth Burke, and Malcolm Cowley. When they tired of the city, Tate and Gordon rented a farmhouse in the country. For four months they shared their home with Hart Crane, but the latter's refusal to help with household chores led to a quarrel, after which they communicated with Crane by slipping notes under his door. Soon Crane moved out, but Tate remained one of his staunchest literary supporters. He had written a foreword to Crane's *White Buildings* (1926) and understood the deeper coherence of Crane's often obscure and difficult poems.

Tate's own poetry could also be difficult—baroque in its diction and densely allusive. Nevertheless, he aimed for what John Frederick Nims would call a "fidelity to the experience of this world, which is the only sign our senses have of any other." Tate said he wanted "to unify religion, morality, and art." But Nims's comment also illuminates Tate's exacting standards as a poet. He began to write his most famous poem, "Ode to the Confederate Dead," in 1925, and revised it for the next twelve years, even after its initial publication. Lacking the headlong Romanticism of Crane's work, Tate's poems were cerebral and classically balanced. His Classicism, however, often served as a necessary force to control the violence and horror of his material.

A Guggenheim fellowship allowed Tate and Gordon to live in France for more than a year, and when they returned they moved into a Tennessee mansion purchased for them by his brother, Ben. They affectionately called it "Benfolly" and hosted many of their literary friends within its walls. Tate's personal life was sometimes troubled. He and Gordon were married and divorced twice; the second divorce, occurring after his conversion to Catholicism, resulted in his excommunication. From 1959 to 1966 he was married to poet Isabelle Gardner. One of his sons by his third wife, Helen Heinz, died accidentally in infancy.

Despite his personal troubles, Tate was steadily productive. *Poems: 1928–1931* appeared in 1932, *The Mediterranean and Other Poems* in 1936, and his one novel, *The Father,* two years later. He was one of the Southern Agrarians who contributed to the reactionary volumes *I'll Take My Stand* (1930) and *Who Owns America?* (1936). It was also in the 1930s that he began teaching at several small colleges, and from 1939 to 1942 he served as Princeton's poet-in-residence. He was an influential editor of the *Sewanee Review* (1944–1946), and in 1951 began teaching at the University of Minnesota, where his colleagues would include Warren, James Wright, and John Berryman. By the time he retired from the post in 1968, he was regarded as one of America's preeminent academic men of letters. He maintained friendships with well-established figures like Malcolm Cowley and T. S. Eliot and also with younger poets, including Randall Jarrell, John Berryman, and Robert Lowell.

Tate was also one of the most articulate and influential poetry critics of his era. His highly regarded critical essays helped to shape the New Criticism. His incisive book reviews contributed to the reception of many modern poets, including Robinson, Pound, Eliot, MacLeish, Ransom, Millay, Cummings, Benét, Auden, Tolson, and Shapiro. If his literary criticism occasionally became abstract or impenetrable, his reviews displayed an uncanny skill at finding essential elements of a poet's work. Not counting such reviews, Tate published more than a hundred essays, many of them collected in books such as *Reason in Madness* (1941), *On the Limits of Poetry* (1948), and *The Man of Letters in the Modern World* (1955).

◄०─────◄०─────◄०►

Ode to the Confederate Dead[1]

Row after row with strict impunity
The headstones yield their names to the element,
The wind whirrs without recollection;
In the riven troughs the splayed leaves
Pile up, of nature the casual sacrament   5
To the seasonal eternity of death;
Then driven by the fierce scrutiny
Of heaven to their election in the vast breath,
They sough the rumour of mortality.

Autumn is desolation in the plot   10
Of a thousand acres where these memories grow
From the inexhaustible bodies that are not
Dead, but feed the grass row after rich row.
Think of the autumns that have come and gone!—
Ambitious November with the humors of the year,   15
With a particular zeal for every slab,
Staining the uncomfortable angels that rot
On the slabs, a wing chipped here, an arm there:
The brute curiosity of an angel's stare
Turns you, like them, to stone,   20

1. In his book *Reason in Madness* (1941), Tate's note on the poem reads: "The structure of the Ode is simple. Figure to yourself a man stopping at the gate of a Confederate graveyard on a late autumn afternoon. The leaves are falling; his first impressions bring him the 'rumor of mortality'; and the desolation barely allows him, at the beginning of the second stanza, the conventionally heroic surmise that the dead will enrich the earth, 'where these memories grow.' From those quoted words to the end of that passage he pauses for a baroque meditation on the ravages of time, concluding with the figure of the 'blind crab.' This figure has mobility but no direction, energy, but from the human point of view, no purposeful world to use it in: in the entire poem there are only two explicit symbols for the locked-in ego; the crab is the first and the less explicit symbol, a mere hint, a planting of the idea that will become overt in its second instance—the jaguar towards the end. The crab is the first intimation of the nature of the moral conflict upon which the drama of the poem develops: the cutoffness of the modern 'intellectual man' from the world.

Transforms the heaving air
Till plunged to a heavier world below
You shift your sea-space blindly
Heaving, turning like the blind crab.

    Dazed by the wind, only the wind   25
    The leaves flying, plunge

You know who have waited by the wall
The twilight certainty of an animal,
Those midnight restitutions of the blood
You know—the immitigable pines, the smoky frieze   30
Of the sky, the sudden call: you know the rage,
The cold pool left by the mounting flood,
Of muted Zeno and Parmenides.[2]
You who have waited for the angry resolution
Of those desires that should be yours tomorrow,   35
You know the unimportant shrift of death
And praise the vision
And praise the arrogant circumstance
Of those who fall
Rank upon rank, hurried beyond decision—   40
Here by the sagging gate, stopped by the wall.[3]

    Seeing, seeing only the leaves
    Flying, plunge and expire

Turn your eyes to the immoderate past,
Turn to the inscrutable infantry rising   45
Demons out of the earth—they will not last.
Stonewall,[4] Stonewall, and the sunken fields of hemp,
Shiloh, Antietam, Malvern Hill, Bull Run.[5]
Lost in that orient of the thick-and-fast
You will curse the setting sun.   50

    Cursing only the leaves crying
    Like an old man in a storm

You hear the shout, the crazy hemlocks point
With troubled fingers to the silence which
Smothers you, a mummy, in time.   55

                     The hound bitch
Toothless and dying, in a musty cellar
Hears the wind only.

2. Greek philosophers of the fifth century B.C.E. who distinguished between the real and the apparent.
3. In *Reason in Madness* Tate goes on to explore the theme of heroism in the poem as "a formal ebullience of the human spirit in an entire society, not private, romantic illusion. . . ."
4. The nickname of Thomas Jackson (1824–1863), one of the most famous Confederate generals in the Civil War.
5. Civil War battles. Shiloh (April 6–7, 1862) was a hard-won Union victory; Antietam (September 17, 1862) and Malvern Hill (July 2) were also Union victories. Two battles at Bull Run in 1861 and 1862 were Confederate victories.

Now that the salt of their blood
Stiffens the saltier oblivion of the sea,
Seals the malignant purity of the flood,
What shall we who count our days and bow   60
Our heads with a commemorial woe
In the ribboned coats of grim felicity,
What shall we say of the bones, unclean,
Whose verdurous anonymity will grow?
The ragged arms, the ragged heads and eyes   65
Lost in these acres of the insane green?
The gray lean spiders come, they come and go;
In a tangle of willows without light
The singular screech-owl's tight
Invisible lyric seeds the mind   70
With the furious murmur of their chivalry.

    We shall say only the leaves
    Flying, plunge and expire

We shall say only the leaves whispering
In the improbable mist of nightfall   75
That flies on multiple wing;
Night is the beginning and the end
And in between the ends of distraction
Waits mute speculation, the patient curse
That stones the eyes, or like the jaguar leaps   80
For his own image in a jungle pool, his victim.
What shall we say who have knowledge
Carried to the heart? Shall we take the act
To the grave? Shall we, more hopeful, set up the grave
In the house? The ravenous grave?   85
                Leave now
The shut gate and the decomposing wall:
The gentle serpent, green in the mulberry bush,
Riots with his tongue through the hush—
Sentinel of the grave who counts us all!

                                        1928

The Subway

Dark accurate plunger down the successive knell
Of arch on arch, where ogives[6] burst a red
Reverberance of hail upon the dead
Thunder like an exploding crucible![7]
Harshly articulate, musical steel shell   5
Of angry worship, hurled religiously
Upon your business of humility
Into the iron forestries of hell:

6. Diagonal ribs of a vault.
7. A melting pot.

Till broken in the shift of quieter
Dense altitudes tangential of your steel,   10
I am become geometries, and glut
Expansions like a blind astronomer
Dazed, while the worldless heavens bulge and reel
In the cold revery of an idiot.

1928

◄ ROBERT FRANCIS ►
(1901–1987)

Robert Churchill Francis was born in Upland, Pennsylvania, the son of a Baptist minister, and grew up in New Jersey, New York, and Massachusetts. In 1923 he took a bachelor's degree from Harvard, and three years later, after a teaching stint in Beirut, a master's degree in education from the same university. He moved to Amherst, Massachusetts, where he taught high school and also gave lessons on the violin, leading a spartan and self-effacing existence. In 1933 he met Robert Frost for the first time; the older poet treated the younger one as a sort of acolyte. Because Francis's poems are usually in meter and often have New England settings, he was for much of his life read as a lesser Frost—and in poems like "By Night" the Frostian influence is certainly present. He was never the narrative poet Frost was, but he made well-turned miniatures. In one poem he observed an earthworm that "has turned more earth than I have with my fork" and would be there "When I am earth again. . . ."

The humility of Francis's poetic stance arose not only from his own ascetic life, but also from an interest in eastern and western religions. He often built his poems from minute observations of art as well as nature, and he developed his own lyrical manner, particularly in his graceful use of repetition. Among his books of poems were *Stand With Me Here* (1936), *The Face Against the Glass* (privately printed in 1950), *The Orb Weaver* (1960) and *Robert Francis: Collected Poems, 1936–1976* (1976). He also published a novel, *We Fly Away* (1948); a book of delightfully eccentric essays, *The Satirical Rogue on Poetry* (1968); and an autobiography, *The Trouble with Francis* (1971), which dealt partly with his homosexuality. He won several honors, including the Rome Prize and the Amy Lowell Traveling Poetry Fellowship. The Juniper Prize, offered by the University of Massachusetts Press for a book of poems, is named for Francis's cottage, Fort Juniper.

Hallelujah: A Sestina

A wind's word, the Hebrew Hallelujah.
I wonder they never give it to a boy
(Hal for short) boy with wind-wild hair.
It means Praise God, as well it should since praise

Is what God's for. Why didn't they call my father   5
Hallelujah instead of Ebenezer?

Eben, of course, but christened Ebenezer,
Product of Nova Scotia (Hallelujah).
Daniel, a country doctor, was his father
And my father his tenth and final boy.   10
A baby and last, he had a baby's praise:
Red petticoat, red cheeks, and crow-black hair.

A boy has little say about his hair
And little about a name like Ebenezer
Except that he can shorten either. Praise   15
God for that, for that shout Hallelujah.
Shout Hallelujah for everything a boy
Can be that is not his father or grandfather.

But then, before you know it, he is a father
Too and passing on his brand of hair   20
To one more perfectly defenseless boy,
Dubbing him John or James or Ebenezer
But never, so far as I know, Hallelujah,
As if God didn't need quite that much praise.

But what I'm coming to—Could I ever praise   25
My father half enough for being a father
Who let me be myself? Sing Hallelujah.
Preacher he was with a prophet's head of hair
And what but a prophet's name was Ebenezer,
However little I guessed it as a boy?   30

Outlandish names of course are never a boy's
Choice. And it takes time to learn to praise.
Stone of Help is the meaning of Ebenezer.
Stone of Help—what fitter name for my father?
Always the Stone of Help however his hair   35
Might graduate from black to Hallelujah.

Such is the old drama of boy and father.
Praise from a grayhead now with thinning hair.
Sing Ebenezer, Robert, sing Hallelujah!

1960

Catch

Two boys uncoached are tossing a poem together,
Overhand, underhand, backhand, sleight of hand, every hand,
Teasing with attitudes, latitudes, interludes, altitudes,
High, make him fly off the ground for it, low, make him stoop,
Make him scoop it up, make him as-almost-as-possible miss it,   5
Fast, let him sting from it, now, now fool him slowly,

Anything, everything tricky, risky, nonchalant,
Anything under the sun to outwit the prosy,
Over the tree and the long sweet cadence down,
Over his head, make him scramble to pick up the meaning,   10
And now, like a posy, a pretty one plump in his hands.

1960

Yes, What?

What would earth do without her blessed boobs
her blooming bumpkins garden variety
her oafs   her louts   her yodeling yokels
and all her Breughel characters
under the fat-faced moon?   5

Her nitwits   numskulls   universal
nincompoops jawohl   jawohl   with all
their yawps   burps   beers   guffaws
her goofs   her goons   her big galoots
under the red-face moon?   10

1976

◦►◄ RICHARD EBERHART ►◄◦
(b. 1904)

Richard Eberhart was born in Austin, Minnesota, the son of Alpha LaRue and
Lena Eberhart. His father was a successful businessman in the meatpacking industry. After graduating from high school in 1921, Eberhart attended the University
of Minnesota, then Dartmouth College, from which he received a bachelor's degree in 1926. As a young man he led a rather colorful existence, sailing on a tramp
steamer, eventually jumping ship and traveling to England, where he studied with
F. R. Leavis at St. John's College, Cambridge, and befriended I. A. Richards. There
he also met the poet and critic William Empson, and for a time he worked as private tutor to a Thai prince. On his return to the United States, Eberhart studied
briefly at Harvard, then took a teaching job at St. Mark's School, where one of his
pupils was Robert Lowell. When World War II broke out, Eberhart served in the
navy, an experience that would lead to his best-known poem, "The Fury of Aerial
Bombardment." Before the war he had married the daughter of a wealthy manufacturer, and at the war's end he entered her father's business, The Butcher Polish
Company (makers of floor wax). Though he would later leave full-time work in
business to teach at Princeton and Dartmouth, Eberhart remained on the company's board of directors.

He began publishing poetry while in England in the early 1930s and would
publish more than thirty collections in his long career, in addition to plays and
criticism. He helped to found the Poets' Theatre in 1950, served on boards, guest-
taught at many universities, won the Bollingen, the Pulitzer Prize, and the National Book Award, and was Poetry Consultant to the Library of Congress.

Eberhart once noted that "poetry is allied to religion and music." It is the visionary quality of his poems for which he is usually praised, rather than their precision of expression.

◄──◆──►

The Fury of Aerial Bombardment

You would think the fury of aerial bombardment
Would rouse God to relent; the infinite spaces
Are still silent. He looks on shock-pried faces.
History, even, does not know what is meant.

You would feel that after so many centuries   5
God would give man to repent; yet he can kill
As Cain could, but with multitudinous will,
No farther advanced than in his ancient furies.

Was man made stupid to see his own stupidity?
Is God by definition indifferent, beyond us all?   10
Is the eternal truth man's fighting soul
Wherein the Beast ravens in its own avidity?

Of Van Wettering I speak, and Averill,
Names on a list, whose faces I do not recall
But they are gone to early death, who late in school   15
Distinguished the belt feed lever from the belt holding pawl.[1]

1947

►◄ ROBERT PENN WARREN ►◄
(1905–1989)

Though he lived most of his adult life in northern states like Minnesota and Connecticut, Robert Penn Warren was born and remained a Southerner. In his hometown of Guthrie, Kentucky, his father was a prominent banker. His maternal grandfather, Gabriel Penn, had served under Nathan Bedford Forrest in the Confederate cavalry, and his stories awakened Warren's lifelong interest in history. Nicknamed "Red" for the color of his hair, Warren also hunted as a boy, and it was a hunting accident that blinded one eye and prevented him from accepting an appointment to the Naval Academy at Annapolis. Instead, Warren attended Vanderbilt University, where his roommate was Allen Tate and two of his professors were John Crowe Ransom and Donald Davidson. From 1922 to 1925 he helped to edit the *Fugitive*, a small magazine that launched or furthered the careers of several important Southern writers. While doing graduate work at Berkeley and Yale, Warren further explored his historical interests in a biography of John Brown. As a Rhodes Scholar at Oxford he wrote his first novel, *Night Rider* (published in 1939).

1. Parts of a .50-caliber Browning machine gun.

He also wrote an essay ("The Briar Patch") he would later repudiate for its segregationist views, and it was published in a book of Southern Agrarian manifestos entitled *I'll Take My Stand*.

In 1930 Warren married Emma Brescia (they divorced twenty years later) and embarked on an academic career. While teaching at Louisiana State University from 1934 to 1942, he observed the rise and fall of politician Huey "Kingfish" Long, who was assassinated in 1939. This resulted in what is usually regarded as Warren's best novel, *All the King's Men* (1946), in which Long becomes a populist demagogue named Willie Stark. Not only did Warren's novel win the Pulitzer Prize, but the film version picked up the Academy Award for Best Picture. It was also at Louisiana State University that Warren, together with Cleanth Brooks and Charles Pipkin, founded a distinguished literary journal, the *Southern Review*. Warren and Brooks collaborated on a number of books, notably two of the century's most important textbooks, *Understanding Poetry* (1938) and *Understanding Fiction* (1943). The first of these went through four editions and was one of the strongest influences upon the classroom teaching of poetry for several generations.

Understanding Poetry presented methods of reading and discussing verse that grew out of what John Crowe Ransom would call New Criticism. In their opening "Letter to the Teacher" the authors write, "This book has been conceived on the assumption that if poetry is worth teaching at all it is worth teaching as poetry." They then point out the weaknesses in three other kinds of criticism: paraphrase of a poem's content, biographical criticism, and didactic or moral interpretations. They do not, as some have suggested, deny any value in these ways of reading; they merely assert that poetry has certain distinctive formal and rhetorical characteristics to which fruitful attention can be paid. Later in the book they write, "Poetry, like all discourse, is a communication—the saying of something by one person to another person." Noting "the insufficiency of the 'message-hunting' approach to poetry," they stress an awareness of language's inner workings, its strategies and effects.

Despite the enormous success of these textbooks, to say nothing of his prolific output as a critic and editor in some thirty other nonfiction volumes, Warren declared that he did not think of himself as a critic. "A real critic, like Cleanth Brooks or I. A. Richards, has a system. . . ." He was more an appreciator and historian.

Warren published more than a dozen books of fiction in his lifetime, and sixteen books of poetry. In addition to his Pulitzer Prize for *All the King's Men*, he twice won that prize for poetry. After his divorce, he married the writer Eleanor Clark in 1952. One of their two children, Rosanna Warren, also became a poet.

Warren's early poetry, influenced by Ransom and his reading of English Renaissance verse, was highly traditional but rather static. Critics have often noted that it was his novel in verse, *Brother to Dragons* (1953, revised 1979), that signaled a new approach. At least one critic found in Warren's narrative poems the influence of Robinson Jeffers, perhaps the most highly regarded narrative poet of an earlier generation. If Warren's poetry was too often marred by lapses into prose locutions and wordiness, it was also striking at times for its focus on history and character. Among the shorter poems in which this tendency appeared was "Last Laugh," a bitter poem about Samuel Clemens (Mark Twain). But Warren's long experience with the novel drew him to larger subjects in poems like *Audubon: A Vision* (1969) and *Chief Joseph of the Nez Perce* (1983). In his novels and narratives Warren made new versions of mankind's fall from grace, a theme that also

pervades his shorter, more personal lyrics, causing at least one critic to fault Warren for persistent nostalgia. His *New and Selected Poems* appeared in 1985.

Whatever the weaknesses of his poetry and fiction, Warren was clearly an important American man of letters. In the variety of writers he championed and taught
(his final post for most of his thirty-nine years was at Yale), and the acuity of his
best essays, stories, and poems, he was a powerful appreciator of literature and life,
and a writer who helped form many of our beliefs about American culture.

Bearded Oaks

The oaks, how subtle and marine,
Bearded, and all the layered light
Above them swims; and thus the scene,
Recessed, awaits the positive night.

So, waiting, we in the grass now lie   5
Beaneath the languorous tread of light:
The grasses, kelp-like, satisfy
Then nameless motions of the air.

Upon the floor of light, and time,
Unmurmuring, of polyp made,   10
We rest; we are, as light withdraws,
Twin atolls on a shelf of shade.

Ages to our construction went,
Dim architecture, hour by hour:
And violence, forgot now, lent   15
The present stillness all its power.

The storm of noon above us rolled,
Of light the fury, furious gold,
The long drag troubling us, the depth:
Dark is unrocking, unrippling, still.   20

Passion and slaughter, ruth,[1] decay
Descend, minutely whispering down,
Silted down swaying streams, to lay
Foundation for our voicelessness.

All our debate is voiceless here,   25
As all our rage, the rage of stone;
If hope is hopeless, then fearless is fear,
And history is thus undone.

Our feet once wrought the hollow street
With echo when the lamps were dead   30

1. Pity.

At windows, once our headlight glare
Disturbed the doe that, leaping, fled.

I do not love you less that now
The caged heart makes iron stroke,
Or less that all that light once gave   35
The graduate dark should now revoke.

We live in time so little time
And we learn all so painfully,
That we may spare this hour's term
To practice for eternity.   40

1944

Evening Hawk

From plane of light to plane, wings dipping through
Geometries and orchids that the sunset builds,
Out of the peak's black angularity of shadow, riding
The last tumultuous avalanche of
Light above pines and the guttural gorge,   5
The hawk comes.

                    His wing
Scythes down another day, his motion
Is that of the honed steel-edge, we hear
The crashless fall of stalks of Time.

The head of each stalk is heavy with the gold of our error.   10

Look! Look! he is climbing the last light
Who knows neither Time nor error, and under
Whose eye, unforgiving, the world, unforgiven, swings
Into shadow.

                    Long now,
The last thrush is still, the last bat   15
Now cruises in his sharp hieroglyphics. His wisdom
Is ancient, too, and immense. The star
Is steady, like Plato, over the mountain.

If there were no wind we might, we think, hear
The earth grind on its axis, or history   20
Drip in darkness like a leaking pipe in the cellar.

1975

What Voice at Moth-Hour

What voice at moth-hour did I hear calling
As I stood in the orchard while the white
Petals of apple blossoms were falling,
Whiter than moth-wing in that twilight?

What voice did I hear as I stood by the stream,   5
Bemused in the murmurous wisdom there uttered,
While ripples at stone, in their steely gleam,
Caught last night before it was shuttered?

What voice did I hear as I wandered alone
In a premature night of cedar, beech, oak,   10
Each foot set soft, then still as stone
Standing to wait while the first owl spoke?

The voice that I heard once at dew-fall, I now
Can hear by a simple trick. If I close
My eyes, in that dusk I again know   15
The feel of damp grass between bare toes,

Can see the last zigzag, sky-skittering, high,
Of a bullbat, and even hear, far off, from
Swamp-cover, the whip-o-will, and as I
Once heard, hear the voice: *It's late! Come home.*   20

1981

Mid-Century Poets

The Gotham Book Mart offered mid-century poets a literary home in New York City; it continues to promote poetry, hosting readings in its upstairs gallery.

HISTORICAL AND CRITICAL OVERVIEW

Hot and Cold Wars

> What is an age but something to complain about?
>
> —*Randall Jarrell*

The year 1939 was a watershed for English-language poetry. William Butler Yeats, one of the greatest of all lyric poets, died in January, and in that same month the young English poet W. H. Auden arrived in New York to begin a new life. (He eventually became an American citizen, just as Eliot had become a British subject.) By the end of that year Auden had written his poem "September 1, 1939," marking Hitler's invasion of Poland and the official beginning of World War II in Europe. Auden's lyric meditation was, however, set in a New York bar, and his diagnosis of Europe's troubles had the advantage of distance.[1] Despite the warnings of poets like Auden and other Europeans, the United States, just emerging from a decade of depression, was still officially neutral, and would remain so, or nearly so, until December 7, 1941, when the Japanese bombed Pearl Harbor.

In 1940 our national population was almost 132 million, much of it urban. Franklin Delano Roosevelt was elected to an unprecedented third term in office, and after his inauguration in 1941 he enacted "lend-lease" policies favoring nations at war with the Axis powers. Pearl Harbor obliterated the last vestiges of American neutrality. In 1940 the United States spent $1.5 billion on armaments; by 1943 that number was $37.5 billion. In 1940 roughly 28 percent of the workforce were women; by 1944 that number had risen to nearly 40 percent, due to the participation of women in occupations once filled by the men who had gone off to war. More than 16 million American men and women served in World War II, and nearly three hundred thousand were killed in action. (Noncombat deaths totaled more than one hundred thousand.) Much of Europe and Asia were decimated by the war.

At the end of World War II in 1945, two American decisions would have a defining impact on subsequent global politics. First, at the Yalta Conference in 1944, just two months before his death, Roosevelt gave tacit approval to the Soviet dictator, Joseph Stalin, for the Russian occupation of Eastern Europe, guaranteeing that the post-war world would be divided into Soviet and American spheres of influence and setting the stage for more than a generation of the Cold War. Second, on assuming the presidency, Harry Truman learned of America's nuclear arms project and authorized the bombing of two Japanese cities, Hiroshima and Nagasaki, ending the Pacific war in the summer of 1945. From then on the image of a mushroom cloud looming over a blast site haunted human consciousness. Poets who served in World War II included Thomas McGrath, Howard Nemerov, James Dickey, Richard Hugo, Anthony Hecht, Richard Wilbur, Louis Simpson, Randall Jarrell, Richard Eberhart, John Haines, and W. D. Snodgrass. Robert Lowell, Kenneth Rexroth, William Everson, and William Stafford were notable conscientious objectors. No matter what part they played in the conflict, these poets and others would be profoundly affected by its aftermath—the Cold War and the increasing threat of global nuclear annihilation.

---

1. Readers may well ask why Auden was not, as an American citizen, included in this anthology. After lengthy consideration, the editors decided that Auden had remained essentially English in his poetic character, though his influence on American poetry has been enormous and has yet to be fully understood.

The era of the Cold War, which would last until the collapse of the Soviet Union in 1990, could be broadly characterized in America as one of fear and prosperity. On the one hand, the prospect of nuclear war loomed over everyone's lives. The United States and the Soviet Union engaged in an arms race that ultimately contributed to the latter's bankruptcy. On the other hand, this apparent deadlock and mutual mistrust created a kind of stability in which many nations' economies thrived, despite the occasional recession. There were, of course, several "hot" wars in this era as well, notably in Korea (1950–1953) and Vietnam (1964–1975)—both of them understood largely in terms of the American policy of containing communist expansion. Both wars engendered considerable protest and protest poetry, contributing to various countercultural movements such as the Beats and the broader but also less-defined hippies. These social convulsions in turn affected poets and poetry across the spectrum. If World War II had united much of the American public, the wars that followed, both hot and cold, contributed to a fragmentation that would also be visible in the arts.

Remaking the American Map

> Of course Americans do not read anything.
> —John Berryman

America after World War II enjoyed several bursts of economic expansion that paralleled the "Baby Boom," a generation-long increase in the nation's birthrate. The G.I. Bill of 1944 enabled thousands of veterans to get a college education, and American colleges and universities entered a phase of unprecedented growth. More women and minorities were getting an education as well; this growth in the education industry would ultimately provide employment for great numbers of American writers, transforming the economics of the arts. The development of new suburbs provided affordable housing for millions of Americans while it began to drain the vitality from inner cities. We also became a larger nation—Alaska and Hawaii were admitted to the Union as states in 1958 and 1959, respectively. And we became a healthier one with developments like the Salk polio vaccine in 1955.

By now transportation was utterly revolutionized. Commercial airline travel was increasingly available and popular, and the automobile became the dominant vehicle of American mobility. The nation's highway systems were rebuilt. In the fifties and sixties a network of state-of-the-art interstate highways was begun, bypassing many towns and small businesses that had flourished beside older roads. The map of America was being redrawn by these advances as Americans became used to faster modes of travel. The drawback, of course, was sprawl—more and more cities oozed into what had formerly been open space. Cities or clusters of cities took up more territory, and the automobile became even more essential just to get around in these vast networks of roads. For most of the sixties, the nation was distracted and inspired by what became known as "the space race." Nineteen sixty-one saw the first manned U.S. space flight, and the following year the first private communications satellite was launched. The program reached its apparent apogee in 1969 with the first moon landing.

Back on earth, as communities were connected by faster roads and airports, other kinds of communication were developed as well. The technology of television existed before the war, but because such resources were needed to perfect our radar capabilities, the production of commercial television equipment was banned from

1942 to 1945. The moment that ban was lifted, however, companies began selling TV sets. In 1946, RCA sold roughly ten thousand units with ten-inch viewing tubes. When in 1951 CBS broadcast a one-hour variety show hosted by Ed Sullivan, it was clear that television, albeit only in black and white at the time, had a real future in American culture. Writers who had formerly snubbed Hollywood, preferring the literary dignity of books and theater, now sometimes spoke of TV as an even lower life form. In the last decades of the twentieth century TV became ubiquitous not only in America but all over the globe. It was another way of exporting American culture in the form of movies, news broadcasts, and serial programs. By the election of 1960, especially during the Kennedy-Nixon debates, television was the single most important force in shaping American public opinion, whether in the choice of a president or the purchase of a new car. This fact would not be lost upon poets, who despaired of competing with such tools of mass communication.

Among the popular arts, the most revolutionary was rock n' roll music, partly rooted in African American forms like the blues and gospel. For the previous generation, forms of jazz like the bebop of Charlie Parker, Dizzy Gillespie, and Thelonius Monk evolved into the neo-bop of the fifties. The thirties had been the heyday of the big bands, making stars of such leaders as Glenn Miller, Tommy Dorsey, and Artie Shaw. The forties saw more swing and bop, and in the fifties there appeared more blends of country and western, spirituals, and the blues. Some critics say that the first genuine rock n' roll hit was "Rock Around the Clock" by Bill Haley and the Comets. Whatever the case, this new music with its steady backbeat made dancing easy and had instant appeal with the young. New hits had always spawned new dance crazes, but now new songs came at an ever faster pace, pushed by radio stations and record companies, bewildering some adults who feared that this new music was immoral. Eventually rock would follow the lead of folk music into new forms of social protest, advocating civil rights and opposing our involvement in Vietnam.

In post-war American poetry, this troubled relationship between popular culture and more "high-brow" views would contribute to new definitions of artistic camps. The Black Mountain poets were an outgrowth of the Modernism of Pound and Williams, while the Beats were Neo-romantics and Transcendentalists, looking back to Blake and Whitman, as well as to non-Western cultures for alternative models. There were also the so-called academic formalists, poets of Robert Lowell's generation who often held secure academic positions and practiced verse according to time-honored techniques, but who in many cases abandoned meter for free verse in the sixties, practicing their own kind of neoromantic poetry—antiestablishmentarian and, like other movements, rife with personality cults.

In the new economics of poetry, more poets could make a living by teaching, giving readings, and to a lesser degree, publishing their work, and the temptations to self-aggrandizement were very strong. At the same time, poets of all camps often felt alienated from society at large. As Randall Jarrell wrote, "The poet lives in a world whose newspapers and magazines and books and motion pictures and radio stations and television stations have destroyed, in a great many people, even the capacity for understanding real poetry." The last traces of American populism seemed to reside only in the then-marginalized Beats, while even the more conventional poets—"crucified on bar stools," as Theodore Roethke put it—were martyrs to their art. The 1952 election, in which former General Dwight D. Eisenhower defeated the more intellectual Adlai Stevenson, only widened this cultural divide. Poets could take money from the establishment in the form of teaching positions and grants, but sometimes wondered whether doing so meant collusion with a corrupt society.

Confessional Poets

> At the end of the open road we come to ourselves.
> —*Louis Simpson*

Early in the nineteenth century the French aristocrat Alexis de Tocqueville had observed that American society would of necessity produce new kinds of art, emphasizing subjects and forms that Europeans would hardly consider appropriate. His dichotomy of aristocratic versus democratic art was an oversimplification—it's hard to imagine Whitman without Wordsworth, Eliot without Baudelaire. But something in the nature of American culture, arising with the middle class, would indeed place new emphasis on the individual and his or her personal life. "I am the man," Whitman wrote. "I suffered. I was there." Modernism seemed to set aside this emphasis upon the personality, as Eliot had suggested in "Tradition and the Individual Talent"—though in hindsight we can see that personality was never really banished from the arts. In post-war American poetry, autobiography became increasingly dominant. Whitman was an influence, of course, but so was William Butler Yeats, who had forged his entire oeuvre by recalling that Keats called life a "vale of soul-making." One made one's art and one made one's self, and one did this in opposition to dehumanizing social and political forces at large. In this atmosphere, the sort of political poetry produced in the thirties would come to seem too topical, schematic, and propagandistic, whereas the psychology of the individual was deeply enigmatic and ambiguous. When these poets took on political subjects, it was often in the context of their own autobiographies.

Robert Lowell, with his intense historical self-consciousness, began as what we might call an impersonal poet. In the fifties, though, influenced by the free verse and American idiom of figures like William Carlos Williams and Allen Ginsberg as well as his own personal troubles, Lowell composed the poems of *Life Studies* (1959). Reviewing that book, the critic M. L. Rosenthal may have coined the phrase "confessional poetry." Whoever first adopted the term, it quickly took on broad usage. Personal subject matter, which had never been absent from poetry, seemed more than ever in the air. The individual and his or her family became commonplace subjects. With surprising and disturbing frequency, too, poets from Roethke to Lowell to John Berryman to Sylvia Plath to Anne Sexton detailed their episodes of madness, some of them making fetishes of their death wish.

This self-destructive impulse may not have been unique to the era, of course. In his book-length study of the subject, *The Confessional Poets* (1973), Robert Phillips reminded readers that the confessional mode in poetry was at least as old as Sappho. But he also could not deny that something verifiably new was afoot:

> It could be argued that we are living in a great Age of Autobiography. We no longer believe in the general truths about human nature, only the subjective ones. *Let me tell you about my wound . . . Let me tell you about my scars and deformities . . .* our writers cry out. Not only poems, but the novel (*Herzog; Portnoy's Complaint*) and journalism (Norman Mailer's *The Prisoner of Sex*; Merle Miller's *On Being Different*) are all part of this current autobiographical frenzy.

Furthermore, the mid-century poets are notable for the high rate of mental problems and early deaths among them, increasing the impression that they were a new Romantic generation. Eileen Simpson even entitled her memoir of John Berryman, Robert Lowell, and others *Poets in their Youth* (1982), borrowing from these lines by Wordsworth:

> We Poets in our youth begin in gladness;
> But thereof come in the end despondency and madness.

Berryman himself said in an interview, "The artist is extremely lucky who is presented with the worst possible ordeal which will not actually kill him."

Among poets in the following sections, an alarming number suffered from mental illness, including Theodore Roethke, John Berryman, Robert Lowell, Randall Jarrell, Weldon Kees, Anne Sexton, and Sylvia Plath. Kees, Berryman, Sexton, and Plath committed suicide, and Jarrell may have done so, depending on how one interprets the circumstances of his death. Problems with alcohol and drugs abounded, though a thorough study of these statistics would have to compare the percentage of poets who had such problems with percentages of people in other walks of life to avoid succumbing to Romantic mythologies. John Frederick Nims observed of Confessional poetry, "The nakedness we see there is not the nakedness of nature lovers under the sun; it is the pasty nakedness of hospital sheets." To be brief, this was an era in which the equation of poetry and madness had a great deal of currency, and later generations of poets often reacted against this apparent Romanticism.

The term "Confessional poetry" is also an oversimplification, as few of these poets were autobiographical in a simple or straightforward manner. Critic Richard Gray associated the "'I' as primitive" with Theodore Roethke, the "'I' as historian" with Lowell, the "'I' as martyr" with Berryman, and the "'I' as prophetess" with Sylvia Plath. All of these poets were mannerists of a sort, dwelling on distortions of style and subject for effect, suggesting that all was not well in the land of plenty. In *Alone with America* (1969) the poet Richard Howard used the ancient myth of King Midas to explain American poetry after 1950: ". . . the myth of a precious order longed for in delirium and chaos, attained in dread, and renounced in longing again."

One of the Boys?

> The pact that we made was the ordinary pact
> of men & women in those days
> —*Adrienne Rich*

Feminist consciousness in American poetry dates at least as far back as the seventeenth-century poet Anne Bradstreet, depending on one's definitions, and surely it reached one high point with the right to vote in 1920. But it would take the post-war era of civil rights activism and the social disruptions of the sixties, including the sexual revolution and the invention of the birth control pill, to bring a thoroughgoing feminist revolution to American literature. Until then, even the most prominent women poets appeared to be valued in part for their ability to fit in to a male-dominated literary milieu.

Elizabeth Bishop, for whom reticence was a psychological necessity, had little interest in public feminism and considered it peripheral to her art, just as she considered her alcoholism and sexuality to be private matters rather than public subjects. She preferred a subtler and more subversive feminist approach in her poetry. Josephine Miles and May Swenson were "liberated women," but were also disinclined to make displays of their ideological commitments. For Muriel Rukeyser, on the other hand, social problems were things to be squarely faced. But Rukeyser's politics were not exclusively feminist in their nature. For a commited leftist such as Rukeyser, problems of poverty and anti-Semitism were just as important as those associated with the rights of women. In other words, post-war American poetry was not immediately a great age of feminism in literature—that would have to wait for poets like Adrienne Rich, who began to transform her poetic stance in the sixties, and for poet-critics like Alicia Ostriker and Sandra M. Gilbert, as well as the increasing emphasis upon feminism in the universities and the culture at large.

Women struggled for legitimacy in the fifties and sixties, to be sure, and wrote of their struggle to balance domestic demands with desire for careers, just as Virginia Woolf had done early in the century. But the liberating explosion of feminist consciousness in American poetry would really come about in the seventies. Meanwhile, even among progressive groups like the Beats, women poets often were undervalued unless they pretended to be "one of the boys." In the mainstream, strong poets like Bishop tried to place their faith in their art, asking little on the basis of gender or politics, although in hindsight, Bishop's poetry is notable for its implicit feminism and concern over class inequalities and poverty in Brazil, where she lived for many years. Despite her frequent refusal to complain openly of her situation, though, it cannot have been easy. During his lifetime, Lowell's notoriety made him seem especially important as a poet, while full appreciation of Bishop arrived only after her death.

Rukeyser's leftist politics were strongly opposed to many post-war American trends. The year 1952, that saw Eisenhower elected, also saw new waves of anti-communist sentiment in American life. Loyalty oaths were commonly demanded and enforced. The House Un-American Activities Committee, at work since the late thirties, became even more vociferous in rooting out communist activity in America. It had investigated the film industry starting in 1947, instigating the infamous "blacklist," dividing the American Left between those willing to name names and those not. In 1950, Senator Joseph McCarthy of Wisconsin began using the tactics of the House committee and collaborated with FBI head J. Edgar Hoover to pursue his own anti-communist campaign, portraying President Truman and his administration as soft on communism. When he continued these attacks even during the Eisenhower administration, however, he alienated former allies in the Republican Party and was in turn attacked by such figures as Richard Nixon. In 1954 McCarthy was censured by Congress; he committed suicide three years later. During this anti-communist era, Rukeyser and Thomas McGrath remained among the few open and outspoken leftist poets. Rukeyser's principles concerned liberation on all fronts, political, racial, and social. Her work is perhaps best thought of as a poetic road between the politics of the thirties and the upheavals of the sixties. Increasingly, poetry was associated with civil liberties and forms of social protest that were no longer the sole province of countercultural movements.

Civil Rights

> A riot is at bottom the language of the unheard.
> —*Martin Luther King, Jr.*

African American soldiers returning from service in World War II found an America still segregated in many states, with fewer opportunities for blacks than for whites. Many Japanese Americans found that they had to start their lives over from scratch, having had their possessions confiscated when they were interned with their families during the war. In 1954, *Brown vs. Topeka Board of Education,* the U.S. Supreme Court declared that segregation in the public schools was illegal, and in 1957 President Eisenhower sent the National Guard to reinforce desegregation in Little Rock, Arkansas. In his short presidency, too, John F. Kennedy found himself compelled to use troops to uphold the law in several Southern communities. By 1963, the year in which Kennedy was assassinated, there were widespread demonstrations for civil rights in many American cities, most of them notable for the nonviolent tactics advocated by the Reverend Martin Luther King, Jr. Nineteen sixty-four saw the passage of new civil rights and antipoverty legislation advocated by President Lyndon Johnson as part of his "Great Society" vision. In 1965 came the assassination of Malcolm X, and the following year Huey P. Newton and Bobby Seale founded the Black Panther Party, advocating the use of force to bring about social change. By now protests of racial inequity were becoming increasingly violent, despite King's eloquent pleas for rationality. There was also unrest in American cities due to growing protests against the war in Vietnam. After race riots broke out in Watts, California, in 1966, it became popular among antiwar demonstrators to comment ironically on their solidarity with the rioters by wearing "Watts Fire Department" t-shirts. The war in Vietnam intensified from 1967 through 1969, and new forms of protest emerged, such as the hippie movement at home; 1968 brought the devastating assassinations of both King and Bobby Kennedy, just three months apart. Progress in civil rights came at great cost on all sides, but it was progress nonetheless.

As feminist movements would later do much to raise the visibility of women writers, the Civil Rights movement brought more minority writers to a mass audience in America. The emphasis on America's largest minority at the time, African Americans, would eventually broaden under the rubric of multiculturalism, including minority populations of all kinds. While arguments about the legitimacy and perimeters of multiculturalism exist to this day, we can at least point to important questions raised about the nature of aesthetic values—which of them are universal, which of them culturally specific—as well as to a variety of important poets whose work has been made possible by multicultural ideals.

By 1970 the United States was a deeply divided nation on the verge of recession. The literary world, increasingly tied to colleges and universities, was still a predominantly white and male bastion. The next thirty years would provide more permutations in American society that would be reflected in radical changes of academic culture and a multiplicity of poetic camps.

Anthology Wars

> Anthologies are perhaps the most important
> harbingers of lastingness that a writer's work
> may know during his lifetime; thus they have come
> to seem a kind of trial immortality for all good poems.
> —*James Dickey*

In the final sections of this anthology you will find quite a few categories of poetry and poets, some of them defined as movements, others not. Sometimes poets fit clearly into these tentative definitions, sometimes they do not, and the editors have given them a place for the provisional convenience of discussion. Literary movements announced themselves with increasing frequency in the twentieth century, defined by aesthetics, politics, generation, gender, ethnicity, or any number of other categories. In every case, these definitions sought to bring poets to the attention of readers—or at least critics. And these pleas for attention were usually accompanied or announced by anthologies. In post-war American poetry, the signal example of the anthology war took place in the fifties, defining a rift between the so-called academic poets and the avant-garde.

New Poets of England and America (1957), edited by Donald Hall, Robert Pack, and Louis Simpson, introduced many poets who have continued to exert influence over American verse. The book's introduction was by Robert Frost, chosen as *paterfamilias* to those who followed, including Robert Lowell, Richard Wilbur, Sylvia Plath, Anne Sexton, J. V. Cunningham, James Dickey, Anthony Hecht, and others. By placing Americans side by side with British poets like Philip Larkin and Ted Hughes, the anthology scoffed at notions of literary nationalism, though its apparent anglophilia bothered some critics. The anthology excluded Beats, Black Mountain poets, and the New York School, who responded with an anthology of their own, *The New American Poetry* (1960), edited by Donald Allen. In the latter book, such poets as Allen Ginsberg, John Ashbery, Robert Duncan, William Everson, and Denise Levertov found a home.

These two distinct "schools" of poetry, which Robert Lowell jokingly decreed "cooked" and "raw," would seem to have little in common. The cooked poets were formal and ironic, the raw informal and at times ecstatic. Nevertheless, the middle course, a combination of both broad tendencies, would to some degree define the poetry emerging from writers' workshops over the next two decades. Later anthologies, such as Hayden Carruth's *The Voice That Is Great Within Us* (1970), attempted to illuminate this middle way, while voices at the extremes declared that never the twain could meet. The seeds of still later movements like New Formalism and Language Poetry can be found in this battle of the books, but by that time the avant-garde would depend on the academy for its survival, while poets writing in meter would sometimes ally themselves with a new populism. American poetry was becoming as various—some would say as cacophonous—as a carnival.

THEODORE ROETHKE

(1908–1963)

Theodore Huebner Roethke was born in Saginaw, Michigan, the son of Otto Theodore Roethke and Helen Marie Huebner Roethke. His father and uncle operated a large commercial florist business, and they owned a block of eight greenhouses, which became seedbeds of the poet's imagination. "They were to me," the poet later wrote, "both heaven and hell, a kind of tropics created in the savage climate of Michigan, where austere German Americans turned their love of order and their terrifying efficiency into something beautiful." Otto Roethke, an industrious and earthy man, displayed little sympathy for his son's artistic sensitivity. As Roethke grew, he felt torn by opposing needs—the desire to make beauty and the compulsion to join in the rough, masculine world of athletics and drinking. As a student at the University of Michigan, he confirmed his love of poetry, yet on his graduation in 1929 he still felt that he needed a more practical career. A brief stint in law school, however, turned him back to literature. Roethke pursued a master's degree in English first at Michigan and later at Harvard where he studied with new Critic I. A. Richards. In 1931 he took a teaching job at Lafayette College in Pennsylvania, where he also served as varsity tennis coach. The poet who had been a sickly child was now a hulking bear of a man, six foot two in height and weighing well over two hundred pounds, whose mixture of toughness and sensitivity often caused him to work himself to exhaustion. While at Lafayette, Roethke met Louise Bogan, whose poetry greatly influenced his early work. They quickly became lovers and remained lifelong friends.

In 1935 Roethke began teaching at Michigan State College (now University), but during his first semester he suffered a nervous breakdown. His resulting hospitalization led to losing his job. From 1936 to 1943 he taught at Pennsylvania State University without another mental episode. Fueled by his fervent literary ambition and genuine hunger for fame, his literary reputation slowly grew. His first collection of poems, *Open House* (1941), was published to mixed reviews. Some critics found it too cautious and formal, but others, most notably W. H. Auden, applauded its accomplishment. The publication of *Open House* allowed Roethke to move on to Bennington College, where in 1945 he suffered his second nervous breakdown. Two years later at Yaddo, an artist's colony, he met Robert Lowell, the poet who would become a fellow sufferer of manic depression, and the two became friends.

Roethke finally found a secure academic position at the University of Washington in Seattle where he taught from 1947 until his untimely death in 1963. There he became well known as a devoted teacher whose students included James Wright, Richard Hugo, Carolyn Kizer, and David Wagoner. He was also known for his frequent breakdowns, manic episodes, and alcoholic binges. By this time, however, Roethke had become a celebrated poet, and the University proved a sympathetic and supportive employer. Roethke tended to exhaust himself as a teacher, which contributed to these breakdowns. He was often theatrical in the classroom, inspiring both worry and delight in his students. Although Roethke did not expect most of them to become poets, he believed that one learned about poetry through observation of the natural world and through the imitation of masters. Rigorously critical and demanding, he based both his teaching and his writing on these principles.

Most critics see Roethke's second book, *The Lost Son* (1948), as his poetic breakthrough. It contains not only the probing title poem—like many of his sequences, pulsing between solipsism, despair, and exultation—but also the sequence of "greenhouse poems" in which plants take on powerful interior lives. The sheer physicality of the "greenhouse poems" conveys a kind of animism and childlike mixture of wonder and fear. Roots, an important metaphor from his father's world, are not used to represent a conventional sense of belonging. Rather, they are the irrational probings of the mind and as much a frightening part of the cemetery where Otto Roethke was buried when the poet was fourteen as they are the source of sustenance. The primal childhood Roethke expressed vacillated among terror, self-loathing, and the desire for transcendence.

With *The Lost Son* Roethke initiated a series of interior monologues that he continued in *Praise to the End!* (1951). In *The Waking* (1953) he began to explore traditional forms again. His personal life also grew more ordered. In 1953 he married a former Bennington student, Beatrice O'Connell. (Auden was his best man and Bogan the matron of honor). A new sensuality and joy entered his poetry, especially in *Words for the Wind* (1957), which contained a section of striking love poems, most notably "I Knew a Woman." A collection of poems for children, *I Am! Says the Lamb*, appeared in 1961. Roethke was at work on the poems that would be posthumously published in *The Far Field* (1964) when he died of a heart attack in a friend's swimming pool on Bainbridge Island in 1963. The last poems include not only lyrics like "In a Dark Time," but also the Whitmanesque "North American Sequence," which is perhaps his most ambitious work. He garnered many awards during his lifetime, including a Pulitzer Prize for *The Waking*, the National Book Award for *Words for the Wind*, and the Bollingen Prize (1959). When his *Collected Poems* (1966) was published, it was hailed as the testament of a major poet. Subsequent editions of his letters and notebooks have confirmed his reputation as both poet and teacher.

Roethke's place in modern American poetry seems simultaneously indisputable and undefinable. His best poems have an irresistible physical immediacy. Yet imitation is one of the most important qualities of Roethke's verse. In a poem called "Four for Sir John Davies" he wrote, "I take this cadence from a man called Yeats; / I take it, and I give it back again." Perhaps no poet of similar stature in American literature was so compulsively imitative. Not only rhythms and forms, but various tropes he used can be traced to poets he had studied closely, including Yeats, Dante, Blake, Donne, Sir John Davies, Whitman, and Eliot. If imitation seemed, at times, to prevent him from finding his own voice, close observation rescued some of his best poems. His work teems with unforgettable images and phrases often drawn from his attentiveness to the natural world.

Roethke was not a poet like Robert Lowell in whose work one can map the social changes of a generation. His poetry was alternately psychologically inward and obstreperously outgoing, obsessively concerned with his own moods and exuberantly fascinated with the workings of nature. These two sides of his poetic character were linked and animated by his mystical concept of spirit. As a college student, the young poet had written in a paper, "When I get alone under an open sky where man isn't too evident—then I'm tremendously exalted and a thousand vivid images and sweet visions flood my consciousness." In this, Roethke was both intensely singular and an heir of the Transcendentalists Emerson and Thoreau.

Cuttings

Sticks-in-a-drowse droop over sugary loam,
Their intricate stem-fur dries;
But still the delicate slips keep coaxing up water;
The small cells bulge;

One nub of growth   5
Nudges a sand-crumb loose,
Pokes through a musty sheath
Its pale tendrilous horn.

1948

Cuttings

(later)

This urge, wrestle, resurrection of dry sticks,
Cut stems struggling to put down feet,
What saint strained so much,
Rose on such lopped limbs to a new life?

I can hear, underground, that sucking and sobbing,   5
In my veins, in my bones I feel it,—
The small waters seeping upward,
The tight grains parting at last.
When sprouts break out,
Slippery as fish,   10
I quail, lean to beginnings, sheath-wet.

1948

Root Cellar

Nothing would sleep in that cellar, dank as a ditch,
Bulbs broke out of boxes hunting for chinks in the dark,
Shoots dangled and drooped,
Lolling obscenely from mildewed crates,
Hung down long yellow evil necks, like tropical snakes.   5
And what a congress of stinks!—
Roots ripe as old bait,
Pulpy stems, rank, silo-rich,
Leaf-mold, manure, lime, piled against slippery planks.
Nothing would give up life: 10
Even the dirt kept breathing a small breath.

1948

Dolor

I have known the inexorable sadness of pencils,
Neat in their boxes, dolor of pad and paper-weight,
All the misery of manilla folders and mucilage,
Desolation in immaculate public places,
Lonely reception room, lavatory, switchboard,   5
The unalterable pathos of basin and pitcher,
Ritual of multigraph, paper-clip, comma,
Endless duplication of lives and objects.
And I have seen dust from the walls of institutions,
Finer than flour, alive, more dangerous than silica,   10
Sift, almost invisible, through long afternoons of tedium,
Dropping a fine film on nails and delicate eyebrows,
Glazing the pale hair, the duplicate grey standard faces.

                                                              1948

My Papa's Waltz

The whiskey on your breath
Could make a small boy dizzy;
But I hung on like death:
Such waltzing was not easy.

We romped until the pans   5
Slid from the kitchen shelf;
My mother's countenance
Could not unfrown itself.

The hand that held my wrist
Was battered on one knuckle;   10
At every step you missed
My right ear scraped a buckle.

You beat time on my head
With a palm caked hard by dirt,
Then waltzed me off to bed   15
Still clinging to your shirt.

                                                              1948

Elegy for Jane

My Student, Thrown by a Horse

I remember the neckcurls, limp and damp as tendrils;
And her quick look, a sidelong pickerel smile;
And how, once startled into talk, the light syllables leaped for her,
And she balanced in the delight of her thought,
A wren, happy, tail into the wind,   5

Her song trembling the twigs and small branches.
The shade sang with her;
The leaves, their whispers turned to kissing;
And the mold sang in the bleached valleys under the rose.

Oh, when she was sad, she cast herself down into such a pure depth,   10
Even a father could not find her:
Scraping her cheek against straw;
Stirring the clearest water.

My sparrow, you are not here,
Waiting like a fern, making a spiny shadow.   15
The sides of wet stones cannot console me,
Nor the moss, wound with the last light.

If only I could nudge you from this sleep,
My maimed darling, my skittery pigeon.
Over this damp grave I speak the words of my love: 20
I, with no rights in this matter,
Neither father nor lover.

                                        1953

The Waking

I wake to sleep, and take my waking slow.
I feel my fate in what I cannot fear.
I learn by going where I have to go.

We think by feeling. What is there to know?
I hear my being dance from ear to ear.   5
I wake to sleep, and take my waking slow.

Of those so close beside me, which are you?
God bless the Ground! I shall walk softly there,
And learn by going where I have to go.

Light takes the Tree; but who can tell us how?   10
The lowly worm climbs up a winding stair;
I wake to sleep, and take my waking slow.

Great Nature has another thing to do
To you and me; so take the lively air,
And, lovely, learn by going where to go.   15

This shaking keeps me steady. I should know.
What falls away is always. And is near.
I wake to sleep, and take my waking slow.
I learn by going where I have to go.

                                        1953

I Knew a Woman

I knew a woman, lovely in her bones,
When small birds sighed, she would sigh back at them;
Ah, when she moved, she moved more ways than one:
The shapes a bright container can contain!
Of her choice virtues only gods should speak,   5
Or English poets who grew up on Greek
(I'd have them sing in chorus, cheek to cheek).

How well her wishes went! She stroked my chin,
She taught me Turn, and Counter-turn, and Stand;
She taught me Touch, that undulant white skin;   10
I nibbled meekly from her proffered hand;
She was the sickle; I, poor I, the rake,
Coming behind her for her pretty sake
(But what prodigious mowing we did make).

Love likes a gander, and adores a goose: 15
Her full lips pursed, the errant note to seize;
She played it quick, she played it light and loose;
My eyes, they dazzled at her flowing knees;
Her several parts could keep a pure repose,
Or one hip quiver with a mobile nose   20
(She moved in circles, and those circles moved).

Let seed be grass, and grass turn into hay:
I'm martyr to a motion not my own;
What's freedom for? To know eternity.
I swear she cast a shadow white as stone.   25
But who would count eternity in days?
These old bones live to learn her wanton ways:
(I measure time by how a body sways).

1958

In a Dark Time

In a dark time, the eye begins to see,
I meet my shadow in the deepening shade;
I hear my echo in the echoing wood—
A lord of nature weeping to a tree.
I live between the heron and the wren,   5
Beasts of the hill and serpents of the den.

What's madness but nobility of soul
At odds with circumstance? The day's on fire!
I know the purity of pure despair,
My shadow pinned against a sweating wall.   10
That place among the rocks—is it a cave,
Or winding path? The edge is what I have.

A steady storm of correspondences!
A night flowing with birds, a ragged moon,
And in broad day the midnight come again!   15
A man goes far to find out what he is—
Death of the self in a long, tearless night,
All natural shapes blazing unnatural light.

Dark, dark my light, and darker my desire.
My soul, like some heat-maddened summer fly,   20
Keeps buzzing at the sill. Which I is I?
A fallen man, I climb out of my fear.
The mind enters itself, and God the mind,
And one is One, free in the tearing wind.

1964

From North American Sequence

The Longing

1

On things asleep, no balm:
A kingdom of stinks and sighs,
Fetor of cockroaches, dead fish, petroleum,
Worse than castoreum[1] of mink or weasels,
Saliva dripping from warm microphones,   5
Agony of crucifixion on barstools.
   Less and less the illuminated lips,
   Hands active, eyes cherished;
   Happiness left to dogs and children—
   (Matters only a saint mentions!)   10
Lust fatigues the soul.
How to transcend this sensual emptiness?
(Dreams drain the spirit if we dream too long.)
In a bleak time, when a week of rain is a year,
The slag-heaps fume at the edge of the raw cities: 15
The gulls wheel over their singular garbage;
The great trees no longer shimmer;
Not even the soot dances.

And the spirit fails to move forward,
But shrinks into a half-life, less than itself,   20
Falls back, a slug, a loose worm
Ready for any crevice,
An eyeless starer.

---

1.   Glandular secretions of animals like the mink or the weasel.

2

A wretch needs his wretchedness. Yes.
O pride, thou art a plume upon whose head?   25

How comprehensive that felicity! . . .
A body with the motion of a soul.
What dream's enough to breath in? A dark dream.
The rose exceeds, the rose exceeds us all.
Who'd think the moon could pare itself so thin?   30
A great flame rises from the sunless sea;
The light cries out, and I am there to hear—
I'd be beyond; I'd be beyond the moon,
Bare as a bud, and naked as a worm.

To this extent I'm a stalk.   35
    —How free; how all alone.
Out of these nothings
    —All beginnings come.

3

I would with the fish, the blackening salmon, and the mad lemmings,
The children dancing, the flowers widening.   40
Who sighs from far away?
I would unlearn the lingo of exasperation, all the distortions of malice and
        hatred;
I would believe my pain: and the eye quiet on the growing rose;
I would delight in my hands, the branch singing, altering the excessive bird;
I long for the imperishable quiet at the heart of form;   45
I would be a stream, winding between great striated rocks in late summer;
A leaf, I would love the leaves, delighting in the redolent disorder of this mortal
        life,
This ambush, this silence,
Where shadow can change into flame,
And the dark be forgotten.   50
I have left the body of the whale, but the mouth of the night is still wide;
On the Bullhead, in the Dakotas, where the eagles eat well,
In the country of few lakes, in the tall buffalo grass at the base of the clay buttes,
In the summer heat, I can smell the dead buffalo,
The stench of their damp fur drying in the sun,   55
The buffalo chips drying.

Old men should be explorers?
I'll be an Indian.
Ogalala?
Iroquois.

1964

Journey to the Interior

1

In the long journey out of the self,
There are many detours, washed-out interrupted raw places
Where the shale slides dangerously
And the back wheels hang almost over the edge
At the sudden veering, the moment of turning.   5
Better to hug close, wary of rubble and falling stones.
The arroyo cracking the road, the wind-bitten buttes, the canyons,
Creeks swollen in midsummer from the flash-flood roaring into the narrow valley.
Reeds beaten flat by wind and rain,
Grey from the long winter, burnt at the base in late summer.   10
—Or the path narrowing,
Winding upward toward the stream with its sharp stones,
The upland of alder and birchtrees,
Through the swamp alive with quicksand,
The way blocked at last by a fallen fir-tree,   15
The thickets darkening,
The ravines ugly.

2

I remember how it was to drive in gravel,
Watching for dangerous down-hill places, where the wheels whined beyond eighty—
When you hit the deep pit at the bottom of the swale,   20
The trick was to throw the car sideways and charge over the hill, full of the
    throttle.
Grinding up and over the narrow road, spitting and roaring.
A chance? Perhaps. But the road was part of me, and its ditches,
And the dust lay thick on my eyelids,—Who ever wore goggles?—
Always a sharp turn to the left past a barn close to the roadside,   25
To a scurry of small dogs and a shriek of children,
The highway ribboning out in a straight thrust to the North,
To the sand dunes and fish flies, hanging, thicker than moths,
Dying brightly under the street lights sunk in coarse concrete,
The towns with their high pitted road-crowns and deep gutters,   30
Their wooden stores of silvery pine and weather-beaten red courthouses,
An old bridge below with a buckled iron railing, broken by some idiot plunger;
Underneath, the sluggish water running between weeds, broken wheels, tires,
    stones.
And all flows past—
The cemetery with two scrubby trees in the middle of the prairie,   35
The dead snakes and muskrats, the turtles gasping in the rubble,
The spikey purple bushes in the winding dry creek bed—
The floating hawks, the jackrabbits, the grazing cattle—
I am not moving but they are,
And the sun comes out of a blue cloud over the Tetons,   40
While, farther away, the heat-lightning flashes.
I rise and fall in the slow sea of a grassy plain,

The wind veering the car slightly to the right,
Whipping the line of white laundry, bending the cottonwoods apart,
The scraggly wind-break of a dusty ranch-house.   45
I rise and fall, and time folds
Into a long moment;
And I hear the lichen speak,
And the ivy advance with its white lizard feet—
On the shimmering road,   50
On the dusty detour.

3

I see the flower of all water, above and below me, the never receding,
Moving, unmoving in a parched land, white in the moonlight:
The soul at a still-stand,
At ease after rocking the flesh to sleep,   55
Petals and reflections of petals mixed on the surface of a glassy pool,
And the waves flattening out when the fishermen drag their nets over the stones.

In the moment of time when the small drop forms, but does not fall,
I have known the heart of the sun,—
In the dark and light of a dry place,   60
In a flicker of fire brisked by a dusty wind.
I have heard, in a drip of leaves,
A slight song,
After the midnight cries.
I rehearse myself for this: 65
The stand at the stretch in the face of death,
Delighting in surface change, the glitter of light on waves,
And I roam elsewhere, my body thinking,
Turning toward the other side of light,
In a tower of wind, a tree idling in air,   70
Beyond my own echo,
Neither forward nor backward,
Unperplexed, in a place leading nowhere.

As a blind man, lifting a curtain, knows it is morning,
I know this change: 75
On one side of silence there is no smile;
But when I breathe with the birds,
The spirit of wrath becomes the spirit of blessing,
And the dead begin from their dark to sing in my sleep.

1964

The Far Field

1

I dream of journeys repeatedly:
Of flying like a bat deep into a narrowing tunnel,
Of driving alone, without luggage, out a long peninsula,

The road lined with snow-laden second growth,
A fine dry snow ticking the windshield,   5
Alternate snow and sleet, no on-coming traffic,
And no lights behind, in the blurred side-mirror,
The road changing from glazed tarface to a rubble of stone,
Ending at last in a hopeless sand-rut,
Where the car stalls,   10
Churning in a snowdrift
Until the headlights darken.

2

At the field's end, in the corner missed by the mower,
Where the turf drops off into a grass-hidden culvert,
Haunt of the cat-bird, nesting-place of the field-mouse,   15
Not too far away from the ever-changing flower-dump,
Among the tin cans, tires, rusted pipes, broken machinery,—
One learned of the eternal;
And in the shrunken face of a dead rat, eaten by rain and ground-beetles
(I found it lying among the rubble of an old coal bin)   20
And the tom-cat, caught near the pheasant-run,
Its entrails strewn over the half-grown flowers,
Blasted to death by the night watchman.

I suffered for birds, for young rabbits caught in the mower,
My grief was not excessive.   25
For to come upon warblers in early May
Was to forget time and death:
How they filled the oriole's elm, a twittering restless cloud, all one morning,
And I watched and watched till my eyes blurred from the bird shapes,—
Cape May, Blackburnian, Cerulean,[2]—   30
Moving, elusive as fish, fearless,
Hanging, bunched like young fruit, bending the end branches,
Still for a moment,
Then pitching away in half-flight,
Lighter than finches,   35
While the wrens bickered and sang in the half-green hedgerows,
And the flicker drummed from his dead tree in the chicken-yard.

—Or to lie naked in sand,
In the silted shallows of a slow river,
Fingering a shell,   40
Thinking:
Once I was something like this, mindless,
Or perhaps with another mind, less peculiar;
Or to sink down to the hips in a mossy quagmire;
Or, with skinny knees, to sit astride a wet log,   45
Believing:

2. All types of warblers, small songbirds found in North America.

I'll return again,
As a snake or a raucous bird,
Or, with luck, as a lion.

I learned not to fear infinity,   50
The far field, the windy cliffs of forever,
The dying of time in the white light of tomorrow,
The wheel turning away from itself,
The sprawl of the wave,
The on-coming water.   55

3

The river turns on itself,
The tree retreats into its own shadow.
I feel a weightless change, a moving forward
As of water quickening before a narrowing channel
When banks converge, and the wide river whitens;   60
Or when two rivers combine, the blue glacial torrent
And the yellowish-green from the mountainy upland,—
At first a swift rippling between rocks,
Then a long running over flat stones
Before descending to the alluvial plain,   65
To the clay banks, and the wild grapes hanging from the elmtrees.
The slightly trembling water
Dropping a fine yellow silt where the sun stays;
And the crabs bask near the edge,
The weedy edge, alive with small snakes and bloodsuckers,—   70
I have come to a still, but not a deep center,
A point outside the glittering current;
My eyes stare at the bottom of a river,
At the irregular stones, iridescent sandgrains,
My mind moves in more than one place,   75
In a country half-land, half-water.

I am renewed by death, thought of my death,
The dry scent of a dying garden in September,
The wind fanning the ash of a low fire.
What I love is near at hand,   80
Always, in earth and air.

4

The lost self changes,
Turning toward the sea,
A sea-shape turning around,—
An old man with his feet before the fire,   85
In robes of green, in garments of adieu.

A man faced with his own immensity
Wakes all the waves, all their loose wandering fire.
The murmur of the absolute, the why

Of being born fails on his naked ears.   90
His spirit moves like monumental wind
That gentles on a sunny blue plateau.
He is the end of things, the final man.

All finite things reveal infinitude:
The mountain with its singular bright shade   95
Like the blue shine on freshly frozen snow,
The after-light upon ice-burdened pines;
Odor of basswood on a mountain-slope,
A scent beloved of bees;
Silence of water above a sunken tree: 100
The pure serene of memory in one man,—
A ripple widening from a single stone
Winding around the waters of the world.

                                                                        1964

⊷◄ ELIZABETH BISHOP ►⊶
(1911–1979)

Some of Elizabeth Bishop's most persistent themes—her outsider's perspective, her
fascination with travel, and her search for an abiding home in a changing world—
were set in motion during her childhood, which was characterized by loss and dis-
placement. Born in Worcester, Massachusetts, Bishop spent her early years in
Great Village, Nova Scotia, where she was raised by her maternal grandparents
after her father died when she was eight months old. Unable to recover from the
grief, her mother was hospitalized intermittently for nervous breakdowns until
she was finally committed to a public sanitarium in 1916. Bishop never saw her
again. In 1917 Bishop's wealthy paternal grandparents brought her to live with
them in Worcester, and their icy propriety and class bias intensified her sense of
dislocation. Lonely and isolated, she developed asthma, eczema, and bronchitis so
severe that after only nine months she was taken in by her mother's sister from
Boston. Although her health improved under her aunt's care, Bishop's illnesses
were serious enough that she had little formal education until high school, and
she experienced chronic asthma for the rest of her life.

 After graduating from the Walnut Hill boarding school, Bishop entered Vassar College, where she encountered the poetry of Marianne Moore and was immediately drawn to its descriptive clarity and precision. In her senior year she met
Moore, who became her friend and mentor. But Moore's supportive criticism of
Bishop's poetry was offered primarily by correspondence, for after she received
her B.A. from Vassar in 1934 Bishop traveled frequently, living on funds from her
father's estate. Between 1935 and 1947 she spent time in Europe, Morocco, Massachusetts, Maine, North Carolina, Mexico, Nova Scotia, and Haiti, and shuttled
between New York and Key West, where she bought a house with her friend and
lover, Louise Crane. The critical esteem generated by her first book, *North &
South* (1946), brought Bishop residencies at the Yaddo artists' colony. On the rec-
ommendation of her new friend Robert Lowell, she was appointed the Poetry Con-

sultant to the Library of Congress (1949–1950). Despite these successes, Bishop suffered increasingly from depression and alcoholism, and she felt uncomfortable with literary life in the United States.

In November 1951, on a traveling fellowship from Bryn Mawr College, she left on a trip that would unexpectedly change her life. Intending to sail around the world, Bishop was stalled in Rio de Janeiro by a severe allergic reaction to cashew fruit. A wealthy Brazilian friend, Lota de Macedo Soares, nursed her back to health, and the two women fell in love. Bishop's stopover evolved into a fifteen-year stay with Soares, who provided her with the emotional security she craved and helped her curb her alcoholism. Under Soares's care, Bishop was very productive, writing poems and prose not only about the landscape and culture of Brazil, but also about her childhood. In 1955, her second book, *A Cold Spring*, appeared together with the work from her first book as *Poems: North & South—A Cold Spring* and won the Pulitzer Prize. *Questions of Travel* appeared in 1965, and *The Complete Poems* (1969) won the National Book Award in 1970.

By 1970, however, Bishop's life had changed again, because Soares had committed suicide in 1967. Although Bishop tried to stay in Brazil, she found life there difficult to manage without her partner, and in 1970 she returned to the United States. Until her death in 1979, she taught at Harvard, and also briefly at the University of Washington and New York University. She also traveled widely with a new partner, Alice Methfessel, and spent summers in Maine. In 1976, she won the Books Abroad/Neustadt International Prize for Literature, and her *Geography III* (1976) received the Pulitzer Prize in 1977. Her work was collected posthumously in *The Complete Poems* (1983), *The Collected Prose* (1984), and *One Art: Selected Letters* (1994).

John Ashbery once jokingly described Bishop as "a poet's poet's poet"—a remark that describes her high reputation among her literary colleagues but low profile among the public during her lifetime. Initially categorized by reviewers as "descriptive" and "reticent," Bishop's poetry has increasingly been recognized for its complexity of thought and emotion and seemingly effortless mastery of form. Rather than present a static view of the world, Bishop adjusts perspectives through shifts of scale, unexpected questions, incremental revisions and repetitions, shifts of verb tenses, and similes that pair markedly different elements. Such strategies enable her to convey a sense of the mind in action. Her descriptions, despite their detailed precision, stress not only the mind's mutability but its efforts to come to terms with an unpredictable world. Bishop prefers disorder to an order that inhibits possibility, and she is attracted to scenes whose pleasant chaos allows for the casual but exact perceptions that make the ordinary things appear extraordinary and the extraordinary feel oddly familiar. Bishop's fascination with surrealistic dreamscapes colors many of the poems in *North & South*, but her later poems often emphasize what she called in a letter to the poet Anne Stevenson the "always-more-successful surrealism of everyday life": incongruities that marked her experience of Brazil and childhood in Nova Scotia, or the "unexpected moments of empathy" discovered in mundane settings such as a gas station, a dentist's waiting room, or on a bus ride.

Although her work became more openly autobiographical as she aged, she disliked the sensationalism of Confessional poetry, arguing in 1967 that, "now the idea is that we live in a horrible and terrifying world, and the worst moments of horrible and terrifying lives are an allegory of the world. . . . The tendency is to overdo the morbidity. You just wish they'd keep some of these things to themselves." Bishop preferred understatement to grand gestures and stove for naturalness of tone. In their unexpected conjunctions of order and irregularity, Bishop's forms often appear casual and unpremeditated even when they adhere to exacting patterns. Likewise, the perspective of the outsider—the traveler, the child, the lesbian—allows Bishop to scrutinize the world close-up, from unaccustomed angles, and yet maintain a sense of foreignness that heightens the clarity of her perceptions. Above all, Bishop mediates between divisions—whether tonal, such as her balance between weariness and lightness, or thematic, such as her longing for permanence and acceptance of change—and never ceases to question complacency.

The Fish

I caught a tremendous fish
and held him beside the boat
half out of water, with my hook
fast in a corner of his mouth.
He didn't fight.   5
He hadn't fought at all.
He hung a grunting weight,
battered and venerable
and homely. Here and there
his brown skin hung in strips   10
like ancient wallpaper,
and its pattern of darker brown
was like wallpaper:
shapes like full-blown roses
stained and lost through age.   15
He was speckled with barnacles,
fine rosettes of lime,
and infested
with tiny white sea-lice,
and underneath two or three   20
rags of green weed hung down.
While his gills were breathing in
the terrible oxygen
—the frightening gills,
fresh and crisp with blood,   25
that can cut so badly—
I thought of the coarse white flesh
packed in like feathers,
the big bones and the little bones,
the dramatic reds and blacks   30
of his shiny entrails,
and the pink swim-bladder
like a big peony.
I looked into his eyes

which were far larger than mine 35
but shallower, and yellowed,
the irises backed and packed
with tarnished tinfoil
seen through the lenses
of old scratched isinglass. 40
They shifted a little, but not
to return my stare.
—It was more like the tipping
of an object toward the light.
I admired his sullen face, 45
the mechanism of his jaw,
and then I saw
that from his lower lip
—if you could call it a lip—
grim, wet, and weaponlike, 50
hung five old pieces of fish-line,
or four and a wire leader
with the swivel still attached,
with all their five big hooks
grown firmly in his mouth. 55
A green line, frayed at the end
where he broke it, two heavier lines,
and a fine black thread
still crimped from the strain and snap
when it broke and he got away. 60
Like medals with their ribbons
frayed and wavering,
a five-haired beard of wisdom
trailing from his aching jaw.
I stared and stared 65
and victory filled up
the little rented boat,
from the pool of bilge
where oil had spread a rainbow
around the rusted engine 70
to the bailer rusted orange,
the sun-cracked thwarts,
the oarlocks on their strings,
the gunnels—until everything
was rainbow, rainbow, rainbow! 75
And I let the fish go.

1946

The Map

Land lies in water; it is shadowed green.
Shadows, or are they shallows, at its edges

showing the line of long sea-weeded ledges
where weeds hang to the simple blue from green.
Or does the land lean down to lift the sea from under,   5
drawing it unperturbed around itself?
Along the fine tan sandy shelf
is the land tugging at the sea from under?

The shadow of Newfoundland lies flat and still.
Labrador's yellow, where the moony Eskimo   10
has oiled it. We can stroke these lovely bays,
under a glass as if they were expected to blossom,
or as if to provide a clean cage for invisible fish.
The names of seashore towns run out to sea,
the names of cities cross the neighboring mountains   15
—the printer here experiencing the same excitement
as when emotion too far exceeds its cause.
These peninsulas take the water between thumb and finger
like women feeling for the smoothness of yard-goods.

Mapped waters are more quiet than the land is,   20
lending the land their waves' own conformation:
and Norway's hare runs south in agitation,
profiles investigate the sea, where land is.
Are they assigned, or can the countries pick their colors?
—What suits the character or the native waters best.   25
Topography displays no favorites; North's as near as West.
More delicate than the historians' are the map-makers' colors.

1946

At the Fishhouses

Although it is a cold evening,
down by one of the fishhouses
and old man sits netting,
his net, in the gloaming almost invisible,
a dark purple-brown,   5
and his shuttle worn and polished.
The air smells so strong of codfish
it makes one's nose run and one's eyes water.
The five fishhouses have steeply peaked roofs
and narrow, cleated gangplanks slant up   10
to storerooms in the gables
for the wheelbarrows to be pushed up and down on.
All is silver: the heavy surface of the sea,
swelling slowly as if considering spilling over,
is opaque, but the silver of the benches,   15
the lobster pots, and masts, scattered
among the wild jagged rocks,
is of an apparent translucence

like the small old buildings with an emerald moss
growing on their shoreward walls.   20
The big fish tubs are completely lined
with layers of beautiful herring scales
and the wheelbarrows are similarly plastered
with creamy iridescent coats of mail,
with small iridescent flies crawling on them.   25
Up on the little slope behind the houses,
set in the sparse bright sprinkle of grass,
is an ancient wooden capstan,
cracked, with two long bleached handles
and some melancholy stains, like dried blood,   30
where the ironwork has rusted.
The old man accepts a Lucky Strike.
He was a friend of my grandfather.
We talk of the decline in the population
and of codfish and herring   35
while he waits for a herring boat to come in.
There are sequins on his vest and on his thumb.
He has scraped the scales, the principal beauty,
from unnumbered fish with that black old knife,
the blade of which is almost worn away.   40

Down at the water's edge, at the place
where they haul up the boats, up the long ramp
descending into the water, thin silver
tree trunks are laid horizontally
across the gray stones, down and down   45
at intervals of four or five feet.

Cold dark deep and absolutely clear,
element bearable to no mortal,
to fish and to seals . . . One seal particularly
I have seen here evening after evening.   50
He was curious about me. He was interested in music;
like me a believer in total immersion,
so I used to sing him Baptist hymns.
I also sang "A Mighty Fortress Is Our God."
He stood up in the water and regarded me   55
steadily, moving his head a little.
Then he would disappear, then suddenly emerge
almost in the same spot, with a sort of shrug
as if it were against his better judgment.
Cold dark deep and absolutely clear,   60
the clear gray icy water . . . Back, behind us,
the dignified tall firs begin.
Bluish, associating with their shadows,
a million Christmas trees stand
waiting for Christmas. The water seems suspended   65
above the rounded gray and blue-gray stones.

I have seen it over and over, the same sea, the same,
slightly, indifferently swinging above the stones,
icily free above the stones,
above the stones and then the world.   70
If you should dip your hand in,
your wrist would ache immediately,
your bones would begin to ache and your hand would burn
as if the water were a transmutation of fire
that feeds on stones and burns with a dark gray flame.   75
If you tasted it, it would first taste bitter,
then briny, then surely burn your tongue.
It is like what we imagine knowledge to be:
dark, salt, clear, moving, utterly free,
drawn from the cold hard mouth   80
of the world, derived from the rocky breasts
forever, flowing and drawn, and since
our knowledge is historical, flowing, and flown.

1955

The Armadillo

For Robert Lowell

This is the time of year
when almost every night
the frail, illegal fire balloons appear.
Climbing the mountain height,

rising toward a saint   5
still honored in these parts,
the paper chambers flush and fill with light
that comes and goes, like hearts.

Once up against the sky it's hard
to tell them from the stars—   10
planets, that is—the tinted ones:
Venus going down, or Mars,

or the pale green one. With a wind,
they flare and falter, wobble and toss;
but if it's still they steer between   15
the kite sticks of the Southern Cross,[1]

receding, dwindling, solemnly
and steadily forsaking us,
or, in the downdraft from a peak,
suddenly turning dangerous.   20

---

1. A constellation visible in the Southern hemisphere.

Last night another big one fell.
It splattered like an egg of fire
against the cliff behind the house.
The flame ran down. We saw the pair

of owls who nest there flying up   25
and up, their whirling black-and-white
stained bright pink underneath, until
they shrieked up out of sight.

The ancient owls' nest must have burned.
Hastily, all alone,   30
a glistening armadillo left the scene,
rose-flecked, head down, tail down,

and then a baby rabbit jumped out,
short-eared, to our surprise.
So soft!—a handful of intangible ash   35
with fixed, ignited eyes.

Too pretty, dreamlike mimicry!
O falling fire and piercing cry
and panic, and a weak mailed fist
clenched ignorant against the sky!   40

                                                1965

Questions of Travel

There are too many waterfalls here; the crowded streams
hurry too rapidly down to the sea,
and the pressure of so many clouds on the mountaintops
makes them spill over the sides in soft slow-motion,
turning to waterfalls under our very eyes.   5
—For if those streaks, those mile-long, shiny, tearstains,
aren't waterfalls yet,
in a quick age or so, as ages go here,
they probably will be.
But if the streams and clouds keep travelling, travelling, 10
the mountains look like the hulls of capsized ships,
slime-hung and barnacled.

Think of the long trip home.
Should we have stayed at home and thought of here?
Where should we be today?   15
Is it right to be watching strangers in a play
in this strangest of theatres?
What childishness is it that while there's a breath of life
in our bodies, were are determined to rush
to see the sun the other way around?   20
The tiniest green hummingbird in the world?

To stare at some inexplicable old stonework,
inexplicable and impenetrable,
at any view,
instantly seen and always, always delightful?   25
Oh, must we dream our dreams
and have them, too?
And have we room
for one more folded sunset, still quite warm?

But surely it would have been a pity   30
not to have seen the trees along this road,
really exaggerated in their beauty,
not to have seen them gesturing
like noble pantomimists, robed in pink.
—Not to have had to stop for gas and heard   35
the sad, two-noted, wooden tune
of disparate wooden clogs
carelessly clacking over
a grease-stained filling-station floor.
(In another country the clogs would all be tested.   40
Each pair there would have identical pitch.)
—A pity not to have heard
the other, less primitive music of the fat brown bird
who sings above the broken gasoline pump
in a bamboo church of Jesuit baroque: 45
three towers, five silver crosses.
—Yes, a pity not to have pondered,
blurr'dly and inconclusively,
on what connection can exist for centuries
between the crudest wooden footwear   50
and, careful and finicky,
the whittled fantasies of wooden cages.
—Never to have studied history in
the weak calligraphy of songbirds' cages.
—And never to have had to listen to rain   55
so much like politicians' speeches:
two hours of unrelenting oratory
and then a sudden golden silence
in which the traveller takes a notebook, writes:

"Is it lack of imagination that makes us come   60
to imagined places, not just stay at home?
Or could Pascal have been not entirely right
about just sitting quietly in one's room?

Continent, city, country, society:
the choice is never wide and never free.   65
And here, or there . . . No. Should we have stayed at home,
wherever that may be?"

1965

Visits to St. Elizabeths[2]

[1950]

This is the house of Bedlam.[3]

This is the man
that lies in the house of Bedlam.

This is the time
of the tragic man   5
that lies in the house of Bedlam.

This is a wristwatch
telling the time
of the talkative man
that lies in the house of Bedlam.   10

This is a sailor
wearing the watch
that tells the time
of the honored man
that lies in the house of Bedlam.   15

This is the roadstead all of board
reached by the sailor
wearing the watch
that tells the time
of the old, brave man   20
that lies in the house of Bedlam.

These are the years and the walls of the ward,
the winds and clouds of the sea of board
sailed by the sailor
wearing the watch   25
that tells the time
of the cranky man
that lies in the house of Bedlam.

This is the Jew in a newspaper hat
that dances weeping down the ward   30
over the creaking sea of board
beyond the sailor
winding his watch

2. The poet Ezra Pound, declared unfit to stand trial for treason after World War II, was kept in St. Elizabeth's hospital as a mental patient from 1946 to 1958. Pound was infamous for his fascism and anti-
Semitism, but was supported by friends who were writers on the basis of his contribution to modern
literature. Many writers have told of their visits to him in the hospital, but Bishop's use of the nursery
rhyme, "This is the House that Jack Built," adds a special layer of irony to the situation.
3. A madhouse or asylum. One of the earliest of these is said to have been St. Mary's of Bethlehem,
founded in London in the thirteenth century.

that tells the time
of the cruel man   35
that lies in the house of Bedlam.

This is a world of books gone flat.
This is a Jew in a newspaper hat
that dances weeping down the ward
over the creaking sea of board   40
of the batty sailor
that winds his watch
that tells the time
of the busy man
that lies in the house of Bedlam.   45

This is a boy that pats the floor
to see if the world is there, is flat,
for the widowed Jew in the newspaper hat
that dances weeping down the ward
waltzing the length of a weaving board   50
by the silent sailor
that hears his watch
that ticks the time
of the tedious man
that lies in the house of Bedlam.   55

These are the years and the walls and the door
that shut on a boy that pats the floor
to feel if the world is there and flat.
This is a Jew in a newspaper hat
that dances joyfully down the ward   60
into the parting seas of board
past the staring sailor
that shakes his watch
that tells the time
of the poet, the man   65
that lies in the house of Bedlam.

This is the soldier home from the war.
These are the years and the walls and the door
that shut on a boy that pats the floor
to see if the world is round or flat.   70
This is a Jew in a newspaper hat
that dances carefully down the ward,
walking the plank of a coffin board
with the crazy sailor
that shows his watch   75
that tells the time
of the wretched man
that lies in the house of Bedlam.

1965

In the Waiting Room

In Worcester, Massachusetts,
I went with Aunt Consuelo
to keep her dentist's appointment
and sat and waited for her
in the dentist's waiting room.   5
It was winter. It got dark
early. The waiting room
was full of grown-up people,
arctics and overcoats,
lamps and magazines.   10
My aunt was inside
what seemed like a long time
and while I waited I read
the *National Geographic*
(I could read) and carefully   15
studied the photographs:
the inside of a volcano,
black, and full of ashes;
then it was spilling over
in rivulets of fire.   20
Osa and Martin Johnson[4]
dressed in riding breeches,
laced boots, and pith helmets.
A dead man slung on a pole
—"Long Pig,"[5] the caption said.   25
Babies with pointed heads
wound round and round with string;
black, naked women with necks
wound round and round with wire
like the necks of light bulbs.   30
Their breasts were horrifying.
I read it right straight through.
I was too shy to stop.
And then I looked at the cover:
the yellow margins, the date.   35

Suddenly, from inside,
came an *oh!* of pain
—Aunt Consuelo's voice—
not very loud or long.
I wasn't at all surprised;   40
even then I knew she was
a foolish, timid woman.
I might have been embarrassed,

---

4. Osa (1894–1953) and Martin (1883–1937) Johnson were popular explorers, authors of travel books and film scripts. Their adventures were often chronicled in the pages of *National Geographic*.
5. Human meat eaten by cannibals.

but wasn't. What took me
completely by surprise   45
was that it was *me:*
my voice, in my mouth.
Without thinking at all
I was my foolish aunt,
I—we—were falling, falling,   50
our eyes glued to the cover
of the *National Geographic,*
February, 1918.

I said to myself: three days
and you'll be seven years old.   55
I was saying it to stop
the sensation of falling off
the round, turning world
into cold, blue-black space.
But I felt: you are an *I,*   60
you are an *Elizabeth,*
you are one of *them.*
Why should you be one, too?
I scarcely dared to look
to see what it was I was.   65
I gave a sidelong glance
—I couldn't look any higher—
at shadowy gray knees,
trousers and skirts and boots
and different pairs of hands   70
lying under the lamps.
I knew that nothing stranger
had ever happened, that nothing
stranger could ever happen.
Why should I be my aunt,   75
or me, or anyone?
What similarities—
boots, hands, the family voice
I felt in my throat, or even
the *National Geographic*   80
and those awful hanging breasts—
held us all together
or made us all just one?
How—I didn't know any
word for it—how "unlikely" . . .   85
How had I come to be here,
like them, and overhear
a cry of pain that could have
got loud and worse but hadn't?

The waiting room was bright   90
and too hot. It was sliding

beneath a big black wave,
another, and another.

Then I was back in it.
The War was on. Outside,   95
in Worchester, Massachusetts,
were night and slush and cold,
and it was still the fifth
of February, 1918.

                                                          1976

The Moose

For Grace Bulmer Bowers

From narrow provinces
of fish and bread and tea,
home of the long tides
where the bay leaves the sea
twice a day and takes   5
the herrings long rides,

where if the river
enters or retreats
in a wall of brown foam
depends on if it meets   10
the bay coming in,
the bay not at home;

where, silted red,
sometimes the sun sets
facing a red sea,   15
and others, veins the flats'
lavender, rich mud
in burning rivulets;

on red, gravelly roads,
down rows of sugar maples,   20
past clapboard farmhouses
and neat, clapboard churches,
bleached, ridged as clamshells,
past twin silver birches,

through late afternoon   25
a bus journeys west,
the windshield flashing pink,
pink glancing off of metal,
brushing the dented flank
of blue, beat-up enamel;   30

down hollows, up rises,
and waits, patient, while
a lone traveller gives
kisses and embraces
to seven relatives   35
and a collie supervises.

Goodbye to the elms,
to the farm, to the dog.
The bus starts. The light
grows richer; the fog,   40
shifting, salty, thin,
comes closing in.

Its cold, round crystals
form and slide and settle
in the white hens' feathers,   45
in gray glazed cabbages,
on the cabbage roses
and lupins like apostles;

the sweet peas cling
to their wet white string   50
on the whitewashed fences;
bumblebees creep
inside the foxgloves,
and evening commences.

One stop at Bass River.   55
Then the Economies—
Lower, Middle, Upper;
Five Islands, Five Houses,
where a woman shakes a tablecloth
out after supper.   60

A pale flickering. Gone.
The Tantramar marshes
and the smell of salt hay.
An iron bridge trembles
and a loose plank rattles   65
but doesn't give way.

On the left, a red light
swims through the dark:
a ship's port lantern.
Two rubber boots show,   70
illuminated, solemn.
A dog gives one bark.

A woman climbs in
with two market bags,
brisk, freckled, elderly.   75

"A grand night. Yes, sir,
all the way to Boston."
She regards us amicably.

Moonlight as we enter
the New Brunswick woods,   80
hairy, scratchy, splintery;
moonlight and mist
caught in them like lamb's wool
on bushes in a pasture.

The passengers lie back.   85
Snores. Some long sighs.
A dreamy divagation
begins in the night,
a gentle, auditory,
slow hallucination. . . .   90

In the creakings and noises,
an old conversation
—not concerning us,
but recognizable somewhere,
back in the bus: 95
Grandparents' voices

uninterruptedly
talking, in Eternity:
names being mentioned,
things cleared up finally;   100
what he said, what she said,
who got pensioned;

deaths, deaths and sicknesses;
the year he remarried;
the year (something) happened.   105
She died in childbirth.
That was the son lost
when the schooner foundered.

He took to drink. Yes.
She went to the bad.   110
When Amos began to pray
even in the store and
finally the family had
to put him away.

"Yes . . ." that peculiar   115
affirmative. "Yes . . ."
A sharp, indrawn breath,
half groan, half acceptance,
that means "Life's like that.
We know *it* (also death)."   120

Talking the way they talked
in the old featherbed,
peacefully, on and on,
dim lamplight in the hall,
down in the kitchen, the dog   125
tucked in her shawl.

Now, it's all right now
even to fall asleep
just as on all those nights.
—Suddenly the bus driver   130
stops with a jolt,
turns off his lights.

A moose has come out of
the impenetrable wood
and stands there, looms, rather,   135
in the middle of the road.
It approaches; it sniffs at
the bus's hot hood.

Towering, antlerless,
high as a church,   140
homely as a house
(or, safe as houses).
A man's voice assures us
"Perfectly harmless. . . ."

Some of the passengers   145
exclaim in whispers,
childishly, softly,
"Sure are big creatures."
"It's awful plain."
"Look! It's a she!"   150

Taking her time,
she looks the bus over,
grand, otherworldly.
Why, why do we feel
(we all feel) this sweet   155
sensation of joy?

"Curious creatures,"
says our quiet driver,
rolling his *r*'s.
"Look at that, would you."   160
Then he shifts gears.
For a moment longer,

by craning backward,
the moose can be seen

on the moonlight macadam;[6]   165
then there's a dim
smell of moose, an acrid
smell of gasoline.

1976

One Art

The art of losing isn't hard to master;
so many things seem filled with the intent
to be lost that their loss is no disaster.

Lose something every day. Accept the fluster
of lost door keys, the hour badly spent.   5
The art of losing isn't hard to master.

Then practice losing farther, losing faster:
places, and names, and where it was you meant
to travel. None of these will bring disaster.

I lost my mother's watch. And look! my last, or   10
next-to-last, of three loved houses went.
The art of losing isn't hard to master.

I lost two cities, lovely ones. And, vaster,
some realms I owned, two rivers, a continent.
I miss them, but it wasn't a disaster.   15

—Even losing you (the joking voice, a gesture
I love) I shan't have lied. It's evident
the art of losing's not too hard to master
though it may look like (*Write* it!) like disaster.

1976

◄ J. V. CUNNINGHAM ►
(1911–1985)

James Vincent Cunningham was born in Cumberland, Maryland, one of four children of a working-class Irish Catholic family. In his early teens his father, a steamshovel operator, moved the family to Billings, Montana. Cunningham there attended St. Vincent's Parochial School, spending summers on a nearby ranch. When he was twelve, his family moved to Denver, where he completed the eighth grade and the following year entered a rigorous Jesuit high school that required four years of Latin and Greek. When Cunningham was fifteen, his father died in an industrial accident,

---

6. A pavement made with compacted stone, named for its inventor, John L. McAdam (1756–1836).

leaving the family in difficult straits. After graduating from high school at sixteen, Cunningham worked for various Denver newspapers and as a delivery boy for a local brokerage house. His literary consciousness was formed not only by the discipline of Catholic schools, but also by the austere emptiness of Montana, the family troubles in Denver, and the deprivations of the Great Depression.

Cunningham spent the first few years of the Depression wandering through the Southwest, looking for work. Meanwhile he satisfied his hunger for education by constant reading. His early grounding in the classics had been strong, but on his own he discovered Eliot and Pound, as well as the satires of Jonathan Swift. With the help of the poet Yvor Winters, Cunningham eventually entered Stanford University. (The impoverished student initially lived in a tiny study shed in Winters's backyard.) Cunningham took is B.A. in 1934 and a Ph.D. eleven years later. Eventually, he taught at a number of universities, including Harvard and the University of Virginia, Charlottesville, before settling at Brandeis in 1953 (where one of his best students was poet Timothy Steele.) The influence of Winters upon Cunningham's life and work may have been overstated by some critics. Certainly Cunningham was grateful for the older poet's help, and the two shared a commitment to formal verse. Yet Cunningham took his own path. His poetry has a remarkable sense of humor, a quality utterly lacking in Winters's work. He also had little appetite for the sort of canon-making criticism in which Winters engaged. He divided his attention between Renaissance scholarship and the careful crafting of his poems. Cunningham was never a prolific writer. The first of his slim poetry collections, *The Helmsman*, appeared in a small hand-printed edition in 1942, and five more small books were published before *The Collected Poems and Epigrams of J. V. Cunningham* in 1971.

Cunningham is the consummate outsider of modern American poetry. His works seems—at least initially—to stand at complete remove from the general trends of his era. He eschewed free verse, rejected stylistic fragmentation, rarely relied on imagery as a structural device, and unabashedly reveled in abstract ideas. And yet in his own idiosyncratic way Cunningham is a thoroughly modern poet. The characteristic compression of his poems and elliptical use of imagery reflect the influence of Pound, Stevens, and the Imagists. His antiromanticism and cultural pessimism show the presence of Eliot. His savage wit and genius for memorable concision, however, are entirely his own. Cunningham is indisputably the finest epigrammatist in American literature, and his best short lyrics are remarkable in their evocative force, especially his masterful 1964 cycle of love poems, *To What Strangers, What Welcome*. In his prose Cunningham writes of "a chastity of diction and a crispness of technique," adding to his values a "sinuous exacting speech." Cunningham held himself to too high a standard to succumb to verbosity and imprecision. If these strictures sometimes seem too confining, too limiting, he nevertheless left behind a small body of masterful poems that, to paraphrase Robert Frost, are difficult to get rid of.

-‹•›——‹•›-

For My Contemporaries

How time reverses
The proud in heart!

I now make verses
Who aimed at art.

But I sleep well.   5
Ambitious boys
Whose big lines swell
With spiritual noise,

Despise me not,
And be not queasy   10
To praise somewhat:
Verse is not easy.

But rage who will.
Time that procured me
Good sense and skill   15
Of madness cured me.

1942

In the Thirtieth Year

In the thirtieth year of life
I took my heart to be my wife,

And as I turn in bed by night
I have my heart for my delight.

No other heart may mine estrange   5
For my heart changes as I change,

And it is bound, and I am free,
And with my death it dies with me.

1950

To My Wife

And does the heart grow old? You know
In the indiscriminate green
Of summer or in earliest snow
A landscape is another scene,

Inchoate and anonymous,   5
And every rock and bush and drift
As our affections alter us
Will alter with the season's shift.

So love by love we come at last,
As through the exclusions of a rhyme,   10
Or the exactions of a past,
To the simplicity of time,

The antiquity of grace, where yet
We live in terror and delight
With love as quiet as regret   15
And love like anger in the night.

1960

To What Strangers, What Welcome

A Sequence of Short Poems

When we parted,
I told her I should see the King again,
And, having seen him, might go back again
To see her face once more. But I shall see
No more the lady Vivian. Let her love
What man she may, no other love than mine
Shall be an index of her memories.
I fear no man who may come after me,
And I see none. I see her, still in green,
Beside the fountain. I shall not go back. . . .
*   If I come not,*
The lady Vivian will remember me,
And say: "I knew him when his heart was young,
Though I have lost him now. Time called him home,
And that was as it was; for much is lost
Between Broceliande and Camelot."
                    Edwin Arlington Robinson, *Merlin*, 7.425–42

[1]

I drive Westward. Tumble and loco weed
Persist. And in the vacancies of need,
The leisure of desire, whirlwinds a face
As luminous as love, lost as this place.

[2]

On either side of the white line
The emblems of a life appear
In turn: purpose like lodgepole pine
Competitive and thin, and fear

Agile as aspen in a storm.   5
And then the twilit harboring
In a small park. The room is warm.
And by the ache of traveling

Removed from all immediacy,
From all time, I as time grows late   10
Sense in disordered fantasy
The sound and smell of love and hate.

[3]

In a few days now when two memories meet
In that place of disease, waste, and desire
Where forms receptive, featureless, and vast
Find occupation, in that narrow dark,
That warm sweat of a carnal tenderness,   5
What figure in the pantheon of lust,
What demon is our god? What name subsumes
That act external to our sleeping selves?
Not pleasure—it is much too broad and narrow—,
Not sex, not for the moment love, but pride,   10
And not in prowess, but pride undefined,
Autonomous in its unthought demands,
A bit of vanity, but mostly pride.

[4]

You have here no otherness,
Unaddressed correspondent,
No gaunt clavicles, no hair
Of bushy intimacy.
You are not, and I write here   5
The name of no signature
To the unsaid—a letter
At midnight, a memorial
And occupation of time.

I'll not summon you, or feel   10
In the alert dream the give
And stay of flesh, the tactile
Conspiracy.
                    The snow falls
With its inveterate meaning,
And I follow the barbed wire   15
To trough, to barn, to the house,
To what strangers, what welcome
In the late blizzard of time.

On the highway cars flashing,
Occasional and random   20
As pain gone without symptom,
And fear drifts with the North wind.
We neither give nor receive:
The unfinishable drink
Left on the table, the sleep   25
Alcoholic and final
In the mute exile of time.

[5]

The soft lights, the companionship, the beers,
And night promises everything you lacked.

The short drive, the unmade bed, and night in tears
Hysteric in the elemental act.

[6]

It was in Vegas. Celibate and able
I left the silver dollars on the table
And tried the show. The black-out, baggy pants,
Of course, and then this answer to romance:
Her ass twitching as if it had the fits,   5
Her gold crotch grinding, her athletic tits,
One clock, the other counter clockwise twirling.
It was enough to stop a man from girling.

[7]

A traveller, the highway my guide,
And a little bastard of a dog
My friend. I have pin-ups for passion
As I go moseying about these scenes,
Myself improbable as yucca,   5
Illusory as the bright desert,
And finally here: the surf breaking,
Repetitive and varied as love
Enacted, and inevitably
The last rim of sunset on the sea.   10

[8]

The night is still. The unfailing surf
In passion and subsidence moves
As at a distance. The glass walls,
And redwood, are my utmost being.
And is there there in the last shadow,   5
There in the final privacies
Of unaccosted grace,—is there,
Gracing the tedium to death,
An intimation? Something much
Like love, like loneliness adrowse   10
In states more primitive than peace,
In the warm wonder of winter sun.

[9]

Innocent to innocent,
One asked, What is perfect love?
Not knowing it is not love,
What is imperfect—some kind
Of love or other, some kind   5
Of interchange with wanting.
There when all else is wanting,
Something by which we make do.

So, impaired, uninnocent,
If I love you—as I do—   10
To the very perfection
Of perfect imperfection,
It's that I care more for you
Than for my feeling for you.

[10]

A half hour for coffee, and at night
An hour or so of unspoken speech,
Hemming a summer dress as the tide
Turns at the right time.
                        Must it be sin,
This consummation of who knows what?   5
This sharp cry at entrance, once, and twice?
This unfulfilled fulfilment?
                              Something
That happens because it must happen.
We live in the given. Consequence,
And lack of consequence, both fail us.   10
Good is what we can do with evil.

[11]

I drive Eastward. The ethics of return,
Like the night sound of coyotes on a hill
Heard in eroded canyons of concern,
Disposes what has happened, and what will.

[12]

Absence, my angel, presence at my side,
I know you as an article of faith
By desert, prairie, and this stonewalled road—
As much my own as is the thought of death.

[13] NESCIT VOX MISSA REVERTI . . .[1]

The once hooked ever after lives in lack,
And the once said never finds it way back.

[14]

I write only to say this,
In a syllabic dryness
As inglorious as I feel:
Sometime before drinking time
For the first time in some weeks   5
I heard of you, the casual

---

1. (Latin) "The word sent out cannot return . . ." from the *Ars Poetica* of Horace.

News of a new life, silence
Of unconfronted feeling
And maples in the slant sun
The gay color of decay.   10
What is unforgivable,
My darling, that you loved me?

[15]

Identity, that spectator
Of what he calls himself, that net
And aggregate of energies
In transient combination—some
So marginal are they mine? Or is   5
There mine? I sit in the last warmth
Of a New England fall, and I?
A premise of identity
Where the lost hurries to be lost,
Both in its own best interests   10
And in the interests of life.

1964

Ten Epigrams

(From *"A Century of Epigrams"*)

12

Time heals not: it extends a sorrow's scope
As goldsmith's gold, which we may wear like hope.

14

On the cover of my first book

This garish and red cover made me start.
I who amused myself with quietness
Am here discovered. In this flowery dress
I read the wild wallpaper of my heart.

21

Grief restrains grief as dams torrential rain,
And time grows fertile with extended pain.

30

Kiss me goodbye, to whom I've only been
Cause for uncloistered virtue, not for sin.

42

Soft found a way to damn me undefended:
I was forgiven who had not offended.

43

This Humanist whom no beliefs constrained
Grew so broad-minded he was scatter-brained.

48

Epigraph to The Judge Is Fury[2]

These the assizes: here the charge, denial,
Proof and disproof: the poem is the trial.
Experience is defendant, and the jury
Peers of tradition, and the judge is fury.

50

Naked I came, naked I leave the scene,
And naked was my pastime in between.

56

On Doctor Drink

A reader (did he buy it, borrow, beg,
Or read it in a bookstore on one leg?)
Dislikes my book; calls it, to my discredit,
A book you can't put down before you've read it.
Yet in this paucity, this drouth of phrases,   5
There are as many as in children phases:
The trivial, vulgar, and exalted jostle
Each other in a way to make the apostle
Of culture and right feeling shudder faintly.
It is a shudder that affects the saintly.   10
It is a shudder by which I am faulted.
I like the trivial, vulgar, and exalted.

60

Here lies New Critic who would fox us
With his poetic paradoxes.
Though he lies here rigid and quiet,
If he could speak he would deny it.

1971

---

2. This poem was written for Cunningham's second collection of poems, *The Judge Is Fury* (1947).

⋙ JOSEPHINE MILES ⋘
(1911–1985)

Born in Chicago, Josephine Miles grew up in Southern California, where her family moved when she was five in the hopes that a desert climate would mitigate the rheumatoid arthritis she had developed. Severely afflicted by the disease throughout her life, Miles was often confined to a wheelchair and sometimes unable even to use it—needing to be carried from place to place. She argued that her disease gave her the time and determination to write, and she excelled as a poet and scholar. After mastering classical languages in high school, she graduated Phi Beta Kappa from the University of California at Los Angeles in 1932. She then earned her Ph.D. from the University of California at Berkeley in 1938.

On the same day in 1940 she received two letters—the first from the famed Pasadena Playhouse offering her a playwright fellowship, the second from the University of California at Berkeley offering her a teaching job. Without hesitation, she chose the academic career. Her decision proved successful, and she taught at Berkeley until her retirement in 1978. In the intervening years she became, in 1947, the first woman to be tenured in the English Department. Her skill as a teacher may be judged by a list of her famous literary students, which includes A. R. Ammons, William Stafford, Jack Spicer, and Diane Wakoski. Except for two years in Michigan, she lived all of her adult life in California. She died in 1985 at seventy-three.

Miles's first book of poetry, *Lines at Intersection* (1939), found her mature style—concise, understated, and exact—already fully formed. Eight volumes of poetry followed before her *Collected Poems: 1930–1983* (1983) appeared. She was a maverick in both her poetry and scholarship, developing her voice and interests into a distinctive, compelling body of work that often chafes against the norms of her era. Oddly enough, in her scholarship she sought to define such norms. Through statistical analysis of patterns in poetic diction and syntax, she mapped stylistic changes and confluences from the Elizabethan age to the twentieth century. Unlike other literature scholars of her generation, who preferred close commentary on individual poems, Miles examined broad trends. In her most important study, *Eras and Modes in English Poetry* (1957; revised and enlarged 1964), she argues, "It seems to me that by specifying certain characteristics within style and era and by tracing their changes within individual and group usage, we may learn more definitely what are the interrelationships of time and manner and what are the qualities and tempos of artistic change." Clearly written and still useful today, her book teaches the reader not only to pay careful attention to a poet's sentence structure and word choice, but to compare and contrast the stylistic habits of different poets as a means of recognizing not individual idiosyncracies but commonalities shared by a generation.

Her preoccupation with diction and syntax extends to her own poetry. She emphasizes in *Eras and Modes* that "Every word is potentially metaphoric, potentially connotative, potentially intensive or normative, potentially ambiguous in all these ways . . . and every sentence as it limits also empowers every word." Miles's poetry, particularly through her deft lineation, centers the reader's attention on her often unexpected diction—words that carry multiple potential—and the shape of her sentences. Though she often writes about ordinary occasions, she sees herself as a public poet—a moral commentator on contemporary society. At the conclusion to *Eras and Modes,* she looks to the future and suggests that what she calls "the poetry of praise" "can be not only personal and ambiguous, but social and magnanimous, in the magnanimity of a poetry which transfigures what it values."

Miles's poetry can be personal, in that it reflects her experience, but she always turns that experience outward into the social domain, seeking both to evaluate and shape the common good. Although her many books of poetry received praise from reviewers, Miles cannot be easily linked to any particular group or school of poets, and thus her work has not often been credited in overviews of twentieth-century American writing. Moreover, her poetry can at first appear unassuming, only to reveal its power after several readings. In going against the grain, Miles would likely see herself as the individual artist she describes in *Eras and Modes,* who "moves away from the hardened strictures" of the current generation and subtly shifts the compass of poetry.

Reason

Said, Pull her up a bit will you, Mac, I want to unload there.
Said, Pull her up my rear end, first come first serve.
Said, Give her the gun, Bud, he needs a taste of his own bumper.
Then the usher came out and got into the act:

Said, Pull her up, pull her up a bit, we need this space, sir.   5
Said, For God's sake, is this still a free country or what?
You go back and take care of Gary Cooper's horse
And leave me handle my own car.

Saw them unloading the lame old lady,
Ducked out under the wheel and gave her an elbow,   10
Said, All you needed to do was just explain;
Reason, Reason is my middle name.

                                                                                    1955

Riddle

You are a riddle I would not unravel,
You are the riddle my life comprehends.
And who abstracts the marvel
Abstracts the story to its sorriest ends.

But not your riddle. It is patent,   5
Never more than it says, and since that is
Impossible, it is the marvel
Nobody, as I am nobody, believes.

                                                                                    1955

Conception

Death did not come to my mother
Like an old friend.
She was a mother, and she must
Conceive him.

Up and down the bed she fought crying   5
Help me, but death
Was a slow child
Heavy. He

Waited. When he was born
We took and tired him, now he is ready   10
To do his good in the world.

He has my mother's features.
He can go among strangers
To save lives.

1974

Album

This is a hard life you are living
While you are young,
My father said,
As I scratched my casted knees with a paper knife.
By laws of compensation   5
Your old age should be grand.

Not grand, but of a terrible
Compensation, to perceive
Past the energy of survival
In its sadness   10
The hard life of the young.

1979

◦►◄ ROBERT HAYDEN ►◄◦
(1913–1980)

Robert Hayden was born Asa Bundy Sheffey, son of Asa and Ruth Sheffey, in Detroit, Michigan. While still an infant, he was given up by his impoverished mother
to William and Sue Ellen Hayden. His new parents renamed him Robert, and the
poet did not discover until he was forty years old that they had never officially
adopted him. Hayden's childhood contained some stability. As a teenager, he knew
his natural mother, who took an interest in his education. His adoptive parents
tried their best to encourage his interests, but the family was riven by domestic
strife and violence. Sue Ellen Hayden was a storyteller who had experienced firsthand the great migration of blacks after the Civil War. But her troubled past, sug-

gested in "The Ballad of Sue Ellen Westerfield," had left her with a burden of disappointment which she carried to her new life in the North. In a 1972 interview Hayden said:

> My family were uneducated, poor. But worse, much worse, than being poor—there were anyway periods when we lived fairly well—worse than the poverty were the conflicts, the quarreling, the tensions that kept us most of the time on the edge of some shrill domestic calamity. This is what the line "the chronic angers of that house" in my poem "Those Winter Sundays" refers to. We had a terrible love-hate relationship with one another, and dreadful things happened I can never forget.

Another difficulty the young Hayden faced was his extreme nearsightedness. Forced to wear thick glasses, he fell victim to the cruelty of other children. In an effort to protect his weak eyes, teachers limited his reading, so books seemed especially precious to him. Music, books, and theater became the consolations he naturally sought for a painful life. By the time he entered high school, he was already familiar with a variety of poets, including Edna St. Vincent Millay, Carl Sandburg, and Langston Hughes. The critic Arnold Rampersad has written, "He was especially taken with the example of Countee Cullen, whose emotional and lyrical blending of race consciousness with traditional poetics left an immediate mark on Hayden's youthful writing."

Hayden grew up in a racially mixed, poor Detroit neighborhood ironically nicknamed Paradise Valley. But race consciousness was not at first a large part of his pain. In an unfinished autobiography he remembered, "I never thought of the people I knew as anything but human." As a student at Detroit City College during the Depression, however, Hayden became radicalized and wrote protest poetry. After college, he joined the Federal Writers' Project, a Depression-era government program to employ out-of-work journalists, editors, and imaginative writers. In addition to reinforcing his leftist politics, the project helped make Hayden an important poet of history by encouraging his research into antislavery activity. His first collection of poems, *Heart-Shape in the Dust,* was published in 1940. In the same year, he married Erma Inez Morris. Their marriage produced a daughter, Maia, born in 1942. Although brought up a Baptist, Hayden eventually turned to the Baha'i faith, which became a major influence on both his life and writing. The Baha'i believe that all religions are one, that the sexes are equal, and that simplicity of lifestyle is a virtue. Already inclined to ecumenism, the poet became a man whom his fellow poet William Meredith would call "as gifted in humanity as he was in poetry."

An important factor in Hayden's literary development was his friendship with W. H. Auden, with whom he had studied as a graduate student at the University of Michigan in the 1940s. Auden's impeccable craftsmanship and deep humanity inspired Hayden. In 1946 Hayden moved to his first full-time teaching position at Fisk University, in Nashville, Tennessee. He remained there until he was given a professorship at the University of Michigan in 1969—the post he held until his death in 1980. Hayden never won any of the major American literary awards such as the Pulitzer, National Book Award, or Bollingen. His poetic path was too independent, and he never actively sought the public limelight. His most significant award was Grand Prize in Poetry at the First World Festival of Negro Arts in Dakar, Senegal. He did earn one signal honor in his native land—in 1976 Hayden became the first African American to serve as Consultant in Poetry to the Library of Congress.

Although Hayden wrote constantly of African American experience, his poetic models were various. From Yeats, for example, he learned that a poet could be steeped in his own culture and speak of his own people while remaining an individual. When Hayden began to publish his best work in the 1960s—just as the Black Power and Black Arts movements were voicing angry condemnation of the white world—his polite, professorial manner and seemingly traditional verse made him an outsider. In "How It Strikes a Contemporary," his final address at the Library of Congress, he had this to say on the subject of race and poetry:

> As a poet I am trying to come to grips with reality, as I perceive it. Isn't that what every poet worthy of the name is attempting to do? Why does a particular racial identity make me any less aware of life, life as human beings live it? What is a poet but a human being speaking to other human beings about things that matter to all of us?

Despite his universalist beliefs, Hayden's first mature collection, *A Ballad of Remembrance* (1962), is nonetheless saturated with African American history—from the personal past in "The Ballad of Sue Ellen Westerfield" and "Those Winter Sundays" to more public matters in "Middle Passage" and "Frederick Douglass." Yet one can also see the influence of Eliot and Auden in "Middle Passage," not only in the Eliotic collage of voices in Parts 1 and 2, but also in the ironic juxtapositions of religious faith and murderous hypocrisy. The poem was first published in a 1945 issue of *Phylon,* edited by W. E. B. DuBois. Hayden's vision of slavery, both here and in lyrics like "O Daedalus, Fly Away Home" and "The Ballad of Nat Turner," is deeply humanizing while squarely facing the horror of such atrocities. A slave trader speaking in part 2 of "Middle Passage" notes the complicity of African peoples in the trade. Hayden does not sentimentalize the trader—only his old age prevents him from continuing the abysmal work—but he does give the man a human voice. Another poem about violence, "The Whipping," begins with unflinching objectivity but offers surprising compassion in its concluding stanza.

In 1966 Hayden published his *Selected Poems,* and he followed it with four important collections in the next twelve years: *Words for the Mourning Time* (1970), *The Night-Blooming Cereus* (1972), *Angle of Ascent* (1975), and *American Journal* (1978). All of these books contain poems characterized by Hayden's social conscience and lyrical grace. These later volumes also reflect Hayden's growing commitment to nonviolence as the only moral means of social change. Although the later poems still deal with historical and individual acts of violence, the author, influenced by his Baha'i faith, now articulates the futility of such action to improve the world. Ultimately, Hayden must be seen as an important American poet, one of the more accomplished and distinctive voices of his generation. He was a writer who understood anger and injustice, but would not allow his art to be consumed by them. His *Collected Prose* was published in 1984, and his *Collected Poems* was published in 1985.

The Ballad of Sue Ellen Westerfield

(For Clyde)

She grew up in bedeviled southern wilderness,
but had not been a slave, she said,

because her father wept and set her mother free.
She hardened in perilous rivertowns
and after The Surrender,[1]   5
went as maid upon the tarnished Floating Palaces.[2]
Rivermen reviled her for the rankling cold
sardonic pride
that gave a knife-edge to her comeliness.

When she was old, her back still straight,   10
her hair still glossy black,
she'd talk sometimes
of dangers lived through on the rivers.
But never told of him,
whose name she'd vowed she would not speak again   15
till after Jordan.[3]
Oh, he was nearer nearer now
than wearisome kith and kin.
His blue eyes followed her
as she moved about her tasks upon the *Memphis Rose.*   20
He smiled and joshed, his voice quickening her.
She cursed the circumstance. . . .

The crazing horrors of that summer night,
the swifting flames, he fought his way to her,
the savaging panic, and helped her swim to shore.   25
The steamer like besieged Atlanta blazing,
the cries, the smoke and bellowing flames,
the flamelit thrashing forms in hellmouth water,
and he swimming out to them,
leaving her dazed and lost.   30
A woman screaming under the raddled trees—
Sue Ellen felt it was herself who screamed.
The moaning of the hurt, the terrified—
she held off shuddering despair
and went to comfort whom she could.   35
Wagons torches bells
and whimpering dusk of morning
and blankness lostness nothingness for her
until his arms had lifted her
into wild and secret dark.   40

How long how long was it they wandered,
loving fearing loving,
fugitives whose dangerous only hidingplace

---

1. The end of the Civil War in 1865.
2. Mississippi riverboats.
3. Since the Jordan River was thought to separate the Promised Land from the wilderness, it also became a metaphor for the crossing over at death. "After Jordan" implies "after death" and the entry into Paradise.

was love?
How long was it before she knew   45
she could not forfeit what she was,
even for him—could not, even for him,
forswear her pride?
They kissed and said farewell at last.
He wept as had her father once.   50
They kissed and said farewell.
Until her dying-bed,
she cursed the circumstance.

1966

Frederick Douglass[4]

When it is finally ours, this freedom, this liberty, this beautiful
and terrible thing, needful to man as air,
usable as earth; when it belongs at last to all,
when it is truly instinct, brain matter, diastole, systole,
reflex action; when it is finally won; when it is more   5
than the gaudy mumbo jumbo of politicians:
this man, this Douglass, this former slave, this Negro
beaten to his knees, exiled, visioning a world
where none is lonely, none hunted, alien,
this man, superb in love and logic, this man   10
shall be remembered. Oh, not with statues' rhetoric,
not with legends and poems and wreaths of bronze alone,
but with the lives grown out of his life, the lives
fleshing his dream of the beautiful, needful thing.

1966

Middle Passage[5]

I

Jesús, Estrella, Esperanza, Mercy:[6]

Sails flashing to the wind like weapons,
sharks following the moans the fever and the dying;
horror the corposant[7] and compass rose.[8]

---

4. Frederick Douglass (1818–1895), autobiographer, abolitionist, journalist, and statesman, was born a slave in Maryland and escaped to freedom in the North, where he became one of the most prominent public intellectuals of his time.
5. Refers to the route taken by slave ships between Africa and the New World.
6. Ironic names for slave ships. *Estrella* means "Star"; *Esperanza* means "Hope."
7. St. Elmo's Fire, in this case an eerie light that appears on a ship's deck during a lightning storm.
8. An indicator of directions printed on a map.

Middle Passage: 5
        voyage through death
                to life upon these shores.

"10 April 1800—
Blacks rebellious. Crew uneasy. Our linguist says
their moaning is a prayer for death,   10
ours and their own. Some try to starve themselves.
Lost three this morning leaped with crazy laughter
to the waiting sharks, sang as they went under."

Desire, Adventure, Tartar, Ann:

Standing to America, bringing home   15
black gold, black ivory, black seed.

        Deep in the festering hold thy father lies,
        of his bones New England pews are made,
        those are altar lights that were his eyes.[9]

Jesus   Saviour   Pilot   Me   20
Over   Life's   Tempestuous   Sea

We pray that Thou wilt grant, O Lord,
safe passage to our vessels bringing
heathen souls unto Thy chastening.

Jesus   Saviour   25

    "8 bells. I cannot sleep, for I am sick
with fear, but writing eases fear a little
since still my eyes can see these words take shape
upon the page & so I write, as one
would turn to exorcism. 4 days scudding,   30
but now the sea is calm again. Misfortune
follows in our wake like sharks (our grinning
tutelary gods). Which one of us
has killed an albatross?[1] A plague among
our blacks—Ophthalmia: blindness—& we   35
have jettisoned the blind to no avail.
It spreads, the terrifying sickness spreads.
Its claws have scratched sight from the Capt.'s eyes
& there is blindness in the fo'c'sle
& we must sail 3 weeks before we come   40
to port."

        What port awaits us, Davy Jones'
        or home? I've heard of slavers drifting, drifting,

9. These lines allude to Shakespeare's *The Tempest* (I. ii. 399–401) in which Ariel sings about a death by drowning: "Full fathom five thy father lies; / Of his bones are coral made; / Those are pearls that were his eyes. . . ."
1. To kill one of these magnificent seabirds was considered bad luck to sailors.

> *playthings of wind and storm and chance, their crews*
> *gone blind, the jungle hatred*   45
> *crawling up on deck.*

Thou   Who   Walked   On   Galilee

"Deponent[2] further sayeth *The Bella J*
left the Guinea Coast
with cargo of five hundred blacks and odd   50
for the barracoons[3] of Florida:

"That there was hardly room 'tween-decks for half
the sweltering cattle stowed spoon-fashion there;
that some went mad of thirst and tore their flesh
and sucked the blood: 55

"That Crew and Captain lusted with the comeliest
of the savage girls kept naked in the cabins;
that there was one they called The Guinea Rose
and they cast lots and fought to lie with her:

"That when the Bo's 'n piped all hands, the flames   60
spreading from starboard already were beyond
control, the negroes howling and their chains
entangled with the flames:

"That the burning blacks could not be reached,
that the Crew abandoned ship,   65
leaving their shrieking negresses behind,
that the Captain perished drunken with the wenches:

"Further Deponent sayeth not."

Pilot   Oh   Pilot   Me

II

Aye, lad, and I have seen those factories,   70
Gambia, Rio Pongo, Calabar;[4]
have watched the artful mongos[5] baiting traps
of war wherein the victor and the vanquished

Were caught as prizes for our barracoons.
Have seen the nigger kings whose vanity   75
and greed turned wild black hides of Fellatah,
Mandingo, Ibo, Kru[6] to gold for us.

2. One who gives testimony in a deposition.
3. Barracks for slaves.
4. All locations in West Africa from which slaves might be taken.
5. Slang for blacks.
6. These are names of African tribes.

And there was one—King Anthracite[7] we named him—
fetish face beneath French parasols
of brass and orange velvet, impudent mouth   80
whose cups were carven skulls of enemies:

He'd honor us with drum and feast and conjo
and palm-oil-glistening wenches deft in love,
and for tin crowns that shone with paste,
red calico and German-silver trinkets   85

Would have the drums talk war and send
his warriors to burn the sleeping villages
and kill the sick and old and lead the young
in coffles to our factories.

Twenty years a trader, twenty years,   90
for there was wealth aplenty to be harvested
from those black fields, and I'd be trading still
but for the fevers melting down my bones.

III[8]

Shuttles in the rocking loom of history,
the dark ships move, the dark ships move,   95
their bright ironical names
like jests of kindness on a murderer's mouth;
plough through thrashing glister toward
fata morgana's lucent melting shore,
weave toward New World littorals[9] that are   100
mirage and myth and actual shore.

Voyage through death,
                              voyage through chartings are unlove.
A charnel stench, effluvium of living death
spreads outward from the hold,   105
where the living and the dead, the horribly dying,
lie interlocked, lie foul with blood and excrement.

   Deep in the festering hold thy father lies,
   the corpse of mercy rots with him,
   rats eat love's rotten gelid eyes.   110

   But, oh, the living look at you
   with human eyes whose suffering accuses you,
   whose hatred reaches through the swill of dark
   to strike you like a leper's claw.

---

7. A racist pun, since anthracite is hard, black coal.
8. This section borrows from an account of the *Amistad* mutiny written by Muriel Rukeyser in a biography of Willard Gibbs, a nineteenth century scientist.
9. Coastal areas.

You cannot stare that hatred down   115
or chain the fear that stalks the watches
and breathes on you its fetid scorching breath;
cannot kill the deep immortal human wish,
the timeless will.

"But for the storm that flung up barriers   120
of wind and wave, *The Amistad*,[1] señores,
would have reached the port of Príncipe in two,
three days at most; but for the storm we should
have been prepared for what befell.
Swift as the puma's leap it came. There was   125
that interval of moonless calm filled only
with the water's and the rigging's usual sounds,
then sudden movement, blows and snarling cries
and they had fallen on us with machete
and marlinspike. It was as though the very   130
air, the night itself were striking us.
Exhausted by the rigors of the storm,
we were no match for them. Our men went down
before the murderous Africans. Our loyal
Celestino ran from below with gun   135
and lantern and I saw, before the cane-
knife's wounding flash, Cinquez,
that surly brute who calls himself a prince,
directing, urging on the ghastly work.
He hacked the poor mulatto down, and then   140
he turned on me. The decks were slippery
when daylight finally came. It sickens me
to think of what I saw, of how these apes
threw overboard the butchered bodies of
our men, true Christians all, like so much jetsam.   145
Enough, enough. The rest is quickly told:
Cinquez was forced to spare the two of us
you see to steer the ship to Africa,
and we like phantoms doomed to rove the sea
voyaged east by day and west by night,   150
deceiving them, hoping for rescue,
prisoners on our own vessel, till
at length we drifted to the shores of this
your land, America, where we were freed
from our unspeakable misery. Now we   155
demand, good sirs, the extradition of
Cinquez and his accomplices to La
Havana. And it distresses us to know

---

1. During the *Amistad* mutiny, the slave Cinquez killed the ship's captain, Celestino. When the case
reached the U.S. Supreme Court in 1841, former president John Quincy Adams defended the mutineers
and secured their release to return to Africa.

there are so many here who seem inclined
to justify the mutiny of these blacks.   160
We find it paradoxical indeed
that you whose wealth, whose tree of liberty
are rooted in the labor of your slaves
should suffer the august John Quincy Adams
to speak with so much passion of the right   165
of chattel slaves to kill their lawful masters
and with his Roman rhetoric weave a hero's
garland for Cinquez. I tell you that
we are determined to return to Cuba
with our slaves and there see justice done. Cinquez—   170
or let us say 'the Prince'—Cinquez shall die."

The deep immortal human wish,
the timeless will:

Cinquez its deathless primaveral image,
life that transfigures many lives.   175

Voyage through death
                        to life upon these shores.

                                                1966

Night, Death, Mississippi

I

A quavering cry. Screech-owl?
Or one of them?
The old man in his reek
and gauntness laughs—

One of them, I bet—   5
and turns out the kitchen lamp,
limping to the porch to listen
in the windowless night.

Be there with Boy and the rest
if I was well again.   10
Time was. Time was.
White robes like moonlight

In the sweetgum dark.
Unbuckled that one then
and him squealing bloody Jesus   15
as we cut it off.

Time was. A cry?
A cry all right.
He hawks and spits,
fevered as by groinfire.   20

Have us a bottle,
Boy and me—
he's earned him a bottle—
when he gets home.

II

Then we beat them, he said,   25
beat them till our arms was tired
and the big old chains
messy and red.

O Jesus burning on the lily cross

Christ, it was better   30
than hunting bear
which don't know why
you want him dead.

O night, rawhead and bloodybones night

You kids fetch Paw   35
some water now so's he
can wash that blood
off him, she said.

O night betrayed by darkness not its own

                                                              1966

Those Winter Sundays

Sundays too my father got up early
and put his clothes on in the blueblack cold,
then with cracked hands that ached
from labor in the weekday weather made
banked fires blaze. No one ever thanked him.   5

I'd wake and hear the cold splintering, breaking.
When the rooms were warm, he'd call,
and slowly I would rise and dress,
fearing the chronic angers of that house,

Speaking indifferently to him,   10
who had driven out the cold
and polished my good shoes as well.
What did I know, what did I know
of love's austere and lonely offices?

                                                              1966

The Whipping

The old woman across the way
  is whipping the boy again
and shouting to the neighborhood
  her goodness and his wrongs.

Wildly he crashes through elephant ears,   5
  pleads in dusty zinnias,
while she in spite of crippling fat
  pursues and corners him.

She strikes and strikes the shrilly circling
  boy till the stick breaks   10
in her hand. His tears are rainy weather
  to woundlike memories:

My head gripped in bony vise
  of knees, the writhing struggle
to wrench free, the blows, the fear   15
  worse than blows that hateful

Words could bring, the face that I
  no longer knew or loved . . . .
Well, it is over now, it is over,
  and the boy sobs in his room,   20

And the woman leans muttering against
  a tree, exhausted, purged—
avenged in part for lifelong hidings
  she has had to bear.

1966

A Plague of Starlings

(Fisk Campus)

Evenings I hear
the workmen fire
into the stiff
magnolia leaves,
routing the starlings   5
gathered noisy and
befouling there.

Their scissoring
terror like glass
coins spilling breaking   10
the birds explode
into mica sky

raggedly fall
to ground rigid
in clench of cold.   15

The spared return,
when the guns are through,
to the spoiled trees
like choiceless poor
to a dangerous   20
dwelling place,
chitter and quarrel
in the piercing dark
above the killed.

1970

JOHN FREDERICK NIMS
(1913–1999)

The son of a rural postman, John Frederick Nims was born in Muskegon, on the
eastern shores of Lake Michigan. His father was of Protestant stock, his mother
Catholic—"a spirited Irish girl." The poet would recall his father reciting Tennyson to him, and how, once the whole family had converted to his mother's faith,
he learned Latin as an altar boy. When he was twelve, the family moved to
Chicago, which took him "from Norman Rockwell Country to Studs Lonigan
turf." There he attended Catholic schools and pursued his interests in tennis and
poetry. Nims studied classics at Notre Dame, graduating in 1937. Various health
problems curbed his tennis playing and kept him out of World War II. By 1945,
when he received his Ph.D. from the University of Chicago, Nims was an accomplished poet and critic, joining the editorial board of *Poetry* magazine for three
years. (He returned as editor from 1978 to 1984.) He married Bonnie Larkin in
1947. They had five children, one of whom, their firstborn son, had Down's syn-
drome and died young. The family moved according to Nims's academic posts in
Canada, Italy, Spain, and the United States.

Nims was best known as an editor and translator, but he was also a remarkably learned poet. A selection of his early poems appeared in *Five Young American
Poets: Third Series* (1944), followed by several distinguished collections, including
The Kiss: A Jambalaya (1982), *Selected Poems* (1982), and *The Six-Cornered
Snowflake* (1990). His brilliant, often funny essays were collected in *A Local Habitation* (1985), and his translations appeared in several volumes, including *Sappho
to Valéry* (1971, revised 1979 and 1990). He also edited anthologies and authored
the highly regarded textbook *Western Wind: An Introduction to Poetry* (first edition 1974). Though he suffered occasional depression, Nims's poems display an
often comic attitude, as well as a fascination with formal patterns in both life and
art. Writing almost to the day of his death, Nims turned out new poems and translations. His last completed books were *The Complete Poems of Michelangelo*
(1998) and *The Powers of Heaven and Earth* (2002), a volume of new and selected
poems. He died in Chicago, across Lake Michigan from where he was born.

Dedication: Love Poem

My clumsiest dear, whose hands shipwreck vases,
At whose quick touch all glasses chip and ring,
Whose palms are bulls in china, burs in linen,
And have no cunning with any soft thing

Except all ill-at-ease fidgeting people: 5
The refugee uncertain at the door
You make at home; deftly you steady
The drunk clambering on his undulant floor.

Unpredictable dear, the taxi drivers' terror,
Shrinking from far headlights pale as a dime   10
Yet leaping before red apoplectic streetcars—
Misfit in any space. And never on time.

A wrench in clocks and the solar system. Only
With words and people and love you move at ease;
In traffic of wit expertly manoeuvre   15
And keep us, all devotion, at your knees,

Forgetting your coffee spreading on our flannel,
Your lipstick grinning on our coat,
So gayly in love's unbreakable heaven
Our souls on glory of spilt bourbon float.   20

Be with me, darling, early and late. Smash glasses—
I will study wry music for your sake.
For should your hands drop white and empty
All the toys of the world would break.

     1947

Epigrams

LOVERS

And here the two by the one grievance haunted
Lie in the dark. But not the dark they wanted.

LOVE AND DEATH

And yet a kiss (like blubber)'d blur and slip,
Without the assuring skull beneath the lip.

VISITING POET

"The famous bard, he comes! The vision nears!"
Now heaven protect your booze. Your wife. Your ears.

PHILOSOPHER

He scowled at the barometer: "Will it rain?"
None heard, with all that pattering on the pane.

BARD ANNOUNCES HE IS TAKING UP SOCIAL ACTION
INSTEAD OF WRITING HIS "LITTLE BOOKS OF VERSE"

Good man! Left letters, to improve the folk.
And made the two worlds better at a stroke.

DISCIPLES

Just one in twelve a traitor? Blessed day!
Since Judas' time, been downhill all the way.

PROTESTATION

"You say so, but will you be faithful? You men!"
But dear, I've been faithful again and again!

CONTEMPLATION

"I'm Mark's alone!" you swore. Given cause to doubt you,
I think less of you, dear. But more about you.

AVANT-GARDE

"A dead tradition! Hollow shell!
Outworn, outmoded—time it fell.
Let's make it new. Rebel! Rebel!"
Said cancer-cell to cancer cell.

1990

◄ MURIEL RUKEYSER ►
(1913–1980)

Born to wealthy Jewish parents in New York City, Muriel Rukeyser led a privileged childhood that included elite schools, summer homes, and country clubs. She joked that she "was expected to grow up and become a golfer." Instead, she broke from her parents to pursue poetry, political activism, journalism, and biography. She attended Vassar College for two years but left in 1932, already sure of her dedication to writing. Along with other intellectuals of her generation, she joined the Communist Party, and during the Depression years of the 1930s she worked as a journalist for leftist publications such as *New Masses*. Her assignments took her to Decatur, Alabama, in 1933, where she witnessed the trial of the Scottsboro boys, and in 1936 to Gauley Bridge, West Virginia, to help expose the life-threatening working conditions countenanced by a silica mining conglomerate. She also traveled to Spain, where her assignment to cover the antifascist Olympics coincided with the start of the Spanish Civil War. By the end of the decade she had left the Party, in part because she refused to conform to its expectations that she write narrow, propagandistic poetry. For the rest of her life, however, she remained committed to political activism and leftist ideals.

By the time she was thirty, she had published extensively, her work including journalism, reviews, poetry, and an ambitious biography. *Theory of Flight* (1935), which won the Yale Series of Younger Poets' Award, was inspired in part by her experiences as an amateur pilot and is notable for presenting socially concerned poetry with a Whitmanesque expansiveness and also experimental techniques derived from Hart Crane. Her next book, *U. S. 1* (1938), continues these juxtapositions; her long poem, "The Book of the Dead," blends documentary realism with Modernist collage through her portraits of workers and their families and her quotations from sources such as congressional subcommittee testimony on the corporate cover-up of the miners' deaths from silicosis. "The Book of the Dead" caused controversy because Rukeyser refused to limit herself to only one perspective on poetry. Critics on the right attacked her for being overly political, while critics on the left complained that her Modernist techniques were obscurantist. Rukeyser continued her independent path in *A Turning Wind* (1939) and *Wake Island* (1942). She never wavered from what she saw as the democratic inclusiveness of her poetry and her goal of crossing boundaries—whether between disciplines or between types of poetry. In a series of lectures that she eventually published as *The Life of Poetry* (1949), she argued against divisions—between human beings, disciplines, modes of poetry, even between poets and readers. While writing out of her own individual consciousness as a woman and a Jew, Rukeyser aimed to expand outward to reach readers everywhere, even though she recognized the obstacles that often impede such exchanges.

An openness to change characterized not only Rukeyser's poetry, but her life as well. By the end of the 1940s she had published four more books of poetry, including *Beast in View* (1944), with a long poem that contained the sonnet, "To Be a Jew in the Twentieth Century." This sonnet would eventually be made part of the Reform Liturgy. In 1945 she moved to California, taught at the California Labor School, and married a painter. But the marriage lasted only two months, and in 1947 she gave birth to a son by another man, whose identity she never made public. Single motherhood sapped some of her writing energy, and her publication rate slowed during the years that she raised her son and worked to support him by teaching at Sarah Lawrence College in New York, where she had returned in 1954. Nevertheless, she was able to complete two books of poetry, *Body of Waking* (1958) and *Waterlily Fire: Poems 1935–1962* (1962).

In the late 1960s she returned full force to poetry writing and political activism, buoyed by the renewed climate for socially responsive poetry and also by the burgeoning feminist movement. She participated in demonstrations against the Vietnam War, and in 1972 traveled to South Vietnam to lobby for peace. Her book publications included *The Speed of Darkness* (1968), *Breaking Open* (1973), *The Gates* (1976), *The Collected Poems of Muriel Rukeyser* (1979), as well as an experimental novel, *The Orgy* (1966).

Although Rukeyser had always emphasized the female perspective, her later work became more explicitly feminist, and women poets found inspiration both in her writing and her uncompromising life. Because of her stubborn independence from the various schools that dominated American poetry, her poetry's strong political content, and her identity as "a she-poet," Rukeyser was often omitted from anthologies and critical surveys. After her death in 1980 her books fell out of print. But the publication of *Out of Silence: Selected Poems* (1992) and *A Muriel Rukeyser Reader* (1994) with an introduction by Adrienne Rich, eventually helped to reestablish her reputation as a twentieth-century innovator.

--◆--

Effort at Speech between Two People

Speak to me.   Take my hand.   What are you now?
I will tell you all.   I will conceal nothing.
When I was three, a little child read a story about a rabbit
who died, in the story, and I crawled under a chair   :
a pink rabbit   :   it was my birthday, and a candle   5
burnt a sore spot on my finger, and I was told to be happy.

Oh, grow to know me.   I am not happy.   I will be open:
Now I am thinking of white sails against a sky like music,
like glad horns blowing, and birds tilting, and an arm about me.
There was one I loved, who wanted to live, sailing.   10

Speak to me.   Take my hand.   What are you now?
When I was nine, I was fruitily sentimental,
fluid   :   and my widowed aunt played Chopin,
and I bent my head on the painted woodwork, and wept.
I want now to be close to you.   I would   15
link the minutes of my days close, somehow, to your days.

I am not happy.   I will be open.
I have liked lamps in evening corners, and quiet poems.
There has been fear in my life.   Sometimes I speculate
On what a tragedy his life was, really.   20

Take my hand.   Fist my mind in your hand.   What are you now?
When I was fourteen, I had dreams of suicide,
and I stood at a steep window, at sunset, hoping toward death   :
if the light had not melted clouds and plains to beauty,
if light had not transformed that day, I would have leapt.   25
I am unhappy.   I am lonely.   Speak to me.

I will be open.   I think he never loved me:
he loved the bright beaches, the little lips of foam
that ride small waves, he loved the veer of gulls:
he said with a gay mouth: I love you.   Grow to know me.   30

What are you now?   If we could touch one another,
if these our separate entities could come to grips,
clenched like a Chinese puzzle . . . yesterday
I stood in a crowded street that was live with people,
and no one spoke a word, and the morning shone.   35
Everyone silent, moving. . . . Take my hand.   Speak to me.

                                                    1935

From "Letter to the Front"

To Be a Jew in the Twentieth Century

To be a Jew in the twentieth century
Is to be offered a gift.   If you refuse,

Wishing to be invisible, you choose
Death of the spirit, the stone insanity.
Accepting, take full life.   Full agonies: 5
Your evening deep in labyrinthine blood
Of those who resist, fail, and resist; and God
Reduced to a hostage among hostages.

The gift is torment.   Not alone the still
Torture, isolation; or torture of the flesh.   10
That may come also.   But the accepting wish,
The whole and fertile spirit as guarantee
For every human freedom, suffering to be free,
Daring to live for the impossible.

                                                                1944

Double Dialogue:

Homage to Robert Frost

In agony saying   :   "The last night of his life,
My son and I in the kitchen   :   At half-past one
He said, 'I have failed as a husband. Now my wife
Is ill again and suffering.' At two
He said, 'I have failed as a farmer, for the sun   5
Is never there, the rain is never there.'
At three he said, 'I have failed as a poet who
Has never not once found my listener.
There is no sense to my life.' But then he heard me out.
I argued point by point. Seemed to win. Won.   10
He spoke to me once more when I was done:
'Even in argument, father, I have lost.'
He went and shot himself. Now tell me this one thing:
Should I have let him win then? Was I wrong?"

To answer for the land for love for song   15
Arguing life for life even at your life's cost.

                                                                1968

The Poem as Mask

Orpheus[1]

When I wrote of the women in their dances and wildness, it was a mask,[2]
on their mountain, gold-hunting, singing, in orgy,
it was a mask; when I wrote of the god,

---

1. In Greek mythology, Orpheus was a Thracian poet who could move even the stones and trees with his song. He rescued his wife Eurydice from the underworld, but lost her again when he looked back to be sure she was with him. The Furies, enraged by his grief at this loss, tore him to pieces and threw his still-singing head into the Hebrus River.
2. Rukeyser refers to her long poem *Orpheus* (1949).

fragmented, exiled from himself, his life, the love gone down with song,
it was myself, split open, unable to speak, in exile from myself.   5

There is no mountain, there is no god, there is memory
of my torn life, myself split open in sleep, the rescued child
beside me among the doctors, and a word
of rescue from the great eyes.

No more masks! No more mythologies!   10

Now, for the first time, the god lifts his hand,
the fragments join in me with their own music.

                                                                      1968

Poem

I lived in the first century of world wars.
Most morning I would be more or less insane,
The newspapers would arrive with their careless stories,
The news would pour out of various devices
Interrupted by attempts to sell products to the unseen.   5
I would call my friends on other devices;
They would be more or less mad for similar reasons.
Slowly I would get to pen and paper,
Make my poems for others unseen and unborn.
In the day I would be reminded of those men and women   10
Brave, setting up signals across vast distances,
Considering a nameless way of living, of almost unimagined values.
As the lights darkened, as the lights of night brightened,
We would try to imagine them, try to find each other.
To construct peace, to make love, to reconcile   15
Waking with sleeping, ourselves with each other,
Ourselves with ourselves. We would try by any means
To reach the limits of ourselves, to reach beyond ourselves,
To let go the means, to wake.

I lived in the first century of these wars.   20

                                                                      1968

◄ JOHN BERRYMAN ►
(1914–1972)

John Berryman was born John Smith in McAlester, Oklahoma. His father, John Allyn Smith, was a small-town banker who moved from one failure to another, resigning or being fired from several jobs. His mother, Martha Little, was a schoolteacher who wanted a better life for the family. During the Florida land boom of the 1920s they moved to Tampa and opened a restaurant, but were forced to close within a year. As Berryman later told the first of his three wives, Eileen Simpson, "One day, Daddy, agitated and depressed, took me on his back and swam far out in the Gulf at Clearwater, threatening to drown us both. Or so mother claimed. . . . Early one morning he got out his gun and put a bullet through his head."

The image of his father's suicide, which took place outside Berryman's window when he was twelve years old, haunted the poet for the rest of his life. He felt responsible for the catastrophe, and his guilt and shame were intensified by his Catholic upbringing. Less than three months after the suicide, his mother remarried—to her landlord, a bond salesman, who was sixteen years older than she. The new family moved to New York and Berryman and his brother took their stepfather's surname. Although this marriage did not last, Berryman's kindly stepfather sent him to preparatory school and helped him attend Columbia University, where he took a bachelor's degree in 1936. He earned a second bachelor's degree at Clare College, Cambridge, two years later.

After trying life as a schoolteacher and journalist, Berryman eventually became a college professor at various institutions, including Harvard and Princeton. He befriended most of the major American literary figures of his generation, including Saul Bellow, Robert Lowell, Elizabeth Bishop, Randall Jarrell, Delmore Schwartz, and the publisher Robert Giroux. His brilliance was widely recognized, though compared to some of his friends he was slow to achieve success as a poet. "I masquerade as a writer," he once said. "Actually I'm a scholar." He wrote penetrating essays on William Shakespeare and Christopher Marlowe as well as on modern poets. He first gathered his poems in the seminal New Directions anthology, *Five Young American Poets* (1940). A slender first volume, *Poems* (1942), soon appeared, followed by more substantial collections such as *The Dispossessed* (1948) and *Homage to Mistress Bradstreet* (1956). The early poems were densely written, difficult, and strictly formal, though they could be wildly playful as well, and scholarly in their wit. Berryman, like his friend Robert Lowell, began with a very elevated notion of what poetry ought to be. He wrote that poetry aimed "at the reformation of the poet, as prayer does. In the grand cases—as in our century Yeats and Eliot—it enables the poet . . . to become almost another man."

This definition not only glorifies the art, but denigrates the self. A profound sense of loss and self-loathing underlaid Berryman's early accomplishments. His personal life during this time was plagued by financial worry, artistic anxiety, and severe alcoholism, making it difficult for him to keep a job or maintain a marriage. Eileen Simpson, in her superb memoir, *Poets in their Youth* (1982), saw Berryman disastrously repeating the patterns of his father's life. She asserted that it was not poetry that created the instability in Berryman, but his private wounds. "It was poetry," she insisted, "that had kept him alive." Perhaps in part because of his own troubles, Berryman made poems that dealt with psychological extremes. In his biography of Stephen Crane (1950), he wrote that Crane's writing captured "a mind at stretch"—and the same can be said of Berryman's best poems. By the 1960s he was turning away from the "transcendent" examples of Yeats and Rilke, and toward the personal testimony and self-mythologizing of Whitman in "Song of Myself." The poems that emerged from this transitional period were some of Berryman's best, especially *77 Dream Songs* (1964). He later described the plan of this work, which he considered a single long poem, in a preface to one of the sequel volumes:

The poem, then, whatever its wide cast of characters, is essentially about an imaginary character (not the poet, not me) named Henry, a white American in early middle age sometimes in blackface, who has suffered an irreversible loss and talks about himself sometimes in the first person, sometimes in the third, sometimes even in the second; he has a friend, never named, who addresses him as Mr. Bones and variants thereof. Requiescat in pace.

The borrowed trappings of the minstrel show, the provisional identities, and tragic-comic role playing, even the obsession with death, are all suggested in this passage. But the best dream songs pulse with vitality in their sometimes jazzy rhythms, their humor, and their mixtures of poetic diction and slang—what James Dickey called "a kind of Berryman Esperanto." For each poem, these contradictory impulses were contained in three six-line stanzas, loosely borrowed from Yeats.

Although still openly tormented by his private demons, Berryman had by his early fifties achieved enormous public success. He had been appointed Regents' Professor at the University of Minnesota and had won the Pulitzer Prize, the National Book Award, and the Bollingen Prize. Widely reviewed and featured in the press, he appeared as the poet shouting into the wind in a *Life* magazine photograph. He continued to publish more poems in his epic dream song series, which were finally collected in *The Dream Songs* (1969). He also issued a steady stream of other verse collections, most notably *Love and Fame* (1970) and a difficult volume, *Berryman's Sonnets* (1967), much of which was written in the 1940s. Increasingly his poetry focused on death or suicide. As his personal problems intensified, he suffered both mental and physical breakdowns. Berryman began to admit his alcoholism in the late 1960s, as his posthumously published novel, *Recovery* (1973), attests. In 1971 he underwent a spiritual crisis and returned to the Catholic faith of his youth, but it could not protect him from his own deepening despair. On January 7, 1972, he jumped to his death from a bridge in Minneapolis, ending his life at the age of fifty-seven.

Since his death, Berryman's reputation has declined from the enormous celebrity he enjoyed during his final years, but the harrowing drama of his life and the vitality of his best poems have kept interest in him alive. Berryman has been the subject of several biographies and memoirs, and his *Collected Poems,* edited by Charles Thornbury, was published in 1989. Berryman's acute scholarly essays have also been published in several collections, notably *Berryman's Shakespeare* (1999), edited by John Haffenden. His critical biography, *Stephen Crane,* has also been reprinted. While he is no longer widely seen as a dominant voice of his generation, his *Dream Songs*—whatever the work's flaws—still stands as one of the most ambitious and original enterprises of mid-century American poetry. Berryman's life remains a cautionary tale about addiction and art; the best of his work both expressed and brilliantly transcended the agonizing trials of his life.

◄─────►

Desires of Men and Women

Exasperated, worn, you conjure a mansion,
The absolute butlers in the spacious hall,
Old silver, lace, and privacy, a house

Where nothing has for years been out of place,
Neither shoe-horn nor affection been out of place,   5
Breakfast in summer on the eastern terrace,
All justice and all grace.

                    At the reception
Most beautifully you conduct yourselves—
Expensive and accustomed, bow, speak French,
That Cinquecento[1] miniature recall   10
The Duke presented to your great-grandmother—

And none of us, my dears, would dream of you
The half-lit and lascivious apartments
That are in fact your goal, for which you'd do
Murder if you had not your cowardice   15
To prop the law; or dream of you the rooms,
Glaring and inconceivably vulgar,
Where now you are, where now you wish for life,
Whence you project your naked fantasies.

                                        1948

FROM The Dream Songs

1

Huffy Henry hid   the day,
unappeasable Henry sulked.
I see his point,—a trying to put things over.
It was the thought that they thought
they could *do* it made Henry wicked & away.   5
But he should have come out and talked.

All the world like a woolen lover
once did seem on Henry's side.
Then came a departure.
Thereafter nothing fell out as it might or ought.   10
I don't see how Henry, pried
open for all the world to see, survived.

What he has now to say is a long
wonder the world can bear & be.
Once in a sycamore I was glad   15
all at the top, and I sang.
Hard on the land wears the strong sea
and empty grows every bed.

                                        1964

---

1. Sixteenth century.

14

Life, friends, is boring. We must not say so.
After all, the sky flashes, the great sea yearns,
we ourselves flash and yearn,
and moreover my mother told me as a boy
(repeatingly) "Ever to confess you're bored   5
means you have no

Inner Resources." I conclude now I have no
inner resources, because I am heavy bored.
Peoples bore me,
literature bores me, especially great literature,   10
Henry bores me, with his plights & gripes
as bad as achilles,

who loves people and valiant art, which bores me.
And the tranquil hills, & gin, look like a drag
and somehow a dog   15
has taken itself & its tail considerably away
into mountains or sea or sky, leaving
behind: me, wag.

1964

29

There sat down, once, a thing on Henry's heart
só heavy, if he had a hundred years
& more, & weeping, sleepless, in all them time
Henry could not make good.
Starts again always in Henry's ears   5
the little cough somewhere, an odour, a chime.

And there is another thing he has in mind
like a grave Sienese face a thousand years
would fail to blur the still profiled reproach of. Ghastly,
with open eyes, he attends, blind.   10
All the bells say: too late. This is not for tears;
thinking.

But never did Henry, as he thought he did,
end anyone and hacks her body up
and hide the pieces, where they may be found.   15
He knows: he went over everyone, & nobody's missing.
Often he reckons, in the dawn, them up.
Nobody is ever missing.

1964

384

The marker slants, flowerless, day's almost done,
I stand above my father's grave with rage,

often, often before
I've made this awful pilgrimage to one
who cannot visit me, who tore his page   5
out: I come back for more,

I spit upon this dreadful banker's grave
who shot his heart out in a Florida dawn
O ho alas alas
When will indifference come, I moan & rave   10
I'd like to scrabble till I got right down
away down under the grass

and ax the casket open ha to see
just how he's taking it, which he sought so hard
we'll tear apart   15
the mouldering grave cloths ha & then Henry
will heft the ax once more, his final card,
and fell it on the start.

1968

⚫◄ RANDALL JARRELL ►⚫
(1914–1965)

In a letter to a college sweetheart, Randall Jarrell once wrote, "I've lived all over, and always been separated from at least half of a very small family, and been alone as children ever are." Childhood and loneliness would become two of his most important subjects. He was born in Nashville, Tennessee, to Owen and Anna Jarrell. When his parents separated, he was shuttled back and forth between his mother in Nashville and his father and grandparents in Southern California. He would remember his grandparents' home in Hollywood as a childhood Eden lost to him through forces beyond his control. As a boy in Nashville, he was befriended by sculptors Belle Kinney and Leopold Scholz, who nearly adopted him. They had been at work on the concrete replica of the Parthenon in Centennial Park, and Jarrell posed for the figure of Ganymede, cup-bearer to the gods.

While at Vanderbilt University (B.A. 1936, M.A. 1939), Jarrell was quickly recognized as a brilliant and somewhat overbearing student. His teachers included men who were then becoming powerful literary figures—John Crowe Ransom and Robert Penn Warren, the Southern Agrarian poets who had helped edit the *Fugitive,* an influential Modernist journal published in Nashville from 1922 to 1925. Ransom and Warren were also key figures in New Criticism, a revisionist movement only beginning to exert what would soon become a decisive influence on the academic study of literature. Although Jarrell's politics were left of center (and his favorite contemporary poet was the Marx- and Freud-inspired early Auden), he was influenced by the *Fugitive* poets who were mostly very conservative in their political views. His literary connections helped him secure early and prestigious publication. Allen Tate, an early mentor, took five of Jarrell's undergraduate poems for a supplement to the *American Review,* and when Warren established the *Southern Review* at Louisiana State University, Jarrell appeared in the premiere issue.

He was invited to review books for the magazine and immediately displayed a prodigious talent for succinctness and wit.

When Ransom moved to Kenyon College, founding the *Kenyon Review* and establishing his "school" of New Critical writers, Jarrell followed him there as instructor and tennis coach. At Kenyon he befriended Robert Lowell and the fiction writer Peter Taylor. From 1939 to 1942, Jarrell taught at the University of Texas at Austin. He was also writing brilliant reviews for Edmund Wilson and Malcolm Cowley at the *New Republic* and beginning to publish poems in prominent magazines. In Texas he began to write poems in what would become his mature style, like "90 North," an uncanny blending of images from polar expeditions and ordinary life. In 1940 he published a selection of poems with an important prose preface, "A Note on Poetry," in the New Directions Anthology *Five Young American Poets*. His ideas in that statement would be extended in his famous essay "The End of the Line" in which he argued that Modernism was not a response to Romanticism but, in fact, Romanticism's last gasp. That same year he married one of his colleagues, Mackie Langham.

In 1942 Jarrell enlisted in the Army Air Corps, just as he published his first collection of poems, *Blood for a Stranger*. That book was followed in his lifetime by nine more collections of poetry, two books of critical prose, several translations, various editions of others writers' work, and four children's books. While in the air corps (he eventually became a celestial navigation tower operator), Jarrell wrote some of his best-known poems, including "Eighth Air Force" and "The Death of the Ball Turret Gunner," frequently imagining combat conditions that he never saw firsthand. After the war there were brief teaching stints at Sarah Lawrence College, which eventually served as the setting for his satirical novel *Pictures from an Institution* (1954), and Princeton University before Jarrell joined the faculty of the Women's College of the University of North Carolina at Greensboro, where he taught for most of his remaining years. His first marriage ended in divorce; in 1952 he married Mary Eloise von Schrader, a divorcée with two daughters. While acting as Poetry Consultant to the Library of Congress, Jarrell began to experience episodes of manic depression. Eventually these events required hospitalization, and it was during one of these hospital stays that Jarrell, out walking along a country highway in the evening, was struck by a car and killed. The coroner ruled Jarrell's death an accident, though several friends assumed it was a suicide.

By the time of his death, Jarrell had worn out some of his prodigious energy as a critic and had begun to discover himself anew as a poet. His final collection, *The Lost World* (1965), showed him at the height of his powers. He had also established himself as a children's writer of unusual lyrical sweep tinged with wonder and melancholy, with books such as *The Bat-Poet* (1964) and *The Animal Family* (1965), which appeared a few weeks after his death. Jarrell's poetry was sometimes faulted for sentimentality—and it is often drenched in nostalgia, sadness, or regret—but at its best it achieves surprising and memorable moments of deep sympathy.

◄◦━━◗━━◦►

Losses

It was not dying: everybody died.
It was not dying: we had died before
In the routine crashes—and our fields
Called up the papers, wrote home to our folks,

And the rates rose, all because of us.   5
We died on the wrong page of the almanac,
Scattered on mountains fifty miles away;
Diving on haystacks, fighting with a friend,
We blazed up on the lines we never saw.
We died like aunts or pets or foreigners.   10
(When we left high school nothing else had died
For us to figure we had died like.)

In our new planes, with our new crews, we bombed
The ranges by the desert or the shore,
Fired at towed targets, waited for our scores—   15
And turned into replacements and woke up
One morning, over England, operational.
It wasn't different: but if we died
It was not an accident but a mistake
(But an easy one for anyone to make).   20
We read our mail and counted up our missions—
In bombers named for girls, we burned
The cities we had learned about in school—
Till our lives wore out; our bodies lay among
The people we had killed and never seen.   25
When we lasted long enough they gave us medals;
When we died they said, "Our casualties were low."

They said, "Here are the maps"; we burned the cities.

It was not dying—no, not ever dying;
But the night I died I dreamed that I was dead,   30
And the cities said to me: "Why are you dying?
We are satisfied, if you are; but why did I die?"

1944

The Death of the Ball Turret Gunner

From my mother's sleep I fell into the State,
And I hunched in its belly till my wet fur froze.
Six miles from earth, loosed from its dream of life,
I woke to black flak and the nightmare fighters.
When I died they washed me out of the turret with a hose.   5

1945

90 North[1]

At home, in my flannel gown, like a bear to its floe,
I clambered to bed; up the globe's impossible sides
I sailed all night—till at last, with my black beard,
My furs and my dogs, I stood at the northern pole.

---

1. The latitude of the North Pole.

There in the childish night my companions lay frozen,   5
The stiff furs knocked at my starveling throat,
And I gave my great sigh: the flakes came huddling,
Were they really my end? In the darkness I turned to my rest.

—Here, the flag snaps in the glare and silence
Of the unbroken ice. I stand here,   10
The dogs bark, my beard is black, and I stare
At the North Pole . . .
               And now what? Why, go back.

Turn as I please, my step is to the south.
The world—my world spins on this final point
Of cold and wretchedness: all lines, all winds   15
End in this whirlpool I at last discover.

And it is meaningless. In the child's bed
After the night's voyage, in that warm world
Where people work and suffer for the end
That crowns the pain—in that Cloud-Cuckoo-Land²   20

I reached my North and it had meaning.
Here at the actual pole of my existence,
Where all that I have done is meaningless,
Where I die or live by accident alone—

Where, living or dying, I am still alone;   25
Here where North, the night, the berg of death
Crowd me out of the ignorant darkness,
I see at last that all the knowledge

I wrung from the darkness—that the darkness flung me—
Is worthless as ignorance: nothing comes from nothing,   30
The darkness from the darkness. Pain comes from the darkness
And we call it wisdom. It is pain.

                                         1945

The Woman at the Washington Zoo

The saris go by me from the embassies.

Cloth from the moon. Cloth from another planet.
They look back at the leopard like the leopard.

And I. . . .
            this print of mine, that has kept its color
Alive through so many cleanings; this dull null   5
Navy I wear to work, and wear from work, and so
To my bed, so to my grave, with no

2. From Aristophanes' comedy *The Birds,* an imaginary city built in the air by birds.

Complaints, no comment: neither from my chief,
The Deputy Chief Assistant, nor his chief—
Only I complain. . . . this serviceable   10
Body that no sunlight dyes, no hand suffuses
But, dome-shadowed, withering among columns,
Wavy beneath fountains—small, far-off, shining
In the eyes of animals, these beings trapped
As I am trapped but not, themselves, the trap,   15
Aging, but without knowledge of their age,
Kept safe here, knowing not of death, for death—
Oh, bars of my own body, open, open!

The world goes by my cage and never sees me.
And there come not to me, as come to these,   20
The wild beasts, sparrows pecking the llamas' grain,
Pigeons settling on the bears' bread, buzzards
Tearing the meat the flies have clouded. . . .
                              Vulture,
When you come for the white rat that the foxes left,
Take off the red helmet of your head, the black   25
Wings that have shadowed me, and step to me as man:
The wild brother at whose feet the white wolves fawn,
To whose hand of power the great lioness
Stalks, purring. . . .
                    You know what I was,
You see what I am: change me, change me!   30

1960

Next Day

Moving from Cheer to Joy, from Joy to All,
I take a box
And add it to my wild rice, my Cornish game hens.
The slacked or shorted, basketed, identical
Food-gathering flocks   5
Are selves I overlook. Wisdom, said William James,

Is learning what to overlook. And I am wise
If that is wisdom.
Yet somehow, as I buy All from these shelves
And the boy takes it to my station wagon,   10
What I've become
Troubles me even if I shut my eyes.

When I was young and miserable and pretty
And poor, I'd wish
What all girls wish: to have a husband,   15
A house and children. Now that I'm old, my wish

Is womanish:
That the boy putting groceries in my car

See me. It bewilders me he doesn't see me.
For so many years   20
I was good enough to eat: the world looked at me
And its mouth watered. How often they have undressed me,
The eyes of strangers!
And, holding their flesh within my flesh, their vile

Imaginings within my imagining,   25
I too have taken
The chance of life. Now the boy pats my dog
And we start home. Now I am good.
The last mistaken,
Ecstatic, accidental bliss, the blind   30

Happiness that, bursting, leaves upon the palm
Some soap and water—
It was so long ago, back in some Gay
Twenties, Nineties, I don't know . . . Today I miss
My lovely daughter   35
Away at school, my sons away at school,

My husband away at work—I wish for them.
The dog, the maid,
And I go through the sure unvarying days
At home in them. As I look at my life,   40
I am afraid
Only that it will change, as I am changing:

I am afraid, this morning, of my face.
It looks at me
From the rear-view mirror, with the eyes I hate,   45
The smile I hate, its plain, lined look
Of gray discovery
Repeats to me: "You're old." That's all, I'm old.

And yet I'm afraid, as I was at the funeral
I went to yesterday.   50
My friend's cold made-up face, granite among its flowers,
Her undressed, operated-on, dressed body
Were my face and body.
As I think of her I hear her telling me

How young I seem; I *am* exceptional;   55
I think of all I have.
But really no one is exceptional,
No one has anything, I'm anybody,
I stand beside my grave
Confused with my life, that is commonplace and solitary.   60

                                                                    1965

◆━ WELDON KEES ━◆
(1914–1955)

Weldon Kees, the mysterious and melancholy Renaissance man of mid-century American poetry, was born in Beatrice, Nebraska, in 1914. His father, a second-generation German American with cultivated literary taste, owned a small hardware factory. His mother, who could trace her ancestry back to the *Mayflower,* was a conventional woman inclined to indulge her only child. A frail but conspicuously talented boy, the young Kees put on puppet shows, played the piano, and published his own magazine on his father's office mimeograph machine. In high school Kees avoided sports, acted in plays, edited the yearbook, and annoyed his teachers. For two years he attended Doane College in Crete, Nebraska, where he wrote and produced five one-act plays before transferring to University of Missouri at Columbia in an unsuccessful search for better writing courses. A year later Kees transferred again to University of Nebraska in Lincoln to study with Lowry C. Wimberly, the editor of *Prairie Schooner,* the preeminent Midwestern literary quarterly of the Depression era. Wimberly, who had already accepted Kees's short story, "Saturday Rain," for the journal, quickly recognized the singular artistic gifts of the impeccably well-dressed and remarkably well-read student.

Graduating in 1935, Kees faced the considerable challenge of starting a literary career in the middle of the Depression. At this point he considered himself primarily a fiction writer. He had already begun a novel and was successfully placing his short stories in journals. (Between 1935 and 1945 he published forty-three stories and sketches before abandoning fiction.) Kees entered graduate school at the University of Chicago but quickly dropped out. "I've never been quite so disappointed in a place in my life," he wrote a friend—sounding a note of bitter disillusionment often to be repeated in his life. In 1936 Kees was invited by Wimberly to join the Federal Writers' Project in Lincoln where he spent two years working on the Nebraska state guide. Finally in 1937 he obtained a job at the Denver Public Library. One month after being hired, Kees married his college girlfriend, Ann Swan.

For the next six years the couple lived in Denver where in 1940 Kees became director for the Rocky Mountain Center for Bibliographical Research. In Colorado Kees finished but was unable to publish two novels, *Slow Parade,* the manuscript of which has been lost, and *Fall Quarter,* a dark academic satire, which appeared posthumously in 1990. Kees also began to work seriously on poetry, and gradually his literary interests shifted decisively from prose to verse. This artistic move transformed his literary work. Although the bleak naturalist vision of his stories continued into the poetry, his style changed remarkably. The deliberately flat and minimalist style of his fiction bloomed into the supple, dramatic, and extravagant language of his poetry.

In March 1943, the twenty-nine-year-old Kees moved to New York City. Assuming he would soon be drafted, he wanted to make a real beginning at a mainstream literary life. Kees was soon hired by *Time* magazine to write on books and music. Meanwhile to his relief, he was declared "psychologically unfit" for military service. Witty, cultivated, and sociable, Kees thrived in Manhattan. He struck up friendships with many distinguished writers, including Edmund Wilson, Conrad Aiken, Malcolm Cowley, Horace Gregory, and Howard Nemerov. Laid off by *Time* in September, he found a job writing for Paramount Pictures newsreels—just as his first collection of poems, *The Last Man* (1943), appeared in a limited edition.

The eight years Kees spent in New York marked the height—at least in public terms—of his artistic and intellectual career. His poems, essays, and reviews appeared in the most influential magazines, the *New Yorker, Time,* the *New Republic,* the *Nation, Partisan Review,* and *Poetry,* as well as the most fashionable small journals. He published his second book of poems, *The Fall of the Magicians* (1947), and won *Poetry's* Blumenthal Award. In 1947 he quit Paramount to freelance as a writer. Meanwhile he became fascinated with contemporary painting, especially the emerging Abstract Expressionist movement. Kees began painting seriously, and he formed friendships with some of the most innovative artists of the time, including Jackson Pollack, Hans Hoffman, Mark Rothko, and Willem de Kooning. Actively involved in the cultural battles of contemporary painting, he was one of the "Irascibles," the eighteen artists who signed a protest letter castigating the Metropolitan Museum of Art for excluding experimental works from their 1950 exhibition of American painting. Kees was very highly regarded in the New York art world. He exhibited his paintings at the Peridot Gallery, and in 1949 he succeeded the prominent and powerful Clement Greenberg as art critic for the *Nation.*

In late 1950 the ever-restless Kees left New York for California. Although he loved the intellectual excitement of Manhattan, he and Ann were tired of living in poverty. "We damn near froze," he complained about his last winter in a shabby Lower East Side loft. He also disliked the intense competition and neurotic angst among artists and writers in New York. Hoping to find a supportive community of artists, he arrived in the Bay Area, full of energy and optimism, and immediately became a significant cultural presence. He made documentary films with anthropologist Gregory Bateson and psychiatrist Jurgen Ruesch, as well as his own experimental films like *Hotel Apex* (1952). The California Palace of the Legion of Honor mounted a solo show of his paintings. He hosted a radio program on film (to which he often invited the young Pauline Kael who would eventually become the *New Yorker's* most celebrated movie critic). Kees also produced *The Poets' Follies of 1955,* a literary cabaret, which attracted national attention and prefigured the Beat gatherings that would soon transform San Francisco literary life. For *The Poets' Follies* he composed songs and sketches. He also wrote the score for James Broughton's film, *Adventures of Jimmy* (1950).

This frenetic activity, however, could not cure the deepening melancholy affecting Kees. Despite his constant work, he could barely make a living. He complained to Kael that even at forty he still had to borrow money from his parents, who reluctantly helped subsidize his final collection, *Poems: 1947–1954* (1954), which appeared in a limited edition. In 1954 Ann had an alcoholic breakdown, and Kees quickly separated and divorced her—a move that increased his manic depressive mood swings. He drank heavily and took both tranquilizers and stimulants. In 1955 he invested his money and energy in creating the Showplace, a performance space in San Francisco's Mission District. He planned and rehearsed an evening of notable one-act plays, which would include the premiere of his own work, *The Waiting Room,* a compelling experimental play. When the Showplace was closed days before the planned premiere for Fire Department violations, Kees despaired. "I wanted to cry 'enough,'" he wrote a friend, "so I did." The company disbanded, the theater's lease was broken, and the already financially strapped Kees bore most of the penalties.

The poet's mood darkened. Uncharacteristically aimless and depressed, he talked about suicide and claimed to be researching a book entitled *Famous Sui-*

cides. He also spoke of going to Mexico to start a new life. On July 18, 1955, his car was found abandoned—with the keys still in the ignition—on the north end of the Golden Gate Bridge. His body was never found. Although a few people have claimed to see him later in Mexico and Southern California, the circumstantial evidence points overwhelmingly toward suicide. At the time of his disappearance, he was forty-one years old.

Five years later, Kees's *Collected Poems,* edited by Donald Justice, was published in a limited edition. In his preface Justice made what might have seemed an extravagant claim for the little-known writer. "He is an important poet, among the three or four best of his generation." Nearly half a century later that bold assessment seems to have been borne out. Although academic critics still mostly neglect his work, Kees has become a major figure and continuing influence—indeed a virtual cult figure—among contemporary poets, both in the United States and abroad.

Kees had a particular genius for formal innovation, which ranged from experimentation with existing patterns to the invention of entirely new shapes of poetry. No poet of his generation, including Robert Lowell, experimented so successfully with the sonnet; Kees created sinuous new variants of this traditional form, as in "For My Daughter." More unexpected and provocative were Kees's many attempts to employ the visual techniques of modern art, especially collage and abstraction, in poetry. In this sense Kees's work prefigures the poetry of the New York School, though his verse usually reflects a more careful and expressive musical structure. His influential poem, "Round," for instance, assembles a collage of historical quotations, biographical facts, and mundane domestic details and arranges them to create a haunting verbal tune. Kees also took ordinary prose forms—concert program notes, dissertation abstracts, diary entries, detective stories, meeting reports—and transformed them into new verse forms. Feverishly inventive, Kees rarely repeated an experiment, preferring to move on to some new idea. His development of novel forms is not mere technical bravado since he characteristically uses them to convey powerful emotional and intellectual effects.

Despite his formal originality, musical brilliance, and technical skill, it is ultimately the dark and brooding vision of Kees's poetry that makes his great claim on posterity. Like T. S. Eliot, who greatly influenced his work, Kees had a deep dread of contemporary civilization. He also shared Eliot's ability to make a nightmarish view of human existence not merely bearable but strangely beautiful by conveying it with lyrical force and mordant humor. One of the most bitter modern American poets, he is also one of the funniest since he grimly delights in the absurdities of human frailty and hypocrisy. He sees modern civilization as a failed experiment—spiritually, culturally, and politically—that has led the world to the brink of apocalypse. Kees's poetry is also suffused with religious longing, but unlike Eliot or W. H. Auden, he found no comfort or reassurance in Christianity. The characters in his poems, like his alter ego Robinson, see no possibility of salvation or transcendence. They can only wait, quietly or hysterically, for the inevitable end.

For My Daughter

Looking into my daughter's eyes I read
Beneath the innocence of morning flesh
Concealed, hintings of death she does not heed.
Coldest of winds have blown his hair, and mesh
Of seaweed snarled these miniatures of hands;   5
The night's slow poison, tolerant and bland,
Has moved her blood. Parched years that I have seen
That may be hers appear: foul, lingering
Death in certain war, the slim legs green.
Or, fed on hate, she relishes the sting   10
Of others' agony; perhaps the cruel
Bride of a syphilitic or a fool.
These speculations sour in the sun.
I have no daughter. I desire none.

1943

Crime Club

No butler, no second maid, no blood upon the stair.
No eccentric aunt, no gardener, no family friend
Smiling among the bric-a-brac and murder.
Only a suburban house with the front door open
And a dog barking at a squirrel, and the cars   5
Passing. The corpse quite dead. The wife in Florida.

Consider the clues: the potato masher in a vase,
The torn photograph of a Wesleyan basketball team,
Scattered with check stubs in the hall;
The unsent fan letter to Shirley Temple,   10
The Hoover button on the lapel of the deceased,
The note: "To be killed this way is quite all right with me."

Small wonder that the case remains unsolved,
Or that the sleuth, Le Roux, is now incurably insane,
And sits alone in a white room in a white gown,   15
Screaming that all the world is mad, that clues
Lead nowhere, or to walls so high their tops cannot be seen;
Screaming all day of war, screaming that nothing can be solved.

1947

River Song

By the public hook for the private eye,
Near the neutral river where the children were,
I was hung for the street, to watch the sky.

When they strung me there, I waved like a flag
Near the bright blue river where the children played,   5
And my smile became part of the cultural lag.

I named three martyrs. My mother came
To the grayish river where the children stared:
"My son, you have honored the family name."

I was happy. Then a parade went by   10
Near the shadowy river where the children waved,
And the uniforms made me shiver and cry.

I tried to get down. What I had learned
Near the sunless river where the children screamed
Was only pain. My ropemarks burned.   15

But I couldn't move. Had I been thrown
By the darkening river where the children failed,
Or had I come there quite alone?

The bands were playing when they cut me down
By the dirty river where the children cried,   20
And a man made a speech in a long black gown.

He called me a hero. I didn't care.
The river ran blood and the children died.
And I wanted to die, but they left me there.

1947

Robinson

The dog stops barking after Robinson has gone.
His act is over. The world is a gray world,
Not without violence, and he kicks under the grand piano,
The nightmare chase well under way.

The mirror from Mexico, stuck to the wall,   5
Reflects nothing at all. The glass is black.
Robinson alone provides the image Robinsonian.

Which is all of the room—walls, curtains,
Shelves, bed, the tinted photograph of Robinson's first wife,
Rugs, vases, panatellas in a humidor.   10
They would fill the room if Robinson came in.

The pages in the books are blank,
The books that Robinson has read. That is his favorite chair,
Or where the chair would be if Robinson were here.

All day the phone rings. It could be Robinson   15
Calling. It never rings when he is here.

Outside, white buildings yellow in the sun.
Outside, the birds circle continuously
Where trees are actual and take no holiday.

1947

Aspects of Robinson

Robinson at cards at the Algonquin;[1] a thin
Blue light comes down once more outside the blinds.
Gray men in overcoats are ghosts blown past the door.
The taxis streak the avenues with yellow, orange, and red.
This is Grand Central,[2] Mr. Robinson.   5

Robinson on a roof above the Heights;[3] the boats
Mourn like the lost. Water is slate, far down.
Through sounds of ice cubes dropped in glass, an osteopath,
Dressed for the links, describes an old Intourist[4] tour.
—Here's where old Gibbons jumped from, Robinson.   10

Robinson walking in the Park, admiring the elephant.
Robinson buying the *Tribune,* Robinson buying the *Times.* Robinson
Saying "Hello. Yes, this is Robinson. Sunday
At five? I'd love to. Pretty well. And you?"
Robinson alone at Longchamps,[5] staring at the wall.   15

Robinson afraid, drunk, sobbing Robinson
In bed with a Mrs. Morse. Robinson at home;
Decisions: Toynbee or luminol?[6] Where the sun
Shines, Robinson in flowered trunks, eyes toward
The breakers. Where the night ends, Robinson in East Side bars.   20

Robinson in Glen plaid jacket, Scotch-grain shoes,
Black four-in-hand[7] and oxford button-down,
The jeweled and silent watch that winds itself, the brief-
Case, covert topcoat, clothes for spring, all covering
His sad and usual heart, dry as a winter leaf.   25

1954

1926

The porchlight coming on again,
Early November, the dead leaves
Raked in piles, the wicker swing
Creaking. Across the lots
A phonograph is playing *Ja-Da.*[8]   5

---

1. A stylish Manhattan hotel favored by writers.
2. Grand Central Station, a major New York City train station.
3. Brooklyn Heights.
4. The official Soviet Union tourist agency.
5. A Manhattan restaurant.
6. Arnold Toynbee (1889–1975) was a British historian. Luminol was a sedative. The implication is that both can put Robinson to sleep.
7. A knot for a necktie.
8. A popular song of the period.

An orange moon. I see the lives
Of neighbors, mapped and marred
Like all the wars ahead, and R.
Insane, B. with his throat cut,
Fifteen years from now, in Omaha.   10

I did not know them then.
My airedale scratches at the door.
And I am back from seeing Milton Sills
And Doris Kenyon.[9] Twelve years old.
The porchlight coming on again.   15

1954

Round[1]

"Wondrous life!" cried Marvell at Appleton House.[2]
Renan[3] admired Jesus Christ "wholeheartedly."
But here dried ferns keep falling to the floor,
And something inside my head
Flaps like a worn-out blind. Royal Cortissoz[4] is dead.   5
A blow to the *Herald-Tribune*. A closet mouse
Rattles the wrapper on the breakfast food. Renan
Admired Jesus Christ "wholeheartedly."

Flaps like a worn-out blind. Cézanne[5]
Would break out in the quiet streets of Aix   10
And shout, "Le monde, c'est terrible!"[6] Royal
Cortissoz is dead. And something inside my head
Flaps like a worn-out blind. The soil
In which the ferns are dying needs more Vigoro.[7]
There is no twilight on the moon, no mist or rain,   15
No hail or snow, no life. Here in this house

Dried ferns keeping falling to the floor, a mouse
Rattles the wrapper on the breakfast food. Cézanne
Would break out in the quiet streets and scream. Renan
Admired Jesus Christ "wholeheartedly." And something inside my head   20

---

9. A pair of popular silent film stars.
1. A round is a type of song (like "Row, Row, Row Your Boat") in which three or four voices follow one another singing the same melody in counterpoint. Kees's poem combines different voices to achieve the same effect in words.
2. English poet Andrew Marvell (1621–1678) wrote his famous celebration of the contemplative rural life, "The Garden," at Appleton House, a Yorkshire country manor.
3. Ernest Renan, a French historian (1823–1892), wrote *The Life of Jesus* (1863), a humanistic study of the origins of Christianity.
4. Royal Cortissoz (1869–1948), a middlebrow art critic for the New York *Herald Tribune*. Presumably, the speaker of the poem has just read his obituary in the newspaper.
5. Paul Cézanne (1839–1906), a French Post-impressionist painter, who was born and died in Aix-en-Provence.
6. (French) "The world, it is terrible!"
7. A commercial brand of plant food.

Flaps like a worn-out blind. Royal Cortissoz is dead.
There is no twilight on the moon, no hail or snow.
One notes fresh desecrations of the portico.
"Wondrous life!" cried Marvell at Appleton House.

1954

◆━ DUDLEY RANDALL ━◆
(1914–2000)

Although often overlooked by the literary establishment during his lifetime, Dudley Randall was a poet of distinction and originality as well as a major figure in the Black Arts movement. The son of a Congregational minister, Randall was born in Washington, D.C., but his family moved to Detroit when he was nine. He began publishing poems on the "Young Poets Page" of the *Detroit Free Press* at thirteen, and by sixteen he graduated from high school. In 1932 he took a job in Ford Motors' River Rouge foundry where he stayed for five years until joining the U.S. Postal Service. In 1943 Randall served in the U.S. Army Air Corps as a supply sergeant in the South Pacific. After World War II, he used the GI Bill to attend Wayne State University where he earned both a bachelor's degree in English and a master's degree in library sciences. In 1951 he began a career as a librarian.

Randall's literary career initially developed slowly—interrupted by the Depression, World War II, a late education, a library career, and two unsuccessful marriages. By early middle age, however, he was settled in both a career and a happy third marriage (which lasted forty-three years until his death), and poetry reasserted itself in his life. His defining moment as a writer came after the 1963 Birmingham, Alabama, church bombing that killed four black girls. The outraged Randall wrote "The Ballad of Birmingham" in their memory, and he published the poem as a single-sheet broadside. In this one passionate gesture Randall not only created his most widely anthologized poem but he also started the Detroit-based Broadside Press, which over the next ten years became the major literary press of the Black Arts movement. Started with twelve dollars in Randall's spare bedroom, it eventually published writers like Alice Walker, Gwendolyn Brooks, Amiri Baraka, Sterling Brown, Etheridge Knight, Audre Lorde, and Margaret Walker. Broadside Press was conceived in idealistic terms. "Black publishers should try to build a stable base in their own communities," Randall declared. He never turned a profit with his community-based press, but its artistic success has never been questioned.

Randall's own poetry flourished in the Broadside Press environment. His first book, *Poem Counterpoem,* a collaboration with Margaret Danner, appeared in 1966. *Cities Burning* (1968) and *Love You* (1970) soon followed. Randall's poetry defied the mainstream poetic fashions of the era. He wrote both free and formal verse, refusing to see the two modes as oppositional. In both modes he uses auditory and musical elements to create a resonant type of public speech. His poems are often political, but they usually make their points indirectly, often with cutting humor, as in "Booker T. and W. E. B."

Randall was also an influential anthologist. His collection *For Malcolm: Poems on the Life and Death of Malcolm X* (1967) gathered a broad spectrum of African American writing on the assassinated black Muslim leader. *The Black Poets* (1971) became one of the defining anthologies of its kind. Both books are still in print decades later. Despite his many accomplishments Randall received little national attention during his long, active career, but he was recognized in Detroit as one of the city's major cultural figures. In 1981 he was appointed Detroit's first Poet Laureate. Randall died in 2000 at the age of eighty-six.

◄◦►═◄█►═◄◦►

Ballad of Birmingham

(On the Bombing of a Church in Birmingham, Alabama, 1963)

"Mother dear, may I go downtown
Instead of out to play,
And march the streets of Birmingham
In a Freedom March today?"

"No, baby, no, you may not go,   5
For the dogs are fierce and wild,
And clubs and hoses, guns and jail
Aren't good for a little child."

"But, mother, I won't be alone.
Other children will go with me,   10
And march the streets of Birmingham
To make our country free."

"No, baby, no, you may not go,
For I fear those guns will fire.
But you may go to church instead   15
And sing in the children's choir."

She has combed and brushed her night-dark hair,
And bathed rose petal sweet,
And drawn white gloves on her small brown hands,
And white shoes on her feet.   20

The mother smiled to know her child
Was in the sacred place,
But that smile was the last smile
To come upon her face.

For when she heard the explosion,   25
Her eyes grew wet and wild.
She raced through the streets of Birmingham
Calling for her child.

She clawed through bits of glass and brick,
Then lifted out a shoe.   30
"O here's the shoe my baby wore,
But, baby, where are you?"

                                                                  1966

Booker T. and W. E. B.[1]

"It seems to me," said Booker T.,
"It shows a mighty lot of cheek
To study chemistry and Greek
When Mister Charlie needs a hand
To hoe the cotton on his land,   5
And when Miss Ann looks for a cook,
Why stick your nose inside a book?"

"I don't agree," said W. E. B.,
"If I should have the drive to seek
Knowledge of chemistry or Greek,   10
I'll do it. Charles and Miss can look
Another place for hand or cook.
Some men rejoice in skill of hand,
And some in cultivating land,
But there are others who maintain   15
The right to cultivate the brain."

"It seems to me," said Booker T.,
"That all you folks have missed the boat
Who shout about the right to vote,
And spend vain days and sleepless nights   20
In uproar over civil rights.
Just keep your mouths shut, do not grouse,
But work, and save, and buy a house."

"I don't agree," said W. E. B.,
"For what can property avail   25
If dignity and justice fail.
Unless you help to make the laws,
They'll steal your house with trumped-up clause.
A rope's as tight, a fire as hot,
No matter how much cash you've got.   30
Speak soft, and try your little plan,
But as for me, I'll be a man."

"It seems to me," said Booker T.—

---

1. Booker T. Washington (1856–1915) was an educator and a founder of the Tuskegee Institute, a leading black educational institution where George Washington Carver was also employed. W. E. B. Du Bois (1868–1963) was a civil rights leader, an author, and the cofounder of the NAACP (National Association for the Advancement of Colored People). His best-known book was *The Souls of Black Folk* (1903).

"I don't agree,"
Said W. E. B.   35

1966

A Different Image

The age
requires this task:
create
a different image;
re-animate   5
the mask.

Shatter the icons of slavery and fear.
Replace
the leer
of the minstrel's burnt-cork face   10
with a proud, serene
and classic bronze of Benin.[2]

1968

◄ WILLIAM STAFFORD ►
(1914–1993)

Born in Hutchinson, Kansas, to parents who loved books, but struggled to survive during the Great Depression, William Edgar Stafford learned early on to value literature, hard work, and independence of mind. As his family moved from town to town during the 1930s looking for work, Stafford took jobs delivering newspapers, raising vegetables to sell from door to door, and serving as an electrician's assistant in an oil refinery. After graduating from high school and spending two years at El Dorado junior college, Stafford enrolled at the University of Kansas, waiting tables to pay his way.

He received his B.A. in 1937 and hoped to become a writer, but his ambition was tested during World War II when he registered as a conscientious objector. Stafford served in C.O. camps in Arkansas, Illinois, and California—an experience he documented in his novel, *Down in My Heart* (1947). Despite the forced isolation and constant labor, Stafford did not put his life on hold; he continued writing and even married in 1944. Because physical exhaustion allowed no time to write at night, Stafford devised a strategy he maintained for the rest of his life: rising at four A.M. "Since those days," he noted, " I have had the habit of writing in the early morning. That dawn time is precious: the world is quiet; no one will interrupt; you are rested and ready."

The habit was especially useful after his release from the camps. He completed his master's degree at the University of Kansas, fathered four children, taught high

---

2. A country in West Africa.

school in California, and then worked for a relief agency. In 1948, he was hired to teach English at Lewis and Clark College in Portland, Oregon, a job he held until his retirement in 1980. From 1950 to 1952, the college granted him a leave to study creative writing at the University of Iowa, where he earned a Ph.D. in 1954. Although he enjoyed having daily exchanges with other writers there, he felt that the competitive climate of the Iowa workshops was antithetical to his goal of making writing a process of discovery rather than dictated by a group's definition of good poetry. After Stafford returned to teaching, this nonconformist attitude shaped his own approach to the classroom, for he tried not to praise or criticize students, but instead to help them discover their own directions. Stafford's faith in the creative process also clarified his own writing—especially his practice of letting poems develop almost by chance, as a means of exploration.

Despite his immense productivity, book publication came late for Stafford. His first collection, *West of Your City* (1960), did not appear until he was forty-six. But he went on to publish twelve volumes of poetry with mainstream presses, as well as numerous broadsides, chapbooks, and full-length collections with small presses. After his second book, *Traveling through the Dark* (1962), won the National Book Award, he continued to receive honors for his poetry: the Shelley Memorial Award (1964), a Guggenheim Fellowship (1966), an appointment to serve as Poetry Consultant to the Library of Congress (1970), the Award in Literature from the American Academy and Institute of Arts and Letters (1981), and—a year before his death—the Western States Book Award for Lifetime Achievement in Poetry (1992). Although academic critics have rarely found Stafford's direct and heartfelt style compelling, his fellow poets admired him greatly. When *Writer's Digest* polled U.S. poets in 1986 to determine their nominations for "the ten major living American poets," Stafford ranked first in votes.

Stafford's belief in the power of "the inner life" to shape his work linked him with the Deep Image poets, for whom poetry was a way of mining the unconscious. His best poems take disquieting turns and offer unsentimental meditations on human limitations and nature's inscrutability. His pared down language and spare syntax are supple enough to echo the forbidding landscapes of the Great Plains and the American West that he often contemplates and also to balance between seriousness and lightness so that his poems develop complex perspectives on ordinary experience.

The Farm on the Great Plains

A telephone line goes cold;
birds tread it wherever it goes.
A farm back of a great plain
tugs an end of the line.

I call that farm every year,   5
ringing it, listening, still;
no one is home at the farm,
the line gives only a hum.

Some year I will ring the line
on a night at last the right one,   10
and with an eye tapered for braille
from the phone on the wall

I will see the tenant who waits—
the last one left at the place;
through the dark my braille eye   15
will lovingly touch his face.

"Hello, is Mother at home?"
No one is home today.
"But Father—he should be there."
No one—no one is here.   20

"But you—are you the one . . . ?"
Then the line will be gone
because both ends will be home:
no space, no birds, no farm.

My self will be the plain,   25
wise as winter is gray,
pure as cold posts go
pacing toward what I know.

                                                                    1960

Traveling through the Dark

Traveling through the dark I found a deer
dead on the edge of the Wilson River road.
It is usually best to roll them into the canyon:
that road is narrow; to swerve might make more dead.

By glow of the tail-light I stumbled back of the car   5
and stood by the heap, a doe, a recent killing;
she had stiffened already, almost cold.
I dragged her off; she was large in the belly.

My fingers touching her side brought me the reason—
her side was warm; her fawn lay there waiting,   10
alive, still, never to be born.
Beside that mountain road I hesitated.

The car aimed ahead its lowered parking lights;
under the hood purred the steady engine.
I stood in the glare of the warm exhaust turning red;   15
around our group I could hear the wilderness listen.

I thought hard for us all—my only swerving—,
then pushed her over the edge into the river.

                                                                    1962

Ask Me

Some time when the river is ice ask me
mistakes I have made. Ask me whether
what I have done is my life. Others
have come in their slow way into
my thought, and some have tried to help   5
or to hurt: ask me what difference
their strongest love or hate has made.

I will listen to what you say.
You and I can turn and look
at the silent river and wait. We know   10
the current is there, hidden; and there
are comings and goings from miles away
that hold the stillness exactly before us.
What the river says, that is what I say.

1975

At the Un-National Monument

along the Canadian Border

This is the field where the battle did not happen,
where the unknown soldier did not die.
This is the field where grass joined hands,
where no monument stands,
and the only heroic thing is the sky.   5

Birds fly here without any sound,
unfolding their wings across the open.
No people killed—or were killed—on this ground
hallowed by neglect and an air so tame
that people celebrate it by forgetting its name.   10

1977

Our Kind

Our mother knew our worth—
not much. To her, success
was not being noticed at all.
"If we can stay out of jail,"
she said, "God will be proud of us."   5

"Not worth a row of pins,"
she said, when we looked at the album:
"Grandpa?—ridiculous."
Her hearing was bad, and that
was good: "None of us ever says much."   10

She sent us forth equipped
for our kind of world, a world of
our betters, in a nation so strong
its greatest claim is no boast,
its leaders telling us all, "Be proud"—   15

But over their shoulders, God and
our mother, signaling: "Ridiculous."

1982

THOMAS MERTON
(1915–1968)

The son of two artists, Thomas Merton was born in southern France but spent his early childhood in New York. After his mother's death when he was six years old, he lived in Bermuda, France, and England with his father and spent time with his mother's relatives on Long Island. Sustained schooling began at age eleven, when he entered the Lycée de Montauban in France. Later he attended Oakham School in England, and then studied at Cambridge for a year before transferring to Columbia University. In his autobiography, *The Seven Storey Mountain* (1948), he confesses that after his father's death from cancer in 1930, "I found myself completely stripped of everything that impeded the movement of my own will to do as it pleased. I imagined that I was free. And it would take me five or six years to discover what a frightful captivity I had got myself into." By the time he received his bachelor's degree in 1938, that freedom felt empty to him. After reading Etienne Gilson's *The Spirit of Medieval Philosophy,* he became increasingly drawn to Catholicism and was baptized into the church in November 1938. The following February he completed his master's degree in English at Columbia. For the next three years, he taught at St. Bonaventure University in upstate New York. Although Merton had schooled himself as a writer, he became so deeply immersed in his new faith that, in December 1941, he entered the Abbey of Gethsemani near Louisville, Kentucky, determined to live a contemplative life as a Trappist monk.

The Trappists, Cistercian monks who follow the strict rules of the French abbey of La Trappe, not only required the three traditional clerical vows—poverty, chastity, and obedience—but also demanded withdrawal from the secular world within the walls of the monastery as well as a vow of silence. The monks slept on boards in unheated cells, and spent their days alternating between prayer and hard physical labor. Although Merton's two vocations, as writer and monk, sometimes conflicted, he spent the remaining twenty-seven years of his life in Gethsemani, and he was ordained a priest in 1949. Once his abbot sanctioned his writing, Merton was remarkably prolific. While maintaining his religious duties, he produced over fifty books—including fifteen collections of poetry—and hundreds of essays. He also carried out a voluminous correspondence. His books of verse include *Thirty Poems* (1944), *Figures for an Apocalypse* (1947), and *The Tears of the Blind Lion* (1949). Merton's *Collected Poems* appeared posthumously in 1977. His autobiography, *The Seven Storey Mountain,* became an international bestseller, and Merton followed it with a series of remarkable books exploring the

Catholic contemplative and mystical traditions—most notably *Seeds of Contemplation* (1949), *The Waters of Siloe* (1949), *No Man Is an Island* (1955), and *The Wisdom of the Desert* (1960). He also explored cultural and political issues in articles and books like *Thoughts in Solitude* (1958) and *The Secular Journal of Thomas Merton* (1959). Sequestered in his monastery (where he eventually lived as a hermit in a small building in the woods), the reclusive author became one of the major public intellectuals of mid-century American letters. Today Merton is often regarded as the most important American Catholic writer of the twentieth century. As he grew older, he became interested in the correspondences between Catholicism and Asian religions, and in the last five years of his life he made trips to Asia to visit other monasteries. He died in Bangkok, Thailand, accidentally electrocuted after he touched the exposed wires of a fan.

Merton's first love was poetry, and he wrote it with ease and enthusiasm. Because of that ease—both with the religious themes he explores and with the forms he employs—his poetry often lacks the sense of struggle that animates the work of his favorite poet, Gerard Manley Hopkins. But at its best, Merton's verse articulates the serenity and sense of security that he found in his faith.

◂•▸━◆━◂•▸

For My Brother:
Reported Missing in Action, 1943

Sweet brother, if I do not sleep
My eyes are flowers for your tomb;
And if I cannot eat my bread,
My fasts shall live like willows where you died.
If in the heat I find no water for my thirst,   5
My thirst shall turn to springs for you, poor traveller.

Where, in what desolate and smokey country,
Lies your poor body, lost and dead?
And in what landscape of disaster
Has your unhappy spirit lost its road?   10

Come, in my labor find a resting place
And in my sorrows lay your head,
Or rather take my life and blood
And buy yourself a better bed—
Or take my breath and take my death   15
And buy yourself a better rest.

When all the men of war are shot
And flags have fallen into dust,
Your cross and mine shall tell men still
Christ died on each, for both of us.   20

For in the wreckage of your April Christ lies slain,
And Christ weeps in the ruins of my spring:
The money of Whose tears shall fall

Into your weak and friendless hand,
And buy you back to your own land: 25

The silence of Whose tears shall fall
Like bells upon your alien tomb.
Hear them and come: they call you home.

1944

The Reader[1]

Lord, when the clock strikes
Telling the time with cold tin
And I sit hooded in this lectern

Waiting for the monks to come,
I see the red cheeses, and bowls   5
All smile with milk in ranks upon their tables.

Light fills my proper globe
(I have won light to read by
With a little, tinkling chain)

And the monks come down the cloister   10
With robes as voluble as water.
I do not see them but I hear their waves.

It is winter, and my hands prepare
To turn the pages of the saints:
And to the trees Thy moon has frozen on the windows   15
My tongue shall sing Thy Scripture.

Then the monks pause upon the step
(With me here in this lectern
And Thee there on Thy crucifix)
And gather little pearls of water on their fingers' ends   20
Smaller than this my psalm.

1949

◄ MARGARET WALKER ►

(1915–1998)

Born in Birmingham, Alabama, in 1915, Margaret Walker absorbed a love of literature, music, and the Bible from her father, a Methodist minister, and her mother, a musician. By the age of eleven, she was reading the poetry of Langston Hughes and Countee Cullen. She graduated from Northwestern University in 1935 and a year

---

1. In Trappist communities the monks eat in silence while one of them reads from Scripture or from writings of the church fathers.

later was hired as a junior writer by the WPA's Writers' Project in Chicago, where she began a friendship with another young writer, Richard Wright, that Walker called a "rare and once-in-a-lifetime association . . . rather uncommon in its strictly literary nature." For the next three years, Wright and Walker commented on each other's writing and supported each other's efforts to publish. After Wright returned to the South, Walker helped him accumulate material on which he based his novel, *Native Son,* and he encouraged her to concentrate on poetry and to delay the novel she was drafting, a story of slavery in the Civil War era, eventually published decades later as *Jubilee* (1966). In 1939, pursuing a career in teaching and writing, Walker enrolled at the University of Iowa, where she received a master's degree in 1940. Steven Vincent Benét chose her thesis, *For My People,* as the winner of the Yale Series of Younger Poets Award in 1942. Walker was the first African American to be given this honor. Praising Walker's achievement, Benét noted: "Straightforwardness, directness, reality are good things to find in a young poet. It is rarer to find them combined with a controlled intensity of emotion and a language that, at times, even when it is most modern, has something of the surge of biblical poetry." *For My People,* which includes protest poems, sonnets, and ballads that depict a range of African American folk characters, enjoyed both critical success and popular acclaim. Its title sums up Walker's goal to write accessible poems that will move readers; she has said that "my books have been popular—that is, they have been successful with the people—and that is all that I could wish."

During the 1940s, Walker took year-long teaching appointments at several Southern colleges, married in 1943, and had the first of her four children soon after. In 1949, she began teaching at Jackson State University in Mississippi, where she remained until her retirement thirty years later. Because of the pressures of teaching and raising a family, she published little during the 1950s, and although she pursued research for *Jubilee,* she could complete the book only by enrolling again at the University of Iowa in 1962, where she developed the novel as her Ph.D. dissertation. Turning back to poetry during the Civil Rights Movement, she published her second full collection, *Prophets for a New Day* (1970), with Broadside Press, Dudley Randall's African American press in Detroit, which also published several pamphlets of her poetry including *The Ballad of the Free* (1966) and *October Journey* (1973). Retirement from teaching in 1979 gave her the time to complete a critical study, *The Daemonic Genius of Richard Wright* (1982), and collect her essays in *How I Wrote Jubilee and Other Essays on Life and Literature* (1989) and *On Being Female, Black, and Free: Essays by Margaret Walker, 1932–1992* (1997). She also gathered her poetry in *This Is My Century: New and Collected Poems* (1989). After a long battle with breast cancer, Walker died in 1998.

◄◦═══►═◦►

For Malcolm X[1]

All you violated ones with gentle hearts;
You violent dreamers whose cries shout heartbreak;
Whose voices echo clamors of our cool capers,
And whose black faces have hollowed pits for eyes.

---

1. Malcolm Little (1925–1965), a militant civil rights leader who converted to Islam. He was assassinated in New York City.

All you gambling sons and hooked children and bowery bums   5
Hating white devils and black bourgeoisie,
Thumbing your noses at your burning red suns,
Gather round this coffin and mourn your dying swan.

Snow-white moslem head-dress around a dead black face!
Beautiful were your sand-papering words against our skins!   10
Our blood and water pour from your flowing wounds.
You have cut open our breasts and dug scalpels in our brains.
When and Where will another come to take your holy place?
Old man mumbling in his dotage, or crying child, unborn?

1970

◦◄ JOHN CIARDI ►◦
(1916–1986)

Poet, translator, critic, anthologist, lexicographer, media celebrity, and eminently successful public man of letters, John Anthony Ciardi was born in Boston's Italian section, the North End. The youngest of four children of Neapolitan immigrants, Ciardi was just three years old when his father died in a car accident. The poet's impoverished mother, who was illiterate, moved her children to nearby Medford to live with her relations. Raised bilingually, speaking an Italian dialect at home and English at school, Ciardi worked from an early age to help support the family—selling vegetables door-to-door and working on a fishing boat. An excellent student, he became the one member of the family chosen to go to college—a common practice among Italian immigrants who could not afford advanced education for all their children. Accepted at Bates College in 1934, Ciardi had to hitchhike to Lewiston, Maine, to begin classes. In 1936 he transferred to Tufts University. Working in construction during his two years at Tufts, he still managed to graduate magna cum laude in 1938. Ciardi won a scholarship for graduate school at the University of Michigan, where his teachers were surprised to meet the big, muscular, dark-haired young man. "No one would have guessed him a poet," commented one instructor.

Ciardi's poetic talent and ambition, however, were never in doubt. He won Michigan's prestigious Avery Hopwood Award in 1939 and used the money to repay family loans. The prize also led to the publication of his first book, *Homeward to America* (1940), his first teaching job at the University of Kansas City, and his first visit to the Bread Loaf Writers' Conference, the influential summer program that Ciardi would eventually direct from 1955 to 1972. In 1942 Ciardi enlisted in the U.S. Army Air Corps, and he served in the Pacific theater as an aerial gunner on a B-29 "superfortress" bomber. He saw combat in dangerous raids on Tokyo and other mainland Japanese cities in which many American soldiers were lost. Returning from the war, Ciardi married Judith Hostetter—to whom he would write numerous love poems, including "Most Like an Arch This Marriage," his joyful allegorical celebration of conjugal love. The couple had three children.

Ciardi's postwar literary career was enormously successful. The poverty of his childhood drove him to compulsive hard work, and he took on an extraordinary number of obligations, which he handled with verve and confidence. After teaching at Harvard for five years, he joined the Rutgers faculty in 1953 and soon became a full professor. (He left in 1961 to be a full-time writer.) In 1956 he became both the poetry editor and a columnist for *Saturday Review,* the nation's best-selling cultural magazine of the period. In 1961 he hosted *Accent,* an arts talk show for CBS television, which ran weekly for thirteen months. (This network production was only the first of several Ciardi television and radio shows.) Capitalizing on his fame, he lectured tirelessly from coast to coast. Ciardi also became an influential anthologist. His *Mid-Century American Poets* (1950) is probably the anthology that first cogently defined the postwar canon of mainstream poets—Robert Lowell, Randall Jarrell, Elizabeth Bishop, Theodore Roethke, Richard Wilbur, Muriel Rukeyser, a list that still pertains today but was by no means conventional then. Meanwhile Ciardi's anthology *How Does a Poem Mean?* (1959) became one of the most widely used literary textbooks in America. No Italian American writer had ever exercised such influence on American letters.

Ciardi's literary output was legendary. He published eighteen books of poetry in his lifetime, most notably *I Marry You* (1958), *Person to Person* (1964), and *Lives of X* (1971). He also published thirteen books of children's verse and more than a dozen volumes of literary essays and books on language. Perhaps most notable was his translation of Dante's *The Divine Comedy* (1977), which appeared volume by volume, *The Inferno* (1954), *The Purgatorio* (1961), and *The Paradiso* (1970). Many critics still consider it the finest poetic version of Dante ever done in English, and readers have overwhelmingly agreed. Ciardi's *Inferno* alone has sold over four million copies—making it perhaps the twentieth century's best-selling book of poetry in America. Not surprisingly, by 1966 Ciardi had become a millionaire from his writing. "The Capitalist of Po Biz," he called himself, and he flaunted his affluence—to the horror of many genteel fellow poets—with the unabashed pleasure of an immigrant who had struck it rich.

Brusque, cocky, and outspoken, Ciardi spent his later years impatient with new literary trends. At Bread Loaf, he argued with younger poets whom he considered ignorant of tradition. At literary gatherings he found himself a respected but unfashionable figure. Despite a stroke in 1982, he kept traveling on the lecture and reading circuit, but he sensed his reputation was in decline. He wrote less about poetry and more on language in lexicographies like *A Browser's Dictionary* (1980). He died of a heart attack at home in 1986.

◂━◆━▸

Most Like an Arch This Marriage

Most like an arch—an entrance which upholds
and shores the stone-crush up the air like lace.
Mass made idea, and idea held in place.
A lock in time. Inside half-heaven unfolds.

Most like an arch—two weaknesses that lean   5
into a strength. Two fallings become firm.
Two joined abeyances become a term
naming the fact that reaches fact to mean.

Not quite that? Not much less. World as it is,
what's strong and separate falters. All I do   10

at piling stone on stone apart from you
is roofless around nothing. Till we kiss

I am no more than upright and unset.
It is by falling in and in we make
the all-bearing point, for one another's sake,   15
in faultless failing, raised by our own weight.

1958

Firsts

At forty, home from traveled intention,
I could no longer speak my mother's dialect.

I had been in Italy rinsing my vowels.
She had been in Medford, Massachusetts

thickening her tongue on English crusts.   5
She had become a patois. What tongue was I?

I understood what I heard her say.
Could say it over and remember—ah, yes—

a taste like cooked wine-lees mushed with snow,
our winter *dolce*[1] once. And how many years   10

not thought of, not forgotten? A taste
that slipped my tongue. Would I still like it, I doubt?

*

At times anywhere someone will say,
"Ah, you're from Boston!" And in Boston,

sooner or later, "Where are you from?"   15
Who in a last dark ever will call from his loss

as Dante was called, known by his cradle sounds
that spoke him to a birth and sharing?

Something still sits my tongue: that long "a"
down from the Hill, that "r" where no "r" is   20

I still catch myself sounding, surprised to hear it.
If anything speaks in Hell, it will be, alas,

the English Departments in whose cubicles
of lettered glass I numbered twenty years.

*

James Baldwin[2] in back-Switzerland where no black man   25
had ever been, and they thought he was the devil,

1. (Italian) "Sweet"; also "soft" or "gentle."
2. James Baldwin (1924–1987), African American novelist, essayist, and expatriate.

sat a mountain, trapped in a Harvard accent,
and listened for months to Billie Holiday records

learning back Mama's cadence, ashamed to have lost
its glazed mornings, their first light of himself;   30

learning what had to be learned over. Like going back
to find a chimney in a wildrose thicket.

*

I remember losing the rifle my uncle gave me,
a single shot .22 from lathes in Heaven

to my twelfth birthday. I damned a dozen friends   35
I *knew* had stolen it. Till, ten years later,

Uncle—tired of his own bad wine, and clear
California gallons selling for less than it cost

to make his silty, cleared out the rack of barrels
—and there was the rifle, rusted shut, behind them.   40

And I put it out on the curb with the trash, and my shame
for what I had done with his gift, once perfect.

1979

❖◄ THOMAS McGRATH ►❖
(1916–1990)

Born on a farm in Sheldon, North Dakota, Thomas McGrath was the grandson of Irish Catholic homesteaders. "I got to poetry," he once said, "by way of my father, who was known far and wide, in a small circle naturally, as a wonderful storyteller." The upper Midwest of his youth was rife with labor politics, and McGrath thoroughly absorbed the communist views of the "Wobblies" (a nickname for the International Workers of the World). But McGrath was also under the spell of literature:

> "I read the *Iliad* and the *Odyssey* when I was in grade school. I read probably most of the *Edda*. Oh hell, and of course I read junk all the time, all the bunkhouse materials that I could get my hands on after the end of the depression. The idea of reading and the idea of writing, I didn't feel was foreign to me at all."

Having begun his education in a one-room schoolhouse, he went on to the University of North Dakota, Louisiana State University, and (on a Rhodes Scholarship) New College, Oxford. He also worked as a dockyard labor organizer in New York, spent two years of World War II stationed in the Aleutian Islands, and worked as a film writer and college teacher until he was blacklisted for his communist associations in the 1950s. He later taught at North Dakota State University and Moorhead State University, spending his last years in the Twin Cities.

Although McGrath had his champions, including Chicago writer Studs Terkel, the relative neglect of his work was remarkable and cannot be entirely explained by his leftist politics, which his critics sometimes found sentimental. He did win awards and fellowships, but his work was rarely anthologized and taught. His poems range from satirical attacks on American society (reminiscent at their best of British poets W. H. Auden and Luis MacNeice) to elegies for the country's war dead, including one of his own brothers. Increasingly he admired the public, political poems of the South Americans. There were Deep Image poems like those of Robert Bly and James Wright (both friends of McGrath), and there was also his extraordinary long poem *Letter to an Imaginary Friend* (first volume, 1970, second volume, 1985; revised edition, 1998), in which McGrath displays a broad verbal range as he moves from pseudo-autobiography to a visionary conclusion. Whatever its failings, the poem contains some of the most vivid writing produced by an American poet of his generation. His shorter work, gathered in *Selected Poems, 1938–1988*, is wildly uneven, but at its best it balances McGrath's formal gifts with his deep compassion for ordinary people.

Jig Tune: Not for Love

Where are you going? asked Manny the Mayor.
What are you doing? asked President Jane.
I'll bet you're a bastard, said Daniel the Deacon;
We'll put you away where you'll never be seen.

There won't be no pardon, said Manny the Murderer.   5
There won't be no stay, said Tommygun Jane.
Said Daniel McBedlam, You won't go no farther;
My father won't even declare you insane.

For a Madman's Way, intoned Manny the Magnate.
The Public Good, shouted Editor Jane.   10
I think he's a Commie, cried Danny O'Garrote;
If he won't do murder, I call it a crime.

It's not a long drop, sang Manny the Hangman.
The rope will stop you, crooned Juryman Jane.
In a box long and black, chanted Danny Le Flack,   15
We'll suit you warm to keep out the rain.

All flesh is grass, sighed Manny the Mourner.
The handsome young man, wept Sob-sister Jane.
R.I.P., prayed Capital Daniel;
If he were alive we could kill him again.   20

1940

Ars Poetica:[1]
or: Who Lives in the Ivory Tower?

Perhaps you'd like a marching song for the embattled prolet-
Ariat, or a realistic novel, the hopeful poet
Said, or a slice of actual life with the hot red heart's blood running,
The simple tale of a working stiff, but better than Jack London?[2]

Nobody wants your roundelay, nobody wants your sestina,   5
Said the housewife, we want Hedy Lamarr and Gable[3] in the cinema,
Get out of my Technicolor dream with your tragic view and your verses;
Down with iambic pentameter and hurray for Louella Parsons.[4]

Of course you're free to write as you please, the liberal editor answered,
But take the red flags out of your poem—we mustn't offend the censor—   10
And change this stanza to mean the reverse, and you must tone down this
        passage;
Thank God for the freedom of the press and a poem with a message!

Life is lousy enough without you should put it into a sonnet,
Said the man in the street, so keep it out of the novel, the poem, the drama;
Give us a paean of murder and rape, or the lay of a willing maiden,   15
And to hell with the Bard of Avalon[5] and to hell with Eliot Auden.[6]

Recite the damn things all day long, get drunk on smoke come Sunday,
I respect your profession as much as my own, but it don't pay off when you're
        hungry;
You'll have to carry the banner instead—said the hobo in the jungle—
If you want to eat; and don't forget: it's my bridge you're sleeping under.   20

Oh it's down with art and down with life and give us another reefer—
They all said—give us a South Sea isle, where light my love lies dreaming;
And who is that poet come in off the streets with a look unleal and lour?
Your feet are muddy, you son-of-a-bitch, get out of our ivory tower.

                                                                  1949

The Buffalo Coat

I see him moving, in his legendary fleece,
Between the superhighway and an Algonquin stone axe;
Between the wild tribes, in their lost heat,
And the dark blizzard of my Grandfather's coat;

---

1. (Latin) "The Art of Poetry," from the Roman poet Horace (65–68 B.C.E.).
2. American novelist (1876–1916), author of *The Call of the Wild* and other books, known for his left-ist politics.
3. Film actors.
4. A famous Hollywood gossip columnist.
5. Author of Arthurian romances.
6. McGrath's whimsical reference to two poets, T. S. Eliot and W. H. Auden, who had found favor among academic critics.

Cold with the outdoor cold caught in the curls,   5
Smelling of the world before the poll tax.[7]

And between the new macadam[8] and the Scalp Act[9]
They got him by the short hair; had him clipped
Who once was wild—and all five senses wild—
Printing the wild with his hoof's inflated script   10
Before the times was money in the bank,
Before it was a crime to be so mild.

But history is a fact, and moves on feet
Sharper than his, toward wallows deeper than.
And the myth that covered all his moving parts,   15
Grandfather's time had turned into a coat;
And what kept warm then, in the true world's cold
Is old and cold in a world his death began.

                                                                        1973

Remembering the Children of Auschwitz[1]

We know the story. The children
Are lost in the deep forest—
Though it is the same forest
In which we all are born.

But somehow it has changed: 5
A new kind of darkness,
Or something they never noticed,
Has colored the pines and the larches.

And now appears the Bird,
(Bird of a strange dreaming)   10
To lead them, as tales foretold,
Over the little streams

Into the garden of order
Where trees no longer menaced,
And a little house was protected   15
Inside its candy fences.

And all seemed perfectly proper:
The little house was covered
with barbwire and marzipan;
And the Witch was there; and the Oven.   20

---

7. A tax paid at the polls before one could vote. Discriminatory against the poor, and by extension against nonwhites.
8. A type of pavement invented by John McAdam (1756–1836).
9. Several laws had this name, but the most famous was enacted in 1756 by Governor Robert Morris of Pennsylvania in declaring war on the Delaware and Shawnee tribes. Bounties were offered for Indians killed or captured.
1. Refers to one of the most infamous concentration camps of World War II.

Perhaps they never noticed—
After all that disorder
Of being lost—that they'd come
To the Place named in the stories.

Perhaps there was even peace—   25
A little—after disorder,
Before they awoke into
A dream of deeper horror.

And now the Bird will never
Take them across the river   30
(Though they knew how to walk on water).
They become part of the weather.

They have become the Ascensions.[2]
When we lift up our eyes,
In any light, we see them: 35
Darkening all our skies.

                                                              1983

◦━◄ GWENDOLYN BROOKS ►━◦
(1917–2000)

Gwendolyn Brooks was born in Topeka, Kansas, but grew up on the south Side of Chicago, where her parents created a sustaining home life despite economic hardship and fostered her love of poetry. Brooks published her first poem at age thirteen, and by the time she was seventeen had contributed over seventy-five poems to the *Chicago Defender,* an African American newspaper. Before graduating from Englewood High School in 1934, she had corresponded with Langston Hughes, who encouraged her to listen to the blues, and James Weldon Johnson, who led her to the work of Modernists such as T. S. Eliot and Ezra Pound.

Brooks graduated from Warren Wilson Junior College in 1936 and joined the NAACP youth council, where she met Henry Blakey II, whom she married in 1939. After the birth of their first child, in 1941 Brooks became a member of a poetry workshop run by Inez Cunningham Stark, a wealthy white woman who, Brooks recalls, "flew in the face of her society tradition, coming among blacks. . . . She gave us an education in modern poetry." Equally important to Brooks's poetry was her experience living in Chicago's South Side ghetto. After her marriage she moved from her parents' home to a small kitchenette apartment in a crowded building, and the vibrant complex life of the South Side (christened "Bronzeville" by the *Chicago Defender*) became the primary subject of her work.

Brooks's poetry is notable for its technical ingenuity, emotional vitality, and nuanced explorations of African American city life. During the early 1940s, the literary world was dominated by the "New Criticism," whose practitioners wrote poetry characterized by complex forms, dense verbal textures, wit, irony, and allusion. Brooks not only mastered this style, but took it to new lengths, for the poetry

---

2. Alludes ironically to the Ascension of Christ (Acts 1:9 and Mark 16:19).

of her first three books depends on word play, heavy alliteration and assonance, and ease with a variety of forms, both traditional and invented. Whereas much New Critical poetry suffers from overemphasis on wit and technique so that it becomes a form of intellectual gamesmanship, Brooks's work is invigorated by her passionate portrayals of ordinary African American women and men and by her arguments against prejudice. And because Brooks deploys irony to attack racial and social inequalities, she implicitly challenges the New Critics' view that poetry should be disengaged from politics. Yet Brooks also continues the traditions of African American folk forms, especially in her ballads and character portraits.

Brooks soon received national recognition. After she won the Midwestern Writers' Conference Poetry Award in 1943, Harper published her first book, *A Street in Bronzeville* (1945), which garnered her the American Academy of Letters Award (1946) and two Guggenheim Fellowships (1946 and 1947). With the publication of *Annie Allen* (1949), Brooks became the first African American to win the Pulitzer Prize. The focus on black women's experience that she developed in *Annie Allen* continued in her lyrical novella, *Maud Martha* (1953). As the 1960s came to a close, African American protests for civil rights intensified, and Brooks's third book of poetry, *The Bean Eaters* (1960), became more openly political than her earlier books, although she still favored traditional forms.

During the first half of the 1960s, Brooks was honored by President John F. Kennedy, who invited her to read at the Library of Congress, and by Columbia College in Chicago (where she began teaching in 1963), which gave her the first of the fifty-one honorary degrees she was to receive from American universities over the next thirty years. But Brooks's most momentous experience of the decade was her participation in the 1967 Second Black Writers' Conference at Fisk University in Nashville, Tennessee. There, she met proponents of the Black Arts movement, including Amiri Baraka and Don L. Lee (Haki R. Madhubuti), who espoused black nationalism and argued that African American poets should write strictly for a black audience, view poetry as a vehicle for community building and social change, and use only forms such as the blues or a free verse based on African American speech rhythms. Their ideas reflected her own growing convictions—so much so that, with the publication of *In the Mecca* (1968), she changed her style to make it more easily accessible to an African American audience. Describing her new work, Brooks stressed that, "my aim . . . is to write poems that will somehow successfully 'call' all black people: black people in taverns, black people in alleys, black people in gutters, schools, offices, factories, prisons, the consulate; I wish to reach black people in pulpits, black people in mines, on farms, on thrones; *not* always to 'teach'—I shall wish often to entertain, to illumine."

In the spirit of community building, after 1969 she broke with Harper and Row and began publishing with African American presses, where she released many small chapbooks of new poems, as well as her autobiography, *Report from Part One* (1972) and *Report from Part Two* (1995), and *Blacks* (1987), a retrospective poetry collection spanning her whole career. Brooks also continued her dedicated involvement in her own community through the workshops and contests for young writers that she sponsored as Poet Laureate of Illinois, a position she held from 1968 to her death in 2000, and through the Gwendolyn Brooks Center for Black Literature and Creative Writing, founded in 1993 by Chicago State University, where she was Distinguished Professor of English. Brooks's many national honors—including being the first black woman elected to the National Institute of Arts and Letters and also the first black woman appointed as Poetry Consultant to the Library of Congress—attest to the broad appeal of her work. When asked in a 1967 interview, "What is your Poet's Premise?" she responded: " 'Vivify the contemporary fact,' said Whitman. I like to vivify the *universal* fact, when it occurs to me. But the universal wears contemporary clothing very well."

The Mother

Abortions will not let you forget.
You remember the children you got that you did not get,
The damp small pulps with a little or with no hair,
The singers and workers that never handled the air.
You will never neglect or beat   5
Them, or silence or buy with a sweet.
You will never wind up the sucking-thumb
Or scuttle off ghosts that come.
You will never leave them, controlling your luscious sigh,
Return for a snack of them, with gobbling mother-eye.   10

I have heard in the voices of the wind the voices of my dim killed children.
I have contracted. I have eased
My dim dears at the breasts they could never suck.
I have said, Sweets, if I sinned, if I seized
Your luck   15
And your lives from your unfinished reach,
If I stole your births and your names,
Your straight baby tears and your games,
Your stilted or lovely loves, your tumults, your marriages, aches, and your deaths,
If I poisoned the beginnings of your breaths,   20
Believe that even in my deliberateness I was not deliberate.
Though why should I whine,
Whine that the crime was other than mine?—
Since anyhow you are dead.
Or rather, or instead,   25
You were never made.
But that too, I am afraid,
Is faulty: oh, what shall I say, how is the truth to be said?
You were born, you had body, you died.
It is just that you never giggled or planned or cried.   30

Believe me, I loved you all.
Believe me, I knew you, though faintly, and I loved, I loved you all.

                                                                 1945

Sadie and Maud

Maud went to college.
Sadie stayed at home.

Sadie scraped life
With a fine-tooth comb.

She didn't leave a tangle in.   5
Her comb found every strand.
Sadie was one of the livingest chits
In all the land.

Sadie bore two babies
Under her maiden name.   10
Maud and Ma and Papa
Nearly died of shame.

When Sadie said her last so-long
Her girls struck out from home.
(Sadie had left as heritage   15
Her fine-tooth comb.)

Maud, who went to college,
Is a thin brown mouse.
She is living all alone
In this old house.   20

1945

Southeast Corner

The School of Beauty's a tavern now.
The Madam is underground.
Out at Lincoln, among the graves
Her own is early found.
Where the thickest, tallest monument   5
Cuts grandly into the air
The Madam lies, contentedly.
Her fortune, too, lies there,
Converted into cool hard steel
And right red velvet lining;   10
While over her tan impassivity
Shot silk is shining.

1945

But Can See Better There, and Laughing There

"pygmies are pygmies still, though percht on Alps"
—*Edward Young*

But can see better there, and laughing there
Pity the giants wallowing on the plain.
Giants who bleat and chafe in their small grass,
Seldom to spread the palm; to spit; come clean.

Pygmies expand in cold impossible air,   5
Cry fie on giantshine, poor glory which
Pounds breast-bone punily, screeches, and has
Reached no Alps: or, knows no Alps to reach.

1949

The Rites for Cousin Vit

Carried her unprotesting out the door.
Kicked back the casket-stand. But it can't hold her,
That stuff and satin aiming to enfold her,
The lid's contrition nor the bolts before.
Oh oh. Too much. Too much. Even now, surmise,   5
She rises in the sunshine. There she goes,
Back to the bars she knew and the repose
In love-rooms and the things in people's eyes.
Too vital and too squeaking. Must emerge.
Even now she does the snake-hips with a hiss,   10
Slops the bad wine across her shantung,[1] talks
Of pregnancy, guitars and bridgework, walks
In parks or alleys, comes haply on the verge
Of happiness, haply hysterics. Is.

1949

The Bean Eaters

They eat beans mostly, this old yellow pair.
Dinner is a casual affair.
Plain chipware on a plain and creaking wood,
Tin flatware.

Two who are Mostly Good.   5
Two who have lived their day,
But keep on putting on their clothes
And putting things away.

And remembering . . .
Remembering, with tinklings and twinges,   10
As they lean over the beans in their rented back room that is full of beads
    and receipts and dolls and cloths, tobacco crumbs, vases and fringes.

1960

---

1. A form of Chinese silk.

We Real Cool

The Pool Players.
Seven at the Golden Shovel.

We real cool. We
Left school. We

Lurk late. We
Strike straight. We

Sing sin. We   5
Thin gin. We

Jazz June. We
Die soon.

                                        1960

The Blackstone Rangers[2]

I
As Seen by Disciplines[3]

There they are.
Thirty at the corner.
Black, raw, ready.
Sores in the city
that do not want to heal.   5

II
The Leaders

Jeff, Gene. Geronimo, And Bop.
They cancel, cure and curry.
Hardly the dupes of the downtown thing
the cold bonbon,
the rhinestone thing. And hardly   10
in a hurry.
Hardly Belafonte, King,
Black Jesus, Stokeley, Malcolm X or Rap.[4]
Bungled trophies.
Their country is a Nation on no map.   15

Jeff, Gene, Geronimo and Bop
in the passionate noon,
in bewitching night

---

2. A Chicago street gang that took its name from Blackstone Street, the eastern edge of the black ghetto in Chicago.
3. Refers to law enforcement.
4. The names refer to heroic figures in African American culture and politics, including singer Harry Belafonte, Martin Luther King, Jr., Stokeley Carmichael, Malcolm X, and H. Rap Brown.

are the detailed men, the copious men.
They curry, cure,   20
they cancel, cancelled images whose Concerts
are not divine, vivacious; the different tins
are intense last entries; pagan argument;
translations of the night.

The Blackstone bitter bureaus   25
(bureaucracy is footloose) edit, fuse
unfashionable damnations and descent;
and exulting, monstrous hand on monstrous hand,
construct, strangely, a monstrous pearl or grace.

III
GANG GIRLS

A Rangerette

Gang Girls are sweet exotics.   30
Mary Ann
uses the nutrients of her orient,
but sometimes sighs for Cities of blue and jewel
beyond her Ranger rim of Cottage Grove.[5]
(Bowery Boys, Disciples, Whip-Birds will   35
dissolve no margins, stop no savory sanctities.)

Mary is
a rose in a whiskey glass.

Mary's
Februaries shudder and are gone. Aprils   40
fret frankly, lilac hurries on.
Summer is a hard irregular ridge.
October looks away.
And that's the Year!
                    Save for her bugle-love.   45
Save for the bleat of not-obese devotion.
Save for Somebody Terribly Dying, under
the philanthropy of robins. Save for her Ranger
bringing
an amount of rainbow in a string-drawn bag.   50
"Where did you get the diamond?" Do not ask:
but swallow, straight, the spirals of his flask
and assist him at your zipper; pet his lips
and help him clutch you.

Love's another departure.   55
Will there be any arrivals, confirmations?
Will there be gleaning?

---

5. A main thoroughfare on Chicago's South Side.

Mary, the Shakedancer's child
from the rooming-flat, pants carefully, peers at
her laboring lover. . . .   60
              Mary! Mary Ann!
Settle for sandwiches! settle for stocking caps!
for sudden blood, aborted carnival,
the props and niceties of non-loneliness—
the rhymes of Leaning.

                                                        1968

The Coora Flower

Today I learned the *coora* flower
grows high in the mountains of Itty-go-luba Bésa.
Province Meechee.
Pop. 39.

Now I am coming home.   5
This, at least, is Real, and what I know.

It was restful, learning nothing necessary.
School is tiny vacation. At least you can sleep.
At least you can think of love or feeling your boy friend against you
(which is not free from grief).   10

But now it's Real Business.
I am Coming Home.

My mother will be screaming in an almost dirty dress.
The crack[6] is gone. So a Man will be in the house.

I must watch myself.   15
I must not dare to sleep.

                                                        1991

━━◄ ROBERT LOWELL ►━━
(1917–1977)

In *Notebook 1967–68*, Robert Lowell wrote a verse account of a conversation
with T. S. Eliot:

> Caught between two streams of traffic, in the gloom
> of Memorial Hall and Harvard's war-dead. . . . And he:
> "Don't you loathe to be compared with your relatives?
> I do. I've just found two of mine reviewed by Poe.
> He wiped the floor with them . . . and I was *delighted*."

The quotation is telling—not only about Eliot, but also about the man who recorded
it in a verse rather than a prose memoir. Robert Lowell could never forget—or let

6. Cocaine.

his readers forget—his own distinguished family and social position. His family had already included two well-known poets. James Russell Lowell was his great-great-uncle, and the Imagist Amy Lowell was a distant cousin. The son of a naval officer father and a socially ambitious mother, Lowell was marked in childhood by pretensions to gentility and a subtle shame. His ineffectual father was never quite successful enough—even when he gave up his military career and went to work for various businesses—while his mother strove to place the family in some proximity to the prominence of its name, and to that of her own family, the Winslows. The poet was born Robert Traill Spence Lowell, Jr., and often felt he was being groomed for a life he did not want. He developed a rebellious side, and as a student at St. Mark's School (one of his teachers was poet Richard Eberhart) he was given the nickname "Cal," derived both from Caliban and Caligula.

It was expected that Lowell would choose Harvard for his college education, but after two years of study there he shocked his family by transferring to Kenyon College in Ohio to study with poet John Crowe Ransom. "The kind of poet I am," Lowell later wrote, "was largely determined by the fact that I grew up in the heyday of the New Criticism. From the beginning I was preoccupied with technique, fascinated by the past and tempted by other languages. It is hard for me (now) to imagine a poet not interested in the classics." After graduating from Kenyon in 1940, Lowell studied at Louisiana State University with two other scions of the New Criticism, Cleanth Brooks and Robert Penn Warren, and befriended the poet Allen Tate.

Lowell had already survived a few awkward romances that annoyed his family when in 1940 he married the Colorado-born novelist Jean Stafford. The marriage was troubled; the previous year he had drunkenly wrecked a car, leaving Stafford's face permanently scarred, and Lowell was more than once physically abusive to her. Stafford's short story, "An Influx of Poets," records some of the trials of their union. Though he was raised Episcopalian and quite conscious of his Puritan heritage, in 1941 Lowell converted, with much publicity, to Roman Catholicism, and for a time adhered fervently to his newfound beliefs. The intensity of his religious feeling was so strong that it frightened or put off some of his friends. In 1943, when he was drafted, he published a letter to President Roosevelt in which he declared his pacifist principles and refused induction. For this impulsive and public act he was sent briefly to the West Street jail in New York City, and then to the Federal Correctional Center in Danbury, Connecticut.

On his release from prison in 1944 he was given a medical deferment, and in the same year he published *Land of Unlikeness,* his first collection of poems, in a limited edition. Reviewing this book in *Poetry,* John Frederick Nims called Lowell's style "imbricated," suggesting just how compact Lowell's early poems were—densely allusive to history and Christian symbols, gnarled in their syntax. These poems, obsessively revised, appeared in his first full-length collection, *Lord Weary's Castle* (1946), which won Lowell the Pulitzer Prize, as well as secured him a Guggenheim Fellowship, an award from the National Institute of Arts and Letters, and the position of Poetry Consultant to the Library of Congress in 1947 and 1948.

Such early and conspicuous success, however, did little to help Lowell with his most disturbing and persistent problem. What had early on seemed merely an emotional instability in his character was gradually understood to be devastating manic depression. Between 1949 and 1965 alone he suffered nine major episodes that required hospitalization. Divorced from Stafford in 1948, Lowell married the novelist and critic Elizabeth Hardwick during the following year. Their marriage had the approval of Lowell's parents and lasted until 1972, but it was severely tested by Lowell's continuing illness and infidelities. Hardwick and Lowell lived in Europe from 1950 to 1954. On their return he taught intermittently at various colleges and universities (among his students at Boston University were Sylvia Plath, Anne Sexton, and George Starbuck). In 1957 their daughter, Harriet Winslow Lowell, was born.

In 1959 Lowell published *Life Studies,* the poetry collection that announced a new style and helped inaugurate the Confessional School of American poetry. The poems of *Life Studies* display the influence of William Carlos Williams's free verse technique, as well as the more personal and domestic ruminations of poets like W. D. Snodgrass. In an acceptance speech for the National Book Award, Lowell referred to two "schools" of American poetry, the "cooked" and the "raw." Academic formalists, such as Ransom, were associated with the "cooked," while free verse poets like Allen Ginsberg and the Beats were among the "raw." *Life Studies* was a kind of negotiation between such styles, and that struggle would continue through Lowell's subsequent collections such as *For the Union Dead* (1964), *Near the Ocean* (1967), and *Day by Day* (1977).

Despite the shifts in style in Lowell's books, critics have noted a thematic consistency in all of his work, namely his obsession with the family and history. This central focus is found even in the 373 unrhymed sonnets in *Notebook 1967–68* (1969), a wide-ranging and idiosyncratic sequence in which Lowell meditates on history and current events, as well as literary friends and family. Lowell conceived of this quickly written rumination in sonnets as a long poem, "jagged in pattern, but not a conglomeration or sequence of related material." Lowell revised the book again in 1970, and then three years later completely reformulated and rearranged the poems in three books: *History* (1973), mostly on public and political themes, and the more personal and indeed confessional volumes, *For Lizzie and Harriet* (1973) and *The Dolphin* (1973). His friend Elizabeth Bishop begged him not to publish such intimate revelations about his family life, but Lowell went ahead, apparently not caring whose feelings he might hurt. Although they are fascinating for their intellectual scope and imaginative ambition, these five interrelated "Notebook" volumes remain generally less satisfying than Lowell's earlier work.

In the later poems the dense muscularity of Lowell's early style relaxes into something more conversational; they mix high and low diction but remain deliberate, crafted objects. They also allude to Lowell's increasing visibility as a public figure. He became more and more active politically, protesting the Vietnam War by publicly refusing Lyndon Johnson's invitation to the White House, and working on Senator Eugene McCarthy's failed campaign for the presidency. His circle of friends was often a privileged and powerful one.

Nevertheless, Lowell rarely lost his sense of the world's cruelties and hypocrisies. He saw friends and students die too young: Plath, Roethke, Jarrell, Schwartz, Sexton—some of these by suicide. And his own mental difficulties, insufficiently relieved by drugs like Thorazine and, later, lithium carbonate, were devastating both to him and to his family. In his manic phases, Lowell swelled with delusions of grandeur and exposed his strange fascination with Hitler. When he was being considered for the Poetry Professorship at Oxford in 1965, W. H. Auden confided "that his supporters should be aware . . . that Cal has times when he has to go to the bin.

The warning signs are three: (a) He announces that he is the *only* living poet; (b) a romantic and usually platonic attraction to a young girl; and (c) he gives a huge party." Lowell was not elected to the professorship, but he had already obtained a position at Harvard where he remained from 1963 till his death.

In 1971 Lowell had a son by English novelist Lady Caroline Blackwood, who was the heiress to the Guinness brewing fortune. They married the following year. That marriage began to dissolve in 1976, and by 1977 he appeared to have decided once and for all to return to Hardwick. He was on his way to her apartment when he died of a heart attack in a taxi from New York's Kennedy Airport. The poetry he left behind is one of the defining cultural statements of his time. It wrestles with tradition and literary sophistication and a desire for candor, for some new way of negotiating between life and art. In his poem "Epilogue" Lowell wrote of his wish "to make / something imagined, not recalled[.]" But he followed those lines with a question: "[W]hy not say what happened?" His art remains disturbingly suspended between those two desires.

Concord

Ten thousand Fords are idle here in search
Of a tradition. Over these dry sticks—
The Minute Man,[1] the Irish Catholics,[2]
The ruined bridge and Walden's[3] fished-out perch—
The belfry of the Unitarian Church   5
Rings out the hanging Jesus. Crucifix,
How can your whited spindling arms transfix
Mammon's unbridled industry, the lurch
For forms to harness Heraclitus' stream!
This Church is Concord—Concord where Thoreau[4]   10
Named all the birds without a gun to probe
Through darkness to the painted man and bow:
The death-dance of King Philip[5] and his scream
Whose echo girdled this imperfect globe.

                                                                    1946

---

1. New England militiamen ready at short notice to fight against the British in the American Revolution.
2. Considered second-class citizens, especially by the British, the Irish immigrants were often blamed for protests such as the one resulting in the Boston Massacre of 1770.
3. Pond near Concord; setting of Thoreau's masterpiece.
4. Henry David Thoreau (1817–1862), an American poet and essayist who was born in Concord and in his lifetime was often at odds with American political and commercial life.
5. The nickname Puritans gave to Metacomet, chief of the Wampanoags in New England. He fought a war against the Puritan settlers in 1675–76 and was killed in its aftermath.

The Quaker Graveyard in Nantucket

(For Warren Winslow,[6] *Dead at Sea)*

Let man have dominion over the fishes of the sea and the fowls of the air and the beasts
and the whole earth, and every creeping creature that moveth upon the earth.[7]

I

A brackish reach of shoal off Madaket,—[8]
The sea was still breaking violently and night
Had steamed into our North Atlantic Fleet,
When the drowned sailor clutched the drag-net. Light
Flashed from his matted head and marble feet,   5
He grappled at the net
With the coiled, hurdling muscles of his thighs:
The corpse was bloodless, a botch of reds and whites,
Its open, staring eyes
Were lustreless dead-lights   10
Or cabin-windows on a stranded hulk
Heavy with sand. We weight the body, close
Its eyes and heave it seaward whence it came
Where the heel-headed dogfish barks its nose
On Ahab's void and forehead;[9] and the name   15
Is blocked in yellow chalk.
Sailors, who pitch this portent at the sea
Where dreadnaughts[1] shall confess
Its hell-bent deity,
When you are powerless   20
To sand-bag this Atlantic bulwark, faced
By the earth-shaker, green, unwearied, chaste
In his steel scales: ask for no Orphean lute
To pluck life back.[2] The guns of the steeled fleet
Recoil and then repeat   25
The hoarse salute.

II

Whenever winds are moving and their breath
Heaves at the roped-in bulwarks of this pier,
The terns and sea-gulls tremble at your death
In these home waters. Sailor, can you hear   30

---

6. Lowell's cousin, who perished when his ship was sunk in World War II. Lowell modeled this elegy on
Milton's "Lycidas," another poem about a young man lost at sea. Other details are from Thoreau's
Cape Cod and Melville's *Moby-Dick*.
7. Genesis 1:26–27.
8. A town on the west side of Nantucket Island.
9. Ahab is the captain of the whaling ship *Pequod* in Melville's *Moby-Dick* (1851). He is obsessed with
killing the eponymous white whale. Whaling ships once put to sea from Nantucket.
1. Battleships.
2. In Greek mythology, the poet-musician Orpheus used music to charm Hades into allowing his wife to
return to earth after her death.

The Pequod's sea wings, beating landward, fall
Headlong and break on our Atlantic wall
Off 'Sconset, where the yawing S-boats[3] splash
The bellbuoy, with ballooning spinnakers,
As the entangled, screeching mainsheet clears   35
The blocks: off Madaket, where lubbers lash
The heavy surf and throw their long lead squids
For blue-fish? Sea-gulls blink their heavy lids
Seaward. The winds' wings beat upon the stones,
Cousin, and scream for you and the claws rush   40
At the sea's throat and wring it in the slush
Of this old Quaker graveyard where the bones
Cry out in the long night for the hurt beast
Bobbing by Ahab's whaleboats in the East.

III

All you recovered from Poseidon[4] died   45
With you, my cousin, and the harrowed brine
Is fruitless on the blue beard of the god,
Stretching beyond us to the castles in Spain,
Nantucket's westward haven. To Cape Cod
Guns, cradled on the tide,   50
Blast the eelgrass about a waterclock[5]
Of bilge and backwash, roil the salt and sand
Lashing earth's scaffold, rock
Our warships in the hand
Of the great God, where time's contrition blues   55
Whatever it was there Quaker sailors lost
In the mad scramble of their lives. They died
When time was open-eyed,
Wooden and childish; only bones abide
There, in the nowhere, where their boats were tossed   60
Sky-high, where mariners had fabled news
Of IS,[6] the whited monster. What it cost
Them is their secret. In the sperm-whale's slick
I see the Quakers drown and hear their cry:
"If God himself had not been on our side,   65
If God himself had not been on our side,
When the Atlantic rose against us, why,
Then it had swallowed us up quick."

IV

This is the end of the whaleroad[7] and the whale
Who spewed Nantucket bones on the thrashed swell   70

3. Racing sailboats of the "S Class."
4. Greek god of the sea. In his anger he did great harm to Odysseus and his crew.
5. A device for telling time by measuring the flow of water.
6. This is thought to mean existence, all that "is." (Compare Exodus 3:14.)
7. A translated Anglo-Saxon term for the sea.

And stirred the troubled waters to whirlpools
To send the Pequod packing off to hell:
This is the end of them, three-quarters fools,
Snatching at straws to sail
Seaward and seaward on the turntail whale,   75
Spouting out blood and water as it rolls,
Sick as a dog to these Atlantic shoals:
Clamavimus,[8] O depths. Let the sea-gulls wail

For water, for the deep where the high tide
Mutters to its hurt self, mutters and ebbs.   80
Waves wallow in their wash, go out and out,
Leave only the death-rattle of the crabs,
The beach increasing, its enormous snout
Sucking the ocean's side.
This is the end of running on the waves;   85
We are poured out like water. Who will dance
The mast-lashed master of Leviathans[9]
Up from this field of Quakers in their unstoned graves?

V

When the whale's viscera go and the roll
Of its corruption overruns this world   90
Beyond tree-swept Nantucket and Wood's Hole[1]
And Martha's Vineyard,[2] Sailor, will your sword
Whistle and fall and sink into the fat?
In the great ash-pit of Jehoshaphat[3]
The bones cry for the blood of the white whale,   95
The fat flukes arch and whack about its ears,
The death-lance churns into the sanctuary, tears
The gun-blue swingle, heaving like a flail,
And hacks the coiling life out: it works and drags
And rips the sperm-whale's midriff into rags,   100
Gobbets of blubber spill to wind and weather,
Sailor, and gulls go round the stoven timbers
Where the morning stars sing out together
And thunder shakes the white surf and dismembers
The red flag hammered in the mast-head. Hide,   105
Our steel, Jonas Messias,[4] in Thy side.

8. (Latin) "We have cried out."
9. In the Bible these are giant sea monsters; here they refer to whales.
1. Southwest tip of Cape Cod.
2. Island west of Nantucket.
3. Compare Joel 3:12. Lowell himself noted that some of the prophets predicted a fiery end for the world.
4. Lowell may be relating the biblical Jonah to the Messiah.

VI

Our Lady of Walsingham[5]

There once the penitents took off their shoes
And then walked barefoot the remaining mile;
And the small trees, a stream and hedgerows file
Slowly along the munching English lane,   110
Like cows to the old shrine, until you lose
Track of your dragging pain.
The stream flows down under the druid tree,
Shiloah's whirlpools gurgle and make glad
The castle of God. Sailor, you were glad   115
And whistled Sion by that stream. But see:

Our Lady, too small for her canopy,
Sits near the altar. There's no comeliness
At all or charm in that expressionless
Face with its heavy eyelids. As before,   120
This face, for centuries a memory,
Non est species, neque decor,[6]
Expressionless, expresses God: it goes
Past castled Sion. She knows what God knows,
Not Calvary's Cross nor crib at Bethlehem   125
Now, and the world shall come to Walsingham.

VII

The empty winds are creaking and the oak
Splatters and splatters on the cenotaph,
The boughs are trembling and a gaff
Bobs on the untimely stroke   130
Of the greased wash exploding on a shoal-bell[7]
In the old mouth of the Atlantic. It's well;
Atlantic, you are fouled with the blue sailors,
Sea-monsters, upward angel, downward fish:
Unmarried and corroding, spare of flash   135
Mart once of supercilious, wing'd clippers,
Atlantic, where your bell-trap guts its spoil
You could cut the brackish winds with a knife
Here in Nantucket, and cast up the time
When the Lord God formed man from the sea's slime   140
And breathed into his face the breath of life,
And blue-lung'd combers lumbered to the kill.
The Lord survives the rainbow[8] of His will.

1946

---

5. Lowell has borrowed here from *Catholic Art and Culture* (1947) by E. I. Watkins. The stream running by the shrine described here suggests both death and resurrection.
6. (Latin) "There's no comeliness, or charm."
7. Buoy warning boats against shallow water.
8. Genesis 9:13, God's promise after the flood not to again destroy mankind.

Memories of West Street and Lepke[9]

Only teaching on Tuesdays, book-worming
in pajamas fresh from the washer each morning,
I hog a whole house on Boston's
"hardly passionate Marlborough Street,"[1]
where even the man   5
scavenging filth in the back alley trash cans,
has two children, a beach wagon, a helpmate,
and is a "young Republican."
I have a nine months' daughter,
young enough to be my granddaughter.   10
Like the sun she rises in her flame-flamingo infants' wear.

These are the tranquillized *Fifties*,
and I am forty. Ought I to regret my seedtime?
I was a fire-breathing Catholic C.O.,[2]
and made my manic statement,   15
telling off the state and president, and then
sat waiting sentence in the bull pen
beside a Negro boy with curlicues
of marijuana in his hair.

Given a year,   20
I walked on the roof of the West Street Jail, a short
enclosure like my school soccer court,
and saw the Hudson River once a day
through sooty clothesline entanglements
and bleaching khaki tenements.   25
Strolling, I yammered metaphysics with Abramowitz,
a jaundice-yellow ("it's really tan")
and fly-weight pacifist,
so vegetarian,
he wore rope shoes and preferred fallen fruit.   30
He tried to convert Bioff and Brown,
the Hollywood pimps, to his diet.
Hairy, muscular, suburban,
wearing chocolate double-breasted suits,
they blew their tops and beat him black and blue.   35

I was so out of things, I'd never heard
of the Jehovah's Witnesses.
"Are you a C.O.?" I asked a fellow jailbird.
"No," he answered, "I'm a J.W."
He taught me the "hospital tuck,"   40

---

9. In 1943 Lowell refused induction into the armed services, and in a public letter to President Roosevelt declared that he was against America's involvement in the war. He was sentenced to a year in jail and spent part of that time at the West Street jail in New York. One of his fellow inmates was Lepke Buchalter, boss of the organized crime syndicate called Murder Incorporated.
1. Quoted from William James's description of a neighborhood where Lowell lived in the 1950s.
2. Conscientious Objector—that is, against the war.

and pointed out the T-shirted back
of *Murder Incorporated's* Czar Lepke,
there piling towels on a rack,
or dawdling off to his little segregated cell full
of things forbidden the common man: 45
a portable radio, a dresser, two toy American
flags tied together with a ribbon of Easter palm.
Flabby, bald, lobotomized,
he drifted in a sheepish calm,
where no agonizing reappraisal   50
jarred his concentration on the electric chair—
hanging like an oasis in his air
of lost connections. . . .

                                                    1959

Skunk Hour

[For Elizabeth Bishop][3]

Nautilus Island's[4] hermit
heiress still lives through winter in her Spartan cottage;
her sheep still graze above the sea.
Her son's a bishop. Her farmer
is first selectman[5] in our village;   5
she's in her dotage.

Thirsting for
the hierarchic privacy
of Queen Victoria's century,
she buys up all   10
the eyesores facing her shore,
and lets them fall.

The season's ill—
we've lost our summer millionaire,
who seemed to leap from an L. L. Bean[6]   15
catalogue. His nine-knot yawl
was auctioned off to lobstermen.
A red fox stain covers Blue Hill.

And now our fairy
decorator brightens his shop for fall;   20
his fishnet's filled with orange cork,
orange, his cobbler's bench and awl;

---

3. See Elizabeth Bishop's poem, "The Armadillo," on p. 466.
4. An island near Castine, Maine, where Lowell spent many summers.
5. An elected town official in New England parlance.
6. A business in Freeport, Maine, that specializes in outdoor clothing and equipment.

there is no money in his work,
he'd rather marry.

One dark night,[7]   25
my Tudor Ford climbed the hill's skull;
I watched for love-cars. Lights turned down,
they lay together, hull to hull,
where the graveyard shelves on the town. . . .
My mind's not right.   30

A car radio bleats,
"Love, O careless Love. . . ."[8] I hear
my ill-spirit sob in each blood cell,
as if my hand were at its throat. . . .
I myself am hell;[9]   35
nobody's here—

only skunks, that search
in the moonlight for a bite to eat.
They march on their soles up Main Street:
white stripes, moonstruck eyes' red fire   40
under the chalk-dry and spar spire
of the Trinitarian Church.

I stand on top
of our back steps and breathe the rich air—
a mother skunk with her column of kittens swills the garbage pail.   45
She jabs her wedge-head in a cup
of sour cream, drops her ostrich tail,
and will not scare.

                                             1959

For the Union Dead

"Relinquunt Omnia Servare Rem Publicam."[1]

The old South Boston Aquarium[2] stands
in a Sahara of snow now. Its broken windows are boarded.
The bronze weathervane cod has lost half its scales.
The airy tanks are dry.

---

7. Lowell said that he had St. John of the Cross's "Dark Night of the Soul" in mind when he wrote lines 25–36.
8. A line from a folk song about seduction, murder, and suicide.
9. Compare Milton's *Paradise Lost* (IV. 75), where Satan says, "Which way I fly is hell; myself am hell."
1. (Latin) "They give up everything to serve the Republic." Lowell takes this quote from the inscription on a monument to the Massachusetts 54th Regiment (the first all-black Union regiment in the Civil War) and its commander, Robert Gould Shaw (1837–1863). The bronze relief was made by the Irish American sculptor, Augustus Saint-Gaudens (1848–1907), and it stands in Boston Common. Lowell has altered the inscription slightly, from the singular "he" to the plural "they," meaning the whole regiment.
2. The poem was written during the reconstruction of the aquarium, which Lowell had known in childhood.

Once my nose crawled like a snail on the glass;   5
my hand tingled
to burst the bubbles
drifting from the noses of the cowed, compliant fish.

My hand draws back. I often sigh still
for the dark downward and vegetating kingdom   10
of the fish and reptile. One morning last March,
I pressed against the new barbed and galvanized

fence on the Boston Common. Behind their cage,
yellow dinosaur steamshovels were grunting
as they cropped up tons of mush and grass   15
to gouge their underworld garage.

Parking spaces luxuriate like civic
sandpiles in the heart of Boston.
A girdle of orange, Puritan-pumpkin colored girders
braces the tingling Statehouse,   20

shaking over the excavations, as it faces Colonel Shaw
and his bell-cheeked Negro infantry
on St. Gaudens' shaking Civil War relief,
propped by a plank splint against the garage's earthquake.

Two months after marching through Boston,   25
half the regiment was dead;
at the dedication
William James[3] could almost hear the bronze Negroes breathe.

Their monument sticks like a fishbone
in the city's throat.   30
Its Colonel is as lean
as a compass-needle.

He has an angry wrenlike vigilance,
a greyhound's gentle tautness;
he seems to wince at pleasure,   35
and suffocate for privacy.

He is out of bounds now. He rejoices in man's lovely,
peculiar power to choose life and die—
when he leads his black soldiers to death,
he cannot bend his back.   40

On a thousand small town New England greens,
the old white churches hold their air
of sparse, sincere rebellion; frayed flags
quilt the graveyards of the Grand Army of the Republic.

---

3. William James (1842–1910) was a philosopher and psychologist, and the brother of novelist Henry
James.

The stone statues of the abstract Union Soldier   45
grow slimmer and younger each year—
wasp-waisted, they doze over muskets
and muse through their sideburns . . .

Shaw's father wanted no monument
except the ditch,   50
where his son's body was thrown
and lost with his "niggers."

The ditch is nearer.
There are no statues for the last war[4] here;
on Boylston Street,[5] a commercial photograph   55
shows Hiroshima[6] boiling

over a Mosler Safe, the "Rock of Ages"[7]
that survived the blast. Space is nearer.
When I crouch to my television set,
the drained faces of Negro school-children rise like balloons.   60

Colonel Shaw
is riding on his bubble,
he waits
for the blesséd break.

The Aquarium is gone. Everywhere,   65
giant finned cars nose forward like fish;
a savage servility
slides by on grease.

                                        1959

Waking Early Sunday Morning

O to break loose, like the chinook
salmon jumping and falling back,
nosing up to the impossible
stone and bone-crushing waterfall—
raw-jawed, weak-fleshed there, stopped by ten   5
steps of the roaring ladder, and then
to clear the top on the last try,
alive enough to spawn and die.

Stop, back off. The salmon breaks
water, and now my body wakes   10
to feel the unpolluted joy
and criminal leisure of a boy—

4. World War II.
5. A street that passes the Common.
6. Japanese city destroyed by the American atomic bomb in 1945.
7. Lowell shows us how the religious phrase has been put to commercial use.

no rainbow smashing a dry fly
in the white run is free as I,
here squatting like a dragon on   15
time's hoard before the day's begun!

Fierce, fireless mind, running downhill.
Look up and see the harbor fill:
business as usual in eclipse
goes down to the sea in ships—   20
wake of refuse, dacron rope,
bound for Bermuda or Good Hope,
all bright before the morning watch
the wine-dark hulls of yawl and ketch.

I watch a glass of water wet   25
with a fine fuzz of icy sweat,
silvery colors touched with sky,
serene in their neutrality—
yet if I shift, or change my mood,
I see some object made of wood,   30
background behind it of brown grain,
to darken it, but not to stain.

O that the spirit could remain
tinged but untarnished by its strain!
Better dressed and stacking birch,   35
or lost with the Faithful at Church—
anywhere, but somewhere else!
And now the new electric bells,
clearly chiming, "Faith of our fathers,"
and now the congregation gathers.   40

O Bible chopped and crucified
in hymns we hear but do not read,
none of the milder subtleties
of grace or art will sweeten these
stiff quatrains shoveled out four-square—   45
they sing of peace, and preach despair;
yet they gave darkness some control,
and left a loophole for the soul.

When will we see Him face to face?
Each day, He shines through darker glass.   50
In this small town where everything
is known, I see His vanishing
emblems, His white spire and flag-
pole sticking out above the fog,
like old white china doorknobs, sad,   55
slight, useless things to calm the mad.

Hammering military splendor,
top-heavy Goliath in full armor—

little redemption in the mass
liquidations of their brass,   60
elephant and phalanx moving
with the times and still improving,
when that kingdom hit the crash:
a million foreskins stacked like trash . . .

Sing softer! But what if a new   65
diminuendo brings no true
tenderness, only restlessness,
excess, the hunger for success,
sanity of self-deception
fixed and kicked by reckless caution,   70
while we listen to the bells—
anywhere, but somewhere else!

O to break loose. All life's grandeur
is something with a girl in summer . . .
elated as the President   75
girdled by his establishment
this Sunday morning, free to chaff
his own thoughts with his bear-cuffed staff,
swimming nude, unbuttoned, sick
of his ghost-written rhetoric!   80

No weekends for the gods now. Wars
flicker, earth licks its open sores,
fresh breakage, fresh promotions, chance
assassinations, no advance.
Only man thinning out his kind   85
sounds through the Sabbath noon, the blind
swipe of the pruner and his knife
busy about the tree of life . . .

Pity the planet, all joy gone
from this sweet volcanic cone;   90
peace to our children when they fall
in small war on the heels of small
war—until the end of time
to police the earth, a ghost
orbiting forever lost   95
in our monotonous sublime.

                                                        1967

History

History has to live with what was here,
clutching and close to fumbling all we had—
it is so dull and gruesome how we die,
unlike writing, life never finishes.

Abel was finished; death is not remote,   5
a flash-in-the-pan electrifies the skeptic,
his cows crowding like skulls against high-voltage wire,
his baby crying all night like a new machine.
As in our Bibles, white-faced, predatory,
the beautiful, mist-drunken hunter's moon ascends—   10
a child could give it a face: two holes, two holes,
my eyes, my mouth, between them a skull's no-nose—
O there's a terrifying innocence in my face
drenched with the silver salvage of the mornfrost.

                                                                              1973

Epilogue

Those blessèd structures, plot and rhyme—
why are they no help to me now
I want to make
something imagined, not recalled?
I hear the noise of my own voice: 5
The painter's vision is not a lens,
it trembles to caress the light.
But sometimes everything I write
with the threadbare art of my eye
seems a snapshot,   10
lurid, rapid, garish, grouped,
heightened from life,
yet paralyzed by fact.
All's misalliance.
Yet why not say what happened?   15
Pray for the grace of accuracy
Vermeer[1] gave to the sun's illumination
stealing like the tide across a map
to his girl solid with yearning.
We are poor passing facts,   20
warned by that to give
each figure in the photograph
his living name.

                                                                              1977

◦◄ WILLIAM JAY SMITH ►◦
(b. 1918)

Poet, translator, children's author, critic, memoirist, anthologist, and sometimes
statesman, William Jay Smith has been one of the most versatile American writers

---

1. Jan Vermeer (1632–1675), Dutch painter known for his skill in depicting stillness, detail, and light.

of his generation. He was born in Winfield, Louisiana, of European and Choctaw Indian ancestry, but soon after his birth, Smith's father, an unsuccessful farmer, reenlisted to become a clarinetist in the U.S. Army band. In 1921 the family moved to Jefferson Barracks near St. Louis, where Smith spent his entire youth—suavely recounted in his elegant memoir, *Army Brat* (1980). After completing a bachelor's and master's degree in French from Washington University, Smith served in the U.S. Navy during World War II as liaison officer onboard a French frigate in both the Atlantic and Pacific theaters of operation. After the war he taught briefly before winning a Rhodes scholarship in 1947 to study at Wadham College, Oxford. That year he also married the poet Barbara Howes. This marriage ended in divorce in 1964. Two years later he married Sonja Haussman of Paris. Smith's career has been remarkably diverse. He taught at several colleges and universities, and also served two years in the Vermont House of Representatives. From 1968 to 1970 he worked as Poetry Consultant to the Library of Congress. He currently divides his time between Paris and Cummington, Massachusetts.

Smith has been a prolific writer, publishing over fifty books of poetry, translation, children's verse, literary criticism, and memoir, in addition to editing several influential anthologies. His best poems are unlike anything else in contemporary American literature. His early lyric poetry is as close as any verse by the French Symbolists to the unattainable ideal of *poésie pure*. Although often based on realistic situations, Smith's compressed, formal lyrics develop language musically in a way that summons an intricate, dreamlike set of images and associations. The poems sometimes use simple syntax and diction—as in "American Primitive"—to create dark and ambiguous effects. Smith likewise uses tight formal patterns—as in "Galileo Galilei"—to present nightmarish scenes that defy rational explanation. Without abandoning formal verse, Smith also explored a unique brand of free verse in later volumes like *The Tin Can* (1966). His recent book, *The Cherokee Lottery* (2000), examines his family roots and tells the story of the "Trail of Tears," the forced removal of southern Indian tribes east of the Mississippi River. Although Smith is often grouped with the formalist poets of his generation (like Richard Wilbur and Howard Nemerov), his work remains original and distinctly personal, ultimately bearing as much relation to French as to American literature.

The World Below the Window: Poems 1937–1997 (1998) is the most comprehensive edition of Smith poetry. *Laughing Time: Collected Nonsense* (1990) is the best gathering of his polished light verse. A substantial selection of his literary criticism can be found in *The Streaks of the Tulips* (1972). A sampling of his voluminous translations appeared in *Collected Translations* (1985).

⊷━◆━⊷

A Note on the Vanity Dresser

The yes-man in the mirror now says no,
No longer will I answer you with lies.
The light descends like snow, so when the snow-
man melts, you will know him by his eyes.

The yes-man in the mirror now says no.   5
Says no. No double negative of pity

Will save you now from what I know you know:
These are your eyes, the cinders of your city.

1947

Galileo Galilei[1]

Comes to knock and knock again
At a small secluded doorway
In the ordinary brain.

Into light the world is turning,
And the clocks are set for six;   5
And the chimney pots are smoking,
And the golden candlesticks.

Apple trees are bent and breaking,
And the heat is not the sun's;
And the Minotaur[2] is waking,   10
And the streets are cattle runs.

Galileo Galilei,
In a flowing, scarlet robe,
While the stars go down the river
With the turning, turning globe,   15

Kneels before a black Madonna
And the angels cluster round
With grave, uplifted faces
Which reflect the shaken ground

And the orchard which is burning,   20
And the hills which take the light;
And the candles which have melted
On the altars of the night.

Galileo Galilei
Comes to knock and knock again   25
At a small secluded doorway
In the ordinary brain.

1950

American Primitive

Look at him there in his stovepipe hat,
His high-top shoes, and his handsome collar;
Only my Daddy could look like that,
And I love my Daddy like he loves his Dollar.

1. Galileo (1564–1642) was an Italian astronomer whose scientific discoveries brought him into conflict with the Catholic Church during the Inquisition.
2. Creature in Greek mythology, half man and half bull, kept by King Minos in the labyrinth on Crete.

The screen door bangs, and it sounds so funny—   5
There he is in a shower of gold;
His pockets are stuffed with folding money,
His lips are blue, and his hands feel cold.

He hangs in the hall by his black cravat,
The ladies faint, and the children holler: 10
Only my Daddy could look like that,
And I love my Daddy like he loves his Dollar.

1953

◄ MAY SWENSON ►
(1919–1989)

The daughter of Swedish immigrants who had converted to Mormonism, Anna Thilda May Swenson was born and raised in Logan, Utah, and spoke only Swedish until she entered the first grade. The eldest of ten children, she helped rear her siblings, and although she was brought up in the Church of Jesus Christ of Latter-Day Saints, she became skeptical of biblical fundamentalism and Mormon scripture when she was a teenager. Out of love and respect for her parents, she made no grand break with the church, but slipped away gradually. After receiving a bachelor's degree in English from Utah State University in 1939, she worked as a journalist for a year and then moved to New York City. Answering an advertisement in the *New York Times,* she was hired as a secretary to an author—but quickly found out that the man who placed the ad had never published and expected her to do more than type for him. Tired of his advances, she found an office job, and later joked, "I had doubted the Word of my religion, but believed implicitly every word of the *New York Times.*"

While working as a secretary, Swenson pursued poetry diligently. She sometimes typed ideas for poems and even her own correspondence on company stationery so that she would appear to be concentrating on office business. From 1942 to 1949 she rose from typist to editor of two trade pharmaceutical journals, and then she took a year off to live on her savings and write. In 1950 she secured a residency at the Yaddo artists' colony where she met Elizabeth Bishop, who remained a lifelong friend, though the friendship was sustained primarily through correspondence after Bishop moved to Brazil. Meanwhile, James Laughlin, the publisher of New Directions Press, gave Swenson part-time employment as a manuscript reader and chief writer of rejection letters, a position that lasted for twelve years and was flexible enough to allow her to concentrate on her own writing. After circulating three poetry manuscripts among presses, Swenson finally found a publisher for her fourth: Scribners released *Another Animal: Poems* (1954). Her second collection was *A Cage of Spines* (1958), which was followed by *To Mix with Time* (1963), *Half Sun Half Sleep* (1967), *Iconographs* (1970), and *New and Selected Things Taking Place* (1978), children's books, translations from the Swedish poet Tomas Tranströmer, and several posthumously published books of poetry, including *The Love Poems of May Swenson* (1991) and *Nature* (1994). She garnered numerous awards, including the Bollingen Prize in 1981, and a MacArthur fellowship. Apart from a 1960 trip to Europe on an Amy Lowell Traveling Fellowship, Swenson lived in or near New York City for most of her life. After leaving Utah, she lived in Greenwich Village, first with Anca Vrbovska, a Czechoslovakian writer, and from 1950 until the late 1960s with Pearl Schwartz. After 1967 Swenson relocated to Sea Cliff, New York, with a new partner, Rozanne Knudson, whom she met while serving as a writer-in-residence at Purdue University in 1966 and 1967. With "Zan" she spent winters in Arizona, Southern California, and Delaware, where she died in December 1989 from heart failure brought on by a severe asthma attack.

Although Swenson has been called "the poet of the perceptible," her best poems do more than annotate the world. She stresses that poetry is "based in a craving to get through the curtains of things as they *appear,* to things as they *are,* and then into the larger, wilder space of things as they *are becoming.*" The realm of Swenson's poetry is not static, but set in motion—often through her relentless questioning of appearances. Skeptical of religion, she does not search for transcendence, but instead evokes change. Fond of riddles and combining visual and verbal dimensions in her shaped poems, Swenson has sometimes been criticized for being too clever and for her choice to write impersonal poetry in an era of confessionalism. Yet the precision of her descriptions and rich sonority of her language allow a broad scope for interpretation, so that her poetry develops not a personal history, but an idiosyncratic vision, intimate in scale and expansive in implication.

Question

Body my house
my horse my hound
what will I do
when you are fallen

Where will I sleep   5
How will I ride
What will I hunt

Where can I go
without my mount
all eager and quick   10
How will I know
in thicket ahead
is danger or treasure
when Body my good
bright dog is dead   15

How will it be
to lie in the sky
without roof or door
and wind for an eye

With cloud for shift   20
how will I hide?

1954

Four-Word Lines

Your eyes are just
like bees, and I
feel like a flower.
Their brown power makes
a breeze go over   5
my skin. When your
lashes ride down and
rise like brown bees'
legs, your pronged gaze
makes my eyes gauze.   10
I wish we were
in some shade and
no swarm of other
eyes to know that
I'm a flower breathing   15
bare, laid open to
your bees' warm stare.
I'd let you wade
in me and seize
with your eager brown   20
bees' power a sweet
glistening at my core.

                                                                  1970

Strawberrying

My hands are murder-red. Many a plump head
drops on the heap in the basket. Or, ripe
to bursting, they might be hearts, matching
the blackbird's wing-fleck. Gripped to a reed
he shrieks his ko-ka-ree in the next field.   5
He's left his peck in some juicy cheeks, when
at first blush and mostly white, they showed
streaks of sweetness to the marauder.

We're picking near the shore, the morning
sunny, a slight wind moving rough-veined leaves   10
our hands rumple among. Fingers find by feel
the ready fruit in clusters. Here and there,
their squishy wounds. . . . Flesh was perfect
yesterday. . . . June was for gorging. . . .
sweet hearts young and firm before decay.   15

"Take only the biggest, and not too ripe,"
a mother calls to her girl and boy, barefoot
in the furrows. "Don't step on any. Don't
change rows. Don't eat too many." Mesmermized

by the largesse, the children squat and pull   20
and pick handfuls of rich scarlets, half
for the baskets, half for avid mouths.
Soon, whole faces are stained.

A crop this thick begs for plunder. Ripeness
wants to be ravished, as udders of cows when hard,   25
the blue-veined bags distended, ache to be stripped.
Hunkered in mud between the rows, sun burning
the backs of our necks, we grope for, and rip loose
soft nippled heads. If they bleed—too soft—
let them stay. Let them rot in the heat.   30

When, hidden away in a damp hollow under moldy
leaves, I come upon a clump of heart-shapes
once red, now spiderspit-gray, intact but empty,
still attached to their dead stems—
families smothered as at Pompeii[1]—I rise   35
and stretch. I eat one more big ripe lopped
head. Red-handed, I leave the field.

                                                    1987

---

1. Ancient Roman city near present-day Naples, destroyed by the eruption of Mt. Vesuvius in 79 C.E.

Open Form: Objectivists, Black Mountain Poets, San Francisco Renaissance, and Beats

Bob Donlin, Neal Cassady, Allen Ginsberg, Robert LaVigne, and Lawrence Ferlinghetti in front of City Lights Bookstore.

HISTORICAL AND CRITICAL OVERVIEW

Opening the Field

> A longing grows to return to the open composition in which the accidents
> and imperfections of speech might awake intimations of human being.
> —*Robert Duncan*

Robert Duncan's equation in 1953 of "open composition" with "human being,"
and particularly with accident, imperfection, longing, and speech (as opposed to
print) heralds a shift in American poetry that began in the early 1950s and grew
in influence over the next several decades. For the Black Mountain, San Francisco
Renaissance, and Beat poets, the polished and urbane "New Critical poem," ubiquitous in mainstream journals of the early postwar era, lacked "intimations of
human being." Seeking to connect poetry to a sense of discovery, these poets valued improvisation for the "accidents and imperfections" that would lend their
work freshness and immediacy. These values increasingly reflected the spirit of the
times, as the country moved from the middle class conformity of the fifties toward
the social upheavals and liberation movements of the sixties. As Duncan later observed in "Towards an Open Universe" (1966), "It is a changing aesthetic, but
also a changing sense of life."

What is "open form"? Some poets and critics link the term with free verse and
contrast it to what Charles Olson, in "Projective Verse" (1950), defined as "the
NON-Projective, or what a French critic calls 'closed' verse, that is, the verse that
print bred and which is pretty much what we have had, in English & American, despite the work of Pound and Williams." Olson's formulation, however, is problematic. Although much of the poetry written in open form derives from the style of
free verse pioneered by Pound and Williams, some open-form poets were also skilled
at writing in rhyme and meter. Likewise, rhyme and meter are aural techniques that
are in fact rarely associated with print culture, whereas free verse is historically
linked with typography and print culture. Moreover, although open form is also
commonly associated with the poetic revolutions incited by the Black Mountain
and Beat poets, poets such as the Objectivists and the maverick Modernist Laura
Riding helped "open the field" through experimental work that focused attention
on language and raised philosophical and ethical questions about perception. Open
form, therefore, should be thought of not simply as free verse, but as a style of writing that calls attention to process and thought, and above all to the act of writing.

The dedication to process and discovery led these poets to experiment with
innovative configurations of lines and stanzas, often through envisioning the page
and white space as part of the poem's meaning, as if the poem—and the mind
along with it—traversed a "field of action." Despite their stated emphasis on
speech, therefore, Black Mountain poets often looked on poetry as largely a visual
and typographic art. In their search for precedents, they turned to poets often underrated by the New Critics, including Pound, Williams, H. D., Gertrude Stein,
Walt Whitman, D. H. Lawrence, and British Romantics such as William Blake
and Percy Shelley. Along with their experiments with free verse, some of the open-
form poets took up rhyme and meter, working with invented stanzas and counting
systems (Laura Riding, Kenneth Rexroth, and Louis Zukofsky); seeking modern
contexts for folk forms such as the ballad and nursery rhyme (Robert Duncan and

Lorine Niedecker); or finding flexible musicality in the strictures of very short poems (Samuel Menashe).

For many open-form poets, the long poem and the poetic sequence or serial poem highlighted process, especially the daily activity of writing, in which the mind incorporated into the poem everything it encountered. As Creeley admiringly quoted Zukofsky, "We write one poem all our lives." The ongoing, often open-ended projects already had a long American heritage from Walt Whitman's *Leaves of Grass* (1855), which changed in each edition the poet published, to Ezra Pound's unfinished and omnivorous *Cantos*. The concept of the all-inclusive sequential poem influenced most of the key writers of this loosely connected group. One sees the idea in Lorine Niedecker's constant rearrangements of her short poems, Jack Spicer's self-published serial poems, A. R. Ammons's *Tape for the Turn of the Year* (1965), which he wrote daily on adding machine tape, and George Oppen's *Discrete Series* (1934). It also guided the expansive, Poundian sequences that took their authors decades to write, such as Louis Zukofsky's *"A,"* Charles Olson's *Maximus Poems,* and Robert Duncan's *Passages.*

For many of the poets committed to "discovering form," writing poetry became both a means of self-exploration and a path toward the Divine. As Denise Levertov suggested, "For me, back of the idea of organic form is the concept that there is a form in all things (and in our experience) which the poet can discover and reveal." Many of the open-form poets sought such mystical illumination through religion, although the routes they chose were far from conventional. William Everson became a Dominican Catholic monk and changed his name to Brother Antoninus. Levertov, who was born Jewish, converted to Catholicism late in life. Gary Snyder studied in Japan for seven years to become a Zen adept, and Allen Ginsberg was a disciple of Tibetan Buddhism. Robert Duncan and Jack Spicer were steeped in occult traditions, and A. R. Ammons adopted an Emersonian Transcendentalist outlook. Samuel Menashe grounded his poetry in his Jewish religious heritage, while Objectivist George Oppen embraced Communism as a sort of secular religion of social responsibility.

Duncan argued in "Towards an Open Universe" that, "Our consciousness, and the poem as a supreme effort of consciousness, comes in a dancing organization between personal and cosmic identity." The "open mind" that these poets associated with open form also encompassed radical politics, including the Marxist worldview of Zukofsky and Oppen, the anarcho-pacifism of Everson and Kenneth Rexroth, who both were interned in conscientious objector work camps during World War II, and the willingness of Duncan and Ginsberg to publicly admit their homosexuality and advocate for gay rights.

The Beat poets also initiated a new candidness about the body and sexuality. Like the Black Mountain poets, the Beats opposed the New Critical emphasis on wit and intellect. Refusing to separate body and mind, they followed Charles Olson in allying their poems with "the breath." Thus Allen Ginsberg saw the form of his poems originating "from a source deeper than the mind, that is to say, it came from the breathing and the belly and the lungs." Favoring the immediacy of speech, the Beats contributed much to the poetry reading as a venue for new work. Like the Deep Image poets, the Beats sought to recover a kind of primal experience, sometimes explicitly linking poetry with primitivism. The alignment of "authentic experience" with nakedness became so commonplace during the period that Stephen Berg and Robert Mezey eventually entitled an anthology *Naked Poetry* (1969) and proudly declared in their foreword, "We begin with the firm conviction that the most alive poetry in America had abandoned or at least broken the grip of traditional meters and had set out, once again, into 'the wilderness of unopened life.' " Seeking such authenticity, at many of his poetry readings during the 1960s Allen Ginsberg often quite literally gave his audience "naked poetry," as he disrobed while intoning his long-lined verses. Likewise Brother Antoninus announced his decision to leave the Dominican order in 1969 by stripping off his religious robes at the end of a reading.

Although the Black Mountain poets and Beats initially published with small presses, after the appearance of Donald Allen's anthology *The New American Poetry* (1960), their work quickly gained mainstream attention. By the end of the decade open form became the norm, especially in university writing programs, rather than an avant-garde alternative. As Olson foresaw in "Projective Verse," "the projective involves a stance toward reality outside a poem as well as a new stance toward the reality of the poem itself." For the poets in this section, new ways of seeing reality demanded new ways of writing about it.

The Objectivists

> One is brought back to the entirety of the single word, which is in itself a relation, an implied metaphor, an arrangement, a harmony, or a dissonance.
> —*Louis Zukofsky*

In 1930, at the urging of Ezra Pound, Harriet Monroe asked Pound's young friend Louis Zukofsky to guest-edit a special issue of *Poetry* magazine. After Zukofsky had solicited contributions from poets he knew, Monroe insisted that he both write an essay discussing his criteria for selection and also give this new group of poets a name. Reluctantly, Zukofsky complied, entitling his essay "Sincerity and Objectification: With Special Reference to the Work of Charles Reznikoff" and referring to the poets as "Objectivists." But throughout his career, when referring to the Objectivists, Zukofsky always put the word in quotation marks, in part to indicate his doubts about defining a poetry movement on request, but also to reflect the group's scrupulous concern for language. As Zukofsky announced in his essay, which he later revised and retitled, "An Objective," every word in a language is laden with meaning, not only in terms of dictionary definitions or etymological ancestry, but through its association with different cultural and historical contexts over time. Putting quotations marks around "Objectivist" drew attention to the word itself. The gesture also raised questions about the group's integrity as a movement, for the poets—Zukofsky, George Oppen, Charles Reznikoff, Carl Rakosi, and Lorine Niedecker (who sought Zukofsky out after she read the February 1931 Objectivist issue of *Poetry*)—did not band together and vigorously promote themselves as a new school of poetry. Even after Zukofsky edited *An "Objectivists" Anthology* (1932), which also included the work of Kenneth Rexroth, the poets instead maintained only a loose association over the years.

Nevertheless, they shared common ideals about poetry, many of which Zukofsky articulated in "An Objective." Compelled by the material reality of the world around them and the complexity of doing justice to that reality in language, they came to see words as objects, weighty yet fallible and subject to decay. On the other hand, they also aimed to register what Zukofsky called "historical and contemporary particulars"—not only the particularity of things in the world and of language, but of milieus not often considered in Modernist poetry, such as the urban Jewish perspectives of Zukofsky and Reznikoff or Niedecker's wry evocations of working-class life in the Midwest.

In voicing those concerns, the Objectivists contended with challenges they inherited from Modernist poets, especially Pound, Williams, and Stein, and from the political philosopher Karl Marx. They examined the problem of seeing things clearly (whether material things in the world, or people and events, or poems and other works of art) when perception is compromised not only by historical and cultural circumstances but by the very language poets use. Zukofsky began his essay by referring to optics, particularly to the "objective lens" found in telescopes and microscopes:

> An Objective: (Optics)—The lens bringing the rays from an object into focus. That which is aimed at. (Use extended to poetry)—Desire for what is objectively perfect, inextricably the direction of historic and contemporary particulars.

The sentence plays on multiple meanings of "object" and "objective" and stresses the desire to see the world "objectively" rather than "subjectively." Yet such a "desire for what is objectively perfect" raises problems for poets and readers. If the poem is a kind of lens, then to what extent can the person who looks through it see the world objectively? Will "historical and contemporary particulars" impede seeing, or will an "objectively perfect" poem throw these into focus?

Despite their skepticism concerning subjectivity, each of the Objectivists wrestled with these questions in different ways. Zukofsky's mathematical approach to poetic form, such as the poems of 80 Flowers (each composed of five lines containing eight words), Oppen's contemplations of the moral dimensions of perception, and Niedecker's attentiveness to vernacular speech are all different, yet equally innovative ways of exploring such questions. As Hugh Kenner observes, "The exacting objectivist ambition was to keep the poem open to the entire domain of fact, and simultaneously to keep it a thing made of words, which have their own laws." The poems that resulted from this difficult goal served as a crucial link between the work of the High Modernist poets such as Pound, Williams, and Stein and the mid- and late-century experimentalists, particularly the Language Poets.

Black Mountain Poets

> Form is never more than an extension of content.
> —*Robert Creeley*

The Black Mountain group of poets gained their name through their association (whether as students, fellow teachers, or dedicated correspondents) with Black Mountain College, a short-lived experimental school in North Carolina where Charles Olson taught from 1948 until its bankruptcy in 1956. Grounded on principles of educational freedom, the small college attracted professors and students who would distinguish themselves as avant-garde innovators, including the composer John Cage, the dancer and choreographer Merce Cunningham, and visual artists such as Josef Albers, Franz Kline, Willem de Kooning, and Robert Rauschenberg. A focus on process and spontaneity, as well as a wish to draw attention to the materials from which their work was constructed, enabled these men to help shift the very ground of their respective disciplines. The Black Mountain writers had a similar effect on the poetry of their time, creating a change of attitudes and aesthetics that spread so broadly across the American poetry scene that by the end of the 1960s open form had become the literary norm.

The writers who came to Black Mountain College were attracted by the charismatic presence of Olson, who soon became rector of the college. In 1950, he published his influential essay, "Projective Verse," a freewheeling, antirationalistic meditation on poetry that to many seemed a welcome contrast to the analytical approach of the New Critics. Like Zukofsky, Olson began his manifesto by drawing attention to the individual words, a series of three words broadly spaced below the essay's title, which was also positioned across the page in an unorthodox way:

PROJECTIVE   VERSE

    (PROJECTILE   (PERCUSSIVE   (PROSPECTIVE

vs.

The NON-Projective

The typographical layout here embodies the opposition Olson presents, for projective verse is associated with the open space of the page while "the NON-Projective" sits tightly closed. Olson's unusual spacing and open parentheses announced his vision of a new poetry: adversarial ("projective" versus "non-projective"), kinetic, and conceived as what William Carlos Williams called "a field of action," in which the lines spread out across the page.

Of course, Olson's ideas were not entirely new, but relied on the typographical playfulness of E. E. Cummings, whom Olson cites in his essay, and the Modernist prosody of Pound and Williams, who write adversarial manifestos, experimented with alternative spacing and typography, and favored "process"—the spontaneity of the mind in motion weaving everything it encounters, whether in intellectual or daily life—in the fabric of the poem. As Olson's word "projectile" implies, he envisioned poetry as thrusting forward, both in terms of how lines were positioned on the page and also in terms of the mind's forward momentum.

Throughout his manifesto, Olson celebrated speed and motion. Beginning with a quotation from his friend, the leftist novelist Edward Dahlberg, he framed his ideas through a style whose acceleration evokes urgency:

> ONE PERCEPTION MUST IMMEDIATELY AND DIRECTLY LEAD TO A FURTHER PERCEPTION. It means exactly what it says . . . get on with it, keep moving, keep in, speed, the nerves, their speed, the perceptions, theirs, the acts, the split second acts, the whole business, keep it moving as fast as you can, citizen. And if you also set up as a poet, USE USE USE the process at all points, in any given poem always, always one perception must must must MOVE, INSTANTER, ON ANOTHER!

Olson's fusion of the movement of the mind with the movement of words on the page led him to ground his poetics not on words or stanzas, but on building blocks he found to be even more basic: "the syllable" and "the line," which he felt corresponded, respectively, to "the ear" and "the breath." Concentrating on syllables, he believed, would help poets achieve spontaneity, for syllables are "the elements and minims of language" whose very meaninglessness would encourage writers to focus on sound patterns rather than on logic. Likewise, he argued that moment-by-moment attention to the line, and especially to its varying movement across the page, would enable the mind to open completely.

A diverse array of poets took Olson's ideas and developed them, through poems and manifestos of their own, into flexible modes of writing. The short lines and heavily qualified sentences of Robert Creeley's poems created a sense of immediacy, of a mind in colloquy with itself, trapped by self-awareness yet also capable of wonder and delight. Robert Duncan "opened the field" of the poem through accretion, growing more and more inclusive in his ongoing *Passages* series, which fused references to his eclectic reading, his dream life, the life of the nation, and his contemplation of what he called "the creative strife" of homosexual desire. Denise Levertov, who saw form as "a revelation," rather than "an extension" of content, charted the mind's consciousness of physical sensations through heavily enjambed free verse that evoked the joy of discovery. Calling form *organic,* she suggested that "the revelation of form itself can be a deep joy; yet I think form *as means* should never obtrude, whether from intention or carelessness, between the reader and the essential force of the poem, it must be so fused with that force." In the best work of the Black Mountain poets, form is never gratuitous, but is instead perfectly fused with thought and feeling.

San Francisco Renaissance and Beats

> America is having a nervous breakdown. San Francisco is one of many places
> where a few individuals, poets, have had the luck and courage and fate to
> glimpse something new through the crack in mass consciousness.
> —*Allen Ginsberg*

In 1957, the last issue of *Black Mountain Review,* edited by Robert Creeley, who then was living in San Francisco, was devoted to the work of Beats such as Allen Ginsberg and the novelist Jack Kerouac. The magazine's shift in focus from Black Mountain College to the San Francisco Bay Area attested not only to Creeley's attraction to the Beat aesthetic, but also to the similar ideals of the two movements, for the Beats' emphasis on spontaneity and process and their equation of "the line" with "the breath," derived in part from Olson's influence. Ginsberg had met Olson in 1946, and although he was never a disciple of the elder poet, they became friends and respected each other's work. Kerouac's essay, "Essentials of Spontaneous Prose," which summed up the Beat approach to writing and deeply influenced Ginsberg, owed much of its inspiration to "Projective Verse." The meeting place for the two movements was San Francisco, where Ginsberg, Kerouac, Lawrence Ferlinghetti, and other Beats had drifted from New York in the early to mid-1950s. Later in the decade Creeley and Levertov took up residence in the city, while Robert Duncan, a Bay Area native, sustained his literary friendship with Olson largely through correspondence.

It was no accident that Creeley and Levertov gravitated to San Francisco, nor that Duncan found his native region more congenial to his imagination than Black Mountain College, where he taught only briefly in 1956. Although San Francisco is popularly associated with the Beat generation, the city nurtured several important groups of poets, who began opening possibilities for poetry a decade before the Beats headed west. Since the 1940s, Kenneth Rexroth had served as an elder statesman of the city's poetry life and a mentor to many younger poets. Intellectually omnivorous, Rexroth was sympathetic toward many different styles of writing, and the clarity and directness of his own poetry, along with that of his translations from Asian poets, influenced the work of the poets who associated with him. His broad reading not only encompassed the literature of Western Europe and Asia, but also science, politics, and philosophy. His eclectic erudition contributed to the cosmopolitan flavor of the San Francisco literary scene. His literary salons focused as much on politics or theology as on poetry and were regularly attended by the city's writers and intellectuals, including Duncan, Jack Spicer, William Everson, and Weldon Kees. (Kees's powerful presence and restless artistic activity, especially in linking poetry, jazz, and the visual arts, helped lay the foundation for the San Francisco Renaissance, but he disappeared in 1955 just before the Beat movement hit national prominence.)

Another important San Francisco literary circle surrounded Spicer, Duncan, and the poet Robin Blaser at the University of California, Berkeley, in the 1940s, and focused not only on poetry but on medievalism, occult lore, and dreams of a utopian homosexual community. In the 1950s, Spicer presided over a series of "Blabbermouth Nights" at North Beach bars, where participants free-associated in front of a microphone, and he also led a workshop on magic at the San Francisco Public Library. Publishing small, inexpensive chapbooks, Spicer refused to distribute his poems beyond his circle. Although his aesthetic of cool, often tongue-in-cheek Surrealism differed from the Beat predilection for self-revelation and media baiting, Spicer, like Duncan, Kees, and Rexroth, was a galvanizing presence in literary San Francisco. His combination of eclectic intellectualism and living "on the edge" through his drinking and homosexual affairs was in tune with the "bohemian" ethos of the era.

But that ethos gained national attention only in the late 1950s, through the agency of Ginsberg, Kerouac, and Ferlinghetti, whose City Lights Bookstore and press gave the Beat writers a stable venue for their work. The name "Beat Generation," deriving from the slang sense of "down and out," was coined by Kerouac, who claimed "we were a generation of furtives. You know, with an inner knowledge . . . a kind of beatness . . . and a weariness with all the forms, all the conventions of the world. So I guess you could say we're a 'Beat Generation.' " After the Beats received negative media attention, including *San Francisco Chronicle* columnist Herb Caen's invention in 1958 of the derogative term "Beatnik," evoking the threatening Russian satellite "Sputnik," Kerouac tried to reclaim "Beat" by associating it with "beatitude" and "beatific."

Kerouac's definitions encapsulated the world-weariness, disgust with convention, and search for spiritual beauty (often through alcohol, drugs, or unconventional religious experiences) that characterized the Beat aesthetic and drew together these temperamentally different writers. Ginsberg and Snyder, along with Michael McClure, Philip Whalen, and Philip Lamantia, inaugurated the Beat era in San Francisco through a poetry reading in October 1955 at the Six Gallery. Although the other poets' contributions were memorable, Ginsberg stole the show with his hypnotic reading of *Howl*, a poem in long, incantatory lines merging personal confession, sexual frankness, and rage at the hypocrisy of America in the Cold War era.

The publication of *Howl and Other Poems* (1956) by City Lights led to seizure of the books on charges of obscenity and a widely publicized trial the following year in which many writers testified in favor of the poem's literary and social merit. Ginsberg was exonerated, and the press coverage made him a national celebrity. In part through his public persona, Ginsberg became the representative Beat. Yet his poetry also exemplified the ideals of performance-oriented, improvisatory composition, opposition to mainstream society, and search for both personal and transcendent revelations that his fellow Beats pursued and that would become an increasingly common approach to American poetry over the next few decades.

⊸◀ LAURA RIDING ▶⊶
(1901–1991)

Laura Riding's several name changes over the course of her life accompany significant milestones in her often tempestuous career. For a poet who sought truth through language, her determination to rename herself reflected her own search for authenticity. She was born Laura Reichenthal to Jewish parents in New York City. Her father, Nathaniel Reichenthal, had emigrated from Austria-Hungary as a child and changed jobs frequently. Her mother, whose health had been ruined by years of sweatshop labor, became an invalid during the poet's childhood. As a socialist and union organizer, Nathaniel Reichenthal engaged his daughter in lively debates, which she credited for helping to hone her mind, even though early in her life she rejected his leftist politics. In 1918, winning three scholarships, she matriculated at Cornell University, where she met Louis Gottschalk, a history instructor, whom she married in 1920.

Finding the married name of Laura Reichenthal Gottschalk cumbersome, Riding revised it to Laura Riding Gottschalk, which became, through 1926, her first-author name. By that time, however, she had divorced her husband, whom she had accompanied on his job changes from college to college, while never earning her own degree. She had, however, begun to write poetry and achieved early success. In 1923 Riding submitted poems to The *Fugitive*, a magazine published by a conservative group of modernist Southern poets, including Allen Tate, John Crowe Ransom, and Robert Penn Warren. The Fugitives championed her work, publishing it in almost every subsequent issue of their magazine. When they gave her their 1924 Nashville Prize for the year's most promising poet, they applauded her work's irony, formal integrity, and intellectual substance, values that they strove to promote in poetry. Although she formally joined the Fugitives in 1925, she had already developed her own ideas about poetry. In her essay, "A Prophecy or a Plea" (1925), she embraces poetry as thought's express culmination and views the poet as a prophet: "By taking the universe apart he [the poet] will have reintegrated it with his own vitality; and it is this reintegrated universe that will in turn possess him and give him rest." Disillusioned with New York literary culture, and having difficulty making a living, she sailed in 1926 to join the poet Robert Graves and his wife Nancy Nicholson in England.

Riding and Graves soon became both lovers and collaborators. During her fourteen-year partnership with Graves, she established herself as an uncompromising literary presence. Living in the Graves household, the poet published her first collection, *The Close Chaplet* (1926), with Virginia and Leonard Woolf's Hogarth Press. In 1927 she changed her name, publishing subsequent books through 1939 (with the exception of those issued under pseudonyms) as Laura Riding. In 1962/63, she reemerged as Laura (Riding) Jackson. With Graves, she wrote the influential *A Survey of Modernist Poetry* (1927), a critical study whose scrupulous attentiveness to form and language and distancing of poetry from the life of the poet helped lay the groundwork for the New Criticism, later promulgated by Tate, Ransom, and Warren. The book's claims about purifying language also came very close to the effects Riding aimed for in her own poetry:

> [In Modernist poetry] language . . . had to be reorganized, used as if afresh, cleansed of its experience: to be as "pure" and "abstract" as colour or stone. Words had to be reduced to their least historical value; the purer they could be made, the more eternally

immediate and present they would be; they could express the absolute at the same time as they expressed the age.

Not surprisingly, at the conclusion of their study Riding and Graves praised Gertrude Stein whose determination to pare poetry down to its essentials, however, only superficially resembled Riding's own meaning-centered aesthetic.

In 1927 Riding and Graves founded Seizin Press, which published her poetry collections, *Love as Love, Death as Death* (1928) and *Poet: A Lying Word* (1933). In 1929 Riding's already complicated domestic life grew even more wrenched. When Irish poet Geoffrey Phibbs tried to convince her to leave the Graves household and live with him, she jumped out of a third-story window. She later claimed that she did so not to commit suicide, but to break the hold that Graves, his wife Nancy, and Phibbs had over her. The incident was sensationally reported in the press, and Graves was questioned by the police on suspicion of attempted murder. For the next several months, Graves nursed her through a difficult convalescence, for she had suffered a compound spinal fracture. Meanwhile, Phibbs took up with Nancy.

After Riding's recovery, she and Graves relocated to Deyá, Mallorca, where they held court among a tight group of disciples until the Spanish Civil War forced them to flee in 1936. After spending time in France, Switzerland, and England, they moved to New Hope, Pennsylvania, in 1939—the year after Riding's *Collected Poems* appeared from Random House. In New Hope, Riding's personal life changed yet again. She met Schuyler B. Jackson, who had written a laudatory review for *Time* magazine of her work. The two fell in love and were married in 1941, moving to Wabasso, Florida, where they cultivated citrus trees. After her move to Florida, Riding stopped writing poems altogether, for she had come to distrust poetry's efficacy as a means of expressing truth. Instead, she worked with Jackson on a long study of language, *Rational Meaning* (1997), which was only published posthumously. She died in 1991 from cardiac arrest.

Riding's contribution to the development of modernist poetry was obscured for two decades after her marriage to Jackson (who died in 1968) by her withdrawal from literary life, her renunciation of poetry, and her refusal to allow her work to be reprinted in anthologies. From 1962, she began to permit her poems to be republished, at first in magazines, later in *Selected Poems: In Five Sets* (1970) and *The Poems of Laura Riding* (1980). These books were framed, however, by intimidating introductions warning the reader against poetry and explaining why she stopped writing. As John Ashbery has commented, "Laura Riding was what we would call today a 'control freak.' Her poetry, hedged about with caveats of every sort in the form of admonitory prefaces and postscripts, presents us with something like a minefield; one reads it always with a sensation of sirens and flashing lights in the background."

Despite Riding's eventual belief—anticipated in her book title, *Poet: A Lying Word* (1933)—that poetry was not the right means to achieve the linguistic ultimate, her best work is original and strangely compelling. Jettisoning the conventional devices of analogy and sensuous description, and using allusion and even metaphor sparingly, Riding disconnected her poetry from the external world to create a realm of pure thought. Equating thought with language, she drew the reader's attention to language through repetition, unconventional usage (such as adopting nouns and adjectives as verbs), and nonce rhyme schemes and stanza patterns. In doing so, she created a unique, though difficult, body of work that served as a stepping-stone for many later poets, including the Objectivists, the New York School, and the Language Poets.

Helen's Burning[1]

Her beauty, which we talk of,
Is but half her fate.
All does not come to light
Until the two halves meet
And we are silent   5
And she speaks,
Her whole fate saying,
She is, she is not, in one breath.

But we tell only half, fear to know all
Lest all should be to tell   10
And our mouths choke with flame
Of her consuming
And lose the gift of prophecy.

                                        1930

The Map of Places

The map of places passes.
The reality of paper tears.
Land and water where they are
Are only where they were
When words read *here* and *here*   5
Before ships happened there.

Now on naked names feet stand,
No geographies in the hand,
And paper reads anciently,
And ships at sea   10
Turn round and round.
All is known, all is found.
Death meets itself everywhere.
Holes in maps look through to nowhere.

                                        1930

The World and I

This is not exactly what I mean
Any more than the sun is the sun.
But how to mean more closely
If the sun shines but approximately?
What a world of awkwardness!   5
What hostile implements of sense!

1. Riding contemplates the fate of Helen of Troy, who left her aging husband Menelaus for the young and handsome Paris, thereby precipitating the Trojan War.

Perhaps this is as close a meaning
As perhaps becomes such knowing.
Else I think the world and I
Must live together as strangers and die—   10
A sour love, each doubtful whether
Was ever a thing to love the other.
No, better for both to be nearly sure
Each of each—exactly where
Exactly I and exactly the world   15
Fail to meet by a moment, and a word.

1933

⊶◄ KENNETH FEARING ►⊶
(1902–1961)

Born in Oak Park, Illinois, Kenneth Fearing was the son of a successful lawyer who could trace his Yankee ancestry back to colonial Massachusetts. His mother came from a family of Bohemian Jews, and one material uncle was the first director of the Institute for Advanced Studies at Princeton. Olive Fearing's obsession with success made her a difficult figure in her son's life. His parents divorced when he was quite young, and Kenneth often lived with his paternal relatives, among whom anti-Semitism was not uncommon. His mother never supported his literary ambitions and was frequently critical of him. Kenneth followed another Oak Park native, Ernest Hemingway, to Oak Park-River Forest High School where his senior class voted him both the wittiest boy and class pessimist. After two years of college at the University of Illinois, Kenneth transferred to the University of Wisconsin, soon after befriending the poet Carl Rakosi. He also began to publish stories and poems in the *Wisconsin Literary Magazine,* which he edited until his financial mismanagement, difficult prose style, and outspoken views on sex forced him to resign.

Upon graduation, Fearing went with his girlfriend, the writer Margery Latimer, to New York City. They scraped by as writers with the help of a small allowance from his family. His unwillingness to get a job or propose marriage strained their relationship. (Latimer would later marry the poet Jean Toomer and die bearing his child.) Fearing not only wrote poetry but also pulp fiction—including soft-core pornography under a pseudonym—for the income it brought. His early poems appeared in such magazines as the Marxist *New Masses,* and his politics were consistently leftist. He probably joined the Communist Party briefly, though he denied it—for obvious reasons—during the postwar "Red Scare" years. Years later when he was subpoenaed in 1950 by the U.S. Attorney's office and asked whether he was a member of the Communist Party, he pointedly replied, "Not yet." Still, when his first collection of poems, *Angel Arms,* appeared in 1929, critics generally associated it with leftist sympathies, failing to notice their irony and archness. This political vision of Fearing is reflected in Alice Neal's surreal 1935 portrait of the poet in which a small skeleton pours blood out of the smiling author's chest "to show," the artist commented, that "his heart bled for the grief of the world."

In 1931 Fearing met Rachel Meltzer, who immediately sensed that the hard-drinking and disorganized poet "needed someone to take care of him." They were married in 1933, and Fearing was soon embarked on a prolific and successful period as a writer. He published almost a book a year, including four distinguished literary thrillers, most notably *The Big Clock* (1946), a brilliantly plotted detective story about a reporter ironically sent in pursuit of himself for a crime he did not commit. He also published his best-received volumes of poems, *Dead Reckoning* (1938) and *Stranger at Coney Island* (1948). He lived in London for eight months with his wife and son on a Guggenheim fellowship, and his poems were now often published in such mainstream periodicals as the *New Yorker*. But during these years Fearing's alcoholism gradually destroyed his professional relationships. In 1944 he and Meltzer divorced, and a year later he married an artist, Nan Lurie. In 1948 *The Big Clock* was made into a celebrated movie with Charles Laughton and Ray Milland. (It was also remade in 1987 as *No Way Out* with Kevin Costner.) Fearing became temporarily wealthy from the novel's commercial success and sale to Hollywood, but he managed his affairs so badly that in the last decade of his life he was often poor. By 1952 his second marriage had failed. In 1961 Fearing died of a malignant melanoma in New York City.

Fearing's poetry was often ironic in tone and scathing in its social vision. After starting as a traditionalist influenced by Edwin Arlington Robinson, he adopted the long free verse line of Whitman and Sandburg. Though he once said that he was in the "Whitman tradition," he was also influenced by the fragmentation of Modernism, especially the work of T. S. Eliot. At least one critic compared Fearing's poetry, with its bits of characterization and dialogue, to Hemingway's prose vignettes. Certainly Fearing was vernacular in diction and populist in subject matter. He provocatively used slang, newspaper headlines, and advertising in his verse. Reviewing the *Collected Poems* (1940), Weldon Kees observed that Fearing had "taken over and extended techniques of the anti-poetic common to both Whitman and Sandburg, supplementing them with more raucous tricks not unknown to the soap-boxer, the radio orator, and the sideshow barker. Principal among these are the device of repetition . . . and the device of listing and cataloguing." Indeed, many of Fearing's poems unfold as inspired lists of images and observations drawn from contemporary urban life.

Fearing helped pave the way for later writers in the New York School and the Beat Movement who used elements drawn from popular culture in their work. Though now best remembered as a suspense novelist, he remains one of the most interesting and original American poets of his generation. His gritty urban sensibility and dark wit reflect the nation's experience during the decisive period between the Depression and World War II.

Dirge

1-2-3 was the number he played but today the number came 3-2-1;
Bought his Carbide at 30 and it went to 29: had the favorite at Bowie[1] but the
    track was slow—

---

1. A race track in Maryland.

O executive type, would you like to drive a floating-power, knee-action, silk-
    upholstered six? Wed a Hollywood star? Shoot the course in 58? Draw to the
    ace, king, jack?
O fellow with a will who won't take no, watch out for three cigarettes on the
    same, single match; O democratic voter born in August under Mars, beware
    of liquidated rails—

Denouement to denouement, he took a personal pride in the certain, certain way
    he lived his own, private life,   5
But nevertheless, they shut off his gas; nevertheless, the bank foreclosed;
    nevertheless, the landlord called; nevertheless, the radio broke,

And twelve o'clock arrived just once too often,
Just the same he wore one gray tweed suit, bought one straw hat, drank one
    straight Scotch, walked one short step, took one long look, drew one deep
    breath,
Just one too many,

And wow he died as wow he lived,   10
Going whop to the office and blooie home to sleep and biff got married and
    bam had children and oof got fired,
Zowie did he live and zowie did he die,

With who the hell are you at the corner of his casket, and where the hell're we
    going on the right-hand silver knob, and who the hell cares walking second
    from the end with an American Beauty[2] wreath from why the hell not,

Very much missed by the circulation staff of the New York Evening Post; deeply,
    deeply mourned by the B.M.T.[3]

Wham, Mr. Roosevelt;[4] pow, Sears Roebuck; awk, big dipper; bop, summer
    rain;   15
Bong, Mr., bong, Mr., bong, Mr., bong.

                                                                                 1935

Literary

I sing of simple people and the hardier virtues, by Associated Stuffed Shirts &
    Company, Incorporated, 358 West 42d Street, New York, brochure enclosed;
Of Christ on the Cross, by a visitor to Calvary, first class;
Art deals with eternal, not current verities, revised from last week's Sunday
    supplement;
Guess what we mean, in *The Literary System;* and a thousand noble answers
    to a thousand empty questions, by a patriot who needs the dough.

And so it goes.   5
Books are the key to magic portals. Knowledge is power. Give the people light.

---

2. An award-winning rose.
3. The Brooklyn Manhattan Transit, a New York City subway line.
4. Franklin Delano Roosevelt (1882–1945), president of the United States from 1932 to 1945.

Writing must be such a nice profession.
Fill in the coupon. How do you know? Maybe you can be a writer, too.

1938

⊷◄ LORINE NIEDECKER ►⊷
(1903–1970)

Born in Fort Atkinson, Wisconsin, Lorine Niedecker grew up on Black Hawk Island, in the southeastern part of the state, where the Rock River empties into Lake Koshkonong. She was the only daughter of parents who grew increasingly alienated from one another. Her father, a carp seiner and owner of an inn and vacation cottages along the Rock River, was outgoing and profligate. He conducted a long-term affair with a local married woman and over the years he divested himself of much of his land as gifts to appease her husband. Niedecker's introverted mother withdrew into bitter silence, which was hastened as she grew older by deafness and incipient blindness. Niedecker, herself quite shy, recalled, "Early in life I looked back of our buildings to the lake and said, 'I am what I am because of all of this—I am what is around me—those woods made me.'" Although as an adult she repeatedly left the island, she always returned, and the place and its people saturated her poetry.

In 1922, she graduated from Fort Atkinson High School and then spent the next two years at Beloit College, but returned home to care for her mother. She married in 1928 and lived with her husband in Fort Atkinson, where she worked at the public library. In 1930, after her husband defaulted on a loan and lost their home, Niedecker moved in with her parents, although she did not officially obtain a divorce until 1942. During these years, she had dedicated herself to writing poetry, begun submitting poems to little magazines, and schooled herself in Modernism, especially Surrealism. But in 1931, after reading the "Objectivist" issue of *Poetry*, guest-edited by the poet Louis Zukofsky, she was so struck by his ideas that she began a correspondence with him, initiating a friendship that would become a literary lifeline for both of them.

Because of her friendship with Zukofsky, Niedecker has often been considered a satellite of his Objectivist group of poets. She admired the Objectivists but maintained her artistic independence. Although their emphasis on linguistic condensation and precise perception appealed to her, she felt that their preoccupation with the external world was so encompassing that they sometimes denied the pull of memory and the unconscious. In the mid-1930s, she complained to a friend:

> Objects, objects. Why are people, artists above all, so terrifically afraid of *themselves?* Thank god for the Surrealist tendency running side by side with Objectivism and toward the monologue tongue. It is my conviction that no one yet, has talked to himself. And until then, what is art? . . . the most important part of memory is its non-expressive, unconscious part. We remember most and longest that which at first perception was unrecognizable, though we are not aware of this. We remember, in other words, a nervesense, a vibration, a colour, a rhythm.

Niedecker developed a distinct, sometimes folksy idiom for her poetry, and her voice is immediately recognizable whether she deploys rhyme and meter or free verse, for she was fluent in both traditional form and open form, especially the enjambed free verse practiced by William Carlos Williams, whose work she admired. Although sharing much of the Objectivist emphasis on careful visual description and fragmentary exposition, Niedecker, as poet-critic Stephen Burt observes, "differs from her peers (especially from her mentor Zukofsky) in her small scales and her fidelity to prose sense. On the one hand she is never programmatically difficult; on the other, she rarely spells everything out." Although her exact descriptions evoke her life by water—the minute details of the river ecosystem and the acute, often wry insights about her family and friends—Niedecker's poetry springs as much from her reading as from her environment. Isolated from the hubs of literary activity, and preferring not to admit to neighbors and co-workers that she wrote poetry, she sustained her work through reading and correspondence, turning often to favorite authors such as Emerson, Thoreau, Dickinson, Henry James, Henry Adams, Thomas Jefferson, the Japanese haiku master Basho, and naturalists such as John Audubon, Linnaeus, and Charles Darwin. Her correspondence with Zukofsky, and later with the poet Cid Corman, gave her the literary companionship that she lacked in daily life.

Niedecker's early relationship with Zukofsky, however, was not limited to correspondence. In 1933, she traveled to New York to meet him and then visited him as often as she could, sometimes staying for months at a time. The romance that swiftly developed between them foundered when she became pregnant and, at Zukofsky's insistence, reluctantly had an abortion. They remained close friends, and after 1939, when he married, they fueled the friendship through letters, sometimes writing to each other several times a week. Over the years, Zukofsky contributed to Niedecker's writing life not only through their discussions of poetry and running commentary on each other's work, but also by introducing her to other poets and helping her gain publication.

The failure of her father's fishing business in the late 1930s made work a necessity for Niedecker. In 1938, she moved to Madison, where she was employed first by the Federal Writers' Project, as a writer and editor for the *Wisconsin Guide,* and then briefly by a radio station as a scriptwriter. She returned to Black Hawk Island and from 1944 to 1950 worked as a stenographer and proofreader for Hoard's, printer of a local journal, *Hoard's Dairyman.* In 1946 a small press in Illinois published her first book, *New Goose,* whose poems sketch working-class life in vernacular permutations of Mother Goose rhymes. In the same year, she built a small cabin on her parents' property beside the Rock River. She lived there for the next fifteen years in spartan conditions, lacking plumbing and inundated each spring by the river's floods. Her mother died in 1951, and after her father's death three years later she inherited several thousand dollars and two cottages, which she rented for income. Because maintenance expenses eroded her funds, she sold the cottages. But failing eyesight prevented her from finding office work, so in 1957 she took a job as a cleaning woman at a local hospital, where she remained until 1963, when she married Albert Millen, an industrial painter, and moved to Milwaukee. The couple returned often to Black Hawk Island and built a retirement home there in 1969, where Niedecker died less than two years later from a stroke.

During her last two decades, Niedecker never stopped writing. In 1955, she completed a series of poems, "For Paul," dedicated to Zukofsky's son, a violin prodigy, and began work on another series of short poems inspired by haiku. Although she had continued to publish in literary journals throughout the decade, her friendship with Cid Corman, who became her literary executor, helped her gain recognition. Corman frequently featured her poems in his magazine, *Origin,* and later edited two posthumous collections of her work: *Blue Chicory* (1976) and *The Granite Pail: The Selected Poems of Lorine Niedecker* (1985). After her second marriage, she completed a series of poems, *North Central* (1968), based on trips she and her husband took around the Great Lakes. Her other late poems include a series on Thomas Jefferson and the autobiographical series of short lyrics, "Paean to Place."

Before her death, Niedecker oversaw publication of *My Life by Water: Collected Poems 1936–1969* (1970). Her complete poetry is available in *Collected Works* (2002), edited by Jenny Penberthy, which gathers all her previously published poems, sometimes in several versions, as well as unpublished poetry and most of her prose pieces. Two volumes of her letters have also appeared: *"Between Your House and Mine": Selected Letters of Lorine Niedecker and Cid Corman* (1986) and *Niedecker and the Correspondence with Zukofsky 1931–1970* (1993). Although she remained virtually unknown during her lifetime, since her death she has been increasingly recognized as one of the century's most original and dedicated American poets.

The Element Mother

I SHE'S GONE

The branches' snow is like the cotton fluff
she wore in her aching ears. In this deaf huff
after storm shall we speak of love?

As my absent father's distrait wife
she worked for us—knew us by sight.   5

We know her now by the way the snow
protects the plants before they go.

II THE GRAVES

You were my mother, thorn apple bush,
armed against life's raw push.
But you my father catalpa tree   10
stood serene as now—he refused to see
that the other woman, the hummer he shaded
          hotly cared
for his purse petals falling—
                    his mind in the air.   15

III KEPLER

Comets you say shoot from nothing?
In heaven's name what other
than matter can be matter's mother.

[c. 1956]

Sorrow Moves in Wide Waves

Sorrow moves in wide waves,
    it passes, lets us be.
It uses us, we use it,
    it's blind while we see.

Consciousness is illimitable,   5
    too good to forsake
tho what we feel be misery
    and we know will break.

[c. 1956]

Poet's Work

Grandfather
    advised me:
        Learn a trade

I learned
    to sit at desk   5
        and condense

No layoff
    from this
        condensery

[c. 1962]

I Knew a Clean Man

I knew a clean man
but he was not for me.
Now I sew green aprons
over covered seats. He

wades the muddy water fishing,   5
falls in, dries his last pay-check
in the sun, smooths it out
in *Leaves of Grass*.[1] He's
the one for me.

[c. 1964]

---

1. Walt Whitman's masterpiece, a book of poetry that expanded with each new edition between its first publication in 1855 and its final version in 1891–1892.

[Autumn Sequence]²

Autumn

Ice
on the minnow bucket

and a school of leaves
moving downstream

．

Last night the trash barrel   5
smoked from lighted paper
This morning
from sun burning
the frost

．

The boy tossed the news   10
and missed
They found it
on the bush

．

Popcorn-can cover
screwed to the wall   15
over a hole
        so the cold
can't mouse in

．

Truth
gives heat   20

He blushed
when I said

before he came
I never wore beads

．

Lights, lifts   25
parts nicely opposed
this white
            lice lithe
pink bird

．

2. Editor's title.

O late fall
marsh—
I
raped by the dry
weed stalk   30

1969

He Lived—Childhood Summers

He lived—childhood summers
  thru bare feet
then years of money's lack
  and heat

beside the river—out of flood   5
  came his wood, dog,
woman, lost her, daughter—
  prologue

to planting trees. He buried carp
  beneath the rose   10
where grass-still
  the marsh rail goes.

To bankers on high land
  he opened his wine tank.
He wished his only daughter   15
  to work in the bank

but he'd given her a source
  to sustain her—
a weedy speech,
  a marshy retainer.   20

1969

◄ LOUIS ZUKOFSKY ►
(1904–1978)

The man whose work Robert Creeley would call a bridge between the Modernist poetry of the 1920s and the experimental poetry of the 1950s learned to bridge cultures from an early age. The son of Jewish immigrants from Lithuania, which was then part of the Russian empire, Louis Zukofsky was born on Manhattan's Lower East Side and initially spoke only Yiddish, learning English in elementary school. Although he soon rebelled against his parents' Orthodox faith, their work ethic and family devotion became central components of his poetry, both in his unstinting dedication to literature and as recurring themes. Despite the financial burden, his parents sent him to Columbia University, where he studied philosophy and English, graduating in 1924 with a master's degree in English. The poetry he wrote during his college years was accomplished enough to appear in *Poetry* magazine. At Columbia he also began reading the work of Karl Marx, and although Zukofsky never joined the Communist Party, Marx's ideas about class, economics, and materialism would deeply influence his poetry.

By 1926 Zukofsky had thoroughly schooled himself in Modernism, displaying his skills in his ambitious "Poem beginning 'The.'" Zukofsky not only built his poem on Modernist techniques such as fragmentation and collage, but styled it both as a parody of *The Waste Land* and an assertion (pitted against Eliot's anti-Semitism) of Jewish identity. In 1927 Zukofsky took the bold step of sending the poem to Ezra Pound, who published it in his journal, *Exile*. The correspondence that developed between Zukofsky and Pound, who was then living in Italy, grew into a lifelong friendship that was strained at times due to Pound's anti-Semitism but remained productive for both writers. Zukofsky apprenticed himself to Pound so studiously that some readers consider his work too derivative. But Zukofsky differentiated himself from his mentor by developing a Marxist, Jewish perspective and by taking Modernist quotation, rapid juxtaposition, and concern with language even further than Pound—using language abstractly as a system like music or mathematics, so that composition became a matter of arrangement (especially of quoted material) that highlighted the building blocks of the system, such as prepositions, articles, and sonic patterns.

Pound was so impressed with Zukofsky's skill and intelligence that he persuaded Harriet Monroe to allow the young poet to edit the February 1931 issue of *Poetry*. Zukofsky included his own verse, along with work by William Carlos Williams, George Oppen, Carl Rakosi, and Charles Reznikoff—the group that was thereafter loosely associated with the name Zukofsky gave to the issue: "Objectivist." At Monroe's request, Zukofsky also wrote an essay that indicated the poets' shared concerns, "Sincerity and Objectification: With Special Reference to the work of Charles Reznikoff," which Zukofsky later revised, merging it with two other early essays, and retitled "An Objective." Opening the essay with a definition that links poetry with optical precision, Zukofsky stressed poetry's need to register the concrete particulars of a world embedded in history. He also drew attention to a poem's identity as an object: a thing made of words.

Although some critics have questioned Objectivism's provenance as a legitimate school of poetry (Zukofsky later claimed that he only created a movement at Monroe's request), there is no doubt that the essay articulated his own aims for poetry. His view of poetry—and even of language itself—as contingent upon history and as a material thing, an object that exists in and of itself, arose from his Marxist perspective. During the course of his career, he worked assiduously to develop the implications of these ideas in numerous volumes of verse, most notably his dense, book-length poem *"A,"* which he began in 1928 and completed in 1974; in experimental translations from Catullus; and in criticism. Much of Zukofsky's work is formalist in the strictest sense possible; for example, he bases a section of *"A"* on a careful count of "n" and "r" sounds, and his translations from Cataullus aim for sonic accuracy, rather than accuracy of meaning. Yet he was also capable of moving lyricism, as in the 1945 elegy for his mother, "A Song for the Year's End."

Apart from teaching at the University of Wisconsin from 1930 to 1931, Zukofsky spent his life in New York City. From 1935 until 1942, he worked for the

Federal Writers' Project of the Works Progress Administration (WPA), and in 1947 he began teaching English at the Polytechnic Institute of Brooklyn, where he remained until his retirement in 1966. After ending an affair with the Wisconsin poet Lorine Niedecker, with whom he remained close friends, in 1939 he married Celia Thaew, a musician and composer, whose work became increasingly important to his poetry. Zukofsky's *Autobiography* (1970) consists almost entirely of her musical settings of his short poems, and the last section of *"A"* features her settings of his poetry and prose to Handel's *Harpsichord Pieces*. Their only child, Paul Zukofsky, was a violin prodigy who debuted at Carnegie Hall in 1956 at the age of thirteen.

The son's fame stood in stark contrast to the father's obscurity, for as Zukofsky aged, he became increasingly reclusive and resentful of his lack of recognition, despite the homage he received from a diverse array of younger poets, including Creeley, Charles Olson, Denise Levertov, Allen Ginsberg, and Robert Duncan. After Zukofsky's death in 1978 his influence increased. Language Poets such as Ron Silliman and Lyn Hejinian acknowledge him as an important forerunner of their work. Although his poetry is not widely read, Zukofsky's ideas have exerted considerable influence on midcentury and contemporary American poetry.

Non Ti Fidar[1]

in opera poetry must be the obedient daughter of music
—Mozart

The hand a shade of moonlight on the pillow
And that a shadowed white would seem above or below
Their heads ear to ear, hearing water
Not like the word, the flickflack of the eye opening on it
With what happiness   5
Where the word is the obedient daughter of music
And Don Giovanni's shapely seat and heart live in hell[2]
Lovable as its fire
As all loves that breathe and kiss
Simply by life   10
Rocking to sleep and flame:
Until mine own voice tired, the sound
A quiet wasting summer's breath

Babylon his flood is stilled
Babel her tower doeth tie my tongue   15
In the willow path that it hath swilled
My spirit, His case, and young.

1949

1. (Italian) "Don't trust him." The poem's title is a quotation from the opening phrase of a celebrated quartet from Mozart's opera *Don Giovanni* (1787). It refers to the infamous seducer Don Giovanni (better known in English as Don Juan).
2. At the end of Mozart's opera, Don Giovanni is pulled down to hell by the haunted statue of a man he killed.

A Song for the Year's End

1

Daughter of music
and her sweet son
so that none rule
the dew to his own hurt
with the year's last sigh   5
awake
the starry sky and bird.

2

I shall go back to my mother's grave after this war
Because there are those who'll still speak of loyalty
In the outskirts of Baltimore   10
Or wherever Jews are not the right sort of people,
And say to her one of the dead I speak to—
There are less Jews left in the world,
While they were killed
I did not see you in a dream to tell you,   15
And that I now have a wife and son.

Then I shall go and write for my country,
Have a job all my life
Seldom write with grace again, be part of the world,
See every man in forced labor,   20
Dawn only where suburbs are *restricted*
To people who take trains every morning,
Never the gentleness that can be,
The hope of the common man, the eyes that love leaves
Any shade, thought or thing that makes all man uncommon,   25

But always the depraved bark
Fight or work,
Dawn the red poster, the advertiser's cock crow,
Sunset a lack of wonder, the lone winged foot of Mercury in
    tie with a tire,[3]   30
The fashion model
Her train stopped in the railroad cut
Looking up to a billboard of herself
As she goes home to her small son asleep,

So early and so late in the fortunes that followed   35
    me from my mother's grave
A lovely air follows her
And the dead President who is worth it:

---

3. Since 1900, the Goodyear Tire and Rubber Company has featured as its logo the winged foot of
Mercury, the swift messenger of the gods in Roman and Greek mythology.

'Dear death, like peace, I end not speaking,
The chitchat has died   40
And the last smile is unwilled
I am dead, I can't talk
To blossoms or spring in the world.'

3

          "Because he was crying
I like him most of all," says my son   45
"Because he was crying,"—the red fox
With three porcupine quills in his paw—
Who brings tears to the eyes,
     button nose against shambles,
Valentines all day, all night, tomorrow   50
The simplest the keyboard can play,
'Pony gay, on your way,' love's hair
With two gray, Papa Bear's Song
     new to renew,
'Who's been sitting in my chair?'   55

                                                                   1956

Starglow[4]

Starglow dwarf china rose shrubthorn
lantern fashion-fare airing car-tire crushed
young's churning old rambler's flown
to sky cane cut back
a crown transplanted patient of   5
drought sun's gold firerimmed branched
greeting thyme's autumn sprig head
happier winter sculpt white rose

                                                                   1978

◄ KENNETH REXROTH ►
(1905–1982)

Poet, critic, translator, anarchist, and cultural impresario, Kenneth Rexroth, who
would occupy the intellectual center of the San Francisco Renaissance, was born in
South Bend, Indiana. The only child of affluent, bohemian parents, Rexroth had a
nourishing but unconventional childhood in a progressive Christian Socialist household. When he was four, his family relocated to Elkhart—the first of many moves
his increasingly erratic parents made as their fortunes rose and fell. Eventually the

---

4. A miniature white rose. This poem is the first of Zukofsky's *80 Flowers* (1978); every poem in the series
consists of eight lines, with each line containing five words.

couple separated, but briefly reunited before his mother's untimely death in 1916. In her final illness she refused to let her ten-year-old son attend school but read to him from her sickbed, urging him to be a writer. Three years later his alcoholic father died suddenly. The orphaned adolescent went to Chicago to live with an aunt, but he quickly rebelled against the conventional new setting. Dropping out of high school at sixteen, Rexroth frequented bohemian Chicago, supporting himself through odd jobs and journalism. Soon he began hitchhiking across the country and later worked his way to Europe and Latin America aboard ships.

In 1927 Rexroth married Andrée Schafer, a painter, and the newlyweds soon moved to San Francisco, the city with which the poet would ever afterwards be associated. "It is the only city in the United States," he observed, "which was not settled overland by the westward-spreading puritan tradition." Deciding to "stay and grow up in the town," Rexroth wrote, painted, and worked in radical politics—usually just scraping by. He briefly joined the Communist Party but left because his own principles were pacifist and anarchist. His marriage also broke up—he would eventually marry four times. In 1932 his poems appeared in Louis Zukofsky's An "Objectivists" Anthology, and his first book, In What Hour (1940), was published to largely hostile reviews by Northeastern critics who either decried his political defection from the organized Left or considered his West Coast subject matter trivial. Despite his growing reputation and readership, Rexroth would never be read sympathetically by Eastern critics, and he never won a major establishment award.

A conscientious objector and pacifist, Rexroth engaged in antiwar activity during the early days of World War II, especially by helping Japanese Americans resist internment, which made him the subject of an FBI investigation. He was eventually granted an exemption from the draft and escaped incarceration, although the strain of the situation contributed to the break-up of his second marriage. In 1944 he published a long poem, The Phoenix and the Tortoise, with New Directions, which was the start of a lifelong partnership with poet James Laughlin, the greatest American publisher of Modernist letters.

Now at the height of his powers, Rexroth published a steady stream of poetry, prose, translations, and drama. His most notable collections of poetry include The Signature of All Things (1950), The Dragon and the Unicorn (1952), In Defense of the Earth (1956), Natural Numbers (1963), and The Heart's Garden, the Garden's Heart (1967). Rexroth also began translating Asian poetry in an influential series of books, most notably One Hundred Poems from the Japanese (1955) and One Hundred Poems from the Chinese (1956).

By 1950 Rexroth had established himself—through hard work and sheer ambition—at the center of San Francisco literary life. He not only published in national journals but also conducted a weekly book-review show on Berkeley's newly established KPFA, the nation's first listener-sponsored radio station. A public spokesman for Modernist literature, political dissent, and alternate lifestyles, Rexroth became the elder statesman of the new Beat movement emerging in San Francisco, which generated huge amounts of media coverage that turned several younger writers he had championed—most notably Allen Ginsberg, Lawrence Ferlinghetti, and Jack Kerouac—into international celebrities. Such fame never came to Rexroth himself; he was too mature, well read, and intellectual to fit the media's definition of the Beat identity. (Instead, Time magazine dubbed him "the Daddy of the Beat Generation," not a particularly cool title.) The media craze did allow Rexroth to develop with the other Beats a new form of poetry reading—not the academic lecture style still prevalent today but a performance spoken to the accompaniment of live jazz.

Rexroth's later years were secure and comfortable. In 1968 he took a teaching position at the University of California at Santa Barbara, which he held until his retirement in 1974. Also in 1974, Rexroth married his longtime companion, Carol Tinker, his fourth and final spouse. He wrote a popular literary column, "Classics Revisited," for *Saturday Review* and a twice-weekly column in the *San Francisco Examiner* in which he was free to discuss any topic from avant-garde art to world politics. Rexroth died at seventy-six in Santa Barbara where, after a Catholic and Buddhist ceremony, he was buried facing the Pacific Ocean.

Although Rexroth's poetic style may have seemed unorthodox early in his career, it prefigured the mainstream American poetry of the 1960s and 1970s. Clarity, simplicity, accessibility, and intensity are the main characteristics of his style. Written in direct, plainspoken free verse, Rexroth's poetry makes its points through image and observation. His lines are usually end-stopped with line breaks coming at an obvious pause of syntax or sense—a technique that heightens their conversational quality without letting them ever appear unduly chatty or verbose. Rexroth is a master of pictorial depiction, especially when describing the western landscape with an easy command of precise naturalist detail. There is also usually a strong sense of personal voice in his work—the "I" in the poem is an attempt to re-create a convincing persona of the poet in words.

Rexroth worked to establish a West Coast identity for American poetry, one that would reflect the unique geographical, historical, cultural, and ethnic qualities of the region. "I am NOT Ivy League," he once asserted, as if anyone could have ever confused his self-educated libertarian anarchism with Ivy League elitism or New Critical detachment. He was both a populist and an intellectual—a potent combination of cultural values in the right circumstances. Rexroth also understood that regional literary identity need not, indeed must not, be provincial. His international sense of literary enterprise led him to translate from Chinese, Japanese, French, Spanish, and Greek, all as relevant sources for a California literary identity.

Rexroth's place in the American literary canon—like that of many Californian poets such as Robinson Jeffers, William Everson, Josephine Miles, Robert Duncan, and Jack Spicer—remains open to debate. Consistently ignored by the Eastern literary establishment, these poets continue to exercise an active influence on West Coast writers, and they continue to be read. Rexroth left a small but enduring body of original poems, elegant translations, and still potent essays out of the huge body of work he created. It remains impossible to discuss the changes in mid-twentieth-century American poetry responsibly without mentioning him.

◄•────►─•►

A Very Early Morning Exercise

Chang Yuen is on the threshold of a remarkable career.
He is a minor official in Nanking;
However he is intimate with the highest circles in the capital.
Great things are predicted for him;
But he has literary tastes.   5
He works listlessly and stays up all night;

He wishes times were quieter;
He wishes he could become a monk;
He longs for what he calls social cohesion;
He wishes he lived in a more positive culture.   10
Anonymously he has published a learned paper,
"On the Precision of Shinto[1] as an Agnostic Cultural Determinant."
At times he believes the world is on the verge
Of a Great Spiritual Rebirth.
He is very fond of Rimbaud,[2] Bertrand Russell [3] and Tu Fu.[4]   15
He wishes he could live in Paris.

He crosses the bridge by the Heavenly Inspiration Textile Works.
The long building quivers all over with the rattle of machinery.
In the windows the greenish lights
Wink as the people pass before them.   20
Porters plunge in and out of vast faint doorways.
Against the fence faces gleam in a heap of rags.
Chang Yuen pauses on the bridge muttering,
"The concubines of the Above One
Dance in transparent gossamer   25
In the evening at the Purple Phoenix Pavilion."
He thinks of the girls he could have bought for ten dollars
In Shantung during the famine.
He says aloud softly,
"Il faisait chaud, dans la vallée   30
Bien que le soleil se fût couché depuis longtemps,"[5]
He thinks of the son of his very important friend Won;
He is fourteen years old and goes out at night in Shanghai,
With rouged cheeks in the streets of the International Settlement.
He decides to take his opium more seriously.   35
Pear blossoms fall in the fog,
The tide stirs in the river,
The first dawn glows at the end of the streets.

1940

Andrée Rexroth[6]

Died October, 1940

Now once more grey mottled buckeye branches
Explode their emerald stars,
And alders smoulder in a rosy smoke
Of innumerable buds.

---

1. A polytheistic religion of Japan emphasizing ancestor worship and veneration for nature.
2. Arthur Rimbaud (1854–1891), French Symbolist poet.
3. (1872–1970) British mathematician and philosopher.
4. Eighth-century Chinese poet whose work Rexroth translated.
5. (French) "It was hot in the valley, although the sun had set a long time ago."
6. Rexroth's first wife, Andrée Schafer, died from epilepsy three years after he divorced her in 1937.

I know that spring again is splendid   5
As ever, the hidden thrush
As sweetly tongued, the sun as vital—
But these are the forest trails we walked together,
These paths, ten years together.
We thought the years would last forever,   10
They are all gone now, the days
We thought would not come for us are here.
Bright trout poised in the current—
The racoon's track at the water's edge—
A bittern booming in the distance—   15
Your ashes scattered on this mountain—
Moving seaward on this stream.

                                                                     1944

Vitamins and Roughage

Strong ankled, sun burned, almost naked,
The daughters of California
Educate reluctant humanists;
Drive into their skulls with tennis balls
The unhappy realization   5
That nature is still stronger than man.
The special Hellenic privilege
Of the special intellect seeps out
At last in this irrigated soil.
Sweat of athletes and juice of lovers   10
Are stronger than Socrates' hemlock;[7]
And the games of scrupulous Euclid[8]
Vanish in the gymnopaedia.[9]

                                                                     1944

The Signature of All Things[1]

My head and shoulders, and my book
In the cool shade, and my body
Stretched bathing in the sun, I lie
Reading beside the waterfall—
Boehme's "Signature of All Things."   5

---

7. Greek philosopher Socrates (469–399 B.C.E.) was found guilty of treason for teaching the young men
of Athens how to think; he fulfilled his death sentence by drinking hemlock, a poison.
8. Greek geometer of the third century B.C.E.
9. A religious choral dance performed at ancient Greek festivals by naked youth.
1. In *The Signature of All Things*, German Lutheran mystic Jacob Boehme (1575–1624) argues that
opposites define each other; therefore good and evil are necessary and even God, like human beings,
encompasses both.

Through the deep July day the leaves
Of the laurel, all the colors
Of gold, spin down through the moving
Deep laurel shade all day. They float
On the mirrored sky and forest   10
For a while, and then, still slowly
Spinning, sink through the crystal deep
Of the pool to its leaf gold floor.
The saint saw the world as streaming
In the electrolysis of love.   15
I put him by and gaze through shade
Folded into shade of slender
Laurel trunks and leaves filled with sun.
The wren broods in her moss domed nest.
A newt struggles with a white moth   20
Drowning in the pool. The hawks scream,
Playing together on the ceiling
Of heaven. The long hours go by.
I think of those who have loved me,
Of all the mountains I have climbed,   25
Of all the seas I have swum in.
The evil of the world sinks.
My own sin and trouble fall away
Like Christian's bundle, and I watch
My forty summers fall like falling   30
Leaves and falling water held
Eternally in summer air.

Deer are stamping in the glades,
Under the full July moon.
There is a smell of dry grass   35
In the air, and more faintly,
The scent of a far off skunk.
As I stand at the wood's edge,
Watching the darkness, listening
To the stillness, a small owl   40
Comes to the branch above me,
On wings more still than my breath.
When I turn my light on him,
His eyes glow like drops of iron,
And he perks his head at me,   45
Like a curious kitten.
The meadow is bright as snow.
My dog prowls the grass, a dark
Blur in the blur of brightness.
I walk to the oak grove where   50
The Indian village was once.
There, in blotched and cobwebbed light
And dark, dim in the blue haze,

Are twenty Holstein heifers,
Black and white, all lying down,   55
Quietly together, under
The huge trees rooted in the graves.

When I dragged the rotten log
From the bottom of the pool,
It seemed heavy as stone.   60
I let it lie in the sun
For a month; and then chopped it
Into sections, and split them
For kindling, and spread them out
To dry some more. Late that night,   65
After reading for hours,
While moths rattled at the lamp—
The saints and the philosophers
On the destiny of man—
I went out on my cabin porch,   70
And looked up through the black forest
At the swaying islands of stars.
Suddenly I saw at my feet,
Spread on the floor of night, ingots
Of quivering phosphorescence,   75
And all about were scattered chips
Of pale cold light that was alive.

1950

───────────── ◦◄ **GEORGE OPPEN** ►◦── ─────────────

(1908–1984)

The son of a diamond merchant, George Oppen was born in New Rochelle, New York. His childhood was materially secure, but emotionally difficult—when he was four his mother committed suicide. Five years later his father remarried, and the family moved to San Francisco in 1918. Oppen later claimed that his step-mother made his life miserable, "My father's second marriage opened upon me an attack totally murderous, totally brutal, involving sexual attack, beatings." He attended the Warren Military Academy, but just before his graduation he was the driver in a car accident that killed a person. After the Academy expelled him for drinking, he traveled in Europe and then enrolled in a small prep school, from which he graduated in 1926. He matriculated at Oregon State University at Corvallis, where in his first semester in a course on modern poetry he met Mary Colby, a fellow student who would become his wife. After they stayed out all night on their first date, the school expelled Mary and suspended George, who then left voluntarily. In her autobiography, *Meaning a Life*, Mary Oppen writes: "I found George Oppen and poetry at one moment, but the college expelled me and suspended George as a result of our meeting. Choice may not have been apparent to some outside our situation, but what happened to us, our joined lives, seems to us both choice and inevitability."

In 1927 the pair began a two-year trek across the United States, often hitchhiking and working short-term jobs to pay their way. In the autobiography, Mary emphasizes that "We were in search of an esthetic within which to live, and we were looking for it in our own American roots, in our own country. We had learned at college that poetry was being written in our own times, and that in order for us to write it was not necessary for us to ground ourselves in the academic; the ground we needed was the roads we were traveling." They were married in Dallas, Texas, in 1927, and the following year they sailed a catboat from the Great Lakes to New York City, where they met Louis Zukofsky and Charles Reznikoff, poets who would become lifelong literary allies.

After receiving an inheritance from Oppen's mother, the couple moved to France and formed a press, To Publishers, which issued Ezra Pound's *How to Read,* William Carlos Williams's *A Novelette and Other Prose (1921–1931),* and Louis Zukofsky's *An "Objectivists" Anthology.* Oppen was also working on his own poetry, some of which appeared in the February 1931 objectivist issue of *Poetry,* edited by Zukofsky, which featured poetry by Oppen, Reznikoff, Carl Rakosi, and Zukofsky himself, who emphasized an "economy of presentation" that would draw attention to a poem as an object made of words. Equally, he argued that a poem should register the material reality of the world outside of it. Deriving from the Imagist concision of Pound's early work and Williams's vernacular language and attentiveness to ordinary things, Objectivist poetics also had a political dimension, for it was grounded on a Marxist orientation toward exposing the historical and material foundations of knowledge—a common concern of many American intellectuals during the 1930s.

Returning to the United States in 1933, the Oppens set up The Objectivist Press and published another influential group of books by Williams and Reznikoff. The press also issued Oppen's own *Discrete Series* (1934), a book that Williams praised for its economy of technique and implicit social consciousness. In a 1969 interview Oppen noted that in his early work he had learned from Zukofsky, "the necessity of forming a poem properly, for achieving form. That's what 'objectivist' really means. . . . People assume it means the psychological objective in attitude. It actually means the objectification of the poem." Because *Discrete Series* offered "empirical statements" about the social conditions of the Depression, rather than overt statements, it chafed against the more aggressive, denunciatory Marxist poetry of the 1930s. Although Oppen and his wife joined the Communist Party in 1935 and became political activists, he refused to write the kind of sloganeering poetry that the Party advocated. He later admitted, "Maybe I admire myself . . . for simply not attempting to write communist verse. That is, to any statement already determined before the verse."

Caught between his high ideals for poetry and his loyalty to the Communist Party, Oppen ceased writing for the next twenty-five years. In a 1980 interview, Oppen said, "Poetry was not the most important thing in the world at that time. . . . And I thought most of the poets didn't know about the world as a life." The Oppens served as Communist Party activists, helping to organize strikes and election campaigns. Their daughter was born in 1940. Two years later Oppen was drafted into the army. Between 1944 and 1945, he fought in Europe as part of an antitank unit. Severely wounded during an April 1945 attack in Alsace, which killed several of his companions, Oppen received the Purple Heart and disability benefits. After the war, he worked as a house contractor and a carpenter in Redondo Beach, California, until 1950, when the family fled to Mexico to avoid investigation by the House Committee on Un-American Activities. In Mexico, he served as a supervisor for a furniture manufacturer and studied woodcarving at an art school, but wrote neither letters nor poems.

After his daughter was admitted to Sarah Lawrence College in 1958, Oppen began writing poetry again at the age of fifty. In the same year, the family was granted passports to return to the United States, and he began corresponding with editors. In 1960 the Oppens moved to Brooklyn Heights, New York, and then relocated to San Francisco in 1966. Apart from occasional trips to Europe and summers in Maine, they remained in San Francisco until Oppen, suffering from Alzheimer's disease, was admitted to a nursing home in Sunnyvale, California. He died in 1984.

Oppen's achievement was recognized in 1969, when he won the Pulitzer Prize for *Of Being Numerous,* and in 1980, when he was given an award from the American Academy and Institute of Arts and Letters. Oppen's later work appeared in seven books: *The Materials* (1962), *This in Which* (1965), *Of Being Numerous* (1968), *Alpine: Poems* (1969), *Seascape: Needle's Eye* (1972), *The Collected Poems of George Oppen* (1975), and *Primitive* (1978). The new poems were invigorated by the experiences he had undergone during his long years of silence, yet still concerned with perception, the material world, and the extent to which language could come to terms with reality. For Oppen, the question of whether language could do justice to the world had profoundly moral dimensions, and the clarity he achieved in his poetry was hard-won, derived from the tension he felt between the rigor of isolated observation and the necessity "of being numerous"—the social responsibilities of belonging to a community.

FROM Discrete Series

The Knowledge Not of Sorrow, You Were

The knowledge not of sorrow, you were
  saying, but of boredom
Is—aside from reading speaking
  smoking——
Of what, Maude Blessingbourne[1] it was,   5
  wished to know when, having risen,
"approached the window as if to see
  what really was going on";
And saw rain falling, in the distance
  more slowly,   10

1. A character from Henry James's "The Story in It" (1903). Oppen explained that "Hemingway's style, the model of all the left-wing writers of the thirties, [was] an essentially and incorrigibly right-wing style,—whereas H James, the very symbol of 'snobbery' to such writers, displayed a style and a sensibility which made possible a political and social critique. In acknowledgment of this, I placed on the first page of Discrete Series the quotation from James."

The road clear from her past the window-
    glass——
Of the world, weather-swept, with which
    one shares the century.

                                                    1934

Leviathan[2]

Truth also is the pursuit of it:
Like happiness, and it will not stand.

Even the verse begins to eat away
In the acid. Pursuit, pursuit;

A wind moves a little,   5
Moving in a circle, very cold.

How shall we say?
In ordinary discourse—

We must talk now. I am no longer sure of the words,
The clockwork of the world. What is inexplicable   10

Is the "preponderance of objects." The sky lights
Daily with that predominance

And we have become the present.

We must talk now. Fear
Is fear. But we abandon one another.   15

                                                    1962

The Bicycles and the Apex

How we loved them
Once, these mechanisms;
We all did. Light
And miraculous,

They have gone stale, part   5
Of the platitude, the gadgets,
Part of the platitude
Of our discontent.

Van Gogh[3] went hungry and what shoe salesman
Does not envy him now? Let us agree   10

2. The leviathan, a "monster of the waters," appears in the Old Testament books of Job, Psalms, and Isaiah. In *Leviathan* (1660), the English political philosopher Thomas Hobbes uses "leviathan" as an analogy for an absolutist government.
3. Vincent Van Gogh (1853–1890), self-taught French painter whose work went unsold during his lifetime.

Once and for all that neither the slums
Nor the tract houses

Represent the apex
Of the culture.
They are the barracks. Food   15

Produced, garbage disposed of,
Lotions sold, flat tires
Changed and tellers must handle money

Under supervision but it is a credit to no one
So that slums are made dangerous by the gangs   20
And suburbs by the John Birch Societies[4]

But we loved them once,
The mechanisms. Light
And miraculous . . .

1965

Psalm

Veritas sequitur . . .[5]

In the small beauty of the forest
The wild deer bedding down—
That they are there!

            Their eyes
Effortless, the soft lips   5
Nuzzle and the alien small teeth
Tear at the grass

            The roots of it
Dangle from their mouths
Scattering earth in the strange woods.   10
They who are there.

            Their paths
Nibbled thru the fields, the leaves that shade them
Hang in the distances
Of sun   15

            The small nouns
Crying faith

---

4. Archconservative anti-communist organization founded in 1958.
5. (Latin) "Truth follows." Oppen quotes the medieval philosopher Thomas Aquinas's assertion that there is a connection between the mind and the world. Aquinas's full sentence translates as "Truth follows upon the being of things."

In this in which the wild deer
Startle, and stare out.

1965

The Building of the Skyscraper

The steel worker on the girder
Learned not to look down, and does his work
And there are words we have learned
Not to look at,
Not to look for substance   5
Below them. But we are on the verge
Of vertigo.

There are words that mean nothing
But there is something to mean.
Not a declaration which is truth   10
But a thing
Which is. It is the business of the poet
"To suffer the things of the world
And to speak them and himself out."

O, the tree, growing from the sidewalk—   15
It has a little life, sprouting
Little green buds
Into the culture of the streets.
We look back
Three hundred years and see bare land.   20
And suffer vertigo.

1965

FROM "Of Being Numerous"

Strange That the Youngest People I Know

Strange that the youngest people I know
Live in the oldest buildings

Scattered about the city
In the dark rooms
Of the past—and the immigrants,   5

The black
Rectangular buildings
Of the immigrants.

They are the children of the middle class.

"The pure products of America—"[6]   10

---

6. Oppen quotes the first line of "To Elsie," a 1923 poem by William Carlos Williams. See p. 155.

Investing
The ancient buildings
Jostle each other

In the half-forgotten, that ponderous business.
This Chinese Wall.   15

                                                                                      1968

⊷◄ CHARLES OLSON ►⊶
(1910–1970)

A poet, theorist, and educator with broad influence, Charles Olson was born in Worcester, Massachusetts. His father, a Swedish immigrant, worked as a postman. His Irish American mother, a devout Catholic, was protective of her only son, and Olson grew up in a supportive and indulgent household. As a senior at the Classical High School, he won third prize in a national oratorical contest. His award was a ten-week trip to Europe, which gave the young Olson the opportunity to meet the Irish poet William Butler Yeats. In 1928 he matriculated at Wesleyan University, where he received his bachelor's degree in 1932 and his master's in 1933. After two years teaching at Clark University in Worcester, Olson began graduate studies at Harvard. At 6'8" he cut an impressive figure, and he was described as both scholarly and absentminded. Although he never completed his doctorate in American Studies, the dissertation he had researched on Herman Melville would eventually become his first book—*Call Me Ishmael* (1947), a critique of American culture.

In 1941 Olson joined the American Civil Liberties Union in New York and became increasingly active in Democratic Party politics. He eventually went to work for the Roosevelt Administration as Assistant Chief of the Foreign Language Division of the Federal Office of War Information. He held that post until 1944 when he quit in a dispute over censorship of his press releases. Discouraged by government protocol and determined to make his mark as a poet, Olson moved to Florida and continued his work on Melville and other projects. In 1948 he joined the faculty of Black Mountain College in rural North Carolina, an experimental school that was becoming well-known for its arts curriculum. Other faculty members included the choreographer Merce Cunningham, painters Franz Kline and Josef Albers, and at various times the poets Robert Duncan and Robert Creeley. The latter two were invited to teach during Olson's tenure as rector of the college, from 1951 until its close in 1956. Creeley founded the *Black Mountain Review,* and a school of poetry emerged, the Black Mountain Poets, including Olson, Creeley, Duncan, Edward Dorn, and Joel Oppenheimer.

In his 1949 poem "The Kingfishers," Olson declared, "What does not change / is the will to change," and much of his teaching was reaction against a perceived status quo in American letters. This was the time in which the academic school of New Criticism was at its height. Olson and other Black Mountain Poets reacted against the stringent advocacy of traditional or "closed" forms in poetry. Olson's famous essay "Projective Verse," published as a pamphlet in 1950, became a manifesto for the movement. It began as an attempt to explain his own poetic practice in "The Kingfishers," in which he had made use of Aztec religious motifs in opposition to European literary inheritance. Olson, who would eventually call rhyme "the dross of verse," sought a reconception of poetry's formal principles. In "Projective Verse" he argued that "the line comes (I swear it) from the breath." These breath units were new measures placed on the "open field" of the page. While stressing oral presentation and breath, Olson saved particular praise for the typewriter as a tool of composition: "It can, for a poet, indicate exactly the breath, the pause, the suspensions even of syllables, the juxtapositions even of parts of phrases, which he intends." Olson's prosodic method was conceived as a new musical form of composition, not to be confused with free verse, although this distinction is admittedly hard to see. He also rejected narrative as a way of organizing verse. *The Mayan Letters* (1953), a collection of his correspondence edited by Creeley, further explores Olson's fascination with cultural alternatives.

Olson's common-law marriage to Constance Wilcock lasted from 1941 to 1956. In 1957, with his new common-law partner, Betty Kaiser, Olson moved to Gloucester, Massachusetts, to devote himself to his poetry. From 1963 to 1965 he taught literature at the State University of New York at Buffalo, and during that time Betty Kaiser was killed in an automobile accident. The trauma of this event contributed to Olson's continued difficulties with alcohol. In late 1969 he was diagnosed with liver cancer, and he died after a brief illness.

As a poet Olson is best known for *The Maximus Poems,* a sequence he began in the 1940s which was finally published in near-complete form only after his death. Loosely modeled on Pound's *Cantos* (although some critics call them a deliberate alternative to Pound), *The Maximus Poems* was conceived as "a poem of a person and a place," spoken by an ancient Phoenician wanderer and writer whose perceptions parallel Olson's own. Discursive, didactic, full of historical, mythological, and scientific references, the sequence accrued in separate volumes in 1953, 1968, and 1974. The entire work, edited by George F. Butterick, appeared in 1983 and won the author a posthumous *Los Angeles Times* Book Award. *The Collected Poems of Charles Olson* appeared in 1987. A number of poets have built upon Olson's literary legacy, including Denise Levertov, Robert Duncan, Robert Creeley, and Jack Foley.

Maximus, to himself

I have had to learn the simplest things
last. Which made for difficulties.
Even at sea I was slow, to get the hand out, or to cross
a wet deck.
        The sea was not, finally, my trade.   5
But even my trade, at it, I stood estranged
from that which was most familiar. Was delayed,
and not content with the man's argument
that such postponement
is now the nature of   10
obedience,

that we are all late
in a slow time,
that we grow up many
And the single   15
is not easily
known

It could be, though the sharpness (the *achiote*)[1]
I note in others,
makes more sense   20
than my own distances. The agilities

they show daily
who do the world's
businesses
And who do nature's   25
as I have no sense
I have done either

I have made dialogues,
have discussed ancient texts,
have thrown what light I could, offered   30
what pleasures
doceat[2] allows

But the known?
This, I have had to be given,
a life, love, and from one man   35
the world.

Tokens.
But sitting here
I look out as a wind
and water man, testing   40
And missing
some proof

I know the quarters
of the weather, where it comes from,
where it goes. But the stem of me,   45
this I took from their welcome,
or their rejection, of me

And my arrogance
was neither diminished
nor increased,   50
by the communication

---

1. The seed of the annatto tree, used in Latin America as a red dye and as a form of pepper for flavor.
2. (Latin) "That he teach."

2

It is undone business
I speak of, this morning,
with the sea
stretching out   55
from my feet.

1956

La Chute[3]

my drum, hollowed out thru the thin slit,
carved from the cedar wood, the base I took
when the tree was felled

o my lute, wrought from the tree's crown

my drum, whose lustiness   5
was not to be resisted
                    my lute,

from whose pulsations
not one could turn away

                              They   10
are where the dead are, my drum fell
where the dead are, who
will bring it up, my lute
who will bring it up where it fell in the face of them
where they are, where my lute and drum have fallen?   15

1967

►◄ WILLIAM EVERSON ►◄
[BROTHER ANTONINUS]
(1912–1994)

William Oliver Everson, who would briefly achieve immense celebrity as Brother
Antoninus at the height of the San Francisco Renaissance while also becoming
one of the greatest letterpress printers in American history, was born in Sacramento, California, the second of three children to a mismatched couple. The poet's
father, a Norwegian immigrant, had come to America alone as a boy and now
worked as a bandmaster and printer. His wife, who was twenty years younger,
grew more emotionally distant from her husband with the birth of each child. "In
the world of the myth," the poet later commented, "my mother was a goddess
and my father was an ogre." A few months after his birth the poet's parents moved

---

3. (French) "The Fall."

to Selma, California a small farming town in the San Joaquin Valley where Everson grew up. A poor student, Everson graduated from Selma Union High School in 1931 and entered Fresno State College but quickly dropped out. Soon he enlisted in the Civilian Conservation Corps, a Roosevelt administration job program, in which he worked building roads in Sequoia National Park.

Returning to Fresno State College in the fall of 1934, Everson made the crucial literary discovery of his life—the poetry of Robinson Jeffers. "Suddenly the whole inner world began to tremble," he later described his first reading of Jeffers's work. The poetic encounter led to Everson's lifelong devotion to the older writer's work— which eventually resulted in two extraordinary and impassioned critical studies, *Robinson Jeffers: Fragments of an Older Fury* (1968) and *The Excesses of God: Robinson Jeffers as a Religious Figure* (1988). The discovery also confirmed the young man's literary vocation. "I couldn't believe it," he recalled. "I began to write other poems and by the end of the semester I knew what I was going to do." He dropped out of college hoping to be a poet while supporting himself as an irrigation-pipe layer. He published his first two volumes of poems, *These Are the Ravens* (1935) and *San Joaquin* (1939), with small California presses. In 1938 he married his high school girlfriend and soon bought a small farm.

In 1940 American males were required to register for possible military conscription—Europe was already at war—but Everson filed as a conscientious objector. After the United States declared war on the Axis powers, the thirty-year-old Everson was called up and sent to Civilian Public Service Camp 56 in Waldport, Oregon, where he worked with other conscientious objectors clearing trails and crushing rocks. The camp, which contained many other intellectuals and artists, including Kenneth Rexroth and Henry Miller, covertly published an underground newsletter, *Untide* (to counter the official publication, *Tide*) and eventually issued an anarchist journal, the *Illiterati*. Everson not only contributed to these illicit publications but also helped print them—his introduction to hand printing, the craft he would soon master. During his three-year incarceration Everson's father died (his mother had died in 1940), and his wife left him for another man. At the time of his demobilization in 1946, Everson moved to Sebastopol, then a small farm town in Sonoma County, California, to set up a letterpress in an arts commune, but he soon moved to Berkeley both to learn more about printing and to court an Italian American artist who was in the process of rediscovering her Catholic faith. She gave Everson a copy of St. Augustine's *Confessions* as a gift—which introduced him to what would prove to be the other decisive author in the poet's life.

At a midnight mass on Christmas Eve, 1948, Everson underwent a mystical experience and the following July he was baptized at St. Augustine's Church in Oakland. He soon began working for Dorothy Day's Catholic Worker on San Francisco's skid row, which provided food and lodging for the homeless. In his private devotions Everson continued to have mystical experiences. "I was seized with a feeling so intense as to exceed anything I had previously experienced," he recorded in a notebook about one such event. "It was a feeling of extreme anguish and joy, of transcendent spirituality and of great, thrilling physical character. . . . From the tabernacle had issued to me something like an intense invisible ray, a dark ray, like a ray of light seen in the mind only." In 1951 Everson joined the Dominican order as a lay brother (a postulate, that is, who had no intention of becoming a priest and who had no obligation to take the vows of poverty, obedience, and chastity). Given the name Brother Antoninus, the poet entered St.

Albert's, a monastery in Oakland. He set up his letterpress in the basement and started designing and printing a Latin *Psalter,* which would eventually be recognized as one of the central masterpieces of American handpress printing.

Everson's conversion unleashed a torrent of poetic creation. Most critics rate the three major collections published under the name of Brother Antoninus as his finest poetic works—*The Crooked Lines of God* (1959), *The Hazards of Holiness* (1962), and *The Rose of Solitude* (1967), which were later collected in *The Veritable Years: 1949–1966* (1978). In this rhapsodic, visionary poetry Everson transcends his earlier influences to create an expansive lyrical mode. The poems often trace the ebb and tide of the poet's religious exhilaration, ecstasy, and despair. William Stafford, the plainspoken and understated poet who in most ways seems Everson's opposite, admiringly described this poetry as offering "a shock and a delight to break free into the heart's unmanaged impulses." As Brother Antoninus, Everson became one of the key figures of the San Francisco Renaissance—the "Beat Friar" featured in *Time* magazine dressed in Dominican monastic robes intoning his poems to huge audiences around the country.

In 1969 Everson left the Dominican order to marry Susanna Rickson. With typical panache he announced his new life by stripping off his religious robes at the end of a poetry reading. Everson took a position as poet-in-residence at Kresge College at the University of California at Santa Cruz and started a new fine press on campus. He continued to publish poetry prolifically, most notably *Man-Fate* (1974), *River Root* (1976), and *The Masks of Drought* (1980). His most important later work, however, was perhaps his critical prose, in which he examined the nature of poetic creation. His critical methods may seem unconventional when compared to contemporary academic criticism, but they are firmly based in Catholic contemplative literature. "Suffice it to say," he explained in the "foreword" to *Birth of Poet: The Santa Cruz Meditations* (1982), "that when I left the monastery for academe the method that I brought with me was meditative rather than discursive. For I had learned how concepts seemingly exhausted by endless repetition could suddenly, under the probe of intuition, blossom into life."

These Are the Ravens[1]

These are the ravens of my soul,
Sloping above the lonely fields
And cawing, cawing.
I have released them now,
And sent them wavering down the sky,   5
Learning the slow witchery of the wind,
And crying on the farthest fences of the world.

1935

1. Whereas in classical literature ravens are birds of ill-omen whose appearance signals death, in Christian iconography ravens symbolize God's providence, for they fed the prophet Elijah in the desert (1 Kings 1–7).

The Making of the Cross

Rough fir,[2] hauled from the hills. And the tree it had been,
Lithe-limbed, wherein the wren had nested,
Whereon the red hawk and the grey
Rested from flight, and the raw-head vulture
Shouldered to his feed—that tree went over   5
Bladed down with a double-bitted axe; was snaked with winches;
The wedge split it; hewn with the adze
It lay to season toward its use.

So too with the nails: milleniums under the earth,
Pure ore; chunked out with picks; the nail-shape   10
Struck in the pelt-lunged forge; tonged to a cask,
And the wait against that work.

Even the thorn-bush flourished from afar,
As do the flourishing generations of its kind,
Filling the shallow soil no one wants.   15
Wind-sown, it cuts the cattle and the wild horse;
It tears the cloth of man, and hurts his hand.

Just as in life the good things of the earth
Are patiently assembled: some from here, some from there;
Wine from the hill and wheat from the valley;   20
Rain that comes blue-bellied out of the sopping sea;
Snow that keeps its drift on the gooseberry ridge,
Will melt with May, go down, take the egg of the salmon,
Serve the traffic of otters and fishes,
Be ditched to orchards . . .   25

So too are gathered up the possibles of evil.

And when the Cross was joined, quartered,
As is the earth; spoked, as is the Universal Wheel—
Those radials that led all unregenerate act
Inward to innocence—it met the thorn-wove Crown;   30
It found the Scourges and the Dice;
The Nail was given and the reed-lifted Sponge;[3]
The Curse caught forward out of the heart corrupt;
The excoriate Foul, stoned with the thunder and the hail—
All these made up that miscellaneous wrath   35
And were assumed.

The evil and the wastage and the woe,
As if the earth's old cyst, back down the slough
To Adam's sin-burnt calcinated bones,
Rushed out of time and clotted on the Cross.   40

---

2. The fir tree, an evergreen, is associated in the Christian tradition with everlasting life.
3. Before the crucifixion, Jesus was whipped with scourges; during the crucifixion, Roman soldiers threw dice to claim his robes and quenched his thirst by lifting to his lips a vinegar-soaked sponge on a reed.

Off there the cougar
Coughed in passion when the sun went out; the rattler
Filmed his glinty eye, and found his hole.

1949

Advent[4]

Fertile and rank and rich the coastal rains
Walked on the stiffened weeds and made them bend;
And stunned November chokes the cottonwood creeks
For Autumn's end.

And the hour of Advent draws on the small-eyed seeds   5
That spilled in the pentacostal[5] drought from the fallen cup:
Swept in the riddled summer-shrunken earth;
Now the eyes look up.

Faintly they glint, they glimmer; they try to see;
They picked at the crust; they touch at the wasted rind.   10
Winter will pinch them back but now they know,
And will not stay blind.

And all Creation will gather its glory up
Out of the clouded winter-frigid womb;
And the sudden Eye will swell with the gift of sight,   15
And split the tomb.

1949

⚫◄ ROBERT DUNCAN ►⚫
(1919–1988)

Robert Duncan's lifelong fascination with myth, signs, wonders, and hidden meanings that exist as "felt presences" and can be revealed through poetry originated in his childhood, which was far from ordinary. Born Edward Howard Duncan in Oakland, California, in 1919, the poet was put up for adoption at the age of six months. His mother died shortly after he was born, and his father, a day laborer already supporting a large family, could not care for the baby. His new parents, who were theosophists, believers in occult mysteries, chose the baby because they found his astrological chart auspicious. He grew up as Robert Edward Symmes but changed his name back to "Duncan" in 1941. Throughout his childhood, he was surrounded by family members steeped in the wisdom literature of many cultures and who saw cosmic significance in everything. In "The Truth and Life of

---

4. In the Christian liturgical calendar, Advent (from the Latin, *adventus,* "arrival") lasts four weeks, from St. Andrew's Day (November 30) until Christmas (December 25).
5. From "Pentecost," a Christian holiday on the seventh Sunday after Easter that commemorates the descent of the Holy Spirit on Christ's apostles.

Myth," Duncan recalls that, for his family, "the truth of things was esoteric (locked inside) or occult (masked by) the apparent, and one needed a 'lost key' in order to piece out the cryptogram of . . . who created the universe and what his real message was." His awareness of inner dimensions, truths that cannot be apprehended through ordinary means, was also heightened by an unfortunate accident. At the age of three, Duncan injured an eye in a fall. For the rest of his life he was cross-eyed and experienced double vision.

By the time Duncan had graduated from Kern High School in Bakersfield, he had already decided to devote his life to poetry, even though he knew that such a decision went against his family's expectations. In another essay, "Man's fulfillment in Order and Strife," he emphasizes the need for "creative strife" and recalls the family conflict that his vocation caused: "Poetry was not in the order of things. One could not earn a living at poetry. Writing poems was not such a bad thing, but to give one's life over to poetry, to become a *poet,* was to evidence a serious social disorder." Also "not in the order of things" was his sexual orientation, and he came to link his feelings of outsiderhood as a poet with those he experienced as a homosexual. "The structure of my life, like the structure of my work," he later remarked, "was to emerge in a series of trials, a problematic identity."

Those trials were pronounced during the next ten years of his life. Although he had entered the University of California at Berkeley in 1936, he left after two years to follow a lover to New York City. There he became part of a bohemian group of writers led by the novelist and diarist Anaïs Nin. In 1941 he was drafted into the army. Refusing to hide his homosexuality, he was soon discharged on psychiatric grounds. He returned to San Francisco in 1942, and then went back to New York in 1943, where he was married for a few months to a painter, Marjorie McKee. Meanwhile he wrote and published poems in journals and helped edit a little magazine, the *Experimental Review.*

In 1944 he was on the verge of breaking into the literary mainstream when John Crowe Ransom accepted a poem of his for the *Kenyon Review.* In the same year, however, Duncan published "The Homosexual in Society" in the journal *Politics.* The essay was important for its bold discussion of homosexuality in terms of individual rights and its equally frank consideration of how sexuality inflects the work of gay writers such as Herman Melville and Hart Crane. Duncan showed his independence not only by identifying homosexuals as a persecuted minority group, but also by criticizing the exclusionary attitudes he observed among them. He also bravely declared his own sexuality in the piece. When Ransom read the essay, he wrote Duncan to say that he had decided not to publish his poem. At least partially because of his sexual candor—aggravated by his West Coast location—Duncan was never fully accepted by mainstream literary culture during his lifetime.

Such exclusion, however, had its benefits, for Duncan was free to make his sexuality one of his major themes. His work explores the variety of gay experience, from the "creative strife" of desire to the rewards of long-term partnership. But his failure to achieve a mainstream audience was also due to the difficulty of his work. Even learned readers are challenged by his eclectic combination of mystical lore, world mythology, and wide-ranging literary allusions. Yet his poetry also offers clear and moving expressions of feeling, which freshen even his difficult poems.

Duncan became an influential figure in the alternative poetry movements of the midcentury. After his return to Berkeley in 1945, he joined with other poets such as Jack Spicer and Kenneth Rexroth to create a poetry "renaissance" in the

Bay Area long before most of the Beat poets moved west. Duncan's first book, *Heavenly City Earthly City* (1947), reflects the studies of medieval history and literature he was pursuing at Berkeley. It also contains his first experiments in process-oriented writing, in which, as he notes in *The Years as Catches*, "The poems are not ends in themselves but forms arising from the final intention of the whole in which they have their form and in turn giving rise anew to that intention." In 1951 he fell in love with a painter and collagist, Jess Collins (known professionally as "Jess"), and the two men soon established a household together in San Francisco. Their partnership lasted until Duncan's death in 1988, and Duncan benefited from the stability of their commitment and from contemplating Jess's collage techniques.

Duncan's fascination with the creative process, interactive patterns of meaning, and energetic motion in poetry was also fostered Charles Olson, whose concept of "Projective Verse" coalesced with Duncan's own ideas. In 1956 Duncan taught for several months at Black Mountain College, where Olson was rector, and Duncan's second full-length book, *The Opening of the Field* (1960), explores the possibilities of Olson's vision of the poem as "a field of action." As Duncan argues in the introduction to his fourth collection, *Bending the Bow* (1968), "The artist, after Dante's poetics, works with all parts of the poem as *polysemous,* taking each thing of the composition as generative of meaning, a response to and a contribution to the building form." Duncan now conceived of his poetry as an ongoing sequence, a "building form," that wove together all elements of his life, including his reading life, dream life, domestic life, and, increasingly, his alarm over the life of the nation.

Many readers of Duncan find his deployment of "Projective Verse" more successful than Olson's experiments, for Duncan succeeds in creating poetry that is supple and energetic in its form, learned in its remarkable breadth of references, yet invigorated by deep feeling and great clarity of description. Moreover, though sometimes long-winded, Duncan convincingly assumes a visionary, prophetic voice, supported by his passionate conviction and his deep knowledge of mysticism. In *Bending the Bow,* his condemnations of U.S. involvement in Vietnam take on an apocalyptic fervor. Unlike many poets who attacked the war, Duncan, who saw connections between all things, argued that all Americans, including himself, were implicated in the violence. In 1972 his linkage of personal and political strife, and his commitment to developing an ongoing sequence of poems led him to announce that he would not publish another book for fifteen years—a decision that surely did not help foster more mainstream attention. His last two books, *Ground Work: Before the War* (1984) and *Ground Work II: In the Dark* (1987), offer sequences that aim for the inclusiveness of Whitman's and Pound's work, and Duncan strikes a balance between his visionary themes and contemplation of the nature of love and war. Although his poetry attracted a small but devoted following during his lifetime, since his death in 1988 many readers have begun to recognize the scope of his accomplishments.

The Temple of the Animals

The temple of the animals has fallen into disrepair.
The pad of the feet has faded.
The panthers flee the shadows of the day.

The smell of musk has faded but lingers there . . .
lingers, lingers. Ah, bitterly in my room.   5
Tired, I recall the animals of last year—
the altars of the bear, tribunals of the ape,
solitudes of elephantine gloom, rare
zebra-striped retreats, prophecies of dog,
sanctuaries of the pygmy deer.   10

Were there rituals I had forgotten? animal calls
to which those animal voices replied,
calld and calld until the jungle stirrd?
Were there voices that I heard?
Love was the very animal made his lair,   15
slept out his winter in my heart.
Did he seek my heart or ever
sleep there?

I have seen the animals depart,
forgotten their voices, or barely remembered   20
—like the last speech when the company goes
or the beloved face that the heart knows,
forgets and knows—
I have heard the dying footsteps fall.
The sound has faded, but lingers here.   25
Ah, bitterly I recall
the animals of last year.

                                                                          1959

Poetry, a Natural Thing

      Neither our vices nor our virtues
further the poem. "They came up
            and died
just like they do every year
            on the rocks."   5

      The poem
feeds upon thought, feeling, impulse,
            to breed itself,
a spiritual urgency at the dark ladders leaping.

This beauty is an inner persistence   10
            toward the source
striving against (within) down-rushet of the river,
            a call we heard and answer
in the lateness of the world
            primordial bellowings   15
from which the youngest world might spring,

salmon not in the well where the
    hazelnut falls
but at the falls battling, inarticulate,
    blindly making it.   20

This is one picture apt for the mind.

A second: a moose painted by Stubbs,[1]
where last year's extravagant antlers
    lie on the ground.
The forlorn moosey-faced poem wears   25
    new antler-buds,
    the same,

"a little heavy, a little contrived,"[2]

his only beauty to be
    all moose.   30

                                                   1960

This Place Rumored to Have Been Sodom[3]

    might have been.
Certainly these ashes might have been pleasures.
Pilgrims on their way to the Holy Places remark
this place. Isn't it plain to all
that these mounds were palaces? This was once   5
a city among men, a gathering together of spirit.
It was measured by the Lord and found wanting.

It was measured by the Lord and found wanting.
destroyed by the angels that inhabit longing.
Surely this is Great Sodom where such cries   10
as if men were birds flying up from the swamp
ring in our ears, where such fears that were once
desires walk, almost spectacular,
stalking the desolate circles, red eyed.

This place rumored to have been a City surely was,   15
separated from us by the hand of the Lord.
The devout have laid out gardens in the desert,
drawn water from springs where the light was blighted.

1. *The Duke of Richmond's First Bull Moose*, painted by English artist George Stubbs in 1770.
2. Duncan drew this phrase from a rejection letter sent to him by New Critic John Crowe Ransom, editor of *The Kenyon Review*.
3. Genesis 18–19 tells the story of the destruction of Sodom and Gomorrah, cities that angered God because of their immorality. Whereas in the sixteenth century, due to the King James translation of the Bible, the term *sodomite* signified any person who engaged in "unnatural" sex acts, by the twentieth century *sodomite* had become a synonym for *homosexual man*.

How tenderly they must attend these friendships
or all is lost. All *is* lost.   20
Only the faithful hold this place green.

Only the faithful hold this place green
where the crown of fiery thorns descends.
Men that once lusted grow listless. A spirit
wrapped in a cloud, ashes more than ashes,   25
fire more than fire, ascends.
Only these new friends gather joyous here,
where the world like Great Sodom lies under fear.

The world like Great Sodom lies under Love
and knows not the hand of the Lord that moves.   30
This the friends teach where such cries
as if men were birds fly up from the crowds
gatherd and howling in the heat of the sun.
In the Lord Whom the friends have named at last Love
the images and loves of the friends never die.   35
This place rumored to have been Sodom is blessd
in the Lord's eyes.

                                                              1960

Roots and Branches

    Sail, Monarchs, rising and falling
orange merchants in spring's flowery markets!
messengers of March in warm currents of news floating,
    flitting into areas of aroma,
tracing out of air unseen roots and branches of sense   5
    I share in thought,
filaments woven and broken where the world might light
    casual certainties of me. There are

    echoes of what I am in what you perform
this morning. How you perfect my spirit!   10
    almost restore
an imaginary tree of the living in all its doctrines
    by fluttering about,
intent and easy as you are, the profusion of you!
awakening transports of an inner view of things.   15

                                                              1964

The Torso   Passages 18

    Most beautiful!   the red-flowering eucalyptus,
      the madrone, the yew

Is he . . .

So thou wouldst smile, and take me in thine arms
The sight of London to my exiled eyes   5
Is as Elysium to a new-come soul[4]

If he be Truth
I would dwell in the illusion of him

His hands unlocking from chambers of my male body

such an idea in man's image   10

rising tides that sweep me towards him

. . . *homosexual?*

and at the treasure of his mouth

pour forth my soul

his soul   commingling   15

I thought a Being more than vast, His body leading
into Paradise,   his eyes
quickening a fire in me,   a trembling

hieroglyph: At the root of the neck

the clavicle, for the neck is the stem of a great artery   20
upward into his head that is beautiful

At the rise of the pectoral muscle,

the nipples, for the breasts are like sleeping fountains
of feeling in man, waiting above the beat of his heart,
shielding the rise and fall of his breath, to be   25
awakend

At the axis of his mid hriff

the navel, for in the pit of his stomach the chord from
which first he was fed has its temple

At the root of the groin   30

the pubic hair, for the torso is the stem in which the man
flowers forth and leads to the stamen of flesh in which
his seed rises

a wave of need and desire over   taking me

cried out my name   35

---

4. From Christopher Marlowe's *Edward the Second* (I.i 9–11). These lines are spoken by King Edward's lover Gaveston, who anticipates moving to court at London and making their relationship public now that the old king has died and Edward has acceded to the throne.

(This was long ago. It was another life)

and said,

What do you want of me?

I do not know, I said. I have fallen in love.   He
has brought me into heights and depths my heart   40
would fear   without him.   His look

pierces my side • fire eyes •

I have been waiting for you, he said:
I know what you desire

you do not yet know   but through me •   45

And I am with you everywhere.   In your falling

I have fallen from a high place.   I have raised myself

from darkness in your   rising

wherever you are

my hand in your hand   seeking   the locks, the keys   50

I am there.   Gathering me, you gather

your Self •

For my Other is not a woman but a man

the King upon whose bosom let me lie.[5]

1968

━━━━━━━━ ◦━◄ **LAWRENCE FERLINGHETTI** ►━◦ ━━━━━━━━
(b. 1919)

The poet who rose to international acclaim as Lawrence Ferlinghetti was born
Lawrence Monsanto Ferling, the youngest son of Charles and Clemence Ferling.
Ferlinghetti has claimed to be of Italian descent, but this assertion is almost certainly a poetic fiction. His mother was a French Sephardic Jew, and the poet's first
language was French. He never knew his father, who purportedly died before he
born, and his mother was soon hospitalized for a nervous disorder. The young
Lawrence Ferling spent several years living with relatives in France, then in an orphanage in New York, and finally with a wealthy family in Bronxville. He studied
journalism at the University of North Carolina and was an officer in the Naval
Reserve during World War II. After the war he took his master's degree at Columbia and his doctorate at the University of Paris. In 1952 he cofounded City Lights

---

5. From Christopher Marlowe's *Edward the Second* (I.i. 14).

Bookstore in the Italian North Beach section of San Francisco. In 1955 he published his first book, *Pictures of the Gone World,* and Italianized his name to Ferlinghetti, a witty pun on his birth name. He has lived in San Francisco ever since. In 1998 he was named the city's first official Poet Laureate.

Co-owner of the City Lights Bookstore and editor-in-chief of City Lights Books, Ferlinghetti became one of the most influential figures of the Beat Movement in the 1950s. He published Allen Ginsberg's *Howl* in 1956, and the following year prevailed over the government, which had charged him with "printing and selling lewd and indecent material." The trial and their victory over censorship lifted publisher and poet to national attention and energized the Beats. A prolific poet, Ferlinghetti made the greatest impression with his early books, especially *A Coney Island of the Mind* (1958), which became one of the best-selling poetry books of the century. He has published more than thirty collections of poems, an autobiographical novel, and several plays. His later books include *Starting from San Francisco* (1961) and *The Secret Meaning of Things* (1968). He also co-authored with Nancy J. Peters a comprehensive history of Northern California literary life, *Literary San Francisco* (1980).

No longer the vocal outsider, Ferlinghetti has become increasingly aware that he is part of mainstream American poetry: "Herbert Marcuse once noted the enormous capacity of society to ingest its own dissident elements. . . . It happens to everyone successful within the system. I'm ingested myself." His poems display an oral performance aesthetic, the best of them offering charming but pointed irreverence reminiscent of E. E. Cummings. As Ferlinghetti wrote in a 1955 essay about getting poetry out of the classroom and into the streets, "The printed word has made poetry so silent." Among his many contributions to American literature perhaps the greatest has been to make poetry speak out loud to a large new audience.

◄●►━━◆━━◄●►

In Goya's Greatest Scenes We Seem to See[1]

In Goya's greatest scenes we seem to see
                                    the people of the world
            exactly at the moment when
                    they first attained the title of
                                            "suffering humanity"   5

    They writhe upon the page
                    in a veritable rage
                            of adversity
        Heaped up
                    groaning with babies and bayonets   10
                            under cement skies
        in an abstract landscape of blasted trees
                bent statues bats wings and beaks
                    slippery gibbets

---

1. Throughout the poem, Ferlinghetti describes scenes from work of Spanish artist Francisco Goya y Lucientes (1746–1828), particularly his series of etchings, *The Disasters of War* (1810–13).

cadavers and carnivorous cocks   15
and all the final hollering monsters
        of the
                "imagination of disaster"
they are so bloody real
                        it is as if they really still existed   20

And they do

        Only the landscape is changed

They still are ranged along the roads
        plagued by legionaires
                        false windmills and demented roosters   25

They are the same people
                only further from home
        on freeways fifty lanes wide
                on a concrete continent
                        spaced with bland billboards   30
                illustrating imbecile illusions of happiness

The scene shows fewer tumbrils
                but more maimed citizens
                        in painted cars
        and they have strange license plates   35
    and engines
                that devour America

                                                                    1958

◆━◀ **DENISE LEVERTOV** ▶━◆
(1923–1997)

Denise Levertov's ancestry and upbringing set her apart from most American poets of her generation. She was born in Ilford, England, the daughter of Paul Philip Levertoff, a Russian Jew who had become an Anglican minister, and Beatrice Adelaide Spooner-Jones; her most famous ancestors were on her mother's side, the Welsh tailor and mystic Angel Jones of Mold and, on her father's side, the Russian rabbi Schneour Zaimon, who was reputed to know the language of birds. Both Denise and her older sister, Olga, were largely educated at home. "As a child," she remembered, "I 'did lessons' at home under the tutelage of my mother and listened to the BBC Schools Programs." She also had a year of nursing school and worked in several London hospitals during World War II.

Denise came early to poetry, and at age twelve had the temerity to send some of her poems to T. S. Eliot, who responded with encouragement and advice—unfortunately his letter was lost. In 1946 she published her first book of poems, *The Double Image,* and quickly found that she had several other champions. One of them, the American poet Kenneth Rexroth, would call Levertov "the baby of the new Romanticism."

The poet Denise Levertov, undated photo.

While still in England, Levertov married an American writer, Mitchell Goodman, in 1947. The couple emigrated to the United States the following year, and
Levertov became a naturalized citizen in 1955. They had one child, a son.

In America, Levertov set about remaking her poetic voice. She retained a
degree of her early romanticism, but almost immediately felt the influence of
Wallace Stevens and William Carlos Williams. Her first significant American publications were in magazines associated with the Black Mountain poets, *Origin* and
Black Mountain Review. The Black Mountain poets, including Charles Olsen,
Robert Creeley, and Robert Duncan, advocated theories of "open" and "organic"
forms for poetry, often modeled on the work of Pound and Williams, but also indebted to the examples of D. H. Lawrence and Walt Whitman. Although Levertov
was never associated with Black Mountain College, she knew several of the poets
in Olson's circle and regarded them (especially Duncan) highly.

But Williams, with whom she corresponded from 1951 until 1962, was her primary American mentor. When asked in a 1967 interview to sum up Williams's influence on her work, she replied:

> Williams's interest in the ordinary, in the present, in local history as microcosm, in the lives and speech of ordinary people; and his unsentimental compassion, which illumined the marvelous in the apparently banal, so deeply affected my "sense of living, of being alive" (which effect is, according to Wallace Stevens [in *Adagia*], one of the main functions of poetry) that it is impossible for me to measure.

Although Williams's example helped Levertov develop her own strongly enjambed free verse, she preferred to emphasize correspondences between style of writing and attitude toward living as the moral foundation of poetry. Beginning with *Here and Now* (1957) and culminating in *The Jacob's Ladder* (1961) and *O Taste and See* (1964), she developed a poetry focused on epiphanies discovered in ordinary moments and grounded on the sensuous perception of concrete particulars. her poems often arose from domestic situations like marriage or motherhood, but were increasingly characterized by a spare lucidity. In one poem she wrote, "The best work is made / from hard, strong materials, / obstinately precise. . . ."

As one of only four women poets included in Donald Allen's influential anthology *The New American Poetry* (1960), Levertov gained notice as a leading proponent of the Black Mountain style, even as her ideas about poetry began to diverge from those of Olson, Creeley, and Duncan. Whereas Creeley and Olsen argued that "form is never more than the extension of content," Levertov stressed in her 1965 essay "Some Notes on Organic Form" that "form is never more than a *revelation* of content." The religious language here suggests that for Levertov, poetry is a form of spiritual discipline whose practice can lead the poet (and reader) to a visionary apprehension of ordinary experience.

As the decade of the 1960s progressed, Levertov and her husband became deeply involved in the antiwar movement, not only protesting American policy in Vietnam but letting their anger and political commitment become a main focus of their writing. With Muriel Rukeyser and others, Levertov founded Writers and Artists Protest against the War in Vietnam. In books such as *The Sorrow Dance* (1967), *Relearning the Alphabet* (1970), *To Stay Alive* (1971), and *Footprints* (1972), she sometimes questioned her poetics of perception even as she used her skills of evoking the concrete to write poems of protest and outrage. Critics had mixed responses to the political turn her career took. But Levertov saw her political orientation as a natural outgrowth of her engagement with the world. In a 1975 essay "On the Edge of Darkness: What Is Political Poetry?" she argued for a poetic melding of the personal and the political.

Her subsequent books reach for this goal, fusing her individual experience and perceptions with her consciousness of speaking as a public poet. In *The Freeing of the Dust* (1975) and *Life in the Forest* (1978), she meditates on death, change, the rhythms of nature, and the return of love following her 1972 divorce from Goodman. Her books of the 1980s and 1990s display an increasing concern for environmental problems in the United States and a renewed spiritual dimension, born of her conversion to Christianity. By the time of her 1997 death from lymphoma in Seattle, she had won numerous awards for her work and published more than fifty books.

-◦-◖▶-◦-

". . . Else a great Prince in prison lies"[1]

All that blesses the step of the antelope
all the grace a giraffe lifts to the highest leaves
all steadfastness and pleasant gazing, alien to ennui,
dwell secretly behind man's misery.

Animal face, when the lines   5
of human fear, knots of a net, become transparent
and your brilliant eyes and velvet muzzle
are revealed, who shall say you are not the face of a man?

In the dense light of wakened flesh
animal man is a prince. As from alabaster   10
a lucency animates him from heel to forehead.
Then his shadows are deep and not gray.

1961

The Ache of Marriage

The ache of marriage:

thigh and tongue, beloved,
are heavy with it,
it throbs in the teeth

We look for communion   5
and are turned away, beloved,
each and each

It is leviathan[2] and we
in its belly
looking for joy, some joy   10
not to be known outside it

two by two in the ark of
the ache of it.

1964

Hypocrite Women

Hypocrite women, how seldom we speak
of our own doubts, while dubiously
we mother man in his doubt!

---

1. Line 68 of John Donne's metaphysical love poem "The Ecstasy."
2. The leviathan, a "monster of the waters," appears in the Old Testament books of Job, Psalms, and Isaiah. Levertov refers here to the "great fish" that swallowed Jonah.

And if at Mill Valley[3] perched in the trees
the sweet rain drifting through western air   5
a white sweating bull of a poet told us

our cunts are ugly—why didn't we
admit we have thought so too? (And
what shame? They are not for the eye!)

No, they are dark and wrinkled and hairy,   10
caves of the Moon . . .   And when a
dark humming fills us, a

coldness towards life,
we are too much women to
own to such unwomanliness.   15

Whorishly with the psychopomp[4]
we play and plead—and say
nothing of this later.   And our dreams,

with what frivolity we have pared them
like toenails, clipped them like ends of   20
split hair.

                                                                    1964

O Taste and See

The world is
not with us enough.
O taste and see

the subway Bible poster said,
meaning **The Lord,** meaning   5
if anything all that lives
to the imagination's tongue,

grief, mercy, language,
tangerine, weather, to
breathe them, bite,   10
savor, chew, swallow, transform

into our flesh our
deaths, crossing the street, plum, quince,
living in the orchard and being

hungry, and plucking   15
the fruit.

                                                                    1964

3. When Levertov first visited San Francisco in 1957, her friend Robert Duncan threw a welcoming party for her at which Jack Spicer read a misogynistic poem called "Admonitions." Levertov wrote "Hypocrite Women" in response to Spicer's poem.
4. A guide of souls to the afterworld.

Our Bodies

Our bodies, still young under
the engraved anxiety of our
faces, and innocently

more expressive than faces:
nipples, navel, and pubic hair   5
make anyway a

sort of face: or taking
the rounded shadows at
breast, buttock, balls,

the plump of my belly, the   10
hollow of your
groin, as a constellation,

how it leans from earth to
dawn in a gesture of
play and   15

wise compassion—
nothing like this
comes to pass
in eyes or wistful
mouths.   20
          I have

a line or groove I love
runs down
my body from breastbone
to waist. It speaks of   25
eagerness, of
distance.

          Your long back,
the sand color and
how the bones show, say   30

what sky after sunset
almost white
over a deep woods to which

rooks are homing, says.

                                                              1964

Prisoners

Though the road turn at last
to death's ordinary door,
and we knock there, ready
to enter and it opens

easily for us,   5
        yet
all the long journey
we shall have gone in chains,
fed on knowledge-apples
acrid and riddled with grubs.   10

We taste other food that life,
like a charitable farm-girl,
holds out to us as we pass—
but our mouths are puckered,
a taint of ash on the tongue.   15

It's not joy that we've lost—
wildfire, it flares
in dark or shine as it will.
What's gone
is common happiness,   20
plain bread we could eat
with the old apple of knowledge.

That old one—it griped us sometimes,
but it was firm, tart,
sometimes delectable . . .   25

The ashen apple of these days
grew from poisoned soil. We are prisoners
and must eat
our ration. All the long road
in chains, even if, after all,   30
we come to
death's ordinary door, with time
smiling its ordinary
long-ago smile.

1984

⚫◄ SAMUEL MENASHE ►⚫
(b. 1925)

Samuel Menashe was born in New York City in 1925, the only child of Jewish Ukrainian immigrants. Raised speaking both Yiddish and English by his well-read, multilingual, and cultivated parents, he attended public schools and finished two years of college before enlisting in the U.S. Army at the age of eighteen during World War II. Menashe saw fierce combat in France, Belgium, and Germany, where his company took enormous losses, especially during the Battle of the Bulge. After the war, he finished a bachelor's degree at Queens College and then earned a doctorate at the Sorbonne. Menashe taught briefly at Bard College and Long Island University before embarking on the bohemian life he has subsequently led—living in California, Spain, England, Ireland, and France, but always returning to his native New York where he has lived in a cold-water flat in Greenwich Village for nearly fifty years. A lifelong bachelor, he has observed, "Since I have never been a father, I am still only a son."

Menashe's literary career has been paradoxical. Largely overlooked by mainstream critics and anthologists, his work has never found a broad audience, even within the confines of academia. Yet almost from the beginning his poetry has attracted the admiration of a diverse band of discerning poets and critics in England, Ireland, and the United States. Menashe's obscurity probably comes from his strict devotion to a single literary enterprise, perfecting the short poem—not the conventional short poem of twenty to forty lines popular among magazine editors, but the very short poem. As anyone studying *The Niche Narrows: New and Selected Poems* (2000) will discover, few of his poems are longer than ten lines. His style is idiosyncratic and utterly original—combining elements of Imagism, epigram, and wisdom literature in ways that defy easy critical categorization.

Menashe is essentially a religious poet, though one without an orthodox creed. Nearly every poem he has published radiates a heightened spiritual awareness. His central themes are the unavoidable concerns of religious poetry—the tension between the soul and body, past and present, time and eternity. Like the Psalms of the Old Testament, his poems are alternately joyous and elegiac. Even his poetic technique—which so strikingly combines Imagist compression with irregular rhyme—focuses words into mystical symbols of perception. A reader senses that Menashe's rhymes exist not only for musical effect but also to freeze two or more words in time and hold them perpetually in spiritual or intellectual harmony. Likewise, his short, dense lines slow down the rhythm to encourage the reader to linger on each word. Menashe's style is not merely compressed and evocative, but talismanic, visionary, and symbolic. He often writes about the human body, but he is a poet who understands physical reality in relation to the metaphysical. Although Menashe's spiritual roots are Hebrew, the soil that nourishes them is the English language. His Old Testament is preeminently the King James Version, and among his sacred poets is Blake as well as David, Isaiah, and Solomon. Although Jewish, he also frequently alludes to the New Testament. His range of allusion is narrow but extraordinarily deep. The Bible permeates his poetry, but he uses his sources in ways that most readers will immediately understand.

O Many Named Beloved

O Many Named Beloved
Listen to my praise
Various as the seasons
Different as the days
All my treasons cease   5
When I see your face

1961

The Shrine Whose Shape I Am

The shrine whose shape I am
Has a fringe of fire
Flames skirt my skin

There is no Jerusalem but this
Breathed in flesh by shameless love   5
Built high upon the tides of blood
I believe the Prophets and Blake[1]
And like David[2] I bless myself
With all my might

I know many hills were holy once   10
But now in the level lands to live
Zion[3] ground down must become marrow
Thus in my bones I am the King's son
And through death's domain I go
Making my own procession   15

                                        1961, revised 1971

Self Employed

For John Smith

Piling up the years
I awake in one place
and find the same face
or counting the time
since my parents died—   5
certain less is left
than was spent—
I am employed
every morning
whose ore I coin   10
without knowing
how to join
lid to coffer
pillar to groin—
each day hinges   15
on the same offer

                                                      1971

1. William Blake (1757–1827), visionary English poet and artist.
2. The second king of the Israelites, David was also a great poet who authored many of the Old Testament Psalms.
3. One of the hills on which Jerusalem, "the city of David," is built. *Zion* is also a synonym for Jerusalem, Israel, the Jewish people, and a utopia.1.   Literally, a résumé. But Menashe also plays on the phrase's Latin meaning, "the race of life."

At a Standstill

That statue, that cast
Of my solitude
Has found its niche
In this kitchen
Where I do not eat   5
Where the bathtub stands
Upon cat feet—
I did not advance
I cannot retreat

1986

Curriculum Vitae[4]

Scribe out of work
At a loss for words
Not his to begin with,
The man life passed by
Stands at the window   5
Biding his time

2

Time and again
And now, once more
I climb these stairs
Unlock this door—   10
No name where I live
Alone in my lair
With one bone to pick
And no time to spare

1986

►◄ JACK SPICER ►◄
(1925–1965)

Jack Spicer was born in Los Angeles in 1925, the elder of two sons of Midwestern parents. His father, a former radical labor unionist, managed hotels and apartment buildings, and the family lived comfortably even during the Great Depression. A bookish and unattractive child with poor eyesight who was teased by other boys, Spicer sought refuge in local libraries where he read escapist detective novels and thrillers. Declared physically unfit to serve in the military during World War II, Spicer attended the University of Redlands for two years before transferring in 1945 to the University of California at Berkeley where he majored in philosophy

4. Literally, a résumé. But Menashe also plays on the phrase's Latin meaning, "the race of life."

and literature. In the thriving nonconformist Berkeley community, the young Spicer gradually reinvented himself as a poet, a bohemian, a radical, and—very slow and timidly—a gay man. His first English teacher at Berkeley was the poet Josephine Miles, who generously encouraged his literary ambitions. Spicer also became interested in radical politics and joined San Francisco's Libertarian Circle, a group of "philosophical anarchists" led by Kenneth Rexroth.

The decisive encounter for Spicer, however, came in 1946 when he met Robert Duncan, whose flamboyant and self-assured public persona as poet and homosexual so dazzled the younger writer that he declared afterwards that 1946 was the true year of his birth. The two young poets soon announced—only half-seriously at first—"The Berkeley Renaissance," which essentially meant the group of their literary friends gathered around bookstore owner George Leite who published the international arts magazine, *Circle*.

Amid this bohemian ferment, Spicer continued his academic studies. After earning a master's degree in linguistics at Berkeley in 1950, he entered a doctoral program in Anglo-Saxon and Old Norse, although he never finished his dissertation. For the rest of his short life Spicer eked out a living as a "research linguist," working on scholarly projects. He taught at the University of Minnesota for two years but returned to California in 1952. A few years later he moved briefly to New York and then to Boston, but in late 1956 he returned to San Francisco. He would never leave the West again.

Working part-time as a researcher in Berkeley, he also taught a "Poetry as Magic" workshop at the San Francisco Public Library. During the next few years Spicer finally came into his own as a poet. The key to his artistic development was his concept of the "serial poem." Unhappy with his earlier work, Spicer decided that it had failed because he had tried to write poems that stood alone. "There is no single poem," he now realized. "Poems should echo and reecho against each other. . . . They should create resonances." Spicer now began to conceive of his work as individual books or booklets of interrelated poems. A serial poem, he explained in a lecture, uses the book as its unit of composition. Unlike traditional poetic sequences, however, these books were not necessarily conceived as progressive sequences of individual poems; rather, they existed as a competitive community of synchronous alternatives.

The first of Spicer's "serial" books was *After Lorca* (1957), an ingenious and moving compilation of genuine translations, fake translations, and prose letters to the dead Spanish poet, Federico García Lorca, who also supposedly provided an introduction from beyond the grave. *After Lorca* was published by the newly created White Rabbit Press, which printed the stapled chapbook on a mimeograph press on a Saturday night at the San Francisco Greyhound Bus offices—a representative genesis for books in bohemian North Beach of the era. Other "books" quickly followed, many of which were published only after Spicer's death. *A Book of Music* was finished in 1958, for example, but not published until 1969. *Billy the Kid* (1959) appeared with drawings by Jess, the Bay Area artist who was Robert Duncan's lover. *The Heads of the Town up to the Aether* (1962), his longest book, was followed by *The Holy Grail* (1964) and *Language* (1965)—as well as half a dozen other "books" that appeared posthumously.

Unreviewed and hardly noticed at the time of their creation, these playful and profoundly inventive collections today provide the most exuberant and accessible entry into the experimental West Coast poetry of the era. Spicer never fell into the common fallacy that experimental art need not be interesting. His poems eagerly charm, cajole, argue, and amuse the reader, and they gleefully adopt every available technique to accomplish their task. Depending on what works one cites, the dexterously diverse Spicer can with equal justice be classified as a Beat or Surrealist, a late Modernist or early Post-Modernist, a proto-Language poet or premature New Formalist.

Until the posthumous publication of *The Collected Books of Jack Spicer* (1975), edited by his friend Robin Blaser, the poet's reputation was confined to San Francisco and Berkeley. This situation was mostly Spicer's doing. He printed his books in tiny editions and did not allow them to be sold outside San Francisco—often giving them away free at readings. He also broke bitterly with Duncan after his mentor joined with the Black Mountain School, which Spicer found abstract and humorless. He was happiest in his small "magic circle" of friends talking drunkenly late into the night at North Beach bars.

As the national media touted the "San Francisco Renaissance" and catapulted many friends and former friends into international fame as Beat poets in the late 1950s, Spicer knew he had become a marginal figure. After being injured in an automobile crash sometime in the winter of 1962–63, the poet increased his already heavy drinking, which eventually led to his being fired from his research job. In July 1965 Spicer collapsed and fell into a coma. Waking only intermittently, he died three weeks later in the alcoholic ward of the public hospital.

Conspiracy

A violin which is following me

In how many distant cities are they listening
To its slack-jawed music? This
Slack-jawed music?
Each of ten thousand people playing it.   5

It follows me like someone that hates me.

Oh, my heart would sooner die
Than leave its slack-jawed music. They
In those other cities
Whose heart would sooner die.   10

It follows me like someone that hates me.

Or is it really a tree growing just behind my throat
That if I turned quickly enough I could see
Rooted, immutable, neighboring
Music.   15

1958

A Book of Music

Coming at an end, the lovers
Are exhausted like two swimmers. Where
Did it end? There is no telling. No love is
Like an ocean with the dizzy procession of the waves' boundaries
From which two can emerge exhausted, nor long goodbye   5
Like death.
Coming at an end. Rather, I would say, like a length
Of coiled rope
Which does not disguise in the final twists of its lengths
Its endings.   10
But, you will say, we loved
And some parts of us loved
And the rest of us will remain
Two persons. Yes,
Poetry ends like a rope.   15

1958

◄ A. R. AMMONS ►
(1926–2001)

Archie Randolph Ammons was born in his parents' small tobacco farm near Whiteville, North Carolina, and grew up during the Depression years as the youngest of three surviving children. His family circumstances were made difficult not only by poverty but also by the early deaths of three siblings—a sister before Ammons was born, and two brothers who were born after him. He has admitted that as "the surviving son, I must have felt guilty for living and also endangered, as the only one left to be next. Mourning the loss of life, in life and in death, has been the undercurrent of much of my verse and accounts for a tone of constraint that my attempts at wit, prolixity, and transcendence merely underscore." But farm life also had its benefits, for Ammons gained a love of the land and an attentiveness to the natural world that sustain his poetry. He attended rural schools and, after graduating from high school, worked for a shipbuilding company in Wilmington, Delaware.

In 1944 the eighteen-year-old Ammons joined the U.S. Navy. Stationed on a destroyer in the South Pacific for nineteen months, he began to write poetry and continued throughout his undergraduate years at Wake Forest College. He recalls that "about a month before I left Wake Forest I finally got up the nerve to show some of my poems to the professors and they were very encouraging. From then on, my mind, my energies, were focused on poetry even though I had to do what everyone else does—try to figure out some way to make a living." After graduation in 1949 with a general science degree, he married and became principal of a small school in Cape Hatteras, North Carolina. The following year, he pursued a master's degree in English at the University of California, Berkeley, where he studied with the poet and critic Josephine Miles, who encouraged him to submit his poems to literary magazines. He returned east in 1952 to work as a sales executive for a south New Jersey medical glass factory owned by his father-in-law.

He issued his first book, *Ommateum with Doxology* (1955), from a vanity press, and it sold so poorly that Ammans's father-in-law, who bought forty copies to send to business associates in South America, was the main purchaser. Seven years passed before Ammons published another book. He recalls that during those years: "I just kept writing, resubmitting manuscripts, tearing them apart, putting them back together, getting rejected, trying again, and so on until I was finally rejected by everybody, I took my work to a vanity publisher in New York City and I was turned down by them, too." In 1963 he published his first trade book, *Expressions of Sea Level*. The next year he left business to teach writing at Cornell University where he remained throughout his academic career.

Ammons's third book, *Corson's Inlet* (1965), finally brought him into critical prominence, and he quickly released another well-received book, *Northfield Poems* (1966). A prolific poet, he went on to publish over twenty books of verse and garnered enough major awards to secure his high reputation. He won the National Book Award for *Collected Poems 1951–1971* (1972); the Bollingen Prize followed for the book-length poem *Sphere: The Form of a Motion* (1974). He received the National Book Critics Circle Award for *A Coast of Trees* (1981) and also won a MacArthur Fellowship. In 1993, he was awarded the Pulitzer Prize and his second National Book Award for another book-length poem, *Garbage*. Ammons retired from Cornell in 1998 and died at his home in Ithaca, New York in 2001.

Despite his continued public acclaim, the concerns of Ammons's poems remained resolutely private: an isolated self's encounters with nature and negotiations of daily life. His obsession with the natural world's ceaseless changes not only led to an emphasis on motion and process as major themes but also shaped his creative process. His poems try to record the mind's shifts just as faithfully as they observe nature's flux. In fact, for Ammons, mind and nature mirror each other, and a poem becomes a way of charting both, especially their similarities and differences, conjunctions and separations. Like the American transcendentalists Ralph Waldo Emerson and Walt Whitman, whose work strongly influenced him, Ammons alternately celebrates the self—sometimes expanding it to vast proportions—and empties the self out into the overwhelming force of nature. Like Whitman, Ammons favors the catalogue, and his poems brim with features of the natural world or objects that he records in a vocabulary that swings from elevated words such as "radiant" to slang or scientific terminology.

Working on a typewriter, Ammons often improvised poems, as in the book-length volume *Tape for the Turn of the Year* (1965), which he typed on a scroll of adding machine tape. Although such improvisation sometimes results in tedium, Ammons more often infused his poems with an anxious urgency that took them in surprising directions. The contradiction that fascinated him above all others was between unity and multiplicity. He sought to celebrate the overarching patterns in nature while also revelling in nature's infinite diversity. Similarly, his poems can both cohere into patterns and dissolve into randomness. Ammons therefore saw a poem as something that moves, yet also opens into a meditative stillness. "Poetry is a verbal means to a non-verbal source," he once remarked. "It is a motion to no-motion, to the still point of contemplation and deep realization."

◄►

Gravelly Run

I don't know somehow it seems sufficient
to see and hear whatever coming and going is,
losing the self to the victory
   of stones and trees,
of bending sandpit lakes, crescent   5
round groves of dwarf pine:

for it is not so much to know the self
as to know it as it is known
   by galaxy and cedar cone,
as if birth had never found it   10
and death could never end it:

the swamp's slow water comes
down Gravelly Run fanning the long
   stone-held algal
hair and narrowing roils between   15
the shoulders of the highway bridge:

holly grows on the banks in the woods there,
and the cedars' gothic-clustered
   spires could make
green religion in winter bones: 20

so I look and reflect, but the air's glass
jails seals each thing in its entity:

no use to make any philosophies here:
   I see no
god in the holly, hear no song from   25
the snowbroken weeds: Hegel[1] is not the winter
yellow in the pines: the sunlight has never
heard of trees: surrendered self among
   unwelcoming forms: stranger,
hoist your burdens, get on down the road.   30

1965

The City Limits

When you consider the radiance, that it does not withhold
itself but pours its abundance without selection into every
nook and cranny not overhung or hidden; when you consider

that birds' bones make no awful noise against the light but
lie low in the light as in a high testimony; when you consider   5
the radiance, that it will look into the guiltiest

---

1. Georg Wilhelm Friedrich Hegel (1770–1831), a German philosopher who argued that all past, present, and future knowledge and experience evolve toward an Absolute Spirit, in which the human mind will reach its full power.

swervings of the weaving heart and bear itself upon them,
not flinching into disguise or darkening; when you consider
the abundance of such resource as illuminates the glow-blue

bodies and gold-skeined wings of flies swarming the dumped 10
guts of a natural slaughter or the coil of shit and in no
way winces from its storms of generosity; when you consider

that air or vacuum, snow or shale, squid or wolf, rose or lichen,
each is accepted into as much light as it will take, then
the heart moves roomier, the man stands and looks about, the 15

leaf does not increase itself above the grass, and the dark
work of the deepest cells is of a tune with May bushes
and fear lit by the breadth of such calmly turns to praise.

1971

The Constant

When leaving the primrose, bayberry dunes, seaward
I discovered the universe this morning,
           I was in no
mood
for wonder,   5
        the naked mass of so much miracle
already beyond the vision
of my grasp:

along a rise of beach, a hundred feet from the surf,
a row of clam shells   10
          four to ten feet wide
          lay sinuous as far as sight:

in one shell—though in the abundance
              there were others like it—upturned,
four or five inches across the wing,   15
a lake
three to four inches long and two inches wide,
all dimensions rounded,
          indescribable in curve:

and on the lake a turning galaxy, a film of sand,   20
co-ordinated, nearly circular (no real perfections),
          an inch in diameter, turning:
turning:
counterclockwise, the wind hardly perceptible from 11 o'clock
              with noon at sea: 25
              the galaxy rotating,
              but also,
at a distance from the shell lip,
revolving
round and round the shell: 30

     a gull's toe could spill the universe:
two more hours of sun could dry it up:
a higher wind could rock it out:

the tide will rise, engulf it, wash it loose:
utterly: 35

the terns, their
   young somewhere hidden in clumps of grass or weed,
were diving *sshik sshik* at me,
        then pealing upward for another round and dive:

I have had too much of this inexhaustible miracle: 40
miracle, this massive, drab constant of experience.

                                                      1966

Cut the Grass

The wonderful workings of the world: wonderful,
wonderful: I'm surprised half the time:
ground up fine, I puff if a pebble stirs:

I'm nervous: my morality's intricate: if
a squash blossom dies, I feel withered as a stained   5
zucchini and blame my nature: and

when grassblades flop to the little red-ant
queens burring around trying to get aloft, I blame
my not keeping the grass short, stubble

firm: well, I learn a lot of useless stuff, meant   10
to be ignored: like when the sun sinking in the
west glares a plane invisible, I think how much

revelation concealment necessitates: and then I
think of the ocean, multiple to a blinding
oneness and realize that only total expression   15

expresses hiding: I'll have to say everything
to take on the roundness and withdrawal of the deep dark:
less than total is a bucketful of radiant toys.

                                                      1971

Viable

Motion's the dead give away,
eye catcher, the revealing risk:
the caterpillar sulls on the hot macadam

but then, risking, ripples to the bush:
the cricket, startled, leaps the   5
quickest arc: the earthworm, casting,

nudges a grassblade, and the sharp robin
strikes: sound's the other
announcement: the redbird lands in

an elm branch and tests the air with   10
cheeps for an answering, reassuring
cheep, for a motion already cleared:

survival organizes these means down to
tension, to enwrapped, twisting suasions:[2]
every act or non-act enceinte[3] with risk or   15

prize: why must the revelations be
sound and motion, the poet, too, moving and
saying through the scary opposites to death.

1972

◦►◄ ROBERT CREELEY ►◄◦
(b. 1926)

Robert Creeley was born in Arlington, Massachusetts, but his family soon relocated to a farm in West Acton, where at the age of two Creeley suffered a laceration
of his left eye so severe that he lost sight in it three years later. After his father died
in 1930, his mother supported the family by resuming her nursing career. Of his
New England upbringing, Creeley has said—playfully quoting Longfellow—that
"life was real and life was earnest, and one had best get on with it," and he attributes the laconic style of his poetry in part to the New England tradition of pithy
speech. He attended high school at a New Hampshire boarding school and then enrolled at Harvard in 1943 but left in 1944 to drive an ambulance in India and
Burma for the American Field Service. He returned to Harvard in the fall of 1945
and soon after married Ann McKinnon, with whom he would have three children.
Afflicted by the anomie experienced by many men returning from the war, Creeley
dropped out of college in the last semester of his senior year, and he and his wife
bought a farm in New Hampshire with the help of money from her trust fund.

Unable to sustain the farm, the Creeleys left for France in 1951, but not before
he had initiated correspondence with Charles Olson of Black Mountain College in
North Carolina. His exchanges with Olson were fruitful, for Olson's influential essay
"Projective Verse" was grounded in part on Creeley's declaration that "form is never
more than an extension of content," and both men became vocal proponents of
"open form," process-oriented free verse that countered what Creeley called the
"closed system, . . . poems patterned on exterior and traditionally accepted models."

After the Creeleys relocated to Majorca in 1952, Olson invited Creeley to edit
the *Black Mountain Review,* an influential little magazine that featured core poets
of the Projectivist group, such as Olson, Robert Duncan, Denise Levertov, and Creeley himself. On his own small printing press, Creeley also began issuing books by

2. Influences.
3. Pregnant.

Projectivist poets. In 1954, Olson asked him to teach at the alternative college, whose faculty included not only poets, but dancers, musicians, and painters, all seeking alternatives to convention and exploring working methods that centered on motion and process rather than representation. Creeley felt a particular affinity for the Abstract Expressionist painters there and later admitted that "the attraction the artist had for people like myself . . . was that lovely, uncluttered directness of perception and act we found in so many of them," qualities he sought in his own poetry.

After divorcing Ann McKinnon in 1955, Creeley grew increasingly restless. Early the next year he resigned from Black Mountain and headed for San Francisco where for three months he imbibed Beat poetics from Allen Ginsberg, Gary Snyder, Jack Kerouac, and others. Moving to Albuquerque, New Mexico, he began teaching at a boys' school, his credentials boosted by Olson's gift of a bachelor's degree from Black Mountain. In January 1957, he met Bobbie Louise Hall and married her within two weeks. With the security provided by his new marriage and job, and the insights into emotional expansiveness that he gained from his sojourn with the Beats, Creeley achieved a new level of intimacy and directness in his poetry. In 1960, he won the Levinson Prize for ten poems published in *Poetry,* and his work was included in Donald Allen's *The New American Poetry: 1945–1960,* a book that introduced the alternative poets of the 1950s to a wide audience. In 1962, Scribners released *For Love,* which included selections from the myriad small press books that Creeley had published in the 1950s. Nominated for the National Book Award and selling over 47,000 copies, *For Love,* with its blend of halting self-examination, restless isolation, and qualified articulations of love, appealed to a generation wrestling with similar misgivings during the sexual revolution.

Finishing a master's degree at the University of New Mexico in 1960, Creeley began an academic career, holding visiting posts at many universities but keeping permanent ties with the State University of New York at Buffalo, where he began teaching in 1966. In 1976 he divorced Bobbie and in 1977 married Penelope Highton, whom he met on a reading tour of New Zealand. Since the 1960s his reputation has been solidified by the many reading tours he has embarked upon and the prizes he has garnered, including two Guggenheim Fellowships, the Shelley Memorial Award (1981), the Poetry Society of America's Frost Medal (1987), and election to the National Academy of Arts and Letters.

In keeping with his emphasis on process and improvisation, Creeley has generated a constant stream of writing throughout his career, producing not only poems, but stories, novels, an autobiography, essays on poetry, and a voluminous correspondence. Like William Carlos Williams, Creeley sees writing as a means of discovery. Taking Williams's work as his model, Creeley aims to create tension through balancing terse lines against often heavily qualified sentences to create the illusion of immediacy. Creeley's poems tend to include spontaneous revisions and consider whether writing aids or inhibits communication with others or even understanding of one's self. For Creeley, love never involves escape from the self, but the opportunity for the self to confirm its subjective existence.

After *For Love,* his books became increasingly experimental; *Words* (1967) and *Pieces* (1968) fragmented language and challenged its sufficiency. Although they were faulted by many reviewers for a lack of coherence, *Words* and *Pieces* have been hailed by other critics as harbingers of Language Poetry. Nevertheless, since the late 1970s Creeley has returned to exploring the boundaries of the self and varied registers of feeling. He emphasizes in the introduction of his *Selected Poems* (1991) that the materials of poetry are "constant, simple, elusive, specific." Poetry, he adds, "costs so little and so much. It preoccupies a life, yet can only find one in living. It is a music, a playful construct of feeling, a last word and communion."

I Know a Man

As I sd to my
friend, because I am
always talking,—John, I

sd, which was not his
name, the darkness sur-   5
rounds us, what

can we do against
it, or else, shall we &
why not, buy a goddamn big car,

drive, he sd, for   10
christ's sake, look
out where yr going.

1954

Heroes

In all those stories the hero
is beyond himself into the next
thing, be it those labors
of Hercules,[1] or Aeneas[2] going into death.

I thought the instant of the one humanness   5
in Virgil's plan of it
was that it was of course human enough to die,
yet to come back, as he said, *hoc opus, hic labor est.*[3]

That was the Cumaean Sibyl speaking.
This is Robert Creeley, and Virgil   10
is dead now two thousand years, yet Hercules
and the *Aeneid,* yet all that industrious wis-

---

1. Greek hero whose remarkable strength enabled him to complete nine labors, dangerous tasks imposed as penance after he slew his wife and children in a fit of madness.
2. Trojan hero of Virgil's *Aeneid* (19 B.C.E.); one of Aeneas's adventures was a journey, led by the Cumaean Sibyl, through the underworld.
3. (Latin) "That is the task, that is the labor." In Virgil's *Aeneid,* the Sibyl warns Aeneas that descending to the underworld is easy, but returning to the world of the living is difficult.

dom lives in the way the mountains
and the desert are waiting
for the heroes, and death also   15
can still propose the old labors.

                                                  1959

Oh No

If you wander far enough
you will come to it
and when you get there
they will give you a place to sit

for yourself only, in a nice chair,   5
and all your friends will be there
with smiles on their faces
and they will likewise all have places.

                                                  1959

For Love

For Bobbie[4]

Yesterday I wanted to
speak of it, that sense above
the others to me
important because all

that I know derives   5
from what it teaches me.
Today, what is it that
is finally so helpless,

different, despairs of its own
statement, wants to   10
turn away, endlessly
to turn away.

If the moon did not . . .
no, if you did not
I wouldn't either, but   15
what would I not

do, what prevention, what
thing so quickly stopped.
That is love yesterday
or tomorrow, not   20

now. Can I eat
what you give me. I

---

4. Bobbie Louise Hall was Creeley's second wife.

have not earned it. Must
I think of everything

as earned. Now love also   25
becomes a reward so
remote from me I have
only made it with my mind.

Here is tedium,
despair, a painful   30
sense of isolation and
whimsical if pompous

self-regard. But that image
is only of the mind's
vague structure, vague to me   35
because it is my own.

Love, what do I think
to say. I cannot say it.
What have you become to ask,
what have I made you into,   40

companion, good company,
crossed legs with skirt, or
soft body under
the bones of the bed.

Nothing says anything   45
but that which it wishes
would come true, fears
what else might happen in

some other place, some
other time not this one.   50
A voice in my place, an
echo of that only in yours.

Let me stumble into
not the confession but
the obsession I begin with   55
now. For you

also (also)
some time beyond place, or
place beyond time, no
mind left to   60

say anything at all,
that face gone, now.
Into the company of love
it all returns.

1962

The Rain

All night the sound had
come back again,
and again falls
this quiet, persistent rain.

What am I to myself   5
that must be remembered,
insisted upon
so often? Is it

that never the ease,
even the hardness,   10
of rain falling
will have for me

something other than this,
something not so insistent—
am I to be locked in this   15
final uneasiness.

Love, if you love me,
lie next to me.
Be for me, like rain,
the getting out   20

of the tiredness, the fatuousness, the semi-
lust of intentional indifference.
Be wet
with a decent happiness.

                                                                  1962

"I Keep to Myself Such Measures . . ."

I keep to myself such
measures as I care for,
daily the rocks
accumulate position.

There is nothing   5
but what thinking makes
it less tangible. The mind,
fast as it goes, loses

pace, puts in place of it
like rocks simple markers,   10
for a way only to
hopefully come back to

where it cannot. All
forgets. My mind sinks.

I hold in both hands such weight   15
it is my only description.

1967

◄ ALLEN GINSBERG ►
(1926–1997)

Allen Ginsberg was born in Newark, New Jersey, the son of Louis Ginsberg, a poet and high school teacher, and his wife Naomi, whose Communist sympathies profoundly influenced her son. As a student in the public schools in Paterson, New Jersey, Ginsberg became acquainted with William Carlos Williams, an early supporter and mentor. In 1945 Ginsberg matriculated at Columbia University, where he received his bachelor's degree in 1948; his part-time and summer jobs included work on cargo ships, washing dishes in an all-night cafeteria, and copyediting for newspapers. In New York he befriended writers William S. Burroughs, Jack Kerouac, and Gregory Corso, all of whom would figure prominently in the Beat Movement.

At Columbia he experienced a vision of William Blake, which he later described in an interview with Bay Area poet Jack Foley:

> 1948. So I'd be 22. . . . I had some sort of auditory hallucination of Blake's voice reciting "The Sunflower" and then later "The Sick Rose"—and with "The Sunflower" a sense of, like, eternal spaciousness and solitude and silence. Alone with the alone, so to speak.

In addition to the visionary poems of Blake, the broad embrace of Walt Whitman was an influence on Ginsberg, especially as he wrestled with the issue of his sexuality. Whitman's expansive, long-lined poetry and emphasis on spontaneity, the body, and the power of the self, seemed to Ginsberg to be the perfect antidote to the New Critical poetry that predominated in the late 1940s and 1950s. Williams had tried introducing Ginsberg to Marianne Moore, who expressed dismay at the negativity of the young man's writing.

In 1954, armed with Williams's letter of introduction to Kenneth Rexroth, Ginsberg went to San Francisco, where he worked as market researcher. There, with the help of a psychiatrist, he accepted his homosexuality and soon after met his lifelong partner, Peter Orlovsky. Ginsberg also experimented with drugs, and, influenced by Kerouac's aphorism "first thought, best thought," he often wrote poems spontaneously without revision. Aiming to write a bardic, Whitmanesque poetry that blended intense subjectivity with a passionate concern for the fate of the nation, Ginsberg voiced outrage at the hypocrisy he saw in American society and articulated a powerful desire for transcendence.

Ginsberg's "Howl" became the seminal poem of the Beat Generation. Famously performed at the Six Gallery in San Francisco, it was published by Lawrence Ferlinghetti's City Lights Books in 1956 with an introduction by Williams. The following year U.S. Customs seized a second printing, and Ferlinghetti was arrested for distributing obscene material. The resulting trial, in which both publisher and poet were exonerated (after testimonials from American writers of all stripes), gave enormous publicity to the Beats. Ever since that time, Ginsberg so closely allied himself with countercultural movements of various kinds that his persona gained more attention than his poetry.

But his poetry was enormously influential. He not only stood at the forefront of the challenge to New Critical orthodoxy but broadened possibilities for Jewish poetry and gay poetry. After his mother died in 1956, Ginsberg wrote "Kaddish," a long and, for its time, shockingly frank elegy that went into great detail about her mental illness and his own efforts to come to terms with her legacy. (His mother had been hospitalized for paranoid schizophrenia, and Ginsberg, who had suffered from depression, often worried about his own mental state.) Published in *Kaddish and Other Poems, 1958–1960* (1961), Ginsberg's elegy, like W. D. Snodgrass's *Heart's Needle* (1959) and Robert Lowell's *Life Studies* (1959), was a precedent-setting book in its exposure of the poet's personal trauma and in the analogies he drew between troubled family history and the tense American political landscape of the 1950s. For Ginsberg, candor—about his difficult childhood, his sexuality, and his radical politics—was the key to his beliefs about health and sanity. "Candor," he asserted, "ends paranoia."

He also made no secret of the link between his drug use and his poetry writing. He wrote Part II of "Howl" under the influence of peyote, "Denver Doldrums" on Benzedrine, "Wales—a Visitation" on LSD. But his experience in India in 1962 to 1963 and his introduction to yoga and meditation gradually turned him away from drugs as sources of liberation and inspiration. Wishing to convey the sacredness and beauty of the human body, he strove to remove guilt from sex and sexuality. Although he remained involved in antiestablishment politics (arrested at an antiwar demonstration in 1967, tear-gassed at the 1968 Democratic Convention in Chicago, jailed at the 1972 Republican Convention in Miami), he nevertheless became increasingly a mainstream populist figure. At different times, he was ousted by two Communist countries (Czechoslovakia and Cuba) where he was officially declared a degenerate for his homosexuality. In 1972 Ginsberg finally declared himself a Buddhist and developed a close relationship wit the Naropa Institute in Colorado. Two years later, Ginsberg and poet Anne Waldman cofounded the Jack Kerouac School of Disembodied Poetics at the Institute, naming it in honor of Ginsberg's Beat compatriot who had died as a result of severe alcoholism.

All of this social activity did little to slow Ginsberg's productivity as a writer. Among the books he published were *Reality Sandwiches* (1963), *Wales—a Visitation, July 29, 1967* (1968), *Planet News* (1968), and *The Fall of America* (1973), for which he won the National Book Award. He had also received a Guggenheim Fellowship and NEA grants, although some critics had begun to find his new books trivial and lacking in the ferocity of his early work. As if to signal his acceptance by mainstream America, his *Collected Poems* (1984) was issued by a major commercial New York publisher, Harper and Row, followed by *White Shroud* (1986), *Cosmopolitan Greetings* (1994), and *Selected Poems, 1947–1995* (1996). In 1994, Stanford University reportedly paid Ginsberg over a million dollars for his papers. He died in 1997 at age seventy in New York City of liver cancer. The irony of his eventual mainstream acceptance was not entirely lost on Ginsberg. He wrote in a late poem,

> Now I'm a Senior Citizen
> and stuck with a million
> books
> a million thoughts a million
> dollars a million

loves
How'll I ever leave my body?

The pun in the last quoted line is typical of the humor in Ginsberg's poetry. Though his commitment to spontaneous composition sometimes compromised the quality of his poems, his best work achieved an anarchic freshness and hypnotic emotional intensity that has remained influential and given pleasure to readers all over the world.

◄═══►═══►

America

America I've given you all and now I'm nothing.
America two dollars and twentyseven cents January 17, 1956.
I can't stand my own mind.
America when will we end the human war?
Go fuck yourself with your atom bomb.   5
I don't feel good don't bother me.
I won't write my poem till I'm in my right mind.
America when will you be angelic?
When will you take off your clothes?
When will you look at yourself through the grave?   10
When will you be worthy of your million Trotskyites?[1]
America why are your libraries full of tears?
America when will you send your eggs to India?
I'm sick of your insane demands.
When can I go into the supermarket and buy what I need with my good looks?   15
America after all it is you and I who are perfect not the next world.
Your machinery is too much for me.
You made me want to be a saint.
There must be some other way to settle this argument.
Burroughs[2] is in Tangiers I don't think he'll come back it's sinister.   20
Are you being sinister or is this some form of practical joke?
I'm trying to come to the point.
I refuse to give up my obsession.
America stop pushing I know what I'm doing.
America the plum blossoms are falling.   25
I haven't read the newspapers for months, everyday somebody goes on trial for
    murder.
America I feel sentimental about the Wobblies.[3]
America I used to be a communist when I was a kid I'm not sorry.
I smoke marijuana every chance I get.
I sit in my house for days on end and stare at the roses in the closet.   30

1. Followers of Russian communist Leon Trotsky (1879–1940) rather than the more brutal Joseph Stalin (1879–1953). One of the several references made in the poem to the anti-communist witch hunts of Senator Joseph McCarthy.
2. The writer William S. Burroughs went to Tangiers to escape prosecution for heroin possession.
3. A nickname for members of the Industrial Workers of the World, a radical labor organization.

When I go to Chinatown I get drunk and never get laid.
My mind is made up there going to be trouble.
You should have seen me reading Marx.
My psychoanalyst thinks I'm perfectly right.
I won't say the Lord's Prayer.   35
I have mystical visions and cosmic vibrations.
America I still haven't told you what you did to Uncle Max after he came over
      from Russia.

I'm addressing you.
Are you going to let your emotional life be run by Time Magazine?
I'm obsessed by Time Magazine.   40
I read it every week.
Its cover stares at me every time I slink past the corner candystore.
I read it in the basement of the Berkeley Public Library.
It's always telling me about responsibility. Businessmen are serious. Movie
      producers are serious. Everybody's serious but me.
It occurs to me that I am America.   45
I am talking to myself again.

Asia is rising against me.
I haven't got a chinaman's chance.
I'd better consider my national resources.
My national resources consist of two joints of marijuana millions of genitals an
      unpublishable private literature that goes 1400 miles an hour and twentyfive-
      thousand mental institutions.   50
I say nothing about my prisons nor the millions of underprivileged who live in my
      flowerpots under the light of five hundred suns.
I have abolished the whorehouses of France, Tangiers is the next to go.
My ambition is to be President despite the fact that I'm a Catholic.[4]

America how can I write a holy litany in your silly mood?
I will continue like Henry Ford my strophes are as individual as his automobiles
      more so they're all different sexes.   55
America I will sell you strophes $2500 apiece $500 down on your old strophe
America free Tom Mooney[5]
America save the Spanish Loyalists[6]
America Sacco & Vanzetti[7] must not die
America I am the Scottsboro boys.   60
America when I was seven momma took me to Communist Cell meetings they
      sold us garbanzos a handful per ticket a ticket costs a nickel and the speeches

4. Alludes to the controversy surrounding Catholics running for high office before the election of John
F. Kennedy in 1960.
5. A labor organizer convicted on false testimony of setting off a bomb during a San Francisco parade.
He was condemned to death.
6. Left-wing members of Ginsberg's family had sympathized with the anti-Franco Loyalists in the Spanish Civil War (1936–39).
7. Nicola Sacco and Bartolomeo Vanzetti were executed in 1927 for a murder and robbery they did not
commit. Their trial was a cause célèbre among American liberals, leftists, and anarchists.

were free everybody was angelic and sentimental about the workers it was all
so sincere you have no idea what a good thing the party was in 1835 Scott
Nearing was a grand old man a real mensch Mother Bloor made me cry I
once saw Israel Amter plain.[8] Everybody must have been a spy.
America you don't really want to go to war.
America it's them bad Russians.
Them Russians them Russians and them Chinamen. And them Russians.
The Russia wants to eat us alive. The Russia's power mad. She wants to take our
   cars from our garages.   65
Her wants to grab Chicago. Her needs a Red Readers' Digest. Her wants our
   auto plants in Siberia. Him big bureaucracy running our fillingstations.
That no good. Ugh. Him make Indians learn read. Him need big black niggers.
   Hah. Her make us all work sixteen hours a day. Help.
America this is quite serious.
America this is the impression I get from looking in the television set.
America is this correct?   70
I'd better get right down to the job.
It's true I don't want to join the Army or turn lathes in precision parts factories,
   I'm nearsighted and psychopathic anyway.
America I'm putting my queer shoulder to the wheel.

                                                                                                    1956

Howl

For Carl Solomon[9]

I

I saw the best minds of my generation destroyed by madness, starving hysterical
   naked,
dragging themselves through the negro streets at dawn looking for an angry fix,
angelheaded hipsters churning for the ancient heavenly connection to the starry
   dynamo in the machinery of night,
who poverty and tatters and hollow-eyed and high sat up smoking in the
   supernatural darkness of cold-water flats floating across the tops of cities
   contemplating jazz,
who bared their brains to Heaven under the El[1] and saw Mohammedan angels
   staggering on tenement roofs illuminated,   5

---

8. Scott Nearing was an economist who left the Communist Party in 1930. Ella Reeve Bloor and Israel
Amter worked for the Party in New York. Ginsberg's line alludes toward the end to the first line of
Robert Browning's "Memorabilia," "Ah, did you once see Shelley plain?"
9. Ginsberg met Carl Solomon at the Columbia Psychiatric Institute in 1949. Solomon helped William
S. Burroughs publish *Junkie*, a book about heroin addiction. The opening of the poem may also allude
to Herbert E. Huncke, a Times Square hipster and drug addict, and Neal Cassady, a Denver hipster who
achieved fame as Dean Moriarty in Kerouac's *On the Road* (1957).
1. The elevated railway in New York City.

who passed through universities with radiant cool eyes hallucinating Arkansas
and Blake-light tragedy among the scholars of war,

who were expelled from the academies for crazy & publishing obscene odes on
the windows of the skull,

who cowered in unshaven rooms in underwear, burning their money in
wastebaskets and listening to the Terror through the wall,

who got busted in their pubic beards returning through Laredo with a belt of
marijuana for New York,

who ate fire in paint hotels or drank turpentine in Paradise Alley,[2] death, or
purgatoried their torsos night after night   10

with dreams, with drugs, with waking nightmares, alcohol and cock and endless
balls,

incomparable blind streets of shuddering cloud and lightning in the mind leaping
toward poles of Canada & Paterson,[3] illuminating all the motionless world
of Time between,

Peyote solidities of halls, backyard green tree cemetery lawns, wine drunkenness
over the rooftops, storefront boroughs of teahead joyride neon blinking
traffic light, sun and moon and tree vibrations in the roaring winter dusks of
Brooklyn, ashcan rantings and kind king light of mind,

who chained themselves to subways for the endless ride from Battery to holy
Bronx on Benzedrine until the noise of wheels and children brought them
down shuddering mouth-wracked and battered bleak of brain all drained of
brilliance in the dear light of Zoo,[4]

who sank, all night in submarine light of Bickford's[5] floated out and sat through
the stale beer afternoon in desolate Fugazzi's,[6] listening to the crack of doom
on the hydrogen jukebox,   15

who talked continuously seventy hours from park to pad to bar to Bellvue[7] to
museum to the Brooklyn Bridge,

a lost battalion of platonic conversationalists jumping down the stoops off fire
escapes off windowsills off Empire State out of the moon,

yacketayakking screaming vomiting whispering facts and memories and
anecdotes and eyeball kicks and shocks of hospitals and jails and wars,

whole intellects disgorged in total recall for seven days and nights with brilliant
eyes, meat for the Synagogue cast on the pavement,

who vanished into nowhere Zen New Jersey leaving a trail of ambiguous picture
postcards of Atlantic City Hall,   20

suffering Eastern sweats and Tangerian bone-grindings and migraines of China
under junk-withdrawal in Newark's bleak furnished room,

who wandered around and around at midnight in the railroad yard wondering
where to go, and went, leaving no broken hearts,

who lit cigarettes in boxcars boxcars boxcars racketing through snow toward
lonesome farms in grandfather night,

2. Part of the slum on New York's Lower East Side.
3. Town in New Jersey where Ginsburg attended school; titular setting of William Carlos Williams's
long poem.
4. The place names are in New York City, including the Bronx Zoo.
5. An all-night cafeteria where Ginsberg worked while in college.
6. A bar in Greenwich Village.
7. A public hospital in New York City that is well-known for its psychiatric ward.

who studied Plotinus Poe St. John of the Cross[8] telepathy and bop kaballa
    because the cosmos instinctively vibrated at their feet in Kansas,

who loned it through the streets of Idaho seeking visionary indian angels who
    were visionary indian angels,   25

who thought they were only mad when Baltimore gleamed in supernatural ecstasy,

who jumped in limousines with the Chinaman of Oklahoma on the impulse of
    winter midnight streetlight smalltown rain,

who lounged hungry and lonesome through Houston seeking jazz or sex or soup,
    and followed the brilliant Spaniard to converse about America and Eternity,
    a hopeless task, and so took ship to Africa,

who disappeared into the volcanoes of Mexico leaving behind nothing but the
    shadow of dungarees and the lava and ash of poetry scattered in fireplace
    Chicago,

who reappeared on the West Coast investigating the F.B.I. in beards and shorts
    with big pacifist eyes sexy in their dark skin passing out incomprehensible
    leaflets,   30

who burned cigarette holes in their arms protesting the narcotic tobacco haze of
    Capitalism,

who distributed Supercommunist pamphlets in Union Square[9] weeping and
    undressing while the sirens of Los Alamos[1] wailed them down, and wailed
    down Wall,[2] and the Staten Island ferry also wailed,

who broke down crying in white gymnasiums naked and trembling before the
    machinery of other skeletons,

who bit detectives in the neck and shrieked with delight in policecars for
    committing no crime but their own wild cooking pederasty and intoxication,

who howled on their knees in the subway and were dragged off the roof waving
    genitals and manuscripts,   35

who let themselves be fucked in the ass by saintly motorcyclists, and screamed
    with joy,

who blew and were blown by those human seraphim, the sailors, caresses of
    Atlantic and Caribbean love,

who balled in the morning in the evenings in rosegardens and the grass of public
    parks and cemeteries scattering their semen freely to whomever come who
    may,

who hiccupped endlessly trying to giggle but wound up with a sob behind a
    partition in a Turkish Bath when the blonde & naked angel came to pierce
    them with a sword,

who lost their loveboys to the three old shrews of fate the one eyed shrew of the
    heterosexual dollar the one eyed shrew that winks out of the womb and the
    one eyed shrew that does nothing but sit on her ass and snip the intellectual
    golden threads of the craftsman's loom,   40

8. Plotinus (205–270) was a Neoplatonic philosopher who synthesized Greek philosophy and eastern mysticism. Edgar Allan Poe (1809–1849) was an American poet and short story writer whose work often dealt with macabre and mysterious subjects. St. John of the Cross (1542–1591) was a Spanish Carmelite friar and poet whose most famous poem is "The Dark Night of the Soul." All three of these writers influenced Ginsberg as a student.
9. A center of radicalism in New York City in the 1930s.
1. Location in New Mexico of the laboratory that developed the atomic bomb during World War II.
2. Might refer both to Wall Street, the financial center of New York City, and the Wailing Wall in Jerusalem.

who copulated ecstatic and insatiate with a bottle of beer a sweetheart a package
of cigarettes a candle and fell off the bed, and continued along the floor and
down the hall and ended fainting on the wall with a vision of ultimate cunt
and come eluding the last gyzym of consciousness,

who sweetened the snatches of a million girls trembling in the sunset, and were
red eyed in the morning but prepared to sweeten the snatch of the sunrise,
flashing buttocks under barns and naked in the lake,

who went out whoring through Colorado in myriad stolen night-cars, N.C.,[3]
secret hero of these poems, cocksman and Adonis of Denver—joy to the
memory of his innumerable lays of girls in empty lots & diner backyards,
moviehouses' rickety rows, on mountaintops in caves or with gaunt
waitresses in familiar roadside lonely petticoat upliftings & especially secret
gas-station solipsisms of johns, & hometown alleys too,

who faded out in vast sordid movies, were shifted in dreams, woke on a sudden
Manhattan, and picked themselves up out of basements hung-over with
heartless Tokay[4] and horrors of Third Avenue iron dreams & stumbled to
unemployment offices,

who walked all night with their shoes full of blood on the snowbank docks
waiting for a door in the East River to open to a room full of steamheat and
opium,   45

who created great suicidal dramas on the apartment cliff-banks of the Hudson
under the wartime blue floodlight of the moon & their heads shall be
crowned with laurel in oblivion,

who ate the lamb stew of the imagination or digested the crab at the muddy
bottom of the Rivers of Bowery,[5]

who wept at the romance of the streets with their pushcarts full of onions and
bad music,

who sat in boxes breathing in the darkness under the bridge, and rose up to build
harpsichords in their lofts,

who coughed on the sixth floor of Harlem crowned with flame under the
tubercular sky surrounded by orange crates of theology,   50

who scribbled all night rocking and rolling over lofty incantations which in the
yellow morning were stanzas of gibberish,

who cooked rotten animals lung heart feet tail borsht & tortillas dreaming of the
pure vegetable kingdom,

who plunged themselves under meat trucks looking for an egg,

who threw their watches off the roof to cast their ballot for Eternity outside of
Time, & alarm clocks fell on their heads every day for the next decade,

who cut their wrists three times successively unsuccessfully, gave up and were
forced to open antique stores where they thought they were growing old and
cried,   55

who were burned alive in their innocent flannel suits on Madison Avenue[6] amid
blasts of leaden verse & the tanked-up clatter of the iron regiments of

---

3. Refers to Neal Cassady, who was briefly Ginsberg's lover.
4. A Hungarian wine.
5. Part of New York City known for its winos and drug addicts.
6. Burroughs had worked for a year as an advertising copywriter. The line also refers to *The Man in the Grey Flannel Suit* (1955), a novel by Sloan Wilson.

fashion & the nitroglycerine shrieks of the fairies of advertising & the
mustard gas of sinister intelligent editors, or were run down by the drunken
taxicabs of Absolute Reality,

who jumped off the Brooklyn Bridge this actually happened and walked away
unknown and forgotten into the ghostly daze of Chinatown soup alleyways
& firetrucks, not even one free beer,

who sang out of their windows in despair, fell out of the subway window, jumped
in the filthy Passaic,[7] leaped on negroes, cried all over the street, danced on
broken wineglasses barefoot smashed phonograph records of nostalgic
European 1930's German jazz finished the whiskey and threw up groaning
into the bloody toilet, moans in their ears and the blast of colossal
steamwhistles,

who barreled down the highways of the past journeying to each other's hotrod-
Golgotha[8] jail-solitude watch or Birmingham jazz incarnation,

who drove crosscountry seventytwo hours to find out if I had a vision or you had
a vision or he had a vision to find out Eternity,   60

who journeyed to Denver, who died in Denver, who came back to Denver &
waited in vain, who watched over Denver & brooded & loned in Denver and
finally went away to find out the Time, & now Denver is lonesome for her
heroes,

who fell on their knees in hopeless cathedrals praying for each other's salvation
and light and breasts, until the soul illuminated its hair for a second,

who crashed through their minds in jail waiting for impossible criminals with
golden heads and the charm of reality in their hearts who sang sweet blues to
Alcatraz,

who retired to Mexico to cultivate a habit, or Rocky Mount to tender Buddha or
Tangiers to boys or Southern Pacific to the black locomotive or Harvard to
Narcissus to Woodlawn[9] to the daisychain or grave,

who demanded sanity trials accusing the radio of hypnotism & were left with
their insanity & their hands & a hung jury,   65

who threw potato salad at CCNY lecturers in Dadaism and subsequently
presented themselves on the granite steps of the madhouse with shaven heads
and harlequin speech of suicide, demanding instantaneous lobotomy,

and who were given instead the concrete void of insulin metrosol electricity
hydrotherapy psychotheraphy occupational therapy pingpong & amnesia,

who in humorless protest overturned only one symbolic pingpong table, resting
briefly in catatonia,

returning years later truly bald except for a wig of blood, and tears and fingers,
to the visible madman doom of the wards of the madtowns of the East,

Pilgrim State's Rockland's and Greystone's[1] foetid halls, bickering with the
echoes of the soul, rocking and rolling in the midnight solitude-bench

---

7. A river that flows through Paterson, New Jersey.
8. Biblical name for "the place of the skulls," the hill where Christ was crucified.
9. Burroughs "retired to Mexico to cultivate a habit" and to escape prosecution. Kerouac lived for a while in Rocky Mount, North Carolina. Burroughs and Ginsberg lived in Tangiers, where they were visited by Kerouac. Neal Cassady worked as a brakeman for the Southern Pacific Railroad. Woodlawn is a cemetery in the Bronx.
1. Names of mental hospitals near New York. Carl Solomon stayed at the first two, Ginsberg's mother at the third.

dolmen-realms of love, dream of life a nightmare, bodies turned to stone as
heavy as the moon,   70
with mother finally ******, and the last fantastic book flung out of the tenement
window, and the last door closed at 4 AM and the last telephone slammed at
the wall in reply and the last furnished room emptied down to the last piece of
mental furniture, a yellow paper rose twisted on a wire hanger in the closet,
and even that imaginary, nothing but a hopeful little bit of hallucination—
ah, Carl, while you are not safe I am not safe, and now you're really in the total
animal soup of time—
and who therefore ran through the icy streets obsessed with a sudden flash of the
alchemy of the use of the ellipse the catalog the meter & the vibrating plane,
who dreamt and made incarnate gaps in Time & Space through images
juxtaposed, and trapped the archangel of the soul between 2 visual images
and joined the elemental verbs and set the noun and dash of consciousness
together jumping with sensation of Pater Omnipotens Aeterna Deus[2]
to recreate the syntax and measure of poor human prose and stand before you
speechless and intelligent and shaking with shame, rejected yet confessing
out the soul to conform to the rhythm of thought in his naked and endless
head,   75
the madman bum and angel beat in Time, unknown, yet putting down here what
might be left to say in time come after death,
and rose reincarnate in the ghostly clothes of jazz in the goldhorn shadow of the
band and blew the suffering of America's naked mind for love into an eli eli
lamma lamma sabacthani[3] saxophone cry that shivered the cities down to the
last radio
with the absolute heart of the poem of life butchered out of their own bodies
good to eat a thousand years.

II

What sphinx of cement and aluminum bashed open their skulls and ate up their
brains and imagination?
Moloch![4] Solitude! Filth! Ugliness! Ashcans and unobtainable dollars! Children
screaming under the stairways! Boys sobbing in armies! Old men weeping in
the parks!
Moloch! Moloch! Nightmare of Moloch! Moloch the loveless! Mental Moloch!
Moloch the heavy judger of men!   80
Moloch the incomprehensible prison! Moloch the crossbone soulless jailhouse
and Congress of sorrows! Moloch whose buildings are judgement! Moloch
the vast stone of war! Moloch the stunned governments!
Moloch whose mind is pure machinery! Moloch whose blood is running money!
Moloch whose fingers are ten armies! Moloch whose breast is a cannibal
dynamo! Moloch whose ear is a smoking tomb!

2. (Latin) "Omnipotent Father, Eternal God." Ginsberg is quoting from a letter written by the French painter Paul Cézanne in 1904: "Lines parallel to the horizon give breadth, that is a section of nature or, if you prefer, of the spectacle that the Pater Omnipotens Aeterna Deus spread out before our eyes." He had studied Cézanne with Professor Meyer Schapiro at Columbia, and had been struck by the idea that the sacred is immanent in the world, and that the artist's job was to pay attention to it.
3. (Hebrew) My God, my God, why hast thou forsaken me?" (Mark 15:34), the last words of Christ.
4. Biblical, the god of the Ammonites. The word has come to refer to anything that demands the sacrifice of what is most precious to us, particularly the young.

Moloch whose eyes are a thousand blind windows! Moloch whose skyscrapers
stand in the long streets like endless Jehovahs! Moloch whose factories
dream and croak in the fog! Moloch whose smokestacks and antennae crown
the cities!

Moloch whose love is endless oil and stone! Moloch whose soul is electricity and
banks! Moloch whose poverty is the specter of genius! Moloch whose fate is
a cloud of sexless hydrogen! Moloch whose name is the Mind!   85

Moloch in whom I sit lonely! Moloch in whom I dream Angels! Crazy in
Moloch! Cocksucker in Moloch! Lacklove and manless in Moloch!

Moloch who entered my soul early! Moloch in whom I am a consciousness without
a body! Moloch who frightened me out of my natural ecstasy! Moloch whom I
abandon! Wake up in Moloch! Light streaming out of the sky!

Moloch! Moloch! Robot apartments! invisible suburbs! skeleton treasuries! blind
capitals! demonic industries! spectral nations! invincible madhouses! granite
cocks! monstrous bombs!

They broke their backs lifting Moloch to Heaven! Pavements, trees, radios, tons!
lifting the city to Heaven which exists and is everywhere about us!

Visions! omens! hallucinations! miracles! ecstasies! gone down the American
river!   90

Dreams! adorations! illuminations! religions! the whole boatload of sensitive
bullshit!

Breakthroughs! over the river! flips and crucifixions! gone down the flood! Highs!
Epiphanies! Despairs! Ten years' animal screams and suicides! Minds! New
loves! Mad generation! down on the rocks of Time!

Real holy laughter in the river! They saw it all! the wild eyes! the holy yells! They
bade farewell! They jumped off the roof! to solitude! waving! carrying
flowers! down to the river! into the street!

III

Carl Solomon! I'm with you in Rockland
    where you're madder than I am
I'm with you in Rockland   95
    where you must feel very strange
I'm with you in Rockland
    where you imitate the shade of my mother
I'm with you in Rockland
    where you've murdered your twelve secretaries
I'm with you in Rockland
    where you laugh at this invisible humor
I'm with you in Rockland
    where we are great writers on the same dreadful typewriter
I'm with you in Rockland   100
    where your condition has become serious and is reported on the radio
I'm with you in Rockland
    where the faculties of the skull no longer admit the worms of the senses
I'm with you in Rockland
    where you drink the tea of the breasts of the spinsters of Utica
I'm with you in Rockland
    where you pun on the bodies of your nurses the harpies of the Bronx

I'm with you in Rockland
> where you scream in a straightjacket that you're losing the game of the
> actual pingpong of the abyss

I'm with you in Rockland   105
> where you bang on the catatonic piano the soul is innocent and immortal it
> should never die ungodly in an armed madhouse

I'm with you in Rockland
> where fifty more shocks will never return your soul to its body again from its
> pilgrimage to a cross in the void

I'm with you in Rockland
> where you accuse your doctors of insanity and plot the Hebrew socialist
> revolution against the fascist national Golgotha

I'm with you in Rockland
> where you will split the heavens of Long Island and resurrect your living
> human Jesus from the superhuman tomb

I'm with you in Rockland
> where there are twentyfive-thousand mad comrades all together singing the
> final stanzas of the Internationale[5]

I'm with you in Rockland   110
> where we hug and kiss the United States under our bedsheets the United
> States that coughs all night and won't let us sleep

I'm with you in Rockland
> where we wake up electrified out of the coma by our own souls' airplanes
> roaring over the roof they've come to drop angelic bombs the hospital
> illuminates itself imaginary walls collapse O skinny legions run outside O
> starry-spangled shock of mercy the eternal war is here O victory forget your
> underwear we're free

I'm with you in Rockland
> in my dreams you walk dripping from a sea-journey on the highway across
> America in tears to the door of my cottage in the Western night.

1956

A Supermarket in California

What thoughts I have of you tonight, Walt Whitman, for I walked down the sidestreets under the trees with a headache self-conscious looking at the full moon.

In my hungry fatigue, and shopping for images, I went into the neon fruit supermarket, dreaming of your enumerations![6]

What peaches and what penumbras! Whole families shopping at night! Aisles full of husbands! Wives in avocados, babies in the tomatoes!—and you, Garcia Lorca,[7] what were you doing down by the watermelons?

5. Anthem of the international Communist Party.
6. Many of Whitman's poems contain lists of observed details.
7. Modern Spanish poet who wrote an "Ode to Walt Whitman" in his book-length sequence *Poet in New York*.

I saw you, Walt Whitman, childless, lonely old grubber, poking among the meats in the refrigerator and eyeing the grocery boys.

I heard you asking questions of each: Who killed the pork chops? What price bananas? Are you my Angel?   5

I wandered in and out of the brilliant stacks of cans following you, and followed in my imagination by the store detective.

We strode down the open corridors together in our solitary fancy tasting artichokes, possessing every frozen delicacy, and never passing the cashier.

Where are we going, Walt Whitman? The doors close in an hour. Which way does your beard point tonight?

(I touch your book and dream of our odyssey in the supermarket and feel absurd.)

Will we walk all night through solitary streets? The trees add shade to shade, lights out in the houses, we'll both be lonely.   10

Will we stroll dreaming of the lost America of love past blue automobiles in driveways, home to our silent cottage?

Ah, dear father, graybeard, lonely old courage-teacher, what America did you have when Charon quit poling his ferry and you got out on the smoking bank and stood watching the boat disappear on the black waters of Lethe?[8]

1956

◦►◄ GARY SNYDER ►◄◦
(b. 1930)

Gary Snyder was born in San Francisco and grew up mostly in Oregon and Washington State. From an early age he was sensitive to the landscape of the Pacific Northwest, the woods, mountains, and tidal flats. While attending public schools in Seattle and Portland he discovered a fondness for Native American lore. In high school he began climbing mountains and learning about wilderness survival. The fine collection of Asian art at the Seattle Art Museum intrigued Snyder when he was a teenager. He took his bachelor's degree in anthropology from Reed College in 1951, studied briefly at Indiana University (where he read Kenneth Rexroth, another West Coast poet who loved the outdoors), and from 1953 to 1956 studied Asian languages at the University of California at Berkeley. His life became an effort to balance physical labor and work in the woods with more intellectual and spiritual pursuits. When not studying he worked as a lumberjack, trail maker, and in a forest fire lookout in the Cascade Mountains. The young Snyder was the model for Japhy Ryder in Jack Kerouac's novel *The Dharma Bums* (1958).

While living in the Bay Area, Snyder became part of the Beat Movement through his friendships with Kerouac, Philip Whalen (his Reed roommate), and Allen Ginsberg. He took part in the famous reading at the Six Gallery in October 1955 when Ginsberg read "Howl" and Snyder read his poem "The Berry Feast."

---

8. Is the poet confusing two underworld rivers? Charon, in Greek and Roman mythology, is the boatman who ferries the souls of the dead across the River Styx. The River Lethe also flows through Hades, and a drink of its waters makes the dead lose their painful memories of loved ones they have left behind.

Snyder's deep interest in Zen Buddhism influenced the reading of his friends, and these poets also benefited from translations of Asian poetry by Ezra Pound, Arthur Waley, Kenneth Rexroth, and others. In 1956, with a scholarship from the First Zen Institute of America, Snyder moved to Japan. He lived abroad most of the next twelve years, writing and studying while the Beat Movement in America progressed into the political and social turmoil of the 1960s. He also visited India and sailed to Istanbul on an oil tanker. After his return to the United States, Snyder built a house in the Sierra Nevada Mountains of Northern California, and he has lived there ever since, except when teaching at various institutions throughout the country. Snyder has been married four times, and has a son, Kai, by his third marriage.

While in Japan, Snyder published his first books of poems, *Riprap* (1959), as well as *Myths and Texts* (1960) and *Riprap & Cold Mountain Poems* (1965) which included his translations of Han Shan, the T'ang dynasty poet. Upon his return to America, his main publisher became New Directions, the influential Modernist house founded by Pound's disciple James Laughlin, who also published Rexroth, Duncan, Levertov, Merton, and many other American poets. New Directions brought out such volumes as *The Back Country* (1968), *Regarding Wave* (1970), and *Turtle Island* (1974). Later collections from other publishers included *Axe Handles* (1983), *No Nature: New and Selected Poems* (1992) and his long poem, *Mountains and Rivers without End* (1996).

For the most part, Snyder's books do not display the sort of notable stylistic or intellectual development that can be traced in the careers of other poets. Snyder's primary concerns—spiritual attunement, nature and the environment, and alternative definitions of community—were very much with him from the start. As for technique, his meditative stance came with a quietude and mistrust of language. The body of the poem was a kind of allusion to the primary experience that engendered it rather than an embodiment of such experience.

In *The Real Work,* a collection of interviews and talks published in 1980, Snyder said:

> I've written some of my best poems working in the engine room of a tanker for months at a time when I didn't see a green leaf, or even a fly. That's not the problem. The problem is, where do you put your feet down, where do you raise your children, what do you do with your hands?

His approach to writing was passive-receptive more than artful and shaping. "I listen to my own interior mind-music closely, and most of the time there's nothing particularly happening," he comments. "But once in a while I hear something which I recognize as belonging in the sphere of poetry."

Unlike Kerouac, who drank himself to death, and Ginsberg, who developed an addiction to publicity, Snyder has led a quieter life. His spiritual stance allowed him to appreciate establishment poets his peers had denigrated, such as T. S. Eliot. He has also been consistent in his devotion to environmental causes. As a result, he became one of the enduring heroes of the literary counterculture and possibly the most widely respected individual in the Beat Generation. He has won grants from the Bollingen and Guggenheim Foundations, the Levinson Prize from *Poetry* magazine, even the Pulitzer Prize in 1975 for *Turtle Island*. Because Snyder did not see his art as a thing apart from his life or the life of the community, it is sometimes difficult to determine whether the admiration of his readers is directed toward the man, his poems, or his principles. He is an emblematic figure of the

American West, a role model for those who share his belief that materialism has endangered the planet. "As a poet," he once wrote in an essay, "I hold the most archaic values on earth. They go back to the late Paleolithic: the fertility of the soil, the magic of the animals, the power-vision in solitude, the terrifying initiation and rebirth; the love and ecstasy of the dance, the common work of the tribe."

Riprap[1]

Lay down these words
Before your mind like rocks.
       placed solid, by hands
In choice of place, set
Before the body of the mind   5
      in space and time:
Solidity of bark, leaf, or wall
      riprap of things:
Cobble of milky way
      straying planets,   10
These poems, people,
      lost ponies with
Dragging saddles—
      and rocky sure-foot trails.
The worlds like an endless   15
      four-dimensional
Game of Go.[2]
      ants and pebbles
In the thin loam, each rock a word
      a creek-washed stone   20
Granite: ingrained
      with torment of fire and weight
Crystal and sediment linked hot
      all change, in thoughts,
As well as things.   25

1959

Mid-August at Sourdough Mountain[3] Lookout

Down valley a smoke haze
Three days heat, after five days rain
Pitch glows on the fir-cones

---

1. Riprap is a loose layer of broken stone used as a building foundation or sustaining wall in water or soft ground.
2. A Japanese board game in which two players move stones across a grid of nineteen vertical and horizontal lines.
3. In the Northern Cascades of Washington State, where Snyder worked as a fire spotter.

Across rocks and meadows
Swarms of new flies.   5

I cannot remember things I once read
A few friends, but they are in cities.
Drinking cold snow-water from a tin cup
Looking down for miles
Through high still air.   10

1959

Water

Pressure of sun on the rockslide
Whirled me in a dizzy hop-and-step descent,
Pool of pebbles buzzed in a Juniper shadow,
Tiny tongue of a this-year rattlesnake flicked,
I leaped, laughing for little boulder-color coil—   5
Pounded by heat raced down the slabs to the creek
Deep tumbling under arching walls and stuck
Whole head and shoulders in the water:
Stretched full on cobble—ears roaring
Eyes open aching from the cold and faced a trout.   10

1959

Why Log Truck Drivers Rise Earlier Than Students of Zen

In the high seat, before-dawn dark,
Polished hubs gleam
And the shiny diesel stack
Warms and flutters
Up the Tyler Road grade   5
To the logging on Poorman creek.
Thirty miles of dust.

There is no other life.

1974

Axe Handles

One afternoon the last week in April
Showing Kai how to throw a hatchet
One-half turn and it sticks in a stump.
He recalls the hatchet-head
Without a handle, in the shop   5
And go gets it, and wants it for his own.
A broken-off axe handle behind the door
Is long enough for a hatchet,
We cut it to length and take it

With the hatchet head   10
And working hatchet, to the wood block.
There I begin to shape the old handle
With the hatchet, and the phrase
First learned from Ezra Pound
Rings in my ears!   15
"When making an axe handle
      the pattern is not far off."
And I say this to Kai
"Look: We'll shape the handle
By checking the handle   20
Of the axe we cut with—"
And he sees. And I hear it again:
It's in Lu Ji's *Wên Fu*, fourth century
A.D. "Essay on Literature"—in the
Preface: "In making the handle   25
Of an axe
By cutting wood with an axe
The model is indeed near at hand."
My teacher Shih-hsiang Chen
Translated that and taught it years ago   30
And I see: Pound was an axe,
Chen was an axe, I am an axe
And my son a handle, soon
To be shaping again, model
And tool, craft of culture,   35
How we go on.

1983

Postwar Formalism and Its Discontents: From Formalism to Feminism and the Confessional Mode

The sixties and seventies were decades in which America saw the greatest social upheaval since the Civil War.

HISTORICAL AND CRITICAL OVERVIEW

Midcentury Formalism

> There's rust on the old truths.
> —*Gregory Corso*

Formalism is a broad literary term with several meanings, but in the context of modern American poetry, it generally refers to work composed in meter, often with rhyme or stanza patterns. Traditional poetic form has been an enduring feature in American poetry from the earliest colonial period, and it has never vanished entirely from the scene. Yet there have been intervals in literary history—particularly in the early Modernist era after World War I and the "Open Form" period in the 1960s and 1970s—in which these traditional techniques have been marginalized. Even today one finds certain readers who consider rhyme and meter elitist, academic, retrograde, un-American, or phallocentric—irredeemably wrong, that is, for some ideological reason. While such condemnations may illuminate the critical concerns of a particular moment, they are not cogent universal observations. No literary technique is inherently wrong. Each style or mode of writing offers certain advantages and disadvantages, which the individual artist must balance and maneuver.

The contemporary poetry world is highly factionalized and combative; numerous aesthetic, ideological, professional, and regional camps busily make a critical case for their own creative enterprise—often at the expense of some real or imaginary rival group. Such debates are as old as poetry itself, but surely the sheer size of the contemporary American poetry world with many thousands of graduate programs, presses, conferences, magazines, and websites is unprecedented. At present American poetry is so vast and diverse as to be virtually unknowable. And yet a contemporary anthology must attempt to provide at least a provisional map of this enormous terrain. Our goal in the final sections of the anthology is to document and clarify the aesthetic arguments and poetic practices of the recent decades. No single style encompasses the full possibilities of poetry. We have tried to offer the best selection of poems possible from each major camp—without losing sight of the essential fact that what matters most is the quality of the individual poem and not the salience of the general trend or school.

Most poets in the following section began their careers by writing in rhyme and meter. Although they were very much aware of the verse experiments of the Modernists, they had largely turned aside from them under the influence of such poets as Thomas Hardy, W. B. Yeats, Robert Frost, and W. H. Auden—all masters of traditional forms. Equally important was the influence of the New Critics, whose ideas dominated university classrooms and literary magazines of the 1940s and '50s. Several of the New Critics, it should be remembered, were also significant poets, most notably John Crowe Ransom, Allen Tate, Yvor Winters, and Robert Penn Warren. New Criticism, elaborating on principles developed by T. S. Eliot, valued not only formal structures like rhyme and meter, but also a highly intellectual style of poetry characterized by wit, irony, and impersonality.

Following these New Critical poets, the midcentury writers made their own fusion of Modernist compression and complexity with traditional rhyme and meter. This merger of old and new created a powerful and original period style best exemplified in the early work of poets like Richard Wilbur, Donald Justice, Anthony Hecht, and Adrienne Rich. The language is rich and musical but the tone generally ironic and understated. Usually written in iambic meter and often rhymed, the poems display quiet erudition and subtle wordplay replete with literary allusion. The poems do not lack emotion, but their emotional content tends to be carefully balanced or qualified by intellection or reflection. (Reading the best poems of this group, one recalls William Wordsworth's famous definition of poetry as "emotion recollected in tranquility.") The total effect of the midcentury style is not unlike that of the *cool jazz* of the period, performed by musicians like Chet Baker, Paul Desmond, and John Lewis of the Modern Jazz Quartet—the poems are lyric, elegant, and evocative rather than raw or passionate, yet at their best still genuinely moving.

American formalism had a parallel phenomenon in postwar Britain with the so-called Movement poets, who included Philip Larkin, Donald Davie, Kingsley Amis, Elizabeth Jennings, and Thom Gunn. Prizing form, wit, and clarity, the Movement openly rejected Modernism in favor of a contemporary version of the English lyric tradition. Using subjects found in everyday modern life and idiomatic current language, the Movement poets also created a "cool," ironic, and sophisticated literary style. The midcentury formalist revival was, therefore, an international trend engaging poets on both sides of the Atlantic.

The midcentury formalist style was so successful and pervasive that its very dominance bred discontent and a hunger for wildness and experimentation. By the mid-1960s many poets of this generation had rejected traditional techniques at least temporarily. In stringent reviews and essays, both James Dickey and Robert Bly (whose work is found in the "American Internationalism" section) lamented the increasing reliance of poets upon a university culture associated with formalism. At the same time they were critical of the Beats, finding a lack of rigor in their work. Bly in particular looked to Europe and South America for new models, his theories leading to such concepts as Deep Image poetry. Dickey ruminated upon "the 'open' poem":

> I was interested most of all in getting an optimum "presentational immediacy," a compulsiveness in the presentation of the matter of the poem that would cause the reader to forget literary judgments entirely and simply experience.

By the mid-1950s, many American poets were groping for a new way of writing. Rigorously trained in traditional techniques, these poets had begun to associate the old methods with an intolerable dishonesty. Modernism appeared to be a dead end in some ways, while the term "Postmodernism" was still hardly a whisper. The New Criticism still dominated discourse in postwar colleges and universities, largely emphasizing a somewhat intellectual (and mostly masculine) canon of poets whose verse could be described as formal, rhetorical works elevating irony and allusion to the highest level of regard. There was a troubling sense, however, that now some of the poetry and much of the criticism generated by the New Critical movement had grown increasingly remote from contemporary experience.

Academic Poets

> God took away our readers and gave us students.
> —*Randall Jarrell*

Many poets in this section made their livings in the universities, including Howard Nemerov, Adrienne Rich, Anthony Hecht, W. D. Snodgrass, Donald Justice, and Louis Simpson. Other writers spent at least substantial portions of their careers teaching. Richard Hugo and James Dickey became professors after having worked in business. Richard Wilbur, X. J. Kennedy, and Donald Hall all taught for many years before making enough money as writers, editors, and translators to retire early from academia. Even Anne Sexton, who never attended college, taught after she had achieved literary fame. There were exceptions to this trend of association with universities. James Merrill's family wealth liberated him from having to pursue an academic career. Howard Moss worked as the poetry editor of the *New Yorker.* Sylvia Plath taught for only one year at Smith College, but left to piece together an income with her husband, Ted Hughes, through writing and clerical work.

Broadly speaking, this generation came of age after the role the writer-in-residence was already institutionalized. The fact that most early poet-professors were male and appeared to represent established aesthetic values, whatever their actual politics, which were usually quite liberal, contributed to the association of such values with conservatism—this despite the richness and innovation of much of their writing. When Beats referred to "academic poets" with contempt, they had in mind such figures as Nemerov and Wilbur. But the accusation "academic poet" was frequently inaccurate, repeatedly used to condemn poets who were not full-time teachers, like Bishop, Moss, and Merrill, simply because of their use of rhyme and meter. It is a further irony that those charges of academicism were often made by poets who themselves held teaching positions—or, like Allen Ginsberg, would eventually become university professors.

Some poets in this section turned away from rhyme and meter under the influence of Robert Lowell's *Life Studies* (1959), the book that began the vogue for Confessional Poetry. The most obvious of these were Anne Sexton, Sylvia Plath, and Louis Simpson. Others like Donald Justice experimented with free verse and surrealism partly as ways of absorbing international influences. Dickey and Simpson turned their attention to narrative verse, though in radically different styles. For Simpson, Walt Whitman and the Russian writer Anton Chekhov became vital examples in new poems about contemporary American life. Dickey was obsessed with narratives of violence from the beginning of his career. Both of these poets brought a prose-writer's sense of character and story to their work, but so did Anthony Hecht and Richard Wilbur in poems of Jamesian opulence. Hecht and Wilbur's narratives were written in lush blank verse, while Dickey and Simpson employed a spare and often conversational free verse. And yet both share a commitment to psychological depth and sociological observation.

In his 1980 essay, "Reflections on Narrative Poetry," Simpson wrote with a convert's conviction, "I can see no reason for writing in the old forms of verse. Finding the form for the poem as one writes is half the joy of poetry." On the other hand, formalists like Hecht and Wilbur would respond that meter and rhyme liberate rather than oppress the imagination. Wilbur has often pointed out that when he begins a poem he never knows what form it will take. His mastery of traditional form helps him climb out of the turmoil of composition.

These midcentury partisans of form versus process were part of an ongoing debate that characterizes twentieth-century American poetry. Despite their arguments, their poetics are not always as opposed as they appear to be, but the heated rhetoric of this debate often reduced the vital claims made in their poems to more schematic formulae. Free verse became associated with genuine or nonacademic experience, while poems that employed rhyme and meter were increasingly dismissed as artificial or academic. Formal poets were stereotyped as hyper-literary and elitist writers who drew their inspiration from books rather than real life. Such easy dichotomies were, of course, crude simplifications. It is worth noting that such poet-professors as Nemerov, Wilbur, Hecht, Simpson, Dickey, and Hugo were all veterans of World War II, some of them having seen horrific combat—the real world at its very worst. They had not spent their entire lives cushioned by tenured positions. Each of these authors wrote poems tackling difficult or dark subject matter, though their detractors sometimes failed to notice the elements of violence, madness, and despair haunting their supposedly calm and rational poems.

Feminism

> We all know that there is another story to be told.
> —*Adrienne Rich*

The feminist revolution is one of the transformative events in modern history, yet it cannot be called complete despite the new freedoms women have gained in Western society. The recognition now afforded women writers is a recent phenomenon. The generation of women represented in this section had to struggle, to varying degrees, for legitimacy in their careers. Robert Frost once wrote, "The English Department may be the poet's best and surest friend," but Frost lived at a time when it was harder for a woman or minority poet to get a job teaching in a university than it was for a white male. That world has now so greatly changed that it might be difficult for new readers to remember the limits still placed upon women's lives in the decades immediately following World War II. While an increasing number of women gained positions in the academic and business worlds, they often felt excluded from decision-making processes or generally treated as second-class citizens.

Of the women poets in this section, none had a consistent academic career. In general, they taught composition early in their careers, often enduring heavy course loads. They secured better teaching appointments only after they gained prominence as poets. Adrienne Rich taught writing in the City College of New York from 1967 until 1975. Only in the mid-1980s did she obtain prestigious appointments at San Jose State and Stanford universities. Maxine Kumin also taught composition early in her career, but eventually she stopped teaching to write full-time, returning to various universities only occasionally as a distinguished visiting professor. Mona Van Duyn worked only part-time at Washington University, because of the university's rules against hiring "faculty wives." Despite such obstacles, these poets helped pave the way for women in university English and Creative Writing Departments.

The rise of feminism, however, often came at great cost. The suicides of Plath and Sexton were sometimes misread as general defeats for the movement rather than as intensely personal events. Rich asked young women not to look in that direction for their models, not to think self-destruction was the only course embattled women could take. As an essayist, poet, and radical activist, Rich tirelessly promoted not only liberation for women, but other forms of political and sexual liberation. "A change in the concept of sexual identity," she maintains, "is essential if we are not going to see the old political order reassert itself." In her poetry, Rich's restless stylistic experimentation has been an attempt to find a mode of writing that will not feel complicit with "the old political order."

For the generation of American poets that came of age in the fifties and sixties, a strong association of aesthetic choices and political beliefs was inevitable. Many postwar poets who began as formalists felt that the old forms were compromised, too easily associated with a white-male–dominated society that repressed women and minorities. Such arguments ignored the fluent formalism of a poet like Emily Dickinson, who combined tradition with experimentation; it was easier to stress the apparent limitations of Dickinson's life instead. (Likewise, these critiques ignored the African American formalist tradition that stretched from Paul Laurence Dunbar and James Weldon Johnson up through Robert Hayden and Gwendolyn Brooks.) But this highly restrictive definition by feminist critics—emphasizing the denial of form and the rejection of social norms—was itself only part of the story. Subject matter was perhaps more significant than style, and feminists introduced new areas of human experience into American poetry. Rich celebrated lesbian love, while Sexton broke taboos to write of abortion and insanity and the female body. Likewise Rich, Kizer, Sexton, Plath, and Stevenson were daring in their expression of negative emotions, too, such as an ambivalence or antipathy toward marriage and motherhood or anger at the hypocrisy of society's double standards for women's behavior.

Even these strong women poets, however, have not all felt the need to make a complete break with traditional form. Rich has occasionally used rhyme in more recent work, while Kizer, Van Duyn, Kumin, and Stevenson have never entirely abandoned meter and rhyme. Stevenson, who has lived in England much of her adult life, has been particularly militant in her retention of any literary technique she desires—formal or free—and frequently brings new vigor to traditional methods. Each of these poets was changed by the massive rejection of traditional forms in American poetry. Yet each in her own way asserted her freedom to choose from the old and the new. They have helped prove that no literary techniques have a monopoly on truth and justice, just as they have shown that literary practice cannot deny the reality of social change.

Social Upheaval and Artistic Change

> It does seem to be the case that the power of free verse has had something
> to do with its revolt against some alternative formal principle that feels fictitious.
> —Robert Haas

The sixties and seventies were decades in which America saw the greatest social upheaval since the Civil War, and to a large extent the formal changes in American poetry were responses to the broader social environment. As our social, political, and cultural reality was being re-formed, poetry in some ways needed to be reformulated with it. These trends reached their climax during the Vietnam War era. "Who represents my body in the Pentagon?" cried Allen Ginsberg. "Who spends / my spirit's billions for war manufacture?" Many of the poets in the following section wrote poems against the Vietnam War or American policies in other regions. The relatively new institution of the poetry reading on college campuses provided the perfect vehicle for a new poetry of protest. The voices of social protest in American poetry were sometimes as complex and multifaceted as America itself, and sometimes those voices were heard in rhyme and meter. In "For the Student Strikers," though (a poem we have excluded for reasons of space), Richard Wilbur memorialized the intense antiwar demonstrations following the shootings at Kent State University in 1970 by reminding protestors that their enemies were human too.

In January 1973 the United States and North Vietnam signed the Paris Peace Agreement, calling for the withdrawal of American troops by the following April. In 1975 South Vietnam fell to the Communists. A mass evacuation of Americans and some Vietnamese loyal to America meant that the war was finally over, and the United States was not victorious. During this time the nation endured another trauma in the Watergate scandal, which led to the resignation of President Richard Nixon in 1974. For more than a decade the country had been torn apart by foreign war, civil strife, assassinations, and political scandal. Much American art of the time expressed profound cynicism, even paranoia, and American poetry drank deeply of these dark emotions. While it was an era of hard-won social progress, it was also one of intense national convulsion and pain.

Perhaps the sheer weight and rapidity of these public events caused many poets to turn inward. What we call "Confessional Poetry" (see the headnote to the section Midcentury Poets) began in an effort to find genuine subject matter by looking candidly at one's personal life. Although so-called Confessional Poets were often public, even political in their stance, it is undeniable that postwar American poetry deals more often with personal psychological and domestic issues than does poetry before the war. Perhaps this tendency occurred because revolutions in sexuality were necessarily psychological to a great degree. Perhaps, too, the lives of many poets in middle-class suburbs felt distanced from public struggles and facilitated a poetry of confession, made of the most private materials of the poet's life.

The return to personal and domestic themes took many different forms. James Merrill made autobiographical scenes from both his privileged childhood and his peripatetic adult life as a gay man central to his work—often using the modern Greek poet C. P. Cavafy as his model. Carolyn Kizer wrote witty and sometimes savage accounts of female domestic life—both personal and historical. Anthony Hecht and Louis Simpson confessed dark psychological states, while Richard Hugo wrote directly to his literary friends in verse epistles. As we have seen, Anne Sexton and Sylvia Plath made their intimate relationships public—though Plath could not have known the impact her final poems, published posthumously in *Ariel,* would eventually have. Anne Stevenson has written about family life from many points of view, including her own, while also stepping away from confession to view the world with Darwinian objectivity. Ironically, one of the least confessional poets in the following section is W. D. Snodgrass, whose "Heart's Needle" is credited by many critics as the beginning of the Confessional movement.

In such an atmosphere, poets struggled to remain relevant or insisted that relevance came from private truth more than public engagement. Meanwhile the art itself appeared to be losing readers to competition from movies, television, pop music, and other media. Some of the era's most private poetry arose from a need poets felt to assert any existence at all in the face of apparent neglect by a reading public. Here, too, free verse was usually considered more contemporary, honest, and closer to the bone than meter, although some critics worried if open form could ever have the wide public appeal that rhyme and meter once offered. Poets who emphasized the virtues of traditional form seemed, in some quarters, as antiquated as neckties and ankle-length dresses. In one of his notebooks, X. J. Kennedy responded, his usual humor tinged with rue: "Woe is me—born just a little too late for the crest of formal poetry that rose in the 1950s, so that my stuff didn't begin to appear till the great stampede out of traditional form was on." Although poets like Nemerov, Wilbur, Justice, and Hecht were still honored with prizes and publication in glossy magazines, the sort of verse they loved had fallen on hard times.

By 1970 most young American poets wrote free verse of one sort or another. To do otherwise was considered nostalgic. There were a few voices that objected to these trends, of course, such as that found in Kennedy's 1972 essay, "Fenced-in Fields," or the magazine, pointedly entitled *Counter/Measures,* that he edited with his wife, Dorothy. In 1978 Philip K. Jason edited a tiny anthology entitled *Shaping,* voicing some of the concerns that would later be associated with the New Formalism, especially a sense that the confessional free verse lyric had run its course. But these were marginalized, minority points of view. The mainstream was moving in the opposite direction. Free verse in its many forms was dominant across the literary scene.

———◦◄ HOWARD NEMEROV ►◦◦———
(1920–1991)

Born in New York City, Howard Stanley Nemerov had a privileged childhood. His family owned Russeks, a Fifth Avenue department store specializing in furs, and could afford private schools for the children, a fine apartment near Central Park, and servants. This affluence reflected the hard work of Nemerov's maternal and paternal grandparents, Eastern European Jews who immigrated to the United States in the late nineteenth century and struggled to establish themselves in their new country. His grandfather, Meyer Nemerov, after working in Lower East Side sweatshops, opened his own grocery store, and eventually went on to found a yeshiva in Crown Heights, Brooklyn. Howard Nemerov admired his grandfather, a Talmudic scholar, as "one of the wisest men I've ever known," and acknowledged him as inspiring the combination of learnedness and sorrow that characterizes his early poetry. Nemerov was also close to his younger sister, Diane, a gifted artist who in adulthood gained international recognition as a photographer under her married name, Diane Arbus. Temperamentally similar, Nemerov and his sister shared an intuitive bond throughout their lives until her suicide in 1971.

Although his family expected him to help run the department store, Nemerov, a precocious reader, never swayed from his dedication to literature. Enrolling at Harvard University in 1937, he achieved academic distinction, publishing short stories in the *Harvard Advocate* and winning the Bowdoin Prize for an essay on the German novelist Thomas Mann. Nemerov was bold enough to send the essay to Mann, who was teaching at Princeton, and the novelist was so impressed by the Harvard student's insights into his work that he agreed to meet him. Throughout his career Nemerov distinguished himself as an essayist as well as a poet, never losing sight of the original purpose of the essay as a trial, or search for knowledge. In his reviews and essays, he consistently challenged conventional opinions and developed surprising yet accurate analogies for how poems achieve their effects. At Harvard, however, and especially in the early years of his career, his search for knowledge and drive for professional accomplishment was carried out with a dedication designed to prove his seriousness to his father, who disapproved of a literary life. In *Journal of the Fictive Life* (1965), Nemerov admitted:

> As well as having its religiously exalted mystique, writing was for me at the beginning sinful and a transgression. That is to say, the emphasis I place to this day on work, on being industrious for the sake of being industrious, contains a guilty acknowledgment that I became a writer very much against the will of my father, who wanted me to go into his business, or, as it used to be called, go to *work*. Of course, a large part of my effort must have gone into showing my father that I was nevertheless a man of good character, that art was just as much work as work was.

Upon graduating from Harvard in 1941, Nemerov volunteered to serve as a pilot in World War II, flying bombing missions first for the Royal Canadian Air Force and then for the United States Air Force. After the war, in 1946, Nemerov and his English wife, Peggy Russell, settled in New York, where he co-edited the literary journal *Furioso* and completed his first book of poetry, *The Image and the Law* (1947). But after only a year he began earning his living as a college teacher, first at Hamilton College and a number of other New England schools, before settling on

Washington University in St. Louis, where he remained from 1964 until his death from cancer in 1991. His wife recalled, "Howard really started to educate himself after he became a teacher. In spite of his Harvard degree, he felt there were gaps in his knowledge and he determined to fill them. I've never seen a man study so. He read Proust, Auden, Yeats, Shakespeare, Montaigne, he reread Thomas Mann, Kierkegaard, Freud."

Erudition underlies all of Nemerov's work, particularly his essays and his early poetry. Yet that erudition was often coupled with a melancholy wit and a remarkable clarity of line and syntax, so that, unlike the work of Eliot or Pound, Nemerov's writing, though it may be full of allusions, never seems forbiddingly difficult or obscure. In fact, over the years Nemerov's style shifted from his early, studious poems in which he imitated Modernist masters, to an ease of argument in which the thought may be complex, but the expression was sometimes deceptively simple. Citing the early influence of T. S. Eliot, W. H. Auden, Wallace Stevens, E. E. Cummings, and W. B. Yeats, Nemerov admitted in "Attentiveness and Obedience" (1966) that his style had changed over the course of his career: "I now regard simplicity and the appearance of ease in the measure as primary values, and the detachment of a single thought from its ambiguous surroundings as a worthier object than the deliberate cultivation of ambiguity." Nemerov's Collected Poems (1977) demonstrates, however, that his books contain a variety of approaches and themes—poems of social satire, often written in tight, epigrammatical forms; visionary, sometimes riddling poems concerned with human destiny and deploying archetypal symbols; and meditative poems, often engaged in testing theological questions or contemplating the nature of thought, especially the complex relationship between the mind and the world. Living in New England in his college years and during his early teaching jobs attuned Nemerov to nature, and many of his nature poems owe a debt to Robert Frost, not only for their dark vision and concrete analogies, but for the liberties they take with the iambic pentameter line. Nemerov's nature poems, however, offer no homespun wisdom, but instead consider the foreignness of the natural world.

In the books that followed his Collected Poems, Nemerov's satirical mode increasingly began to prevail over his visionary and meditative tendencies. Although some of his satires seem glib, even the late books contain poems in which Nemerov characteristically balances wit and sadness. During his lifetime, he received many awards, most notably the Pulitzer Prize and National Book Award in 1978 for Collected Poems, and the Bollingen Prize in 1981. In 1963 and 1964 he served as Poetry Consultant to the Library of Congress, and he was the U.S. Poet Laureate from 1988 to 1990. Although currently his work is not studied or written about as frequently as that of his contemporaries such as Elizabeth Bishop and Robert Lowell, his achievement, if not his influence, equals theirs.

◄•►━◄ ►━•►

A Primer of the Daily Round

A peels an apple, while B kneels to God,
C telephones to D, who has a hand
On E's knee, F coughs, G turns up the sod
For H's grave, I do not understand

But J is bringing one clay pigeon down   5
While K brings down a nightstick on L's head,
And M takes mustard, N drives into town,
O goes to bed with P, and Q drops dead,
R lies to S, but happens to be heard
By T, who tells U not to fire V   10
For having to give W the word
That X is now deceiving Y with Z,
   Who happens just now to remember A
   Peeling an apple somewhere far away.

                        1958

The Blue Swallows

Across the millstream below the bridge
Seven blue swallows divide the air
In shapes invisible and evanescent,
Kaleidoscopic beyond the mind's
Or memory's power to keep them there.   5

"History is where tensions were,"
"Form is the diagram of forces."
Thus, helplessly, there on the bridge,
While gazing down upon those birds—
How strange, to be above the birds!—   10
Thus helplessly the mind in its brain
Weaves up relation's spindrift web,
Seeing the swallows' tails as nibs
Dipped in invisible ink, writing . . .

Poor mind, what would you have them write?   15
Some cabalistic history
Whose authorship you might ascribe
To God? to Nature? Ah, poor ghost,
You've capitalized your Self enough.
That villainous William of Occam[1]   20
Cut out the feet from under that dream
Some seven centuries ago.
It's taken that long for the mind
To waken, yawn and stretch, to see
With opened eyes emptied of speech   25
The real world where the spelling mind
Imposes with its grammar book
Unreal relations on the blue
Swallows. Perhaps when you will have
Fully awakened, I shall show you   30

---

1. Franciscan scholastic philosopher (d. 1349). An advocate of nominalism, he is famous for a statement known as "Occam's Razor" because it cuts away superfluities: "Beings ought not to be multiplied except out of necessity."

A new thing: even the water
Flowing away beneath those birds
Will fail to reflect their flying forms,
And the eyes that see become as stones
Whence never tears shall fall gain.   35

O swallows, swallows, poems are not
The point. Finding again the world,
That is the point, where loveliness
Adorns intelligible things
Because the mind's eye lit the sun.   40

                                                              1967

The Western Approaches

As long as we look forward, all seems free,
Uncertain, subject to the Laws of Chance,
Though strange that chance should lie subject to laws,
But looking back on life it is as if
Our of Book of Changes[2] never let us change.   5

Stories already told a time ago
Were waiting for us down the road, our lives
But filled them out; and dreams about the past
Show us the world is post meridian
With little future left to dream about.   10

Old stories none but scholars seem to tell
Among us any more, they hide the ways,
Old tales less comprehensible than life
Whence nonetheless we know the things we do
And do the things they say the fathers did.   15

When I was young I flew past Skerryvore
Where the Nine Maidens[3] still grind Hamlet's meal,
The salt and granite grain of bitter earth,
But knew it not for twenty years and more.
My chances past their changes now, I know   20

How a long life grows ghostly towards the close
As any man dissolves in Everyman[4]
Of whom the story, as it always did, begins
In a far country, once upon a time,
There lived a certain man and he had three sons . . .   25

                                                              1975

---

2. Also known as *I Ching*, a classic Chinese book of prophetic wisdom.
3. These are locations in the Scottish Hebrides, including the Skerryvore lighthouse once written about by Robert Louis Stevenson.
4. Central character in a medieval English morality play (c. 1529), Everyman is summoned by Death and invites his friends to accompany him.

Because You Asked about the Line between Prose and Poetry

Sparrows were feeding in a freezing drizzle
That while you watched turned into pieces of snow
Riding a gradient invisible
From silver aslant to random, white, and slow.

There came a moment that you couldn't tell.   5
And then they clearly flew instead of fell.

1980

The Makers

Who can remember back to the first poets,
The greatest ones, greater even than Orpheus?
No one has remembered that far back
Or now considers, among the artifacts
And bones and cantilevered inference   5
The past is made of, those first and greatest poets,
So lofty and disdainful of renown
They left us not a name to know them by.

They were the ones that in whatever tongue
Worded the world, that were the first to say   10
Star, water, stone, that said the visible
And made it bring invisibles to view
In wind and time and change, and in the mind
Itself that minded the hitherto idiot world
And spoke the speechless world and sang the towers   15
Of the city into the astonished sky.

They were the first great listeners, attuned
To interval, relationship, and scale,
The first to say above, beneath, beyond,
Conjurors with love, death, sleep, with bread and wine,   20
Who having uttered vanished from the world
Leaving no memory but the marvelous
Magical elements, the breathing shapes
And stops of breath we build our Babels of.

1980

The War in the Air

For a saving grace, we didn't see our dead,
Who rarely bothered coming home to die
But simply stayed away out there
In the clean war, the war in the air.

Seldom the ghosts came back bearing their tales   5
Of hitting the earth, the incompressible sea,
But stayed up there in the relative wind,
Shades fading in the mind,

Who had no graves but only epitaphs
Where never so many spoke for never so few: 10
Per ardua, said the partisans of Mars,
Per aspera, to the stars.[5]

That was the good war, the war we won
As if there were no death, for goodness' sake,
With the help of the losers we left out there   15
In the air, in the empty air.

1987

◦◄ MONA VAN DUYN ►◦
(b. 1921)

A poet who has spent her life in the Midwest, Mona Van Duyn was born in Waterloo, Iowa, and raised in nearby Eldora. She received her bachelor's degree from Iowa State Teachers College (now the University of Northern Iowa) in 1942 and went on to earn her master's in English from the University of Iowa in 1943. That same year she married Jarvis Thurston, who was also a graduate student in English. She took additional graduate courses and taught at Iowa until 1946, when she moved with Thurston to the University of Louisville, Kentucky. At Louisville, she and Thurston founded the little magazine *Perspective: A Quarterly of Literature,* which they co-edited for the next twenty years. In 1950, the couple moved to St. Louis, where Thurston worked as a professor in the English Department at Washington University. Van Duyn also taught occasional courses at the university and became part of its active community of writers there who eventually included the poets Howard Nemerov, Donald Finkel, John N. Morris, and the novelists Stanley Elkin and William H. Gass. Van Duyn's first poetry book, *Valentines to the Wide World,* appeared in 1959, and she has published steadily since then: several individual collections—*A Time of Bees* (1964), *To See, To Take* (1970), *Bedtime Stories* (1972), *Letters from a Father and Other Poems* (1982), *Near Changes* (1990), and *Firefall* (1993)—two comprehensive collections, *Merciful Disguises: Poems Published and Unpublished* (1973) and *If It Be Not I: Collected Poems* (1993), and a new *Selected Poems* (2002). She has been honored with many important awards, including the Bollingen Prize and a National Book Award in 1971, and a Pulitzer Prize for poetry in 1991. In 1992, she became the first woman to serve as Poet Laureate of the United States.

Despite the major awards that she has won, Van Duyn has not received much critical attention. Although many of her poems arise from the details of her life in St. Louis, she is not a confessional poet. Writing about personal experiences such as the rewards and travails of married love, or the difficulty of watching parents age, she offers a balanced perspective, weighing the pain and pleasure of human experience. In "Matters of Poetry," her 1993 address as Poet Laureate given to the Library of Congress, she emphasizes the importance of privacy as a means of nurturing the imagination:

5. *Per ardua ad astra* is the Latin motto of Britain's Royal Air Force: "Through strife to the stars."

Though some few professional poets have felt free to express outwardly their quirky
selfness, it is the strong inner sense of self, usually protected from the public eye, saved
from and dedicated to the poems, that is characteristic of most successful publishing
poets. Most of them are happy to be indistinguishable in public, leading quiet, domestic lives. The private aspects of the wild and the unique are saved for the poems. Icono-
clasm is saved, hoarded, for language—for forms on the page.

Van Duyn here offers a key not only to the sources of poetic inspiration, but to
her own work. Although reviewers have classified her as a domestic poet because
she often writes about daily experience, her poems are not tame as the term *domestic* implies, but, to use her own terms of praise, *wild* and *iconoclastic*. Her language, for example, is often colloquial, yet she favors intricate rhyme schemes and
unorthodox rhymes. Likewise, although her poems seem to deal with ordinary experience, she develops extended analogies, so that a Ferris wheel provides the
means for a complex meditation on the vicissitudes of love, or a first trip through
an automatic car wash allows Van Duyn to consider the tension between selfhood
and the need for love. Her elaborate analogies owe much to the example of metaphysical poets such as John Donne, and yet her language, although witty, is em-
phatically contemporary. Her poems are also "wild" in their attraction to the
grotesque, especially in Van Duyn's unflinching attention to physical processes
and the body's deterioration over time. For Van Duyn, human experience, and
above all the experience of married love, is mixed, a cycle in which the joys of
mind, emotion, and body are always intertwined with suffering. Rather than dwell
extensively on suffering, as many of her contemporaries do, Van Duyn instead
stresses that the experience of suffering can intensify life's pleasure, and that pleasure cannot be separated from pain. Her poems therefore often run through many
levels of emotion, integrating humor with hard-earned wisdom.

⋯⊶⟩⊷⋯

Earth Tremors Felt in Missouri

The quake last night was nothing personal,
you told me this morning. I think one always wonders,
unless, of course, something is visible: tremors
that take us, private and willy-nilly, are usual.

But the earth said last night that what I feel,   5
you feel; what secretly moves you, moves me.
One small, sensuous catastrophe
makes inklings letters, spelled in a worldly tremble.

The earth, with others on it, turns in its course
as we turn toward each other, less than ourselves, gross,   10
mindless, more than we were. Pebbles, we swell
to planets, nearing the universal roll,
in our conceit even comprehending the sun,
whose bright ordeal leaves cool men woebegone.

1964

Causes

"Questioned about why she had beaten her spastic child to death,
the mother told police, 'I hit him because he kept falling off his crutches.'"

—*News Item*

Because one's husband is different from one's self,
the pilot's last words were "Help, my God, I'm shot!"
Because the tip growth on a pine looks like Christmas tree candles,
cracks appear in the plaster of old houses.

And because the man next door likes to play golf,   5
a war started up in some country where it is hot,
and whenever a maid waits at the bus-stop with her bundles,
the fear of death comes over us in vacant places.

It is all foreseen in the glassy eye on the shelf,
woven in the web of notes that sprays from a trumpet,   10
announced by a salvo of crackles when the fire kindles,
printed on the nature of things when a skin bruises.

And there's never enough surprise at the killer in the self,
nor enough difference between the shooter and the shot,
nor enough melting down of stubs to make new candles   15
as the earth rolls over, inverting billions of houses.

1982

◂ RICHARD WILBUR ▸
(b. 1921)

One of the most accomplished poets and translators in American literature,
Richard Wilbur has never wavered from the pursuit of excellence. There was a
time when some critics found his poetry too genteel or ornamental, but discerning
readers now see that he has always been a poet with a realistic view of life. Rather
than dwelling on gritty or nightmarish images, however, Wilbur makes his art a
compensating grace. His pursuit of order occurs in poems laden with knowledge
of life's disorder. His poems for children, too, suggest a world of uncertainty and
contradiction, but they do so in joyful, even hilarious terms. While the terrors of
life and death are palpable in many Wilbur poems, a strong faith underlies them,
as when the poet asserts that the world is "[n]ot governed by me only."

He was born in New York City, the oldest son of Lawrence Lazear and Helen
Ruth Wilbur. His father was a painter who made his living doing magazine covers
and eventually as a portraitist. In a recent interview, Wilbur recalled, "I spent my
childhood in a New Jersey country town called North Caldwell which was twenty
miles from New York and has now been wiped out by spreading suburbs." This
bucolic life in New Jersey was made possible by Joshua Dickinson Armitage, a
wealthy industrialist who offered the Wilburs a stone house on his estate for a low
rent. "My childhood," the poet remembered, "left me with a preference for living
in the sticks, for long walks, for physical work and the raising of great crops of
herbs and vegetables. It made me a fair amateur naturalist and gave me an abil-

ity—essential in a poet, I should think—to make something of solitude." Wilbur was not unaffected by the nation's tribulations in the thirties, however, and he records that his early political leanings were distinctly leftist.

One summer before college he struck out on his own, riding the rails through much of the United States—he much later related a small part of this adventure in his poem "Piccola Commedia." While at Amherst College (B.A., 1942), Wilbur wrote for student publications, but he did not begin to write poetry seriously until, like so many others of his generation, he was caught up in World War II. The year of his college graduation he married Mary Charlotte Hayes Ward—nicknamed Charlee—and enlisted in the army. In 1943 he was sent to Europe with the 36th (Texas) Infantry Division, eventually becoming a cryptographer, a job that made good use of his talent for solving puzzles. His division saw deadly combat in Italy at Monte Cassino and Anzio before taking part in the invasion of France. With typical understatement, he explained his writing poetry in foxholes, "One does not use poetry for its major purposes, as a means to organize oneself and the world, until one's world somehow gets out of hand."

After the war, Wilbur attended Harvard University, where he took a master's degree in 1947 and was elected to the Society of Fellows for the next three years. He would eventually teach for nearly forty years at colleges such as Wellesley, Wesleyan, and Smith. In 1947 he also published his first collection of poems, *The Beautiful Changes*, which was generally very well received. The title of that first book is notable for its grammatical ambiguity: Is *beautiful* an adjective, *changes* a noun, or is the former a noun with the latter a verb? Both ways of reading the title suggest important aspects of Wilbur's poetry. Another element of his work in evidence from the start was his attitude toward traditional form. Though he would write in and translate fixed forms like the sonnet from time to time, Wilbur tended to deploy meter and his superb facility with rhyme to move a poem toward his own stanzaic inventions. He discovered his form through composition rather than imposing it from the outset. Wilbur also avoided, for the most part, the "confessional" mode that dominated American poetry a decade later. Though personal subjects and interior dream states would always be part of his work, he tended not to dwell on autobiography or his own psychological preoccupations, but to emphasize the complex beauties and mysteries of the world outside himself. Some critics have argued that Wilbur has always been a devotional Christian poet, aware like George Herbert of the limits of human understanding, but founding his worldview on a belief in God. Wilbur's formalism, then, despite the dark subjects of some poems, reflects the bountiful forms of creation in defiance of the predominantly pessimistic tenor of the times.

His second collection, *Ceremony and Other Poems*, appeared in 1950, but it was Wilbur's third book of poems, *Things of This World* (1956), that solidified his reputation as a contemporary master, winning both the Pulitzer Prize and the National Book Award for poetry. Despite his confident lyric gift, however, Wilbur wished to extend his range by writing dramatic works. In the fifties he discovered that the creative outlet most available to him for this extension was translation. His version of Molière's *The Misanthrope* premiered and was published in 1955. It was republished, together with his translation of *Tartuffe*, in 1965. Wilbur went on to translate more plays by Molière and Racine—by far the most successful versions of both playwrights ever done in English. His translations, unlike most, feel like original verse creations despite their faithfulness to the originals. He brought the same talent for verse translation to lyrics by François Villon, Charles Baudelaire,

Gerard de Nerval, Jorge Luis Borges, Anna Akhmatova, Andrei Voznesensky, Stéphane Mallarmé, and others. The added income from theatrical works proved a boon to Wilbur, eventually allowing him to lighten the burden of teaching and maintain a winter home in Florida's Key West. His biggest financial success in the theater came when he collaborated on the lyrics for Leonard Bernstein's comic operetta *Candide,* which premiered on Broadway in 1956. Wilbur found himself in the enviable position of having the solitary pursuit of lyric poetry and the more gregarious life of the theater.

His next major collection of poems, *Advice to a Prophet* (1961), showed him extending his range in both form and content. It was followed by *Walking to Sleep* (1969) and *The Mind-Reader* (1976), each of which contained verse translations and at least one extended and ambitious blank verse poem exploring characters and dream states. Despite the richness and variety of these volumes, however, some critics found Wilbur so much at odds with broader trends in American poetry, so much the gentleman in a roomful of rebels, that he seemed increasingly insignificant as an artist. It was the publication of *New and Collected Poems* in 1988 that prompted a reassessment of Wilbur's work. Readers could see a progression from the more baroque style of his early poems to less affected work. Just as a previous generation had discovered a dark side in Robert Frost and valued him more as a result, critics began to notice the instability apparent in Wilbur's world, the way his lines compensated for troubling experience. Manners and decorum remained important elements of his poetry in part because of the implied brutality of a world in which those things could not save anyone from pain. *New and Collected Poems* earned Wilbur his second Pulitzer Prize among numerous other awards. Twelve years would pass before he published another collection, the slender but excellent *Mayflies* (2000), where again one could see Wilbur's vision of life's ephemeral nature.

Wilbur has also authored lighter verse, particularly in his books for children, each of which offers pleasures for adult readers as well. Among the most important of these are *Opposites* (1973), *More Opposites* (1991), *A Game of Catch* (1994), *Runaway Opposites* (1995), *The Disappearing Alphabet* (1998), and *The Pig in the Spigot* (2000). The humor in these books builds upon genuine anxieties, and critics might profitably compare them to Wilbur's "grown-up" collections. This talent for making games out of anxieties underlies his fondness for riddles and puzzles. Like Emerson, he sees the world as a coded place. And, like Frost, he sees our confusion in such a place as only momentarily stayed by poetry. These and other matters are explored in Wilbur's two major collections of essays, *Responses* (1976; reprinted 2000) and *The Catbird's Song* (1997).

Wilbur served as United States Poet Laureate from 1987 to 1988. He splits the seasons between Key West and Cummington, Massachusetts, with his wife of more than sixty years.

-=o=-◆-=o=-

The Beautiful Changes

One wading a Fall meadow finds on all sides
The Queen Anne's Lace lying like lilies
On water; it glides

So from the walker, it turns
Dry grass to a lake, as the slightest shade of you   5
Valleys my mind in fabulous blue Lucernes.

The beautiful changes as a forest is changed
By a chameleon's turning his skin to it;
As a mantis, arranged
On a green leaf, grows   10
Into it, makes the leaf leafier, and proves
Any greenness is deeper than anyone knows.

Your hands hold roses always in a way that says
They are not only yours; the beautiful changes
In such kind ways,   15
Wishing ever to sunder
Things and things' selves for a second finding, to lose
For a moment all that it touches back to wonder.

                                                          1947

The Pardon

My dog lay dead five days without a grave
In the thick of summer, hid in a clump of pine
And a jungle of grass and honeysuckle-vine.
I who had loved him while he kept alive

Went only close enough to where he was   5
To sniff the heavy honeysuckle-smell
Twined with another odor heavier still
And hear the flies' intolerable buzz.

Well, I was ten and very much afraid.
In my kind world the dead were out of range   10
And I could not forgive the sad or strange
In beast or man. My father took the spade

And buried him. Last night I saw the grass
Slowly divide (it was the same scene
But now it glowed a fierce and mortal green)   15
And saw the dog emerging. I confess

I felt afraid again, but still he came
In the carnal sun, clothed in a hymn of flies,
And death was breeding in his lively eyes.
I started in to cry and call his name,   20

Asking forgiveness of his tongueless head.
. . . I dreamt the past was never past redeeming:
But whether this was false or honest dreaming
I beg death's pardon now. And mourn the dead.

                                                          1950

Love Calls Us to the Things of This World[1]

The eyes open to a cry of pulleys,
And spirited from sleep, the astounded soul
Hangs for a moment bodiless and simple
As false dawn.
             Outside the open window
The morning air is all awash with angels.   5

Some are in bed-sheets, some are in blouses,
Some are in smocks: but truly there they are.
Now they are rising together in calm swells
Of halcyon[2] feeling, filling whatever they wear
With the deep joy of their impersonal breathing;   10

Now they are flying in place, conveying
The terrible speed of their omnipresence, moving
And staying like white water; and now of a sudden
They swoon down into so rapt a quiet
That nobody seems to be there.
                The soul shrinks   15

From all that it is about to remember,
From the punctual rape of every blessèd day,
And cries
       "Oh, let there be nothing on earth but laundry,
Nothing but rosy hands in the rising steam
And clear dances done in the sight of heaven."   20

Yet, as the sun acknowledges
With a warm look the world's hunks and colors,
The soul descends once more in bitter love
To accept the waking body, saying now
In a changed voice as the man yawns and rises,   25

"Bring them down from their ruddy gallows;
Let there be clean linen for the backs of thieves;
Let lovers go fresh and sweet to be undone,
And the heaviest nuns walk in a pure floating
Of dark habits,[3]
          keeping their difficult balance."   30

                            1956

Cottage Street, 1953

Framed in her phoenix fire-screen, Edna Ward
Bends to the tray of Canton, pouring tea
For frightened Mrs. Plath; then, turning toward
The pale, slumped daughter, and my wife, and me,

---

1. The poet has said that he found the title in St. Augustine's commentary on the Psalms.
2. Peaceful or happy, from Greek mythology.
3. In addition to the usual meaning, Wilbur intends us to think of the gowns worn by nuns.

Asks if we would prefer it weak or strong.   5
Will we have milk or lemon, she enquires?
The visit seems already strained and long.
Each in his turn, we tell her our desires.

It is my office to exemplify
The published poet in his happiness,   10
Thus cheering Sylvia, who has wished to die;
But half-ashamed, and impotent to bless,

I am a stupid life-guard who has found,
Swept to his shallows by the tide, a girl
who, far from shore, has been immensely drowned,   15
And stares through water now with eyes of pearl.

How large is her refusal; and how slight
That genteel chat whereby we recommend
Life, of a summer afternoon, despite
The brewing dusk which hints that it may end.   20

And Edna Ward shall die in fifteen years,
After her eight-and-eighty summers of
Such grace and courage as permit no tears,
The thin hand reaching out, the last word *love*,

Outliving Sylvia who, condemned to live,   25
Shall study for a decade, as she must,
To state at last her brilliant negative
In poems free and helpless and unjust.

                                                    1976

Piccola Commedia[4]

He is no one I really know,
The sun-charred, gaunt young man
By the highway's edge in Kansas
Thirty-odd years ago.

On a tourist-cabin veranda   5
Two middle-aged women sat;
One, in a white dress, fat,
With a rattling glass in her hand,

Called "Son, don't you feel the heat?
Get up here into the shade."   10
Like a good boy, I obeyed,
And was given a crate for a seat

---

4. (Italian) "Small Comedy." The poem is based upon Wilbur's recollection of a year in which he tramped through much of the United States, prior to his service in World War II.

And an Orange Crush and gin.
"This state," she said, "is hell."
Her thin friend cackled, "Well, dear,   15
You've gotta fight sin with sin."

"No harm in a drink; my stars!"
Said the fat one, jerking her head.
"And I'll take no lip from Ed,
Him with his damn cigars."   20

Laughter. A combine whined
On past, and dry grass bent
In the backwash; liquor went
Like an ice-pick into my mind.

Beneath her skirt I spied   25
Two sea-cows on a floe.
"Go talk to Mary Jo, son,
She's reading a book inside."

As I gangled in at the door
A pink girl, curled in a chair,   30
Looked up with an ingénue stare.
Screenland[5] lay on the floor.

Amazed by her starlet's pout
And the way her eyebrows arched,
I felt both drowned and parched.   35
Desire leapt up like a trout.

"Hello," she said, and her gum
Gave a calculating crack.
At once, from the lightless back
Of the room there came the grumble   40

Of someone heaving from bed,
A Zippo's click and flare,
Then, more and more apparent,
The shuffling form of Ed,

Who neither looked nor spoke   45
But moved in profile by,
Blinking one gelid eye
In his elected smoke.

This is something I've never told,
And some of it I forget.   50
But the heat! I can feel it yet,
And that conniving cold.

1976

---

5. A movie magazine.

To the Etruscan Poets[6]

Dream fluently, still brothers, who when young
Took with your mothers' milk the mother tongue,

In which pure matrix, joining world and mind,
You strove to leave some line of verse behind

Like a fresh track across a field of snow,   5
Not reckoning that all could melt and go.

1976

The Writer

In her room at the prow of the house
Where light breaks, and the windows are tossed with linden,
My daughter is writing a story.

I pause in the stairwell, hearing
From her shut door a commotion of typewriter-keys   5
Like a chain hauled over a gunwale.

Young as she is, the stuff
Of her life is a great cargo, and some of it heavy:
I wish her a lucky passage.

But now it is she who pauses,   10
As if to reject my thought and its easy figure.
A stillness greatens, in which

The whole house seems to be thinking,
And then she is at it again with a bunched clamor
Of strokes, and again is silent.   15

I remember the dazed starling
Which was trapped in that very room, two years ago;
How we stole in, lifted a sash

And retreated, not to affright it;
And how for a helpless hour, through the crack of the door,   20
We watched the sleek, wild, dark

And iridescent creature
Batter against the brilliance, drop like a glove
To the hard floor, or the desk-top.

And wait then, humped and bloody,   25
For the wits to try it again; and how our spirits
Rose when, suddenly sure,

6. No trace of the language of the Etruscans, who inhabited part of Italy before the advent of Rome, survives.

It lifted off from a chair-back,
Beating a smooth course for the right window
And clearing the sill of the world.   30

It is always a matter, my darling,
Of life or death, as I had forgotten. I wish
What I wished you before, but harder.

                                                        1976

Hamlen Brook

At the alder-darkened brink
Where the stream slows to a lucid jet
I lean to the water, dinting its top with sweat,
    And see, before I drink,

A startled inchling trout   5
Of spotted near-transparency,
Trawling a shadow solider than he.
    He swerves now, darting out

To where, in a flicked slew
Of sparks and glittering silt, he weaves   10
Through stream-bed rocks, disturbing foundered leaves,
    And butts then out of view

Beneath a sliding glass
Crazed by the skimming of a brace
Of burnished dragon-flies across its face,   15
    In which deep cloudlets pass

And a white precipice
Of mirrored birch-trees plunges down
Toward where the azures of the zenith drown.
    How shall I drink all this?   20

Joy's trick is to supply
Dry lips with what can cool and slake,
Leaving them dumbstruck also with an ache
    Nothing can satisfy.

                                                        1987

The Ride

The horse beneath me seemed
To know what course to steer
Through the horror of snow I dreamed,
And so I had no fear,

Nor was I chilled to death   5
By the wind's white shudders, thanks
To the veils of his patient breath
And the mist of sweat from his flanks.

It seemed that all night through,
Within my hand no rein   10
And nothing in my view
But the pillar of his mane,

I rode with magic ease
At a quick, unstumbling trot
Through shattering vacancies   15
On into what was not,

Till the weave of the storm grew thin,
With a threading of cedar-smoke,
And the ice-blind pane of an inn
Shimmered, and I awoke.   20

How shall I now get back
To the inn-yard where he stands,
Burdened with every lack,
And waken the stable-hands

To give him, before I think   25
That there was no horse at all,
Some hay, some water to drink,
A blanket and a stall?

1987

◆►◄ HOWARD MOSS ►◄◆
(1922–1987)

Howard Moss was born in New York City, the only son of a prosperous importer
and manufacturer. He was a sickly infant, and for the sake of his health Moss's
parents moved to nearby Rockaway Beach, Long Island, where he spent his childhood and adolescence. He entered the University of Michigan but was expelled
after one year for participating in a dormitory workers' labor protest. Upon graduation from the University of Wisconsin in 1943, he worked for the War Information Office. After the war he took various editorial jobs and taught for one year at
Vassar College before joining the *New Yorker* as a fiction editor in 1948. Two
years later he became the magazine's first full-time poetry editor, a position he
held for nearly four decades until his death.

Before Moss's tenure, the *New Yorker* was not a prestigious venue for poetry
and was best known for light verse. Under his discriminating leadership it became
the most important showcase for new poetry in America. As an editor, Moss often
published sophisticated, polished, intellectually demanding poetry, but his taste
was remarkably diverse. He championed many poets early in their careers and
helped establish the reputation of Theodore Roethke, Elizabeth Bishop, Richard
Wilbur, Anne Sexton, Sylvia Plath, Mark Strand, James Dickey, James Merrill,
John Ashbery, W. S. Merwin, Donald Justice, Charles Wright, and May Swenson.

Moss's fame as an editor often obscured his substantial achievement as a poet.
Maturing early, he wrote prolifically, and his published poetry spans forty years

and twelve major collections. His early work—influenced by Auden, Yeats, and Stevens—was tight, formal, and lucid, but it did not share the ironic intellectuality or emotional detachment that characterize the verse of his 1950s contemporaries like Howard Nemerov or Anthony Hecht. Moss's best early poems like "Burning Love Letters" or "Elegy for My Father" frequently talked about love and loss in colloquial but musically precise language. Moss later experimented with free verse, often writing compressed psychological narratives, but the lyric and elegy remained his most characteristic forms. He also excelled at light verse, though he published only one collection, *A Swim off the Rocks* (1976). Moss's first *Selected Poems* (1972) won the National Book Award. His *New Selected Poems* (1985), which remains the definitive collection of his verse, won the Lenore Marshall Prize from the *Nation*.

In addition to his poetry, Moss was a diversely talented man of letters. He wrote two plays, *The Folding Green* (for the Cambridge Poets' Theater in 1958), and *The Palace at 4 A.M.* (1964). He collaborated with the artist Edward Gorey on *Instant Lives* (1974), a sophisticated literary satire, and edited several anthologies, most notably *New York: Poems* (1980), which celebrates his native city in verse. He was also an active critic, but because of his influential position at the *New Yorker,* he eventually refused to review the work of living poets (a rule he only broke each time his idol, Elizabeth Bishop, published a new volume). In 1987 Moss died of heart failure at the age of sixty-five in—how could it be otherwise?—New York City.

◆—▶—◆

The Pruned Tree

As a torn paper might seal up its side,
Or a streak of water stitch itself to silk
And disappear, my wound has been my healing,
And I am made more beautiful by losses.
See the flat water in the distance nodding   5
Approval, the light that fell in love with statues,
Seeing me alive, turn its motion toward me.
Shorn, I rejoice in what was taken from me.

What can the moonlight do with my new shape
But trace and retrace its miracle of order?   10
I stand, waiting for the strange reaction
Of insects who knew me in my larger self,
Unkempt, in a naturalness I did not love.
Even the dog's voice rings with a new echo,
And all the little leaves I shed are singing,   15
Singing to the moon of shapely newness.

Somewhere what I lost I hope is springing
To life again. The roofs, astonished by me,
Are taking new bearings in the night, the owl

Is crying for a further wisdom, the lilac   20
Putting forth its strongest scent to find me.
Butterflies, like sails in grooves, are winging
Out of the water to wash me, wash me.
Now, I am stirring like a seed in China.

1965

Tourists

Cramped like sardines on the Queens, and sedated,
The sittings all first, the roommates mismated,

Three nuns at the table, the waiter a barber,
Then dumped with their luggage at some frumpish harbor,

Veering through rapids in a vapid *rapido*   5
To view the new moon from a ruin on the Lido,[1]

Or a sundown in London from a rundown Mercedes,
Then high-borne to Glyndebourne[2] for Orfeo[3] in Hades,

Embarrassed in Paris in Harris tweed, dying to
Get to the next museum piece that they're flying to,   10

Finding, in Frankfurt, that one indigestible
Comestible makes them too ill for the Festival,

Footloose in Lucerne, or taking a pub in in
Stratford or Glasgow, or maudlin in Dublin, in-

sensitive, garrulous, querulous, audible,   15
Drunk in the dolomites, tuning a portable,

Homesick in Stockholm, or dressed to toboggan
At the wrong time of the year in too dear Copenhagen,

Generally being too genial or hostile—
Too grand at the Grand, too old at the Hostel—   20

Humdrum conundrums, what's to become of them?
Most will come home, but there will be some of them

Subsiding like Lawrence in Florence, or crazily
Ending up tending shop up in Fiesole.[4]

1976

1. An outdoor bathing place, the most famous of which is in Venice.
2. An English opera house.
3. One of several operas devoted to the Greek mythological figure Orpheus.
4. A town near Florence, Italy.

JAMES DICKEY
(1923–1997)

Well before his best-selling novel, *Deliverance* (1970), became a popular film in 1972, James Dickey was one of the most highly regarded poets of his generation. His often-sensational subjects and rhetorical style were markedly different from the cool formality of more academic poets, the painful personal testimony of the Confessionals, or the social revolutionary prophecy of the Beats. His aggressively masculine and exuberantly Southern voice sounded a novel note in contemporary poetry. Dickey wrote about extreme situations where heroism was possible, passions ran high, and violence was common. By the time his first selected poems were published in 1968, Dickey was already widely discussed as a major American poet.

Such literary success had a long and unusual prelude. Born a lawyer's son in Buckhead, Georgia, Dickey grew up in a privileged household. His parents had lost a son before James was born, and the image of the lost brother haunts a number of his poems. His Southern bourgeois milieu instilled a strong work ethic, a devotion to practicality, and a suspicion of dreamy aestheticism. "Yet even in my high school days I also began to be aware of a connection—a very disturbing and apparently necessary one—between words in a certain order and the events of my own life." As Henry Hart makes clear in his biography, *James Dickey: The World as a Lie* (2000), Dickey was notorious for fabricating the details of his life. As an adult, for example, Dickey often mentioned his impoverished childhood, but his wealthy parents had a cook, a chauffeur, two nannies, and maids. His many autobiographical statements ranged from self-flattering exaggeration to outright lies. For that reason, most biographical profiles of the poet contain errors and inconsistencies. A self-proclaimed football star in high school, Dickey would later claim to have been interested in poetry from an early age, although he only began to write it at twenty-four, after serving in World War II. (He served as a radar operator in the U.S. Army Air Corps in the Pacific and flew some combat bombing missions—though less often and less dangerous than he later boasted.)

After World War II, Dickey earned a belated bachelor's degree at Vanderbilt University in 1949 and a master's in 1950. He also re-enlisted for the Korean War, although he never actually went to Korea, as he sometimes claimed. He married Maxine Syerson, a flight attendant, in 1948, and when not in the military he supported his young family by teaching at colleges in Texas and Florida. In 1956, however, he left teaching to join the McCann-Erickson advertising firm in New York as a copywriter for their Coca-Cola account. When that account was moved to the company's Atlanta office, Dickey moved with it. His success in the business world can be measured by the fact that he twice changed firms, each time negotiating a significant promotion and raise. However, he would later insist, "My commitment always was to writing, not to commerce." He kept up his writing in evenings after work and on weekends. In 1960 his first collection, *Into the Stone and Other Poems*, won a prize and was published by Scribner's. On the strength of that book, Dickey received a Guggenheim Fellowship. He left his secure but demanding job in business and took the family to Europe, determined to sustain his success as a writer.

Throughout the sixties, Dickey made his living with short-term faculty positions, fellowships, and increasing fees for his public readings. A second collection, *Drowning with Others*, appeared in 1962, a third, *Helmets* in 1964, and a fourth, the National Book Award–winning *Buckdancer's Choice*, in 1965. He was now modestly famous, featured as "The Unlikeliest Poet" in *Life* magazine for his unorthodox career path. One reason for Dickey's popularity was the dramatic content of his poems. "Most of my earlier work," he said in a later interview, "has some sort of narrative element in it because I like stories." This narrative quality caused some critics to compare Dickey to Edwin Arlington Robinson, whose poems he had edited, and also to other southern writers like William Faulkner and Flannery O'Conner. He once wrote in a journal, "Poetry occurs when the utmost reality and the utmost strangeness coincide." This imaginative juxtaposition is the formula of "The Sheep Child," a strangely beautiful poem in which he sympathetically imagines a taboo subject.

The success of *Deliverance* as both a novel and film launched Dickey to a level of fame few contemporary American poets ever know. The story of four middle-class businessmen whose canoe trip down a southern river turns into a nightmare of rape, murder, and revenge, the novel also contributed to Dickey's image as a man's man, a Hemingwayesque figure who lived by a code adapted to the world's inherent violence. Despite his increasing eminence as a man of letters—he had served two years as Poetry Consultant to the Library of Congress and in 1969 became writer-in-residence at the University of South Carolina, Columbia—Dickey was combative in defense of his reputation. His private life was also often sacrificed to his career and his public persona as a hard-drinking, guitar-picking, he-man of a poet. He became estranged from his first wife and two sons, and when Maxine died in 1976, he quickly married Deborah Dodson, with whom he would have a daughter, but who would do little to increase the emotional stability of his life.

Although Dickey continued to write and publish at a prolific rate despite the ravages of alcohol, critics have often noted a decline in the power and precision of his later work. Important poems like "The Firebombing," which opened *Buckdancer's Choice,* had signaled a relaxation of form and structure in Dickey's work. Even many critics who dislike the later work still find poems to praise in books such as *The Zodiac* (1976) and *The Strength of Fields* (1979). *Puella* (1982), however, is generally regarded as one of Dickey's weakest volumes, and the numerous collections that followed it do not reverse the impression of a poet who has lost control of his medium. Dickey's health was in steady decline throughout the nineties, and in 1997 he died of complications from lung disease.

◄◦═══◄►═══◦►

The Performance

The last time I saw Donald Armstrong
He was staggering oddly off into the sun,
Going down, of the Philippine Islands.[1]
I let my shovel fall, and put that hand
Above my eyes, and moved some way to one side   5
That his body might pass through the sun,

1. The poem is set after General MacArthur abandoned the islands to the Japanese and probably after the Bataan Death March, in which many captured Americans were sent to prison camps.

And I saw how well he was not
Standing there on his hands,
On his spindle-shanked forearms balanced,
Unbalanced, with his big feet looming and waving   10
In the great, untrustworthy air
He flew in each night, when it darkened.

Dust fanned in scraped puffs from the earth
Between his arms, and blood turned his face inside out,
To demonstrate his suppleness   15
Of veins, as he perfected his role.
Next day, he toppled his head off
On an island beach to the south,

And the enemy's two-handed sword
Did not fall from anyone's hands   20
At that miraculous sight,
As the head rolled over upon
Its wide-eyed face, and fell
Into the inadequate grave

He had dug for himself, under pressure.   25
Yet I put my flat hand to my eyebrows
Months later, to see him again
In the sun, when I learned how he died,
And imagined him, there,
Come, judged, before his small captors,   30

Doing all his lean tricks to amaze them—
The back somersault, the kip-up—
And at last, the stand on his hands,
Perfect, with his feet together,
His head down, evenly breathing,   35
As the sun poured up from the sea

And the headsman broke down
In a blaze of tears, in that light
Of the thin, long human frame
Upside down in its own strange joy,   40
And, if some other one had not told him,
Would have cut off the feet

Instead of the head,
And if Armstrong had not presently risen
In kingly, round-shouldered attendance,   45
And then knelt down in himself
Beside his hacked, glittering grave, having done
All things in this life that he could.

                                                    1960

The Heaven of Animals

Here they are. The soft eyes open.
If they have lived in a wood
It is a wood.
If they have lived on plains
It is grass rolling   5
Under their feet forever.

Having no souls, they have come,
Anyway, beyond their knowing.
Their instincts wholly bloom
And they rise.   10
The soft eyes open.

To match them, the landscape flowers,
Outdoing, desperately
Outdoing what is required:
The richest wood,   15
The deepest field.

For some of these,
It could not be the place
It is, without blood.
These hunt, as they have done,   20
But with claws and teeth grown perfect,

More deadly than they can believe.
They stalk more silently,
And crouch on the limbs of trees,
And their descent   25
Upon the bright backs of their prey

May take years
In a sovereign floating of joy.
And those that are hunted
Know this as their life,   30
Their reward: to walk

Under such trees in full knowledge
Of what is in glory above them,
And to feel no fear,
But acceptance, compliance.   35
Fulfilling themselves without pain

At the cycle's center,
They tremble, they walk
Under the tree,
They fall, they are torn,   40
They rise, they walk again.

1962

The Lifeguard

In a stable of boats I lie still,
From all sleeping children hidden.
The leap of a fish from its shadow
Makes the whole lake instantly tremble.
With my foot in the water, I feel   5
The moon outside.

Take on the utmost of its power.
I rise and go through the boats.
I set my broad sole upon silver,
On the skin of the sky, on the moonlight,   10
Stepping outward from earth onto water
In quest of the miracle

This village of children believed
That I could perform as I dived
For one who had sunk from my sight.   15
I saw his cropped haircut go under.
I leapt, and my steep body flashed
Once, in the sun.

Dark drew all the light from my eyes.
Like a man who explores his death   20
By the pull of his slow-moving shoulders,
I hung head down in the cold,
Wide-eyed, contained, and alone
Among the weeds,

And my fingertips turned into stone   25
From clutching immovable blackness.
Time after time I leapt upward
Exploding in breath, and fell back
From the change in the children's faces
At my defeat.   30

Beneath them I swam to the boathouse
With only my life in my arms
To wait for the lake to shine back
At the risen moon with such power
That my steps on the light of the ripples   35
Might be sustained.

Beneath me is nothing but brightness
Like the ghost of a snowfield in summer.
As I move toward the center of the lake,
Which is also the center of the moon,   40
I am thinking of how I may be
The savior of one

Who has already died in my care.
The dark trees fade from around me.

The moon's dust hovers together. 45
I call softly out, and the child's
Voice answers through blinding water.
Patiently, slowly,

He rises, dilating to break
The surface of stone with his forehead. 50
He is one I do not remember
Having ever seen in his life.
The ground I stand on is trembling
Upon his smile.

I wash the black mud from my hands. 55
On a light given off by the grave
I kneel in the quick of the moon
At the heart of a distant forest
And hold in my arms a child
Of water, water, water. 60

1962

The Sheep Child

Farm boys wild to couple
With anything   with soft-wooded trees
With mounds of earth   mounds
Of pinestraw   will keep themselves off
Animals by legends of their own: 5
In the hay-tunnel dark
And dung of barns, they will
Say   I have heard tell

That in a museum in Atlanta
Way back in a corner somewhere 10
There's this thing that's only half
Sheep   like a woolly baby
Pickled in alcohol   because
Those things can't live   his eyes
Are open   but you can't stand to look 15
I heard from somebody who . . .

But this is now almost all
Gone. The boys have taken
Their own true wives in the city,
The sheep are safe in the west hill 20
Pasture   but we who were born there
Still are not sure. Are we,
Because we remember, remembered
In the terrible dust of museums?

Merely with his eyes, the sheep-child may 25

Be saying   saying

> *I am here, in my father's house.*
> *I who am half of your world, came deeply*
> *To my mother in the long grass*
> *Of the west pasture, where she stood like moonlight*   30
> *Listening for foxes. It was something like love*
> *From another world that seized her*
> *From behind, and she gave, not lifting her head*
> *Out of dew, without ever looking, her best*
> *Self to that great need. Turned loose, she dipped her face*   35
> *Farther into the chill of the earth, and in a sound*
> *Of sobbing   of something stumbling*
> *Away, began, as she must do,*
> *To carry me. I woke, dying,*
>
> *In the summer sun of the hillside, with my eyes*   40
> *Far more than human. I saw for a blazing moment*
> *The great grassy world from both sides,*
> *Man and beast in the round of their need,*
> *And the hill wind stirred in my wool,*
> *My hoof and my hand clasped each other,*   45
> *I ate my one meal*
> *Of milk, and died*
> *Staring. From dark grass I came straight*
>
> *To my father's house, whose dust*
> *Whirls up in the halls for no reason*   50
> *When no one comes   piling deep in a hellish mild corner,*
> *And, through my immortal waters,*
> *I meet the sun's grains eye*
> *To eye, and they fail at my closet of glass.*
> *Dead, I am most surely living*   55
> *In the minds of farm boys: I am he who drives*
> *Them like wolves from the hound bitch and calf*
> *And from the chaste ewe in the wind.*
> *They go into woods   into bean fields   they go*
> *Deep into their known right hands. Dreaming of me,*   60
> *They groan   they wait   they suffer*
> *Themselves, they marry, they raise their kind.*

1967

◄ ANTHONY HECHT ►
(b. 1923)

Anthony Hecht was born in New York City and attended three schools there, including the Horace Mann School for Boys. His father had quit college to take over
the family business, the New England Enamel Company. In a book-length series

of interviews with the British critic Philip Hoy, Hecht talks about his family's financial difficulties:

> [My father] hated business and was not good at it. In the course of my lifetime he lost every cent he had, not once but three times. . . . Each time this happened he attempted suicide. . . . When I was six the stock market collapsed, and I can remember seeing on New York's sidewalks the bodies of those, covered for decency's sake with blankets, who had thrown themselves from windows. Our own condition went down noticeably in the world, though we were never seriously in want. Each time my father lost his shirt . . . my mother's family bailed him out. But her rage about this . . .came close to unhinging her.

There were also other family troubles, especially the ailments of his younger brother, Roger (also a poet), which included severe epilepsy. As a result, Hecht grew up with a strong sense of the frailty of social privilege and personal happiness.

While a student at Bard College, then a part of Columbia University, Hecht fell in love with poetry, including such influential modern figures as T. S. Eliot, Wallace Stevens, and W. H. Auden. His formal education, however, was interrupted at age twenty when he was drafted into the U.S. Army. He went overseas with the 97th Infantry Division and fought in France, Germany, and Czechoslovakia, where his company suffered heavy casualties. In his long poem, "The Venetian Vespers," Hecht's troubled narrator recalls a soldier who carried "A book of etiquette by Emily Post" into battle:

> He haunts me here, that seeker after law
> In a lawless world, in rainsoaked combat boots,
> Oil-stained fatigues and heavy bandoleers.
> He was killed by enemy machine-gun fire.
> His helmet had fallen off. They had sheared away
> The top of his cranium like a soft-boiled egg,
> And there he crouched, huddled over his weapon,
> His brains wet in the chalice of his skull.

He also participated in the liberation of a concentration camp called Flossenburg, near the German-Czech border. "The place," he recalled, "the suffering, the prisoner's accounts were beyond comprehension. For years after I would wake shrieking." After serving an additional eight months in occupied Japan, Hecht was discharged in 1946.

Having been awarded a bachelor's degree in absentia from Bard, Hecht attended Kenyon College as a "special student" on the GI Bill. Among his teachers at Kenyon was the poet John Crowe Ransom, who would publish some of Hecht's early poems in the *Kenyon Review*. Hecht did his early teaching at Kenyon, New York University, and the University of Iowa. In 1951, he was awarded the Prix de Rome, which allowed him to spend a year in Italy, a country for which he developed lifelong fascination. There he met Auden, who became a friend and eventually the subject of one of Hecht's critical books. His first collection of poems, *A Summoning of Stones,* appeared in 1954, after which he returned to Italy on a Guggenheim Fellowship.

From 1956 to 1959, Hecht taught at Smith College, where he came to know Sylvia Plath and Ted Hughes. This was also the period of his first marriage, to Patricia Harris, which lasted five and a half years and produced two sons. When the marriage ended in divorce, his exwife left for Europe with their children, and the poet was hospitalized for three months, undergoing treatment for depression. (His poem "Adam" dramatizes his painful separation from his sons.) Mental illness has been a subject of several of Hecht's poems, and he has more than once acknowledged the relative lack of health and happiness in his work. Hecht is a dark poet, to say the least, yet the compensations of his elegant and magisterial technique prevent his poems from descending into hysteria.

After the failure of his first marriage, Hecht remained single until 1971, when he married Helen D'Alessandro, who had once been his student at Smith. (Their marriage produced another son.) He taught at Bard again, then at the University of Rochester, where, after receiving the Pulitzer Prize for his second book, *The Hard Hours* (1967), he was promoted to an endowed chair. Thirteen years had elapsed between the publication of his first two books, and it would be another ten years before his third, *Millions of Strange Shadows* (1977), appeared. With this volume, the formerly unprolific Hecht entered an amazingly productive period that continues through to the present. Two years later he published *The Venetian Vespers* (1979). His *Collected Earlier Poems* appeared in 1990, the same year in which he published a new book, *The Transparent Man*. His sixth collection, *Flight among the Tombs,* followed in 1996. During this period he also published a selection of George Herbert's poetry, an edition of Shakespeare's sonnets, and three books of criticism: *Obbligati* (1986), *The Hidden Law: The Poetry of W. H. Auden* (1993), and *On the Laws of the Poetic Art* (1995). He also served as Poetry Consultant to the Library of Congress from 1982 to 1984, and in 1985 joined the faculty of Georgetown University. Since his retirement from teaching in 1993, Hecht has won still more honors—to date almost every significant prize it is possible for an American poet to win—and has continued to produce poems, essays, and book reviews.

Although Hecht is a dark poet whose subjects include madness, war, and the Holocaust, subjects upon which he has written with undeniable authority, he is also a writer of great range. "There is a clear contrast in the diction of my poems," he remarked, "between elaborate and subtle speech, between the ornate, the compressed, the densely worded passage and the fluent, colloquial and straight-forward mode of parlance. This is conscious and deliberate." In his work one can find the formal invention of "Sestina d'Inverno," the directness and horror of "The Book of Yolek," the comedy of "The Dover Bitch," the grandeur of "Adam." Hecht has also proven a master of narrative poetry. Even a short narrative like "The Mysteries of Caesar" movingly evokes an entire human life with its pleasures and sorrows.

Hecht is a poet for whom the close examination of the world seems almost a saving grace: "The soul being drenched in fine particulars." If some critics find these particulars on occasion too precious, others argue that his knowledge of life's potential horrors underlies them. His sense of art's attempted compensation for life's difficulties results in a deliberate complexity of tone, which he described in his 1965 essay "On the Methods and Ambitions of Poetry": "the devices which poetry summons to its aid are fundamentally discontinuous, representing incoordinate orders of experiences, which the poem, ever so briefly and tentatively, suggests must find their place in one constituent universe; and though not logically related, and not always delighted by one another's company, they move to accommodate each other, and in Kant's words, display 'a certain purposiveness . . .

which is not, within our act of judging, referred to any end.'" What Hecht wrote about the poems of Joseph Brodsky is true of his own:

> Underneath
> Their gaiety and music, note the chilled strain
> Of irony, of felt and mastered pain,
> The sound of someone laughing through clenched teeth.

Adam[1]

Hath the rain a father? or who hath begotten the drops of dew?[2]

"Adam, my child, my son,
These very words you hear
Compose the fish and starlight
Of your untroubled dream.
When you awake, my child,   5
It shall all come true.
Know that it was for you
That all things were begun."

Adam, my child, my son,
Thus spoke Our Father in heaven   10
To his first, fabled child,
The father of us all.
And I, your father, tell
The words over again
As innumerable men   15
From ancient times have done.

Tell them again in pain,
And to the empty air.
Where you are men speak
A different mother tongue.   20
Will you forget our games,
Our hide-and-seek and song?
Child, it will be long
Before I see you again.

Adam, there will be   25
Many hard hours,
As an old poem says,
Hours of loneliness.
I cannot ease them for you;

---

1. According to Genesis 2:6–7, God created Adam from the dust of the earth. Adam is also the name of Anthony Hecht's first son from a marriage that ended in divorce.
2. In Job 38:28, God speaks these words to Job.

They are our common lot.   30
During them, like as not,
You will dream of me.

When you are crouched away
In a strange clothes closet
Hiding from one who's "It"   35
And the dark crowds in,
Do not be afraid—
O, if you can, believe
In a father's love
That you shall know some day.   40

Think of the summer rain
Or seedpearls of the mist;
Seeing the beaded leaf,
Try to remember me.
From far away   45
I send my blessing out
To circle the great globe.
It shall reach you yet.

                                                          1967

The Dover Bitch[3]   *A Criticism of Life?*

For Andrews Wanning

So there stood Matthew Arnold and this girl
With the cliffs of England crumbling away behind them,
And he said to her, "Try to be true to me,
And I'll do the same for you, for things are bad
All over, etc., etc."   5
Well now, I knew this girl. It's true she had read
Sophocles in a fairly good translation
And caught that bitter allusion to the sea,
But all the time he was talking she had in mind
The notion of what his whiskers would feel like   10
On the back of her neck. She told me later on
That after a while she got to looking out
At the lights across the channel, and really felt sad,
Thinking of all the wine and enormous beds
And blandishments in French and the perfumes.   15
And then she got really angry. To have been brought
All the way down from London, and then be addressed
As a sort of mournful cosmic last resort
Is really tough on a girl, and she was pretty.
Anyway, she watched him pace the room   20
And finger his watch-chain and seem to sweat a bit,

---

3. Compare Matthew Arnold's poem "Dover Beach."

And then she said one or two unprintable things.
But you mustn't judge her by that. What I mean to say is,
She's really all right. I still see her once in a while
And she always treats me right. We have a drink   25
And I give her a good time, and perhaps it's a year
Before I see her again, but there she is,
Running to fat, but dependable as they come.
And sometimes I bring her a bottle of *Nuit d'Amour*.[4]

1967

A Hill

In Italy, where this sort of thing can occur,
I had a vision once—though you understand
It was nothing at all like Dante's, or the visions of saints,
And perhaps not a vision at all. I was with some friends,
Picking my way through a warm sunlit piazza   5
In the early morning. A clear fretwork of shadows
From huge umbrellas littered the pavement and made
A sort of lucent shallows in which was moored
A small navy of carts. Books, coins, old maps,
Cheap landscapes and ugly religious prints   10
Were all on sale. The colors and noise
Like the flying hands were gestures of exultation,
So that even the bargaining
Rose to the ear like a voluble godliness.
And then, when it happened, the noises suddenly stopped,   15
And it got darker; pushcarts and people dissolved
And even the great Farnese Palace[5] itself
Was gone, for all its marble; in its place
Was a hill, mole-colored and bare. It was very cold,
Close to freezing, with a promise of snow.   20
The trees were like old ironwork gathered for scrap
Outside a factory wall. There was no wind,
And the only sound for a while was the little click
Of ice as it broke in the mud under my feet.
I saw a piece of ribbon snagged on a hedge,   25
But no other sign of life. And then I heard
What seemed the crack of a rifle. A hunter, I guessed;
At least I was not alone. But just after that
Came the soft and papery crash
Of a great branch somewhere unseen falling to earth.   30

And that was all, except for the cold and silence
That promised to last forever, like the hill.

---

4. (French) "Night of Love," an ironic name for the bottle of wine.
5. One home of an aristocratic Italian family. Allessandro Farnese became Pope Paul III (1534–1549).
The family ruled Parma and Piacenza from 1545 to 1731.

Then prices came through, and fingers, and I was restored
To the sunlight and my friends. But for more than a week
I was scared by the plain bitterness of what I had seen.   35
All this happened about ten years ago,
And it hasn't troubled me since, but at last, today,
I remembered that hill; it lies just to the left
Of the road north of Poughkeepsie;[6] and as a boy
I stood before it for hours in wintertime.   40

                                                              1967

The Book of Yolek

Wir haben ein Gesetz,
Und nach dem Gesetz soll er sterben.[7]

The dowsed coals fume and hiss after your meal
Of grilled brook trout, and you saunter off for a walk
Down the fern trail, it doesn't matter where to,
Just so you're weeks and worlds away from home,
And among midsummer hills have set up camp   5
In the deep bronze glories of declining day.

You remember, peacefully, an earlier day
In childhood, remember a quite specific meal:
A corn roast and bonfire in summer camp.
That summer you got lost on a Nature Walk;   10
More than you dared admit, you thought of home;
No one else knows where the mind wanders to.

The fifth of August, 1942.
It was morning and very hot. It was the day
They came at dawn with rifles to The Home   15
For Jewish Children, cutting short the meal
Of bread and soup, lining them up to walk
In close formation off to a special camp.

How often you have thought about that camp,
As though in some strange way you were driven to,   20
And about the children, and how they were made to walk,
Yolek who had bad lungs, who wasn't a day
Over five years old, commanded to leave his meal
And shamble between armed guards to his long home.

We're approaching August again. It will drive home   25
The regulation torments of that camp
Yolek was sent to, his small, unfinished meal,

---

6. A town on the Hudson River in eastern New York State.
7. (German) "We have a law, / and according to the law he must die." This is the Jews' response to Pontius Pilate in John 19:7.

The electric fences, the numeral tattoo,
The quite extraordinary heat of the day
They all were forced to take that terrible walk.   30

Whether on a silent, solitary walk
Or among crowds, far off or safe at home,
You will remember, helplessly, that day,
And the smell of smoke, and the loudspeakers of the camp.
Wherever you are, Yolek will be there, too.   35
His unuttered name will interrupt your meal.

Prepare to receive him in your home some day.
Though they killed him in the camp they sent him to,
He will walk in as you're sitting down to a meal.

                                                                   1990

The Mysteries of Caesar

Known to the boys in his Latin class as "Sir,"
Balding, cologned, mild-mannered Mr. Sypher
Defied his sentence as a highschool lifer
With a fresh, carefully chosen boutonniere

As daily he heard the Helvetians plead their cause   5
In chains while captives were brought face to face
With the impositions of the ablative case,
The torts and tortures of grammatic laws.

Gracelessly stalled by vast impediments
Of words and baggage as by a conqueror's shackles,   10
O'Rourke, his face a celestial sphere of freckles
(One Gaul brought down by the pluperfect tense)

Submitted to all the galls and agonies
Of pained sight-readings from the *Gallic Wars*.[8]
They all bore dark, dishonorable scars   15
From what their textbook called an "exercise"

At least as draining as the quarter-mile.
But Mr. Sypher listened with superb
Imperial hauteur, with imperturb-
able patience, and a somewhat cryptic smile.   20

"Thompson," he'd murmur, "please instruct our class."
And Thompson would venture, timidly, much rattled,
"Caesar did withhold his men from battle,
And he did have enough in presentness

To prohibit the enemy from further wastings,   25
From foragings and rapines." And through a long

---

8. A chronicle of Julius Caesar's campaigns (58–51 B.C.E.) against the tribes of Gaul (early France).

Winter campaign of floundering, grief, and wrong,
That little army force-marched without resting.

"Please aid us, Jones," Mr. Sypher would beseech;
And Jones would tremulously undertake   30
To decipher the old Caesarian mystique
In the mixed medium of cracked parts of speech.

"Which things being known, when surest things accede,
He did deem enough of cause . . .," Jones volunteered.
Invariably it came out sounding weird,   35
The garbled utterance of some lesser breed

Without the law of common intercourse.
Long weeks of rain, followed by early frost
Had not improved morale, and yet the worst
Is not when there can always still be worse.   40

They rather liked Mr. Sypher, who was kind,
An easy grader. Was he a widower?
It was thought he had lost a child some years before.
Often they wondered what passed through his mind

As he calmly attended to their halt and crude   45
Efforts, not guessing one or another boy
Served as Antinous⁹ to that inward eye
Which is the pitiless bliss of solitude.

                                                             1996

Sarabande¹⁰ on Attaining the Age of Seventy-seven

> *The harbingers are come. See, see their mark:*
> *White is their colour, and behold my head.*¹¹

Long gone the smoke-and-pepper childhood smell
Of the smoldering immolation of the year,
Leaf-strewn in scattered grandeur where it fell,
Golden and poxed with frost, tarnished and sere.

And I myself have whitened in the weathers   5
Of heaped-up Januarys as they bequeath
The annual rings and wrongs that wring my withers,
Sober my thoughts and undermine my teeth.

The dramatis personae of our lives
Dwindle and wizen; familiar boyhood shames,   10
The tribulations one somehow survives,
Rise smokily from propitiatory flames

---

9. Author's note: "Antinous was the favorite of the emperor Hadrian, by whose command statues of the young man, after his death, were set up in major cities throughout the empire."
10. A sarabande was a stately dance of the seventeenth and eighteenth centuries.
11. From George Herbert (1593–1633), English religious poet.

Of our forgetfulness until we find
It becomes strangely easy to forgive
Even ourselves with his clouding of the mind,   15
This cinerous blur and smudge in which we live.

A turn, a glide, a quarter-turn and bow,
The stately dance advances; these are airs
Bone-deep and numbing as I should know by now,
Diminishing the cast, like musical chairs.   20

2001

RICHARD HUGO
(1923–1982)

In 1964, the University of Washington Press published *Five Poets of the Pacific Northwest*, edited by Robin Skelton, a volume that sampled the work of Kenneth O. Hanson, Richard Hugo, Carolyn Kizer, William Stafford, and David Wagoner. Each of these writers made significant contributions to the poetry of the region. Hugo, who spent most of his life in Washington State and Montana, left a body of work that is full of that area's flavor before the land was transformed by developers. Often describing sites of human failure, the poems are also enriched by the place names and colloquial language of the coast.

Hugo was born in Seattle and raised in particularly painful circumstances. His father, Richard Franklin Hogan, abandoned the family, and his mother, remarried to a man named Hugo, felt unable to care for her children. Richard was raised largely by his maternal grandparents, who did little to assuage his feelings of guilt for being such a burden at birth. His education was interrupted by World War II, where he saw service in Italy as a bombardier in the Army Air Corps. A modest man, he would recall not being very good at the job: "One day I missed not only the target in the Brenner Pass, but the entire Brenner Pass itself, thirteen miles wide at that point." However, in the course of the war he was promoted to First Lieutenant, and awarded both the Distinguished Flying Cross and the Air Medal.

After his discharge, Hugo returned to Seattle and matriculated at the University of Washington, where he studied with Theodore Roethke, who became a hugely important figure in his life and work. He earned a bachelor's degree in 1948, and in 1951 he married Barbara Williams. He also began to work for the Boeing Aircraft Company, taking classes in his spare time. He earned a master's degree in 1952, but would wait years to make professional use of it. He worked at Boeing as a technical writer until 1963, when he had established himself sufficiently as a poet to try teaching creative writing at the University of Montana in Missoula. Hugo taught at Montana from 1964 until his death from leukemia at age fifty-eight in 1982. His first marriage ended in divorce in 1966, and he married Ripley Schemm in 1974.

Often writing in conversational blank verse stanzas, Hugo found most of his subjects close to home. As he wrote in his important critical book, *The Triggering Town* (1979), "I suspect that the true or valid subject is one in which physical characteristics or details correspond to attitudes the poet has toward the world and himself. For me, a small town that has seen better days often works." These locations of communal tragedy no doubt reflected Hugo's inner psychological state, his own feelings of failure or inadequacy. The Northwest where Hugo grew up was far less settled and sophisticated than it is today, and his Seattle still had some of the atmosphere of a frontier city. He also came to know small towns from the Skagit Valley and the Cascade Mountains to the plains of eastern Montana— their transience, their ruggedness, and their spare survivals.

Among his books of poems were *A Run of Jacks* (1961), *Death of the Kapowsin Tavern* (1965), *The Lady in Kicking Horse Reservoir* (1973), *What Thou Lovest Well, Remains American* (1975), and the openly confessional *31 Letters and 13 Dreams* (1977). His wartime service informed the collection called *Good Luck in Cracked Italian* (1969), and his travels largely in Scotland on a Guggenheim Fellowship resulted in the poems of *The Right Madness on Skye* (1980). *White Center* (1980) revisited landscapes of his earlier poems in a somewhat happier mood. Following his posthumous collection, *Sea Lanes Out* (1983), W. W. Norton published *Making Certain It Goes On: The Collected Poems of Richard Hugo* (1984). His mystery novel, *Death and the Good Life,* appeared in 1981. After his death another novel and a volume of autobiography appeared.

Hugo's legacy is partly in the poems and prose he left behind, and partly in his influence as a teacher. His essays in *The Triggering Town* are about teaching as well as writing and are full of practical advice from a man who had known several different careers. Impatient with some forms of avant-garde art, he wrote, "Quest for self is fundamental to poetry. What passes for experimentation is often an elaborate method of avoiding one's feelings at all costs." But Hugo was equally impatient with certain acknowledged masters in the mainstream. The voice he sought in poem after poem was somewhere between formality and the natural speech of an ordinary man.

◄◦►━━◄◦►

Degrees of Gray in Philipsburg

You might come here Sunday on a whim.
Say your life broke down. The last good kiss
you had was years ago. You walk these streets
laid out by the insane, past hotels
that didn't last, bars that did, the tortured try   5
of local drivers to accelerate their lives.
Only churches are kept up. The jail
turned seventy this year. The only prisoner
is always in, not knowing what he's done.

The principal supporting business now   10
is rage. Hatred of the various grays
the mountain sends, hatred of the mill,
the Silver Bill repeal, the best liked girls
who leave each year for Butte. One good
restaurant and bars can't wipe the boredom out.   15
The 1907 boom, eight going silver mines,
a dance floor built on springs—
all memory resolves itself in gaze,

in panoramic green you know the cattle eat
or two stacks high above the town,   20
two dead kilns, the huge mill in collapse
for fifty years that won't fall finally down.

Isn't this your life? That ancient kiss
still burning out your eyes? Isn't this defeat
so accurate, the church bell simply seems   25
a pure announcement: ring and no one comes?
Don't empty houses ring? Are magnesium
and scorn sufficient to support a town,
not just Philipsburg, but towns
of towering blondes, good jazz and booze   30
the world will never let you have
until the town you came from dies inside?

Say no to yourself. The old man, twenty
when the jail was built, still laughs
although his lips collapse. Someday soon,   35
he says, I'll go to sleep and not wake up.
You tell him no. You're talking to yourself.
The car that brought you here still runs.
The money you buy lunch with,
No matter where it's mined, is silver   40
And the girl who serves you food
Is slender and her red hair lights the wall.

                                                             1973

Driving Montana

The day is a woman who loves you. Open.
Deer drink close to the road and magpies
spray from your car. Miles from any town
your radio comes in strong, unlikely
Mozart from Belgrade, rock and roll   5
from Butte. Whatever the next number,
you want to hear it. Never has your Buick
found this forward a gear. Even
the tuna salad in Reedpoint is good.

Towns arrive ahead of imagined schedule.   10
Absorakee at one. Or arrive so late—
Silesia at nine—you recreate the day.
Where did you stop along the road
and have fun? Was there a runaway horse?
Did you park at that house, the one   15
alone in a void of grain, white with green
trim and red fence, where you know you lived
once? You remembered the ringing creek,
the soft brown forms of far off bison.

You must have stayed hours, then drove on.   20
In the motel you know you'd never seen it before.

Tomorrow will open again, the sky wide
as the mouth of a wild girl, friable
clouds you lose yourself to. You are lost
in miles of land without people, without   25
one fear of being found, in the dash
of rabbits, soar of antelope, swirl
merge and clatter of streams.

1973

◦━◄ LOUIS SIMPSON ►━◦
(b. 1923)

Louis Simpson's life and work are marked by frequent changes. Like many other
poets of his generation, he began as a formalist, often using rhyme and meter, but
in midcareer he underwent a radical aesthetic transformation. For a while associated with deep image poets like James Wright and Robert Bly, he has in recent
decades emerged as a poet of free verse suburban narratives, frequently told with
a Chekhovian obliqueness and humor. As such, he has produced his most distinctive and original work—understated, even prosaic, conveying aspects of contemporary American life most poets rarely touch upon.

    Yet Simpson had the upbringing of an English colonial schoolboy. Born in Ja-
maica, he was the second son of Aston Simpson, a prosperous lawyer, and Ros-
alind Marantz Simpson, a Russian Jewish immigrant who had been a dancer and
aspiring opera singer. (His mother later called herself De Marantz to give an aristocratic air to her business ventures.) His privileged childhood did not impede his
awareness of racial and class differences on the island, and his mother's stories of
Russia were fraught with poverty and suffering. When Simpson was seven, his parents divorced. "No one explained it to me—one day I had a mother, the next she
was gone." She moved away to Toronto and New York. In addition to this trauma,
Louis and his brother did not get along with their stepmother and her children.
They were soon alienated from their own home. At age nine he began to attend
Munro college, a boarding school a hundred miles away. In various memoirs he
described the strict, traditional curriculum and his budding love of literature.

    When his father died suddenly of complications from diabetes, Louis and his
brother learned that they had been left out of the family estate. While publishing
poems as a teenager, Simpson thought of joining his mother in New York. At age
seventeen, Louis left Jamaica for New York and a new life. At Columbia University he studied with Lionel Trilling and Mark Van Doren. When America entered
World War II, Simpson decided to ignore his foreign birthright, registered for the
draft, and in 1943 was inducted into the U.S. Army. For the next three years he
served in the 101st Airborne Division, seeing combat in Normandy, Holland, Belgium, and Germany. He was awarded both the Purple Heart and the Bronze Star
with Oak Leaf for valor, and he left the army a sergeant. The shock of war was
not easy to shrug off, however. While back at Columbia to finish his degree, Simpson suffered a nervous breakdown that required hospitalization.

A disability pension and the G.I. Bill allowed him to travel to France, where he briefly studied at the Sorbonne. There he began to recall the war in dreams and poems, starting with the ballad "Carentan O Carentan." His first collection, *The Arrivistes* (French for "go-getters"), was privately printed in 1949. He acquired a New York distributor for the book and it was favorably reviewed by Randall Jarrell. Yet six difficult years would pass before Simpson published his second collection, *Good News of Death and Other Poems,* in a Scribner's series called *Poets of Today.* During this time he continued his studies toward a Ph.D. at Columbia and worked as a book editor at Bobbs-Merrill in New York (1950–1955). With Donald Hall and Robert Pack, he co-edited *New Poets of England and America* (1957), an important anthology that showcased a new generation of poets writing in rhyme and meter. Simpson's third collection of poems, *A Dream of Governors,* appeared in 1959. That same year he began to teach at the University of California, Berkeley, where he remained until 1967. His one novel, the highly autobiographical *Riverside Drive,* appeared in 1962.

By this time, critics had begun to notice changes in Simpson's verse style. "At the end of the 1950s," he recalled, "I felt the need to express my thoughts more intimately, and began writing in free forms and a conversational style." Simpson had been reading Whitman, and he combined the earlier poet's vision with his own experience in a searching reexamination of his adoptive country. His new collection, *At the End of the Open Road* (1963), won the Pulitzer Prize. A *Selected Poems* appeared two years later. In 1967 Simpson began to teach on Long Island at SUNY Stony Brook. He remained there until his retirement from teaching in 1993. Among his many poetry collections since winning the Pulitzer, the most significant were *Searching for the Ox* (1976) and *Collected Poems* (1988). Between these two volumes, Simpson had perfected the minimalist verse narrative that defined his later poetry. Narrative has always interested him—in addition to his novel there have been several volumes of autobiographical prose, and early in his career he published "The Runner," a narrative in blank verse about a soldier in combat during World War II.

Early in the Morning

Early in the morning
The dark Queen said,
"The trumpets are warning
There's trouble ahead."
Spent with carousing,   5
With wine-soaked wits,
Antony drowsing
Whispered, "It's
Too cold a morning
To get out of bed."   10

The army's retreating.
The fleet has fled,
Caesar is beating
His drums through the dead.

"Antony, horses!   15
We'll get away,
Gather our forces
For another day . . ."
"It's a cold morning,"
Antony said.   20

Caesar Augustus
Cleared his phlegm.
"Corpses disgust us.
Cover them."
Caesar Augustus   25
In his time lay
Dying, and just as
Cold as they,
On the cold morning
Of a cold day.   30

                                                  1955

The Man Who Married Magdalene

The man who married Magdalene
Had not forgiven her.
God might pardon every sin . . .
Love is no pardoner.

Her hands were hollow, pale, and blue,   5
Her mouth like watered wine.
He watched to see if she were true
And waited for a sign.

It was old harlotry, he guessed,
That drained her strength away,   10
So gladly for the dark she dressed,
So sadly for the day.

Their quarrels made her dull and weak
And soon a man might fit
A penny in the hollow cheek   15
And never notice it.

At last, as they exhausted slept,
Death granted the divorce,
And nakedly the woman leapt
Upon that narrow horse.   20

But when he woke and woke alone
He wept and would deny
The loose behavior of the bone
And the immodest thigh.

                                                  1955

To the Western World

A siren sang, and Europe turned away
From the high castle and the shepherd's crook.
Three caravels went sailing to Cathay
On the strange ocean, and the captains shook
Their banners out across the Mexique Bay.   5

And in our early days we did the same.
Remembering our fathers in their wreck
We crossed the sea from Palos where they came
And saw, enormous to the little deck,
A shore in silence waiting for a name.   10

The treasures of Cathay were never found.
In this America, this wilderness
Where the axe echoes with a lonely sound,
The generations labor to possess
And grave by grave we civilize the ground.   15

1959

American Poetry

Whatever it is, it must have
A stomach that can digest
Rubber, coal, uranium, moons, poems.

Like the shark, it contains a shoe.
It must swim for miles through the desert   5
Uttering cries that are almost human.

1963

My Father in the Night Commanding No

My father in the night commanding No
Has work to do. Smoke issues from his lips;
        He reads in silence.
The frogs are croaking and the street lamps glow.

And then my mother winds the gramophone;   5
The Bride of Lammermoor begins to shriek—
        Or reads a story
About a prince, a castle, and a dragon.

The moon is glittering above the hill.
I stand before the gateposts of the King—   10
        So runs the story—
Of Thule, at midnight when the mice are still.

And I have been in Thule! It has come true—
The journey and the danger of the world,
        All that there is   15
To bear and to enjoy, endure and do.

Landscapes, seascapes . . . where have I been led?
The names of cities—Paris, Venice, Rome—
    Held out their arms.
A feathered god, seductive, went ahead.   20

Here is my house. Under a red rose tree
A child is swinging; another gravely plays.
    They are not surprised
That I am here; they were expecting me.

And yet my father sits and reads in silence,   25
My mother sheds a tear, the moon is still,
    And the dark wind
Is murmuring that nothing ever happens.

Beyond his jurisdiction as I move
Do I not prove him wrong? And yet, it's true   30
    They will not change
There, on the stage of terror and of love.

The actors in that playhouse always sit
In fixed positions—father, mother, child
    With painted eyes.   35
How sad it is to be a little puppet!

Their heads are wooden. And you once pretended
To understand them! Shake them as you will,
    They cannot speak.
Do what you will, the comedy is ended.   40

Father, why did you work? Why did you weep,
Mother? Was the story so important?
    "Listen!" the wind
Said to the children, and they fell asleep.

                           1963

The Unwritten Poem

You will never write the poem about Italy.
What Socrates said about love
is true of poetry—where is it?
Not in the beautiful faces and distant scenery
but the one who writes and loves.   5

In your life here, on this street
where the houses from the outside
are all alike, and so are the people.
Inside, the furniture is dreadful—
floc on the walls, and huge color television.   10

To love and write unrequited
is the poet's fate. Here you'll need

all your ardor and ingenuity.
This is the front and these are the heroes—
a life beginning with "Hi!" and ending with "So long!"   15

You must rise to the sound of the alarm
and march to catch the 6:20—
watch as they ascend the station platform
and, grasping briefcases, pass beyond your gaze
and hurl themselves into the flames.   20

1983

A Clearing

I had come to Australia
for ten weeks, as a guest of the state.
My duties were light: to confer
with students. They didn't want to—
they came once or twice, that was all.   5

One night someone knocked: a student
with some poems she'd like me to see.
The next day I observed her
in the dining room, and went over.
"I liked" I began to say . . .   10
She lifted her hands, imploring me
not to speak. All around her
they were talking about the usual subjects,
motorbikes and football.
If it got around that she wrote poems . . .   15

At night I would sit in my room
reading, keeping a journal,
and, with the aid of a map,
trying to learn the positions
of the southern constellations.   20
I'd look at them on the map,
then go outside and try to find them
in the sky, before I forgot.

I had recently been divorced
and was starting a new life,   25
as they say. The world lies before you,
where to live and what to be.
A fireman? An explorer?
An astronaut? Then you look in the mirror.
It was night sweats. Listening   30
to an echo of the end.

✦

Roger had a live-in girlfriend.
They asked if I'd like to go with them
to a party, and sleep over.

He drove. I looked at the gum trees.   35
Not the Outback, but country . . .
cattle and kangaroos,
and flies, getting in your eyes,
ears, nose, and mouth.
Once, talking to a sheepherder,   40
I watched a fly crawl over his face
from his eye to his mouth,
and start walking back
before he brushed it off.
They learn to put up with nature   45
and not make a fuss like us.

We arrived. I was introduced,
and they made up a bed for me
on the porch at the back.
Then the party began to arrive: 50
Australians, lean and athletic.
They put a tape on the stereo,
turned it up full blast,
and danced, or stood and shouted
to each other above the noise,   55

I danced with two or three women
and tried shouting. Then I went
and sat on the bed on the porch.
There was nowhere to go, no door
I could close to shut out the noise.   60

♦

So I went for a walk
in the dark, away from the sound.
There were gum trees, wind rustling
the leaves. Or was it snakes?

There are several venomous kinds.   65
The taipan. There's a story
about a child who was sitting
on a log and fell backward
onto a taipan. It struck him
twenty-three times.   70
There's the tiger snake and the brown.
When they have finished telling you
about snakes, they start on spiders.

You don't need these—you have only to walk
into the bush. There are stories   75

about campers who did, and were lost
and never seen again.

All this was on my mind.
I stepped carefully, keeping the lights
of the house behind me in sight.   80
And when I saw a clearing
in the trees, I walked to it.

I stood in the middle of the clearing
looking at the sky. It was glittering
with unknown constellations.   85
Everything I had ever known
seemed to have disappeared.
And who was I, standing there
in the middle of Australia
at night? I had ceased to exist.   90
There was only whatever it was
that was looking at the sky
and listening to the wind.

After a while I broke away
and went back to the lights and the party.   95
A month later I left Australia.

But ever since, to this day,
there has been a place in my mind,
a clearing in the shadows,
and above it, stars and constellations   100
so bright and thick they seem to rustle.
And beyond them . . . infinite space,
eternity, you name it.

There's nothing that stands between me
and it, whatever it is.   105

1995

◄ DONALD JUSTICE ►
(b. 1925)

One of the most distinctive and accomplished poets of his generation, Donald Justice is also a painter and composer, and those two arts have exerted profound influences upon his writing. His quiet, carefully wrought poems seem composed with a musician's touch for tonality and a painter's deliberate eye. A Southerner, he evokes nostalgia for the lost world of childhood, but he manages to summon powerful emotions without sentimentality. Often impersonal and avoiding overt autobiography, Justice's poems nonetheless convey their highly personal emotions as musical compositions do, working on our nerves in ways we might not fully comprehend. His poems are often haunted by a rueful sense of lost possibility and passing time.

Justice was born in Miami, Florida, where his father worked as a carpenter. While attending public schools, he took piano lessons and developed a serious interest in music. At the University of Miami, where he received his bachelor's degree in 1945, he studied with the Modernist composer Carl Ruggles, but poetry gradually became his primary interest. He was especially attracted to the works of Charles Baudelaire, Wallace Stevens, and W. H. Auden, and he ultimately decided to continue his studies in English, although he never abandoned his interest in musical composition.

Justice earned a master's degree at the University of North Carolina in 1947, and that same summer married Jean Catherine Ross, a writer, with whom he had one son. The following academic year, Justice studied with Yvor Winters at Stanford, then moved on to the what is now the University of Iowa in Iowa city, earning a Ph.D. in English in 1954. Iowa already had the first major program in creative writing, and in 1957 Justice returned there to teach. Except for sabbaticals or visiting professorships at other institutions, Justice remained primarily at the Iowa Writers' Workshop for a quarter-century, becoming perhaps the most influential poetry teacher of the postwar era. His students would include Mark Strand, Charles Wright, Jorie Graham, William Logan, and Mark Jarman. In 1982 he returned to this native Florida, finishing his teaching career at the University of Florida, Gainesville. After retiring in 1992, he returned to Iowa City where he writes, paints, and composes.

Justice's first collection of poems, *The Summer Anniversaries* (1960), won the Lamont Award from the Academy of American Poets. Although he would later appear to criticize his early poems in a line of verse—"How fashionably sad those early poems are!"—several of them are among his best works, such as "On the Death of Friends in Childhood" and "Counting the Mad." *The Summer Anniversaries* is notable not only for its formal range, but also for the restless experimentation that characterizes Justice's work. Few poets of equal distinction have ever shown such a strong disinclination to repeat themselves. Another characteristic that arose early is Justice's delight in borrowing from other poets—demonstrating T. S. Eliot's dictum, "Immature poets imitate; mature poets steal; bad poets deface what they take, and good poets make it into something better or at least different."

Never a prolific poet, always as demanding of himself as he was of his students, Justice waited seven years to publish another collection, although these gaps between full-length books were punctuated by the publication of important chapbooks in limited editions. *Night Light* (1967) contains poems of darker moods and freer range, and *Departures* (1973) provides further extensions of both form and content. Written almost entirely in free verse, it contains poems in the surrealist mode as well as others composed by aleatory, or chance, procedures. Critics who objected to rhyme and meter were happy to see Justice writing in seemingly open forms, but many failed to understand that he always regarded any formal technique as a viable means to achieve memorable utterance. In an interview he said, "Probably more than other poets I know I play games in my poems (as I do in my life), and one of the unwritten rules of the game for me, as I like it played, is that you can risk this much personality or that much confession if the voice is promised to be that of someone else to start with." Thus, in his "Variations on a Text by Vallejo," Justice used a literary borrowing to compel new music that was at some level personal.

When Justice won the Pulitzer Prize for his *Selected Poems* (1979), the award seemed an acknowledgment that he had become one of the country's indispensable poets, a master of what Emily Grosholz would call "illusionless wit." His next collection, *The Sunset Maker* (1987), concluded with two prose pieces building on his themes of music and memory. *A Donald Justice Reader: Selected Poetry and Prose*, appeared in 1991, the same year in which he won the Bollingen Prize. His *New and Selected Poems* (1995) led to a Lannan Literary Award in 1996. The fifteen new poems collected in that volume convey again Justice's strong sense of the ephemeral, but also his faith in what endures. The book begins with the ironic epigram "On a Picture by Burchfield": "Writhe no more, little flowers. Art keeps long hours. / Already your agony has outlasted ours."

Those who know Justice often recount his love of high-stakes poker as well as music and painting, and perhaps there is something of the card-player's skill in his poems—the ability to mask himself, revealing only what is necessary for a given effect. It should also be remarked that he has always been a generous supporter of good poetry where he finds it and has championed several poets in danger of neglect. He was the first to champion the posthumous reputation of the important poet Weldon Kees by editing and introducing Kees's *Collected Poems* (1960)—a service Justice has performed for several other dead writers. With Robert Mezey he edited *The Collected Poems of Henri Coulette* (1990) and with others *The Comma after Love: Selected Poems of Raeburn Miller* (1994). He also collected *The Last Nostalgia* (1999), poems of Joe Bolton, a former student who committed suicide. To have rescued these poets from oblivion is by itself no small contribution.

Counting the Mad

This one was put in a jacket,
This one was sent home,
This one was given bread and meat
But would eat none,
And this one cried No No No No   5
All day long.

This one looked at the window
As though it were a wall,
This one saw things that were not there,
This one things that were,   10
And this one cried No No No No
All day long.

This one thought himself a bird,
This one a dog,
And this one thought himself a man,   15

An ordinary man,
And cried and cried No No No No
All day long.

1960

In Bertram's Garden

Jane looks down at her organdy skirt,
As if *it* somehow were the thing disgraced,
For being there, on the floor, in the dirt,
And she catches it up about her waist,
Smooths it out along one hip,   5
And pulls it over the crumpled slip.

On the porch, green-shuttered, cool,
Asleep is Bertram, that bronze boy,
Who, having wound her around a spool,
Sends her spinning like a toy   10
Out to the garden, all alone,
To sit and weep on a bench of stone.

Soon the purple dark must bruise
Lily and bleeding heart and rose,
And the little Cupid lose   15
Eyes and ears and chin and nose,
And Jane lie down with others soon
Naked to the naked moon.

1960

On the Death of Friends in Childhood

We shall not ever meet them bearded in heaven,
Nor sunning themselves among the bald of hell;
If anywhere, in the deserted schoolyard at twilight,
Forming a ring, perhaps, or joining hands
In games whose very names we have forgotten.   5
Come, memory, let us seek them there in the shadows.

1960

But That Is Another Story

I do not think the ending can be right.
How can they marry and live happily
Forever, these who were so passionate
At chapter's end? Once they are settled in
The quiet country house, what will they do,   5
So many miles from anywhere?
Those blond ancestral ghosts crowding the stair,
Surely they disapprove? Ah me,
I fear love will catch cold and die

From pacing naked through those drafty halls   10
Night after night. Poor Frank! Poor Imogene!
Before them now their lives
Stretch empty as great Empire beds
After the lovers rise and the damp sheets
Are stripped by envious chambermaids.   15

And if the first night passes brightly enough,
What with the bonfires lit with old love letters,
That is no inexhaustible fuel, perhaps?
God knows how it must end, not I.
Will Frank walk out one day   20
Alone through the ruined orchard with his stick,
Strewing the path with lissome heads
Of buttercups? Will Imogene
Conceal in the crotches of old trees
Love notes for beardless gardeners and such?   25
Meanwhile they quarrel and make it up
Only to quarrel again. A sudden storm
Pulls the last fences down. Now moonstruck sheep
Stray through the garden all night peering in
At the exhausted lovers where they sleep.   30

1967

Men at Forty

Men at forty
Learn to close softly
The doors to rooms they will not be
Coming back to.

At rest on a stair landing,   5
They feel it moving
Beneath them now like the deck of a ship,
Though the swell is gentle.

And deep in mirrors
They rediscover   10
The face of the boy as he practices tying
His father's tie there in secret,

And the face of that father,
Still warm with the mystery of lather.
They are more fathers than sons themselves now.   15
Something is filling them, something

That is like the twilight sound
Of the crickets, immense,
Filling the woods at the foot of the slope
Behind their mortgaged houses.   20

1967

Variations on a Text by Vallejo[1]

Me moriré en Paris con aguacero . . .

I will die in Miami in the sun,
On a day when the sun is very bright,
A day like the days I remember, a day like other days,
A day that nobody knows or remembers yet,
And the sun will be bright then on the dark glasses of strangers   5
And in the eyes of a few friends from my childhood
And of the surviving cousins by the graveside,
While the diggers, standing apart, in the still shade of the palms,
Rest on their shovels, and smoke,
Speaking in Spanish softly, out of respect.   10

I think it will be on a Sunday like today,
Except that the sun will be out, the rain will have stopped,
And the wind that today made all the little shrubs kneel down;
And I think it will be Sunday because today,
When I took out this paper and began to write,   15
Never before had anything looked so blank,
My life, these words, the paper, the gray Sunday;
And my dog, quivering under a table because of the storm,
Looked up at me, not understanding,
And my son read on without speaking, and my wife slept.   20

Donald Justice is dead. One Sunday the sun came out,
It shone on the bay, it shone on the white buildings,
The cars moved down the street slowly as always, so many,
Some with their headlights on in spite of the sun,
And after awhile the diggers with their shovels   25
Walked back to the graveside through the sunlight,
And one of them put his blade into the earth
To lift a few clods of dirt, the black marl[2] of Miami,
And scattered the dirt, and spat,
Turning away abruptly, out of respect.

1973

Psalm and Lament

Hialeah, Florida
in memory of my mother (1897–1974)

The clocks are sorry, the clocks are very sad.
One stops, one goes on striking the wrong hours.

---

1. César Vallejo (1895–1938), Peruvian poet. The original Vallejo text says that the poet will die in
Paris on a rainy Thursday.
2. Soil rich in clay.

And the grass burns terribly in the sun,
The grass turns yellow secretly at the roots.

Now suddenly the yard chairs look empty, the sky looks empty,   5
The sky looks vast and empty.

Out on Red Road the traffic continues; everything continues.
Nor does memory sleep; it goes on.

Out spring the butterflies of recollection,
And I think that for the first time I understand   10

The beautiful ordinary light of this patio
And even perhaps the dark rich earth of a heart.

(The bedclothes, they say, had been pulled down.
I will not describe it. I do not want to describe it.

No, but the sheets were drenched and twisted.   15
They were the very handkerchiefs of grief.)

Let summer come now with its schoolboy trumpets and fountains.
But the years are gone, the years are finally over.

And there is only
This long desolation of flower-bordered sidewalks   20

That runs to the corner, turns, and goes on,
That disappears and goes on

Into the black oblivion of a neighborhood and a world
Without billboards or yesterdays.

Sometimes a sad moon comes and waters the roof tiles.   25
But the years are gone. There are no more years.

1987

◄ CAROLYN KIZER ►
(b. 1925)

Well-respected for her witty feminist perspective and sophisticated poetic style, Carolyn Ashley Kizer grew up in a cultivated household that helped foster her gifts. She was born in Spokane, Washington, the only child of parents who married late and dedicated themselves to her education. Although Kizer's literary interests were encouraged by her father, a successful civil liberties lawyer, her accomplished mother—who before her marriage had earned a doctorate in biology from Stanford University, studied art and philosophy at Harvard University, and worked as a union organizer—was an even stronger influence. Kizer later claimed that she developed her own identity as a poet only after her mother's death. But she also acknowledges that her habits and goals as a poet were shaped by her mother's high expectations and love for literature. Kizer's intellectual curiosity was also stimulated by her parents' friendships with the poet Vachel Lindsay, the social philosopher and architect

Lewis Mumford, the composer and pianist Percy Grainger, and a host of visiting diplomats and intellectuals from Asia and Europe.

Kizer worked on her writing at Sarah Lawrence College, and in her sophomore year she had a poem accepted by the *New Yorker*. In an autobiographical essay, "The Stories of My Life," she remarks that the poem wasn't very good but that "I began, very tentatively and shyly, to think of myself as someone who might become a poet. The materials were all in place: my family, my imagination, my reading. Now all I needed was to learn how to do it.

After receiving her bachelor's degree from Sarah Lawrence in 1945, Kizer received a Chinese cultural fellowship to do graduate work for a year in comparative literature at Columbia University, and she spent some of that time studying in Taiwan. Returning to the Pacific Northwest in 1946, she did graduate work for a year at the University of Washington, coming back in 1953 to study poetry with Theodore Roethke. In 1948 she married Charles Bullitt, with whom she had three children. After a divorce in 1954 she intensified her literary activities, founding the literary journal *Poetry Northwest* in 1959 (which she edited until 1965) and writing the poems that would appear in her first full-length book, *The Ungrateful Garden* (1961). From 1964 to 1965, she lived in Pakistan as a literature specialist under the auspices of the U.S. State Department, and her government affiliation continued in 1970 when she served as the first director of literary programs sponsored by the National Endowment for the Arts. From 1970 to 1974 she taught at the University of North Carolina, Chapel Hill, and in 1975 she married the architect John Marshall Woodbridge and gave up full-time teaching. Relocating to California in 1977, the couple lived first in Berkeley and then in 1987 moved to Sonoma.

Kizer has published many books of poetry, including *Knock upon Silence* (1965), *Midnight Was My Cry* (1971), *Yin* (1984), *Mermaids in the Basement: Poems for Women* (1984), *The Nearness of You: Poems for Men* (1986), *Harping On* (1996), and *Cool, Calm & Collected: Poems 1960–2000* (2000). She has also edited several anthologies, published a collection of her translations, *Carrying Over: Poems from the Chinese, Urdu, Macedonian, Yiddish and French African* (1988), and released two books of essays and reviews, *Proses: On Poems & Poets* (1993) and *Picking and Choosing: Essays on Prose* (1995). Characterized by intelligence, humane wit, graceful style, and a poised clarity gained from long familiarity with Asian literature, Kizer's poems often explore feminist themes such as relationships between mothers and daughters, female friendship, and women's perspectives on men. Although Kizer's two 1984 books, *Mermaids in the Basement*, which reprinted poems about women from her previous collections, and *Yin*, solidified her reputation as a feminist poet, her feminist slant was evident early on in the themes she chose to address and the conclusions she drew.

Receiving the Pulitzer Prize in 1985 for *Yin*, Kizer's literary prominence increased substantially over the next decade, culminating in her 1995 appointment as a Chancellor of the Academy of American Poets. But Kizer, along with Maxine Kumin, resigned from this prestigious post in 1998 to protest the absence of women and minorities on the board and among the recipients of the Academy's major awards. The resulting public controversy led to reforms in the Academy's system and management. Kizer's other honors include the American Academy and Institute of Arts and Letters Award and the Poetry Society of America's Frost Medal for Lifetime Achievement.

Whether writing in free verse or traditional form, Kizer is a perfectionist whose complex verbal harmonies and rich diction deepen the implications of the arguments she develops. Unlike many poets of her generation, Kizer feels comfortable making explicit arguments in her poetry, not only in her satirical work such as her best-known poem, "Pro Femina," but also in her lyrics and poems about personal experience. Her choice to reprint in *Proses* not one but two reviews of Maynard Mack's biography of Alexander Pope reveals her affinity for Pope's combination "of satiric with lyric" modes of writing and also for his exacting habits of revision. "Pope was quite aware," she remarked, "as most working poets are, that the lines which seem to the reader or critic most spontaneous, graceful and natural are often the ones laboriously revised, far into the night, with an obbligato of curses and an outpouring of sweat." Like Pope, Kizer also merges the satiric with the lyric, tempering her wit through sensuous description and precise observations of human feeling and the natural world. Although Kizer is not often described as a nature poet, the workings of the natural world provide a background against which she contemplates human behavior.

<hr>

FROM Pro Femina

I.

From Sappho[1] to myself, consider the fate of women.
How unwomanly to discuss it! Like a noose or an albatross necktie
The clinical sobriquet hangs us: cod-piece coveters.[2]
Never mind these epithets; I myself have collected some honeys.
Juvenal[3] set us apart in denouncing our vices   5
Which had grown, in part, from having been set apart:
Women abused their spouses, cuckolded them, even plotted
To poison them. Sensing, behind the violence of his manner—
"Think I'm crazy or drunk?"—his emotional stake in us,
As we forgive Strindberg and Nietzsche,[4] we forgive all those   10
Who cannot forget us. We *are* hyenas. Yes, we admit it.

While men have politely debated free will, we have howled for it,
Howl still, pacing the centuries, tragedy heroines.
Some who sat quietly in the corner with their embroidery
Were Defarges,[5] stabbing the wool with the names of their ancient   15
Oppressors, who ruled by the divine right of the male—
I'm impatient of interruptions! I'm aware there were millions

1. Greek poetess of the 7th century B.C.E.
2. Cloth covering for male genitalia, worn in the Renaissance.
3. Roman satirist, 60?–140? C.E.
4. August Strindberg (1849–1912), Swedish dramatist known for dark portrayals of marriage; Friedrich Nietzsche (1844–1900), German philosopher.
5. Madame Defarge, character in Charles Dickens' novel *A Tale of Two Cities,* known for knitting during executions.

Of mutes for every Saint Joan or sainted Jane Austen,
Who, vague-eyed and acquiescent, worshiped God as a man.
I'm not concerned with those cabbageheads, not truly feminine   20
But neutered by labor. I mean real women, like *you* and like *me*.

Freed in fact, not in custom, lifted from furrow and scullery,
Not obliged, now, to be the pot for the annual chicken,
Have we begun to arrive in time? With our well-known
Respect for life because it hurts so much to come out with it;   25
Disdainful of "sovereignty," "national honor" and other abstractions;
We can say, like the ancient Chinese to successive waves of invaders,
"Relax, and let us absorb you. You can learn temperance
In a more temperate climate." Give us just a few decades
Of grace, to encourage the fine art of acquiescence   30
And we might save the race. Meanwhile, observe our creative chaos,
Flux, efflorescence—whatever you care to call it!

II.

I take as my theme "The Independent Woman,"
Independent but maimed: observe the exigent neckties
Choking violet writers; the sad slacks of stipple-faced matrons;   35
Indigo intellectuals, crop-haired and callous-toed,
Cute spectacles, chewed cuticles, aced out by full-time beauties
In the race for a male. Retreating to drabness, bad manners
And sleeping with manuscripts. Forgive our transgressions
Of old gallantries as we hitch in chairs, light our own cigarettes,   40
Not expecting your care, having forfeited it by trying to get even.

But we need dependency, cosseting and well-treatment.
So do men sometimes. Why don't they admit it?
We will be cows for a while, because babies howl for us,
Be kittens or bitches, who want to eat grass now and then   45
For the sake of our health. But the role of pastoral heroine
Is not permanent, Jack. We want to get back to the meeting.

Knitting booties and brows, tartars or termagants,[6] ancient
Fertility symbols, chained to our cycle, released
Only in part by devices of hygiene and personal daintiness,   50
Strapped into our girdles, held down, yet uplifted by man's
Ingenious constructions, holding coiffures in a breeze,
Hobbled and swathed in whimsy, tripping on feminine
Shoes with fool heels, losing our lipsticks, you, me,
In ephemeral stockings, clutching our handbags and packages.   55

Our masks, always in peril of smearing or cracking,
In need of continuous check in the mirror or silverware,
Keep us in thrall to ourselves, concerned with our surfaces.
Look at man's uniform drabness, his impersonal envelope!

6. Barbarians and shrewish women.

Over chicken wrists or meek shoulders, a formal, hard-fibered assurance.   60
The drape of the male is designed to achieve self-forgetfulness.
So, Sister, forget yourself a few times and see where it gets you:
Up the creek, alone with your talent, sans everything else.
You can wait for the menopause, and catch up on your reading.
So primp, preen, prink, pluck and prize your flesh,   65
All posturings! All ravishment! All sensibility!
Meanwhile, have you used your mind today?
What pomegranate raised you from the dead?[7]
Springing, full-grown, from your own head, Athena?

III.

I will speak about women of letters, for I'm in the racket.   70
Our biggest successes to date? Old maids to a woman.
And our saddest conspicuous failures? The married spinsters
On loan to the husbands they treated like surrogate fathers.
Think of that crew of self-pitiers, not-very-distant,
Who carried the torch for themselves and got first-degree burns.   75
Or the sad sonneteers, toast-and-teasdales we loved at thirteen;
Middle-aged virgins seducing the puerile anthologists
Through lust-of-the-mind; barbiturate-drenched Camilles[8]
With continuous periods, murmuring softly on sofas
When poetry wasn't a craft but a sickly effluvium,   80
The air thick with incense, musk, and emotional blackmail.

I suppose they reacted from an earlier womanly modesty
When too many girls were scabs to their stricken sisterhood,
Impugning our sex to stay in good with the men,
Commencing their insecure bluster. How they must have swaggered   85
When women themselves endorsed their own inferiority!
Vestals, vassals and vessels, rolled into several,
They took notes in rolling syllabics, in careful journals,
Aiming to please a posterity that despises them.
But we'll always have traitors who swear that a woman surrenders   90
Her Supreme Function, by equating Art with aggression
And failure with Femininity. Still, it's just as unfair
To equate Art with Femininity, like a prettily-packaged commodity
When we are the custodians of the world's best-kept secret:
Merely the private lives of one-half of humanity.   95

But even with masculine dominance, we mares and mistresses
Produced some sleek saboteuses, making their cracks
Which the porridge-brained males of the day were too thick to perceive,
Mistaking young hornets for perfectly harmless bumblebees.
Being thought innocuous rouses some women to frenzy;   100

---

7. The pomegranate was a food of the underworld, and because she had eaten its seeds Persephone had to
return there to live for three months of each year; thus the fruit is associated with death and resurrection.
8. *Camille* was both a novel and a play by Alexander Dumas, *fils* (1824–1895), and the basis of the
opera *La Traviata* by Guiseppe Verdi (1813–1901).

They try to be ugly by aping the ways of the men
And succeed. Swearing, sucking cigars and scorching the bedspread,

Slopping straight shots, eyes blotted, vanity-blown
In the expectation of glory: *she writes like a man!*
This drives other women mad in a mist of chiffon.   105
(One poetess draped her gauze over red flannels, a practical feminist.)

But we're emerging from all that, more or less,
Except for some lady-like laggards and Quarterly priestesses
Who flog men for fun, and kick women to maim competition.
Now, if we struggle abnormally, we may almost seem normal;   110
If we submerge our self-pity in disciplined industry;
If we stand up and be hated, and swear not to sleep with editors;
If we regard ourselves formally, respecting our true limitations
Without making an unseemly show of trying to unfreeze our assets;
Keeping our heads and our pride while remaining unmarried;   115
And if wedded, kill guilt in its tracks when we stack up the dishes
And defect to the typewriter. And if mothers, believe in the luck of our children,
Whom we forbid to devour us, whom we shall not devour,
And the luck of our husbands and lovers, who keep free women.

                                                        1965

Bitch

Now, when he and I meet, after all these years,
I say to the bitch inside me, don't start growling.
He isn't a trespasser anymore,
Just an old acquaintance tipping his hat.
My voice says, "Nice to see you,"   5
As the bitch starts to bark hysterically.
He isn't an enemy now,
Where are your manners, I say, as I say,
"How are the children? They must be growing up."
At a kind word from him, a look like the old days,   10
The bitch changes her tone; she begins to whimper.
She wants to snuggle up to him, to cringe.
Down, girl! Keep your distance
Or I'll give you a taste of the choke-chain.
"Fine, I'm just fine," I tell him.   15
She slobbers and grovels.
After all, I am her mistress. She is basically loyal.
It's just that she remembers how she came running
Each evening, when she heard his step;
How she lay at his feet and looked up adoringly   20
Though he was absorbed in his paper;
Or, bored with her devotion, ordered her to the kitchen
Until he was ready to play.
But the small careless kindnesses
When he'd had a good day, or a couple of drinks,   25

Come back to her now, seem more important
Than the casual cruelties, the ultimate dismissal.
"It's nice to know you are doing so well," I say.
He couldn't have taken you with him;
You were too demonstrative, too clumsy,   30
Not like the well-groomed pets of his new friends.
"Give my regards to your wife," I say. You gag
As I drag you off by the scruff,
Saying, "Goodbye! Goodbye! Nice to have seen you again."

1971

►◄ MAXINE KUMIN ►◄
(b. 1925)

Born Maxine Winokur, the poet was raised in Philadelphia, the city of her birth, and attended a Roman Catholic convent school next to her home even though she was Jewish. After graduation from high school, she studied history and literature at Radcliffe College, receiving a bachelor's degree in 1946 and a master's degree in 1948. In 1946 she married Victor Kumin, an engineer, with whom she had three children. After her third child went to kindergarten, she began teaching part-time at Tufts College in 1958. She has said in an interview that, "I began as a poet in the Dark Ages of the fifties with very little sense of who I was—a wife, a daughter, a mother, a college instructor, a swimmer, a horse lover, a hermit." Her vocation for poetry intensified in the late 1950s after she enrolled in a writing workshop at the Boston Center for Adult Education, where she met and became close friends with Anne Sexton. The poems that she wrote over the next five years appeared in *Halfway* (1961). That same year she began a two-year fellowship at Radcliffe's prestigious Bunting Institute, then continued to teach at Tufts from 1965 to 1986. *Halfway* was followed by *The Privilege* (1965), *The Nightmare Factory* (1970), and *Up Country: Poems of New England, New and Selected* (1972), which won the Pulitzer Prize.

The poems of *Up Country* reflect on Kumin's life in Warner, New Hampshire, where she and her husband spent weekends and summers on a farm they had purchased. In the late 1970s, Kumin moved permanently to the farm, and her books since then have continued to focus on the rhythms of country life, including her experiences as a breeder of thoroughbred horses. Her prolific publications include novels, children's books, short stories, several collections of essays, and prose memoirs of her New Hampshire life, including *Inside the Halo and Beyond: The Anatomy of a Recovery* (2000), which details her difficult recovery from a near-fatal riding accident. The recipient of numerous honors and awards, she served as the Poetry Consultant to the Library of Congress (1981–1982), Poet Laureate of the state of New Hampshire (1989–1994), and a Chancellor of the Academy of American Poets (1995–1999).

Kumin's poetry is largely elegiac, yet also optimistic, focusing on loss and survival. Although she is not an overtly confessional poet like her friend Anne Sexton, she often contemplates the intertwining difficulties and joys of family life and considers these in the context of the cyclical rhythms of nature. She has also written poems exploring her Jewish identity, although, because of her convent education, her poems sometimes include symbols drawn from Christianity as well. Her early books often display a mastery of traditional form. In an interview she claimed that form helps her approach emotionally charged material: "The tougher the form the easier it is for me to handle the poem, because the form gives permission to very gut-honest about feelings. . . . I almost always put some sort of formal stricture on a deeply-felt poem, maybe not rhyme, but at least a stanzaic pattern." Over the decades, however, she loosened her language, writing more and more in free verse, adopting colloquial diction, and focusing on concrete details. Throughout her career, she has examined the process of change, whether in nature or in human life, and has considered how change creates endurance.

At the End of the Affair

That it should end in an Albert Pick[1] hotel
with the air conditioner gasping like a carp
and the bathroom tap plucking its one-string harp
and the sourmash bond half gone in the open bottle,

that it should end in this stubborn disarray   5
of stockings and car keys and suitcases,
all the unfoldings that came forth yesterday
now crammed back to overflow their spaces,

considering the hairsbreadth accident of touch
the nightcap leads to—how it protracts   10
the burst of colors, the sweetgrass of two tongues,
then turns the lock in Hilton or in Sheraton,
in Marriott or Holiday Inn for such
a man and woman—bearing in mind these facts,

better to break glass, sop with towels, tear   15
snapshots up, pour whiskey down the drain
than reach and tangle in the same old snare
saying the little lies again.

1970

How It Is

Shall I say how it is in your clothes?
A month after your death I wear your blue jacket.
The dog at the center of my life recognizes
you've come to visit, he's ecstatic.
In the left pocket, a hole.   5
In the right, a parking ticket

1. An American hotel chain.

delivered up last August on Bay State Road.
In my heart, a scatter like milkweed,
a flinging from the pods of the soul.
My skin presses your old outline.   10
It is hot and dry inside.

I think of the last day of your life,
old friend, how I would unwind it, paste
it together in a different collage,
back from the death car idling in the garage,   15
back up the stairs, your praying hands unlaced,
reassembling the bits of bread and tuna fish
into a ceremony of sandwich,
running the home movie backward to a space
we could be easy in, a kitchen place   20
with vodka and ice, our words like living meat.

Dear friend, you have excited crowds
with your example. They swell
like wine bags, straining at your seams.
I will be years gathering up our words,   25
fishing out letters, snapshots, stains,
leaning my ribs against the durable cloth
to put on the dumb blue blazer of your death.

                                                     1978

The Retrieval System

It begins with my dog, now dead, who all his long life
carried about in his head the brown eyes of my father,
keen, loving, accepting, sorrowful, whatever;
they were Daddy's all right, handed on, except
for their phosphorescent gleam tunneling the night   5
which I have to concede was a separate gift.

Uncannily when I'm alone these features
come up to link my lost people
with the patient domestic beasts of my life. For example,
the wethered goat who runs free in pasture and stable 10
with his flecked, agate eyes and his minus-sign pupils
blats in the tiny voice of my former piano teacher

whose bones beat time in my dreams and whose terrible breath
soured "Country Gardens," "Humoresque," and unplayable Bach.
My elderly aunts, wearing the heads of willful   15
intelligent ponies, stand at the fence begging apples.
The sister who died at three has my cat's faint chin,
my cat's inscrutable squint, and cried catlike in pain.

I remember the funeral. *The Lord is my shepherd,*
we said. I don't want to brood. Fact: it is people who fade,   20

it is animals that retrieve them. A boy
I loved once keeps coming back as my yearling colt,
cocksure at the gallop, racing his shadow
for the hell of it. He runs merely to be.
A boy who was lost in the war thirty years ago   25
and buried at sea.

Here, it's forty degrees and raining. The weatherman
who looks like my resident owl, the one who goes out and in
by the open haymow, appears on the TV screen.
With his heart-shaped face, he is also my late dentist's double,   30
donnish, bifocaled, kind. Going a little gray,
advising this wisdom tooth will have to come out someday,
meanwhile filling it as a favor. Another save.
It outlasted him. The forecast is nothing but trouble.
It will snow fiercely enough to fill all these open graves.

                                                                        35
                                                              1978

Noted in the New York Times

Lake Buena Vista, Florida, June 16, 1987

Death claimed the last pure dusky seaside sparrow
today, whose coastal range was narrow,
as narrow as its two-part buzzy song.
From hummocks lost to Cape Canaveral
this mouselike skulker in the matted grass,   5
a six-inch bird, plain brown, once thousands strong,
sang *toodle-raeeee azhee,* ending on a trill
before the air gave way to rocket blasts.

It laid its dull white eggs (brown specked) in small
neat cups of grass on plots of pickleweed,   10
bulrushes, or salt hay. It dined
on caterpillars, beetles, ticks, the seeds
of sedges. Unremarkable
the life it led with others of its kind.

Tomorrow we can put it on a stamp,   15
a first-day cover with Key Largo rat,
Schaus swallowtail, Florida swamp
crocodile, and fading cotton mouse.
How simply symbols replace habitat!
The tower frames at Aerospace   20
quiver in the flush of another shot
where, once indigenous, the dusky sparrow
soared trilling twenty feet above its burrow.

                                                              1989

◄ W. D. SNODGRASS ►
(b. 1926)

When William DeWitt Snodgrass published his first collection, *Heart's Needle*, in 1959, he was immediately recognized as a leading poet of his generation. *Heart's Needle* won the Pulitzer Prize for 1960, beating out Robert Lowell's *Life Studies*. Nevertheless, appreciations of Snodgrass rarely failed to mention Lowell or to lump the two poets together under the newly coined rubric of "Confessional Poetry." But where Lowell's technique became less formal while his autobiographical obsessions increased, Snodgrass remained relatively reticent about personal matters, never completely abandoned rhyme and meter, and was more frequently inclined to write dramatic monologues. Though as one critic noted, the poems of *Heart's Needle* were "jaunty and assertive on the surface but somber and hurt beneath," Snodgrass was never a confessional poet in the quite the same way that Lowell, Sylvia Plath, and Anne Sexton would be. He was instead a poet seeking the compensations of formality for a life he rarely revealed in blatant terms.

Snodgrass was born in Wilkinsburg, Pennsylvania, the son of a successful accountant, and in *After Images: Autobiographical Sketches* (1999), he compared his verse writing to his father's profession: "When I make a poem, I erect a column of words much like those words on my father's page markers or the figures on his balance sheet. Like him, I intend in this an act of inventory and mastery." Despite their prosperity, Snodgrass's family was in a constant state of clutter and disarray—even filth, since his mother refused to clean up after her pet dogs and cats. These unsanitary conditions went beyond mere eccentricity; they resulted in the death of Snodgrass's sister, who had suffered from asthma. The poet admits that he grew up feeling increasingly remote from other people and had difficulty connecting with others for much of his early life.

After a brief period of college study, Snodgrass joined the navy, serving in the Pacific (1944–1946). Eventually he went to the University of Iowa, then becoming known for its writers' workshop. He earned a bachelor's degree in 1949, and stayed on for two master's degrees, (1951) and an M.F.A. (1953). Among his teachers there were the poets Randall Jarrell, John Berryman, and Robert Lowell, who would champion Snodgrass's poetry. Reacting to the "Confessional" label, Lowell would eventually call Snodgrass "the American Philip Larkin," suggesting that like the British poet he was formal, colloquial, and deeply ironic, rather than strictly autobiographical.

As Snodgrass's career progressed, his personal life was often in disarray—he married four times, and frequently sought help from psychotherapists to grow beyond his traumatic childhood. As a poet who had once desired to be a playwright, Snodgrass found fertile ground in the lives of others, and his second major collection, *After Experience* (1968), contained dramatic monologues as well as lyrics. There was also something of an escape from autobiography in the work he published under an anagrammatic pseudonym, S. S. Gardons, *Remains: A Sequence of Poems* (1970; 1985). This dramatic tendency would find its fullest expression in Snodgrass's most controversial book, *The Fuehrer Bunker* (1977), in which prominent Nazis soliloquized while the Allies closed in on Berlin in the last month of the European war. Alternately praised and vilified by critics, this book continues to find champions and detractors who usually argue about whether it goes too far in humanizing figures like Hitler and Goebbels. It has also been presented in a stage version.

Selected Poems, 1957–1987, contains much of Snodgrass's best work from ten collections, large and small. He has published limited editions and chapbooks over the years, as well as volumes of translations, introductions to books by others, light verse, and poems for children. His *Selected Translations* appeared in 1998. He has taught widely, his longest-held appointments being those at Wayne State University, Syracuse University, and the University of Delaware, where he is now Distinguished Professor Emeritus. He currently divides his time between upstate New York and Mexico.

◄●►━━◀━━►●►

April Inventory

The green catalpa tree has turned
All white; the cherry blooms once more.
In one whole year I haven't learned
A blessed thing they pay you for.
The blossoms snow down in my hair;   5
The trees and I will soon be bare.

The trees have more than I to spare.
The sleek, expensive girls I teach,
Younger and pinker every year,
Bloom gradually out of reach.   10
The pear tree lets its petals drop
Like dandruff on a tabletop.

The girls have grown so young by now
I have to nudge myself to stare.
This year they smile and mind me how   15
My teeth are falling with my hair.
In thirty years I may not get
Younger, shrewder, or out of debt.

The tenth time, just a year ago,
I made myself a little list   20
Of all the things I'd ought to know,
Then told my parents, analyst,
And everyone who's trusted me
I'd be substantial, presently.

I haven't read one book about   25
A book or memorized one plot.
Or found a mind I did not doubt.
I learned one date. And then forgot.
And one by one the solid scholars
Get the degrees, the jobs, the dollars.   30

And smile above their starchy collars.
I taught my classes Whitehead's[1] notions;
One lovely girl, a song of Mahler's.[2]
Lacking a source-book or promotions,
I showed one child the colors of   35
A luna moth and how to love.

I taught myself to name my name,
To bark back, loosen love and crying;
To ease my woman so she came,
To ease an old man who was dying.   40
I have not learned how often I
Can win, can love, but choose to die.

I have not learned there is a lie
Love shall be blonder, slimmer, younger;
That my equivocating eye   45
Loves only by my body's hunger;
That I have forces, true to feel,
Or that the lovely world is real.

While scholars speak authority
And wear their ulcers on their sleeves,   50
My eyes in spectacles shall see
These trees procure and spend their leaves.
There is a value underneath
The gold and silver in my teeth.

Though trees turn bare and girls turn wives,   55
We shall afford our costly seasons;
There is a gentleness survives
That will outspeak and has its reasons.
There is a loveliness exists,
Preserves us, not for specialists.   60

                                                            1959

Leaving the Motel

Outside, the last kids holler
Near the pool: they'll stay the night.
Pick up the towels; fold your collar
Out of sight.

Check: is the second bed   5
Unrumpled, as agreed?
Landlords have to think ahead
In case of need,

1. Alfred North Whitehead (1861–1947), British mathematician and philosopher.
2. Gustav Mahler (1860–1911), Austrian composer.

Too. Keeps things straight: don't take
The matches, the wrong keyrings—   10
We've nowhere we could keep a keepsake—
Ashtrays, combs, things

That sooner or later others
Would accidentally find.
Check: take nothing of one another's   15
And leave behind

Your license number only,
Which they won't care to trace;
We've paid. Still, should things get lonely;
Leave in their vase   20

An aspirin to preserve
Our lilacs, the wayside flowers
We've gathered and must leave to serve
A few more hours;

That's all. We can't tell when   25
We'll come back, can't press claims;
We would no doubt have other rooms then,
Or other names.

                                        1967

Disposal

The unworn long gown, meant for dances
She would have scarcely dared attend,
Is fobbed off on a friend—
Who can't help wondering if it's spoiled
But thinks, well, she can take her chances.   5

We roll her spoons up like old plans
Or failed securities, seal their case,
Then lay them back. One lace
Nightthing lies in the chest, unsoiled
By wear, untouched by human hands.   10

We don't dare burn those canceled patterns
And markdowns that we actually wore,
Yet who do we know so poor
They'd take them? Spared all need, all passion,
Saved from loss, she lies boxed in satins   15

Like a pair of party shoes
That seemed to never find a taker;
We send back to its maker
A life somehow gone out of fashion
But still too good to use.   20

                                        1970

—•◄ JAMES MERRILL ►•—
(1926–1995)

The son of Charles E. Merrill, a founder of the investment firm known today as Merrill Lynch, James Ingram Merrill was born in New York City into a life of privilege. Raised on Long Island and Palm Beach, Merrill was educated in his early years by a European nanny who taught him French and German. After his parents' difficult divorce in 1939, he was sent to Lawrenceville, an elite New Jersey boarding school near Princeton. Although he had begun writing poetry at an early age, his interest in it quickened at Lawrenceville, where he edited the literary magazine. In his senior year, his father privately published *Jim's Book* (1942), a selection of his son's poems, which, Merrill recalls, "thrilled me for days, then mortified me for a quarter-century." In the same essay, "Acoustical Chambers," he adds that the book motivated him to study literature seriously at Amherst College, which he entered in 1943. "I opened my eyes enough at least to see how much remained to learn about writing," he remembers. "Presently I was at Amherst, reading Proust, Dante, and *Faust* in their various originals, Jane Austen and Pope . . . Shakespeare and Darwin."

After serving as a private in the U.S. Army infantry from 1944 to 1945, Merrill returned to Amherst, graduating summa cum laude in 1947, with a senior thesis on Marcel Proust. For two years he lived in New York City and taught at Bard College. In 1950 he set off on the first of the many trips to Europe he would take during his life. His brilliantly written and deeply observant memoir, *A Different Person* (1993), describes his experiences as a young man living in Europe, a formative period when he committed himself to his vocation as a poet and fully accepted his homosexuality despite familial opposition. As the memoir's title suggests, during these years he was learning to live as "a different person"—a poet, a gay man, and a person whose great wealth set him apart from others, yet whose dedication to art clashed with the attitudes of the wealthy society in which he was raised. He emphasizes in a 1992 interview:

> I suppose early on I began to understand the relativity, even the reversibility, of truths. At the same time as I was being given a good education I could feel, not so much from my parents, but from the world they moved in, that kind of easygoing contempt rich people have for art and scholarship—"these things are all right *in their place,* and their place is to ornament a life rather than to nourish or to shape it." Or when it came to sex, I had to face it that the worst iniquity my parents (and many of my friends) could imagine was for me a blessed source of pleasure and security—as well as suffering, to be sure. There was truth on both sides. . . . I believe the secret lies primarily in the nature of poetry—and of science too, for that matter—and that the ability to see both ways at once isn't merely an idiosyncrasy but corresponds to how the world needs to be seen: cheerful *and* awful, opaque *and* transparent.

Merrill's poetry, in its multiple perspectives on experience and its tendency to be both "opaque *and* transparent" reflects this complex understanding of experience. His early work, *The Black Swan* (1946) and *First Poems* (1951), established his reputation as a meticulous master of traditional verse forms. Although reviewers admired Merrill's wit and verbal dexterity in describing the objets d'art that served as his primary subjects, most found the poems static and his sensibility too rarified. After receiving these mixed reviews, Merrill tried his hand at other genres, publishing a novel, *The Seraglio* (1957), and writing a play, *The Immortal Husband,* that was produced in New York in 1955. His next poetry book, *The Country of a Thousand Years of Peace* (1959), encompassed European settings from his travels and gained in human scale through elegizing a Dutch friend, Hans Lodeizen, who had died of leukemia in 1950.

Merrill's great breakthrough as a poet came with his third mature collection, *Water Street* (1962), which demonstrated greater openness of theme, casual ease with form, and increased variety of tones. The title refers to the street in Stonington, Connecticut, on which Merrill had shared a house since 1955 with his partner, the novelist David Jackson. The book, which ends with a poem describing the move into the couple's new house, meditates on the conjunctions and conflicts between home and eros. *Water Street*'s autobiographical bent reflects the shift toward self-revelation that swept American poetry in the early 1960s, but unlike the Confessional poets, Merrill maintained a sense of lightness through irony and wit, and his memoiristic narratives raised questions—learned from Proust and Henry James—about the extent to which anyone can separate a "real life" from the constantly shifting views of it that a person develops over time. Merrill aimed in his autobiographical poetry not for lyric intensity, but for a sophisticated range of tones. As he remarked in a 1967 interview:

> I've enjoyed reading novels more often—or more profoundly—than I've enjoyed reading poems. There seems to be no poet except perhaps Dante whose work has the extraordinary richness of Tolstoy or Proust; and there are very few poets whose work gives as much fun as James. . . . You hear a voice talking in prose, often a very delightful voice which can say all kinds of odd things. For me, to get something of that into poetry was a pleasure and even perhaps an object.

Merrill's increasing stature as a poet was confirmed when his next book, *Nights and Days* (1966), won a National Book Award. Through further autobiographical narratives and exquisite lyrics, the book continued his exploration of time's power to change memory and perception. Merrill sometimes thickened his narratives, and particularly his poems that contemplated erotic desire, with allusions to mythology that deftly paralleled the stories he developed. Several of the poems in this book and his next two, *The Fire Screen* (1969) and *Braving the Elements* (1972), were set in Athens, where he and Jackson spent six months out of every year in a house they owned there.

With his Pulitzer Prize-winning volume *Divine Comedies* (1976), Merrill took a step beyond his mastery of short lyric and narrative poems. The volume closes with "The Book of Ephraim," a brilliant ninety-page narrative poem, which describes how he and Jackson consult a Ouija board and converse with spirits. Told in twenty-six sections (one for each letter of the alphabet), this loosely autobiographical novella-in-verse demonstrates Merrill's mastery at combining lyric charm, narrative ingenuity, and intellectual ambition. Determined to extend this material into an epic poem, he extended the project in his next two books, *Mirabell: Books of Number* (1978), which won a National Book Award, and *Scripts for the Pageant* (1980). These two books and "The Book of Ephraim" were ultimately consolidated, with a new epilogue, as *The Changing Light at Sandover* (1982). The bulky trilogy, which is nearly as long as *Paradise Lost,* does not take on Milton's epic aim "to justifie the ways of God to man," but instead proposes to create a twentieth-century myth to explain the universe. Merrill develops a complicated and idiosyncratic cosmology that incorporates diverse topics such as nuclear fission, reincarnation, population control, and the purpose of art. The trilogy's scope is both dazzling and intimidating, yet Merrill tempered the poem by including ordinary details about his daily life with Jackson and even by admitting his own skepticism of the Ouija board project from time to time as the narrative progresses. The epic thus enabled him to continue his autobiographical probings, yet expand beyond the self, as he explained in a 1982 interview:

> Don't you think there comes a time when everyone, not just a poet, wants to get beyond the self? Or reach, if you like, the "god" within you? The board, in however clumsy or absurd a way, allows for precisely that. Or if it's still *yourself* you're drawing on, then that self is much stranger and freer and more farseeing than the one you thought you knew.

In the last decade of his life, Merrill returned to writing short lyric and narrative poems, striking a fine balance between lightness and seriousness as he furthered his exploration of time, memory, and desire—particularly the revival of desire in old age. *Late Settings* (1985) includes many poems set in Key West, where he and Jackson wintered after they sold their Athens home in 1979. His late poems also appear in *The Inner Room* (1988) and posthumously published *A Scattering of Salts* (1995). During the early 1990s Merrill also learned that he was HIV-positive, though his condition was kept secret. Weakened by AIDS, he died of cardiac arrest in Tucson, Arizona, in February 1995. Dying at the height of his fame, Merrill was mourned as one of the most important American poets of the century.

◄•►━━◄▮►━━◄•►

The Broken Home[1]

Crossing the street,
I saw the parents and the child
At their window, gleaming like fruit
With evening's mild gold leaf.

In a room on the floor below,   5
Sunless, cooler—a brimming
Saucer of wax, marbly and dim—
I have lit what's left of my life.

I have thrown out yesterday's milk
And opened a book of maxims.   10
The flame quickens. The word stirs.

Tell me, tongue of fire,
That you and I are as real
At least as the people upstairs.

My father, who had flown in World War I,   15
Might have continued to invest his life

---

1. This sonnet sequence deals with the divorce of the poet's parents. His father was a famous investor, the Merrill in Merrill Lynch.

In cloud banks well above Wall Street and wife.
But the race was run below, and the point was to win.

Too late now, I make out in his blue gaze
(Through the smoked glass of being thirty-six)   20
The soul eclipsed by twin black pupils, sex
And business; time was money in those days.

Each thirteenth year he married. When he died
There were already several chilled wives
In sable orbit—rings, cars, permanent waves.   25
We'd felt him warming up for a green bride.

He could afford it. He was "in his prime"
At three score ten. But money was not time.

When my parents were younger this was a popular act:
A veiled woman would leap from an electric, wine-dark car   30
To the steps of no matter what—the Senate or the Ritz Bar—
And bodily, at newsreel speed, attack

No matter whom—Al Smith[2] or José Maria Sert[3]
Or Clemenceau[4]—veins standing out on her throat
As she yelled *War mongerer! Pig! Give us the vote!*,   35
And would have to be hauled away in her hobble skirt.

What had the man done? Oh, made history.
Her business (he had implied) was giving birth,
Tending the house, mending the socks.

Always that same old story—   40
Father Time and Mother Earth,
A marriage on the rocks.

One afternoon, red, satyr-thighed
Michael, the Irish setter, head
Passionately lowered, led   45
The child I was to a shut door. Inside,

Blinds beat sun from the bed.
The green-gold room throbbed like a bruise.
Under a sheet, clad in taboos
Lay whom we sought, her hair undone, outspread,   50

And of a blackness found, if ever now, in old
Engravings where the acid bit.
I must have needed to touch it

---

2. A governor of New York and, in 1928, a candidate for President.
3. Spanish painter (1876–1945). In 1930 he decorated part of the Waldorf Astoria Hotel in New York City.
4. Georges Clemenceau (1841–1929), premier of France during World War I.

Or the whiteness—was she dead?
Her eyes flew open, startled strange and cold.   55
The dog slumped to the floor. She reached for me. I fled.

Tonight they have stepped out onto the gravel.
The party is over. It's the fall
Of 1931. They love each other still.

She: Charlie, I can't stand the pace.   60
He: Come on, honey—why, you'll bury us all!

A lead soldier guards my windowsill:
Khaki rifle, uniform, and face.
Something in me grows heavy, silvery, pliable.

How intensely people used to feel!   65
Like metal poured at the close of a proletarian novel,
Refined and glowing from the crucible,
I see those two hearts, I'm afraid,
Still. Cool here in the graveyard of good and evil,
They are even so to be honored and obeyed.   70

. . . Obeyed, at least, inversely. Thus
I rarely buy a newspaper, or vote.
To do so, I have learned, is to invite
The tread of a stone guest[5] within my house.

Shooting this rusted bolt, though, against him,   75
I trust I am no less time's child than some
Who on the heath impersonate Poor Tom[6]
Or on the barricades risk life and limb.

Nor do I try to keep a garden, only
An avocado in a glass of water   80
Roots pallid, gemmed with air. And later,

When the small gilt leaves have grown
Fleshy and green, I let them die, yes, yes,
And start another. I am earth's no less.

A child, a red dog roam the corridors,   85
Still, of the broken home. No sound. The brilliant
Rag runners halt before wide-open doors.
My old room! Its wallpaper—cream, medallioned
With pink and brown—brings back the first nightmares,
Long summer colds, and Emma, sepia-faced,   90
Perspiring over broth carried upstairs
Aswim with golden fats I could not taste.

5. Refers to the statue in Mozart's opera *Don Giovanni* who returns to get revenge on the title character.
6. In Shakespeare's *King Lear* Edgar pretends to be this madman.

The real house became a boarding school.
Under the ballroom ceiling's allegory
Someone at last may actually be allowed   95
To learn something; or, from my window, cool
With the unstiflement of the entire story,
Watch a red setter stretch and sink in cloud.

1966

The Mad Scene

Again last night I dreamed the dream called Laundry.
In it, the sheets and towels of a life we were going to share,
The milk-stiff bibs, the shroud, each rag to be ever
Trampled or soiled, bled on or groped for blindly,
Came swooning out of an enormous willow hamper   5
Onto moon-marbly boards. We had just met. I watched
From outer darkness. I had dressed myself in clothes
Of a new fiber that never stains or wrinkles, never
Wears thin. The opera house sparkled with tiers
And tiers of eyes, like mine enlarged by belladonna,   10
Trained inward. There I saw the cloud-clot, gust by gust,
Form, and the lightning bite, and the roan mane unloosen.
Fingers were running in panic over the flute's nine gates.
Why did I flinch? I loved you. And in the downpour laughed
To have us wrung white, gnarled together, one   15
Topmost mordent of wisteria,
As the lean tree burst into grief.

1966

Last Words

My life, your light green eyes
Have lit on me with joy.
There's nothing I don't know
Or shall not know again,
Over and over again.   5
It's noon, it's dawn, it's night,
I am the dog that dies
In the deep street of Troy
Tomorrow, long ago—
Part of me dims with pain,   10
Becomes the stinging flies,
The bent head of the boy.
Part looks into your light
And lives to tell you so.

1969

Casual Wear

Your average tourist: Fifty. 2.3
Times married. Dressed, this year, in Ferdi Plinthbower
Originals. Odds 1 to 9^{10}
Against her strolling past the Embassy

Today at noon. Your average terrorist: 5
Twenty-five. Celibate. No use for trends,
At least in clothing. Mark, though, where it ends.
People have come forth made of colored mist

Unsmiling on one hundred million screens
To tell of his prompt phone call to the station,   10
"Claiming responsibility"—devastation
Signed with a flourish, like the dead wife's jeans.

1985

◦◀ DONALD HALL ▶◦
(b. 1928)

Author or editor of more than eighty books, Donald Hall is one of the preeminent American men of letters of the last fifty years. He appears to have known everyone and written about them with compassion, accuracy, and wit. His textbooks and anthologies have been among the most important of his generation, his memoirs are classics of American prose, his essays are judiciously outspoken and wide ranging, and the best of his poems give significant voice to concerns of family, history, and creativity.

Hall was born in New Haven, Connecticut, to a middle-class family. His father was a businessman, often frustrated with his career. Hall reports that his father once vowed that his son would never have to endure such humiliations. Perhaps because of this, Hall was encouraged by his parents when, at the age of twelve, he showed an interest in writing. At sixteen, he attended the prestigious Bread Loaf Writers' Conference, where he met Robert Frost for the first time. It was a precocious start for a memoirist. Among his classmates at Harvard were Robert Bly, John Ashbery, Kenneth Koch, and Adrienne Rich. He won prizes for poetry at Harvard, where he also edited the undergraduate literary magazine, the *Advocate,* and studied under Archibald MacLeish. After graduating in 1951, Hall went on to Oxford, learning a great deal about the British literary establishment and winning the Newdigate Prize for his poem "Exile." From 1953 to 1961 he served as poetry editor for the *Paris Review,* and in that capacity he conducted important interviews with T. S. Eliot, Ezra Pound, and Marianne Moore. He also attended Stanford University in 1953–1954, studying with Yvor Winters. In short, Hall seems to have set out to become a poet in part by developing a personal relationship with almost every significant poet and critic of his time.

His first full-length collection of poems, *Exiles and Marriages,* won the Lamont Poetry Prize from the Academy of American Poets and was published by Viking in 1955. The book was precocious, but only a few of its poems now seem to transcend the conventions of the period. Hall's subsequent early collections often suggest that he felt pressured to publish too quickly. These poems sometimes seem to drift in search of a style or subject he could call his own. For a while, work of various kinds interfered with his full self-realization as a poet. Married, a father, he joined the faculty of the University of Michigan, Ann Arbor, where he taught from 1957 to 1975. By almost any measure Hall enjoyed immense literary success, with six full-length collections of poems to his name by 1971, a highly regarded book of memoirs called *String Too Short to Be Saved* (1979), books on sculptor Henry Moore and poet Marianne Moore, and several influential anthologies. One of these, *New Poets of England and America* (1957), co-edited with Robert Pack and Louis Simpson, with a preface by Robert Frost, was a landmark of the fifties, often contrasted to Donald Allen's *The New American Poetry* (1960). Hall also edited the influential *Contemporary American Poetry* for Penguin (1962).

Despite these public successes and the approbation of older writers, Hall felt that something essential was lacking from his own poetry. He also underwent the trauma of a divorce from his first wife in 1969 and married the poet Jane Kenyon in 1972. In 1975, frustrated by the compromises of academic life, Hall decided to change his life. He purchased his grandparents' farm in New Hampshire, a place he remembered fondly from childhood summers, left his teaching position, and, with Kenyon, set out to live by his wits. This liberating gesture was made possible only because of his prodigious industry. "In the culture I was born to," he once wrote, "'work' is a golden syllable." Hall made a habit of rising early, devoting his first and best hours to poems, then turning to prose, much of it done for hire.

The move proved decisive for his poetry, which developed and deepened in his new life. Among the important collections he published were *Kicking the Leaves* (1978), *The Happy Man* (1986), *The One Day* (1988), and *Old and New Poems* (1990). *The Museum of Clear Ideas* (1993) celebrated his favorite sport, baseball, just as he had done in his popular book of essays, *Fathers Playing Catch with Sons* (1985). Early in the nineties, however, Hall was diagnosed with cancer, and in the course of treatment lost two-thirds of his colon to surgery. It was widely reported in literary circles that he was dying. Ironically, Hall lived on while the young Kenyon succumbed rapidly to leukemia in 1995. Hall's 1996 collection, *The Old Life,* comprised poems based upon old memoirs. Then in 1998 he published *Without,* his poems dealing with grief over the loss of his wife. A prolific writer of children's books, Hall has also written plays and has won numerous awards, including the National Book Critics Circle Award, the *Los Angeles Times* Book Prize, and the Robert Frost Silver Medal from the Poetry Society of America. He continues to live and write on his family's farm.

◄●━━◄●━►●►

My Son My Executioner

My son, my executioner,
   I take you in my arms,
Quiet and small and just astir
   And whom my body warms.

Sweet death, small son, our instrument   5
  Of immortality,
Your cries and hungers document
  Our bodily decay.

We twenty-five and twenty-two,
  Who seemed to live forever,   10
Observe enduring life in you
  And start to die together.

1955; Revised 1969

Names of Horses

All winter your brute shoulders strained against collars, padding
and steerhide over the ash hames, to haul
sledges of cordwood for drying through spring and summer,
for the Glenwood stove next winter, and for the simmering range.

In April you pulled cartloads of manure to spread on the fields,   5
dark manure of Holsteins, and knobs of your own clustered with oats.
All summer you mowed the grass in meadow and hayfield, the mowing machine
clacketing beside you, while the sun walked high in the morning;

and after noon's heat, you pulled a clawed rake through the same acres,
gathering stacks, and dragged the wagon from stack to stack,   10
and the built hayrack back, up hill to the chaffy barn,
three loads of hay a day, hanging wide from the hayrack.

Sundays you trotted the two miles to church with the light load
of a leather quartertop buggy, and grazed in the sound of hymns.
Generation on generation, your neck rubbed the window sill   15
of the stall, smoothing the wood as the sea smooths glass.

When you were old and lame, when your shoulders hurt bending to graze,
one October the man who fed you and kept you, and harnessed you every
    morning,
led you through corn stubble to sandy ground above Eagle Pond,
and dug a hole beside you where you stood shuddering in your skin,   20

and lay the shotgun's muzzle in the boneless hollow behind your ear,
and fired the slug into your brain, and felled you into your grave,
shoveling sand to cover you, setting goldenrod upright above you,
where by next summer a dent in the ground made your monument.

For a hundred and fifty years, in the pasture of dead horses,   25
roots of pine trees pushed through the pale curves of your ribs,
yellow blossoms flourished above you in autumn, and in winter
frost heaved your bones in the ground—old toilers, soil makers:

O Roger, Mackerel, Riley, Ned, Nellie, Chester, Lady Ghost.

1978

Ox Cart Man

In October of the year,
he counts potatoes dug from the brown field,
counting the seed, counting
the cellar's portion out,
and bags the rest on the cart's floor.   5

He packs wool sheared in April, honey
in combs, linen, leather
tanned from deerhide,
and vinegar in a barrel
hooped by hand at the forge's fire.   10

He walks by his ox's head, ten days
to Portsmouth Market, and sells potatoes,
and the bag that carried potatoes,
flaxseed, birch brooms, maple sugar, goose
feathers, yarn.   15

When the cart is empty he sells the cart.
When the cart is sold he sells the ox,
harness and yoke, and walks
home, his pockets heavy
with the year's coin for salt and taxes,   20

and at home by fire's light in November cold
stitches new harness
for next year's ox in the barn,
and carves the yoke, and saw planks
building the cart again.   25

1978

▰ ANNE SEXTON ▰
(1928–1974)

Anne Sexton was the third daughter of Ralph Harvey, a successful wool merchant, and Mary Gray Staples, who gave up her own literary aspirations to become a suburban housewife. The family had a large house in Weston, Massachusetts, as well as a summer home on Squirrel Island. Never comfortable with her parents' ideas about social position, Anne felt closer to her affectionate maiden great-aunt, nicknamed "Nana." Her parents ignored much of the trouble she had with concentration and discipline in school, even after her teachers suggested counseling. At sixteen she was sent to a boarding school in Lowell, where she enjoyed theatricals and poetry, but she did not take college preparatory or career-oriented classes. Instead, on graduating from high school Sexton had a year at the Garland School in Boston, a private finishing school for young women. At Garland the strikingly beautiful young poet became even more aware of the power of physical attraction. "I was born doing reference work in sin," she later wrote, "and born confessing it." At age nineteen she eloped with Alfred "Kayo" Sexton II. They lived together while he attended college, and she moved in with her parents while he fought in Korea.

In 1953 Sexton gave birth to their first daughter, Linda Gray, and almost immediately fell into a state of depression. She spent the better part of two years hospitalized. Her depression deepened further when Nana died in 1954. A year later, Sexton gave birth to her second daughter, Joyce Ladd, but her mother-in-law had taken on most of the early care of the children. Sexton herself was too incapacitated by illness to be of much help. It was her psychotherapist, Dr. Martin Orne, who suggested in 1957 that she write poetry as a form of therapy. She later told an interviewer that a televised lecture on the sonnet by I. A. Richards energized her even more: "I thought maybe I could do that," she recalled. "Oh, I was turned on. I wrote two or three a day for about a year." She also enrolled in a creative writing workshop taught by John Holmes, where she met Maxine Kumin and other aspiring poets. Sexton's early poems displayed a facility with traditional forms and a penchant for personal subject matter. She studied with W. D. Snodgrass in the summer of 1958 and credited his collection, *Heart's Needle* (1959), with influencing her confessional approach. She also took workshops from Robert Lowell at Boston University, where she met the poets Sylvia Plath and George Starbuck. Several important journals, including the *Hudson Review,* began to publish her early poems—and then came the books in rapid succession.

Sexton's first two collections, *To Bedlam and Part Way Back* (1960) and *All My Pretty Ones* (1962) were notable for strong rhythmic qualities and playful rhymes as well as their frankness about her hospital stays and fascination with suicide. A selection of her early work was well received in England, and her third American collection, *Live or Die* (1966), won the Pulitzer Prize. As Sexton's forms became freer and her stance toward shocking subjects even less inhibited, some critics began to complain about the increasing self-indulgence and lack of stylistic control in her work. Others have stated that her willingness to write about abortion, sex, and women's bodies was her strongest contribution to poetry. Perhaps sensing that blunt confession of one's private life had its limits, Sexton turned to myth and narrative in her collection *Transformations* (1971), which was based mostly on Grimms' *Fairy Tales.* Her title was apt, as she transformed these traditional stories into witty feminist allegories and parables of sexuality, her style closer to the prose of Kurt Vonnegut than to her own early verse.

Her many successes, however, barely masked a profoundly troubled personal life. Not only was she taking Thorazine for depression, but her marriage to Kayo had long been falling apart. Sexton became a popular performer on college campuses, often touring with a rock band called Her Kind (from the title of one of her best poems). Her last collections, *The Book of Folly* (1972) and *The Death Notebooks* (1974), were generally less well regarded than earlier books. In late 1973 she and Kayo divorced. In October of 1974 she committed suicide by inhaling carbon monoxide in the garage of her home. A posthumous collection of poems, *The Awful Rowing toward God* (1975), revealed that she had begun to search for religious sustenance, though her sincere but unfocused spiritual yearning failed to provide a stable center for her increasingly desperate life.

As a significant literary figure of her generation, Sexton's precise contribution to poetry has been difficult to characterize fairly. Her posthumous *Complete Poems*

(1981) contains wildly uneven work, and her early poetry along with *Transformations* constitutes her most compelling claim to posterity. Her carefully cultivated image as a glamorous social rebel has troubled feminists like Adrienne Rich, who argue that too many young women are attracted to the image of the suicidal poet. Like an alarming number of poets in her time, Sexton's personal troubles fed her art but also ultimately defeated her. The smart, edgy, and candid writing she left behind, however, remains an important part of feminist consciousness.

✦

Her Kind

I have gone out, a possessed witch,
haunting the black air, braver at night;
dreaming evil, I have done my hitch
over the plain houses, light by light:
lonely thing, twelve-fingered, out of mind.   5
A woman like that is not a woman, quite.
I have been her kind.

I have found the warm caves in the woods,
filled them with skillets, carvings, shelves,
closets, silks, innumerable goods;   10
fixed the suppers for the worms and the elves:
whining, rearranging the disaligned.
A woman like that is misunderstood.
I have been her kind.

I have ridden in your cart, driver,   15
waved my nude arms at villages going by,
learning the last bright routes, survivor
where your flames still bite my thigh
and my ribs crack where your wheels wind.
A woman like that is not ashamed to die.   20
I have been her kind.

                                                1960

The Abortion

Somebody who should have been born
is gone.

Just as the earth puckered its mouth,
each bud puffing out from its knot,
I changed my shoes, and then drove south.   5

Up past the Blue Mountains, where
Pennsylvania humps on endlessly,
wearing, like a crayoned cat, its green hair,

its roads sunken in like a gray washboard;
where, in truth, the ground cracks evilly,   10
a dark socket from which the coal has poured,

Somebody who should have been born
is gone.

the grass as bristly and stout as chives,
and me wondering when the ground would break,   15
and me wondering how anything fragile survives;

up in Pennsylvania, I met a little man,
not Rumpelstiltskin, at all, at all . . .
he took the fullness that love began.
Returning north, even the sky grew thin   20
like a high window looking nowhere.
The road was as flat as a sheet of tin.

Somebody who should have been born
is gone.

Yes, woman, such logic will lead   25
to loss without death. Or say what you meant,
you coward . . . this baby that I bleed.

1962

The Truth the Dead Know

For my mother, born March 1902, died March 1959,
and my father, born February 1900, died June 1959

Gone, I say and walk from church,
refusing the stiff procession to the grave,
letting the dead ride alone in the hearse.
It is June. I am tired of being brave.

We drive to the Cape. I cultivate   5
myself where the sun gutters from the sky,
where the sea swings in like an iron gate
and we touch. In another country people die.

My darling, the wind falls in like stones
from the whitehearted water and when we touch   10
we enter touch entirely. No one's alone.
Men kill for this, or for as much.

And what of the dead? They lie without shoes
in their stone boats. They are more like stone
than the sea would be if it stopped. They refuse   15
to be blessed, throat, eye and knucklebone.

1962

Wanting to Die

Since you ask, most days I cannot remember.
I walk in my clothing, unmarked by that voyage.
Then the almost unnameable lust returns.

Even then I have nothing against life.
I know well the grass blades you mention,   5
the furniture you have placed under the sun.

But suicides have a special language.
Like carpenters they want to know *which tools*.
They never ask *why build*.

Twice I have so simply declared myself,   10
have possessed the enemy, eaten the enemy,
have taken on his craft, his magic.

In this way, heavy and thoughtful,
warmer than oil or water,
I have rested, drooling at the mouth-hole.   15

I did not think of my body at needle point.
Even the cornea and the leftover urine were gone.
Suicides have already betrayed the body.

Still-born, they don't always die,
but dazzled, they can't forget a drug so sweet   20
that even children would look on and smile.

To thrust all that life under your tongue!—
that, all by itself, becomes a passion.
Death's a sad bone; bruised, you'd say,

and yet she waits for me, year after year,   25
to so delicately undo an old wound,
to empty my breath from its bad prison.

Balanced there, suicides sometimes meet,
raging at the fruit, a pumped-up moon,
leaving the bread they mistook for a kiss,   30

leaving the page of the book carelessly open,
something unsaid, the phone off the hook
and the love, whatever it was, an infection.

1966

⊷◄ X. J. KENNEDY ►⊶
(b. 1929)

Joseph Charles Kennedy, who publishes under the pseudonym X. J. Kennedy, was
born in Dover, New Jersey, the only child of a Roman Catholic father and Methodist

mother. As a boy, he so loved science fiction and horror stories and films that at twelve he published his own mimeograph magazines, *Vampire* and *Terrifying Test-Tube Tales*. Raised Catholic, he took an undergraduate degree at Seton Hall and then completed a master's degree at Columbia in 1951. Knowing he would be drafted during the Korean War, he soon enlisted in the U.S. Navy. Much to the amusement of his fellow sailors, he once served on the navy destroyer, USS *Joseph P. Kennedy, Jr.*—perhaps an early impetus to use a nom de plume for his writing. Returning to civilian life in 1955, he attended the Sorbonne in Paris before entering a Ph.D. program at the University of Michigan where he completed all the work for his doctorate except the dissertation. In Ann Arbor, Kennedy found a supportive community of poets, which included W. D. Snodgrass, Donald Hall, Anne Stevenson, and Keith Waldrop. He won Michigan's Hopwood Award in 1959 in both poetry and nonfiction. In 1961 he published his first collection, *Nude Descending a Staircase*, which won the Lamont Prize.

In 1962 Kennedy married Dorothy Mintzlaff. The couple has had five children—four sons and a daughter. From 1963 to 1979 Kennedy taught at Tufts University, eventually becoming a full professor; but the success of his many books, especially his best-selling anthologies, *An Introduction to Poetry* (first edition 1966, now in its tenth edition) and *Literature* (1976, now in its eighth edition), allowed him to leave academia. His subsequent collections of poetry include *Growing into Love* (1969), *Breaking and Entering* (1971), *Emily Dickinson in Southern California* (1974), *Cross-Ties: Selected Poems* (1985), and *Dark Horses* (1992). In 2001 he was awarded the Aiken Taylor Award for lifetime achievement in poetry. Kennedy has also been an inspired writer of children's poetry and nonsense verse with collections such as *One Winter Night in August* (1975), *The Phantom Ice Cream Man* (1979), *The Beasts of Bethlehem* (1992)—as well as his hilarious series *Brats* (1986), *Fresh Brats* (1990), and *Drat These Brats!* (1993).

Already in his first collection, *Nude Descending a Staircase,* Kennedy had developed a mature and distinctive style, rooted in tradition but markedly personal and contemporary. His poetry characteristically employs rhyme and meter usually in a fixed form like the sonnet, ballad, or quatrain, but the effect is rarely smooth or elegant in the manner of Anthony Hecht or Richard Wilbur. A master satirist, Kennedy favors a rough, heterogeneous style, mixing high and low diction, with the rude and vernacular elements usually gaining the upper hand. For comedy and satire, this obstreperous style has its obvious advantages, but Kennedy's poems are not always humorous. He sometimes pursues dark and painful effects, though even these poems often seem tinged with corrosive irony or bitter satire.

In contemporary letters Kennedy played an important role in the preservation of formal verse during the free verse revolution of the 1970s. Identifying himself as, "One of an endangered species: people who still write in meter and rime," Kennedy took an unfashionable stand in defending these traditional techniques when they were widely considered—at least among poets and critics—as retrograde. In 1972 with his wife he founded *Counter/Measures: A Magazine of Rime, Meter, and Song*. Although the journal expired in 1974, it proved a lively and influential gathering place for formal poets both young and old during a crucial moment in literary history. Likewise his popular anthologies have exerted a quiet but powerful influence on the contemporary canon of American poetry. Still an active poet, children's writer, anthologist, and critic, Kennedy lives with his wife in Lexington, Massachusetts.

In a Prominent Bar in Secaucus One Day

To the tune of "The Old Orange Flute"
or the tune of "Sweet Betsy from Pike"

In a prominent bar in Secaucus one day
Rose a lady in skunk with a topheavy sway,
Raised a knobby red finger—all turned from their beer—
While with eyes bright as snowcrust she sang high and clear:

"Now who of you'd think from an eyeload of me   5
That I once was a lady as proud as could be?
Oh I'd never sit down by a tumbledown drunk
If it wasn't, my dears, for the high cost of junk.

"All the gents used to swear that the white of my calf
Beat the down of the swan by a length and a half.   10
In the kerchief of linen I caught to my nose
Ah, there never fell snot, but a little gold rose.

"I had seven gold teeth and a toothpick of gold,
My Virginia cheroot was a leaf of it rolled
And I'd light it each time with a thousand in cash—   15
Why the bums used to fight if I flicked them an ash.

"Once the toast of the Biltmore, the belle of the Taft,
I would drink bottle beer at the Drake, never draft,
And dine at the Astor[1] on Salisbury steak
With a clean tablecloth for each bite I did take.   20

"In a car like the Roxy I'd roll to the track,
A steel-guitar trio, a bar in the back,
And the wheels made no noise, they turned over so fast,
Still it took you ten minutes to see me go past.

"When the horses bowed down to me that I might choose,   25
I bet on them all, for I hated to lose.
Now I'm saddled each night for my butter and eggs
And the broken threads race down the backs of my legs.

"Let you hold in mind, girls, that your beauty must pass
Like a lovely white clover that rusts with its grass.   30
Keep your bottoms off barstools and marry you young
Or be left—an old barrel with many a bung.[2]

"For when time takes you out for a spin in his car
You'll be hard-pressed to stop him from going too far
And be left by the roadside, for all your good deeds,   35
Two toadstools for tits and a face full of weeds."

1. Names of upscale hotels.
2. A stopper for a hole.

All the house raised a cheer, but the man at the bar
Made a phonecall and up pulled a red patrol car
And she blew us a kiss as they copped her away
From that prominent bar in Secaucus, N.J.

40

1961

Little Elegy

For a child who skipped rope

Here lies resting, out of breath,
Out of turns, Elizabeth
Whose quicksilver toes not quite
Cleared the whirring edge of night.

Earth whose circles round us skim   5
Till they catch the lightest limb,
Shelter now Elizabeth
And for her sake trip up Death.

1961

Loose Woman

Someone who well knew how she'd toss her chin
    Passing the firehouse oglers, at their taunt,
    Let it be flung up higher than she'd want,
Just held fast by a little hinge of skin.
Two boys come from the river kicked a thatch   5
    Of underbrush and stopped. One wrecked a pair
    Of sneakers blundering into her hair
And that day made a different sort of catch.

Her next-best talent—setting tongues to buzz—
    Lasts longer than her best. It still occurs   10
    To wonder had she been our fault or hers
And had she loved him. Who the bastard was,
Though long they asked and notebooked round about
    And turned up not a few who would have known
    That white inch where her neck met shoulderbone,   15
Was one thing more we never did find out.

1969

The Waterbury Cross

Fall. You're driving 84 southwest—
A hillock scarlet as a side of beef
Accosts your eyes. Gigantic on its crest,
An outstretched cross stands waiting for its thief.

Your fingers as though hammered to the wheel   5
Clench hard. Frost-kindled sumac blazes down
Like true gore pouring from a bogus crown.
The earth grows drizzled, dazzled, and bedrenched.

Did even Wallace Stevens at the last,
Having sown all his philosophe's wild oats,   10
Gape for the sacred wafer and clutch fast
To Mother Church's swaddling petticoats?

Connecticut's conversions stun. Is there
Still a pale Christ who clings to hope for me,
Who bides time in a cloud? Choking, my car   15
Walks over water, across to Danbury.

1992

◄ ADRIENNE RICH ►
(b. 1929)

One of the most influential American writers of the past half-century, Adrienne Rich has consciously evolved over the course of her career, revising both her style and her ideas in response to changing times. Her searching changes arise from her determination to chart new territory opened by feminist perspectives. In her essay, "Blood, Bread, and Poetry" (1984), she described her goal and its consequences: "To write directly and overtly as a woman, out of a woman's experience, to take women's existence seriously as theme and source for art, was something I had been hungering to do, needing to do, all my writing life. It placed me nakedly face to face with both terror and anger; it did indeed *imply the breakdown of the world as I had always known it. . . .*" The risks Rich has taken, both artistic and political, have involved not only the intellectual and spiritual evolution that fueled her poetry and prose, but life changes as well.

Adrienne Cecile Rich was born in Baltimore to Arnold Rice Rich, a doctor and professor of pathology at Johns Hopkins University, and Helen Jones Rich, who gave up her dream of a career as a concert pianist to devote all of her attention to her family. In addition to this strain on the family, which Rich herself would later experience and document, the family also struggled with its religious identity. In "Split at the Root: An Essay on Jewish Identity" (1982), Rich describes household frictions resulting from her father's Judaism and her mother's Southern Protestantism and traces her own intimations of a Jewish identity that surfaced despite her family's efforts to live a life of assimilation.

Rich took an early interest in poetry, and her father encouraged her love of literature, directing her reading and offering serious criticism of the poems she wrote. By the time she graduated from Radcliffe College, Rich had already won the Yale Series of Younger Poets Prize for her first book, *A Change of World* (1951). The prize helped her earn a Guggenheim fellowship the next year to travel in Europe. After her return in 1953, she married Alfred Conrad, a young professor of economics at Harvard University. Her second book, *The Diamond Cutters*, appeared in 1955, but, due to the demands of caring for her three young sons, she did not publish her next collection, *Snapshots of a Daughter-in-Law*, until 1963.

In *Of Woman Born: Motherhood as Experience and Institution* (1976), a substantial prose study of motherhood, Rich recalled the difficulties she had in raising three small children while trying to sustain her writing life. She concluded that, during these years, "I knew I was fighting for my life through, against, and with the lives of my children. . . . I had been trying to give birth to myself."

That second birth resulted in crucial changes both to her poetry and her worldview. In "Blood, Bread, and Poetry," she acknowledged her indebtedness to the work of Mary Wollstonecraft, Simone de Beauvoir, and James Baldwin:

> Each of them helped me to realize that what had seemed simply "the way things are" could actually be a social construct, advantageous to some people and detrimental to others, and that these constructs could be criticized and changed. The myths and obsessions of gender, the myths and obsessions of race, the violent exercise of power in these relationships could be identified, their territories mapped. They were not simply part of my private turmoil, a secret misery, an individual failure.

Beginning with *Snapshots of a Daughter-in-Law,* Rich set out to map those territories. The title poem's challenges to traditional literary views of women and its portrayal of a dissatisfied wife and mother drew criticism from reviewers, who expected Rich to exhibit the polish and emotional poise of her first two books. In 1966, she moved to New York City with her husband so that he could work at City College, and they both became active in social justice movements. Her opposition to the war in Vietnam, her commitment to the women's movement, and her job teaching remedial English to minority students taught her lessons that were vital to her poetry. "As a poet," she remarked, "I had learned much about both the value and the constraints of convention: the reassurances of traditional structures and the necessity to break from them in recognition of new experience. I felt more and more urgently the dynamic between poetry as language and poetry as a kind of action, probing, burning, stripping, placing itself in dialogue with others out beyond the individual self."

Her vision of poetry as action, a means of bringing about both individual and social change, governed the books following *Necessities of Life* (1966). In *Leaflets* (1969), *The Will to Change* (1971), and *Diving into the Wreck* (1973), Rich revised her views of herself and the world. The need to reimagine her identity was given added impetus by difficult events in her life. Her father died in 1968, and by 1969 Rich had also become estranged from her husband, who committed suicide the following year.

With *The Dream of a Common Language* (1978), which included a series of lesbian love poems, "Twenty-One Love Poems," her earlier emphasis on anger and fragmentation shifted to a search for human connection, especially through relationships with women. In her later poetry, Rich continued to emphasize women's experience, while opening her inquiry to include race relations, class conflict, and radical economics, especially the inequalities fostered by corporate domination of American politics. Above all, she balances a public voice, witnessing to injustice and envisioning change, against her own private experience and considers how that experience is inseparable from her public concerns. Her own achievement of these goals has been honored through many awards, including the National Book Award (1974), the Robert Frost Silver Medal for Lifetime Achievement in Poetry (1992), and a MacArthur Foundation Fellowship (1994). But her strongest measure of achievement is her large, devoted readership and her enduring influence in the cultural debates of her era.

Aunt Jennifer's Tigers

Aunt Jennifer's tigers prance across a screen,
Bright topaz denizens of a world of green.
They do not fear the men beneath the tree;
They pace in sleek chivalric certainty.

Aunt Jennifer's fingers fluttering through her wool   5
Find even the ivory needle hard to pull.
The massive weight of Uncle's wedding band
Sits heavily upon Aunt Jennifer's hand.

When Aunt is dead, her terrified hands will lie
Still ringed with ordeals she was mastered by.   10
The tigers in the panel that she made
Will go on prancing, proud and unafraid.

                                                    1951

The Diamond Cutters

However legendary,
The stone is still a stone,
Though it had once resisted
The weight of Africa,
The hammer-blows of time   5
That wear to bits of rubble
The mountain and the pebble—
But not this coldest one.

Now, you intelligence
So late dredged up from dark   10
Upon whose smoky walls
Bison took fumbling form
Or flint was edged on flint—
Now, careful arriviste,
Delineate at will   15
Incisions in the ice.

Be serious, because
The stone may have contempt
For too-familiar hands,
And because all you do   20
Loses or gains by this:
Respect the adversary,
Meet it with tools refined,
And thereby set your price.

Be hard of heart, because   25
The stone must leave your hand.
Although you liberate
Pure and expensive fires
Fit to enamor Shebas,

Keep your desire apart.   30
Love only what you do,
And not what you have done.

Be proud, when you have set
The final spoke of flame
In that prismatic wheel,   35
And nothing's left this day
Except to see the sun
Shine on the false and the true,
And know that Africa
Will yield you more to do.   40

1955

Living in Sin

She had thought the studio would keep itself;
no dust upon the furniture of love.
Half heresy, to wish the taps less vocal,
the panes relieved of grime. A plate of pears,
a piano with a Persian shawl, a cat   5
stalking the picturesque amusing mouse
had risen at his urging.
Not that at five each separate stair would writhe
under the milkman's tramp; that morning light
so coldly would delineate the scraps   10
of last night's cheese and three sepulchral bottles;
that on the kitchen shelf among the saucers
a pair of beetle-eyes would fix her own—
envoy from some village in the moldings . . .
Meanwhile, he, with a yawn,   15
sounded a dozen notes upon the keyboard,
declared it out of tune, shrugged at the mirror,
rubbed at his beard, went out for cigarettes;
while she, jeered by the minor demons,
pulled back the sheets and made the bed and found 20
a towel to dust the table-top,
and let the coffee-pot boil over on the stove.
By evening she was back in love again,
though not so wholly but throughout the night
she woke sometimes to feel the daylight coming   25
like a relentless milkman up the stairs.

1955

Diving into the Wreck

First having read the book of myths,
and loaded the camera,
and checked the edge of the knife-blade,
I put on
the body-armor of black rubber   5

the absurd flippers
the grave and awkward mask.
I am having to do this
not like Cousteau[1] with his
assiduous team   10
aboard the sun-flooded schooner
but here alone.

There is a ladder.
The ladder is always there
hanging innocently   15
close to the side of the schooner.
We know what it is for,
we who have used it.
Otherwise
it's a piece of maritime floss   20
some sundry equipment.

I go down.
Rung after rung and still
the oxygen immerses me
the blue light   25
the clear atoms
of our human air.
I go down.
My flippers cripple me,
I crawl like an insect down the ladder   30
and there is no one
to tell me when the ocean
will begin.

First the air is blue and then
it is bluer and then green and then   35
black I am blacking out and yet
my mask is powerful
it pumps my blood with power
the sea is another story
the sea is not a question of power   40
I have to learn alone
to turn my body without force
in the deep element.

And now: it is easy to forget
what I came for   45
among so many who have always
lived here
swaying their crenellated fans

1. Jacques-Yves Cousteau (1910–1997), French undersea explorer and film producer.

between the reefs
and besides   50
you breathe differently down here.

I came to explore the wreck.
The words are purposes.
The words are maps.
I came to see the damage that was done   55
and the treasures that prevail.
I stroke the beam of my lamp
slowly along the flank
of something more permanent
than fish or weed   60

the thing I came for:
the wreck and not the story of the wreck
the thing itself and not the myth
the drowned face always staring
toward the sun   65
the evidence of damage
worn by salt and sway into this threadbare beauty
the ribs of the disaster
curving their assertion
among the tentative haunters.   70

This is the place.
And I am here, the mermaid whose dark hair
streams black, the merman in his armored body
We circle silently
about the wreck   75
we dive into the hold.
I am she: I am he

whose drowned face sleeps with open eyes
whose breasts still bear the stress
whose silver, copper, vermeil cargo lies   80
obscurely inside barrels
half-wedged and left to rot
we are the half-destroyed instruments
that once held to a course
the water-eaten log   85
the fouled compass

We are, I am, you are
by cowardice or courage
the one who find our way
back to this scene   90
carrying a knife, a camera
a book of myths
in which
our names do not appear.

1973

From a Survivor

The pact that we made was the ordinary pact
of men & women in those days

I don't know who we thought we were
that our personalities
could resist the failures of the race   5

Lucky or unlucky, we didn't know
the race had failures of that order
and that we were going to share them

Like everybody else, we thought of ourselves as special

Your body is as vivid to me   10
as it ever was: even more

since my feeling for it is clearer:
I know what it could and could not do

it is no longer
the body of a god   15
or anything with power over my life

Next year it would have been 20 years
and you are wastefully dead
who might have made the leap
we talked, too late, of making   20

which I live now
not as a leap
but a succession of brief, amazing movements

each one making possible the next

                                                                     1973

Rape

There is a cop who is both prowler and father:
he comes from your block, grew up with your brothers,
had certain ideals.
You hardly know him in his boots and silver badge,
on horseback, one hand touching his gun.   5

You hardly know him but you have to get to know him:
he has access to machinery that could kill you.
He and his stallion clop like warlords among the trash,
his ideals stand in the air, a frozen cloud
from between his unsmiling lips.   10

And so, when the time comes, you have to turn to him,
the maniac's sperm still greasing your thighs,
your mind whirling like crazy. You have to confess

to him, you are guilty of the crime
of having been forced.   15

And you see his blue eyes, the blue eyes of all the family
whom you used to know, grow narrow and glisten,
his hand types out the details
and he wants them all
but the hysteria in your voice pleases him best.   20

You hardly know him but now he thinks he knows you:
he has taken down your worst moment
on a machine and filed it in a file.
He knows, or thinks he knows, how much you imagined;
he knows, or thinks he knows, what you secretly wanted.   25

He has access to machinery that could get you put away;
and if, in the sickening light of the precinct,
and if, in the sickening light of the precinct,
your details sound like a portrait of your confessor,
will you swallow, will you deny them, will you lie your way home?   30

                                                              1973

Power

Living   in the earth-deposits   of our history

Today a backhoe divulged   out of a crumbling flank of earth
one bottle   amber   perfect   a hundred-year-old
cure for fever   or melancholy   a tonic
for living on this earth   in the winters of this climate   5

Today I was reading about Marie Curie:[2]
she must have known she suffered   from radiation sickness
her body bombarded for years   by the element
she had purified
It seems she denied to the end   10
the source of the cataracts on her eyes
the cracked and suppurating skin   of her finger-ends
till she could no longer hold   a test-tube or a pencil

She died   a famous woman   denying
her wounds   15
denying
her wounds   came   from the same source as her power

                                                              1978

(Dedications)

I know you are reading this poem
late, before leaving your office

---

2. The Polish scientist (1867–1934) who helped discover polonium and radium. She was the first person to win two Nobel Prizes.

of the one intense yellow lamp-spot and the darkening window
in the lassitude of a building faded to quiet
long after rush-hour.   I know you are reading this poem   5
standing up in a bookstore far from the ocean
on a grey day of early spring, faint flakes driven
across the plains' enormous spaces around you.
I know you are reading this poem
in a room where too much has happened for you to bear   10
where the bedclothes lie in stagnant coils on the bed
and the open valise speaks of flight
but you cannot leave yet.   I know you are reading this poem
as the underground train loses momentum and before running
                    up the stairs   15
toward a new kind of love
your life has never allowed.
I know you are reading this poem by the light
of the television screen where soundless images jerk and slide
while you wait for the newscast from the *intifada*.   20
I know you are reading this poem in a waiting-room
of eyes met and unmeeting, of identity with strangers.
I know you are reading this poem by fluorescent light
in the boredom and fatigue of the young who are counted out,
count themselves out, at too early an age.   I know   25
you are reading this poem through your failing sight, the thick
lens enlarging these letters beyond all meaning yet you read on
because even the alphabet is precious.
I know you are reading this poem as you pace beside the stove
warming milk, a crying child on your shoulder, a book in your   30
                    hand
because life is short and you too are thirsty.
I know you are reading this poem which is not in your language
guessing at some words while others keep you reading
and I want to know which words they are.   35
I know you are reading this poem listening for something, torn
                    between bitterness and hope
turning back one again to the task you cannot refuse.
I know you are reading this poem because there is nothing else
                    left to read   40
there where you have landed, stripped as you are.

                                                                1991

Tattered Kaddish³

Taurean reaper of the wild apple field
messenger from earthmire gleaning
transcripts of fog

---

3. The title refers to a Jewish prayer recited after the death of a close relative.

in the nineteenth year and the eleventh month
speak your tattered Kaddish for all suicides: 5

Praise to life though it crumbled in like a tunnel
on ones we knew and loved

    Praise to life though its windows blew shut
    on the breathing-room of ones we knew and loved

Praise to life though ones we knew and loved   10
loved it badly, too well, and not enough

    Praise to life though it tightened like a knot
    on the hearts of ones we thought we knew loved us

Praise to life giving room and reason
to ones we knew and loved who felt unpraisable   15

    Praise to them, how they loved it, when they could.

1991

❧ SYLVIA PLATH ❧
(1932–1963)

Sylvia Plath was born in Boston, the daughter of Otto Emil Plath, a German immigrant who taught German and biology at Boston University, and Aurelia
Schober Plath, whose parents were Austrian immigrants. When Plath was four,
the family moved to the seaside town of Winthrop, Massachusetts, to be near her
maternal grandparents, for her father's health was declining. After Otto Plath died
in 1940 from the effects of undiagnosed diabetes, Mrs. Plath moved inland to
Wellesley, Massachusetts, and supported herself and her two children—Sylvia and
her younger brother, Warren—through teaching clerical courses at Boston University. Interested in writing from an early age, Sylvia published her first poem when
she was only eight years old. By the time she graduated from high school in 1950,
she had published a short story and a poem in *Seventeen* and a poem in the *Christian Science Monitor.*

    A driven student, Plath won a fellowship to attend Smith College. In the sum-
mer of her junior year, she served as a student guest editor in New York City for
the college issue of *Mademoiselle* magazine—an experience that would eventually
serve as the background for her novel, *The Bell Jar.* Afflicted by depression after
her return home, she attempted suicide by taking an overdose of sleeping pills.
She was then hospitalized at Massachusetts General Hospital and transferred to
McLean Hospital in Belmont, Massachusetts, where her treatment program included psychotherapy and electroshock therapy. She returned to Smith in early
1954 and graduated summa cum laude in 1955, with an honors thesis on "The
Double in Dostoevsky."

    In the fall of 1955 Plath traveled on a Fulbright Fellowship to England to
study at Cambridge University. There, in February 1956, she met and fell in love
with the poet Ted Hughes and married him four months later. In Hughes, Plath

believed she had found a soul mate—a man who was her equal creatively and intellectually. The two ambitious young artists supported each other's writing and did their best to forge a life in which the demands of making a living would not compromise their literary aspirations. After Plath earned a bachelor's degree from Cambridge in 1957, she and Hughes moved to Massachusetts. Plath taught freshman English for the next academic year at Smith. The couple relocated to Boston determined to live on the proceeds of their writing, but Plath supplemented their income with part-time work as a secretary at the psychiatric ward of Massachusetts General Hospital. She also took a writing class taught by Robert Lowell at Boston University, where she befriended Anne Sexton, a fellow student. After a summer touring the United States and a residency at the Yaddo Artists' Colony, Plath and Hughes returned to England in late 1959.

They settled in London, and the following year Plath gave birth to a daughter. She also saw the publication of her first book, *The Colossus* (1960). Issued only in England, the volume received few reviews—in contrast to Hughes's highly acclaimed and prize-winning two books, *The Hawk in the Rain* (1957) and *Lupercal* (1960). Returning to fiction, Plath began work on an autobiographical novel, *The Bell Jar,* that framed her 1953 breakdown and recovery in terms of death and rebirth and also cast a satirical eye on the gender double standards of midcentury America. She completed the novel in only eight months, despite suffering a miscarriage, an appendectomy, and buying a new home with Hughes, a thatched-roof cottage in Devon. There, she gave birth to a second child in 1962.

Plath's marriage, however, soon began to deteriorate as she discovered that Hughes was seeing another woman. Plath and Hughes separated in September, and she stayed on in the Devon house, caring for the children and writing poems at a rapid rate. She wrote to a friend: "When I was 'happy' domestically I felt a gag in my throat. Now that my domestic life . . . is chaos, I am living like a Spartan, writing through huge fevers and producing free stuff I had locked in me for years. I feel astounded and very lucky." Yet she also felt increasingly isolated in Devon, so she moved to a London apartment, where she continued her new habit of writing from 4 A.M. to 8 A.M., before the children awoke and demanded her attention. In January 1963 *The Bell Jar* was published in England under a pseudonym, "Victoria Lucas." Although Plath had struggled to maintain her equilibrium as she tried to rebuild her life, she succumbed to depression. On the morning of February 11, 1963, she committed suicide in her apartment kitchen by inhaling gas from the oven.

Because Plath died without a will, Hughes, whom she had not yet divorced at the time of her death, became her literary executor. In November 1962, Plath had completed a new poetry manuscript, carefully arranging the poems so that the book, *Ariel* (1965) developed according to an archetypal pattern of death and rebirth and whose purview included the disintegration of her marriage. When Hughes prepared the book for publication, however, he changed the manuscript. He admitted in his introduction to Plath's *Collected Poems* (1981) that the published version of *Ariel* "omitted some of the more personally aggressive poems of 1962, and might have omitted one or two more if [Plath] had not already published them herself in magazines." Along with deleting poems that were "personally aggressive" against him, he included at the end of the collection poems of despair that Plath had written immediately before her suicide. As Marjorie Perloff notes in her essay, "The Two *Ariels*: the (Re) Making of the Sylvia Plath Canon," in the published version of *Ariel* "the poems that make only too clear that

Hughes's desertion was the immediate cause of Plath's depression are expunged; instead, the volume now culminates in ten death poems, poems written, as it were, from beyond rage, from someone who no longer blames anyone for her condition and reconciles herself to death."

When *Ariel* appeared, first in England in 1965 and then in the United States in 1966, it caused a sensation. Reviewers interpreted the book as a suicide note. Whether they praised Plath for her courage or dismissed her as angry and self-destructive, they tended to judge Plath personally rather than the poems. Mostly, reviewers sensationalized the book, framing Plath, in the words of *Time* magazine, as a "literary dragon who . . . breathed a burning river of bale across the literary landscape." Little recognized during her life, in death Plath had become a new cultural icon, a mythic figure—depending on the reader—of either self-destructive genius or female martyrdom.

Speculation about Plath's life continued in the decades after her death, as Hughes edited additional books: *Crossing the Water: Transitional Poems* (1971), *Winter Trees* (1971), and *Johnny Panic and the Bible of Dreams and Other Prose Writings* (1977). Plath's mother also published *Letters Home: Correspondence 1950–1963* (1975). Plath's *Collected Poems* posthumously won the Pulitzer Prize. *The Journals of Sylvia Plath* (1982) provided another "portrait of the artist as a young woman" that Plath paints of herself. In its introduction Hughes admitted his abridgments and his destruction of the journals she kept during the last three years of her life. Only two years after Hughes's death was *The Unabridged Journals of Sylvia Plath* (2000) published.

Because Plath mined painful personal experiences in many of her poems, she has been considered an exemplar of the Confessional School of poetry. Following Hughes's lead in his essays about Plath, critics have often seen her poetry as her attempt to find her "true" self. This relentlessly biographical approach was reinforced by A. Alvarez's international best-selling study of poetry and suicide, *The Savage God* (1971), which focused on Plath. On the other hand, feminist critics have made Plath a cause célèbre, applauding her freedom to express bitter anger in her poetry, her exploration of the female psyche, and her portrayal of the challenges of domestic life, especially the confinement of an oppressive marriage.

Plath's poetry strikes a complex range of tones. Its emotional intensity encompasses not just rage but also acerbic wit, maternal tenderness, sheer joy at the strange beauty of life, and triumphant declarations of poetic power. In the last year of her life, she honed a style in which her poems shifted swiftly, from image to image, through deft line breaks and simple, declarative sentences that exert a tense control over the breakneck pace of her disquieting insights. Because her poems register inner experience in ways that raise the events she describes to the level of myth, strictly biographical approaches to her work fail to do justice to its sophistication. As Plath herself argues in a BBC interview from October 1962:

> I think my poems immediately come out of the sensuous and emotional experiences I have, but I must say I cannot sympathize with these cries from the heart that are informed by nothing except a needle or a knife, or whatever it is. I believe that one should be able to control and manipulate experiences, even the most terrifying, like madness, being tortured, this sort of experience, and one should be able to manipulate these experiences with an informed and an intelligent mind. I think that personal experience is very important, but certainly it shouldn't be a kind of shut-box and mirror-looking, narcissistic experience. I believe it should be *relevant,* and relevant to larger things.

The Colossus[1]

I shall never get you put together entirely,
Pieced, glued, and properly jointed.
Mule-bray, pig-grunt and bawdy cackles
Proceed from your great lips.
It's worse than a barnyard.   5

Perhaps you consider yourself an oracle,
Mouthpiece of the dead, or of some god or other.
Thirty years now I have labored
To dredge the silt from your throat.
I am none the wiser.   10

Scaling little ladders with gluepots and pails of Lysol
I crawl like an ant in mourning
Over the weedy acres of your brow
To mend the immense skull-plates and clear
The bald, white tumuli of your eyes.   15

A blue sky out of the Oresteia[2]
Arches above us. O father, all by yourself
You are pithy and historical as the Roman Forum.
I open my lunch on a hill of black cypress.
Your fluted bones and acanthine hair are littered   20

In their old anarchy to the horizon-line.
It would take more than a lightning-stroke
To create such a ruin.
Nights, I squat in the cornucopia
Of your left ear, out of the wind,   25

Counting the red stars and those of plum-color.
The sun rises under the pillar of your tongue.
My hours are married to shadow.
No longer do I listen for the scrape of a keel
On the blank stones of the landing.   30

1959

Metaphors

I'm a riddle in nine syllables,
An elephant, a ponderous house,
A melon strolling on two tendrils.
O red fruit, ivory, fine timbers!
This loaf's big with its yeasty rising.   5

1. The bronze Colossus of Rhodes, completed in the third century B.C.E., was one of the Seven Wonders of the World.
2. A trilogy of plays by Greek dramatist Aeschylus (525–456 B.C.E.), each concerned with murder, revenge, and justice in a single family.

Money's new-minted in this fat purse.
I'm a means, a stage, a cow in calf.
I've eaten a bag of green apples,
Boarded the train there's no getting off.

1960

Blackberrying

Nobody in the lane, and nothing, nothing but blackberries,
Blackberries on either side, though on the right mainly,
A blackberry alley, going down in hooks, and a sea
Somewhere at the end of it, heaving. Blackberries
Big as the ball of my thumb, and dumb as eyes   5
Ebon in the hedges, fat
With blue-red juices. These they squander on my fingers.
I had not asked for such a blood sisterhood; they must love me.
They accommodate themselves to my milkbottle, flattening their sides.

Overhead go the choughs in black, cacophonous flocks—   10
Bits of burnt paper wheeling in a blown sky.
Theirs is the only voice, protesting, protesting.
I do not think the sea will appear at all.
The high, green meadows are glowing, as if lit from within.
I come to one bush of berries so ripe it is a bush of flies,   15
Hanging their bluegreen bellies and their wing panes in a Chinese screen.
The honey-feast of the berries has stunned them; they believe in heaven.
One more hook, and the berries and bushes end.

The only thing to come now is the sea.
From between two hills a sudden wind funnels at me,   20
Slapping its phantom laundry in my face.
These hills are too green and sweet to have tasted salt.
I follow the sheep path between them. A last hook brings me
To the hills' northern face, and the face is orange rock
That looks out on nothing, nothing but a great space   25
Of white and pewter lights, and a din like silversmiths
Beating and beating at an intractable metal.

[1961] 1971

Mirror

I am silver and exact. I have no preconceptions.
Whatever I see I swallow immediately
Just as it is, unmisted by love or dislike.
I am not cruel, only truthful—
The eye of a little god, four-cornered.   5
Most of the time I meditate on the opposite wall.
It is pink, with speckles. I have looked at it so long
I think it is a part of my heart. But it flickers.
Faces and darkness separate us over and over.

Now I am a lake. A woman bends over me,   10
Searching my reaches for what she really is.
Then she turns to those liars, the candles or the moon.
I see her back, and reflect it faithfully.
She rewards me with tears and an agitation of hands.
I am important to her. She comes and goes.   15
Each morning it is her face that replaces the darkness.
In me she has drowned a young girl, and in me an old woman
Rises toward her day after day, like a terrible fish.

[1961] 1971

Daddy[3]

You do not do, you do not do
Any more, black shoe
In which I have lived like a foot
For thirty years, poor and white,
Barely daring to breathe or Achoo.   5

Daddy, I have had to kill you.
You died before I had time—
Marble-heavy, a bag full of God,
Ghastly statue with one grey toe
Big as a Frisco seal   10

And a head in the freakish Atlantic
Where it pours bean green over blue
In the waters off beautiful Nauset.
I used to pray to recover you.
Ach, du.[4]   15

In the German tongue, in the Polish town
Scraped flat by the roller
Of wars, wars, wars.
But the name of the town is common.
My Polack friend   20

Says there are a dozen or two.
So I never could tell where you
Put your foot, your root,
I never could talk to you.
The tongue stuck in my jaw.   25

It stuck in a barb wire snare.
Ich, ich, ich, ich,[5]

3. Introducing this poem in a reading, Sylvia Plath remarked:
     The poem is spoken by a girl with an Electra complex. Her father died while she
   thought he was God. Her case is complicated by the fact that her father was also a Nazi
   and her mother very possibly part Jewish. In the daughter the two strains marry and par-
   alyze each other—she has to act out the awful little allegory before she is free of it.
4. (German) Oh, you.
5. (German) I, I, I, I.

I could hardly speak.
I thought every German was you.
And the language obscene   30

An engine, an engine
Chuffing me off like a Jew.
A Jew to Dachau, Auschwitz, Belsen.
I began to talk like a Jew.
I think I may well be a Jew.   35

The snows of the Tyrol, the clear beer of Vienna
Are not very pure or true.
With my gypsy ancestress and my weird luck
And my Taroc pack and my Taroc pack
I may be a bit of a Jew.   40

I have always been scared of *you*,
With your Luftwaffe, your gobbledygoo.
And your neat moustache
And your Aryan eye, bright blue,
Panzer-man, panzer-man, O You—   45

Not God but a swastika
So black no sky could squeak through.
Every woman adores a Fascist,
The boot in the face, the brute
Brute heart of a brute like you.   50

You stand at the blackboard,[6] daddy,
In the picture I have of you,
A cleft in your chin instead of your foot
But no less a devil for that, no not
Any less the black man who   55

Bit my pretty red heart in two.
I was ten when they buried you.
At twenty I tried to die
And get back, back, back to you.
I thought even the bones would do.   60

But they pulled me out of the sack,
And they stuck me together with glue.
And then I knew what to do.
I made a model of you,
A man in black with a Meinkampf[7] look   65

And a love of the rack and the screw.
And I said I do, I do.
So daddy, I'm finally through.

6. Otto Plath had been a professor of biology at Boston University.
7. Adolf Hitler entitled his autobiography *Mein Kampf* ("My Struggle").

The black telephone's off at the root,
The voices just can't worm through.   70

If I've killed one man, I've killed two—
The vampire who said he was you
And drank my blood for a year,
Seven years, if you want to know.
Daddy, you can lie back now.   75

There's a stake in your fat black heart
And the villagers never liked you.
They are dancing and stamping on you.
They always *knew* it was you.
Daddy, daddy, you bastard, I'm through.   80

                                                                 1965

Morning Song

Love set you going like a fat gold watch.
The midwife slapped your footsoles, and your bald cry
Took its place among the elements.

Our voices echo, magnifying your arrival. New statue.
In a drafty museum, your nakedness   5
Shadows our safety. We stand round blankly as walls.

I'm no more your mother
Than the cloud that distils a mirror to reflect its own slow
Effacement at the wind's hand.

All night your moth-breath   10
Flickers among the flat pink roses. I wake to listen:
A far sea moves in my ear.

One cry, and I stumble from bed, cow-heavy and floral
In my Victorian nightgown.
Your mouth opens clean as a cat's. The window square   15

Whitens and swallows its dull stars. And now you try
Your handful of notes;
The clear vowels rise like balloons.

                                                                 1965

Lady Lazarus

I have done it again.
One year in every ten
I manage it—

A sort of walking miracle, my skin
Bright as a Nazi lampshade,   5
My right foot

A paperweight,
My face a featureless, fine
Jew linen.

Peel off the napkin   10
O my enemy.
Do I terrify?—

The nose, the eye pits, the full set of teeth?
The sour breath
Will vanish in a day.   15

Soon, soon the flesh
The grave cave ate will be
At home on me

And I a smiling woman.
I am only thirty.   20
And like the cat I have nine times to die.

This is Number Three.
What a trash
To annihilate each decade.

What a million filaments.   25
The peanut-crunching crowd
Shoves in to see

Them unwrap me hand and foot—
The big strip tease.
Gentleman, ladies,   30

These are my hands,
My knees.
I may be skin and bone,

Nevertheless, I am the same, identical woman.
The first time it happened I was ten.   35
It was an accident.

The second time I meant
To last it out and not come back at all.
I rocked shut

As a seashell.   40
They had to call and call
And pick the worms off me like sticky pearls.

Dying
Is an art, like everything else.
I do it exceptionally well.   45

I do it so it feels like hell.
I do it so it feels real.
I guess you could say I've a call.

It's easy enough to do it in a cell.
It's easy enough to do it and stay put.   50
It's the theatrical

Comeback in broad day
To the same place, the same face, the same brute
Amused shout:

"A miracle!"   55
That knocks me out.
There is a charge

For the eyeing of my scars, there is a charge
For the hearing of my heart—
It really goes.   60

And there is a charge, a very large charge,
For the word or a touch
Or a bit of blood

Or a piece of my hair or my clothes.
So, so, Herr Doktor.   65
So, Herr Enemy.

I am your opus,
I am your valuable,
The pure gold baby

That melts to a shriek.   70
I turn and burn.
Do not think I underestimate your great concern.

Ash, ash—
You poke and stir.
Flesh, bone, there is nothing there—   75

A cake of soap,
A wedding ring,
A gold filling,

Herr God, Herr Lucifer,
Beware   80
Beware.

Out of the ash
I rise with my red hair.
And I eat men like air.

                                                        1965

Edge

The woman is perfected.
Her dead

Body wears the smile of accomplishment,
The illusion of a Greek necessity

Flows in the scrolls of her toga,　　　　　5
Her bare

Feet seem to be saying:
We have come so far, it is over.

Each dead child coiled, a white serpent,
One at each little　　　　　　　　　　10

Pitcher of milk, now empty.
She has folded

Them back into her body as petals
Of a rose close when the garden

Stiffens and odours bleed　　　　　　15
From the sweet, deep throats of the night flower.

The moon has nothing to be sad about,
Staring from her hood of bone.

She is used to this sort of thing.
Her blacks crackle and drag.　　　　　20

　　　　　　　　　　　　　　　　1965

◦►◄ ANNE STEVENSON ►◄◦
(b. 1933)

Although an American citizen, Anne Stevenson has lived much of her life in Britain. "This has meant a measure of flexibility," she once wrote, "and a constant state of flux." She was born in Cambridge, England, where her father, the American philosopher Charles Leslie Stevenson, was studying with G. E. Moore and Ludwig Wittgenstein. Growing up in America, Stevenson lived in a cultivated household. Her father, a prominent professor at the University of Michigan in Ann Arbor, was also an accomplished musician who played both piano and cello—instruments that Anne, too, would take up.

　　After graduating from University High School in Ann Arbor in 1950, Stevenson entered the University of Michigan. While an undergraduate, she won the prestigious Hopwood Literary Award three times. She received her bachelor's degree from Michigan in 1954, and that same year moved to England and married Robin Hitchcock, with whom she would have a daughter. The marriage lasted just a few years. Returning to Michigan, she earned her master's degree in 1962 and married Mark Elvin, with whom she would have two sons. By that time she was back in England composing the poems she would collect in *Living in America* (1965) and doing research for the first full-length study of Elizabeth Bishop. Her correspondence with Bishop has proved an irreplaceable archive for scholars.

　　A second collection, *Reversals* (1969), offered both light and troubling views of domesticity and sex spoken fearlessly from a woman's point of view. By this time it was clear that Stevenson was a relentlessly honest poet; like Sylvia Plath she was frank even about her negative emotions. In 1974 Stevenson published *Correspondences: A Family History in Letters,* which would later be the basis of a radio play for the BBC. This long, ambitious work, which uses both verse and prose, is a sprawling family saga that moves from early nineteenth-century America to the present. Although *Correspondences* is fictional, its sense of family psychology is personal, and its conclusion displays some of the transatlantic complexity of her work: "It is a poem I can't continue. / It is America I can't contain."

Stevenson's poetic stance—fiercely intelligent, formally rigorous but not hide-bound, negotiating personal and public subjects—characterizes the poetry she has published in more than a dozen collections. In her preface to the *Collected Poems* (1996) she wrote, "It may be possible to descry in these peregrinations stages in 'the growth to the poet's mind'; on the other hand, I myself regard most of these poems as experiments in words and sounds." Yet the poems are often philosophi-cal and always intellectually lucid, whether in free verse or meter. Her most recent collection, *Granny Scarecrow* (2000), is among her strongest, and it continues to develop Stevenson's sense of the world outside herself—a Darwinian vision she has adapted partly from Elizabeth Bishop. Now regarded in England as one of po-etry's senior eminences, Stevenson currently divides her time between two houses—one in northern England, the other in Wales—with her fourth husband, historian Peter Lucas.

◄◦━━◗━━◦►

The Victory

I thought you were my victory
though you cut me like a knife
when I brought you out of my body
into your life.

Tiny antagonist, gory,   5
blue as a bruise. The stains
of your cloud of glory
bled from my veins.

How can you dare, blind thing,
blank insect eyes?   10
You barb the air. You sting
with bladed cries.

Snail. Scary knot of desires.
Hungry snarl. Small son.
Why do I have to love you?   15
How have you won?

1970

Generations

Know this mother by her three smiles:
A grey one drawn over her mouth by frail hooks,
A hurt smile under each eye.

Know this mother by the frames she makes.
By the silence in which she suffers each child   5
To scratch out the aquatints in her mind.

Know this mother by the way she says
"Darling" with her teeth clenched,
By the fabulous lies she cooks.

1974

The Marriage

They will fit, she thinks,
but only if her backbone
cuts exactly into his rib cage,
and only if his knees
dock exactly under her knees   5
and all four
agree on a common angle.

All would be well
if only
they could face each other.   10

Even as it is,
there are compensations
for having to meet
nose to neck
chest to scapula   15
groin to rump
when they sleep.

They look, at least,
as if they were going
in the same direction.   20

1974

Making Poetry

"You have to inhabit poetry
if you want to make it."

And what's "to inhabit"?

To be in the habit of, to wear
words, sitting in the plainest light,   5

in the silk of morning, in the shoe of night;
a feeling bare and frondish in surprising air;
familiar . . . rare.

And what's "to make"?

To be and to become words' passing   10
weather; to serve a girl on terrible
terms, embark on voyages over voices,
evade the ego-hill, the misery-well,
the siren hiss of *publish, success, publish,*
success, success, success.   15

And why inhabit, make, inherit poetry?

Oh, it's the shared comedy of the worst
blessed; the sound leading the hand;
a wordlife running from mind to mind
through the washed rooms of the simple senses;   20
one of those haunted, undefendable, unpoetic
crosses we have to find.

                                              1985

Alas

The way you say the world is what you get.
What's more, you haven't time to change or choose.
The words swim out to pin you in their net

Before you guess you're in the TV set,
Lit up and sizzling in unfriendly news.   5
The mind's machine—and you invented it—

Grinds out the formulae you have to fit,
The ritual syllables you need to use
To charm the world and not be crushed by it.

This cluttered motorway, that screaming jet,   10
Those crouching skeletons whose eyes accuse;
O see and say them, make yourself forget

The world is vaster than the alphabet,
And profligate, and meaner than the muse.
A bauble in the universe? Or shit?   15

Whichever way, you say the world you get.
Though what there is is always there to lose.
No crimson name redeems the poisoned rose,
The absolute's irrelevant. And yet . . .

                                              1994

American Internationalism: Surrealism, Deep Image Poetry, and the New York School

At an exhibition of paintings by Abstract Expressionist Mark Rothko

HISTORICAL AND CRITICAL OVERVIEW

Alternatives to America

> I feel very much part of a new international style.
> —*Mark Strand*

In "The Day Lady Died," when Frank O'Hara describes his lunch hour stroll through Manhattan on a muggy July afternoon in 1959, he seems to have the world at his fingertips. He buys French cigarettes and Italian liqueur, peruses the literary journal *New World Writing* "to see what the poets / in Ghana are doing these days," and buys a book of French Symbolist poetry—after considering as alternatives recent French and Irish plays and a new translation of ancient Greek poetry. International in scope, O'Hara's interests and opportunities reflected the expansion of U.S. political, economic, and cultural influence after World War II. But O'Hara's eclecticism also epitomized an impulse common among poets of his generation. He sought alternatives to the cultural conventions and constrictions of America during the Cold War. For the poets featured in this section, the literatures of Europe and Latin America, especially surrealism, became a lifeline from which they wove what Strand called "a new international style."

To James Wright and the other "American Internationalists," this cultural exploration meant not only reading the work of European and Latin American poets, but imitating it, translating it, and gaining firsthand experience of the world through foreign travel. One reflection of the United States' new spirit of internationalism in the aftermath of World War II was the Fulbright scholarship program established by Congress in 1946 to foster cultural exchange. John Ashbery, Robert Bly, Mark Strand, Charles Wright, and James Wright all lived and worked in Europe on Fulbright scholarships early in their careers. Several of the American Internationalists spent significant portions of their lives in Europe. Charles Simic grew up in Yugoslavia and immigrated to the United States at age fifteen, and Ashbery lived in Paris for eight years, earning his living as an art critic. W. S. Merwin spent much of his twenties and thirties in Europe. Living in Portugal, Spain, and England, and eventually purchasing a farmhouse in the French countryside, Merwin earned his living first as a tutor, then as a translator. As perhaps the most gifted translator among the American Internationalists, Merwin set the standard for adapting techniques he learned from the many authors he translated.

Translation was not a new enterprise for American poets. In the mid-nineteenth century Henry Wadsworth Longfellow proved a formidable translator from nearly a dozen languages, and his grandnephew Ezra Pound made translation central to the poetic vocation. But never had poetic translation occupied so central a place in a new generation as it did with the poets of the 1960s. For them, translation served as a passport to becoming a poet. James Wright, John Ashbery, Edward Field, Philip Levine, Charles Simic, Mark Strand, and Charles Wright all published translations, but foremost among them was Robert Bly who used translation to proselytize for the new style. He recalled in a 1966 interview that the poets he discovered during his Fulbright years in Norway, "Pablo Neruda, Juan Ramon Jiménez, Cesar Vallejo, Georg Trakl . . . were well known in Europe, even in little countries, but totally ignored or unheard of in the United States." In 1958, he founded *The Fifties* (which, as the decades passed, became *The Sixties* and *The Seventies*) as a platform not only for his translations and incendiary essays, but also for what came to be known as "Deep Image" poetry. (The term was coined in a 1961 essay, "Notes on the Poetry of Deep Image," by the poet Robert Kelly.) Bly proudly offered his poetry and that of his peers alongside translations of European and Latin American poets as an antidote for what he called, in the title of his best-known essay, "A Wrong Turning in American Poetry."

Although Bly was a more vocal proponent of the new style than his fellow American Internationalists, particularly the urbane poets of the New York School, they shared a common goal. They wanted to enliven American poetry, which many felt had reached a dead end, and to offer an alternative to the views of the New Critics, who dominated both the literary magazines of the 1940s and '50s and the teaching of poetry at American universities. Like many of the Open Form poets, the American Internationalists attended college during the heyday of the New Criticism, when textbooks such as Cleanth Brooks and Robert Penn Warren's *Understanding Poetry* trained students in analytical "close reading." In a 1966 interview, Bly expressed the frustration of many poets of his generation when he condemned "the isolationist New Criticism" of Cleanth Brooks, Allen Tate, and John Crowe Ransom. "They broke abruptly," Bly asserted, "with Eliot's and Pound's fertile internationalism which looked to the French and to other foreign poets."

To find sustenance, many American poets of the period turned not to an eclectic range of European and Asian writers, as did Pound and Eliot, but primarily to European and Latin American surrealists, whose opposition to rationalism seemed the perfect antidote to the New Criticism. Overall, the legacy of surrealism was claimed by many midcentury poets, including Elizabeth Bishop, Lorine Niedecker, Thomas McGrath, Donald Justice, Louis Simpson, Donald Hall, Weldon Kees, William Stafford, Allen Ginsberg, A. R. Ammons, Jack Spicer, Sylvia Plath, John Berryman, and Amiri Baraka (who was associated with the New York School before he went on to help found the Black Arts Movement in the late 1960s). The poets included in this section, however, helped to define a period style whose core elements were largely drawn from surrealist precedents and assumptions. Not only through their poems, but also through essays, translations, and teachings, these American Internationalists gave their brand of surrealism a wide currency during the second half of the century.

Surrealism: French Roots

> A story is told according to which Saint-Pol-Roux, in times gone by, used to have a notice posted on the door of his manor house in Camaret, every evening before he went to sleep, which read: THE POET IS WORKING.
> —*André Breton*

When asked to define the term *surrealism,* most educated Americans would associate it primarily with the visual arts, especially the work of painters such as Salvador Dalí, Jóan Miró, and René Magritte, filmmakers such as Luis Buñuel, and the sculptures and "ready-mades" of Marcel Duchamp (such as the urinal he labeled "Fountain" and displayed at the 1915 Armory Show in New York City). But from its inception in the early twentieth century, the movement galvanized writers as well as visual artists, often inspiring cross-disciplinary collaborations, and surrealism has deeply influenced the course of modern poetry in the Western world. In fact, the term *surrealism* was originally coined in 1917 by a French poet, Guillaume Apollinaire, and then defined at length by his compatriot, the poet André Breton, who ceaselessly championed the movement until his death in 1966.

In his first "Manifesto of Surrealism" (1924), Breton argued that the movement could help artists break away from the dead-end patterns of thinking he associated with rationalism by gaining access to the mysteries of the unconscious mind. Acknowledging his debt to Sigmund Freud, he urged writers to seek inspiration in dreams and practice automatic writing and free association. Although the term *surrealism* translates literally as "above or beyond reality," Breton and his followers felt that the techniques they adopted enhanced experience, whether combining it with marvelous images from the dream world or illuminating an elemental, authentic form of reality that conventional modes of perception occluded. Breton proposed a two-part definition:

> SURREALISM, *n.* Psychic automatism in its pure state, by which one proposes to express—verbally, by means of the written word, or in any other manner—the actual functioning of thought. Dictated by thought, in the absence of any control exercised by reason, exempt from any aesthetic or moral concern.

> ENCYCLOPEDIA. *Philosophy.* Surrealism is based on the belief in the superior reality of certain forms of previously neglected associations, in the omnipotence of dream, in the disinterested play of thought. It tends to ruin once and for all all other psychic mechanisms and to substitute itself for them in solving all the principle problems of life.

Breton's view of surrealism as a panacea reflected his revolutionary stance. Despite its roots in the earlier anarchic and apolitical movement known as Dada, Breton began in the late twenties to link surrealism with Marxist opposition to bourgeois culture. (A fervent Communist, Breton repeatedly tried to link his surrealist agenda with that of the French Communist Party, which not surprisingly rejected his avant-garde proposals, causing the poet eventually to leave the Party in 1935.) In later manifestos, Breton would claim that surrealism could help undermine fascism. He was not the first, nor would he be the last, to see nonpopulist artistic techniques as a way of getting around official authority and censorship. But his first manifesto focused on seeing the world anew through chance-based techniques, particularly automatic writing and free association; probing the mysterious realm of the unconscious to tap the raw power of the imagination; and, in pursuit of these goals, loosening "any control exercised by reason."

Surrealism: American Branches

> My heart is in my
> pocket, it is Poems by Pierre Reverdy.
> —*Frank O'Hara*

The American Internationalists absorbed the core principles of surrealism from many sources. They not only drew on French poetry by Breton and his circle, but also the variations of surrealism that arose in the poetry of Spain, Germany and Austria, Italy, and Latin America. Whether they practiced free association or simply concentrated on creating disjunctive images, faith in chance and the power of the unknown helped them escape the poetic conventions they associated with the New Criticism. As Charles Simic argued in his 1978 essay, "Negative Capability and Its Children":

> Dada and then surrealism made Chance famous, made it ontological. They turned it into a weapon. Cause and effect as the archenemies. . . . So the project became one of

using Chance to break the spell of our habitual literary expectations and to approach the condition of what has been called "free association."

In the same essay, Simic suggests that the work of visual artists such as Marcel Duchamp led to "a fundamental revision of what we mean by creativity. In that view, the poet was not a *maker,* but someone able to detect the presence of poetry in the accidental." The poet was someone with superior perception, able to see the "surreality" of the world around him. Whether they practiced free association or adopted other strategies to dismantle "the archenemy cause and effect," the American Internationalists sought "the presence of poetry in the accidental."

Of course American approaches and attitudes toward these ideals varied widely, depending on which surrealist tradition they looked to for inspiration. The New York School poets gravitated toward French surrealism, finding intellectual sophistication, disjunctive humor, and tantalizing irresolution in French experiments with collage, free association, and chance-based forms. John Ashbery, for example, did research in France toward a doctoral dissertation on Raymond Roussel, an early twentieth-century surrealist poet and novelist whose work depended on pun, non sequitur, tenuous plot lines, labyrinthine descriptions, and sentences qualified by multiple parentheses. In an essay on Roussel, Ashbery championed a style of surrealism in which meaning was both infinitely suggested and infinitely thwarted, and in which complex structure techniques drew attention to themselves as forms, rather than reflecting any easily definable content. But Ashbery disliked surrealist work that resulted from automatic writing, preferring instead the elaborate surfaces of Roussel, or the poetry of Pierre Reverdy. Both Ashbery and O'Hara adapted to their own ends Reverdy's experiments with line and syntax and his disjunctive shifts between registers of language, especially human speech and fragments of popular culture such as advertising slogans.

Other American Internationalists found the surrealism of Spanish and Latin American poets more congenial than French surrealism. Spanish surrealists adopted the rapid juxtapositions of disjunctive images familiar from French surrealism, but they concentrated as well on evoking intense emotion. Poets associated with the Deep Image school found a new passion and authenticity in Spanish and Latin American poetry. John Haines, for example, complained in "A Hole in the Bucket" (1978) that contemporary American poetry lacked substance, and he urged readers to "look elsewhere for the most authentic voice of the period. In [Miguel] Unamuno, in [Antonio] Machado, in [Juan Ramon] Jiménez, and in [Octavio] Paz, the fire of the idea, the passion of it, lights up the best poems." Likewise, in "The Delicacy of Walt Whitman" (1962), James Wright found "the spirit of Whitman" absent from poetry in the United States, but

> everywhere present among Spanish and South American poets: in the form which rejects external rhetoric in order to discover and reveal a principle of growth; in the modesty and simplicity of diction; in the enormously courageous willingness to leap from one image into the unknown, in sheer faith that the next image will appear in the imagination; in the sensitive wholeness of the single poems that appear from such imaginative courage; and, above all, in the belief in the imagination as the highest flowering of human life (the phrase belongs to Jorge Guillén), not just a rhetorical ornament.

Although he had studied with John Crowe Ransom at Kenyon College and respected the intellectual seriousness of the New Critics, Wright nonetheless joined his friend Robert Bly in reframing his style along the lines of Spanish models and in translating poetry from Spanish and German. Bly, who displayed a fierce, even religious fervor in his embrace of Spanish poetry, trumpeted its virtues in his essays, often creating a reductive "black and white" dichotomy between North American poetry and the poetry of other countries. But in advocating surrealism, he too linked it with emotion and authenticity. For poets such as Bly, Wright, and Haines, surrealism was attractive not only because its associative "leaps of thought" provided a counter to the rationalism of the New Critics, but because those leaps evoked deep emotion and gave the poet access to the unconscious mind.

Imagism Revised: The Deep Image School

> A man cannot turn his face at the same moment toward the inward world
> and the outer world: he cannot face both south and north at the same moment.
> —*Robert Bly*

For the American poets of the deep image school, "the unconscious mind" was not the Freudian unconscious, site of Oedipal sexual dramas, but "the collective unconscious" as envisioned by the psychologist Carl Jung—the archetypal images that Jung believed reflect the deepest recesses of the unconscious in all people, regardless of culture. In an influential 1930 essay, Jung argued that, as a seeker of these archetypes, the poet sets out on a heroic journey inward. Jung saw the poet as a shaman, or conscience figure, simultaneously exploring the mysteries of his own unconscious mind, while also bringing into focus archetypes and primal experiences, such as those surrounding birth and death, shared by everyone. Certain words and concepts, therefore, became totemic for the Deep Image poets—silence, blood, water, stone, shadow, fire, ash, and bone. Bly, Merwin, Haines, Wright, and other proponents of the style pared down their poems—even sometimes jettisoning punctuation—to evoke primal experiences that go beyond what they saw as the dulling influence of civilization.

The Deep Image poets therefore drew their surrealistic images not from urban life, but from the natural world, often evoking the American Midwest and using its vast spaces as an analogy for existential emptiness (in the 1960s, Bly and Wright lived in Minnesota, and several poets who adopted the Deep Image styled studied or taught creative writing at the University of Iowa). Additionally, Bly and Merwin took the concept of poet as prophet seriously enough that in the late 1960s they began to write political poems. Bly used this new surrealist-influenced style to condemn the Vietnam War, while Merwin took an environmentalist stance and lamented the industrialized world's destruction of nature.

Above all, the Deep Image poets favored what Bly called "inwardness"—so much so that the word became a kind of mantra repeated by many poets of the period. Likewise, poets advanced exploration of "the unknown" as a primary goal of poetry. James Wright combined both concepts in praising the Austrian poet Georg Trakl, whose work he translated. Describing Trakl's poems as "molded from within," Wright emphasized that Trakl

> did not write according to any "rules of construction," traditional or other, but rather
> waited patiently and silently for the worlds of his poems to reveal their own natural
> laws. . . . I cannot imagine any more difficult tasks than these, either for a poet or for a
> reader of poetry. They are, ultimately, attempts to enter and to recognize one's very self.

These goals—attainment of silence, the journey inward, the recognition of "one's very self" through the unknown "interior universe" of primal archetypes—

became important not just for writers of Deep Image poetry, but for readers of it as well. As Charles Wright concluded in an exchange of correspondence with Simic: "Poetry is at least as important for what is not said as for what is. The secret of poetry is silence, the unheard echoes of utterances that wash through us with their solitary innuendoes."

Urban Surrealism: The New York School

> It wasn't a question of New York subject matter. . . . New York
> was where it was happening and it was these people living in
> New York who said "That's what we want to do."
> —*Edwin Denby*

Whereas the Deep Image poets plumbed the depths of the unconscious mind and attuned readers to the mysteries of primal experience, the New York School poets celebrated the strangeness of urban life. In contrast to the Deep Image poets' spareness and faith in silence, the New York School poets were voluble, pouring forth a dazzling abundance of words. Moving surrealistic dissonance beyond the realm of the image, the New York School poets juxtaposed not only discordant images, but also erudite diction and slang, and references to high and popular culture. A New York School poem might jostle references to French symbolist poetry, everyday American phrases, advertising slogans, B-movies, psychoanalysis, and cartoons.

In the spirit of the French surrealists, the New York School poets forged connections with other arts, particularly painting, through friendships and collaborations with painters and through working in the art world. John Ashbery, Barbara Guest, and Frank O'Hara, all wrote art criticism. (A decade earlier, poet Weldon Kees, whose work prefigures the New York School in significant ways, had also written art criticism and exhibited his paintings with the major Abstract Expressionists.) O'Hara rose from selling tickets at the Museum of Modern Art to curating major exhibitions. In fact, the term "New York School poets," was coined in 1961 by an art gallery director, John Bernard Myers, as a counterpart of the "New York School" of Abstract Expressionist painters. Ashbery disliked the name, especially because it proposed New York City as the center of the movement, whereas for him Paris was equally important. He therefore emphasized the importance not of New York City alone, but of "modern French poetry, modern music, and modern painting" as formative influences on himself and his peers.

Although O'Hara was the only major figure in the group who made New York City itself a consistent theme, New York School poetry overall displayed a distinctively urban sensibility. The work was sophisticated, self-aware, and more interested in the energetic play of thought than in the dramatic revelations characteristic of the Confessional school. New York School poems are often laced with irony, a fondness for parody, and a tendency to undercut seriousness with mocking wit. Many of these proclivities, especially a heightened concern with artifice and parody, fit the definition of "Camp" proposed by cultural critic Susan Sontag. In her 1964 essay, "Notes on Camp," Sontag declared, "The hallmark of Camp is the spirit of extravagance. . . . The whole point of Camp is to dethrone the serious." Although Camp was an important dimension of the urban gay aesthetic cultivated by Ashbery, O'Hara, and Edward Field, the New York School poets also raised serious existential questions about postwar American culture and the individual's place within it. For Ashbery, O'Hara, Guest, and other members of the group, such as Kenneth Koch and James Schuyler, experience was open-ended, both meaningless and meaningful. As O'Hara admitted in a note on his poems published in Donald Allen's 1960 anthology, *The New American Poetry* (the anthology through which many of the New York School poets received their first mainstream exposure),

> What is happening to me, allowing for lies and exaggerations which I try to avoid, goes into my poems. I don't think my experiences are clarified or made beautiful for myself or anyone else, they are just there in whatever form I can find them.

Like the Abstract Expressionist painters with whom they associated, the New York School poets were dedicated to process—showing the mind in action—which led them to give equal importance to banal and revelatory experiences. Yet the focus on process also brought with it a concern with language as a source of endless, often self-referential, play. These postmodern ideas have continued to resonate through contemporary American poetry, particularly in the work of the Language Poets. As David Lehman argues in *The Last Avant-Garde: The Making of the New York School of Poets* that after O'Hara's death in 1966 the group lost its "dominant personality." But by then the New York School had established a sphere of influence beyond its initial milieu."

Devolution of a Style: Surrealism as Mannerism

> What we have seen, I suppose, is the domestication of Surrealism.
> —*John Haines*

During the late fifties and the sixties, surrealist techniques enabled the American Internationalist poets to create new possibilities for contemporary poetry, but by the mid-seventies those possibilities had narrowed considerably. So many poets had incorporated surrealism into their work—and, in particular, the Deep Image style was so easily imitated that American surrealism became a form of mannerism. In reviews and essays, poet-critics such as Paul Breslin, Robert Pinsky, and Alan Williamson challenged the linguistic and intellectual assumptions of the American Internationalist styles. Williamson attacked surrealism in a 1975 essay, calling it "easily the most formulaic style we have had since the 'academic' poetry of the 1950s." Questioning the foundations of Deep Image poetry, Breslin concluded: "It has a stock rhetoric of portentousness, and all too often its mysteries are only the trivial mystifications of cant and code."

In the face of such criticism, some of the American Internationalist poets began to deny their allegiance to surrealism or else to voice reservations. By 1978 James Wright had called the influence of surrealism on contemporary poetry "dangerous" and admitted that when his poems "sound surrealistic, all that means is my attempt to be clear has failed." Haines, in a 1979 letter to *Kayak,* complained of the American "talent . . . for trivializing everything, . . . for turning even the most innovative idea into clichés" and suggested that "the problem with surrealism, as with many another modern mode, is that it is partial, a piece of the whole." Among the New York School poets, Ashbery always resisted being categorized as what he terms "a late blooming umbilical cord between the French Surrealists and the Americans," but his resistance grew stronger in the 1980s, after he became less reliant on surrealistic techniques than he was early in his career. Defending the style, however, W. S. Merwin suggested that some of the seemingly surrealistic images in his poetry were instead attentive observations of a natural world whose details had become foreign to contemporary American readers. Merwin countered his critics by looking back to the roots of surrealism and suggesting that the startling juxtapositions in his poems were not mannerisms but ways of perceiving the world as it really was, in all of its strangeness.

For the American Internationalists, especially those like Merwin, Simic, Haines, Guest, and Ashbery who have continued to develop as poets, even as they build on their surrealist foundations, fidelity to the world's strangeness is paramount. What Ashbery claims for early European surrealism in a 1968 essay, "The Heritage of Dada and Surrealism," can also be applied to the surrealism of American poetry during the sixties and seventies, especially the Deep Image movement. Surrealism, "like all revolutions, substituted some new restrictions for old ones, limiting its direct effectiveness and eventually bringing about its own decay as a movement, though its effectiveness as a catalyst continues."

◦━◄ BARBARA GUEST ►━◦
(b. 1920)

Born Barbara Ann Pinson in Wilmington, North Carolina, and raised in Los Angeles, the poet moved to New York City at age twenty-three, soon after graduating from the University of California, Berkeley. Although she had begun writing poetry in college, her vocation took hold in New York. As she notes in a 1992 interview, the city "seemed like civilization [after] coming from the west coast." For Guest, civilization centered on literature and the visual arts. From 1951 to 1954 she worked as an editorial associate at *ARTnews*. Fueled by friendship with other New York poets and painters, she developed a distinctive style that, like the work of other New York School poets such as her friends Frank O'Hara and John Ashbery, drew its inspiration from the disjunctions of French Surrealist poetry and the energy of Abstract Expressionist painting. Her early work appeared in avant-garde magazines, and her first book, *The Location of Things* (1960), was published by an art gallery. After she was featured as only one of four women poets in Donald Allen's 1960 anthology, *The New American Poetry*, Guest found a mainstream publisher for her second book, *Poems: The Locations of Things, Archaics, The Open Skies* (1960), which included all of the poems from her first volume and many new ones. Since then, she has published over eighteen books, including several collaborations with artists and a well-respected biography, *Herself Defined: The Poet H. D. and Her World* (1984).

Like H. D., Guest infuses her poetry with a rapturous attention to visual details and great faith in the power of the unconscious mind. Attracted by mystery, Guest believes that poems should not be "solvable," as if they were puzzles made for interpretation, but that they should open the writer (and the reader) to possibility. She therefore adopts an associative approach to writing, mixing references to different, and sometimes contradictory, realms of experience. Like the other New York School poets, she sometimes shifts between slang, educated speech, and obsolete "poetic" diction during the course of a single poem. Although Guest loves to surprise her readers by exhibiting wry humor in her poems and focusing on unexpected subjects, throughout her long career she has returned to characteristic themes, such as distance and the relationships of people and objects in space, through developing analogies to travel or architecture. Influenced by painters as well as poets, she has also written poems that aim for abstraction through treating language as a kind of object that can be arranged. The view of poetry that she proposes in "Invisible Architecture" (2000), a piece of writing whose own "architecture" balances between poem and essay, reveals her primary concerns:

> An invisible architecture upholds the poem while allowing a moment of relaxation for the unconscious.. A period of emotional suggestion,   of lapse,   of reliance on the conscious substitute words pushed toward the bridge of the architecture. An architecture in the period before the poem finds an exact form and vocabulary—

Eschewing confessional modes of poetry, Guest has been reticent about revealing the details of her personal life, whether in her work or in interviews. She changed her name to "Guest" after marrying Lord Stephen Haden-Guest in 1949. After their divorce in 1954, she married again, to Trumbull Higgins, a military historian, in the same year. She had a daughter by her first marriage and a son by her second. Although her early work was not celebrated as widely as the poetry of her male compatriots in the New York School, in the 1980s she began to gain recognition from feminist scholars, who drew attention to the question her poems raise about gender, and from Language poets, who admired her linguistic experiments. Her *Selected Poems* (1995) won an America Award for literature, and in 1999 Guest received the Frost Medal for Distinguished Lifetime Achievement from the Poetry Society of America.

Green Revolutions

Being drunk upstairs and listening
to voices downstairs. The roll of the sea
sounding calm
                after the voices
and the machinery   5
                Tibet with Monaco
thrown in for measure

                Distant greens
they appear on walls when one is tired
the dark background greens then the light ones   10
bringing us closer. As landscape appears
with its fresh basket approaching the car
then relinquishing, going away, telling us
something that is secret, not even whispering,
but indicating as if an ear of corn might be over there   15
choice and ripe, but neglected.

                The cars go away. The voices
go away. For lunch. At noon.
It's harsh with old Donne[1] in his steeple.
I'm upstairs "looking at a picture"   20
like a Bostonian in Florence, "looking at a picture."
Now it's green. Now it isn't.

                                                1995

Poem

Disturbing to have a person
So negative beside you
I dreamed last night
The Mississippi Belle[2] rolled over
We were all drowned.   5

---

1. The metaphysical poet John Donne (1572–1631) served as a minister in the Church of England from 1615 until his death.
2. A riverboat.

I promise to do better.
Look I have a net here
Filled with trout.

Ain't nothin' like river trout.

1995

━━━◦◂ EDWARD FIELD ▸◦━━━
(b. 1924)

Edward Field was born in Brooklyn, New York, to parents who were Russian and
Polish immigrants. His childhood in Lynbrook, Long Island, was often unhappy,
mostly due to other children teasing him about being Jewish and his awkwardness
at sports. Music provided a refuge for the boy. He played cello in the Field Family
Trio and was broadcast on the radio. He enrolled at New York University, but soon
left to join the U.S. Air Force. Field flew twenty-five missions over Europe during
World War II, one of which he barely survived after crashing into the North Sea.
After the war, he attempted to resume his education at New York University, but
he quickly dropped out and began a string of brief jobs in factories and warehouses,
ranging from a machinist to a clerk-typist. In his early thirties Field studied method
acting with Vera Soloviova of the Moscow Art Theater. This apprenticeship not
only sparked Field's amateur acting career, but also fostered his dramatic style in
public poetry readings, which made him a popular performer on the college circuit.

Field's first collection of poetry, *Stand Up, Friend, with Me* (1963), was published to strong reviews, and the book won the Lamont Award. Field also received
a Guggenheim Fellowship and was commissioned to write the narrative for *To Be
Alive!* (1964), an Academy Award–winning documentary short. *Stand Up, Friend,
with Me* comprised more than a decade of writing, during some of which Field had
lived in Greece and discovered the poetry of Constantine Cavafy, who became a
central influence on his work and artistic sensibility. Field's poetry is characteristically candid, conversational, and comic—often using humor to explore the embar-
rassing aspects of the self, especially personal rejection, homosexuality, childhood,
and his mixed feelings about his Jewish heritage. In the author's preface to his volume of selected poems, *Counting Myself Lucky* (1992), Field discusses the personal and confiding voice found in his work:

> Writing for me is such a private act that when I see my poems in print, they embarrass
> me, like the dream of being the only one naked in a crowd. My poems expose me to the
> world. And they're so easy to understand, which makes it all the more embarrassing, as
> if some part of me, too, wished to observe the rules of polite discourse. How I envy
> poets who keep buttoned up! But as Cavafy said, that has nothing to do with poetry.

Field's second collection, *Variety Photoplays* (1967), celebrated the author's
love of popular culture with a series of poems inspired by old movies, silver-screen
film stars, and Sunday comics. Some of these poems like "Curse of the Cat
Woman" or "The Bride of Frankenstein" amusingly interweave subversive subtexts into retellings of the plots of popular B-budget movies. Field's poetry reflects
the "camp" style of the urban gay males of mid-century, a deeply ironic sensibility

that simultaneously mocked and adored stylized and out-of-date cultural artifacts. Field is unapologetic about his allegiance to "poetry for the voice." "I was immediately attracted to poets who sounded like recognizable human beings," he confesses. "Without undervaluing elaborate syntax and elegant language, I prefer to explore the poetry of everyday expression." Although Field's work has sometimes been criticized for its simple and conversational style, his best poetry is witty, honest, and insightful—revealing general truths about humankind, especially New Yorkers, who never cease to fascinate him.

In *Contemporary Poets,* Field describes himself as "a survivor from the time before universities took over American poetry. Poetry then belonged to what might be called a 'bohemian' world of artists and social misfits and eccentrics." Although he has occasionally taught writing workshops at places such as Sarah Lawrence College and YMHA Poetry Center, Field has largely avoided academia. He has won a Shelley Memorial Award, the Prix de Rome, and a Lambda Literary Award. Field has also published a group of popular novels, most notably *Village* (1982), under the pseudonym Bruce Elliot, written in conjunction with his longtime partner Neil Derrick. He and Derrick reside in New York City.

Curse of the Cat Woman[1]

It sometimes happens
that the woman you meet and fall in love with
is of that strange Transylvanian people
with an affinity for cats.

You take her to a restaurant, say, or a show,   5
on an ordinary date, being attracted
by the glitter in her slitty eyes and her catlike walk,
and afterwards of course you take her in your arms
and she turns into a black panther
and bites you to death.   10

Or perhaps you are saved in the nick of time
and she is tormented by the knowledge of her tendency:
That she daren't hug a man
unless she wants to risk clawing him up.

This puts you both in a difficult position—   15
panting lovers who are prevented from touching
not by bars but by circumstance:
You have terrible fights and say cruel things
for having the hots does not give you a sweet temper.

One night you are walking down a dark street   20
and hear the pad-pad of a panther following you,

---

1. Field's poem borrows much of its story from Val Lewton's classic B movie *Cat People* (1942).

but when you turn around there are only shadows,
or perhaps one shadow too many.

You approach, calling, "Who's there?"
and it leaps on you.   25
Luckily you have brought along your sword
and you stab it to death.

And before your eyes it turns into the woman you love,
her breast impaled on your sword,
her mouth dribbling blood saying she loved you   30
but couldn't help her tendency.

So death released her from the curse at last,
and you knew from the angelic smile on her dead face
that in spite of a life the devil owned,
love had won, and heaven pardoned her.   35

1967

Roaches

An old decrepit city like London
doesn't have any.
They ought to love it there
in those smelly, elegant buildings.
Surely I myself have smuggled some in in my luggage   5
but they obviously don't like the English—
for that alone I should love them.

They are among the brightest
and most attractive of small creatures
though you have to be prepared   10
for the look of horror
on the faces of out-of-town guests
when a large roach walks across the floor
as you are sipping drinks.
You reach out and swat,   15
and keeping the conversation going
pick up the corpse and drop it into an ashtray
feeling very New Yorky doing it.
After all, you've got to be tough to live here—
the visitor didn't make it.   20

Roaches also thrive on it here:
They set up lively communes
in open boxes of rice, spaghetti, and matzohs.
You come in to make coffee in the morning
and find a dead one floating in the kettle   25
and dots of roach shit on the dishes,
hinting at roachy revels the night before.

If you let them alone
they stop running at the sight of you
and whisker about   30
taking a certain interest in whatever you are doing,
and the little ones, expecting like all babies to be adored,
frolic innocently in the sink,
even in daytime when grownup roaches rest
after a night of swarming around the garbage bag.   35
The trouble with this approach is
they outbreed you and take over,
even moving sociably right into your bed.

Which brings up the question, Do they bite?
Some say yes, and if yes,   40
do they carry Oriental diseases?
Even though you have tried to accept them
there comes a point when you find your eyes
studying labels of roach killers on supermarket shelves,
decide to try a minimal approach, buy one,   45
but when you attack with spray can aimed
they quickly learn to flee.
The fastest of course live to multiply
so they get cleverer all the time
with kamikaze leaping into space,   50
or zigzagging away,
race into far corners of the apartment
where they drop egg-sacs in their last throes
to start ineradicable new colonies.

When you light the oven   55
they come out and dance on the hot stove top
clingin with the tips of their toes,
surviving by quick footwork until you swat them.
Or if you spray it first
you have the smell of roaches roasting slowly.   60

And when you wash them down the drain
without their being certifiably dead
do they crawl up when the coast is clear?
Some even survive the deadliest poisons devised by man
and you have weird, white mutations running about.   65
Dying, they climb the walls, or up your legs, in agony,
making you feel like a dirty rat,
until they fall upside down with frail legs
waving in the air.

No more half-measures—   65
it's them or us you finally realize
and decide on nothing less than total fumigation:
The man comes while you are out
and you return to a silent apartment, blissfully roach-free.

You vacuum up the scattered bodies of the unlucky,   70
pushing down guilty feelings, lonely feelings,
and congratulate yourself.

                              You booby,
they have only moved over to the neighbor's
who is now also forced to fumigate,   75
and just when you are on the princess phone crowing to your friends,
back they come, the whole tribe of them,
many gone now
due to their trivial life span and chemical adversaries
but more numerous than ever with the newborn   80
and all the relatives from next door and the neighborhood with them,
you standing there outraged, but secretly relieved
as they swarm into the kitchen from every crevice,
glad to be home, the eternal innocents,
greeting you joyfully.   85

                                                              1977

◦━◄ JOHN HAINES ►━◦
(b. 1924)

John Haines has forged one of the most independent lives of any contemporary
American poet. He never followed a traditional career, but instead was a home-
steader in the Alaska wilderness for almost a quarter of a century. More recently he
has been a freelance writer and itinerant teacher. The poems of his first books sometimes resemble the "Deep Image" school of Robert Bly, but over time Haines's own
idiosyncratic vision and technique have prevailed. Frequently hailed as a major nature poet, he has also written many poems about art, politics, and other matters.

   From the start, Haines has been mobile. Born in Norfolk, Virginia, the son of
a naval officer and a schoolteacher, he grew up on naval bases on both the East
and West coasts. The family's frequent moves prevented him from establishing
friendships easily, and he developed a facility for solitude. His education was interrupted by World War II. From 1943 to 1946 he served in the U.S. Navy, earning several battle stars in the Pacific while operating sonar on a destroyer. Haines
was a talented artist, and when he left the navy he tried the National Art School
in Washington, D.C. for a year, but his own restlessness made institutional learning difficult. In the spring of 1947 he moved to Alaska and began building a cabin
on a homestead claim seventy miles southeast of Fairbanks. He later wrote in *Living Off the Country* (1981) that in Alaska he was "born" as a poet, "overlooking
the Tanana River. . . ."

   Still Haines felt divided, not only between art and poetry, but also between
his Alaskan solitude and the desire for a cultural life he could only find in the great
cities. He moved back to Washington, D.C., then to New York, where he attended
the Hans Hofmann School of Fine Art for two years, from 1950 to 1952. In New
York he became acquainted with many of the most important painters and poets
of the time, including Franz Kline, Willem de Kooning, and Weldon Kees. He was

not temperamentally suited to the New York art scene, however. By 1954 he was back at his Alaskan homestead, where he would remain until 1969, making his living by hunting, trapping, and occasional jobs as a carpenter. He was writing new poems, encouraged by a 1964 prize from the *Massachusetts Review* and a Guggenheim Fellowship the following year.

In 1966 Haines published *Winter News,* a collection of short free verse lyrics. These spare, quiet poems announced a new talent, but they were criticized by reviewers who could not empathize with Haines's remote experience. One poet who had early recognized the strengths of Haines's free verse technique was William Carlos Williams, with whom he had corresponded in the 1950s. Building on the older poet's advice, as well as his affection for maverick poets like Robinson Jeffers, Haines developed poems of subtle but undeniable craft. He was also writing about more than the snowbound solitude of a backwoodsman, as subsequent collections like *The Stone Harp* (1971) and *Cicada* (1977) proved. When he published *News from the Glacier: Selected Poems 1960–1980* (1982), he gained significant critical attention as an important American poet. Having become the "token Alaskan" of American poetry, he was by then on the move again, teaching in Montana and Ohio, and returning to Fairbanks when he could. He was also building sequences of lyrics, often centered on themes such as mortality and the passage of time.

Although Haines has acknowledged the influence of poets such as Tu Fu, W. B. Yeats, T. S. Eliot, Edwin Muir, Federico García Lorca, Rainer Maria Rilke, Octavio Paz, Antonio Machado, and Georg Trakl, in general, he has remained outside dominant trends in American poetry. His liberal politics have no doubt contributed to an apocalyptic tone in some of his poems, a satirical edge in others. Here, perhaps, he would note a kinship with another maverick poet, Thomas McGrath. Both Haines and McGrath had Catholic upbringings, resulting in an allegorical turn of mind. For Haines, this attitude is most evident in *New Poems* (1990), winner of the Western States Book Award and other prizes. As Haines's reputation has grown, he has also been honored with fellowships from the Academy of American Poets and other powerful institutions, but the lack of a conventional career has also meant sacrifices. Three of his marriages have failed, and he has frequently had to take short-term teaching positions to make ends meet. In the 1990s he moved to Helena, Montana. *The Owl in the Mask of the Dreamer: Collected Poems* (1993) consolidated Haines's position as one of the most distinctive poets of his generation. *At the End of This Summer,* a collection of his early poems about Alaska was published in 1997. He is also well known for his prose about Alaska, collected principally in *Living Off the Country: Essays on Poetry and Place* (1981) and *The Stars, the Snow, the Fire: Twenty-five Years in the Northern Wilderness* (1989). His essays, reviews, and memoirs have appeared in numerous magazines over the years, and some were gathered in *Fables and Distances: New and Selected Essays* (1996).

◄─◦─◀━▶─◦─►

Winter News

They say the wells
are freezing
at Northway where
the cold begins.

Oil tins bang   5
as evening comes on,
and clouds of
steaming breath drift
in the street.

Men go out to feed   10
the stiffening dogs,

the voice of the snowman
calls the white-
haired children home.

1966

The Flight

It may happen again—this much
I can always believe
when our dawn fills with frightened neighbors
and the ancient car refuses to start.

The gunfire of locks and shutters   5
echoes next door to the house
left open
for the troops that are certain to come.

We shall leave behind nothing but cemeteries,

and our life like a refugee cart   10
overturned in the road,
a wheel slowly spinning . . .

1971

The Ghost Towns

"The North is strewn with cities
of one winter . . ."

I have seen them, the tinderboxes
stacked upon each other,
their wind-structures fallen,   5
no way to enter now but the gates of frost.

They were lighted by the pressure
lamps of fever, by lamp-men
trimming soot and breaking coal,
reading by the fire of their wicks   10
the cold logic of the snow.

It was all dream and delirium,
the amazed rumor of gold—a letter
carried in a stampeder's pocket,
unread, and the homeland long forgotten.   15

As I have held my hand above a candle,
seen the red flesh glow
and the knotted bones darken,

so will these buildings leave
their trusses charred and crossed,   20
the graveyards lettered
with a script no one can read . . .

And over the bleak and gutted land
no wall to stop the wind—
one space, one frame for all.   25

1978

Night

Do not wake me, for I am not ready
to speak, to break the spell
fixed in these sleeping stones.

Go quietly here. Whisper to wise men
what you cannot speak aloud.   5
Quiet the metal of doors.

It is the time of earth-changes,
of vanishing rainfall,
and the restless barking of dogs.

Divided is the man of hidden   10
purpose, and evil his redemption.

Harness the wind and drive the water,
you that govern,
who yoke and stride the world . . .

And then be still.   15

Leaves of the one standing tree
fall through the twilight;
the nightborn images rise, the owl

in the mask of the dreamer wakes:
Who is the guest?   20
Who is it who knocks and whispers?

As one calmed in his death-dream
would never return
to this hunted world—

one more key to the clockwork   25
that drives the stunned machine,
another cry under the wheel . . .

But calmed and stationed aloft,
delight in his distance,
to see on the star-pavilions   30

the bright, imperial creatures rise,
ascend their thrones, rule
and prosper. The thrones darken,

earth in the moon-shadow fails,
and he alone in that cold   35
and drifting waste keeps alight

memorial constellations . . .

So I in this quiet sleep of stone
can say to you: Leave to me
this one sustaining solace—   40

my night that has more night
to come. To the sun that has set,
whose dawn I cannot see . . .

Mute in my transformation,
and do not wake me.   45

1993

•—◄ ROBERT BLY ►—•
(b. 1926)

Although he became a media celebrity for his best-selling study of male identity, *Iron John: A Book about Men* (1990), Robert Bly had already long exerted influence upon the culture of contemporary American poetry. Through his poetry, translations, criticism, editing, and public appearances, Bly not only inspired many poets of his own generation, but built a large following among general readers. Often criticized for his prophetic posturing, literary dogmatism, and occasionally slapdash writing, Bly nonetheless played an indispensable role in the significant change of sensibility in American poetry during the 1960s, and he remained a pivotal figure in the literary world during the last three decades of the twentieth century.

Robert Elwood Bly was born into a Norwegian Lutheran farming family in Madison, Minnesota, close to the Lac Qui Parle River and the lake of the same name. He would later speak and write about the emotional isolation he felt in his early years, partly due to his father's alcoholism, partly to the family's Nordic stoicism. He and his old brother attended a small one-room country schoolhouse where they were sometimes the only students.

Graduating from high school during World War II, Bly postponed college and enlisted in the U.S. Navy. He served from 1944 to 1946, but never left the United States or saw combat. After the war he attended St. Olaf College for a year before transferring to Harvard, where his fellow students included the poets Donald Hall, Adrienne Rich, John Ashbery, Kenneth Koch, L. E. Sissman, and Frank O'Hara. His lifelong friend Hall has described meeting Bly in 1948, "He was skinny, never smiled, and wore three-piece suits with narrow striped ties; he was very intelligent."

The severity and isolation of Bly's early experience would to some degree be reinforced by years spent far from cultural centers. After graduating from Harvard magna cum laude, he spent some time in New York City and his ancestral Norway and also earned a master's degree from the University of Iowa in 1956. But Bly's determined independence was most exemplified by his return to the family farm, where he has lived on his own parcel of land most of his adult life. In 1955 he married Carolyn McLean (now well known as the writer Carol Bly). Although they would divorce twenty-four years later, they were for the duration of their marriage an influential literary couple, often entertaining writers and artists at the farm. Among the poets who came to see Bly on his farm were Donald Hall, Louis Simpson, and James Wright.

Bly named his farmhouse Odin House and soon created what would prove to be one of the most innovative, influential, and openly combative small magazines of the postwar era, the *Fifties* (Named for the decades in which it was published, the journal was regularly rechristened the *Sixties,* the *Seventies,* the *Eighties,* and the *Nineties.*) The journal, subtitled "A Magazine of Poetry and Opinion," declared open warfare on the New Critical orthodoxy then dominant in academic English departments. Often writing under the pseudonym "Crunk," Bly promoted his own poetic agenda, attacked American provincialism, and mercilessly ridiculed his opponents—sometimes awarding them the "Order of the Blue Toad," a mock literary prize for stupidity, crassness, and commercialism. Through this journal Bly gradually became well known nationally.

Decrying the ignorance of monolingual American literati, Bly championed and translated modern Latin American and European poetry including the work of Antonio Machado, Juan Ramón Jiménez, Federico García Lorca, and Tomas Tranströmer.

Although he had begun as a traditional poet, writing in rhyme and meter, and continued to admire masters of form like W. B. Yeats and Rainer Maria Rilke, Bly increasingly associated poetic meter and form with literary rationalism and stale academicism. Under Bly's influence, James Wright changed his style and became a predominantly free verse poet with a visionary bent. The two men became associated with what was called "Deep Image" poetry.

Once Bly had abandoned meter in his own poems, having shown little talent for it in the first place, he fashioned a quiet, direct voice of his own, effectively displayed in his first important book, *Silence in the Snowy Fields* (1962). This volume announced a flat, imagistic, and minimalist style that would exercise enormous influence on American poetry for the next twenty years. Bly's main objection to the academic poetry of the 1950s had been that its rationality became a formal and psychological straitjacket. Strongly influenced by Jung's method of associating archetypes, Bly developed poetry intended to speak from a source deep in the unconscious. "Inward poetry deepens all life around it," he declared, and his essays began to use such terms as "inwardness," "association," "leaping," and "revolutionary feeling." Although it differed from the more exuberant and expansive Beat poetry, Bly's quiet and introspective work moved on a parallel countercultural path.

Bly's activism against the Vietnam War provided another career high point. When his second full-length collection, *The Light around the Body* (1967), won the National Book Award in 1968, the poet used the ceremony to publicly donate the award money to an antiwar organization. Such bold acts contributed to Bly's image as a courageous and generous public figure. He published his best antiwar poems in *The Teeth Mother Naked at Last* (1971).

Many volumes of translations followed, including a version of the Norwegian Knut Hamsun's classic novel *Hunger* (1967) and the work of Persian ecstatic poet Kabir. He also edited a series of short polemical anthologies like *The Sea and the Honeycomb* (1971) and *Leaping Poetry* (1975) to proselytize his new aesthetic. Many of his essays were collected in *American Poetry: Wildness and Domesticity* (1990).

Increasingly, Bly was reaching beyond the poetry audience to a broader readership of people experimenting with New Age mysticism and alternative lifestyles. For these readers, Bly has become less a poet than a secular priest or shaman, whose ideas about male grief, the loss of wildness, and the power of myths have been guiding principles.

◄◦►━━◄ ►━◄◦►

Waking from Sleep

Inside the veins there are navies setting forth,
Tiny explosions at the waterlines,
And seagulls weaving in the wind of the salty blood.

It is the morning. The country has slept the whole winter.
Window seats were covered with fur skins, the yard was full   5
Of stiff dogs, and hands that clumsily held heavy books.

Now we wake, and rise from bed, and eat breakfast!
Shouts rise from the harbor of the blood,
Mist, and masts rising, the knock of wooden tackle in the sunlight.

Now we sing, and do tiny dances on the kitchen floor.   10
Our whole body is like a harbor at dawn;
We know that our master has left us for the day.

1962

The Busy Man Speaks

Not to the mother of solitude will I give myself
Away, not to the mother of love, nor to the mother of conversation,
Nor to the mother of art, nor the mother
Of tears, nor the mother of the ocean;
Not to the mother of sorrow, nor the mother   5
Of the downcast face, nor the mother of the suffering of death;
Not to the mother of the night full of crickets,
Nor the mother of the open fields, nor the mother of Christ.

But I will give myself to the father of righteousness, the father
Of cheerfulness, who is also the father of rocks,   10
Who is also the father of perfect gestures;
From the Chase National Bank
An arm of flame has come, and I am drawn
To the desert, to the parched places, to the landscape of zeros;
And I shall give myself away to the father of righteousness,   15
The stones of cheerfulness, the steel of money, the father of rocks.

1967

Counting Small-Boned Bodies

Let's count the bodies over again.

If we could only make the bodies smaller,
the size of skulls,
we could make a whole plain white with skulls in the moonlight.

If we could only make the bodies smaller,   5
maybe we could fit
a whole year's kill in front of us on a desk.

If we could only make the bodies smaller,
we could fit
a body into a finger ring, for a keepsake forever.   10

1967

Johnson's[1] Cabinet Watched by Ants

I

It is a clearing deep in a forest: overhanging boughs
Make a low place. Here the citizens we know during the day,
The ministers, the department heads,
Appear changed: the stockholders of large steel companies
In small wooden shoes; here are the generals dressed as gamboling lambs.   5

II

Tonight they burn the rice supplies; tomorrow
They lecture on Thoreau;[2] tonight they move around the trees;
Tomorrow they pick the twigs from their clothes;
Tonight they throw the firebombs; tomorrow
They read the Declaration of Independence; tomorrow they are in church.   10

III

Ants are gathered around an old tree.
In a choir they sing, in harsh and gravelly voices,
Old Etruscan[3] songs on tyranny.
Toads nearby clap their small hands, and join
The fiery songs, their five long toes trembling in the soaked earth.   15

1967

Romans Angry about the Inner World

What shall the world do with its children?
There are lives the executives

1. During his term as president of the United States (1963–68), Lyndon Baines Johnson sharply escalated the Vietnam War. The escalation included extensive bombing of North Vietnam and a commitment of 500,000 American troops by 1968.
2. Henry David Thoreau (1817–1862), author of *Walden* (1854) and "Civil Disobedience" (1849), an
essay that influenced the strategies of the Civil Rights and peace movements of the 1960s.
3. A civilization that flourished in northwestern Italy from 950–300 B.C.E., before the rise of the Roman
Empire.

Know nothing of:
A leaping of the body
The body rolling—I have felt it—   5
And we float
Joyfully toward the dark places.
But the executioners
Move toward Drusia. They tie her legs
On the iron horse. "Here is a woman   10
Who has seen our Mother
In the other world." Next they warm
The hooks. The two Romans had put their trust
In the outer world. Irons glowed
Like teeth. They wanted her   15
To assure them. She refused. Finally
They took burning
Pine sticks, and pushed them
Into her sides. Her breath rose
And she died. The executioners   20
Rolled her off onto the ground.
A light snow began to fall from the clear sky
And covered the mangled body.
And the executives, astonished, withdrew.
The inner world is a thorn   25
In the ear of a tiny beast!
The fingers of the executive are too thick
To pull it out.
It is a jagged stone
Flying toward us out of the darkness.   30

1967

⚫◄ FRANK O'HARA ►⚫
(1926–1966)

Frank O'Hara was so attached to the variety and hectic pace of New York City life that he once claimed, "I can't even enjoy a blade of grass, unless I know there's a subway handy, or a record store or some other sign that people do not totally *regret* life." Yet this exuberantly urban poet grew up in rural Grafton, in central Massachusetts, where his father oversaw three farms and a dealership for farm machinery. Art became the young O'Hara's refuge. In "Autobiographical Fragments," O'Hara recalls that "I was sent against my will to Catholic schools, but fortunately I also began at the age of seven to study music. A lot of my aversions to Catholicism dumped themselves into my musical enthusiasms." Although he still hoped to pursue a career as a concert pianist, O'Hara joined the navy immediately after his 1944 graduation from St. John's High School in Worcester. During the next two years, he worked as a shore patrolman in San Francisco, where he kept up his studies in piano, attended symphony concerts, and served on the destroyer USS *Nicholas*, which was stationed in the South Pacific. During the long months at sea, the young O'Hara turned to literature and music for solace, and he began to write poetry.

After his military service ended in 1946, O'Hara enrolled at Harvard University where he initially majored in music but soon changed to English. He read French and German poetry as well and published poems and stories in the *Harvard Advocate*. Although John Ashbery, whose work is often linked to O'Hara's, also attended Harvard at the same time, the two poets did not meet until their senior year, when at a party Ashbery overhead O'Hara rank the twentieth-century French composer Francis Poulenc's eighteen-minute cantata, *Les Sécheresses,* over Richard Wagner's four-hour opera, *Tristan und Isolde.* In a 1978 essay paying tribute to O'Hara, Ashbery remarked that "Frank didn't really believe that *Les Sécheresses* was greater than *Tristan* . . . but at the same time he felt . . . that art is already serious enough; there is no point in making it seem even more serious by taking it too seriously."

After graduation from Harvard in 1950, O'Hara spent a year at the University of Michigan, where he earned a master's degree in comparative literature, winning the university-sponsored Hopwood Award for a manuscript of poems and a play. In 1951 he settled permanently in New York City. Until his premature death fifteen years later, he thrived on the city's energy and liberality, for in New York he was free to live an openly homosexual life and to become part of the avant-garde art scene. Both the rhythms of city life and the details of his social life became subjects of his poems. O'Hara was gregarious and maintained an extensive network of friendships, especially with painters. He made his living as an editorial assistant for *ARTnews,* to which he contributed reviews, and later at the Museum of Modern Art, where he began in 1951 by selling tickets and postcards at the information desk, rising to the rank of curator by 1960. His friendships with painters gave him an understanding of new trends in art. This knowledge, combined with his energy and enthusiasm, led to his achievements as a curator, for he helped organize traveling exhibitions that introduced Abstract Expressionism to Europe.

As a poet, O'Hara achieved fluency, generosity, and expansiveness through a lack of premeditation that is the result of knowledge and constant practice, rather than mere accident. O'Hara wanted to embrace all dimensions of experience in his poetry, whether momentous or banal. He included allusions to high culture alongside references to popular culture, particularly movies and advertising. Although his poems often chronicled his feelings and experiences, O'Hara is not considered a "confessional poet," for rather than focus on "the self" as his main subject, he gave equal value to the self and to the world and imbued his work with wry humor. His humility led not only to his habit of writing quickly, but also to a casual attitude toward publication. Ashbery recalls, "Dashing the poems off at odd moments—in his office at the Museum of Modern Art, in the street at lunchtime or even in a room full of people—he would then put them away in drawers and cartons and half forget them."

For O'Hara, the process of writing mattered more than the pursuit of literary fame. His poems often appeared in limited editions that were sometimes printed by art galleries and included artwork by his friends. Only two short collections of poems, *Second Avenue* (1960) and *Lunch Poems* (1964), received wide distribution during his lifetime. After his sudden death in 1966 from injuries sustained when he was hit by a dune buggy on Fire Island, his friends began gathering his poems. *The Collected Poems of Frank O'Hara* appeared in 1971 and won the National Book

Award. It was followed by additional volumes of poetry, plays, and art criticism, most notably *Art Chronicles: 1954–1966* (1975). Today, O'Hara remains one of the most influential mid-twentieth-century poets. His work is much imitated, especially by young poets, but his idiosyncratic combination of attentive spontaneity, disjunctive wit, and openness to all levels of experience is seldom matched.

Today

Oh! kangaroos, sequins, chocolate sodas!
You really are beautiful! Pearls,
harmonicas, jujubes, aspirins! all
the stuff they've always talked about

still makes a poem a surprise!   5
These things are with us every day
even on beachheads and biers. They
do have meaning. They're strong as rocks.

                                                    1950

Poem

The eager note on my door said "Call me,
call when you get in!" so I quickly threw
a few tangerines into my overnight bag,
straightened my eyelids and shoulders, and

headed straight for the door. It was autumn   5
by the time I got around the corner, oh all
unwilling to be either pertinent or bemused, but
the leaves were brighter than grass on the sidewalk!

Funny, I thought, that the lights are on this late
and the hall door open; still up at this hour, a   10
champion jai-alai[1] player like himself? Oh fie!
For shame! What a host, so zealous! And he was

there in the hall, flat on a sheet of blood that
ran down the stairs. I did appreciate it. There are few
hosts who so thoroughly prepare to greet a guest   15
only casually invited, and that several months ago.

                                                    1952

To the Harbormaster

I wanted to be sure to reach you;
though my ship was on the way it got caught
in some moorings. I am always tying up

---

1. A Spanish game, played on a court, in which players with wicker rackets hit a ball off of a wall.

and then deciding to depart. In storms and
at sunset, with the metallic coils of the tide   5
around my fathomless arms, I am unable
to understand the forms of my vanity
or I am hard alee with my Polish rudder
in my hand and the sun sinking. To
you I offer my hull and the tattered cordage   10
of my will. The terrible channels where
the wind drives me against the brown lips
of the reeds are not all behind me. Yet
I trust the sanity of my vessel; and
if it sinks, it may well be in answer   15
to the reasoning of the eternal voices,
the waves which have kept me from reaching you.

                                                                        1954

The Day Lady[1] Died

It is 12:20 in New York a Friday
three days after Bastille day,[2] yes
it is 1959 and I go get a shoeshine
because I will get off the 4:19 in Easthampton[3]
at 7:15 and then go straight to dinner   5
and I don't know the people who will feed me

I walk up the muggy street beginning to sun
and have a hamburger and a malted and buy
an ugly NEW WORLD WRITING[4] to see what the poets
in Ghana are doing these days   10
            I go on to the bank
and Miss Stillwagon (first name Linda I once heard)
doesn't even look up my balance for once in her life
and in the GOLDEN GRIFFIN I get a Little Verlaine[5]
for Patsy with drawings by Bonnard[6] although I do   15
think of Hesiod,[7] trans. Richmond Lattimore or
Brendan Behan's new play[8] or Le Balcon or Les Nègres
of Genet,[9] but I don't, I stick with Verlaine
after practically going to sleep with quandariness

---

1. "Lady" refers to "Lady Day," the nickname of the great jazz singer Billie Holiday (1915–1959).
2. July 14, known as the Independence Day in France in commemoration of Parisian citizens' storming of the Bastille prison, which started the French Revolution.
3. A resort town and artists' enclave on Long Island.
4. Literary and cultural magazine (1957–1963).
5. French poet Paul Verlaine (1844–1896), associated with the symbolist movement.
6. French painter Pierre Bonnard (1867–1947).
7. Greek poet, eighth century B.C.E., author of *Works and Days*. Richmond Lattimore's translation appeared in 1959.
8. The Irish playwright Brendan Behan (1923–1964); O'Hara probably refers to *The Hostage*, which was published in New York by Grove Press in 1959.
9. Gay French writer (1910–1986); O'Hara refers to Genet's plays *The Balcony* (1956) and *The Blacks* (1958).

and for Mike I just stroll into the PARK LANE   20
Liquor Store and ask for a bottle of Strega[1] and
then I go back where I came from to 6th Avenue
and the tobacconist in the Ziegfeld Theatre [2] and
casually ask for a carton of Gauloises[3] and a carton
of Picayunes,[4] and a NEW YORK POST with her face on it   25

and I am sweating a lot by now and thinking of
leaning on the john door in the 5 SPOT[5]
while she whispered a song along the keyboard
to Mal Waldron[6] and everyone and I stopped breathing

                                                    1964

Autobiographia Literaria

When I was a child
I played by myself in a
corner of the schoolyard
all alone.

I hated dolls and I   5
hated games, animals were
not friendly and birds
flew away.

If anyone was looking
for me I hid behind a   10
tree and cried out "I am
an orphan."

And here I am, the
center of all beauty!
writing these poems!   15
Imagine!

                                                    1967

Homosexuality

So we are taking off our masks, are we, and keeping
our mouths shut? as if we'd been pierced by a glance!

The song of an old cow is not more full of judgment
than the vapors which escape one's soul when one is sick;

so I pull the shadows around me like a puff   5
and crinkle my eyes as if at the most exquisite moment

1. Italian liquor.
2. Popular Broadway theater built in 1927 by William Randolph Hearst.
3. French cigarettes.
4. Southern regional cigarettes marketed as "The Pride of New Orleans."
5. Greenwich Village jazz club.
6. Billie Holiday's pianist from 1957 until her death.

of a very long opera, and then we are off!
without reproach and without hope that our delicate feet

will touch the earth again, let alone "very soon."
It is the law of my own voice I shall investigate.   10

I start like ice, my finger to my ear, my ear
to my heart, that proud cur at the garbage can

in the rain. It's wonderful to admire oneself
with complete candor, tallying up the merits of each

of the latrines. 14th Street is drunken and credulous,   15
53rd tries to tremble but is too at rest. The good

love a park and the inept a railway station,
and there are the divine ones who drag themselves up

and down the lengthening shadow of an Abyssinian head
in the dust, trailing their long elegant heels of hot air   20

crying to confuse the brave "It's a summer day,
and I want to be wanted more than anything else in the world."

[c. 1954] 1971

Why I Am Not a Painter

I am not a painter, I am a poet.
Why? I think I would rather be
a painter, but I am not. Well,

for instance, Mike Goldberg[7]
is starting a painting. I drop in.   5
"Sit down and have a drink" he
says. I drink; we drink. I look
up. "You have SARDINES in it."
"Yes, it needed something there."
"Oh." I go and the days go by   10
and I drop in again. The painting
is going on, and I go, and the days
go by. I drop in. The painting is
finished. "Where's SARDINES?"
All that's left is just   15
letters, "It was too much," Mike says.

But me? One day I am thinking of
a color: orange. I write a line
about orange. Pretty soon it is a
whole page of words, not lines.   20
Then another page. There should be

---

7. New York artist who collaborated with O'Hara on a number of projects, most notably O'Hara's *Odes*, for which he provided silk screen prints. Goldberg's painting *Sardines* was done in 1955.

so much more, not of orange, of
words, of how terrible orange is
and life. Days go by. It is even in
prose, I am a real poet. My poem   25
is finished and I haven't mentioned
orange yet It's twelve poems, I call
it ORANGES. And one day in a gallery
I see Mike's painting, called SARDINES.

1971

◄— JOHN ASHBERY —►
(b. 1927)

Born in Rochester, New York, John Ashbery grew up in Sodus, a small town in upstate New York on the shores of Lake Ontario. While his father was a fruit farmer and his mother a former high school biology teacher, both fostered Ashbery's interest in painting and literature, as did his maternal grandfather, a professor of physics at the University of Rochester. After Ashbery graduated from Deerfield Academy in 1945, he entered Harvard University, where he majored in English and wrote an honors thesis on W. H. Auden, whose urbane wit deeply influenced his own poetry.

After graduation in 1949, Ashbery moved to New York City to pursue a master's degree in literature at Columbia University, which he received in 1951. Along with his Harvard friends, the poets Kenneth Koch and Frank O'Hara, he kept company with painters, and the world of avant-garde art inspired him to take new risks in his poetry. In an essay on the work of his friend, the painter Jane Frielicher, he recalls:

> I hadn't realized it, but my arrival in New York coincided with the cresting of the "heroic" period of Abstract Expressionism, as it was later to be known, and somehow we all seemed to benefit from this strong movement even if we paid little attention to it and seemed to be going our separate ways.

Interested in capturing in words the energetic disjunctions and emphasis on artistic process that he witnessed in nonrepresentational painting, as well as in the music and theater scenes of midcentury Manhattan, Ashbery became increasingly experimental in his poetry. In the same essay, he notes that, in response to a 1950 exhibit of the Lithuanian painter, Chaim Soutine, he, like many of the abstract expressionist painters, saw Soutine's work as "full of possibilities. . . . The fact that the sky could come crashing joyously into the grass, that trees could dance upside down and houses roll over like cats eager to have their tummies scratched was something I hadn't realized before, and I began pushing my poems around and standing words on end."

The "possibilities" that he absorbed from his immersion in the art world and from modern poets such as Auden, Wallace Stevens, Marianne Moore, and Gertrude Stein nurtured his imagination. In 1955, Ashbery submitted the manuscript of his first book to the prestigious Yale Series of Younger Poets contest, only to have it rejected in the initial screening process. But W. H. Auden, who was then judge of the series, disliked the work of the twelve finalists. Against the advice of the press personnel, Auden asked two young poets he knew whose work had been rejected—Ashbery and Frank O'Hara—to resubmit their manuscripts. A few days later he chose Ashbery's book as the winner. For the collection, retitled *Some Trees* (1956), Auden wrote a foreword praising Ashbery's linguistic virtuosity and elegant lyrics, but warned the young poet against his tendencies toward surrealism.

Although Ashbery was influenced by surrealist writers and painters, and in his next book, *The Tennis Court Oath* (1962), his poems grew increasingly experimental, he was never a disciple of surrealism. He came to believe, as he argues in an essay on the poet David Schubert, that "surrealism, in abandoning itself to the unconscious, can never accurately reflect experience in which both the conscious and the unconscious play a role." Instead, in his poetry Ashbery tries to chart the interplay between the unconscious and conscious minds, to show how the mind, in the process of thinking, responds both to its own fluctuations and to the often random occurrences of everyday life. "My poetry is disjunct," he remarked in an interview, "but then so is life."

Aware that disjunction alone can easily descend into mannerism, throughout his career Ashbery sought new forms in which to explore the patterns of consciousness. Thus, in many of the seventeen new books of poetry that followed *Some Trees*, Ashbery tries out different forms. In *The Tennis Court Oath*, for example, he includes a long collage poem, "Europe," intercut with quotations from *Beryl of the Bi-plane*, a 1917 British detective novel. *Three Poems* (1972) consists entirely of prose poems. Written on two sides of a notebook, the sixty-page poem "Litany," from *As We Know* (1979), appears in two columns, which Ashbery describes as "simultaneous but independent monologues." But his books, regardless of their forms, all explore the poetic process, extending almost to their limits Modernist practice of writing poems about poetry and the shifts of perspective that he adapted from his study of experimental poets and painters.

His engagement with the fine arts, in fact, has continued to nourish his poetry over the years. From 1959 to 1967 he lived in France, earning his living by writing art criticism for the European edition of the *New York Herald Tribune* and contributing articles on European exhibitions to *ARTnews* and *Art International*. After the death of his father in 1965, he returned to the United States and became the executive editor of *ARTnews*. Even after he began teaching in the creative writing program at Brooklyn College in 1972, he continued to contribute art criticism to various magazines, including *New York* and *Newsweek*.

Since winning the Pulitzer Prize, the National Book Award, and the National Book Critics Circle Award in 1976 for *Self Portrait in a Convex Mirror* (1975), critics have acknowledged him as one of the most important and influential poets writing in the United States, and he has continued to receive many other important awards, including the Bollingen Prize (1985) and a MacArthur fellowship (1985–1990). Whether in book-length poems or short lyrics, Ashbery's poetry depends on techniques that make it both difficult and strangely compelling. The poems often contain abrupt shifts of tense, pronouns, and levels of diction, so that within the space of a few lines Ashbery will coast from gorgeous, "poetic" language and allusions to high culture into slang, clichés, and references to popular culture, such as movies and cartoons. In a 1993 interview he claims that, "My idea is to democratize all forms of expression, an idea which comes to me from afar, perhaps from Whitman's *Democratic Vistas*—the idea that both the most demotic and the most elegant forms of expression deserve equally to be taken into account. It seems to me that there is something of this in postmodernism." Ashbery's dislocated grammar and syntax, his shifting allusions, and his habit of addressing an unspecified "you," have angered some critics of his work while inspiring legions of younger poets to imitate him. All of these techniques create a poetry that is open to interpretation from multiple perspectives. Although Ashbery did not make his homosexuality an overt theme, as Frank O'Hara did, some of his poetry can be interpreted as homoerotic. Overall, his techniques draw attention to the process of writing and create poems that seem always on the verge of disclosing a meaning, but that also seem to withhold and frustrate meaning.

When asked to explain his poems, Ashbery usually demurs. In the introduction to *Other Traditions* (2000), his book of essays based on his series of Charles Eliot Norton lectures at Harvard, he admits that:

> Unfortunately, I'm not very good at "explaining" my work. I once tried to do this in a question-and-answer period with some students of my friend [the poet] Richard Howard, after which he told me: "They want the key to your poetry, but you presented them with a new set of locks." That sums up for me and my feelings on the subject of "unlocking" my poetry. I am unable to do so because I feel that my poetry is the explanation. The explanation of what? Of my thought, whatever that is.

‹◦———◗———◦›

Some Trees

These are amazing: each
Joining a neighbor, as though speech
Were a still performance.
Arranging by chance

To meet as far this morning   5
From the world as agreeing
With it, you and I
Are suddenly what the trees try

To tell us we are:
That their merely being there   10
Means something; that soon
We may touch, love, explain.

And glad not to have invented
Such comeliness, we are surrounded:
A silence already filled with noises,   15
A canvas on which emerges

A chorus of smiles, a winter morning.
Placed in a puzzling light, and moving,
Our days put on such reticence
These accents seem their own defense.   20

1956

These Lacustrine[1] Cities

These lacustrine cities grew out of loathing
Into something forgetful, although angry with history.
They are the product of an idea: that man is horrible, for instance,
Though this is only one example.

They emerged until a tower   5
Controlled the sky, and with artifice dipped back
Into the past for swans and tapering branches,
Burning, until all that hate was transformed into useless love.

Then you are left with an idea of yourself
And the feeling of ascending emptiness of the afternoon   10
Which must be charged to the embarrassment of others
Why fly by you like beacons.

The night is a sentinel.
Much of your time has been occupied by creative games
Until now, but we have all-inclusive plans for you.   15
We had thought, for instance, of sending you to the middle of the desert,

To a violent sea, or of having the closeness of the others be air
To you, pressing you back into a startled dream
As sea-breezes greet a child's face.
But the past is already here, and you are nursing some private project.   20

The worst is not over, yet I know
You will be happy here. Because of the logic
Of your situation, which is something no climate can outsmart.
Tender and insouciant by turns, you see

You have built a mountain of something,   25
Thoughtfully pouring all your energy into this single monument,
Whose wind is desire starching a petal,
Whose disappointment broke into a rainbow of tears.

1966

My Erotic Double

He says he doesn't feel like working today.
It's just as well. Here in the shade
Behind the house, protected from street noises,
One can go over all kinds of old feeling,
Throw some away, keep others.
                                    The wordplay   5
Between us gets very intense when there are
Fewer feelings around to confuse things.
Another go-round? No, but the last things

---

1. Of or from a lake.

You always find to say are charming, and rescue me
Before the night does. We are afloat   10
On our dreams as on a barge made of ice,
Shot through with questions and fissures of starlight
That keep us awake, thinking about the dreams
As they are happening. Some occurrence. You said it.

I said it but I can hide it. But I choose not to.   15
Thank you. You are a very pleasant person.
Thank you. You are too.

                                                                1979

Paradoxes and Oxymorons

This poem is concerned with language on a very plain level.
Look at it talking to you. You look out a window
Or pretend to fidget. You have it but you don't have it.
You miss it, it misses you. You miss each other.

The poem is sad because it wants to be yours, and cannot be.   5
What's a plain level? It is that and other things,
Bringing a system of them into play. Play?
Well, actually, yes, but I consider play to be

A deeper outside thing, a dreamed role-pattern,
As in the division of grace these long August days   10
Without proof. Open-ended. And before you know it
It gets lost in the steam and chatter of typewriters.

It has been played once more. I think you exist only
To tease me into doing it, on your level, and then you aren't there
Or have adopted a different attitude. And the poem   15
Has set me softly down beside you. The poem is you.

                                                                1981

At North Farm

Somewhere someone is traveling furiously toward you,
At incredible speed, traveling day and night,
Through blizzards and desert heat, across torrents, through narrow passes.
But will he know where to find you,
Recognize you when he sees you,   5
Give you the thing he has for you?

Hardly anything grows here,
Yet the granaries are bursting with meal,
The sacks of meal piled to the rafters.
The streams run with sweetness, fattening fish;   10
Birds darken the sky. Is it enough
That the dish of milk is set out at night,
That we think of him sometimes,
Sometimes and always, with mixed feelings?

                                                                1984

Just Walking Around

What name do I have for you?
Certainly there is no name for you
In the sense that the stars have names
That somehow fit them. Just walking around,

An object of curiosity to some,   5
But you are too preoccupied
By the secret smudge in the back of your soul
To say much, and wander around,

Smiling to yourself and others.
It gets to be kind of lonely   10
But at the same time off-putting,
Counterproductive, as you realize once again

That the longest way is the most efficient way,
The one that looped among islands, and
You always seemed to be traveling in a circle.   15
And now that the end is near

The segments of the trip swing open like an orange.
There is light in there, and mystery and food.
Come see it. Come not for me but it.
But if I am still there, grant that we may see each other.   20

1984

⊷ W. S. MERWIN ⊶
(b. 1927)

Author of more than fifty books of poetry and translations, W. S. Merwin is one of the most prolific poets of his generation. Given the multiple forms in which his poems have been written, he is also one of the most protean and difficult poets to pin down. Three primary obsessions in his work are translation, narrative, and, as subject matter, the environment, or the place of the human in the natural setting. What links these matters is a mind aware of lost or neglected connections and a belief that nothing exists entirely in isolation.

He was born William Stanley Merwin, the son of a Presbyterian minister in New York City, and grew up in New Jersey and Pennsylvania. "I started writing hymns for my father almost as soon as I could write at all, illustrating them. But the first writers that held me were not the poets: Conrad first, and then Tolstoy, and it was not until I had received a scholarship and gone away to the university that I began to read poetry steadily and try incessantly, and with abiding desperation, to write it." He was a precocious if unruly student and took his bachelor's degree from Princeton at the age of twenty, followed by an additional year of graduate study in modern languages. R. P. Blackmur and John Berryman were two particularly important teachers for him at Princeton. While a student, Merwin also corresponded with Ezra Pound, who was in St. Elizabeth's hospital in Washington, D.C. During an Easter recess, the young poet traveled to Washington and visited Pound "a couple of times." It was Pound who advised Merwin to read the seeds, not the twigs, of poetry.

Pound's twin examples of erudition and independence were models for Merwin's subsequent career. Unlike so many postwar American poets, he never had an academic career, despite sporadic teaching, but made a living by translating, by writing for the BBC in the 1950s, and by giving readings and workshops in many different places. He has had a colorful life. Living in France and Portugal in 1949, he worked as a tutor; the following year he tutored Robert Graves's son in Majorca. From 1951 to 1954 he lived in London, and he has often been to France, having bought a house there with a small family inheritance. He has also spent time living in Boston and New York, but since the late '70s Merwin has made his home in Hawaii. One is tempted to see in his life a movement geographically from east to west, Europe to Hawaii, and also notice a movement culturally from west to east in the works he has chosen to translate over his long career. Important early translations include *The Poem of the Cid* (1959), *Spanish Ballads* (1961), and *The Song of Roland* (1963), while more recently he published *East Window: The Asian Translations* (1998). Between these collections there were translations of Pablo Neruda, Jean Follain, Osip Mandelstam, and many other writers.

Merwin's own poetic career got off to a strong start when W. H. Auden selected his first book, *A Mask for Janus* (1952), for the Yale Series of Young Poets. The book showed a traditional formality common to poets of the time. It was followed by *The Dancing Bears* (1954), *Green with Beasts* (1956), and *The Drunk in the Furnace* (1960), which many regard as the best of his early collections. Merwin's grounding in medieval poetry and ancient mythology was clear in all of these books, though he also made use of North American landscapes. But he had already decided he wanted to change his style, and the title of his next collection, *The Moving Target* (1963), suggests this formal restlessness. He was beginning to make his poetry out of archetypal correspondences and to remove embroideries. He even went so far as to remove punctuation for reasons he gave in his prose statement "On Open Form." These formal concerns, coupled with a growing environmentalism and pessimism, resulted in what may be his most powerful book, *The Lice* (1967). Here his verse technique was so reduced, so deliberately simplified, that many critics were reminded of Samuel Beckett. There was humor in the work of this period, but *The Lice* was a dark enough book that Merwin claimed it nearly made him consider not writing again.

The Carrier of Ladders (1970) won Merwin the Pulitzer Prize and contained a sequence of poems meditating on American expansion. In the same year Merwin published *The Miner's Pale Children*, his collection of short fiction. By 1979, when he won the Bollingen Prize for his work, he had published another important book of prose, *Houses and Travellers*; a collection of poems, *The Compass Flower*; and several more volumes of translations. His move to Hawaii was reflected in the poems of *Finding the Islands* (1982), *Opening the Hand* (1983), and *The Rain in the Trees* (1988). By the latter volume, Merwin was working his way out of the minimalism that had characterized some of his poetry from *The Moving Target* on. *The River Sound* (1999) contains narrative poems, and in 1998 Merwin published *The Folding Cliffs*, a book-length narrative about Hawaii. Yet another indication of Merwin's renewed interest in narrative, among other things, was his translation of Dante's *Purgatorio* (2000).

Air

Naturally it is night.
Under the overturned lute with its
One string I am going my way
Which has a strange sound.

This way the dust, that way the dust.   5
I listen to both sides
But I keep right on.
I remember the leaves sitting in judgment
And then winter.

I remember the rain with its bundle of roads.   10
The rain taking all of its roads.
Nowhere.

Young as I am, old as I am,

I forget tomorrow, the blind man.
I forget the life among the buried windows.   15
The eyes in the curtains.
The wall
Growing through the immortelles.[1]
I forget silence
The owner of the smile.   20

This must be what I wanted to be doing,
Walking at night between the two deserts,
Singing.

1963

The Animals

All these years behind windows
With blind crosses sweeping the tables

And myself tracking over empty ground
Animals I never saw

I with no voice   5

Remembering names to invent for them
Will any come back will one

Saying yes

Saying look carefully yes
We will meet again   10

1967

---

1. Literally, the poem refers to a Mediterranean plant with long-lasting flowers that keep their shape
and color even when dried. But Merwin also puns on the French word *immortelle*, a feminine adjective
meaning "immortal."

For a Coming Extinction

Gray whale
Now that we are sending you to The End
That great god
Tell him
That we who follow you invented forgiveness   5
And forgive nothing

I write as though you could understand
And I could say it
One must always pretend something
Among the dying   10
When you have left the seas nodding on their stalks
Empty of you
Tell him that we were made
On another day

The bewilderment will diminish like an echo   15
Winding along your inner mountains
Unheard by us
And find its way out
Leaving behind it the future
Dead   20
And ours

When you will not see again
The whale calves trying the light
Consider what you will find in the black garden
And its court   25
The sea cows the Great Auks the gorillas
The irreplaceable hosts ranged countless
And foreordaining as stars
Our sacrifices

Join your word to theirs   30
Tell him
That it is we who are important

                                                    1967

For the Anniversary of My Death

Every year without knowing it I have passed the day
When the last fires will wave to me
And the silence will set out
Tireless traveler
Like the beam of a lightless star   5

Then I will no longer
Find myself in life as in a strange garment
Surprised at the earth

And the love of one woman
And then shamelessness of men   10
As today writing after three days of rain
Hearing the wren sing and the falling cease
And bowing not knowing to what

1967

The Last One

Well they'd made up their minds to be everywhere because why not.
Everywhere was theirs because they thought so.
They with two leaves they whom the birds despise.
In the middle of stones they made up their minds.
They started to cut.   5

Well they cut everything because why not.
Everything was theirs because they thought so.
It fell into its shadows and they took both away.
Some to have some for burning.

Well cutting everything they came to the water.   10
They came to the end of the day there was one left standing.
They would cut it tomorrow they went away.
The night gathered in the last branches.
The shadow of the night gathered in the shadow on the water.
The night and the shadow put on the same head.   15
And it said Now.

Well in the morning they cut the last one.
Like the others the last one fell into its shadow.
It fell into its shadow on the water.
They took it away its shadow stayed on the water.   20

Well they shrugged they started trying to get the shadow away.
They cut right to the ground the shadow stayed whole.
They laid boards on it the shadow came out on top.
They shone lights on it the shadow got blacker and clearer.
They exploded the water the shadow rocked.   25
They built a huge fire on the roots.
They sent up black smoke between the shadow and the sun.
The new shadow flowed without changing the old one.
They shrugged they went away to get stones.

They came back the shadow was growing.   30
They started setting up stones it was growing.
They looked the other way it went on growing.
They decided they would make a stone out of it.
They took stones to the water they poured them into the shadow.
They poured them in they poured them in the stones vanished.   35
The shadow was not filled it went on growing.
That was one day.

The next day was just the same it went on growing.
They did all the same things it was just the same.
They decided to take its water from under it.   40
They took away water they took it away the water went down.
The shadow stayed where it was before.
It went on growing it grew onto the land.
They started to scrape the shadow with machines.
When it touched the machines it stayed on them.   45
They started to beat the shadow with sticks.
Where it touched the sticks it stayed on them.
They started to beat the shadow with hands.
Where it touched the hands it stayed on them.
That was another day.   50

Well the next day started about the same it went on growing.
They pushed lights into the shadow.
Where the shadow got onto them they went out.
They began to stomp on the edge it got their feet.
And when it got their feet they fell down.   55
It got into eyes the eyes went blind.

The ones that fell down it grew over and they vanished.
The ones that went blind and walked into it vanished.
The ones that could see and stood still
It swallowed their shadows.   60
Then it swallowed them too and they vanished.
Well the others ran.

The ones that were left went away to live if it would let them.
They went as far as they could.
The lucky ones with their shadows.   65

                                                      1967

Some Last Questions

What is the head
            A. Ash
What are the eyes
            A. The wells have fallen in and have
                Inhabitants   5
What are the feet
            A. Thumbs left after the auction
No what are the feet
            A. Under them the impossible road is moving
                Down which the broken necked mice push   10
                Balls of blood with their noses
What is the tongue
            A. The black coat that fell off the wall
                With sleeves trying to say something
What are the hands   15
            A. Paid

No what are the hands
   A. Climbing back down the museum wall
   To their ancestors the extinct shrews that will
   Have left a message   20
What is the silence
   A. As though it had a right to more
Who are the compatriots
   A. They make the stars of bone

              1967

Rain Travel

I wake in the dark and remember
it is the morning when I must start
by myself on the journey
I lie listening to the black hour
before dawn and you are   5
still asleep beside me while
around us the trees full of night lean
hushed in their dream that bears
us up asleep and awake then I hear
drops falling one by one into   10
the sightless leaves and I
do not know when they began but
all at once there is no sound but rain
and the stream below us roaring
away into the rushing darkness   15

              1992

⊷◄ JAMES WRIGHT ►⊶
(1927–1980)

Although he lived only fifty-two years, James Wright had an enormous impact on American poetry. Partly this was stylistic. Like many poets of his generation, he began writing poems in meter and rhyme—he credited Edwin Arlington Robinson and Robert Frost as influences—but in midcareer switched predominantly to free verse. Wright's impact was even stronger, perhaps, in his stance toward his subjects, his profound sympathy for outsiders or people who had somehow been harmed by society at large, and his visionary sense of ordinary experience. In a 1959 review of *Saint Judas,* Wright's second book, Anthony Hecht observed: "James Wright is a gifted young poet who is trying to write the most difficult kind of poetry: the poetry of wisdom." Wright was also a translator, discerning critic, and voluminous correspondent who offered sympathy and help to other writers. His death was lamented in elegies by dozens of other poets.

  Wright was born the second of three sons in Martins Ferry, Ohio, across the Ohio River from Wheeling, West Virginia. Much of his work concerns this and other Midwestern locales. "My father," he wrote in a memoir, "worked as a die-setter at the Hazel-Atlas Glass Company in Wheeling. . . . He was a handsome man of great physical strength and the greatest human strength of all, an enduring gentleness in the presence of the hardship that the Great Depression brought to everyone." Economic struggles framed much of Wright's childhood and contributed to his portrayals of drifters, drunks, prostitutes, criminals, and others who appeared to have failed at life. His friend Donald Hall would later write, "Jim's whole life was compelled by his necessity to leave the blighted valley, to escape his father's fate, never to work at Hazel-Atlas Glass." But Wright himself would also remember the Ohio Valley for its pastoral beauty, comparing it to rivers he later knew in Europe.

Wright's personal sensitivity—he began to write poetry as early as age eleven—was accompanied by occasional nervous breakdowns. The first of these occurred when he was only sixteen, causing him to miss a year of high school. Graduating in 1946, he joined the army and served in Japan with the U.S. occupation forces. Always interested in other cultures, Wright began to absorb Japanese poetry at this time. After his honorable discharge from the army, he attended Kenyon College from January 1948 to January 1952, where he studied with John Crowe Ransom and wrote a thesis on Thomas Hardy. He was also publishing early poems and widening his acquaintanceship with writers of his own generation. A month after his graduation he married a former high school classmate, Liberty Kardules, and the couple were soon on their way to Europe on a Fulbright Fellowship for 1952–1953. The first of their two sons, Franz (now also a poet), was born in Vienna in March 1953. Wright's interest in such German-language poets as Georg Trakl began during this year abroad.

On their return to the United States, the Wrights moved to Seattle, where the writer studied at the University of Washington with Theodore Roethke and Stanley Kunitz, and befriended Richard Hugo. He took a master's degree there in 1954 and a doctorate with a dissertation on Charles Dickens in 1959. By then he had already joined the faculty of the University of Minnesota, where he taught from 1957 to 1964. He was now becoming an established poet. In 1956, W. H. Auden had chosen Wright's first collection, *The Green Wall* (1957), for the Yale Series of Younger Poets. Two years later he published *Saint Judas* (1959). These early books were "the work of a 1950s formalist chafing against formal disciplines," according to poet and critic Robert B. Shaw. But they were also notable for his sympathetic approach to subjects such as the convicted and executed murderer, George Doty, and Judas, the betrayer of Christ. Although his first books were respectfully reviewed, Wright found himself listed by James Dickey among poets who were playing it too safe, hiding behind their sense of decorum. Dickey's charge may have been too strong, but Wright took it seriously. As he later put it, "It is true that I wrote to my publisher after *St. Judas* and said I don't know what I am going to do after this but it will be completely different."

A big influence in this sea-change was his meeting with Robert Bly after discovering Bly's magazine, *The Fifties*. Bly's antiacademic stance, rejection of rhyme, and interest in translation were attracting poets who wanted to change the way they wrote. While in Minnesota, Wright visited Bly's farm and found friendship and acceptance, meeting poets such as Thomas McGrath, Louis Simpson, and John Logan. His family was changing—a second son, Marshall, was born in 1958. He was also struggling with alcoholism and marital difficulties, and his friendship with other poets were increasingly important to him.

The poems he wrote after *Saint Judas* were in free verse and a plainer style. They included "A Blessing" and "Lying in a Hammock at William Duffy's Farm in Pine Island, Minnesota"—the latter closing famously, "I have wasted my life." The need for renewal and change was palpable in this work, though Wright would later wonder about the veracity of some poems, telling one interviewer, "'I have wasted my life'—well, that's the way I happened to feel at the moment. Actually, I haven't wasted my life."

Divorced from Liberty in 1962, Wright published *The Branch Will Not Break* (1963), his most critically admired volume. While some critics objected to his abandonment of meter and rhyme, most welcomed what they considered a more genuine voice. His problems with drinking, however, contributed to his being denied tenure at the University of Minnesota. He taught for two years at Macalester College in St. Paul, took a year off with a Guggenheim Fellowship, and in 1966 accepted a position at Hunter College in New York, where he would teach for the rest of his life.

Soon after moving to New York, Wright met Edith Anne Runk, "Annie," whom he married in 1967. A new collection, *Shall We Gather at the River* (1968), soon appeared, followed by his *Collected Poems* (1971). The latter volume earned Wright both the Pulitzer Prize and a $10,000 fellowship from the Academy of American Poets. During the 1970s the Wrights often traveled to Europe, especially Italy. The influence of European landscapes and poetry continued to be felt in his work, but he was also very knowledgeable about Asian writers. He liked "the effort the Japanese writers make to get rid of the clutter of language, to conceive of a poem as something which, with the greatest modesty, is brought up close to its subject so that it can be suggestive and evocative." Wright's literary criticism is notable for its range of affections, its catholic taste, its unwillingness to throw out the old in order to engage the new. Wright also published several volumes of translations, sometimes in collaboration with Bly and others, of poets such as Trakl, Cesar Vallejo, and Pablo Neruda.

Two Citizens, one of his weaker collections, appeared in 1973. In 1975, after suffering another nervous breakdown, Wright joined Alcoholics Anonymous. In the last collection published in his lifetime, *To a Blossoming Pear Tree* (1977), Wright appeared to be returning to humility in a clear, plain style, although critics were still undecided about how to read him. Some disliked his lack of irony and his tendency to become maudlin, while others considered him genuinely visionary. In 1979 Wright was diagnosed with cancer of the tongue. He died at Calvary Hospital in the Bronx on March 25, 1980.

Anticipating his death, Wright had begun circulating a new manuscript of poems among his friends. *This Journey,* widely regarded as one of his best books, was published posthumously in 1982. His *Collected Prose,* edited by Anne Wright, was published in 1983, and *Above the River: The Complete Poems,* with an introduction by Donald Hall, appeared in 1990.

◄○►━◄○►━◄○►

Complaint

She's gone. She was my love, my moon or more.
She chased the chickens out and swept the floor,
Emptied the bones and nut-shells after feasts,
And smacked the kids for leaping up like beasts.
Now morbid boys have grown past awkwardness;   5

The girls let stitches out, dress after dress,
To free some swinging body's riding space
And form the new child's unimagined face.
Yet, while vague nephews, spitting on their curls,
Amble to pester winds and blowsy girls,   10
What arm will sweep the room, what hand will hold
New snow against the milk to keep it cold?
And who will dump the garbage, feed the hogs,
And pitch the chickens' heads to hungry dogs?
Not my lost hag who dumbly bore such pain: 15
Childbirth and midnight sassafras and rain.
New snow against her face and hands she bore,
And now lies down, who was my moon or more.

                                                          1959

Saint Judas[1]

When I went out to kill myself, I caught
A pack of hoodlums beating up a man.
Running to spare his suffering, I forgot
My name, my number, how my day began,
How soldiers milled around the garden stone   5
And sang amusing songs; how all that day
Their javelins measured crowds; how I alone
Bargained the proper coins, and slipped away.

Banished from heaven, I found this victim beaten,
Stripped, kneed, and left to cry. Dropping my rope   10
Aside, I ran, ignored the uniforms:
Then I remembered bread my flesh had eaten,
The kiss that ate my flesh. Flayed without hope,
I held the man for nothing in my arms.

                                                          1959

Autumn Begins in Martins Ferry, Ohio

In the Shreve High football stadium,
I think of Polacks nursing long beers in Tiltonsville,
And gray faces of Negroes in the blast furnace at Benwood,
And the ruptured night watchman of Wheeling Steel,
Dreaming of heroes.   5

All the proud fathers are ashamed to go home.
Their women cluck like starved pullets,[2]
Dying for love.

---

1. After Jesus was condemned to death, Judas, who had betrayed him for thirty pieces of silver, felt such
remorse that he returned the money and then committed suicide by hanging himself (Matthew 27:3–10
and Acts 1:18–19).
2. Chickens.

Therefore,
Their sons grow suicidally beautiful   10
At the beginning of October,
And gallop terribly against each other's bodies.

                                                                                        1963

A Blessing

Just off the highway to Rochester, Minnesota,
Twilight bounds softly forth on the grass.
And the eyes of those two Indian ponies
Darken with kindness.
They have come gladly out of the willows   5
To welcome my friend and me.
We step over the barbed wire into the pasture
Where they have been grazing all day, alone.
They ripple tensely, they can hardly contain their happiness
That we have come.   10
They bow shyly as wet swans. They love each other.
There is no loneliness like theirs.
At home once more,
They begin munching the young tufts of spring in the darkness.
I would like to hold the slenderer one in my arms,   15
For she has walked over to me
And nuzzled my left hand.
She is black and white,
Her mane falls wild on her forehead,
And the light breeze moves me to caress her long ear   20
That is delicate as the skin over a girl's wrist.
Suddenly I realize
That if I stepped out of my body I would break
Into blossom.

                                                                                        1963

Lying in a Hammock
at William Duffy's Farm
in Pine Island, Minnesota

Over my head, I see the bronze butterfly,
Asleep on the black trunk,
Blowing like a leaf in green shadow.
Down the ravine behind the empty house,
The cowbells follow one another   5
Into the distances of the afternoon.
To my right.
In a field of sunlight between two pines,
The droppings of last year's horses
Blaze up into golden stones.   10

I lean back, as the evening darkens and comes on.
A chicken hawk floats over, looking for home.
I have wasted my life.

1963

Twilights

The big stones of the cistern behind the barn
Are soaked in whitewash.
My grandmother's face is a small maple leaf
Pressed in a secret box.
Locusts are climbing down into the dark green crevices   5
Of my childhood. Latches click softly in the trees. Your hair is gray.

The arbors of the cities are withered.
Far off, the shopping centers empty and darken.

A red shadow of steel mills.

1963

The Life

Murdered, I went, risen,
Where the murderers are,
That black ditch
Of river.

And if I come back to my only country   5
With a white rose on my shoulder,
What is that to you?
It is the grave
In blossom.

It is the trillium of darkness,   10
It is hell, it is the beginning of winter,
It is a ghost town of Etruscans[1] who have no names
Any more.

It is the old loneliness.
It is.   15
And it is
The last time.

1968

1. Members of a civilization that flourished in northwestern Italy from 950–300 B.C.E., before the rise of the Roman Empire.

PHILIP LEVINE
(b. 1928)

A celebrated poet of the working-class experience, Philip Levine was born in Detroit, Michigan, the son of middle-class Russian Jewish immigrants. His father was a businessman, his mother a bookseller. When Levine and his twin brother were five years old, their father died without leaving adequate insurance, and the family began a slow decline in its fortunes. The poet's childhood memories were colored by financial strain and family anxiety during the Great Depression. He would also recall the radical politics of adults overheard in conversation and his early fascination with the Spanish Civil War. He was educated locally, receiving a bachelor's degree from Wayne State College (now University) in 1950. In the early '50s he worked in several factories, including Chevrolet Gear and Axle and Detroit Transmission, while earning his master's degree "through the mails with a thesis on Keats's 'Indolence' ode" in 1954. Those few years of factory work provided Levine with characters and images for much of his poetry of the next forty-five years. A self-described "anarchist," Levine has eloquently spoken for the working man even while leading the bourgeois life of a college professor.

In 1953 Levine went to the University of Iowa to study with Robert Lowell and ended up taking an influential class with the lesser-known John Berryman, "the most brilliant, intense, articulate man I've ever met." Among his fellow students were poets Donald Justice, Henri Coulette, and Jane Cooper. The following year he met and married Frances Artley, went with her to Florida while she taught drama for a year, then returned with his small family to Iowa, where he taught until he received another master's degree in 1957. Following a year of study with Yvor Winters at Stanford, Levine moved to Fresno. From 1958 to 1992 he taught English and writing at California State University, Fresno, occasionally taking appointments at Tufts and other universities. (Under Levine's guidance Fresno became a major graduate center for creative writing.) He was twice able to live with his wife and sons for a year in Spain (1965–66 and 1968–69), deepening his affinity both for Spanish poets Federico García Lorca and Antonio Machado and for Spanish anarchism.

Levine's poetry had long appeared in magazines and limited editions when, at forty, he published his first full-length collection *Not This Pig* (1968). He had a reputation for poems in a street-wise vernacular, an early version of the mythologized working-class persona he would create. Following several more limited edition collections, Levine brought out *They Feed They Lion* (1972) with the prestigious New York publishing firm Atheneum. (Its title poem distorts grammar to achieve a powerful surreal effect.) Levine's next book, *1933* (1974), took its title from the year of his father's death and dealt more directly with memories of his Detroit childhood. Levine's leftist sympathies and fascination with the Spanish Civil War led him to compose the poems of *The Names of the Lost* (1976). Collections that followed were *7 Years from Somewhere* (1979), *Ashes: Poems New and Old* (1979), *One for the Rose* (1981), and *Selected Poems* (1984).

As his later poetry evolved, Levine's voice became more direct and his lines less energetic and ironic, which caused some critics to express disappointment even though Levine's readership and reputation continued to grow. *A Walk with Tom Jefferson* (1988) concerned an African American factory worker, not the

Founding Father, and *New Selected Poems* (1991) gained Levine an even wider following. *What Work Is* (1991) won the National Book Award (his second), while *The Simple Truth* (1994) won the Pulitzer Prize. While still finding material in his Detroit past, Levine has also set recent poems in California and Europe. One of the most honored poets of his generation, he has toured widely, giving popular readings of his poems.

On the Edge

My name is Edgar Poe and I was born
in 1928 in Michigan.
Nobody gave a damn. The gruel I ate
Kept me alive, nothing kept me warm,
But I grew up, almost to five foot ten,   5
And nothing in the world can change my weight.

I have been watching you these many years,
There in the office, pencil poised and ready,
Or on the highway when you went ahead.
I did not write; I watched you watch the stars   10
Believing that the wheel of fate was steady;
I saw you rise from love and go to bed;

I heard you lie, even to your daughter.
I did not write, for I am Edgar Poe,
Edgar the mad one, silly, drunk, unwise,   15
But Edgar waiting on the edge of laughter,
And there is nothing that he does not know
Whose page is blanker than the raining skies.

                                                        1964

Animals Are Passing from Our Lives

It's wonderful how I jog
on four honed-down ivory toes
my massive buttocks slipping
like oiled parts with each light step.

I'm to market. I can smell   5
the sour, grooved block, I can smell
the blade that opens the hole
and the pudgy white fingers

that shake out the intestines
like a hankie. In my dreams   10
the snouts drool on the marble,
suffering children, suffering flies,

suffering the consumers
who won't meet their steady eyes
for fear they could see. The boy   15
who drives me along believes

that any moment I'll fall
on my side and drum my toes
like a typewriter or squeal
and shit like a new housewife   20

discovering television,
or that I'll turn like a beast
cleverly to hook his teeth
with my teeth. No. Not this pig.

                                        1968

To a Child Trapped in a Barber Shop

You've gotten in through the transom
          and you can't get out
till Monday morning or, worse,
          till the cops come.

That six-year-old red face   5
          calling for mama
is yours; it won't help you
          because your case

is closed forever, hopeless.
          So don't drink   10
the Lucky Tiger,[1] don't
          fill up on grease

because that makes it a lot worse,
          that makes it a crime
against property and the state   15
          and that costs time.

We've all been here before,
          we took our turn
under the electric storm
          of the vibrator   20

and stiffened our wills to meet
          the close clippers
and heard the true blade mowing
          back and forth

1. Hair ointment and dandruff cure.

on a strip of dead skin,   25
  and we stopped crying.
You think your life is over?
  It's just begun.

1968

They Feed They Lion

Out of burlap sacks, out of bearing butter,
Out of black bean and wet slate bread,
Out of the acids of rage, the candor of tar,
Out of creosate, gasoline, drive shafts, wooden dollies,
They Lion grow.   5

  Out of the grey hills
Of industrial barns, out of rain, out of bus ride,
West Virginia to Kiss My Ass, out of buried aunties,
Mothers hardening like pounded stumps, out of stumps,
Out of the bones' need to sharpen and the muscles' to stretch,   10
They Lion grow.

  Earth is eating trees, fence posts,
Gutted cars, earth is calling her little ones,
"Come home, Come home!" From pig balls,
From the ferocity of pig driven to holiness,   15
From the furred ear and the full jowl come
The repose of the hung belly, from the purpose
They Lion grow.

  From the sweet glues of the trotters[1]
Come the sweet kinks of the fist, from the full flower   20
Of the hams the thorax of caves,
From "Bow Down" come "Rise Up,"
Come they Lion from the reeds of shovels,
The grained arm that pulls the hands,
They Lion grow.   25

  From my five arms and all my hands,
From all my white sins forgiven, they feed,
From my car passing under the stars,
They Lion, from my children inherit,
From the oak turned to a wall, they Lion,   30
From they sack and they belly opened
And all that was hidden burning on the oil-stained earth
They feed they Lion and he comes.

1972

1. Pigs' feet.

You Can Have It

My brother comes home from work
and climbs the stairs to our room.
I can hear the bed groan and his shoes drop
one by one. You can have it, he says.

The moonlight streams in the window   5
and his unshaven face is whitened
like the face of the moon. He will sleep
long after noon and waken to find me gone.

Thirty years will pass before I remember
that moment when suddenly I knew each man   10
has one brother who dies when he sleeps
and sleeps when he rises to face this life,

and that together they are only one man
sharing a heart that always labors, hands
yellowed and cracked, a mouth that gasps   15
for breath and asks, Am I gonna make it?

All night at the ice plant he had fed
the chute its silvery blocks, and then I
stacked cases of orange soda for the children
of Kentucky, one gray box-car at a time   20

with always two more waiting. We were twenty
for such a short time and always in
the wrong clothes, crusted with dirt
and sweat. I think now we were never twenty.

In 1948 in the city of Detroit, founded   25
by de la Mothe Cadillac[1] for the distant purposes
of Henry Ford, no one wakened or died,
no one walked the streets or stoked a furnace,

for there was no such year, and now
that year has fallen off all the old newspapers,   30
calendars, doctors' appointments, bonds,
wedding certificates, drivers licenses.

The city slept. The snow turned to ice.
The ice to standing pools or rivers
racing in the gutters. Then bright grass rose   35
between the thousands of cracked squares,

and that grass died. I give you back 1948.
I give you all the years from then

---

1. The French explorer Antoine de la Mothe Cadillac (1658–1730) built Fort Ponchartrain in 1701 at the site of what is now Detroit.

to the coming one. Give me back the moon
with its frail light falling across a face.   40

Give me back my young brother, hard
and furious, with wide shoulders and a curse
for God and burning eyes that look upon
all creation and say, You can have it.

1979

◆►◄ MARK STRAND ►◄◆
(b. 1934)

Mark Strand was born on Prince Edward Island in Canada. Because of his father's work as a salesman, he was raised in a succession of cities, Halifax, Montreal, New York, Philadelphia, and Cleveland, and during his teenage years he lived in Latin America. After graduation from Antioch College with a bachelor's degree in 1957, he studied painting at Yale with Josef Albers and earned another bachelor's in 1959. But soon he shifted his main interest from painting to poetry. He studied poetry in Italy on a Fulbright Fellowship from 1960 to 1961 and then attended the University of Iowa, where he worked with Donald Justice and received a master's degree in 1962. After teaching at Iowa from 1962 to 1965, he served from 1965 to 1966 as a Fulbright lecturer at the University of Brazil in Rio de Janeiro. His first book, *Sleeping with One Eye Open,* appeared in 1964 from a small press; but his next book, *Reasons for Moving* (1968), was issued by Atheneum, a press notable for its poetry books, and from the late 1960s onward Strand's poetry received great acclaim. His work was not only widely anthologized, but much imitated by young poets attracted by his stylistic directness, existential isolation, and surrealistic juxtapositions of odd images. He pursued a teaching career, working at numerous universities before settling at the University of Utah from 1981 to 1993 and then moving to Johns Hopkins University in 1994. His books of poetry have garnered him many honors and awards, including a MacArthur Foundation fellowship in 1987, a term as U.S. Poet Laureate from 1990 to 1991, the Bollingen Prize in 1993, and the Pulitzer Prize for *Blizzard of One* (1998). He edited many anthologies and published children's books, short stories, art criticism, and translations of poetry from a variety of languages, including Spanish, Portuguese, and Quechua. He has been married twice and has two children, one from each marriage.

In his poetry, interviews, and essays about poetry, Strand often looks to "the unknown" for inspiration, arguing that poets should find their sources and methods in the unconscious. In a 1978 essay, "The Craft of Poetry," he observes: "The purpose of the poem is not disclosure or storytelling or the telling of a daydream, nor is a poem a symptom. A poem is itself and is the act by which it is born; it is self-referential and is not necessarily preceded by any known order." Thus, he has demurred from offering any insights into how poetry should be written. In the same essay he proposes: "The poems that are of greatest value are those that break rules so that they may exist, whose urgency make rules about how to write or not write poems irrelevant." Despite his distaste for rules, Strand relies in his poetry of the 1960s and 1970s on tactics that he honed with great skill. These poems are spare, grounded on simple, declarative sentences, short, end-stopped lines, and stark discontinuities of tone and imagery. He learned some of the these strategies from American poets he admires, such as Wallace Stevens, Elizabeth Bishop, his teacher Donald Justice, and his contemporary W. S. Merwin. Strand has also borrowed strategies from poets whose work he has translated, particularly the Spanish poet Rafael Alberti and the Brazilian poet Carlos Drummond de Andrade. In his early poetry, Strand cultivates an aura of mystery and explores the dark side of the psyche, for his dreamlike disjunctions explore the dimensions of a consciousness alienated from itself and the world. Despite the isolation the poems project, many of them display a wry humor that helps Strand modulate the tone of his books. In his later work, Strand began varying his style somewhat, lengthening his lines, experimenting with the prose poetry he inaugurated in *The Monument* (1978), and even writing a book-length poem, *Dark Harbor* (1993). Moreover, as the title of his book, *The Continuous Life* (1990), suggests, he became less interested in a poetry of extreme isolation and more concerned with the interconnections between self and others. Evoking life's strangeness and the self's continual surprise at its own existence, Strand's poems have appealed to mid- and late-century readers searching for dreamscapes that reflect their own feelings of unease.

Keeping Things Whole

In a field
I am the absence
of field.
This is
always the case.   5
Wherever I am
I am what is missing.

When I walk
I part the air
and always   10
the air moves in
to fill the spaces
where my body's been.

We all have reasons
for moving.   15
I move
to keep things whole.

1964

Eating Poetry

Ink runs from the corners of my mouth.
There is no happiness like mine.
I have been eating poetry.

The librarian does not believe what she sees.
Her eyes are sad   5
and she walks with her hands in her dress.

The poems are gone.
The light is dim.
The dogs are on the basement stairs and coming up.

Their eyeballs roll,   10
their blond legs burn like brush.
The poor librarian begins to stamp her feet and weep.

She does not understand.
When I get on my knees and lick her hand,
she screams.   15

I am a new man.
I snarl at her and bark.
I romp with joy in the bookish dark.

                                                              1968

◄ CHARLES WRIGHT ►
(b. 1935)

Charles Penzel Wright, Jr., was born in Pickwick Dam, Tennessee. His father was a civil engineer for the Tennessee Valley Authority, and during the poet's childhood the family lived in several rural towns built at dam sites in eastern Tennessee and western North Carolina. Eventually the family settled in Kingsport, Tennessee. In the tenth grade, Wright attended an Episcopalian boarding school, where he was one of only eight students. He finished high school at another religious boarding school in Arden, Tennessee. The Christian doctrine he absorbed from his family and teachers underlies the religious vocabulary he often deploys in his poetry. Likewise, the lush landscape of the rural South also became a persistent focus of his poems, one that he entwines with searching questions about the presence and absence of divinity. In a 1992 interview he remarked, "There are three things, basically, that I write about—language, landscape, and the idea of God." His Southern religious upbringing helped to instill two of those themes, although as an adult he eventually left the Episcopalian faith.

Along with the rural South of his childhood, the landscape of Italy also figures prominently in Wright's poetry. After graduating from Davidson College in 1957 with a bachelor's degree in history, Wright served for four years in the U.S. Army Intelligence Corps. Stationed in Verona, Italy, for three years, he experienced an epiphany while sightseeing. In a 1977 interview he recalled,

> I was given a book, *The Selected Poems of Ezra Pound* . . . and I was told to go out to Sirmione, on Lake Garda, where the Latin poet, Catullus, supposedly had a villa. It's still one of the most beautiful places I have ever been to. . . . Lake Garda in front of you, the Italian Alps on three sides of you, the ruined and beautiful villa around you, and I read a poem that Pound has written about the place, about Sirmione being more beautiful than Paradise, and my life was changed forever.

The Italy he looks back to in his adult poetry is, indeed, a romanticized one, what he calls in another interview "the 'idea' of Italy," a fictional place of scenic land-scapes, picturesque architecture, and great works of art. This idealized perspective of Italy merged in the young Wright's mind with the sense of discovery he experienced when reading poetry, especially the poetry of Pound. He has claimed that "reading Pound showed me there was a way to do what I had always wanted to do—to write—and Italy somehow allowed me to do it." He began writing poetry in Italy and, after his discharge from the army in 1961, enrolled in the Writers' Workshop at the University of Iowa, where he received a master's degree in 1963. The Iowa poetry workshops, taught in the early 1960s by Donald Justice, gave Wright an important foundation for his poetry. "I am," he admits, "almost a 100 percent product of the writing workshop system. And it was not only good for me, but necessary as well."

After finishing his degree, Wright returned to Italy for two years on a Fulbright Fellowship, working on translations from the poetry of Eugenio Montale, Pier Paolo Pasolini, and Cesare Pavese, modern poets whose style influenced his own. From 1966 to 1983, he taught in the English Department at the University of California, Irvine. In 1969, he married Holly McIntire, a photographer, with whom he had a son. After becoming the Souder Family Professor in English in 1983 at the University of Virginia, he sojourned in Italy again in 1992 when he served as a distinguished visiting professor at the Universita Degli Studi in Florence. Wright achieved professional success early for his poetry. His second collection, *Hard Freight* (1973), was nominated for a National Book Award, and he won the award ten years later for *Country Music: Selected Early Poems* (1982). *Black Zodiac* (1997) won both the Pulitzer Prize and the National Book Critics Circle Award, and he has received many other honors.

Styling himself as a poet of visionary epiphanies, Wright looks for inspiration to poets such as Dante, William Blake, Emily Dickinson, Gerard Manley Hopkins, and Hart Crane. Although the short lyrics of his first books inclined toward the surrealism popular in American poetry during the late 1960s, his poems have grown more expansive from volume to volume—so much so that he has presented his life's work as a "trilogy." The first part consists of selected poems culled from his early collections of the '70s and reprinted in *Country Music*. The middle phase of his career is collected in *The World of the Ten Thousand Things: Poems 1980–1990*. The third part of the trilogy incorporates his most recent volumes—*Chicamauga* (1995), *Black Zodiac*, and *Appalachia* (1998)—reincorporated in *Negative Blue: Selected Later Poems* (2000).

Throughout his career, Wright's work has been characterized by gorgeous descriptions and an imagistic, associative structure derived from his early reading of Pound. Wright favors two basic approaches to depicting landscape: (1) contrasting its permanence to the impermanence of human life and consciousness, and (2) finding analogues in the landscape—and especially in evanescent phenomena such as mists and the play of light on water—for mutability. As he has aged, Wright has become increasingly concerned with mortality and memory, and he often juxtaposes an ephemeral landscape that glows in his memory with a present landscape he scrutinizes. This technique makes his work simultaneously abstract and concrete and also leads him to contemplate in many poems the limitations of language, a preoccupation that has led critics to classify Wright's work as post-modernist.

The New Poem

It will not resemble the sea.
It will not have dirt on its thick hands.
It will not be part of the weather.

It will not reveal its name.
It will not have dreams you can count on.   5
It will not be photogenic.

It will not attend our sorrow.
It will not console our children.
It will not be able to help us.

1973

Clear Night

Clear night, thumb-top of a moon, a back-lit sky.
Moon-fingers lay down their same routine
On the side deck and the threshold, the white keys and the black keys.
Bird hush and bird song. A cassia flower falls.

I want to be bruised by God.   5
I want to be strung up in a strong light and singled out.
I want to be stretched, like music wrung from a dropped seed.
I want to be entered and picked clean.

And the wind says "What?" to me.
And the castor beans, with their little earrings of death, say "What?" to me. 10
And the stars start out on their cold slide through the dark.
And the gears notch and the engines wheel.

1977

Stone Canyon Nocturne

Ancient of Days, old friend, no one believes you'll come back.
No one believes in his own life anymore.

The moon, like a dead heart, cold and unstartable, hangs by a thread
At the earth's edge,
Unfaithful at last, splotching the ferns and the pink shrubs.   5

In the other world, children undo the knots in their tally strings.
They sing songs, and their fingers blear.

And here, where the swan hums in his socket, where bloodroot
And belladonna insist on our comforting,
Where the fox in the canyon wall empties our hands, ecstatic for more, 10

Like a bead of clear oil the Healer revolves through the night wind,
Part eye, part tear, unwilling to recognize us.

1977

California Dreaming

We are not born yet, and everything's crystal under our feet.
We are not brethren, we are not underlings.
We are another nation,
                        living by voices that you will never hear,
Caught in the net of splendor   5
                        of time-to-come on the earth.
We shine in our distant chambers, we are golden.

———————

Midmorning, and Darvon[1] dustfall off the Pacific
Stuns us to ecstasy,
                        October sun   10
Stuck like a tack on the eastern drift of the sky,
The idea of God on the other,
                        body by body
Rinsed in the Sunday prayer-light, draining away
Into the undercoating and slow sparks of the west,   15
                        which is our solitude and our joy.

———————

I've looked at this ridge of lights for six years now
                        and still don't like it,
Strung out like Good Friday along a cliff
That Easters down to the ocean,   20
A dark wing with ruffled feathers as far out as Catalina
Fallen from some sky,
                        ruffled and laid back by the wind,
Santa Ana[2] that lisps its hot breath
                        on the neck of everything.   25

———————

What if the soul indeed is outside the body,
                        a little rainfall of light
Moistening our every step, prismatic, apotheosizic?[3]
What if inside the body another shape is waiting to come out,
White as a quilt, loose as a fever,   30
                        and sways in the easy tides there?
What other anagoge[4] in this life but the self?
What other ladder to Paradise
                        but the smooth handholds of the rib cage?
High in the palm tree the orioles twitter and grieve.   35

———

1. A narcotic drug related to methadone.
2. A dry, hot wind that arises in the desert region of Southern California and blows toward the Pacific during the winter.
3. Adjective form of the noun *apotheosis*, the deification or exaltation of a person or thing.
4. The mystical or allegorical meaning of a text, especially a passage from the Bible.

We twitter and grieve, the spider twirls the honey bee.
Who twitters and grieves, around in her net,
                                 then draws it by one leg
Up to the fishbone fern leaves inside the pepper tree
                                 swaddled in silk   40
And turns it again and again until it is shining.

———————

Some nights, when the rock-and-roll band next door has quit playing,
And the last helicopter has thwonked back to the Marine base,
And the dark lets all its weight down
                             to within a half inch of the ground,   45
I sit outside in the gold lamé of the moon
                      as the town sleeps and the country sleeps
Like flung confetti around me,
And wonder just what in the hell I'm doing out here
So many thousands of miles away from what I know best.   50
And what I know best
                   has nothing to do with Point Conception
And Avalon and the long erasure of ocean
Out there where the landscape ends.
What I know best is a little thing.   55
It sits on the far side of the simile,
                       the like that's like the like.

———————

Today is sweet stuff on the tongue.
The question of how we should live our lives in this world
Will find no answer from us   60
                   this morning,
Sunflick, the ocean humping its back
Beneath us, shivering out
                 wave after wave we fall from
And cut through in a white scar of healed waters,   65
Our wet suits glossed slick as seals,
                   our boards grown sharp as cries.
We rise and fall like the sun.

———————

Ghost of the Muse and her dogsbody
Suspended above the beach, November 25th,   70
Sun like a Valium[1] disc, smog like rust in the trees.
White-hooded and friar-backed,
                  a gull choir eyeballs the wave reach.
Invisibly pistoned, the sea keeps it up,
                plunges and draws back, plunges and draws back,   75

———————

1. A tranquilizer.

Yesterday hung like a porcelain cup behind the eyes,
Sonorous valves, insistent extremities,
                              the worm creeping out of the heart . . .

Who are these people we pretend to be,
                              untouched by the setting sun?   80
They stand less stiffly than we do, and handsomer,
First on the left foot, and then the right.
Just for a moment we see ourselves inside them,
                              peering out,
And then they go their own way and we go ours,   85
Back to the window seat above the driveway,
Christmas lights in the pepper tree,
                    black Madonna
Gazing out from the ailanthus.
Chalk eyes downcast, heavy with weeping and bitterness,   90
Her time has come round again.

Piece by small piece the world falls away from us like spores
From a milkweed pod,
                    and everything we have known,   95
And everyone we have known,
Is taken away by the wind to forgetfulness,
Somebody always humming,
                    California dreaming . . .

1984

━━━━ ◅•◄ CHARLES SIMIC ►•▻ ━━━━
(b. 1938)

Charles Simic was born in Belgrade, Yugoslavia, and his early years were spent in
that city as it endured World War II and the beginnings of the Tito regime. Much
of his poetry is colored by the fear, violence, and hunger he experienced at that
time. This dark perspective even shades his recent work, like his brief 1996 poem
"Slaughterhouse Flies," which begins: "Evenings, they ran their bloody feet / Over
the pages of my schoolbooks." And yet humor also plays an important role in his
work. In one of his notebooks, Simic observes: "I grew up among some very witty
people, I now realize. They knew how to tell stories and how to laugh, and that
has made all the difference." The echo of Robert Frost in Simic's last phrase here
may be indicative of his poetry's bridge between Europe and America.

Simic was a poor student and troubled youth who often had difficulty with
authority. When he was fifteen, his family was allowed to travel to Paris, and in
1954 they joined his father, now living in Chicago. Simic had studied English while
in France, and his high school experience in America seems to have been positive,
awakening his interest in literature. Later, Simic worked as an office boy for the

Chicago Sun Times and took night classes toward a college degree. But his college career was interrupted by service in the U.S. Army from 1961 to 1963. He received his bachelor's degree from New York University in 1966 and became a naturalized citizen in 1971. He currently teaches at the University of New Hampshire.

Simic published his first volume of poems, *What the Grass Says,* in 1967, and a second, *Somewhere among Us a Stone is Taking Notes,* two years later—both published by Kayak, a small San Francisco press. These early books already show the mixture of humor and violence that would characterize much of his work. The early work also displays Simic's allegiances to surrealism and an absurdist sense of humor that seems particularly European. Surrealism has its own roots in Europe between the two world wars partly as a reaction against both bourgeois complacency and state terror. In America, Simic's brand of surrealism became popular during the political upheavals of the Vietnam era. The fact that he has never entirely abandoned such tendencies is one aspect of his distinctiveness as an American poet. "To be an exception to the rule is my sole ambition," he has written. At least one critic, Vernon Young, has argued that Simic's poetic stance may be due as much to the memory of European folklore as to a mature artist's theories, and it is true that Simic's poems often prove to be fables or parables. Brevity is another consistent characteristic of Simic's verse. As he wrote in his notebooks, "Little said, much meant, is what poetry is all about."

Among the collections for which he is best known are *Classic Ballroom Dances* (1980), *Selected Poems 1963–1983* (1985), *The World Doesn't End* (1989), which won the Pulitzer Prize, *The Book of Gods and Devils* (1990), and *Jackstraws* (2000). His prose books include *Dime-Store Alchemy: The Art of Joseph Cornell* (1992) and *The Unemployed Fortune-Teller: Essays and Memoirs* (1994). Simic has translated many Yugoslavian poets, including Tomaz Salamun and Nicola Tadic, and has also championed jazz, the great art of his adoptive country.

◄●▬▬●▬▬●►

Fear

Fear passes from man to man
Unknowing,
As one leaf passes its shudder
To another.

All at once the whole tree is trembling.   5
And there is no sign of the wind.

1967

My Shoes

Shoes, secret face of my inner life:
Two gaping toothless mouths,
Two partly decomposed animal skins
Smelling of mice nests.

My brother and sister who died at birth   5
Continuing their existence in you,
Guiding my life
Toward their incomprehensible innocence.

What use are books to me
When in you it is possible to read   10
The Gospel of my life on earth
And still beyond, of things to come?

I want to proclaim the religion
I have devised for your perfect humility
And the strange church I am building   15
With you as the altar.

Ascetic and maternal, you endure:
Kin to oxen, to Saints, to condemned men,
With your mute patience, forming
The only true likeness of myself.   20

1967

Fork

This strange thing must have crept
Right out of hell.
It resembles a bird's foot
Worn around the cannibal's neck.

As you hold it in your hand,   5
As you stab with it into a piece of meat,
It is possible to imagine the rest of the bird:
Its head which like your fist
Is large, bald, beakless, and blind.

1969

Eyes Fastened with Pins

How much death works,
No one knows what a long
Day he puts in. The little
Wife always alone
Ironing death's laundry.   5
The beautiful daughters
Setting death's supper table.
The neighbors playing
Pinochle in the backyard
Or just sitting on the steps   10
Drinking beer. Death,
Meanwhile, in a strange
Part of town looking for
Someone with a bad cough,

But the address is somehow wrong,   15
Even death can't figure it out
Among all the locked doors . . .
And the rain beginning to fall.
Long windy night ahead.
Death with not even a newspaper   20
To cover his head, not even
A dime to call the one pining away,
Undressing slowly, sleepily,
And stretching naked
On death's side of the bed.   25

1977

Classic Ballroom Dances

Grandmothers who wring the necks
Of chickens; old nuns
With names like Theresa, Marianne,
Who pull schoolboys by the ear;

The intricate steps of pickpockets   5
Working the crowd of the curious
At the scene of an accident; the slow shuffle
Of the evangelist with a sandwich board;

The hesitation of the early-morning customer
Peeking through the window grille   10
Of a pawnshop; the weave of a little kid
Who is walking to school with eyes closed;

And the ancient lovers, cheek to cheek,
On the dance floor of the Union Hall,
Where they also hold charity raffles   15
On rainy Monday nights of an eternal November.

1980

━━⋗ JAMES TATE ⋗━━
(b. 1943)

James Tate, the *enfant terrible* of American surrealist poetry, was born in Kansas City, Missouri, in 1943. His father, a pilot, was killed the following year in a combat mission over Germany when his son was only five months old—a loss that would haunt the poet's early work. Tate attended University of Missouri, Kansas City, and Kansas State College, Pittsburgh, Kansas, from which he graduated in 1965. He then entered the University of Iowa Writing Workshop where he studied with Donald Justice. At Iowa Tate quickly distinguished himself as a literary prodigy by publishing two chapbooks and then winning the Yale Series of Younger Poets competition for his first full-length collection, *The Lost Pilot* (1967). One of the youngest writers to win this award, he was only twenty-two when the book was accepted for publication—the age at which his father had died, a coincidence not lost on the author.

Tate's debut made an enormous impression on other young poets. *The Lost Pilot* struck an ummistakably new and original note. Tate had developed a vernacular American style for surrealism, a modernist European movement that had mostly sounded foreign and awkward in earlier English-language poets. His language and images were not from the cafés of Paris or Barcelona but from the streets of Iowa City. Although Tate claimed he often wrote in a trance, his poems gave no hint of automatic writing. The poems were tightly constructed, the language clean and sharply chiseled. What Tate borrowed from surrealism was the use of dream logic and free association. In *The Lost Pilot* Tate usually created a clear narrative line in his poems. Only as the details of the story and situation unfolded in an increasingly bizarre fashion, did one realize that the speaker inhabited some private landscape of dream or hallucination. Often he would incorporate these surrealist principles into something very similar to the standard confessional poem, as in the book's title poem, "The Lost Pilot," a visionary fantasy about his dead father.

While still in his mid-twenties Tate emerged as a central figure in the low-key surrealism that would become one of the mainstream styles of American poetry in the 1970s and probably the most influential style among male poets. (Robert Bly, James Wright, and Donald Hall were among the many established writers who would adopt—at least temporarily—what came to be called the "deep image" style.) In contrast to the austere minimalism of the deep image school, Tate created a quirky, inclusive, and often zany style that mixed absurdist comedy with bewildering juxtapositions of image and mood. His tone was at once understated and aggressive. Everything, including violent or tragic subjects, was presented with dark, detached humor.

To his detriment, Tate proved an unrestrainedly prolific poet. By 1979 when he reached the age of thirty-five, he had already published over twenty books and pamphlets—some with purposely bizarre titles like *The Oblivion Ha-Ha* (1970), *Row with Your Hair* (1969), and *Riven Doggeries* (1979), which reflect desire to surprise or puzzle typical of that restless and rebellious moment in American culture. As Surrealism and Deep Image poetry fell from popularity, Tate gradually became a whipping boy for reviewers. Yet he remained true to his imaginative roots and slowly grew more selective and self-critical in his publications. His work also deepened and darkened in its vision, and his reputation was slowly rehabilitated. In 1992 he won the Pulitzer Prize for his carefully chosen and pruned *Selected Poems,* and in 1994 he received the National Book Award for *Worshipful Company of Fletchers.* Tate has taught creative writing at Columbia University and Emerson College. Since 1971 he has been a faculty member at the University of Massachusetts, Amherst.

◦━◆━◦

The Lost Pilot

For my father, 1922–1944

Your face did not rot
like the others—the co-pilot,
for example, I saw him

yesterday. His face is corn-
mush: his wife and daughter,
the poor ignorant people, stare   5

as if he will compose soon.
He was more wronged than Job.[1]
But your face did not rot

like the others—it grew dark,   10
and hard like ebony;
the features progressed in their

distinction. If I could cajole
you to come back for an evening,
down from your compulsive   15

orbiting, I would touch you,
read your face as Dallas,
your hoodlum gunner, now,

with the blistered eyes, reads
his braille editions. I would   20
touch your face as a disinterested

scholar touches an original page.
However frightening, I would
discover you, and I would not

turn you in; I would not make   25
you face your wife, or Dallas,
or the co-pilot, Jim. You

could return to your crazy
orbiting, and I would not try
to fully understand what   30

it means to you. All I know
is this: when I see you,
as I have seen you at least

once every year of my life,
spin across the wilds of the sky   35
like a tiny, African god,

I feel dead. I feel as if I were
the residue of a stranger's life,
that I should pursue you.

My head cocked toward the sky,   40
I cannot get off the ground,
and, you, passing over again,

1. In the Old Testament book, Job's faith was tested by God through an increasingly severe series of disasters.

fast, perfect, and unwilling
to tell me that you are doing
well, or that it was mistake   45

that placed you in that world,
and me in this; or that misfortune
placed these worlds in us.

                                                              1967

Teaching the Ape to Write Poems

They didn't have much trouble
teaching the ape to write poems:
first they strapped him into the chair,
then tied the pencil around his hand
(the paper had already been nailed down).   5
Then Dr. Bluespire leaned over his shoulder
and whispered into his ear:
"You look like a god sitting there.
Why don't you try writing something?"

                                                              1972

The Chaste Stranger

All the sexually active people in Westport[1]
look so clean and certain, I wonder
if they're dead. Their lives are tennis
without end, the avocado-green Mercedes
waiting calm as you please. Perhaps it is   5
my brain that is unplugged, and these
shadow-people don't know how to drink
martinis anymore. They are suddenly and
mysteriously not in the least interested
in fornicating with strangers. Well,   10
there are a lot of unanswered questions
here, and certainly no dinner invitations
where a fella could probe Buffy's inner-
mush, a really complicated adventure,
in a 1930ish train station, outlandish   15
bouquets, a poisonous insect found
burrowing its way through the walls
of the special restaurant and into one
of her perfect nostrils—she was reading
Meetings with Remarkable Men,[2] needing   20
succor, dreaming of a village near Bosnia,

1. An upscale town in Connecticut.
2. Autobiography of the Russian guru G. I. Gurdjieff, who advocated equality, harmony, and antimaterialism.

when a clattering of carts broke her thoughts—
"Those billy goats and piglets, they are
all so ephemeral . . ." But now, in Westport
Connecticut, a boy, a young man really,   25
looking as if he had just come through
a carwash, and dressed for the kind of success
that made her girlfriends froth and lather,
can be overheard speaking to no one
in particular: "That *Paris Review*[1] crowd,   30
I couldn't tell if they were bright or
just overbred." Whereupon Buffy swings
into action, pinning him to the floor:
"I will unglue your very being from this
planet, if ever . . ." He could appreciate   35
her sincerity, not to mention her spiffy togs.
Didymus the Blind[2] has put three dollars
on Total Departure, and I am tired of pumping
my own gas. I'm Lewis your aluminum man, and
we are whirling in a spangled frenzy toward   40
a riddle and a doom—here's looking up

your old address.

1986

---

1. Literary magazine founded in 1953.
2. An Alexandrian layman with a prodigious memory, Didymus (313–398 C.E.), blind from age four, headed a Christian school and became known as one of the most learned men of his era through his extensive biblical commentaries.

Return to Realism: Regionalism and Cultural Identity

New views have emerged of both urban and rural settings.

HISTORICAL AND CRITICAL OVERVIEW

American Places

> It wasn't a place—time is where I came from.
> —*William Stafford*

Most American literature can be defined in terms of regional identity. Think of New England writers from Anne Bradstreet to Robert Frost, Southerners from Mark Twain to James Dickey, or New Yorkers from Walt Whitman to Frank O'Hara. Other regions and subregions that have developed unmistakable literary accents and identities include the Midwest, the Rockies, the Southwest, the Northwest, and California. In the United States even avant-garde movements have often announced their regional or local identities, as in the Harlem Renaissance, San Francisco Renaissance, and New York School. Regionalism supposes that the imagination is forged in a writer's earliest associations, including landscape (or cityscape), history, dialect, climate, and culture. As John Haines has asserted, "I think there is a spirit of place, a presence asking to be expressed." The poetry of Robinson Jeffers, for example, could have developed as it did nowhere but from the coast of northern California.

Regionalism, of course, is not the only impulse in modern American poetry. There is also a radically different orientation evident in the works of certain writers, who display a deep anxiety about the artist's relationship to any one place, culture, or community. As we have seen earlier in this anthology, many authors from Modernists like Pound, Eliot, and H. D. to the present have been such internationalists, expressing a frustration with the parochial aspects of American life and art. Some of these writers have literally uprooted themselves from their native soil to live abroad—like the members of the so-called "Lost Generation" of the 1920s who lived in Paris, a group that included Pound, Ernest Hemingway, F. Scott Fitzgerald, Gertrude Stein, and Archibald MacLeish. Likewise certain literary movements like Imagism and Surrealism have generally tended to be internationalist in their flavor. In some ways, modern American literary history can be seen as an unresolvable dialectic between regionalism and internationalism, as two competing identities for the writer.

Regionalism, however, must not be understood in reductive terms as small-minded provincialism. To draw inspiration from a specific place, time, and culture does not mean that an artist closes himself or herself from wider concerns. While it is difficult to imagine William Faulkner, Flannery O'Connor, or Robert Penn Warren without reference to the particular storytelling heritage of the South, all three writers were also influenced by numerous European and American literary models. It is equally hard to imagine Allen Ginsberg, Kenneth Rexroth, and Gary Snyder without picturing the bohemian San Francisco in the fifties, yet these three Beat poets each originally came from three different regions of the country. Did Kansas-born William Stafford, who lived much of his life in Oregon, ever stop being a Midwest poet in some fundamental way? N. Scott Momaday can hardly be understood without taking his Southwestern background into account, but his Kiowa heritage is surely even more important to his literary identity. Regionalism is a difficult and evasive concept to analyze in isolation from other sociological and historical factors. Certainly, region, race, and culture are sometimes hard to tell apart.

Regional identity also does not limit a writer's audience. Artists rooted in one place do not cease being broadly appealing elsewhere. James Joyce, Thomas Hardy, Constantine Cavafy, Chinua Achebe, and Willa Cather—to cite only five major modern figures—are all explicitly regional writers. Their enormous artistry, however, made the concerns of their place and time universal. Homer and Shakespeare are writers of the world, yet both were equally the products of small regions—the Aegean and England, respectively—as well as specific moments in history. As the Stafford epigraph suggests, regionalism alone will not explain the development of the literary imagination. Time is part of the equation. He suggests that he was defined by his era as much as by his place—by the Depression, World War II, and the cold war as much as by Kansas and Oregon.

The writers in the following section were all born in the thirties, which might be their strongest common bond. But each of them is powerfully associated with regional and cultural identity as well. Some cases are more obvious than others. Miller Williams and Fred Chappell are clearly Southern writers, Jared Carter and Ted Kooser Midwesterners. N. Scott Momaday and Bernice Zamora are from the Southwest, while the New York–New Jersey area produced writers as diverse as Amiri Baraka, Audre Lorde, Lucille Clifton, and Stephen Dunn. The fact that each of these poets spent some part of infancy and childhood in the era of Franklin Delano Roosevelt, with its Depression-era sense of social inequities, matters a great deal. These poets were young during World War II, which they remember to varying degrees. In each subsequent decade they were influenced by new movements in the arts as well as by the various social movements of the Cold War era.

The Civil Rights Movement of the 1960s, for example, fostered African American pride, anger, and interest in renewing a Black literary heritage. Drawing on African American traditions such as blues, jazz, and vernacular preaching, the poets who founded the Black Arts Movements, particularly Amiri Baraka and Ishmael Reed, voiced that pride and anger in poems directed toward a Black audience. Although the new poetry was published in book form, often by small Black presses like Dudley Randall's Broadside Press, the poets grounded it on oral tradition and disseminated it through performance, merging the liberationist political spirit of the times with the heritage of both the African storyteller and the African American preacher. Influenced by sources as diverse as the tall tale and surrealism, Black Arts poetry was not always realistic in a strict sense. Yet, in their desire to expose the truths of African American life, including the effects of racism and urban poverty, the Black Arts poets perfected an edgy realism whetted by political protest and steeped in a regionalism that reflected each writer's experience. Etheridge Knight's region is partly that of the prison, Amiri Baraka's the theater of rage and urban angst, and Lucille Clifton's the tenement.

The poets in this section were born at a time when American poetry was still mostly published in the cultural centers of New York and Boston—a situation that gradually changed during their lifetimes. Most of them felt by heritage and predilection estranged from the very idea of a cultural center. They knew that American poetry could be found in their own back yards, as it were, sometimes in surprising ways. They owed something to earlier poets like William Carlos Williams who had written in the American grain, and they took up the obligation of the poet to speak for the local, carrying it abroad. Jared Carter has used the landscape and history of his native Indiana as the raw material for lyric poetry, and Bernice Zamora has written out of the hills and arroyos of Colorado. In his recent prose book, *Local Wonders* (2002), Ted Kooser recorded the following verse notation:

> If you can awaken
> inside the familiar
> and discover it new
> you need never
> leave home

Not every writer in this section has remained at home, literally or metaphorically, but each of them would know and react to the idea of locality conveyed in Kooser's poem.

Endangered Places

> Shall I not have intelligence with the earth?
> Am I not partly leaves and vegetable mold myself?
> —*Henry David Thoreau*

In his groundbreaking study, *The Environmental Imagination* (1996), the critic Lawrence Buell observed, "In literary history since World War II, the resurgence of environmental writing is as important as the rise of magical realist fiction." He meant that environmental consciousness has pervaded even the work of writers where we might least expect it. Buell's study points out that awareness of environmental issues, of human relations to what we call nature or wilderness, goes back very far in American literature. The issue of environmentalism is surely a complex one, involving perceptions and choices in urban as well as rural settings. But it is difficult for poets to conceive of such things without the sense of place we have discussed here, whatever that place might be. John Haines, who homesteaded in Alaska for twenty-five years, wrote, "The extreme and growing transience of persons, places, and things makes even more difficult the task of discovering who and what we are." The sense of place—wanting to have it or wanting to leave it—provides both anxiety and satisfaction in American poetry. It is often indistinguishable from a sense of self.

Furthermore, the belief that our place, our world, might be endangered, though not new by any means, animates the ecological consciousness in recent poetry. It is perhaps most vivid for poets born after World War II, who came of age when national and international debates about environmental policies intensified. But one can turn the pages of this entire anthology and find an environmental consciousness at some level—most obviously in poets we could label regional, like Robinson Jeffers, Robert Penn Warren, Theodore Roethke, William Stafford, Thomas McGrath, Lorine Niedecker, Kenneth Rexroth, and Gary Snyder, to name only a few. In this section on Regionalism there are obvious cases of poets with a strong environmental focus, like N. Scott Momaday, C. K. Williams, Ishmael Reed, and Ted Kooser. We can also broaden our definitions of environmentalist concerns, relating them to all struggles for civil rights as part of a larger vision of sustainable life on the planet. The sections that follow this one will also provide plenty of poets who think in these terms. Increasingly, poets would agree with John Haines that "If we exceed the capacity of the land to support and contain us, whether we are rabbits or men, we die." This is as true in the cities as it is in the countryside.

Regionalism, then, is only one way of understanding the sense of place, and the sense of place is only part of an environmentalist consciousness. But writers with a strong sense of place have an advantage over those who do not when it comes to finding a language, either in protest or of affirmation, for this struggle to sustain life on earth.

Engagements with the Real

> The ambition of literary realism is to plagiarize God's creation.
>
> —*Charles Simic*

In the opening pages of this anthology we discussed Realism and Naturalism as literary modes. In a general sense, the term *Realism* refers to the literary representation of characters, events, and settings in ways that readers consider plausible—an approach which often means using a conventional framework of social, economic, and psychological reality, even if the author intends ultimately to reject or re-form that framework. Realism, therefore, is more an attitude than a style. Naturalism, however, usually refers to a specific literary movement, an extreme form of Realism that tried to explain human and social behavior by postulating a set of quasi scientific laws. Developed by the French novelist Émile Zola, Naturalism was quickly adopted by American writers like Jack London, Frank Norris, and Edwin Markham. Naturalism went in and out of fashion throughout the twentieth century—culminating in the work of Theodore Dreiser, Zora Neale Hurston, Richard Wright, and Robinson Jeffers—but the Realist impulse has rarely gone far away. The Realist mode, however, necessarily changes with history, reflecting the social, economic, cultural, political, and technological conditions of the times. In general, Realism gives great scope to the individual, showing how people negotiate the complex social, political, and economic realities of their lives without allowing their existences to be wholly determined by external forces.

The 1930s, when poets in this section were born, was—despite the prevalence of escapist mass entertainment—notably an era of Realism in the arts, such as the cinema of John Ford and the fiction of John Steinbeck. The notion that literature could not and should not be entirely divorced from the economic and social realities of the time was pervasive. This impulse to represent the tough realities of the American experience resurfaces in the poetry of writers born in the thirties. It is evident in the characters found in the work of Knight and C. K. Williams, the political issues raised by Baraka and Reed, and the domestic problems conveyed by Linda Pastan and Miller Williams. Realism as a mode—not always conveyed in conventional literary terms that "plagiarize God's creation"—binds these writers in fascinating ways. In terms of literary style this section offers a broad range of approaches, from Reed's satire to the metaphorical precision of Kooser to the narrative mastery of Carter. Despite this array of voices and techniques, the *stance* of Realism is nearly everywhere in evidence.

One of the most powerful elements in any sense of regional or cultural identity is language, and these poets can also be described as taking a realistic approach to diction in their poems, Pastan, Williams, Dunn, and Kooser use a plain style with great felicity. Lorde, Baraka, Clifton, and Reed have all made use of African American rhythms and inflections as sources of vigor and authenticity in poems, which are also informed by personal and public histories. Espaillat and

Zamora give voice to the immigrant, steeped both in the native Spanish and adoptive American idioms.

One can argue that any poet's true homeland is language, and in these poets language is a growth of the soil or the streets of their regions. Some of these authors like Carter and Momaday draw heavily on local history and lore, despite their broad reading. They convey a personal version of regional culture and tradition. They refuse to see individual experience in any sort of social or historical vacuum. Despite certain similarities, the poets in this section are perhaps best characterized by their diversity, but something beyond the decade of their birth seems to connect them. They are poets of social consciousness, interested in characters and stories as well as lyric techniques. Part of the explosive diversity of postwar American poetry, they nonetheless work together toward discovering the varied sources of our common humanity.

◄ MILLER WILLIAMS ►
(b. 1930)

Miller Williams was born in Hoxie, Arkansas, the son of a Methodist minister. His father moved the family often, as his assignments changed to different congregations, so young Miller never settled in one town for long. Williams's parents were liberal activists in a conservative, volatile South. His father fought for desegregation and preached against the racist policies of Arkansas Governor Orville Faubus. Williams was influenced by his father's politically active spirit. Recalling his time at Hendrix College, the poet commented, "I was invited to leave Hendrix at the end of my sophomore year after I had joined others in a scheme to have a young Negro student enrolled before his race could be found out." Williams transferred to Arkansas State Teachers College for a year, before moving on to Arkansas State College.

In 1950 Williams earned a bachelor's degree from Arkansas State in biology. He went on to study zoology and anthropology at the University of Arkansas at Fayetteville (M.A., 1952). While there, he married Lucille Day, a pianist. They had three children together, the first of whom would become a successful country musician, Lucinda Williams. The marriage ended in divorce after fifteen years.

Williams didn't begin writing poetry seriously until later in his life. After completing his studies, he taught biology for nine years before moving on to a variety of occupations in the early 1960s. Those jobs, and others he had held while still a teenager, included work in a popsicle factory, as a drugstore manager, a movie-house projectionist, a field man with a New York publishing house, a manager for a Sears furniture department, and a tire salesman for Montgomery Ward. During that time, Williams met John Ciardi and Howard Nemerov, who would prove vital to his career as a poet and a teacher. The two poets helped Williams obtain a position teaching English at Louisiana State University in 1962, even though his academic training and experience had been in the sciences. Two years later Williams published his first book, *A Circle of Stone* (1964), inaugurating the LSU Press poetry series. Although this early book was uneven, it contained many moments of originality and sharp observation that reflected the ironic and skeptical worldview of his later volumes.

In 1964 Williams won an Amy Lowell Traveling Scholarship, allowing him to teach as a guest professor at the University of Chile. Two years later Williams took an associate professorship at Loyola University, where in 1968 he founded the *New Orleans Review.* Williams had married Rebecca Jordan Hall in 1969, and the following year they moved back to his native state so he could join the graduate creative writing faculty of the University of Arkansas. In 1980 Williams founded and became director of the University of Arkansas Press. He retired from the press in 1997.

Having made a late start in literature, Williams has made up for lost time by publishing a steady stream of books since *A Circle of Stone* and has earned some impressive honors. In 1970 he was awarded both a Fulbright Lectureship at the National University of Mexico and the New York Arts Fund Award. *Living on the Surface* (1989) earned him the Poets' Prize, and in 1994 Williams received the John William Corrington Award. His many collections of poetry include *Halfway from Hoxie* (1973), *The Boys on Their Bony Mules* (1983), and *The Ways We*

Touch (1997). In 1999 the University of Illinois Press published Williams's collected poems, *Some Jazz a While.*

Williams has enjoyed rare connections with the Washington political world. He became former President Jimmy Carter's poetry mentor. The two had met in 1981 when Williams presented Carter with a poem he had written about the President's term in the White House. The former President invited Williams to his Georgia home to lecture and teach him about poetic composition, an interest of Carter's since childhood. Williams also had a long-standing friendship with Bill Clinton, former governor of Arkansas. In 1997 President Clinton invited Williams to deliver a poem at his second inauguration. This public honor is a distinction shared by only two other poets—Robert Frost for John F. Kennedy and Maya Angelou for Clinton's first inauguration. Williams's inaugural poem was a fitting high point to the career of a poet who had always sought to connect poetry to a broader audience and speak of the concerns of common people.

◄•——◄►——•►

On a Photograph of My Mother at Seventeen

How come to town she was, tied bright and prim,
with not a thought of me nor much of him.

Now, tied to a chair, she tries to pull free
of it and the world. Little is left of me,

I think, or him, inside her teetering head   5
where we lie with the half-remembered dead.

Her bones could be as hollow as a bird's,
they are so light. Otherness of words.

They could be kite sticks. She could be a kite;
that's how thin her skin is. But now some light   10

from somewhere in the brain comes dimly through
then flickers and goes out. Or it seems to.

Maybe a door opened, where other men
and women come and go, and closed again.

How much we need the metaphors we make   15
to say and still not say, for pity's sake.

1986

Ruby Tells All

When I was told, as Delta children were,
that crops don't grow unless you sweat at night,
I thought that it was my own sweat they meant.
I have never felt as important again
as on those early mornings, waking up,   5

my body slick, the moon full on the fields.
That was before air-conditioning.
Farm girls sleep cool now and wake up dry
but still the cotton overflows the fields.
We lose everything that's grand and foolish;   10
it all becomes something else. One by one,
butterflies turn into caterpillars
and we grow up, or more or less we do,
and, Lord, we do lie then. We lie so much
truth has a false ring and it's hard to tell.   15

I wouldn't take crap off anybody
if I just knew that I was getting crap
in time not to take it. I could have won
a small one now and then if I was smarter,
but I've poured coffee here too many years   20
for men who rolled in in Peterbilts,
and I have gotten into bed with some
if they could talk and seemed to be in pain.

I never asked for anything myself;
giving is more blessed and leaves you free.   25
There was a man, married and fond of whiskey.
Given the limitations of men, he loved me.
Lord, we laid concern upon our bodies
but then he left. Everything has its time.
We used to dance. He made me feel the way   30
a human wants to feel and fears to.
He was a slow man and didn't expect.
I would get off work and find him waiting.
We'd have a drink or two and kiss awhile.
Then a bird-loud morning late one April   35
we woke up naked. We had made a child.
She's grown up now and gone though God knows where.
She ought to write, for I do love her dearly
who raised her carefully and dressed her well.

Everything has its time. For thirty years   40
I never had a thought about time.
Now, turning through newspapers, I pause
to see if anyone who passed away
was younger than I am. If one was
I feel hollow for a little while   45
but then it passes. Nothing matters enough
to stay bent down about. You have to see
that some things matter slightly and some don't.
Dying matters a little. So does pain.
So does being old. Men do not.   50
Men live by negatives, like don't give up,
don't be a coward, don't call me a liar,

don't ever tell me don't. If I could live
two hundred years and had to be a man
I'd take my grave. What's a man but a match,   55
a little stick to start a fire with?

My daughter knows this, if she's alive.
What could I tell her now, to bring her close,
something she doesn't know, if we met somewhere?
Maybe that I think about her father,   60
maybe that my fingers hurt at night,
maybe that against appearances
there is love, constancy, and kindness,
that I have dresses I have never worn.

1986

⊶◄ ETHERIDGE KNIGHT ►⊶
(1931–1991)

Etheridge Knight was born in Corinth, Mississippi, one of seven children of Bushie
and Belzora Knight. Although he attended high school for two years, he was
largely self-educated. He served in the army from 1947 to 1951 and was wounded
in combat during the Korean War. While recuperating from the injury, Knight,
who had often used drugs before, became addicted to morphine. Narcotics would
remain a serious problem for him the rest of his life. In 1960 he was sentenced to
ten to twenty-five years in Indiana State Prison for robbery. Before being released
on parole in 1968, he had begun to make his name as a writer. Dudley Randall,
poet and founder of the Broadside Press, frequently visited Knight in prison and
encouraged his writing. Meanwhile Knight had fallen in love with poet Sonia
Sanchez, who had encouraged his work. The couple married soon after his release
but divorced a few years later.

Broadside Press published Knight's first book, *Poems from Prison* (1968),
with a preface by Gwendolyn Brooks, as well as two other significant collections—
A Poem for Brother/Man (after His Recovery from an O.D.) (1972) and *Belly
Song and Other Poems* (1973), which was nominated for the National Book
Award. With other publishers, Knight brought out *Born of a Woman: New and
Selected Poems* (1980) and *The Essential Etheridge Knight* (1986). He taught at
several universities, including University of Pittsburgh, University of Hartford,
and Lincoln University. Charismatic and amiable, he was adored by audiences at
his frequent poetry readings. Knight was particularly well known as a reciter of
"toasts," an African American tradition in which long narrative and satirical
poems are performed from memory. Despite his considerable literary success,
Knight's personal troubles continued through his later life, and he repeatedly spent
time in veterans' hospitals recovering from drug addiction. He died at age fifty-
nine of lung cancer.

Knight is one of the most popular and populist poets associated with the Black
Arts Movement. His style is direct, graphic, and vernacular, full of slang and con-

versational elisions. His punctuation is often unconventional—designed perhaps more as cues for oral performance than as standard syntactical markings. His best poems cry out to be spoken aloud, and his aesthetic remains rooted in the African American oral tradition. His lucid narratives offer a humane but unromanticized view of prison life. He also frequently wrote of his own personal troubles, including his three marriages that all ended in divorce and the difficulties caused by a life of addiction and recovery. Through his art, Knight attempted to join rather than separate people, contrary to what he saw white society doing. He believed that the black artist should "through his art form give back to the people the truth that he has gotten from them." Where the white artist might edify and prettify, he asserted, the black artist must present the unadorned truth even when it is ugly.

Haiku

1

Eastern guard tower
glints in sunset; convicts rest
like lizards on rocks.

2

The piano man
is stingy, at 3 A.M.
his songs drop like plum.

3

Morning sun slants cell.
Drunks stagger like cripple flies
On jailhouse floor.

4

To write a blues song
is to regiment riots
and pluck gems from graves.

5

A bare pecan tree
slips a pencil shadow down
a moonlit snow slope.

6

The falling snow flakes
Cannot blunt the hard aches nor
Match the steel stillness.

7

Under moon shadows
A tall boy flashes knife and
Slices star bright ice.

8

In the August grass
Struck by the last rays of sun
The cracked teacup screams.

9

Making jazz swing in
Seventeen syllables AIN'T
No square poet's job.

1968

Hard Rock Returns to Prison from the Hospital for the Criminal Insane

Hard Rock / was / "known not to take no shit
From nobody," and he had the scars to prove it:
Split purple lips, lumbed ears, welts above
His yellow eyes, and one long scar that cut
Across his temple and plowed through a thick   5
Canopy of kinky hair.

The WORD / was / that Hard Rock wasn't a mean nigger
Anymore, that the doctors had bored a hole in his head,
Cut out part of his brain, and shot electricity
Through the rest. When they brought Hard Rock back,   10
Handcuffed and chained, he was turned loose,
Like a freshly gelded stallion, to try his new status.
And we all waited and watched, like a herd of sheep,
To see if the WORD was true.

As we waited we wrapped ourselves in the cloak   15
Of his exploits: "Man, the last time it took eight
Screws to put him in the Hole." "Yeah, remember when he
Smacked the captain with his dinner tray?" "He set
The record for time in the Hole—67 straight days!"
"Ol Hard Rock! man, that's one crazy nigger."   20
And then the jewel of a myth that Hard Rock had once bit
A screw on the thumb and poisoned him with syphilitic spit.

The testing came, to see if Hard Rock was really tame.
A hillbilly called him a black son of a bitch
And didn't lose his teeth, a screw who knew Hard Rock   25
From before shook him down and barked in his face.
And Hard Rock did *nothing*. Just grinned and looked silly,
His eyes empty like knot holes in a fence.

And even after we discovered that it took Hard Rock
Exactly 3 minutes to tell you his first name,   30
We told ourselves that he had just wised up,
Was being cool; but we could not fool ourselves for long,
And we turned away, our eyes on the ground. Crushed.

He had been our Destroyer, the doer of things
We dreamed of doing but could not bring ourselves to do,   35
The fears of years, like a biting whip,
Had cut deep bloody grooves
Across our backs.

                                                                    1968

The Idea of Ancestry

I

Taped to the wall of my cell are 47 pictures: 47 black
faces: my father, mother, grandmothers (1 dead), grand
fathers (both dead), brothers, sisters, uncles, aunts,
cousins (1st & 2nd), nieces, and nephews. They stare
across the space at me sprawling on my bunk. I know   5
their dark eyes, they know mine. I know their style,
they know mine. I am all of them, they are all of me;
they are farmers, I am a thief, I am me, they are thee.

I have at one time or another been in love with my mother,
1 grandmother, 2 sisters, 2 aunts (1 went to the asylum),   10
and 5 cousins. I am now in love with a 7 yr old niece
(she sends me letters written in large block print, and
her picture is the only one that smiles at me).

I have the same name as 1 grandfather, 3 cousins, 3 nephews,
and 1 uncle. The uncle disappeared when he was 15, just took   15
off and caught a freight (they say). He's discussed each year
when the family has a reunion, he causes uneasiness in
the clan, he is an empty space. My father's mother, who is 93
and who keeps the Family Bible with everybody's birth dates
(and death dates) in it, always mentions him. There is no   20
place in her Bible for "whereabouts unknown."

II

Each Fall the graves of my grandfathers call me, the brown
hills and red gullies of mississippi send out their electric
messages, galvanizing my genes. Last yr/like a salmon quitting
the cold ocean—leaping and bucking up his birthstream/I   25
hitchhiked my way from L.A. with 16 caps in my pocket and a
monkey on my back, and I almost kicked it with the kinfolks.

I walked barefoot in my grandmother's backyard/I smelled the old
land and the woods/I sipped cornwhiskey from fruit jars with the men/

I flirted with the women/I had a ball till the caps ran out   30
and my habit came down. That night I looked at my grandmother
and split/my guts were screaming for junk/but I was almost
contented/I had almost caught up with me.
    The next day in Memphis I cracked a croaker's crib[1] for a fix.

This yr there is a gray stone wall damming my stream, and when   35
the falling leaves stir my genes, I pace my cell or flop on my bunk
and stare at 47 black faces across the space. I am all of them,
they are all of me, I am me, they are thee, and I have no sons
to float in the space between.

1968

The Warden Said to Me the Other Day

The warden said to me the other day
(innocently, I think), "Say, etheridge,
why come the black boys don't run off
like the white boys do?"
I lowered my jaw and scratched my head   5
and said (innocently, I think), "Well, suh,
I ain't for sure, but I reckon it's cause
we ain't got no wheres to run to."

1968

A Poem for Myself

(Or Blues for a Mississippi Black Boy)

I was born in Mississippi;
I walked barefooted thru the mud.
Born black in Mississippi,
Walked barefooted thru the mud.
But, when I reached the age of twelve   5
I left that place for good.
Said my daddy chopped cotton
And he drank his liquor straight.
When I left that Sunday morning
He was leaning on the barnyard gate.   10
Left her standing in the yard
With the sun shining in her eyes.
And I headed North
As straight as the Wild Goose Flies,
I been to Detroit & Chicago   15
Been to New York city too.
I been to Detroit and Chicago
Been to New York city too.

1. A drug dealer's home.

Said I done strolled all those funky avenues
I'm still the same old black boy with the same old blues.   20
Going back to Mississippi
This time to stay for good
Going back to Mississippi
This time to stay for good—
Gonna be free in Mississippi   25
Or dead in the Mississippi mud.

1973

◦► RHINA ESPAILLAT ►◦
(b. 1932)

Rhina Espaillat was born in 1932 in the Dominican Republic, which was then ruled by the dictator, Rafael Trujillo. When her father, who was part of the Dominican diplomatic mission in Washington, D.C., was exiled for opposing the Trujillo regime, the family emigrated to the United States. In 1939 they came to New York where the young Espaillat was suddenly immersed in a new language and culture. She attended New York City public schools, as she has remarked, "from grade to graduate school." After finishing her bachelor's degree at Hunter College in 1953, she taught English for a year in the city's high school system. In 1952 she married Alfred Moskowitz, an industrial arts teacher, and had three sons. Once the children were older, she earned a master's degree in English in 1964 from Queen's College and taught English for fifteen years at Jamaica High School in Queens, New York. In 1990, she and her husband moved to Newburyport, Massachusetts, to be near two of their sons.

After retiring Espaillat had the opportunity to work more assiduously on poetry, which she had written all her life—first in Spanish, then in English. Having published in a major journal as a high school junior in 1943, she had been invited to join the Poetry Society of America, the youngest member ever accepted into the organization. Her first volume, *Lapsing to Grace*, appeared in 1992. Shortly thereafter she won both the Howard Nemerov and the *Sparrow* sonnet awards. A second collection, *Where Horizons Go* (1998), appeared after having won the T. S. Eliot award. As X. J. Kennedy, the judge for the prize, noted, "I'm won over by the way the poet writes of the most commonplace experience—she's a warm affirmer of life. Keen intelligence, keen feeling."

◦►◄►◦

Agua[1]

Mother, the trees you loved are dense with water,
alive with wings darting through stippled blue
of recent and imminent rain. And that old street
you mistook for water—remember?—is flowing still,

---

1. (Spanish) "Water."

as when we walked between its banks of pickets   5
down to the river, which you knew was water
and spoke to, leaning over it last summer.

Mother, those cracks in pavement you stepped over,
avoiding water you imagined, are cradling
eddies of clover, tufted islands of moss;   10
and look how the roots of that locust are pouring into
every crevice, joining water to water,
look how its trunk is a fountain, a tower of water
out to the tips of its fussy, feathery branches.

Mother, balmy old Thales,[2] how true your sight was   15
that pierced every disguise, uncovered the water
that links us, the current that bears us
from season to season, whose tide you greeted
in the mindless music you spoke, ocean departing,
returning, into whose keeping, Mother,   20
you slipped from your body's mooring and out before me.

                                                        1998

Bilingual/Bilingüe[3]

My father liked them separate, one there,
one here (allá y aquí), as if aware

that words might cut in two his daughter's heart
(el corazón) and lock the alien part

to what he was—his memory, his name   5
(su nombre)—with a key he could not claim.

"English outside this door, Spanish inside,"
he said, "y basta." But who can divide

the world, the word (mundo y palabra) from
any child? I knew how to be dumb   10

and stubborn (testaruda); late, in bed,
I hoarded secret syllables I read

until my tongue (mi lengua) learned to run
where his stumbled. And still the heart was one.

I like to think he knew that, even when,   15
proud (orgulloso) of his daughter's pen,

he stood outside mis versos, half in fear
of words he loved but wanted not to hear.

                                                        1998

---

2. Thales (c. 636–546 B.C.E.) was a pre-Socratic philosopher who theorized that water was the most essential of the elements.
3. The Spanish words in parentheses are translated in the context of the poem.

Bra

What a good fit! But the label says Honduras:
Alas, I am Union forever, yes, both breasts
and the heart between them committed to U.S. labor.

But such a splendid fit! And the label tells me
the woman who made it, bronze as the breasts now in it,   5
speaks the language I dream in; I count in Spanish

the pesos she made stitching this breast-divider:
will they go for her son's tuition, her daughter's wedding?
The thought is a lovely fit, but oh, the label!

And oh, those pesos that may be pennies, and hard-earned.   10
Was it son or daughter who made this, unschooled, unwedded?
How old? Fourteen? Ten? That fear is a tight fit.

If only the heart could be worn like a breast, divided,
nosing in two directions for news of the wide world,
sniffing here and there for justice, for mercy.   15

How burdened every choice is with politics, guilt,
expensive with duty, heavy as breasts in need of
this perfect fit whose label says Honduras.

1998

◄ LINDA PASTAN ►
(b. 1932)

Linda Pastan did not publish her first collection of poetry until she was thirty-nine
years old. Seventeen years earlier, however, she had come briefly to national attention when she won *Mademoiselle*'s Dylan Thomas Poetry Award while a senior at
Radcliffe College. (The runner-up for the contest was Sylvia Plath.) After marrying
Ira Pastan, a molecular biologist, in 1953, Pastan put aside her writing career to
raise three children. She explained that long hiatus from poetry to Michael Kernan
in the *Washington Post:* "I was into the whole '50s thing, kids and the clean floor
bit. I was unhappy because I knew what I should be doing." When Pastan finally
committed herself to writing with the publication of *A Perfect Circle of Sun* (1971),
domesticity and the female experience were her most prominent themes.

Another important subject for Pastan is her Jewish heritage and upbringing.
She was born in the Bronx, New York, in 1932 into a traditional Jewish extended
family. During her childhood, Pastan held her origins at bay, even revolting against
them, although the sounds and characters that would combine to create her identity were present from the start. In her essay, "Root Systems," Pastan explains:

> How I despised the housewives with their soap opera eyes, their elastic stockings, and
> their accents that lacked even the grating energy of Brooklyn speech. It is difficult for me,
> so many years later, to confess to that early snobbery; certainly it troubles me now. Yet
> out of it grew not only my earliest concern with the exact sounds of language but also
> some of the tensions, the ambivalence, the guilt that many second and third generation

Americans feel about their own ethnicity, their own root systems. . . . [Those roots] give us not only a sense of our deepest selves but some of our best material.

After graduating from Radcliffe College in 1954 Pastan earned her M.L.S. from Simmons College (1955). In 1957 she earned a master's degree from Brandeis University, where she worked individually with J. V. Cunningham. Pastan has published more than ten volumes of poetry. Her fourth collection, *The Five Stages of Grief* (1978), won the Di Castagnola Award. Pastan was also nominated for a *Los Angeles Times* Book Award for her 1988 collection, *The Imperfect Paradise*. From 1991 to 1995 she served as the Poet Laureate of Maryland. She has taught at American University in Washington, D.C., and was on the faculty of the Bread Loaf Writers' Conference for twenty years.

Pastan's work has often been compared to the poetry of Emily Dickinson for its attention to the "dailiness" of life. Dick Allen, in the *Hudson Review*, commented on Pastan's poetic voice: "It is a poetry of acceptance with serious irony, of wonder rather than rattle, a relaxed poetry and phrasing which signifies satisfactions and regrets, not one that clenches the teeth and thrusts the head forward. Always interesting, balanced, seldom profound, this is a poetry we return to more for content than form, a poetry of the whole poem rather than the individual line."

◄◦►━◗━◄◦►

Journey's End

How hard we try to reach death safely,
luggage intact, each child accounted for,
the wounds of passage quickly bandaged up.
We treat the years like stops along the way
of a long flight from the catastrophe   5
we move to, thinking: home free all at last.
Wave, wave your hanky towards journey's end;
avert your eyes from windows grimed with twilight
where landscapes rush by, terrible and lovely.

1971

Ethics

In ethics class so many years ago
our teacher asked this question every fall:
if there were a fire in a museum
which would you save, a Rembrandt painting
or an old woman who hadn't many   5
years left anyhow? Restless on hard chairs
caring little for pictures or old age
we'd opt one year for life, the next for art
and always half-heartedly. Sometimes
the woman borrowed my grandmother's face   10
leaving her usual kitchen to wander
some drafty, half imagined museum.

One year, feeling clever, I replied
why not let the woman decide herself?
Linda, the teacher would report, eschews   15
the burdens of responsibility.
This fall in a real museum I stand
before a real Rembrandt, old woman,
or nearly so, myself. The colors
within this frame are darker than autumn,   20
darker even than winter—the browns of earth,
though earth's most radiant elements burn
through the canvas. I know now that woman
and painting and season are almost one
and all beyond saving by children.   25

                                                          1981

                    1932–

I saw my name in print the other day
with 1932 and then a blank
and knew that even now some grassy bank
just waited for my grave. And somewhere a gray

slab of marble existed already   5
on which the final number would be carved—
as if the stone itself were somehow starved
for definition. When I went steady

in high school years ago, my boyfriend's name
was what I tried out, hearing how it fit   10
with mine; then names of film stars in some hit.
My husband was anonymous as rain.

There is a number out there, odd or even
that will become familiar to my sons
and daughter. (They are the living ones   15
I think of now: Peter, Rachel, Stephen.)

I picture it, four integers in a row
5 or 7, 6 or 2 or 9:
a period; silence; and end-stopped line;
a hammer poised . . . delivering its blow.   20

                                                          1991

—◄ **AMIRI BARAKA/LeROI JONES** ►—
(b. 1934)

Poet, essayist, playwright, anthologist, music critic, and political activist, Amiri
Baraka helped to define African American poetry of the 1960s through his prolific
publications, forceful readings, and dramatic shifts in ideals. Consistent throughout

his poetry, along with his articulation of black consciousness, is his exploration of the vexed relationship between the self and the world, especially in the political sense of whether the self can change the world. Thus Baraka's poetry swings from isolated speakers who recognize injustice but feel powerless to change it, to speakers who demand change and aim to initiate it through often violent denunciation, testifying against racial and social inequities.

Born Everett LeRoy Jones in Newark, New Jersey, Baraka (in college he altered the spelling of his middle name to LeRoi) grew up in a middle-class home and excelled in the integrated but primarily white public schools he attended—so much so that he graduated from high school at the age of fifteen. In 1951 he began college at Rutgers, but transferred to Howard University in 1952, where he studied with Sterling Brown. From Brown, Baraka gained not only a historical understanding of African American poetry, but, through the senior poet's vast collection of jazz and blues records, began to explore the connections between African American poetry and music. After flunking out of Howard in 1954, he enrolled in the air force, and three years later received an "undesirable" discharge. Back in civilian life, he settled in Greenwich Village and quickly became active in the Beat scene. Influenced by William Carlos Williams's emphasis on an American idiom that breaks from traditional metrics, Charles Olson's Projectivism, and the surrealism of the Spanish poet Federico García Lorca, Baraka crafted a free verse that was casual in its approximations of common speech, sometimes oblique in its imagery, yet modernist in its focus on an isolated self. But because that self was African American, Baraka's early poetry begins to develop the political concerns that would characterize his later work. He points out in a 1963 interview: "Mostly it's the *rhythms* of speech that I utilize, trying to get closer to the way I sound *peculiarly*, as opposed to somebody else. . . . There are certain influences on me, as a Negro person, that certainly wouldn't apply to a poet like Allen Ginsberg. . . . Everything applies—everything in your life."

Baraka's life in Greenwich Village was steeped in music. The Village was ground zero for the jazz explorations of John Coltrane, Thelonious Monk, and Ornette Coleman, whose work Baraka reviewed for *Downbeat*, the *Jazz Review*, and *Metronome*. His musical passions led to his influential study, *Blues People: Negro Music in White America* (1963). With his white wife, Hettie Roberta Cohen, whom he married in 1958, Baraka edited the influential journal *Yugen*, publishing poetry by members of the Beat, New York, and Black Mountain schools. His first book, *Preface to a Twenty Volume Suicide Note* (1961), displays the spontaneity and individualism shared by both Beat poetry and improvisatory jazz, as well as the surrealism associated with the New York School.

As the Civil Rights Movement gathered force, politics became increasingly central to Baraka's mission. A trip to Cuba in 1961 shook his bohemian allegiances, and he began to question his life in Greenwich Village and the scope of his poetry. After his return, he shifted his purview to Harlem and devoted his energy to community organizing and playwriting, which meshed when he founded the Black Repertory Theater in Harlem in 1964. His play *The Dutchman* won an Obie award for Best Off-Broadway Play of 1964, and Guggenheim and National Endowment for the Arts grants soon followed. The assassination of Malcolm X in 1965 accelerated Baraka's turn to black nationalism. He left his white wife and two young daughters and moved to Harlem, relocating to Newark in 1966, where he opened Spirit House Theater and married a black woman, Sylvia Robinson.

For Baraka, black nationalism meant not only immersing himself in political protests and community activism, but reconfiguring his poetics. One of the leading figures in the Black Arts Movement of the late 1960s, Baraka advocated a poetry that was written for a black audience, developed to instill black pride and solidarity, and grounded on black traditions such as jazz, the blues, and African American speech rhythms. His publication of *Black Magic: Collected Poetry, 1961–1967* (1967) and *Black Fire: An Anthology of Afro-American Writing,* co-edited with Larry Neal (1968), helped lift the movement into the national spectrum. Changing his name in 1968 to Imamu ("spiritual leader") Amiri ("prince") Baraka ("the blessed one"), the poet completed his transition—only to change again in the 1970s, when he adopted Marxism and repudiated black nationalism. His ideological fervor sometimes resulted in antiwhite, anti-Semitic, and antigay statements that mar both his later poetry and prose. Muting his Marxist rhetoric in the late 1980s, Baraka remains committed to the African American community and to attacking the status quo. Although his ultimate place in the literary canon has seemed increasingly problematic, his place in recent American cultural history remains indisputable.

◂•▬◖▬•▸

Preface to a Twenty Volume Suicide Note

(For Kellie Jones, born 16 May 1959)

Lately, I've become accustomed to the way
The ground opens up and envelops me
Each time I go out to walk the dog.
Or the broad edged silly music the wind
Makes when I run for a bus . . .   5

Things have come to that.

And now, each night I count the stars,
And each night I get the same number.
And when they will not come to be counted,
I count the holes they leave.   10

Nobody sings anymore.

And then last night, I tiptoed up
To my daughter's room and heard her
Talking to someone, and when I opened
The door, there was no one there . . .   15
Only she on her knees, peeking into

Her own clasped hands.

1961

Legacy

(For Blues People)

In the south, sleeping against
the drugstore, growling under
the trucks and stoves, stumbling
through and over the cluttered eyes
of early mysterious night. Frowning   5
drunk waving moving a hand or lash.
Dancing kneeling reaching out, letting
a hand rest in shadows. Squatting
to drink or pee. Stretching to climb
pulling themselves onto horses near   10
where there was sea (the old songs
lead you to believe). Riding out
from this town, to another, where
it is also black. Down a road
where people are asleep. Towards   15
the moon or the shadows of houses.
Towards the songs' pretended sea.

1967

Black Bourgeoisie,

has a gold tooth, sits long hours
on a stool thinking about money.
sees white skin in a secret room
rummages his sense for sense
dreams about Lincoln(s)   5
conks his daughter's hair
sends his coon to school
works very hard
grins politely in restaurants
has a good word to say   10
never says it
does not hate ofays[1]
hates, instead, him self
him black self

1969

---

1. Slang for whites.

AUDRE LORDE
(1934–1992)

Born in New York City, Audre Geraldine Lorde grew up in Harlem, the youngest of three daughters. Her parents, immigrants from the West Indies, hoped to return to their native Grenada, but their plans were halted by the Depression. Overweight, tongue-tied, and so nearsighted that she was legally blind without her thick glasses, Lorde developed a fierce independence that she depended on for survival throughout her life. She stresses in *The Cancer Journals* (1980) that "growing up Fat Black Female and almost blind in america [*sic*] requires so much surviving that you have to learn from it or die." She attended Catholic schools and began writing poetry in eighth grade. In her autobiography, *Zami: A New Spelling of My Name* (1982), she contrasts the strict atmosphere of her home life with the "lifeline" she found at Hunter High School: "It was in high school that I came to believe that I was different from my white classmates, not because I was Black, but because I was me. . . . For the first time I met young women my own age, Black and white, who spoke a language I could usually understand and reply within." Publishing a poem in *Seventeen* while she was still in high school, Lorde was elected editor of the literary magazine. "Writing poetry became an ordinary effort," she observed about Hunter High School, "not a secret and rebellious vice." For a poet who would grow up to advocate overcoming silences, the discovery that poetry could be not only an "ordinary effort," but a public means to have her voice heard and respected, was immensely empowering.

Lorde matriculated at Hunter College and paid her way by working at a wide variety of jobs, including social worker, factory worker, X-ray technician, medical clerk, ghost writer, and library clerk. She received her bachelor's degree in English and philosophy in 1959 and then attended Columbia University, earning her master's degree in library science in 1961. Despite her active lesbianism, the following year she married an attorney, Edwin Ashley Rollins, with whom she had two children. They divorced in 1970, and Lorde renewed her commitment to women with her new partner Frances Clayton, whom she had met while serving in 1968 as poet-in-residence at Tougaloo College, a black college in Mississippi. After publishing her debut volume, *The First Cities* (1968), she decided to teach rather than continue on as a librarian, for teaching complemented her poetry writing and her dedication to feminism and civil rights. During the 1970s, she published six more books of poetry and taught at John Jay College of Criminal Justice. Her third book, *From a Land Where Other People Live* (1973), was nominated for a National Book Award, and her fourth collection, *Coal* (1976), was published by W. W. Norton, which gave her work wider distribution.

In 1978 Lorde was diagnosed with breast cancer and underwent a radical mastectomy, an experience she documents in *The Cancer Journals,* a book whose combination of autobiography and polemic examined not only her own battle against cancer, but also raised difficult questions about black women and cancer and attacked the medical establishment's infantilization of breast cancer patients. The book solidified her reputation as an activist writer, whose unflinching examination of being black, lesbian, and feminist helped change the course of feminist thought in the United States. She also taught at Hunter College, founded Kitchen Table Press, which published works by women of color, and released her selected poems, *Chosen Poems—Old and New* (1982), and *Our Dead behind Us* (1986). Lorde served as Poet Laureate of New York in 1991. Her cancer returned in 1984, and she decided to reject conventional medical treatment in favor of homeopathy. By the end of the decade the cancer had spread, and she faced death with courage and equanimity, moving to St. Croix in the Virgin Islands, where she worked on gathering together and revising her poems for *Undersong: Chosen Poems Old and New* (1992) and writing new poems which appeared in *The Marvelous Arithmetics of Distance* (1993). She died in November 1992, and Norton released *The Collected Poems* in 1997.

In her essay "Poetry Is Not a Luxury" (1977), Lorde views poetry as:

> a revelatory distillation of experience, not the sterile word play that, too often, the white fathers distorted *poetry* to mean—in order to cover a desperate wish for imagination without insight. For women, then, poetry is not a luxury. It is a vital necessity of our existence. It forms the quality of the light within which we predicate our hopes and dreams toward survival and change, first made into language, then into idea, then into tangible action. Poetry is the way we help give name to the nameless so that it can be thought. The farthest horizons of our hopes and fears are cobbled by our poems, carved from the rock experiences of our daily lives.

For Lorde, as for other contemporary feminist poets, poetry is capable of igniting personal and political change. Lorde therefore explored a wide range of approaches. She shows her lyrical introspection in lesbian love poems, poems on motherhood, and meditations on coming to terms with death. She also shows defiance and outrage in poems that attack racism, poverty, and the oppression of women, while voicing affirmation in poems asserting black pride, her African and Caribbean roots, lesbian identity, and survival against terrible odds. Yet all of her poems are marked by realism, honesty, and urgency. Arguing at every stage in her career that differences should be celebrated rather than ignored, Lorde refused to fit herself into solitary categories such as "feminist" or "lesbian" or "African American," preferring instead to claim all of her identities simultaneously. Her poetry, in its merging of various approaches, embodies her complex sense of self and her dedication to social change.

Father Son and Holy Ghost

I have not ever seen my father's grave.

Not that his judgment eyes
have been forgotten
nor his great hands' print
on our evening doorknobs   5
    one half turn each night
    and he would come
    drabbled with the world's business
    massive and silent

as the whole day's wish 10
ready to redefine
each of our shapes
but now the evening doorknobs
wait   and do not recognize us
as we pass. 15

Each week a different woman
regular as his one quick glass
each evening
pulls up the grass his stillness grows
calling it weed. 20
Each week   a different woman
has my mother's face
and he
who time has   changeless
must be amazed 25
who knew and loved
but one.

My father died in silence
loving creation
and well-defined response 30
he lived   still judgments
on familiar things
and died   knowing
a January 15th that year me.

Lest I go into dust 35
I have not ever seen my father's grave.

1960, revised 1992

Coal

I   is the total black
being spoken
from the earth's inside.

There are many kinds of open
how a diamond comes 5
into a knot of flame
how sound comes into a word
colored
by who pays what for speaking.

Some words are open 10
diamonds on a glass window
singing out within the crash
of passing sun
other words are stapled wagers
in a perforated book 15

buy and sign and tear apart
and come whatever wills all chances
the stub remains
an ill-pulled tooth
with a ragged edge.   20

Some words live in my throat
breeding like adders
others
know sun
seeking like gypsies   25
over my tongue
to explode through my lips
like young sparrows
bursting from shell.

Some words   30
bedevil me.

Love is a word, another kind of open.
As the diamond comes
into a knot of flame
I am Black   35
because I come from the earth's inside
take my word for jewel
in the open light.

1976, revised 1992

October

Spirits of the abnormally born
live on in water
of the heroically dead
in the entrails of snake.

Now I span my days like a wild bridge   5
swaying in place   caught
between poems like a vise
I am finishing my piece of this bargain
and how shall I return?

Seboulisa   mother of power   10
keeper of birds   fat and beautiful
give me the strength of your eyes
to remember what I have learned
help me attend with passion
these tasks at my hand for doing.   15

Carry my heart to some shore
my feet will not shatter
do not let me pass away

before I have a name
for this tree   20
under which I am lying

Do not let me die   still
needing to be a stranger.

1982, revised 1992

◦—◄ N. SCOTT MOMADAY ►—◦

(b. 1934)

N. Scott Momaday is one of the most influential and accomplished Native American writers of the twentieth century. His Pulitzer Prize-winning novel, *House Made of Dawn* (1968), was instrumental in bringing about the American Indian literary renaissance of the following decades. Although Momaday has written fiction, essays, and children's literature, and is an accomplished painter, he remains first and foremost a poet. His carefully crafted work skillfully blends Native American and European elements using forms as dissimilar as rhymed pentameter and litanylike tribal chants. That merging of cultures in Momaday's poetry parallels his family history. His father, Alfred Morris Momaday, was a full-blooded Kiowa and a well-known painter. His mother, Mayme Natachee Scott Momaday, was a teacher and writer descending from French, Scottish, and Cherokee origins.

Momaday was born Navarro Scott Mammedaty in Lawton, Oklahoma, in 1934. (His father changed the spelling of the family name when the poet was a boy.) Momaday's family moved often, as his parents followed teaching opportunities, which allowed the young boy to observe many cultures and landscapes, although most of his youth was spent in New Mexico. After graduating from a military academy in Virginia, Momaday returned to the Southwest and entered the University of New Mexico at Albuquerque as a political science major with minors in English and speech. While still an undergraduate, he spent a year studying law at the University of Virginia where he met William Faulkner, who considerably influenced Momaday's early work. After graduating from the University of New Mexico, Momaday took a teaching position on an Apache reservation, and there he met his first wife, Gaye Mangold.

In 1959 Momaday won a Wallace Stegner Fellowship at Stanford and began studying with the man who would have the most profound influence over his work and career, the poet-critic Yvor Winters. Although Winters did not live to see Momaday win the Pulitzer Prize, he passionately championed the young writer and predicted his success. Momaday left Stanford in 1963 with a Ph.D. (He returned a decade later to teach in Stanford's English Department for nine years.) Momaday has taught at many other universities, including the University of California at Berkeley, the University of Arizona, and the University of Regensberg in Germany, where he met his second wife, Regina Heitzer.

Momaday's work is thematically diverse. He has explored Native American sources, but his work rarely takes an overtly autobiographical turn. When he addresses personal subjects, he characteristically universalizes both the voice and situation. His poetry often addresses philosophical issues, especially death and man's relationship with nature. For Momaday a poem about nature is not simply descriptive, it must show the mind coming to terms with what it describes. His work is also varied in its style and structure. Metered verse is found next to chants, and syllabics next to prose poems. Momaday has been labeled a postsymbolist, and his poetry often uses sound, image, metaphor, and symbol to create an elusive structure of associative meaning that augments the surface meaning of the text.

Acting as a link between cultures, Momaday's poetry often explains one society's ideals to another. He sometimes assumes the role of a memoirist. "When I was growing up on the reservations of the Southwest," he recalls, "I saw people who were deeply involved in their traditional life, in the memories of their blood. They had, as far as I could see, a certain strength and beauty that I find missing in the modern world at large. I like to celebrate that involvement in my writing."

A fastidious writer, Momaday has published relatively little poetry, considering the length of his career. He produced two early, short volumes, *Angle of Geese* (1974) and *The Gourd Dancer* (1976), and then years later released *In the Presence of the Sun: Stories and Poems, 1961–1991* (1992). While Momaday has published work in other genres, he seems to have taken his mentor Winters's advice from a 1964 letter, "Any poet with a critical conscience will publish a small body of work." Momaday is a poet conspicuously more concerned with quality than quantity.

Momaday has been recognized with numerous awards and honors throughout his career. Besides the Pulitzer Prize, he has received a Guggenheim fellowship, a National Institute of Arts and Letters grant, and the *Premio Letterario Internazionale Mondelo,* Italy's highest literary award. Bridging cultures with his art, Momaday's greatest success has been in establishing a large and serious international audience for Native American letters.

Simile

What did we say to each other
that now we are as the deer
who walk in single file
with heads high
with ears forward   5
with eyes watchful
with hooves always placed on firm ground
in whose limbs there is latent flight

1974

Carriers of the Dream Wheel[1]

This is the Wheel of Dreams
Which is carried on their voices,

---

1. Dream visions are of central importance to Native American societies. Plains Indians sometimes used objects such as dream hoops to catch and hold the power of their dreams.

By means of which their voices turn
And center upon being.
It encircles the First World,   5
This powerful wheel.
They shape their songs upon the wheel
And spin the names of the earth and sky,
The aboriginal names.
They are old men, or men   10
Who are old in their voices,
And they carry the wheel among the camps,
Saying: Come, come,
Let us tell the old stories,
Let us sing the sacred songs.   15

1976

The Delight Song of Tsoai-talee[2]

I am a feather on the bright sky
I am the blue horse that runs in the plain
I am the fish that rolls, shining, in the water
I am the shadow that follows a child
I am the evening light, the lustre of meadows   5
I am an eagle playing with the wind
I am a cluster of bright beads
I am the farthest star
I am the cold of the dawn
I am the roaring of the rain   10
I am the glitter on the crust of the snow
I am the long track of the moon in a lake
I am a flame of four colors
I am a deer standing away in the dusk
I am a field of sumac and the pomme blanche[3]   15
I am an angle of geese in the winter sky
I am the hunger of a young wolf
I am the whole dream of these things
You see, I am alive, I am alive
I stand in good relation to the earth   20
I stand in good relation to the gods
I stand in good relation to all that is beautiful
I stand in good relation to the daughter of Tsen-tainte[4]
You see, I am alive, I am alive

1976

2. Tsoai-talee is the poet's Kiowa name.
3. White apple, or prairie turnip.
4. The great Kiowa chief White Horse (d. 1892).

The Eagle-Feather Fan

The eagle is my power,
And my fan is an eagle.
It is strong and beautiful
In my hand. And it is real.
My fingers hold upon it   5
As if the beaded handle
Were the twist of bristlecone.
The bones of my hand are fine
And hollow; the fan bears them.
My hand veers in the thin air   10
Of the summits. All morning
It scuds on the cold currents;
All afternoon it circles
To the singing, to the drums.

1976

Headwaters

Noon in the intermountain plain:
There is scant telling of the marsh—
A log, hollow and weather-stained,
An insect at the mouth, and moss—
Yet waters rise against the roots,   5
Stand brimming to the stalks. What moves?
What moves on this archaic force
Was wild and welling at the source.

1976

━━━ ⊷◄ FRED CHAPPELL ►◦━ ━━━
(b. 1936)

Fred Davis Chappell, who became poet laureate of his native state, was born in
Canton, a mill town in the mountains of western North Carolina. He has remained
in North Carolina for his entire life, with the exception of a year in Italy on a
Rockefeller grant in 1967. The landscape, people, and culture of the South, especially the Appalachians, have figured strongly in Chappell's writing. Although
Chappell has claimed poetry as his "first allegiance," he initially made his name as
a novelist. Only after publishing three early novels—all with major New York
houses—did he bring out his first volume of poetry, *The World between the Eyes*
(1971). He has continued to publish an impressive volume of work—many novels, more than a dozen collections of verse, books of essays, short fiction, and
countless articles and book reviews.

　　Both of Chappell's parents were schoolteachers, although his father quit
teaching to sell furniture and work the family farm. Chappell enrolled at Duke
University, but took three years off before completing a bachelor's degree in 1961.

In a profile in *Duke Magazine,* the writer recalled his time away from school: "I worked in a farmer's supply store. Worked at my father's furniture store. Farmed. Collected bills. You know, what most guys do and what all writers do—just a variety of jobs and chores. And I got married." In 1959, Chappell married Susan Nicholls, with whom he had attended Canton High School.

Chappell stayed at Duke for his graduate studies. During that time, Hiram Haydn of Atheneum Press happened upon one of Chappell's short stories and asked the young student to write a novel for the press. The result was *It Is Time, Lord* (1963), published a year before Chappell finished his master's degree. The University of North Carolina, Greensboro, had already offered him a faculty position, which Chappell accepted in 1965. Now a full professor, he teaches there still. His subsequent works of fiction include *I Am One of You Forever* (1985), *Brighten the Corner Where You Are* (1989), and *More Shapes Than One* (1991). His new and selected poems, *Spring Garden,* appeared in 1995. Chappell has been awarded the *Prix de Meilleur des Livres Etrangers* from the French Academy, a Bollingen Prize, the Aiken Taylor Award, and was named North Carolina Poet Laureate for 1997 to 2002.

Perhaps Chappell's beginnings in fiction helped him develop a talent for storytelling and characterization in his verse. His long poem, *Midquest* (1981), is a complex quasi-autobiographical epic that borrows its structure from Dante's *Divine Comedy* to give an allegorical version of the poet's life. His collection *Family Gathering* (2000) is a book-length sequence focusing on members of a large extended family. His wit is at its sharpest here, as he presents poetic snapshots of relative after relative. Chappell's satiric gift is also apparent in *C* (1993), which as its Roman numeral title suggests, presents one hundred short poems and epigrams. Despite the folksy persona he sometimes adopts, Chappell is a deeply literary writer who often draws his subject matter and inspiration from classical European literature, especially Latin and French writers. Of his literary goals, he has written: "To be serious but not ponderous, or to be light but not frivolous: these are the qualities I strive for. They require clarity, and this is my strongest ambition."

Narcissus and Echo[1]

Shall the water not remember	*Ember*	
my hand's slow gesture, tracing above		*of*
its mirror my half-imaginary	*airy*	
portrait? My only belonging	*longing;*	
is my beauty, which I take	*ache*	5
away and then return, as love	*of*	
teasing playfully the one being	*unbeing.*	

1. This poem is an example of echo verse, a form (which dates back to the late classical Greek poetry) in which the final syllables of the lines are repeated back as a reply or commentary, often a punning one. In Greek mythology, Narcissus was a beautiful young man who fell in love with his own reflection in the water of a well. He gradually pined away because he could not reach his love; upon dying he changed into the flower that bears his name. Echo was a nymph who, according to Roman tradition, loved Narcissus. When her love was not returned, she pined away until only her voice was left.

whose gratitude I treasure   *Is your*
moves me. I live apart   *heart*
from myself, yet cannot   *not*   10
live apart. In the water's tone,   *stone?*
that brilliant silence, a flower   *Hour,*
whispers my name with such slight   *light:*
moment, it seems filament of air,   *fare*
the world become cloudswell.   *well.*   15

1985

The Epigrammatist

Mankind perishes. The world goes dark.
He racks his brain for a tart remark.

1993

Televangelist

He claims that he'll reign equally
With Jesus in eternity.
But it's not like him to be willing
To give a partner equal billing.

1993

Overheard in the Tearoom

"Marianne, my dear,
I'll say this for Ruth:
Though she never tells the truth
Her lies are quite sincere."

1993

⤞ LUCILLE CLIFTON ⤝
(b. 1936)

Since 1969, when she published her first book, *Good Times*, Lucille Clifton has been recognized for her skill in crafting poems that are succinct yet ripe with implications, particularized in their evocations of African American experience, and universal in their celebration of endurance. Born Thelma Lucille Sayles in Depew, New York, she grew up listening to stories about her family, especially of her great-great-grandmother Caroline Donald, born in Dahomey, West Africa, and abducted by slave traders, and her great-grandmother Lucille, who, according to Clifton's father, became the first African American woman to be legally hanged in Virginia after shooting the white father of her son. The family chronicle that she often traces in her work, as well as the strong African American women she portrays in her poems, took root from such stories. Enriched by the supportive home life created by her father, a steelworker, and her mother, a laundress (and amateur poet),

Clifton enrolled at Howard University as a drama major in 1953 and studied with Sterling Brown. Shifting her focus to education, she transferred to Fredonia State Teachers College in 1955 but did not complete a degree. Between her marriage to Fred J. Clifton in 1958 and the publication of *Good Times* (1969) eleven years later, she worked in Buffalo and Washington, D.C., and had six children. Both *Good Times* and her next book, *Good News about the Earth* (1972), display the stylistic clarity and emotional directness as well as the emphasis on urban African American family life that would characterize her subsequent collections.

Her next books, *An Ordinary Woman* (1974) and the prose memoir *Generations* (1976), explore the personal, historical, and social trials of her family, especially the lives of her great-grandmothers and also of her mother, sisters, and daughters. Her interest in the female experience is explored in *Two-Headed Woman* (1980), with its often witty poems such as "Homage to My Hips" that combine humor, realism, and frank assertiveness. *Next* (1987), *Quilting* (1991), *The Book of Light* (1993), and *The Terrible Stories* (1996) solidified her reputation not only as an important African American writer, but also as a significant feminist writer. In these recent volumes, she develops brief but emotionally complex poems that offer bold considerations of women's lives—particularly in *Next*, where she elegizes her husband, who died in 1984, and *The Terrible Stories*, where she comes to terms with having breast cancer. Although she never denies the brutality of suffering, in all of her books she champions perseverance. In the conclusion to *Generations*, she affirms: "Things don't fall apart. Things hold. Lines connect in thin ways that last and last and lives become generations made out of pictures and words just kept. . . . our lives are more than the days in them, our lives are our line and we go on."

Clifton has taught at a number of universities, including the University of California at Santa Cruz and St. Mary's College in Maryland. From 1976 to 1985 she was the Poet Laureate of Maryland, and she has received many awards, including the Juniper Prize (1980), the American Library Association's Coretta Scott King Award (1984), and a Lannan Award (1996). She currently lives in Columbia, Maryland.

◄•>━━◖▶━━<•►

good times

My Daddy has paid the rent
and the insurance man is gone
and the lights is back on
and my uncle Brud has hit
for one dollar straight   5
and they is good times
good times
good times

My Mama has made bread
and Grampaw has come   10
and everybody is drunk
and dancing in the kitchen

and singing in the kitchen
oh these is good times
good times   15
good times

oh children think about the
good times

                                                1969

---

homage to my hips

these hips are big hips.
they need space to
move around in.
they don't fit into little
petty places, these hips   5
are free hips.
they don't like to be held back.
these hips have never been enslaved,
they go where they want to go
they do what they want to do.   10
these hips are mighty hips.
these hips are magic hips.
i have known them
to put a spell on a man and
spin him like a top!   15

                                                1991

---

to my last period

well girl, goodbye,
after thirty-eight years.
thirty-eight years and you
never arrived
splendid in your red dress   5
without trouble for me
somewhere, somehow.

now it is done,
and i feel just like
the grandmothers who,   10
after the hussy has gone,
sit holding her photograph
and sighing, *wasn't she*
beautiful? wasn't she beautiful?

                                                1991

⊷ C. K. WILLIAMS ►⊷
(b. 1936)

Charles Kenneth Williams was born and raised in Newark, New Jersey. Although his father had read poems to him and encouraged him to memorize them, Williams did not develop a sense of his poetic vocation until the age of nineteen. In the essay "Beginnings" (1983), he writes about the mixture of intense concentration and inspiration he experienced when writing poetry:

> I started writing one day, for no real reason . . . but once I did, I knew, I can't remember exactly how, that the realities poetry offered me differed in essential and splendid ways from those of every day. . . . There was something about the way poetry isolated experience, its powers of demarcation, that promised a way to endow experience with forms that if nothing else would be at least more dramatically exciting.

After spending his first year of college at Bucknell University, he transferred to the University of Pennsylvania, where he received a bachelor's degree in 1959. He remained in Philadelphia, marrying Sarah Dean Jones in 1966 and divorcing her in 1975. He remarried the same year to Catherine Mauger, a Frenchwoman, and began spending half of each year living in Paris.

Since 1975 Williams has earned his living as a college professor, serving as a visiting writer at a number of universities before attaining more stable appointments at Columbia University, from 1981 to 1985, George Mason University, from 1985 to 1995, and, beginning in 1996, at Princeton. He has received many honors and awards, most notably the National Book Critics Circle Award for *Flesh and Blood* (1987) and the Pulitzer Prize for *Repair* (1999). Along with over ten books of poetry, he has also published a collection of critical essays, *Poetry and Consciousness* (1998), a memoir, *Misgivings: My Mother, My Father, Myself* (2000), and several translations, including Sophocles' *Women of Trachis* (1978) and Euripides' *The Bacchae* (1990).

Throughout his career, Williams has searched for alternatives to the subjective, first-person lyric, even as many of his poems explore the consciousness of a first-person speaker. Williams's speakers, however, engage in intense self-scrutiny prompted by their encounters with people and events outside themselves, over which they have no control. That sense of powerlessness, and rage at authority, whether government authority or a deterministic God unconcerned with human suffering, defines his first two books, *Lies* (1969) and *I Am the Bitter Name* (1972). Although the nihilism and surrealistic tendencies of both books, as well as the protest poems against the Vietnam War that he includes in *I Am the Bitter Name,* were common features of poetry during the period, Williams's early poems are both energetic and economical. The books earned Williams the reputation of an "angry young man," yet the poems are surprisingly nuanced, especially *Lies*'s "A Day for Anne Frank," a Holocaust meditation in which Williams, prompted by his own Jewish heritage, addresses Frank as his sister. For Williams, the poem was crucial to his development, for he used the encounter with Frank to revise his own limited perspective. As he notes in "Beginnings":

> Without understanding how, I'd created a method of composition for myself that, no matter what stylistic changes my work has gone through, has remained basic to the way I conceive poems. Having to balance two apparently contradictory ethical attitudes at

the same time, having to realize the contingency of my own convictions, however apparently heartfelt they might be; to confront them and force them to a more rigorous, more honest level . . . allowed me to bring the poems to a central position in relation to my own experience, my own sense of the struggle to be fully human. My poems have a double function for me: they are about consciousness, in a more or less direct way, and they're involved just as much with the social, moral world with which my consciousness is necessarily concerned.

His next two books, *With Ignorance* (1977) and *Tar* (1983), inaugurated a major stylistic change for Williams. Eschewing the short, free verse lines of his first books, he lengthened his line to Whitmanesque proportions. Shifting his purview to narrative, Williams reveled in moments when an observer, often the voyeuristic first-person speaker of the poem, is forced to change his view of himself and of the world. The long lines enabled Williams to develop an elaborate syntax, in which qualifications and incremental revisions reflect the shifts of the speaker's consciousness. His long sentences also encompassed unflinchingly detailed descriptions, whether of complex human relationships or of gritty urban scenes. Williams achieved a realism in which he could contemplate large moral and ethical dilemmas without being abstract, for, like Whitman, he includes an endless array of concrete details and raises important questions about the self's limitations.

In subsequent books, Williams's long-lined style became increasingly flexible, as in the eight-line vignettes of *Flesh and Blood* or the long title poem of *A Dream of Mind* (1992), in which he contemplates the shifting nature of consciousness. In *The Vigil* (1997) he focuses on specifically human concerns by presenting short meditations on suffering and endurance. Thus, despite the stylistic similarity of his later poetry, his thematic scope has grown more varied with each new collection. In all of his poems, however, he strives to fulfill the definition of poetry he proposed in "Poetry and Consciousness" (1986): "Poetry confronts in the most clear-eyed way just those emotions that consciousness most wishes to slide by, and it deals with them in their greatest profundity, with the most refined moral sensibility."

Hood

Remember me? I was the one
in high school you were always afraid of.
I kept cigarettes in my sleeve, wore
engineer's boots, long hair, my collar
up in back and there were always   5
girls with me in the hallways.

You were nothing. I had it in for you—
when I peeled rubber at the lights
you cringed like a teacher.
And when I crashed and broke both lungs   10
on the wheel, you were so relieved
that you stroked the hard Ford paint
like a breast and your hands shook.

1969

From My Window

Spring: the first morning when that one true block of sweet, laminar, complex
    scent arrives
from somewhere west and I keep coming to lean on the sill, glorying in the
    end of the wretched winter.
The scabby-barked sycamores ringing the empty lot across the way are
    budded—I hadn't noticed—
and the thick spikes of the unlikely urban crocuses have already broken
    the gritty soil.
Up the street, some surveyors with tripods are waving each other left and
    right the way they do.   5
A girl in a gym suit jogged by a while ago, some kids passed, playing hooky,
    I imagine,
and now the paraplegic Vietnam vet who lives in a half-converted warehouse
    down the block
and the friend who stays with him and seems to help him out come weaving
    towards me,
their battered wheelchair lurching uncertainly from one edge of the sidewalk
    to the other.
I know where they're going—to the "Legion": once, when I was putting
    something out, they stopped,   10
both drunk that time, too, both reeking—it wasn't ten o'clock—and we
    chatted for a bit.
I don't know how they stay alive—on benefits most likely. I wonder if they're
    lovers?
They don't look it. Right now, in fact, they look a wreck, careening hap-
    hazardly along,
contriving, as they reach beneath me, to dip a wheel from the curb so that
    the chair skewers, teeters,
tips, and they both tumble, the one slowly, almost gracefully sliding in
    stages from his seat,   15
his expression hardly marking it, the other staggering over him, spinning
    heavily down,
to lie on the asphalt, his mouth working, his feet shoving weakly and fruit-
    lessly against the curb.
In the storefront office on the corner, Reed and Son, Real Estate, have come
    to see the show.
Gazing through the golden letters of their name, they're not, at least, thank
    god, laughing.
Now the buddy, grabbing at a hydrant, gets himself erect and stands there
    for a moment, panting.   20
Now he has to lift the other one, who lies utterly still, a forearm shielding
    his eyes from the sun.
He hauls him partly upright, then hefts him almost all the way into the chair,
    but a dangling foot
catches a support-plate, jerking everything around so that he has to put him
    down,
set the chair to rights, and hoist him again and as he does he jerks the grimy
    jeans right off him.

No drawers, shrunken, blotchy thighs: under the thick, white coils of
belly blubber,   25
the poor, blunt pud, tiny, terrified, retracted, is almost invisible in the
sparse genital hair,
then his friend pulls his pants up, he slumps wholly back as though he
were, at last, to be let be,
and the friend leans against the cyclone fence, suddenly staring up at me
as though he'd known,
all along, that I was watching and I can't help wondering if he knows that
in the winter, too,
I watched, the night he went out to the lot and walked, paced rather, almost
ran, for how many hours.   30
It was snowing, the city in that holy silence, the last we have, when the
storm takes hold,
and he was making patterns that I thought at first were circles, then realized
made a figure eight,
what must have been to him a perfect symmetry but which, from where I
was, shivered, bent,
and lay on its side: a warped, unclear infinity, slowly, as the snow came
faster, going out.
Over and over again, his head lowered to the task, he slogged the path he'd
blazed,   35
but the race was lost, his prints were filling faster than he made them now
and I looked away,
up across the skeletal trees to the tall center city buildings, some, though it
was midnight,
with all their offices still gleaming, their scarlet warning beacons signaling
erratically
against the thickening flakes, their smoldering auras softening portions of
the dim, milky sky.
In the morning, nothing: every trace of him effaced, all the field pure white,   40
its surface glittering, the dawn, glancing from its glaze, oblique, relentless,
unadorned.

                                                                              1983

Elms

All morning the tree men have been taking down the stricken elms skirting
the broad sidewalks.
The pitiless electric chain saws whine tirelessly up and down their piercing,
operatic scales
and the diesel choppers in the street shredding the debris chug feverishly,
incessantly,
packing truckload after truckload with the feathery, homogenized, inert
remains of heartwood,
twig and leaf and soon the block is stripped, it is as though illusions of
reality were stripped: 5
the rows of naked facing buildings stare and think, their divagations more
urgent than they were.

"The winds of time," they think, the mystery charged with fearful clarity:
    "The winds of time . . ."
All afternoon, on to the unhealing evening, minds racing, "Insolent,
    unconscionable, the winds of time . . ."

1987

BERNICE ZAMORA
(b. 1938)

Bernice Zamora was born Bernice Ortiz in the small village of Aguilar, Colorado, where her family had been farmers for many generations. Community life in Aguilar centered on the Catholic Church and she attended parochial school. After high school she worked in a bank in Denver. At twenty-eight, married with two daughters, she began undergraduate work at Southern Colorado University. She has also studied at Colorado State University (M.A., 1972) and Stanford University (Ph.D., 1986). Zamora's work often recasts Jungian archetypes through a feminist perspective.

Zamora's principal themes include the sexual roles of women and the ways women participate in the rituals of culture. The following poem, from her best-known collection, *Restless Serpents* (1976), recounts the celebrated Southwestern Catholic penitential ritual performed during Holy Week prior to Easter in which a cult of devout men secretly reenact the Passion and Crucifixion of Christ. Traditionally, the *penitentes* exclude women from their ritual.

Penitents

Once each year *penitentes* in mailshirts
journey through arroyos Seco, Huerfano,
to join *"edmanos"* at the *morada.*[1]

Brothers Carrasco, Ortiz, Abeyta
prepare the Cristo for an unnamed task.   5
Nails, planks and type O blood are set
upon wooden tables facing, it is decreed,
the sacred mountain range to the Southwest.

Within the dark *morada*[2] average
chains rattle and clacking prayer wheels jolt   10
the hissing spine to uncoil wailing tongues

---

1. The poem is set in southern Colorado and deals with a ritual of sacrifice performed by secret groups of *penitentes*. Arroyos are washes or gulleys in the West, and these are named Seco (Dry) and Huerfano (Orphan). *Edmanos* is possibly a mispronunciation of *hermanos*, or "brothers."
2. A dwelling or abode where the ceremony will be performed—usually flagellation, but sometimes a form of crucifixion.

of Nahuatl[3] converts who slowly wreath
rosary whips to flog one another.

From the mountains *alabados*[4] are heard:
"En una columna atado se   15
hallo el Rey de los Cielos,
herido y ensangrentado,
y arrastrado por los suelos."[5]

The irresistible ceremony
beckoned me many times like crater lakes   20
and desecrated groves. I wished to swim
arroyos and know their estuaries
where, for one week, all is sacred in the valley.

1976

━━━━◄ ISHMAEL REED ►━━━━
(b. 1938)

Satirist, innovator, and iconoclast, Ishmael Reed was born in Chattanooga, Tennessee, but grew up in the working-class neighborhoods of Buffalo, New York. After graduating from high school in 1956, he attended the University of Buffalo but left in his junior year. Reed then worked as a journalist—first for Buffalo's *Empire Star Weekly,* a black community newspaper, and then in New York City where in 1965 he helped establish the *East Village Other,* one of America's earliest "underground" newspapers. In 1967 Reed published his first novel, *The Free-Lance Pallbearers.* That same year he moved to the West Coast to teach at the University of California at Berkeley. Establishing himself as one of the leading African American novelists of his generation with books like *Mumbo Jumbo* (1972), *The Last Days of Louisiana Red* (1974), and *Flight to Canada* (1976), Reed developed an audacious and experimental approach, mixing elements from high and low culture with comic ingenuity, a combination one also finds in his poetry. Although best known as a novelist, Reed is quintessentially a man of letters, adept at the full range of literary enterprises—fiction, poetry criticism, editing, and organizing. He is undoubtedly one of the most active and resourceful figures in contemporary literary life.

Reed played an early, continuing, and decisive role in articulating the literary ethos now known as multiculturalism. He founded *Yardbird Reader* (1972–76), a highly influential and inclusive African American literary journal, which represented a lively forum for what Reed's co-editor, Al Young, called "a non-white establishment." In the United States bicentennial year of 1976 Reed also co-founded the Before Columbus Foundation, a "multi-ethnic organization dedicated to promoting a pan-cultural view of America." These values were further articulated in 1995 when Reed served as general editor for HarperCollins's four-volume Liter-

---

3. Refers to the descendants of Aztecs in Mexico.
4. A song of praise.
5. (Spanish) "In a bundled formation is met / the King of the Sky, / wounded and bloodstained, / and poverty-stricken for the low ones."

ary Mosaic Series anthologies. "Once these voices have been heard," Reed remarked in his preface to the groundbreaking multicultural series, "there is no turning back." His career has frequently been characterized by public controversy. Reed's sharp satire and outspoken views have outraged critics on the political Right, Left, and middle, though he has usually handled these literary battles with a humor and grace not always found among his detractors.

Reed's first collection of poems, *Catechism of D Neoamerican Hoodoo Church* (1970), parodied everything from Marx and Engels's *Communist Manifesto* and Eurocentric literary standards to Ralph Ellison and other mainstream black intellectuals. The volume's most celebrated poem, "I Am a Cowboy in the Boat of Ra," presents a black gunslinger outlaw journeying to battle the ancient Egyptian deity, Set, a symbol of the repressive and moribund in Western culture. His subsequent collections, *Conjure* (1972), *Chattanooga* (1973), *A Secretary to the Spirits* (1978), and *New and Collected Poems* (1988), demonstrate Reed's eclectic aesthetic and restless energy. He currently lives in Oakland, California.

—◦◦▶◦—

I am a cowboy in the boat of Ra

> The devil must be forced to reveal any such physical evil (potions,
> charms, fetishes, etc.) still outside the body and these must be burned.
> *(Rituale Romanun, published 1947, endorsed by the coat-of-arms
> and introductory letter from Francis Cardinal Spellman[1])*

I am a cowboy in the boat of Ra,[2]
sidewinders in the saloons of fools
bit my forehead   like   ○
the untrustworthiness of Egyptologists
who do not know their trips. Who was that   5
dog-faced man?[3] they asked, the day I rode
from town.

School marms with halitosis[4] cannot see
the Nefertiti[5] fake chipped on the run by slick
germans, the hawk behind Sonny Rollins'[6] head or   10
the ritual beard of his axe; a longhorn winding
its bells thru the Field of Reeds.

---

1. (1889–1967) Catholic archbishop and cardinal of New York, famous for his conservative opinions.
2. The ancient Egyptian sun god, important to creation myths.
3. The Egyptian mortuary god Anubis looked like a dog or jackal. "Who was that masked man?" was frequently asked of the Lone Ranger on radio and television.
4. Bad breath.
5. Egyptian queen. A head of Nefertiti was removed by the Germans and is now in Berlin.
6. (b. 1929) Jazz saxophonist, influenced by Coleman Hawkins (1901–1969)—hence the hawk reference in this line.

I am a cowboy in the boat of Ra. I bedded
down with Isis,[7] Lady of the Boogaloo,[8] dove
down deep in her horny, stuck up her Wells-Far-ago[9]   15
in daring midday getaway. 'Start grabbing the
blue', I said from top of my double crown.

I am a cowboy in the boat of Ra. Ezzard Charles[1]
of the Chisolm Trail.[2] Took up the bass but they
blew off my thumb. Alchemist in ringmanship but a   20
sucker for the right cross.

I am a cowboy in the boat of Ra. Vamoosed from
the tempe i bide my time. The price on the wanted
poster was a-going down, outlaw alias copped[3] my stance
and moody greenhorns were making me dance; while my mouth's   25
shooting iron got its chambers jammed.

I am a cowboy in the boat of Ra. Boning-up in
the ol West i bide my time. You should see
me pick off these tin cans whippersnappers. I
write the motown[4] long plays for the comeback of   30
Osiris. Make them up when stars stare at sleeping
steer out here near the campfire. Women arrive
on the backs of goats and throw themselves on
my Bowie.

I am a cowboy in the boat of Ra. Lord of the lash,[5]   35
the Loup Garou[6] Kid. Half breed son of Pisces and
Aquarius. I hold the souls of men in my pot. I do
the dirty boogie[7] with scorpions. I make the bulls
keep still and was the first swinger to grape the taste.

I am a cowboy in his boat. Pope Joan[8]of the   40
Ptah[9] Ra. C/mere a minute willya doll?
Be a good girl and
bring me my Buffalo horn of black powder
bring me my headdress of black feathers
bring me my bones of Ju-Ju[1] snake   45

---

7. Egyptian fertility goddess.
8. Popular dance of the 1960s. The term *boogaloo* was sometimes used as a racist epithet for a black person.
9. Refers to an American banking company, Wells Fargo, but plays on the word "farago," which can refer to a jumble of unrelated matters, a mixture of truth and fiction, etc.
1. (1922–1975) An African American prizefighter.
2. A route used to drive cattle from Texas to Kansas.
3. Slang, meaning "stole," "understood," or "admitted."
4. Highly successful record label from Detroit that helped put many black musicians in the spotlight in the 1960s.
5. May refer to Lash LaRue, an actor in cowboy films.
6. Werewolf.
7. A style of piano blues. To boogie can mean either to dance or to have sex.
8. Apocryphal female pope in the ninth century.
9. A rival Egyptian god to Ra and patron of craftsmen.
1. Charm to ward off evil spirits.

go get my eyelids of red paint.
Hand me my shadow

I'm going into town after Set[2]

I am a cowboy in the boat of Ra

look out Set	here i come Set	50
to get Set	to sunset Set	
to unseat Set	to Set down Set	

usurper of the Royal couch
imposter RAdio of Moses' bush
party pooper O hater of dance   55
vampire outlaw of the milky way

                                      1972

Oakland Blues

Well it's six o'clock in Oakland
and the sun is full of wine
I say, it's six o'clock in Oakland
and the sun is red with wine
We buried you this morning, baby   5
in the shadow of a vine

Well, they told you of the sickness
almost eighteen months ago
Yes, they told you of the sickness
almost eighteen months ago   10
You went down fighting, daddy. Yes
You fought Death toe to toe

O, the egrets fly over Lake Merritt
and the blackbirds roost in trees
O, the egrets fly over Lake Merritt   15
and the blackbirds roost in trees
Without you little papa
what O, what will become of me

O, it's hard to come home, baby
To a house that's still and stark   20
O, it's hard to come home, baby
To a house that's still and stark
All I hear is myself
thinking
and footsteps in the dark.   25

                                      1988

---

2. Egyptian god of chaos who killed his brother, Osiris. Reed also puns on "a set," a portion of a musical performance.

◦►◄ JARED CARTER ►◄◦
(b. 1939)

Jared Carter, the son of a general contractor, was born and raised in Elwood, Indiana, a small town northeast of Indianapolis. His maternal grandmother, who read to him and his three siblings, introduced him to literature—not only children's fare, such as Lang's *Blue Fairy Book,* but classics such as the Greek myths, Nathaniel Hawthorne's *House of the Seven Gables,* and Jonathan Swift's *Gulliver's Travels.* In high school, he extended his literary interests to journalism, by working on the school newspaper, and to printing, by getting to know the local printers who set type for the paper. After graduating from high school in 1956, he attended Yale University on a scholarship and majored in English, but dropped out in his junior year to work as a reporter for a newspaper in Huntington, Indiana. Returning to Yale the next year, Carter won the Academy of American Poets Prize, but left again without taking a degree. He married in 1961, and the following year he was drafted into the army. Stationed in Fontainebleau, France, he spent three years living with his wife in a nearby village, Thomery. Discharged in 1965, he traveled in Europe and then returned to Indiana, where he worked odd jobs and focused on his writing. In 1967 he completed his bachelor's degree through enrolling in a nonresident program at Vermont's Goddard College. His daughter, Selene, was born in 1969. Carter and his wife moved to Indianapolis, where he began working at Bobbs-Merrill, a publishing firm. He became managing editor of the textbook division in 1973. He and his wife divorced in 1974, and he left Bobbs-Merrill in 1976, working as a freelance editor and book designer. He remarried in 1979 to Diane Haston, a teacher who encouraged him to devote himself to his poetry.

Although he had published many poems in literary magazines and anthologies, Carter did not receive national attention until he was forty-two when his first book, *Work, for the Night Is Coming* (1981), was published as the winner of the Walt Whitman Award, sponsored by the Academy of American Poets. First published by Macmillan and then reissued by Cleveland State University Press, the book has sold over 10,000 copies and is still in print. The book's strong critical reception gave Carter the opportunity to give many readings of his work around the country. He also guest-taught at Purdue University and won additional awards, including the Poets' Prize for his second full-length collection, *After the Rain* (1993). A third collection, *Les Barricades Mysterieuses* (1999), is a series of thirty-two villanelles set in and around a nineteenth-century midwestern farmhouse. His interest in printing and small artisan presses has led him to publish many chapbooks as well.

Focusing on the rural Midwest and often set in his fictional Mississinewa County, Carter's books offer vignettes of small-town life. Although he has been celebrated as a masterful narrative poet, his work depends less on storytelling in the narrow sense than on evoking the details of specific places, characters, and moments in time, aims that depend on the compression, repetition, and attention to evocative detail that are also hallmarks of lyric poetry. In an interview, Carter stresses the importance of these techniques: "Years ago I heard Robert Bly speak, and he said something I've always remembered. He said that poetry has to 'come up close to its object.' That made a great deal of sense to me—coming up close. I'm a great believer in careful observation, along with extensive background study."

By drawing the reader's attention to concrete details and the minute changes in them, Carter transmutes them into emblems for the passage of time. Yet, although his poems evoke small-town ways of life that are dying or already obsolete, Carter avoids sentimentalized nostalgia. Instead, he shows the vitality of the past and its relevance to the present. In the same interview, he describes the way the past can still speak to us:

> Henry James has that wonderful phrase, in his preface to *The Aspern Papers*, about how he delights "in a palpable imaginable visitable past." He goes on to say that it is "the past fragrant of all . . . the poetry of the thing outlived and lost and gone." And yet somehow the artist can make it "appreciable."

Deeply conscious of both change and tradition, Carter strives to make the past—and the Midwestern life he loves—palpable to the reader.

Work, for the Night Is Coming

On the road out of town past the old quarry
I watched a light rain darkening ledges
Blocked and carded by the drill's bit

Twenty years back. Within those stiff lines,
Places half-stained with damp, the rock face   5
Opened to a deeper grain—the probable drift

Of the entire ridge outlined for a moment
By the rain's discoloring. Then all turned dim—
Grass holding to the seams, redbud scattered

Across the cliff, dark pool of water   10
Rimmed with broken stones, where rain, now
Falling steadily, left no lasting pattern.

                                        1981

The Gleaning

All day long they have been threshing
and something breaks: the canvas belt
that drives the separator flies off,
parts explode through the swirl
of smoke and chaff, and he is dead   5
where he stands—drops the pitchfork
as they turn to look at him—and falls.
They carry him to the house and go on
with the work. Five wagons and their teams
stand waiting, it is still daylight,   10
there will be time enough for grieving.

When the undertaker comes from town
he brings the barber, who must wait
till the women finish washing the body.

Neighbors arrive from the next farm   15
to take the children. The machines
shut down, one by one, horses
are led away, the air grows still
and empty, then begins to fill up
with the sounds of cicada and mourning dove.   20
The men stand along the porch, talking
in low voices, smoking their cigarettes;
the undertaker sits in the kitchen
with the family.
                    In the parlor
the barber throws back the curtains   25
and talks to this man, whom he has known
all his life, since they were boys
together. As he works up a lather
and brushes it onto his cheeks,
he tells him the latest joke. He strops   30
the razor, tests it against his thumb,
and scolds him for not being more careful.
Then with darkness coming over the room
he lights a lamp, and begins to scrape
at the curve of the throat, tilting the head   35
this way and that, stretching the skin,
flinging the soap into a basin, gradually
leaving the face glistening and smooth.

And as though his friend had fallen asleep
and it were time now for him to stand up   40
and stretch his arms, and look at his face
in the mirror, and feel the closeness
of the shave, and marvel at his dreaming—
the barber trims the lamp, and leans down,
and says, for a last time, his name.   45

                                                              1993

STEPHEN DUNN
(b. 1939)

Stephen Dunn has had an atypical career for a contemporary poet. A serious athlete during his youth, he never expected he would become a writer. While earning his bachelor's degree at Hofstra University, Dunn was a star player of a basketball team that went 25–1 (and is still ranked as the best team in the school's history). He spent 1962 in the U.S. Army stationed at Fort Jackson, South Carolina, where he did sports reporting for a regimental newspaper. Upon leaving the service, Dunn played professional basketball for a year with the Williamsport Billies in Pennsylvania.

Stephen Dunn was born in New York City where his father, Charles Francis Dunn, worked as a salesman. Although his family was not particularly bookish,

Dunn recalled influential memories of his grandfather in an interview: "My maternal grandfather, who lived with us, was the only reader in the family. Though we had no books in the house, he borrowed one almost every day from the lending library and—with a bottle of gin by his side—would read it before he fell asleep in his chair. . . . He was also a wonderful storyteller, a Jew who had been in the Merchant Marines and ended up as a theatrical agent. I may have learned from him that reading and storytelling were valuable."

After an uninspiring stint writing promotional brochures for Nabisco, in 1964 Dunn married Lois Ann Kelly, a yoga teacher, and began graduate studies at the New School for Social Research. The couple moved to Spain two years later so Dunn could focus on writing. After a failed attempt at a novel, Dunn began to write poetry. Upon returning to the States, he enrolled at Syracuse University (M.A., 1970) where he studied with Donald Justice and W. D. Snodgrass. Dunn has had a secure and steady teaching career. He has held a professorship of creative writing at Richard Stockton College in New Jersey since 1974. He has also lectured and guest taught at many universities, including the University of Michigan, Columbia University, and Syracuse.

Although he has published more than a dozen collections of poetry, it was not until Dunn's fourth full-length volume, *Work and Love* (1981), that the direct and candid voice that characterizes his mature work began to emerge. His subsequent volumes, including *Local Time* (1986), *Between Angels* (1989), and *Landscape at the End of the Century* (1991), confirmed his position as one of the most personable and accessible poets of his generation. Reviewing *Loosestrife* (1996) in *Poetry* magazine, David Baker discussed Dunn's use of clear and common language, "which, by lesser poets, often shakes me with tedium these days: plain-spoken, in an easygoing method of personal anecdote, homely in its formal strategies, wistful in tone." Dunn's identity is distinctly male. His narrative strategy is often to contrast the external identity that society requires males to show—strength, reserve, and responsibility—with the hidden inner-self full of doubt, longing, and unarticulated feeling. Dunn, as Baker observes, is a poet who writes "from the nearly paralyzed districts of American suburbia and middle age." Dunn also has a comic side to his work, which exhibits sly and gentle satire. His humor, however, usually has a serious undertone, and his jokes become ways of revealing certain truths that cannot quite be conveyed convincingly in any other way.

Dunn has earned three fellowships from the National Endowment of the Arts, a Levinson Prize, and the Pulitzer Prize for *Different Hours* (2000). He lives in Port Republic, New Jersey.

◄•►━━◄•►

Beautiful Women

More things come to them,
and they have more to hide.
All around them: mirrors, eyes.
     In any case
they are different from other women
and like great athletes have trouble

making friends, and trusting a world
quick to praise.

I admit without shame
I'm talking about superficial beauty,   10
the beauty unmistakable
to the honest eye, which causes
some of us to pivot and to dream,
to tremble before we dial.

        Intelligence warmed by generosity   15
is inner beauty, and what's worse
some physically beautiful women have it,
and we have to be strapped and handcuffed
to the mast, or be ruined.

But I don't want to talk of inner beauty,   20
it's the correct way to talk
and I'd feel too good
about myself, like a parishioner.
        Now, in fact,
I feel like I'm talking   25
to a strange beautiful woman at a bar, I'm
animated, I'm wearing that little fixed
smile, I might say anything at all.

Still, it's better to treat a beautiful woman
as if she were normal, one of many.   30
She'll be impressed that you're unimpressed,
might start to lean your way.
This is especially true if she has aged
into beauty, for she will have learned
the sweet gestures one learns   35
in a lifetime of seeking love.
Lucky is the lover of such a woman
and lucky the woman herself.

Beautiful women who've been beautiful girls
are often in some tower of themselves   40
waiting for us to make the long climb.

But let us have sympathy for the loneliness
of beautiful women.
Let us have no contempt for their
immense privilege, or for the fact   45
that they never can be wholly ours.

        It is not astonishing
when the scared little girl in all of them
says here I am, or when they weep.
But we are always astonished by what   50
beautiful women do.

"Boxers punch harder when women are around,"
Kenneth Patchen said. Think what happens
when *beautiful* women are around.
We do not question   55
that a thousand ships were launched.

In the eye of the beholder? A platitude.
A beautiful woman enters a room,
and everyone beholds. Geography changes.
We watch her everywhere she goes.   60

1994

Decorum[1]

She wrote, "They were making love
up against the gymnasium wall,"
and another young woman in class,
serious enough to smile, said

"No, that's fucking, they must   5
have been fucking," to which many
agreed, pleased to have the proper fit
of word with act.

But an older woman, a wife, a mother,
famous in the class for confusing grace   10
with decorum and carriage,
said the F-word would distract

the reader, sensationalize the poem.
"Why can't what they were doing
just as easily be called making love?"   15
It was an intelligent complaint,

and the class proceeded to debate
what's fucking, what's making love,
and the importance of the context, tact,
the *bon mot*.[2] I leaned toward those   20

who favored fucking; they were funnier
and seemed to have more experience
with the happy varieties of their subject.
But then a young man said, now believing

he had permission, "What's the difference,   25
you fuck 'em and you call it making love;
you tell 'em what they want to hear."
The class jeered, and another man said

1. Manners.
2. (French) "Good word."

"You're the kind of guy who gives fucking
a bad name," and I remembered how fuck   30
gets dirty as it moves reptilian
out of certain minds, certain mouths.

The young woman whose poem it was,
small-boned and small-voiced,
said she had no objection to fucking,   35
but these people were making love, it was

her poem and she herself up against
that gymnasium wall, and it felt like love,
and the hell with all of us.
There was silence. The class turned   40

to me, their teacher, who they hoped
could clarify, perhaps ease things.
I told them I disliked the word fucking
in a poem, but that fucking

might be right in this instance, yet   45
I was unsure now, I couldn't decide.
A tear formed and moved down
the poet's cheek. I said I was sure

only of "gymnasium," sure it was
the wrong choice, making the act seem   50
too public, more vulgar than she wished.
How about "boat house?" I said.

                                                         1994

◄ TED KOOSER ►
(b. 1939)

Born in Ames, Iowa, Ted Kooser has spent all his life in the Midwest, which in his best poems becomes as universal as Constantine Cavafy's Alexandria. His father, who managed a department store, was a good storyteller, and he credits his mother with teaching him "to see the life at play in everything." Recalling his student days at Iowa State College (now University), he once wrote, "When I was a nineteen-year-old freshman in college, it suddenly struck me that I should set out to become a famous poet, and I fell upon this aspiration with typical adolescent single-mindedness." It was also in college that he discovered the poetry of William Carlos Williams, which taught him that genuine writing could be fashioned out of local materials. Williams's poems displayed some of the strong visual sense and deceptively simple diction that would characterize Kooser's work.

Kooser is a talented visual artist, and over the years he has pursued an interest in painting along with his poetry. After college he tried teaching high school, then entered a master's degree program at the University of Nebraska, where one of his professors was the poet Karl Shapiro. Now married and the father of a son, Kooser supported his family by working for an insurance company, taking his classes at night. By the time he received his master's degree in 1968, he had decided against an academic career. Instead, he continued working in the insurance business, eventually becoming a vice president of Lincoln Benefit Life Company. His first marriage ended in divorce in 1969. He remarried in 1977 and now lives in a remodeled old farmhouse outside Lincoln, Nebraska, with his second wife, Kathleen Rutledge, a newspaper editor. Kooser took early retirement in 1998 while undergoing treatment for cancer.

The wry title of his first book of poems, *Official Entry Blank* (1969), is indicative not only of Kooser's humor, but also of his bemused vision of the poetry world. As a midwesterner, a businessman, and a writer who prefers short, lucid poems, Kooser has bucked the literary establishment, which often measures ambition by difficulty and length. His poems can usually be understood in a single reading, though they draw readers back for the pleasure of their precise insights. Critics looking for arcane interpretations found little to chew on in Kooser's work, and he has generally been championed by readers and writers who understand that popular appeal and artistic merit are not incompatible qualities in poetry.

Kooser's poetry was slow to achieve recognition. After the publication of his first full-length volume, he spent the next decade issuing a series of small press chapbooks. Although limited in circulation, these modestly produced books, including *Grass Country* (1971), *A Local Habitation and a Name* (1974), and *Not Coming to Be Barked At* (1976), demonstrated the remarkable development of his individual voice and style. The singular quality and consistent vision of his poetry signaled the emergence—though initially only to a small audience—of a major new midwestern writer. Critics noticed an affinity for the small-town portraits of Edwin Arlington Robinson and Edgar Lee Masters, reinforcing an impression of Kooser as a regional writer at a time when postmodern internationalism was in vogue. Nevertheless, Kooser's readership grew steadily. *Sure Signs: New and Selected Poems* (1980), *One World at a Time* (1985), *Weather Central* (1994), and *Winter Morning Walks: One Hundred Postcards to Jim Harrison* (2000) have gradually consolidated his reputation as one of the most quietly original poets of his generation.

An heir to the Imagist dedication to compression, exactitude, and sensory physicality, Kooser has created a personal style wonderfully suited for his imaginative enterprise—to capture the small towns and family farms of the Great Plains in poetry that is at once local and universal. Considered separately, his poems offer brief but brilliant moments of illumination. Read together, however, the poems acquire a cumulative resonance and present a sweeping vision of a vast American rural landscape that is disappearing into history. A regional writer in the best sense of the term—like Willa Cather or William Faulkner—Kooser writes out of a specific place to investigate the larger human condition.

◄◦━━◄▶►━━◦►

Abandoned Farmhouse

He was a big man, says the size of his shoes
on a pile of broken dishes by the house;
a tall man too, says the length of the bed
in an upstairs room; and a good, God-fearing man,
says the Bible with a broken back   5

on the floor below the window, dusty with sun;
but not a man for farming, say the fields
cluttered with boulders and the leaky barn.

A woman lived with him, says the bedroom wall
papered with lilacs and the kitchen shelves   10
covered with oilcloth, and they had a child,
says the sandbox made from a tractor tire.
Money was scarce, say the jars of plum preserves
and canned tomatoes sealed in the cellar hole.
And the winters cold, say the rags in the window frames.   15
It was lonely here, says the narrow country road.

Something went wrong, says the empty house
in the weed-choked yard. Stones in the fields
say he was not a farmer; the still-sealed jars
in the cellar say she left in a nervous haste.   20
And the child? Its toys are strewn in the yard
like branches after a storm—a rubber cow,
a rusty tractor with a broken plow,
a doll in overalls. Something went wrong, they say.

                                                      1969/1974

The Blind Always Come as Such a Surprise

The blind always come as such a surprise,
suddenly filling an elevator
with a great white porcupine of canes,
or coming down upon us in a noisy crowd
like the eye of a hurricane.   5
The dashboards of cars stopped at crosswalks
and the shoes of commuters on trains
are covered with sentences
struck down in mid-flight by the canes of the blind.
Each of them changes our lives,   10
tapping across the bright circles of our ambitions
like cracks traversing the favorite china.

                                                            1974

Tom Ball's Barn

For Bill Kloefkorn

The loan that built the barn
just wasn't big enough
to buy the paint, so the barn
went bare and fell apart
at the mortgaged end of twelve   5
nail-popping, splintering winters.
Besides the Januaries,

the barber says it was
five-and-a-half percent,
three dry years, seven wet,   10
and two indifferent,
the banker (dead five years),
and the bank (still open
but deaf, or *deef* as it were), *and*
poor iron in the nails that   15
were all to blame for the barn's collapse
on everything he owned, thus
leading poor Tom's good health
to diabetes and
the swollen leg that threw him   20
off the silo, probably
dead (the doctor said)
before he hit that board pile.

                                                          1971

Spring Plowing

West of Omaha the freshly plowed fields
steam in the night like lakes.
The smell of the earth floods over the roads.
The field mice are moving their nests
to the higher ground of fence rows,   5
the old among them crying out to the owls
to take them all. The paths in the grass
are loud with the squeak of their carts.
They keep their lanterns covered.

                                                          1974

Carrie

"There's never an end to dust
and dusting," my aunt would say
as her rag, like a thunderhead,
scudded across the yellow oak
of her little house. There she lived   5
seventy years with a ball
of compulsion closed in her fist,
and an elbow that creaked and popped
like a branch in a storm. Now dust
is her hands and dust her heart.   10
There's never an end to it.

                                                          1980

Contemporary Voices

Since 1973, Nuyorican Poets Cafe has been an important venue for Spoken Word and multicultural poetry in New York City.

HISTORICAL AND CRITICAL OVERVIEW

Generations and Changes

> Countries, like people,
> Cannot be told or known in final terms.
> —*Robert Pinsky*

In the latter half of this anthology we have surveyed local and international strains in recent poetry. There is obviously more to be said, and once again we want to set our observations in broader contexts.

Of the fifty-one poets gathered in this final section, the eldest, Robert Pinsky, was nearly thirty years old in 1969 when the first astronauts walked on the moon. The youngest, Kevin Young, had not even been born. The social and historical experiences of these two poets, one Jewish, the other African American, could hardly be more different, though both have made similar careers as writers, editors, and teachers. Pinsky is one of four recent Poets Laureate of the United States (the others are Rita Dove, Robert Hass, and Billy Collins) who have made the once largely ceremonial office an effective public pulpit for poetry. At present, American poetry is experiencing a renewal that might not have been dreamed of when men first walked on the moon. In addition to the range of poetries now being written and performed, there are now modes for "publication"—from CDs and videos to desktop publishing and Internet websites—that have taken the art form in new directions. Meanwhile venues for poetry readings, once largely confined to college campuses, have increased exponentially. The audience for poetry is large, diverse, and growing.

Not long ago most poets and critics did not think such a rebirth of public interest was possible. Writing in 1988, the poet-critic Bruce Bawer noted, "Thirty-five years have passed since Randall Jarrell complained, in the lead essay of his book, *Poetry and the Age,* about the indifference of the American public toward the American poet, and it is safe, I think, to say that the situation has not changed appreciably since." That same year essayist Joseph Epstein published his shrewd but caustic article, "Who Killed Poetry?" suggesting that the art had lost most of its cultural power and allure. Epstein's critical obituary whipped up a storm of protest—mostly from poets who made a living from the supposedly dead art.

The debate on the current state of poetry continued to rage through the next decade, inspiring dozens of books and essays along with innumerable newspaper articles. Many essays, including Dana Gioia's "Can Poetry Matter?" examined the rise of master of fine arts programs in creative writing and the ways that such programs may have generated an insular audience for poetry. In his collection of essays, *The Castle of Indolence* (1995), Thomas M. Disch lamented the influence of creative writing programs: "The art of poetry is poorly served by its bureaucratization, and only the trade is advanced." Meanwhile Language poet Charles Bernstein attacked the mediocrity of what he termed years earlier as "official verse culture." Many poets dismissed populist notions of a wide audience for poetry as antithetical to the art. Poetry, they argued, has always been a learned art created by writers mostly for a discerning audience of other writers. But the majority of readers seemed not to agree with this elitist vision and continued to long for a deeper relationship between American poetry and its diverse audiences.

The argument about poetry's place in society was not new, but rarely had it occupied such a prominent position in public culture. For much of the twentieth century there had been enormous anxiety about the future of the art. Despite the emergence of a large and vital poetry subculture in university writing programs during the last decades of the century, this concern about poetry's decline grew deeper with each passing decade among almost every group of poets, causing old questions to be asked all over again. What is poetry and who is it for? What kinds of poems should be advocated? What cultural conditions are best for the art? The answers to such questions, which have been asked for thousands of years, have been multiple and often contradictory. Despite their ferocity, the "poetry wars" that arose at the end of the twentieth century from this crisis of confidence in verse as a contemporary medium were ultimately good for the art. By bringing basic issues about the place and purpose of the art into public debate, they expanded the audience and increased support for poetry outside the academy.

In the 1990s there began a slow but steady increase of poetry's public presence. Poems started appearing regularly on radio and television—and were frequently quoted in films—while also receiving broader coverage in mainstream newspapers and magazines. Meanwhile there was greater local support in the form of public or civic poetry festivals and book fairs as well as state or local laureateships. Poetry readings in libraries, museums, and bookstores as well as bars and cafes became commonplace. Certain poets like Billy Collins, Maya Angelou, Sharon Olds, and Robert Pinsky achieved minor celebrity status. Poetry's heightened presence in American public culture and the mass media gradually contributed to the elevated public position the art now enjoys.

Poetry and Public Events

> Man is a history-making creature who can
> neither repeat his past nor leave it behind.
> —W. H. Auden

History has also affected the course of recent poetry. Poets like Rafael Campo, Marisa de los Santos, Larissa Szporluk, and Diane Thiel, all born in the 1960s, would have known continued racial division in the United States even as opportunities for minority poets increased. They would have spent their early years as the country endured the end of the Vietnam War, Watergate, Gerald Ford's pardon of Richard Nixon, and Jimmy Carter's pardon of most Vietnam-era draft dodgers. They would have been teenagers during the Iran hostage crisis that helped bring an end to Carter's presidency and elect Ronald Reagan in 1980. They would have seen the attempted assassination of President Reagan in 1981. They would have come to maturity in economic recession and the dawning of the AIDS crisis in the eighties. The president during their thirties would have been Bill Clinton, whose administration was marked by economic prosperity and recurrent scandals. All of the poets in this section lived through the events outlined here, though few of them have chosen to reflect such public moments in their work. All have witnessed the turn of a new century, horribly punctuated by terrorist attacks on New York and Washington, D.C., on September 11, 2001. All have lived with anxiety about global population, which in 2000 had topped 6 billion people, or the population of the United States at nearly 290 million in the same year, or global warming. All have witnessed the apparent time of peace at the end of the Cold War in the early 1990s turn into a newly dangerous and uncertain era.

There has been no uniform poetic response to these historical trends. The events of September 11, 2001, caused a huge outpouring of poems—with one website alone listing and linking nearly forty thousand individual works. Some writers like Carolyn Forché and Wendy Rose have long advocated a poetry of political engagement with the world. Other poets like Lyn Hejinian and Ron Silliman have formed worlds out of private mythologies or delved into the very grammar of English in a new poetry of mind. Quite a few have found their poetic stance in social or sexual identity. Others have explored narrative or formal strategies. Many have differed about what makes poetry *new*. Those arguments, however bitter, have been a sign of the art's continuing relevance. Poetry's vitality depends upon its ability to articulate not one point of view but the full range of contemporary experience.

No More Mainstream

> I dislike the idea that a single mind, or even a collective bound
> together by common theory, should determine what is called best.
> —*Louise Glück*

As we have said, contemporary American poetry is an enormously diverse and crowded field. No one really knows the full extent of what is now being published. Each year several thousand new books of verse appear, but that traditional measure represents only a small amount of what is being written and published in one form or another. The prodigious growth of small presses, small magazines, publishing collectives, and websites, along with the continuing presence of numerous mainstream presses and journals (both commercial and academic), has probably brought the number of published living U.S. poets into the hundreds of thousands. A few dozen of these writers command large audiences. Most probably have no readership beyond a small coterie of friends and associates. But read or unread, they collectively represent a significant cultural presence in American society. Any attempt to summarize this complex and vibrant field will be both reductive and inadequate, but there are certainly a few general observations that might provide a starting point for future explorations.

There is at present no "mainstream" in contemporary American poetry. The art is too diverse, dynamic, and divided to be explained by any single dominant trend. Yet amid the immense flux of current poetic activity it is possible to discern certain major trends—stylistic, cultural, or philosophical—that link large numbers of individual writers into common groups. At present, four of the most influential and pervasive trends in recent American poetry are Identity poetics, Language poetry, New Formalism, and Spoken Word. None of these movements consist of a single tightly knit group of writers who share a specific, unitary aesthetic. Instead, each of these trends represents a common set of issues and concerns that unite what can best be seen as a loose coalition of individual poets, many of whom have differing aims and allegiances. While one finds much in common among various Language poets or New Formalists, for example, one also recognizes crucial distinctions between writers who seemingly occupy the same camp. Likewise, there is as much diversity in the styles and concerns of various Identity poets as there is in their personal backgrounds. In each school poets may share certain basic assumptions, but they distinguish themselves by the individuality of their excellence.

Identity Poetry and Multiculturalism

> What am I? Who am I? What shall I call myself?
> —*Sandra M. Gilbert*

Of the current schools or movements, surely the largest is "Identity poetics," a general term that encompasses the various types of poetry that focus on the personal, cultural, ethnic, or sexual identity of the speaker. Emerging out of the multicultural and diversity movements that became prominent in the final quarter of the twentieth century, Identity poetry comprises such individual traditions as Hispanic American poetry, Asian American poetry, African American poetry, Native American poetry, and feminist poetry, as well as gay and lesbian poetry—all movements insisting that how one writes and speaks is shaped by the author's gender, race, sexual orientation, class, and culture.

There has been an autobiographical element in Western poetry since Greek and Roman classical authors like Sappho and Catullus, but American poetry (like American society in general) has offered an unprecedented range of personal expression. This impulse unites many aspects of our national culture, especially the radical individualism that differentiates modern American society from most traditional societies elsewhere in the world. Individualism has also been a prevalent trend in American poetry since Walt Whitman and Ralph Waldo Emerson, who took the deeply private and internal aspects of American Protestantism and reformulated them into secular and universal terms. In the Emersonian and Whitmanian traditions, the artist (and ultimately the reader) becomes in some sense divine or connected to divinity outside the self. Other countries have great national epics that express their unique character and identity, but only the United States has one titled "Song of Myself"—a poem which, moreover, exists in eight different versions, each revised by the author to reflect his personal vision at a different age.

Identity poetry postulates the continuity between the author's life and work that Whitman famously asserted in "Song of Myself," "Camerado, this is no book, / Who touches this, touches a man." The autobiographical impulse has been central to English-language poetry at least since Romanticism. In *The Prelude,* for example, William Wordsworth made his own psychological, social, and philosophical struggles the central subject of his epic-length work. Modernism, however, rejected the autobiographical impulse that governed such poetry. Anti-Romantics like T. S. Eliot and Marianne Moore prized "impersonality" in art and praised a type of poem that would seemingly exist as an expressive verbal work independent of its author. Some modern American poets like Edna St. Vincent Millay continued to write autobiographical poetry, but they were often marginalized by critics as a consequence. Not until the Confessional poets of the 1960s did autobiography regain a central and critically respected place in American poetry. Developing this trend, Identity poetry has taken the Romantic autobiographical aesthetic of self-discovery and put it to new personal and political uses.

Identity poetry may have grown out of Confessional poetry, but there are significant differences. Identity poetry typically cultivates a communal as well as a personal level of meaning. In exploring her own identity as a Native American poet, for example, Wendy Rose also speaks in some sense for her community. Likewise when Shirley Geok-lin Lim describes her personal past she also articulates the difficult social and psychological transitions of other Asian immigrants. Whereas the Confessional poetry of Anne Sexton, Robert Lowell, and Sylvia Plath focused on the self-definition of the individual poets, including candid admission of painful and intimate experiences—like adultery, family violence, and suicide—Identity poetry generally tends to move beyond merely the individual and to explore group as well as individual consciousness. Whereas Confessional poetry shocked its initial readers through new subject matter, Identity poetry not only explores new subjects but goes one step further by bringing in new voices with life experience outside those traditionally presented—or at least presented openly—in poetry.

The Civil Rights and multicultural movements in late twentieth-century America opened doors for poets who might not have been heard had they lived at another time. While this opening has brought significant vitality and change to the art, it has also contributed to arguments about aesthetic values from many points of view. The late A. Poulin, Jr., in his essay "Contemporary American Poetry: The Radical Tradition," charted the sociological fragmentation of American poetry into constituencies based upon race, gender, sexuality, and other criteria:

> Thus certain poetry is sometimes published or celebrated not for its aesthetic achievement *as poetry,* but rather for the extent to which it serves a given sociopolitical objective. And that may well be the most radical departure from tradition that has occurred in American poetry since 1945.

As a rule, Poulin celebrated the poet's freedom to depart from tradition, however it was defined; but here he seems to imply that some departures were better than others, that poets who were published because they suited a sociopolitical agenda were inferior to those poets who were at least partly defined in purely aesthetic terms.

There are philosophical and ideological points of view from which Poulin's point could be disputed. Many contemporary theorists have asserted that there can be no aesthetic values apart from all other human values, political or otherwise. Still, humanists claim it is possible to read points of view other than one's own—to try to understand experience other than one's own. Literature's power to enlarge and refine our sense of life is, after all, one compelling reason for the human value of the art. In "The Transformation of Silence into Language and Action," Audre Lorde urged "that we not hide behind the mockeries of separations that have been imposed upon us and which so often we accept as our own: for instance, 'I can't possibly teach black women's writing—their experience is so different from my own,' yet how many years have you spent teaching Plato and Shakespeare and Proust?" Vitality and accuracy in language can be found in many places, and the engaged reader recognizes those virtues even when they articulate life experience different from his or her own.

In the following section, some poets ask to be read in multicultural terms—but they also hope the particulars of their poems will not prevent them from achieving a form of universality. We have Asian poets like Shirley Geok-lin Lim, Marisa de los Santos, Amy Uyematsu and Cathy Song; Hispanic poets like Judith Ortiz Cofer, Francisco X. Alarcón, Benjamin Alire Sáenz, Rafael Campo; African American poets like Marilyn Nelson, Yusef Komunyakaa, Rita Dove, and Kevin Young; Native Americans like Adrian C. Louis, Wendy Rose, Joy Harjo, and Sherman Alexie. Some poets like Ai, Dana Gioia, Shirley Geok-lin Lim, and Naomi Shihab Nye come from unusual combinations of ethnic and cultural backgrounds—new admixtures that are characteristic of the American "melting pot"—which will certainly become more common in the multicultural twenty-first century. Religion is also a powerful form of personal and cultural identity, and there is a religious dimension in some of these poets. Christianity informs the work of Mark Jarman, Andrew Hudgins, and Benjamin Alire Sáenz, and Jewish traditions stand behind Robert Pinsky, David Lehman, and Jacqueline Osherow. There are also poets who define themselves at least partly by their gay identity, such as Rafael Campo, Francisco X. Alarcón, and Mark Doty, as well as others in this final section who are gay but do not define their literary identity in terms of sexual orientation.

Such categories are important, and reading contemporary poetry from a multicultural perspective or in terms of personal identity can be enriching in many ways. But even poets with less overt identity concerns can be read in social contexts. Like Edna St. Vincent Millay and Anne Sexton before them, Sharon Olds and Kim Addonizio have made sexual openness an important dimension of their poetry. Carolyn Forché has forged some of the most overtly political poetry of her generation, particularly from an internationalist perspective. Ai, Andrew Hudgins, Mark Jarman, David Mason and others have written narratives in the voices of characters whose circumstances are often very different from their own. In the work of the poets gathered here, no matter what aesthetic they espouse, one can find representation of multiple social, political, and religious points of view. Contemporary American poetry varies not only in its forms, but in its voices.

Language Poetry and Postmodernism

> Poetry is the orphan of silence.
> —*Charles Simic*

In the twentieth century, the study of linguistics had a profound impact upon many disciplines, including criticism and poetry. To think of words not as organically rooted entities but as arbitrary signs, floating signifiers, was frightening to some, liberating to others. In postwar American poetry, interest in approaching language itself from a position of radical skepticism, informed by philosophy, semiotics, and literary theory, has been broad. It can be found in the most extreme articulation in the poetics of Language poetry and the New York School. But one also sees it even in the more mainstream poetics of a figure like Robert Hass, who once wrote, "A word is elegy to what it signifies." Taken to its most extreme, "Language writing" as it is also sometimes called, changes the focus of poetry by moving it away from the purported subject and drawing attention to the verbal system, the signifiers. In theory, Language poets would be less interested in whether they had painful childhoods or enjoyed the flavor of an orange, more in the impossibility of knowing experience outside language.

As a definable movement Language poetry emerged in 1978 with the first issue of the journal *L=A=N=G=U=A=G=E*, edited by Bruce Andrews and Charles Bernstein. Filled with essays and reviews, the journal focused, in the words of the editors, on "exploring the numerous ways that meanings and values can be (& are) realized—revealed—produced in writing." Motivated by Marxist politics and deconstructionist literary theory, many contributors were particularly interested in stripping away the conventional ways in which words convey meanings in a commercialized, capitalistic society. By exploring new forms of meanings—or refusing to mean anything at all in conventional terms—these writers hoped to critique and even transform culture. *L=A=N=G=U=A=G=E* lasted only four years, but its impact was enormous. Although it did not create the political revolution its contributors longed for, Language poetry did revolutionize the avant-garde poetry scene and inspire a number of small journals and anthologies to wage war against "official verse culture." Based initially in the San Francisco Bay Area and New York City, the movement quickly spread nationally.

No poetic movement in American history has been so deeply concerned with literary theory as Language poetry—not even the High Modernism of Pound and Eliot. In a very real sense, the poetic practice of this movement grows out of postmodern literary skepticism and linguistic theory. "Postmodernism" is a slippery term that has multiple meanings. Its definitions differ by art form and often even within the same discipline. In architecture, for instance, postmodernism encompasses everything from the eclectic neoclassicism of Michael Graves to the organic expressionism of Frank Gehry. In literature, the term generally refers to several concepts: a conviction that Modernism is over as a historical period; a notion that all previous literary styles are valuable but that none has precedence or authority; a suspicion of traditional literary values; and a tendency to distrust the ability of language to convey truth. These concepts have all proved central to Language poetry.

In his 1979 essay, "The New Sentence," Ron Silliman concludes, "If 'language writing' means anything, it means writing which does focus the reader onto the level of the sentence and below, as well as those units above." Silliman has been interested in language as subject, and has even produced whole books devoted to letters of the alphabet. But Language poets also voice overt social and political aims, which they address in many forms and forums, and poets like Lyn Hejinian and Michael Palmer have used autobiography in their work, suggesting that "words alone" are not the whole of their concern. Furthermore, the playful skepticism of Language poetry can be related to the work of diverse mainstream writers like Heather McHugh, H. L. Hix, Alice Fulton, Larissa Szporluk, and Jorie Graham.

New Formalism

> I feel subversive in formal verse.
> —*Julia Alvarez*

If Language poetry has been a controversial movement of recent decades, so has another trend which appears to be its polar opposite—New Formalism. The term "New Formalism" came into vogue in the 1980s when critics noticed that some younger American poets were adopting the unfashionable techniques of rhyme, meter, and narrative, which had been dismissed by most established schools of American poetry. There was something simultaneously traditional and rebellious about these younger poets. On the one hand, they seemed retrograde in revitalizing traditional meters and fixed forms like the sonnet, villanelle, and sestina—not to mention championing the narrative mode, which had been largely moribund since the time of E. A. Robinson and Robert Frost. Yet there was also an undeniable element of generational rebellion in their brash repudiation of current poetic fashions. The New Formalists were all members of the first generation to come of age after the free-verse revolution of the 1960s, when Beat, Confessional, Black Mountain, and Deep Image poetry dominated the literary scene, so their stylistic choices represented a deliberate and overt rejection of the aesthetic authority of their elders. If there was any doubt about this dismissal of the literary status quo, these younger poets made their rejection of Confessional free verse and Deep Image obscurantism unambiguously clear in their essays and manifestos, which incited enormous controversy in the poetry world. Not surprisingly, the first significant New Formalist anthology was entitled, *Rebel Angels* (1996).

Most New Formalists, however, are not merely distinguished by their stylistic choice to write in rhyme and meter; they also emphasized the importance of subject matter. Unlike Language poetry, New Formalist work characteristically treats definable subjects, accessible to the common reader, though the topics range widely and unpredictably from alien visitations or drug use to sexuality, race, or any other aspect of American life. The New Formalists have argued that traditional techniques are not incompatible with contemporary experience, citing examples from pop music as well as poetry to make their case. (Many New Formalists are not dogmatic about meter, often choosing to write in free verse as well.) Among poets directly or indirectly associated with this stance are Charles Martin, R. S. Gwynn, Timothy Steele, Dana Gioia, Marilyn Nelson, Mark Jarman, Kim Addonizio, Mary Jo Salter, and Rafael Campo. Initially attacked by many mainstream critics as retrograde, New Formalist poets have proven a diverse and durable group.

The revival of narrative poetry has united both formal and free verse poets in trying to recapture some of the creative ground poetry lost to fiction in the modern period. Contemporary narrative poets include B. H. Fairchild, Marilyn Nelson, Ai, Carolyn Forché, Rita Dove, Andrew Hudgins, Mark Jarman, David Mason, Kim Addonizio, and Christian Wiman. Some of these writers have learned from the narratives of Frost, Jeffers, Hecht, and Simpson, while others have felt compelled by more immediate social pressure to tell stories in verse. Due to problems of space, the range and vitality of contemporary narrative poems cannot be fully represented in this anthology, especially since some of the finest work is in the form of book-length poems. Readers are urged to seek out books by these and other poets.

The odd thing about the New Formalist revolt was that it had so much in common with that of the Language poets. Although each movement was based on aesthetic premises that were irreconcilable with the other, both New Formalism and Language poetry made essentially the same critique of mainstream poetry. Both camps defined themselves in opposition of what they claimed—fairly or unfairly—was the unreflective and loose Confessional free verse style that had become "commodified" and "standardized" in academic writing programs. Both camps considered themselves more intellectually rigorous and technically proficient than the mainstream. Both defined themselves in terms of technological changes, especially the development of electronic mass media like film, radio, television, and recorded music, albeit in radically different ways. Both movements saw themselves as reforming and revitalizing American poetry with their aesthetic agenda.

The differences between the two movements, however, can hardly be overstated, despite some ingenious critical arguments to the contrary. New Formalism tends to define poetry primarily as an auditory medium—a type of heightened and impassioned speech that is shaped and intensified by aural techniques like meter, rhyme, stanza, and other forms of repetition. Language poetry, by contrast, characteristically defines poetry as "writing" or a "text," usually with reference to "the white page" or mechanically printed production. Of course, these tendencies are not absolute. New Formalists also pay careful attention to the visual appearance of their poems, and Language poets attend to sound. Each group also has a radically different sense of audience. New Formalists have repeatedly stated their populist aim to recapture the larger audience that poetry once commanded. This ambition to expand poetry's appeal has led the movement to be termed "Expansive Poetry" by poet-critics like Wade Newman, Kevin Walzer, and Frederick Turner. Language poets, by contrast, have characteristically addressed their work largely to a coterie of artists, intellectuals, and academics, whom they see (in traditional Marxist terms) as the vanguard of social change. Finally, New Formalists claim there is much to learn from popular culture, especially film and music—which embody the contemporary lyric and narrative impulses—whereas Language poets often view those media with suspicion as examples of commercialized and commodified capitalist culture.

Ultimately, such designations as "Language poetry" and "New Formalism" are helpful only to the degree that they do not prejudice or obscure our reading of the individual poets associated with those movements. The philosopher and poet H. L. Hix has sought in his critical essays to bridge perceptual gaps between traditionalists and the avant-garde. In "New Formalism among the Postmoderns" he concludes, "The dynamic *tension* between traditional forms and nontraditional, between New Formalist and postmodern, can be vivifying and productive."

Spoken Word and the Populist Revival

> The intelligent young have grown impatient with the silence of books.
> —*Jack Foley*

"Spoken Word poetry" is a blanket term used to describe a range of literary phenomena from poetry slams to performance poetry that share a common commitment to the auditory nature of the art. By insisting that the material identity of poetry is spoken language rather than written or typographic language, the Spoken Word movement brings the art back to its ancient form as an oral and performative medium. Like the oral poetry found in preliterate cultures, Spoken Word poetry also tends to include improvisational elements. Consequently, there is sometimes no fixed text of the work but one that is adjusted slightly in performance. In other cases, there is a fixed text, but it depends heavily on the skill of the performer to convey its full expressive possibilities. This auditory, performative aesthetic unites Spoken Word poetry with contemporary forms of popular poetry like rap and cowboy poetry as well as avant-garde forms like performance art and literary trends like New Formalism.

Spoken Word poetry is not aligned to any particular literary style. Spoken Word artists employ virtually every literary style from the traditional rhymed ballad stanzas of cowboy poetry and the syncopated rhyme of rap to the verbal experiments of performance poetry. It is not style that differentiates spoken word from traditional literary poetry; it is the medium of performance and transmission. Because the nature of this poetry is auditory, it lies mostly outside the scope of this anthology, which focuses on those forms of contemporary poetry that can be fully portrayed by printed texts; but it would be irresponsible to attempt a description of the contemporary poetry world without taking it into account. And its impact is increasingly evident on contemporary American poetry of every school. One sees its impact strongly on both Identity poetry and New Formalism.

The subject of Spoken Word poetry, however, touches on a more general literary trend that transcends any specific camp or aesthetic—the reemerging populist impulse in American poetry. Poetry has historically been a medium with a broad and mixed audience. Although the continuity of poetic texts and techniques has historically depended on a learned clerical class, the art itself has usually sought to engage an audience beyond a narrow coterie of literary intellectuals. Modernism broke the deep connections that American poetry had traditionally enjoyed with the general reader (who historically found poetry in newspapers, magazines, almanacs, and other print-era mass media.) That break was reinforced in the decades after World War II by the increasing institutionalization of contemporary poetry and poetry criticism in the university. The enormous cultural anxiety about the loss of poetry to the general culture articulated by critics and poets Edmund Wilson, Randall Jarrell, Delmore Schwartz, Joseph Epstein, and others reflected the increasingly isolated situation of American poetry in the postmodern era. The populist revival of the 1990s reconnected poetry with the nonspecialist audience, and the chief means of that rapprochement was the public reading—the spoken performance of verse.

It is still too early to assess the ultimate impact of the populist revival in American poetry, but it is already clear how profoundly it has changed the literary environment. Poetry has suddenly become prominent in cultural life—quoted on television or in the newspaper, introduced in public events, even appearing on the bestseller list. In major cities one cannot ride the subways, buses, or trains without encountering public poetry. As poet and anthologist David Lehman has quipped, "Poetry's invasion of space formerly verse-free continues apace." This prominent trend will not necessarily invalidate or marginalize more challenging forms of contemporary poetry. The avant-garde is never healthier than when popular artistic norms exist for it to violate. Whatever the future holds for American poetry, one thing is certain. It has entered the twenty-first century as a vital and dynamic art.

ROBERT PINSKY
(b. 1940)

As a critic, teacher, and one of the most active Poets Laureate of the United States, Robert Pinsky has had an enormous impact on the contemporary poetry scene. He is a writer who honors the past but enlivens the present with American idioms. In its ambitious range of subjects, his poetry presents a dialectic of private moments and public voices.

Born the son of an optician in Long Branch, New Jersey, Pinsky grew up in "this half-dead but still gaudy and once glorious setting," a town of "beachfront hotels and penny arcades." While a student at Rutgers University, where one of his professors was the critic and historian Paul Fussell, Pinsky discovered his vocation as a poet. It was also there that he met and married Ellen Jane Bailey, who would become a psychologist, and with whom he would have three daughters. He went on to the doctoral program in English at Stanford, where he was given a one-on-one tutorial in Yvor Winters's "History of the Lyric" course. Later he recalled that "most of my graduate education consisted of reading English and American poetry with Winters as a series of these Directed Readings." Among his fellow graduate students at Stanford was the poet Robert Hass, who became a close friend and occasional collaborator.

After earning his Ph.D. in 1966, Pinsky took teaching jobs, first at the University of Chicago, then at Wellesley College, where one colleague, poet and translator David Ferry, introduced him to Frank Bidart. Through his friendship with Bidart, Pinsky met Robert Lowell and Elizabeth Bishop, the latter of whom he credits as an important influence on his own work. By the time he left Wellesley for a position at Berkeley in 1980, he had published two collections of poems, *Sadness and Happiness* (1975) and *An Explanation of America* (1979). He taught at Berkeley until 1988, then moved to his present position at Boston University, a tenure interrupted in 1997 when he served as Poet Laureate for an unprecedented three terms.

Always an advocate of a public stance for poets, Pinsky has also displayed a more private range in such books as *History of My Heart* (1984), *The Want Bone* (1990), *The Figured Wheel: New and Collected Poems* (1996), and *Jersey Rain* (2000). As a translator, he is particularly well known for his collaborations with Robert Hass on translations of Nobel Prize–winner Czeslaw Milosz in *The Separate Notebooks* (1984) and for his version of Dante's *Inferno* (1994).

Shirt

The back, the yoke, the yardage. Lapped seams,
The nearly invisible stitches along the collar
Turned in a sweatshop by Koreans or Malaysians

Gossiping over tea and noodles on their break
Or talking money or politics while one fitted
This armpiece with its overseam to the band   5

Of cuff I button at my wrist. The presser, the cutter,
The wringer, the mangle. The needle, the union,
The treadle, the bobbin. The code. The infamous blaze

At the Triangle Factory in nineteen-eleven.   10
One hundred and forty-six died in the flames
On the ninth floor, no hydrants, no fire escapes—

The witness in a building across the street
Who watched how a young man helped a girl to step
up to the windowsill, then held her out   15

Away from the masonry wall and let her drop.
And then another. As if he were helping them up
To enter a streetcar, and not eternity.

A third before he dropped her put her arms
Around his neck and kissed him. Then he held   20
Her into space, and dropped her. Almost at once

He stepped to the sill himself, his jacket flared
And fluttered up from his shirt as he came down,
Air filling up the legs of his gray trousers—

Like Hart Crane's Bedlamite, "shrill shirt ballooning."[1]   25
Wonderful how the pattern matches perfectly
Across the placket and over the twin bar-tacked

Corners of both pockets, like a strict rhyme
Or a major chord. Prints, plaids, checks,
Houndstooth, Tattersal, Madras. The clan tartans   30

Invented by mill-owners inspired by the hoax of Ossian,[2]
To control their savage Scottish workers, tamed
By a fabricated heraldry: MacGregor,

Bailey, MacMartin. The kilt, devised for workers
To wear among the dusty clattering looms.   35
Weavers, carders, spinners. The loader,

The docker, the navvy. The planter, the picker, the sorter
Sweating at her machine in a litter of cotton
As slaves in calico headrags sweated in fields:

George Herbert,[3] your descendant is a Black   40
Lady in South Carolina, her name is Irma
And she inspected my shirt. Its color and fit

---

1. From Crane's "To Brooklyn Bridge': see page 423, line 19.
2. In 1760–63, Scottish poet James Macpherson published poems purporting to be translated from the Gaelic bard Ossian, who lived in the third century. Samuel Johnson was among those who exposed the "translations" as a hoax.
3. George Herbert (1593–1633), English poet and Anglican priest.

And feel and its clean smell have satisfied
Both her and me. We have culled its cost and quality
Down to the buttons of simulated bone,   45

The buttonholes, the sizing, the facing, the characters
Printed in black on neckband and tail. The shape,
The label, the labor, the color, the shade. The shirt.

1990

ABC

Any body can die, evidently. Few
Go happily, irradiating joy,

Knowledge, love. Many
Need oblivion, painkillers,
Quickest respite.   5

Sweet time unafflicted,
Various world:

X = your zenith.

2000

◆━ BILLY COLLINS ━◆
(b. 1941)

In 2001 Billy Collins was named the nation's eleventh Poet Laureate—or forty-first, if one counts the earlier Poetry Consultants to the Library of Congress. The press was immediately full of praise for Collins's comic and accessible poems. While some literary critics have disparaged his popularity, Collins has rightly been recognized as a highly imaginative comic writer who has steered an independent course throughout his career. He has criticized the self-congratulatory pose of sincerity and the nearly automatic reliance on autobiographical themes that characterize much contemporary American poetry, finding in it a residue of stale Romanticism. A relatively early poem of his like "Personal History" portrays the love-live of a couple as though it were played out across hundreds of years:

> Now we find ourselves in the post-modern age,
> using one of its many Saturday nights
> to drive to the movies in a Volkswagen.

The very term "Personal History" becomes the conceit of the poem, its rationale and its method, but we have no way of knowing whether any of its detail is rooted in autobiography.

William James Collins was born in New York City, the son of an electrician and a nurse. Both of his grandfathers had been Irish immigrants, and Collins has remained a New Yorker with close ties to his Irish heritage. Raised Roman Catholic, he went to parochial schools and attended Archbishop Stepinac High School in White Plains, New York. After receiving a bachelor's degree from the

College of the Holy Cross in 1963, he studied literature—particularly Romantic poetry—at the University of California, Riverside, where he earned a Ph.D. in 1971. That same year he joined the English Department of Lehman College, a part of the City University of New York in the Bronx, and he has taught there ever since. He has also more recently been a writer-in-residence at Sarah Lawrence College. Married since 1979, Collins lives with his wife, an architect, in a farmhouse in Somers, New York.

Much of Collins's poetry is disarmingly simple, not only in its conceits, but also in its diction and free verse technique. Frequently literary and playfully rhetorical, his poems arise from reading as much as from other life experiences. Often they are about poetry, poets, or other literary subjects. Although they sometimes use material from his personal life, they are rarely Confessional, instead turning personal details into archetypes of everyday life. "I start out on a sociable, welcoming note," he once told the *New York Times,* "standing at the door to the poem." But "by the end of the poem the reader should be in a different place from where he started. I would like him to be slightly disoriented at the end, like I drove him outside of town at night and dropped him off in a cornfield."

Collins's rise to fame was slow in coming. His first collection, *Pokerface,* appeared in a limited edition in 1977, and was followed by *Video Poems* (1980), *The Apple That Astonished Paris* (1988), *Questions About Angels* (1991), and *The Art of Drowning* (1995). The crucial turn in his reputation came with the publication of *Picnic, Lightning* (1998) when Garrison Keillor invited Collins to appear on his popular National Public Radio show, *A Prairie Home Companion,* which led to other NPR appearances. As a broad new audience discovered his work on the radio, Collins's books, which had long sold well by university press standards, suddenly began selling at an extraordinary rate. In 2000 he made headlines when Random House offered him a six-figure advance for a three-book deal—an unprecedented offer for an American poet. For the first of these books Collins wanted to use poems selected from his university press collections, but the University of Pittsburgh Press nearly nixed the deal. Amid the abundant publicity Collins had to deal with the jealousy of his fellow poets as well as the strain of negotiations. In the end, his *Sailing Alone Around the Room: New and Selected Poems* (2001), appeared from Random House and achieved remarkable sales. His appointment as Poet Laureate served to increase his already considerable popularity, making him one of the most successful public figures in contemporary American poetry.

◄◦►━━◄►━━◄◦►

Embrace

You know the parlor trick.
Wrap your arms around your own body
and from the back it looks like
someone is embracing you,
her hands grasping your shirt,   5
her fingernails teasing your neck.

From the front it is another story.
You never looked so alone,
your crossed elbows and screwy grin.

You could be waiting for a tailor   10
to fit you for a straitjacket,
one that would hold you really tight.

                                                                1988

Lowell, Mass.

Kerouac was born in the same town
as my father, but my father never
had time to write *On the Road*

let alone drive around the country
in circles.   5

He wrote notes for the kitchen table
and a novel of checks
and a few speeches to lullaby
businessmen after a fat lunch

and some of his writing is within   10
me for I house catalogues of jokes
and handbooks of advice
on horses, snow tires, women,

along with some short stories
about the deadbeats at the office,   15
but he was quicker to pick up
a telephone than a pen.

Like Jack, he took a drink but
beatific to him meant the Virgin Mary.

He called jazz jungle music   20
and he would have told Neal Cassady
to let him off at the next light.

                                                                1988

The Dead

The dead are always looking down on us, they say,
while we are putting on our shoes or making a sandwich,
they are looking down through the glass-bottom boats of heaven
as they row themselves slowly through eternity.

They watch the tops of our heads moving below on earth,   5
and when we lie down in a field or on a couch,
drugged perhaps by the hum of a warm afternoon,
they think we are looking back at them,

which makes them lift their oars and fall silent
and wait, like parents, for us to close our eyes.   10

                                                                1991

➤◄ ROBERT HASS ➤◄
(b. 1941)

Serving as Poet Laureate of the United States from 1995 to 1997, Robert Hass set a highly activist standard for the position. Recognizing that poetry had acquired a new grassroots popularity that was often unreported in the mass media, he worked to elevate the public profile of the art. As the first Poet Laureate from the West Coast, Hass also signaled that new attention ought to be paid to the literary life of that region.

Hass (whose surname rhymes with "grass") was born in San Francisco, the son of a businessman, and he was raised a short distance to the north in San Rafael where he attended Catholic school. In 1962, while still a student at St. Mary's College, he married Earlene Leif, and they raised three children together. After graduating from college in 1963, Hass went on to Stanford, where one of his professors was Yvor Winters. "He bullied, cajoled, ignored, and laid down the law," Hass remembers. "He did everything I now associate with bad pedagogy—and it was the most powerful course I can ever remember." He completed his Ph.D. in 1971, while teaching at the State University of New York at Buffalo, then moved back to California to teach at his alma mater, St. Mary's, from 1971 to 1989, after which he became a professor at the University of California, Berkeley. Among his numerous awards was a MacArthur Foundation "Genius" Grant in 1984. Except for a few years on the East Coast, Hass has lived most of his life in his native state.

Hass's West Coast identity shaped much of his work. The proximity of wilderness and the sea influenced his writing about nature and his environmentalist consciousness. His West Coast eclecticism has also made him a sympathetic reader of diverse poetries. His first collection of poems, *Field Guide* (1973), won the Yale Series of Younger Poets Award. It was followed by *Praise* (1979), the book containing his most often anthologized poem, "Meditation at Lagunitas." In both of these books, Hass's lucid and sensual meditations convey questions about the *how* of writing. "A word is elegy to what it signifies," he says in his best-known poem, wondering whether the experience of the body can be fully conveyed in language. Sensory and sensual pleasure has been a significant theme for Hass. He frequently writes about happiness, especially the sheer pleasure of existence in the physical world.

Another enormous influence upon Hass's work has been his collaborative translation of the great Polish émigré poet, Czeslaw Milosz, who happened to be his neighbor and to share his publisher. Among the books of Milosz translations to which Hass has contributed are *The Separate Notebooks* (1984), *Unattainable Earth* (1986), *Collected Poems, 1931–1987* (1988), *Road-Side Dog* (1998), and *Treatise on Poetry* (2001). Milosz's example may have contributed to the social and political concerns of poems in his fourth collection, *Human Wishes* (1989). His most recent book of poems, *Sun Under Wood* (1996), which explored painful confessional themes like his mother's alcoholism and the poet's divorce, won the National Book Critics Circle Award. In 1995 Hass married a second time—the poet Brenda Hillman.

➤◄━◆━►◄

Black Mountain, Los Altos

Clumps of ghostly buckeye
    bleached bones
weirdly grey in the runoff
between ridges, the flats
in fog. Five deer grazing   5
on the long hill, the soft
cluck of mourning doves,
creeks running. I feel
furry as sage here
after an hour's walk   10
in clear midmorning air.
                 Only
three species of tree in
all these hills: blue oak,
buckeye, and patches of   15
wind-rasped laurel.
In the old quiet the Indians
could have heard bells
at Mission Santa Clara
where the brown-cowled padres   20
taught the sorrowful mysteries
with a whip. They
manufacture napalm
in the fog where Redwood
City sprawls into the bay.   25
I think of the village
of Bien Hoa, the early spring
death in the buckeyes
and up the long valley
my eyes flash, another   30
knife, clean as malice.

                                1973

Heroic Simile

When the swordsman fell in Kurosawa's *Seven Samurai*[1]
in the gray rain,
in Cinemascope and the Tokugawa dynasty,
he fell straight as a pine, he fell
as Ajax fell in Homer   5
in chanted dactyls and the tree was so huge
the woodsman returned for two days
to that lucky place before he was done with the sawing
and on the third day he brought his uncle.

---

1. Renowned Japanese director Akira Kurosawa made *Seven Samurai* in 1954. The film is famous for its swordplay.

They stacked logs in the resinous air,   10
hacking the small limbs off,
tying those bundles separately.
The slabs near the root
were quartered and still they were awkwardly large;
the logs from midtree they halved: 15
ten bundles and four great piles of fragrant wood,
moons and quarter moons and half moons
ridged by the saw's tooth.

The woodsman and the old man his uncle
are standing in midforest   20
on a floor of pine silt and spring mud.
They have stopped working
because they are tired and because
I have imagined no pack animal
or primitive wagon. They are too canny   25
to call in neighbors and come home
with a few logs after three days' work.
They are waiting for me to do something
or for the overseer of the Great Lord
to come and arrest them.   30

How patient they are!
The old man smokes a pipe and spits.
The young man is thinking he would be rich
if he were already rich and had a mule.
Ten days of hauling   35
and on the seventh day they'll probably
be caught, go home empty-handed
or worse. I don't know
whether they're Japanese or Mycenaean
and there's nothing I can do.   40
The path from here to that village
is not translated. A hero, dying,
gives off stillness to the air.
A man and a woman walk from the movies
to the house in the silence of separate fidelities.   45
There are limits to imagination.

                                                                        1979

Meditation at Lagunitas

All the new thinking is about loss.
In this it resembles all the old thinking.
The idea, for example, that each particular erases
the luminous clarity of a general idea. That the clown-
faced woodpecker probing the dead sculpted trunk   5
of that black birch is, by his presence,
some tragic falling off from a first world

of undivided light. Or the other notion that,
because there is in this world no one thing
to which the bramble of *blackberry* corresponds,   10
a word is elegy to what it signifies.
We talked about it late last night and in the voice
of my friend, there was a thin wire of grief, a tone
almost querulous. After a while I understood that,
talking this way, everything dissolves: *justice,*   15
pine, hair, woman, you and *I.* There was a woman
I made love to and I remembered how, holding
her small shoulders in my hands sometimes,
I felt a violent wonder at her presence
like a thirst for salt, for my childhood river   20
with its island willows, silly music from the pleasure boat,
muddy places where we caught the little orange-silver fish
called *pumpkinseed.* It hardly had to do with her.
Longing, we say, because desire is full
of endless distances. I must have been the same to her.   25
But I remember so much, the way her hands dismantled bread,
the thing her father said that hurt her, what
she dreamed. There are moments when the body is as numinous
as words, days that are the good flesh continuing.
Such tenderness, those afternoons and evenings,   30
saying *blackberry, blackberry, blackberry.*

1979

◦━◄ LYN HEJINIAN ►◄━◦
(b. 1941)

One of the founding members of the Language poetry movement, Hejinian was born Lyn Hall in San Francisco and raised in Alameda, California. She graduated from Harvard University in 1963, the year she began publishing poems in literary magazines. Her 1961 marriage to John Hejinian, with whom she had two children, lasted until 1972. Five years later she married a Bay Area jazz musician, Larry Ochs, a member of the ROVA Saxophone Quartet. During the seventies, she gave increased attention to her writing and founded Tuumba Press in 1976, with which she published several chapbooks, *A Thought Is the Bride of What Thinking* (1976), *Gesualdo* (1978), and *The Guard* (1978), as well as books by other Bay Area Language writers. Her first full collection, *Writing Is an Aid to Memory* (1978), explores the disjunctions of memory through correspondingly disjunctive lines and syntax. Her prose poem, *My Life* (1980), continues these explorations through its open-ended approach to autobiography. Hejinian gives many possible versions of her childhood self, stresses the instability of adult recollections of childhood, and, by omitting transitions between most of her sentences, invites the reader to participate in her narrative. In 1987 she made *My Life* even more open-ended by publishing a significantly revised and expanded edition, which effectively gave critics two versions to consider. Since *My Life* Hejinian has continued to focus on "a flow of contexts," the "transitions, transmutations, the endless radiating of denotation into relation" that she defines as the essential properties of language in the introduction to her book of essays, *The Language of Inquiry* (2000).

Although her early poetry was political in calling "the self" into question, her many visits to Russia in the 1980s increased her concern with poetry's social and political dimensions, and her subsequent books have raised even more explicit questions about identity. In particular, Hejinian challenges national identities and gender identities while continuing to highlight language's fluidity in *Oxota: A Short Russian Novel* (1991), *The Cell* (1992), and *A Border Comedy* (1999).

FROM My Life

It was only a coincidence

The tree rows in orchards are capable of patterns. What were Caesar's battles but Caesar's prose. A name trimmed with colored ribbons. We "took" a trip as if that were part of the baggage we carried. In other words, we "took our time." The experience of a great passion, a great love, would remove me, elevate me, enable me at last to be both special and ignorant of the other people around me, so that I would be free at last from the necessity of appealing to them, responding to them. That is, to be nearly useless but at rest. There were cut flowers in vases and some arrangements of artificial flowers and ceramic bouquets, but in those days they did not keep any living houseplants. The old fragmentary texts, early Egyptian and Persian writings, say, or the works of Sappho, were intriguing and lovely, a mystery adhering to the lost lines. At the time, the perpetual Latin of love kept things hidden. It was not his fate to be as famous as Segovia. Nonetheless, I wrote my name in every one of his books. Language is the history that gave me shape and hypochondria. And followed it with a date, as if by my name I took the book and by the date, historically, contextualized its contents, affixed to them a reading. And memory a wall. My grandmother had been a great beauty and she always won at cards. As for we who "love to be astonished," the ear is less active than the eye. The artichoke has done its best, armored, with scales, barbed, and hiding in its

interior the soft hairs so aptly called the choke. I
suppose I had always hoped that, through an act
of will and the effort of practice, I might be
someone else, might alter my personality and   35
even my appearance, that I might in fact create
myself, but instead I found myself trapped in the
very character which made such a thought possible and such a wish mine. Any work dealing
with questions of possibility must lead to new   40
work. In between pieces, they shuffled their feet.
The white legs of the pear trees, protected from
the sun. Imagine, please: morbid myopia. The
puppy is perplexed by the lizard which moves
but has no smell. We were like plump birds   45
along the shore, unable to run from the water.
Could there be swans in the swamp. Of course,
one continues to write, and thus to "be a writer,"
because one has not yet written that "ultimate"
work. Exercise will do it. I insert a description: 50
of agonizing spring morning freshness, when
through the open window a smell of cold dust
and buds of broken early grass, of schoolbooks
and rotting apples, trails the distant sound of an
airplane and a flock of crows. I thought that for 55
a woman health and comfort must come after
love. Any photographer will tell you the same.
So I wouldn't wear boots in the snow, nor socks
in the cold. Shufflers scuff. That sense of responsibility was merely the context of the search for 60
a lover, or, rather, for a love. Let someone from
the other lane in. Each boat leaned toward us
as it turned and we, pretending to know more
than we did, identified each class as it was blown
by. Politics get wider as one gets older. I was   65
learning a certain geometry of purely decorative
shapes. One could base a model for form on a
crystal or the lungs. She showed the left profile,
the good one. Foghorns is that you can't see
them, need to hear them. More by hive than by   70
heart the mathematics of droves makes it notice-
able. It was May, 1958 and reading was anti-
anonymous. She disapproved of background
music.

[1980] 1987

Nostalgia is the elixir drained

Nostalgia is the elixir drained
from guilt . . . I've been writing . . .

with the fingers of my non-writing hand
I patted the dashboard. "Hi, car."
It responded "Hello Mommy."   5

The city is uncarlike. She who had lived
all her life in the city and absorbed
all its laws in her blood . . . madness, really
. . . she waited for the light
to change and stepped into the traffic   10

on red. Objects always flicker.
Rain threatens but what can it do.
Knocking, buzzing, sloshing . . .
somewhere between empty and full . . .
the excitement is mental, internal   15

as they remain urgently still.
We have stayed in the city
over which it really is raining.
Reflections water the gardens.
The fields that pressed in the passing   20

landscapes were immobilized by trees.
Uneven individual glowing.
The photograph craves history.
The automobile drove to the photograph.
It faces me as I awake.   25

                                                              1985

◄ CHARLES MARTIN ►
(b. 1942)

Charles Martin was born in the Bronx, of German and Irish descent. Raised
Catholic, he attended parochial school and a Marist high school where he began
studying Latin in ninth grade. He took a bachelor's degree in English with a minor
in classics at Fordham University in 1964, and then attended graduate school at
the State University of New York at Buffalo from 1964 to 1968. He completed all
of his coursework for his doctorate but did not finish his dissertation (on Ezra
Pound and the Latin poet Catullus) until 1985. He married Leslie Barnett in 1966,
with whom he had two children. (The couple divorced in 1998.) At Buffalo Martin began writing poetry seriously and once shared a house with Robert Hass. Returning to New York City, Martin taught briefly at Notre Dame of Staten Island,
and then in 1971 he joined the faculty of Queensborough Community College in
their basic education program, often teaching English as a Second Language. Although Martin has taught as a visiting professor at Johns Hopkins and at various
writing conferences, he remains at Queensborough.

    In 1978 Martin published his first poetry collection, *Room for Error*, a remark-
able debut that combined Modernist proclivities with traditional rhyme and meter,
both tempered by a classical sense of detachment. Mixing high and low culture, Martin wrote about everything from Roman literature and French cinema to cunnilingus

and flying saucers. Although *Room for Error* attracted little critical notice at the time, it is now recognized as one of the earliest manifestations of what came in the next decade to be called New Formalism. The following year Martin published his translation of the *Poems of Catullus* (1979) in a limited edition. Once again his book garnered little attention at the time, but when a slightly revised trade edition appeared in 1989, it was hailed as a major accomplishment. Martin's position as an erudite and innovative interpreter of the Latin classics was consolidated in 1992 with his critical volume, *Catullus,* a brilliantly revisionist view of the ancient lyric poet as an artistic innovator in a time of cultural ferment not unlike early Modernism.

Martin's second full-length collection, *Steal the Bacon* (1987), offered the most complete and accomplished expression of his style. Mordant, urbane, and deeply skeptical, Martin favors language that is both resonantly musical and slyly allusive. He almost always employs traditional forms, but he uses them for decidedly untraditional ends. His frequent use of classical myth is usually satiric or ironic. Most often he takes an everyday situation or setting and uses it to reflect on larger moral or imaginative issues. In "E.S.L.," for example, he turns a classroom discussion of English grammar into a meditation on the idea of America among non-native speakers, from the perspective of its recent immigrants. Martin is a moralist in the old literary sense of the word, a poet concerned with defining human values in a changing society, making his points with both wit and compassion. His third full-length volume, *What the Darkness Proposes,* appeared in 1996 and his selected poems, *Starting from Sleep,* in 2002. Martin lives in Manhattan with his second wife, the poet J. B. Keller.

◄◦►━━◄◦►

Taken Up

Tired of earth, they dwindled on their hill,
Watching and waiting in the moonlight until
The aspens' leaves quite suddenly grew still,

No longer quaking as the disc descended,
That glowing wheel of lights whose coming ended   5
All waiting and watching. When it landed

The ones within it one by one came forth,
Stalking out awkwardly upon the earth,
And those who watched them were confirmed in faith:

Mysterious voyagers from outer space,   10
Attenuated, golden—shreds of lace
Spun into seeds of the sunflower's spinning face—

Light was their speech, spanning mind to mind:
We come here not believing what we find—
Can it be your desire to leave behind   15

The earth, which those called angels bless,
Exchanging amplitude for emptiness?
And in a single voice they answered *Yes,*

Discord of human melodies all blent
To the unearthly strain of their assent.   20
Come then, the Strangers said, and those that were taken, went.

1978

E.S.L.[1]

My frowning students carve
   Me monsters out of prose:
This one—a gargoyle—thumbs its contemptuous nose
At how, in English, subject must agree
With verb—for any such agreement shows   5
   Too great a willingness to serve,
      A docility

   Which wiry Miss Choi
   Finds un-American.
She steals a hard look at me. I wink. Her grin   10
Is my reward. *In his will, our peace, our Pass:*
Gargoyle erased, subject and verb now in
   Agreement, reach object, enjoy
      Temporary truce.

   Tonight my students must   15
   Agree or disagree:
America is still a land of opportunity.
The answer is always, uniformly, *Yes*—even though
"It has no doubt that here were to much free,"
   As Miss Torrico will insist.   20
      She and I both know

   That Language binds us fast,
   And those of us without
Are bound and gagged by those within. Each fledgling polyglot
Must shake old habits: tapping her sneakered feet,   25
Miss Choi exorcises incensed ancestors, flout-
   ing the ghosts of her Chinese past.
      Writhing in the seat

   Next to Miss Choi, Mister
   Fedakis, in anguish   30
Labors to express himself in a tongue which
Proves *Linear B*[2] to me, when I attempt to read it
Later. They're here for English as a Second Language,
   Which I'm teaching this semester.
      God knows they need it,   35

---

1. Academic shorthand for "English as a Second Language."
2. A form of writing dating back to the Mycenaean civilization of Crete from 1400 to 1200 B.C.E.

And so, thank God, do they.
    The night's made easier
By our agreement: I am here to help deliver
Them into the good life they write me papers about.
English is pre-requisite for that endeavor,   40
    Explored in their nightly essays
        Boldly setting out

    To reconnoiter the fair
    New World they would enter:
Surburban Paradise, the endless shopping center   45
Where one may browse for hours before one chooses
Some new necessity—gold-flecked magenta
    Wallpaper to re-do the spare
        Bath no one uses,

    Or a machine which can,   50
    In seven seconds, crush
A newborn calf into such seamless mush
As a *mousse* might be made of—or our true sublime:
The gleaming counters where frosted cosmeticians brush
    Decades from the allotted span,   55
        Abrogating Time

    As the spring tide brushes
    A single sinister
Footprint from the otherwise unwrinkled shore
Of America the Blank. In absolute confusion   60
Poor Mister Fedakis rumbles with despair
    And puts the finishing smutches
        To his conclusion

    While Miss Choi erases:
One more gargoyle routed.   65
Their pure, erroneous lines yield an illuminated
Map of the new found land. We will never arrive there,
Since it exists only in what we say about it,
    As all the rest of my class is
        Bound to discover.   70

                    1987

Metaphor of Grass in California

The seeds of certain grasses that once grew
Over the graves of those who fell at Troy
Were brought to California in the hooves
Of Spanish cattle. Trodden into the soil,

They liked it well enough to germinate,   5
Awakening into another scene
Of conquest: blade fell upon flashing blade
Until the native grasses fled the field,

And the native flowers bowed to their dominion.
Small clumps of them fought on as they retreated   10
Toward isolated ledges of serpentine,
Repellent to their conquerors. . . .
                              In defeat,

They were like men who see their city taken,
And think of grass—how soon it will conceal   15
All of the scattered bodies of the slain;
As such men fall, these fell, but silently.

                                        1987

◄ SHARON OLDS ►
(b. 1942)

Sharon Olds was born in San Francisco and raised in Berkeley, California. Although her autobiographical poetry would suggest that she was the victim of prolonged child abuse at the hands of a violent, alcoholic father, she has not corroborated the vivid scenarios of her poems with detailed biographical information. In a 1996 interview she stated, "Ten years ago, I made a vow not to talk about my life. Obviously, the apparently very personal nature of my writing made this seem to me like . . . a good idea, for both sides of the equation—for both the muses and the writer." She did, however, in the same interview describe her family's religion as "hellfire Episcopalian," grounded on a staunchly patriarchal system of power. She attended high school in an East Coast boarding school and then matriculated at Stanford, graduating with a bachelor's degree in 1964. She went on to earn a Ph.D. from Columbia University in 1972, where she wrote a dissertation on Emerson.

After completing her degree, Olds decided not to pursue a scholarly career, opting instead to focus on writing poetry. In interviews, she describes a moment when, having received her degree, she stood on the university steps and made a devil's bargain, "I would give up all I learned if I could just write my own poems." Olds's determination to seek her own path as a poet, however, owes much to the examples of Emerson—and his eminent disciple, Walt Whitman, whom she also admires. Olds was also inspired by Muriel Rukeyser, with whom she took a workshop in 1976 at the YMHA in New York City. Olds's devotion to breaking conventional silences on certain uncomfortable topics and writing a poetry of witness that merges her personal experience as a woman with her political concerns about social injustice owes much to Rukeyser's example. Like both Rukeyser and Whitman, Olds has worked hard to bring poetry to a wide audience, arguing that poetry is not a rarified enterprise fit only for an academic elite, but an art capable of strengthening the lives of all people. Thus, despite her full-time job as a professor and director of the graduate creative writing program at New York University, she runs a poetry workshop at New York's Goldwater Hospital for the severely disabled, and she encourages her graduate students to teach workshops in schools and prisons. From 1998 till 2000, she served as New York State's Poet Laureate. But it is through her poetry books that Olds has reached the widest audience. Her second collection, *The Dead and the Living* (1984), which won the National Book Critics Circle Award, has sold over 50,000 copies, and high sales figures for her other books—*Satan Says* (1980), *The Gold Cell* (1987), *The Father* (1992), *The*

Wellspring (1996), and *Blood, Tin, Straw* (1999)—attest to the popularity of her work, especially among women.

Following the example of earlier Confessional poets like Robert Lowell and Anne Sexton, Olds makes her family life the primary subject of her poetry. The poems usually present some version of the author as persona, but that self is inevitably refracted through its relationships to others—parents, spouse, children. Writing as a daughter, wife, lover, mother, Olds explores these identities and considers how they influence one another. Like Whitman, Olds writes a poetry of the body. Her work is strongly visceral, whether she celebrates sex or relentlessly details child abuse or the death of her father from cancer. Interested in breaking taboos, Olds tests the limits of subject matter in poetry, shocking some readers with graphic descriptions of violent family life.

Despite the charged personal content of her poems, Olds insists on the concept of artistic distance and stresses in interviews that readers should think of the self in her work as "a speaker," rather than the real "Sharon Olds." Such a term, she argues, "frees each maker of art . . . from being dealt with as an autobiographer, perhaps making it possible for us to try for more accuracy—with a less anxious self-consciousness." Indeed, some of her seemingly autobiographical poems are almost certainly carefully constructed fictions spoken by skillfully invented voices. For Olds, accuracy arises not simply from sincerity, but from language, for she grounds her poems on striking figurative language, especially similes. Her work has sparked controversy, mostly for her use of political analogies to describe child abuse. In one poem, for example, she compares the abusive father to the Shah of Iran and his children to the Shah's torture victims. Olds is one of the most widely read of contemporary American poets, inspiring her audience through her insightful depictions of sexual love and motherhood and setting an example for young poets who admire her skill with language and her bold approach to subject matter.

◄●──◆──●►

The Language of the Brag

I have wanted excellence in the knife-throw,
I have wanted to use my exceptionally strong and accurate arms
and my straight posture and quick electric muscles
to achieve something at the center of a crowd,
the blade piercing the bark deep,   5
the haft slowly and heavily vibrating like the cock.

I have wanted some epic use for my excellent body,
some heroism, some American achievement
beyond the ordinary for my extraordinary self,
magnetic and tensile, I have stood by the sandlot   10
and watched the boys play.

I have wanted courage, I have thought about fire
and the crossing of the waterfalls, I have dragged around

My belly big with cowardice and safety,
my stool black with iron pills,   15

my huge breasts oozing mucus,
my legs swelling, my hands swelling,
my face swelling and darkening, my hair
falling out, my inner sex
stabbed again and again with terrible pain like a knife.   20
I have lain down.

I have lain down and sweated and shaken
and passed blood and feces and water and
slowly alone in the center of a circle I have
passed the new person out   25
and they have lifted the new person free of the act
and wiped the new person free of that
language of blood like praise all over the body.

I have done what you wanted to do, Walt Whitman,
Allen Ginsberg, I have done this thing,   30
I and the other women this exceptional
act with the exceptional heroic body,
this giving birth, this glistening verb,
and I am putting my proud American boast
right here with the others.   35

1980

The One Girl at the Boys' Party

When I take my girl to the swimming party
I set her down among the boys. They tower and
bristle, she stands there smooth and sleek,
her math scores unfolding in the air around her.
They will strip to their suits, her body hard and   5
indivisible as a prime number,
they'll plunge in the deep end, she'll subtract
her height from ten feet, divide it into
hundreds of gallons of water, the numbers
bouncing in her mind like molecules of chlorine   10
in the bright blue pool. When they climb out,
her ponytail will hang its pencil lead
down her back, her narrow silk suit
with hamburgers and french fries printed on it
will glisten in the brilliant air, and they will   15
see her sweet face, solemn and
sealed, a factor of one, and she will
see their eyes, two each,
their legs, two each, and the curves of their sexes,
one each, and in her head she'll be doing her   20
wild multiplying, as the drops
sparkle and fall to the power of a thousand from her body.

1984

Rites of Passage

As the guests arrive at my son's party
they gather in the living room—
short men, men in first grade
with smooth jaws and chins.
Hands in pockets, they stand around   5
jostling, jockeying for place, small fights
breaking out and calming. One says to another
How old are you? Six. I'm seven. So?
They eye each other, seeing themselves
tiny in the other's pupils. They clear their   10
throats a lot, a room of small bankers,
they fold their arms and frown. *I could beat you
up*, a seven says to a six,
the dark cake, round and heavy as a
turret, behind them on the table. My son,   15
freckles like specks of nutmeg on his cheeks,
chest narrow as the balsa keel of a
model boat, long hands
cool and thin as the day they guided him
out of me, speaks up as a host   20
for the sake of the group.
We could easily kill a two-year-old,
he says in his clear voice. The other
men agree, they clear their throats
like Generals, they relax and get down to   25
playing war, celebrating my son's life.

1984

Sex Without Love

How do they do it, the ones who make love
without love? Beautiful as dancers,
gliding over each other like ice-skaters
over the ice, fingers hooked
inside each other's bodies, faces   5
red as steak, wine, wet as the
children at birth whose mothers are going to
give them away. How do they come to the
come to the   come to the   God   come to the
still waters, and not love   10
the one who came there with them, light
rising slowly as steam off their joined
skin? These are the true religious,
the purists, the pros, the ones who will not
accept a false Messiah, love the   15
priest instead of the God. They do not
mistake the lover for their own pleasure,

they are like great runners: they know they are alone
with the road surface, the cold, the wind,
the fit of their shoes, their over-all cardio-   20
vascular health—just factors, like the partner
in the bed, and not the truth, which is the
single body alone in the universe
against its own best time.

1984

━━━•◄ LOUISE GLÜCK ►•━━━
(b. 1943)

Born in New York City, Louise Elisabeth Glück (pronounced "Glick") grew up on
Long Island. Her father was a successful businessman who had unfulfilled dreams
of being a writer. In "Education of the Poet," Glück observes, "Both my parents
admired intellectual accomplishment; my mother, in particular, revered creative
gifts." As to her own literary development, Glück remarks, "I read early, and
wanted, from a very early age, to speak in return. When, as a child, I read Shakespeare's songs, or later, Blake and Yeats and Keats and Eliot, I did not feel exiled,
marginal. I felt, rather, that this was the tradition of my language: *my* tradition, as
English was my language. My inheritance. My wealth." In the same autobiographical essay, Glück notes the impact of psychoanalysis on her thinking.

After beginning her undergraduate education at Sarah Lawrence College,
Glück transferred to Columbia University. There she eventually studied with Stanley Kunitz, to whom she would dedicate her first collection of poems, *Firstborn*
(1968). She has since taught at Goddard College, the University of California at
Los Angeles, Harvard, Brandeis, and since 1984 at Williams College in Vermont.
Among the many awards her work has received are the National Book Critics Circle Award and the Pulitzer Prize. Her early collections include *The House on the
Marshland* (1975); *Descending Figure* (1980), which she called her favorite among
her early books; *The Triumph of Achilles* (1985); and *Ararat* (1990).

Glück's early work flirts with surrealism and occasionally employs grotesque
imagery but already displays the austere and deliberate manner for which Glück's
poetry is now known. She slowly but unmistakably perfected a deeply expressive
lyric style in which emotion seems simultaneously repressed and evoked. Although
autobiography—in subjects like divorce and family life—enters her poems, Glück
is characteristically concerned with universalizing from personal experience. She
often pursues a problem she has set in terms of grammar or subject matter or images derived from mythological archetypes. She has also quite frequently adopted
personae, from the voice of a figure in a painting to that of a wildflower. Critics
have noted the plainness of her diction while praising her subtle uses of sound
echoes and off-rhymes. They have called her "direct" in her intimacy, yet have
also noted a mysterious and philosophical quality in her work, a kind of distance,
probing and provocative.

In Glück's later books like *The Wild Iris* (1992), *Meadowlands* (1996), *Vita
Nova* (1999), and *The Seven Ages* (2001), a kind of metaphysical yearning
emerges. Her introduction to *The Best American Poetry 1993* begins: "The world

is complete without us. Intolerable fact. To which the poet responds by rebelling, wanting to prove otherwise."

The School Children

The children go forward with their little satchels.
And all morning the mothers have labored
to gather the late apples, red and gold,
like words of another language.

And on the other shore   5
are those who wait behind great desks
to receive these offerings.

How orderly they are—the nails
on which the children hang
their overcoats of blue or yellow wool.   10

And the teachers shall instruct them in silence
and the mothers shall scour the orchards for a way out,
drawing to themselves the gray limbs of the fruit trees
bearing so little ammunition.

                                                             1975

The Gift

Lord, you may not recognize me
speaking for someone else.
I have a son. He is
so little, so ignorant.
He likes to stand   5
at the screen door, calling
oggie, oggie, entering
language, and sometimes
a dog will stop and come up
the walk, perhaps   10
accidentally. May he believe
this is not an accident.
At the screen
welcoming each beast
in love's name, Your emissary.   15

                                                             1980

Mock Orange[1]

It is not the moon, I tell you.
It is these flowers
lighting the yard

I hate them.
I hate them as I hate sex,   5
the man's mouth
sealing my mouth, the man's
paralyzing body—

and the cry that always escapes,
the low, humiliating   10
premise of union—

In my mind tonight
I hear the question and pursuing answer
fused in one sound
that mourns and mounts and then   15
is split into the old selves,
the tired antagonisms. Do you see?
We are made fools of.
And the scent of mock orange
drifts through the window.   20

How can I rest?
How can I be content
where there is still
that odor in the world.

1985

The Gold Lily

As I perceive
I am dying now and know
I will not speak again, will not
survive the earth, be summoned
out of it again, not   5
a flower yet, a pine only, raw dirt
catching my ribs, I call you,
father and master: all around,
my companions are failing, thinking
you do not see. How   10
can they know you see
unless you save us?
In the summer twilight, are you
close enough to hear

1. A shrub with white or gold flowers, sometimes quite fragrant.

your child's terror? Or   15
are you not my father,
you who raised me?

1992

Circe's Power[2]

I never turned anyone into a pig.
Some people are pigs; I make them
look like pigs.

I'm sick of your world
that lets the outside disguise the inside.   5

Your men weren't bad men;
undisciplined life
did that to them. As pigs,

under the care of
me and my ladies, they   10
sweetened right up.

Then I reversed the spell,
showing you my goodness
as well as my power. I saw

we could be happy here,   15
as men and women are
when their needs are simple. In the same breath,

I foresaw your departure,
your men with my help braving
the crying and pounding sea. You think   20

a few tears upset me? My friend,
every sorceress is
a pragmatist at heart; nobody

sees essence who can't
face limitation. If I wanted only to hold you   25

I could hold you prisoner.

1996

◄ MICHAEL PALMER ►
(b. 1943)

Michael Palmer was born in New York City in an Italian American family. His father, Giuseppe Palmerini, who had immigrated as a young man from Italy, worked as a hotel manager, and the young poet grew up in Manhattan hotels. Determined that his son receive the finest education possible, his father sent him to the Choate

---

2. In Homer's *Odyssey,* Circe was a witch who turned men into pigs.

Academy, an exclusive boarding school in Wallingford, Connecticut. Palmer then attended Harvard, where he majored in French history and literature. After graduation in 1965, he spent a year in Europe, mostly in Florence where he learned Italian, before returning to Harvard to earn a master's degree in comparative literature in 1968. At Harvard he attended courses by the famous Russian linguist Roman Jakobson who proved influential on Palmer's ideas of language, poetry, and prosody.

In 1969 Palmer moved to San Francisco to escape "the institutional weight" of the Boston literary world. For several years he taught at California State University at San Jose. He also worked as a gardener and landscaper, a trade he had learned from his maternal Italian grandfather. In 1972 he married Cathy Simon, an architect. Although he has taught at New College of California, University of California at Berkeley, and San Francisco State University, Palmer has avoided a full-time academic career. A prolific poet, he published sixteen books and chapbooks between his debut volume, *Plan of the City of O* (1971), and *The Promises of Glass* (2000), as well as many translations and essays. He served as a contributing editor to *Sulfur,* a literary journal committed to experimental writing. Palmer has also worked for thirty years writing words and narration for San Francisco's Margaret Jenkins Dance Company.

Of the many writers associated with Language poetry, Palmer has often seemed the one who most successfully merges the movement's restlessly deconstructive urge with its more familiar Modernist roots. Palmer's poems often seem deliberately obscure or elusive, but they are also lyrical and powerfully evocative. Part of Palmer's expressive force comes from his carefully shaped and highly compressed poetic language—a concision that stands in sharp contrast to the loosely expansive style of much Language poetry. Although distinctively personal, his poetic style clearly announces its allegiance to Modernist models like George Oppen, Louis Zukofsky, Wallace Stevens, and Ezra Pound, as well as earlier European masters like Arthur Rimbaud and Charles Baudelaire (whose prose poetry seems to have been a special touchstone for Palmer's work).

Palmer's poetic concerns are primarily philosophical, even epistemological. He eschews the autobiographical mode as well as all linear narrative strategies of writing. His characteristic method is suggestive and elliptical. "The problem is that poetry, at least my poetry and much that interests me," he has written, "tends to concentrate on primary functions and qualities of language such as naming and the arbitrary structuring of a code." Such concerns place Palmer among postmodernists in general and Language poets in particular, but his work rarely seems abstract or generically ideological. For him, the fundamental issues of language and meaning are genuine and personal concerns. However dense and difficult Palmer's poetry can be, it is above all playful in its approach to puzzling questions of meaning. It is this notion of poetry as a verbal game played for both pleasure and insight that makes his potentially intimidating work both attractive and engaging.

Autobiography

All clocks are clouds.
Parts are greater than the whole.
A philosopher is starving in a rooming house, while it rains outside.

He regards the self as just another sign.
Winter roses are invisible.   5
Late ice sometimes sings.

A and *Not-A* are the same.
My dog does not know me.
Violins, like dreams, are suspect.
I come from Kolophon,[1] or perhaps some small island.   10
The strait has frozen, and people are walking—a few skating—across it.
On the crescent beach, a drowned deer.

A woman with one hand, her thighs around your neck.
The world is all that is displaced.
Apples in a stall at the streetcorner by the Bahnhof, pale yellow to blackish red. 15
Memory does not speak.
Shortness of breath, accompanied by tinnitus.
The poet's stutter and the philosopher's.

The self is assigned to others.
A room from which, at all times, the moon remains visible.   20
Leningrad cafe: a man missing the left side of his face.
Disappearance of the sun from the sky above Odessa.
True description of that sun.
A philosopher lies in a doorway, discussing the theory of colors

with himself   25
the theory of self with himself, the concept of number, eternal return, the
    sidereal pulse
logic of types, Buridan[2] sentences, the *lekton*.
Why now that smoke off the lake?
Word and thing are the same.
Many times white ravens have I seen.   30

That all planes are infinite, by extension.
She asks, Is there a map of these gates?
She asks, Is this the one called Passages, or is it that one to the west?
Thus released, the dark angels converse with the angels of light.
They are not angels.   35
Something else.

For Poul Borum

1995

All those words we once used . . .

All those words we once used for things but have now discarded
in order to come to know things. There in the mountains I
discovered the last tree or the letter A. What it said to me was
brief, "I am surrounded by the uselessness of blue falling away

1. A colophon is a publisher's emblem or description in a book, so the poet implies that he comes from
a country of book(s).
2. Jean Buridan was a fourteenth-century philosopher, much of whose work had to do with categorization.

on all sides into fields of bitter wormwood, all-heal and centaury.   5
If you crush one of these herbs between your fingers the scent will
cling to your hand but its particles will be quite invisible. This is
a language you cannot understand." Dismantling the beams of
the letter tree I carried them one by one down the slope to our
house and added them to the fire. Later over the coals we grilled   10
red mullets flavored with oil, pepper, salt and wild oregano.

                                                                    1984

Of this cloth doll which

(Sarah's fourth)

Of this cloth doll which
says Oh yes
and then its face changes
to Once upon a time
to Wooden but alive   5
to Like the real
to Late into the night
to There lived an old
to Running across ice
(but shadows followed)   10
to Finally it sneezed
to The boat tipped over
to Flesh and blood
to Out of the whale's mouth

                                                                    1984

◄ MARY KINZIE ►
(b. 1944)

Born in Montgomery, Alabama, Mary Kinzie received her bachelor's degree from
Northwestern University in 1967 and then pursued graduate work at the Free University of Berlin and Johns Hopkins University on Fulbright and Woodrow Wilson Fellowships. From Johns Hopkins University, she earned her master's degree
in 1970 and her Ph.D. in 1980. Since 1975, she has taught at Northwestern, where
she directs the English Department's undergraduate creative writing major. Kinzie
has published five books of poetry: *The Threshold of the Year* (1982), *Summers of
Vietnam and Other Poems* (1990), *Masked Women* (1990), *Autumn Eros and
Other Poems* (1991), and *Ghost Ship* (1996). She developed many of her critical
essays into a book-length study, *The Cure of Poetry in an Age of Prose: Moral Essays on the Poet's Calling* (1993), and collected other reviews in *The Judge Is Fury:
Dislocation and Form in Poetry* (1994). Her third book of criticism, *A Poet's
Guide to Poetry* (1999), is more than just a handbook of versification and poetics.
In addition to introducing basic concepts, it develops an extended and challenging
meditation on the arts of writing and reading poetry.

For Kinzie, the arts of poetry and literary criticism coalesce: she believes that good readers of poetry must learn to think like writers, not only through developing a knowledge of tradition and a sensitivity to the possibilities of language, but through experiencing the process of uncertainty and discovery that the poet undergoes. In *A Poet's Guide to Poetry*, she argues, "Reading, like writing, requires us to uncover a poem that is in the process of uncovering itself."

Although she often grounds her poetry in traditional forms, her deployment of form is never predictable but tends to pull against the norms of meter and rhyme scheme and unfold through complex syntax and unexpected shifts in diction. Whether writing autobiographical poetry, describing a landscape, or reframing a mythic tale, Kinzie explores the inner reaches of the psyche where knowledge—especially self-knowledge—arises through ventures into uncertain terrain. Kinzie's exacting attention to detail and skill at conveying complex states of feeling give her poems a sense of severity and strangeness even when she focuses on ordinary experience. In *The Cure of Poetry in an Age of Prose*, Kinzie's summation of Louise Bogan's achievement reveals much about her own artistic aims. Bogan's poem, "Cassandra," Kinzie maintains, "moves the reader to extremes, as perhaps all great lyrical art must, as if to persuade us that poetry's only cure—the one concocted by its prophetic sources—is radical, a permanent alienation from ordinary life and conventional intonations."

◄•►——◄ ►——◄•►

The Tattooer

After the story by Tanizaki

Her toenail and the pearly heel
dissolved by the dark grin of the retreating
palanquin were all he'd seen,
sufficient for his whole career,

Imagination's view of her   5
complete: the sense of endless thigh
milky as the ponies of the Emperor
above their slender slicing hooves,

his expectation of her skin
a wilderness of intercostal   10
ice on which her sanguine soul
could be engraved in Ryukyu cinnabar.

Years later—since our fate in these accounts
is after all the fruit of our desires
and sentences in which we crave are those   15
by which we're doomed—he found her at his door.

Master of a beauty that is pain,
he waited for the ivory girl to wake:
his last and lethal muse with history ahead,
whips in her hair, and from her ribs   20

to find her breasts, two threads of trembling jet
from the titanic spider he'd emblazoned down her back.

1982

The Same Love

There is the love that makes you feel
Your life will never end; and then the one—
Embrace of bright mortality
In warm metal come

Between brazen surface and descending lake—   5
When the voice you could identify from any
Other whispers at your cheek
The old drowning endearments of the many.

Love alters when it finds
That it must mask its reasons as it goes;   10
With a hard eye
By their less snowfall trace the standing roads;

But lifting a poor brilliance to the glass
Can read no word of how the thirst of love would pass.

1990

SHIRLEY GEOK-LIN LIM
(b. 1944)

Shirley Geok-lin Lim was born in the small town of Malacca, Malaysia. Her childhood was difficult. Lim's Malay mother abandoned the family when Lim was eight
years old, leaving her Chinese father—a failed businessman who became a parale-
gal—to raise her and her five brothers. Lim's father was an avid reader, and his
passion soon rubbed off on his daughter. "Growing up when I did," Lim recalled,
"there weren't many other recreational alternatives, and I had a pretty unhappy
childhood. Reading was a huge solace, retreat, escape. I was a really obsessive
reader." Although her first language was Malay and her second the Hokkin dialect of Chinese, Lim could read English by age six. She began devouring fairy
tales and, later, novels and poetry, especially Tennyson and the Georgian poets.

Living under the British colonial system, Lim attended a missionary convent
school run by Irish nuns. By age ten she had a poem published in the *Malacca
Times*. Soon after, she discovered a book on versification and poetic technique
that sparked her interest in poetic form. Lim won a federal scholarship to the University of Malaya, where she received a bachelor's degree in English in 1969. Im-
migrating then to America, she studied with J. V. Cunningham at Brandeis
University, earning a Ph.D. in British and American literature in 1973.

Lim's first collection, *Crossing the Peninsula and Other Poems* (1980), earned
the Commonwealth Poetry Prize. (She was the first woman and the first Asian to
receive the award.) She has won two American Book Awards, one for co-editing
The Forbidden Stitch: An Asian-American Women's Anthology (1989) and the

other for her memoir *Among the White Moon Faces: An Asian-American Memoir of Homelands* (1996). Lim has published collections of short fiction, a novel, and numerous books of poetry, including *Monsoon History: Selected Poems* (1994) and *What the Fortune Teller Didn't Say* (1998). She married Charles Bozerman in 1972 and has a son. Lim is currently a professor of English and chair of women's studies at the University of California, Santa Barbara.

To Li Po[1]

I read you in a stranger's tongue,
Brother whose eyes were slanted also.
But you never left to live among
Foreign devils. Seeing the rice you ate grow
In your own backyard, you stayed on narrow   5
Village paths. Only your mind travelled
Easily: east, north, south and west
Compassed in observation of field
And family. All men were guests
To one who knew traditions, the best   10
Of race. Country man, you believed to be Chinese
No more than a condition of human history.
Yet I cannot speak your tongue with ease,
No longer from China. Your stories
Stir griefs of dispersion and find   15
Me in simplicity of kin.

                                        1980

My Father's Sadness

My father's sadness appears in my dreams.
His young body is dying of responsibility.
So many men and women march out of his mouth
each time he opens his heart for fullness,
he is shot down; so many men and women   5
like dragons' teeth rising in the instance
of his lifetime. He is an oriental. He claims
paternity. But in his dreams he is a young body
with only his life before him.

My father's sadness masks my face. It is hard   10
to see through his tears, his desires drum in my chest.
I tense like a young man with a full moon
and no woman in sight. My father broke
with each child, finer and finer, the clay

---

1. Li Po, also known as Li T'ai-po (701–762), was one of the great Chinese poets of the T'ang dynasty.

of his body crumbling to a drizzle of silicone   15
in the hour-glass. How hard it is
to be a father, a bull under the axle,
the mangrove netted by lianas, the host
perishing of its lavishness.

                                                                        1994

Learning to Love America

because it has no pure products

because the Pacific Ocean sweeps along the coastline
because the water of the ocean is cold
and because land is better than ocean

because I say we rather than they   5

because I live in California
I have eaten fresh artichokes
and jacarandas bloom in April and May

because my senses have caught up with my body
my breath with the air it swallows   10
my hunger with my mouth

because I walk barefoot in my house

because I have nursed my son at my breast
because he is a strong American boy
because I have seen his eyes redden when he is asked who he is   15
because he answers I don't know

because to have a son is to have a country
because my son will bury me here
because countries are in our blood and we bleed them

because it is late and too late to change my mind   20
because it is time.

                                                                        1998

⤞ B. H. FAIRCHILD ⤝
(b. 1945)

Bertram Harry Fairchild, Jr., was born in Houston but grew up mostly in small towns in west Texas, Oklahoma, and southwest Kansas. Fairchild was called "Pete" by his family since he was named against his father's wishes—while his father was in service during World War II. The poet only discovered his real name when he was nine. Fairchild's father managed a machine shop in Liberal, Kansas, where the teenage boy also worked. The men who ran the lathes, milling machines, and drill-presses made a decisive impression on the young poet's imagination and provided inspiration for much of his later work. Fairchild attended the University of Kansas where he received a bachelor's degree in 1964 and a master's degree in 1968. That same year he married Patricia Gillespie. He earned a Ph.D. in 1975 from the University of Tulsa (writing his dissertation on William Blake).

Although Fairchild wrote poems in high school and college, he stopped writing during his mid-twenties while he began his teaching career at several institutions, including University of Nebraska at Kearney and Southwest Texas State University. He began writing poems again in his early thirties. After publishing two chapbooks, Fairchild brought out his first full-length collection, *The Arrival of the Future* (1985). His second collection, *Local Knowledge* (1991) appeared in the *Quarterly Review of Literature* series. By then Fairchild had moved west to become a professor at California State University, San Bernardino, where he has taught since 1983.

Fairchild's first two collections attracted little notice. His third volume, *The Art of the Lathe* (1998), however, which had an introduction by Anthony Hecht, dramatically and decisively changed his situation. This tough-minded but oddly tender volume garnered more literary prizes than any other poetry book of that year—winning five major awards, including the William Carlos Williams Award, the California Book Award, and the $50,000 Kingsley Tufts Award, as well as becoming a finalist for the National Book Award. Like his earlier work, *The Art of the Lathe* centers on the working-class world of midwestern men, isolated in small towns and caught in demanding jobs. Fairchild shows the pride, dignity, and passion these blue-collar characters bring to their outwardly ordinary lives. He finds beauty in odd and unexpected places in the tough masculine world of machine shops, neighborhood bars, and sandlot sports fields. Many of his poems have a simple narrative structure, a realistic story that rises slowly to a quietly epiphanic climax. As Kate Daniels commented in a review of *The Art of the Lathe*, "Fairchild's ability not only to choose a story, but to pace it and to reveal its meaning through unfolding of the narrative is probably unmatched in contemporary American poetry."

Fairchild also has a special talent for creating memorable characters who seem both plausibly ordinary and meaningfully individual. These protagonists often seem like versions of the poet's younger self but slightly fictionalized for the purposes of the poem. This gift for characterization is further displayed in *Early Occult Memory Systems of the Lower Midwest* (2002), which contains the imaginative investigations of memory and experience of his earlier work. Across his four volumes, Fairchild has created a moving depiction of small-town American life and labor, the community and loneliness of a particular human landscape now passing into history.

◄◦══◄►══◦►

The Death of a Small Town

It's rather like snow: in the beginning,
immaculate, brilliant, the trees shocked
into a crystalline awareness of something

remarkable, like them, but not of them,
perfectly formed and yet formless.   5
You want to walk up and down in it,

this bleak, maizeless field of innocence
with its black twigs and blue leaves.
You want to feel the silence crunching

beneath your houseshoes, but soon everyone   10
is wallowing in it, the trees no longer
bear sunlight, the sky has dragged down

its gray dream, and now it's no longer snow
but something else, not water or even
its dumb cousin, mud, but something used,   15

ordinary, dull. Then one morning at 4 a.m.
you go out seeking that one feeble remnant,
you are so lonely, and of course you find

its absence. An odd thing, to come upon
an absence, to come upon a death, to come upon   20
what is left when everything is gone.

1998

A Starlit Night

All over America at this hour men are standing
by an open closet door, slacks slung over one arm,
staring at wire hangers, thinking of taxes
or a broken faucet or their first sex: the smell
of back-seat Naugahyde, the hush of a maize field   5
like breathing, the stars rushing, rushing away.

And a woman lies in an unmade bed watching
the man she has known twenty-one, no,
could it be? twenty-two years, and she is listening
to the polonaise climbing up through the radio static   10
from the kitchen where dishes are piled
and the linoleum floor is a great, gray sea.

It's the A-flat polonaise she practiced endlessly,
never quite getting it right, though her father,
calling from the darkened TV room, always said,   15
"Beautiful, kiddo!" and the moon would slide across
the lacquered piano top as if it were something
that lived underwater, something from far below.

They both came from houses with photographs,
the smell of camphor in closets, board games   20
with missing pieces, sunburst clocks in the kitchen
that made them, each morning, a little sad.
They didn't know what they wanted, every night,
every starlit night of their lives, and now they have it.

2002

❮ KAY RYAN ❯
(b. 1945)

Kay Ryan was born Kay Peterson in San Jose, California, but was raised mostly in the small, working-class towns of the San Joaquin Valley and Mojave Desert. Her father, the son of Danish immigrants, was a well-driller and farmhand. Her mother had taught elementary school briefly before marriage but stayed at home to raise Ryan and her brother. The poet grew up in the hot, rural landscape of interior California—an irrigated desert transformed into farmland. (Something of Ryan's harsh and hard-worked native terrain is reflected in her carefully cultivated minimalist aesthetic.) She completed her bachelor's and master's degrees in English literature at University of California at Los Angeles, but she never took a creative writing course. She has lived in Marin County, north of San Francisco, since 1971 where she teaches basic English skills at College of Marin, a public two-year college, and occasionally at San Quentin Prison.

An outsider to literary circles, Ryan was slow in establishing her literary career. Her first book, *Dragon Acts to Dragon Ends* (1983), was privately published by a subscription of friends and attracted no critical attention. *Strangely Marked Metal* (1985), a more mature and distinctive volume, followed from Copper Beech Press of Rhode Island—a small publisher from America's smallest state with a knack for discovering literary talent—but it gained little notice. When *Flamingo Watching* (1994) appeared nine years later, Ryan had fully emerged as a poet of unmistakable originality and expressive power. Slowly and steadily her literary reputation has risen—supported by frequent appearances in the *New Yorker*. Her recent volumes, *Elephant Rocks* (1996) and *Say Uncle* (2000), have confirmed her position as one of the finest poets of her generation.

Ryan's poems characteristically take the shape of an observation or idea in the process of clarifying itself. Although the poems are brightly sensual and imagistic, there is often a strongly didactic sense at work. As Andrew Frisardi observed in *Poetry*, Ryan's poems usually say "something useful and important." But the didactic impulse inevitably takes a surprisingly lyric form. The language reflects the shaping hand of a quick and skeptical intelligence often pulling some general notion from the arresting particulars—a process sometimes prefigured in the poem's title. In "Paired Things" from *Flamingo Watching*, for example, image and abstraction dance so consummate a pas de deux that one wonders why modern poetics ever considered the two imaginative impulses at odds.

Ryan's characteristic style usually employs dense figurative language, varied diction, internal rhyme, the interrogative mode, and playful free verse, which elusively alternates between iambic and unmetered lines. One of Ryan's signature devices is the counterpoint of sight and sound in the placement of her poetic language. Her hidden rhymes and metrical passages only become fully apparent when the poem is spoken aloud. The central images become emblematic of a larger truth, but they usually slip away before the interpretation becomes fixed. Ryan's style is zestfully contemporary, but there is something almost eighteenth-century about her sensibility. She is a *moraliste* in the expansive and exemplary sense of the French *philosophes*—a theorist of human conduct. In this way, as in several others, Ryan resembles Emily Dickinson, who is surely the presiding genius loci of her poetry. Like Dickinson, Ryan has found a way of exploring ideas without losing either the musical impulse or imaginative intensity necessary to lyric poetry. She is one of the genuinely original talents in contemporary American poetry.

Paired Things

Who, who had only seen wings,
could extrapolate the
skinny sticks of things
birds use for land,
the backward way they bend,   5
the silly way they stand?
And who, only studying
birdtracks in the sand,
could think those little forks
had decamped on the wind?   10
So many paired things seem odd.
Who ever would have dreamed
the broad winged raven of despair
would quit the air and go
bandylegged upon the ground,   15
a common crow?

                                     1994

Turtle

Who would be a turtle who could help it?
A barely mobile hard roll, a four-oared helmet,
she can ill afford the chances she must take
in rowing toward the grasses that she eats.
Her track is graceless, like dragging   5
a packing-case places, and almost any slope
defeats her modest hopes. Even being practical,
she's often stuck up to the axle on her way
to something edible. With everything optimal,
she skirts the ditch which would convert   10
her shell into a serving dish. She lives
below luck-level, never imagining some lottery
will change her load of pottery to wings.
Her only levity is patience,
the sport of truly chastened things.   15

                                     1994

Bestiary

A bestiary catalogs
bests. The mediocres
both higher and lower

are suppressed in favor
of the singularly savage
or clever, the spectacularly   5
pincered, the archest
of the arch deceivers
who press their advantage
without quarter even after   10
they've won as of course they would.
Best is not to be confused with *good*—
a different creature altogether,
and treated of in the goodiary—
a text alas lost now for centuries.   15

1996

Chemise

What would the self
disrobed look like,
the form undraped?
There is a flimsy cloth
we can't take off—   5
some last chemise
we can't escape—
a hope more intimate
than paint
to please.   10

2000

Don't Look Back

This is not
a problem
for the neckless.
Fish cannot
recklessly   5
swivel their heads
to check
on their fry;
no one expects
this. They are   10
torpedoes of
disinterest,
compact capsules
that rely
on the odds   15
for survival,
unfollowed by
the exact and modest
number of goslings

the S-necked   20
goose is—
who if she
looks back
acknowledges losses
and if she does not   25
also loses.

                                        2000

Mockingbird

Nothing whole
is so bold,
we sense. Nothing
not cracked is
so exact and   5
of a piece. He's
the distempered
emperor of parts,
the king of patch,
the master of   10
pastiche, who so
hashes other birds'
laments, so minces
their capriccios, that
the dazzle of dispatch   15
displaces the originals.
As though brio
really does beat feeling,
the way two aces
beat three hearts   20
when it's cards
you're dealing.

                                        2000

◄ ADRIAN C. LOUIS ►
(b. 1946)

Adrian C. Louis, a self-described "half-breed Native American," was born and raised the eldest of twelve children. His family was part of the Lovelock Paiute Indian tribe in northern Nevada. Louis's interest in writing was sparked by a Native American high school literature teacher, and he already had his first poem published by the time he was a junior. After flunking out of the University of Nevada at Reno, Louis spent some time on the road, living first in San Francisco's Haight-Ashbury district and later in Boston during the late 1960s. Deciding to return to school, Louis enrolled at Brown University, where he received his master's degree in creative writing in 1980. He began working as an editor and journalist for Native American newspapers in Los Angeles and eventually in Pine Ridge, South Dakota. Louis later accepted a position teaching English and creative writing at Oglala Lakota College on the Pine Ridge Reservation.

Louis's poetry addresses his personal conflicts and struggles—especially his long-standing battle with alcoholism—yet he seeks to universalize his experience into a broader investigation of his community, his country, and indeed, human nature in general. "The overall theme in my work is personal survival," Louis has asserted. "I'm writing about my life. I guess deep down I sort of fancy myself as speaking for certain kinds of people who don't have a voice—for the downtrodden." Although Louis's work explores Native American themes and concerns, he approaches them from a more complex and critical perspective than many of his contemporaries. He refuses to romanticize either reservation life or Native American lore. His poems speak in a skeptical and candid voice—with no shortage of irony and painful honesty—both about himself and American Indian culture. Yet his work is suffused with his deep, if troubled, love for his community. Leslie Ullman, in a review of Louis's collection *Among the Dog Eaters* (1992), describes the poet as "a thorny, passionate presence, at once angry at his people, angry on their behalf, and very much a part of them. In other words, he speaks as both an observer and a prime example of a condition, as both the accuser and the accused."

Louis has been the recipient of the Lila Wallace–Reader's Digest Writer's Award, as well as of fellowships from the Bush Foundation and the National Endowment for the Arts. He has published many volumes of poetry including *Fire Water World* (1989), *Vortex of Indian Fevers* (1995), *Ceremonies of the Damned* (1997), and *Bone and Juice* (2001). His novel, *Skins* (1995), was made into a film. In 1999 Louis joined the English Department at Southwest State University in Marshall, Minnesota, where he currently teaches.

◄◆►

Without Words

Farewell from this well is impossible.
Man is composed mainly of water.
I lower a frayed rope into the depths and hoist
the same old Indian tears to my eyes.
The liquid is pure and irresistible.   5
We have nothing to live for, nothing to die for.
Each day we drink and decompose into a different flavor.
Continuity is not fashionable
and clashing form is sediment
obscuring the bottom of thirst.   10
the parched and cracking mouths
of our Nations do not demand
a reason for drinking
so across America
we stagger and stumble with contempt for the future   15
and with no words of pride for our past.

1989

Looking for Judas

Weathered gray, the wooden walls
of the old barn soak in the bright
sparkling blood of the five-point mule
deer I hang there in the moonlight.
Gutted, skinned, and shimmering in eternal   5
nakedness, the glint in its eyes could
be stolen from the dry hills of Jerusalem.
They say before the white man
brought us Jesus, we had honor.
They say when we killed the Deer People,   10
we told them their spirits
would live in our flesh.
We used bows of ash, not spotlights, no rifles,
and their holy blood became ours.
Or something like that.   15

1995

◄ MARILYN NELSON ►
(b. 1946)

Well known as a poet of formal grace and narrative breadth, Marilyn Nelson has
also brought quiet but undeniable power to poems of social conviction and spirituality. Born in Cleveland, Ohio, the eldest child of an air force officer and a
schoolteacher, Nelson moved often throughout her childhood. The necessity of
making friends in varied circumstances may have contributed to the compassion
and humor of her work. Her father was one of the Tuskegee Airmen, a famous
African American squadron, and her mother's family had preserved its stories
from slave times. Her legacy was thus one of pride in the face of adversity. When
she was born her father drove a cab while her mother studied toward a master's
degree, but when the Korean War broke out her father was recalled to active service. Thereafter, Nelson and her younger siblings moved constantly—to Maine,
California, and many points between. They were often the only black family on
base, and Nelson grew up bookish and relatively protected from racism, though
she experienced a few incidents that shocked her into awareness of the prejudice
most African Americans faced.

Nelson finished high school in Sacramento, California, then attended the University of California, Davis, where she took a bachelor's degree in 1968. By that
time she was also involved in the antiwar and Civil Rights movements, developing
spiritual and political convictions that remain important to her. While working toward a master's degree at the University of Pennsylvania, she met her first husband,
Erdmann Waniek. After they married, she taught in Oregon while he pursued his
doctorate, then the two lived in Denmark and later Minnesota, where they both
taught at St. Olaf College while Nelson worked toward her Ph.D. at the University
of Minnesota. The couple eventually divorced, and in 1978 Nelson began teaching
at the University of Connecticut, Storrs. With her second husband, scholar Roger
Wilkenfield, she had a son and a daughter.

Her first book of poems, *For the Body* (1978), which was published under the name Marilyn Nelson Waniek, involved personal and familial subjects, while her second, *Mama's Promises* (1985), grew out of an attempt to create a "black feminist theology." In her third book, *The Homeplace* (1990), Nelson went back to family stories, retelling them in sequences of lyrics, both in free and fixed forms. This book, which was a finalist for the National Book Award, established Nelson (still publishing under the name Waniek) as one of the most assured and compassionate voices of her generation. She followed it with *Magnificat* (1994), a more overtly spiritual book in which she introduced her character Abba Jacob, a Benedictine monk. She also made translations from Euripides and Rilke. Nelson's *The Fields of Praise: New and Selected Poems* (1997), another finalist for the National Book Award and winner of the Poets' Prize, revisited earlier collections but removed many of her poems from their original sequences. An author or translator of several books for children, Nelson has recently published *Carver, A Life in Poems* (2001), a sequence of poems for younger readers that is also compelling reading for adults.

The Ballad of Aunt Geneva

Geneva was the wild one.
Geneve was a tart.
Geneva met a blue-eyed boy
and gave away her heart.

Geneva ran a roadhouse.   5
Geneva wasn't sent
to college like the others:
Pomp's pride her punishment.

She cooked out on the river,
watching the shore slide by,   10
her lips pursed into hardness,
her deep-set brown eyes dry.

They say she killed a woman
over a good black man
by braining the jealous heifer   15
with an iron frying pan.

They say, when she was eighty,
she got up late at night
and sneaked her old, white lover in
to make love, and to fight.   20

First, they heard the tell-tale
singing of the springs,
then Geneva's voice rang out:
I need to buy some things,

So next time, bring more money.   25
And bring more moxie, too.

I ain't got no time to waste
on limp white mens like you.

Oh yeah? Well, Mister White Man,
it sure might be stone-white,   30
but my thing's as white as it is.
And you know damn well I'm right.

Now listen: take your heart pills
and pay the doctor mind.
If you up and die on me,   35
I'll whip your white behind.

They tiptoed through the parlor
on heavy, time-slowed feet.
She watched him, from her front door,
walk down the dawnlit street.   40

Geneva was the wild one.
Geneva was a tart.
Geneva met a blue-eyed boy
and gave away her heart.

                                                    1990

How I Discovered Poetry

It was like soul-kissing, the way the words
filled my mouth as Mrs. Purdy read from her desk.
All the other kids zoned an hour ahead to 3:15,
but Mrs. Purdy and I wandered lonely as clouds borne
by a breeze off Mount Parnassus. She must have seen   5
the darkest eyes in the room brim: The next day
she gave me a poem she'd chosen especially for me
to read to the all except for me white class.
She smiled when she told me to read it, smiled harder,
said oh yes I could. She smiled harder and harder   10
until I stood and opened my mouth to banjo playing
darkies, pickaninnies, disses and dats. When I finished
my classmates stared at the floor. We walked silent
to the buses, awed by the power of words.

                                                    1990

Thus Far by Faith

Thomas Chapel C.M.E., Hickman, Kentucky

I SERMON IN THE COTTON FIELD

Philippians 2:12b–15a

His heart's upwelling of its own accord
slackens the reins, stopping the plow mid-row

beside a sea of furrows, as the word
whirling within takes shape: *Whoa, brothers, whoa.*
One mule cranes questioningly; the other nips 5
his neck, ears back. They bray against the hitch
which matches them. And Uncle Warren wraps
his arms around the sky and starts to preach.

Beloved, stop your grumbling. Be the stars
what give a twisted generation light. 10
That's what the book say. But old Satan roars
louder, sometimes, than Master. He say, Hate
the whip-hand and the yoke: Why be a fool?
The Lord Hisself were tempted, Brother Mule.

II SERMON IN THE WOODLOT

1 Corinthians 9:24–27

The Lord Himself was tested, Brother Mule, 15
but y'all would try the patience of a saint.
There's only a few more loads of lumber to haul;
Git up, there! You know Master don't know no cain't.
The Book say, Run so as to win the crown
imperishable. That mean man must grunt 20
and sweat from first light til the sun sink down,
same as a mule. We can run lightfoot with praise
or toting a croaker sack of dead-weight sins around.
Come on now, git.
                        The wagon creaks and sways,
a mockingbird trills from a branch almost overhead. 25
Uncle Warren nods to a quietly working slave
whose bare brown back is criss-crossed with black and red.
The mules meander into sunshine, leaving the wood.

III SERMON IN THE RUINED GARDEN

James 2:14–18

A mule meanders into sunshine from the wood
near Sally's garden. Almost nothing left 30
after the locust tides of the bereft
swept north. Some die for truth; some died for food.
Uncle Warren plucks a few choice stalks of grass,
chirrups and holds it in an outstretched hand.
The mule flinches just out of reach, to stand 35
flat-eared, tail flickering, willful as an ass.
Uncle Warren says, *Uh-huh: You think you smart.*
Well, don't hee-haw to me about how faith
helped you survive the deluge. Save your breath.
Show me. Faith without works ain't worth a fart. 40
People is hungry. Act out your faith now
by hitching your thanks for God's love to my plow.

IV MEDITATION OVER THE WASHTUB

Exodus 19:4–6a

Oh, I'm hitching my love for Jesus to my plow;
Aunt Sally hums thanksgiving to her Lord,
pausing occasionally to wipe her brow,   45
scrubbing wet, soapy darks on the washboard.
The clean whites undulate against a breeze
scented with hyacinth and simmering greens.
So this is freedom: the peace of hours like these,
and wages, now, for every house she cleans.   50
Her singing starts as silence, then her throat
fills with a bubble of expanding praise.
A deeper silence underlies each note:
a lifting mystery, the sky of grace.
Aunt Sally sings, *Yes, Jesus is my friend.*   55
Hosannas rise like incense on the wind.

V PALM SUNDAY, 1866

1 Peter 2:22–24

Make our hosannas incense on the wind;
may we wave palms of welcome . . . Listening
from the colored pew, Aunt Sally nods amen.
From beside her, T.T., bored and fidgeting,   60
chases his rubber ball into the aisle.
The front pew kneels at the communion rail,
heads bowed. Aunt Sally, reaching for the child,
bumps into Captain Randall. He goes pale
with cursing rage, jumps up, and knocks her down.   65
In the hush that follows, the minister proclaims,
Coloreds aren't welcome here, from this day on.
T.T.'s blue eyes meet hers, sharing her shame.
The colored worshippers, silent and grim,
file out as the organist strikes up a hymn.   70

VI GOOD FRIDAY PRAYER

Psalm 51

Defy him! Tear his organ off! Strike him
with righteous lightning! Make the devil pay!
Uncle Warren paces, has paced since Sunday,
wrestling with demons and with cherubim,
reaching for heaven, balancing on hell's rim.   75
Life's promise seems to him a vast array
of shit and more shit, followed by decay.
Now, on Friday evening, he kneels to pray a psalm,
remembering *His* unearned suffering,
and how He said, forgive them. Poor, poor fools.   80
The spade of prayer cuts stone, untaps a spring

of clear compassion. Uncle Warren feels
God present again. *Help ME do no wrong.*
The others? Well, it's like preaching to mules.

VII EASTER SERMON, 1866

Acts 10:40–43

Others might think it's like preaching to mules   85
to preach to dark-faced people who sign X
laboriously. They listen on cotton bales
as Uncle Warren reads from the book of Acts.
A rose-gold dawnlight streams in through the chinks
and roosters halleloo the sun's return.   90
In a makeshift church reeking with familiar stinks,
field hands, bricklayers, and domestics yearn
toward Jesus.
                    Well, sir, like the gospels say,
only a handful saw the risen Lord:
What was true in them days still holds true today.   95
Be a witness. Pull the plow and sow His word.
Come harvest you'll have love you can give away,
and a heart that wells up of its own accord.

1990

◦—◄ RON SILLIMAN ►—◦
(b. 1946)

A leading proponent and practitioner of Language poetry, Ron Silliman was born
in Pasco, Washington, and grew up in Northern California. He once recalled that
there were few cultural amenities in his family's home; yet by the age of eighteen he
was publishing poems in magazines. After high school, his education was sporadic,
a curious fact in the life of a poet whose theories seemingly demand an academic
audience. He attended Merritt College in Oakland, San Francisco State University,
and the University of California, Berkeley, but never completed a degree. Although
he has worked at several colleges and universities, both as a poet and an adminis-
trator, his more recent jobs have been nonacademic. For years he worked as the
managing editor of *Computer Land*. In 1995 he moved to Pennsylvania where he
works as a computer market analyst, while continuing to write at a prolific pace.
    Silliman's poetic stance has been influenced by such figures as Gertrude Stein,
Ezra Pound, William Carlos Williams, and Jack Spicer. Although he has experimented with different prosodies in his many books, his fundamental project has
been an assault on conventional poetic values along broadly poststructuralist lines,
especially by rejecting conventional concepts of value and meaning. A committed
leftist and former editor of the *Socialist Review,* Silliman associates his efforts to
deconstruct poetic hierarchies with social egalitarianism. Yet his revolutionary attack on the literary status quo has found its most positive reception in the heart of
the literary establishment, university English departments, where poststructuralist
thinking has most deeply taken root.

Silliman's work is not concerned with aural structure or verbal musicality as traditionally conceived, but with visual and conceptual prosodies. His book, *Nox* (1974), for example, presents readers with pages divided into a simple grid, with a word or linguistic fragment visually placed in each quadrant of the page. The impact of the work is primarily visual and conceptual, as each text creates a field of interpretations and squarely denies efforts to impose narrative or discursive meaning.

Silliman's most ambitious project appears to be concerned with language at its most minute level. Since 1979 he has been writing *The Alphabet*, a multivolume work with a book-length poem for each letter of the alphabet, each book published without concern for conventional sequence. This approach has been called "formalist and conceptual," by critic T. C. Marshall, and while this is literally true, that sober assessment perhaps misses some of the sincere and inspired mischief in Silliman's tactics.

Whatever cogency underlies his denial of cogency, Silliman's work stands as a challenge to most commonly held ideas about language and poetry. His abstract language is a far cry from the demotic energy of Ezra Pound's early Modernist manifestos, but Silliman's earnest and imaginative means of assertion reveals the same passion for radical reform of the art.

FROM The Chinese Notebook

1.   Wayward, we weigh words. Nouns reward objects for meaning. The chair in the air is covered with hair. No part is in touch with the planet.

2. Each time I pass the garage of a certain yellow house, I am greeted with barking. The first time this occurred, an instinctive fear seemed to run through me. I have never been attacked. Yet I firmly believe that if I opened the door to the garage I should confront a dog.

3. Chesterfield, sofa, divan, couch—might these items refer to the same object? If so, are they separate conditions of a single word?

4. My mother as a child would call a potholder a "boppo," the term becoming appropriated by the whole family, handed down now by my cousins to their own children. Is it a word? If it extends, eventually, into general usage, at what moment will it become one?

5. Language is, first of all, a political question.

6. I wrote this sentence with a ballpoint pen. If I had used another would it have been different sentence?

7. This is not philosophy, it's poetry. And if I say so, then it becomes painting, music or sculpture, judged as such. If there are variables to consider, they are at least partly economic—the question of the distribution, etc. Also differing critical traditions. Could this be good poetry, yet bad music? But yet I do not believe I would, except in jest, posit this as dance or urban planning.

8. This is not speech. I wrote it.

9. Another story, similar to 2: until well into my twenties the smell of cigars repelled me. The strong scent inevitably brought to mind the image of warm, wet shit. That is not, in retrospect, an association I can rationally explain. Then I worked as a legislative advocate in the state capitol and was around cigar smoke constantly. Eventually the odor seemed to dissolve. I no longer noticed it. Then I began to notice it again, only now it was an odor I associated with suede or leather. This was how I came to smoke cigars.

10. What of a poetry that lacks surprise? That lacks form, theme, development? Whose language rejects interest? That examines itself without curiosity? Will it survive?

11. Rose and maroon we might call red.

12. Legalistic definitions. For example, in some jurisdictions a conviction is not present, in spite of a finding of guilt, without imposition of sentence. A suspension of sentence, with probation, would not therefore be a conviction. This has substantial impact on teachers' credentials, or the right to practice medicine or law.

13. That this form has a tradition other than the one I propose, Wittgenstein,[1] etc., I choose not to dispute. But what is its impact on the tradition proposed?

14. Is Wittgenstein's contribution strictly formal?

15. Possibility of a poetry analogous to the paintings of Rosenquist[2]—specific representational detail combined in non-objective, formalist systems.

16. If this were theory, not practice, would I know it?

17. Everything here tends away from an aesthetic decision, which, in itself, is one.

18. I chose a Chinese notebook, its thin pages not to be cut, its six redline columns which I turned 90°, the way they are closed by curves at both top and bottom, to see how it would alter the writing. Is it flatter, more airy? The words, as I write them, are larger, cover more surface on this two-dimensional picture plane. Shall I, therefore, tend toward shorter terms—impact of page on vocabulary?

19. Because I print this, I go slower. Imagine layers of air over the planet. One closer to the center of gravity moves faster, while the one above it tends to drag. The lower one is thought, the planet itself the object of the thought. But from space what is seen is what filters through the slower outer air of representation.

20. Perhaps poetry is an activity and not a form at all. Would this definition satisfy Duncan?[3]

21. Poem in a notebook, manuscript, magazine, book, reprinted in an anthology. Scripts and contexts differ. How could it be the same poem?

22. The page intended to score speech. What an elaborate fiction that seems!

---

1. Ludwig Wittgenstein (1889–1951), Austrian-born philosopher.
2. James Rosenquist (b. 1933), an American painter.
3. Robert Duncan (1919–1988), American poet.

23. As a boy, riding with my grandparents about Oakland or in the country, I would recite such signs as we passed, directions, names of towns or diners, billboards. This seems to me now a basic form of verbal activity.

24. If the pen won't work, the words won't form. The meanings are not manifested.

25. How can I show that the intentions of this work and poetry are identical?

1986

◄ AI ►
(b. 1947)

Ai was born Florence Anthony in Albany, Texas. Of mixed Japanese, African American, Native American, and Irish ancestry, Ai never knew her natural father, a Japanese man with whom her mother had a brief liaison. Growing up, she struggled with questions of racial identity and eventually resolved not to align herself with any conventional racial category but to explore her individuality as a multiracial person. Renouncing her birth name, she chose "Ai," which means "love" in Japanese, to express her new identity. She took a bachelor's degree in Japanese from the University of Arizona in 1969 and then went on to complete a master's at the University of California at Irvine in 1971. She has taught at Wayne State, George Mason, and Arizona State University.

Ai's poetry often takes the form of the dramatic monologue in which characters explore the anguish of frustrated, desperate, or dangerous lives. The names of her first five collections vividly express Ai's thematic concerns: *Cruelty* (1973), *Killing Floor* (1979), *Sin* (1986), *Fate* (1991), and *Greed* (1993). Her poems both dramatize and investigate the situations of people—often including real historical figures like Elvis Presley, J. Edgar Hoover, Jack Ruby, and Lee Harvey Oswald—caught up in extreme circumstances of violence, drugs, sex, or destructive fame. Poetic technique is less her concern than the narrative energy of addressing important issues of racism, politics, and sexuality. Her work has been widely recognized. *Killing Floor* won the Lamont Prize, and *Sin* was given the American Book Award. In 1999 Ai published *Vice: New and Selected Poems*, which won the National Book Award. She currently lives in Tucson, Arizona.

Child Beater

Outside, the rain, pinafore of gray water, dresses the town
and I stroke the leather belt,
as she sits in the rocking chair,
holding a crushed paper cup to her lips.
I yell at her, but she keeps rocking;   5
back, her eyes open, forward, they close.
Her body, somehow fat, though I feed her only once a day,
reminds me of my own just after she was born.

It's been seven years, but I still can't forget how I felt.
How heavy it feels to look at her.   10

I lay the belt on a chair
and get her dinner bowl.
I hit the spoon against it, set it down
and watch her crawl to it,
pausing after each forward thrust of her legs   15
and when she takes her first bite,
I grab the belt and beat her across the back
until her tears, beads of salt-filled glass, falling,
shatter on the floor.

I move off. I let her eat,   20
while I get my dog's chain leash from the closet.
I whirl it around my head.
O daughter, so far, you've only had a taste of icing,
are you ready now for some cake?

1973

◆◄ YUSEF KOMUNYAKAA ►◆
(b. 1947)

The first African American man to win a Pulitzer Prize for poetry, Yusef Komun-yakaa was born James Willie Brown, Jr., in Bogalusa, Louisiana, a quiet mill town seventy miles northeast of New Orleans. He was the son of a carpenter whose violence and misunderstandings are the subjects of several poems, especially "Songs for My Father":

> You banged a crooked nail
> Into a pine slab,
> Wanting me to believe
> I shouldn't have been born
> With hands & feet
> If I didn't do
> Your kind of work.
> You hated my books.

But in the same world, Komunyakaa began to develop a fondness for cultural consolations, such as jazz and the blues. Early poems of his would concern such figures as Leadbelly, Thelonious Monk, and Charles Mingus. There were hardly any books in the house, but his mother bought him an inexpensive encyclopedia set—one volume at a time—at the local supermarket, and the young poet read the Bible.

Komunyakaa's interest in poetry arose almost by accident in high school, when he volunteered to write a poem for his graduating class, an experience that suddenly and surprisingly instilled a desire to be a poet. Komunyakaa went on to serve in the U.S. Army, including a tour in Vietnam. There he was an information specialist and editor of *Southern Cross*, a military paper. He was awarded the Bronze Star, but on his return to the United States he found the rejection of Vietnam veterans by many Americans as painful as the racism he had always known.

These social concerns occupied him as he began his studies toward a bachelor's degree at the University of Colorado. "In the early 1970s," he recalls, "those years I entertained the idea of becoming a psychiatrist, I believed that racism was a mental illness. Perhaps this idea had a lot to do with a kind of elemental hope. A faith in knowledge and one's capacity to change. If it was an illness, it could be cured, right?" He compiled copious notes on the subject, "a treatise," he now calls it, covering, "Sex. Environment. Cultural and social indoctrination. Fear. Envy. Nonverbal gestures that pass down racism to the cradle. Language. Literature." These concerns stayed with him as he worked toward a master's degree at Colorado State University (1978) and then a second master's at the University of California at Irvine (1980). Komunyakaa's early collections such as *Lost in the Bonewheel Factory* (1979), *Copacetic* (1984) and *I Apologize for the Eyes in My Head* (1986) deal with issues of race and racism.

Race consciousness also informs the poems of Komunyakaa's Vietnam experience—his most powerful work to date—published in two collections: *Toys in a Field* (1986) and *Dien Cai Dau* (1988). The latter title is a term used by the Vietnamese to refer to the "crazy" Americans fighting in their country. Poet-critic Wayne Kostenbaum noted of *Dien Cai Dau* that "The book works through accretion, not argument; the poems are all in the present tense, which furthers the illusion that we are receiving tokens of a reality untroubled by language." Elliot Goldenthan, a composer, set some of these poems to music for "Fire Water Paper: A Vietnam Oratorio," and said of them, "These poems are out there; they are not poetic or arty, but right there."

In terms of poetic technique, Komunyakaa rarely varies from the short free verse lines and colloquial diction that are his trademark, yet within those formal limitations he conveys a supple intelligence and a variety of rhythmic effects. "This is how poems happen for me," he wrote in a notebook. "Bits and pieces, glimpses and strokes, hints and imagistic nudges, and at some almost-accidental moment it all flies together—not to make sense but to induce a feeling. I call these *gifts*." His fascination with jazz improvisation has also led him to edit (with poet and jazz saxophonist Sascha Feinstein) *The Jazz Poetry Anthology* (1991) and *The Second Set: The Jazz Poetry Anthology, Volume 2* (1996).

Komunyakaa's *Neon Vernacular: New and Selected Poems* (1993) won both the Pulitzer Prize and the $50,000 Kingsley Tufts Award. More recent collections include *Thieves of Paradise* (1998), *Talking Dirty to the Gods* (2000), and *Pleasure Dome: New & Collected Poems, 1975–1999* (2001). A selection of his prose can be found in *Blues Notes: Essays, Interviews & Commentaries* (2000). Married to fiction writer Mandy Sayer, he has taught at several colleges and universities. He currently teaches at Princeton and serves as a Chancellor of the Academy of American Poets.

◄●►

Facing It

My black face fades,
hiding inside the black granite.
I said I wouldn't,
dammit: No tears.
I'm stone. I'm flesh.   5

My clouded reflection eyes me
like a bird of prey, the profile of night
slanted against morning. I turn
this way—the stone lets me go.
I turn that way—I'm inside   10
the Vietnam Veterans Memorial
again, depending on the light
to make a difference.
I go down the 58,022 names,
half-expecting to find   15
my own in letters like smoke.
I touch the name Andrew Johnson;
I see the booby trap's white flash.
Names shimmer on a woman's blouse
but when she walks away   20
the names stay on the wall.
Brushstrokes flash, a red bird's
wings cutting across my stare.
The sky. A plane in the sky.
A white vet's image floats   25
closer to me, then his pale eyes
look through mine. I'm a window.
He's lost his right arm
inside the stone. In the black mirror
a woman's trying to erase names: 30
No, she's brushing a boy's hair.

1988

Starlight Scope Myopia

Gray-blue shadows lift
shadows onto an oxcart.

Making night work for us,
the starlight scope brings
men into killing range.   5

The river under Vi Bridge
takes the heart away

like the Water God
riding his dragon.
Smoke-colored   10

Viet Cong
move under our eyelids,

lords over loneliness
winding like coral vine through
sandalwood & lotus,   15

inside our lowered heads
years after this scene

ends. The brain closes
down. What looks like
one step into the trees,   20

they're lifting crates of ammo
& sacks of rice, swaying

under their shared weight.
Caught in the infrared,
what are they saying?   25

Are they talking about women
or calling the Americans

beaucoup dien cai dau?[1]
One of them is laughing.
You want to place a finger   30

to his lips & say "shhhh."
You try reading ghost talk

on their lips. They say
"up-up we go," lifting as one.
This one, old, bowlegged,   35

you feel you could reach out
& take him into your arms. You

peer down the sights of your M-16,
seeing the full moon
loaded on an oxcart.   40

                                                         1988

Tu Do Street

Music divides the evening.
I close my eyes & can see
men drawing lines in the dust.
America pushes through the membrane
of mist & smoke, & I'm a small boy   5
again in Bogalusa. *White Only*
signs & Hank Snow. But tonight
I walk into a place where bar girls
fade like tropical birds. When
I order a beer, the mama-san   10
behind the counter acts as if she
can't understand, while her eyes
skirt each white face, as Hank Williams
calls from the psychedelic jukebox.
We have played Judas where   15

1. Mixed French and Vietnamese, meaning "very crazy."

only machine-gun fire brings us
together. Down the street
black GIs hold to their turf also.
An off-limits sign pulls me
deeper into alleys, as I look   20
for a softness behind these voices
wounded by their beauty & war.
Back in the bush at Dak To
& Khe Sanh, we fought
the brothers of these women   25
we now run to hold in our arms.
There's more than a nation
inside us, as black & white
soldiers touch the same lovers
minutes apart, tasting   30
each other's breath,
without knowing these rooms
run into each other like tunnels
leading to the underworld.

                                                   1988

Banking Potatoes

Daddy would drop purple-veined vines
Along rows of dark loam
& I'd march behind him
Like a peg-legged soldier,
Pushing down the stick   5
With a V cut into its tip.

Three weeks before the first frost
I'd follow his horse-drawn plow
That opened up the soil & left
Sweet potatoes sticky with sap,   10
Like flesh-colored stones along a riverbed
Or diminished souls beside a mass grave.

They lay all day under the sun's
Invisible weight, & by twilight
We'd bury them under pine needles   15
& then shovel in two feet of dirt.
Nighthawks scalloped the sweaty air,
Their wings spread wide

As plowshares.   But soon the wind
Knocked on doors & windows   20
Like a frightened stranger,
& by mid-winter we had tunneled
Back into the tomb of straw,
Unable to divide love from hunger.

                                                   1992

————————— •»—◄ **AMY UYEMATSU** ►—•» —————————

(b. 1947)

Amy Uyematsu was born in Pasadena, California, in 1947. Her father owned a nursery with her grandfather. Writing was a family tradition. Her paternal grandmother wrote haiku and tanka in Japanese. Her mother wrote a newspaper column. Her parents and grandparents had been interned in the Japanese relocation camps during World War II, an experience that gave Uyematsu a powerful sense of her ethnic identity. A member of the *sansei*, the third generation of Japanese Americans, Uyematsu was raised in Sierra Madre, an attractive suburban community where she lived directly behind the public library, which she would walk to from her own backyard. Although living in a homogenous Southern California suburb, the family often drove to Los Angeles's thriving Little Tokyo section. (The distance between Sierra Madre and Little Tokyo provided the title for Uyematsu's first collection, *30 miles from J-Town.*)

Growing up in middle-class Southern California, Uyematsu sought to reconcile her Japanese identity with the "bleached blond culture of Los Angeles." How did one "stay Japanese and cool?" she and her friends wondered. She attended University of California at Los Angeles where she took a master's degree in mathematics in 1969, and later a master's in education in 1972. While at UCLA she also helped pioneer the Asian American Studies program, an experience that shaped her literary achievement. "My poetry roots," she has remarked, "can be traced back to my 'yellow power' period of political activism." Uyematsu teaches mathematics at Grant High School in Van Nuys, California, and lives with her son in Culver City.

Uyematsu's first collection, *30 Miles from J-Town* (1992) won the Nicholas Roerich first book competition from Story Line Press. Incorporating both a Japanese and Japanese American slang, Uyematsu's book chronicled the poet's emotional and intellectual coming-of-age amid the complex and contradictory cultural forces of contemporary California. Uyematsu's second collection, *Nights of Fire, Nights of Rain* (1998) portrays a darker vision of California with the use of fire—the flames of the Watts riots, the inferno of Western wildfires, the emotional fires of violence—as its central metaphor and symbol.

•»—◄ ►—•»

Deliberate

So by sixteen we move in packs
learn to strut and slide
in deliberate lowdown rhythm
talk in a syn/co/pa/ted beat
because we want so bad   5
to be cool, never to be mistaken
for white, even when we leave
these rowdier L.A. streets—
remember how we paint our eyes
like gangsters   10

flash our legs in nylons
sassy black high heels
or two inch zippered boots
stack them by the door at night
next to Daddy's muddy gardening shoes.   15

                                                          1992

The Ten Million Flames of Los Angeles

—a New Year's poem, 1994

I've always been afraid of death by fire,
I am eight or nine when I see the remnants of a cross
burning on the Jacobs' front lawn,
seventeen when Watts[1] explodes in '65,
forty-four when Watts blazes again in 1992.   5
For days the sky scatters soot and ash which cling to my skin,
the smell of burning metal everywhere. And I recall
James Baldwin's warning about the fire next time.

> *Fires keep burning in my city of the angels,*
> *from South Central to Hollywood,*   10
> *burn, baby, burn.*

In '93 LA's Santana winds incinerate Laguna and Malibu.
Once the firestorm begins, wind and heat regenerate
on their own, unleashing a fury so unforgiving
it must be a warning from the gods.   15

> *Fires keep burning in my city of the angels,*
> *how many does it take,*
> *burn, LA, burn.*

Everybody says we're all going to hell.
No home safe   20
from any tagger, gangster, carjacker, neighbor.
LA gets meaner by the minute
as we turn our backs
on another generation of young men,
become too used to this condition   25
of children killing children.
I wonder who to fear more.

> *Fires keep burning in my city of angels,*
> *but I hear someone whisper,*
> *"Mi angelita, come closer."*   30

Though I ready myself for the next conflagration,
I feel myself giving in to something I can't name.

---

1. The predominantly black neighborhood in Los Angeles, torn apart by riots in 1965 and 1992.

I smile more at strangers, leave big tips to waitresses,
laugh when I'm stuck on the freeway, content
just listening to B.B. King's "Why I Sing the Blues."   35

    "Mi angelita, mi angelita."

I'm starting to believe in a flame
which tries to breathe in each of us.
I see young Chicanos fasting one more day
in a hunger strike for education,   40
read about gang members preaching peace in the 'hood,
hear Reginald Denny[2] forgiving the men
who nearly beat him to death.
I look at people I know, as if for the first time,
sure that some are angels. I like the unlikeliness   45
of this unhandsome crew—then men losing their hair,
needing a shave, those with dark shining
eyes, and the grey-haired women, rage
and grace in each sturdy step.
What is this fire I feel, this fire which breathes freely   50
inside without burning them alive?

    Fires keep burning in my city of angels,
    but someone calls to me,
    "Angelita, do not run from the flame."

                    1998

◄ DAVID LEHMAN ►
(b. 1948)

David Lehman was born in New York City. Both of his parents were European
Jewish refugees who had fled the Nazis—his father from Germany, his mother
from Austria. Raised in an orthodox Jewish home, Lehman was taught to respect
both learning and hard work—two qualities that have distinguished his literary
career. He attended Columbia University where he took a bachelor's degree in
1970. Originally intending an academic career, Lehman earned a master's degree
at Cambridge University in England and then returned to Columbia to complete a
Ph.D. in English in 1978. (He wrote his dissertation on the prose poem in English
and American poetry.) From 1976 to 1980 he taught at Hamilton College before
quitting to become a freelance writer and editor. From 1982 to 1989 Lehman
served as book reviewer and cultural critic for *Newsweek*. He then published a series of influential critical studies, including *The Perfect Murder* (1989), a study of
detective fiction, *Signs of the Times* (1991), a skeptical analysis of deconstruction-
ism, and *The Last Avant-Garde* (1998), a celebration of the New York School of
poets. He also issued two books of literary essays, *The Line Forms Here* (1992)
and *The Big Question* (1995). Lehman also emerged as a prolific and influential

---

2. A white truck driver who was badly beaten during the 1992 riots.

editor. In 1988 he founded the annual anthology, *The Best American Poetry,* which would quickly become a fixture of U.S. literary life. Lehman also returned to teaching on a part-time basis, serving as a core faculty member for both Bennington's Writing Seminars and the New School graduate writing program.

Lehman's prominence as an editor has often obscured his idiosyncratic but genuine achievements as a poet. His first collection, *An Alternative to Speech* (1986), announced his witty, urbane, and elusive voice. Working consciously in the traditions of the New York School, Lehman has been drawn more deeply to the movement's humor and intelligence than to its philosophical concerns. His poetry is above all else playful. Generally unconcerned with personal revelation or autobiography, Lehman creates verbal games, and by pushing his ingenious narrative or linguistic diversions to their furthest conclusions, he creates a curiously accessible and entertaining sort of experimental poetry. Although Lehman the critic idolizes the ambiguous and often obscure work of John Ashbery, Lehman the poet instinctively reaches for a more inclusive, though equally sophisticated, style. Especially in his collections *Operation Memory* (1990) and *Valentine Place* (1996), he often uses form in his poetry, but it is no sense central to his style, which can best be described as poised, eclectic, and provisional; each new poem seems determined to depart from its predecessors.

Lehman's most recent books, *The Daily Mirror* (2000) and *The Evening Sun* (2002), are drawn from a daily poem journal the author started keeping in 1996. Written quickly in free verse, these new poems emphasize the process of perception and imagination—in the urbane but casual style of the New York School. Rather than aiming for verbal polish or rhetorical finish, they create an open-ended intellectual portrait of the poet as a living contemporary, a sort of Frank O'Hara *de nos jours.* Lehman's work often parodies or alludes to other works of art—not only poems and fiction but also movies and television shows. Worldly but never world-weary, he represents the contemporary New York sensibility at its most appealingly cosmopolitan.

Rejection Slip

"Oh, how glad I am that she
Whom I wanted so badly to want me
Has rejected me! How pleased I am, too,
That my Fulbright to India fell through!

The job with the big salary and the perks   5
Went to a toad of my acquaintance, a loathsome jerk
Instead of to me! I deserved it! Yet rather than resent
My fate, I praise it: heaven-sent

It is! For it has given me pain, prophetic pain,
Creative pain that giveth and that taketh away again!   10
Pain the premonition of death, mother of beauty,
Refinement of all pleasure, relief from duty!

Pain that you swallow and nurture until it grows
Hard like a diamond or blooms like a rose!
Pain that redoubles desire! Pain that sharpens the sense!   15
Of thee I sing, to thee affirm my allegiance!"

The audience watched in grim anticipation
Which turned into evil fascination
And then a standing ovation, which mesmerized the nation,
As he flew like a moth into the flames of his elation.   20

1990

First Lines

Mother was born today. I traveled back to watch her
In the school play, crying because her mother wasn't there.
There was always a crisis in the tailor shop in Vienna.
Father smoked cigars. What he liked about his life was
The chance to do the same thing twice—to lose the lady   5
A second time, flee from Europe, and live in a grand hotel,
Looking sharp in a tuxedo among the gambling tables.
If childhood is a foreign country, his had armed guards
At the barbed-wire border. "Don't you remember me,"
The lady asked plaintively. He shook his head no, grinning   10
Like a soldier before combat, "But I'm willing to learn."
Sometimes the memory of her face was all that kept him going.
He had to see her again. It didn't matter where or when.
They would go to Coney Island, eat hot dogs, be American.
America was young then, naïve, brash, confident.   15
The immigrants were pouring in: new blood, old guts.
And when the market crashed, and banks started failing,
My old man gave me a piece of advice that I've never
Forgotten, though I never did manage to follow it.
Get the money. Cut your losses. Always look your partner   20
In the eye, except when kissing her warm red lips,
Drunk on her aroma, surprised to be alive.

1996

◄ R. S. GWYNN ►
(b. 1948)

A critic in the *Los Angeles Times* called R. S. Gwynn "a low-key Texas Fellini who brings to American popular culture—movies, talk shows, circuses, lounge acts, even community theatre—some of the Italian maestro's knack for wonder, world-weariness and a satirical anger." This odd description is apt. Gwynn's special ability as a poet has been to bridge cultural categories—high and low, popular and academic, serious and comic—to produce a distinctly personal poetry that is at once highly entertaining and deeply felt. A master of verse forms and a darkly satiric commentator on American life, Gwynn has emerged as one of the most strongly individual poets of his generation.

Robert Samuel Gwynn was born the middle of three sons in Leaksville (now Eden), North Carolina. His father, a former air corps cadet and merchant seaman, ran several local movie theaters, including the Eden Drive-In pictured on the cover of Gwynn's first trade book. The poet's mother was a kindergarten teacher and day care worker. Gwynn played football in high school, winning a partial scholarship to Davidson College in 1965. During spring practice in 1967, however, a serious knee injury ended his football career. It also disqualified him from military service in the Vietnam War. After taking a bachelor's degree at Davidson in 1969, where one of his teachers was George Core, later editor of the *Sewanee Review,* Gwynn entered the University of Arkansas. There he studied with poets James Whitehead and Miller Williams, taking two master's degrees by 1973. It was also in graduate school that he befriended the poets Leon Stokesbury and Frank Stanford. Gwynn's first marriage ended in divorce, and in 1977 he married Donna Kay Simon. After teaching briefly at Southwest Texas State, Gwynn moved to Lamar University in Beaumont, Texas, where he has taught ever since.

Gwynn has been an active critic, translator, and anthologist. For five years he wrote the massive "The Year in Poetry" article for the *Dictionary of Literary Biography,* an entry that covered almost every significant book of verse published in America during each year. He edited a two-volume critical survey of *American Poets since World War II,* as well as a variety of other successful literary anthologies, including *Poetry: A Pocket Anthology* (1993, revised 1998, 2002). He also edited *The Advocates of Poetry: A Reader of American Poet-Critics of the Modernist Era* (1996) and *New Expansive Poetry* (1999), a volume of essays concerned with the New Formalism.

Gwynn's first chapbook of poems, *Bearing and Distance* (1977), was followed by *The Narcissiad* (1981), a long work that revealed a poet almost entirely at odds with the literary temper of his times. Formal and satiric, this mock epic in heroic couplets pilloried the excesses of contemporary American poetry by recounting the adventures of Narcissus, an ambitious but talentless poet. In Gwynn's mercilessly satiric tale American poets simultaneously realize that to achieve artistic fame in the overcrowded field of contemporary verse they must kill all competitors. After a series of outrageous comic battles fought by recognizable caricatures of fashionable American poets, Narcissus ineptly triumphs. Gwynn's irreverent poem cannot have pleased the influential targets of his humor, but it enjoyed a lively underground life and has been repeatedly reprinted.

Gwynn's first full-length collection, *The Drive-In* (1986), stands as one of the representative volumes of the New Formalist movement. Gwynn's meters are traditional, but his language is aggressively contemporary and colloquial. The volume is a small encyclopedia of historical forms and genres—elegy, satire, anacreontic, epistle, dialogue, ode, sonnet-sequence—but Gwynn usually employs them in deliberately irreverent, even obscene ways. The early cynicism of *The Narcissiad* is balanced by a lyrical impulse. *The Drive-In*'s signature piece, "Among Philistines," retells Samson's downfall in a lurid American setting of shopping malls and tabloid journalism. This dark, comic poem unexpectedly rises to a lyric epiphany as the captive hero finds redemption in his mutilations.

Gwynn's new and selected poems, *No Word of Farewell* (2001), confirmed his position as a unique talent—a masterful formal poet who is at once ingeniously funny yet able to rise to lyricism. No American poet of his generation has written better sonnets, and few can equal him in the "French" forms, like the ballade, rondeau, and pantoum—not to mention half a dozen new forms he has invented. Gwynn's great distinction is to use these forms for powerful expressive ends. One can read "Body Bags," the heartbreaking story of three lives destroyed in different ways by the Vietnam War, several times without noticing it is a short sonnet sequence. The dark side of Gwynn's imagination has grown more evident in his recent work. (His painful bout with cancer in the mid-1990s casts a shadow across the later poems.) The satire is still evident, but now he offers a brooding nightmarish vision only made bearable by humor. An often skeptical, even cynical observer of the human scene, Gwynn cannot mock his subjects without feeling a common human sympathy.

◆━━◆━━◆

Untitled

> In the morning light a line
> Stretches forever. There my unlived life
> Rises, and I resist . . .
> —*Louis Simpson*

In which I rise untroubled by my dreams,
In which my unsung theories are upheld
By massive votes, in which my students' themes
Move me, in which my name is not misspelled;

In which I enter strangers' rooms to find,   5
Matched in unbroken sets, immaculate,
My great unwritten books, in which I sign
My name for girls outside a convent gate;

In which I run for daylight and my knee
Does not fold up, in which the home teams win,   10
In which my unwed wife steeps fragrant tea
In clean white cups, in which my days begin
With scenes in which, across unblemished sands,
Unborn, my children come to touch my hands.

1986

Body Bags

I

Let's hear it for Dwayne Coburn, who was small
And mean without a single saving grace
Except for stealing—home from second base
Or out of teammates' lockers, it was all
The same to Dwayne. The Pep Club candy sale,   5
However, proved his downfall. He was held
Briefly on various charges, then expelled
And given a choice: enlist or go to jail.

He finished basic and came home from Bragg
For Christmas on his reassignment leave   10
With one prize in his pack he thought unique,
Which went off prematurely New Year's Eve.
The student body got the folded flag
And flew it in his memory for a week.

II

Good pulling guards were scarce in high school ball.
The ones who had the weight were usually slow
As lumber trucks. A scaled-down wild man, though,
Like Dennis "Wampus" Peterson, could haul
His ass around right end for me to slip   5
Behind his blocks. Played college ball a year—
Red-shirted when they yanked his scholarship
Because he majored, so he claimed, in Beer.

I saw him one last time. He'd added weight
Around the neck, used words like "grunt" and "slope,"   10
And said he'd swap his Harley and his dope
And both balls for a 4-F[1] knee like mine.
This happened in the spring of '68.
He hanged himself in 1969.

III

Jay Swinney did a great Roy Orbison
Impersonation once at Lyn Rock Park,
Lip-synching to "It's Over" in his dark
Glasses beside the jukebox. He was one
Who'd want no better for an epitaph   5
Than he was good with girls and charmed them by
Opening his billfold to a photograph:
Big brother. The Marine. Who didn't die.

He comes to mind, years from that summer night,
In class for no good reason while I talk   10
About Thoreau's remark that one injustice
Makes prisoners of us all. The piece of chalk
Splinters and flakes in fragments as I write,
To settle in the tray, where all the dust is.

1990

1-800

Credit cards out, pencil and notepad handy,
    The insomniac sinks deeply in his chair,
Begging swift needles in his glass of brandy
    To knit once more the raveled sleeve of care,

---

1. A medical deferment from the draft.

As with control, remotely, in one hand he   5
  Summons bright visions from the midnight air:

The six-way drill! The eight-way folding ladder!
  Knives that pierce coins or thin-slice loaves of bread!
Devices that will make one's tummy flatter,
  Rout car thieves, or purge household taps of lead!   10
All made of stuff no earthly force can shatter!
  Their lauds ascend Olympus in his head.

And yet how little will his days be brightened
  By *Opera Favorites* or, if he feels lewd,
Even THE SWIMSUIT ISSUE. Briefly heightened,   15
  His hopes, ephemeral as stir-fried food,
Vanish like screws his six-way grill has tightened,
  Leaving him just like them—completely screwed.

"Buy houses and apartments with no money!
  Discover how today! Write this address!"   20
Snapping alert and clicking with his gun, he
  Draws a bead on the forehead of Success,
Whose orchid leis are fresh, whose teeth are sunny,
  Whose tapes will wing their way via UPS.

But anger, with succeeding snifters, passes   25
  and soon all softens in an amber hue;
As through a pair of UV/blue-block glasses,
  Doubt fades before the testimony—true
Accounts of hair sprouting like jungle grasses!
  Of lifeless penises lifting anew!   30

Of bags and wrinkles blotted out! Of dumber
  Than average kids who, spared the wrath and rod
Have learned to multiply! He fights off slumber
  The moment that his head begins to nod
And resolutely punches the first number   35
  Of what may be the area code of God.

                                        1993

------------ ●━◄ **HEATHER McHUGH** ►━● ------------
(b. 1948)

The daughter of Canadian parents, Heather McHugh was born in San Diego, California, and raised in Virginia. Nurtured by gifts of poetry books from her parents, she began writing poetry as a child. In the preface to *Hinge & Sign, Poems 1968–1993* (1994), which was a finalist for a National Book Award, she recalls, "As the world's shyest child, I was the one who never spoke in school but who registered, with uncalled-for intensity, every twist of tone and talk; who, at home, went directly to her room to write, because writing proposed a fellow-listener, though things seemed quite unspeakable." Fascinated by the nuances of language, in her adult work McHugh continues to explore the tension between "every twist of tone and talk" and the "unspeakable," working the full range of American English to approach ideas and experiences that go beyond words.

McHugh entered Harvard-Radcliffe in 1965 where she studied with Robert Lowell, a poet whose sensitivity to the heft of language, and skill at mixing levels of diction, from conversational vernacular to learned speech, mirrored her own proclivities. Unlike Lowell, however, McHugh has never adopted a confessional approach to poetry, preferring instead to ponder consciousness through word play. After her graduation from Harvard, cum laude, in 1970, she continued her studies at the University of Denver, where she earned a master's in English literature in 1972.

Beginning with her first book, *Dangers* (1977), McHugh has published six books of her own poetry and a collection of essays, *Broken English: Poetry and Partiality* (1993). Her fascination with language has led to numerous translation projects from a variety of languages: French, classical Greek, Bulgarian, and German. Several of these projects have been collaborations with her husband, Nikolai Popov, whom she married in 1987. Together, they published *Because the Sea is Black* (1989), translations from the work of Blaga Dimitrova, a Bulgarian poet, and *Glottal Stop: 101 Poems by Paul Celan* (2000). She has served as a core faculty member of Warren Wilson College's M.F.A. program, and in 1983 she began teaching at the University of Washington at Seattle, where she now holds the titles of Milliman Distinguished Writer in Residence and Professor of English. Her awards and honors include a Lila Wallace–Reader's Digest Writers' Award and election in 1999 as a Chancellor of the Academy of American Poets.

Moving from an ebullient exploration of life's strangeness to an increasing preoccupation with love and mortality, McHugh's poetry depends on the interplay between linguistic density and unexpected silences. Often skeptical of her own tendency toward verbal density, McHugh favors puns and etymological puzzles, yet also questions the extent to which language can fathom experience, for she believes that poetry's "brokenness," its dependence upon multiplicity and implication, derives as much from calculated silence as from the power of words themselves. In these aims, she follows the examples of Rainer Maria Rilke, Paul Celan, Samuel Beckett, and Jorge Luis Borges, writers who can make even ordinary language feel unfamiliar, yet whose complex word play allows them to approach the mysteries of human experience, especially suffering.

McHugh has been a perceptive critic of contemporary American poetry, opposing its tendency toward self-congratulation and nostalgia. In her introduction to *Broken English,* she argues that poetry is:

> not for burying the terror, salving the sorrow, buying a balm. No salesman's music or easy analgesic, it is not in the comforter business. For its regards are not formalities: they require us to notice what we might otherwise most wish to overlook. Imagination isn't needed, says Valéry, to see what isn't; it is needed to see what *is*. That's what we most deeply miss.

Deeply attentive to the mind's engagement with the world, McHugh strives to break through the mind's self-absorption and to shake the reader (and herself) out of complacency. Thus, she concludes, "the position of poetry is THAT imposition: it requires you to face the difficulty, the unfathomability, of your life." Throughout her career, she has aimed to "fathom" such difficulties of life and language.

The Trouble with "In"

In English, we're in trouble,
Love's a place
we fall into, so
sooner or later they ask

How deep? Time's a measure   5
of extent, so sooner or later
they ask How long? We keep
some comforters inside a box,
the heart inside a chest,

but still it's there the trouble with the dark   10
accumulates the most. The end of life
is said to be
a boat to a tropic,
good or bad. The suitor wants
to size up what he's getting into, so he gets   15
her measurements. But how much

is enough? The best man cannot
help him out—he's given to his own
uncomfortable cummerbund. Inside the mirror,
several bridesmaids look   20
and look, in the worst
half-light,

too long, too little, not enough alike.
And who can stand to be
made up for good? And who can face   25
being adored? I swear

there is no frame
that I would keep you in.
I didn't love a shape
and later find you fit it—   30
every day your sight was a surprise.
You made my taste, made sense,
made eyes. But when you set me up

in high esteem, I was a star
that's bound, in time,   35
to fall. The bound's
the sorrow of the song.

I loved you to no end,
and when you said, "So far,"
I knew the idiom: it meant So long.   40

                                                    1987

Earthmoving Malediction

Bulldoze the bed where we made love,
bulldoze the goddamn room.
Let rubble be our evidence
and wreck our home.

I can't give touching up by inches,   5
can't give beating up
by heart. So set
the comforter on fire and turn the dirt

to some advantage—palaces of
pigweed, treasuries of turd. The fist   10
will vindicate the hand; the tooth
and nail refuse to burn, and I

must not look back, as
Mrs. Lot was named for such
a little—something   15
in a cemetery,

or a man. Bulldoze the coupled
ploys away, the cute exclusives
in the social mall. We dwell

on earth, where beds are brown,   20
where swoops are fell. Bulldoze
it all, up to the pearly gates:

if paradise comes down
there is no other hell.

                                                    1988

◄ TIMOTHY STEELE ►
(b. 1948)

One of the foremost practitioners of formal verse in the United States today, Timothy Reid Steele was born in Burlington, Vermont. Since the late sixties, however, when he entered Stanford University, his life and work have been rooted in California. When he took his bachelor's degree at Stanford in 1970, the English Department was still very much under the influence of the poet-critic Yvor Winters and his disciples. Steele then went to Brandeis University, where he did graduate work with one of Winters's strongest advocates, J. V. Cunningham, earning his Ph.D. in 1977. Steele returned to Stanford twice—first as a Stegner Fellow

(1972–1973) and later as a lecturer (1975–1977). He has taught at California State University, Los Angeles, since 1987. Steele's first brief marriage ended in divorce, and in 1979 he married Victoria Erpelding.

The mark of strong teachers like Winters and Cunningham reveals itself in Steele's skill with meter, his lucid style, and his tendency toward rationalism. He has even published epigrammatic verse. But unlike Cunningham's epigrams, his poems tend not to reflect bitter personal difficulties. Rather, like another mentor, Richard Wilbur, Steele often conveys a sense of the joy and awe of living. This is not to say that there is no sadness in his poems, only that Steele's emotions are usually hidden beneath burnished verbal surfaces.

The title of Steele's first book, *Uncertainties and Rest* (1979), suggests something of his dual vision in which the poet's formal poise becomes a stay against undeniable transience. Although the book was respectfully reviewed, it seemed to many an anomaly in a world where most poets had abandoned rhyme and meter. At about this time, the term New Formalism began to enter critical parlance, and Steele has since been identified with that movement. Like many other poets given this distinction, Steele has found the term misleading. "Meter's always been around for anyone wishing to explore it," he remarked, "the only true New Formalist in English is Geoffrey Chaucer." His next small book, *The Prudent Heart* (1983), was followed by more chapbooks and then a very successful full-length volume, *Sapphics Against Anger* (1986), where again form was perceived as a way of living with one's human passions. *The Color Wheel* (1994) was followed by *Sapphics and Uncertainties: Poems 1970–1986* (1995), which reprinted and slightly corrected his first two volumes.

◄◦►━━◄▶━━◄◦►

Sapphics Against Anger

Angered, may I be near a glass of water;
May my first impulse be to think of Silence,
Its deities (who are they? do, in fact, they
　　　　Exist? etc.).

May I recall what Aristotle says of   5
The subject: to give vent to rage is not to
Release it but to be increasingly prone
　　　　To its incursions.

May I imagine being in the *Inferno*,
Hearing it asked: "Virgilio mio, who's   10
That sulking with Achilles there?" and hearing
　　　　Virgil say: "Dante,

That fellow, at the slightest provocation,
Slammed phone receivers down, and waved his arms like
A madman. What Attila did to Europe,   15
　　　　what Genghis Khan did

To Asia, that poor dope did to his marriage."
May I, that is, put learning to good purpose,
Mindful that melancholy is a sin, though
      Stylish at present.   20

Better than rage is the post-dinner quiet,
The sink's warm turbulence, the streaming platters,
The suds rehearsing down the drain in spirals
      In the last rinsing.

For what is, after all, the good life save that   25
Conducted thoughtfully, and what is passion
If not the holiest of powers, sustaining
      Only if mastered.

                                          1986

The Sheets

From breezeway or through front porch screen
You'd see the sheets, wide blocks of white
Defined against a backdrop of
A field whose grasses were a green
      Intensity of light.   5

How fresh they looked there on the line,
Their laundered sweetness through the hours
Gathering richly in the air
While cumulus clouds gathered in
      Topheavily piled towers.   10

We children tightroped the low walls
Along the garden; bush and bough
And the washed sheets moved in the wind;
And thinking of this now recalls
      Vasari's tale of how   15

Young Leonardo, charmed of sight,
Would buy in the loud marketplace
Caged birds and set them free—thus yielding
Back to the air which gave him light
      Lost beauty and lost grace.   20

So with the sheets: for as they drew
Clear warming sunlight from the sky,
They gave to light their rich, clean scent.
And when, the long day nearly through,
      My cousin Anne and I   25

Would take the sheets down from the line,
We'd fold in baskets their crisp heat,

Absorbing, as they had, the fine
Steady exchange of earth and sky,
  Material and sweet.   30

1986

Summer

Voluptuous in plenty, summer is
Neglectful of the earnest ones who've sought her.
She best resides with what she images:
Lakes windless with profound sun-shafted water;
Dense orchards in which high-grassed heat grows thick; 5
The one-lane country road where, on his knees,
A boy initials soft tar with a stick;
Slow creeks which bear flecked light through depths of trees.

And he alone is summer's who relents
In his poor enterprisings; who can sense, 10
In alleys petal-blown, the wealth of chance;
Or can, supine in a deep meadow, pass
Warm hours beneath a moving sky's expanse,
Chewing the sweetness from long stalks of grass.

1986

◄ WENDY ROSE ►
(b. 1948)

A painter and anthropologist as well as a writer, Wendy Rose was born Bronwen
Elizabeth Edwards in Oakland, California. Her father was a full-blooded Hopi
from Arizona, her mother of mixed Scots, Irish, and Miwok Indian blood. "The
Hopi side of my family is more sympathetic to my situation," Rose said in an interview, "but our lineage is through the mother, and because of that, having a
Hopi father means that I have no real legitimate place in Hopi society." This feeling of alienation was increased by the fact that she grew up in an urban environment. Much of her life and work have involved the recovery of identity—a theme
that appeals to many Americans of diverse backgrounds—and coming to terms
with what she has called "halfbreedness."

  Rose studied at several colleges before completing her bachelor's degree in
1976 at the University of California at Berkeley—the same year in which she married magician and judo instructor Arthur Murata. Both in college and in graduate
school, working toward her master's degree, she managed the bookstore of the
Lowie Museum of Anthropology. From 1979 to 1983 she lectured in Native American Studies at Berkeley, and she has since held similar positions at the California
State University, Fresno, and Fresno City College. While teaching, she continues
to work as a painter, book illustrator, anthropologist, and poet. With regard to
her poetry, however, Rose clearly wishes to be considered in literary more than
anthropological terms, and she has objected strenuously to having her work categorized in bookstores under nonliterary headings.

A prolific writer, Rose has published many literary books in addition to her works of history and anthropology. Her collections of poetry include *Hopi Roadrunner Dancing* (1973), *Lost Copper* (1980), *The Halfbreed Chronicles* (1985), *Going to War with All My Relations* (1993), *Bone Dance: New and Selected Poems, 1965–1993* (1994), and *Itch Like Crazy* (2002). In both prose and verse she has inveighed against what she calls "whiteshamanism," a term referring to whites who romanticize and adopt Native American rituals and beliefs to which they have no birthright. A social advocate, academic, and artist, Rose is deeply concerned with intersections of the personal and political.

◆━◆━◆

Vanishing Point: Urban Indian

It is I in the cities, in the bars,
in the dustless reaches of cold eyes
who vanishes, who leans underbalanced

into nothing; it is I
without learning, I without song   5
who dies & cries the death-time

who blows from place to place on creosote dust,
dying over & over. It is I who had to search
& turn the stones, half-dead crawl

through the bones, let tears dissolve in dry caves   10
where women's ghosts roll *piki*[1]
& insects move to keep this world alive.

It is I who hold the generous bowl
that flows over with shell & stone
& buries its future in blood, places its shape   15

within rock wall carvings. It is I who die
bearing cracked turquoise & making noise
so as to protect your fragile immortality,

O medicine ones.

1976

For the White Poets Who Would Be Indian

just once
just long enough
to snap up the words
fish-hooked
from our tongues.   5
You think of us now
when you kneel

---

1. Corn rolls.

on the earth,
turn holy
in a temporary tourism   10
of our souls.
With words
you paint your faces,
chew your doeskin,
touch breast to tree   15
as if sharing a mother
were all it takes,
could bring
instant and primal
knowledge.   20
You think of us only
when your voice
wants for roots,
when you have sat back
on your heels   25
and become primitive.
You finish your poem
and go back.

1980

◄ CAROLYN FORCHÉ ►
(b. 1950)

Born and raised in Detroit, Michigan, Carolyn Louise Sidlosky, the oldest of seven children, was the daughter of a tool- and dyemaker. Her interests in literature and language were nurtured by her mother and by the example of her grandmother, Anna Bassar Sidlosky, a Czechoslovakian immigrant. The grandmother's approximations of English words and phrases, along with her earthy strength and imagination, taught the young poet to look at language from a fresh perspective. Through her grandmother, Forché also began the fascination with agrarian cultures and folk wisdom that characterizes her early poetry and with the plight of refugees and other victims of political oppression, a subject that permeates her later work. She credits her grandmother with teaching her to extend her imagination beyond confines of the self, a perspective that was reinforced by her education at Catholic schools and her coming of age during the Vietnam War era. She married Bruce Charles Forché in 1969, but this early union quickly ended in divorce the next year. In 1972 she graduated from Michigan State University with a major in creative writing, and she went on to study writing at Bowling Green State University, receiving a master's degree in 1974.

Forché achieved professional success early when she won the Yale Series of Younger Poets Prize at twenty-five for *Gathering the Tribes* (1976). The book garnered such acclaim that within two years it had gone into three printings. *Gathering the Tribes* reflected many of the concerns of Forché's generation, for the book details the poet's search for alternatives to mainstream American culture. In spare, lyrical language, Forché contemplates time spent hiking in the wilderness, life among the Pueblo Indians, and the experiences of her Czech grandmother. The book's celebration of a life lived close to nature, as well as poems about reaching sexual maturity, balance the personal lyric against the poet's need to escape the self through making connections with others.

Her second book, *The Country between Us* (1981), which won the Lamont Prize, shifts these concerns to the political arena. In 1978 Forché won a Guggenheim Fellowship, which she used to travel to El Salvador to observe the political oppression and atrocities practiced by the Salvadoran military government. In a 1986 essay, "A Lesson in Commitment," Forché describes the poems that resulted from her travels:

> The poetry which came of my time [in Central America] was written out of a private grief and a dark vision of historical repetition to which I could not reconcile myself. I approached the page, as I always have, in the wakeful reverie of impassioned remembrance, this time with more sadness than joy, but never with the intention to persuade, inspire, or define the war which could not be stopped and which was to become the most significant influence on my life and the education of my heart.

Blending stark lyricism with documentary aims, *The Country between Us* provoked controversy, with admirers extolling Forché's moral courage and detractors accusing her of political opportunism. Forché responded to her critics by writing essays on the moral obligations of the poet and by intensifying her dedication to human rights causes, traveling to Northern Ireland, Israel, Lebanon, Guatemala, and making what she describes as "pilgrimages" to Hiroshima, Nagasaki, and Jerusalem.

Changes in Forché's personal life brought her nomadic period to an end. Divorcing her second husband, James Turner, a Milton scholar whom she had wedded in 1981, she married news photographer Harry Mattison in 1984. Since 1994 she has taught creative writing at George Mason University.

Forché did not publish another book of poetry for thirteen years after *The Country between Us*. In the meantime she worked on an anthology, *Against Forgetting: Twentieth-Century Poetry of Witness* (1993). In her introduction she argued against separating "the personal" from "the political," but she nonetheless steered clear of writing personal lyrics in her third collection of poems, *The Angel of History* (1994). The book takes on a global perspective by meditating on the scars of modern war, genocide, and political oppression in many countries. Forché fragments language, using a variety of voices in a technique, similar to T. S. Eliot's *The Waste Land*, of juxtaposing quotations from many sources against brief monologues spoken by witnesses of war and oppression. In all three of her books Forché challenges both heself and her readers to develop an engaged moral conscience and to reevaluate the boundaries between self and community.

◄◦▬▬◖▬▬◦►

The Morning Baking

Grandma come back, I forgot
How much lard for these rolls?

Think you can put yourself in the ground
Like plain potatoes and grow in Ohio?

I am damn sick of getting fat like you   5
Think you can lie through your Slovak?

Tell filthy stories about the blood sausage?
Pish-pish nights at the virgin in Detroit?

I blame your raising me up for my Slav tongue
You beat me up out back, taught me to dance   10

I'll tell you I don't remember any kind of bread
Your wavy loaves of flesh

Stink through my sleep
The stars on your silk robe

But I'm glad I'll look when I'm old   15
Like a gypsy dusha hauling milk

1976

The Colonel

What you have heard is true. I was in his house. His wife carried a tray of
coffee and sugar. His daughter filed her nails, his son went out for the night.
There were daily papers, pet dogs, a pistol on the cushion beside him. The
moon swung bare on its black cord over the house. On the television was a
cop show. It was in English. Broken bottles were embedded in the walls   5
around the house to scoop the kneecaps from a man's legs or cut his hands
to lace. On the windows there were gratings like those in liquor stores. We
had dinner, rack of lamb, good wine, a gold bell was on the table for calling
the maid. The maid brought green mangoes, salt, a type of bread. I was
asked how I enjoyed the country. There was a brief commercial in Spanish.   10
His wife took everything away. There was some talk then of how difficult
it had become to govern. The parrot said hello on the terrace. The colonel
told it to shut up, and pushed himself from the table. My friend said to me
with his eyes: say nothing. The colonel returned with a sack used to bring
groceries home. He spilled many human ears on the table. They were like   15
dried peach halves. There is no other way to say this. He took one of them
in his hands, shook it in our faces, dropped it into a water glass. It came
alive there. I am tired of fooling around he said. As for the rights of anyone,
tell your people they can go fuck themselves. He swept the ears to the floor
with his arm and held the last of his wine in the air. Something for your   20
poetry, no? he said. Some of the ears on the floor caught this scrap of his
voice. Some of the ears on the floor were pressed to the ground.

(May 1978) 1982

◄ DANA GIOIA ►
(b. 1950)

Michael Dana Gioia (pronounced JOY-a) was born in Los Angeles, the oldest child
in a working-class family of Italian, Mexican, and Native American heritage. His

father, Micheal Gioia, was a cab driver who later owned a shoe store. His mother, Dorothy Ortiz, was a telephone operator. "I was raised in a tightly-knit Sicilian family," he once told an interviewer. "We lived in a triplex next to another triplex. Five of these six apartments were occupied by relatives. Conversations among adults were usually in their Sicilian dialect." In the same interview Gioia recalled his Catholic education: "I was in the last generation that experienced Latin as a living language." Although he was expelled three times from his all-boys Catholic high school for conduct, Gioia graduated in 1969 as valedictorian.

Receiving a scholarship to Stanford, Gioia became the first person in his family to attend college. At Stanford he wrote music and book reviews for the *Stanford Daily* and later edited the literary magazine, *Sequoia*. He also spent his sophomore year in Vienna, Austria, studying German and music. After taking his bachelor's degree with highest honors in 1973, he went to Harvard, receiving a master's degree in comparative literature in 1975, having studied with two influential poet-teachers, Robert Fitzgerald and Elizabeth Bishop, as well as the critics Northrop Frye and Edward Said. At Harvard, Gioia decided his ambitions to be a writer had little to do with an academic career. Leaving the doctoral program, he returned to Stanford to earn a master's degree in business administration. "I am probably the only person in history," he has remarked, "who went to Stanford Business School to be a poet." Moving to New York after graduation in 1977, Gioia worked for the next fifteen years as an executive at General Foods, eventually becoming a vice president. In 1980 he married Mary Hiecke, whom he had met at business school.

Despite his arduous career, Gioia devoted several hours a night to writing. His poems, essays, reviews, and memoirs gradually appeared in such magazines as the *Hudson Review, Poetry,* and the *New Yorker*. His first full-length collection of poems, *Daily Horoscope,* appeared in 1986. Although the book contained poems in both free verse and metrical forms, Gioia's formal work caught the attention of critics who began debating the merits of what they termed the "New Formalism," and the volume was widely reviewed—winning both high praise and bitter condemnation from different poetic camps.

In 1987 the sudden death in infancy of his first son compelled Gioia to stop writing for nearly a year. When he resumed, he composed the darkly personal lyrics and narratives that made up his second collection, *The Gods of Winter* (1991), which was also published in England where it was chosen as the main selection by the Poetry Book Society. A decade passed before the publication of his third book of poems, *Interrogations at Noon* (2001), which won the American Book Award. That same year saw his verse libretto for *Nosferatu* (2001), an opera by Neo-Romantic composer Alva Henderson. To many readers Gioia is best known as an iconoclastic literary critic. When his essay, "Can Poetry Matter?," first appeared in the *Atlantic Monthly* in 1991, it ignited an international debate on poetry's place in contemporary culture. The essay became the title piece in his collection, *Can Poetry Matter?: Essays on Poetry and American Culture* (1992), which was a finalist for the National Book Critics Circle Prize.

In 1992 Gioia left business to become a full-time writer. Although he has occasionally taught as a visiting poet at universities and colleges, including Johns Hopkins, Wesleyan, Sarah Lawrence, Mercer, and Colorado College, he has never taken a full-time academic appointment. Instead, he has modeled his new life after the careers of public intellectuals of an earlier era—writing, reviewing, editing, and lecturing. In 1996 he returned to California and now lives in Santa Rosa. Since leaving the business world, Gioia has published many other books, including translations from Italian, German, and Latin, and numerous anthologies. He is also the music critic for *San Francisco* magazine and a commentator on American culture for BBC Radio. In 2003 he was named Chairman of the National Endowment for the Arts.

The Next Poem

How much better it seems now
than when it is finally done—
the unforgettable first line,
the cunning way the stanzas run.

The rhymes soft-spoken and suggestive   5
are barely audible at first,
an appetite not yet acknowledged
like the inkling of a thirst.

While gradually the form appears
as each line is coaxed aloud—   10
the architecture of a room
seen from the middle of a crowd.

The music that of common speech
but slanted so that each detail
sounds unexpected as a sharp   15
inserted in a simple scale.

No jumble box of imagery
dumped glumly in the reader's lap
or elegantly packaged junk
the unsuspecting must unwrap.   20

But words that could direct a friend
precisely to an unknown place,
those few unshakeable details
that no confusion can erase.

And the real subject left unspoken   25
but unmistakable to those
who don't expect a jungle parrot
in the black and white of prose.

How much better it seems now
than when it is finally written.   30
How hungrily one waits to feel
the bright lure seized, the old hook bitten.

1991

Planting a Sequoia

All afternoon my brothers and I have worked in the orchard,
Digging this hole, laying you into it, carefully packing the soil.
Rain blackened the horizon, but cold winds kept it over the Pacific,
And the sky above us stayed the dull gray
Of an old year coming to an end.   5

In Sicily a father plants a tree to celebrate his first son's birth—
An olive or a fig tree—a sign that the earth has one more life to bear.
I would have done the same, proudly laying new stock into my father's orchard,
A green sapling rising among the twisted apple boughs,
A promise of new fruit in other autumns.   10

But today we kneel in the cold planting you, our native giant,
Defying the practical custom of our fathers,
Wrapping in your roots a lock of hair, a piece of an infant's birth cord,
All that remains above earth of a first-born son,
A few stray atoms brought back to the elements.   15

We will give you what we can—our labor and our soil,
Water drawn from the earth when the skies fail,
Nights scented with the ocean fog, days softened by the circuit of bees.
We plant you in the corner of the grove, bathed in western light,
A slender shoot against the sunset.   20

And when our family is no more, all of his unborn brothers dead,
Every niece and nephew scattered, the house torn down,
His mother's beauty ashes in the air,
I want you to stand among strangers, all young and ephemeral to you,
Silently keeping the secret of your birth.   25

                                                                    1991

❦ WILLIAM LOGAN ❦
(b. 1950)

William Logan was born in Boston, Massachusetts, the son of a marketing executive and a realtor. His family moved several times, from Boston to Pittsburgh and then to Long Island where Logan attended high school. He was educated at Yale (B.A., 1972) and the University of Iowa (M.F.A., 1975), where he studied with Donald Justice. After leaving Iowa, Logan worked as a book critic, reviewing both fiction and poetry. Since 1983 he has been the director of creative writing at the University of Florida at Gainesville, where he lives with the poet Debora Greger. The couple also keep a house in Cambridge, England, where they spend their summers.

Logan's first collection was a chapbook, *Dream of Dying* (1980). Written in the high style with dense word play, frequent allusions, and sharply pointed phrasing, Logan's poems have from the start approached personal subject matter as if armed for battle. They overtly distrust the confessional territory most American poets of his generation take for granted. Often his poems use other people's lives—including those of historical and literary figures—for his personal imaginative ends. The poets he has most admired have often been Englishmen—W. H. Auden, Philip Larkin, and Geoffrey Hill—or Americans whose aesthetic is impersonal and formal, like Justice and Amy Clampitt. There is something essentially dark and sorrowfully stoic about Logan's sensibility, which is evident even from the titles of his five full-length collections of verse: *Sad-Faced Men* (1982), *Difficulty* (1985), *Sullen Weedy Lakes* (1988), *Vain Empires* (1995), and *Night Battle* (1999).

In his most characteristic poems, Logan often seems to view his subjects from a great height—a technique of clinical detachment borrowed perhaps from Auden. This approach provides the author with both emotional distance from the scene and a more expansive vision of his imaginative terrain. In "Small Bad Town," for example, Logan assumes an almost omniscient perspective. This narrative method might prove antiseptic in other hands, but Logan unexpectedly combines it with a welter of darkly satiric puns, double-edged images, comic allusion, and idiosyncratic word play. The carefully contrived surfaces of his poems miss no opportunity for expressive effect.

Despite his poetic accomplishments, Logan is far better known as America's most astringent critic and book reviewer. Like one of his literary heroes, Randall Jarrell, Logan is often more passionate in his prose than in his verse. Parsimonious with praise and savage with his wit, he is fiercely independent in his opinions, willing to alienate any constituency. Poet-critic Robert McDowell has accurately summarized Logan's position, "I have heard writers refer to him as 'the most hated man in American poetry,' a title one could be proud of in this time of fawning and favor-trading." Even poets who have been "Loganized," to use a private parlance among poets, by having their work raked over his fiery wit, usually admit his intelligence if not his taste. His two critical collections are *All the Rage: Prose on Poetry 1976–1992* (1998) and *Reputations of the Tongue: On Poets and Poetry* (1999). He also co-edited (with Dana Gioia) the critical Festschrift, *Certain Solitudes: On the Poetry of Donald Justice* (1997). Logan contributes a regular "Verse Chronicle" to the *New Criterion*—a column that has become both famous and infamous in the poetry world for its mordant evaluations of new books.

◄•═══◄▌►═══•►

After a Line by F. Scott Fitzgerald

Southampton, Hot Springs, and Tuxedo Park:
lost in the backwash of the Crash, the War,
the refugees of grace were washed ashore.
The girls who once were "miffed" or "truly vexed"
would soon acquire the morals of a shark,   5
waltzing the railroad barons round the floor,
their cold, triumphant necks a jewelry store.
And in the shadows the next drink, and the next.
Where does it go, the moment of desire?
Lost, rattling down the Special's corridor,   10
the distance vein of lights in semaphore;
lost, the champagne glasses tossed against the fire,
the bullet laid inside a lower drawer.
And there is love, cruel love, the last to bore.

1999

Small Bad Town

The fractional white moons
of the satellite dishes
bother the broken noons
and the mortal wishes

of the local housewife   5
burning from her soaps.
Time sends invitations
in little envelopes.

The Spanish moss like hunger
hangs from the dogwood tree,   10
and no one pays the phone bill
of eternity.

Worship the devil of plenty,
worship the devil of wrath,
whose lovesick Brahma thunders   15
up the garden path.

O Protestant God, forgive us,
you Age of Steam antique.
The river floods its banks
and the flesh is weak.   20

Look! An egret launches
high above the oak,
like a Pershing missile.
The cows drink Diet Coke.

Too near, white churches tower,   25
like chalk cliffs of Dover.
In our small bad town
the cold war's never over.

1999

━◅ JORIE GRAHAM ▻━
(b. 1951)

The rarified atmosphere of Jorie Graham's childhood in Europe gave her rich
sources to mine when she decided to become a poet. She was born in New York
City to Curtis Bill Pepper, a scholar specializing in Catholic history and theology,
and Beverly Stoll Pepper, a painter and sculptor. Raised in the south of France and
Italy, Graham was exposed to religious art through the churches her father studied
and to modern art through watching her mother work. Fluent in English, French,
and Italian, Graham attended French schools and matriculated at the Sorbonne.
After being expelled for her participation in the student strikes of 1968, Graham
enrolled at New York University, intending to study filmmaking. She claims, how-

ever, that one day she passed by a classroom and overheard the professor reading lines from T. S. Eliot's "The Love Song of J. Alfred Prufrock": "I have heard the mermaids singing, each to each. / I do not think that they will sing to me." Enchanted by the siren song, Graham sneaked into the classroom and was so enthralled that she changed her focus from film to poetry. After graduating from NYU with a bachelor's degree in 1973, she was accepted into the creative writing program at the University of Iowa, where she earned her master's degree in 1978. She began her teaching career at Murray State University, in Kentucky, in 1978 and then moved to Arcata, California, where she taught at Humboldt State University. Her first book, *Hybrids of Plants and of Ghosts* (1980), earned her invitations to teach at Columbia University and to work as a Bunting Fellow at Radcliffe in 1982. With the successful reception of her second book, *Erosion* (1983), she returned to teach at the University of Iowa and married the poet James Galvin. Over the next sixteen years, Graham published six more books of poetry and collected so many major prizes, grants, and awards that she became one of the most celebrated contemporary American poets of her generation. Her honors include a MacArthur Foundation grant, the Pulitzer Prize for *The Dream of the Unified Field: Poems 1974–1994* (1995), and election in 1997 to serve as a Chancellor of the Academy of American Poets. In 1999, she left Iowa to teach at Harvard University as a Boylston Professor of Rhetoric and Oratory.

Graham has earned critical admiration for her relentless exploration of contemporary aesthetic concerns, particularly the dilemma of how to write poetry in a postmodern society where ideals such as "beauty," "truth," "individuality," and even "morality" have deteriorated. In her first two books, *Hybrids of Plants and of Ghosts* and *Erosion*, she approached such questions through lush descriptive poems that contemplated works of art or through the expansion of an individual consciousness enmeshed in domestic activities. Taking as her model poets such as Emily Dickinson and Wallace Stevens, Graham found "mystery and power" in secular experience, although she often applied a religious vocabulary to describe such moments of illumination. Aiming to write a poetry that fuses physical and mental experience, she also questioned divisions between body and spirit. In subsequent books, her work became self-consciously informed by postmodern literary theory, as she began to emphasize the boundaries where language—and even Western culture itself—fails to equal the transcendence (and, sometimes, the failure of transcendence) that she strove to articulate. Thus, in her introduction to *The Best American Poetry 1990*, she emphasizes that poetry "attempts to render aspects of experience that occur outside the provinces of logic and reason."

In *The End of Beauty* (1987), *Region of Unlikeness* (1991), *Materialism* (1993), *The Errancy* (1997), *Swarm* (2000), and *Never* (2002) she has defined those "boundary areas" more and more ambitiously in an attempt to blur divisions not only between body and spirit, but between individual consciousness and history. These later volumes have proved increasingly controversial among critics, some of whom praise her bold investigation of the far limits of language and others who decry the deliberate obscurity and incoherence of the work. Graham's poems are strongest when she grounds these investigations on concrete analogies. Sometimes, she will expand her meditations through incremental revisions and hesitations, so that the poems' arguments risk implosion through their severe self-scrutiny. This habit enriches some of her poems, but degrades others, especially when she loads her texts with multiple abstractions. But for Graham, such techniques approximate ideas and feelings that go beyond language. As she has remarked, poetry blends "irrational procedures with the rational nature of language."

Mind

The slow overture of rain,
each drop breaking
without breaking into
the next, describes
the unrelenting, syncopated   5
mind. Not unlike
the hummingbirds
imagining their wings
to be their heart, and swallows
believing the horizon   10
to be a line they lift
and drop. What is it
they cast for? The poplars,
advancing or retreating,
lose their stature   15
equally, and yet stand firm,
making arrangements
in order to become
imaginary. The city
draws the mind in streets,   20
and streets compel it
from their intersections
where a little
belongs to no one. It is
what is driven through   25
all stationary portions
of the world, gravity's
stake in things. The leaves,
pressed against the dank
window of November   30
soil, remain unwelcome
till transformed, parts
of a puzzle unsolvable
till the edges give a bit
and soften. See how   35
then the picture becomes clear,
the mind entering the ground
more easily in pieces,
and all the richer for it.

1980

Over and Over Stitch

Late in the season the world digs in, the fat blossoms
hold still for just a moment longer.
Nothing looks satisfied,
but there is no real reason to move on much further:
this isn't a bad place;   5
why not pretend

we wished for it?
The bushes have learned to live with their haunches.
The hydrangea is resigned
to its pale and inconclusive utterances.   10
Towards the end of the season
it is not bad

to have the body. To have experienced joy
as the mere lifting of hunger
is not to have known it   15
less. The tobacco leaves
don't mind being removed
to the long racks—all uses are astounding

to the used.
There are moments in our lives which, threaded, give us heaven— 20
noon, for instance, or all the single victories
of gravity, or the kudzu vine,
most delicate of manias,
which has pressed its luck

this far this season.   25
It shines a gloating green.
Its edges darken with impatience, a kind of wind.
Nothing again will ever be this easy, lives
being snatched up like dropped stitches, the dry stalks of daylilies
marking a stillness we can't keep.   30

                                                    1980

Erosion

I would not want, I think, a higher intelligence, one
simultaneous, cut clean
of sequence. No,
it is our slowness I love, growing slower,
tapping the paintbrush against the visible,   5
tapping the mind.
We are, ourselves, a mannerism now,
having fallen
out of the chain
of evolution.   10
So we grow fat with unqualified life.

Today, on this beach
I am history to these fine
pebbles. I run them
through my fingers. Each time   15
some molecules rub off
evolving into
the invisible. Always
I am trying to feel
the erosion—my grandfather, stiffening   20
on his bed, learning
to float on time, his mind like bait presented
to the stream ongoing, or you, by my side,
sleep rinsing you always a little less
clean, or daily   25
the erosion
of the right word, what it shuts,
or the plants coming forth as planned out my window, row
after row, sealed
into here. . . .   30
I've lined all our wineglasses up on the sill,
a keyboard, a garden. Flowers of the poles.
I'm gifting each with a little less water.
You can tap them
for music.   35
Outside the window it's starting to snow.
It's going to get colder.
The less full the glass, the truer
the sound.
This is my song   40
for the North
coming toward us.

                                                    1983

◦◄ JOY HARJO ►◦
(b. 1951)

A member of the Muscogee Creek tribe, Joy Harjo was born in Tulsa, Oklahoma.
Her father was of Muscogee descent and her mother's origins were a mixture of
French, Irish, and Cherokee. Harjo's great-great-grandfather was the war chief and
orator Menewa, who led his people in the Red Stick War against Andrew Jackson.
Attending high school at the Institute of American Indian Arts in Santa Fe, New
Mexico, Harjo first studied painting and theater. At age seventeen she had a son,
and as a single mother worked at various jobs before the birth of her daughter four
years later. Harjo has supported herself as a waitress, a service-station attendant, a
nursing assistant, and a dance instructor.

Harjo did not begin writing poetry until she was twenty-two years old. When
she eventually enrolled at the University of New Mexico, she continued her stud-

ies in painting and theater before switching to creative writing during her senior year. After earning a bachelor's degree in 1976, Harjo did graduate work at the University of Iowa (M.F.A., 1978). She then became an instructor at the Institute of American Indian Arts in Santa Fe.

Asked about the influence of her Creek heritage on her work, Harjo has commented, "It provides the underlying psychic structure, within which is a wealth of memory. I was not brought up traditionally Creek; [I] was raised in the north side of Tulsa in a neighborhood where there lived many other mixed-blood Indian families. My neighbors were Seminole Indian, Pawnee, other tribes, and white. I know when I write there is an old Creek within me that often participates." Harjo's poetry has been influenced not only by those Creek traditions but also by the Navajo memory poems of Luci Tapahonso and the Pueblo stories of Native Americans such as Simon Ortiz.

With a mixture of incantatory language and melancholy atmosphere, Harjo explores her physical and spiritual relationship to the mountains and mesas of the Southwestern landscapes. "Song for the Deer and Myself to Return On" typifies Harjo's evocative mixture of the familial, the spiritual, and the mythopoetic. Critic John Scarry in *World Literature Today* observed, "Harjo is clearly a highly political and feminist Native American, but she is even more the poet of myth and the subconscious; her images and landscapes owe as much to the vast stretches of our hidden mind as they do to her native Southwest."

Perhaps Harjo's best-known collection of poems is *In Mad Love and War* (1990) for which she won many awards, including the Josephine Miles Award, the William Carlos Williams Award, and an American Book Award. Other collections include *She Had Some Horses* (1983), *The Woman Who Fell From the Sky* (1994), *A Map to the Next World* (2000), and *How We Became Human* (2002). As lead singer and saxophonist, the poet fronts the rock–jazz–tribal fusion band Joy Harjo and the Real Revolution. She has taught in several universities, including University of Colorado at Boulder, University of Arizona at Tucson, and University of New Mexico at Albuquerque. Harjo currently lives in Honolulu, Hawaii.

--◦—◀▶—◦--

She Had Some Horses

She had some horses.

She had horses who were bodies of sand.
She had horses who were maps drawn of blood.
She had horses who were skins of ocean water.
She had horses who were the blue air of sky.   5

She had horses who were fur and teeth.
She had horses who were clay and would break.
She had horses who were splintered red cliff.

She had some horses.

She had horses with long, pointed breasts.   10
She had horses with full, brown thighs.

She had horses who laughed too much.
She had horses who threw rocks at glass houses.
She had horses who licked razor blades.

She had some horses.   15

She had horses who danced in their mothers' arms.
She had horses who thought they were the sun and their bodies shone
      and burned like stars.
She had horses who waltzed nightly on the moon.
She had horses who were much too shy, and kept quiet in stall of
      their own making.

She had some horses.   20

She had horses who liked Creek Stomp Dance songs.
She had horses who cried in their beer.
She had horses who spit at male queens who made them afraid
      of themselves.
She had horses who said they weren't afraid.
She had horses who lied.   25
She had horses who told the truth, who were stripped bare of their
      tongues.

She had some horses.

She had horses who called themselves, "horse."
She had horses who called themselves, "spirit," and kept their voices
      secret and to themselves.
She had horses who had no names.   30
She had horses who had books of names.

She had some horses.

She had horses who whispered in the dark, who were afraid
      to speak.
She had horses who screamed out of fear of the silence, who carried
      knives to protect themselves from ghosts.
She had horses who waited for destruction.   35
She had horses who waited for resurrection.

She had some horses.

She had horses who got down on their knees for any savior.
She had horses who thought their high price had saved them.
She had horses who tried to save her, who climbed in her bed at
      night and prayed as they raped her.   40

She had some horses.

She had some horses she loved.
She had some horses she hated.

These were the same horses.

1983

Song for the Deer and Myself to Return On

This morning when I looked out the roof window
before dawn and a few stars were still caught
in the fragile weft of ebony night
I was overwhelmed. I sang the song Louis taught me:
a song to call the deer in Creek, when hunting,   5
and I am certainly hunting something as magic as deer
in this city far from the hammock of my mother's belly.
It works, of course, and deer came into this room
and wondered at finding themselves
in a house near downtown Denver.   10
Now the deer and I are trying to figure out a song
to get them back, to get all of us back,
because if it works I'm going with them.
And it's too early to call Louis
and nearly too late to go home.   15

(For Louis Oliver)

1990

·◄ ANDREW HUDGINS ►·
(b. 1951)

Andrew Hudgins, one of the leading narrative poets of his generation, was born
in Killeen, Texas, the oldest surviving child of an air force officer. "Two of my uncles were Methodist ministers and I, being Southern Baptist, was surrounded by
preachers—people of The Word." As a military family, they moved often, and Andrew, who would later write most about the South, spent his childhood years in
many places, including North Carolina, California, France, and Alabama, where
he attended Sidney Lanier High School in Montgomery. A voracious reader from
an early age, Hudgins recalls the way he would disappear into books, especially
those of which his parents disapproved: "I learned early that reading, which I saw
as a pure pleasure, was seen by my parents as work."

   At Huntingdon College, where he earned his bachelor's degree in 1974, Hudgins discovered poetry, and soon was writing seriously enough to consider entering
the Iowa Writers' Workshop—an aspiration he would have to postpone. In the
meantime he tried teaching elementary school, took a master's degree at the University of Alabama, and did additional postgraduate work at Syracuse University.
Once accepted at Iowa, however, he applied himself to his poetry with renewed attention, completing many of the poems that would comprise his first book, *Saints
and Strangers* (1985), which appeared with an introduction by John Frederick
Nims. This book, particularly the title poem, a complex narrative sequence about
the daughter of an evangelical preacher, immediately earned Hudgins high praise
for his empathetic range, mordant humor, and emotional intensity. He followed
that successful debut with *After the Lost War* (1988), which he has called "an historical novel in verse that masquerades as a biography of the Civil War veteran and
poet Sidney Lanier." On the strength of this work he won the Poets' Prize and an

Alfred Hodder Fellowship at Princeton. Hudgins's poems are often characterized by colloquial, even crude, humor and a rigorous attention to daily life.

Hudgins joined the faculty of the University of Cincinnati in 1985, then moved to Ohio State University in 2001. He has steadily produced new work, including the meditative poems of *The Never-Ending* (1991), the autobiographical lyrics of *The Glass Hammer: A Southern Childhood* (1994), *Babylon in a Jar* (1998), and a collection of essays, *The Glass Anvil* (1997). Married to fiction writer Erin McGraw, Hudgins is the recipient of many awards and fellowships.

The Hereafter[1]

Some people as they die grow fierce, afraid.
They see a bright light, offer frantic prayers,
and try to climb them, like Jacob's ladder, up
to heaven. Others, never wavering,
inhabit heaven years before they die,   5
so certain of their grace they can describe,
down to the gingerbread around the eaves,
the cottage God has saved for them. For hours
they'll talk of how the willow will not weep,
the flowering Judas not betray. They'll talk   10
of how they'll finally learn to play the flute
and speak good French.
                                   Still others know they'll rot
and their flesh turn to earth, which will become
live oaks, spreading their leaves in August light.
The green cathedral glow that shines through them   15
will light grandchildren playing hide-and-seek
inside the grove. My next-door neighbor says
he's glad the buzzards will at last give wings
to those of us who've envied swifts as they
swoop, twist, and race through tight mosquito runs.   20

And some—my brother's one—anticipate
the grave as if it were a chair pulled up
before a fire on winter nights. His ghost,
he thinks, will slouch into the velvet cushion,
a bourbon and branchwater in its hand.   25
I've even met a man who says the soul
will come back in another skin—the way
a renter moves from house to house. Myself,
I'd like to come back as my father's hound.
Or something fast: a deer, a rust-red fox.   30

1. This poem is the final section of Hudgins's book-length narrative, *After the Lost War*, which deals with the life of Southern poet Sidney Lanier.

For so long I have thought of us as nails
God drives into the oak floor of this world,
it's hard to comprehend the hammer turned
to claw me out. I'm joking, mostly. I love
the possibilities—not one or two   35
but all of them. So if I had to choose,
pick only one and let the others go,
my death would be less strange, less rich, less like
a dizzying swig of fine rotgut. I roll
the busthead, slow, across my tongue and taste   40
the copper coils, the mockingbird that died
from fumes and plunged, wings spread, into the mash.
And underneath it all, just barely there,
I find the scorched-nut hint of corn that grew
in fields I walked, flourished beneath a sun   45
that warmed my skin, swaying in a changing wind
that tousled, stung, caressed, and toppled me.

                                                                        1988

Dead Christ

There seems no reason he should've died. His hands
are pierced by holes too tidy to have held,
untorn, hard muscles as they writhed on spikes.
And on the pink, scrubbed bottom of each foot
a bee-stung lip pouts daintily.   5
No reason he should die—and yet, and yet
Christ's eyes are swollen with it, his mouth
hangs slack with it, his belly taut with it,
his long hair lank with it, and damp;
and underneath the clinging funeral cloth   10
his manhood's huge and useless with it: Death.

One blood-drop trickles toward his wrist. Somehow
the grieving women missed it when they bathed,
today, the empty corpse. Most Christs return.
But this one's flesh. He isn't coming back.   15

                                                                        1991

Elegy for My Father, Who Is Not Dead

One day I'll lift the telephone
and be told my father's dead. He's ready.
In the sureness of his faith, he talks
about the world beyond this world
as though his reservations have   5
been made. I think he wants to go,
a little bit—a new desire
to travel building up, an itch
to see fresh worlds. Or older ones.
He thinks that when I follow him   10

he'll wrap me in his arms and laugh,
the way he did when I arrived
on earth. I do not think he's right.
He's ready. I am not. I can't
just say good-bye as cheerfully   15
as if he were embarking on a trip
to make my later trip go well.
I see myself on deck, convinced
his ship's gone down, while he's convinced
I'll see him standing on the dock   20
and waving, shouting, *Welcome back.*

1991

◄ JUDITH ORTIZ COFER ►
(b. 1952)

Judith Ortiz Cofer was born in the small town of Hormigueros, Puerto Rico, where the famous sanctuary of the Virgin of Monserrate is located. Her father joined the U.S. Navy and brought his family to Paterson, New Jersey, close to the Brooklyn Navy Yard where he was stationed. The family would move back and forth between Puerto Rico and Paterson whenever Cofer's father would leave on assignment, typically every six months. This culturally divided upbringing had a significant effect on the poet as a child and became the focus of much of her writing. A captivating storyteller, she found a wealth of material from her own family lore. In an interview Cofer recalls:

> In our apartment we spoke only Spanish, we listened only to Spanish music, we talked about *la casa* (back home in Puerto Rico) all the time. We practiced a very intense Catholic religion, with candles in the bathtub, pictures of the Virgin and Jesus everywhere. . . . So I would come home from the "outside world," where I really had to practice street survival (Paterson is a tough town and I used to get harassed by other kids occasionally) into this apartment where I was supposed to be a proper *señorita.* You had to sit right, behave right, say your prayers before you went to bed at night.

Cofer's father retired from the navy in 1968, and the family relocated to Augusta, Georgia, where the poet attended high school and Augusta College (B.A., 1974). Her father died in a car accident in 1976, and Cofer's mother moved back to Puerto Rico. At Florida Atlantic University, Cofer earned a master's degree and a fellowship from the English Speaking Union of America to study for a summer at Oxford University. She did not begin to write seriously until she was a graduate student. Her first two books of poetry were published almost simultaneously—*Terms of Survival* (1987) and *Reaching for the Mainland* (1987). Cofer then began writing fiction, and her first novel, *The Line of the Sun* (1989), soon appeared. Her subsequent collections have included a mix of poetry and prose, mostly involving the stories of her childhood and her ancestors. Interviewed in the *Kenyon Review,* Cofer discussed the presence of folklore and cultural identity in her work: "How can I separate my national background from my artistic impulse? I am a Puerto Rican woman possessing knowledge of that fact in a very intimate, personal, and intrinsic way. When I use a Puerto Rican tale, my story reflects that identity. I don't like to claim rhetoric or to tag my stories. I claim folklore because it belongs to all of us."

Cofer has received fellowships from the National Endowment for the Arts and the Witter Bynner Foundation. She is a professor of English and the director of the creative writing program at the University of Georgia. Cofer lives with her husband on a farm in the rural community of Louisville, Georgia.

Quinceañera[1]

My dolls have been put away like dead
children in a chest I will carry
with me when I marry.
I reach under my skirt to feel
a satin slip bought for this day. It is soft   5
as the inside of my thighs. My hair
has been nailed back with my mother's
black hairpins to my skull. Her hands
stretched my eyes open as she twisted
braids into a tight circle at the nape   10
of my neck. I am to wash my own clothes
and sheets from this day on, as if
the fluids of my body were poison, as if
the little trickle of blood I believe
travels from my heart to the world were   15
shameful. Is not the blood of saints and
men in battle beautiful? Do Christ's hands
not bleed into your eyes from His cross?
At night I hear myself growing and wake
to find my hands drifting of their own will   20
to soothe skin stretched tight
over my bones.
I am wound like the guts of a clock,
waiting for each hour to release me.

                                                        1987

The Lesson of the Sugarcane

My mother opened her eyes wide
at the edge of the field
ready for cutting.
"Take a deep breath,"

                   she whispered,   5
"There is nothing as sweet:
Nada más dulce."
                  Overhearing,

---

1. A fifteen-year-old girl's coming-out party in Latin cultures.

Father left the flat he was changing
in the road-warping sun,   10
and grabbing my arm, broke my sprint
toward a stalk:
"Cane can choke a little girl: snakes hide
where it grows over your head."

And he led us back to the crippled car   15
where we sweated out our penitence,
for having craved more sweetness
than we were allowed,
more than we could handle.

                                                        1993

RITA DOVE
(b. 1952)

In a memoir of her family life and early career, Rita Dove recalled, "Both sets of grandparents were blue-collar workers who had moved Up North as part of the Great Migration of rural southern blacks to the northern urban centers during the 1910s and '20s. My parents were the first in their working-class families to achieve advanced degrees." Growing up middle class in Akron, Ohio, Dove and her three siblings learned that they were "expected to carry 'the prize'—the respect that had been earned—a little further along the line." With time, Dove became aware that class and race had provided hardships for both her parents and her grandparents, but she herself met strong encouragement for her talents. One supportive high school teacher took her to a book signing by poet John Ciardi, an event that helped Dove realize her own interest in writing.

Dove matriculated at Ohio's Miami University, graduating summa cum laude in 1973. A Fulbright Fellowship to Germany (1974–1975) broadened her sense of language, culture, and history. On her return to the United States, while pursuing a master's degree at the Iowa Writers' Workshop, she met the German novelist Fred Viebahn. They were married in 1979 and have a daughter, Aviva.

The poetry Dove would write over the next decades would explore the themes of personal and national history, travel and language, motherhood and domesticity. Her first full-length collection, *The Yellow House on the Corner,* appeared in 1980, followed by *Museum* (1983), and a collection of short stories, *Fifth Sunday* (1985). It was her third collection of poems, *Thomas and Beulah* (1986), a sequence of lyrics based on the lives of her maternal grandparents, that proved a critical breakthrough. Championed by new advocates of narrative poetry, as well as established critics like Helen Vendler, it won the Pulitzer Prize, and established Rita Dove, at age thirty-five, as one of her generation's most visible poets.

Although Dove's poetry squarely faces issues of race in America, she has never felt that this was her only subject and has openly expressed a desire to speak for humanity in broader terms. The public success of *Thomas and Beulah* enabled her to move from her first teaching position in Arizona to a chair at the University of Virginia and to gain increased public notice not only as a poet, but as an advocate of poetry. From 1993 to 1995 she served as the youngest-ever and first African American Poet Laureate of the United States.

Her important collections after *Thomas and Beulah* include *Grace Notes* (1989), *Selected Poems* (1993), *Mother Love* (1995), a book dedicated to her daughter that melds personal experience with Greek mythology, and *On the Bus with Rosa Parks* (1999). Dove has also published a novel, *Through the Ivory Gate* (1992), and a successful verse drama, *The Darker Face of the Earth* (1994), in which she reimagines the tragedy of Oedipus in the antebellum South.

Adolescence—I

In water-heavy nights behind grandmother's porch
We knelt in the tickling grasses and whispered:
Linda's face hung before us, pale as a pecan,
And it grew wise as she said:
    "A boy's lips are soft,   5
      As soft as baby's skin."
The air closed over her words.
A firefly whirred near my ear, and in the distance
I could hear streetlamps ping
Into miniature suns   10
Against a feathery sky.

            1980

Adolescence—II

Although it is night, I sit in the bathroom, waiting.
Sweat prickles behind my knees, the baby-breasts are alert.
Venetian blinds slice up the moon; the tiles quiver in pale strips.

Then they come, the three seal men with eyes as round
As dinner plates and eyelashes like sharpened tines.   5
They bring the scent of licorice. One sits in the washbowl,

One on the bathtub edge; one leans against the door.
"Can you feel it yet?" they whisper.
I don't know what to say, again. They chuckle,

Patting their sleek bodies with their hands.   10
"Well, maybe next time." And they rise
Glittering like pools of ink under moonlight,

And vanish. I clutch at the ragged holes
They leave behind, here at the edge of darkness.
Night rests like a ball of fur on my tongue.   15

            1980

Adolescence—III

With Dad gone, Mom and I worked
The dusky rows of tomatoes.
As they glowed orange in sunlight

And rotted in shadow, I too
Grew orange and softer, swelling out   5
Starched cotton slips.

The texture of twilight made me think of
Lengths of Dotted Swiss. In my room
I wrapped scarred knees in dresses
That once went to big-band dances;   10
I baptized my earlobes with rosewater.
Along the window-sill, the lipstick stubs
Glittered in their steel shells.

Looking out at the rows of clay
And chicken manure, I dreamed how it would happen: 15
He would meet me by the blue spruce,
A carnation over his heart, saying,
"I have come for you, Madam;
I have loved you in my dreams."
At his touch, the scabs would fall away.   20
Over his shoulder, I see my father coming toward us:
He carries his tears in a bowl,
And blood hangs in the pine-soaked air.

                                                                        1980

Daystar

She wanted a little room for thinking:
but she diapers steaming on the line,
a doll slumped behind the door.

So she lugged a chair behind the garage
to sit out the children's naps.   5

Sometimes there were things to watch—
the pinched armor of a vanished cricket,
a floating maple leaf. Other days
she stared until she was assured
when she closed her eyes   10
she'd see only her own vivid blood.

She had an hour, at best, before Liza appeared
pouting from the top of the stairs.
And just *what* was mother doing
out back with the field mice? Why,   15

building a palace. Later
that night when Thomas rolled over and
lurched into her, she would open her eyes
and think of the place that was hers
for an hour—where   20
she was nothing,
pure nothing, in the middle of the day.

                                                                        1986

ALICE FULTON
(b. 1952)

Alice Fulton was born and raised in Troy, New York. She received her bachelor's degree in creative writing in 1978 from New York Empire State College and her master's in 1982 from Cornell University, where she studied with A. R. Ammons. In the late 1970s she worked briefly for an advertising firm in New York City, and in 1980 she married Hank De Leo, a painter. In 1983 she began teaching at the University of Michigan. After *Dance Script with Electric Ballerina* (1983), she published four more poetry collections—*Palladium* (1986), *Powers of Congress* (1990), *Sensual Math* (1995), and *Felt* (2001)—and a book of essays, *Feeling as a Foreign Language: The Good Strangeness of Poetry* (1999). Among her many awards, she has received a MacArthur Foundation grant.

In her drive to freshen poetic diction, avoid cliché and sentimentality, and create "skewed domains" in her poetry, Fulton has distinguished herself as one of the most original American poets writing today. She has succeeded in challenging not only assumptions about gender roles, but also the assumptions underlying current modes of poetry such as the autobiographical, first-person lyric or the experimental "Language poem." Rather than follow any prescriptive method for writing, she mixes her techniques, so that poems of hers that appear to be autobiographical are often concerned with how the mind comes to terms with experience through language, and poems that call attention to her linguistic virtuosity through puns and sudden shifts of diction are never abstract products of the mind, but invest themselves in feeling and celebrate the quirky details that she observes in the world around her.

Although many of the poems from *Dance Script with Electric Ballerina* refer to details of her Catholic girlhood, she has voiced skepticism about autobiographical poetry, pointing out that such poems are constructs whose pose of sincerity readers rarely question. Her later books have tended more and more toward emphasizing texture and variety of language and poses that call attention to themselves as poses—dramatic monologue, poems in which several voices arise and often contradict one another, and active enjambments that make words do double duty as different parts of speech. In particular, she often refuses to gender her speakers, forcing her readers to reconsider their assumptions about what constitutes male or female identity. Like the Language poets, Fulton is interested in linguistic play and artifice, and also in critical theory and philosophy, although the theories most evident in her poetry and essays are those of science and mathematics.

What I Like

Friend—the face I wallow toward
through a scrimmage of shut faces.
Arms like towropes to haul me home, aide-
memoire, my lost childhood docks, a bottled ark
in harbor. *Friend*—I can't forget
how even the word contains an *end*.   5

We circle each other in a scared bolero,
imagining stratagems: postures and imposters.
Cold convictions keep us solo. I ahem
and hedge my affections. Who'll blow the first kiss,   10
land it like the lifeforces we feel
tickling at each wrist? It should be easy
easy to take your hand, whisper down this distance
labeled hers or his: what I like about you is

                                                    1983

The Expense of Spirit[1]

The credits and debits of cold sex:
Release, power, what the back-to-basics fuck-
You on the subway adds up to.

Are we making love yet?

Look, fingers speak and shine the world. They count.   5
I'd think twice before bagging them
To pass for guns, or cocking
Them through the flesh of some
Likely one whose hand you wouldn't hold.
Endearments ease the deal. Which sounds callous,   10

Though neither she who guns her reproductive
Engine, whining "Can he be *niced?*"
Nor he who speaks of sex as "making *like,*"
Damning the heart till it rankles, playing with ashes,
Exchange the compliment I mean; to praise the otherness   15
Rising or widening next to one's own
Nude dilations. We care to an hygienic extent. No more, though
Earth and self get ugly when unloved. Cellulite
Skies where heaven stared! Suffer, but don't let me
See: that's the dearest, cheapest prayer.   20

                                                    1990

◄ MARK JARMAN ►
(b. 1952)

Born in Mount Sterling, Kentucky, Mark Foster Jarman spent his childhood in places as dissimilar as Southern California and Scotland. When Jarman was six years old, his father, a minister of the Christian Church (Disciples of Christ), moved the family to Kircaldy, Scotland, as part of the U.S. Christian Church Fraternal Aid to British Churches. Returning to America a few years later, the Jarmans settled in Redondo Beach, California, in the South Bay district of Los

---

1. Fulton draws her title from William Shakespeare's Sonnet 129, "Th' expense of spirit in a waste of shame."

Angeles, where Jarman grew up participating in the surfer culture of his new hometown. Choosing to remain near the coast at college, Jarman attended the University of California at Santa Cruz, where he studied with Raymond Carver. At Santa Cruz, he met his future wife, a singer and music professor, and befriended classmate and fellow aspiring poet, Robert McDowell, with whom he would later collaborate on the *Reaper,* a little magazine that championed narrative poetry. After receiving his bachelor's degree in 1974, Jarman enrolled at the Iowa Writers' Workshop, where he earned his master's degree in 1976. He taught at a number of universities before settling at Vanderbilt in 1983. By that time, he had published two collections of poetry, *North Sea* (1978) and *The Rote Walker* (1981), and was developing his ideas about narrative poetry through his co-editorship of the *Reaper,* which he and McDowell founded in 1980.

Frustrated by the increasing prevalence of poems about poetry and by poets who seemed to envision an audience consisting only of other poets and academic commentators, in their *Reaper* editorials Jarman and McDowell proposed narrative as a means of drawing poets' attention outward, away from "the self" or "the mind" as primary themes. In their opinion, narrative could help recapture the general readers who kept up with contemporary fiction but did not read poetry. Although the magazine had a small circulation, it became known for the questions it raised about trends in contemporary poetry and for the black humor that tempered the magazine's adversarial stance. Jarman and McDowell invented a persona, "The Reaper," who made tongue-in-cheek, apocalyptic proclamations condemning the mannerism, sloppy technique, and solipsism that the editors found in the work of their contemporaries. When the magazine folded in 1989, it had succeeded in drawing attention to narrative poetry, which became an increasingly viable option for poets writing in the last two decades of the century. Jarman and McDowell's criticism from the *Reaper* was eventually collected by Story Line Press in *The Reaper Essays* (1996).

In his own poetry, Jarman began to focus on short narratives in *The Rote Walker, Far and Away* (1985), and *The Black Riviera* (1990), and also tried his hand at a book-length narrative poem, *Iris* (1992). The narratives of these books often center on the beachtown culture of Southern California. In the 1990s, he shifted his focus in *Questions for Ecclesiastes* (1997) and *Unholy Sonnets* (2000) to religious poetry exploring Christian faith and doubt. The poems of these two collections search for language to describe God and wrestle with the problem of unredemptive suffering, as the poems' speakers swing between anger over God's absence to celebrating the mystery of the Divine. Throughout his career Jarman has felt the need to identify himself with a specific kind of poetry, first narrative and then religious. He documents his evolving perspective in the essays and reviews collected in *The Secret of Poetry* (2001) and *Body and Soul* (2002). He has also co-edited (with David Mason) an anthology, *Rebel Angels: 25 Poets of the New Formalism* (1996).

Ground Swell

Is nothing real but when I was fifteen,
Going on sixteen, like a corny song?

I see myself so clearly then, and painfully—
Knees bleeding through my usher's uniform
Behind the candy counter in the theater   5
After a morning's surfing; paddling frantically
To top the brisk outsiders coming to wreck me,
Trundle me clumsily along the beach floor's
Gravel and sand; my knees aching with salt.
Is that all that I have to write about?   10
You write about the life that's vividest.
And if that is your own, that is your subject.
And if the years before and after sixteen
Are colorless as salt and taste like sand—
Return to those remembered chilly mornings,   15
The light spreading like a great skin on the water,
And the blue water scalloped with wind-ridges,
And—what was it exactly?—that slow waiting
When, to invigorate yourself, you peed
Inside your bathing suit and felt the warmth   20
Crawl all around your hips and thighs,
And the first set rolled in and the water level
Rose in expectancy, and the sun struck
The water surface like a brassy palm,
Flat and gonglike, and the wave face formed.   25
Yes. But that was a summer so removed
In time, so specially peculiar to my life,
Why would I want to write about it again?
There was a day or two when, paddling out,
An older boy who had just graduated   30
And grown a great blonde moustache, like a walrus,
Skimmed past me like a smooth machine on the water,
And said my name. I was so much younger,
To be identified by one like him—
The easy deference of a kind of god   35
Who also went to church where I did—made me
Reconsider my worth. I had been noticed.
He soon was a small figure crossing waves,
The shawling crest surrounding him with spray,
Whiter than gull feathers. He had said my name   40
Without scorn, just with a bit of surprise
To notice me among those trying the big waves
Of the morning break. His name is carved now
On the black wall in Washington, the frozen wave
That grievers cross to find a name or names.   45
I knew him as I say I knew him, then,
Which wasn't very well. My father preached
His funeral. He came home in a bag
That may have mixed in pieces of his squad.
Yes, I can write about a lot of things   50
Besides the summer that I turned sixteen.

But that's my ground swell. I must start
Where things began to happen and I knew it.

1997

Hands Folded

Hands folded to construct a church and steeple,
A roof of knuckles, outer walls of skin,
The thumbs as doors, the fingers bent within
To be revealed, wriggling as "all the people,"
All eight of them, enmeshed, caught by surprise,   5
Turned upward blushing in the sudden light,
The nails like welders' masks, the fit so tight
Among them you can hear their half-choked cries
To be released, to be pried from this mess
They're soldered into somehow—they don't know.   10
But stuck now they are willing to confess,
If that will ease your grip and let them go,
Confess the terror they cannot withstand
Is being locked inside another hand.

1997

After the Praying

After the praying, after the hymn-singing,
After the sermon's trenchant commentary
On the world's ills, which make ours secondary,
After communion, after the hand-wringing,
And after peace descends upon us, bringing   5
Our eyes up to regard the sanctuary
And how the light swords through it, and how, scary
In their sheer numbers, motes of dust ride, clinging—
There is, as doctors say about some pain,
Discomfort knowing that despite your prayers,   10
Your listening and rejoicing, your small part
In this communal stab at coming clean,
There is one stubborn remnant of your cares
Intact. There is still murder in your heart.

1997

➤◄ NAOMI SHIHAB NYE ►◄
(b. 1952)

Naomi Shihab Nye was born in 1952 to parents of diverse cultural backgrounds.
Nye's father was Palestinian, and her American mother was of Swiss and German
descent. The poet spent her early childhood in St. Louis before moving to Jerusalem
for a year of high school. When the family returned to the United States they settled in San Antonio, Texas, where Nye presently lives with her husband and son.

Nye earned a bachelor's degree from Trinity University in English and world religions. Her studies, extensive travel, and varied ethnic origins stimulated Nye's interest in international cultures and issues—a common subject of her poetry and prose. Nye's poetry also contains significant local and regional influences. In the *Dictionary of Literary Biography*, Nye remarked, "For me the primary source of poetry has always been local life, random characters met on the streets, our own ancestry sifting down to us through small essential daily tasks." Nye writes both free verse and prose poems, using simple language and imagery, elegantly phrased for expressive effect. Mary Logue observed in the *Village Voice* that in Nye's work, "Sometimes the fabric is thin and the mundaneness of the action shows through. But, in an alchemical process of purification, Nye often pulls gold from the ordinary."

Nye has won four Pushcart Prizes and the Lavan Award from the Academy of American Poets in 1988. Her first full-length collection, *Different Ways to Pray* (1980), was awarded the Voertman Poetry Prize. Other collections include *Hugging the Jukebox* (1982), *Yellow Glove* (1986), and *Fuel* (1998). Nye has been a visiting writer at schools such as University of Hawaii, University of Alaska at Fairbanks, University of Texas at Austin, and has guest-taught at the University of California, Berkeley. Besides poetry, she has published children's literature, fiction, essays, and anthologies of juvenile and international literature.

◦━━◗▶━◦

Famous

The river is famous to the fish.

The loud voice is famous to silence,
which knew it would inherit the earth
before anybody said so.

The cat sleeping on the fence is famous to the birds   5
watching him from the birdhouse.

The tear is famous, briefly, to the cheek.

The idea you carry close to your bosom
is famous to your bosom.

The boot is famous to the earth,   10
more famous than the dress shoe,
which is famous only to floors.

The bent photograph is famous to the one who carries it
and not at all famous to the one who is pictured.

I want to be famous to shuffling men   15
who smile while crossing streets,
sticky children in grocery lines,
famous as the one who smiled back.

I want to be famous in the way a pulley is famous,
or a buttonhole, not because it did anything spectacular,   20
but because it never forgot what it could do.

1982

The Traveling Onion

"It is believed that the onion originally came from India. In Egypt it was an object of worship—why I haven't been able to find out. From Egypt the onion entered Greece and on to Italy, thence into all of Europe."

Better Living Cookbook

When I think how far the onion has traveled   5
just to enter my stew today, I could kneel and praise
all small forgotten miracles,
crackly paper peeling on the drainboard,
pearly layers in smooth agreement,
the way knife enters onion   10
and onion falls apart on the chopping block,
a history revealed.

And I would never scold the onion
for causing tears.
It is right that tears fall   15
for something small and forgotten.
How at meal, we sit to eat,
commenting on texture of meat or herbal aroma
but never on the translucence of onion,
now limp, now divided,   20
or its traditionally honorable career:
For the sake of others,
disappear.

1986

◄ MARK DOTY ►
(b. 1953)

Mark Doty moved often during his childhood, raised in suburban towns in Tennessee, Florida, Southern California, and Arizona. His father was an army engineer whose work frequently required him to relocate his family. Doty's mother was from a family of Irish immigrants who settled in Sweetwater, Tennessee. In an interview, the poet recalled his childhood:

> I grew up in a very disconnected suburban landscape, in town after town, and it seems to me that there was very little that existed in order to enchant, to instruct us in our larger possibilities, to engage the spirit. There was, in other words, little art, and a great deal of practicality, of ways of life determined by social and economic necessity, or social and economic ambition.

Doty's memoir, *Firebird* (1999), recounts his slow and difficult discovery of his sexual identity. His mother was a heavy drinker, and there was no shortage of tension between young Doty and his unsympathetic parents. *Firebird* tells of Doty returning home one night to overhear his mother drunkenly ranting to his father that their son was a homosexual and their daughter a whore. "But you go on past their door," he tells himself, "into your room, the lights are out, and you're hoping you're not visible at all, not even a shadow." Still denying his sexuality, Doty married poet Ruth Dawson at age eighteen, a marriage that would last for nine years. After completing his undergraduate work at Drake University, he divorced his wife and set out for Manhattan with $600 in his pocket. There he worked in temporary office jobs while attending Goddard College in Vermont part time, earning a master's degree (1980). In New York Doty met Wally Roberts, a department store window-dresser, who would become his longtime partner. The couple lived together in Manhattan and in Provincetown, Massachusetts.

Roberts tested HIV-positive in 1989 and died of AIDS five years later. The experience of the decline and death of Doty's lover became the central focus and transformative event of his life and work. His third collection of poetry, *My Alexandria* (1993), addressed AIDS and its victims personally and directly. The critically acclaimed book garnered the *Los Angeles Times* Book Award, the National Book Critics Circle Award, and Britain's T. S. Eliot Prize, which Doty was the first American to receive. Following the success of *My Alexandria,* Doty has published a steady stream of new poetry collections, including *Atlantis* (1995), *Sweet Machine* (1998), *Source* (2001), and *Still Life with Oysters and Lemon* (2001), as well as two memoirs, *Heaven's Coast* (1996) and *Firebird.* Doty has taught poetry and creative writing in various schools, including Columbia University, Sarah Lawrence College, the University of Utah, and Goddard College. He has also been the recipient of a Guggenheim fellowship, a National Endowment for the Arts fellowship and a Rockefeller Foundation fellowship. Doty was given a three-year Lila Wallace–Reader's Digest Writer's Award in 2000.

Often confessional in tone and subject matter, Doty's poetry calls to mind the work of Robert Lowell, a poet he particularly admires. His poems are generally long, full of detailed descriptions, memorable characters, and an acute awareness of mortality. Although his critics claim his work often bogs down in ornate writing and emotional excess, he has achieved a distinct personal style that—like Robert Lowell's work—mixes political and personal passions. Doty has remarked, "The sort of beauty that interests me now is something more revealing of character—a very personal sort of beauty, often a failed sort. I am drawn to the ways people reinvent themselves—how they make order and harmony out of the chaos or uncertainty that surrounds them." Doty currently teaches poetry and memoir-writing at the University of Houston, splitting his time between Texas and Provincetown.

Fog

The crested iris by the front gate waves
its blue flags three days, exactly,

then they vanish. The peony buds'
tight wrappings are edged crimson;

when they open, a little blood-color   5
will ruffle at the heart of the flounced,

unbelievable white. Three weeks after the test,
the vial filled from the crook

of my elbow, I'm seeing blood everywhere:
a casual nick from the garden shears,   10

a shaving cut and I feel the physical rush
of the welling up, the wine-fountain

dark as Siberian iris. The thin green porcelain
teacup, our homemade Ouija's planchette,

rocks and wobbles every night, spins   15
and spells. It seems a cloud of spirits

numerous as lilac panicles vie for occupancy—
children grabbing for the telephone,

happy to talk to someone who isn't dead yet?
Everyone wants to speak at once, or at least   20

these random words appear, incongruous
and exactly spelled: *energy, immunity, kiss.*

Then: *M. has immunity. W. has.*
And that was all. One character, Frank,

distinguishes himself: a boy who lived   25
in our house in the thirties, loved dogs

and gangster movies, longs for a body,
says he can watch us through the television,

asks us to stand before the screen
and kiss. *God in garden,* he says   30

Sitting out on the back porch at twilight,
I'm almost convinced. In this geometry

of paths and raised beds, the green shadows
of delphinium, there's an unseen rustling:

some secret amplitude   35
seems to open in this orderly space.

Maybe because it contains so much dying,
all these tulip petals thinning

at the base until any wind takes them.
I doubt anyone else would see that, looking in,   40

and then I realize my garden has no outside, only *is*
subjectively. As blood is utterly without

an outside, can't be seen except out of context,
the wrong color in alien air, no longer itself.

Though it submits to test, two,   45
to be exact, each done three times,

though not for me, since at their first entry
into my disembodied blood

there was nothing at home there.
For you they entered the blood garden over   50

and over, like knocking at a door
because you know someone's home. Three times

the Elisa Test, three the Western Blot,
and then the incoherent message. We're

the public health care worker's   55
nine o'clock appointment,

she is a phantom hand who forms
the letters of your name, and the word

that begins with *P.* I'd lie out
and wait for the god if it weren't   60

so cold, the blue moon huge
and disruptive above the flowering crab's

foaming collapse. The spirits say *Fog*
when they can't speak clearly

and the letters collide; sometimes   65
for them there's nothing outside the mist

of their dying. Planchette,
peony, I would think of anything

not to say the word. Maybe the blood
in the flower is a god's. Kiss me,   70

in front of the screen, please,
the dead are watching.

They haven't had enough yet.
Every new bloom is falling apart.

I would say anything else   75
in the world, any other word.

1993

Homo Will Not Inherit

Down anywhere and between the roil
of bathhouse steam—up there the linens of joy
and shame must be laundered again and again,

all night—downtown anywhere
and between the column of feathering steam   5
unknotting itself thirty feet above the avenue's

shimmered azaleas of gasoline,
between the steam and the ruin
of the Cinema Paree (marquee advertising

its own milky vacancy, broken showcases sealed,   10
ticketbooth a hostage wrapped in tape
and black plastic, captive in this zone

of blackfronted bars and bookstores
where there's nothing to read
but longing's repetitive texts,   15

where desire's unpoliced, or nearly so)
someone's posted a xeroxed headshot
of Jesus: permed, blonde, blurred at the edges

as though photographed through a greasy lens,
and inked beside him, in marker strokes: 20
HOMO WILL NOT INHERIT. *Repent & be saved.*

I'll tell you what I'll inherit: the margins
which have always been mine, downtown after hours
when there's nothing left to buy,

the dreaming shops turned in on themselves,   25
seamless, intent on the perfection of display,
the bodegas and offices lined up, impenetrable:

edges no one wants, no one's watching. Though
the borders of this shadow-zone (mirror and dream
of the shattered streets around it) are chartered   30

by the police, and they are required,
some nights, to redefine them. But not now, at twilight,
permission's descending hour, early winter darkness

pillared by smoldering plumes. The public city's
ledgered and locked, but the secret city's boundless;   35
from which do these tumbling towers arise?

I'll tell what I'll inherit: steam,
and the blinding symmetry of some towering man,
fifteen minutes of forgetfulness incarnate.

I've seen flame flicker around the edges of the body,   40
pentecostal, evidence of inhabitation.
And I have been possessed of the god myself,

I have been the temporary apparition
salving another, I have been his visitation, I say it
without arrogance, I have been an angel   45

for minutes at a time, and I have for hours
believed—without judgement, without condemnation—
that in each body, however obscured or recast,

is the divine body—common, habitable—
the way in a field of sunflowers   50
you can see every bloom's

the multiple expression
of a single shining idea,
which is the face hammered into joy.

I'll tell you what I'll inherit: 55
stupidity, erasure, exile
inside the chalked lines of the police,

who must resemble what they punish,
the exile you require of me,
you who's posted this invitation   60

to a heaven nobody wants.
You who must be patrolled,
who adore constraint, I'll tell you

what I'll inherit, not your pallid temple
but a real palace, the anticipated   65
and actual memory, the moment flooded

by skin and the knowledge of it,
the gesture and its description
—do I need to say it?—

the flesh *and* the word. And I'll tell you,   70
you who can't wait to abandon your body,
what you want me to, maybe something

like you've imagined, a dirty story:
Years ago, in the baths,
a man walked into the steam,   75

the gorgeous deep indigo of him gleaming,
solid tight flanks, the intricately ridged abdomen—
and after he invited me to his room,

nudging his key toward me,
as if perhaps I spoke another tongue   80
and required the plainest of gestures,

after we'd been, you understand,
worshipping a while in his church,
he said to me, *I'm going to punish your mouth.*

I can't tell you what that did to me.   85
My shame was redeemed then;
I won't need to burn in the afterlife.

It wasn't that he hurt me,
more than that: the spirit's transactions
are enacted now, here—no one needs   90

your eternity. This failing city's
radiant as any we'll ever know,
paved with oily rainbow, charred gates

jeweled with tags, swoops of letters
over letters, indecipherable as anything   95
written by desire. I'm not ashamed

to love Babylon's scrawl. How could I be?
It's written on my face as much as on
these walls. This city's inescapable,

gorgeous, and on fire. I have my kingdom.   100

1995

⚫◄ GJERTRUD SCHNACKENBERG ►⚫
(b. 1953)

Reviewing Gjertrud Schnackenberg's third collection, *A Gilded Lapse of Time*
(1992), the usually acerbic critic William Logan called her "the most talented
American poet under the age of forty." What dazzled Logan was the poet's intellectual range in a book that embroidered upon the ruins of ancient and modern
empires. Schnackenberg has also been praised for her formal acuity and her use of
verse sequences to broaden the possibilities of her art.

Born in Tacoma, Washington, the daughter of second-generation Norwegian
Lutherans, her father a history professor, Schnackenberg was educated in public
schools and went on to college at Mount Holyoke (B.A., 1975), where she won
the prestigious intercollegiate Glascock poetry prize (which had earlier been
awarded to Robert Lowell, James Merrill, and Sylvia Plath). While still at Mount
Holyoke, the twenty-year-old Schnackenberg received the devastating news of her
father's death, an event that would inspire her most deeply felt early poetry. Her
first collection, *Portraits and Elegies* (1982; revised 1986), contains the twelve-
part sequence entitled "Laughing with One Eye," which recalls her childhood and
her close relationship with her father. From her second book, *The Lamplit Answer* (1985), critics have most often praised another elegy on the same subject,
"Supernatural Love." Schnackenberg's first marriage to poet Paul Smyth ended in
divorce. In 1987 she married the philosopher Robert Nozick who taught at Harvard University. The couple lived in Cambridge, Massachusetts, until Nozick's
death in 2002.

A master of the high style, Schnackenberg is a deeply literary poet whose work
always expresses an overt consciousness of tradition. Her earliest work reflected
the influence of W. B. Yeats, who was soon displaced by Robert Lowell, Elizabeth
Bishop, and Joseph Brodsky, whose various presences haunt both *Portraits and
Elegies* and *The Lamplit Answer*. Although some reviewers have found her too
beholden to her models, especially Lowell, this criticism is unfair in any general

sense. Allusion and historical echo are a fundamental part of her poetic method, and her poems acknowledge their allegiances without ever losing command of their individual aims and emotions. Her best work, especially *The Lamplit Answer,* has demonstrated the viability of ambitious and demanding poetry written in a traditional style during an era that has privileged experimental poetics.

Critics have been more divided about *The Gilded Lapse of Time* (1992) and her latest collection, a verse meditation on the meaning of classical tragedy called *The Throne of Labdacus* (2000), though her intelligence and ambition continue to be praised. The verbal ornateness of both recent books, as well as their unapologetically Eurocentric concerns, make them highly unusual contributions to contemporary American poetry. Her first three collections have been republished under one cover as *Supernatural Love* (2000). While Schnackenberg's later poems have generally become more allusive and intellectual, her work remains important for its rigorous exploration of profound aesthetic concerns. "In each of her books so far," the critic Adam Kirsch has written, "Schnackenberg is reaching towards a more comprehensive work of art." Unabashedly literary and learned, she remains one of the most ambitious and skillful contemporary American poets.

The Paperweight

The scene within the paperweight is calm,
A small white house, a laughing man and wife,
Deep snow. I turn it over in my palm
And watch it snowing in another life,

Another world, and from this scene learn what   5
It is to stand apart: she serves him tea
Once and forever, dressed from head to foot
As she is always dressed. In this toy, history

Sifts down through the glass like snow, and we
Wonder if their single deed tells much   10
Or little of the way she loves, and whether he
Sees shadows in the sky. Beyond our touch,

Beyond our lives, they laugh, and drink their tea.
We look at them just as the winter night
With its vast empty spaces bends to see   15
Our isolated little world of light,

Covered with snow, and snow in clouds above it,
And drifts and swirls too deep to understand.
Still, I must try to think a little of it,
With so much winter in my head and hand.   20

1982

Supernatural Love

My father at the dictionary-stand
Touches the page to fully understand
The lamplit answer, tilting in his hand

His slowly scanning magnifying lens,
A blurry, glistening circle he suspends   5
Above the word "Carnation." Then he bends

So near his eyes are magnified and blurred,
One finger on the miniature word,
As if he touched a single key and heard

A distant, plucked, infinitesimal string,   10
"The obligation due to every thing
That's smaller than the universe." I bring

My sewing needle close enough that I
Can watch my father through the needle's eye,
As through a lens ground for a butterfly   15

Who peers down flower-hallways toward a room
Shadowed and fathomed as this study's gloom
Where, as a scholar bends above a tomb

To read what's buried there, he bends to pore
Over the Latin blossom. I am four,   20
I spill my pins and needles on the floor

Trying to stitch "Beloved" X by X.
My dangerous, bright needle's point connects
Myself illiterate to this perfect text

I cannot read. My father puzzles why   25
It is my habit to identify
Carnations as "Christ's flowers," knowing I

Can give no explanation but "Because."
Word-roots blossom in speechless messages
The way the thread behind my sampler does   30

Where following each X I awkward move
My needle through the word whose root is love.
He reads, "A pink variety of Clove,

Carnatio, the Latin, meaning flesh."
As if the bud's essential oils brush   35
Christ's fragrance through the room, the iron-fresh

Odor carnations have floats up to me,
A drifted, secret, bitter ecstasy,
The stems squeak in my scissors, *Child, it's me,*

He turns the page to "Clove" and reads aloud: 40
"The clove, a spice, dried from a flower-bud."
Then twice, as if he hasn't understood,

He reads, "From French, for *clou*, meaning a nail."
He gazes, motionless. "Meaning a nail."
The incarnation blossoms, flesh and nail,   45

I twist my threads like stems into a knot
And smooth "Beloved," but my needle caught
Within the threads, *Thy blood so dearly bought,*

The needle strikes my finger to the bone.
I lift my hand, it is myself I've sewn,   50
The flesh laid bare, the threads of blood my own,

I lift my hand in startled agony
And call upon his name, "Daddy daddy"—
My father's hand touches the injury

As lightly as he touched the page before,   55
Where incarnation bloomed from roots that bore
The flowers I called Christ's when I was four.

1985

●━◄ KIM ADDONIZIO ►━●
(b. 1954)

Kim Addonizio was born in Washington, D.C., the daughter of Bob Addie, a sports writer, and Pauline Betz, a tennis champion. When she was seventeen she learned that her surname had been shortened after her paternal grandparents immigrated from Italy, and she would later change it back to its original form. She grew up Catholic and Italian American in Bethesda, Maryland. "I got straight A's in school and felt superior and alienated." After a brief flirtation with undergraduate studies at Georgetown University, she spent a few years leading a rambling and disconnected life, experimenting with drugs and sex in ways that would later inform her poetry. By the late seventies she had made her way to the Bay Area, where she has lived ever since. She earned her bachelor's degree summa cum laude at San Francisco State University in 1982, a master's degree four years later. Twice married and divorced, and the mother of a daughter, Addonizio has taught at several colleges and universities.

Her poetry is characterized by its high-spirited energy and raucous refusal of conventional literary gentility. *The Philosopher's Club* (1994), her first full-length collection, is notable for its mixture of sexual candor and lively use of traditional forms, especially the sonnet. Her next volume was a hard-edged urban verse novel, *Jimmy and Rita* (1997), which recounts the lives of two lovers in the drug-filled and crime-ridden streets of San Francisco's Tenderloin district. Written in lyric bursts and told with unsparing realism, it is one of the more notable experiments in recent verse narrative. Addonizio's third book of poems, *Tell Me* (2000), a finalist for the

National Book Award, displays less formality in the verse and an even greater attention to sex. Her Catholic upbringing is evident not only in her rebellious stance in some poems, but also in her relentless drive toward honest interrogation of life. She is the author of a novel, *In the Box Called Pleasure* (1999), and, with Dorianne Laux, *The Poet's Companion: A Guide to the Pleasures of Writing Poetry* (1997).

First Poem for You

I like to touch your tattoos in complete
darkness, when I can't see them. I'm sure of
where they are, know by heart the neat
lines of lightning pulsing just above
your nipple, can find, as if by instinct, the blue   5
swirls of water on your shoulder where a serpent
twists, facing a dragon. When I pull you
to me, taking you until we're spent
and quiet on the sheets, I love to kiss
the pictures in your skin. They'll last until   10
you're seared to ashes; whatever persists
or turns to pain between us, they will still
be there. Such permanence is terrifying.
So I touch them in the dark; but touch them, trying.

1994

Stolen Moments

What happened, happened once. So now it's best
in memory—an orange he sliced: the skin
unbroken, then the knife, the chilled wedge
lifted to my mouth, his mouth, the thin
membrane between us, the exquisite orange,   5
tongue, orange, my nakedness and his,
the way he pushed me up against the fridge—
Now I get to feel his hands again, the kiss
that didn't last, but sent some neural twin
flashing wildly through the cortex. Love's   10
merciless, the way it travels in
and keeps emitting light. Beside the stove
we ate an orange. And there were purple flowers
on the table. And we still had hours.

1999

◄ FRANCISCO X. ALARCÓN ►
(b. 1954)

Francisco X. Alarcón was born in Wilmington, California, but during his childhood he moved back and forth between Los Angeles and Mexico. Being educated in both English and Spanish, Alarcón developed an early sense of his double identity. "I consider myself bi-national," he claims, but that duality has made him both an outsider and insider in each culture. (In Mexico he was called "Pancho," an insulting name for an Americanized Mexican.) Returning to California, he worked briefly as a dishwasher and grape-picker before finishing his high school diploma at an adult school. Alarcón eventually completed a bachelor's degree at California State University at Long Beach in 1977 and a master's degree at Stanford. He also obtained a Fulbright Fellowship to study in Mexico City.

In adulthood Alarcón came to terms with another sort of double identity, the alienation of being a gay man in the Hispanic community. In 1984 he was publicly put under suspicion of a young boy's murder in San Francisco, although he had been giving a poetry reading at the time of the crime. Until the actual murderer was apprehended months later, Alarcón was the subject of prolonged police persecution. This humiliating experience served as the impetus for his first book of poems, *Tattoos* (1985).

Alarcón has been a prolific poet. His later books include *Body in Flames* (1990), *Snake Poems* (1992), which won the American Book Award, *No Golden Gate for Us* (1993), *Sonnets to Madness and Other Misfortunes* (2001), and *From the Other Side of Night* (2002). He has also written several bilingual books for children. His poetry is characteristically taut and compressed; the utterance is reduced to the fewest words possible with much being left to implication. The title poem of *Tattoos,* for instance, is only seven words long: "poems / fill up / pages / tattoos / puncture / flesh." Much of his poetry is also written bilingually with the English and Spanish texts side by side. Alarcón is currently a professor of Spanish and classics at the University of California at Davis.

◄►────◄►

The X in My Name

the poor
signature
of my illiterate
and peasant
self   5
giving away
all rights
in a deceiving
contract for life

1993

Frontera	Border
ninguna	no
frontera	border
podrá	can ever
separarnos	separate us

1999

◄ DAVID MASON ►
(b. 1954)

David Mason was born in Bellingham, Washington, the second of three sons in a well-educated, middle-class family. His father was a pediatrician and his mother a psychologist. After graduating from high school in 1973, Mason entered Colorado College but left a year later to travel to Europe—the first of the many peregrinations that would characterize his adult life. (He financed his trip by working in an Alaskan fish cannery for seven months.) Returning to Colorado College a year later, he completed a bachelor's degree in 1978 and married his college girlfriend, Jonna Heinrich. Determined to be a writer, Mason spent the next six years supporting himself in a variety of jobs—from gardener to harbormaster—while working on his fiction and poetry. He and his wife also went abroad to Greece where they lived in a small stone cottage.

Tired of the frustration and isolation of his bohemian literary life, Mason entered graduate school in 1984 at the University of Rochester where he studied with poet Anthony Hecht. Slowly his literary interests moved more exclusively toward poetry. Finishing his Ph.D. in 1989 with a dissertation on W. H. Auden, Mason took a teaching position at Moorhead State University in Minnesota. In 1998 he returned to Colorado College where he codirects the creative writing program. The long years of searching and defining his literary identity were not without emotional turbulence. In 1979 his older brother was killed in a mountain climbing accident—an event that has reverberated in Mason's poetry. In 1986 his first marriage ended in divorce. In 1988 Mason married Anne Lennox, a photographer, with whom he now lives in Woodland Park, Colorado.

Mason has published two full-length collections of poetry, *The Buried Houses* (1991), which won the Nicholas Roerich Award, and *The Country I Remember* (1996), the winner of the Alice Fay Di Castagnola Award. The title poem of *The Country I Remember*, a long narrative in two voices that runs from the Civil War across the Oregon Trail to contemporary California, has been produced and broadcast as a verse drama. Mason has also published several poetry chapbooks and two poetry anthologies, *Rebel Angels: 25 Poets of the New Formalism* (1996), which he co-edited with Mark Jarman, and *Western Wind: An Introduction to Poetry* (2000), which he co-edited with John F. Nims. His collection of critical essays, *The Poetry of Life and the Life of Poetry*, also appeared in 2000.

Mason's poetry is characterized by subtle musicality and psychological penetration. His most influential work is surely his midlength narrative poems like "Spooning," "Blackened Peaches," "The Collector's Tale," and preeminently "The

Country I Remember." These quietly innovative works borrow from the largely neglected examples of Edwin Arlington Robinson, Robert Frost, and Robinson Jeffers to explore the possibilities of the contemporary narrative poem.

Spooning[1]

After my grandfather died I went back home
to help my mother sell his furniture:
the old chair he did his sitting on,
the kitchen things. Going through his boxes
I found letters, cancelled checks, the usual   5
old photographs of relatives I hardly knew
and grandmother, clutching an apron in both hands.
And *her.* There was an old publicity still
taken when she wore her hair like a helmet,
polished black. Posed before a cardboard shell   10
and painted waves, she seemed unattainable,
as she was meant to.

         For years we thought he lied
about his knowing her when he was young,
but grandfather was a man who hated liars,
a man who worshipped all the tarnished virtues,   15
when daily to his shop at eight, until
the first of three strokes forced him to retire.

He liked talking. Somebody had to listen,
so I was the listener for hours after school
until my parents called me home for dinner.   20
We'd sit on his glassed-in porch where he kept a box
of apples wrapped in newsprint.

He told me about the time he lost a job
at the mill. Nooksack seemed to kill its young
with boredom even then, but he owned a car,   25
a '24 Ford. He drove it east to see
America, got as far as Spokane's desert,
sold the car and worked back on the railroad.

Sometimes he asked me what I liked to do.
I told him about the drive-in movies where   30
my brother, Billy, took me if I paid.
In small towns everyone goes to the movies.
Not grandfather. He said they made them better when

---

1. All references in this poem are fictional. The title is an old slang term for "making out," kissing and caressing, that may be used euphemistically here.

nobody talked, and faces told it all.
"I knew Lydia Truman Gates," he said,　　　　35
"back when she was plain old Lydia Carter
down on Water Street. One time her old man
caught us spooning out to the railroad tracks.
Nearly tanned my hide. He was a fisherman—
that is, till she moved her folks to Hollywood."　　40

I don't know why, but I simply couldn't ask
what spooning was. He seemed to talk then
more to his chair's abrasions on the floor,
more to the pale alders outside his window.
The way he said her name I couldn't ask　　　45
who was Lydia Truman Gates.

*

　　　　　　　　"Nonsense,"
was all my mother said at dinner. "His mind
went haywire in the hospital. He's old.
He makes things up and can't tell the difference."　　50

I think my father's smile embarrassed her
when he said, "The poor guy's disappointed.
Nothing went right for him, so he daydreams."

"Nonsense," my mother said. "And anyway
no Lydia Truman Gates ever came　　　　55
from a town like this."

　　　　　　　　　"It's not so bad a place."
I make a pretty decent living here."

My mother huffed. While I stared past my plate
Billy asked, "Who is Lydia Truman Gates?"

*

It wasn't long before we all found out.　　　　60
The papers ran a story on her. How
she was famous in the twenties for a while,
married the oil billionaire, Gates, and retired.
She was coming back home to Nooksack. The mayor
would give a big award and ask her help　　　65
to renovate our landmark theatre.

Our mother said we had better things to spend
our money on than some old movie house,
though she remembered how it used to look.
She said that people living in the past　　　70
wouldn't amount to much.
Billy and I pretended we didn't care.
We didn't tell our parents where we went
that night, riding our bikes in a warm wind

past the fishhouses on the Puget Sound,   75
and up Grant Street to the Hiawatha.

Inside, Billy held my hand, and showed me
faded paintings of Indians on the walls
and dark forest patterns in the worn carpet.
The place smelled stale like old decaying clothes   80
shut up in a trunk for twenty years,
but Nooksack's best were there, some in tuxes,
and women stuffed into their evening gowns.
We sat in the balcony looking down
on bald heads, high hair-dos and jewels.   85
Near the stage they had a twenty-piece band—
I still remember when the lights went out
the violins rose like a flock of birds
all at once. The drums sounded a shudder.

We saw *Morocco Gold, The Outlaw, Colonel Clay*   90
and the comic short, *A Bird in the Hand,*
flickering down to the screen
where Lydia Truman Gates arose in veils,
in something gossamer
astonishing even in 1965.   95
Lydia Truman Gates was like a dream
of lithe attention, her dark eyes laughing
at death, at poverty or a satin bed.
And when they brought her on the stage, applause
rising and falling like a tidal wave,   100
I had to stand up on my seat to see
a frail old woman assisted by two men,
tiny on that distant stage.

                    My brother
yanked me past what seemed like a hundred pairs
of knees for all the times I said, "Excuse us."   105
We ran out where the chauffeur
waited by her limousine, his face painted
green by the light from Heilman's Piano Store,
breathing smoke. "You guys keep your distance."

"Is she coming out?"

                    He crushed his cigarette: 110
"No, she's gonna die in there. What do you think?"

More people joined us, pacing in the alley,
watching the chauffeur smoke by the door propped
open with a cinderblock.
And then the door half-opened, sighed back,   115
opened at last on the forearm of a man.

Behind him, Lydia Truman Gates stepped out
with her cane—hardly the woman I had seen

enduring all the problems of the world
with such aplomb. She stared down at the pavement,   120
saying, "Thank you, I can see it clearly now."

"Mrs. Gates," Billy stuttered. "Mrs. Gates."

The chauffeur tried to block us, but she said,
"That's all right, Andrew. They're just kids. I'm safe."

"Our grandpa says hello," I blurted out.   125

She paused for half a beat, glanced at Billy,
then peered at me as if to study terror,
smiling. "Well I'll be damned. And who's he?"

"Don't listen to him," Billy said. "He's nuts."

"George McCracken," I said, "the one you spooned with   130
down by the railroad tracks."

                    "George McCracken."
She straightened, looked up at the strip of sky.
"Spooned. Well, that's one way to talk about it."
She laughed from deep down in her husky lungs.
"Old Georgie McCracken. Is he still alive?   135
Too scared to come downtown and say hello?"
She reached out from her furs and touched my hair.
"Thanks for the message, little man. I knew him.
I knew he'd never get out of this town.
You tell your grampa Hi from Liddy Carter."   140

The man at her elbow said they had to leave.
She nodded, handing her award and purse
to the chauffeur.

                    Then flashbulbs started popping.
I saw her face lit up, then pale and caving
back into the darkness. "Christ," she whispered,   145
"get me out of here."

                    I stumbled, or was pushed.
My eyes kept seeing her exploding at me,
a woman made entirely of light
beside the smaller figure who was real.
Two men tipped her into the limousine   150
and it slid off like a shark, parting the crowd.

                              *

A picture ran in the next day's *Herald*—
the great actress touches a local boy.
For two weeks everybody talked about me,
but I kept thinking, "Is he still alive?   155
Too scared to come downtown and say hello?"

I thought of her decaying on a screen,
her ribs folding like a silk umbrella's rods,
while all the men who gathered around her
clutched at the remnants of her empty dress.   160

1991

Song of the Powers

Mine, said the stone,
mine is the hour.
I crush the scissors,
such is my power.
Stronger than wishes,   5
my power, alone.

Mine, said the paper,
mine are the words
that smother the stone
with imagined birds,   10
reams of them, flown
from the mind of the shaper.

Mine, said the scissors,
mine all the knives
gashing through paper's   15
ethereal lives;
nothing's so proper
as tattering wishes.

As stone crushes scissors,
as paper snuffs stone   20
and scissors cut paper,
all end alone.
So heap up your paper
and scissor your wishes
and uproot the stone   25
from the top of the hill.
They all end alone
as you will, you will.

1996

BENJAMIN ALIRE SÁENZ
(b. 1954)

Born the fourth of seven children, Benjamin Alire Sáenz was raised on a cotton
farm in the village of Old Picacho, New Mexico. He spoke only Spanish until he
began public school. Sáenz's mother spent her days cleaning houses and working
in a factory, while Sáenz's father returned to his job as a cement finisher once they
lost their farm. To help support the growing family, young Benjamin also found
employment—roofing houses, picking onions, and doing janitorial work. At eighteen, Sáenz entered St. Thomas Seminary in Denver to study philosophy (B.A.,

1977), after which he moved to the University of Louvain in Belgium to receive his theological training. Sáenz was ordained a Catholic priest four years later, and he returned to the States to settle in the border regions of Texas and New Mexico, which would become the central subject of his writing.

Sáenz left the clergy after serving for three years, and took a job waiting tables. Eventually returning to school, he earned his master's degree from the University of Texas at El Paso and began Ph.D. work at the University of Iowa. He was soon given a prestigious Wallace Stegner Fellowship at Stanford, where he worked with Denise Levertov for two years and assembled his first collection of poems, the American Book Award-winning *Calendar of Dust* (1991). He also won a poetry prize from the Lannan Foundation in 1993. Sáenz has since returned to the University of Texas at El Paso where he teaches in the bilingual graduate writing program. He has published novels, short fiction, essays, children's books, and more poetry, including *Dark and Perfect Angels* (1995) and *Elegies in Blue* (2002).

The Southwestern landscape and people pervade Sáenz's poetry, in which he grapples with questions of Chicano identity, the lessons of history, and political issues. He has vowed never to move from the Southwest, and that culturally complex region is a particularly appropriate home for Sáenz. His poetry and prose examines the lines separating English and Spanish, America and Mexico, the rich and the poor. When asked in an interview if he felt that writers should address society's problems, Sáenz stated that writers should, "Do what they have to do. And I am a political animal. With no apologies." Catholicism also remains a central influence on the poetry of the former priest. Although one rarely finds explicit Christian allusions in Sáenz's poetry, a sacramental sense of the world suffuses his work. Catholicism, he claims, "affects my sense of ritual, the way I look at things. What I love about Catholicism is that it's so sensual. You taste, you see, you smell; all of the senses are involved in Catholic ritual."

◄►

To the Desert

I came to you one rainless August night.
You taught me how to live without the rain.
You are thirst and thirst is all I know.
You are sand, wind, sun, and burning sky,
The hottest blue. You blow a breeze and brand   5
Your breath into my mouth. You reach—then *bend*
Your force, to break, blow, burn, and make me new.[1]
You wrap your name tight around my ribs
And keep me warm. I was born for you.
Above, below, by you, by you surrounded.   10
I wake to you at dawn. Never break your
Knot. Reach, rise, blow, *Sálvame, mi dios,*
Trágame, mi tierra. Salva, traga,[2] Break me,
I am bread. I will be the water for your thirst.

1995

1. The italicized lines are from "Batter my heart, three-personed God; for you," the 14th "Holy Sonnet" of John Donne (1572–1631).
2. (Spanish) "Save me, my God, / Swallow me, my earth. Save, swallow."

Resurrections

California
Lent, 1990

The stones themselves will sing.[3]

Broken, Incan roads. The stones laid perfect
on mountains of snow so stubborn
not even blazing suns could beat it into water.
But the Incans could tame such mountains. With a fire
of their own, they knew how to melt that ice.   5
Stone by stone, step by step, the ancients
walked the highest paths of earth. Stones,
tight knots that tied the world together. Roads, higher—
now stones are buried deep like bones
of Incan lords. I walked there barefoot   10
on cold stones. Those roads were perfect once again
until I woke. Those roads, like Incan hands
who built them, refuse to lie still
in the ground. They loosen the wasted land.

•

My mother lost him young, her older brother. She gave   15
my brother his name "because the moment he was born
his name rose to my lips." Ricardo, "A friend
took a stone, and broke his skull wide open—
and broke my mother's heart." She walks with him
on a path they took to school. There, in the sun, he laughs   20
until she wakes. Been forty years,
and grief is glued to her. Anger rises
in her voice: "But *here*," she grabs his picture,
"*Here* he is perfect. *Here* he is not broken."

•

The beer I drink is good tonight,   25
almost sweet, but cold. The dead are close.
Calm, I sit, touch the photographs of those
I walked with. Grandparents, uncles, not one
generation was spared. A brother. A niece.
In the country of their final exile   30
their legs will not cross the border.
Their feet will not touch my earth again
but tonight I hear their steps. I swallow,
must finish the beer I have started. *Take this
all of you and drink. This is my blood.* Tired,   35
I drink from the cup, take the cold, within me now,
and wrap myself in faces of the dead:
stones which form a path where I walk still.

---

3. From an 1816 hymn by James Montgomery, "When Jesus Left His Father's Throne."

•

The Mimbres buried their dead beneath their homes.
At night, softly, the buried   40
rose, re-entered the rooms of the living
as blankets woven with the heavy threads of memory,
blankets on which the Mimbres rested,
on which they slept, and dreamed.

1991

◄ MARY JO SALTER ►
(b. 1954)

Known for the verbal elegance, astute perception, and quiet intellectual assurance
of her poetry, Mary Jo Salter grew up in Grand Rapids, Michigan. Her father, Albert Salter, was an advertising executive. Her mother, Lorima Paradise Salter, was
a painter. While a student in a Harvard writing workshop taught by Elizabeth
Bishop, Salter met her future husband, the poet and novelist Brad Leithauser. She
received a bachelor's degree from Harvard in 1976 and a master's degree from
New Hall, Cambridge University, in 1978. Returning to the United States she
taught at Harvard briefly where she found herself in proximity with Leithauser
again, who was now at Harvard Law School. They married in 1980 and then set
off for a three-year residency in Japan where Salter taught conversational English.
Salter and Leithauser have continued to travel with extended stays in Italy, France,
and Iceland, finally settling down to share a teaching appointment at Mount
Holyoke College and raise their two daughters.

Salter has published four collections of poems—*Henry Purcell in Japan* (1985),
Unfinished Painting (1989), *Sunday Skaters* (1994), and *A Kiss in Space* (1999).
From the start her work has displayed an attraction to traditional subjects as well
as traditional technique. She often writes in rhyme and meter, though she also employs free verse. Salter has written of historical events and personages such as
Thomas Jefferson, Robert Frost, Helen Keller, and Alexander Graham Bell. These
poems of graceful intellectual range are accompanied as well by more intimate evocations of domestic life, often combined with grief at actual or potential losses.

Salter's poetry has sometimes been criticized as too emotionally restrained—
perhaps because the tone of so many contemporary poets is strident and emphatic
by comparison—but that objection ignores the complex emotional depth of her
work. The understated, mannerly style of her poems is achieved in the face of an
awareness of just how horrific and devastating life can be. In her poem, "Welcome
to Hiroshima," for example, the speaker admits her difficulty as a foreigner in
fully comprehending the city's tragedy as the Japanese themselves experienced it,
especially as she tries to learn about it in commercialized modern Japan. Her candor and humility before the enormity of the historic disaster, however, eventually
allow her—and the reader—to feel its impact on a personal level. Salter's poem
may be quiet, but it is also quietly impassioned.

Salter has served as poetry editor of the *New Republic* and is one of the editors of the *Norton Anthology of Poetry*. She has also published a children's book,
The Moon Comes Home (1989). Her own work has received numerous awards,

including a Discovery Award from the *Nation,* an Amy Lowell Poetry Traveling Scholarship, and the Lamont Prize for *Unfinished Painting,* which included an elegy for her mother, who died young. An eloquent critic, Salter has been a passionate advocate of the poetry of Emily Dickinson, Elizabeth Bishop, and Amy Clampitt. She has also written searchingly of the problematic position of the contemporary woman poet, especially in her 1991 essay, "A Poem of One's Own," in which she stresses the writer's freedom to transcend gender and personal history. "Has there ever been a mature, great poet of any stripe," she asks, "who did not seek access to something greater than him or herself?" Although often rooted in the author's everyday life as wife, mother, and daughter, Salter's poetry has calmly, cunningly, and cogently explored themes and subjects larger than herself.

Welcome to Hiroshima

is what you first see, stepping off the train:
a billboard brought to you in living English
by Toshiba Electric. While a channel
silent in the TV of the brain

projects those flickering re-runs of a cloud   5
that brims its risen columnful like beer
and, spilling over, hangs its foamy head,
you feel a thirst for history: what year

it started to be safe to breathe the air,
and when to drink the blood and scum afloat   10
on the Ohta River. But no, the water's clear,
they pour it for your morning cup of tea

in one of the countless sunny coffee shops
whose plastic dioramas advertise
mutations of cuisine behind the glass: 15
a pancake sandwich; a pizza someone tops

with a maraschino cherry. Passing by
the Peace Park's floral hypocenter (where
how bravely, or with what mistaken cheer,
humanity erased its own erasure),   20

you enter the memorial museum
and through more glass are served, as on a dish
of blistered grass, three mannequins. Like gloves
a mother clips to coatsleeves, strings of flesh

hang from their fingertips; or as if tied   25
to recall a duty for us, *Reverence*
the dead whose mourners too shall soon be dead,
but all commemoration's swallowed up

in questions of bad taste, how re-created
horror mocks the grim original,   30
and thinking at last *They should have left it all*
you stop. This is the wristwatch of a child.

Jammed on the moment's impact, resolute
to communicate some message, although mute,
it gestures with its hands at eight-fifteen   35
and eight-fifteen and eight-fifteen again

while tables of statistics on the wall
update the news by calling on a roll
of tape, death gummed on death, and in the case
adjacent, an exhibit under glass   40

is glass itself: a shard the bomb slammed in
a woman's arm at eight-fifteen, but some
three decades on—as if to make it plain
hope's only as renewable as pain,

and as if all the unsung   45
debasements of the past may one day come
rising to the surface once again—
worked its filthy way out like a tongue.

                                                                          1985

The Age of Reason

"When can we have *cake?*" she wants to know.
And patiently we explain: when dinner's finished.
Someone wants seconds; and wouldn't she like to try,
while she's waiting, a healthful lettuce leaf?
     The birthday girl can't hide her grief—   5

worse, everybody laughs. That makes her sink
two rabbity, gapped teeth, acquired this year,
into a quivering lip, which puts an end
to tears but not the tedium she'll take
     in life before she's given cake: 10

"When I turned seven, now," her Grandpa says,
"the priest told me I'd reached the age of reason.
That means you're old enough to tell what's right
from wrong. Make decisions on your own."
     Her big eyes brighten. "So you mean   15

I can decide to open presents first?"
Laughter again (she joins in) as the reward
of devil's food is brought in on a tray.
"You know why we were taught that?" asks my father.
     "No." I light a candle, then another   20

in a chain. "—So we wouldn't burn in Hell."
A balloon pops in the other room; distracted,
she innocently misses talk of nuns'
severities I never knew at seven.
    By then, we were Unitarian   25

and marched off weekly, dutifully, to hear
nothing in particular. "Ready!"
I call, and we huddle close to sing
something akin, you'd have to say, to prayer.
    Good God, her hair—   30

one beribboned pigtail has swung low
as she leans to trade the year in for a wish;
before she blows it out, the camera's flash
captures a mother's hand, all hope, no blame,
    saving her from the flame.   35

                                         1994

◄ CATHY SONG ►
(b. 1955)

Cathy Song was born in Honolulu in a mixed Asian marriage—a personal and social background that has provided much material for her work. Her father was a
Korean American airline pilot, and her mother a Chinese American seamstress.
Song lived during her early childhood in Wahiawa, a small plantation town in
central Oahu, Hawaii, and later moved to Honolulu. She studied with poet-critic
John Unterecker at the University of Hawaii at Manoa for two years, then transferred to Wellesley College where she earned a bachelor's degree in 1977. She took
her master's degree at Boston University in 1981.

    Although Song is quick to dispel the labels of "Asian American writer" or
"Hawaiian writer," her subject matter concentrates largely on exploring precisely
those identities. Her debut collection, *Picture Bride* (1983), which was chosen by
Richard Hugo for the Yale Series of Younger Poets Award, contains a long narrative
that tells the true story of Song's paternal grandmother leaving Korea to marry a
man who had only seen her photograph. Other poems address the plantation culture of Hawaii that Song knew as a girl. Her work is strongly focused on the stories
of her ancestry as well as her immediate family—Song married Dr. Douglas Daven-
port and returned to Hawaii in 1987, where the couple has raised three children.

    Song's later poetry develops the themes of place, heritage, and identity initi-
ated in *Picture Bride. Frameless Windows, Squares of Light* (1988) explores the
primal but problematic relationship between parent and child. *School Figures*
(1994) also investigates the changing social and cultural environment in Hawaii as
her generation enters parenthood and middle-class life. Her explorations of mater-
nity show how grief, resentment, and even madness lie beneath the seemingly quiet
surface of domestic life. Song won the Hawaii Award for Literature in 1993 and
the Shelley Memorial Award from the Poetry Society of America the following year.

Beauty and Sadness

For Kitagawa Utamaro[1]

He drew hundreds of women
in studies unfolding
like flowers from a fan.
Teahouse waitresses, actresses,
geishas, courtesans and maids.   5
They arranged themselves
before this quick, nimble man
whose invisible presence
one feels in these prints
is as delicate   10
as the skinlike paper
he used to transfer
and retain their fleeting loveliness.

Crouching like cats,
they purred amid the layers of kimono   15
swirling around them
as though they were bathing
in a mountain pool with irises
growing in the silken sunlit water.
Or poised like porcelain vases,   20
slender, erect and tall; their heavy
brocaded hair was piled high
with sandalwood combs and blossom sprigs
poking out like antennae.
They resembled beautiful iridescent insects,   25
creatures from a floating world.

Utamaro absorbed these women of Edo
in their moments of melancholy
as well as of beauty.
He captured the wisp of shadows,   30
the half-draped body
emerging from a bath; whatever
skin was exposed
was powdered white as snow.
A private space disclosed.   35
Portraying another girl
catching a glimpse of her own vulnerable
face in the mirror, he transposed
the trembling plum lips
like a drop of blood   40
soaking up the white expanse of paper.

1. (1753–1806) Japanese painter famous for portraits of court ladies.

At times, indifferent to his inconsolable
eye, the women drifted
through the soft gray feathered light,
maintaining stillness, the moments in between.   45
Like the dusty ash-winged moths
that cling to the screens in summer
and that the Japanese venerate
as ancestors reincarnated;
Utamaro graced these women with immortality   50
in the thousand sheaves of prints
fluttering into the reverent hands of keepers:
the dwarfed and bespectacled painter
holding up to a square of sunlight
what he had carried home beneath his coat   55
one afternoon in winter.

1983

Stamp Collecting

The poorest countries
have the prettiest stamps
as if impracticality were a major export
shipped with the bananas, t-shirts, and coconuts.
Take Tonga, where the tourists,   5
expecting a dramatic waterfall replete with birdcalls,
are taken to see the island's peculiar mystery:
hanging bats with collapsible wings
like black umbrellas swing upside down from fruit trees.
The Tongan stamp is a fruit.   10
The banana stamp is scalloped like a butter-varnished seashell.
The pineapple resembles a volcano, a spout of green on top,
and the papaya, a tarnished goat skull.

They look impressive,
these stamps of countries without a thing to sell   15
except for what is scraped, uprooted and hulled
from their mule-scratched hills.
They believe in postcards,
in portraits of progress: the new dam;
a team of young native doctors   20
wearing stethoscopes like exotic ornaments;
the recently constructed "Facultad de Medicina,"
a building as lack-lustre as an American motel.

The stamps of others are predictable.
Lucky is the country that possesses indigenous beauty.   25
Say a tiger or a queen.
The Japanese can display to the world
their blossoms: a spray of pink on green.
Like pollen, they drift, airborne.
But pity the country that is bleak and stark.   30

Beauty and whimsy are discouraged as indiscreet.
Unbreakable as their climate, a monument of ice,
they issue serious statements, commemorating
factories, tramways and aeroplanes;
athletes marbled into statues.   35
They turn their noses upon the world, these countries,
and offer this: an unrelenting procession
of a grim, historic profile.

                                                             1988

⫸ JACQUELINE OSHEROW ⫷
(b. 1956)

Jacqueline Osherow was born and raised in Philadelphia, and her fascination with
the power and mystery of language began early, through listening to Hebrew at
her synagogue and to the Yiddish spoken by both sets of grandparents, immigrants
who had earned their livings in the United States as garment workers. Osherow
grounds her poetry on her religious and cultural heritage, emphasizing in an essay:

> It was surely hearing the psalms in synagogue as a child that gave me my first sense of
> what poetry is and my desire to write it must have something to do with the extremely
> appealing notion—even to a six-or-seven-year-old—that there is such a thing as a holy
> language. Surely if I write out of a specific poetic tradition, it is the Jewish poetic tradi-
> tion, American poet though I am.

Although her root sense of poetry springs from Judaism, she nurtured her understanding of the English and American poetic tradition at prestigious universities.
At Radcliffe, she studied with Robert Lowell and Robert Fitzgerald, graduating
magna cum laude in 1978. As a Fiske Scholar sponsored by Harvard, she attended
Trinity College in Cambridge from 1978 to 1979 and then pursued graduate study
at Princeton, earning her Ph.D. in 1990. She now lives in Salt Lake City with her
husband and three children, where she teaches at the University of Utah in the
English Department and Jewish Studies Program.

Osherow explores her Jewish heritage through poems that are notable for her
deft mastery of forms such as the sonnet, blank verse, and terza rima, and for her
equally impressive fluency in merging casual, conversational diction, with high-
toned language drawn from the Old Testament and Latinate diction culled from a
variety of sources. Admiring the work of American Yiddish poets, Osherow admits, "I can't tell you how often I have found in their work the voice I have longed
for—born of tradition, but irreverent, deadly serious, but funny, self-mocking, but
full of mastery." Osherow strikes these notes in her poetry, along with contemplating the power and majesty of the Old Testament God from a distinctly twentieth-
century perspective. That perspective involves reevaluating the place of women in
Jewish tradition and asking difficult questions about God's place in a secular world.

Osherow often focuses on the Holocaust in poems that revisit the concentration camps or detail the lives of survivors. The Holocaust haunts all of her books:
Looking for Angels in New York (1988), *Conversations with Survivors* (1994),
With a Moon in Transit (1996), and *Dead Men's Praise* (1999). In her second
book, however, she redefines the concept of "survivors," for many of the victims

she considers did not survive the Holocaust, yet survive in her memory and in her poems. For Osherow, poetry becomes both a memorial and a testament in which she bears witness to the Holocaust. As she points out in the preface to *Conversations with Survivors:* "For my generation—those born in the aftermath of war—the horror is a fact of life. Indeed, it defined the world to us."

Song for the Music in the Warsaw Ghetto[1]

Pity the tune bereft of singers
Pity the tone bereft of chords
Where shall we weep? By which waters?
Pity the song bereft of words

Pity the harps hung on rifles   5
The unsuspected cunning in each hand
Pity the shrill, bewildered nightingales
How could they sing in that strange land?

Pity the string that has no bow
Pity the flute that has no breath   10
Pity the rifle's muted solo
Pity its soundless aftermath

1996

Ghazal:[2] Comet

Amidst our troubles, a sudden blessing:
Look up. There's a comet in the evening sky.

An omen for a pharaoh, caught retracing
Its half-forgotten summit in the evening sky;

Two burning tails—one gas, one ice—arousing   5
Ancient tumult in the evening sky;

Debris of a lost planet decomposing,
Gypsy diplomat in the evening sky;

Debut of life on earth, its ice dispersing
Facts too intimate for the evening sky. . . .   10

1. By 1942 the Nazis had forced some 500,000 Jews to live in a ghetto of Warsaw in Poland. In the winter of 1943, sensing that they were doomed if they did nothing, a large number of Jews staged an armed uprising against the German army. Some 40,000 Jews were killed in immediate retaliation and many more starved or died in the camps. By the time Soviet troops liberated Warsaw in 1945 there were only about 200 Jews left in the city.
2. The *ghazal* is a medieval Persian poetic form that has recently become more popular in America, thanks to the efforts of the late Agha Shahid Ali.

Traces of comet in us. This burning, this freezing?
Let's just blame it on the evening sky,

The music of the spheres in us, rehearsing
Across the gamut of the evening sky.

But—see?—the comet's already devising   15
A shortcut past the limit in the evening sky,

And when it comes again, we won't be witnessing.
Who will even claim it in the evening sky?

What's left of us may well be improvising
Our own last-minute plummet in the evening sky.   20

1999

◄ H. L. HIX ►
(b. 1960)

Although now a noted poet, critic, and philosopher, H. L. Hix did not have a particularly bookish childhood. Born in Stillwater, Oklahoma, Harvey Lee Hix moved often during his early years, living in many southern and midwestern towns. Although his journalist parents ran a weekly newspaper for fifteen years in Millington, Tennessee, Hix argued tirelessly with them about the importance of reading literature. By the time he graduated from high school, Hix had read only two novels—Madeleine L'Engle's *A Wrinkle in Time* and Nathaniel Hawthorne's *The Scarlet Letter,* and the latter book was a classroom assignment. He did, however, devotedly study car magazines like *Road and Track* and *Motor Trends.* After a year at Georgia Tech, Hix transferred to Belmont University in Nashville, where, ironically, he discovered he loved reading books and soon double-majored in philosophy and literature (B.A., 1982). He also began writing poetry and met his wife, Sheila Pedigo, whom he married in 1983. Hix spent one year in English graduate study at Baylor University before deciding to pursue philosophy as a career. He earned his Ph.D. in philosophy at the University of Texas (1987), and accepted a position at the Kansas City Art Institute, where he taught for fifteen years. In 2002 Hix became the Vice President for Academic Affairs at the Cleveland Institute of Art. He currently lives in Shaker Heights, Ohio.

Hix has published books of philosophy, translations, and literary criticism, including book-length studies of poet W. S. Merwin and novelist William H. Gass. He has written philosophical critiques of literary theory, including *Morte d'Author: An Autopsy* (1990), and has published *As Easy as Lying: Essays on Poetry* (2002). Most important, however, are Hix's three remarkable and ambitious books of poetry. His first collection, *Perfect Hell* (1996), won the Peregrine Smith Contest, and was chosen as one of the best poetry books of the year by the *Washington Post Book World.* Hix followed this debut with the T. S. Eliot-winning *Rational Numbers* (2000), which contained a pair of intricate long poems. Most recently, *Surely as Birds Fly* (2002) has appeared.

Postmodern in sensibility and experimental in approach, Hix's poems simultaneously affirm and question their own meaning. Unlike much postmodern writing, however, his poems relentlessly work to keep the reader engaged. Hix has an astounding ability to fashion a haunting phrase or breathtaking image. The surfaces of his poems bristle with obstreperous verbal effects—puns, allusions, quotations, double entendres—while obscure and troubling motives seem to lurk in his subtexts. His poems are often deliberately mysterious and inconclusive, often suffused by dark sexuality and covert sadism. Informed by contemporary literary theory, his poetry is highly intellectual—often incorporating ideas from mathematics, science, linguistics, and philosophy—but at its frequent best, it is also intimate, emotional, and sensual. Still at the start of his career, Hix is a significant and original talent.

No Less Than Twenty-Six Distinct Necronyms

Father dead, we will call her, or *Niece dead*.
Cousin in car crash. So many names fit.
Sister cut wrists, Brother shot in the head.
*Grandfather wandered off, Great uncle hit
By train while drunk. Aunt dead. Aunt dead. Aunt dead*.   5
Brother stillborn. Uncle had heart attack.
Niece murdered. Great-grandmother died in bed.
Nephew dead. Sister drowned in frozen lake.
*Sister burned in trailer home fire. Brother
Overdosed. Sister, crib death*. Every breath   10
Matters. *Cousin fell from window. Cancer
Ate colons of two uncles, lungs of both
Grandmothers. Cousin had kidney failure
After going blind. Mother died giving birth*.

1996

Reasons

Because when I look back, she disappears.
Because I look back.
Because retreat can be wiser than attack.
Because one can be harder than two careers.
Because the crows are calling.   5
Because I can muster so little tragedy.
Because it wounds to hear the word *petty*.
Because I want to be worth a reckoning.
Because revisions are not always corrections.
Because paper is altered easily, easily burned.   10
Because some promises should not stay obligations.
Because the moon is up, because the earth turned.
Because there are no good reasons.
Because unlike this joy, guilt must be earned.

1996

RAFAEL CAMPO
(b. 1964)

The son of immigrants who fled Cuba after the rise of Fidel Castro, Rafael Campo was born in Dover, New Jersey. In an autobiographical essay, "A Case of Mistaken Identities," Campo describes the self-consciousness he felt about being Latino in a white suburb: "I mostly grew up in an affluent New Jersey suburb. I was the darkest note in the white harmony of classroom after antiseptic classroom—I worried that I made discordant sounds when I smiled or played." Campo began writing poetry in grade school, perhaps as a way to help him come to terms with his awareness of his differences. "I wonder whether my obsessive impulse to write," he has speculated, "was even at its earliest manifestation a rebellious one, engendered by an unconscious desire to revise the world according to a discordant internal reality I was trying so desperately to decipher." After graduation from high school, he matriculated at Amherst College, drawn by its rigorous premed program and its venerable reputation for poetry. He received a bachelor's degree in 1987, with a double major in neuroscience and English.

By the time of his graduation, Campo had also accepted his homosexual identity, for at Amherst he met Jorge Arroyo, the young man who would become his life partner. Campo went on to earn a master's degree in creative writing in 1991 at Boston University and an M.D. from Harvard Medical School in 1992. There, under pressure to dedicate himself wholly to becoming a doctor, he felt more anxiety over admitting that he wrote poetry than he did about telling his classmates of his homosexuality. He now practices and teaches internal medicine at Harvard Medical School and Beth Israel Deaconess Medical Center in Boston and lives in Jamaica Plain with Arroyo, who is also a doctor, and their adopted son.

Since the publication of his first book, *The Other Man Was Me: A Voyage to the New World* (1994), Campo has explored the connections between his experiences as a gay man, a Latino, and a doctor. In a 1999 interview, he remarks: "There is a transcending theme in my work that has to do with shared humanity. Whether I am the physician in the emergency room taking care of a patient who has OD'd on heroin; whether I am the gay son thinking about my relationship to my parents; or whether I am the expatriate imagining visiting Cuba some day—all these experiences are linked by a sense of trying to connect across differences. . . . Poetry has so much to do with healing, and healing has so much to do with poetry, that they become one and the same thing." For Campo, poetry inspires empathy through enabling both poet and reader to inhabit the voices of others, and he often teaches poetry to his medical students to help them see patients as full human beings rather than as medical problems to be solved. From the largely autobiographical poetry of his first book, Campo has increasingly focused on medical narratives in his subsequent volumes, *What the Body Told* (1996), *Diva* (1999), and *Landscape with Human Figure* (2002). Whether writing about AIDS and cancer patients, homosexual desire, or the Cuban diaspora, Campo crafts intimate, plain-style narratives that, while focusing on physical experience, also stress the ways in which people distance themselves from the body. Campo believes that poetry can help merge body and mind, especially through the visceral pleasures of rhyme and meter. He therefore prefers writing in traditional forms such as the sonnet, pantoum, and villanelle, for he believes that these forms, particularly the sonnet, embody the kinds of connections that he strives to develop in his poetry. In a 1997 interview, he remarks:

The sonnet has always stood at the imagined intersection of the romance languages and English. . . . as a bilingual writer, I've always longed for ways to make English sound somehow like Spanish, to re-create the musicality of my first language in my adopted tongue. Second, I find the erotics of the form terribly compelling—as a gay writer, I relish the paradox of claiming this traditional medium of the love song as my own, playing by the rules and yet crossing boundaries, and thus demonstrating that the rhythms and pleasures of lovemaking truly are universal. Lastly, I would say of the sonnet that no other way of writing poetry so completely mirrors what I discover in my patients' occupying of their physical bodies—the undercurrent of iambs in the beating heart and breathing lungs, the gorgeousness of rhyme akin to dressing up the body in layers of clothes, the replication of the same patterns across centuries a kind of literary genetics.

For Campo, the sonnet and other poetic forms allow him to work both with and against literary tradition. His poetry and essays have reached a diverse audience, achieving the kind of links that Campo seeks to make among different communities.

My Childhood in Another Part of the World

The world was quiet then.
A child was playing dead,
Avoiding being immunized.
I lived in Venezuela when

Democracies could kill.   5
A child was turning red,
Beneath a sun he understood
Was angry. Miracle

Of miracles, the world
Was children taking guns   10
Away from soldiers—run!
Through streets like mental wards.

The world confused me then.
A child was clenching in
His fist the Ritalin[1]
He would not take. In mine,   15

I shielded a secret thing:
A large, bright-emerald beetle.
Revealed, it would startle
Adults, who thought it menacing.   20

My childhood, my childhood,
Returning to me. I was
Too dumb to be unwise,
Too young to be so unafraid.

1996

---

1. A medication given to hyperactive children.

What the Body Told

Not long ago, I studied medicine.
It was terrible, what the body told.
I'd look inside another person's mouth
And see the desolation of the world.
I'd see his genitals and think of sin.   5

Because my body speaks the stranger's language,
I've never understood those nods and stares.
My parents held me in their arms, and still
I think I've disappointed them; they care
And stare, they nod, they make their pilgrimage   10

To somewhere distant in my heart, they cry.
I look inside their other-person's mouths
And see the sleek interior of souls.
It's warm and red in there—like love, with teeth.
I've studied medicine until I cried   15

All night. Through certain books, a truth unfolds.
Anatomy and physiology,
The tiny sensing organs of the tongue—
Each nameless cell contributing its needs.
It was fabulous, what the body told.   20

1996

SHERMAN ALEXIE
(b. 1966)

Sherman Alexie, one of the major young Native American voices of contemporary letters, was born in Spokane, Washington, to a Coeur d'Alene father and a mother of Colville, Flathead, Spokane, and European descent. Alexie's alcoholic father was absent for much of the boy's youth, and the poet himself would struggle with alcohol during his college years. After growing up on the reservation, Alexie spent two years at Spokane's Jesuit-run Gonzaga University, then transferred to Washington State University to rejoin his high school girlfriend, but dropped out in 1991 shortly before earning his bachelor's degree. By then his work had already begun appearing in literary journals. The university gave him an honorary degree in 1995.

Alexie's literary breakthrough occurred soon after leaving Washington State, when his first book, *The Business of Fancydancing: Stories and Poems* (1992), was lauded in the *New York Times Book Review* in an article on contemporary Native American writers. "Mr. Alexie," the review proclaimed, "is one of the major lyric voices of our time." Following his quick rise to national attention, Alexie's literary output was staggering—nine more books in less than five years: poetry, novels, and short fiction—among them *First Indian on the Moon* (1993) and *The Lone Ranger and Tonto Fistfight in Heaven* (1993), which received the PEN/Hemingway Award for best first book of fiction. His novel *Reservation Blues* (1995) won an American Book Award. Alexie also wrote the screenplay for the film, *Smoke Signals* (1998), which was based on *The Lone Ranger and Tonto Fist-fight in Heaven,* and he both wrote and directed *Business of Fancydancing* (2002), based on his first book. Alexie has received a national endowment for the Arts grant and a Lila Wallace–Reader's Digest Writer's Award.

Alexie's work typically addresses reservation life and Native American issues. His poems are often political, and his identification with his ancestry informs every aspect of his work. In *Contemporary Authors* Alexie asserts, "I am a Spokane/Coeur d'Alene Indian from Wellpinit, Washington, where I live on the Spokane Indian Reservation. Everything I do now, writing and otherwise, has its origin in that."

◄◦────◀▶────◦►

Indian Boy Love Song (#2)

I never spoke
the language
of the old women

visiting my mother
in winters so cold   5
they could freeze
the tongue whole.

I never held my head
to their thin chests
believing in the heart.   10

Indian women, forgive me.
I grew up distant
and always afraid.

1992

From "The Native American Broadcasting System"

9.

I am the essence of powwow, I am
toilets without paper, I am fry bread
in sawdust, I am bull dung
on rodeo grounds at the All-Indian
Rodeo and Horse Show, I am   5

the essence of powwow, I am
video games with braids, I am spit
from toothless mouths, I am turquoise
and bootleg whiskey, both selling
for twenty bucks a swallow, I am   10

the essence of powwow, I am
fancydancers in flannel, I am host drum
amplified, I am *Fuck you
don't come back* and *Leave me*

the last hard drink. I am 15
the essence of powwow, I am the dream
you lace your shoes with, I am
the lust between your toes, I am
the memory you feel across the bottom
of your feet whenever you walk too close. 20

1993

The Powwow at the End of the World

I am told by many of you that I must forgive and so I shall
after an Indian woman puts her shoulder to the Grand Coulee Dam
and topples it. I am told by many of you that I must forgive
and so I shall after the floodwaters burst each successive dam
downriver from the Grand Coulee. I am told by many of you 5
that I must forgive and so I shall after the floodwaters find
their way to the mouth of the Columbia River as it enters the Pacific
and causes all of it to rise. I am told by many of you that I must forgive
and so I shall after the first drop of floodwater is swallowed by that salmon
waiting in the Pacific. I am told by many of you that I must forgive and so I shall 10
after that salmon swims upstream, through the mouth of the Columbia
and then past the flooded cities, broken dams and abandoned reactors
of Hanford. I am told by many of you that I must forgive and so I shall
after that salmon swims through the mouth of the Spokane River
as it meets the Columbia, then upstream, until it arrives 15
in the shallows of a secret bay on the reservation where I wait alone.
I am told by many of you that I must forgive and so I shall after
that salmon leaps into the night air above the water, throws
a lightning bolt at the brush near my feet, and starts the fire
which will lead all of the lost Indians home. I am told 20
by many of you that I must forgive and so I shall
after we Indians have gathered around the fire with that salmon
who has three stories it must tell before sunrise: one story will teach us
how to pray; another story will make us laugh for hours;
the third story will give us reason to dance. I am told by many 25
of you that I must forgive and so I shall when I am dancing
with my tribe during the powwow at the end of the world.

1996

⤚•◄ MARISA DE LOS SANTOS ►•⤛
(b. 1966)

Marisa de los Santos, born in Baltimore, Maryland, was raised in northern Virginia. Her father was a surgeon and her mother worked as a nurse before managing her husband's office. The poet's father emigrated from the Philippines, although de los Santos did not visit her ancestral homeland until she was a young woman. She has written, "Unlike many writers I know, I didn't grow up steeped in family lore. I think my writing was fueled more by the lack of family stories, by the fact that my parents have always seemed vaguely mysterious to me, despite the day-to-day closeness we have." De los Santos began writing poetry her senior year at the University of Virginia. At the suggestion of her workshop professor, she applied and was accepted to the master of fine arts program at Sarah Lawrence College, and later earned her Ph.D. in creative writing at the University of Houston in 1996.

De los Santos has published one collection of poetry, *From the Bones Out* (2000). Her poems employ a mix of formal and free verse techniques and address family and love relationships, her various landscapes, and, most poignantly, the female body. She married David Teague in 1992 and the couple both began teaching at the University of Delaware two years later, where they remain. De los Santos has won a Rona Jaffe Writers Award, which goes to eight women of national promise, and a Delaware Division of the Arts grant.

Perfect Dress

It's here in a student's journal, a blue confession
in smudged, erasable ink: "I can't stop hoping
I'll wake up, suddenly beautiful," and isn't it strange
how we want it, despite all we know? To be at last

the girl in the photograph, cobalt-eyed, hair puddling   5
like cognac, or the one stretched at the ocean's edge,
curved and light-drenched, more like a beach than
the beach. I confess I have longed to stalk runways,

leggy, otherworldly as a mantis, to balance a head
like a Fabergé egg[1] on the longest, most elegant neck.   10
Today in the checkout line, I saw a magazine
claiming to know "How to Find the Perfect Dress

for that Perfect Evening," and I felt the old pull, flare
of the pilgrim's twin flames, desire and faith. At fifteen,
I spent weeks at the search. Going from store to store,   15
hands thirsty for shine, I reached for polyester satin,

machine-made lace, petunia- and Easter egg–colored,
brilliant and flammable. Nothing *haute* about this
couture but my hopes for it, as I tugged it on
and waited for my one, true body to emerge.   20

(Picture the angel inside uncut marble, articulation
of wings and robes poised in expectation of release.)
What I wanted was ordinary miracle, the falling away
of everything wrong. Silly maybe or maybe

1. Peter Carl Fabergé (1846–1920) was a Russian designer and jeweler famous for his elaborately decorated eggs.

I was right, that there's no limit to the ways eternity   25
suggests itself, that one day I'll slip into it, say
floor-length plum charmeuse. Someone will murmur,
"She is sublime," will be precisely right, and I will step,

with incandescent shoulders, into my perfect evening.

2000

◄ CHRISTIAN WIMAN ►
(b. 1966)

Born in Abilene, Texas, Christian Wiman was raised in the small oil town of Snyder, and the imagery of Wiman's poetry reflects the flat, dry landscape of his native region. He attended Washington and Lee University in Virginia where he became an All-American tennis player who helped win his school the national championship. Graduating in 1988, Wiman spent the next seven years traveling while mastering the craft of writing. He taught English at the Prague School of Economics in the Czech Republic and worked as a translator in Mexico City. In 1992 he won a Wallace Stegner fellowship to Stanford where in 1996 he became the Jones Lecturer in Poetry. He also lived in England and Guatemala. In 1998 his first book, *The Long Home,* won the Nicholas Roerich Prize in poetry. He has taught at Lynchburg College in Virginia and at Northwestern University in Evanston, Illinois.

Wiman is one of the most eloquent and authoritative poetry critics of his generation. His essays and reviews have appeared in *Poetry, Sewanee Review,* and the *Hudson Review.* He has also reviewed widely for newspapers, especially the *Dallas Morning News* and *Austin American-Statesman.* The experience of poetry, he has written, "is to be given an image of life that you have lost or long dreamed of, to hear as sound something of the farthest sorrows that you are, and to know in that moment that what you've been given is not enough." In 2003, Wiman was named editor of *Poetry* magazine in Chicago.

◄─────►

What I Know

These fields go farther than you think they do.
That darkness is my father walking away.
It is my shadow that I tell this to.

This stillness is not real. The cloud that grew
Into an old man's face didn't stay.   5
These fields go farther than you think they do.

The sun loves shattered things, and loves what's new.
I love you so much more than I can say.
It is my shadow that I tell this to.

He is not sleeping, that bird the bugs crawl through.   10
Don't touch. Don't cry. Think good things. Pray.
These fields go farther than you think they do.

Some darknesses breathe, look back at you.
Under the porch a pair of eyes waits all day.
It is my shadow that I tell this to.   15

The things my father told me must be true:
There are some places that you cannot play.
These fields go farther than you think they do.
It is my shadow that I tell this to.

1998

◄ LARISSA SZPORLUK ►
(b. 1967)

Larissa Szporluk was born and raised in Ann Arbor, Michigan. A champion long-distance runner during her childhood, she won several cross-country state competitions and a national meet in 1982. She earned a bachelor's degree at the University of Michigan, where her father, who was raised in Ukraine and Poland, taught history. He now teaches at Harvard. Szporluk's mother worked for years as an editor at Ardis Publishers and currently translates Russian literature into English. Szporluk took a master's degree at the University of California at Berkeley in 1992, and another master's at the University of Virginia in 1994. She was married the following year to Carlo Celli, an Italian citizen with whom she has had two children. She teaches creative writing and literature at Bowling Green State University and spends summers in Italy with her husband's family.

Szporluk's first full-length collection, *Dark Sky Question* (1998), won the Barnard New Women's Poetry Prize. She followed this with *Isolato* (2000), which was awarded the Iowa Poetry Prize. In *Contemporary Authors,* Szporluk describes herself as an "escapist writer." She explains, "Most of my poems are invented in an amorphous, intangible space that never includes details from my personal life. In realizing that I am using my poems as vehicles for escape, I am trying to explore a variety of escapes that would allow readers to accompany me; in other words, my ambition is to create a fleet of spaceships, as opposed to a single rocket."

Vertigo

Sing now.
Sing from on high, high roof
you're afraid of
losing. Sing yourself into
a tiny blue worm,   5
maybe no eyes,

squeezing its mite
through a tinier
passage, maybe no
outlet, maybe   10
no light, maybe you'll never
ever find light,
and the stars that you think
in a world of height
there should be   15
aren't even stars, only actors
that swing in the dark
like paper lanterns
and don't serve as guides
as you peer from the edge   20
at the people below
without nets;
they don't know who you are,
but they're waiting
in droves   25
for your butterfly nerves
to tuck in their tails
and fold.

                                          2000

⇥ DIANE THIEL ⇤
(b. 1967)

Diane Thiel was born in Coral Gables, Florida, in 1967, the second of five children, and grew up in Miami Beach. Her father had been a child in Germany during World War II and came to the United States in his twenties. The traumas he experienced as a child affected him deeply, and he grew increasingly unstable in his adulthood. Thiel's mother, a teacher, was from West Virginia, the daughter of a coal miner and the only one of ten children to attend college. Thiel's poetry often reflects her tense, oppressive, and sometimes violent childhood home, though her frank portrayals never lack compassion.

Thiel's German grandmother and aunt came to the United States to live with the family when she was a child, and the young poet grew up bilingually. Her grandmother often recited poems in German to her, and Thiel began writing poetry during childhood. Living in Miami, Thiel also learned Spanish from the age of five and eventually became fluent. Thiel received tuition scholarships to attend Brown University but had to work nearly full time to pay for other expenses. She waitressed, managed an inn, and worked on university publications during her undergraduate years. In 1987, she studied abroad and lived in East Germany. She received both her bachelor's degree (1988) and master's degree (1990) from Brown University. Thiel then taught at various universities and lived in both Europe and Latin America, including extensive periods doing environmental work in Columbia, Peru, Nicaragua, Britain, and Greece. In 1997 she married Costa Hadjilambrinos, a Greek native.

Thiel has received numerous literary prizes, including the Robert Frost Award and the Robinson Jeffers Award. Her chapbook *Cleft in the Wall* was published by Aralia Press in 1999. Her first full-length book, *Echolocations* (2000), received the Nicholas Roerich Poetry Prize from Story Line Press. Her writing guide *Writing Your Rhythm: Using Nature, Culture, Form and Myth* appeared in 2001. Thiel was a Fulbright Scholar from 2001 to 2002 in Odessa, Ukraine, on the Black Sea. She often teaches and writes on ecological subjects, particularly in her nonfiction. She is a professor of English and creative writing at the University of New Mexico.

Memento Mori[1] in Middle School

When I was twelve, I chose Dante's *Inferno*
in gifted class—an oral presentation
with visual aids. My brother, *il miglior fabbro*,[2]

said he would draw the tortures. We used ten
red posterboards. That day, for school I dressed   5
in pilgrim black, left earlier to hang them

around the class. The students were impressed.
The teacher, too. She acted quite amused
and peered too long at all the punishments.

We knew by reputation she was cruel.   10
The class could see a hint of twisted forms
and asked to be allowed to round the room

as I went through my final presentation.
We passed the first one, full of poets cut
out of a special issue of *Horizon*.   15

The class thought these were such a boring set,
they probably deserved their tedious fates.
They liked the next, though—bodies blown about,

the lovers kept outside the tinfoil gates.
We had a new boy in our class named Paolo   20
and when I noted Paolo's wind-blown state

and pointed out Francesca, people howled.
I knew that more than one of us not-so-
covertly liked him. It seemed like hours

before we moved on to the gluttons, though,   25
where they could hold the cool fistfuls of slime
I brought from home. An extra touch. It sold

---

1. (Latin) "Remember you must die."
2. (Italian) "The better maker." Dante's tribute to poet Arnaut Daniel in the *Purgatorio*. Also borrowed by T. S. Eliot in his dedication of *The Waste Land* to Ezra Pound.

in canisters at toy stores at the time.
The students recognized the River Styx,
the logo of a favorite band of mine.   30

We moved downriver to the town of Dis,
which someone loudly re-named Dis and Dat.
And for the looming harpies and the furies,

who shrieked and tore things up, I had clipped out
the shrillest, most deserving teacher's heads   35
from our school paper, then thought better of it.

At the wood of suicides, we quieted.
Though no one in the room would say a word,
I know we couldn't help but think of Fred.

His name was in the news, though we had heard   40
he might have just been playing with the gun.
We moved on quickly by that huge, dark bird

and rode the flying monster, Geryon,
to reach the counselors, each wicked face,
again, I had resisted pasting in.   45

To represent the ice in that last place,
where Satan chewed the traitors' frozen heads,
my mother had insisted that I take

an ice-chest full of popsicles—to end
my gruesome project on a lighter note.   50
"It *is* a comedy, isn't it," she said.

She hadn't read the poem, or seen our art,
but asked me what had happened to the sweet,
angelic poems I once read and wrote.

The class, though, was delighted by the treat,   55
and at the last round, they all pushed to choose
their colors quickly, so they wouldn't melt.

The bell rang. Everyone ran out of school,
as always, yelling at the top of their lungs,
The *Inferno* fast forgotten, but their howls   60

showed off their darkened red and purple tongues.

                                                                        2000

◂—◂ KEVIN YOUNG ▸—▸
(b. 1970)

Kevin Young was born in Lincoln, Nebraska, the only child of a professional couple. His father was an ophthalmologist, his mother a chemist who worked in public health. His parents' careers led the family to move frequently, and the poet

changed addresses six times before he was ten when they finally settled in Topeka, Kansas. Young's literary interests developed seriously at age thirteen when he took a summer writing class at Washburn University. A varsity wrestler in high school, he went on to attend Harvard University where he took a bachelor's degree in 1992 after having studied with Irish poet Seamus Heaney. He won a Stegner fellowship to Stanford where he attended Denise Levertov's final course before going to Brown University to receive a master's degree in 1996.

Young's first collection of poems, *Most Way Home* (1995), was chosen for the National Poetry Series by Lucille Clifton, and the first printing sold out after Young was featured on National Public Radio. It also won the John Zacharis Award for best first book of the year from *Ploughshares* magazine. Critics have noted Young's talent for assuming a wide variety of voices and personae, from slave times to the present day, and his mixture of social conscience and verbal facility. Young has also edited an anthology of younger African American writers, *Giant Steps* (2000), taking his title from one of John Coltrane's breakthrough albums. The anthology, he wrote in his introduction, "hopes to counter our expectations of what black writing should be with what it be." Connecting the writing of his generation to hip-hop, he added, "Hip-hop is more than just rap: It is an aesthetic approach, a flexible form, which, at its best, is unafraid to take from any source. . . . It is hip-hop's premise—'hear it new'—that matches modernism's urging the writer to 'make it new.'" Young's second collection, *To Repel Ghosts* (2001), was a lengthy homage to painter Jean-Michel Basquiat, which has been called "an encyclopedic take on twentieth-century black and popular culture, from Jack Johnson to Muhammad Ali, from entertainer Bert Williams to Billie Holiday." Young has taught at the University of Georgia and is now Ruth Lilly Professor of Poetry at Indiana University.

◄◦──◆──◦►

Quivira City Limits

For Thomas Fox Averill

Pull over. Your car with its slow
breathing. Somewhere outside Topeka

it suddenly all matters again,
those tractors blooming rust

in the fields only need a good coat   5
of paint. Red. You had to see

for yourself, didn't you; see that the world
never turned small, transportation

just got better; to learn
we can't say a town or a baseball   10

team without breathing in
a dead Indian. To discover why Coronado

pushed up here, following the guide
who said he knew fields of gold,

north, who led them past these plains,   15
past buffaloes dark as he was. Look.

Nothing but the wheat, waving them
sick, a sea. While they strangle

him blue as the sky above you
The Moor must also wonder   20

when will all this ever be enough?
this wide open they call discovery,

disappointment, this place my
thousand bones carry, now call home.

1995

Selected Bibliographies

HISTORICAL SURVEYS

Norman F. Cantor, *The American Century: Varieties of Culture in Modern Times* (1997).

Henry Steele Commager, *The American Mind: An Interpretation of American Thought and Character since the 1880s* (1950).

Horace Gregory and Marya Zaturenska, *A History of American Poetry, 1900–1940* (1946).

Alfred Kazin, *On Native Grounds: An Interpretation of Modern America* (1942).

Alfred Kreymborg, *A History of American Poetry: Our Singing Strength* (1934).

Jay Parini and Brett C. Millier, eds., *The Columbia History of American Poetry* (1993).

Roy Harvey Pearce, *The Continuity of American Poetry* (1961).

David Perkins, *A History of American Poetry* (1976).

Louis Untermeyer, *The New Era in American Poetry* (1919).

———, *Lives of the Poets* (1959).

Hyatt H. Waggoner, *American Poets from the Puritans to the Present* (1984).

REALISM AND NATURALISM

Henry James, *The Art of Fiction and Other Essays*, introduction by Morris Roberts (1948).

Amy Kaplan, *The Social Construction of American Realism* (1988).

Donald Pizer and Earl N. Herbert, eds., *American Realists and Naturalists* (1982).

Peter Quartermain, ed., *American Poets 1880–1945* (1986).

———, *American Poets 1880–1945* (1987).

Larzer Ziff, *The American 1890s: Life and Times of a Lost Generation* (1966).

EARLY MODERNISM

World War I and Its Aftermath

Paul Fussell, *The Great War and Modern Memory* (1975).

Paul Johnson, *Modern Times: The World from the Twenties to the Eighties* (1983).

Barbara Tuchman, *The Guns of August* (1962).

Mark W. Van Wienan, *Partisans and Poets: The Political Work of American Poetry* (1997).

———, *In the Great War* (1997).

Critical and Scholarly Studies

Bruce Bawer, *Prophets and Professors* (1995).

Christopher Beach, *ABC of Influence: Ezra Pound and the Remaking of American Poetic Tradition* (1992).

Michael André Bernstein, *The Tale of the Tribe: Ezra Pound and the Modern Verse Epic* (1980).

R. P. Blackmur, *Form and Value in Modern Poetry* (1957).

Harold Bloom, ed., *American Poetry 1915 to 1945* (1987).

Louise Bogan, *The Achievement in American Poetry, 1900–1950* (1951).

Malcolm Bradbury and James McFarlane, eds., *Modernism 1890–1930* (1991).

Suzanne Clark, *Sentimental Modernism: Women Writers and the Revolution of the Word* (1991).

Stanley K. Coffman, *Imagism: A Chapter for the History of Modern Poetry* (1951).

Paul DeMan, *Blindness and Insight* (1983).

Babette Deutsch, *This Modern Poetry* (1935).

Margaret Dickie, *On the Modernist Long Poem* (1986).

Denis Donoghue, *Connoisseurs of Chaos: Ideas of Order in Modern American Poetry* (1965).

William Doreski, *The Modern Voice in American Poetry* (1995).

Elizabeth Drew, *Directions in Modern Poetry* (1941).

Albert Gelpi, ed., *Wallace Stevens and the Poetics of Modernism* (1985).

Donald Hall, *Their Ancient, Glittering Eyes* (1992).

Gillian E. Hanscombe and Virginia L. Smyers, *Writing for Their Lives: The Modernist Women 1910–1940* (1987).

Randall Jarrell, *Kipling, Auden & Co.* (1980).

——, *Poetry and the Age* (1980).

Martin A. Kayman, *The Modernism of Ezra Pound: The Science of Poetry* (1986).

Hugh Kenner, *The Pound Era* (1971).

Michael Levenson, *A Genealogy of Modernism* (1984).

James Longenbach, *Stone Cottage: Pound, Yeats, and Modernism* (1988).

——, *Wallace Stevens: The Plain Sense of Things* (1991).

Louis Menand, *Discovering Modernism: T. S. Eliot and His Context* (1987).

J. Hillis Miller, *The Linguistic Moment* (1985).

Harriet Monroe, *Poets & Their Art* (1926).

William Pritchard, *Lives of the Modern Poets* (1980).

Ricardo J. Quinones, *Mapping Literary Modernism* (1985).

Lisa Rado, ed., *Rereading Modernism: New Directions in Feminist Criticism* (1994).

Patricia Rae, *The Practical Muse: Pragmatist Poetics in Hume, Pound, and Stevens* (1997).

Lawrence S. Rainey, *Institutions of Modernism: Literary Elites and Public Culture* (1998).

Joan Reardon and Kristine A. Thorsen, *Poetry By Women, 1900–1975: A Bibliography* (1979).

M. L. Rosenthal and Sally M. Gall, *The Modern Poetic Sequence: The Genius of Modern Poetry* (1983).

Vincent Sherry, *Ezra Pound, Wyndham Lewis, and Radical Modernism* (1993).

William Jay Smith, *The Spectra Hoax* (2000).

Monroe K. Spears, *Dionysus and the City: Modernism in Twentieth Century American Poetry* (1970).

Donald E. Stanford, *Revolution and Convention in Modern Poetry* (1983).

Timothy Steele, *Missing Measures: Modern Poetry and the Revolt against Meter* (1990).

Walter Sutton, *American Free Verse: The Modern Revolution in Poetry* (1973).

René Taupin, *The Influence of French Symbolism of Modern American Poetry* (1985).

Edmund Wilson, *Axel's Castle* (1931).

Yvor Winters, *In Defense of Reason* (1947).

Alan Young, *Dada and After: Extremist Modernism and English Literature* (1981).

THE HARLEM RENAISSANCE

Jervis Anderson, *This Was Harlem: A Cultural Portrait, 1900–1950* (1981).

Houston A. Baker, Jr., *Afro-American Poetics: Revisions of Harlem and the Black Aesthetic* (1988).

———, *Modernism and the Harlem Renaissance* (1987).

Sterling Brown, *Negro Poetry and Drama* and *The Negro in American Fiction* (1937, 1969).

Countee Cullen, ed., *Caroling Dusk: An Anthology of Verse by Black Poets* (1927, 1993).

James De Jongh, *Vicious Modernism: Black Harlem and the Literary Imagination* (1990).

Ann Douglas, *Terrible Honesty: Mongrel Manhattan in the 1920s* (1995).

Samuel A. Floyd, Jr., ed., *Black Music in the Harlem Renaissance: A Collection of Essays* (1990).

Nathan Irvin Huggins, ed., *Voices from the Harlem Renaissance* (1976).

Gloria Hull, *Color, Sex, and Poetry: Three Women Writers of the Harlem Renaissance* (1987).

George Hutchinson, *The Harlem Renaissance in Black and White* (1995).

James Weldon Johnson, *Black Manhattan* (1930, 1968).

Bruce Kellner, ed., *The Harlem Renaissance: A Historical Dictionary for the Era* (1984).

Robert T. Kerlin, ed., *Negro Poets and Their Poems* (1923, 1947).

Victor A. Kramer and Robert A. Russ, eds., *Harlem Renaissance Re-examined: A Revised and Expanded Edition* (1997).

David Levering Lewis, ed., *When Harlem Was in Vogue* (1981).

———, *The Portable Harlem Renaissance Reader* (1994).

Alain Locke, ed., *The New Negro: An Interpretation* (1925, 1968).

Gilbert Osofsky, *Harlem: The Making of a Ghetto: Negro New York, 1890–1930* (1971).

Roi Ottley and William J. Weatherby, *The Negro in New York: An Informal Social History* (1967).

Michael W. Peplow and Arthur P. Davis, eds., *The New Negro Renaissance: An Anthology* (1975).

Cheryl A. Wall, *Women of the Harlem Renaissance* (1995).

Steven Watson, *The Harlem Renaissance: Hub of African-American Culture, 1920–1930* (1995).

Cary D. Wintz, *Black Culture and the Harlem Renaissance* (1988).

MODERNIST ALTERNATIVES

John Merrill Bradbury, *The Fugitives: A Critical Account* (1958).

Paul Keith Conkin, *The Southern Agrarians* (1988).

Louise Cowan, *The Fugitive Group: A Literary History* (1959).

Margaret Dickie and Thomas Travisano, eds., *Gendered Modernisms: American Women Poets and Their Readers* (1996).

William Drake, *The First Wave: Women Poets in America 1914–1945* (1987).

Jen Gould, *Modern American Women Poets* (1984).

Alfred Kazin, *Contemporaries* (1962).

————, *Starting Out in the Thirties* (1965).

R. W. B. Lewis, *The Poetry of Hart Crane: A Critical Study* (1967).

Jan Montefiore, *Feminism and Poetry* (1987).

John Lincoln Steward, *The Burden of Time: The Fugitives and the Agrarians* (1965).

Twelve Southerners, *I'll Take My Stand: The South and the Agrarian Tradition* (1930).

Edmund Wilson, *The Thirties*, ed. Leon Edel (1980).

————, *The Twenties,* ed. Leon Edel (1975).

MIDCENTURY POETS

General Criticism

Donald Allen and Warren Tallman, eds., *The Poetics of the New American Poetry* (1984).

Bruce Bawer, *The Middle Generation: The Lives and Poetry of Delmore Schwartz, Randall Jarrell, John Berryman and Robert Lowell* (1986).

————, *Prophets and Professors* (1995).

Mutlu K. Blasing, *American Poetry: the Rhetoric of Its Forms* (1989).

Harold Bloom, *The Anxiety of Influence* (1973).

James Breslin, *From Modern to Contemporary Poetry* (1984).

Christopher Clausen, *The Place of Poetry* (1981).

Thomas M. Disch, *The Castle of Indolence* (1995).

Dana Gioia, *Can Poetry Matter?* (1992).

Paul Goodman, *Speaking and Language: A Defense of Poetry* (1971).

Robert von Hallberg, *American Poetry and Culture, 1945–1980* (1985).

Richard Howard, *Alone with America: Essays on the Art of Poetry in the United States Since 1950* (1969).

Mark Jarman, *The Secret of Poetry* (2001).

Mark Jarman and Robert McDowell, eds., *The Reaper Essays* (1996).

David Kalstone, *Becoming a Poet: Elizabeth Bishop, Marianne Moore and Robert Lowell* (1989).

————, *Five Temperaments: Elizabeth Bishop, Robert Lowell, James Merrill, Adrienne Rich, John Ashbery* (1977).

Martin Lammon, ed., *Written in Water, Written in Stone* (1996).

James Longenbach, *Modern Poetry after Modernism* (1997).

David Mason, *The Poetry of Life and the Life of Poetry* (2000).

J. D. McClatchy, *White Paper* (1989).

James McCorkle, ed., *Conversant Essays: Contemporary Poets on Poetry* (1990).

Robert McDowell, ed., *Poetry after Modernism* (1991, rev. 1998).

Diane Middlebrook and Marilyn Yalom, eds., *Coming to Light: American Women Poets in the Twentieth Century* (1985).

Ralph J. Mills, *Creation's Very Self* (1988).

————, *Cry of the Human: Essays on Contemporary American Poetry* (1974).

Charles Molesworth, *The Fierce Embrace: A Study of Contemporary American Poetry* (1979).

Alicia Ostriker, *Stealing the Language: The Emergence of Women's Poetry in America* (1986).

Jay Parini, ed., *The Columbia History of American Poetry* (1993).

Robert Phillips, *The Confessional Poets* (1973).

Wyatt Prunty, *Fallen from the Symboled World: Precedents for the New Formalism* (1990).

M. L. Rosenthal, *The New Poets: American and British Poetry since World War II* (1967).

Robert B. Shaw, ed., *American Poetry since 1960* (1974).

Vernon Shetley, *After the Death of Poetry: Poet and Audience in Contemporary America* (1993).

Eileen Simpson, *Poets in Their Youth* (1982).

Willard Spiegelman, *The Didactic Muse: Scenes of Instruction in Contemporary American Poetry* (1989).

Peter Stitt, *Uncertainty and Plenitude: Five American Poets* (1997).

———, *The World's Hieroglyphic Beauty: Five American Poets* (1987).

Alan Williamson, *Eloquence and Mere Life* (1994).

Anthologies

Donald Allen, ed., *The New American Poetry* (1960).

Hayden Carruth, ed., *The Voice That Is Great within Us* (1983).

Donald Hall, Robert Pack, and Louis Simpson, eds., *New Poets of England and America* (1957).

Donald Hall, ed., *Contemporary American Poetry* (1963).

A. Poulin, Jr., and Michael Waters, eds., *Contemporary American Poetry* (2001).

OPEN FORM

Donald Allen and Warren Tallman, eds., *The Poetics of the New American Poetry* (1973).

Charles Altieri, *Enlarging the Temple: New Directions in American Poetry during the 1960s* (1979).

James E. B. Breslin, *From Modern to Contemporary: American Poetry 1945–1965* (1983).

Ann Charters, *Beats & Company: A Portrait of a Literary Generation* (1986).

———, *The Portable Beat Reader* (1992).

Joseph M. Conte, *Unending Design: The Forms of Postmodern Poetry* (1991).

Michael Davidson, *The San Francisco Renaissance: Poetics and Community at Mid-Century* (1989).

Rachel Blau DuPlessis and Peter Quartermain, *The Objectivist Nexus: Essays in Cultural Poetics* (1999).

Ekbert Faas, ed., *Towards a New America Poetics: Essays and Interviews* (1978).

Edward Halsey Foster, *Understanding the Beats* (1992).

———, *Understanding the Black Mountain Poets* (1995).

Stephen Fredman, *The Grounding of American Poetry: Charles Olson and the Emersonian Tradition* (1993).

Warren French, *The San Francisco Poetry Renaissance 1955–1960* (1991).

Nancy M. Grace, *Girls Who Wore Black: Women Writing the Beat Generation* (2002).

Burton Hatlen, "A Poetics of Marginality and Resistance: The Objectivist Poets in Context," *The Objectivist Nexus: Essays in Cultural Poetic,* ed. Rachel Blau DuPlessis and Peter Quartermain, 37–55 (1999).

Hugh Kenner, "Oppen, Zukofsky, and the Poem as Lens," *Literature at the Barricades: The American Writer in the 1930s,* ed. Ralph F. Bogardus and Fred Hobson, 161–171 (1982).

Brenda Knight, ed., *Women of the Beat Generation: The Writers, Artists, and Muses at the Heart of a Revolution* (1996).

William Lawlor, *The Beats: A Bibliographical Teaching Guide* (1998).

David Meltzer, ed., *San Francisco Beat: Talking with the Poets* (2001).

———, ed., *The San Francisco Poets* (1971).

———, *Sustainable Poetry: Four American Ecopoets* (1999).

Rod Phillips, *"Forest Beatniks" and "Urban Thoreaus": Gary Snyder, Jack Kerouac, Lew Welch and Michael McClure* (2000).

Libbie Rifkin, *Career Moves: Olson, Creeley, Zukofsky, Berrigan, and the American Avant-Garde* (2000).

John Tytell, *Paradise Outlaws: Remembering the Beats* (1999).

Ann Waldman, *The Beat Book: Writings from the Beat Generation* (1999).

Steven Watson, *The Birth of the Beat Generation: Visionaries, Rebels, and Hipsters 1944–1960* (1995).

Tim Woods, *The Poetics of the Limit: Ethics and Politics in Modern and Contemporary American Poetry* (2002).

POSTWAR FORMALISM AND ITS DISCONTENTS

General Criticism

Calvin Bedient, *Eight Contemporary Poets* (1974).

Robert Bly, *American Poetry: Wildness and Domesticity* (1990).

Robert Boyers, ed., *Contemporary Poetry in America: Essays and Interviews* (1974).

James Breslin, *From Modern to Contemporary: American Poetry, 1945–1965* (1984).

Peter Davison, *One of the Dangerous Trades* (1991).

Terrence Des Pres, *Praises and Dispraises* (1988).

Richard Gray, *American Poetry of the Twentieth Century* (1990).

Donald Hall, ed., *Claims for Poetry* (1982).

Charles O. Hartman, *Free Verse: An Essay on Prosody* (1980).

Lawrence Lieberman, *Unassigned Frequencies: American Poetry in Review, 1964–1977* (1977).

James Longenbach, *Modern Poetry after Modernism* (1997).

Samuel Maio, *Creating Another Self: Voice in Modern American Poetry* (1995).

Jerome Mazzaro, *Postmodern American Poetry* (1980).

Diane Wood Middlebrook and Marilyn Yalom, eds., *Coming to Light: American Women Poets in the Twentieth Century* (1985).

Ralph J. Mills, *Contemporary American Poetry* (1965).

———, *Creation's Very Self: On the Personal Element in Recent American Poetry* (1969).

———, *Cry of the Human: Essays on Contemporary American Poetry* (1975).

Jan Montefiore, *Feminism and Poetry* (1994).

Wyatt Prunty, *"Fallen from the Symboled World": Precedents for the New Formalism* (1990).

Nathan A. Scott, Jr., *Visions of Presence in Modern American Poetry* (1993).

Thomas Simmons, *Erotic Reckonings: Mastery and Apprenticeship in the Work of Poets and Lovers* (1994).

Louis Simpson, *A Revolution in Taste* (1978).

Peter Stitt, *The World's Hieroglyphic Beauty* (1985).

Robert Von Hallberg, *American Poetry and Culture, 1945–1980* (1985).

Alan Williamson, *Introspection and Contemporary Poetry* (1984).

Anthologies

Stephen Berg and Robert Mezey, eds., *The New Naked Poetry* (1976).

Hayden Carruth, ed., *The Voice That Is Great within Us* (1983).

Donald Hall, ed., *Contemporary American Poetry* (1963).

Stephen Kuusisto, Deborah Tall, and David Weiss, eds., *The Poet's Notebook: Excerpts from the Notebooks of 26 American Poets* (1995).

J. D. McClatchy, ed., *The Vintage Book of Contemporary American Poetry* (1990).

Mark Strand, *The Contemporary American Poets: American Poetry since 1940* (1967).

AMERICAN INTERNATIONALISM

Charles Altieri, *Self and Sensibility in Contemporary American Poetry* (1984).

Dore Ashton, *The New York School: A Cultural Reckoning* (1992).

Philip Auslander, *The New York School Poets as Playwrights: O'Hara, Ashbery, Koch, Schuyler, and the Visual Arts* (1989).

Mutlu Konuk Blasing, *Politics and Form in Postmodern Poetry: O'Hara, Bishop, Ashbery, and Merrill* (1995).

Paul Breslin, *The Psycho-Political Muse: American Poetry since the 1950s* (1987).

André Breton, *Manifestoes of Surrealism*, trans. Richard Seaver and Helen R. Lane (1969).

Andrew P. Debicki, *Spanish Poetry of the Twentieth Century: Modernity and Beyond* (1994).

Terrence Diggory and Stephen Paul Miller, *The Scene of My Selves: New Work on New York School Poets* (2001).

Gérard Durozoi, *History of the Surrealist Movement* (2002).

Wallace Fowlie, *Age of Surrealism* (1950).

Edward B.Germain, ed., *English and American Surrealist Poetry* (1978).

Lawrence Goldstein, *The American Poet at the Movies* (1994).

Edward Hoeppner, *Echoes and Moving Fields: Structure and Subjectivity in the Poetry of W. S. Merwin and John Ashbery* (1994).

C. G. Jung, *The Essential Jung*, ed. Anthony Storr (1983).

David Lehman, *The Last Avant-Garde: The Making of the New York School of Poets* (1998).

George S. Lensing and Ronald Moran, *Four Poets and the Emotive Imagination: Robert Bly, James Wright, Louis Simpson, and William Stafford* (1976).

J. H. Matthews, *An Introduction to Surrealism* (1965).

Robert Pinsky, *The Situation of Poetry: Contemporary Poetry and Its Traditions* (1976).

Susan Sontag, *A Susan Sontag Reader* (1982).

Peter Stitt, *Uncertainty and Plenitude: Five Contemporary American Poets* (1997).

Geoff Ward, *Statutes of Liberty: The New York School of Poets* (2001).

Alan Williamson, "Language against Itself: The Middle Generation of Contemporary Poets" *American Poetry since 1960: Some Critical Perspectives*, ed. Robert B. Shaw (1973).

RETURN TO REALISM

John Westerdale Bowker, *Hallowed Ground: Religions and the Poetry of Place* (1993).

Lawrence Buell, *The Environmental Imagination* (1995).

————, *Writing for an Endangered World* (2001).

Frank Deodene and William P. French, *Black American Poetry since 1944: A Preliminary Checklist* (1971).

John Haines, *Living Off the Country: Essays on Poetry and Place* (1981).

Jonathan Holden, *The Old Formalism: Character in Contemporary American Poetry* (1999).

————, *Style and Authenticity in Postmodern Poetry* (1986).

Analouise Keating, *Women Reading Women Writing: Self-Invention in Paula Gunn Allen, Gloria Anzuldúa, and Audre Lorde* (1996).

Wesley McNair, *Mapping the Heart: Reflections on Place and Poetry* (2003).

John O'Brien, *Interviews with Black Writers* (1973).

Bernard W. Quetchenbach, *Back from the Far Field: American Nature Poetry in the Late Twentieth Century* (2002).

David Rigsbee and Steven Ford Brown, eds., *Invited Guest: An Anthology of Twentieth-Century Southern Poetry* (2001).

Joan Rita Sherman, ed., *Collected Black Women's Poetry* (1988).

Wallace Stegner and Richard W. Etulain, *Conversations with Wallace Stegner on Western History and Literature* (1990).

Leon Stokesbury, ed., *The Made Thing: An Anthology of Contemporary Southern Poetry* (1999).

Brian Swann and Arnold Krupat, eds., *Recovering the Land: Essays on Native American Literature* (1987).

Thom Tammaro and Mark Vinz, eds., *Imagining Home: Writing from the Midwest* (1995).

————, *Inheriting the Land: Contemporary Voices from the Midwest* (1993).

Claudia Tate, ed., *Black Women Writers at Work* (1983).

Norma C. Wilson, *The Nature of Native American Poetry* (2001).

CONTEMPORARY VOICES

General Criticism

Gloria Anzaldúa, *Borderlands/La frontera: The New Mestiza* (1987).

Charles Bernstein, ed., *The Politics of Poetic Form: Poetry and Public Policy* (1990).

Juan Bruce-Novoa, *RetroSpace: Collected Essays on Chicano Literature* (1990).

Joseph M. Conte, *Unending Design: The Forms of Postmodern Poetry* (1991).

Thomas M. Disch, *The Castle of Indolence* (1995).

Anthony Easthope, *Poetry as Discourse* (1983).

Sascha Feinstein, *Jazz Poetry: From the 1920s to the Present* (1997).

Annie Finch, ed., *After New Formalism: Poets on Form, Narrative, and Tradition* (1999).

Dana Gioia, *Can Poetry Matter?* (1990; 2002).

R. S. Gwynn, ed., *New Expansive Poetry: Theory/Criticism/History* (1999).

George Hartley, *Textual Politics and the Language Poets* (1989).

H. L. Hix, *As Easy as Lying: Essays on Poetry* (2002).

Frederic Jameson, *Postmodernism, or, The Cultural Logic of Late Capitalism* (1991).

Mark Jarman, *Body and Soul* (2002).

Bridget Kevane and Juanita Heneda, eds., *Latina Self-Portraits: Interviews with Contemporary Women Writers* (2000).

Mary Kinzie, *The Judge Is Fury: Dislocation and Form in Poetry* (1994).

Shirley Geok-lin Lim and Amy Ling, eds., *Reading the Literatures of Asian America* (1992).

José E. Limón, *Mexican Ballads, Chicano Poems: History and Influence in Mexican-American Social Poetry* (1992).

April Lindner, *New Formalist Poets of the American West* (2001).

Deborah L. Madson, *Understanding Contemporary Chicana Literature* (2000).

David Mason, *The Poetry of Life and the Life of Poetry* (2000).

James McCorkle, ed., *Conversant Essays: Contemporary Poets on Poetry* (1990).

Robert McDowell and Mark Jarman, eds., *The Reaper Essays* (1996).

Robert McDowell, ed., *Poetry after Modernism* (1998).

Emmanuel S. Nelson, ed., *Critical Essays: Gay and Lesbian Writers of Color* (1993).

Aldon Lynn Nielsen, ed., *Reading Race in American Poetry* (2000).

Alicia Ostriker, *Stealing the Language: The Emergence of Women's Poetry in America* (1986).

Bob Perelman, *The Marginalization of Poetry: Language Writing and Literary History* (1996).

Marjorie Perloff, *The Poetics of Indeterminacy: Rimbaud to Cage* (1981).

Linda Reinfeld, *Language Poetry: Writing as Rescue* (1992).

Sherod Santos, *The Poetry of Two Minds* (2000).

Vernon Shetley, *After the Death of Poetry: Poets and Audience in Contemporary America* (1993).

Timothy Steele, *Missing Measures: Modern Poetry and the Revolt against Meter* (1990).

Kevin Walzer, *The Ghost of Tradition: Expansive Poetry and Postmodernism* (1998).

William Watkin, *In the Process of Poetry: The New York School and the Avant-Garde* (2001).

San-ling Cynthia Wong, *Reading Asian American Literature: From Necessity to Extravagance* (1993).

Anthologies

Bruce Andrews and Charles Bernstein, eds., *The L=A=N=G=U=A=G=E Book* (1984).

Annie Finch, ed., *A Formal Feeling Comes: Poems in Form by Contemporary Women* (1994).

Garrett Hongo, *Open Boat: Poems from Asian America* (1993).

Mark Jarman and David Mason, eds., *Rebel Angels: 25 Poets of the New Formalism* (1996; 1998).

Tony Medina and Louis Reyes Rivera, eds., *Bum Rush the Page: A Def Poetry Jam* (2001).

A. Poulin, Jr. and Michael Waters, eds., *Contemporary American Poetry* (2001).

Kevin Young, ed., *Giant Steps* (2001).

KIM ADDONIZIO

Poetry
The Philosopher's Club (1994); *Jimmy & Rita* (1997); *Tell Me* (2000).

Prose
The Poet's Companion: A Guide to the Pleasures of Writing Poetry (with Dorianne Laux, 1997); *In the Box Called Pleasure* (1999).

AI

Poetry
Cruelty (1973); *Killing Floor* (1979); *Sin* (1986); *Fate* (1991); *Greed* (1993); *Vice: New and Selected Poems* (1999).

Critical Studies
Claudia Ingram, "Writing the Crises: The Deployment of Abjection in Ai's Dramatic Monologues" (*Lit: Literature, Interpretation, Theory* 8.2, Oct. 1997: 173–91); Karen L. Kilcup, "Dialogues of the Self: Toward a Theory of (Re)Reading Ai" (*Journal of Gender Studies* 7.1, 1998: 5–20); Susannah B. Mintz, " 'A Descent Toward the Unknown' in the Poetry of Ai" (*Sage: A Scholarly Journal on Black Women* 9.2, Summer 1995: 36–46).

CONRAD AIKEN

Poetry
Collected Poems (1970).

Prose
The Collected Novels of Conrad Aiken: Blue Voyage, Great Circle, King Coffin, A Heart for the Gods of Mexico, and Conversation (1964); *Collected Criticism (formerly A Reviewer's ABC)* (1968); *The Collected Short Stories of Conrad Aiken* (1982); *Selected Letters of Conrad Aiken* (ed. Joseph Killorin, 1978).

Books Edited
Modern American Poets (1922); *Twentieth-Century American Poetry* (1963).

Bibliography
Catherine Kirk Harris, *Conrad Aiken, Critical Recognition 1914–1981: A Bibliographic Guide* (1983).

Biographical and Critical Studies
Edward Butscher, *Conrad Aiken, Poet of White Horse Vale* (1988); Frederick John Hoffman, *Conrad Aiken* (1962); Clarissa M. Lorenz, *Lorelei Two: My Life with Conrad Aiken* (1983); Harry Marten, *The Art of Knowing: The Poetry and Prose of Conrad Aiken* (1988); Jay Martin, *Conrad Aiken, A Life of His Art* (1962); Ted Ray Spivey, *Time's Stop in Savannah: Conrad Aiken's Inner Journey* (1997).

FRANCISCO X. ALARCÓN

Poetry
Tattoos (1985); *Quake Poems* (1989); *Body in Flames/Cuerpo en llamas* (1990); *Loma Prieta* (1990); *De amor oscuro/Of Dark Love* (1991); *Snake Poems: An Aztec Invocation* (1992); *No Golden Gate for Us* (1993); *Sonnets to Madness and Other Misfortunes* (2001); *From the Other Side of Night* (2002).

Critical Studies
George Hartley, "Hegemony and Identity: The Chicano Hybrid in Francisco X. Alarcón's Snake Poems" (*Studies in Twentieth Century Literature* 25.1, Winter 2001: 281–305).

SHERMAN ALEXIE

Poetry
The Business of Fancydancing: Stories and Poems (1992); *First Indian on the Moon* (1993); *Old Shirts and New Skins* (1993); *The Summer of Black Widows* (1996); *One Stick Song* (2000).

Prose
The Lone Ranger and Tonto Fistfight in Heaven (1993); *Reservations Blues* (1995); *The Toughest Indian in the World* (2000).

Critical Studies
Susan Berry Brill de Ramirez, "Fancy Dancer: A Profile of Sherman Alexie" (*Poets and Writers* 25.1, Jan/Feb 1999: 54–59); Stephen F. Evans, "'Open Containers': Sherman Alexie's Drunken Indians" (*American Indian Quarterly* 25.1, Winter 2001: 46–72); John Newton, "Sherman Alexie's Autoenthography" (*Contemporary Literature* 42.2, Summer 2001: 413–28).

JULIA ALVAREZ

Poetry
Homecoming: New and Collected Poems (1996).

Prose
How the Garcia Girls Lost Their Accents (1991); *In the Time of the Butterflies* (1994); *YO!* (1996); *Something to Declare* (1998); *In the Name of Salome* (2000).

Critical Studies
Alicia G. Andreu, "Julia Alvarez and the Reconstruction of the Self" (*Torre de Papel* 8.3, Fall 1998: 49–56); Kathrine Varnes, "'Practising for the Real Me': Form and Authenticity in the Poetry of Julia Alvarez" (*Antipodas: Journal of Hispanic and Galician Studies* 10, 1998: 67–77); Richard Vela, "Daughter of Invention: The Poetry of Julia Alvarez" (*Postscript: Publication of the Philological Association of the Carolinas* 16, 1999: 33–42).

A. R. AMMONS

Poetry
Collected Poems 1951–1971 (1971); *Selected Longer Poems* (1980); *The Selected Poems* (1987); *The Really Short Poems of A. R. Ammons* (1990); *Brink Road: Poems* (1996); *Glare* (1997); *Worldly Hopes* (2001).

Prose
Set in Motion: Essays, Interviews, and Dialogues (ed. Zofia Burr, 1996).

Critical Studies
Harold Bloom, ed., *A. R. Ammons* (1986); Alan Holder, *A. R. Ammons* (1978); Robert Kirschten, *Approaching Prayer: Ritual and the Shape of Myth in A. R. Ammons and James Dickey* (1998); Steven P. Schneider, *A. R. Ammons and the Poetics of Widening Scope* (1994) and as editor, *Complexities of Motion: New Essays on A. R. Ammons's Long Poems* (1999).

JOHN ASHBERY

Poetry
Selected Poems (1985); *Flow Chart* (1991); *Hotel Lautréamont* (1992); *And the Stars Were Shining* (1994); *Can You Hear Me, Bird* (1995); *The Mooring of Starting Out: The First Five Books of Poetry* (1997); *Wakefulness* (1998); *Girls on the Run: A Poem* (1999); *Your Name Here: Poems* (2000).

Prose
Reported Sightings: Art Chronicles, 1957–1987 (ed. David Bergman, 1989); *Other Traditions* (2000).

Bibliography
David K. Kermani, *John Ashbery: A Comprehensive Bibliography* (1976).

Critical Studies
David Herd, *John Ashbery and American Poetry* (2001); David Lehman, ed., *Beyond Amazement: New Essays on John Ashbery* (1980); Susan M. Schultz, ed., *The Tribe of John: Ashbery and Contemporary Poetry* (1995); David Shapiro, *John Ashbery: An Introduction to the Poetry* (1979); John Shoptaw, *On the Outside Looking In: John Ashbery's Poetry* (1994).

AMIRI BARAKA

Poetry
Transbluesency: The Selected Poetry of Amiri Baraka/LeRoi Jones, 1961–1995 (ed. Paul Vangelisti, 1995); *Funk Lore: New Poems 1984–1995* (ed. Paul Vangelisti, 1996).

Prose
Home: Social Essays (1966); *Daggers and Javelins, Essays 1974–1979* (1984); *The Music: Reflections on Jazz and Blues* (1987); *The Autobiography of LeRoi Jones/Amiri Baraka* (1997).

Poetry, Prose, and Plays
The LeRoi Jones/Amiri Baraka Reader (ed. William J. Harris in collaboration with Baraka, 1991).

Book Edited
Black Fire: An Anthology of Afro-American Writing (with Larry Neal, 1969).

Interviews
Conversations with Amiri Baraka (ed. Charles Reilly, 1994).

Bibliography
Letitia Dace, *LeRoi Jones (Imamu Amiri Baraka): A Checklist of Works by and about Him* (1971).

Critical Studies
Kemberly W. Bentson, *Baraka: The Renegade and the Mask* (1976) and as editor, *Imamu Amiri Baraka (LeRoi Jones): A Collection of Critical Essays* (1978); Bob Bernatos, *Amiri Baraka* (1991); William J. Harris, *Poetry and Poetics of Amiri Baraka: The Jazz Aesthetic* (1985); Theodore Hudson, *From LeRoi Jones to Amiri*

Baraka: The Literary Works (1973); Werner Sollers, Amiri Baraka/LeRoi Jones: The Quest for a "Populist Modernism" (1978); Jerry Gaffio Watts, Amiri Baraka: The Politics and Art of a Black Intellectual (2001); K. Komozi Woodard, A Nation within a Nation: Amiri Baraka (LeRoi Jones) and Black Power Politics (1999).

STEPHEN VINCENT BENÉT

Poetry
John Brown's Body (1928); Ballads and Poems, 1915–1930 (1931); A Book of Americans (with Rosemary Carr Benét, 1933); Western Star (1943).

Prose
The Devil and Daniel Webster (1937); Selected Letters (ed. Charles A. Fenton, 1960).

Biographical and Critical Studies
Charles A. Fenton, Stephen Vincent Benét: The Life and Times of an American Man of Letters (1978); Parry Stroud, Stephen Vincent Benét (1962).

JOHN BERRYMAN

Poetry
The Dream Songs (1969); Love and Fame (1970; 1972); Delusions, Etc. (1972); Henry's Fate and Other Poems, 1967–1972 (ed. John Haffenden, 1977); Collected Poems, 1937–1971 (ed. Charles Thornbury, 1988).

Prose
Stephen Crane (1950); Recovery (1973); The Freedom of the Poet (1976); We Dream of Honor: John Berryman's Letters to his Mother (ed. Richard J. Kelly, 1988); Berryman's Shakespeare (ed. John Haffenden, 1999).

Bibliography
Richard J. Kelly, John Berryman: A Checklist (1972) and John Berryman's Personal Library: A Catalogue (1998).

Biography
Paul Mariani, Dream Song: The Life of John Berryman (1996); Eileen Simpson, Poets in Their Youth (1982).

ELIZABETH BISHOP

Poetry
The Complete Poems, 1929–1979 (1983).

Prose
One Art: Letters (ed. Robert Giroux, 1994); The Collected Prose (1984).

Translation
Alice Brant, The Diary of "Helena Morley" (1957, 1977).

Book Edited
An Anthology of Twentieth-Century Brazilian Poetry (with Emanuel Brasil, 1972).

Paintings
Exchanging Hats: Paintings (ed. William Benton, 1996).

Bibliography
Candace McMahon, *Elizabeth Bishop: A Bibliography, 1927–1979* (1980); Diane E. Wylie, *Elizabeth Bishop and Howard Nemerov: A Reference Guide* (1983).

Biographical and Critical Studies
Bonnie Costello, *Elizabeth Bishop: Questions of Mastery* (1991); Gary Fountain and Peter Brazeau, *Remembering Elizabeth Bishop: An Oral Biography* (1994); David Kalstone, *Becoming a Poet: Elizabeth Bishop with Marianne Moore and Robert Lowell* (1989); Marilyn May Lombardi, ed., *Elizabeth Bishop: The Geography of Gender* (1993); Jeredith Merrin, *An Enabling Humility: Marianne Moore, Elizabeth Bishop, and the Uses of Tradition* (1990); Brett C. Millier, *Elizabeth Bishop: Life and the Memory of It* (1993); Lloyd Schwartz and Sybil Estess, eds., *Elizabeth Bishop and Her Art* (1983); Anne Stevenson, *Elizabeth Bishop* (1966); Thomas Travisano, *Elizabeth Bishop: Her Artistic Development* (1988).

JOHN PEALE BISHOP

Poetry
The Collected Poems of John Peale Bishop (ed. Allen Tate, 1948).

Prose
Many Thousands Gone (1931); *Act of Darkness* (1935); *The Collected Essays of John Peale Bishop* (ed. Edmund Wilson, 1948); *The Republic of Letters in America: The Correspondence of John Peale Bishop and Allen Tate* (ed. Thomas D. Young, 1981).

Biography
Elizabeth Carroll Spindler, *John Peale Bishop: A Biography* (1980).

ROBERT BLY

Poetry
Selected Poems (1986); *Loving a Woman in Two Worlds* (1987); *What Have I Ever Lost by Dying?: Collected Prose Poems* (1992); *Morning Poems* (1997); *Snowbanks North of the House* (1999).

Prose
American Poetry: Wildness and Domesticity (1990); *Iron John: A Book about Men* (1990); *The Sibling Society* (1996).

Translations
Knut Hamsun, *Hunger* (1967); Neruda and Vallejo, *Selected Poems* (1971); Kabir, *The Kabir Book: Forty-Four of the Ecstatic Poems of Kabir* (1977); Machado, *I Never Wanted Fame* (1979); *Lorca and Jimenez: Selected Poems* (1997).

Books Edited
David Ignatow, *Selected Poems* (1975); *The Rag and Bone Shop of the Heart: Poems for Men* (with James Hillman, 1992); William Stafford, *The Darkness around Us Is Deep: Selected Poems* (1994).

Biographical and Critical Studies
Kate Daniels and Richard Jones, eds., *On Solitude and Silence: Writings on Robert Bly* (1982); William V. Davis, *Understanding Robert Bly* (1989); Howard Nelson, *Robert Bly: An Introduction to the Poetry* (1984); Joyce Peseroff, ed., *Robert Bly: When Sleepers Awake* (1984); Thomas R. Smith, ed., *Walking Swiftly: Writings and Images on the Occasion of Robert Bly's 65th Birthday* (1992).

LOUISE BOGAN

Poetry
The Blue Estuaries: Poems 1923–1968 (1968, 1996).

Prose
Journey around My Room: The Autobiography of Louise Bogan (ed. Ruth Limmer, 1980); *What the Woman Lived: Selected Letters of Louise Bogan, 1920–1970* (ed. Ruth Limmer, 1973); *A Poet's Alphabet: Reflections on the Literary Art and Vocation* (ed. Ruth Limmer and Robert Phelps, 1970); *Achievement in American Poetry, 1900–1950* (1951).

Bibliography
Claire E. Knox, *Louise Bogan: A Reference Source* (1990).

Biographical and Critical Studies
Gloria Bowles, *Louise Bogan's Aesthetic of Limitation* (1987); Martha Collins, ed., *Critical Essays on Louise Bogan* (1984); Elizabeth Frank, *Louise Bogan: A Portrait* (1985); Jacqueline Ridgeway, *Louise Bogan* (1984); Lee Upton, *Repression and Release: Rereading the Poetry of Louise Bogan* (1996).

GWENDOLYN BROOKS

Poetry
Selected Poems (1963; 1999); *The World of Gwendolyn Brooks* (1971); *Blacks* (1987; 1991).

Prose
Maud Martha, A Novel (1954); *Report from Part One* (1972); *Report from Part Two* (1996).

Bibliography
R. Baxter Miller, *Langston Hughes and Gwendolyn Brooks: A Reference Guide* (1978).

Biographical and Critical Studies
Harold Bloom, ed., *Gwendolyn Brooks* (2000); B. J. Bolden, *Urban Rage in Bronzeville: Social Commentary in the Poetry of Gwendolyn Brooks, 1945–1960* (1998); George Kent, *A Life of Gwendolyn Brooks* (1987); D. H. Melhem, *Gwendolyn Brooks: Poetry and the Heroic Voice* (1987); Maria K. Mootry and Gary Smith, eds., *A Life Distilled: Gwendolyn Brooks: Her Poetry and Fiction* (1987);

Harry Shaw, *Gwendolyn Brooks* (1980); Stephen Caldwell Wright, ed., *On Gwendolyn Brooks: Reliant Contemplation* (1996).

STERLING BROWN

Poetry
The Collected Poems of Sterling A. Brown (ed. Michael S. Harper, 1980; 1996).

Prose
A Son's Return: Selected Essays of Sterling A. Brown (ed. Mark Sanders, 1996); *The Negro in American Fiction* (1937; 1968); *Negro Poetry and Drama* (1937; 1968); *Outline for the Study of Poetry of American Negroes* (1931).

Book Edited
The Negro Caravan: Writings by American Negroes (with Arthur P. Davis and Ulysses Lee, 1941).

Biographical and Critical Studies
Black History Museum Committee, *Sterling Brown: A UMUM Tribute* (1976); Joanne Gabbin, *Sterling A. Brown: Building the Black Aesthetic Tradition* (1985; 1994); Mark A Sanders, *Afro-Modernist Aesthetics and the Poetry of Sterling Brown* (1999).

RAFAEL CAMPO

Poetry
The Other Man Was Me: A Voyage to the New World (1994); *What the Body Told* (1996); *Diva* (1999); *Landscape with Human Figure* (2002).

Prose
The Poetry of Healing: A Doctor's Education in Empathy, Identity, and Desire (1997).

Critical Studies
S. W. Henderson, "Identity and Compassion in Rafael Campo's 'The Distant Moon'" (*Literature and Medicine* 19.2, Fall 2000: 262–79); Lazaro Lima, "Haunting the Corpus Delicti: Rafael Campo's *What the Body Told* and Wallace Stevens's Modernist Body" (*Wallace Stevens Journal* 25.2, Fall 2001: 220–32); Joanne Rendell, "Drag Acts: Performativity, Subversion, and the AIDS Poetry of Rafael Campo and Mark Doty" (*Critical Survey* 14.2, 2002: 89–100).

JARED CARTER

Poetry
Work, For the Night Is Coming (1981); *After the Rain* (1993); *Les Barricades Mysterieuses: Thirty-Two Villanelles* (1999).

Critical Studies
Dana Gioia, "Jared Carter," *Can Poetry Matter?* (1992: 188–90); Mark Jarman and Robert McDowell, "How to Write Narrative Poetry," *The Reaper Essays* (1996: 131–38); Helen Vendler, "Adrienne Rich, Jared Carter, Philip Levine," *The Music of What Happens: Poets, Poems, Critics* (1988: 374–78).

FRED CHAPPELL

Poetry
The World between the Eyes (1971); *The Man Twice Married to Fir* (1977); *Midquest* (includes *River, Bloodfire, Wind Mountain,* and *Earthsleep*) (1981); *Castle Tzingal* (1984); *Source* (1986); *First and Last Words* (1989); *C: Poems* (1993); *Spring Garden: New and Selected Poems* (1995); *Family Gathering: Poems* (2000).

Prose
Plow Naked: Selected Writings on Poetry (1993); *A Way of Happening: Observations of Contemporary Poetry* (1998).

Other
The Fred Chappell Reader (1987).

Critical Studies
Patrick Bizzaro, ed., *Dream Garden: The Poetic Vision of Fred Chappel* (1997); George Garrett, ed., *Craft So Hard to Learn: Conversations with Poets and Novelists about the Teaching of Writing* (1972); John Lang, *Understanding Fred Chappell* (2001).

JOHN CIARDI

Poetry
The Collected Poems of John Ciardi (ed. Edward M. Cifelli, 1997).

Prose
How Does a Poem Mean? (1959); *Saipan: The War Diary of John Ciardi* (1988); *Ciardi Himself: Fifteen Essays on the Reading, Writing, and Teaching of Poetry* (1989); *The Selected Letters of John Ciardi* (ed. Edward M. Cifelli, 1991).

Translation
Dante Alighieri, *The Divine Comedy* (1970).

Biographical and Critical Studies
Edward Cifelli, *John Ciardi: A Biography* (1997); Vincent Clemente, *John Ciardi: A Measure of the Man* (1987); Edward Francis Krickel, *John Ciardi* (1980).

SARAH CLEGHORN

Poetry and Prose
Portraits and Protest (1917); *Poems of Peace and Freedom* (1945); *Threescore. The Autobiography of Sarah N. Cleghorn* (introduction by Robert Frost, 1936).

LUCILLE CLIFTON

Poetry
Good Woman: Poems and a Memoir, 1969–1980 (1987); *Quilting: Poems 1987–1990* (1991); *The Terrible Stories: Poems* (1996); *Blessing the Boats: New and Selected Poems, 1988–2000* (2000).

Interviews
With Michael Glaser (*Antioch Review* 58.3, Summer 2000: 310–28); with Charles
H. Rowell (*Callaloo* 22.1, Winter 1999: 56–72).

Critical Studies
Akasha Hull, "In Her Own Images: Lucille Clifton and the Bible," *Dwelling in
Possibility: Women Poets and Critics on Poetry* (ed. Yopie Prins and Maeera
Schreiber, 1997); Alicia Ostriker, "Kin and Kin: The Poetry of Lucille Clifton"
(*American Poetry Review* 22, Nov./Dec. 1993: 41–48); Cheryl Wall, "Sifting Lega-
cies in Lucille Clifton's *Generations*" (*Contemporary Literature* 40.4, Winter 1999:
552–74); Mark Bernard White, "Sharing the Living Light: Rhetorical, Personal,
and Social Identity in Lucille Clifton" (*College Language Association Journal* 40,
Mar. 1977: 288–304).

JUDITH ORTIZ COFER

Poetry
Terms of Survival (1987); *The Latin Deli: Prose and Poetry* (1993); *Reaching for
the Mainland and Selected New Poems* (1995); *The Year of Our Revolution: New
and Selected Stories and Poems* (1998).

Prose
The Line of the Sun (1989); *Woman in Front of the Sun: On Becoming a Writer*
(2000).

Critical Studies
Juan Bruce Novoa, "Judith Ortiz Cofer's Rituals of Movement" (*The Americas
Review: A Review of Hispanic Literature and Art of the USA* 19.3–4, Winter
1991: 88–99); Viviana Rangil, "Pro-Claiming a Space: The Poetry of Sandra Cis-
neros and Judith Ortiz Cofer" (*MultiCultural Review* 9.3, Sept. 2000: 48–51,
54–55).

BILLY COLLINS

Poetry
Video Poems (1980); *The Apple That Astonished Paris* (1988); *Questions about
Angels* (1991); *The Art of Drowning* (1995); *Picnic, Lightning* (1998); *Sailing
Alone around the Room: New and Selected Poems* (2001).

HART CRANE

Poetry
The Poems of Hart Crane (ed. Marc Simon, 1986).

Prose
O My Land, My Friends: The Selected Letters of Hart Crane (ed. Langdon Hammer and Brom Weber, 1997); *Hart Crane and Yvor Winters: Their Literary Correspondence* (ed. Thomas Parkinson, 1978); *The Letters of Hart Crane and His
Family* (ed. Thomas S. W. Lewis, 1974).

Bibliography
Joseph Schwartz, *Hart Crane: An Annotated Critical Bibliography* (1970) and *Hart Crane: A Reference Guide* (1983).

Biographical and Critical Studies
Susan Jenkins Brown, *Robber Rocks: Letters and Memories of Hart Crane, 1923–1932* (1969); Lee Edelman, *Transmemberment of Song: Hart Crane's Anatomies of Rhetoric and Desire* (1987); Allen Grossman, "Hart Crane and Poetry: A Consideration of Crane's Intense Poetics with Reference to 'The Return,'" *Critical Essays on Hart Crane* (ed. David R. Clark, 1983); Langdon Hammer, *Hart Crane and Allen Tate: Janus Faced Modernism* (1993); Herbert Leibowitz, *Hart Crane: An Introduction* (1968); R. W. B. Lewis, *The Poetry of Hart Crane: A Critical Study* (1967); Paul Mariani, *The Broken Tower: A Life of Hart Crane* (1999); John Unterecker, *Voyager: A Life of Hart Crane* (1969); Thomas Yingling, *Hart Crane and the Homosexual Text: New Thresholds, New Anatomies* (1990).

STEPHEN CRANE

Poetry
The Complete Poems of Stephen Crane (ed. Joseph Katz, 1972).

Prose
The Complete Short Stories and Sketches (ed. Thomas A. Gullason, 1963); *The Complete Novels* (ed. Thomas A. Gullason, 1967); *The Works of Stephen Crane*, 10 vols. (ed. Fredson Bowers, 1969–1975); *Stephen Crane: Prose and Poetry* (ed. J. C. Levenson, 1984).

Biographical and Critical Studies
John Berryman, *Stephen Crane* (1950); Daniel Hoffman, *The Poetry of Stephen Crane* (1957); Joseph Katz, ed., *Stephen Crane in Transition: Centenary Essays* (1973) and *Stephen Crane in the West and Mexico* (1970); James Nagel, *Stephen Crane and Literary Impressionism* (1980); R. M. Weatherford, ed., *Stephen Crane, The Critical Heritage* (1973).

ADELAIDE CRAPSEY

Poetry and Prose
A Study in English Metrics (1918); *The Complete Poems and Collected Letters of Adelaide Crapsey* (ed. Susan Sutton Smith, 1977).

Biographical and Critical Studies
Karen Alkalay-Gut, *Alone in the Dawn: The Life of Adelaide Crapsey* (1988); Edward Butscher, *Adelaide Crapsey* (1979).

ROBERT CREELEY

Poetry
Collected Poems of Robert Creeley, 1945–1975 (1982); *Selected Poems* (1991); *Echoes* (1994); *Life and Death* (1998).

Prose
Charles Olson and Robert Creeley: The Complete Correspondence (ed. George F. Butterick, 1980–1996); *The Collected Essays of Robert Creeley* (1989); *Irving Layton and Robert Creeley: The Complete Correspondence, 1973–1978* (ed. Ekbert Faas and Sabrina Reed, 1990); *Collected Prose* (ed. Donald Allen and Benjamin Friedlander, 2001).

Bibliography
Willard Fox, *Robert Creeley, Ed Dorn, and Robert Duncan: A Reference Guide* (1989); Mary Novik, *Robert Creeley: An Inventory, 1945–1970* (1973).

Biographical and Critical Studies
Tom Clark, *Robert Creeley and the Genius of the American Common Place: Together with the Poet's Own Autobiography* (1993); Cynthia Dubin Edelbert, *Robert Creeley: A Critical Introduction* (1978); Ekbert Faas, *Robert Creeley: A Biography* (2001); Arthur Ford, *Robert Creeley* (1978); Carroll F. Terrell, ed., *Robert Creeley: The Poet's Workshop* (1984); John Wilson, ed., *Robert Creeley's Life and Work: A Sense of Increment* (1987).

COUNTEE CULLEN

Poetry
On These I Stand: An Anthology of the Best Poems of Countee Cullen (1947).

Biographical and Critical Studies
Houston A. Baker, Jr., *A Many-Colored Coat of Dreams: The Poetry of Countee Cullen* (1974); Blanche E. Ferguson, *Countee Cullen and the Negro Renaissance* (1966); Margaret Perry, *A Bio-Bibliography of Countee Cullen, 1903–1946* (1971); Alan R. Shucard, *Countee Cullen* (1984).

E. E. CUMMINGS

Poems
Complete Poems: 1913–1962 (1972).

Prose
The Enormous Room (1938); *Selected Letters* (ed. F. W. Dupee and George Stade, 1969).

Bibliography
George J. Firmage, *E. E. Cummings: A Bibliography* (1960).

Biographical and Critical Studies
Norman Friedman, *E. E. Cummings: The Art of His Poetry* (1960), *E. E. Cummings: The Growth of a Writer* (1964), and *E. E. Cummings: A Collection of Critical Essays* (1972); Rushworth M. Kidder, *E. E. Cummings: An Introduction to the Poetry* (1979); Gary L. Rotella, *E. E. Cummings: A Reference Guide* (1979); Eve Triem, *E. E. Cummings* (1969).

J. V. CUNNINGHAM

Poetry
The Poems of J. V. Cunningham (ed. Timothy Steele, 1997).

Prose
Tradition and Poetic Structure: Essays in Literary History and Criticism (1960);
The Collected Essays of J. V. Cunningham (1976).

Bibliography
Charles Gullans, *A Bibliography of the Published Works of J. V. Cunningham, 1931–1988* (1988).

Biographical and Critical Studies
R. L. Barth, "The Vacancies of Need: Particularity in J. V. Cunningham's *To What Strangers, What Welcome*" (*Southern Review*, Spring 1982: 286–98); "Cunningham Memorial Issue" (*Sequoia*, Spring 1985); Denis Donoghue, *The Connoisseurs of Chaos* (1965); Steven Helmling, "J. V. Cunningham" (*Dictionary of Literary Biography* 5.1, 1980: 159–65); Robert Pinsky, "The Poetry of J. V. Cunningham" (*New Republic* Jan. 28, 1978: 25–26, 28–29); Timothy Steele, "An Interview with J. V. Cunningham" (*Iowa Review* Fall 1985: 1–24); Henry Taylor, *Compulsory Figures* (1992: 1–17); Yvor Winters, *The Poetry of J. V. Cunningham* (1961) and *Forms of Discovery* (1967: 299–311).

MARISA DE LOS SANTOS

Poetry
From the Bones Out (2000).

JAMES DICKEY

Poetry
The Whole Motion: Collected Poems, 1945–1992 (1992); *Selected Poems* (ed. Robert Kirschten, 1998).

Novels
Deliverance (1970); *Alnilam* (1987); *To the White Sea* (1993).

Prose
Babel to Byzantium: Poets and Poetry Now (1968); *Self-Interviews* (1970); *Sorties: Journals and New Essays* (1971).

Bibliographies
Matthew J. Bruccoli and Judith S. Baughman, *James Dickey: A Descriptive Bibliography* (1990); J. Elledge, *James Dickey: A Bibliography, 1947–1974* (1979).

Biographical and Critical Studies
Matthew Bruccoli and Judith Baughman, eds., *Crux: The Letters of James Dickey* (2000); Christopher Dickey, *Summer of Deliverance: A Memoir of Father and Son* (1998); Henry Hart, *James Dickey: The World as a Lie* (2000); Robert and Calhoun Hill, *James Dickey* (1983); Robert Kirschten, *Critical Essays on James Dickey*

(1994) and as editor, *Struggling for Wings: The Art of James Dickey* (1997); Bruce Weigl and Terry Hummer, eds., *James Dickey: The Imagination of Glory* (1984).

MARK DOTY

Poetry
My Alexandria (1993); *Atlantis* (1995); *Sweet Machine* (1998); *Turtle, Swan & Bethlehem in Broad Daylight: Two Volumes of Poetry* (2000); *Source* (2001); *Still Life with Oysters and Lemon* (2001).

Memoirs
Heaven's Coast (1996); *Firebird* (1999).

Critical Studies
James Fenton, "On the Frontier" (*New York Review of Books* 43.4, Feb. 29, 1996: 52–53); David R. Jarraway, "'Creatures of the Rainbow': Wallace Stevens, Mark Doty, and the Poetics of Androgyny" (*Mosaic,* 30, Sept. 1997: 169–83); Deborah Landau, "'How to Live, What to Do': The Poetics and Politics of AIDS" (*American Literature* 68.1, Mar. 1996: 193–225).

RITA DOVE

Poetry
Selected Poems (1993); *Mother Love: Poems* (1995); *On the Bus with Rosa Parks* (1999).

Play
The Darker Face of the Earth (1994).

Prose
Fifth Sunday (1985); *Through the Ivory Gate* (1992).

Critical Study
Helen Vendler, *The Given and the Made: Strategies of Poetic Redefinition* (1995).

PAUL LAURENCE DUNBAR

Poetry
The Complete Poems (1913); *The Paul Laurence Dunbar Reader* (ed. Gossie H. Hudson and Jay Martin, 1975).

Bibliography
E. W. Metcalf, Jr., *Paul Laurence Dunbar: A Bibliography* (1975).

Biographical and Critical Studies
Addison Gayle, Jr., *Oak and Ivy: A Biography of Paul Laurence Dunbar* (1971); Peter Revell, *Paul Laurence Dunbar* (1979).

ROBERT DUNCAN

Poetry
The Years as Catches: First Poems, 1939–1946 (1966); *The Opening of the Field* (1960; 1973); *Roots and Branches* (1964, 1969); *Bending the Bow* (1968); *Ground Work: Before the War* (1984); *Ground Work II: In the Dark* (1987); *Selected Poems* (ed. Robert J. Bertholf, 1997).

Prose
Fictive Certainties: Essays (1985); *Selected Prose* (ed. Robert. J. Bertholf, 1995).

Bibliographies
Robert J. Bertholf, *Robert Duncan: A Descriptive Bibliography* (1986); Willard Fox, *Robert Creeley, Ed Dorn, and Robert Duncan: A Reference Guide* (1989).

Biographical and Critical Studies
Robert J. Bertholf and Ian W. Reid, eds., *Robert Duncan: Scales of the Marvelous* (1979); Michael Davidson, "Marginality in the Margins: Robert Duncan's Textual Politics" (*Contemporary Literature* 33, Summer 1992: 275–301); Ekbert Faas, *Young Robert Duncan: Portrait of the Poet as Homosexual in Society* (1983); Thom Gunn, "Homosexuality in Robert Duncan's Poetry," *The Occasions of Poetry: Essays in Criticism and Autobiography* (ed. Clive Wilmer, 1985), "The High Road: A Last Collection," and "Adventurous Song: Robert Duncan as Romantic Modernist," *Shelf Life: Essays, Memoirs, and an Interview* (1993: 129–170, 118–134); Mark Johnson, *Robert Duncan* (1988); Sherman Paul, *The Lost America of Love: Rereading Robert Creeley, Edward Dorn, and Robert Duncan* (1981).

STEPHEN DUNN

Poetry
Looking for Holes in the Ceiling (1974); *Full of Lust and Good Usage* (1976); *A Circus of Needs* (1978); *Work and Love* (1981); *Not Dancing* (1984); *Local Time* (1986); *Between Angels* (1989); *Landscape at the End of the Century* (1991); *New & Selected Poems: 1974–1994* (1994); *Loosestrife: Poems* (1996); *Different Hour* (2000).

Prose
Walking Light: Essays & Memoirs (1993).

Critical Studies
Jeanne Andree Nelson, "Of Sand and Storm in the Poetry of Stephen Dunn" (*Southern Humanities Review* 36.3, Summer 2002: 229–38); David Wojahn, "Four from Prospero" (*Georgia Review* 43, Fall 1989: 589–601).

RICHARD EBERHART

Poetry
Collected Verse Plays (1962); *Collected Poems, 1930–1986* (1988).

Prose
Of Poetry and Poets (1979).

Biographical and Critical Studies
Bernard F. Engle, *Richard Eberhart* (1972); Ralph J. Mills, Jr., *Richard Eberhart* (1966).

T. S. ELIOT

Poetry
Complete Poems and Plays (1952); *The Waste Land: A Facsimile and Transcript of the Original Drafts including the Annotations of Ezra Pound* (ed. Valerie Eliot, 1971).

Prose
The Sacred Wood (1920); *Homage to John Dryden* (1924); *For Lancelot Andrewes* (1928); *The Use of Poetry and the Use of Criticism* (1932); *To Criticize the Critic* (1965); *The Letters of T. S. Eliot* vol. 1, 1898–1922 (ed. Valerie Eliot, 1988).

Bibliography
Donald Gallup, *T. S. Eliot: A Bibliography* (1969).

Biographical and Critical Studies
Peter Ackroyd, *T. S. Eliot: A Life* (1984); Ronald Bush, *T. S. Eliot: A Study in Character and Style* (1983); Denis Donoghue, *Words Alone: The Poet T. S. Eliot* (2000) Helen Gardner, *The Art of T. S. Eliot* (1950) and *The Composition of Four Quartets* (1978); Lyndall Gordon, *Eliot's Early Years* (1977) and *Eliot's New Life* (1988); Hugh Kenner, ed., *T. S. Eliot: The Invisible Poet* (1959) and *T. S. Eliot: A Collection of Critical Essays* (1962); A. David Moody, ed., *The Cambridge Companion to T. S. Eliot* (1994); Christopher Ricks, *T. S. Eliot and Prejudice* (1988); Tate, Allen, ed., *T. S. Eliot: The Man and His Work* (1966).

RHINA ESPAILLAT

Poetry
Lapsing to Grace (1992); *Where Horizons Go* (1998); *Mundo y Palabra / The World and the Word* (*Walking to Windward: 21 New England Poets* 4, 2001); *Rehearsing Absence* (2001).

WILLIAM EVERSON/BROTHER ANTONINUS

Poetry
The Residual Years: Poems 1939–1948 (1997); *The Veritable Years: Poems 1949–1966* (1998); *The Integral Years: Poems 1966–1994* (2000).

Prose
Earth Poetry: Selected Essays and Interviews of William Everson 1950/1977 (ed. Lee Bartlett, 1980); *Birth of a Poet: The Santa Cruz Meditations* (ed. Lee Bartlett, 1982); *William Everson on Writing the Waterbirds and Other Presentations: Collected Forewords and Afterword, 1935–1981* (ed. Lee Bartlett, 1983); *The Excesses of God: Robinson Jeffers as a Religious Figure* (1988); *Take Hold upon the Future: Letters on Writers and Writing, 1938–1946* (ed. William R. Eshelman, 1994); *Prodigious Thrust* (1996).

Bibliography
Lee Bartlett and Allen Campo, *William Everson: A Descriptive Bibliography, 1934–1976* (1977)

Biographical and Critical Studies
Lee Bartlett, *William Everson: The Life of Brother Antoninus* (1988); James B. Hall, Bill Hotchkiss, and Judith Shears, eds., *Perspectives on William Everson: A Collection of Essays, Poems, and Reflections in Honor of the Poet in His Eighty-Fifth Year* (1992); Felicia Rice, *The Poet as Printer: William Everson and the Fine Press Art Book* (*Quarry West* Special Issue, Fall 1995: 32).

B. H. FAIRCHILD

Poetry
The Arrival of the Future (1985); *The Art of the Lathe* (1998); *Early Occult Memory Systems of the Lower Midwest* (2002).

KENNETH FEARING

Poetry
Complete Poems (ed. Robert M. Ryley, 1994).

Novels
The Hospital (1939); *Dagger of the Mind* (1941); *Clark Gifford's Body* (1942); *The Big Clock* (1946); *As No Way Out* (1980); *The Generous Heart* (1954).

LAWRENCE FERLINGHETTI

Poetry
These Are My Rivers: New and Selected Poems, 1955–1993 (1993); *A Far Rockaway of the Heart* (1997).

Prose
Literary San Francisco: A Pictorial History from its Beginnings to the Present Day (1980); *Love in the Days of Rage* (1988).

Translations
Jacques Prevert: Selections from Paroles (1958); *Nicanor Parra: Antipoems* (With others, 1985).

Books Edited
Beatitude Anthology (1960); *City Lights Anthology* (1974, 1995) *City Lights Pocket Poets Anthology* (1995).

Biographical and Critical Studies
Neeli Cherkovski, *Ferlinghetti: A Biography* (1979); Kenneth Rexroth, *Assays* (1961); Barry Silesky, *Ferlinghetti: The Artist in His Time* (1990); Larry Smith, *Lawrence Ferlinghetti: Poet-at-Large* (1983).

EDWARD FIELD

Poetry
New and Selected Poems from the Book of My Life (1987); *Counting Myself Lucky: Selected Poems, 1963–1992* (1992); *A Frieze for a Temple of Love* (1998).

Books Edited
A Geography of Poets: An Anthology of New Poetry (1979).

Critical Study
Franklin Abbott, "Homage to Edward Field" (*RFD: A Country Journal for Gay-men Everywhere* Winter 1998–1999, 96: 19–23).

CAROLYN FORCHÉ

Poetry
Gathering the Tribes (1976); *The Country between Us* (1981); *The Angel of History* (1994).

Book Edited
Against Forgetting: Twentieth Century Poetry of Witness (1993).

Critical Studies
Joann Gardner, "The Mirrored Self: Images of Kinship in Carolyn Forché's Poetry" (*Women's Studies* 18.4, 1991: 405–19); Michael Greer, "Politicizing the Modern: Carolyn Forché in El Salvador and America" (*Centennial Review* 30.2, Spring 1986: 160–80); Leonora Smith, "Carolyn Forché: Poet of Witness," *Still the Frame Holds: Essays on Women Poets and Writers* (ed. Sheila Roberts and Yvonne Pacheco Tevis, 1993: 15–28).

ROBERT FRANCIS

Poetry
Collected Poems, 1936–1976 (1976); *Late Fire, Late Snow: New and Uncollected Poems* (1992).

Prose
The Satirical Rogue on Poetry (1968); *The Trouble with Francis* (1971).

ROBERT FROST

Poetry
Collected Poems (1930); *Selected Poems* (Introduction by Robert Graves, 1963); *Complete Poems of Robert Frost* (1968); *Collected Poems, Plays, and Prose* (1995).

Prose
Selected Prose of Robert Frost (ed. Hyde Cox and Edward Connery Lathem, 1966); *Robert Frost on Writing* (ed. Elaine Barry, 1972); *Robert Frost: Poetry and Prose* (ed. Lawrance Thompson and Edward Connery Lathem, 1972).

Letters

The Letters of Robert Frost to Louis Untermeyer (ed. Louis Untermeyer, 1963); *Robert Frost and John Bartlett: The Record of a Friendship* (ed. Margaret Bartlett Anderson, 1963); *Selected Letters of Robert Frost* (ed. Lawrance Thompson, 1964); *Family Letters of Robert and Elinor Frost* (ed. Arnold Grade, 1972); *Robert Frost and Sidney Cox: Forty Years of Friendship* (ed. William R. Evans, 1981).

Interviews

Interviews with Robert Frost (ed. Edward Connery Lathem, 1966).

Bibliography

Marshall Louis Mertins and Esther Mertins, *Intervals of Robert Frost: A Critical Bibliography* (1947).

Biographical Studies

Meyers, Jeffrey. *Robert Frost: A Biography* (1996); Jay Parini, *Robert Frost: A Life* (1999); Elizabeth Shepley Sergeant, *Robert Frost: The Trial by Existence* (1960); Lawrance Thompson, *Robert Frost: The Early Years, 1874–1915* (1966); Lawrance Thompson, *Robert Frost: The Years of Triumph, 1915–1938* (1970); Lawrance Thompson and R. H. Winnick, *Robert Frost: The Later Years, 1938–1963* (1976).

Critical Studies

Harold Bloom, ed., *Robert Frost* (1998); Reuben A. Brower, *The Poetry of Robert Frost: Constellations of Intention* (1963); James M. Cox, ed., *Robert Frost: A Collection of Critical Essays* (1962); Sidney Cox, *Swinger of Birches: A Portrait of Robert Frost* (1957); Jefferey S. Cramer, *Robert Frost among His Poems: A Literary Companion to the Poet's Own Biographical Contexts and Associations* (1996); Lesley Lee Francis, *The Frost Family's Adventure in Poetry* (1994); Elizabeth Jennings, *Frost* (1966); Katherine Kearns, *Robert Frost and a Poetics of Appetite* (1994); Karen L. Kilcup, *Robert Frost and Feminine Literary Tradition* (1998); Edward C. Lathem, ed., *A Concordance to the Poetry of Robert Frost* (1971); Frank Lentricchia, *Robert Frost: Modern Poetics and the Landscapes of Self* (1975); H. A. Maxson, *On the Sonnets of Robert Frost* (1997); George W. Nitchie, *Human Values in the Poetry of Robert Frost* (1960); Richard Poirier, *Robert Frost* (1977); William H. Pritchard, *Frost: A Literary Life Reconsidered* (1984); Mark Richardson, *The Ordeal of Robert Frost: The Poet and His Poetic* (1997); Radcliffe Squires, *Major Themes of Robert Frost* (1969); Linda Welshimer Wagner, ed., *Robert Frost: The Critical Reception* (1977).

ALICE FULTON

Poetry

Dance Script with Electric Ballerina (1983); *Palladium* (1986); *Powers of Congress* (1990); *Sensual Math: Poems* (1995); *Felt: Poems* (2001).

Prose

Feeling as a Foreign Language: The Good Strangeness of Poetry (1999).

Critical Studies

Emily Grosholz, "Distortion, Explosion, and Embrace: The Poetry of Alice Fulton" (*Michigan Quarterly Review* 34, Spring 1995: 213–29); Lynn Keller, "The 'then some inbetween': Alice Fulton's Feminist Experimentalism" (*American Literature* 71.2, June 1999: 311–40); Cristanne Miller, "'The Erogenous Cusp': Or Intersections of Science and Gender in Alice Fulton's Poetry," *Feminist Measures: Soundings in Poetry and Theory* (ed. Lynn Keller and Cristanne Miller, 1994: 317–43).

CHARLOTTE PERKINS GILMAN

Poetry
In This Our World (1898); *Suffrage Songs and Verses* (1911); *The Later Poetry of Charlotte Perkins Gilman* (ed. Denise D. Knight, 1996).

Prose
Charlotte Perkins Gilman: A Nonfiction Reader (ed. Larry Ceplair, 1991); *The Living of Charlotte Perkins Gilman: An Autobiography* (ed. Ann J. Lane, 1991); *Herland and Selected Stories* (ed. Barbara H. Solomon, 1992); *The Diaries of Charlotte Perkins Gilman* (ed. Denise Knight, 1994); *The Charlotte Perkins Gilman Reader: The Yellow Wallpaper, and Other Fiction* (ed. Ann J. Lane, 1999).

Bibliography
Gary Scharnhorst, *Charlotte Perkins Gilman: A Bibliography* (1985).

Biographical and Critical Studies
Cathy N. Davidson, *Charlotte Perkins Gilman: The Woman and Her Work* (1989); Mary Hill, *Charlotte Perkins Gilman: The Making of a Radical Feminist, 1860–1896* (1980); Ann J. Lane, *To Herland and Beyond: The Life and Work of Charlotte Perkins Gilman* (1991); Gary Scharnhorst, *Charlotte Perkins Gilman* (1985).

ALLEN GINSBERG

Poetry
Cosmopolitan Greetings: Poems, 1986–1992 (1994); *Collected Poems: 1947–85* (1995); *Selected Poems, 1947–1995* (1996).

Prose
Indian Journals: Mar. 1962–May 1963: Notebooks, Diary, Blank Pages, Writings (1970, 1996); *Allen Verbatim: Lectures on Poetry, Politics, and Consciousness* (ed. Gordon Ball, 1975); *Journals: Early Fifties, Early Sixties* (ed. Gordon Ball, 1977); *Journals Mid-Fifties, 1954–1958* (ed. Gordon Ball, 1995).

Bibliographies
Michell P. Kraus, *Allen Ginsberg: An Annotated Bibliography, 1967–1977* (1980); Bill Morgan, *The Works of Allen Ginsberg, 1941–1994: A Descriptive Bibliography* (1995) and *The Response to Allen Ginsberg, 1926–1994: A Bibliography of Secondary Sources* (1996).

Biographical and Critical Studies
Jack Foley, *O Powerful Western Star!* (2000) and *Foley's Books* (2000); Jane Kramer, *Allen Ginsberg in America* (1969); Thomas F. Parkinson, *A Casebook on the Beats* (1961); Michael Schumacher, *Dharma Lion* (1994); Louis Simpson, *A Revolution in Taste* (1978).

DANA GIOIA

Poetry
Daily Horoscope (1986); *The Gods of Winter* (1991); *Interrogations at Noon* (2001).

Libretto
Nosferatu (2001).

Prose
Can Poetry Matter? (1992); "Fallen Western Star: The Decline of San Francisco as a Literary Region" (*Hungry Mind Review* 52, Winter 1999–2000: 17–21); *The Barrier of a Common Language* (2004).

Translations
Eugenio Montale, *Mottetti: Poems of Love* (1990); Seneca, *The Madness of Hercules* (1995).

Books Edited
Weldon Kees, *The Ceremony and Other Stories* (1984); *Poems from Italy* (with William Jay Smith, 1985); *New Italian Poets* (with Michael Palma, 1990); *Certain Solitudes: On the Poetry of Donald Justice* (with William Logan, 1997); *The Longman Anthology of Short Fiction* (with R. S. Gwynn, 2001); Weldon Kees, *Selected Stories of Weldon Kees* (2003).

Biographical and Critical Studies
April Lindner, *Dana Gioia* (2000) and *New Formalist Poets of the American West* (2001); David Mason, *The Poetry of Life and the Life of Poetry* (2000); Lewis Turco, "Dana Gioia," *American Poets since World War II, D. L. B.,* vol. 120 (ed. R. S. Gwynn, 1992); Kevin Walzer, "Still Waters: Gioia, Mason, McDowell, Salter," *The Ghost of Tradition: Expansive Poetry and Postmodernism* (1998).

LOUISE GLÜCK

Poetry
The Triumph of Achilles (1985); *Ararat* (1990); *The Wild Iris* (1992); *The First Four Books of Poems* (1995); *Meadowlands* (1996); *Vita Nova* (2001).

Prose
Proofs and Theories: Essays on Poetry (1994).

Critical Study
Elizabeth Caroline Dodd, *The Veiled Mirror and the Woman Poet: H. D., Louise Bogan, Elizabeth Bishop, and Louise Glück* (1992).

JORIE GRAHAM

Poetry
The Dream of the Unified Field: Selected Poems 1974–1994 (1995); *The Errancy: Poems* (1997); *Swarm* (2000); *Never: Poems* (2002).

Biographical and Critical Studies
Stephen Schiff, "Big Poetry" (*New Yorker,* July 14, 1997: 60–67); Willard Spiegel-man, "Jorie Graham's 'New Way of Looking'" (*Salmagundi* 120, Fall 1998: 224–75); Helen Vendler, *The Breaking of Style: Hopkins, Heaney, Graham* (1995).

ANGELINA WELD GRIMKÈ

Poetry and Prose
The Selected Works of Angelina Weld Grimkè (ed. Carolivia Herron, 1991).

Biographical and Critical Studies
Katherine Henry, "Angelina Weld Grimkè's Rhetoric of Exposure" (*American Quarterly* 49, June 1997: 328–55); Akasha (Gloria) Hull, *Color, Sex, and Poetry: Three Women Writers of the Harlem Renaissance* (1987) and "'Under the Days': The Buried Life and Poetry of Angelina Weld Grimkè," *Home Girls: A Black Feminist Anthology* (ed. Barbara Smith, 2000).

BARBARA GUEST

Poetry
Poems: The Location of Things, Archaics, the Open Skies (1964); *Selected Poems* (1995); *Rocks on a Platter: Notes on Literature* (1999); *Miniatures and Other Poems* (2002).

Prose
Herself Defined: The Poet H.D. and Her World (1984).

Critical Studies
Catherine Kasper, ed., "Barbara Guest: This Art" (*Women's Studies: An Interdisciplinary Journal,* Special Issue, 2001).

R. S. GWYNN

Poetry
The Drive-In (1986); *No Word of Farewell: Poems 1970–2000* (2001).

Books Edited
The Advocates of Poetry: A Reader of American Poet-Critics of the Modernist Era (1996); *New Expansive Poetry* (1999); *Poetry: A Pocket Anthology* (2001); *Fiction: A Pocket Anthology* (2001); *Drama: A Pocket Anthology* (2001); *The Longman Anthology of Short Fiction* (with Dana Gioia, 2001).

Critical Studies
Betty Adcock, "A Formal Feeling Comes" (*Tar River Poetry* 41.1, Fall 2001: 44–48); Jonathan Holden, "The Public Nature of End-Rhymed Poems" (*Writer's Chronicle* Dec. 1999: 10–14); Allan M. Jalon, "A Texas Poet Skewers American Pop Culture" (*San Francisco Chronicle,* 26 Aug. 2001: 79); Dave Oliphant, "The New Formalism in Texas" (*Texas Observer,* 3 Aug. 2001: 26–28); Clay Reynolds, "Cause to Sing" (*Texas Books in Review* 21.2, Summer/Fall 2001: 17); Leon Stokesbury, "As If the Axeman's Sorrows Were His Own" (*Sewanee Review* 109,

2001: xxiii–xxv); Lewis Turco, "R. S. Gwynn: A Southern Melancholic" (*Hollins Critic* 39.1, Feb. 2002: 1–14); Kevin Walzer, "The Sword of Wit: Disch, Feirstein, Gwynn, Martin," *The Ghost of Tradition* (1998).

H. D. [HILDA DOOLITTLE]

Poetry
Hermetic Definition (1972); *Helen in Egypt* (1974); *Collected Poems, 1912–1944* (ed. Louis Martz, 1983); *Trilogy: The Walls Do Not Fall, Tribute to the Angels, The Flowering of the Rod* (ed. Aliki Barnstone, 1998).

Prose
Tribute to Freud (1956); *Bid Me to Live (A Madrigal)* (1960); *End to Torment: A Memoir of Ezra Pound* (ed. Norman Holmes Pearson and Michael King, 1979); *HERmione* (1981); *Notes on Thought and Vision and the Wise Sappho* (1982); *Richard Aldington and H. D.: The Early Years in Letters* (ed. Caroline Zilboorg, 1992); *Richard Aldington and H. D.: The Later Years in Letters* (1995); *Between History and Poetry: The Letters of H. D. and Norman Holmes Pearson* (ed. Donna Krolik Hollenberg, 1997); *The Gift: The Complete Text* (ed. Jane Augustine, 1999).

Bibliography
Michael Boughn, *H. D.: A Bibliography, 1905–1990* (1993).

Biographical and Critical Studies
Winifred Bryher, *The Heart to Artemis—A Writer's* (1962); Diana Collecott, *H. D. and Sapphic Modernism, 1910–1950* (1999); Susan Stanford Friedman, *Penelope's Web: Gender, Modernity, H. D.'s Fiction* (1990) and *Psyche Reborn: The Emergence of H. D.* (1981); Susan Stanford Friedman and Rachel Blau DuPlessis, eds., *Signets: Reading H. D.* (1990); Eileen Gregory, *H. D. and Hellenis: Classic Lines* (1997); Barbara Guest, *Herself Defined: The Poet H. D. and Her World* (1984); Michael King, *H. D., Woman and Poet* (1986); Cassandra Laity, *H. D. and the Victorian Fin de Siécle: Gender, Modernism, Decadence* (1996); Janice S. Robinson, *H. D.: The Life and Work of an American Poet* (1982).

JOHN HAINES

Poetry
The Owl in the Mask of the Dreamer: Collected Poems (1993); *Where the Twilight Never Ends* (1994); *At the End of This Summer: Poems 1948–1954* (1997).

Prose
Living Off the Country: Essays on Poetry and Place (1981); *The Stars, the Snow, the Fire: Twenty-five Years in the Northern Wilderness: A Memoir* (1989); *Fables and Distances: New and Selected Essays* (1996).

Critical Studies
Kevin Bezner and Kevin Walzer, eds., *The Wilderness of Vision: On the Poetry of John Haines* (1996); David Mason, "The Tenacity of John Haines," *The Poetry of Life and the Life of Poetry* (2000); Peter Wild, *John Haines* (1985).

DONALD HALL

Poetry
Old and New Poems (1990); *The Museum of Clear Ideas* (1993); *The Old Life* (1996); *Without* (1998).

Prose
Henry Moore: The Life and Work of a Great Sculptor (1966); *Marianne Moore: The Cage and the Animal* (1970); *The Pleasures of Poetry* (1971); *Goatfoot Milk-tongue Twinbird* (1978); *String Too Short to be Saved* (1979); *The Weather for Poetry* (1982); *Poetry and Ambition* (1987); *Their Ancient Glittering Eyes* (1992); *Life Work* (1993); *Principal Products of Portugal* (1995).

Books Edited
The New Poets of England and America (with Robert Pack and Louis Simpson, 1957); *Contemporary American Poetry* (1963); *Claims for Poetry* (1982).

Critical Study
Liam Rector, ed., *The Day I Was Older: Collected Writings on the Poetry of Donald Hall* (1989).

JOY HARJO

Poetry
She Had Some Horses (1983); *In Mad Love and War* (1990); *The Woman Who Fell from the Sky* (1994); *A Map to the Next World* (2000); *How We Became Human: New and Selected Poems 1975–2001* (2002).

Critical Studies
Nancy Lang, "'Twin Gods Bending Over': Joy Harjo and Poetic Memory" (*MELUS* 18, Fall 1993: 41–49); Mary Leen, "An Art of Saying: Joy Harjo's Poetry and the Survival of Storytelling" (*American Indian Quarterly* 19, Winter 1995: 1–16); Rhonda S. Pettit, *Joy Harjo* (1998).

ROBERT HASS

Poetry
Field Guide (1973); *Praise* (1979); *Human Wishes* (1989); *Sun under Wood* (1996).

Prose
Twentieth Century Pleasures (1984).

Translations
Czeslaw Milosz, *The Separate Notebooks* (with Robert Pinsky, 1983), *Unattainable Earth* (1986), *Collected Poems, 1931–1987* (with Louis Iribarne and Peter Scott, 1988), *Facing the River: New Poems* (1995), *Road-Side Dog* (1998), and *Treatise on Poetry* (2001).

Books Edited
Rock and Hawk: A Selection of Shorter Poems by Robinson Jeffers (1987); *Selected Poems of Tomas Transtroemer, 1954–1986* (translated by May Swenson

and others, 1989); *The Essential Haiku: Versions of Basho, Buson, and Issa* (1994); *American Poetry: The Twentieth Century* (with John Hollander, Carolyn Kizer, Nathaniel Mackey, and Marjorie Perloff, 2000).

ROBERT HAYDEN

Poetry
Collected Poems (ed. Frederick Glaysher, 1985, 1996).

Prose
Collected Prose (ed. Frederick Glaysher, 1984).

Book Edited
Kaleidoscope: Poems by American Negro Poets (1967).

Critical and Biographical Studies
Fred M. Feltrow, *Robert Hayden* (1984); Michael S. Harper, "Remembering Robert Hayden" (*Michigan Quarterly Review*, Winter 1982: 182–86); John Hatcher, *From the Auroral Darkness: The Life and Poetry of Robert Hayden* (1984); John O'Brien, *Interviews with Black Writers* (1973); Pontheolla Taylor Williams, *Robert Hayden: A Critical Analysis of His Poetry* (1987).

ANTHONY HECHT

Poetry
Collected Earlier Poems (1990); *The Transparent Man* (1990); *Flight among the Tombs* (1996); *The Darkness and the Light* (2001); *Collected Later Poems* (2003).

Prose
Obbligati (1986); *On the Laws of the Poetic Art* (1992); *The Hidden Law: The Poetry of W. H. Auden* (1993); *Melodies Unheard* (2003).

Books Edited
Jiggery-Pokery: A Compendium of Double-Dactyls (with John Hollander, 1967); *The Essential George Herbert* (1987).

Interviews
Langdon Hammer, "Efforts of Attention: An Interview with Anthony Hecht" (*Sewanee Review*, Winter 1996: 94–107); Philip Hoy, *Anthony Hecht in Conversation* (1999); J. D. McClatchy, "The Art of Poetry XXXX: Anthony Hecht" (*Paris Review*, Fall 1988: 160–205).

Biographical and Critical Studies
Norman German, *Anthony Hecht* (1989); Sydney Lea, ed., *The Burdens of Formality: Essays on the Poetry of Anthony Hecht* (1989); David Mason, "In Praise of Artifice" (*Hudson Review*, Winter 2001: 687–96).

LYN HEJINIAN

Poetry
My Life (1980, 1987, 2002); *Writing Is an Aid to Memory* (1978, 1996); *The Cell* (1992); *The Cold of Poetry* (1994).

Prose
Oxota: A Short Russian Novel (1991); *The Language of Inquiry* (2000).

Critical Studies
Charles Altieri, "Lyn Hejinian and the Possibilities of Postmodernism in Poetry" (*Women Poets of the Americas: Toward a Pan-American Gathering*, ed. Jacqueline Vaught and Cordelia Chavez Candelaria, 1999: 146–55); Rae Armentrout, "Feminist Poetics and the Meaning of Clarity" (*Artifice and Indeterminacy: An Anthology of New Poetics*, ed. Christopher Beach, 1998: 287–96); Craig Douglas Dworkin, "Penelope Reworking the Twill: Patchwork, Writing, and Lyn Hejinian's *My Life*" (*Contemporary Literature* 36, Spring 1995: 58–81); Juliana Spahr, "Resignifying Autobiography: Lyn Hejinian's *My Life*" (*American Literature* 68, Mar. 1996: 139–59).

H. L. HIX

Poetry
Perfect Hell (1996); *Rational Numbers* (2000); *Surely as Birds Fly* (2002).

Prose
Morte d'Author: An Autopsy (1990); *Spirits Hovering over the Ashes: Legacies of Post Modern Theory* (1995); *As Easy as Lying: Essays on Poetry* (2002).

ANDREW HUDGINS

Poetry
Saints and Strangers (1985); *After the Lost War* (1988); *The Never-Ending* (1991); *The Glass Hammer* (1994).

Prose
The Glass Anvil (1999).

LANGSTON HUGHES

Poetry
The Collected Poems of Langston Hughes (ed. Arnold Rampersad and David Roessel, 1994).

Prose
The Big Sea: An Autobiography (1940); *I Wonder as I Wander* (1956); *Langston Hughes and the Chicago Defender: Essays on Race, Politics, and Culture, 1942–62* (ed. Christopher C. De Santis, 1995); *Short Stories of Langston Hughes* (1996).

Bibliography
R. Baxter Miller, *Langston Hughes and Gwendolyn Brooks: A Reference Guide* (1978).

Biographical and Critical Studies
Faith Berry, *Langston Hughes, before and after Harlem* (1995); Montrew Dunham, *Langston Hughes: Young Black Poet* (1995); James Emanuel, *Langston*

Hughes (1967); Donna Sullivan Harper, *Not So Simple: The "Semple" Stories by Langston Hughes* (1985); Milton Meltzer, *Langston Hughes: A Biography* (1968); Alice Walker, *Langston Hughes, American Poet* (1988).

RICHARD HUGO

Poetry
Making Certain It Goes On: The Collected Poems of Richard Hugo (1984).

Prose
The Triggering Town (1979): *Death and the Good Life* (1981); *The Real West Marginal Way: A Poet's Autobiography* (ed. Ripley Hugo and James Welch, 1986).

MARK JARMAN

Poetry
North Sea (1978); *The Rote Walker* (1981); *Far and Away* (1985); *The Black Riviera* (1990); *Iris* (1992); *Questions for Ecclesiastes* (1997); *Unholy Sonnets* (2000).

Prose
The Reaper Essays (with Robert McDowell, 1996); *The Secret of Poetry* (2001).

Book Edited
Rebel Angels: 25 Poets of the New Formalism (with David Mason, 1996).

Biographical and Critical Studies
Meg Schoerke, "Introduction," *The Reaper Essays* (1996); Kevin Walzer, "Bold Colors: Jarman, Nelson, Peacock, Turner," *The Ghost of Tradition: Expansive Poetry and Postmodernism* (1998).

RANDALL JARRELL

Poetry
Complete Poems (1968, 1980); *Selected Poems* (ed. William H. Pritchard, 1990).

Prose
Poetry and the Age (1953, 1972); *The Third Book of Criticism* (1969); *Kipling, Auden & Co: Essays and Reviews 1935–1964* (1979); *Jarrell's Letters: An Autobiographical and Literary Selection* (ed. Mary Jarrell and Stuart Wright, 1985); *No Other Book: Selected Essays* (ed. Brad Leithauser, 1995).

Translations
Ludwig Bechstein, *The Rabbit Catcher and Other Fairy Tales of Ludwig Bechstein* (1962); Ferdinand Gregorovius, *The Ghetto and the Jews of Rome* (1948); Johann Wolfgang von Goethe, *Faust, Part I* (1976); Jakob and Willem Grimm, *The Golden Bird and Other Fairy Tales of the Brothers Grimm* (1962) and *The Juniper Tree and Other Fairy Tales from the Brothers Grimm* (1973).

Novels and Children's Books
Pictures from an Institution (1954); *The Gingerbread Rabbit* (1963); *The Bat-Poet* (1964); *The Animal Family* (1965); *Fly By Night* (1976).

Biographical and Critical Studies
Suzanne Ferguson, *The Poetry of Randall Jarrell* (1971); Robert Lowell, Peter Taylor, and Robert Penn Warren, eds., *Randall Jarrell: 1914–1965* (1967); William H. Pritchard, *Randal Jarrell: A Literary Life* (1990); Sister Bernetta Quinn, *Randall Jarrell* (1981); M. L. Rosenthall, *Randall Jarrell* (1972).

ROBINSON JEFFERS

Poetry
The Collected Poetry of Robinson Jeffers, 5 vols. (ed. Tim Hunt, 1988–2002).

Drama
Medea (1946, first produced Oct. 1947); *The Tower Beyond Tragedy* (first produced Nov. 1950); *The Cretan Woman* (first produced 1954).

Prose
Poetry, Gongorism and a Thousand Years (1949); *Themes in My Poems* (1956); *The Selected Letters of Robinson Jeffers, 1897–1962* (ed. Ann N. Ridgeway, 1968).

Biographical and Critical Studies
Terry Beers, *"A Thousand Graceful Subtleties": Rhetoric in the Poetry of Robinson Jeffers* (1995); Robert Brophy, *Robinson Jeffers* (1975), *Robinson Jeffers: Dimensions of a Poet* (1995), and *Robinson Jeffers: Myth, Ritual, and Symbol in His Narrative Poems* (1973); Frederic I. Carpenter, *Robinson Jeffers* (1962); William Everson, *The Excesses of God: Robinson Jeffers as a Religious Figure* (1988) and *Robinson Jeffers: Fragments of an Older Fury* (1968); James Karman, ed., *Critical Essays on Robinson Jeffers* (1990) and *Robinson Jeffers: Poet of California* (1995); Radcliffe Squires, *The Loyalties of Robinson Jeffers* (1956); Alexander Vardamis, *The Critical Reputation of Robinson Jeffers* (1972); Robert Zaller, *The Cliffs of Solitude: A Reading of Robinson Jeffers* (1983) and ed., *Centennial Essays for Robinson Jeffers* (1991).

JAMES WELDON JOHNSON

Poetry
Complete Poems (2000).

Prose
Autobiography of an Ex-Colored Man (1927, 1979); *Black Manhattan* (1930, 1988); *Along This Way: The Autobiography of James Weldon Johnson* (1933, 1990); *The Selected Writings of James Weldon Johnson* (ed. Sondra Kathryn Wilson, 1995).

Books Edited
The Book of American Negro Spirituals (1925); *The Second Book of Negro Spirituals* (1926); *The Book of American Negro Poetry* (1930, 1983).

Bibliography
Robert E. Fleming, *James Weldon Johnson and Arna Bontemps: A Reference Guide* (1978).

Biographical and Critical Studies
Robert E. Fleming, *James Weldon Johnson* (1987); Eugene Levy, *James Weldon Johnson: Black Writer, Black Voice* (1973); Kenneth M. Price and Lawrence J. Oliver, eds., *Critical Essays on James Weldon Johnson* (1997).

DONALD JUSTICE

Poetry
The Sunset Maker: Poems / Stories / A Memoir (1987); *A Donald Justice Reader: Selected Poetry and Prose* (1991); *New and Selected Poems* (1995).

Prose
Platonic Scripts (1984); *Oblivion* (1998).

Books Edited
The Collected Poems of Henri Coulette (with Robert Mezey, 1990); *The Collected Poems of Weldon Kees* (1992); Joe Bolton, *The Last Nostalgia: Poems, 1982–1990* (1999).

Critical Study
Dana Gioia and William Logan, eds., *Certain Solitudes: On the Poetry of Donald Justice* (1998).

WELDON KEES

Poetry
The Collected Poems of Weldon Kees (ed. Donald Justice, 1960; exp ed. 1962; rev. ed. 1975, 1993).

Fiction
The Ceremony and Other Stories (ed. Dana Gioia, 1984); *Fall Quarter* (ed. James Reidel, 1990); *Selected Short Stories of Weldon Kees* (ed. Dana Gioia, 2002).

Play
The Waiting Room (1999).

Other
Nonverbal Communication: Notes on the Visual Perception of Human Relations (with Jurgen Ruesch, 1956); *Reviews and Essays, 1936–1955* (ed. James Reidel, 1988).

Bibliography
Danny Gillane and Robert Niemi, *The Bibliography of Weldon Kees* (1997).

Biographical and Critical Studies
Jim Elledge, ed., *Weldon Kees: A Critical Introduction* (1985); Robert L. Knoll, *Weldon Kees and the Midcentury Generation: Letters, 1935–1955* (1986); James Reidel, *Vanished Act: The Life and Art of Weldon Kees* (2003); William T. Ross, *Weldon Kees* (1985).

X. J. KENNEDY

Poetry
Cross Ties: Selected Poems (1985); *The Lords of Misrule: Poems 1992–2001* (2002).

Books Edited
An Introduction to Poetry (with Dana Gioia, 2004); *An Introduction to Fiction* (with Dana Gioia, 2004); *Literature: An Introduction to Poetry, Fiction, and Drama* (with Dana Gioia, 2004).

Critical Study
Michael J. Collins, "The Poetry of X. J. Kennedy" (*World Literature Today* Winter 1987, 61: 55–8).

MARY KINZIE

Poetry
The Threshold of the Year (1982); *Summers of Vietnam and Other Poems* (1990); *Autumn Eros and Other Poems* (1991); *Ghost Ship: Poems* (1998).

Prose
The Cure of Poetry in an Age of Prose: Moral Essays on the Poet's Calling (1993); *The Judge Is Fury: Dislocation and Form in Poetry* (1994); *A Poet's Guide to Poetry* (1999).

Books Edited
Prose for Borges (with Charles Newman, 1974); *The Little Magazine in America: A Modern Documentary History* (with Elliott Anderson, 1978); *Tales of Arturo Vivante* (1990).

CAROLYN KIZER

Poetry
Cool, Calm and Collected: Poems 1960–2000 (2001).

Prose
Proses: On Poems and Poets (1993); *Picking and Choosing: Essays on Prose* (1995).

Translations
Carrying Over: Poems from the Chinese, Urdu, Macedonian, Yiddish, and French African (1988).

Book Edited
100 Great Poems by Women (1995).

Biographical and Critical Studies
David Rigsbee, ed., *An Answering Music: On the Poetry of Carolyn Kizer* (1990); Annie Finch, Johanna Keller, and Candace McClelland, eds., *Carolyn Kizer: Perspectives on Her Life and Work* (2001).

ETHERIDGE KNIGHT

Poetry
Poems from Prison (1968); *Born of a Woman: New and Selected Poems* (1980); *The Essential Etheridge Knight* (1986).

Critical Study
Dudley Randall, *Broadside Memories: Poets I Have Known* (1975).

YUSEF KOMUNYAKAA

Poetry
Pleasure Dome: New and Collected Poems (2001).

Prose
Blue Notes: Essays, Interviews & Commentaries (2000).

Translation
Nguyen Quang Thieu, *The Insomnia of Fire* (with Martha Collins, 1995).

Books Edited
The Jazz Poetry Anthology (with Sascha Feinstein, 1991); *The Second Set: The Jazz Poetry Anthology*, vol. 2 (with Sascha Feinstein, 1996).

TED KOOSER

Poetry
Official Entry Blank (1969); *Sure Signs: New and Selected Poems* (1980); *One World at a Time* (1985); *Weather Central* (1994); *Winter Morning Walks: 100 Postcards to Jim Harrison* (2000).

Critical Study
Dana Gioia, "The Anonymity of the Regional Poet," *Can Poetry Matter?* (1992).

MAXINE KUMIN

Poetry
Looking for Luck: Poems (1992); *Connecting the Dots* (1996); *Selected Poems 1960–1990* (1997); *Inside the Halo and Beyond: The Anatomy of a Recovery* (2000); *The Long Marriage: Poems* (2002).

Prose
To Make a Prairie: Essays on Poets, Poetry, and Country Living (1979); *In Deep: Country Essays* (1987); *Women, Animals, and Vegetables: Essays and Stories* (1994); *Always Beginning: Essays on a Life in Poetry* (2000).

Critical Study
Emily Grosholz, ed., *Telling the Barn Swallow: Poets on the Poetry of Maxine Kumin* (1997).

DAVID LEHMAN

Poetry
An Alternative to Speech (1986); *Operation Memory* (1990); *Valentine Place* (1996); *The Daily Mirror* (2000); *The Evening Sun* (2002).

Prose
Signs of the Times (1991); *The Line Forms Here* (1992); *The Big Question* (1995); *The Last Avant-Garde* (1998).

Book Edited
The Best American Poetry (annually since 1988).

DENISE LEVERTOV

Poetry
Collected Earlier Poems, 1940–1960 (1979); *Poems, 1960–1967* (1983); *Poems, 1968–1972* (1987); *The Life around Us: Selected Poems on Nature* (1997); *The Stream and the Sapphire: Selected Poems on Religious Themes* (1997); *This Great Unknowing: Last Poems* (1999); *Poems 1972–1982* (2001).

Prose
The Poet in the World (1973); *Light Up the Cave* (1981); *New & Selected Essays* (1992); *Tesserae: Memories and Suppositions* (1995); *The Letters of Denise Levertov and William Carlos Williams* (ed. Christopher MacGowan, 1998).

Biographical and Critical Studies
Harry Marten, *Understanding Denise Levertov* (1988); Kenneth Rexroth, *Assays* (1961); Kenneth Rexroth, *With Eye and Ear* (1970); Audrey T. Rodgers, *Denise Levertov: The Poetry of Engagement* (1993); Linda W. Wagner, *Denise Levertov* (1967) and *Critical Essays on Denise Levertov* (1990).

PHILIP LEVINE

Poetry
New Selected Poems (1991); *What Work Is* (1991); *The Simple Truth* (1994); *The Mercy* (1999).

Prose
The Bread of Time: Toward an Autobiography (1994); *So Ask: Essays, Conversations, Interviews* (2001).

Critical Studies
Christopher Buckley, ed., *On the Poetry of Philip Levine: Stranger to Nothing* (1991); Edward Hirsch, "Naming the Lost: The Poetry of Philip Levine" (*Michigan Quarterly Review* Spring 1989, 28: 258–66); Wyatt Prunty, *Fallen From the Symboled World* (1990); David St-John, "Where Angels Come toward Us: The Poetry of Philip Levine" (*Antioch Review* Spring 1986, 44: 176–91); Kevin Stein, *Private Poets, Worldly Acts* (1996).

SHIRLEY GEOK-LIN LIM

Poetry
Crossing the Peninsula and Other Poems (1980); *Monsoon History: Selected Poems* (1994); *What the Fortune Teller Didn't Say* (1998).

Prose
Among the White Moon Faces: An Asian-American Memoir of Homelands (1996); *Two Dreams: Short Stories* (1997); *Joss and Gold* (novel) (2001).

VACHEL LINDSAY

Poetry
Selected Poems of Vachel Lindsay (1963); *The Poetry of Vachel Lindsay: Complete & With Lindsay's Drawings* (1984).

Prose
Letters of Vachel Lindsay (1979); *The Prose of Vachel Lindsay: Complete & With Lindsay's Drawings* (1988).

Biographical and Critical Studies
John E. Hallwas and Dennis J. Reader, eds., *The Vision of This Land: Studies of Vachel Lindsay, Edgar Lee Master, and Carl Sandberg* (1976); Ann Massa, *Vachel Lindsay, Fieldworker for the American Dream* (1970); Eleanor Ruggles, *The West-Going Heart: A Life of Vachel Lindsay* (1959).

WILLIAM LOGAN

Poetry
Dream of Dying (1980); *Sad-faced Men* (1982); *Difficulty* (1985); *Sullen Weedy Lakes* (1988); *Vain Empires* (1995); *Night Battle* (1999).

Prose
All the Rage: Prose on Poetry, 1976–1992 (1998); *Reputations of the Tongue: On Poets and Poetry* (1999).

Book Edited
Certain Solitudes: On the Poetry of Donald Justice (with Dana Gioia, 1997).

AUDRE LORDE

Poetry
The Collected Poems of Audre Lorde (1997).

Prose
The Cancer Journals (1980); *Zami: A New Spelling of My Name* (1983); *Sister Outsider: Essays and Speeches* (1984); *A Burst of Light: Essays* (1988).

Biographical and Critical Studies
Zofia Burr, *Of Women, Poetry, and Power: Strategies of Address in Dickinson, Miles, Brooks, Lorde, and Angelou* (2002); AnaLouise Keating, *Women Reading Women Writing: Self-Invention in Paula Gunn Allen, Gloria Anzaldua, and Audre*

Lorde (1996); Cassie Primo Steele, *We Heal from Memory: Sexton, Lorde, Anzaldua and the Poetry of Witness* (2000).

ADRIAN C. LOUIS

Poetry
Fire Water World (1989); *Among the Dog Eaters* (1992); *Vortex of Indian Fevers* (1995); *Ceremonies of the Damned* (1997); *Bone and Juice* (2001).

Prose
Skins (1995); *Wild Indians & Other Creatures* (1996).

AMY LOWELL

Poetry
Complete Poetical Works (1955).

Prose
Poetry and Poets: Essays (ed. Ferris Greenslet, 1930).

Books Edited
Some Imagist Poets, 1916: An Annual Anthology (1916); *Some Imagist Poets, 1917: An Annual Anthology* (1917).

Biographical and Critical Studies
Richard Benvenuto, *Amy Lowell* (1985); Mary E. Galvin, "Imagery and Invisibility: Amy Lowell and the Erotics of Particularity," *Queer Poetics: Five Modernist Women Writers* (1999); Jean Gould, *Amy: The World of Amy Lowell and the Imagist Movement* (1975); Glenn Richard Ruihley, *The Thorn of a Rose: Amy Lowell Reconsidered* (1975).

ROBERT LOWELL

Poetry
Collected Poems (ed. Frank Bidart and David Gewanter, 2002).

Prose
Robert Lowell: Interviews and Memoirs (ed. Jeffrey Meyers, 1988); *Collected Prose* (ed. Robert Giroux, 1990).

Translations
Imitations (1961).

Biographical and Critical Studies
Ian Hamilton, *Robert Lowell: A Biography* (1983); Philip Hobsbaum, *A Reader's Guide to Robert Lowell* (1988); Eileen Simpson, *Poets in their Youth* (1982); Richard Tillinghast, *Robert Lowell's Life and Work: Damaged Grandeur* (1995); Alan Williamson, *Pity the Monsters: The Political Vision of Robert Lowell* (1974); Stephen Yenser, *Circle to Circle: The Poetry of Robert Lowell* (1975).

ARCHIBALD MacLEISH

Poetry
J. B.: A Play in Verse (1958); *Collected Poems 1917–1982* (1985).

Prose
A Continuing Journey (1968); *Riders on the Earth: Essays and Recollections* (1978); *Letters of Archibald MacLeish, 1907–1982* (ed. R. H. Winnick, 1983).

Bibliographies
Helen E. Ellis, *Archibald MacLeish: A Selectively Annotated Bibliography* (1995); Edward J. Mullaly, *Archibald MacLeish: A Checklist* (1973).

Biographical and Critical Studies
Scott Donaldson, *Archibald MacLeish: An American Life* (1992); William H. MacLeish, *Up with Archie: A Son's Journey* (2001); Grover Cleveland Smith, *Archibald MacLeish* (1971).

EDWIN MARKHAM

Poetry
The Man with the Hoe and Other Poems (1899); *Lincoln and Other Poems* (1901); *The Shoes of Happiness and Other Poems* (1915); *Gates of Paradise and Other Poems* (1920); *New Poems: Eighty Songs at Eighty* (1932); *Poems of Edwin Markham* (ed. Charles L. Wallis, 1950).

Prose
The Octopus (1901); *Children in Bondage* (1914); *California the Wonderful: Her Romantic History, Her Picturesque People, Her Wild Shores, Her Desert Mystery, Her Valley Loveliness, Her Mountain Glory* (1915).

Bibliography
Sophie K. Shields, *Edwin Markham: A Bibliography*, 3 vols. (1952–1955).

Biographical and Critical Studies
George Truman Carl, *Edwin Markham: The Poet for Preachers* (1977); Louis Filler, *The Unknown Edwin Markham: His Mystery and Its Significance* (1966); William L. Stidger, *Edwin Markham* (1933).

CHARLES MARTIN

Poetry
Room for Error (1978); *Steal the Bacon* (1987); *What the Darkness Proposes* (1996); *Starting from Sleep* (2002).

Translation
Poems of Catullus (1990).

Prose
Catullus (1992).

Critical Studies
Paul Lake, "Return to Metaphor: From Deep Imagist to New Formalist," *New Expansive Poetry: Theory, Criticism, History* (ed. R. S. Gwynn, 1999); Kevin Walzer, "The Sword of Wit: Disch, Feirstein, Gwynn, Martin," *The Ghost of Tradition* (1998).

DAVID MASON

Poetry
The Buried Houses (1991); *The Country I Remember* (1996).

Prose
The Poetry of Life and the Life of Poetry (2000).

Books Edited
Rebel Angels: 25 Poets of the New Formalism (with Mark Jarman, 1996); *Western Wind: An Introduction to Poetry* (with John F. Nims, 2000).

Critical Studies
Bruce Bennett, "A Limped Medium: The Poetry of David Mason" (*Light: A Quarterly of Verse*, Autumn 2002); Thomas M. Disch, "North American Addresses: Three Verse Narratives," *New Expansive Poetry: Theory, History, Criticism* (ed. R. S. Gwynn, 1999); Jack Foley, "David Mason, the Poetry of Life and the Life of Poetry," <www.alsopreview.com/foley/jfdmason.html;>; H. L. Hix, "David Mason," *Dictionary of Literary Biography* 280 (2003); April Lindner, *New Formalist Poets of the American West* (2001); Kevin Walzer, "Still Waters: Gioia, Mason, McDowell, Salter," *The Ghost of Tradition: Expansive Poetry and Postmodernism* (1998).

EDGAR LEE MASTERS

Poetry
Spoon River Anthology *(1916);* The New Spoon River *(Introduction by Willis Barnstone, 1968);* Spoon River Anthology *(annotated ed. by John E. Hallwas, 1992).*

Prose
Vachel Lindsay: A Poet in America (1935).

Biographical and Critical Studies
John T. Flanagan, *Edgar Lee Masters: The Spoon River Poet and His Critics* (1974); Hilary Masters, *Last Stands: Notes from Memory* (1982); Ronald Rimeau, *Beyond Spoon River—The Legacy of Edgar Lee Masters* (1981).

THOMAS McGRATH

Poetry
The Movie at the End of the World: Collected Poems (1972); *Selected Poems, 1938–1988* (ed. Sam Hamill, 1988); *Death Song* (ed. Sam Hamill, 1991); *Letter to an Imaginary Friend* (1997).

Prose
The Gates of Ivory, the Gates of Horn (1957, 1987); *This Coffin Has No Handles* (1988).

Biographical and Critical Studies
Jack Beeching, *A Memoir of Thomas McGrath* (1993); Robert Bly, *American Poetry: Wildness and Domesticity* (1990); Terrence Des Pres, *Praises and Dispraises* (1988); Reginald Gibbons and Terrence Des Pres, eds., *Thomas McGrath: Life and the Poem* (1992); Frederick C. Stern, ed., *He Revolutionary Poet in the United States: The Poetry of Thomas McGrath* (1988); Fred Whitehead, ed., "Dream Champ—A Festschrift in Honor of Thomas McGrath" (*North Dakota Quarterly* 50. 4, 1982).

HEATHER McHUGH

Poetry
Hinge & Sign: Poems 1968–1993 (1994); *The Father of the Predicaments* (1999).

Prose
Broken English: Poetry and Partiality (1993).

CLAUDE McKAY

Poetry
Selected Poems (1953); *The Passion of Claude McKay: Selected Poetry and Prose, 1912–1948* (ed. Wayne F. Cooper, 1973).

Biographical and Critical Studies
Wayne F. Cooper, *Claude McKay: Rebel Sojourner in the Harlem Renaissance* (1987); Addison Gayle, Jr., *Claude McKay: The Black Poet at War* (1972); Tyrone Tillery, *Claude McKay: A Black Poet's Struggle for Identity* (1992).

SAMUEL MENASHE

Poetry
Collected Poems (1986); *The Niche Narrows: New and Selected Poems* (2000).

Critical Studies
Barry Ahern, "Poetry and Synthesis: The Art of Samuel Menashe" (*Twentieth Century Literature* 42.2, Summer 1996: 294–308); Donald Davie, "The Poetry of Samuel Menashe" (*Iowa Review* 1.3, 1970: 107–15).

JAMES MERRILL

Poetry
The Changing Light at Sandover: Including the Whole of the Book of Ephraim, Mirabell's Books of Number, Scripts for the Pageant, and a New Coda, the Higher Keys (1982, 1992); *Collected Poems* (2001).

Prose
Recitative: Prose (1986); *A Different Person: A Memoir* (1997).

Biographical and Critical Studies
Don Adams, *James Merrill's Poetic Quest* (1997); Alison Lurie, *Familiar Spirits: A Memoir of James Merrill and David Jackson* (2001); Timothy Materer, *James Merrill's Apocalypse* (2000); Guy Rotella, ed., *Critical Essays on James Merrill* (1996); Stephen Yenser, *The Consuming Myth: The Work of James Merrill* (1987).

THOMAS MERTON

Poetry
The Collected Poems of Thomas Merton (1979).

Prose
The Seven Storey Mountain (1948); *The Literary Essays of Thomas Merton* (ed. Patrick Hart, 1981); *The Hidden Ground of Love: The Letters of Thomas Merton on Religious Experience and Social Concerns* (ed. William Shannon, 1985).

Biographical and Critical Studies
Monica Furlong, *Merton: A Biography* (1980); Thérèse Lentfoehr, *Words and Silence: On the Poetry of Thomas Merton* (1979); Robert G. Waldron, *Walking with Thomas Merton: Discovering His Poetry, Essays, and Journals* (2002).

W. S. MERWIN

Poetry
The Moving Target (1963); *The Lice* (1969); *The Carrier of Ladders* (1970); *The First Four Books of Poems* (1975); *The Compass Flower* (1977); *The Rain in the Trees* (1988); *Selected Poems* (1988); *Travels* (1993); *The Vixen* (1996); *The Folding Cliffs* (1998); *The River Sound* (1999).

Prose
The Miner's Pale Children (1970); *Houses and Travellers* (1977); *Unframed Originals: Recollections* (1982).

Translations
The Poem of the Cid (1959); *Some Spanish Ballads* (1961); *Selected Translations, 1948–1968* (1969); Pablo Neruda, *Twenty Love Poems and a Song of Despair* (1969); Osip Mandelstam, *Selected Poems* (with Clarence Brown, 1974); *Selected Translations, 1968–78* (1979); *East Window: The Asian Poems* (1998); Dante Alighieri, *Purgatorio* (2000).

Critical Studies
H. L. Hix, *Understanding W. S. Merwin* (1997); Cary Nelson and Ed Folsom, eds., *W. S. Merwin: Essays on the Poetry* (1987).

JOSEPHINE MILES

Poetry
Collected Poems, 1930–83 (1983).

Prose
Eras and Modes in English Poetry (1957, rev. and enlarged ed., 1964); *Style and Proportion: The Language of Prose and Poetry* (1967); *Poetry and Change: Donne, Milton, Wordsworth, and the Equilibrium of the Present* (1974).

Biographical and Critical Studies
Marjorie Larney, *Josephine Miles, Teaching Poet: An Oral Biography* (1993); Julia Randall, "Dickinson with a Difference: The Poetry of Josephine Miles" (*Hollins Critic* 17.3, 1980: 1–12); Carolyn Smith, "Old Age and Freedom in Josephine Miles's Late Poems, 1973–1979," *Aging and Gender in Literature: Studies in Creativity* (ed. Anne M. Wyatt-Brown and Janice Rossen, 1993); Lisa Steinman, "Putting on Knowledge with Power: The Poetry of Josephine Miles" (*Chicago Review* 37, Winter 1990: 130–138).

EDNA ST. VINCENT MILLAY

Poetry
Collected Lyrics of Edna St. Vincent Millay (1981); *Collected Sonnets of Edna St. Vincent Millay* (1988); *Early Poems* (ed. Holly Peppe, 1998); *The Selected Poetry of Edna St. Vincent Millay* (ed. Nancy Milford, 2001).

Prose
Letters (ed. Allan Ross MacDougal, 1952); *Distressing Dialogues* (published under the pseudonym Nancy Boyd, 1924).

Bibliography
Judith Nierman, *Edna St. Vincent Millay: A Reference Guide* (1977).

Biographical and Critical Studies
Norman A. Brittan, *Edna St. Vincent Millay* (1982); Suzanne Clark, *Sentimental Modernism: Women Writers and the Revolution of the Word* (1991); Daniel Mark Epstein, *What My Lips Have Kissed: The Loves and Love Poems of Edna St. Vincent Millay* (2001); Diane F Freedman, *Millay at 100: A Critical Reappraisal* (1995); Nancy Milford, *Savage Beauty: The Life of Edna St. Vincent Millay* (2001); William B. Thesing, ed., *Critical Essays on Edna St. Vincent Millay* (1993).

N. SCOTT MOMADAY

Poetry
Angle of Geese (1974); *The Gourd Dancer* (1976); *In the Presence of the Sun: Stories and Poems, 1961–1991* (1992).

Prose
House Made of Dawn (1968); *The Way to Rainy Mountain* (1969); *The Names: A Memoir* (1976); *The Man Made of Words: Essays, Stories, Passages* (1997); *In the Bear's House* (1999).

Biographical and Critical Studies
Matthias Schubnell, ed., *Conversations with N. Scott Momaday* (1997) and *N. Scott Momaday: the Cultural and Literary Background* (1986); Martha Scott Trimble, *N. Scott Momaday* (1973); Alan R. Velie, *Four American Literary Masters: N. Scott*

Momaday, James Welch, Leslie Marmon Silko, and Gerald Vizenor (1982); Charles L.Woodard, *Ancestral Voice: Conversations with N. Scott Momaday* (1989).

MARIANNE MOORE

Poetry
The Complete Poems of Marianne Moore (1981); *Becoming Marianne Moore: Early Poems 1907–1924* (ed. Robin G. Schulze, 2002).

Prose
The Complete Prose of Marianne Moore (ed. Patricia Willis, 1986); *The Selected Letters of Marianne Moore* (ed. Bonnie Costello, Celeste Goodrich, and Cristanne Miller, 1997).

Bibliographies
Craig S. Abbot, *Marianne Moore: A Descriptive Bibliography* (1977) and *Marianne Moore: A Reference Guide* (1978).

Biographical and Critical Studies
Bonnie Costello, *Marianne Moore: Imaginary Possessions* (1981); Jeanne Heuving, *"Omissions Are Not Accidents": Gender in the Art of Marianne Moore* (1992); Linda Leavell, *Marianne Moore and the Visual Arts: Prismatic Color* (1995); Cristanne Miller, *Marianne Moore: Questions of Authority* (1995); Lawrence Stapleton, *Marianne Moore: The Poet's Advance* (1978).

HOWARD MOSS

Poetry
A Winter Come, A Summer Gone: Poems 1946–1960 (1960); *Selected Poems* (1971); *New Selected Poems* (1985).

Prose
Writing against Time: Critical Essays and Reviews (1969); *Minor Monuments: Selected Essays* (1986).

Book Edited
The Poet's Story (1973).

Critical Studies
Bruce Bawer, "The Passing of an Elegist" (*New Criterion* 6.3, Nov. 1987: 35–37); Amy Clampitt, "Between the Lines: Rereading Howard Moss" (*Parnassus: Poetry in Review* 15.1, 1989: 341–9; Dana Gioia, "The Difficult Case of Howard Moss," *Can Poetry Matter?* (1992).

MARILYN NELSON

Poetry
For the Body (1978); *Mama's Promises* (1985); *The Homeplace* (1990); *Magnificat* (1994); *The Fields of Praise* (1997); *Carver: A Life in Poems* (2001).

Translation
Halfden Rasmussen, *Hundreds of Hens, and Other Poems for Children* (1982).

Contributor
With Rita Dove, "A Black Rainbow: Modern Afro-American Poetry," *Poetry after Modernism* (ed. Robert McDowell, 1991); *A Formal Feeling Comes: Poems in Form by Contemporary Women* (ed. Annie Finch, 1994).

HOWARD NEMEROV

Poetry
Collected Poems (1977); *Sentences* (1980); *Inside the Onion* (1984); *Trying Conclusions: New and Selected Poems, 1961–1991* (1991).

Prose
Poetry and Fiction: Essays (1963); *Reflexions on Poetry and Poetics* (1972); *Figures of Thought: Speculations on the Meaning of Poetry and Other Essays* (1978); *Journal of the Fictive Life* (1981); *New and Selected Essays* (1985); *The Oak in the Acorn: On Remembrance of Things Past and on Teaching Proust, Who Will Never Learn* (1987).

Bibliography
Diane E. Wylie, *Elizabeth Bishop and Howard Nemerov: A Reference Guide* (1983).

Biographical and Critical Studies
Patricia Bosworth, *Diane Arbus: A Biography* (1984); Duncan Bowie, ed., *The Critical Reception of Howard Nemerov: A Selection of Essays and a Bibliography* (1971); Mary Kinzie, "The Signatures of Things: On Howard Nemerov," *The Cure of Poetry in an Age of Prose* (1993); Ross Labrie, *Howard Nemerov* (1980); William Mills, *The Stillness in Moving Things: The World of Howard Nemerov* (1975); Donna Potts, *Howard Nemerov and Objective Idealism: The Influence of Owen Barfield* (1994); Willard Spiegelman, "The Tempered Tone of Howard Nemerov" (*The Didactic Muse*, 1989, 25–59).

LORINE NIEDECKER

Poetry
The Granite Pail: The Selected Poems of Lorine Niedecker (ed. Cid Corman, 1985, 1996); *Lorine Niedecker: Collected Works* (ed. Jenny Lynn Penberthy, 2002).

Prose
"Between Your House and Mine": The Letters of Lorine Niedecker to Cid Corman (ed. Lisa Pater Faranda, 1986); *Niedecker and the Correspondence with Zukofsky, 1931–1970* (ed. Jenny Lynn Penberthy, 1993).

Biographical and Critical Study
Jenny Lynn Penberthy, ed., *Lorine Niedecker: Woman and Poet* (1998).

JOHN FREDERICK NIMS

Poetry
The Powers of Heaven and Earth: New and Selected Poems (2002).

Prose
A Local Habitation: Essays on Poetry (1985).

Translations
The Complete Poems of Michelangelo (1998); *Sappho to Valéry* (rev. and exp. ed., 1990).

Books Edited
Poetry: A Magazine of Verse (1978–1984); *The Harper Anthology of Poetry* (1981); *Western Wind: An Introduction to Poetry* (4th ed. with David Mason, 2000).

YONE NOGUCHI

Poetry and Prose
From the Eastern Sea (1903); *The Story of Yone Noguchi Told by Himself* (1914); *Japanese Hokkus* (1920); *Selected Poems* (1921); *Yone Noguchi: Collected English Letters* (ed. Ikuko Atsumi, 1975); *Selected Writings of Yone Noguchi: An East-West Literary Assimilation*; vol. 1, Poetry; vol. 2, Prose (ed. Yoshinobu Hakutani, 1990, 1992).

Critical Studies
Essays on Yone Noguchi (1963).

NAOMI SHIHAB NYE

Poetry
Hugging the Jukebox (1982); *Yellow Glove* (1986); *The Red Suitcase* (1994); *The Words Under the Words: Selected Poems* (1995); *Fuel* (1998).

Critical Studies
Ibis Gomez Vega, "The Art of Telling Stories in the Poetry of Naomi Shihab Nye" (*MELUS* 26.4, Winter 2001: 245–52); Gregory Orfalea, "Doomed by Our Blood to Care: The Poetry of Naomi Shihab Nye" (*Paintbrush: A Journal of Contemporary Multicultural Literature* 18.35, Spring 1991: 56–66).

FRANK O'HARA

Poetry
The Collected Poems of Frank O'Hara (ed. Donald Allen, 1995).

Prose
Standing Still and Walking in New York (1975); *Art Chronicles: 1954–1966* (rev. ed., 1990).

Bibliography
Alexander Smith, ed., *Frank O'Hara: A Comprehensive Bibliography* (1979).

Biographical and Critical Studies
John Ashbery, "Introduction," *The Collected Poems of Frank O'Hara* (1971); Jim Elledge, ed., *Frank O'Hara: To Be True to a City* (1990); Brad Gooch, *City Poet: The Life and Times of Frank O'Hara* (1993); Russell Ferguson, *In Memory of My*

Feelings: Frank O'Hara and American Art (1999); Marjorie Perloff, *Frank O'Hara: Poet among Painters* (1977).

SHARON OLDS

Poetry
Satan Says (1980); *The Dead and the Living: Poems* (1984); *The Gold Cell: Poems* (1987); *The Father* (1992); *The Wellspring: Poems* (1996); *Blood, Tin, Straw* (1999); *The Unswept Room* (2002).

Critical Studies
Suzanne Matson, "Talking to Our Fathers: The Political and Mythical Appropriations of Adrienne Rich and Sharon Olds" (*American Poetry Review* 18, Nov–Dec 1989: 35–41); Alicia Ostriker, "I Am (Not) This: Erotic Discourse in Bishop, Olds, and Stevens" (*Wallace Stevens Journal* 19, Fall 1995: 234–54); Laura E. Tanner, "Death Watch: Terminal Illness and the Gaze in Sharon Olds's The Father" (*Mosaic* 29, Mar. 1996: 103–21).

CHARLES OLSON

Poetry
The Collected Poems of Charles Olson (ed. George F. Butterick, 1987).

Prose
Call Me Ishmael (1947, 1958); *Charles Olson and Robert Creeley: The Complete Correspondence*, 10 vols. (1980–1996); *Collected Prose* (ed. Donald Allen and Benjamin Friedlander, 1997).

Biographical and Critical Studies
Tom Clark, *Charles Olson: The Allegory of a Poet's Life* (2000); Jack Foley, "Projective Verse at Fifty" (http://www.flashpointmag.com); Edward Halsey Foster, *Understanding the Black Mountain Poets* (1995); Ralph Maud, *Charles Olson's Reading: A Biography* (1996); Ralph Maud, *What Does Not Change: The Significance of Charles Olson's "The Kingfishers"* (1998); Thomas F. Merrill, *The Poetry of Charles Olson: A Primer* (1982).

GEORGE OPPEN

Poetry
New Collected Poems (ed. Michael Davidson, 2002).

Prose
The Selected Letters of George Open (ed. Rachel Blau DuPlessis, 1990).

Biographical and Critical Studies
Jonathan Griffin, et. al., *Not Comforts, But Vision: Essays on the Poetry of George Oppen* (1985); Burton Halten, *George Oppen, Man and Poet* (1981); Mary Oppen, *Meaning a Life: An Autobiography* (1978); Susan Thackrey, *George Oppen: A Radical Practice* (2001).

JACQUELINE OSHEROW

Poetry
Looking for Angels in New York (1988); *Conversations with Survivors* (1994); *With a Moon in Transit* (1996); *Dead Men's Praise* (1999).

MICHAEL PALMER

Poetry
Codes Appearing: Poems 1979–1988 (1988); *The Lion Bridge: Selected Poems 1972–1995* (1998); *The Promises of Glass* (2000).

Critical Studies
Calvin Bedient, "Breath and Blister: the Word-Burns of Michael Palmer and Leslie Scalapino" (*Parnassus: Poetry in Review* 24.2, 2000: 170–96); P. Michael Campbell, ed., *Palmer/Davidson: Poets and Critics Respond to the Poetry of Michael Palmer and Michael Davidson* (1992); Norman Finkelstein, "The Case of Michael Palmer" (*Contemporary Literature* Winter 29, 1988: 518–37).

DOROTHY PARKER

Poetry
Not Much Fun: The Lost Poems of Dorothy Parker (1996); *Complete Poems* (1999).

Poetry and Prose
The Portable Dorothy Parker (1973).

Prose
The Collected Stories of Dorothy Parker (1942); *Constant Reader* (1970).

Biographical and Critical Studies
Randall Calhoun, *Dorothy Parker: A Bio-Bibliography* (1993); Arthur F. Kinney, *Dorothy Parker* (Rev. 1998); Marion Meade, *Dorothy Parker: What Fresh Hell Is This?* (1988); Rhonda S. Pettit, *A Gendered Collision: Sentimentalism and Modernism in Dorothy Parker's Poetry and Fiction* (2000).

LINDA PASTAN

Poetry
A Perfect Circle of Sun (1971); *Aspects of Eve* (1975); *The Five Stages of Grief* (1978); *Waiting for My Life* (1981); *PM/AM: New and Selected Poems* (1983); *A Fraction of Darkness* (1985); *The Imperfect Paradise* (1988); *Heroes in Disguise* (1991); *An Early Afterlife* (1995); *Carnival Evening: New and Selected Poems 1968–1998* (1998); *The Last Uncle* (2002).

Critical Studies
Benjamin V. Franklin, "Form and Structure in Linda Pastan's Poetry" (*Poet-Lore* 75.4, Winter 1981: 234–41); Sheila Murnaghan, "Penelope's Song: The Lyric Odysseys of Linda Pastan and Louise Glück" (*Classical and Modern Literature* 22.1, Spring 2002: 1–33); Sanford Pinsker, "Family Values and the Jewishness of

Linda Pastan's Poetic Vision," *Women Poets of the Americas: Toward a Pan-American Gathering* (ed. Jacqueline Vaught Brogan and Cordelia Chavez Candelaria, 1999).

ROBERT PINSKY

Poetry
The Figured Wheel: New and Collected Poems, 1966–1996 (1996); *Jersey Rain* (2000).

Prose
Landor's Poetry (1968); *Poetry and the World* (1988); *The Sounds of Poetry: A Brief Guide* (1998).

Translations
Czeslaw Milosz, *The Separate Notebooks* (with Robert Hass, 1983); *The Inferno of Dante: A New Verse Translation* (1994).

SYLVIA PLATH

Poetry
The Collected Poems (1981).

Prose
The Bell Jar (1971); *Letters Home: Correspondence 1950–1963* (ed. Aurelia S. Plath, 1975); *Johnny Panic and the Bible of Dreams: Short Stories, Prose, and Diary Excerpts* (1979); *The Unabridged Journals of Sylvia Plath, 1950–1962* (ed. Karen V. Kukil, 2000).

Bibliographies
Stephen Gould Axelrod, *Sylvia Plath: The Wound and the Cure of Words* (1990); Sheryl L. Meyering, *Sylvia Plath: A Reference Guide* (1990).

Biographical and Critical Studies
Caroline King Barnard Hall, *Sylvia Plath* (rev., 1998); Janet Malcolm, *The Silent Woman: Sylvia Plath and Ted Hughes* (1994); Marjorie Perloff, "The Two Ariels: The (Re)Making of the Sylvia Plath Canon," *Poems in Their Place: The Intertextuality and Order of Poetic Collections* (1986); Jacqueline Rose, *The Haunting of Sylvia Plath* (1992); Anne Stevenson, *Bitter Fame: A Life of Sylvia Plath* (1989).

EZRA POUND

Poetry
Selected Poems (ed. with introduction by T. S. Eliot, 1928); *Personnae: The Collected Poems of Ezra Pound* (1950); *Selected Cantos of Ezra Pound* (1970); *The Collected Early Poems of Ezra Pound* (1982).

Prose
How to Read (1931); *ABC of Reading* (1934); *Make It New* (1934); *Jefferson and/or Mussolini* (1935); *Polite Essays* (1937); *The Letters of Ezra Pound, 1907–1941* (ed. D. D. Paige, 1950); *Patria Mia* (1950); *Literary Essays of Ezra*

Pound (edited with introduction by T. S. Eliot, 1954); *Pound-Joyce: The Letters of Ezra Pound to James Joyce* (ed. Forrest Read, 1967); *Selected Prose, 1909–1965* (ed. William Cookson, 1973); *Ezra Pound and Music: The Complete Criticism* (ed. R. Murray Schafer, 1977); *Pound-Ford, The Story of a Literary Friendship: The Correspondence between Ezra Pound and Ford Madox Ford and Their Writings about Each Other* (1982); *Ezra Pound and Dorothy Shakespear: Their Letters, 1909–1914* (1985); *Pound-Lewis: The Letters of Ezra Pound and Wyndham Lewis* (1985); *Selected Letters of Ezra Pound and Louis Zukofsky* (1987); *Ezra Pound and James Laughlin: Selected Letters* (ed. David Gordon, 1994); *Pound-Cummings: The Correspondence of Ezra Pound and E. E. Cummings* (ed. Betty Ahearn, 1996); *Pound-Williams: Selected Letters of Ezra Pound and William Carlos Williams* (ed. Hugh Witemeyer, 1996).

Translations
The Translations of Ezra Pound (ed. Hugh Kenner, 1953; enlarged ed. published as *Translations*, 1963).

Books Edited
(and contributor) *Des Imagistes* (1914); (and contributor) *Catholic Anthology, 1914–1915* (1915); (and contributor) *Active Anthology* (1933); Ernest Fenollosa, *The Chinese Written Character as a Medium for Poetry* (1936); *Confucius to Cummings: An Anthology of Poetry* (with Marcella Spann, 1964).

Bibliography
Donald Gallup, *Ezra Pound: A Bibliography* (1983).

Biographical and Critical Studies
Massimo Bacigalupo, *The Formèd Trace: The Later Poetry of Ezra Pound* (1980); *Humphrey Carpenter, Serious Character: The Life of Ezra Pound* (1988); William M. Chace, *The Political Identities of Ezra Pound and T.S. Eliot* (1973); William Cookson, *A Guide to the Cantos of Ezra Pound* (rev. ed., 2002); Donald Davie, *Ezra Pound* (1976) and *Ezra Pound: Poet as Sculptor* (1964); Mary de Rachewiltz, *Discretions* (1971); T. S. Eliot, *Ezra Pound: His Metric and Poetry* (1917); Hugh Kenner, *The Poetry of Ezra Pound* (1951) and *The Pound Era* (1971); Charles Norman, *Ezra Pound* (rev. ed., 1969); William Pratt, ed., *Ezra Pound, Nature and Myth* (2002); Sister Bernetta Quinn, *Ezra Pound: An Introduction to the Poetry* (1973); Peter Russell, *An Examination of Ezra Pound* (1950); Noel Stock, *The Life of Ezra Pound* (1970); John Tytell, *Ezra Pound: The Solitary Volcano* (rep., 2001); J. P. Sullivan, *Ezra Pound and Sextus Propertius: A Study in Creative Translation* (1964); Carroll F. Terrell, *A Companion to the Cantos of Ezra Pound* (1993); Ming Xie and Ming Hsieh, *Ezra Pound and the Appropriation of Chinese Poetry: Cathay, Translation, and Imagism* (1998); Wai-lim Yip, *Ezra Pound's Cathay* (1969).

DUDLEY RANDALL

Poetry
More to Remember: Poems of Four Decades (1971); *A Litany of Friends: New and Selected Poems* (1981).

Prose
Broadside Memories: Poets I Have Known (1975).

Books Edited
Black Poetry: A Supplement to Anthologies Which Exclude Black Poets (1969); *The Black Poets* (1971).

Biographical and Critical Studies
R. Baxter Miller, *Black American Poets between Worlds, 1940–1960* (1986); Julius Eric Thompson, *Dudley Randall, Broadside Press, and the Black Arts Movement in Detroit, 1960–1995* (1999); Mark V. Waters, "Dudley Randall and the Liberation Aesthetic: Confronting the Politics of 'Blackness'" (*CLA Journal* 44.1, Sept. 2000: 111–32).

JOHN CROWE RANSOM

Poetry
Selected Poems (1945).

Prose
The New Criticism (1941); *Beating the Bushes: Selected Essays, 1941–1970* (1972); *Selected Letters of John Crowe Ransom* (ed. George Core and Thomas D. Young, 1985).

Bibliography
Thomas D. Young, *John Crowe Ransom: An Annotated Bibliography* (1982).

Biographical and Critical Studies
Thornton H. Parsons, *John Crowe Ransom* (1969); Miller Williams, *The Poetry of John Crowe Ransom* (1972); Thomas D. Young, *Gentleman in a Dustcoat: A Biography of John Crowe Ransom* (1976).

ISHMAEL REED

Poetry
New and Collected Poems (1988).

Novels
The Free-Lance Pallbearers (1967); *Mumbo Jumbo* (1972); *The Last Days of Louisiana Red* (1974); *Flight to Canada* (1976).

Books Edited
Calafia, the California Poetry (1979); *From Totems to Hip Hop: A Multicultural Anthology of Poetry Across America* (2003).

Bibliography
Elizabeth A. Settle, *Ishmael Reed, A Primary and Secondary Bibliography* (1982).

Critical Studies
Jay Boyer, *Ishmael Reed* (1993); Bruce Allen Dick, ed., *The Critical Response to Ishmael Reed* (1999); Reginald Martin, *Ishmael Reed and the New Black Aesthetic Critics* (1988); Patrick McGee, *Ishmael Reed and the Ends of Race* (1997).

KENNETH REXROTH

Poetry
The Complete Poems of Kenneth Rexroth (ed. Sam Hamill and Bradford Marrow, 2002).

Drama
Beyond the Mountains (1951).

Prose
Bird in the Bush: Obvious Essays (1959); *Assays* (1961); *An Autobiographical Novel* (1966, rev. and enlarged ed., Linda Hamalian, 1991); *Classics Revisited* (1968); *The Alternative Society: Essays from the Other World* (1970); *American Poetry in the Twentieth Century* (1971); *The Elastic Retort: Essays in Literature and Ideas* (1973); *Communalism: From Its Origins to the Twentieth Century* (1974); *World outside the Window: The Selected Essays of Kenneth Rexroth* (ed. Bradford Morrow, 1987); *More Classics Revisited* (ed. Bradford Morrow, 1989); *Kenneth Rexroth and James Laughlin: Selected Letters* (ed. Lee Bartlett, 1991).

Translations
One Hundred Poems from the Japanese (1955); *One Hundred Poems from the Chinese* (1956); *Thirty Spanish Poems of Love and Exile* (1956); *Poems from the Greek Anthology* (1962).

Biographical and Critical Studies
Lee Bartlett, *Kenneth Rexroth* (1988); Linda Hamalian, *A Life of Kenneth Rexroth* (1991).

ADRIENNE RICH

Poetry
The Fact of a Doorframe: Poems Selected and New, 1950–1984 (1984); *Your Native Life, Your Land* (1986); *Time's Power: Poems, 1985–1988* (1988); *An Atlas of the Difficult World: Poems 1988–1991* (1991); *Collected Early Poems, 1950–1970* (1993); *Dark Fields of the Republic, Poems 1991–1995* (1995); *Midnight Salvage: Poems 1995–1998* (1999); *Fox Poems, 1998–2000* (2001).

Prose
Of Woman Born: Motherhood as Experience and Institution (1975, 1986); *On Lies, Secrets, and Silence: Selected Prose, 1966–1978* (1979); *Blood, Bread, and Poetry: Selected Prose, 1975–1985* (1986); *What Is Found There: Notebooks on Poetry and Politics* (1993); *Arts of the Possible: Essays and Conversations* (2001).

Critical Studies
Jane Roberta Cooper, ed., *Reading Adrienne Rich: Reviews and Revisions, 1955–1981* (1984); Margaret Dickie, *Stein, Bishop, and Rich: Lyrics of Love, War, and Place* (1997); Barbara Gelpi and Albert Gelpi, eds., *Adrienne Rich's Poetry and Prose: Poems, Prose, Reviews, and Criticism* (2nd ed. 1993); Claire Keyes, *The Aesthetics of Power: The Poetry of Adrienne Rich* (1986); Alice Templeton, *The Dream and the Dialogue: Adrienne Rich's Feminist Poetics* (1994).

LAURA RIDING (JACKSON)

Poetry
The Poems of Laura Riding: A Newly Revised Edition of the 1938/1980 Collection (2001).

Prose
A Survey of Modernist Poetry (with Robert Graves, 1929); *The Word "Woman" and Other Related Writings* (ed. Elizabeth Friedmann and Alan J. Clark, 1993); *Rational Meaning: A New Foundation for the Definition of Words, and Supplementary Essays* (with Schuyler B. Jackson, William Harmon, 1997); *Essays from "Epilogue" 1935–1937* (with Robert Graves, Mark Jacobs, 2001).

Bibliography
Joyce Piell Wexler, *Laura Riding: A Bibliography* (1981).

Biographical and Critical Studies
Barbara Block Adams, *The Enemy Self: Poetry and Criticism of Laura Riding* (1990); Deborah Baker, *In Extremis: The Life of Laura Riding* (1993); Richard Perceval Graves, *Robert Graves: The Years with Laura, 1926–1940* (1990); Joyce Piell Wexler, *Laura Riding's Pursuit of Truth* (1979).

EDWIN ARLINGTON ROBINSON

Poetry
Collected Poems (1937); *Uncollected Poems and Prose of Edwin Arlington Robinson* (ed. Richard Cary, 1975); *The Poetry of Edwin Arlington Robinson* (selected with an intro. by Robert Mezey, 1999).

Prose
Selected Letters (intro. by Ridgely Torrence, 1940).

Bibliographies
Jeanetta Boswell, *Edwin Arlington Robinson & the Critics: A Bibliography of Secondary Sources with Selective Annotations* (1988); Charles Hogan, *Bibliography of Edwin Arlington Robinson* (1936).

Biographical and Critical Studies
Ellsworth Barnard, *Edwin Arlington Robinson: A Critical Study* (1952); Anna S. Blumenthal, *The New England Oblique Style: The Poetry of Ralph Waldo Emerson, Emily Dickinson and Edwin Arlington Robinson* (1998); Denis Donoghue, *Connoisseurs of Chaos* (1984); Edwin Sill Fussell, *Philosophy in the Poetry of Edwin Arlington Robinson* (1954); Frances Murphy, ed., *Edwin Arlington Robinson: A Collection of Critical Essays* (1970); Emory Neff, *Edwin Arlington Robinson* (1948); Louis Untermeyer, *Edwin Arlington Robinson: A Reappraisal* (Catalogue of exhibit at the Library of Congress, 1963); Yvor Winters, *Edwin Arlington Robinson* (1946).

THEODORE ROETHKE

Poetry
The Collected Poems of Theodore Roethke (1966).

Prose
On the Poet and His Craft (ed. Ralph J. Mills, Jr., 1965); *Selected Letters of Theodore Roethke* (ed. Ralph J. Mills, Jr., 1968); *Straw for the Fire* (ed. David Wagoner, 1972).

Bibliography
James R. McLeod, *Theodore Roethke: A Bibliography* (1973).

Biographical and Critical Studies
Richard Blessing, *Theodore Roethke's Dynamic Vision* (1974); Neal Bowers, *Theodore Roethke: The Journey from I to Otherwise* (1982); Karl Malkoff, *Theodore Roethke: An Introduction to the Poetry* (1966); Ralph J. Mills, *Theodore Roethke* (1963); Jay Parini, *Theodore Roethke: An American Romantic* 1979); George Wolff, *Theodore Roethke* (1981).

WENDY ROSE

Poetry
Hopi Roadrunner Dancing (1973); *Lost Copper* (1980); *The Halfbreed Chronicles and Other Poems* (1985); *Going to War with All My Relations: New and Selected Poems* (1993); *Bone Dance: New and Selected Poems, 1965–1993* (1994).

Prose
Long Division: A Tribal History (1976); *Academic Squaw* (1977); *Aboriginal Tattooing in California* (1979).

Biographical and Critical Studies
Paula Gunn Allen, *The Sacred Hoop: Recovering the Feminine in American Indian Traditions* (1986); Laura Coltelli, *Winged Words: American Indian Women Writers Speak* (1990); Brian Swann and Arnold Krupat, eds., *I Tell You Now: Autobiographical Essays of Native American Writers* (1987).

MURIEL RUKEYSER

Poetry
Collected Poems (1978); *Out of Silence: Selected Poems* (ed. Kate Daniels, 1994).

Poetry and Prose
A Muriel Rukeyser Reader (ed. Jan Heller Levi, 1994).

Prose
Willard Gibbs (1942, 1988); *The Life of Poetry* (1949, 1996); *One Life* (1957); *The Traces of Thomas Hariot* (1971).

Biographical and Critical Studies
Anne F. Herzog and Janet E. Kaufman, *"How Shall We Tell Each Other of the Poet?"*: *The Life and Writing of Muriel Rukeyser* (1999); Louise Kertesz, *The Poetic Vision of Muriel Rukeyser* (1980).

KAY RYAN

Poetry
Strangely Marked Metal (1985); *Flamingo Watching* (1994); *Elephant Rocks* (1996); *Say Uncle* (2000).

Critical Studies
Paul Lake, "The Poetry of Kay Ryan" (*Threepenny Review* 82, Summer 2000).

BENJAMIN ALIRE SÁENZ

Poetry
Calendar of Dust (1991); *Dark and Perfect Angels* (1995); *Elegies in Blue* (2002).

MARY JO SALTER

Poetry
Henry Purcell in Japan (1985); *Unfinished Painting* (1989); *Sunday Skaters* (1994); *A Kiss in Space* (1999).

For Children
The Moon Comes Home (1989).

Book Edited
The Norton Anthology of Poetry (with Margaret Ferguson and John Stallworthy, 1996).

CARL SANDBURG

Poetry
Complete Poems (1970).

Prose
Lincoln, 6 vols. (1926–1939).

Letters
The Letters of Carl Sandburg (ed. Herbert Mitgang, 1968); *Carl Sandburg, Philip Green Wright, and the Asgard Press, 1900–1910* (ed. Joan St. C. Crane, 1975).

Bibliographies
Thomas S. Shaw, *Carl Sandburg: A Bibliography* (1948); Mark Van Doren, *Carl Sandburg: With a Bibliography of S Material in the Collections of the Library of Congress* (1969).

Biographical and Critical Studies
Gay Wilson Allen, *Carl Sandburg* (Pamphlets on American Writers 101, 1972); Richard Crowder, *Carl Sandburg* (1964); Gladys Zehnpfennig, *Carl Sandburg, Poet and Patriot* (1963).

GJERTRUD SCHNACKENBERG

Poetry
Supernatural Love (2000); *The Throne of Labdacus* (2000).

Critical Studies
Dorothy Barresi, "A Gilded Lapse of Time" (*Parnassus* 18.2, 1993: 296–315).
Daniel Mendelson, "Breaking Out" (*New York Review of Books*, 29 Mar. 2001).

ALAN SEEGER

Poetry and Letters
Alan Seeger: The Complete Works (ed. Amanda Harlech, photographs Karl Lager-feld, 2001).

Biographical and Critical Studies
M. A. de Wolfe Howe, *Memories of the Harvard Dead in the War against Germany* (1920); Paul Ayers Rockwell, *American Fighters in the Foreign Legion, 1914–1918* (1930); Irving Werstein, *Sound No Trumpet: The Life and Death of Alan Seeger* (1967).

ANNE SEXTON

Poetry
Complete Poems (1981); *Selected Poems of Anne Sexton* (ed. Diane W. Middle-brook and Diana H. George, 1988).

Prose
Anne Sexton: A Self Portrait in Letters (ed. Linda Gray Sexton and Lois Ames, 1977); *No Evil Star: Selected Essays, Interviews, and Prose* (ed. Stephen E. Col-burn, 1985).

Drama
45 Mercy Street (ed. Linda Gray Sexton, 1976).

Bibliography
Cameron Northouse and Thomas P. Walsh, *Sylvia Plath and Anne Sexton: A Reference Guide* (1974).

Biographical and Critical Studies
David Mason, "Anne Sexton and Her Times," *The Poetry of Life and the Life of Poetry* (2000); J. D. McClatchy, ed., *Anne Sexton: The Artist and Her Critics* (1978); Diane Wood Middlebrook, *Anne Sexton: A Biography* (1991); Linda Gray Sexton, *Searching for Mercy Street: My Journey Back to My Mother, Anne Sexton* (1994).

RON SILLIMAN

Poetry
Nox (1974); *Ketjak* (1978); *Tjanting* (1981); *ABC* (1983); *Paradise* (1985); *LIT* (1987); *The New Sentence* (1987); *N/O* (1994); *Xing* (1996).

Critical Studies
Tom Beckett, ed., *The Difficulties: Ron Silliman Issue* (1985); George Hartley, *Textual Politics & the Language Poets* (1989); Jerome McGann (as Anne Mack and J. J. Rome), "The Alphabet, Spelt from Ron Silliman's Leaves" (*South Atlantic Quarterly* 89, Fall 1990: 736–59); Jerome McGann, *Social Values and Poetic Acts: The Historical Judgment of Literary Work* (1988); Marjorie Perloff, *The Dance of the Intellect: Studies in the Poetry of the Pound Tradition* (1985).

CHARLES SIMIC

Poetry
Selected Poems, 1963–1983 (1985); *Unending Blues* (1986); *Hotel Insomnia* (1990); *Walking the Black Cat* (1994); *Jackstraws* (1999); *Selected Early Poems* (1999).

Prose
The Uncertain Certainty (1985); *The Unemployed Fortune-Teller* (1994); *Orphan Factory* (1997).

Translations
Tomaz Salamun, *Selected Poems* (1987); *Horse Has Six Legs: Contemporary Serbian Poetry* (1992).

Critical Studies
Bruce Weigl, ed., *Charles Simic: Essays on the Poetry* (1996).

LOUIS SIMPSON

Poetry
Collected Poems (1988); *In the Room We Share* (1990); *There You Are: Poems* (1995).

Prose
Riverside Drive (1962); *James Hogg: A Critical Study* (1962); *Three on the Tower: The Lives and Works of Ezra Pound, T. S. Eliot and William Carlos Williams* (1975); *A Revolution in Taste: Studies of Dylan Thomas, Allen Ginsberg, Sylvia Plath and Robert Lowell* (1979); *A Company of Poets* (1981); *The Character of the Poet* (1986); *Ships Going into the Blue: Essays and Notes on Poetry* (1994); *The King My Father's Wreck* (1995).

Translations
Modern Poets of France: A Bilingual Anthology (1997); *François Villon's The Legacy & Testament* (2000).

Bibliography
William H. Roberson, *Louis Simpson: A Reference Guide* (1972).

Biographical and Critical Studies
Hank Lazer, ed., *On Louis Simpson: Depths Beyond Happiness* (1988); David Mason, "Louis Simpson's Singular Charm," *The Poetry of Life and the Life of Poetry* (2000); Ronald Moran, *Louis Simpson* (1972).

WILLIAM JAY SMITH

Poetry
The World Below the Window: Poems 1937–1997 (1998).

Prose
Army Brat: A Memoir (1980).

Translations
Collected Translations: Italian, French, Spanish, Portuguese (1985).

Biographical and Critical Studies
Fred Chappell, *A Way of Happening* (1998); Robert Phillips, "William Jay Smith at Eighty" (*New Letters* 65.3, 1999: 90–119); Henry Taylor, *Compulsory Figures: Essays on Recent American Poets* (1992).

W. D. SNODGRASS

Poetry
Selected Poems, 1957–1987 (1987); *Each in His Season* (1993).

Prose
In Radical Pursuit (1975); *After-Images: Autobiographical Sketches* (1999).

Translations
Selected Translations (1998).

Bibliography
William White, ed., *W. D. Snodgrass: A Bibliography* (1960).

Critical Studies
Paul Gaston, *W. D. Snodgrass* (1978); Steven Haven, ed., *The Poetry of W. D. Snodgrass: Everything Human* (1993); Robert Phillips, *The Confessional Poets* (1973); Philip Raisor, *Tuned and Under Tension: The Recent Poetry of W. D. Snodgrass* (1998); M. L. Rosenthal, The *New Poets* (1967).

GARY SNYDER

Poetry
No Nature: New and Selected Poems (1992); *Mountains and Rivers without End* (1996).

Prose
The Real Work: Interviews & Talks, 1964–1979 (ed. Scott McLean, 1980); *The Practice of the Wild* (1990); *A Place in Space: Ethics, Aesthetics and Watersheds* (1995).

Biographical and Critical Studies
Bert Almon, *Gary Snyder* (1979); Bruce Cook, *The Beat Generation* (1971); Charles Molesworth, *Gary Snyder's Vision: Poetry and the Real World* (1983); Bob Steuding, *Gary Snyder* (1976).

CATHY SONG

Poetry
Picture Bride (1983); *Frameless Windows, Squares of Light* (1988); *School Figures* (1995); *The Land of Bliss* (2001).

Critical Studies
Gayle K. Fujita Sato, "'Third World' as Place and Paradigm in Cathy Song's *Picture Bride*" (*MELUS* 15, Spring 1988: 49–72); Masami Usui, "Women Disclosed: Cathy Song's Poetry and Kitagawa Ukiyoe" (*Studies in Culture and the Humanities* 1995: 1–19); Patricia Wallace, "Divided Loyalties: Literal and Literary in the Poetry of Lorna Dee Cervantes, Cathy Song, and Rita Dove" (*MELUS* 18, Fall 1993: 3–19).

JACK SPICER

Poetry and Prose
The Collected Books of Jack Spicer (ed. Robin Blaser 1975); *Collected Poems: 1945–1946* (1981); *Collections: The House That Jack Built: The Collected Lectures of Jack Spicer* (ed. Peter Gizzi, 1998).

Bibliography
Larry Keller, *Jack Spicer: A Bibliography* (1985).

Biographical Studies
Robert Duncan, As Testimony: The Poem & the Scene (1964); Lewis Ellingham and Kevin Killian, *Poet Be Like God: Jack Spicer and the San Francisco Renaissance* (1998); Edward Halsey Foster, *Jack Spicer* (1991); Joanne Kyger, *The Dharma Committee* (1986).

WILLIAM STAFFORD

Poetry
The Darkness around Us Is Deep: Selected Poems of William Stafford (ed. Robert Bly, 1993); *Learning to Live in the World: Earth Poems* (1994); *The Way It Is: New and Selected Poems* (1998).

Prose
Crossing Unmarked Snow: Further Views on the Writer's Vocation (ed. Paul Merchant and Vincent Wixon, 1998); *You Must Revise Your Life* (1986).

Biographical and Critical Studies
Tom Andrews, *On William Stafford: The Worth of Local Things* (1993); Jonathan Holden, *To Mark the Turn: A Reading of William Stafford's Poetry* (1976); Judith Kitchen, *Writing the World: Understanding William Stafford* (1999); Sanford Pinsker, *Three Pacific Northwest Poets: William Stafford, Richard Hugo, and David Wagoner* (1987).

TIMOTHY STEELE

Poetry
The Color Wheel (1994); *Sapphics and Uncertainties: Poems 1970–1986* (1995).

Prose
Missing Measures: Modern Poetry and the Revolt against Meter (1990); *All the Fun's in How You Say a Thing: An Explanation of Meter and Versification* (1999).

Book Edited
The Poems of J. V. Cunningham (1997).

Biographical and Critical Studies
X. J. Kennedy, "Timothy Steele," *American Poets since World War II, Dictionary of Literary Biography* 120 (1992); April Lindner, *New Formalist Poets of the American West* (2001); Kevin Walzer, "Strumming the Lyre: Grosholz, Hadas, Steele," *The Ghost of Tradition: Expansive Poetry and Postmodernism* (1998) and "The Poetry of Timothy Steele" *(Tennessee Quarterly* 2/3, Winter 1996: 16–30) and "An Interview with Timothy Steele" *(Edge City Review* 6, Sept. 1996: 3–6).

GERTRUDE STEIN

Poetry and Prose
The Yale Edition of the Unpublished Writings of Gertrude Stein, 8 vols. (ed. Carl Van Vechten, 1956–1958); *The Yale Gertrude Stein* (ed. Richard Kostelanetz, 1980); *Gertrude Stein: Writings 1903–1932: Q.E.D.; Three Lives, Portraits and Other Short Works; The Autobiography of Alice B. Toklas* (ed. Catherine R. Stimpson, 1998); *Writings 1932–1946: Stanzas in Meditation, Lectures in America, The Geographical History of America, Ida, Brewsie and Willie, Other Works* (ed. Catherine R. Stimpson, 1998); *Selected Writings of Gertrude Stein* (ed. Carl Van Vechten, 1946, 1990).

Bibliography
Maureen R. Liston, *Gertrude Stein: An Annotated, Critical Bibliography* (1979).

Biographical and Critical Studies
John Malcolm Brinnin, *The Third Rose: Gertrude Stein and Her World* (1959); Marianne DeKoven, *A Different Language: Gertrude Stein's Experimental Writing* (1983); Michael J. Hoffman, *Critical Essays on Gertrude Stein* (1986); Bruce Kellner, ed., *A Gertrude Stein Companion: Content with the Example* (1988); James R. Mellow, *Charmed Circle: Gertrude Stein and Company* (1974); Lisa Ruddick, *Reading Gertrude Stein: Body, Text, Gnosis* (1990).

WALLACE STEVENS

Poetry
The Collected Poems of Wallace Stevens (1954); *Opus Posthumous* (ed. Samuel French Morse, 1957); *The Palm at the End of the Mind: Selected Poems and a Play by Wallace Stevens* (ed. Holly Stevens, 1971); *Collected Poetry and Prose* (1997).

Prose
The Necessary Angel: Essays on Reality and the Imagination (1951); *Letters of Wallace Stevens* (ed. Holly Stevens, 1966).

Bibliography
J. M. Edelstein, *Wallace Stevens: A Descriptive Bibliography* (1973).

Biographical and Critical Studies

Milton J. Bates, *Wallace Stevens: A Mythology of Self* (1985); Richard Allen Blessing, *Wallace Stevens' "Whole Harmonium"* (1970); Peter Brazeau, *Parts of A World: Wallace Stevens Remembered: An Oral Biography* (1983); Ashley Brown and Robert S. Haller, eds., *The Achievement of Wallace Stevens* (1962); Irvin Ehrenpreis, ed., *Wallace Stevens: A Critical Anthology* (1973); George Lensing, *Wallace Stevens and the Seasons* (2001); A. Walton Litz, *Introspective Voyager: The Poetic Development of Wallace Stevens* (1972); Samuel French Morse, *Wallace Stevens: Poetry as Life* (1970); Joan Richardson, *Wallace Stevens: The Early Years* (1986); Kristine Santilli, *Poetic Gesture: Myth, Wallace Stevens, and the Motions of Poetic Language* (2002); Melita Schaum, ed., *Wallace Stevens and the Feminine* (1993); Holly Stevens, *Souvenirs and Prophecies: The Young Wallace Stevens* (1977); Helen Hennessy Vendler, *On Extended Wings: Wallace Stevens' Longer Poems* (1969).

ANNE STEVENSON

Poetry

The Collected Poems of Anne Stevenson (1996); *Granny Scarecrow* (2000).

Prose

Elizabeth Bishop (1966); *Bitter Fame: A Life of Sylvia Plath* (1989); *Between the Iceberg and the Ship: Selected Essays* (1998); *Five Looks at Elizabeth Bishop* (1998).

Interview

Cynthia Haven, "Anne Stevenson," http://www.cortlandreview.com/issue/14/stevenson.

TRUMBULL STICKNEY

Poetry

The Poems of Trumbull Stickney (ed. George Cabot Lodge, William Vaughn Moody, and John Ellerton Lodge, 1905); *Homage to Trumbull Stickney: Poems* (ed. James Reeves and Sean Haldane, 1968); *The Poems of Trumbull Stickney* (ed. Amberys R. Whittle, 1972); *Dramatic Verses* (1994).

Bibliography

J. William Myers, "A Complete Stickney Bibliography" (*Twentieth-Century Literature 9*, Jan. 1964: 209–12).

Biographical and Critical Studies

Sean Haldane, *The Fright of Time: Joseph Trumbull Stickney, 1874–1904* (1970); Amberys R. Whittle, *Trumbull Stickney* (1973).

MARK STRAND

Poetry

The Continuous Life: Poems (1990); *Selected Poems* (1990); *Dark Harbor: A Poem* (1993); *Blizzard of One: Poems* (1998); *Chicken, Shadow, Moon, & More* (2000); *Looking for Poetry: Poems* (2002); *The Story of Our Lives; with, The Monument; and, The Late Hour: Poems* (2002).

Prose
The Weather of Words: Poetic Invention (2000).

Critical Studies
David K. Kirby, *Mark Strand and the Poet's Place in Contemporary Society* (1990).

MAY SWENSON

Poetry
New and Selected Things Taking Place (1978); *The Love Poems of May Swenson* (1991); *Nature: Poems Old and New* (1994); *May Out West: Poems of May Swenson* (1998).

Prose
Made with Words (ed. Gardner McFall, 1998); *Dear Elizabeth: Five Poems and Three Letters to Elizabeth Bishop* (ed. Kirsten Hotelling Zona, 2000).

Biographical and Critical Studies
Mark Doty, "Sweet, Queer Thrills: Reading May Swenson" (*Yale Review* 88.1, Jan. 2000: 86–110); Jean Gould, "May Swenson" (*Modern American Women Poets*, 1984); Roxanne Knudson, *May Swenson: A Poet's Life in Photos* (1996); Kirsten Hotelling Zona, "A 'Dangerous Game of Change'": Images of Desire in the Love Poems of May Swenson" (*Twentieth Century Literature* 44.2, Summer 1998: 219–41).

LARISSA SZPORLUK

Poetry
Dark Sky Question (1998); *Isolato* (2000).

ALLEN TATE

Poetry
Collected Poems, 1919–1976 (1977).

Prose
Reactionary Essays on Poetry and Ideas (1936); *Reason in Madness: Critical Essays* (1941); *The Man of Letters in the Modern World: Selected Essays 1928–1955* (1955); *Essays of Four Decades* (1968).

Biographical and Critical Studies
Ferman Bishop, *Allen Tate* (1967); John M. Bradbury, *The Fugitives: A Critical Account* (1958); Robert S. Dupree, *Allen Tate and the Augustinian Imagination* (1983); Langdon Hammer, *Hart Crane & Allen Tate: Janus-Faced Modernism* (1993); Radcliffe Squires, *Allen Tate: A Literary Biography* (1971); Radcliffe Squires, ed., *Allen Tate and His Work: Critical Evaluations* (1972).

JAMES TATE

Poetry
Memoir of the Hawk (2001).

Prose
Selected Poems (1991); *Worshipful Company of Fletchers* (1994); *Shroud of the Gnome* (1997); *The Route as Briefed* (1999).

Critical Studies
Craig McDaniel, "James Tate's Secret Co-Pilot" (*New England Review* 23.2, Spring 2002: 55–72 and *Denver Quarterly, Special Issue on James Tate* 33.3, Fall 1998); Lee Upton, *The Muse of Abandonment: Origin, Identity, Mastery in Five American Poets* (1998); Carolyne Wright, "On James Tate" (*Iowa Review* 26.1, Spring 1996: 183–88).

SARA TEASDALE

Poetry
The Collected Poems of Sara Teasdale (1937, 1996).

Book Edited
The Answering Voice: One Hundred Love Lyrics by Women (1917, enlarged ed. 1928).

Biographical and Critical Studies
Margaret Haley Carpenter, *Sara Teasdale, A Biography* (1979); William Drake, *Sara Teasdale: Woman and Poet* (1979); Carol Schoen, *Sara Teasdale* (1986); Cheryl Walker, "Women and Selfhood: Sara Teasdale and the Passionate Virgin Persona," *Masks Outrageous and Austere* (1991).

DIANE THIEL

Poetry
Echolocations (2000).

Prose
Writing Your Rhythm: Using Nature, Culture, Form and Myth (2001).

MELVIN B. TOLSON

Poetry
Rendezvous with America (1944); *Libretto for the Republic of Liberia* (1953); *A Gallery of Harlem Portraits* (ed. Robert M. Farnsworth, 1979); *Harlem Gallery and Other Poems* (ed. Raymond Nelson, 1999).

Prose
Caviar and Cabbage: Selected Columns by Melvin B. Tolson from the Washington Tribune 1937–1944 (ed. Robert M. Farnsworth, 1982); *The Harlem Group of Negro Writers* (ed. Edward J. Mullen, 2001).

Biographical and Critical Studies
Robert M. Farnsworth, *Melvin B. Tolson 1898–1968: Plain Talk and Poetic Prophecy* (1984); Joy Flasch, *Melvin B. Tolson* (1972); Mariann Russell, *Melvin B. Tolson's Harlem Gallery: A Literary Analysis* (1980).

JEAN TOOMER

Poetry
The Collected Poems of Jean Toomer (ed. Robert B. Jones and Margery Toomer Latimer, 1988).

Poetry and Prose
Cane (1923, 1993); *A Jean Toomer Reader: Selected Unpublished Writings* (ed. Frederik L. Rusch, 1993).

Prose
Jean Toomer: Selected Essays and Literary Criticism (ed. Robert B. Jones, 1996).

Biographical and Critical Studies
Genevieve Fabre and Michel Feith, *Jean Toomer and the Harlem Renaissance* (2001); Robert B. Jones, *Jean Toomer and the Prison-House of Thought: A Phenomenology of the Spirit* (1993); Cynthia Earl Kerman, *The Lives of Jean Toomer: A Hunger for Wholeness* (1987); Charles Scruggs, *Jean Toomer and the Terrors of American History* (1998); Jon Woodson, *To Make a New Race: Gurdjieff, Toomer, and the Harlem Renaissance* (1999).

AMY UYEMATSU

Poetry
30 Miles from J-Town (1992); *Nights of Fire, Nights of Rain* (1998).

Critical Studies
King Kok Cheung, *Words Matter: Conversations with Asian American Writers* (2000); Masami Usui, "Coloring Her Own Garden Yellow: Amy Uyematsu's Poems" (*Chu Shikoku Studies in American Literature* 31, June 1995: 41–57).

MONA VAN DUYN

Poetry
Firefall: Poems (1993); *If It Be Not I: Collected Poems 1959–1982* (1993); *Selected Poems* (2002).

Critical Studies
Michael Burns, ed., *Discovery and Reminiscence: Essays on the Poetry of Mona Van Duyn* (1998).

MARGARET WALKER

Poetry
This Is My Century: New and Collected Poems (1989).

Prose
Jubilee (1966, 1999); *How I Wrote Jubilee and Other Essays on Life and Literature* (1990); *On Being Black, Female, and Free: Essays 1932–1992* (ed. Maryemma Graham, 1997).

Biographical and Critical Studies
Nancy Beke, *Women Poets on the Left: Lola Ridge, Genevieve Taggard, Margaret Walker* (2001); Maryemma Graham, *Fields Watered with Blood: Critical Essays on Margaret Walker* (2001).

ROBERT PENN WARREN

Poetry
The Collected Poems of Robert Penn Warren (ed. John Burt, 1998).

Prose
Understanding Poetry (with Cleanth Brooks, 1938); *All the King's Men* (1946); *Who Speaks for the Negro?* (1965); *Democracy and Poetry* (1975); *New and Selected Essays* (1989).

Bibliography
James A. Grimshaw, Jr., *Robert Penn Warren: A Descriptive Bibliography, 1922–1979* (1981).

Biographical and Critical Studies
Joseph Leo Blotner, *Robert Penn Warren: A Biography* (1997); William Bedford Clark, ed., *Critical Essays on Robert Penn Warren* (1981); Malcolm Cowley, ed., *Writers at Work: The Paris Review Interviews* (1959); Alfred Kazin, *Contemporaries* (1962).

RICHARD WILBUR

Poetry
New and Collected Poems (1988); *Mayflies* (2000).

Prose
Responses: Prose Pieces 1953–1976 (1976, 2000); *The Catbird's Song: Prose Pieces 1963–1995* (1997).

Translations
Moliére, *The Misanthrope and Tartuffe* (1965), *The School for Wives* (1971), *The Learned Ladies* (1978), *Four Comedies* (1982), *The School for Husbands & Siganarelle, or the Imaginary Cuckold* (1994), and *Amphitryon* (1995); Racine, *Andromache* (1982) and *Phaedra* (1986).

For Children
Opposites (1973); *More Opposites* (1991); *Runaway Opposites* (1995); *The Disappearing Alphabet* (1997).

Bibliographies
Frances Bixler, *Richard Wilbur: A Reference Guide* (1991); John Field, *Richard Wilbur: A Bibliographical Checklist* (1971).

Critical Studies
Paul Cummins, *Richard Wilbur: A Critical Essay* (1971); Rodney Edgecombe, *A Reader's Guide to the Poetry of Richard Wilbur* (1995); Donald L. Hill, *Richard Wilbur* (1967); Bruce Michelson, *Wilbur's Poetry: Music in a Scattering Time* (1991).

Interviews
William Butts, ed., *Conversations with Richard Wilbur* (1990); Peter Dale, *Richard Wilbur in Conversation* (2000).

C. K. WILLIAMS

Poetry
Selected Poems (1994); *The Vigil* (1998); *Repair* (1999); *Love About Love* (2001).

Prose
Poetry and Consciousness (1998); *Misgivings: My Mother, My Father, Myself* (2000).

Critical Studies
Charles Altieri, "Contemporary Poetry as Philosophy: Subjective Agency in John Ashbery and C. K. Williams" (*Contemporary Literature* 33.2, Summer 1992: 214–42); Alan Shapiro, *In Praise of the Impure: Poetry and the Ethical Imagination: Essays, 1981–1991* (1993).

MILLER WILLIAMS

Poetry
A Circle of Stone (1964); *Halfway from Hoxie: New and Selected Poems* (1973); *The Boys on Their Bony Mules* (1983); *Living on the Surface: New and Selected Poems* (1989); *Adjusting to the Light: Poems* (1992); *Points of Departure: Poems* (1995); *Some Jazz a While: Collected Poems* (1999).

Prose
The Achievement of John Ciardi (1969); *The Poetry of John Crowe Ransom* (1972); *How Does a Poem Mean?* (with John Ciardi, 1975); *Why God Permits Evil* (1977); *Patterns of Poetry: An Encyclopedia of Forms* (1986).

Books Edited
Southern Writing in the Sixties: Poetry (with John William Corrington, 1967); *Contemporary Poetry in America* (1973).

Critical Studies
Irv Broughton, *The Writer's Mind* (1990); Michael Burns, ed., *Miller Williams and the Poetry of the Particular* (1991); Richard Jackson, *Acts of Mind: Conversations with Contemporary Poets* (1983).

WILLIAM CARLOS WILLIAMS

Poetry
Collected Poems of William Carlos Williams, 2 vols. (ed. A. Walton Litz and Christopher MacGowan, 1986); *Paterson*, rev. ed. (ed. Christopher MacGowan, 1992).

Prose
In the American Grain (1925, 1956); *Selected Essays of William Carlos Williams* (1954, 1969); *Imaginations: Five Experimental Prose Pieces* (ed. Webster Schott, 1970).

Bibliography
Linda W. Wagner, *William Carlos Williams: A Reference Guide* (1978).

Biographical and Critical Studies
Stephen Gould Axelrod and Helen Deese, eds., *Critical Essays on Williams Carlos Williams* (1995); James E. Breslin, *William Carlos Williams: An American Artist* (1970); Stephen Cushman, *William Carlos Williams and the Meaning of Measure* (1985); Paul Mariani, *William Carlos Williams: A New World Naked* (1981); Carl Rapp, *William Carlos Williams and Romantic Idealism* (1984).

CHRISTIAN WIMAN

Poetry
The Long Home (1998).

YVOR WINTERS

Poetry
Collected Poems (1960, 1962); *The Poetry of Yvor Winters* (1980).

Prose
Edwin Arlington Robinson (1946, rev. ed. 1971); *In Defense of Reason* (1947); *The Function of Criticism* (1957); *On Modern Poets: Stevens, Eliot, Ransom, Crane, Hopkins, Frost* (1959); *Forms of Discovery: Critical and Historical Essays on the Forms of the Short Poem in English* (1967); *Uncollected Essays and Reviews* (ed. Francis Murphy, 1973).

Books Edited
Twelve Poets of the Pacific (1937); *Poets of the Pacific* (1949); *Quest for Reality* (with Kenneth Fields, 1969).

Bibliographies
Kenneth A. Lohf and Eugene P. Sheehy, *Yvor Winters: A Bibliography* (1959); Grosvenor Powell, *Yvor Winters: An Annotated Bibliography, 1919–1982* (1983).

Critical Studies
Elizabeth Isaacs, *An Introduction to the Poetry of Yvor Winters* (1981); Thomas Parkinson, *Hart Crane and Yvor Winters: Their Literary Correspondence* (1978); Grosvenor Powell, *Language as Being in the Poetry of Yvor Winters* (1980).

CHARLES WRIGHT

Poetry
Country Music: Selected Early Poems (1982); *The World of the Ten Thousand Things: Poems 1980–1990* (1990); *Negative Blue: Selected Later Poems* (2000); *A Short History of the Shadow* (2002).

Prose
Halflife: Improvisations and Interviews 1977–1987 (1988); *Quarter Notes: Improvisations and Interviews* (1995).

Critical Studies
Tom Andrews, ed., *The Point Where All Things Meet: Essays on Charles Wright* (1995); Bonnie Costello, "Charles Wright's Via Negative: Language, Landscape, and the Idea of God" (*Contemporary Literature* 42.2, Summer 2001: 325–46).

JAMES WRIGHT

Poetry
Above the River: The Complete Poems (1992).

Prose
Collected Prose (ed. Anne Wright, 1982).

Translations
Herman Hesse, *Poems* (1970) and *Wandering: Notes and Sketches* (1972); *Neruda and Vallejo: Selected Poems* (with Robert Bly and John Knoepfle, 1971).

Bibliography
William H. Roberson, *James Wright: An Annotated Bibliography* (1995).

Biographical and Critical Studies
Robert Bly, et al., eds., *James Wright: A Profile* (1988); Saundra Maley, *Solitary Apprenticeship: James Wright and German Poetry* (1996).

JOHN ALLAN WYETH, JR.

Poetry
This Man's Army: A War in Fifty-Odd Sonnets (1928).

ELINOR WYLIE

Poetry
Collected Poems (1932); *Last Poems of Elinor Wylie* (1943, 1982).

Prose
Jennifer Lorn: A Sedate Extravaganza (1923); *Collected Prose* (1933).

Biographical and Critical Studies
Thomas A. Gray, *Elinor Wylie* (1969); Stanley Olson, *Elinor Wylie, A Life Apart: A Biography* (1979); Judith Farr, *The Life and Art of Elinor Wylie* (1983); Cheryl Walker, "Women and Aggression: Elinor Wylie and the Woman Warrior Persona," *Masks Outrageous and Austere* (1991).

KEVIN YOUNG

Poetry
Most Way Home (1995); *To Repel Ghosts* (2001).

Book Edited
Giant Steps (2001).

BERNICE ZAMORA

Poetry
Restless Serpents (1976); *Releasing Serpents* (1994).

Critical Studies
Juan Bruce-Novoa, *Chicano Poetry: A Response to Chaos* (1982); Marta Ester Sanchez, *Contemporary Chicana Poetry: A Critical Approach to an Emerging Literature* (1985); Joseph Sommers and Tomas Ybarra-Frausta, eds., *Modern Chicano Writers: A Collection of Critical Essays* (1979).

LOUIS ZUKOFSKY

Poetry
Complete Short Poetry (1991); *"A"* (1978, 1993).

Prose
Prepositions+: The Collected Critical Essays (ed. Mark Scroggins, 2000); *A Test of Poetry* (2000).

Bibliography
Celia Thaew Zukofsky, *A Bibliography of Louis Zukofsky* (1969).

Biographical and Critical Studies
Barry Ahearn, *Zukofsky's "A": An Introduction* (1983); Mark Scroggins, *Louis Zukofsky and the Poetry of Knowledge* (1998) and as ed., *Upper Limit Music: The Writing of Louis Zukofsky* (1997); Sandra Kumamoto Stanley, *Louis Zukofsky and the Transformation of Modern American Poetics* (1994); Clark Terrell, *Louis Zukofsky: Man and Poet* (1979).

Acknowledgments

KIM ADDONIZIO "First Poem for You" from *The Philosopher's Club*. Copyright © 1994 by Kim Addonizio. Reprinted with the permission of BOA Editions, Ltd. "Stolen Moments" from *Poetry*, September 1999. Copyright © 1999 by Kim Addonizio. Reprinted by the permission of the Editor of Poetry and the author.

AI "Child Beater" from *Vice*. Copyright © 1999 by Ai. Used by permission of W. W. Norton & Company, Inc.

FRANCISCO ALARCON "Frontera/Border" from *From the Other Side of Night/Del otro lado de la luna*, © 1999 Francisco A. Alarcon. "The X in My Name" from *No Golden Gate for Us*, Pennywhistle Press. © 1993 Francisco A. Alarcon. Reprinted with permission of the author.

SHERMAN ALEXIE "The Powwow at the End of the World" from *The Summer of Black Widows*. © 1996 by Sherman Alexie, by permission of Hanging Loose Press. "Indian Boy Love Song #2" and "I am the essence of powwow, I am" from *The Business of Fancydancing: Stories & Poems*. © 1992 by Sherman Alexie, by permission of Hanging Loose Press.

A. R. AMMONS "The City Limits," "The Constant," "Cut the Grass" and "Gravelly Run" from *Collected Poems 1951–1971*. Copyright © 1960 by A. R. Ammons. "Viable" from *Collected Poems 1951–1971*. Copyright © 1972 by A. R. Ammons. Used by permission of W. W. Norton & Company, Inc.

JOHN ASHBERY "Paradoxes and Oxymorons" from *Shadow Train*. Copyright © 1980, 1981 by John Ashbery. "At North Farm" and "Just Walking Around" from *A Wave*. Copyright © 1981, 1982, 1983, 1984 by John Ashbery. "Some Trees" from *Some Trees*. Copyright © 1956 by John Ashbery. "My Erotic Double" from *As We Know*. Copyright © 1979 by John Ashbery. "These Lacustrine Cities" from *Rivers and Mountains* by John Ashbery. Reprinted by permission of Georges Borchardt, Inc., for the author.

AMIRI BARAKA "Preface to a Twenty Volume Suicide Note" from *Selected Poetry*. "Legacy" and "Black Bourgeoisie" from *Black Magic*. Copyright by Amiri Baraka. Reprinted by permission of Sterling Lord Literistic, Inc.

STEPHEN VINCENT BENÉT "American Names" by Stephen Vincent Benét, copyright © 1927 by Stephen Vincent Benét, copyright renewed © 1955 by Rosemary Carr Benét. "1936" from "The Devil and Daniel Webster" from the *Selected Works of Stephen Vincent Benét*, copyright © 1936 by Stephen Vincent Benét, copyright renewed © 1964 by Stephen Vincent Benét. Reprinted by permission of Brandt & Hochman Literary Agents, Inc.

GWENDOLYN BENNETT "Hatred" and "To a Dark Girl" reprinted courtesy of the Literary Representative for the Works of Gwendolyn Bennett, Schomburg Center for Research in Black Culture, New York Public Library, Astor, Lenox and Tilden Foundations.

JOHN BERRYMAN "Desires of Men and Women" from *Collected Poems: 1937–1971*. Copyright © 1989 by Kate Donahue Berryman. Dream Songs "#1 Huffy Henry," "#14 Life, friends," "#22 Of 1826," "#29 There sat down, once," "#384 The marker slants" from *The Dream Songs*. Copyright © 1969 by John Berryman.

BOA Editions, Ltd. "homage to my hips" first appeared in *Good Woman: Poems and a Memoir 1969–1980,* published by BOA Editions. Copyright © 1988 by Lucille Clifton. Reprinted by permission of Curtis Brown, Ltd.

JUDITH ORTIZ COFER "The Lesson of the Sugarcane" from *The Latin Deli: Prose and Poetry.* Copyright © 1993 by Judith Ortiz Cofer. Reprinted by permission of The University of Georgia Press. "Quinceañera" from *Terms of Survival.* Copyright © 1987 by Judith Ortiz Cofer. Reprinted by permission of Arte Publico Press, University of Houston.

BILLY COLLINS "Embrace" and "Lowell, Mass." from *The Apple That Astonished Paris.* Copyright © 1988 by Billy Collins. Reprinted by permission of the University of Arkansas Press. "The Dead" from *Questions About Angels.* Copyright © 1991 by Billy Collins. Reprinted by permission of the University of Pittsburgh Press.

HART CRANE "At Melville's Tomb," "Voyages I, II, III, IV, V, VI," by Marc Simon, Editor, "The Wine Menagerie" by Marc Simon, editor, "To Brooklyn Bridge" by Marc Simon, editor, "Royal Palm" by Marc Simon, editor, "The Broken Tower," from *Complete Poems of Hart Crane* by Hart Crane, edited by Marc Simon. Copyright 1933, © 1958, 1966 by Liveright Publishing Corporation. Copyright © 1986 by Marc Simon. Used by permission of Liveright Publishing Corporation.

ROBERT CREELEY "I Know a Man," "Heroes," "Oh No," "For Love," "The Rain" and "'I Keep to Myself Such Measures...'" from *Collected Poems of Robert Creeley.* Copyright © 1983 The Regents of the University of California. Reprinted by permission of the University of California Press.

COUNTEE CULLEN "For a Lady I Know," "For Paul Lawrence Dunbar," "Incident," "Yet Do I Marvel," "To Certain Critics" and "Heritage" from *My Soul's High Song* by Countee Cullen. Copyright © 1991 Doubleday, New York. Copyrights held by Amistad Research Center, administered by Thompson and Thompson, New York, NY.

E. E. CUMMINGS "next to of course god america i," "i sing of Olaf glad and big," "somewhere i have never travelled,gladly beyond," "may i feel said he," "r-p-o-p-h-e-s-s-a-g-r," "you shall above all things be glad and young.," "anyone lived in a pretty how town," "my father moved through dooms of love," "pity this busy monster,manunkind," "o purple finch/ please tell me why" from *Complete Poems: 1904–1962* by E. E. Cummings, edited by George J. Firmage. Copyright 1923, 1925, 1926, 1931, 1935, 1938, 1939, 1940, 1944, 1945, 1946, 1947, 1948, 1949, 1950, 1951, 1952, 1953, 1954, © 1955, 1956, 1957, 1958, 1959, 1960, 1961, 1962, 1963, 1966, 1967, 1968, 1972, 1973, 1974, 1975, 1976, 1977, 1978, 1979, 1980, 1981, 1982, 1983, 1984, 1985, 1986, 1987, 1988, 1989, 1990, 1991 by the Trustees for the e. e. cummings Trust. Copyright © 1973, 1976, 1978, 1979, 1981, 1983, 1985, 1991 by George James Firmage. Used by permission of Liveright Publishing Corporation.

J. V. CUNNINGHAM "For My Contemporaries," "In the Thirtieth Year," "To My Wife," "To What Strangers, What Welcome" and epigrams from *The Poems of J. V. Cunningham.* Swallow Press/Ohio University Press, 1997. Reprinted with permission of Swallow Press/Ohio University Press, Athens, Ohio.

JAMES DICKEY "The Performance," "The Heaven of Animals," "The Lifeguard" and "The Sheep Child" from *Poems 1957–1967.* Copyright © 1968 by James Dickey. Reprinted by permission of Wesleyan University Press.

H. D. DOOLITTLE "Helen," "The Walls Do Not Fall [1]," "The Walls Do Not Fall [2]" and "The Flowering of the Rod" from *Collected Poems, 1912–1944* by H. D. Doolittle. Copyright © 1944, 1945, 1946 by Oxford University Press, renewed 1973 by Norman Holmes Pearson. Reprinted by permission of New Directions Publishing Corp.

MARK DOTY "Fog" from *My Alexandria: Poems.* Copyright © 1993 by Mark Doty. Used with permission of the poet and the University of Illinois Press. "Homo will Not Inherit" from *Atlantis.* Copyright © 1995 by Mark Doty. Reprinted by permission of HarperCollins Publishers Inc.

RITA DOVE "Adolescence-I," "Adolescence-II" and "Adolescence-III" from *The Yellow House on the Corner,* Carnegie-Mellon University Press. Copyright © 1980 by Rita Dove. "Daystar" from *Thomas and Beulah,* Carnegie-Mellon Press. Copyright © 1986 by Rita Dove. Reprinted by permission of the author.

ROBERT DUNCAN "The Torso, Passages 18" from *Bending the Bow.* Copyright © 1968 by Robert Duncan. "Roots and Branches" from *Roots and Branches.* Copyright © 1964 by Robert Duncan. "Poetry, A Natural Thing" and "This Place Rumored To Have Been Sodom" from *The Opening of the Field.* Copyright © 1960 by Robert Duncan. Reprinted by New Directions Publishing Corp. "The Temple of the Animals" from *Selected Poems.* Copyright © 1959 by Robert Duncan. Reprinted by permission of City Lights Books.

STEPHEN DUNN "Beautiful Women" and "Decorum" from *New and Selected Poems 1974–1994.* Copyright © 1994 by Stephen Dunn. Used by permission of W. W. Norton & Company, Inc.

RICHARD EBERHART "The Fury of Aerial Bombardment" from *Selected Poems, 1930–1965* by Richard Eberhart. Copyright © 1965 by Richard Eberhart. Reprinted by permission of New Directions Publishing Corp.

T. S. ELIOT "The Hollow Men," and "Journey of the Magi" from *Collected Poems 1909–1962* by T. S. Eliot, copyright 1936 by Harcourt, Inc., copyright © 1964, 1963 by T. S. Eliot. "Ash Wednesday" copyright 1930 and renewed 1958 by T. S. Eliot. "Burnt Norton" from *Four Quartets* by T. S. Eliot, copyright 1936 by Harcourt, Inc. and renewed 1964 by T. S. Eliot. Reprinted by permission of the publisher. Reprinted by permission of Faber and Faber Ltd., London.

RHINA ESPAILLAT "Agua," "Bilingual/Bilingue" and "Bra" from *Where Horizons Go: Poems.* Copyright © 1998 by Truman State University Press. Reproduced with permission of Truman State University Press in the format Textbook via Copyright Clearance Center.

WILLIAM EVERSON/BROTHER ANTONINUS "These Are the Ravens" from *The Residual Years.* Copyright © 1935 by William Everson. "Advent" and "The Making of the Cross" from *The Veritable Years.* Copyright © 1978 by William Everson. Reprinted by permission of Jude Everson.

B. H. FAIRCHILD "The Death of a Small Town" from *The Art of the Lathe.* Copyright © 1998 by B. H. Fairchild. Reprinted with the permission of Alice James Books. "A Starlit Night" from *Early Occult Memory Systems of the Lower Midwest: Poems.* Copyright © 2003 by B. H. Fairchild. Used by permission of W. W. Norton & Company, Inc.

KENNETH FEARING "Dirge" and "Literary" from *Kenneth Fearing: Complete Poems.* Copyright © 1994 by Kenneth Fearing. Reprinted by permission of The National Poetry Foundation.

LAWRENCE FERLINGHETTI "In Goya's Greatest Scenes We Seem to See" from *Pictures of the Gone World.* Copyright © 1955 by Lawrence Ferlinghetti. Reprinted by permission of City Lights Books.

EDWARD FIELD "Curse of the Cat Woman" and "Roaches" from *Counting Yourself Lucky: Selected Poems 1963–1992*, Black Sparrow Press. Copyright © 1992 by Edward Field. Reprinted by permission of the author.

CAROLYN FORCHÉ "The Morning Baking" from *Gathering the Tribes,* Yale University Press, 1976. Copyright © 1976 by Carolyn Forché. Reprinted by permission of the publisher. "The Colonel" from *The Country Between Us.* Copyright © 1981 by Carolyn Forché. Originally appeared in *Women's International Resource Exchange.* Reprinted by permission of HarperCollins Publishers Inc.

ROBERT FRANCIS "Yes, What?" from *Robert Francis Collected Poems 1936–1976* by Robert Francis. Copyright © 1976 Robert Francis. Reprinted by permission of the University of Massachusetts Press. "Catch" and "Hallelujah: A Sestina" from *The Orb Weaver* by Robert Francis. Copyright © 1961 by Robert Francis. Reprinted by permission of Wesleyan University Press.

ROBERT FROST "Fire and Ice," "The Need of Being Versed in Country Things," "Nothing Gold Can Stay," "Stopping by Woods on a Snowy Evening," "To Earthward," "Acquainted with the Night," "Once by the Pacific," "Desert Places," "Design," "Neither Out Far Nor in Deep," "Provide, Provide," "Come In," "The Gift Outright," "The Silken Tent" and "Directive" from *The Poetry of Robert Frost,* edited by Edward Connery Lathem, © 1936, 1942, 1951, 1956 by Robert Frost. Copyright 1964, 1971, 1975 by Lesley Frost Ballantine. Copyright 1923, 1928, 1947, 1969 by Henry Holt and Company, LLC. Reprinted by permission of Henry Holt and Company, LLC.

ALICE FULTON "The Expense of Spirit" from *Powers of Congress.* Copyright © 1989, 1990, 2001, 2003 by Alice Fulton. Reprinted by permission of Sarabande Books and the author. "What I Like" from *Dance Script with Electric Ballerina: Poems.* Copyright © 1983 by Alice Fulton. Used with permission of the poet and the University of Illinois Press.

ALLEN GINSBERG "A Supermarket in California" and "Howl" from *Collected Poems 1947–1980.* Copyright © 1955 by Allen Ginsberg. "America" from *Collected Poems 1947–1980.* Copyright © 1956, 1959 by Allen Ginsberg. Reprinted by permission of HarperCollins Publishers Inc.

DANA GIOIA "Planting a Sequoia" and "The Next Poem" from *The Gods of Winter.* Copyright © 1991 by Dana Gioia. Reprinted by permission of Graywolf Press, Saint Paul, Minnesota.

LOUISE GLÜCK "The School Children" "The Gift," "Mock Orange," "The Gold Lily" and "Circe's Power" from *The First Four Books of Poems.* Copyright © 1968, 1971, 1972, 1973, 1974, 1975, 1976, 1977, 1978, 1979, 1980, 1985, 1995 by Louise Glück. Reprinted by permission of HarperCollins Publishers, Inc.

JORIE GRAHAM "Mind" and "Over and Over Stitch" from *Hybrids of Plants and of Ghosts.* Copyright © 1980 by Jorie Graham. "Erosion" from *Erosion.* Copyright © 1983 by Jorie Graham. Reprinted by permission of Princeton University Press.

ANGELINA WELD GRIMKÉ "The Black Finger," "Tenebris," "A Mona Lisa" and "Fragment" by Angelina Weld Grimké reprinted by permission of Moorland-Springarn Research Center, Howard University.

BARBARA GUEST "Green Revolutions" and "Poem" from *Moscow Mansions Poems.* Copyright © 1993 by Barbara Guest. Reprinted by permission of Viking Press/Penguin Putnam and the author.

("Dream Deferred")," "Theme for English B," "Homecoming" and "Dinner Guest: Me" from *The Collected Poems of Langston Hughes* by Langston Hughes. Copyright © 1994 by The Estate of Langston Hughes. Used by permission of Alfred A. Knopf, a division of Random House, Inc.

RICHARD HUGO "Degrees of Gray in Phillipsburg" from *Making Certain It Goes On: Collected Poems of Richard Hugo.* Copyright © 1973 by Richard Hugo. "Driving Montana" from *Making Certain It Goes On: Collected Poems of Richard Hugo.* Copyright © 1984 by The Estate of Richard Hugo. Used by permission of W. W. Norton & Company, Inc.

MARK JARMAN "Ground Swell," "Hands Folded" and "After the Praying" from *Questions for Ecclesiastes.* Copyright © 1997 by Mark Jarman. Reprinted by permission of the author and Story Line Press (www.storylinepress.com).

RANDALL JARRELL "The Death of the Ball Turret Gunner," "Losses," "Next Day," "90 North," and "The Woman at the Washington Zoo" from *The Complete Poems.* Copyright © 1969, renewed 1997 by Mary von S. Jarrell. Reprinted by permission of Farrar, Straus and Giroux, LLC.

ROBINSON JEFFERS "Boats in a Fog" by Robinson Jeffers, copyright 1925 and renewed 1953 by Robinson Jeffers, "To the Stone-Cutters" by Robinson Jeffers, copyright 1924 and renewed 1952 by Robinson Jeffers, "Love the Wild Swan" by Robinson Jeffers, copyright 1935 and renewed 1963 by Donnan Jeffers and Garth Jeffers, "Hurt Hawks" by Robinson Jeffers, copyright 1928 and renewed 1956 by Robinson Jeffers, "Carmel Point" by Robinson Jeffers, copyright 1954 by Robinson Jeffers, "Shine, Perishing Republic" and "Rock and Hawk" from *The Selected Poems of Robinson Jeffers* by Robinson Jeffers, copyright 1925, 1929 and renewed 1953, 1957 by Robinson Jeffers. Used by permission of Random House, Inc. "Fawn's Foster Mother" from *The Collected Poetry of Robinson Jeffers, Volume 1, 1920–1928,* edited by Tim Hunt. Copyright © 1938 and renewed 1966 by Donnan and Garth Jeffers. Editorial matter © 1988 by the Board of Trustees of the Leland Stanford Jr. University. "Ave Caesar," "New Mexican Mountain," "Hands," "Shane O'Neill's Cairn" and "November Surf" from *The Collected Poetry of Robinson Jeffers, Volume 2, 1928–1938,* edited by Tim Hunt. Copyright © 1938 and renewed 1966 by Donnan Jeffers and Garth Jeffers. Editorial matter © 1989 by the Board of Trustees of the Leland Stanford Jr. University. With the permission of Stanford University Press, www.sup.org.

DONALD JUSTICE "Counting the Mad," "In Bertram's Garden," "On the Death of Friends in Childhood," "But That Is Another Story," "Men at Forty," "Variations on a Text by Vallejo" and "Psalm and Lament." Copyright © 2003 by Donald Justice. Reprinted by permission of the author.

WELDON KEES "For My Daughter," "Robinson," "Round," "Crime Club," "Aspects of Robinson," "River Song" and "1926" from *The Collected Poems of Weldon Kees* edited by Donald Justice. Copyright © 1975 by the University of Nebraska Press. Reprinted by permission of the University of Nebraska Press.

ETHERIDGE KNIGHT "Haiku," "Hard Rock Returns to Prison from the Hospital for the Criminal Insane," "The Idea of Ancestry," "The Warden Said to Me the Other Day" and "A Poem for Myself" from *Born of Woman: New and Selected Poems.* Copyright ©1980 by Etheridge Knight. Reprinted by permission of The Estate of Etheridge Knight.

X. J. KENNEDY "The Waterbury Cross" from *Dark Horses: New Poems,* p. 7. Copyright © 1992 by X. J. Kennedy. Reprinted with permission of The Johns Hopkins

WILLIAM LOGAN "After a Line by F. Scott Fitzgerald" and "Small Bad Town" from *Night Battle*, Penguin Putnam, Inc. Copyright © 1999 by William Logan. Reprinted by permission of the author.

AUDRE LORDE "Coal" from *Undersong: Chosen Poems Old and New.* Copyright © 1973, 1970, 1968 by Audre Lorde. "Father Son and Holy Ghost" from *Undersong: Chosen Poems Old and New.* Copyright © 1992, 1982, 1976, 1974, 1973, 1970, 1968 by Audre Lorde. "October" from *Chosen Poems: Old and New.* Copyright © 1982, 1976, 1974, 1973, 1970, 1968 by Audre Lorde. Used by permission of W. W. Norton & Company, Inc.

ADRIAN C. LOUIS "Looking for Judas" from *Vortex of Indian Fevers.* Copyright © 1995 by Adrian C. Louis. Reprinted by permission of Northwestern University Press. "Without Words" from *Fire Water World*, West End Press. Copyright © 1989 by Adrian C. Louis. Reprinted by permission of the author.

ROBERT LOWELL "Concord," and "The Quaker Graveyard in Nantucket" from *Lord Weary's Castle.* Copyright © 1946 and renewed 1974 by Robert Lowell. Reprinted by permission of Harcourt, Inc. "Epilogue" from *Day by Day.* Copyright © 1977 by Robert Lowell. Reprinted by permission of Farrar, Straus and Giroux, LLC. "For the Union Dead," "History," "Memories of West Street and Lepke," "Skunk Hour," "Waking Early Sunday Morning" from *Selected Poems.* Copyright © 1976 by Robert Lowell. Reprinted by permission of Farrar, Straus and Giroux, LLC.

ARCHIBALD MacLEISH "Ars Poetica," "The End of the World," "The Silent Slain," "You, Andrew Marvell" from *Collected Poems 1917–1982* by Archibald MacLeish. Copyright © 1985 by The Estate of Archibald MacLeish. Reprinted by permission of Houghton Mifflin Company. All rights reserved.

THOMAS McGRATH "Ars Poetica: Who Lives in the Ivory Tower?," "The Buffalo Coat" and "Remembering the Children of Auschwitz" from *Selected Poems 1938–1988.* Copyright © 1988 by Thomas McGrath. Reprinted with the permission of Copper Canyon Press, POB 271, Port Townsend, WA 98368-0271. "Jig Tune: Not For Love" from *The Dialectics of Love.* Reprinted by permission of the Estate of Thomas McGrath.

HEATHER McHUGH "The Trouble with 'In'" and "Earthmoving Malediction" from *Hinge & Sign: Poems 1968–1993.* Copyright © 1994 by Heather McHugh. Reprinted by permission of Wesleyan University Press.

CHARLES MARTIN "E.S.L." and "Metaphor of Grass in California" from *Steal the Bacon*, p. 21. Copyright © 1987 by Charles Martin. Reprinted with permission of The Johns Hopkins University Press. "Taken Up" from *Martin's Room for Error.* Copyright © 1978 by Charles Martin. Reprinted by permission of the University of Georgia Press.

DAVID MASON "Spooning" from *The Buried Houses.* Copyright © 1991 by David Mason. "Song of the Powers" from *The Country I Remember.* Copyright © 1996 by David Mason. Reprinted by permission of the author and Story Line Press (www.storylinepress.com).

SAMUEL MENASHE "O Many Named Beloved," "The Shrine Whose Shape I Am," "Self Employed," "At a Standstill" and "Curriculum Vitae" from *The Niche Narrows: New & Selected Poems*, Talisman House Publishers, 2000. Copyright © 2000 Samuel Menashe. Reprinted by permission of the author.

JAMES MERRILL "The Broken Home," "The Mad Scene," "Last Words," and "Casual Wear" from *Collected Poems*, eds. J. D. McClatchy and Stephen Yenser. Copyright © 2001 by the Literary Estate of James Merrill at Washington University. Used by permission of Alfred A. Knopf, a division of Random House, Inc.

THOMAS MERTON "For My Brother: Reported Missing in Action, 1943" from *The Collected Poems of Thomas Merton*. Copyright © 1948 by New Directions Publishing Corp., 1977 by The Trustees of the Merton Legacy Trust. "The Reader" from *The Collected Poems of Thomas Merton*. Copyright © 1949 by Our Lady of Gethsemani Monastery. Reprinted by permission of New Directions Publishing Corp.

W. S. MERWIN "Rain Travel" from *Travels*. Copyright © 1992 by W. S. Merwin. Used by permission of Alfred A. Knopf, a division of Random House, Inc. "Air," "For a Coming Extinction," "The Animals," "For the Anniversary of My Death," "The Last One" and "Some Last Questions" from *The Second Four Books of Poems*, Copper Canyon Press, 1993. Copyright © 1993 by W. S. Merwin. Reprinted with permission from the Wylie Agency.

JOSEPHINE MILES "Conception," "Riddle," "Album" and "Reason" from *Collected Poems 1930–83*. Copyright © 1983 by Josephine Miles. Used with permission of the University of Illinois Press.

EDNA ST. VINCENT MILLAY "What lips my lips have kissed," Sonnet XXX and Sonnet XXXVI of *Fatal Interview* by Edna St. Vincent Millay. From *Collected Poems*, HarperCollins. Copyright © 1923, 1931, 1951, 1958 by Edna St. Vincent Millay and Norma Millay Ellis. All rights reserved. Reprinted by permission of Elizabeth Barnett, Literary executor.

N. SCOTT MOMADAY "Simile" and "Headwaters" from *Angle of Geese and Other Poems*. Copyright © 1972 by Scott Momaday. Reprinted by permission of David R. Godine, Publisher, Inc. "Carriers of the Dream Wheel" and "The Delight Song of Tsaoi-talee" from *In the Presence of the Sun: Stories & Poems 1961–1991*. Copyright © 1992 by N. Scott Momaday. Reprinted by permission of St. Martin's Press, LLC.

MARIANNE MOORE "Poetry," "Marriage," "Silence," and "The Steeple Jack" from *The Collected Poems of Marianne Moore* by Marianne Moore. Copyright © 1935 by Marianne Moore; copyright renewed © 1963 by Marianne Moore and T. S. Eliot. "What Are Years?" from *The Collected Poems of Marianne Moore* by Marianne Moore. Copyright © 1941 by Marianne Moore; copyright renewed © 1969 by Marianne Moore. "In Distrust of Merits" and "The Mind Is An Enchanting Thing" from *The Collected Poems of Marianne Moore* by Marianne Moore. Copyright © 1944 by Marianne Moore; copyright renewed © 1972 by Marianne Moore. Author's Notes – "Omissions are not accidents" from *The Collected Poems of Marianne Moore* by Marianne Moore. Copyright © 1967 by Marianne Moore. Reprinted with the permission of Scribner, a Division of Simon & Schuster, Inc.

HOWARD MOSS "The Pruned Tree" and "Tourists" from *New Selected Poems* by Howard Moss, New York: Atheneum, 1985.

MARILYN NELSON "The Ballad of Aunt Geneva," "How I Discovered Poetry" and "Thus Far by Faith" from *The Fields of Praise: New and Selected Poems*. Copyright © 1997 by Marilyn Nelson. Reprinted by permission of Louisiana State University Press.

HOWARD NEMEROV "A Primer of the Daily Round," "The Blue Swallows" and "The Western Approaches" from *The Collected Poems of Howard Nemerov*. Copyright © 1977 Howard Nemerov. "The Makers" and "Because You Asked about the Line between Prose and Poetry" from *Sentences*. Copyright © 1980 by Howard Nemerov. "The War in the Air" from *War Stories*. Copyright © 1987 by Howard Nemerov. Reprinted by permission of Margaret Nemerov.

LORINE NIEDECKER "The Element Mother," "Sorrow moves in wide waves," "Poet's work," "I knew a clean man," "Autumn" and " He lived – childhood summers" from *Lorine Niedecker: Collected Works*, edited by Jenny Lynn Penberthy.

Pastan. "Journey's End" from *PM/AM: New and Selected Poems*. Copyright © 1982 by Linda Pastan. Used by permission of W. W. Norton & Company, Inc.

ROBERT PINSKY "ABC" from *Jersey Rain*. Copyright © 2000 by Robert Pinsky. Reprinted by permission of Farrar, Straus and Giroux, LLC. "Shirt" from *The Want Bone*. Copyright © 1990 by Robert Pinsky. Reprinted by permission of Ecco/Harper-Collins Publishers Inc.

SYLVIA PLATH "Blackberrying," "Metaphors" and "Mirror" from *Crossing the Water*. Copyright © 1971 by Ted Hughes. "Edge," "Morning Song," and "Lady Lazarus from *Ariel*. Copyright © 1961, 1962, 1963, 1964, 1965, 1966 by Ted Hughes. "Colossus" from *The Collected Poems of Sylvia Plath*. Copyright © 1962, 1965, 1971, 1981 by the Estate of Sylvia Plath. Editorial material copyright © 1981 by Ted Hughes. Reprinted by permission of HarperCollins Publishers Inc. "Daddy" from *Collected Poems*. Copyright © 1992 by Ted Hughes. Used by permission of Alfred A. Knopf, a division of Random House, Inc. Reprinted by permission of Faber & Faber Limited, London.

EZRA POUND "Canto XLV" and "Canto LXXI" from *The Cantos of Ezra Pound*. Copyright © 1948 by Ezra Pound. Reprinted by permission of New Directions Publishing Corp.

DUDLEY RANDALL "Ballad of Birmingham" and "Booker T. and W.E.B." from *Poem Counterpoem*. "A Different Image" from *Cities Burning*. By permission of Broadside Press.

JOHN CROWE RANSOM "Bells for John Whiteside's Daughter," "Blue Girls," "Dead Boy," "Piazza Piece" from *Selected Poems, Third Edition, Revised and Enlarged* by John Crowe Ransom. Copyright 1924 by Alfred A. Knopf, a division of Random House, Inc. and renewed 1952 by John Crowe Ransom. Used by permission of Alfred A. Knopf, a division of Random House, Inc.

ISHMAEL REED "I am a cowboy in the boat of Ra" and "Oakland Blues" from *New and Collected Poems*. Copyright © 1989 by Ishmael Reed. Reprinted by permission of Lowenstein Associates.

KENNETH REXROTH "Vitamins and Roughage" from *Collected Shorter Poems*. Copyright © 1944, 1963 by Kenneth Rexroth. "A very early morning exercise" from *Collected Shorter Poems*. Copyright © 1940 by Kenneth Rexroth. "Andrée Rexroth" and "The Signature of all Things" from *Collected Shorter Poems*. Copyright © 1949 by Kenneth Rexroth. Reprinted by permission of New Directions Publishing Corp.

ADRIENNE RICH "Aunt Jennifer's Tigers," "Living in Sin," "Diving into the Wreck," "From a Survivor," "Rape," "Power," Part XIII "(Dedications)" and "Tattered Kaddish" originally from *An Atlas of the Difficult World*, from *The Fact of a Doorframe: Selected Poems 1950–2001* by Adrienne Rich. Copyright © 2002 by Adrienne Rich. Copyright © 2001, 1999, 1995, 1991, 1989, 1986, 1984, 1981, 1967, 1963, 1962, 1961, 1960, 1959, 1958, 1957, 1956, 1955, 1954, 1953, 1952, 1951 by Adrienne Rich. Copyright © 1978, 1975, 1973, 1971, 1969, 1966 by W. W. Norton & Company, Inc. Used by permission of W. W. Norton & Company, Inc. "The Diamond Cutters" from *Collected Early Poems: 1950–1970* by Adrienne Rich. Copyright © 1993, 1955 by Adrienne Rich. Used by permission of W. W. Norton & Company, Inc.

LAURA RIDING "Helen's Burning," "The Map of Places" and "The World and I" from *The Poems of Laura Riding*. Copyright © 2001 by The Board of Literary Management of the late Laura (Riding) Jackson. Reprinted by permission of Persea Books, Inc. "In conformity with the late author's wish, her Board of Literary Management asks us to record that, in 1940, Laura (Riding) Jackson renounced, on grounds of linguistic principal, the writing of poetry: she had come to hold that 'poetry obstructs general attainment to something better in our linguistic way-of-life than we have.'"

EDWIN ARLINGTON ROBINSON "New England" and "The Sheaves" from *The Collected Poems of Edwin Arlington Robinson*, revised by Edwin Arlington Robinson. Copyright © 1925 by Edwin Arlington Robinson; copyright renewed © 1953 by Ruth Nivison and Barbara R. Holt. Reprinted with the permission of Scribner, a Division of Simon & Schuster, Inc.

THEODORE ROETHKE "Cuttings" and "Cuttings (Later)" copyright © 1948 by Theodore Roethke, "Root Cellar" and "Dolor" copyright © 1943 by Modern Poetry Association, Inc., "My Papa's Waltz" copyright © 1942 by Hearst Magazines, Inc., "Elegy for Jane" copyright © 1950 by Theodore Roethke, "The Waking" copyright © 1953 by Theodore Roethke, "I Knew a Woman" copyright © 1954 by Theodore Roethke, "In A Dark Time" copyright © 1960 by Beatrice Roethke, Administratrix of the Estate of Theodore Roethke, "The Longing" and "The Far Field" copyright © by Beatrice Roethke, Administratrix of the Estate of Theodore Roethke, "Journey to the Interior" copyright © 1961 by Beatrice Roethke, Administratrix of the Estate of Theodore Roethke from *Collected Poems of Theodore Roethke*. Used by permission of Doubleday, a division of Random House, Inc.

WENDY ROSE "Vanishing Point: Urban Indian" from *Lost Copper: Poems by Wendy Rose*. Copyright © 1980 by the Malki Museum, Inc., Morongo Indian Reservation, Banning, California, 92220. "For the White Poets Who Would Be Indian" copyright © 1980 by Wendy Rose, Fresno Public Affairs.

MURIEL RUKEYSER "Double Dialogue: Homage to Robert Frost" from *A Muriel Rukeyser Reader*, W. W. Norton, 1994. "Effort at Speech Between Two People," "To Be a Jew in the Twentieth Century," "The Poem as Mask" and "Poem" from *Out of Silence*, Northwestern University Press, 1992. Copyright © 1992, 1994 by William Rukeyser. Reprinted by permission of International Creative Management, Inc.

KAY RYAN "Paired Things" and "Turtle" from *Flamingo Watching*. Copyright © 1994 by Kay Ryan. Used by permission of Copper Beech Press. "Bestiary" from *Elephant Rocks*. Copyright © 1996 by Kay Ryan. "Chemise," "Don't Look Back" and "Mockingbird" from *Say Uncle*. Copyright © 2000 by Kay Ryan. Used by permission of Grove/Atlantic, Inc.

BENJAMIN ALIRE SÁENZ "To the Desert" from *Dark and Perfect Angels*. Copyright © 1995 by Benjamin Alire Sáenz. Reprinted by permission of Cinco Puntos Press. "Resurrections" from *Calendar of Dust*. Copyright © 1994 by Benjamin Alire Sáenz. Used by permission of Broken Moon Press.

MARY JO SALTER "The Age of Reason" from *Sunday Skaters*. Copyright © 1994 by Mary Jo Salter. "Welcome to Hiroshima" from *Henry Purcell in Japan*. Copyright © 1984 by Mary Jo Salter. Used by permission of Alfred A. Knopf, a division of Random House, Inc.

MARISA DE LOS SANTOS "Perfect Dress" from *From the Bones Out*. Copyright © 2000 by Marisa de los Santos. Reprinted by permission of the University of South Carolina Press.

GJERTRUD SCHNACKENBERG "The Paperweight" and "Supernatural Love" from *Supernatural Love: Poems 1976–1992*. Copyright © 2000 by Gjertrud Schnackenberg. Reprinted by permission of Farrar, Straus and Giroux, LLC.

ANNE SEXTON "Her Kind" from *To Bedlam and Part Way Back*. Copyright © 1960 by Anne Sexton, renewed 1988 by Linda G. Sexton. "Wanting to Die" from *Live or Die*. Copyright © 1966 by Anne Sexton, renewed 1994 by Linda G. Sexton. "The

Truth the Dead Know" and "The Abortion" from *All My Pretty Ones*. Copyright © 1962 by Anne Sexton, renewed 1990 by Linda G. Sexton. Reprinted by permission of Houghton Mifflin Company. All rights reserved.

RON SILLIMAN "The Chinese Notebook" from *Ketjak*. Copyright © 1992 by Ron Silliman. Reprinted by permission of the author.

CHARLES SIMIC "Fear," "My Shoes," "Fork," "Eyes Fastened with Pins," "Classic Ballroom Dances" from *Selected Early Poems*. Copyright © 1999 by Charles Simic. Reprinted by permission of George Braziller, Inc.

LOUIS SIMPSON "Early in the Morning," "The Man Who Married Magdalene," "To the Western World," "American Poetry," "My Father in the Night Commanding No," "The Unwritten Poem" and "A Clearing" copyright © 1988, 1995 by Louis Simpson. Reprinted by permission of the author.

WILLIAM JAY SMITH "A Note on the Vanity Dresser," "Galileo Galilei" and "American Primitive" from *The World Below the Window: Poems 1937–1997*. Copyright © 1998 by William Jay Smith. Reprinted with permission of The Johns Hopkins University Press.

W. D. SNODGRASS "April Inventory," "Leaving the Motel" and "Disposal" from *Selected Poems 1957–1987*. Copyright © 1987 by W. D. Snodgrass. Reprinted by permission of Soho Press.

GARY SNYDER "Why Log Truck Drivers Rise Earlier than Students of Zen" from *Turtle Island*. Copyright © 1974 by Gary Snyder. Reprinted by permission of New Directions Publishing Corp. "Mid-August at Sourdough Mountain Lookout," "Riprap," "Water," "Axe Handles" from *The Gary Snyder Reader*. Copyright © 1959, 1983 by Gary Snyder. Used by permission of the author.

CATHY SONG "Stamp Collecting" from *Frameless Windows, Squares of Light: Poems*. Copyright © 1988 by Cathy Song. Used by permission of W. W. Norton & Company, Inc. "Beauty and Sadness" from *Picture Bride*, Yale University Press, 1983. Copyright © 1983 by Cathy Song. Reprinted by permission of the publisher.

JACK SPICER "Conspiracy" and "A Book of Music" from *The Collected Books*. Copyright © 1975 by the Estate of Jack Spicer. Used with permission of Wesleyan University Press.

WILLIAM STAFFORD "The Farm on the Great Plains," "Traveling through the Dark," "At the Un-National Monument along the Canadian Border," "Ask Me" and "Our Kind" from *The Way It Is: New & Selected Poems*. Copyright © 1959, 1962, 1975, 1977, 1982, 1998 by the Estate of William Stafford. Reprinted by permission of Graywolf Press, Saint Paul, Minnesota.

TIMOTHY STEELE "Sapphics Against Anger," "The Sheets," and "Summer" from *Sapphics Against Anger*. Copyright © 1986 by Timothy Steele. Used by permission of University of Arkansas Press.

WALLACE STEVENS "Sunday Morning," "Evening Without Angels," "The Idea of Order at Key West," "A Postcard From the Volcano," from *Notes Toward a Supreme Fiction*, "Final Soliloquy of the Interior Paramour," "Of Modern Poetry," "The Plain Sense of Things," "The Course of a Particular" and "Of Mere Being" from *The Collected Poems of Wallace Stevens* by Wallace Stevens. Copyright 1954 by Wallace Stevens. Used by permission of Alfred A. Knopf, a division of Random House, Inc.

ANNE STEVENSON "The Victory," "Generations," "The Marriage," "Making Poetry" and "Alas" from *The Collected Poems 1955–1995*. Copyright © 1996 by Anne Stevenson. Reprinted by permission of Bloodaxe Books, U.K.

MARK STRAND "Eating Poetry" and "Keeping Things Whole" from *Reasons for Moving, Darker, and the Sargentville Notebook.* Copyright © 1992 by Mark Strand. Used by permission of Alfred A. Knopf, a division of Random House, Inc.

MAY SWENSON "Question" and "Four-Word Lines" from *Things Taking Place: New & Selected.* Copyright © 1978 by May Swenson. "Strawberrying" from *In Other Words.* Copyright © 1987 by May Swenson. Used with permission of The Literary Estate of May Swenson.

LARISSA SZPORLUK "Vertigo" from Isolato. Copyright © 2000 by Larissa Szporluk. Reprinted by permission of the University of Iowa Press.

ALLEN TATE "Ode to the Confederate Dead," "The Subway," from *Collected Poems 1919–1976* by Allen Tate. Copyright © 1977 by Allen Tate. Reprinted by permission of Farrar, Straus and Giroux, LLC.

JAMES TATE "The Lost Pilot," "Teaching the Ape to Write Poems" and "The Chaste Stranger" from *Selected Poems.* Copyright © 1991 by James Tate. Reprinted by permission of Wesleyan University Press.

SARA TEASDALE "In a Darkening Garden" from *The Collected Poems of Sara Teasdale* by Sara Teasdale. Copyright © 1933 by The Macmillan Company. Reprinted with the permission of Scribner, a Division of Simon & Schuster, Inc.

DIANE THIEL "*Memento Mori* in Middle School" from *Echolocations.* Copyright © 2000 by Diane Thiel. Reprinted by permission of the author and Story Line Press (www.storylinepress.com)

MELVIN B. TOLSON "An Ex-Judge at the Bar" and "Dark Symphony" from A Gallery of Harlem Portraits from *Harlem Gallery and Other Poems of Melvin B. Tolson* by Melvin Tolson. Reprinted with permission of the University Press of Virginia. "Sootie Joe" from *A Gallery of Harlem Portraits* by Melvin B. Tolson, by permission of the University of Missouri Press. Copyright © 1979 by the Curators of the University of Missouri.

JEAN TOOMER "Seventh Street," "November Cotton Flower," "Georgia Dusk" and "Reapers" from *Cane* by Jean Toomer. Copyright 1923 by Boni & Liveright, renewed 1951 by Jean Toomer. Used by permission of Liveright Publishing Corporation.

ROBERT PENN WARREN "Bearded Oaks," "Evening Hawk" and "What Voice at Moth-Hour" copyright © 1985 by Robert Penn Warren. Reprinted by permission of William Morris Agency, Inc. on behalf of the author.

AMY UYEMATSU "Deliberate" from *30 Miles from J-Town.* Copyright © 1992 by Amy Uyematsu. "The Ten Million Flames of Los Angeles" from *Night of Fire, Nights of Rain.* Reprinted by permission of the author and Story Line Press (www.storylinepress.com)

MONA VAN DUYN "Earth Tremors Felt in Missouri" and "Causes" from *Selected Poems.* Copyright © 2002 by Mona Van Duyn. Used by permission of Alfred A. Knopf, a division of Random House, Inc.

MARGARET WALKER "For Malcolm X" from *This Is My Century: New and Collected Poems.* Copyright © 1989 by Margaret Walker Alexander. Reprinted by permission of The University of Georgia Press.

RICHARD WILBUR "The Ride" and "Hamlen Brook" from *New and Collected Poems.* Copyright © 1988 by Richard Wilbur. "The Writer," "Cottage Street, 1953," "Piccola Commedia" and "To the Etruscan Poets" from *The Mind-Reader.* Copyright © 1975 by Richard Wilbur. "Love Calls Us to Things of This World" from *Things of This World.* Copyright © 1956 and renewed 1984 by Richard Wilbur. "The Pardon" from *Ceremony and Other Poems.* Copyright © 1950 and renewed 1978 by Richard Wilbur. "The Beautiful Changes" from *The Beautiful Changes and*

Other Poems. Copyright © 1947 and renewed 1975 by Richard Wilbur. Reprinted by permission of Harcourt, Inc.

C. K. WILLIAMS "Elms," "From My Window" and "Hood" from *Selected Poems*. Copyright © 1994 by C. K. Williams. Reprinted by permission of Farrar, Straus and Giroux, LLC.

MILLER WILLIAMS "On a Photograph of My Mother at Seventeen" and "Ruby Tells All" from *Imperfect Love: Poems*. Copyright © 1986 by Miller Williams. Reprinted by permission of Louisiana State University Press.

WILLIAM CARLOS WILLIAMS "Spring and All, section I," "The Right of Way," "To Elsie, XVIII," "The Red Wheelbarrow," "The Last Words of My English Grandmother," "This is Just to Say," "Flowers by the Sea," "The Yachts," "The Dance," "The Descent" and "Asphodel, That Greeney Flower, Book I" from *Collected Poems 1939–1962, Volume II* by William Carlos Williams. Copyright © 1963 by William Carlos Williams. Reprinted by permission of New Directions Publishing Corp.

CHRISTIAN WIMAN "What I Know" from *The Long Home*. Copyright © 1998 by Christian Wiman. Reprinted by permission of the author and Story Line Press (www.storylinepress.com).

CHARLES WRIGHT "The New Poem," "Clear Night" and "Stone Canyon Nocturne" from *Country Music: Selected Early Poems*. Copyright © 1982 by Charles Wright. Reprinted by permission of Wesleyan University Press. "California Dreaming" from *The World of Ten Thousand Things: Poems 1980–1990*. Copyright © 1990 by Charles Wright. Reprinted by permission of Farrar, Straus and Giroux, LLC.

JAMES WRIGHT "Complaint," " Saint Judas," "Autumn Begins in Martins Ferry, Ohio," "A Blessing," "Lying in a Hammock at William Duffy's Farm in *Pine Island, Minnesota*." "Twilights" and "The Life" from *Above the River: The Complete Poems*. Copyright © 1990 by James Wright. Reprinted by permission of Wesleyan University Press.

KEVIN YOUNG "Quivira City Limits" from *Most Way Home*. Copyright © 1995 by Kevin Young/Fisted Pick Productions. Reprinted by permission of William Morrow/HarperCollins Publishers Inc.

BERNICE ZAMORA "Penitents" from *Releasing Serpents*. Copyright © 1994 by Bilingual Press/Editorial Bilingue, Arizona State University, Tempe, AZ. Reprinted by permission.

LOUIS ZUKOFSKY "Non Ti Fidar," "A Song for the Year's End" and " Starglow" from *Complete Short Poetry*, pp. 111, 123, 325. Copyright © 1991 by Louis Zukofsky. Reprinted with permission of The Johns Hopkins University Press.

Photo Credits

Index of Authors and Titles